DISORDERS OF THE SCHIZOPHRENIC SYNDROME

Edited by

LEOPOLD BELLAK, M.D.

Basic Books, Inc., Publishers

NEW YORK

The material on pp. 244–45 is reprinted by permission of the Publisher from the chapter "Schizophrenia in Children of Schizophrenic Mothers," in *Child Personality and Psychopathology—Current Topics*, ed. A. Davids (New York: John Wiley & Sons, Inc., 1975), pp. 244–45.

Library of Congress Cataloging in Publication Data
Main entry under title:

Disorders of the schizophrenic syndrome.

Includes bibliographies and index.
 1. Schizophrenia. I. Bellak, Leopold, 1916–
RC514.D53   616.8'982   78–19814
ISBN: 0–465–01675–8

Contents

PART I

Research Aspects

PART II
Clinical Aspects

MY SIXTY YEARS WITH
SCHIZOPHRENICS

Manfred Bleuler, M.D.

I was born and spent my entire childhood in a psychiatric hospital of which my father was the director. Altogether I have lived with schizophrenics for sixty years. After graduation from medical school I spent ten years as a resident physician. Eventually I served as the director of a psychiatric hospital, Burghölzli, in Zurich, Switzerland, for twenty-seven years. The remainder of my time was spent either in general hospitals or in general practice. These many years of day-to-day contact with schizophrenics have contributed to the development of the following views regarding this pathology.

The obvious symptomatology is but one level of the schizophrenic's personality. A healthy life exists buried beneath this confusion. Somewhere deep within himself the schizophrenic is in touch with reality despite his hallucinations. He has common sense in spite of his delusions and confused thinking. He hides a warm and human heart behind his sometimes shocking affective behavior. We must know how to approach the schizophrenic. We must enter and feel with him his vision of reality. We must never relinquish this endeavor. With perseverance there will come a time when the schizophrenic is as we are, when there is mutual understanding and sharing of feelings and mood. This short but invaluable moment might well result in a lasting improvement or even in recovery.

I began my work with schizophrenics before the introduction of insulin, electroshock therapy (EST), and neuroleptics into the field. Consequently I was able to observe the effects of various physical, psychotherapeutic, and analytic treatments. I have come to the following formulations regarding the essentials in the treatment of schizophrenics. There must be an active communion with the patient, a communion founded upon the patient-therapist relationship. This relationship is necessary but not sufficient. A community, whether it be in a hospital or in a family, is of paramount importance. In this community the schizophrenic must reach a state of equilibrium between an optimal amount of activity which stimulates him, and an optimal amount of routine and order which helps to calm and control him. When ready, the patient needs to be confronted with new situations and responsibilities which encourage him to mobilize his vital forces. During certain phases of his illness he will require a calming agent such as psychotherapy or drugs. The success of a therapy is contingent upon the organization of an active community, opportunities for the patient to become involved, and possibilities for tranquilization. A social environment, and the ability to deal effectively with stress at times and to relax at other times, are of unparalleled importance in the development and formation of our personality from birth to old age. It is precisely the control of these elements which permits the healthy individual to inhibit his prelogical, unrealistic, and disordered mental life from overflowing.

Schizophrenic thinking is a part of every human being's life. It occurs in our everyday functioning as daydreams, dreams, art, fantasy, and fanatic thinking, among other phenomena. In a normal person this type of thinking prevails in a small part of life and is under control; in a schizophrenic it has become the predominant way of dealing with life and of communicating with oneself and with others. Furthermore, we now recognize that certain types of brain damage can elicit a psychosis similar to schizophrenia. Intoxications, infections, tumors, and temporal epilepsy have been known to produce schizophrenialike symptoms.

Over the years I have asked myself if schizophrenic patients were physical patients, and vice versa. The answer is clearly that the overwhelming majority of schizophrenics are physically, and particularly endocrinologically, healthy, and that the overwhelming majority of physical and endocrine patients are not schizophrenic. To this day a physical process in the etiology of schizophrenia has not been discovered; but we should definitely not discount the possibility of a future discovery in this area. We are at a loss to give a physical interpretation of human intelligence, of human genius, of the understanding of beauty and of the sublime, and of human love and goodness. Biology has contributed to an understanding of the physical basis of human life but not to the human mind in its complexity or to schizophrenic life.

I have always been impressed by the degree of suffering experienced by my schizophrenic patients, as seen through their family and personal history. The schizophrenic female has suffered predominantly from her relationships with parents, siblings, other children, and beloved ones. The schizophrenic male has suffered most frequently from competition with other men. The mental suffering of future schizophrenics is, however, not essentially different from the suffering of future normals. For this reason among others, the development of a schizophrenic psychosis cannot be explained without postulating an inherited disposition. Nevertheless I have found no proof that such a disposition might be accounted for by a single error of metabolism or by some other single inherited defect. The following assumption seems much more probable: the inherited traits for the personal disposition of a future schizophrenic are not in harmony with each other. Such a disharmony, coupled with the disharmony of the social environment, is conducive to loss of a peaceful inner life and an integrated ego at the beginning of psychosis.

I have worked with the families of many schizophrenic patients. In most cases, I was touched by the parents' love and care for their schizophrenic child, and by the child's love for his parents. Assuredly there are schizophrenics who have suffered from their relatives' hate, rejection, aggression, and cruelty. However, this is the exception rather than the rule. Communication within the families of both the parents of the schizophrenic and of the schizophrenic himself is bizarre and idiosyncratic. Furthermore, the nonpsychotic family member's negative attitude toward the development of the schizophrenic member affects the schizophrenic and the other family members. Conversely, the nonpsychotic member develops peculiar attitudes or even neurotic problems as a result of his contact with the future schizophrenic.

In considering schizophrenics, we are dealing essentially with the same problems facing us all regarding heredity, environmental factors, and psychopathology. The schizophrenic is involved in the same struggle each of us is: the struggle to be an integrated person with the ability to adapt one's inner drives and desires to reality. Because of this similarity we must understand the schizophrenic and be hopeful. We must never lose faith. There is no doubt that some cases will be cruel disappointments. On the other hand, 50 percent of our schizophrenic patients are completely or socially recovered some years after the onset of psychosis, and a substantive percentage of the rest are at least improved.

In conclusion, it is realistic to be hopeful in working with schizophrenics; and our faith is an ingredient immensely helpful to the patient in his treatment. In this volume the editor and the many expert contributors present our latest knowledge of the many-faceted disorders of schizophrenia.

DISORDERS OF THE

SCHIZOPHRENIC SYNDROME

Introduction

AN IDIOSYNCRATIC OVERVIEW

Leopold Bellak, M.D.

Unlike Professor Bleuler I have had only forty years of experience with schizophrenics, if I don't count my brief exposure at the Wagner-Jauregg Clinic in Vienna as a student but start with my two years of experience as a psychiatric aide in 1938 and 1939. In 1948 I published my first book on schizophrenia, *Dementia Praecox* (3),* which reviewed close to three thousand papers published in the preceding ten years. Ten years later I edited and contributed to my 1958 volume (4) and did so again (with Loeb) in 1968 (15). It is ten years later once again, and time to present this volume.

I would like to offer a very broad personal overview of the developments that I have had a chance to observe in these forty years, and then follow with more specific ones covering the last ten years. Much more complete coverage of the specific aspects of the schizophrenic syndrome will, of course, be provided by the authors of the subsequent chapters. What I would like to offer is a frame of reference for each of the subsequent chapters as well as some conceptual bridges between them and a few overall conclusions.

Schizophrenia Now

To start with, the current phenotype of schizophrenia—that is, what the 1979 resident can observe today in most hospitals as compared with what he might have observed forty, or twenty-five, or even ten years ago—is quite different. Drug therapy and the varied aspects of community psychiatry are primarily responsible for this change. Above all, we should appreciate the interaction between these two modalities even

---

* Numbers that appear within parentheses refer to references cited in the bibliography found at the end of each chapter.

with all their limitations, for open wards and the early return of schizophrenics to the community would not be possible without psychoactive
drugs. Legal developments have further changed the picture.

Because of the widespread use of our psychoactive drugs, one can
hardly ever see, at least in an acute admitting hospital, catatonics frozen
into bizarre transfigurations conversing loudly with their private voices—
a scene that was once a daily occurrence. Now by the time acutely disturbed patients are admitted, at least to metropolitan hospitals, they
have usually already been medicated by some physician in the community. It is a standing joke that on the psychiatric wards of a general
hospital with a staff in street clothes, it may require an acute observer
to tell who is a patient and who is a staff member (unless, of course, the
patients are identifiable by drug-induced parkinsonism!), because at
least superficially most patients behave rather rationally most of the
time. Only close observation can usually reveal that basically these
patients are not so different from schizophrenics of forty years ago. They
may be less manneristic, and quieter about their hallucinations and delusions, and less often hebephrenic, but their thought processes are still
often dominated by symbolization, overinclusiveness, and ideas of reference. Occasionally, of course, they still behave in a markedly bizarre
fashion.

In state hospitals the patients more closely resemble the ones from
forty years ago, especially if the institutional care is poor. But for the
most part the bizarre extremes of schizophrenic behavior are rarely seen
(few patients pull their hair out and eat it—trichotillomania). It was
once quite common for patients to swallow foreign objects or to have
to be tube-fed. There were patients who fed themselves by tube for years,
having learned to slide the tube down, hold the funnel, and pour down
malted milk. The majority of them used to sit on the floor in lonely
corridors; they were more or less in rags and looked vacantly around
and shuffled to their meals, or when put to some work, moved like mechanical ghosts.

One of my jobs as a young resident assigned to a chronic psychotic
service was to stand at the entrance of the dining hall to watch as many
as I could of the two hundred patients in that particular building (of
the ten thousand in the institution) shuffle by; I was looking for any who
appeared severely physically ill, especially any who might be suffering
from tuberculosis. I am sure the scene could have been filmed any day
as Dante's *Inferno*, and it was the immediate precipitating factor for my
starting to review all I could read on schizophrenia.

I have already suggested elsewhere (7) that what used to be considered pathognomonic "schizophrenic regression" is probably largely
"iatrogenic." Patients were often sent to state hospitals as far away as
thirty miles from their family and from the community in which they
had lived. They lived isolated existences on the wards in conditions
approximating *perceptual isolation* and *sensory deprivation*, and they
suffered from *disuse atrophy of their ego functions*. Under these circumstances bizarre regressions were not at all surprising. The utter sense of
hopelessness fostered in institutions run in very poor and dictatorial
fashion by an ill-trained staff was often hardly better than that described
in *One Flew Over the Cuckoo's Nest*. Acts of sadism were tolerated, if

not encouraged. On my first day as a psychiatric aide in a high-class sanitarium, I was put under the tutelage of an experienced psychiatric aide. Among his first words of wisdom to me were that if I should find it necessary to hit a patient, I should hit him in the abdomen in order to leave no telltale marks. Seeing a patient put into wet packs was the closest thing I could imagine to a rape. Visiting privileges were limited. Telephone privileges were rare, and all mail was censored.

Luckily, community psychiatry, pharmacotherapy, and the civil rights-consumerism movement have changed this picture, at least to a large extent. In fact, much of this change, except the "right to treatment" legal decisions and other recent civil rights issues, had already made itself felt when I edited the 1968 volume.

More characteristic of the last decade is the fact that community psychiatry has passed its zenith and left some disappointment in its wake. Most recently pharmacotherapy has been a source of disappointment even to its most enthusiastic adherents. Among other things, its theoretical basis—in the form of the dopamine hypothesis—is arousing more skepticism rather than less. Generally the impression is growing that the neuroleptics may affect some neurotransmitters and neuroreceptors in such a way that they interfere with hallucinations and delusions and even thought disorders but do not affect schizophrenia per se; they do not affect underlying personality. Their therapeutic effect, that is, is nonspecific; they leave schizophrenics without acute symptoms of schizophrenia. These patients often remain peculiar, seclusive, self-centered people. In addition, the drugs have immediate and long-term side effects, of often serious nature. On the other hand, patients' non-compliance—that is, their not taking drugs—is a serious practical problem, especially in after-care programs.

Civil rights legislation, generally so valuable, has also almost brought as many problems as it has tried to solve. Trying to protect the patients' interests, it often makes it impossible to administer drugs because informed consent, especially a voluntary patient's, may be necessary when that patient's judgment is too impaired to give it.

Drugs, legislation, and community psychiatry have combined to bring us to the current revolving-door phenomenon, in which many patients are discharged after a brief hospital stay, only to return after a short while. This brings up the limitations and the misuse of drugs, legislation, and community psychiatry. The libertarian idea of returning patients to the community because the hospital has nothing more to offer them in actual treatment, has led to the discharge of many patients who are not well able to look after themselves. Many have no friends or relatives with whom to live and as a result have suffered miseries and in turn disrupted communities. Nowhere has this been more dramatic than in Suffolk County in New York where three large state hospitals were legally obliged to discharge thousands of their patients into communities which had no facilities for them.

Community mental health was something like the third revolution in psychiatry, after those of Pinel and Freud. Regrettably, enthusiasm outran facilities and resources; and careful study of the role and the effect of community psychiatry coupled with conservative federal policies have led to an increasing loss of national support. Above all (as I mentioned in my earlier *Handbook of Community Psychiatry and Community Mental Health* [5]), community psychiatry has taken on the characteristics of an ideological movement, with all the implications thereof. A vanguard of community mental health workers became understandably concerned with the social aspects of psychopathology and involved themselves with the common inequalities of daily life—for example, poor housing and low income—in other words, with politics. This aroused enmity in the community, was seen as an intrusion of nonprofessional activities in the work of professionals by others, and, above all, diluted professional effectiveness. There is no question that many factors other than psychiatric care per se—such as economic and occupational status—are crucial for mental health; but this reality should not affect or interfere with the professional effort and attitude involved in patient care. Political problems must be attacked politically, not psychiatrically, and in our role as citizens.

One result of community psychiatry's operating as an *ideology* was the common perception of psychiatry as a tool of the Establishment, and the antipsychiatry movement was one dubious offspring of this perception. Even an institution as enlightened as the American Civil Liberties Union attempted to do away with nearly all legal commitments. California led the way in the attempt to do away with state hospitals, primarily for economic reasons, and was fortunate in being aided by its hospitable climate. New York State then tried to follow suit, with disastrous results. As is well known, many psychotic patients were simply discharged from state facilities and dispersed, frequently with inadequate support, into exploiting communities. They often roamed the streets night and day, and the absence of state hospital care became simply the lack of any care.

The pendulum has just begun to swing to a more reasonable midpoint. Some New York State psychiatric hospitals will be maintained, but many will also provide outreach and other outpatient programs in clinics in the community, coexisting with other community psychiatric facilities. It is recognized again that a hard core, probably about 10 per cent of all schizophrenics, do need prolonged custodial care.

Some of the more reactionary professional and nonprofessional circles responded to some of the failures of community psychiatry with a condemnation of all community psychiatry and community mental health. This attitude is quite inappropriate, in view of community psychiatry's solid achievements and improvements over the past, as commented on above. Emphasis on the legal rights of and legal counsel for patients and insistence on open wards are basic human rights, which too often have been neglected.

It would be a mistake to do away with community psychiatry and community mental health, just because they have in part overreached themselves or failed in their higher expectations. In the final assessment of community psychiatry and community mental health, it is important to stress the measure of dignity, relief, and improved socialization that this movement's humanistic approach has won. The emphasis on treating patients in the acute phase, preferably for a brief period, in a general hospital and on ensuring the patient's right to treatment rather than simply custodial care, has been invaluable. Open wards, halfway houses, follow-up clinics, and rehabilitation services are likely to return a vast number of schizophrenics to relatively more useful lives in the community.

On the other hand, some aspects of community psychiatry have not been adequately studied. What effect do psychotic individuals have on their families and on their community when living with them in a fairly disturbed state? Anthony has studied the effect of psychotic parents on their children (1). He found three groups of disturbances among the children of such parents. In one group the disturbances of the children seemed to stem genetically from the parental psychosis. In a second group the disturbances of the children resulted from the impact of the parents on children who were overly susceptible. Third, there were transient maladjustments, antisocial behavior, or neurotic reactions to the parental psychosis. Anthony found that the latter two groups were likely to respond to separation from the psychotic influence of the parent—and that even the third group may possibly show some mitigation with therapeutic intervention. However, his findings should certainly give one thought about the maintenance in the community—or early return from the hospital to the home—of psychotics with young children. At the least, advantages and disadvantages for both the patient and the family deserve careful consideration.

From my own clinical experience there is no doubt that the siblings of psychotics suffer, certainly at least from the obsessive constraints they adopt to protect themselves against their own impulses, as they realistically perceive their siblings' impulses and illnesses as very threatening and dangerous. The question of just how disorganizing the psychotic individual is to the total family and to the community he dwells in needs to be seriously investigated. Important as it is to ensure the rights of these patients, to give them a chance to function in a community at the highest level they can manage, and not to lock them away to rot, it is also important to protect the community from *mental health pollution* by the deleterious effects on their families and the general society around them.

These concerns bring us close to the matter of the legal and ethical problems of the schizophrenic. The line between individual rights and society's rights is one that changes with the times and with the functions, ethics, and laws of the social structure. In these times of expanding technology, society is increasingly interfering in all aspects of our lives. Wiretapping, computerized data banks, and gene manipulation are but some examples of that interference. One of the thorny questions in our field is that of the role of electroshock therapy (EST) and lobotomy. There is currently heated debate over whether EST does or does not produce any long-term deficits. The history of lobotomy has been more alarming. Some of us remember patients who simply showed up on the ward one day with black eyes; they had had "icepick lobotomies" after anesthesia by EST without apparently either themselves or their families knowing exactly what had happened. Increasingly, and fortunately, regulations for the use of lobotomy have become much tighter. A review board should probably be required to determine whether every other therapeutic modality has really been tried and whether lobotomy is appropriate; in addition, the procedure itself could benefit from a great deal of technical improvement. EST is still very much a mystery with regard to its mode of action, and yet I have no doubt that at times its use is clearly indicated. It should also be recalled by critics of EST that even relatively short periods of pharmacological intervention may produce the long-lasting syndrome of tardive dyskinesia, and that use of long-acting drugs, such as Prolixin Decanoate, also involve issues of undue control. In essense, patients are potentially affected permanently by all of these interventions. The balance between the protection of rights and the opportunity for full and appropriate treatment is a delicate one.

Once upon a time, during my residency, I performed sodium pentothal interviews without much ado. The patient would lie down on the bed, the nurse would fill the syringe with 7½ grains of sodium pentothal and 10 cubic centimeters of distilled water, and I would try my best to understand what was going on beneath the hallucinations and delusions; in time I would generally succeed in having the patient maintain contact with reality by continuing with an oral administration of drugs. Luckily I never had a patient suffer a single complication or an undesirable side effect. On the other hand, when I want to perform a sodium pentothal interview today, written consent by the patient is required, and arrangements must be made in advance to have the patient taken to an operating room and to have an anesthetist in attendance, who usually insists on not only inserting the needle but administering the pentothal, according to my directions, in conjunction with caffeine to reach an optimal mental status. Although intravenous barbiturates are valuable for enabling a mute patient to communicate vital preoccupations that he may be withholding, the difficulties of arranging this type of interview are such that very often we simply have to forego it.

A similar situation holds true for research. While there is absolutely no question that patients were in the past appallingly abused as veritable guinea pigs, it is now almost impossible to conduct any psychiatric research—even administering simple questionnaires—without informed consent and written permission, which is often denied for irrational reasons. This makes potentially informative studies frustrating and often impossible to accomplish.

The Schizophrenic Syndrome

My originating and championing the use of the term "schizophrenic syndrome" and my hypothesis that the syndrome has many etiologic and pathogenic subgroups which share a variable disturbance of ego functions as the final common path, have been so successful that the literature usually makes no further reference to me as the source of the term. The idea that the syndrome may consist of several increasingly distinct subgroups of disorders is now commonly held and discussed (except by the American Psychiatric Associations's Task Force on DSM-III—

the proposed new *Diagnostic and Statistical Manual for Psychiatric Disorders*).

In most research efforts, however, this idea is not sufficiently carried through; most researchers still look for one particular disorder in all schizophrenics, even though recent research, especially as presented in the chapters of this volume, now supports the hypothesis of multiple etiology for this syndrome (31,39,43).

In 1972 I designed a multidisciplinary research project with the goal of trying to sort out such subgroups from a large sample population (6). Such subgroups might be characterized by different types of variables culled from a careful history, examination, and various testing procedures. Thus, one might posit by a priori "hunches" from history and symptomatology that one subgroup might be primarily characterized by a genetic load, another might demonstrate a more prominent experiential load, a third might be remarkable predominantly for abnormal biochemical factors, while still another subgroup might be distinguished by unusual neurophysiological findings. As an alternative to being led specifically by a priori hunches, one might instead investigate the sample population by putting it through several research "sieves." Although I was unable to obtain grant support at that time for this project, I still believe that it is, at least in principle, a sound and desirable strategic approach.

Thus, I would still suggest examining a large sample of schizophrenics for subgroups: in some of whom, for example, the genetic aspects may play a prominent role, with experiential factors of less demonstrable importance. In another part of the population sample, neurophysiological factors, such as delay in some components of the cortical evoked-response potential, might be the specific distinguishing characteristic. In a third group sociopsychological factors might be particularly outstanding, clearly showing pathological family interactions and disturbed communication patterns. Examining the whole sample of patients for evidence of biochemical disturbances, one might find a subgroup with this disorder in transmethylation or another with peculiarities of the dopamine metabolism. In some patients, for example, the history might reveal familial genetic factors with little indication that experiential factors play a role. If all patients are also carefully examined for neurophysiological factors, some may show delayed cortical evoked-response potentials or neuropsychological abnormalities, while others do not. In distinction to the first subgroup's positive family history, these latter may show no familial incident but a personal history of a difficult birth or an infantile episode of long and high fevers. I spoke of this model for research of the schizophrenic syndrome as the "mini-max model"*: a model in which in a particular subgroup one factor plays the maximum characterizing role, and other factors are of *minimal* or intermediate importance. One might, in fact, rank these four or more contributing factors according to their importance in a given patient. Careful statistical analysis might reveal subgroups distinguishable by clusters of interrelated factors with shared specific prognosis and response to therapy.

---

* The term "mini-max" is used in mathematics with a specific technical meaning, not related to its usage in the present context.

This sort of "research sieve" could provide a guide to very definite leads for subgrouping instead of the confusing and contradictory data we have now. Too many researchers have found one variable significant, and others another, while both groups probably unnecessarily invalidate each other, because they have looked for the one distinguishing factor which would characterize *all* "schizophrenics."

Another research approach of the same logical order, however, might consist of "triangulating" from various data. For instance, one might select a group of schizophrenics born in the winter months and see if, indeed, this group has a higher incidence of small capillaries in the fingernail bed (see chapter 2). The rest of the schizophrenic sample, if that were so, might possibly support the contention that their particular schizophrenic phenotype is due to viral factors, because viral infection is more frequent in winter. If so, other aspects of a viral infection should be identifiable. Similar triangulation could be used to test other hypotheses concerning etiology and pathogenesis.

A pilot study of ours, now underway, is concerned with the diagnosis and therapy of one possible subgroup of schizophrenics who also suffer from minimal brain dysfunction (MBD). The existence of this subgroup was suggested partly by ego function profiles from an extensive five-year study, which I shall discuss, and partly by clinical experience with patients who have symptomatologies and personal histories of MBD. These patients seem to be quite different from other schizophrenics. They are outstanding in their poor impulse control, which often manifests itself in their being "management problems" on the ward. Their thought processes are concrete but do not usually show overinclusiveness or excessive symbolization. From the pilot study it is not quite clear whether or not their sense of self is disturbed. Therapeutically this group, very much like hyperkinetic children, appears to respond well to imipramine, often in small doses, and usually immediately, in distinction to the therapeutic delay seen with depressed patients. On the other hand, phenothiazines do not seem to help this group; on the contrary, these patients often seem to respond to them by feeling more disorganized (28).

As a further personal progress report: I offered a detailed ego function conceptualization and assessment of the schizophrenic syndrome in my 1958 volume on schizophrenia, and presented a preliminary report on the ensuing research in my 1968 volume. Since then a five-year study by a large team under my direction culminated in the monograph, *Ego Functions in Schizophrenics, Neurotics, and Normals* (14). Besides presenting a detailed review of the literature on ego functions and discussing the problems involved in this research project in this book, we essentially showed that statistical reliability and discriminant validity in rating and distinguishing a group of schizophrenics, neurotics, and normals could be achieved with regard to their ego functions. These three diagnostic categories were clearly distinguished statistically. A factor analysis applied to the small sample of schizophrenics yielded four ego function factors; also a preliminary further statistical analysis suggested possible subgroups based on ego function profiles, although a larger schizophrenic population will apparently be needed to evaluate these subgroups. The interview guide and comprehensive scoring manual makes it possible to utilize this form of assessment, which attempts to bridge the descriptive and the dynamic aspects of psychiatry. The further theoretical goal remains: to use this assessment in an attempt to establish subgroups characterized phenomenologically by ego function, with the hope that they will eventually be shown to relate to etiologic and pathogenic ones.*

My collaborators (Dr. H. Conte, Dr. B. Meyers, and Cynthia Fielding, M.A.) and I are currently attempting to construct a scale which will be easier to administer and more subtle with regard to questions which may suggest socially desirable and undesirable answers and will at the same time be significantly shorter. We are experimenting with a specific questionnaire form and want to try to make it analogous to the form and administration of the Wechsler Adult Intelligence Scale (WAIS), for increased practical and clinical utility.

One of the EFA hypotheses currently under investigation is whether a clinical hunch of mine can be substantiated—namely, that schizophrenics, however disturbed they may be with respect to certain particular ego functions (reality testing, judgment, sense of reality, and regulation and control of drives, affects, and impulses), may have a good long-range prognosis if four other ego functions (thought processes, autonomous functioning, synthetic-integrative functioning, and mastery competence) are good.† I believe that even if the latter four functions are poor, these schizophrenics may possibly have a good short-range prognosis, but that most likely they would not have a good long-range one. The first four variables would represent primarily an indication of the severity of the acute disorder; the latter four should relate more to the biological matrix or profound early experiences.

The Center for Schizophrenia Research

To the extent to which this first chapter serves as a personal account, I would also like to report on the progress of one of my long-standing interests, the Center for Schizophrenia Research at the National Institute of Mental Health (NIMH). Ever since my 1948 book *Dementia Praecox*, I have felt strongly that a center for the coordination of schizophrenia research and dissemination of information was essential, and I pressed again for it in 1958. I was very pleased at being able to play a

---

* Actually our ego function assessment (EFA) instrument has been used for a wide variety of endeavors other than assessing schizophrenics. For example, Bellak and Meyers discussed its use in determining analyzability (16); Ciompi et al. (25) found it reliable and valid in rating assessment and progress in a group of thirty analytic patients; and significant differences in ego function were demonstrated by Milkman and Frosch (40) between amphetamine addicts and heroin addicts—among a variety of other papers and studies, some of them still in progress. The general broad scope of ego function assessment has been discussed by Bellak and Sheehy (17) with suggestions for its use in outcome studies, in forensic psychiatry, and in evaluation for third-party funding and Professional Standards Review Organization applications.

† In a personal communication Professor Dr. Luc Ciompi, chief of the Social Psychiatric University Clinic, Bern, Switzerland, reports that in a study of the predictive value of successful rehabilitation, mastery competence, synthetic functioning, and drive control were the best predictors of success.

role in the center's ultimate realization in 1968, as described in my 1968 volume.*

It has been gratifying to observe that the center's *Schizophrenia Bulletin* has come to serve the constructive and important role I had hoped for. Many of its articles and special reports are now widely reprinted.

It is also relevant to take note of the funding of research grants in the years since the center came into existence (41). Figure 1 shows that research grants primarily involving schizophrenia jumped from 6.2 million dollars in 1971 to 10.1 million in 1975, while the total NIMH funding remained at the same level of 62 million. Specifically, in 1971, 9.9 percent of the total NIMH funds went toward research in schizophrenia, while in 1975 it was 16.1 percent.

FIGURE 1

Research Grants Funding by Year in Millions

	1971	1972	1973	1974	1975
NIMH total funding	$62.5	$63.1	$56.8	$69.3	$62.8
Schizophrenia—primary involvement	$6.2	$6.6	$7.2	$10.2	$10.2

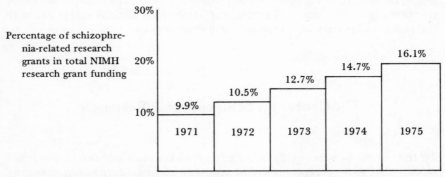

Percentage of schizophrenia-related research grants in total NIMH research grant funding

Source: Data prepared by the staff of the Center for Schizophrenic Research at the National Institute of Mental Health (Fall 1975).

The center is almost certainly the single most important international clearinghouse for work on all aspects of the schizophrenic syndrome, and possibly also the most important catalyst for systematic studies and their cross-fertilization. The importance of prompt reporting of all work in the field can hardly be overestimated.

The center still lacks one function which I had outlined in my original proposal for such a structure: it cannot play an active enough role in the spawning of new research projects. It should, however, be able to "cross-pollinate" research findings or, where important, to supplement,

---

* Bellak and Loeb (15), pp. 8, 9, 10.

modify, or reject important hypotheses. To perform this role, the center needs funds it can allocate solely at its discretion. As of now the center plays a role in research grants only by virtue of its being part of the Extramural Research Branch of the NIMH. The arguments against such independent funding are no better than the ones I heard for years against the creation of an independent center for schizophrenia research in the first place. The latter has proven its value by the role it has come to play. It is extremely likely that discretionary funds, allocated to the responsible individuals who stay most informed about the week-to-week progress of schizophrenia research, would be of seminal value.

Some Specifics

Much, if not all, of Part One of this volume might well have appeared under the heading of "Etiology" in previous volumes. It speaks for the increasing sophistication and complexity of attempts to conceptualize the etiology and the pathogenesis of the schizophrenic syndrome that this time no such single chapter heading can do the subject justice.

Sophisticated investigators are perfectly clear about the close interrelationships of biochemical and neurophysiological factors, possibly influenced by genetic instructions as well as experiential input—all of them interacting with each other.

Numerous factors have been investigated in attempts to find correlations with schizophrenic illness. The relevance of the *birth date* for the *epidemiology* of schizophrenia has alternately been accepted and rejected over the past four decades, which demonstrates in a small fashion the vicissitudes of research and the difficulty of determining when a fact is a fact. In accordance with recent epidemiological studies of the birth date of schizophrenics, it appears quite likely that even meteorological or other seasonal conditions may be a part of this input: since there seem to be more schizophrenics born in the inclement months, the possibility of some viral infection's playing a role has been considered. Some somatic findings are consistent with such a theory.

Biochemical studies of the schizophrenic syndrome show increased sophistication and improved methodology. On the other hand, we must note that the transmethylation hypothesis has celebrated its twenty-fifth anniversary without finding itself on a sounder foundation than it was years ago, and that the dopamine hypothesis—and, for that matter, the catecholamine hypothesis as related to affective illness—specifically offer less firm ground for understanding the action of psychotropic drugs today than they were believed to do only a few years ago. We must be impressed, however, by the fact that the field until recently was dominated by knowledge of only three or four neurotransmitters, while at present more than twenty-five are under investigation.

The *genetic studies* have probably caused the greatest excitement in the last ten years. While certain data concerning genetic transmission of the schizophrenic syndrome in a percentage of those so afflicted seem at present to be generally accepted and on a sounder basis than ever before, the fervor for exclusive or primary genetic determination seems to have passed its high point under repeated scrutiny. The genetic aspect is about to take its proper place as one of the etiological components in a subgroup of the schizophrenic syndrome.

The most ambitious and influential work in this field has been performed by Kety, Rosenthal, Wender, et al. (34) on a Danish population. The excellent medical records kept in that country aided their dogged efforts to study index cases, the biological and adoptive relatives of early-age adoptees, and enabled them to make several studies supporting the hypothesis of a genetic role in the transmission of schizophrenia. These studies have also uncovered a number of possible methodological difficulties, of which many were controlled for statistically by the authors, but also of which various others have been stressed by recent skeptical and critical reviewers. Benjamin (20), for example, in reviewing these studies was struck by questionable statistical techniques and by the relatively insignificant correlations found between index cases, full siblings, and parents as compared with the significant results found between index cases and half siblings. Lidz (37) pointed out that not only did a very high percentage of control adoptees also become schizophrenic (out of keeping with the incidence in the general population), but that there were significant differences in the psychopathology of the adopted index group's biological parents and the cross-fostered group's adoptive parents in the cross-fostering study (a much higher percentage of chronic schizophrenia in the former).

Benjamin's particular statistical arguments were rejected by Kety (32), who, however, readily added in the process that:

In fact, there is no doubt in our minds that important environmental determinants exist and should be elucidated by well-designated and rigorous research . . . [and] The results of all our studies have permitted us to conclude only that genetic factors operate significantly in the schizophrenic syndrome, a conclusion that should disturb only those who assume, without acceptable evidence, that schizophrenia is not a mental illness and is entirely psychosocial in origin. [p. 1136]

Just as I would be loath to ignore the genetic factors in the etiology of schizophrenia, it is certainly difficult to explain the fact that only 40 to 60 percent of monozygotic twins are concordant for schizophrenia on any exclusively genetic grounds. Kety et al. (33) attempted to approach this problem in conceptualizing a schizophrenic *spectrum* of psychopathology, including, for example, "schizoid" personalities, inadequate personalities, borderline or uncertain schizophrenia. The concept of schizophrenia as a "spectrum disorder" seems to me no different from saying that a certain degree of emotional instability, of one kind or another, is part of the common genetic pool. In that sense I think it is reasonable only to say that the *human condition* is a spectrum disorder, of which schizophrenia is a part. In chapter 3 of the present volume Cancro tackles the intricate problem of genetics in lucid detail.

In the area of *neurophysiology* increased numbers of dopamine receptors have recently been found in the mesolimbic and caudate nucleus regions of the brains of schizophrenics, which suggests that such individuals might therefore be "supersensitive" to this neurotransmitter (27). Furthermore, other research suggests that the number of such receptors and the quantitative production of neurotransmitters are affected by environmental input (27). If such findings are further supported, we may be on the verge of ceasing to view the brain as a rigid structure, and indeed we may see it as a structure more in the sense that psychoanalysts have appreciated "psychic structures"—namely, "as processes with a slow rate of change" (42).

These findings may also eventually lead us to a new neurophysiological-biochemical basis for the psychodynamic concept of "low-stimulus barrier" or, perhaps more specifically, for a susceptibility for overloading with subsequent adaptive malfunctioning. The concepts of stimulus barrier and overload have played an increasing role in my own concepts of psychopathology (10,9). I also expect that we shall eventually have a neurophysiological-biochemical basis that will correlate with the psychoanalytic concept of the synthetic-integrative function of the ego, so central to our psychodynamic understanding of psychopathology. I believe that this basis will be experimentally testable. Furthermore, just as Carpenter and Strauss in this volume (chapter 8) point out that many diagnostic and prognostic indicators of schizophrenia overlap with psychopathological conditions other than this syndrome, I believe it is likely that the neurophysiological and biochemical factors which might be commonly found in schizophrenia will also turn out not to be specific for this syndrome. Rather, I expect that they will be found to be more widely distributed, but in differing degree, over the range of our *diagnostic spectrum*. This is the sense in which I discussed in my 1958 volume* a quantitative continuum of psychopathology, with overlapping of diagnostic entities and with more quantitative, rather than qualitative, differences in evidence.

From the *psychological* point of view, a notable change in trend involves the concept of thought disorders. Ever since the early studies of Bleuler and of Cameron, thought disorders have stood in the foreground of interest in the study of schizophrenia and were considered by many as pathognomonic of the disorder. In my own research 10 percent of schizophrenics have not shown a thought disorder (14). These results were by no means isolated findings; in the literature there are numerous reports (14) of schizophrenics without thought disorders and of non-schizophrenics with thought disorders.† It appears that the strength of the concept of thought disorder was closely related to the notion of schizophrenia as a unitary "disease." As the appreciation of schizophrenia as a multifaceted syndrome has been gaining support from many areas—as several chapters in this volume also point out—it has also become obvious that we are not dealing with a clearly circumscribed group that can invariably be characterized by the unitary phenomenon of "thought disorder."

An area of considerable theoretical *and* therapeutic import is that of the *high-risk* studies, involved with identifying and following children at high risk for schizophrenia with psychological and neurophysiological

---

* Bellak (4), p. 56.
† Cancro continues to hold that a thought disorder is pathognomonic of schizophrenia, but his approach is prognostic and sophisticated, rather than relying on simple dogma (chapter 3).

measures. Longitudinal studies of this sort promise to help fill in perhaps the most embarrassing gap in our knowledge: the fact that we rarely see schizophrenic individuals much or at all before their "first break" or before generally advanced psychopathology leaves us with a terrible paucity of understanding as to what they were like before they became seriously ill, and how we might hope to identify such individuals early and allow for very *early intervention.* One potential failing in these studies has been that the means of identifying children at "high risk" has generally been the genetic technique of identifying children who have one or two schizophrenic parents. However, only a subgroup of 10 percent of all individuals labeled "schizophrenic" have a parent similarly diagnosed, and our understanding of schizophrenia as a syndrome implies that it might be dangerous to generalize findings from such studies to the entire population.

The concepts of identifiable high risk and of *prevention* are closely related. While some investigators are pessimistic about our chances for prevention, Anthony, in chapter 15, takes a highly informed and yet mildly optimistic view of this problem.

Family studies have become much more sophisticated since Frieda Fromm-Reichmann's concept of the schizophrenogenic mother and have in the last several years focused more specifically on particular aspects of deviant communication patterns in families. Unfortunately, because of considerable practical methodological obstacles, the field itself has been unable to design studies which can adequately test whether such communication patterns are more appropriately considered as the cause of an offspring's having psychopathology or as the result of this situation. It would seem that this difficulty might be better overcome if such family studies were incorporated into future planned high-risk studies.

Researchers and clinicians both have had a lively time this last decade debating the problems involved with the *diagnosis* of schizophrenia. Chronic patients on back wards probably would fulfill criteria which everyone could agree upon, if for no other reason than that their symptoms are largely *iatrogenic* and induced by *perceptual isolation*, sensory deprivations and their general social situation (7). This diagnosis is of little practical help to either researcher or clinician, however.

One of the most ambitious undertakings in the last decade was the international World Health Organization study (30), which demonstrated that clinicians trained to agree on the same symptoms as indicative of schizophrenia may show at least intracenter reliability and a moderate degree of intercenter agreement. An analogous state of affairs could have been obtained a hundred years ago regarding, for example, the diagnosis of a fever. Independent observers in different countries could have agreed at that time that the condition diagnosed as "fever" was characterized by high temperature, dehydration, fast pulse, fast respiration, etc.—but this would have brought them no closer to the many different etiologies of high fevers and the need for different treatment and different prognosis. This is not to say that once fever is diagnosed today, it is not useful to prescribe extra fluids and bed rest, but these measures are no substitute for penicillin in some cases and of an antimalarial drug in others (8).

Probably the single most relied-upon set of diagnostic criteria in the last ten years has been Schneider's first rank symptoms (FRS). Interestingly, they seemed to become the touchstone of many primarily biological psychiatrists in the United States almost fifty years after Schneider first introduced them, and after German psychiatry had lost interest in them; however, they soon enough failed to represent a theoretical or clinical salvation. Among others, Carpenter et al. demonstrated the unreliability of Schneider's FRS (23). (See chapter 8.) They were found to be present in nonschizophrenics and were not found in some schizophrenics, as diagnosed by other theoretical and clinical tools, and seem to offer no clear advantage over other criteria. Schneider's FRS were even found to give statistically significant different diagnostic rates in several strongly Schneider-oriented German clinics (two of which Schneider himself was chief of at the time of this study [36]).

It is, in fact, remarkable that there are such continuing attempts to diagnose schizophrenia when almost all authorities tend to agree now that there is probably no circumscribed entity called "schizophrenia," but rather, as I have long said, a schizophrenic syndrome with many different subgroups of different etiological and pathogenic natures contributing to a final common path. It seems pure folly to use computer diagnosis and all the sophisticated hardware of our electronic age to try to establish the nature of something that most likely does not exist. Since there is no single valid criterion, it certainly is impossible to establish construct validity for any of the many scales that have been devised to diagnose schizophrenia. Of course, a point can be made that if one wants to diagnose schizophrenia very simplemindedly—for example, by deciding that everyone who has delusions and hallucinations and does not have gross organic neurological disturbances will be called a schizophrenic—one can attain a rather high degree of agreement. On the other hand, even these criteria are likely to include cases of what at least most of European psychiatry would consider to be affective disorders. It also does not solve therapeutic and prognostic problems.

It is regrettable that as yet DSM-III just lists "schizophrenia," instead of "schizophrenic syndrome," as this makes it difficult for us to think in terms of different subgroups of schizophrenics. While the broad attempt to establish operational definitions is commendable (even if not attained), and the idea of introducing multiple axes is useful, this entire effort has been expended in the direction of diagnostic *reliability*, with almost no work toward diagnostic validity.

For myself, I favor a hierarchical diagnosis, beginning with a nomothetic one, "schizophrenic syndrome," perhaps elaborated by the several axes of DSM-III and adding ideographic information (such as ego functions) and etiological hunches (see the Epilogue).

In the past ten years we have seen crucial tests of the value and the limitations of *pharmacotherapy*. Regrettably, pharmacotherapy has not proven itself to be a cure for the schizophrenic syndrome. In most instances it affects prominently what Eugene Bleuler called the secondary symptoms—that is, delusions, hallucinations, and possibly thought disorders—but it does not affect the personality structure of schizophrenics. In fact, recent research suggests that neuroleptics may affect neurotransmitters and neuroreceptors involved in hallucinations and delusions, but that they may not significantly affect the schizophrenic personality at all. The patient often remains withdrawn, peculiar, etc., or what we might call a "silent schizophrenic." At times the neuroleptic seems to block the overloading which enables *vis medicatrix naturae*, the healing forces of nature, to do their reparative work. Whatever role the biological matrix may play in some sufferers of the schizophrenic syndrome, currently available drugs are unable to reverse the lack of cognitive development and psychosocial structure which seem to play such a critical role in the syndrome's pathogenesis. It seems unlikely that pharmacotherapy will ever effect such reversals, but we may fervently hope that someday a drug will be found which can interfere with some biological pathogenesis in children who have been identified early as high risk. Unless and until such drugs are invented, psychotherapy and psychosocial methods will get increased impetus from the disappointment with pharmacotherapy, despite the latter's great contributions to current "management" of people suffering from the schizophrenic syndrome.

Although *other somatic therapeutic* modalities for the schizophrenic syndrome are often controversial and/or not given their due, I considered it of great importance to include such a chapter in the present volume.

There is no good reason to neglect other somatic therapies, including EST in properly selected instances, merely because drug therapy is available and easy to administer, especially in view of the latter's complications, limitations, and sequelae. On the other hand, many of the favorable reports on the effects of EST and its safety were the result of studies by investigators deeply committed to EST. One could feel more reassurance if EST results and the absence of undesirable side effects were reported in double-blind studies.

The modality of *psychotherapy* of the schizophrenic syndrome sustained its most severe critique in this past decade. May (38) suggested that, in the population and setting studied, and with the personnel used, psychotherapy was of little or no value for the treatment of schizophrenics. Subsequent studies, as Gunderson and Mosher point out in chapter 12, have thrown considerable doubts on this finding.

It is still the daily experience of many of us that psychotherapy can be beneficial to schizophrenics; that is, we have been led to accept our subjective evidence as well as both the internal consistency of treatment hypotheses and the apparent relationships between therapeutic interventions and improvement in the patients so treated. Though I have treated a sizable number of schizophrenics with subjectively satisfying results over the past thirty-five years, I have never published case material or, regrettably, engaged in controlled studies. The intensive design technique which I have used for the study of psychoanalytic and psychotherapeutic effects in other patients would be a potentially powerful study tool here (19,12,13). Furthermore, I consider even brief psychotherapy of the acute exacerbations of chronic schizophrenics not only possible but extremely useful for maintaining their level of social functioning and often avoiding hospitalization (18).

On the theoretical side it is still hotly debated whether schizophrenics are qualitatively different, as those writers hold who speak of schizophrenics as having a *defect*—specifically a structural ego defect, for example, as stated in Gunderson and Mosher (29)—or whether the schizophrenic condition is primarily a result of *conflict* only quantitatively different from the conflict and symptom formation in neurotics, as, for example, stated by Arlow and Brenner (2). To my mind, this is a totally unnecessary division. Even if some schizophrenics should have a structural defect described in psychodynamic terms (that is, poor introjects, poor identification figures, poor ego structure), or even a physical structural defect (such as those seen in individuals with minimal brain dysfunction), the fact is that they still have to adapt and attempt to solve the conflict between drives, reality, and superego. Symptom formation will ensue psychodynamically whether there is a structural psychodynamic or a structural neurological defect, or when no such defect is present and we are dealing exclusively with a severe conflict between drive, superego, and reality.

Along this line I am also frankly amazed that apparently many of my contemporaries consider the interpretation of psychotic material—that is, delusions, hallucinations, and nonverbal content—as being of little value. I find that this material is both as essential and as easy to interpret as are dreams and characterological features in neuroses and character disorders and of great therapeutic value.

As for *psychosocial* treatment methods, I personally am primarily acquainted with rehabilitation workshops, which I long ago described as workshops for "habilitation" and "rehabilitation" of various ego functions (11). In a broader sense, the acquisition and the reacquisition of social roles and of object relations in such other settings seem crucial to me in both an etiologic and a pathogenic sense.

The hopes and travails of *community psychiatric* treatment of the schizophrenic syndrome were a dramatic part of the past decade, as has been briefly discussed; they will be treated in detail in chapter 13. Trial and error, overgeneralizations, and polarized "black and white" thinking unfortunately spare no human endeavor.

Prognosis, as will be pointed out in chapter 14, has made great methodological strides; but in my opinion this so far holds true mostly for actuarial pronouncements rather than for individual ones concerning a given patient. It is my personal hope that the proposed ego function assessment of the four variables I mentioned earlier may facilitate an effective individual approach for prognosis.

With regard to prognosis, a recent study by Ciompi and Müller (26, 24) is of particular interest. These authors examined a total of 5,661 psychiatric patients who had been referred by the University Clinic at Lausanne, Switzerland, and were derived from a circumscribed geographic region—namely, Kanton Waadt—of about half a million inhabitants. Their sample consists of all those above age sixty-five who had had their first hospitalization prior to their sixty-fifth year. Of the total, 1,642 were diagnosed as schizophrenic, and at the time of examination 289 were still alive and could be carefully studied.

Only a few of the highlights of their complex findings can be mentioned here as of particular relevance for the picture of the schizophrenic syndrome. The average number of years between first admission and follow-up study for this sample was thirty-seven years. In this time 47 percent of the sample was hospitalized only that one time in their life, and for two-thirds of the patients hospitalization did not last longer than six months. Similarly, the total duration of hospitalization for the entire sample was, surprisingly, less than a year for 47 percent of the probands but over twenty years for nearly a quarter of them. This shows indeed a very marked polarization, but the authors do not find any single identifiable factor or any combination of factors (including onset, type of illness, genetic or other variables) which could provide discriminant validity. Significantly, their data also definitely ran counter to any notion of schizophrenia as a progressively deteriorating process. These data hold true in the face of figures which indicate that, to start with, there were about equally as many acute as chronic patients. At the final evaluation of the total sample, 27 percent were considered as cured, 22 percent as mildly disturbed, 24 percent as moderately disturbed, and 18 percent as severely disturbed, with 9 percent of undecided outcome. Again, this adds up to the fact that just about half of all schizophrenic patients fared well eventually, though with varying courses of their illnesses. Qualitatively, the authors stress that even in advanced age the schizophrenic picture does not take on features of an organic disorder. They reported that schizophrenics tended not only not to deteriorate, but to improve, five years after first admission. This study by Ciompi and Müller almost entirely supports the findings reported earlier by Bleuler (21) and by Bleuler, Huber et al. (22)—namely, the essentially favorable course of the disorder for a majority of patients, and the highly variable nature of the course, with single or recurrent episodes. Regrettably, they also agreed that not a single factor or any combination of factors could be reliably considered prognostic.

Childhood schizophrenia was left for one of the last chapters in this volume because even its relevance for, and relationship to, the adult schizophrenic syndrome is often questioned, as is cogently pointed out in chapter 16. Its relationship to autism, which generally occurs earlier, has been particularly complex, and its lifelong course is of special interest and concern.

The *legal* and *ethical* problems related to schizophrenia are carefully considered in chapter 17, and they are certainly no less thorny than the theoretical and clinical conundrums in earlier chapters. In the end, the legal and ethical situation is perhaps most poignantly presented as the balancing of an ill individual's civil and human rights against those of his family and community.

As editor I see myself as a host presiding over a symposium, a festive gathering around a richly laden table. My overview, I hope, has served as an appetizer for the solid food for thought offered in subsequent chapters by specialized experts in the various fields of importance for the schizophrenic syndrome.

I will return with a final word as epilogue to this volume—"What the Clinician Can Do Until the Scientist Comes"—with the hope of providing a digestive in case the fare was found a bit too rich for immediate satisfaction.

BIBLIOGRAPHY

1. Anthony, J. 1969. A clinical evaluation of children with psychotic parents. *American Journal of Psychiatry* 126:177–84.

2. Arlow, J., and Brenner, C. 1964. *Psychoanalytic concepts and the structural theory* (New York: International Universities Press).

3. Bellak, L. 1948. *Dementia praecox* (New York: Grune & Stratton).

4. Bellak, L., ed. 1958. *Schizophrenia: A review of the syndrome* (New York: Logos; now distributed by Grune & Stratton).

5. Bellak, L., ed. 1964. *A handbook of community psychiatry and community mental health* (New York: Grune & Stratton).

6. Bellak, L. 1970. *A multidisciplinary etiologic study of the schizophrenic syndrome.* National Institute of Mental Health Grant MH 18395-01, 03.

7. Bellak, L., ed. 1974. *A concise handbook of community psychiatry and community mental health* (New York: Grune & Stratton).

8. Bellak, L. 1975. Intercultural studies in search of a disease. *Schizophrenia Bulletin, no. 12:* 6–9.

9. Bellak, L. 1975. *Overload: The new human condition* (New York: Behavioral Publications).

10. Bellak, L., and Berneman, N. 1971. A systematic view of depression. *American Journal of Psychiatry* 3:385–93.

11. Bellak, L.; Black, B. J.; Lurie, A.; and Miller, J. S. 1956. Rehabilitation of the mentally ill through controlled transitional employment. *American Journal of Orthopsychiatry* 26:285–96.

12. Bellak, L., and Chassan, J. B. 1964. An approach to the evaluation of drug effect during psychotherapy: A double-blind study of a single case. *Journal of Nervous and Mental Disease* 139: 20–30.

13. Bellak, L.; Chassan, J. B.; Gediman, H.; and Hurvich, M. 1973. Ego function assessment of analytic psychotherapy combined with drug therapy. *Journal of Nervous and Mental Disease* 6:465–69.

14. Bellak, L.; Hurvich, M.; and Gediman, H. 1973. *Ego functions in schizophrenics, neurotics, and normals* (New York: John Wiley).

15. Bellak, L., and Loeb, L., eds. 1968. *The schizophrenic syndrome* (New York: Grune & Stratton).

16. Bellak, L., and Meyers, B. 1975. Ego function assessment and analyzability. (*International Review of Psycho-Analysis* 2:413–27.

17. Bellak, L., and Sheehy, M. 1976. The broad role of ego function assessment. *American Journal of Psychiatry* 133:1259–64.

18. Bellak, L., and Small, L. 1965. *Emergency psychotherapy and brief psychotherapy*, 2nd ed. (New York: Grune & Stratton, 1978).

19. Bellak, L., and Smith, B. M. 1956. An experimental exploration of the psychoanalytic process: Exemplification of a method. *Psychoanalytic Quarterly* 25:385–414.

20. Benjamin, L. S. 1976. A reconsideration of the Kety and associates study of genetic factors in the transmission of schizophrenia. *American Journal of Psychiatry* 133:1129–33.

21. Bleuler, M. 1968. A 23-year longitudinal study of 208 schizophrenics and impressions in regard to the nature of schizophrenia. In *The transmission of schizophrenia*, eds. D. Rosenthal and S. S. Kety (Oxford: Pergamon Press), pp. 3–12.

22. Bleuler, M.; Huber, G.; Gross, G.; and Schuttler, R. 1976. Der langfristige Verlauf schizophrener Psychosen. Gemeinsame Ergebnisse zweier Untersuchungen. *Nervenarzt* 47:477–81.

23. Carpenter, W. T.; Strauss, J. S.; and Muleh, S. 1973. Are there pathognomonic symptoms in schizophrenia? *Archives of General Psychiatry* 28:847–52.

24. Ciompi, L. Hauptergebnisse Einer Katamnestischen Langzeituntersuchung Zum Lebensweg und Alter der Schizophrenen. *Schizophrenia Bulletin*, in press.

25. Ciompi, L.; Agué, C.; and Dauwalder, J. P. 1976. L'Objectivation de changements psychodynamiques: Expériences avec une version simplifiée des "Ego Strength Rating Scales: de Bellak et al. Communication to the Tenth International Congress of Psychotherapy (Paris, July 10, 1976).

26. Ciompi, L., and Müller, C. 1976. *Lebensweg und Alter der Schizophrenen. Eine katamnestische Langzeitstudie bis ins Senium.* (Heidelberg: Springer).

27. Edson, Lee. 1977. 4,000 scientists in California find the universe in the brain. *The New York Times*, November 13, 1977.

28. Goldstein, M. J. 1970. Premorbid adjustment, paranoid status, and patterns of response to phenothiazine in acute schizophrenia. *Schizophrenia Bulletin* 3:24–37.

29. Gunderson, J. G., and Mosher, L. R., eds. 1975. *Psychotherapy of schizophrenia.* (New York: Jason Aronson).

30. International Pilot Study of Schizophrenia. 1973. (Geneva: World Health Organization Press), vol. 1.

31. Keith, S., et al. 1976. Special report: Schizophrenia 1976. *Schizophrenia Bulletin* 2:509–65.

32. Kety, S. S. 1976. Studies designed to disentangle genetic and environmental variables in schizophrenia: Some epistemological questions and answers. *American Journal of Psychiatry*, 133: 1134–37.

33. Kety, S. S.; Rosenthal, D.; Wender, P.; et al. 1968. The types and prevalence of mental illness in the biological and adoptive families of adopted schizophrenics. In *The transmission of schizophrenia*, eds. D. Rosenthal and S. S. Kety (New York: Pergamon Press), pp. 345–62.

Chapter 1

EPIDEMIOLOGY

E. Fuller Torrey, M.D.

The epidemiology of schizophrenia is like the man of whom it has always been said: "He shows much promise!" Now approaching middle age, there is evidence that the man's perpetually latent promise may at last be ready to bloom. If it does, it will be most welcome for the schizophrenia research field. Epidemiological studies of schizophrenia have contributed remarkably little to our understanding of the disease, especially when contrasted with the contributions of epidemiological studies of chronic diseases in general (e.g., cancers) and of chronic neurological diseases in particular (e.g., multiple sclerosis).

This chapter will review developments in the epidemiology of schizophrenia over the past ten years. It will first review briefly those areas which have been of traditional concern: socioeconomic status, ethnicity, and migration. It will then discuss in more detail four areas of epidemiological research which have emerged more strongly in the past decade and which appear likely to contribute to our understanding of disorders of the schizophrenic syndrome: (1) areas of high schizophrenia prevalence; (2) areas of low schizophrenia prevalence; (3) areas with changed prevalence over time; and (4) the seasonality of births of people who become schizophrenic.

Traditional Areas of Concern

Ever since Hollingshead and Redlich published their *Social Class and Mental Illness* in 1958 (41), schizophrenia researchers in the United States have been intrigued with the question of whether or not there really is more schizophrenia among people in the lower socioeconomic classes, and if so whether it is simply a product of "drift" of schizophrenia-prone individuals to the lower classes. Hare in 1962 (35) and Mishler

and Scotch in 1963 (64) reviewed the question extensively, and Sanua
nicely summarized the conflicting evidence in the last volume of this
series (89). The question is not yet resolved, and very little new light
has been shed on it in the last decade. Ødegaard verified that in Norway
there is a relationship between schizophrenia and lower socioeconomic
class and showed that this relationship remained relatively unchanged
between 1926 and 1965 (73). On the other hand, much evidence has
come to light that the opposite is true in India, and that schizophrenia
in that country is most prevalent among the upper socioeconomic classes;
these studies are reviewed below.

Differential prevalence rates of schizophrenia in various ethnic groups
is another area of traditional epidemiological concern. Like socioeconomic status, however, the last decade has seen primarily reviews of
previous studies, with very little new data being introduced. The black-
white question in particular has been discussed; Kramer et al. (49) reviewed the many studies showing a higher schizophrenia admission rate
for blacks; while Fischer (31) strongly defended the thesis that the
apparent differences are merely the product of differential access to
hospital care and of racist diagnostic practices.

Murphy's work in fourteen Canadian villages is the major recent piece
of work in this research area (67,70). He found a significantly higher
prevalence of schizophrenia in Old French villages compared with either
"New French" (less traditional) villages or those whose major ethnic
composition was Anglo-Protestant, Irish Catholic, Polish, or German. He
also found more schizophrenia among Catholics compared with non-
Catholics, most marked for males. Murphy's own explanation of his findings is a sociocultural one: "namely that there is some element of Roman
Catholic tradition which is more conducive to schizophrenia in Canada
than the corresponding aspect of Protestant tradition" (67).

Finally, patterns of schizophrenia among migrants have continued to
be of interest to epidemiologically inclined researchers; although as in
the other areas of traditional concern, there have been remarkably few
recent studies to push the field forward. Excellent reviews of studies up
to 1969 are contained in two reviews by Sanua (89,90). He summarizes
the findings showing "that overseas emigration, and intracontinental
emigration, with some exceptions is related to an increase of mental
illness" including schizophrenia (89). A recent review by Morrison (66)
summarizes the difficulties and variables inherent in migrant studies,
including various reasons for leaving an old environment, reasons for
choosing a new environment, the stress of the move, attitudes of people
in the new environment toward the migrant, and homogeneity of the
new environment, as well as the differences in the personalities and
life experiences of the migrants themselves. It is little wonder that
migrant studies have yielded contradictory results.

Two recent developments in this area are noteworthy. First, Rosenthal
et al. (87) reported that in Denmark there is evidence that individuals
who are preschizophrenic do not tend to emigrate in disproportionate
numbers; indeed, if the data points in any direction at all, it is in the
opposite direction. The question of preselection for emigration of schizophrenia-prone individuals has been hotly debated for years, with little
hard data available until this study.

The other development is an extension of the work of Krupinski and Stoller on the schizophrenia rate among European immigrants to Australia. Previously they had shown that Eastern European immigrants had a schizophrenia admission rate at least twice that for immigrants from Southern or Western Europe, five times that for British immigrants, and up to seven times that for Australians (50,51). The most likely explanation was thought to be the wartime experiences of the Eastern European immigrants. Recently, however, they tested this hypothesis and found that it was incorrect: "the Jewish refugees who had suffered the most severe war experiences had the lowest prevalence of schizophrenia in both sexes" (52). Thus there is currently no satisfactory explanation for their striking findings.

In contrast to the relative paucity of new research in the areas of socioeconomic status, ethnicity, and migration, the last decade has seen the publication of several important papers opening up new areas of concern. It now appears that there are areas of high schizophrenia prevalence, other areas of low prevalence, and still others in which the prevalence has changed. In addition, it is now clear that there is a seasonality of schizophrenia births. Both the ideas of differing prevalence and seasonality of birth are old ideas in schizophrenia research, which had long since been discarded. They have returned from the old clothes box, however, garbed in shiny new chi squares.

Areas of High Prevalence

Since 1970 two separate studies have been published suggesting that there are areas of the world in which the prevalence of schizophrenia is unusually high. If such studies are confirmed, they could provide clues to the etiology of schizophrenia and be major boons to research.

The first of these studies is the work of Lemkau, Kulcar, Crocetti, and Kesic in Yugoslavia, which was published in 1971 following ten years of research (11,54,and57). The high-prevalence area consists of portions of the Croatian coast including the Istrian peninsula, the area around Rijeka, and adjacent islands such as Krk and Susak. The area is quite wealthy by Yugoslav standards and contains a genetically mixed population of approximately 400,000 Croats, Italians, Austrians, Hungarians, Czechs, and Rumanians (10). The population has not been isolated or inbred and has had longstanding cultural ties to nearby Trieste and to Austria.

Belief in a high prevalence of insanity in this area dates back at least one hundred years (10). These beliefs received additional impetus from a 1933 study showing high schizophrenia rates in this area (10), a World War II rejection rate for schizophrenia in this area twice that for the rest of Croatia (10), and a 1957 study showing a high prevalence of schizophrenia on the island of Susak (89).

The confirmatory research was carried out in three phases beginning in 1961 (57). First, all hospitalized psychiatric patients in Croatia were identified, and a case register was set up. It was found that the prevalence rate for hospitalized psychotic patients was approximately twice as high in the study area compared with the rest of Croatia. Schizophrenia was elevated, but so, too, were all other psychoses; the differences were significant at a level of p<.001.

The second phase was to determine whether the twofold difference in hospitalization rates accurately reflected differences in prevalence in the community. Labin, a village from the study area, was selected for a house-to-house survey by medical students and then compared with surveys of three villages from the rest of Coatia (54). Survey techniques were standardized, and all suspected cases were interviewed by a psychiatrist. Over a two-year period 26,327 interviews were completed.

The village survey revealed that Labin had a prevalence rate for schizophrenia more than twice as high as the three control villages (p<.001). Even more surprising was the fact that manic-depressive psychosis was almost four times higher in Labin as in the control villages. This confirmed the findings of the hospitalization rates and showed that not only was schizophrenia elevated but so also was manic-depressive psychosis.

The third phase of the research was to determine whether the findings in Labin were true for other parts of the study area, or whether they were idiosyncratic in a single village. Therefore, a probability sample of Croatia was determined, and twenty-two cluster samples (each with about two hundred households) were selected for house-to-house interviews (11). The methodology and interview techniques were carefully monitored. Again, it was found that schizophrenia and manic-depressive psychosis were elevated (p<.025) in the study area compared with the rest of Croatia, although the differences were not quite twofold. In this phase, data was also collected on place of birth and migration status, and it was found that the higher schizophrenia and manic-depressive rates applied only to the indigenous population and not to those who had immigrated.

Thus, it appears clear that one part of Croatia has a schizophrenia prevalence rate roughly twice the rate of the remainder of the province. The same difference appears to be true for manic-depressive psychosis as well, implying that whatever the etiology of the difference, it is not unique to schizophrenia. This is particularly interesting in view of recent biochemical and genetic research indicating that schizophrenia and manic-depressive psychosis are probably quite distinct diseases. The Yugoslavia study indicates that in-migration is not the cause of the differences in rate, although selective concentration of the schizophrenic population through out-migration has not been ruled out. Genetic explanations for the differences seem unlikely because of the genetic diversity and small amount of inbreeding in the affected area, but genetics must be further explored. Similarly sociocultural and biological (e.g., nutritional) factors remain to be explored.

The work in Ireland is still in progress but is equally intriguing. The belief that Ireland produces an excess number of insane persons dates to at least 1894 when both Tuke (104) and Drapes (22) noted it. The latter concluded that:

> Ireland, alone of all civilized countries . . . possesses the unique and un-enviable distinction of a continuously increasing amount of insanity with a continuously decreasing population . . . the proportional rate of increase in Ireland is far beyond what exists elsewhere. [p. 519]

Dawson in 1911 noted the same thing (15); he further attempted to correlate insanity rates by county with emigration rates and concluded that there was no relationship.

Meanwhile, in the United States, Irish immigrants were turning up strikingly often in mental hospitals; they were diagnosed as having both schizophrenia and alcoholism. Murphy reviewed the many studies of Pollock, Malzberg, and others demonstrating this situation (69), and concluded that Irish immigrants to the United States did indeed have a very high admission rate for schizophrenia from 1911 to 1930, and that after that date their rate slowly decreased. A recent study of Irish immigrants in London confirmed that their schizophrenia hospitalization rate is not elevated at this time (2).

Then in the 1970s Walsh and O'Hare published figures indicating that the first-admission rate for schizophrenia in Ireland is still very high, be-tween two and five times the rate in England and Wales (76,107). The excess came predominantly from western Irish counties, which are principally rural. Work is currently in progress to ascertain whether these geographical differences are also reflected in cases of schizophre-nia in the community; in addition, the seasonality and place of birth of schizophrenics is being examined.

Despite Dawson's inability to relate schizophrenia rates to emigration rates in 1911, it has been customary on both sides of the Atlantic to ascribe the high schizophrenia rate among the Irish to the unusually extensive emigration of their population. In the United States it was said that schizophrenics from Ireland selectively immigrated and so produced the high rates. In Ireland it was said that schizophrenics were selectively left behind (or selectively returned from the United States) and that this produced the high rates. One thing is clear: both cannot be true. Whether either is true remains to be ascertained.

Several other explanations for the apparently high schizophrenia rate in western Ireland have been proposed. Genetic explanations proposed by some (75) have been denied by others (69) because of the genetic diversity and strong sanctions against inbreeding among the Irish. Dalen (14) suggested that a partial explanation may be associated with advanced maternal age at birth. Excess numbers of available hospital beds (6) and excess numbers of schizophrenogenic mothers (69) have also been proposed, and Murphy (67) elaborated a theoretical explana-tion based on communication patterns in Irish families and villages:

> It will be seen, I think, that the type of confrontation which appears to be schizophrenia-evoking in these communities has some similarities to the types of confrontation which are believed to be schizophrenogenic within families. [p. 145]

Except for an attempt to correlate schizophrenia with celiac disease in Ireland, which proved negative (16), biological explanations of the apparently excessive schizophrenia rate have not been undertaken.

The fact that there are areas of high schizophrenia prevalence should not be too surprising. Book's methodologically very careful study of northern Sweden twenty years ago revealed a schizophrenia prevalence rate of 9.6 per 1,000, approximately two to three times the rate for the rest of Sweden (5). And Field's study of a small area of rural Ghana found a similarly high rate (30). Given the recent work in Yugoslavia and Ireland, it is now necessary to take these older studies more seriously.

Areas of Low Prevalence

Less conclusively documented but more numerous in numbers are studies of areas of apparent low prevalence of schizophrenia. Since virtually all such areas are in less technologically advanced regions, they are necessarily much less productive of accurate epidemiological research. Prior to 1970 there were a plethora of reports of low prevalence of schizophrenia in Brazil (17), Ghana (100), Zaire (29,30), Malawi (94), Tanzania (98), Kenya (9,21,34), the Marshall Islands (59), Saipan (44), and the rural Soviet Union (1); but most of these studies were anecdotal or, at best woefully deficient in epidemiological methodology. Two studies which showed a low prevalence and whose methodology was relatively sound, however, were Eaton and Weil's study of the Hutterite communities in the United States (27) and Rin and Lin's study of Formosan aborigines (86): the schizophrenia prevalence rate in the former was 1.0 per 1,000 and in the latter 0.9 per 1,000. Both studies have been reviewed in previous volumes.

In the past ten years another study has emerged showing an apparently very low prevalence of schizophrenia in a developing area, and further data has been published from India highlighting the unusual prevalence pattern of schizophrenia in that country. The first is the work of Torrey et al. in Papua, New Guinea (101). This work was stimulated by Seligman's 1929 observation there that "in the villages among the natives leading their own normal life" there was no psychosis (92). Seligman, who was both physician and anthropologist, did note six cases of psychosis among "natives" who were living along the coast in close contact with European settlers. More recently Burton-Bradley, a psychiatrist who has been in Papua, New Guinea, for two decades, noted that "bush" individuals from rural areas rarely present with schizophrenia, although they may present as acute reactive psychoses (7,8).

To ascertain the validity of these observations, all psychiatric records for mainland Papua, New Guinea, were examined for the period January 1970 through May 1973, a total of 1,450 records. Only cases in which overtly psychotic signs and symptoms were present were selected out. Psychoses with fever or organic disease, postpartum psychoses, and mixed diagnoses (e.g., schizophrenia with mental retardation, schizophrenia with epilepsy) were not included. Mixed-race individuals were also excluded.

The result was 478 individuals admitted at least once during the study period. They were then divided into three groups:

1. Acute psychosis (332 cases): One or two admissions, each lasting less than three months, with rapid and apparently complete recovery. The majority of these occurred in contract laborers brought from one area to another to work.
2. Schizophrenia (121 cases): Hospitalization for longer than three months, or more than two hospitalizations, with classical signs and symptoms of schizophrenia.
3. Manic-depressive psychosis (25 cases): Multiple admissions for mania and/or depression.

The cases of psychosis were then divided by district of birth of the person. This information was available on the records and is considered to be accurate since it is the person's primary identification. Mainland Papua, New Guinea is divided into thirteen mainland districts, of which the nine coastal districts have had intermittent contact with Western influence and technology for approximately seventy-five years, and the four highland districts for only half that time. There are some areas of the highlands where first contact between natives and Europeans occurred only in the last ten years.

The results of the division of schizophrenic patients by district revealed a concentration greater than expected in four coastal districts (Gulf, Central, Morobe, and Milne Bay), approximately the expected number in two other coastal districts (Western and Northern), and a striking paucity of schizophrenic patients in the four highland districts and in three other coastal districts (Madang, East Sepik, West Sepik). Of the seven districts with too few schizophrenic patients, four were statistically significant at a level of $p<.01$ and three at $p<.05$. Prevalence in the highest district (Morobe) was twenty-two times that in the lowest (East Sepik); in the Madang district, with a population of 150,000, there was not a single case. Also interesting is the comparison of two contiguous districts, both with populations of approximately 200,000 people: Morobe, which is coastal and was colonized by Germany in the nineteeth century, had thirty-one cases; whereas Eastern Highlands, which is mountainous and was contacted only three decades ago, had but three cases.

Even if all the cases of acute psychosis are assumed to have really been schizophrenia, the picture does not change very much; low-prevalence districts have less than one-fifth the number of patients compared with high-prevalence districts. The population of the four highland districts at the time of the study was 842,000. If schizophrenia occurred with approximately the same prevalence in these districts as it occurs in Northern Europe (4–5 per 1,000), then they should have had between 3,000 and 4,000 schizophrenic patients there. Yet over three and one-half years only 18 cases of definite schizophrenia and 87 cases of acute psychosis were hospitalized.

Because of these dramatic differences, possible sources of error were carefully examined. The case records were examined for regional bias and differential accessibility to medical care; the possibility that schizophrenic patients had been killed in some areas was considered; and the effects of migration were examined. None of these factors were found sufficient to explain the markedly low prevalence of schizophrenia in some parts of Papua, New Guinea.

It should also be noted that the Papua, New Guinea, study found suggestions of schizophrenic case-clustering in some subdistricts. As far as is known to the author, the only other suggestions of such clustering in the literature are an old study from England (60) and a recent one from Malaysia (48).

The other significant work on low prevalence of schizophrenia to emerge in the past decade comes from India and shows that the disease is differentially concentrated in certain castes. Among other castes schizophrenia appears to have a very low prevalence.

The antecedents of the recent work date to 1930, when a British-trained psychiatrist in Ranchi (Bihar State) noted (18) that

those Indian communities highly advanced in Western civilization and culture, such as the Anglo-Indians, Parsees, the educated section of the Bengalis etc., are more prone to this form of psychosis [schizophrenia]. [p. 260]

Simultaneously, in Poona (Maharashtra State) another psychiatrist was independently making the same observation (91).

Since 1966 these observations have been confirmed five separate times. A study by Rao in Ranchi provided the breakdown of first-admission schizophrenic patients by caste. Out of ten castes the highest numbers of schizophrenic patients came from the brahmins (the aristocracy), the bania (the traders), the rajputs (the landowners), and the kayasthas (the civil servants). The brahmins and the kayasthas are the castes with the highest literacy, and the banias have the highest socioeconomic status and are the most urbanized (82,83). Rao's work was confirmed by Saxena et al. (91) in the same hospital in 1972, with the brahmins and kayasthas again found to be overrepresented among schizophrenia patients.

Five years later Rao participated in a psychiatric survey of a village in West Bengal State. Six cases of schizophrenia were found, all from the two highest castes. By contrast other forms of mental disorder were found to be more prevalent among the lower castes. The authors concluded (28) that "it is noteworthy that the highest prevalence of schizophrenia is in the socially and economically advanced groups."

Two other village surveys found the same thing. Dube in Agra (Uttar Pradesh State) found 64 persons with schizophrenia in a survey of 29,468 Indians (23,24). The highest prevalence rates by castes were among the vaish (business or trade) and the brahmins (aristocracy and priests), both high-ranking castes educationally and socioeconomically. This caste distribution for schizophrenia was not found for "other psychoses," however. Thus, "the distribution of schizophrenia according to caste is different from the distribution of other psychoses." Another interesting finding was that whereas the schizophrenic patients as a group tended to come from more highly educated castes, the schizophrenics themselves were not highly educated. The trend, in fact, was in the opposite direction, although it was not significant. This finding contradicts that of Dhunjibhoy (18) and may be explained by postulating that early symptoms of the disease may force the preschizophrenic person to drop out of the educational system.

A final village survey, not yet completed, is the work of Kapur, a British-trained psychiatrist and epidemiologist, in Kota (Karnataka State) in South India (45). With an Indian Psychiatric Survey Schedule as an interview instrument, the plan was to sample approximately 4,500 persons in the town. As of 1975, nine cases of psychosis (including all schizophrenic patients) had been identified and all nine were from the brahmin caste, the wealthiest and best educated caste, despite the fact that they comprised less than one-third of the study group.*

What do these findings mean? Why should schizophrenic patients be concentrated in more highly educated and/or wealthier castes? If only hospitalized schizophrenic patients were included in these studies, it would be reasonable to dismiss the results as a biased sample of those who utilize the limited hospital facilities in India. Since field studies of nonhospitalized schizophrenic patients (see references 24, 28, and 45) have found the same thing, however, the findings cannot be so lightly dismissed. And their unanimity over almost forty years is impressive.

Change in Prevalence

Perhaps even more intriguing than areas of high- or low-schizophrenia prevalence is the possibility that there are areas where the prevalence dramatically changes. The past decade has seen an awakening of this idea in epidemiological research.

One apparent example is the case of the Achinese people in northern Sumatra. Although originally published in 1920 by Van Loon in German, it has recently been extensively summarized by H. B. M. Murphy (68, 105). The Achinese people were visited around the turn of the century by a Dutch physician with an interest in anthropology; and he noted that serious mental disorders were rare among them. According to Murphy (68):

Twenty years later, after a period of continuous war and attrition, a psychiatrist was commissioned to do a survey of mental illness in the same people, the reason for his commission being that the local governor had been struck by the unusual frequency with which he encountered insane people during his local travels. The psychiatrist, Van Loon, found that in a neighboring, non-Achinese people that had taken little part in the war the prevalence of mental illness was very low, namely five cases in a population of twenty-six thousand, but that in the Achinese it was very high, reaching twenty cases per thousand in places. Most of the mental illness which he found was schizophrenia of many years' duration, and it affected men much more than women. When we ask what changes had occurred between these two visits one answer is that venereal disease had become widespread thanks to the misuse of the Achinese women by the conquering soldiery, but the other thing is that the Achinese warriors had been defeated and now had little role in their own land, the women running most of the communal affairs. If the Achinese had had roughly the same level of schizophrenia as other Malaysian peoples in Sumatra before this war, as seems likely from the earlier report and from other clues, then one must think of at least a five-fold increase in the disease over the period. . . . [p. 409]

* R. L. Kapur 1973: personal communication.

Murphy explains this apparent rise in schizophrenia on psychosocial grounds. Whatever the case, it does appear to be an example of a group with a low prevalence of schizophrenia, followed by a rapidly rising rate after twenty years of continuous warfare.

A more carefully documented example of change is the work of Meyer Fortes, an anthropologist also trained in psychology, in Ghana. From 1934 to 1937 he spent two and one-half years studying Tallensi villages in northern Ghana. During that period he observed in a population of approximately 5,000, only one psychotic individual, a twenty-two-year-old man who had become ill in adolescence. When talking to Fortes, the man's attention "frequently wandered and a vacuous look spread over his face" (32). Although more clinical information is not given, it appears that he might have had schizophrenia.

In 1963 Fortes returned to the Tallensi villages for two and one-half months, this time accompanied by his wife, Doris Mayer, who was a board-certified psychiatrist. In the same villages where twenty-seven years earlier there had been a single psychotic, there now were seventeen. Of these Dr. Mayer diagnosed thirteen as having schizophrenia, and one each with manic-depressive psychosis and involutional depression. Borderline or doubtful cases were excluded. A history was obtained from a family member, and each patient was interviewed in his or her own home. Of the thirteen patients with schizophrenia, nine were from the same Tallensi villages and four were Gorensi from nearby areas. The symptoms of the nine Tallensi schizophrenic patients, on which more data are supplied, included thought disorder, flat or inappropriate affect, bizarre behavior, delusions, and hallucinations (nine in all). Ages of onset for the nine were 14, 21, 22, 23, 27, 28, 31, 33, and 45. Trypanosomiasis (which may mimic schizophrenia) and neurological diseases were specifically examined for, "and so far as I could tell by crude clinical methods [trypanosomiasis] was not a factor in any of these cases." Two cases had predominantly paranoid symptoms, and another was catatonic. Thus, it seems likely that these patients did indeed have schizophrenia.

Drs. Mayer and Fortes themselves were convinced that the dramatic rise in schizophrenia in the twenty-seven-year period was real, and that it could not be explained by population growth (32):

> What was quite startling, from my point of view, is that several of these cases occurred in families which were basically the same in structure in 1963 as in the early period. I knew some of the patients as young wives or youths or children. These were the families of my best friends and informants, some of whom are still living. Had such cases occurred among them in 1934–37 I could not have missed them. [p. 50]

Tallensi elders were also convinced that there had been a sharp rise in insanity.

The authors rejected the possibility that cases of schizophrenia had simply been missed in the earlier study: "I doubt this, since sufferers are never hidden from public knowledge." Similarly they rejected the explanation that schizophrenic patients in the earlier period had simply been allowed to starve:

> This view is not tenable, for then, as now, food and shelter were always available to a madman even if he was so violent as to require putting "in log"

[putting his foot through a log, so that he could not run around and be destructive]. [p. 52]

The villages under study had of course become much more developed and exposed to technology in the interim between the studies. Schools, missions, bicycles, radios, canned goods, and gin had all become prevalent. In addition to this influx of technology into the Tallensi villages, the authors noted that an unsual number of those who became psychiatrically ill had traveled to southern Ghana (the more urbanized and technologically advanced area) prior to the onset of their illness: Overall, ten of the seventeen "had become ill during or soon after a trip to Southern Ghana for work." H. B. M. Murphy (68) believes that the psychosocial stress encountered on this trip is the key to understanding the rapid increase in schizophrenia among these people:

> On that trip they might have met new foods or new infections, but the one thing we know them to have met was a new social orientation which severely challenged Tallensi traditional values. It seems likely that this trip to the coast was relevant to the development of the schizophrenia and that of the various environmental changes experienced there the social one was the most stressful. At the earlier period the Tallensi travelled less and met less challenging conditions when they did so. [p. 414]

Biological factors must of course be considered as well, but they have not been explored to date.

One final observation by Drs. Mayer and Fortes is of interest. Despite the large number of schizophrenic patients they observed among the Tallensi people in 1963, it was their impression that schizophrenics were even more numerous among the neighboring Gorensi. This group, according to the authors, had become even more westernized than the Tallensi.

In the literature there are few other documented examples of apparent abrupt change in schizophrenia prevalence. In 1957 Shepherd published an analysis of schizophrenia admission rates for Buckinghamshire County in England; this analysis showed that the schizophrenia rate dropped from 9.7 admissions per 100,000 in 1931–33 to 5.3 per 100,000 in 1945–47 (95). The 1931–33 figure he believes is very conservative and probably was actually 14 or 15. Although he examined a variety of possibilities which might explain the drop, none of them provided a satisfactory answer, and to date Shepherd continues to believe that the decrease was real.*

An unexplained decrease in admissions for schizophrenia was also reported by Dohan in Finland, Sweden, and to a lesser extent, Norway during World War II (20). Diagnostic changes, administrative changes, deferred admissions, and decreased population at risk were all examined and found to provide inadequate explanations for the decrease. Ødegaard (72) also believed the decrease was real in Norway but said that, except for this brief period, there was not a significant change in the prevalence of schizophrenia in Norway between 1926 and 1955 (73).

In the United States it is now generally acknowledged that there has not been any significant change in the prevalence of schizophrenia in this century, despite earlier reports to the contrary. In recent years Dun-

---

* M. Shepherd 1977: personal communication.

ham has published data showing no change in seven states between 1910 and 1950 (25). And Kuriansky et al. have shown that when diagnostic standards were controlled for, there was no change in schizophrenia prevalence in New York State between 1932 and 1941 and between 1947 and 1956 (55). It would appear, then, that epidemiologists looking for changes in the prevalence of schizophrenia should look elsewhere than the United States.

Seasonality of Schizophrenic Births

Another important area of epidemiological investigation which has opened up in the last few years is the seasonal birth patterns for those people who later in life are diagnosed as schizophrenic. The basis for such an idea dates to Hippocrates:

Whoever wishes to pursue properly the science of medicine must proceed thus. First he ought to consider what effects each season of the year can produce; for the seasons are not all alike, but differ widely both in themselves and at their changes.*

However it was not until the early 1970s that Hippocrates' idea began to bear fruit in the field of psychiatry.

Scattered reports of a seasonal pattern of schizophrenic births, with an excess number having occurred in the winter and spring months, have appeared in the psychiatric literature since 1929. These early studies were marked by inadequate sampling and controls and, for these reasons, do not appear to have had a significant impact on schizophrenia research. In the United States in particular they were ignored, and this tendency was further exacerbated by Barry and Barry's 1964 paper in the *Archives of General Psychiatry* (3), in which the seasonality was attributed to social-class differences of the sampled and control populations. As late as 1974 a paper, published in the *American Journal of Psychiatry*, ridiculed the notion of a seasonality of schizophrenic births; signs of the zodiac were used instead of calendar months, and the total schizophrenic N of the study was an absurdly low 22 (109).

Meanwhile in Europe the idea was being pursued seriously. Beginning in 1968, in a careful, well-controlled study, Hare (36,37) demonstrated that there was a significant excess of schizophrenic births in between January and March in England and Wales. Dalen (12,13) was simultaneously getting almost identical results in a large study in Sweden, and by 1974 these results had also been replicated by Ødegaard (74) in Norway and by Videbech et al. (106) in Denmark. In 1975 Diebold (19) published an analysis of a small sample of schizophrenic births in Germany with slightly different results: the significant birth peak for schizophrenia occurred in November, December, and January, with February and March actually having a deficit of schizophrenic births. Thus, if this

---

* Hippocrates, *Airs, Waters and Places.*

study is replicated in a larger sample, it would appear that the peak occurs earlier in the winter months in Germany than it does in Scandinavia or England and Wales.

In the United States an analysis of 53,584 schizophrenia births in nineteen eastern and southern states was published by Torrey et al. (103) in 1977. The controls were the general births in the same states for the same years. A highly significant peak in schizophrenic births was found from December to May, most marked for the months of March and April. However, there appeared to be regional differences in the pattern, with the seasonality most marked in the New England and midwestern states and much less pronounced in southern states.

Most recently Shimura et al. (96) analyzed data on schizophrenic births in Japan. They found a pattern strikingly similar to that in the United States, with a significant excess of such births in April. For schizophrenics born prior to 1900 the maximum excess was in May, which raises the possibility that there has been a shift in the seasonal pattern of schizophrenic births over the last one hundred years.

Findings in Northern Hemisphere countries immediately raised the question whether or not there were unique factors above the equator. Thus Dalen and Roche (13) published findings on a sample of schizophrenic births in South Africa where the seasons are reversed. They found that there was indeed a predominance of schizophrenic births from May to October during the South African winter, but that this excess achieved statistical significance only for female schizophrenic births. Parker and Neilson (77), looking at the same issue in New South Wales, Australia, also reported a significant winter excess for female schizophrenics but not for males. On the other hand, Krupinski et al. (53) found no significant seasonal pattern of schizophrenic births in Victoria, Australia.

To date this epidemiological line of inquiry is raising more questions than it is answering, but the questions are fascinating ones. Furthermore, the data are available to answer most of them, if we make the effort to pursue them. Some of the questions are:

1. Do mental disorders other than schizophrenia also show a pattern of seasonality of birth? The answer to date is very unclear, with data available on both sides of the question. The majority of studies have found little or no excess in winter births for other psychiatric conditions, although some have found an excess for manic-depressive psychosis (37) or neurotic disorders (77). What is clear is that until this question is settled, other hospitalized mental patients should not be used as the sole control group when analyzing schizophrenic birth patterns.

2. Has there been a change in schizophrenic birth seasonality over time? The recent study from Japan (96) suggests that this is a possibility. And in the United States there is evidence in Illinois that the maximum excess of schizophrenic births in patients born between 1860 and 1915 was December and January, whereas for patients born between 1922 and 1955, it was March and April (81,103).

3. What is the magnitude of the seasonal excess in schizophrenic births? This question is also not resolved, but most studies estimate it to be between 7 percent and 10 percent. There are exceptions, however. Dalen reported a June excess for northern Sweden of 17 percent (13), and

Torrey et al. found that June schizophrenic births in South Carolina were actually 91 percent in excess (70 expected, 134 occurred) (103). Moreover, it is not known whether the factors causing the excess are exclusively seasonal or just more prevalent during certain seasons, so it is not possible to say how many schizophrenic births are actually affected by the seasonal factor or factors.

4. Is the seasonality only found for certain subgroups of schizophrenic patients? This is also relatively virgin ground. Paranoid schizophrenics were compared with other schizophrenic births in two states by Torrey et al. (103), but no differences were found. On the other hand, Kinney and Jacobsen (47) found more evidence of excessive winter births among schizophrenics without a family history of the disease ("low risk") than among those with a family history ("high risk"). Since it is generally accepted now that schizophrenia is probably a heterogeneous condition, a next logical step would appear to be to look for common factors in those schizophrenic patients who show a pronounced seasonality of birth.

5. The biggest question, of course, is the etiology of the observed seasonality. Some of the possibilities include:

a. *Selection of patients:* Since most state hospitals have a disproportionate number of patients from the lower socioeconomic class, it may be hypothesized that the apparent seasonality of schizophrenic births is merely a function of a different general birth pattern for the lower socioeconomic class, as concluded by Barry and Barry (3). Contrary to this hypothesis, however, are the findings in England (38), Norway (74), and the United States (103).

b. *Different pattern of conception* of parents likely to give birth to schizophrenic children: A recent study in Sweden of the births of well siblings of schizophrenic patients indicated that the siblings had a seasonal birth pattern similar to the schizophrenics (62). In England the results were less clear, because manic-depressive patients were mixed with schizophrenic patients in the study (39). Thus, this remains open as one, at least partial, explanation.

c. *Nutritional factors:* Since the nutrition of pregnant mothers and infants varies in different seasons, it is reasonable to hypothesize that such variations, by causing brain damage, could account for the seasonality of schizophrenic births. Pasamanick and Knobloch (79) proposed that protein deficiency occurs most commonly in summer months, the first trimester for winter births, and that this produces both more schizophrenic and more mentally retarded individuals. They even claimed to have found more schizophrenics born in the winters following hotter summers rather than cooler summers. An attempt to replicate this study among schizophrenic patients in Sweden produced negative results (62). Other nutritional theories proposed have included a deficiency of vitamin C (71) or of vitamin K (13) during the winter months; the latter is associated with an increased bleeding tendency (hemorrhagic disease of the newborn) which could cause brain damage.

d. *Environmental factors:* It is quite possible that a seasonal environmental factor, affecting the brain of the fetus or infant, could account for the seasonality of schizophrenic births. Petersen, for example, explained the findings in his 1934 study by postulating that spring (the time of conception for the peak midwinter schizophrenic births in his study) was a particularly unstable time meteorologically, and that this somehow affected the products of conception and produced schizophrenia (81). A more sophisticated version of this theory was used by Jongbloet when, in an attempt to explain the seasonality of birth of children with chromosomal aberrations, he suggested that climatological factors influence the estrous cycle in women and interfere with the maturation of the egg (43).

An interesting study of the possible effect of exposure to organophosphorus compounds producing schizophrenia was published by Gershon and Shaw in 1961 (33). Although Stoller et al. failed to replicate their findings (99), this kind of approach would seem to be appropriate in view of the seasonality of schizophrenic births.

Environmental factors which have been postulated as causing seasonality in congenital anomalies should also be considered in schizophrenia. LeVann studied radioactivity (fallout from nuclear bomb tests) and rainfall in Alberta in an attempt to explain the seasonality of congenital anomalies there (58). Record postulated that the seasonality of anencephaly in Scotland was related to the amount of sunshine (84). And Renwick's study of anencephaly and its possible relationship to the seasonality of alkaloids in blighted potato tubers, ingested by the mother, is a classic in the search for teratogens (85).

Environmental factors which produce mental retardation should also be kept in mind. A recent report suggested that high levels of lead in the drinking water ingested by pregnant mothers may cause mental retardation (4). Another study found that high blood-lead levels in children were related to lower intelligence (56). Presumably exposure to heavy metals such as lead can vary seasonally and therefore must be considered in exploring the seasonality of schizophrenic births.

e. *Genetic factors:* If genetic damage occurs more in certain seasons, then a genetic mechanism might account for the seasonality of schizophrenic births. For example, children born in March and April are conceived in June and July, which are among the hotter months. Furthermore, there may be a genetic predisposition to schizophrenia which makes individuals more susceptible to seasonal environmental factors. Both the gene and the environmental factor would be necessary but not sufficient factors in themselves. Alternatively, Hare and Price have suggested that the theoretical schizophrenic genotype may confer an increased robustness on the child (e.g., greater resistance to infection), leading to increased survival of affected babies who would otherwise have died in the harsh winter months (36).

f. *Infectious agents:* Since many infectious agents have a seasonality, they must also be considered as possible explanations for the seasonality of schizophrenic births. Viruses in particular are of interest because of their ability to remain latent for twenty years or longer, of their ability to disrupt cell function without affecting cell structure (110), and of the neurotropism which many of them exhibit (42). At least fifteen viruses are known which cause infections in fetuses (65), and rubella, measles, and varicella-zoster in particular have seasonal peaks in the late winter and early spring. An interesting model of viral-induced seasonality of disease is the October-January peak of children born with congenital ductus arteriosus, thought to be related to the spring peak of rubella (88). Other evidence for a viral causation of some cases of schizophrenia has been summarized elsewhere (102).

It is also of interest that seasonality has been described for some complications of pregnancy and for some congenital anomalies. Uterine bleeding during pregnancy in New York City was found to occur disproportionately in the first three months of the year (78). Spontaneous abortions have an increased frequency in late winter and early spring in New York City (40), and in March to June in Montreal (61). Stillbirths in the United States have a peak seasonality in winter and spring, especially in March and April (26,40,80,97). And specific congenital anomalies with a peak seasonality in March or April in the United States include cleft lip, cleft palate, hypospadias, and positional foot defects (108). Such seasonal patterns in complications of pregnancy and congenital anomalies may or may not be related to the same etiological factors which produce the seasonality of schizophrenic births.

Discussion

Epidemiological approaches to schizophrenia have not been very productive in the past. I would like to suggest that the principal reason for this is that psychosocial explanations for the epidemiological findings were not adequate. Schizophrenogenic mothers, disordered patterns of communication, and theories of social and cultural stress may all be interesting applied to a single individual, but none of them has proven very helpful for determining epidemiological patterns of this disease. One consequence of this has been the gradual discreditation of epidemiological studies and their relegation to second-class status.

With the recent resurgence of biological approaches to schizophrenia, this situation is likely to change. Insofar as schizophrenia is believed to be an actual disease and not a reaction of an individual to psychosocial stress, then the epidemiological indices of disease (e.g., prevalence, seasonality) will be taken seriously and pursued. Actually schizophrenia will probably turn out to be heterogeneous; that is, many diseases and epidemiological patterns could well be decisive in delineating different subgroups. The genetically predisposed will probably be one such subgroup.

The potential fertility of this field is, without question, very rich. Just as there are biological explanations for differential rates of some cancers, heart disease, or hypertension by socioeconomic status and ethnic group, so too there may be for schizophrenia. The differential rate of multiple sclerosis among immigrants provided invaluable clues toward an infectious etiology; this could conceivably be the case for schizophrenia as well. Why do areas such as northern Sweden, western Ireland, northern Yugoslavia, or rural Ghana have schizophrenia prevalence rates of 10 or more per 1,000, whereas the rural Hutterites, Formosan aborigines, or

Papua New Guineans have less than one-tenth that much? Why are schizophrenics in the Northern Hemisphere born disproportionately in the late winter and early spring months? When we can answer these questions, we will probably be able to definitively treat, or at least prevent, this disease.

Summary

In this review of epidemiological advances in schizophrenia research over the past decade, it has been noted that areas of traditional focus—socioeconomic status, ethnicity, and migration—have provided relatively little new material. New findings, however, have reopened previously discarded ideas and show that there appear to be areas with a high prevalence of schizophrenia, other areas with a low prevalence, and still other areas where the prevalence appears to have changed dramatically. Additionally, it is now clear that there is a seasonality to schizophrenic births.

Socioeconomic status, ethnicity, migration, prevalence, and seasonality research may all hold valuable clues to the etiologies of schizophrenic disorders; and it is suggested that biologists pay as much attention to these clues as geneticists and social scientists.

BIBLIOGRAPHY

1. Ackerknecht, E. H. 1943. Psychopathology, primitive medicine and primitive culture. *Bulletin of the History of Medicine* 14:50–67.

2. Bagley, C. 1971. The social aetiology of schizophrenia in immigrant groups. *International Journal of Social Psychiatry* 17:292–304.

3. Barry, H., and Barry, H., Jr. 1964. Season of birth in schizophrenics: Its relation to social class. *Archives of General Psychiatry* 11:385–91.

4. Beattie, A. D.; Moore, M. R.; Goldberg, A., et al. 1975. Role of chronic low-level lead exposure in the aetiology of mental retardation. *Lancet* 1:589–92.

5. Book, J. A. 1959. Genetical etiology in mental illness. In *Causes of mental disorders: A review of epidemiological knowledge*. New York: Milbank Memorial Fund.

6. Browne, I. W. 1963. Psychiatry in Ireland. *American Journal of Psychiatry* 119:816–19.

7. Burton-Bradley, B. G. 1963. Culture and mental disorder. *Medical Journal of Australia* 15:539–40.

8. Burton-Bradley, B. G. 1969. Papua and New Guinea—transcultural psychiatry. The first one thousand referrals. *Australian and New Zealand Journal of Psychiatry* 3:130–36.

9. Carothers, J. C. 1948. A study of mental derangement in Africans and especially an attempt to explain its peculiarities, more especially in relation to the African attitude to life. *Psychiatry* 11:47–85.

10. Crocetti, G. M.; Kulcar, Z.; Kesic, B.; and Lemkau, P. V. 1964. Differential rates of schizophrenia in Croatia, Yugoslavia. *American Journal of Public Health* 54:196–206.

11. Crocetti, G. M.; Lemkau, P. V.; Kulcar, Z.; and Kesic, B. 1971. Selected aspects of the epidemiology of psychoses in Croatia, Yugoslavia. III. The cluster sample and results of the pilot survey. *American Journal of Epidemiology* 94:2, 126–34.

12. Dalén, P. 1968. Month of birth and schizophrenia. *Acta Psychiatrica Scandinavia Supplementum* 203:55–60.

13. Dalén, P. 1974. *Season of birth in schizophrenia and other mental disorders* (Göteborg: University of Göteborg).

14. Dalén, P. 1977. Maternal age and incidence of schizophrenia in the Republic of Ireland. *British Journal of Psychiatry* 131:301–5.

15. Dawson, W. R. 1911. The relation between the geographical distribution of insanity and that of certain social and other conditions in Ireland. *Journal of Mental Science* 57:571–97.

16. Dean, G.; Hanniffy, L.; Stevens, F.; et al. 1975. Schizophrenia and coeliac disease. *Journal of the Irish Medical Association* 68:545–46.

17. Demerath, N. J. 1942. Schizophrenia among primitives. *American Journal of Psychiatry* 98:703–7.

18. Dhunjibhoy, J. E. 1930. A brief résumé of the types of insanity commonly met with in India, with a full description of "Indian Hemp Insanity" peculiar to the country. *Journal of Mental Science* 76:254–64.

19. Diebold, K. 1975. The relationship between month of birth and psychic disorder. *Fortschritte der Neurologie, Psychiatrie, und Ihrer Grenzgebiete* 43:71–81.

20. Dohan, F. C. 1966. Wartime changes in hospital admissions for schizophrenia. A comparison of admissions for schizophrenia and other psychoses in six countries during World War II. *Acta Psychiatrica Scandinavia* 42:1–23.

21. Donnison, C. P. 1937. *Civilization and disease* (London: Bailliere Tindall and Cox).

22. Drapes, T. 1894. On the alleged increase of insanity in Ireland. *Journal of Mental Science* 40:519–48.

23. Dube, K. C. 1970. A study of prevalence and biosocial variables in mental illness in a rural and an urban community in Uttar Pradesh, India. *Acta Psychiatrica Scandinavia* 46:327–59.

24. Dube, K. C., and Kumar, N. 1972. An epidemiological study of schizophrenia. *Journal of Biosocial Science* 4:187–95.

25. Dunham, H. W. 1976. Society, culture and mental disorder. *Archives of General Psychiatry* 33:147–56.

26. Eastman, P. R. 1945. Infant mortality in relation to month of birth. *American Journal of Public Health* 35:913–22.

27. Eaton, J. W., and Weil, R. J. 1955. *Culture and mental disorders. A comparative study of the Hutterites and other populations* (Glencoe, Ill.: Free Press).

28. Elnagar, M. N.; Maitra, P.; and Rao, M. N. 1971. Mental health in an Indian rural community. *British Journal of Psychiatry* 118:499–503.

29. Faris, R. E. L. 1934. Some observations on the incidence of schizophrenia in primitive society. *Journal of Abnormal and Social Psychology* 29:30–31.

30. Field, M. J. 1960. *Search for security: An ethno-psychiatric study of rural Ghana* (Evanston, Ill.: Northwestern University Press).

31. Fischer, J. 1969. Negroes and whites and rates of mental illness: reconsideration of a myth. *Psychiatry* 32:428–46.

32. Fortes, M., and Mayer, D. Y. 1969. Psychosis and social change among the Tallensi of Northern Ghana. In *Psychiatry in a changing society*, eds. S. H. Foulkes and G. S. Prince (London: Tavistock).

33. Gershon, S., and Shaw, F. H. 1961. Psychiatric sequelae of chronic exposure to organophosphorus insecticides. *Lancet* 1:1371–74.

34. Gordon, H. L. 1936. An inquiry into the correlation of civilization and mental disorders in the Kenya native. *East African Medical Journal* 12:327–35.

35. Hare, E. H. 1962. The distribution of mental illness in the community. In *Aspects of psychiatric research*, eds. D. Richter, J. M. Tanner, L. Taylor, and O. L. Zangwill (New York: Oxford University Press).

36. Hare, E. H., and Price, J. S. 1968. Mental disorder and season of birth: Comparison of psychoses with neuroses. *British Journal of Psychiatry* 115:533–40.

37. Hare, E. H.; Price, J. S.; and Slater, E. 1974. Mental disorder and season of birth. *British Journal of Psychiatry* 124:81–86.

38. Hare, E. H. 1975. Season of birth in schizophrenia and neurosis. *American Journal of Psychiatry* 132:1168–71.

39. Hare, E. H. 1976. The season of birth of siblings of psychiatric patients. *British Journal of Psychiatry* 129:49–54.

40. Hewitt, D. 1962. A study of temporal variations in the risk of fetal malformations and death. *American Journal of Public Health* 52:1676–88.

41. Hollingshead, A. B,. and Redlich, F. C. 1958. *Social class and mental illness* (New York: John Wiley).

42. Johnson, R. T. 1972. Effects of viral infection on the developing nervous system. *New England Journal of Medicine* 287:599–604.

43. Jongbloet, P. H. 1971. Month of birth and gametopathy. *Clinica Genetic* 2:315–30.

44. Joseph, A., and Murray, V. F. 1951. *Chamorros and Carolinians of Saipan: Personality studies* (Cambridge: Harvard University Press).

45. Kapur, R. L. 1975. An illustrative presentation of a population survey of mental illness in South India. In *Mental health services in developing countries*, eds. T. A. Baasher et al. (Geneva: World Health Organization).

46. Kelleher, M. J.; Copeland, J. R. M.; and Smith, A. J. 1974. High first admission rates for schizophrenia in the west of Ireland. *Psychological Medicine* 4:460–62.

47. Kinney, D. K., and Jacobsen, B. 1978. Environmental factors in schizophrenia: new adoption study evidence and its implications for genetic and environmental research. In *The nature of schizophrenia*, eds. L. Wynne et al. (New York: John Wiley).

48. Kinzie, J. D., and Bolton, J. M. 1973. Psychiatry with the aborigines of West Malaysia. *American Journal of Psychiatry* 130:769–73.

49. Kramer, M.; Rosen, B. M.; and Willis, E. M. 1973. Definitions and distribution of mental

disorders in a racist society. In *Racism and mental health*, eds. C. V. Willie, B. M. Kramer, and B. S. Brown (Pittsburgh: University of Pittsburgh Press).

50. Krupinski, J., and Stoller, A. 1965. Incidence of mental disorders in Victoria, according to country of birth. *Medical Journal of Australia* 2:265–70.

51. Krupinski, J., and Stoller, A. 1969. Patterns of schizophrenia: State mental health services, Victoria. *Australia and New Zealand Journal of Psychiatry* 3:22–30.

52. Krupinski, J.; Stoller, A.; and Wallace, L. 1973. Psychiatric disorders in East European refugees now in Australia. *Social Science and Medicine* 7:31–49.

53. Krupinski, J.; Stoller, A.; and King, D. 1976. Season of birth in schizophrenia: An Australian study. *Australia and New Zealand Journal of Psychiatry* 10:311–14.

54. Kulcar, Z.; Crocetti, G. M.; Lemkau, P. V.; and Kesic, B. 1971. Selected aspects of the epidemiology of psychosis in Croatia, Yugoslavia. II. Pilot studies of communities. *American Journal of Epidemiology* 94:2, 118–25.

55. Kuriansky, J. B.; Gurland, B. J.; Spitzer, R. L.; and Endicott, J. 1977. Trends in the frequency of schizophrenia by different diagnostic criteria. *American Journal of Psychiatry* 134:631–36.

56. Landrigan, P. J.; Whitworth, R. H.; Baloh, R. W.; et al. 1975. Neuropsychological dysfunction in children with chronic low-level lead absorption. *Lancet* 1:708–12.

57. Lemkau, P. V.; Kulcar, Z.; Crocetti, G. M.; and Kesic, B. 1971. Selected aspects of the epidemiology of psychoses in Croatia, Yugoslavia. I. Background and use of psychiatric hospital statistics. *American Journal of Epidemiology* 94:112–17.

58. LeVann, L. J. 1963. Congenital abnormalities in children born in Alberta during 1961: A survey and a hypothesis. *Canadian Medical Association Journal* 89:120–26.

59. McCartney, J. L. 1947. Paradise lost: The psychology of the Marshall Islanders. *Journal of Clinical Psychopathology* 8:405–21.

60. MacDermott, W. R. 1908. The topographical distribution of insanity. *British Medical Journal* 2:950.

61. McDonald, A. D. 1971. Seasonal distribution of abortions. *British Journal of Preventive and Social Medicine* 25:222–24.

62. McNeil, T.; Dalen, P.; Dzierzykray-Rogalska, M.; and Kaij, L. 1975. Birthrates of schizophrenics following relatively warm versus relatively cool summers. *Archiv fuer Psychiatrie und Nervenkrankheiten* 221:1–10.

63. McNeil, T.; Kaij, L.; and Dzierzylkray-Rogalska, M. 1976. Season of birth among siblings of schizophrenics. *Acta Psychiatrica Scandinavia* 54:267–74.

64. Mishler, E. G., and Scotch, N. A. 1963. Sociocultural factors in the epidemiology of schizophrenia: A review. *Psychiatry* 26:315–51.

65. Monif, G. R. G. 1969. *Viral infections of the human fetus* (New York: Macmillan).

66. Morrison, S. D. 1973. Intermediate variables in the association between migration and mental illness. *International Journal of Social Psychiatry* 19:60–65.

67. Murphy, H. B. M. 1968. Cultural factors in the genesis of schizophrenia. In *The transmission of schizophrenia*, eds., D. Rosenthal and S. S. Kety (Oxford: Pergamon Press).

68. Murphy, H. B. M. 1972. The schizophrenia-evoking role of complex social demands. In *Genetic factors in schizophrenia*, ed. A. R. Kaplan (Springfield, Ill.: Charles C Thomas).

69. Murphy, H. B. M. 1975. Alcoholism and schizophrenia in the Irish: A review. *Transculture Psychiatric Research Review* 12:116–39.

70. Murphy, H. B. M. N.D. Community management of rural mental patients. Part II. The schizophrenias. Final Report. (Unpublished.)

71. Nolting, W. W. J. 1954. Vitamin C and the schizophrenic syndrome. *Folla Psychiatrica, Neurologica, et Neurochirugica Neerlandica* 57:347–55. Quoted in Dalen, P. 1968. Month of birth and schizophrenia. *Acta Psychiatrica Scandinavia Supplementum* 203:55–60.

72. Ødegaard, O. 1954. The incidence of mental diseases in Norway during World War II. *Acta Psychiatrica et Neurologica Scandinavia* 29:333–453.

73. Ødegaard, O. 1971. Hospitalized psychoses in Norway: Time trends 1926–1965. *Social Psychiatry* 6:53–58.

74. Ødegaard, O. 1974. Season of birth in the general population and in patients with mental disorder in Norway. *British Journal of Psychiatry* 125:397–405.

75. O'Doherty, E. F. 1965. The high proportion of mental hospital beds in the republic. *Transcultural Psychiatric Research Review* 2:134–36.

76. O'Hare, A., and Walsh, D. 1974. Further data on activities of Irish psychiatric hospitals and units, 1965–1969. *Journal of the Irish Medical Association* 67:57–63.

77. Parker, G., and Neilson, M. 1976. Mental disorder and season of birth—a southern hemisphere study. *British Journal of Psychiatry* 129:355–61.

78. Pasamanick, B., and Knobloch, H. 1958. Seasonal variation in complications of pregnancy. *Obstetrics and Gynecology* 12:110–12.

79. Pasamanick, B., and Knobloch, H. 1961. Epidemiologic studies on the complications of pregnancy and the birth process. In *Prevention of mental disorders in children*, ed. G. Caplan (New York: Basic Books).

80. Perlstein, M. A., and Hood, P. N. 1967. Seasonal variation in congenital cerebral palsy. *Developmental Medicine and Child Neurology* 9:673–91.

81. Petersen, W. F. 1934. *The patient and the weather: Mental and nervous diseases* (Ann Arbor: Edwards Bros.).

82. Rao, S. 1966. Case and mental disorders in Bihar. *American Journal of Psychiatry* 122:1045–55.

83. Rao, S. 1966. Culture and mental disorder: A study in an Indian mental hospital. *International Journal of Social Psychiatry* 12:139–48.

84. Record, R. G. 1961. Anencephalus in Scotland. *British Journal of Preventive and Social Medicine* 15:93–105.

85. Renwick, J. H. 1972. Hypothesis—Anencephaly and spina bifida are usually preventable by avoidance of a specific but unidentified substance present in certain potato tubers. *British Journal of Preventive Medicine* 26:67–88.

86. Rin, H., and Lin, T. Y. 1962. Mental illness among Formosan aborigines as compared with the Chinese in Taiwan. *Journal of Mental Science* 108:134–46.

87. Rosenthal, D.; Goldberg, I.; Jacobsen, B.; Wender, P. H.; Kety, S. S.; Schulsinger, F.; and Eldred, C. E. 1974. Migration, heredity, and schizophrenia. *Psychiatry* 37:321–39.

88. Rutstein, D. D.; Nickerson, R. J.; and Heald, F. P. 1952. Seasonal incidence of patent ductus arteriosus and maternal rubella. *American Journal of Diseases of Children* 84:199–213.

89. Sanua, V. D. 1969. Socio-cultural aspects. In *The schizophrenic syndrome*, eds. L. Bellak and L. Loeb (New York: Grune & Stratton).

90. Sanua, V. D. 1970. Immigration migration and mental illness. In *Behavior in New Environments*, ed. E. B. Brody (Beverly Hills: Sage Publications).

91. Saxena, B. M.; Bhaskaran, K.; and Ananth, J. V. 1972. Social class and schizophrenia: A study based on the caste system in India. *Transcultural Psychiatric Research Review* 9:130–33.

92. Seligman, C. G. 1929. Temperament, conflicts, and psychosis in a stone age population. *British Journal of Medical Psychology* 9:187–202.

93. Shaw, W. S. J. 1930. Some observations on the etiology of dementia praecox. *Journal of Mental Science* 76:505–11.

94. Shelley, H. M., and Watson, W. H. 1936. An investigation concerning mental disorder in the Nyasaland native. *Journal of Mental Science* 82:701–30.

95. Shepherd, M. 1957. *A study of the major psychoses in an English county.* Maudsley Monographs, no. 3 (London: Chapman & Hall).

96. Shimura, M.; Nakamura, I.; and Miura, T. 1977. Season of birth of schizophrenics in Tokyo, Japan. *Acta Psychiatrica Scandinavia* 55:225–32.

97. Slatis, H. M., and DeCloux, R. J. 1967. Seasonal variation in stillbirth frequencies. *Human Biology* 39:284–94.

98. Smartt, C. G. F. 1956. Mental maladjustment in the East African. *Journal of Mental Science* 102:441–66.

99. Stoller, A.; Krupinski, J.; Christopers, A. J.; et al. 1965. Organophosphorus insecticides and major mental illness. *Lancet* 1:1387–88.

100. Tooth, G. 1950. *Studies in mental illness in the Gold Coast.* Colonial Research Publications, no. 6 (London: His Majesty's Stationery Office).

101. Torrey, E. F.; Torrey, B. B.; and Burton-Bradley, B. G. 1974. The epidemiology of schizophrenia in Papua, New Guinea. *American Journal of Psychiatry* 131:567–73.

102. Torrey, E. F., and Peterson, M. R. 1976. The viral hypothesis of schizophrenia. *Schizophrenia Bulletin* 2:136–46.

103. Torrey, E. F.; Torrey, B. B.; and Peterson, M. R. 1977. Seasonality of schizophrenic births in the U. S. *Archives of General Psychiatry* 34:1065–70.

104. Tuke, D. H. 1894. Increase of insanity in Ireland. *Journal of Mental Science* 40:549–58.

105. Van Loon, F. G. H. 1920. The problem of lunacy in Acheen. Quoted by H. B. M. Murphy, Sociocultural factors in schizophrenia: A compromise theory, in *Social Psychiatry*, eds. J. Zubin and F. A. Fryhan, Proceedings of the American Psychopathological Association (New York: Grune & Stratton, 1968).

106. Videbech, T. H.; Weeke, A.; and Dupont, A. 1974. Endogenous psychoses and season for birth. *Acta Psychiatrica Scandinavia* 50:202–18.

107. Walsh, D., and Walsh, B. 1970. Mental illness in the Republic of Ireland: First admissions. *Journal of the Irish Medical Association* 63:365–70.

108. Wehrung, D. A., and Hay, S. 1970. A study of seasonal incidence of congenital malformations in the United States. *British Journal of Preventive and Social Medicine* 24:24–32.

109. Woodruff, R. A.; Guze, S. B.; and Clayton, P. J. 1974. Psychiatric illness and season of birth. *American Journal of Psychiatry* 131:925–26.

110. Zeman, W., and Lennette, E. H. 1974. *Slow virus diseases* (Baltimore: Williams & Wilkins).

111. Zubin, J., and Freyhan, F. A. 1968. *Social Psychiatry.* Proceedings of the American Psychopathological Association (New York: Grune & Stratton).

Chapter 2

BIOCHEMICAL STUDIES
IN SCHIZOPHRENIA*

Herbert Y. Meltzer, M.D.

Introduction

During the last decade, since Kety's review of the biochemistry of schizophrenia for this series (311), there have been enormous strides in our understanding of the chemistry of the nervous system and the mechanism of action of drugs which alleviate psychosis or which produce altered states of consciousness that have certain features in common with schizophrenia. The evidence accumulated in the last decade for an inherited genetic predisposition to the development of schizophrenia implies that schizophrenics have some abnormal body chemistry which plays a significant role in the pathogenesis of their disorder. Along with these advances have come a series of studies of the body fluids and tissues of psychotic patients, including brain and skeletal muscles, which have provided provocative clues to the chemical dysfunction in the schizophrenic syndrome. However, it is unlikely that we have correctly discerned the core pathophysiology of schizophrenia via findings such as the identification of apparent dopaminergic hyperactivity (96,416,569), decreased platelet monoamine oxidase (MAO) (673), or decreased skeletal muscle MAO activity (395). It is highly probable that we are still short of an understanding of the variety of deficits which underlie the schizophrenic syndrome and which would provide a biological basis for identification of vulnerable individuals and prevention of any disability or, failing that, a biological means of diagnosis and rapid, effective treatment without serious side effects.

A measure of the relevance of the increase in knowledge of basic neurobiology to our understanding of schizophrenia and the mechanism

* This review utilized a portion of a previous review by the author and S. Stahl. The excellent secretarial help of Ms. Kathy Hicks is greatly acknowledged. Preparation of this review was assisted by United States Public Health Service grants MH 30938, MH 16127, MH 18396, MH 25116, and MH 29206 and the Illinois Department of Mental Health.

of action of antipsychotic drugs is that no mention of such major foci of contemporary research in schizophrenia as dopamine (DA), MAO, endorphins, neuromuscular dysfunction, the neuroendocrine strategy or viruses, is to be found in the last review of the biochemistry of schizophrenia in this series (311). Of continuing interest from the 1960s have been the roles of methylated indoleamines or catecholamines and autoimmune defects in the etiology of schizophrenia. It is likely that some of the research to be reviewed here, particularly that related to DA and viruses, will be of enduring interest for schizophrenia research; but it is also safe to predict that there will be many new areas of relevance to the biochemistry of schizophrenia in the next decade, because it is likely that the fundamental defect, or defects, in the schizophrenia syndrome have not yet been identified.

Throughout this review, as well as throughout the clinical literature to be cited, schizophrenia is at times referred to as a single disease entity with a unified etiology, and at other times it is divided into various subtypes, with fairly common dimensions such as paranoid/nonparanoid and chronic/acute. It should be stated at the outset that it is the author's view, shared by most other researchers in this area, that schizophrenia, even when diagnosed by precise and relatively narrow research criteria (102), is composed of numerous disease entities which produce similar clinical states that respond fairly similarly to the currently available antipsychotic drugs. This heterogeneity makes for great difficulty in discerning biochemical deficits in groups of schizophrenic patients. Considerable progress has been made in the investigation of major depressive illness by the appreciation of subgroups, such as hyposerotonergic depressions (27,28). When biochemical differences of an unusual magnitude are found in even one apparently schizophrenic patient in a research study, it will be of importance to pursue the relationship between psychopathology and that deficit in the deviant individual. Investigations into the biochemical basis of schizophrenia must characterize accurately the psychopathology of research subjects on multiple axes—such as phenomenology, social functioning, response to treatment, duration of illness, family psychiatric history, etc.—in order to relate biochemical data to those characteristics which may validly subdivide the schizophrenic syndrome into discrete disease entities. It is likely that none of these by themselves or in combination will be adequate for the task of identifying subgroups of psychotic patients with common pathogenesis, but they may help toward the achievement of that goal. It should be clear that we are searching not for *the* cause of schizophrenia but for a variety of biochemical defects which produce similar but rarely identical phenotypes. However, Hartmann (254) has challenged the prevailing view of the heterogeneity of schizophrenia and argued for a single genetically determined predispositional factor which can vary in intensity and which produces a vulnerability to stress.

As pointed out by Blass, Milne, and Rodnight (62), there is no simple and constant relationship between a variety of metabolic disorders and psychiatric abnormalities. A given metabolic defect may produce various types of behavioral disturbances or none at all. These authors summarize the criteria which have been important for the study of various inherited metabolic abnormalities and may be usefully applied to psychiatry. These include: (1) increased incidence of excessive levels of abnormal substances in patients compared to controls; (2) increased synthesis or decreased metabolism of these compounds preferably in tissue culture; (3) demonstration that the enzymatic abnormality was distributed among the patient's relatives in accordance with the known genetics of the disorder; (4) evidence that the defect can produce the specific impairments associated with schizophrenia; and (5) evidence that correction of the metabolic abnormalities was clinically useful. Several of the areas of research in the biochemistry of schizophrenia to be reviewed here, particularly the dopamine hypothesis, fulfill at least some of these criteria.

This review of the biochemistry of schizophrenia will be selective, focusing on the major developments of the last decade and on some promising new areas of inquiry. The interested reader will surely find it of value to consult other review articles and collections of papers which deal with the biochemistry of schizophrenia.*

The Dopamine Hypothesis

The predominant biological hypothesis for a neurochemical defect in schizophrenia during the last decade has been the dopamine hypothesis. In its simplest form this hypothesis states that some forms of the schizophrenic syndrome may be caused by or associated with a relative excess of dopamine-dependent neuronal activity. The initial development of the theory can be credited to Drs. Arvid Carlsson of Sweden, Axel Randrug of Denmark, and Solomon Snyder of the United States. This theory is largely derived from pharmacological evidence that drugs which decrease dopamine (DA) activity (e.g., the neuroleptics, alpha-methylparatyrosine) may be antipsychotic, and that drugs which promote DA activity (e.g., amphetamine and phencyclidine) may be psychotomimetic. The biochemical basis for "too much dopamine" in schizophrenia is not yet known. There are several possibilities, as will be discussed subsequently.

If, as Karl Popper says, the value of a hypothesis lies not so much in whether it is right or wrong, but in its capacity to stimulate attempts to refute it (480), then the DA hypothesis of schizophrenia has been extraordinarily successful. Indeed, this hypothesis has stimulated a legion of basic scientists to investigate the anatomy, the biochemistry, and the function of central DA neurons as well as the relationship between DA neurons and other neurotransmitter systems. On the clinical front there has been a lesser effort to provide evidence for and against the hypothesis, but it is a rather safe assertion that clinical studies related to the DA hypothesis comprise the major group of biological studies in schizophrenia research during the last decade.

---

* See references 4, 67, 88, 127, 166, 192, 312, 379, 391, 392, 415, 424, 478, 498, 508, 515, 526, 543, 609, 622, 624, 625, 629, and 674.

Some of the evidence for the DA hypothesis has been reviewed previously.* Significant segments of recent symposiums on catecholamines or DA are devoted to this topic or are highly relevant.† This review includes some of the material previously covered elsewhere (416) as well as more recent studies.

GROSS ANATOMY AND FUNCTION OF DOPAMINERGIC NEURONAL TRACTS

DA is not present uniformly throughout the brain but is localized in a number of discrete pathways which are still being identified and characterized in the brains of laboratory animals as well as in postmortem human brains (638). The proportion of neurons in the brain which utilize DA as a neurotransmitter is approximately 1 percent. There is good evidence from histofluorescence and biochemical studies for at least six distinct DA neuronal tracts: (1) retinal DA fibers; (2) the incerto-hypothalamic DA tracts; (3) the nigro-striatal DA tracts; (4) the tubero-infundibular DA tracts; (5) the mesolimbic DA tract; and (6) the mesocortical DA neurons (123,343,616). The functional anatomy of the nigro-striatal, tubero-infundibular, mesolimbic, and mesocortical tracts and their possible relation to schizophrenia will now be reviewed, because they have played a major role in schizophrenia research. A schematic presentation of their location and connections is given in figure 2–1.

The largest and by far most thoroughly investigated central DA tract is the nigro-striatal system. The cell bodies for this tract are located in the pars compacta of the substantia nigra. These cells give rise to a large pathway which ascends through the lateral hypothalamus and terminates in the caudate-putamen of the neostriatum (616). The neurons in the neostriatum, upon which the nigro-striatal DA neurons terminate, contain the receptors for DA and are themselves thought to be small interneurons which employ acetylcholine (ACh) as neurotransmitter (360). These cholinergic interneurons may ultimately feed back upon the cell bodies of nigral dopaminergic neurons (86) possibly through GABA neurons—that is, neurons which utilize GABA as a neurotransmitter.

The major function of the nigro-striatal DA tract is to regulate the extrapyramidal nervous system in its control of certain motor movements. Stimulation of DA release from these nigral neurons by amphetamine and a direct effect of apomorphine upon these striatal DA receptors is believed to underlie the stereotyped motor behavior which develops in animals given these drugs (309,491). Degeneration of nigral DA neurons is believed to be the cause of Parkinson's disease (269,270). Blockade of DA receptors in the neostriatum is thought to be the cause of extrapyramidal side effects (EPS) of neuroleptic drugs (268,315).

While it is generally held that the striatum is not involved in producing psychotic symptoms in schizophrenia, Klawans, Goetz, and Westheimer (318) and Wiesel and Sedvall (660) have proposed that this region

---

* See references 54, 318, 354, 371, 372, 416, 526, 567, 568, 569, and 632.
† See references 90, 127, 192, 312, 543, 622, 623, 624, and 625.

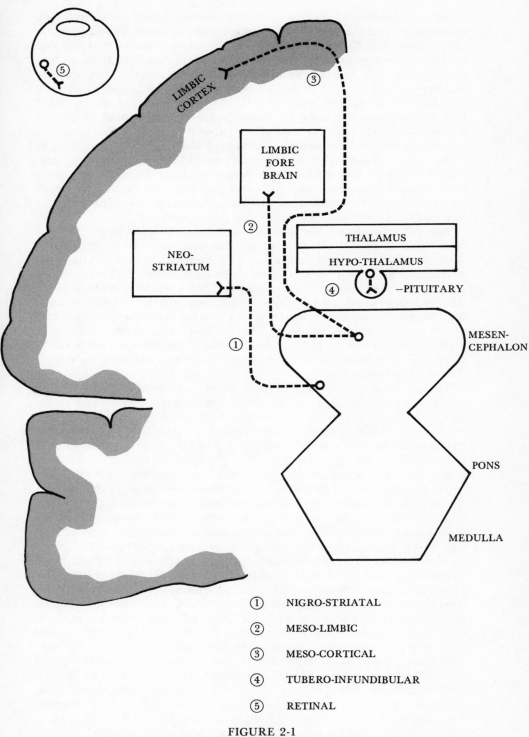

FIGURE 2-1

Major Dopaminergic Pathways in Mammalian Brain

should be considered, along with the mesolimbic region to be discussed subsequently, as the site of the antipsychotic action of the neuroleptic drugs. Crow and Gillbe (134) have raised the possibility that the cell bodies of the nigro-striatal and mesolimbic DA neurons form a continuous sheet and function as a single unit whose purpose is to promote a variety of goal-directed, appetitive behaviors. Antelman and Szechtman (23) have found that the nigro-striatal DA system may play an important role in regulating the organism's responsiveness to a wide variety of environmental stimuli. The role of the substantia nigra in certain types of memory has been stressed by Routtenberg and Holzman (523). Farley, Price, and Hornykiewicz (181) studied DA and homovanillic acid (HVA) levels in the caudate and putamen of six controls and three neuroleptic-treated schizophrenics who had suicided. No difference in mean levels of either substance was found, although the schizophrenics had relatively more DA, possibly due to drug treatment.

The tubero-infundibular DA tract consists of dopaminergic neurons which have their cell bodies in the arcuate nucleus of the hypothalamus and terminals in the external layer of the median eminence. The dopaminergic cells of this system have some morphological characteristics which resemble classical neurosecretory cells (198,260). A major function of tubero-infundibular dopaminergic neurons is to exert a tonic inhibitory effect upon the secretion of prolactin from the posterior lobe of the pituitary gland (199,261). This action of DA has been utilized to considerable advantage for the study of the dopamine-receptor-blocking effects of neuroleptics in both man and laboratory animals, as will be discussed subsequently.

The mesolimbic DA neuronal cell bodies are located dorsal to the interpenduncular nucleus in the ventral tegmental area (VTA) designated A10 in the rat and project to terminals just anterior to the head of the caudate nucleus in the nucleus accumbens septi, the bed nucleus of the stria terminalis, and the deep portion of the olfactory tubercle and the septal nuclei (31,137,616). The nucleus accumbens, the stria terminalis, and the olfactory tubercle are important elements of limbic forebrain structures. The outflow of the limbic nuclei is to the septum, the hypothalamus, and the frontal lobe and other cortical areas (340, 664). The broad distribution of limbic outflow is illustrated by the report that the majority of rat nucleus accumbens efferent fibers terminate in the diencephelon, but there are also projections to cortical and brain stem structures. Among the areas innervated are cingulum, lateral hypothalamus, globus pallidus, thalamus, and substantia nigra (661). This is an indication of the important role the limbic system could serve in influencing many aspects of behavior. The entire limbic system includes the cingulate and hippocampal gyri, the amygdala, the septal area, and, according to Isaacson (277), the hypothalamus as well, because of the extensive interconnections it has to the other areas. Recent studies have called attention to the anterior, dorsal, and median raphe, and the dorsal and ventral tegmental nuclei as a system which could be considered a limbic midbrain area (203). DA concentrations vary among the areas which comprise the limbic system. DA levels are high in the rat olfactory tubercle and the anterior amygdaloid area (82). The nucleus accumbens has much higher DA levels in the human than other mesolimbic areas

(181). No statistically significant differences in the mean levels of DA or HVA were found in the nucleus accumbens of three suicided schizophrenics compared with six controls (181). Lee and Seeman (337) have reported significantly increased DA receptors in the nucleus accumbens, the caudate, and the putamen of schizophrenics.

The function of the limbic system has not been completely ascertained. On the basis of chemical injection, lesion and electrical stimulation studies in animals, and human disease, ablation, and stimulation studies, there is circumstantial evidence that the limbic system mediates various autonomic neuroendocrine, memory learning, affective, motoric, and appetitive functions.* Recent evidence suggests that the mesolimbic DA system is also important in controlling and mediating the increased locomotor activity which develops in rats after treatment with apomorphine or amphetamine. The nucleus accumbens septi may be especially involved in the motor responses to amphetamine and apomorphine (309, 473). It has recently been reported that electric foot shocks in rats activate DA turnover in the nucleus accumbens and the frontal cortex but not the striatum or olfactory tubercle (605).

The mesolimbic tract has been suggested to be the dopaminergic tract most relevant to the pathogenesis of the amphetamine-induced psychosis (567). Snyder, Aghajanian, and Matthysse (568), Stevens (588), and Torrey and Peterson (608) have reviewed the evidence that the mesolimbic DA system may be the DA tract involved in schizophrenia. This evidence will only be briefly cited here. Impairment of the ability to filter out multiple stimuli and disturbances in behavior and affect may be the result of lesions of the limbic system in animals and are important aspects of some types of schizophrenia (565). Injection of small doses of 6-hydroxydopamine into the VTA (A10) of rats leads to selective destruction of DA neurons and increased locomotor activity, increased food spillage, which was attributed to behavioral instability and reduction of attention, and impairment of passive avoidance responses (204). The authors speculated that the A10 area may have a general inhibitory role in behavior, particularly with regard to selective attention and arousal. Electrical stimulation of the dorsal hippocampus (part of the outflow of the limbic striatum) has been reported to produce disturbances in thinking and hallucinations (271). Other changes produced by stimulation or ablation of the limbic system in humans includes paranoia, depersonalization, perceptual distortion, motor retardation, and disturbances of mood and emotion (608). In a study of eighteen patients with intracranial neoplasms affecting limbic structures, Melamud (378) found that all had been originally diagnosed as having a psychiatric disorder, ten of whom were thought to be schizophrenic. It is well known that prominent behavioral symptoms are often the presenting complaint of patients with subacute and chronic forms of viral encephalitis. This is particularly true of viral infections involving the temporal lobe (76,162,219,259).

Another intriguing finding linking schizophrenia to pathology of the limbic system is the relationship between seizure disorders and psychosis. Some clinical manifestations of psychomotor epilepsy (which is believed

---

° See references 5, 14, 44, 277, 342, 363, and 474.

to be predominantly a temporal lobe disorder) are reminiscent of the symptoms of psychosis: subjective feelings of forced, repetitive, and disturbing thoughts, alterations of mood, sensations of impending disaster and anxiety, *déjà vu*, *jamais vu*, episodes of depersonalization, dreamlike states, visual and auditory distortions, and olfactory and gustatory hallucinations (474). Gibbs (215) found that psychiatric disorders were three times more common in patients with anterior temporal seizure foci than those with seizure foci located elsewhere in the brain.

The presence of cortical DA fibers was first demonstrated with biochemical methods by Thierry et al. (603). After destruction of the ascending norepinephrine (NE) pathways, these investigators still observed the presence of an appreciable amount of DA and a persistent synthesis of DA in synaptosomes from rat cortex, while the synthesis of NE was completely abolished. Hokfelt et al. (263) were first to characterize the histochemical distribution of dopaminergic terminals in rat limbic cortex. They described terminal plexuses in gyrus cinguli, entorhinal cortex, hippocampus, amygdaloid cortex (especially in basal lateral nuclei), in the most basal layers of dorsal frontal cortex, and to a minor extent the prepyriform cortex. According to Berger et al. (53, 55), the rat cortical dopaminergic system is distributed in two main areas. The area of highest density was a medial field which spread in the medial cortex anterior and dorsal to the genu of the corpus callosum. In addition, a moderately dense band of dopaminergic fibers was observed between the corpus callosum and the anterior commissure, besides the nucleus accumbens. Fuxe et al. (200) postulated that the cell bodies for these terminals were located not in the cortex itself but probably in the A9 and A10 areas. Lindvall et al. (344) characterized the neocortical DA projections from mesencephalon and found that the projection to frontal cortex arises in the A10 cell group, and that the projection to anterior cingulate cortex arises from the lateral part of the substantia nigra (A9). There is evidence that the cell bodies of the mesolimbic and mesocortical DA neurons are different (605).

The rat prefrontal cortex has been shown to have a role in the response to noxious stimulation (124) and complex behaviors including spatial orientation and response to novel stimuli (152,324).

It is tempting to assume that the disturbances of thinking and symbolic processes which are an essential feature of many, if not all, patients in the schizophrenia spectrum (488), are based on dysfunction of these dopaminergic cerebral cortical neurons.

There is clearly a great need at the present time to define further the function of the mesolimbic and the mesocortical dopaminergic tracts in man and to determine if there is dysfunction, particularly increased activity, in these areas in schizophrenics. Conceivably, human postmortem histofluorescence studies may be useful (54,453,454,455), particularly if techniques specific for DA neurons are developed and if the post-mortem specimens come from well-diagnosed schizophrenics who are relatively young, have no intercurrent illnesses, and have not received drugs for a considerable interval prior to death. Olson's studies (453,454, 455) have so far revealed no differences between chronic schizophrenic and control brains in catecholamine and serotonin terminals in cortical and subcortical areas. Recording of the electrical activity of these regions in schizophrenics might also be of great value, but it is difficult to conceive of situations in which such data could be ethically obtained.

DOPAMINE AND BEHAVIOR

The preceding discussion of DA tracts primarily focused on their anatomy, what little is known of their function in man, and their possible role in schizophrenia. The purpose of this section is to highlight some of the major behavioral functions in animals which are believed to be, at least in part, under dopaminergic control.

Before describing the evidence for the role of DA in these behaviors, it is useful to call attention to the thoughtful discussion of Reis (497) on the difficulty in making linkages between transmitters and behavior. Only a multiplicity of biochemical and pharmacological studies can establish the participation of a central neurotransmitter in a specific behavior. Reis points out that it is unlikely that a single behavior is subserved by a single transmitter.

A variety of stimulant drugs (of which amphetamine is the prototype) administered to several animal species in high doses can induce a syndrome of motor hyperactivity, with sniffing behavior followed by repetitive licking, biting, and gnawing (490). This syndrome is known as "stereotypy" and is somewhat reminiscent of the repetitive purposeless behavior (e.g., continual dismantling and reassembling of objects) observed in human amphetamine abusers (525). The possibility that sterotypy may be mediated by DA receptors is based, in part, upon the findings that drugs which cause the stimulation of DA receptors (e.g., amphetamine, L-DOPA, apomorphine) all induce or enhance stereotyped behavior, whereas drugs which block DA receptors (phenothiazines, haloperidol) inhibit amphetamine-induced stereotypy (491). A series of recent anatomical studies have provided evidence that the nigro-striatal and mesolimbic dopaminergic tracts are important in stereotypy (see Creese and Iversen [133] for additional references and discussion).

Another form of animal behavior for which there is a prominent dopaminergic influence is the rotational behavior of rats which develops after unilateral destruction of the nigro-striatal DA system (308,617). In a series of investigations based on the selective depletion of NE or DA by varying the conditions of administration of the neurotoxic agent 6-hydroxydopamine (6-OHDA) to rats, Breese, Cooper, Grant, and collaborators (74,75) have provided evidence for the importance of DA for normal growth and development, activity, avoidance responding, consumatory behavior, and food-reinforced operant responding. Zis and Fibiger (688) have reported additional evidence, based on neuroleptic-induced blockade of food and water intake, that DA is important to consumatory behavior in rats and that the lateral hypothalamic syndrome in rats is the result of damage to the nigro-neostriatal system. The report by Antelman and Szechtman (23) that nigro-striatal ablation with 6-OHDA abolished eating, gnawing, or licking behavior in rats, may be related to these studies. Rolls et al. (513) and Mora et al. (429) have proposed that DA receptors are involved in self-stimulation in the rat and the monkey, and that the effect of neuroleptics on self-stimulation, eating, and drinking is due to an interference with volitional motor behavior but not to simple motor incapacitation. Evidence has recently been presented that DA may have a tonic facilitatory effect on memory consolidation in the rat (234).

Crow and Gillbe (134), in their discussion of the role of DA in behavior, have attempted to formulate a synthetic concept of the role of dopaminergic mechanisms in overall behavioral control. First, dopaminergic mechanisms facilitate motor behavior; second, the behaviors promoted are "appetitive" in that they seek out food; and finally, they are "rewarding" in so far as self-stimulation experiments may be interpreted in this way. Crow and Gillbe then discuss how this view of the function of DA pathways can be reconciled with the hypothesis of increased DA in schizophrenia. They describe schizophrenia as usually characterized by decreased activity, lack of drive, and lack of pleasure. To reconcile these characteristics with the three principles of DA function mentioned above, they postulate the schizophrenic syndrome as an increase of stereotypic, nonadaptive motor activity seeking goals which give no pleasure.

EFFECTS OF DRUGS WHICH INFLUENCE DOPAMINERGIC NEURONS IN SCHIZOPHRENIA

It should be apparent from the preceding discussion that if schizophrenia is associated with a relative hyperactivity of some DA neurons, a consideration of the functions of the various DA tracts indicates that the mesolimbic, the mesocortical, and perhaps the nigro-striatal tracts are the most likely candidates as tracts which might initiate the perceptual, cognitive, and affective disturbances characterizing this group of disorders. Hyperactivity of all tracts might be present, however, although there is now some evidence that this is not the case.

An understanding of the effect of drugs on DA mechanisms can provide a framework for consideration of many clinical pharmacological studies in schizophrenia. The next section will review this important area of research.

RESERPINE

DA is stored in a physiologically inactive form within synaptic vesicles as a chelate with adenosine triphosphate (ATP) and $Mg++$. These vesicles serve the dual purposes of protecting DA from intracellular deamination by monoamine oxidase (MAO) and storing extra DA for subsequent release during nerve impulse transmission. Thus, it is theoretically possible that a deficit in the storage of DA in granules might underlie at least some cases of schizophrenia. There is as yet no experimental evidence for or against this hypothesis.

Reserpine and tetrabenazine block vesicular storage of norepinephrine (NE) and DA and therefore cause catecholamine depletion due to increased deamination of the unbound amines by MAO (99,265). If schizophrenia is associated with excessive DA activity, one might expect blockers of amine storage, such as reserpine, to have antipsychotic efficacy. In summarizing the results of twenty-nine double-blind clinical trials of the antipsychotic action of reserpine, Davis and Cole (143) list twenty studies which found reserpine to be more effective than placebo, and nine studies which found it to be only equally effective as placebo. The high incidence of extrapyramidal side effects and depression at the doses needed for antipsychotic effects limits the therapeutic utility of reserpine. Thus, the results of clinical trials are consistent with the DA hypothesis, but because reserpine affects storage of biogenic amines such as NE and 5-HT, and most likely other amines that are stored in vesicles, the antipsychotic effects of reserpine cannot be specifically related to DA.

AMANTADINE

Amantadine is a drug which has been successfully used to treat neuroleptic-induced extrapyramidal side effects (418). Some have claimed that amantadine increases brain dopaminergic activity via increased DA release, decreased DA uptake, direct DA agonist effect, and increased synthesis.* Several clinical investigations are consistent with some effect of amantadine to increase brain dopaminergic activity (238, 465). Were amantadine to increase dopaminergic activity at post-synaptic receptor sites in the limbic cortical or mesolimbic regions, one might expect it to exacerbate schizophrenia, but this is not the case (418). However, some reports have disputed that amantadine affects dopaminergic activity significantly (79,626). Further, amantadine might selectively increase presynaptic dopaminergic activity, which could have a clinically useful effect by inhibiting the firing of dopaminergic neurons.

ALPHA-METHYLPARATYROSINE

Alpha-methylparatyrosine (AMPT) inhibits tyrosine hydroxylase, the usual rate-limiting step in the synthesis of DA and NE (577). If schizophrenia is associated with excessive DA activity, inhibition of dopamine synthesis by AMPT might be clinically effective in schizophrenia. Gershon et al. (213) treated ten acute paranoid schizophrenics and three chronic undifferentiated schizophrenics, free of all other drugs, with doses of 800 to 2,000 milligrams of AMPT per day for periods of one day to eight weeks. Two patients improved, five did not change, and two became more psychotic. Levels of NE and two of its metabolites did decrease in the urine of three patients, which suggests that tyrosine hydroxylase inhibition had occurred, at least peripherally. The effect of AMPT, in doses of 2 grams per day for thirty-three to forty-three days, on fifteen chronic schizophrenics (type unspecified), who were off all other drugs for ten days, was also studied by Charalempous and Brown (108). A slight sedative effect was noted in most subjects, but no significant improvement occurred. Nine of the fifteen subjects became progressively worse. A decrease in catecholamine metabolites was noted. It is possible that the inhibition of tyrosine hydroxylase achieved by these dose levels did not interfere with DA synthesis to an extent sufficient to produce an interference with dopaminergic transmission, or that this

---

* See references 39, 182, 532, 599, and 600.

degree of synthesis inhibition was compensated for by receptor supersensitivity and other adaptive changes (649).

Carlsson et al. (97) reported that five chronic schizophrenic patients
with stable symptomatology could be maintained on lower doses of
neuroleptics after adding up to 2 grams of AMPT per day. Stopping the
AMPT produced an exacerbation of the psychosis. Carlsson et al. (98)
replicated this in six other chronic schizophrenic patients. AMPT produced a 70 to 90 percent decrease in spinal-fluid HVA levels in all but one
case, which indicates a marked inhibition of tyrosine hydroxylase. Both
of these studies lasted only about two weeks. Walinder et al. (649) found
that AMPT potentiated the effects of thioridazine for a six-month period,
in a double-blind, crossover trial. No tolerance to the antipsychotic effects
of AMPT were noted. The fact that AMPT potentiated the antipsychotic
effect of neuroleptics is consistent with the hypothesis of excessive DA
as a factor in schizophrenia.

We have treated four chronic schizophrenics with AMPT, with and
without neuroleptic therapy. In one patient AMPT was dramatically
successful in eliminating auditory hallucinations in a double-blind design. In the other three patients AMPT proved of limited clinical value.
This trial is continuing, so that mixed results must be considered preliminary. The striking effect in one patient suggests that the heterogeneity in etiology of schizophrenia, as well as stages of the illness,
must be considered in evaluating the theoretical significance of drug
trials.

The chronic administration of phenothiazines probably leads to increased DA synthesis because of the feedback activation of presynaptic
DA neurons (95,201). The addition of AMPT to a neuroleptic regimen
could produce sufficient diminution of DA synthesis to synergize with
the DA-blocking properties of the neuroleptics, leading to an enhanced
antipsychotic effect (98). No compensatory mechanisms, such as supersensitivity of postsynaptic receptors, could overcome this block.

AMPT tends to produce crystalluria and is too toxic for routine clinical
use. If other inhibitors of tyrosine hydroxylase with much less toxicity
could be developed, they should be tested as antipsychotic agents with
and without neuroleptic treatment. Such inhibitors might be quite useful
in the treatment of schizophrenia by permitting a reduction in neuroleptic dosage.

L-DOPA AND DRUGS WHICH INHIBIT IMPULSE FLOW
IN DOPAMINE NEURONS: PRESYNAPTIC DA NEURONS

One means of determining the effects of increased central dopaminergic activity on behavior is to administer large doses of the DA precursor,
L-DOPA. L-DOPA is also the precursor of NE, but peripheral administration of L-DOPA causes only small and variable changes in brain NE
levels (107,177,440). Although the predominant central effect of L-
DOPA is to increase brain DA levels, several other biochemical changes
can also result, including decreases in brain serotonin levels, competition
with tryptophan for transport into brain, and displacement of other
endogenous amines such as NE and serotonin (see reference 93 for review). One must keep these several biochemical changes in mind when
attempting to explain the behavioral effects of L-DOPA administration.

The mental effects of L-DOPA in Parkinsonian patients, normals, and depressed patients as well as the behavioral effects of L-DOPA in animals have been reviewed by Murphy (430) and will not be extensively dealt with here. Briefly, the average incidence of specific psychiatric problems after L-DOPA treatment in Parkinsonian patients is approximately 15 percent, of which one-fifth to one-third may have some psychotic features, mainly of an organic character, but also with paranoid ideation and auditory hallucinations that are indistinguishable from those in some schizophrenic patients. L-DOPA was noticed to produce an intensification of psychotic symptomatology in six patients who were primarily depressed but also had previously documented or concomitantly present psychotic symptoms (227,228). Normals and patients with narcolepsy, impotency, or migraine did not suffer adverse behavioral effects after L-DOPA.

There are several reported studies of the effects of administration of high doses of L-DOPA to schizophrenic patients. Yayura-Tobias, Diamond, and Merlis (678), and Yayura-Tobias et al. (679) administered relatively low doses of L-DOPA (2 to 3 grams per day) to nine chronic schizophrenic patients who were also receiving neuroleptics. Seven of the nine patients developed an exacerbation of their psychosis, including increased paranoia and auditory hallucinations. Since the neuroleptics might be expected to block the effects of the DA produced from L-DOPA, this may be an indication of increased sensitivity of schizophrenics to DA, or it may indicate that the L-DOPA-induced exacerbation of the psychosis is mediated by non-DA mechanisms. Angrist, Sathananthan, and Gershon (19) administered 3 to 6 grams of L-DOPA per day for a mean of twenty-one days to ten chronic schizophrenic patients who had been on neuroleptics for an unspecified period of time and then on a placebo for five to ten days prior to beginning L-DOPA. All patients were mildly to severely symptomatic prior to L-DOPA treatment. Seven of the ten patients showed a worsening of pre-existing psychotic symptomatology. All ten patients showed signs of stimulation of motor activity. After discontinuing L-DOPA, the patients returned to baseline functioning; however, some required neuroleptic treatment in order to do so. The authors discussed the possibility that the exacerbation of psychosis by L-DOPA could be due either to a nonspecific mental activation or to a specific dopaminergic stimulation. In a later report Sathananthan, Angrist, and Gershon (531) proposed that the effect of L-DOPA in schizophrenics was likely to be specifically dopaminergic. The interpretation of this latter study is clouded by the fact that its patients had recently received neuroleptic drugs which could have made dopaminergic receptors supersensitive to the effects of DA produced from L-DOPA. Thus, it is not yet possible to conclude from these latter two studies that schizophrenics are more susceptible to specific dopaminergic activation than are patients with other types of psychiatric illness. This type of study, however, is potentially most informative and should be repeated in a variety of unmedicated schizophrenic patients, psychiatric controls, and normal controls, with appropriate attention to informed consent and subject well-being.

There is a group of studies on the effects of administration of low doses of L-DOPA to schizophrenics also receiving phenothiazines. Kawamura et al. (299), Inanaga et al. (274,276), Nishikawa, Higasayama, and Kasarhara (445), Yamauchi (676), Asano et al. (26), Sarai et al. (530), Ogura et al. (451), and Otsuka (457) have reported the results of uncontrolled, open studies in which doses of 300 to 1,000 milligrams of L-DOPA per day orally produced additional *improvement* in about 50 percent of schizophrenics treated with phenothiazines. Bruno and Bruno (83) reported that the administration of L-DOPA—2 milligrams per kilogram intravenously—to schizophrenic patients treated with neuroleptics improved motor activity, extended social participation, and produced a feeling of well-being. The beneficial effects of low-dose L-DOPA was also demonstrated in a double-blind controlled study of 104 schizophrenic patients (275). According to these investigators, 200 to 600 milligrams of L-DOPA produced fair to excellent improvement in 26 of 52 patients (50 percent) whose neuroleptic treatment was supplemented with L-DOPA, whereas fair to moderate improvement (no instances of excellent improvement) occurred in 19 of 52 patients (36 percent) of patients supplemented with placebo. The differences were reported to be statistically significant. Benefit was greatest in patients ill for less than five years who had symptoms of loss of spontaneity, abulia, apathy, and autism. Treatment lasted for eight weeks. Some patients relapsed after the L-DOPA was discontinued. The authors proposed that the improvement with L-DOPA might be understood in terms of the theory of Stein and Wise (586) that schizophrenics are deficient in brain dopamine-β-hydroxylase and hence NE. However, there is evidence that L-DOPA is a poor precursor of brain NE.

Gerlach and Luhdorf (210) reported that L-DOPA (300 to 900 mg per day) plus a peripheral decarboxylase inhibitor (benserazide) had a beneficial effect on emotional withdrawal, blunted affect, tendency to isolation, and apathy, without producing or aggravating productive, accessory psychotic symptoms. Increased motor activity was also noted. Higher doses of L-DOPA (900 mg per day plus 225 mg of benserazide) sometimes produced feelings of anxiety, restlessness, and unreality.

Similar results were reported by Cesarec, Eberhard, and Nordgen (105) using d-amphetamine to supplement low-dose neuroleptic treatment. Van Kammen et al. (631) recently reported that intravenous d-amphetamine caused improvement in ten of twenty-seven drug-free schizophrenics, an effect which was subsequently blocked by pimozide treatment. On the other hand, nonresponders to pimozide had a worsening of their symptoms after amphetamine while drug-free or on pimozide. Bromocryptine and piribedil are two dopamine agonists which have not produced an exacerbation of schizophrenia or any improvement in psychotic symptoms (423,507). Smith, Tamminga, and Davis (564) administered apomorphine to chronic schizophrenics receiving butaperazine and noted clinical improvement in the form of decreased productive symptoms. They made no comment on any activating effect of this direct-acting dopamine agonist.

There are several ways to interpret this apparently paradoxical effect of dopamine-agonist-induced improvement in some schizophrenic patients. First, it is possible that some schizophrenics, particularly chronic patients receiving neuroleptics, are suffering from too little dopaminergic activity in specific neuronal areas. This could be due to dysfunction of these neurons or to the effect of neuroleptic drugs. The rapid H-reflex recovery curve reported by our group in some unmedicated chronic schizophrenic patients is consistent with this hypothesis (226). The lack of effect of low-dose oral amphetamine on sleep and performance of chronic schizophrenics may also be explained on this basis (325,425). Neuroleptic treatment might too greatly reduce dopaminergic activity— an effect that might be overcome by supplemental L-DOPA, d-amphetamine, or apomorphine.

Alternatively, these DA-stimulating drugs might have relatively greater effects on presynaptic DA mechanisms. In the last few years very strong evidence has been offered in support of DA receptors on DA neurons which, when stimulated by DA or appropriate agonists, lead to inhibition of the activity of those neurons via inhibition of DA synthesis.* Because most dopamine agonists and antagonists can stimulate or block both presynaptic and postsynaptic receptors, it is very difficult to predict which effects predominate in man. There are various methods to predict this in animals (648). The development of agents which selectively stimulate presynaptic dopamine receptors, or of drugs which inhibit impulse flow in presynaptic dopaminergic neurons, will likely be one of the major strategies exploited in the next decade. Gamma-hydroxybutyric acid and baclofen (p-chlorophenyl GABA) are examples of drugs which inhibit impulse flow in presynaptic DA neurons (140,214,519). Both drugs have been tried in the treatment of schizophrenia with mixed results.† It should be pointed out that baclofen and γ-hydroxybutyrate, though both are chemically related to GABA, may not have any direct gabergic effects, so that results of studies with these drugs are not entirely relevant to the possible role of GABA in schizophrenia, a subject we shall briefly review subsequently.

However, before too much attention is devoted to exploring the mechanism of DA-agonist-induced improvement in schizophrenic symptoms, there is an urgent need to determine how real this phenomenon is. We have not observed any effect of 0.75 milligrams of apomorphine on the mental status of acutely disturbed schizophrenics.‡

DOPA DECARBOXYLASE INHIBITION

The administration of alpha-methyldopa in high doses leads to a marked depletion of NE, DA, and serotonin (5-HT) in the brain (95, 258). Part of the difficulty in predicting the antipsychotic effects of this drug is due to limited understanding of the biochemical mechanism of its amine-depleting effects. Two different hypotheses have been proposed to account for its depletion of brain DA and NE. First, it has been suggested that alpha-methyldopa is itself decarboxylated to alpha-methyldopamine, which is then bound to the storage sites for endogenous amines; thus, it would displace the endogenous amines and cause their subsequent breakdown and depletion (160,161). A second hypothesis is that the decrease in brain catecholamines after alpha-methyldopa is due to a reduction in catecholamine biosynthesis (154,619,620).

Whatever the mechanism of decreased catecholamine levels after

---

° See references 6, 94, 305, 520, 648, and 654.
† See references 190, 243, 326, 338, 345, 540, and 630.
‡ According to unpublished data of Meltzer, Young, and Strahilevitz.

alpha-methyldopa, administration of this drug to schizophrenics might be expected to exert an antipsychotic effect due to a decrease in DA activity. Alpha-methyldopa by itself has been showed to have only occasional beneficial effects in the treatment of schizophrenia, and not infrequently it causes a worsening (257,466,575,579). However, Chouinard et al. (113) have found, in an uncontrolled study, that alpha-methyldopa plus chlorpromazine produced significant improvement in eight of ten chronic schizophrenic patients (type of schizophrenia and diagnostic criteria not clearly stated) who had not previously responded to antipsychotic medication. A more rigorous study of the clinical potential of this combination was reported to be under way.

The failure of alpha-methyldopa to be clinically effective by itself may be due to inadequate depletion of DA by the doses of alpha-methyldopa employed, or to other biochemical effects of this drug. It depletes NE more than DA and also depletes 5-HT. Nevertheless, potentiation of antipsychotic effects of neuroleptics by alpha-methyldopa is consistent with the hypothesis of excessive DA activity in schizophrenia.

DECARBOXYLATION OF L-DOPA BY ERYTHROCYTES IN SCHIZOPHRENIA

Tran, Laplante, and Lebel (612) studied the rate of decarboxylation of radiolabeled L-DOPA by erythrocytes in nine schizophrenics and seven normals. No specific criteria for schizophrenia were cited. Eight of the schizophrenics had received phenothiazines prior to the study. Five patients were hallucinating and had thought disorders, and these five patients had a significantly more rapid, sustained decarboxylation of ^{14}C-DOPA than the four schizophrenics who were in remission, or than the seven controls. The possibility of a phenothiazine effect on DOPA decarboxylase activity could not be ruled out. DOPA decarboxylase is already present in great excess in rat brain in relation to tyrosine hydroxylase, which is rate-limiting in the synthesis of DA. It therefore seems unlikely that increased DOPA decarboxylase activity could account for increased DA activity in schizophrenia.

DOPAMINE TURNOVER AND STRESS

The role of stress in the pathogenesis of the acute psychotic state in schizophrenia is generally accepted and has been discussed in relation to a biological basis of schizophrenia by Pollin (478) and Strahilevitz (593). It is well established that stress increases the turnover of brain noradrenaline, serotonin, and histamine. However, the effect of stress on DA turnover in mice or rats is not as clear.

Intense muscular exercise and cold exposure did not affect the synthesis of DA (230). Thierry et al. (604) found no effect of 180 minutes of electric shocks to the feet on the disappearance of ^{3}H-DA from the striatum. As previously noted, Thierry et al. (605) found that 20 minutes of stress increased DA turnover in the nucleus accumbens and the frontal cortex but not in the striatum or the olfactory tubercle. Corrodi et al. (126) found that in rats restraint stress decreased disappearance of whole brain DA from AMPT-treated rats, which suggests that stress *decreases* DA turnover. They also reported that stress decreased DA turnover in the hypothalamus, as indicated by fluorescence disappearance. They attributed this to a decrease in impulse flow in DA neurons. On the other hand, Bliss and Ailon (63) and Brown, Snider, and Carlsson (80) reported an increase in the turnover of DA in mice subjected to foot shocks or grid shocks. While the reason for the discrepancies may be intensity of stress and species variations, it is of interest that acute revolving-drum stress had no effect on DA turnover in mice, although it markedly raised DA levels, whereas it markedly increased DA turnover in mice that had been given several daily exposures to drum stress and had become more tolerant to what would be lethal amounts of this stress in naïve animals (223). This points out that previous exposure to stress can affect DA turnover in response to additional stress in mice. It is tempting to speculate that the same process occurs in man, and that in schizophrenics it is even more marked—that is, that DA turnover is greatly accelerated with recurrent stress. This does not appear to be the case with neostriatal DA, as evidenced by the lack of increase in CSF HVA in acute schizophrenics,* but it might be the case in other brain areas.

DOPAMINE RELEASE AND AMPHETAMINE PSYCHOSIS

The major pharmacological effect of the psychotomimetic drug amphetamine is believed to be catecholamine release (92,489,524), although it can also inhibit catecholamine neuronal uptake, can weakly inhibit MAO, and may have very weak catecholamine agonist effects.

Clinical observations in human amphetamine addicts have revealed that high doses of amphetamines can produce a florid psychosis bearing certain striking similarities to acute paranoid schizophrenia (120). Careful clinical studies have shown that this "model psychosis," which may be associated with thought disorder, affective changes, and auditory hallucinations, could be produced at high amphetamine doses in normal individuals who were not prepsychotic (18,129). These studies have essentially eliminated the possibility that amphetamine merely activates latent psychosis. The reproduction of the fundamental symptoms of schizophrenia in these volunteers also helps to rule out the possibility that amphetamine acts by nonspecific excitation or sleep deprivation (567). Phenothiazines and haloperidol ameliorate amphetamine psychosis and thus strengthen the analogy to true schizophrenia (17). Janowsky et al. (286) recently reported that primary symptoms of schizophrenia—such as audible thoughts, somatic passivity, thought insertion, thought broadcasting, and widespread bizarre delusions—may be present in psychostimulant-induced psychoses; this possibility challenges one of the major objections to the amphetamine model of schizophrenia.

In schizophrenic patients, amphetamine activates or worsens preexisting psychotic symptoms (17,281). Janowsky et al. (283) found that administering small intravenous doses of methylphenidate, an isomer of amphetamine, to actively ill schizophrenics produced a marked worsening of preexisting psychotic symptoms but did not have a major psychotogenic effect in remitted patients or normals. A wide range of psychotic symptoms—not simply paranoia—were promoted.

---

* See references 70, 71, 73, 109, 481, and 505.

The authors caution against using methylphenidate for diagnostic purposes.

We have previously reviewed the reports of Cesarec et al. (105) and Van Kammen et al. (631) which claim d-amphetamine has a therapeutic effect on some symptoms in some schizophrenics. Possible explanations for this paradoxical effect have been provided. It is likely that the explanation of the divergent effects of amphetamine lie in the heterogeneity of schizophrenia as well as individual variations in response to amphetamine because of underlying metabolic differences in both pharmacokinetics of amphetamine and DA metabolism.

The studies of Randrug and Munkvard (490) and Ellinwood and colleagues (172) have contributed extensively to our understanding of amphetamine-mediated behavioral effects and their relationship to DA metabolism and schizophrenia. Space precludes a detailed review of their studies, which are available in the references cited. Garver et al. (208) have rated the behavior of primates who were administered amphetamine chronically. These investigators have called attention to the hypervigilance, hyperactivity, fragmented and repetitive behavior, and progressive social withdrawal which occurs in primates, in addition to stereotyped behaviors, after chronic amphetamine administration.

The effects of d- and 1-amphetamine on mental status have been studied in normal controls (563), in human amphetamine abusers (20, 245), and in schizophrenic patients (281). These studies reported respectively a 1.3:1, 4:1, 3–7:1, and 2:1 greater potency of the d-isomer than the 1-isomer in producing changes in mental status. These data were used to conclude that increased dopamine activity was the basis of the exacerbation. However, both conclusion and data have been challenged (416,563).

However, other types of evidence suggest a dopaminergic basis for amphetamine-induced psychosis. On the basis of neurophysiologic evidence, it would appear that DA mediates the euphoria and the acute paranoid psychosis in abusers as well as the activation of schizophrenia, since all are more sensitive to d-amphetamine (87). The fact that the ability of neuroleptic drugs to antagonize the effects of amphetamine in man and stereotyped behavior in laboratory animals correlates with clinical potency is further evidence that these effects of amphetamine are due to increased DA. There is additional evidence that DA is relevant to the psychotomimetic effects of amphetamine. As we have indicated, it is well established that the neuroleptics are potent antidotes both to human amphetamine psychosis (18) and to the amphetamine effects upon primate behavior (208). The reasons for concluding that neuroleptic blockade indicates a dopaminergic mechanism for amphetamine psychosis have been reviewed by these authors and by Snyder (567) and will not be repeated here. However, the neuroleptic drugs also have antiadrenergic properties, albeit weaker than their anti-DA effects. The recent report that pimozide, formerly thought to be a neuroleptic specific for DA blockade, is a potent inhibitor of a NE-stimulated adenylate cyclase, a possible NE receptor, has prompted the speculation that NE blockade may be relevant to antipsychotic effects (65). Nevertheless, the evidence in favor of an anti-DA mechanism for the neuroleptics is very strong and does support the contention that increased DA is the mechanism of amphetamine psychosis. This conclusion is also strengthened by the report that the α-adrenergic blocker, phenoxybenzamine, and the β-blocker, propranolol, did *not* inhibit the euphoriant effects of high-dose amphetamine in detoxified amphetamine addicts (245). Their finding that AMPT pretreatment blocked the amphetamine effect is consistent with either a DA or a NE hypothesis. The report by Janowsky et al. (283) that methylphenidate, which is more potent as a central DA releaser than a NE releaser (183), can activate schizophrenia more potently than d-amphetamine, supports the idea that activation of psychosis was due to DA rather than NE.

The finding that amphetamine stimulates brain DA turnover in man —as demontrated by an increased CSF HVA after probenecid without an increase in CSF 3-methoxy-4-hydroxy-phenyl glycol (MHPG), the major metabolite of NE—suggests that amphetamine has a more potent effect on brain DA than NE (18). However, this does not specifically link the increased DA turnover to the central effects of amphetamine.

All evidence considered, it is reasonable to conclude that increased DA plays a significant role in the induction of euphoria, an acute paranoid state, and an exacerbation of schizophrenia by amphetamine.

NEUROLEPTICS AND THE DA HYPOTHESIS OF SCHIZOPHRENIA

The belief that the mechanism of the antipsychotic effect of the neuroleptic drugs is interference with neuronal DA activity is one of the cornerstones of the DA hypothesis of schizophrenia. The older evidence which relates their antipsychotic action to DA has been reviewed by Snyder et al. (569) and will not be repeated here. Selected aspects of pharmacology of the neuroleptics, as well as their clinical effects, are discussed throughout this review. Here we wish to discuss several important areas of research concerning the neuroleptic drugs which have direct relevance to schizophrenia: (a) DA-stimulated adenylate cyclase; (b) DA and neuroleptic binding sites in brain; (c) acute versus long-term effects of neuroleptics on striatal DA receptors; (d) the relationship between dopaminergic and cholinergic neurons in the striatum and the existence of a DA-ACh balance relevant to schizophrenia, Parkinson's disease, and tardive dyskinesia; (e) DA receptor supersensitivity. Other aspects of the biochemistry of neuroleptics have been reviewed elsewhere (416,669).

Dopamine-Stimulated Adenylate Cyclase. The neurotransmitters such as DA bring about their effects by interacting with a receptor and thereby initiating a metabolic process. The identification and characterization of the DA receptor, or receptors, which may be relevant to the antipsychotic effect of the neuroleptics is a major aim of current research. There is considerable interest in the hypothesis that the DA receptor is a dopamine-stimulated adenylate kinase (237). The increase in cyclic adenosine monophosphate (AMP) is brought about by the hormone's stimulation of adenylate cyclase, a membrane-bound enzyme. When activated by a chemical messenger, adenylate cyclase catalyzes the conversion of adenosine triphosphate (ATP) to cyclic AMP, which in turn participates in a host of cellular processes. Cyclic AMP acts as a second chemical messenger and causes various intracellular enzymes to increase their activity. Most commonly, the enzymes are phosphorylated, and the resulting chemical changes bring about the major cellular effects of the original hormone. It is believed that in the nervous system a variety of neurotransmitters such as DA, 5-HT, NE, and histamine can act like hormones and stimulate the production of cyclic AMP in the postsynaptic neuron (139).

The existence of DA-stimulated adenylate cyclase was first demonstrated in the superior cervical ganglion of the rabbit (303). Later studies have found DA-stimulated adenylate cyclases in the basal ganglia (304, 421,551) and in the limbic forebrain (116,421). The adenylate cyclases of the caudate and the limbic regions are sensitive to very low concentrations of dopamine: half-maximal stimulation occurs at 4 to 5 micromoles (μM), and effects are detectable at concentrations as low as 0.3 μM. Dopamine produces a twofold increase in caudate adenylate cyclase, whereas it produces an 80 to 100 percent increase above basal level in the limbic region (422). Although these are relatively small increases, they could be physiologically significant. The low concentration of dopamine necessary to stimulate adenylate cyclase activity also supports the physiologic significance of this process.

The neuroleptics competitively inhibit brain DA sensitive adenylate cyclase at extremely low concentrations—for example, 10^{-9} moles (M) for fluphenazine (116,296,304,421). In general the capacity of phenothiazine drugs to inhibit this enzyme parallels their clinical potency. Thus, fluphenazine is ten to twenty times as potent an inhibitor as chlorpromazine, whereas promazine and chlorpromazine sulfoxide, which are not antipsychotic, do not significantly inhibit the enzyme at concentrations of less than 10^{-7}M. Only the isomers of thioxanthenes which are antipsychotic are potent inhibitors (422). However, the butyrophenones are exceptions. All studies agree that haloperidol, spiroperidol, and the related drug pimozide are far less potent inhibitors of DA-stimulated adenylate cyclases than might be expected from their clinical potency (296,304,421). This apparent discrepancy with the hypothesis that interaction with this enzyme is the basis for antipsychotic effects of the neuroleptics could be due to problems with the *in vitro* assay with the butyrophenones, which are not water-soluble, or because of selective absorption, metabolism, and distribution of these drugs *in vivo* (279). Rat-striatal DA-sensitive adenylate kinase is not inhibited by sulpiride, a dopamine antagonist with no antipsychotic action, or by metoclopramide, a structurally related central DA antagonist which may not be antipsychotic (522). On the other hand, still another discrepancy exists in that several tricyclic antidepressants, particularly amitriptyline and doxepin, which completely lack antipsychotic activity, are as potent inhibitors of DA-stimulated adenylate cyclase as are pimozide (116) or haloperidol (297). A possible explanation for their lack of antipsychotic properties, in addition to the factors cited above for the butyrophenones, is that the central antimuscarinic effects of the antidepressant drugs antagonize the effects of these drugs on the DA receptor (420).

Supersensitivity to DA or DA agonists is not accompanied by an increase in DA-stimulated adenylate cyclase activity (640,641). This does not necessarily mean the DA-stimulated adenylate cyclase is not the DA receptor or part of the DA receptor. However, supersensitivity must be medicated by a mechanism other than an action on this enzyme.

Carenzi et al. (91) obtained autopsy brains from seven chronic schizophrenics and control subjects. DA-stimulated striatal adenylate cyclase activity in both groups was not significantly different and was inhibited equally by haloperidol. The same was true for basal adenylate cyclase activity. In the schizophrenics, but not the controls, there was a significant ($r=-.817$, $p<.05$) negative correlation between baseline and DA-stimulated adenylate cyclase activity. The authors speculated on the existence of two groups of schizophrenic patients with markedly different baseline adenylate cyclase activity and sensitivity to DA. This needs to be verified in additional autopsy specimens.

Baseline cyclic adenosine monophosphate (AMP) levels and probenecid-induced accumulations of cyclic-AMP in the lumbar CSF of schizophrenic patients were not significantly different from those of other psychiatric patients and normal controls (562). Neuroleptic treatment significantly reduces CSF cyclic levels in schizophrenic patients who show clinical improvement (61). This reduction is consistent with inhibition of DA-stimulated cyclase by these drugs.

A group of NE-sensitive adenylate cyclases which are widely distributed in rat brain are also inhibited by the neuroleptics (65, 462). It has been suggested that this adenylate cyclase may also be relevant to the antipsychotic actions of the neuroleptics, as pimozide and clozapine are both very potent inhibitors of this enzyme (65). However, the neuroleptic inhibition of the NE-stimulated adenylate cyclases studied by Palmer and Manian (462) did not correlate well with antipsychotic potency, Furthemore, the α receptor-blocker phenoxybenzamine is not antipsychotic, and the central noradrenergic agonist clonidine does not induce psychosis.

DA and Neuroleptic Binding Sites in Brain. Recently DA and neuroleptic receptors in the brain have been identified by radioactive labeling with forms of DA, other DA agonists, or antagonists. Stereospecific binding of high specific-activity ligands to distinguish specific and nonspecific binding is essential for success with this method. Using this method, Seeman and Snyder and their colleagues have identified what they believe is the authentic dopamine receptor in rat, calf, and human brain regions which are rich in postsynaptic DA nerve terminals (89,131, 546). DA's affinity for specific ^{3}H-DA binding sites is one hundred times its apparent affinity for the DA-sensitive adenylate cyclase. The Hopkins group believe that the DA receptor exists in two states, an agonist and an antagonist state (131). This would account for the fact that DA agonists have about fifty times greater ability to compete with ^{3}H-DA than ^{3}H-haloperidol for binding, whereas the reverse is true for antagonists. There is good agreement between the ability of neuroleptics to bind to the receptor and some of their pharmacological action, including inhibition of apomorphine stereotypy and antipsychotic effects (132, 174,332,547). Lee and Seeman (337) reported increased amounts of haloperidol binding sites in post-mortem brain material from several schizophrenic patients, some of whom were receiving neuroleptics at the time of death. Although preliminary, these results are encouraging about the usefulness of further study of DA receptors in schizophrenia. Possible relationships between the dopamine binding site and the DA-sensitive cyclase have been discussed (570). Interaction of DA with the binding site could be needed for activation of the cyclase.

Cools and Van Rossum (122) have—on the basis of extensive histochemical, electrophysiological, and pharmacological data which they have reviewed and synthesized—proposed that there are two distinct types of DA receptor: excitation-mediating DA receptors and inhibition-mediating DA receptors, each with its own agonists and antagonists. They suggest the existence of excitatory DA receptors which may be presynaptic and sensitive to apomorphine and haloperidol. The inhibition-mediating DA receptors may be postsynaptic and have a low dopamine turnover and thereby they may be insensitive to inhibitors of tyrosine hydroxylase. DPI (3,4-dihydroxy-phenylamine-2-imidazoline) may be an agonist, and ergometrine, piribedil, and noradrenaline may be antagonists for these excitatory receptors (121). The normal function of brain nuclei which contain both types of receptors will depend in part upon the relative balance of the two receptors. Drug effects would depend upon their differential ability to affect each type of receptor.

This provocative theory serves the useful purpose of challenging the assumption of uniform dopamine receptors throughout the central nervous system. It provides an impetus for further development of selective DA agonists and antagonists and a possible basis for explaining the heterogeneous response to drugs which affect DA in psychiatric patients and normals.

Acute and Long-Term Effects of Neuroleptics on Striatal Dopamine Receptors. As first demonstrated by Carlsson and Lindquist (96), acute administration of phenothiazines increases dopamine metabolites in rat brain. This has generally been attributed to postsynaptic blockade of DA receptors by the phenothiazines which activate the DA neurons to release more DA. This activation may be mediated by a cholinergic-GABAminergic loop which is disinhibited when the striatal DA receptors are blocked. Recently Arbuthnott et al. (24) have presented evidence that the feedback loop may not be required for the increased DA turnover produced by neuroleptics in the striatum. They found that lesions in the striatal-nigral pathway did not affect the increase in DA metabolites in the striatum. This could suggest that effects on presynaptic DA receptors mediate the increase in DA turnover produced by neuroleptics.

All classes of neuroleptics can raise striatal HVA or di-hydroxyphenylacetic acid (DOPAC) in the neostriatum following acute administration. Nyback et al. (447) have shown that synthesis and turnover of DA is increased acutely by antipsychotic neuroleptic drugs in a manner roughly proportional to their clinical efficacy. Anden et al. (13) found that chlorpromazine, haloperidol, and spiroperidol (clinically effective), but not promethazine (not clinically effective), can acutely increase striatal HVA in the rat. However, Stawarz et al. (584), using a broader series of antipsychotic drugs, recently found no correlation between antipsychotic potency and capacity to increase striatal HVA acutely. In particular, clozapine and thioridazine were less potent than would have been expected on clinical grounds. This may be the result of their anticholinergic properties. There is an extensive literature, which will not be reviewed here, on the comparative effects of classical neuroleptics and atypical neuroleptics on DA turnover in the striatum and the limbic regions. The aim of these studies has been to determine if those agents which produce low extrapyramidal symptoms, such as clozapine and thioridazine, have a relatively weaker effect on DA turnover in the striatum (11,15,372,660). Since clozapine increases DA turnover in the striatum as much as or more than it does in the nucleus accumbens or olfactory tubercle, it is unlikely that such selectivity is of clinical significance.

Scatton, Garret, and Joulu (533) reported differences in the acute and long-term effects of neuroleptics on striatal DA turnover. These investigators have found that twenty-four hours following daily injection of animals for twelve days of any of three different neuroleptics, or in young animals treated repeatedly with classical neuroleptics immediately after birth (637), there is a significant decrease in striatal DA turnover. In the former group, however, DA turnover is still stimulated for about four hours after the last dose. Scatton, Garret, and Joulu have speculated about a second feedback loop which inhibits DA turnover and which is sensitive to the low concentrations of DA blockers which are present twenty-four hours, but not four hours, after administration. Tolerance to the effects of chronic haloperidol administration on rabbit brain DA turnover was noted in the striatal and limbic regions but not in the frontal cortex (331). The effects of long-term administration of neuroleptics on tyrosine hydroxylase activity of rat striatum were recently studied by Lerner et al. (339). After eight to fourteen days of treatment, the maximum velocity (Vmax) of the enzyme was increased, which suggests an increase in the number of enzyme molecules. There is a time-dependent change in the rate constant (Km) for the enzyme cofactor. At twenty-three hours after the last dose, the enzyme is deactivated, due either to a change in the enzyme itself or to an accumulation of a competitive inhibitor. They, too, observed decreased DA turnover with long-term administration.

Some studies of schizophrenics given neuroleptics acutely and chronically have shown that the increases of CSF HVA after acute phenothiazine administration are diminished after chronic phenothiazine administration. These studies will be reviewed subsequently. Thus, there is evidence that tolerance develops to the capacity of these phenothiazine drugs to increase striatal dopamine turnover in schizophrenics. As will be discussed subsequently, no tolerance develops to the effect of neuroleptics on hypothalamo-pituitary DA receptors, as indicated by continued elevation of serum prolactin in phenothiazine-treated patients. The explanation for the lack of tolerance to the antipsychotic effects of the neuroleptics probably lies in the difference between the effects of neuroleptics on cortical DA receptors or perhaps of mesolimbic DA receptors compared with striatal DA receptors. The limbic receptors show no tolerance, whereas the striatal receptors do.

Dopaminergic-Cholinergic Interregulation. Numerous investigations of the role of neurotransmitters in the regulation of discrete behaviors in laboratory animals have demonstrated that frequently two or more neurotransmitters oppose or synergize with each other. Thermoregulation which is under noradrenergic, serotonergic, cholinergic, and probably dopaminergic control is a classic example (351, 437, 496). Such complexity allows for more precise regulation of biological processes. Considerable research has been carried out to determine the neuronal tracts, the neurotransmitters, and other influences which interact with DA activity of the nigro-striatal, mesolimbic, and tubero-infundibular pathways.

There is increasing evidence that nigro-striatal dopaminergic neurons synapse upon striatal cholinergic interneurons, which in turn can feed back upon the nigral neurons, perhaps by means of a GABAminergic striato-nigral neuron. Other cholinergic neurons of unknown origin also synapse on nigral dopaminergic neurons (12,288). Thus, dopaminergic neurons in the substantia nigra and cholinergic neurons in the neostriatum and elsewhere interact in such a way that the net outflow from the system leads to smooth regulation of a variety of motor activities (128).

Interference with striatal dopaminergic-cholinergic balance is relevant to the etiology of extrapyramidal symptoms (EPS)—for example, tremor, rigidity, and akinesia—which are seen both in Parkinson's disease and after treatment with neuroleptic drugs. The findings of decreased levels of endogenous DA in the striatum of patients with Parkinson's disease and the therapeutic efficacy of L-DOPA have prompted the major hypothesis for the etiology of EPS which characterized them as a "DA deficiency syndrome" (269,270). Furthermore, drugs which *increase* the availability of DA or stimulate DA receptors (e.g., L-DOPA, amphetamine, apomorphine) all improve EPS (41,164,419), whereas drugs which decrease the availability of DA or block DA receptors (e.g., reserpine, phenothiazines) all exacerbate EPS (269). However, EPS are not merely a "DA deficiency syndrome" but also, at least in part, an "ACh excess syndrome." Thus, drugs which decrease ACh action by blocking central muscarinic receptors (e.g., atropine) improve EPS (167); while the centrally active cholinesterase-inhibitor physostigmine aggravates EPS (167,635). The pharmacology of EPS thus represents a combination of both DA deficiency and ACh excess. The hypothesis of a DA-ACh imbalance in EPS states that the mutual antagonism between DA and ACh in the striatum is so altered that the balance tips in favor of ACh. This paradigm accounts for the simultaneous presence of ACh excess and DA deficiency.

Classically, the antipsychotic potency of the neuroleptic drugs has been thought to be directly proportional to their ability to produce EPS. In fact, as the derivation of their name suggests, the neuroleptic drugs were originally screened for their antipsychotic effects according to their ability to produce EPS. The possibility that the capacity of neuroleptic drugs to produce EPS is directly correlated with blockade of striatal DA receptors (590) gave rise to the hypothesis that the antipsychotic effects of these drugs could also be directly correlated with blockade of central DA receptors. However, when it was found that the two potent antipsychotic drugs clozapine and thioridazine produced only weak EPS (34, 591), it appeared that the theory might have to be rejected or modified. The lack of EPS produced by these antipsychotic drugs has recently been attributed to their cholinolytic (anticholinergic) properties (420,571). Thus, clozapine and thioridazine, which produce few EPS, are relatively potent cholinolytics, while fluphenazine and haloperidol, which produce a high incidence of EPS, have relatively weak anticholinergic effects.

These data are all consistent with the ACh-DA paradigm proposed for Parkinson's disease, and exemplify the extreme caution one must employ when extrapolating findings in one central DA system, such as the nigrostriatal system, to any other DA system.

Tardive dyskinesia consists of involuntary, rhythmic, stereotyped movements usually occurring in the oral area (the so-called bucco-linguomasticatory syndrome) (33,129,316). They develop during prolonged treatment with a neuroleptic drug or shortly after a reduction in dosage or discontinuation of such treatments. It has been proposed that, analogous to the situation in Parkinson's disease, tardive dyskinesia can also be conceived as an imbalance in striatal dopaminergic and cholinergic activity, only with the balance tipped in the opposite direction to parkinsonism; thus, increased DA or decreased ACh can promote symptoms of tardive dyskinesia, while decreased dopaminergic activity or increased cholinergic activity relieves symptoms of tardive dyskinesia (180,211, 318). Klawans (316) has summarized the evidence that tardive dyskinesia may be the result of increased responsiveness of DA receptors due to neuroleptic-induced "denervation supersensitivity": that is, prolonged blockade of DA receptors by neuroleptic drugs, and thus a prolonged reduction of dopaminergic stimulation, may cause postsynaptic DA receptors to become more sensitive to DA in order to compensate for DA loss. This receptor supersensitivity causes DA to dominate over ACh in the striatum and thereby to produce dyskinesia.

Tardive dyskinesia might then be expected to exhibit almost the opposite pharmacology from Parkinson's disease, and a good deal of data suggest that this is so. For example, drugs which *decrease* DA activity—such as reserpine, tetrabenazine, AMPT, and even higher doses of neuroleptics—tend to *reduce* tardive dyskinesia, while L-DOPA, which *increases* DA availability, also *exacerbates* tardive dyskinesia (211,300, 301,302). On the other hand, physostigmine and 2-dimethylaminoethanol (Deanol), drugs which *increase* ACh, also *improve* tardive dyskinesia; whereas anticholinergic drugs, which *decrease* ACh action, exacerbate symptoms (103,178,211,316). No beneficial clinical effect or significant side effects with Deanol treatment were found in four chronic schizophrenics, two of whom had tardive dyskinesia. Nevertheless, it has been proposed that tardive dyskinesia might represent both a "DA excess syndrome" and an "ACh deficiency syndrome" (144).

It has been tentatively proposed that psychosis might have a DA-ACh balance tipped in the same direction as in tardive dyskinesia and in the opposite direction to that in Parkinson's disease, so that increased DA or decreased ACh can promote psychotic symptoms, while decreased DA or increased ACh can relieve psychotic symptoms (142,195,283).

There is mixed pharmacologic evidence for a cholinergic-dopaminergic balance in man which is relevant to schizophrenia (464). Acute administration of arecoline and physostigmine (drugs which increase ACh activity) to schizophrenics has been reported to improve some symptoms of schizophrenia (472,628). Rosenthal and Bigelow (517) found that chronic administration of low doses of physostigmine was moderately helpful clinically. However, acute intravenous administration of physostigmine does not seem to have any antipsychotic properties (426) and may even cause schizophrenic patients to become more depressed (283).

Janowsky, El-Yousef, and Davis (282) have found that physostigmine prevented the methylphenidate-induced activation of schizophrenia. Cholinolytic agents may themselves produce a psychosis when given in high doses—for example, Ditran (1) and benztropine (173). The psychoses produced by these cholinolytics are not as similar to schizophrenia as is amphetamine psychosis, but they resemble toxic confusional states with disorientation and memory loss. When given to schizophrenics, Ditran can activate schizophrenic symptoms (214). However, these cholinolytic agents do *not* usually activate psychosis when they are given to schizophrenics to alleviate the extrapyramidal symptoms which develop during treatment with neuroleptics. This finding could relate to the report of Anden (10) that cholinergic receptors of limbic dopaminergic neurons may not be as responsive to cholinolytic agents as are those of the substantia nigra. Therefore, antiparkinsonian effects of cholinolytic drugs might be seen at lower doses than those required to activate psychosis.

There is some evidence linking cyclic guanosine monophosphate (GMP) accumulation with the activity of cholinergic neurons (209). Several investigators have sought to use CSF cyclic GMP levels as an index of brain cholinergic activity in schizophrenia. However, there is evidence from animal studies that brain cyclic GMP levels are sensitive to dopaminergic mechanisms (244). Thus, the results of cyclic-GMP-level studies are not necessarily related to acetylcholine. Ebstein et al. (169) reported that mean CSF cyclic GMP levels of twenty-seven drug-free schizophrenics was lower than that of controls, but this difference did not attain statistical significance. Phenothiazine treatment for two months produced a 50 percent increase in cyclic GMP levels. These investigators concluded that the results could indicate decreased activity of central cholinergic neurons in the drug-free schizophrenics, possibly due to increased dopaminergic activity. The increase due to neuroleptics is consistent with the dopamine-blocking action of neuroleptics which disinhibits postsynaptic cholinergic neurons. Interestingly, anticholinergic drugs had no apparent effect on the increase in CSF cyclic GMP levels. Smith et al. (562) also found a tendency for low CSF cyclic GMP levels in schizophrenics. There was no difference in patients who were receiving pimozide and those who were drug-free. These results and their interpretation, if confirmed, require further study.

In a series of recent reports Singh and collaborators (555,556,557, 558) have reported that anticholinergics can reverse the therapeutic effects of neuroleptics, particularly those such as chlorpromazine, which have some anticholinergic activity of their own which summates with the effects of the more potent anticholinergics prescribed for alleviation of EPS. On this basis they propose that the basic abnormality in schizophrenia may be a relative decrease in cholinergic activity, and that the capacity of neuroleptics to promote cholinergic activity may be the basis of their therapeutic effect. These studies require additional confirmation.

Receptor Supersensitivity. Receptor supersensitivity is a concept of growing importance in neuropharmacology; it refers to variations of receptor response in accordance with the availability of its neurotransmitter: that is, in the absence of neurotransmitter, a receptor becomes "supersensitive" so as to respond maximally to any remaining transmitter. Conversely, when neurotransmitter exists in excess, the receptor sensitivity is diminished. The fluctuation of receptor sensitivity has been demonstrated most elegantly for the adrenergic receptors of the cat nictitating membrane (335).

Recently many investigators have demonstrated changes in the sensitivities of central DA receptors after various pharmacologic agents or brain lesions. The turning behavior which develops in rats after unilateral destruction of the substantia nigra has been attributed to a form of "behavioral supersensitivity," presumably due to supersensitivity of postsynaptic DA receptors which develops after structural denervation (617). When DA receptors are chronically blocked by neuroleptic drugs (i.e., pharmacologically denervated), the stereotypy resulting from DA agonists is much enhanced (534). However, a similar supersensitivity of stereotyped motor behavior develops as well after chronic stimulation of DA receptors (317). These and other complexities in interpreting behavioral assays of DA function make it difficult to equate "behavioral supersensitivity" to postsynaptic neuronal receptor supersensitivity. Behavioral aspects of drug-induced dopaminergic supersensitivity are fully discussed by Moore and Thornburg (427) and Ungerstedt et al. (618).

More direct investigation of neuronal sensitivity has been made by studying the depression of neuronal firing caused by DA. A microiontophoretic study of the caudate nucleus depleted of DA by intraventricular 6-hydroxydopamine showed an increase in the ability of DA to depress neuronal firing which was induced by excitant amino acids in animals under general anesthesia (553).

Supersensitivity of DA receptors may be relevant to dopaminergic hyperactivity in schizophrenia. This has been discussed by Bowers (72) on the basis of a lack of increase in CSF HVA. Klawans (317) has also advocated this concept as the basis of schizophrenia as well as of amphetamine psychosis based on the reports of Janowsky et al. (283), Connell (120), Johnson and Milner (289), and West (653) that schizophrenics are unusually sensitive to methylphenidate or amphetamine. Dose-response curves for selected effects of a DA agonist such as apomorphine or a DA-releasing agent such as amphetamine will be needed in untreated schizophrenics and controls to test this hypothesis.

ENZYMATIC BREAKDOWN

The enzymatic breakdown of DA can be divided into two independent pathways, namely deamination by MAO (516) and O-methylation by catechol-O-methyltransferase (COMT) (32). These two enzymes can act consecutively upon DA or the ensuing catabolite and in either order.

COMT is a soluble enzyme and ubiquitous throughout the brain. The physiologic role of COMT is uncertain; it may serve to increase tyrosine hydroxylase activity by reducing the concentration of deaminated catecholamines which can inhibit tyrosine hydroxylase (287). COMT is located in glial cells, which suggests it may serve to inactivate the DA and the NE taken up from the synaptic cleft by glial cells (298). Matthysse and Baldessarini (373) studied the activity of this enzyme in the red blood cells of schizophrenics and controls and found no significant difference. COMT activity in red blood cells may not correlate with COMT activity in dopaminergic brain regions.

Dill and Campbell (151) have reported that 3-methoxytyramine (O-methyl-dopamine), the product of O-methylation of DA, can produce effects on the basal ganglia similar to those of known hallucinogens, such as mescaline; and they proposed that 3-methoxytyramine could be an endogenous psychotoxin in schizophrenia. No direct evidence for this hypothesis has been presented. O-methyl-dopamine might be likely to accumulate in some cases of schizophrenia, if there is indeed a deficiency in the MAO which inactivates DA in some areas of schizophrenia. The role of MAO in schizophrenia will be discussed subsequently.

DOPAMINE METABOLITES IN CEREBROSPINAL FLUID (CSF) OF SCHIZOPHRENIC PATIENTS

Homovanillic acid (HVA), the major metabolite of DA, is formed as a result of both O-methylation and deamination. Dihydroxyphenylacetic (DOPAC) is an intermediate in the formation of HVA, the product of deamination without O-methylation. It is believed to reflect intraneuronal metabolism of DA (512). Under some circumstances DOPAC may be a better index than HVA of the functional activity of nigro-striatal DA neurons (519). It has been proposed that DOPAC may be an endogenous inhibitor of the enzyme which forms psychotomimetic methylated indoleamines, and that the antipsychotic effect of neuroleptics may be related to the rise in the intraneuronal content of DOPAC acting as a methylation regulator (644).

It is believed that the major contributor to CSF HVA is the caudate nucleus and other dopaminergic structures which border on the lateral ventricles (206,563,576). The increase in dopamine turnover which occurs when dopamine receptors are blocked with neuroleptic drugs is reflected in an increase in lumbar CSF HVA levels (202,469). HVA, as well as other acid metabolites, can be actively transported from the CSF to the blood via the choroid plexus (29). This transport can be inhibited by high concentrations of the drug probenecid (242). Recent studies of CSF HVA have therefore included pretreatment with probenecid to diminish the efflux of HVA from CSF and thereby abolish the 5:1 concentration gradient which exists from ventricular to lumbar CSF. The probenecid technique requires that probenecid levels be measured in CSF, since the degree of inhibition of acid metabolite efflux varies as a function of probenecid concentration (118), especially at low concentrations of probenecid (467). HVA from the blood is believed ordinarily not to enter the CSF (475) but may do so when blood HVA levels are increased, as after L-DOPA administration (485).

If schizophrenia were associated with a generalized increase in brain DA turnover, HVA in unmedicated schizophrenics should be increased. The absence of an increase would not, however, rule out the possibility of increased DA turnover in dopaminergic neurons which do not significantly contribute to the CSF HVA. For example, the contribution of HVA to CSF by the mesolimbic and limbic cortical dopaminergic neurons (which, as mentioned previously, may be the critical ones for the pathophysiology of schizophrenia) may be too small, in part because these neurons may be too far from the lateral ventricles to contribute much HVA to the CSF relative to that of the caudate.

Chase, Schur, and Gordon (109) found normal HVA levels in six chronic schizophrenic patients who had been drug-free for at least two weeks. No probenecid was employed. The fact that these patients had recently been receiving neuroleptics diminishes the significance of this finding. Rimon et al. (505) compared CSF HVA levels (no probenecid) in thirty-one untreated, acute schizophrenics and twenty-seven non-schizophrenic psychiatric patients. There were no significant differences in the groups as a whole. However, patients with paranoid states had significantly higher CSF HVA levels than nonparanoid schizophrenics plus a small control group. The basis for selecting the small control group (nine out of a possible twenty-seven) was not stated.

Bowers and Van Woert (73) using relatively low doses of probenecid, found levels of CSF HVA in acute schizophrenics which were not different from controls. Bowers (70) studied CSF levels of HVA and the serotonin metabolite 5-hydroxyindole-acetic acid (5-HIAA) after probenecid administration in three different groups: (1) twelve patients who developed psychotic episodes following self-administration of psychotomimetic drugs (probably LSD); (2) eighteen nondrug-induced schizophrenic patients; and (3) fifteen prison inmate controls. He found that CSF HVA was not significantly different in the three groups. However, 5-HIAA levels were decreased in the drug-induced psychotic patients—a decrease which was attributed to a direct effect of LSD on the activity of serotonergic neurons. In a later study Bowers (71) measured CSF HVA and 5-HIAA in eighteen untreated acute psychotics (with probenecid, but without measuring probenecid in CSF) and compared the levels with those of depressive patients and prison inmates. For all psychotics HVA and 5-HIAA levels were not significantly different from either control group. However, when the schizophrenics were subdivided into Schneider positive or Schneider negative—that is, according to the presence or absence, respectively, of one or more first-rank symptoms of schizophrenia as defined by Schneider (538)—5-HIAA tended to be high and HVA low in the Schneider-positive group. The ratio of 5-HIAA to HVA was significantly elevated in Schneider-positive psychotics when compared with Schneider-negative psychotics, depressed patients, and inmates. Specific psychotic symptoms were better correlated with 5-HIAA levels than with HVA levels. In a fourth study Bowers (72) utilized high doses of probenecid and corrected for the amount of probenecid in CSF. Subdividing patients on the basis of Stephens-Astrup prognosis ratings, poor-prognosis schizophrenics had significantly lower mean HVA levels [95 ± Sample Error (S.E.) 12 nanograms (ng)/ml] than did eight good-prognosis schizophrenics (124 ± S.E. 20 ng/ml). Eleven patients with affective psychosis had mean CSF HVA levels (142 ± S.E. 14 ng/ml) which were significantly higher than those in poor-prognosis schizophrenics but not in good-prognosis schizophrenics. There were no differences in 5-HIAA levels or probenecid values of the three groups.

Fyro et al. (202) found normal levels of HVA in CSF of twelve untreated schizophrenics. This group consistently finds CSF HVA levels higher in females than in males.

Post et al. (481) studied 5-HIAA and HVA in twenty acutely psychotic unmedicated schizophrenics, patients with affective psychoses, and controls, with and without probenecid. No significant differences in 5-HIAA and HVA levels in the acute schizophrenics, affective psychoses, and controls were found. Patients with more Schneider-positive symptoms had lower 5-HIAA accumulations and lower HVA accumulations. The latter finding is in agreement with Bowers (71), but the former is the opposite of Bowers's findings. Following recovery from the acute episode, probenecid-induced accumulations of HVA were reduced compared with those in the acute stage in schizophrenics but not in patients recovered from acute mania. Patients who had been ill longer than one month prior to hospitalization tended to have lower HVA levels after recovery than patients ill for less than one month. This difference was taken as preliminary evidence that dopamine turnover might be reduced in the prepsychotic phase and relatively increased in the acute stage. It is difficult to evaluate this finding because only twelve of seventeen schizophrenic patients and six of sixteen manic patients were studied in the recovered phase; yet the mean levels were compared with the entire sample of schizophrenic and manic patients. Nevertheless, this is a most important lead and points up the need for longitudinal studies in unmedicated patients, through as many cycles of health and illness as possible, with collection of a variety of behavioral data to correlate with the biological data.

Van Praag and Korpf (633) studied CSF HVA with probenecid pretreatment and measurement of CSF probenecid in thirty-three psychotic patients, most of whom would be diagnosed as schizophrenic, and controls (number not specified). Van Praag and Korpf divided the psychotic patients into those with (1) motor agitation and anxiety, (2) anxiety but no motor agitation, and (3) neither motor agitation nor anxiety. They found that HVA levels were significantly increased in the group with motor agitation when compared with the controls or with the other two psychotic groups; and they postulated that increased dopamine turnover must be related to motor activity and not to "true" psychotic symptoms. It is not possible to evaluate this report fully, since the differences in HVA levels between the motor-agitation group and the other was relatively small, the standard deviation was rather large, and an inappropriate statistical test was utilized: students' t without correction for the number of comparisons performed rather than an analysis of variance. Sedvall et al. (545) found no relationship between motor activity and CSF HVA in manic patients.

Van Praag and Korpf (634) reported that the percentage increase in CSF HVA following one week's neuroleptic treatment correlated with overall clinical improvement or improvement in delusions, hallucinations, and anxiety, and that the percentage increase in HVA was greatest in those with severe extrapyramidal side effects. There was no difference in dose-corrected incidence of extrapyramidal side effects with low- or high-potency neuroleptics. The CSF HVA response to probenecid was less in those patients who developed a "hypokinetic-rigid" syndrome. This provocative study needs further replication, which must include measurement of blood levels of the parent drug and active metabolites.

Markianos, Ruther, and Gluba (368) determined DOPAC and HVA levels in the serum and CSF of thirteen drug-free psychotic patients who were not further described. DOPAC levels were higher than HVA levels in both specimens for most patients, but the DOPAC/HVA ratio varied from 0.5 to 10.6, mean 2.6 for serum and 1.8 for CSF. No comparison with levels in normal controls was made.

With the exception of the studies of Post et al. (481) and with Van Praag and Korpf (633), all other studies of lumbar CSF HVA in unmedicated acute schizophrenics (total N>100) have found low-normal HVA levels. Thus, it seems likely that there is no increase in dopamine turnover, at least in the caudate nucleus of acute schizophrenic patients. As stated previously, this conclusion should not be used to reject the hypothesis of increased DA turnover in schizophrenia, since the functional activity of DA relevant to schizophrenia may not be measured by the method. Furthermore, Bowers (72) has cited unpublished data demonstrating that initial HVA levels in untreated schizophrenics are negatively correlated with the dose of a phenothiazine necessary to produce remission. This could indicate that increased transmission in DA pathways such as the mesolimbic or the mesocortical systems is associated with decreased turnover of DA in the striatum. Bowers (72) and Curzon (136) have pointed out that supersensitivity of DA receptors might permit an increased DA activity in the face of low or normal HVA levels.

GABA AND SCHIZOPHRENIA

Roberts (508) has hypothesized that the inhibitory neurotransmitter gamma-aminobutyric acid (GABA) may be deficient in schizophrenia. He has theorized that there may be pacemaker or command neurons which utilize GABA as a neurotransmitter and which inhibit complex preprogramed neuronal circuits that regulate discrete bits of behavior. A decrease in the activity of these GABA neurons might initiate hyperactivity of dopaminergic neurons. There is accumulating evidence that GABAminergic neurons with cell bodies in the globus pallidus, and possibly the putamen, synapse on the dopaminergic neuronal cell bodies in the substantia nigra and inhibit the activity of these neurons (314, 362,680). Fonnum, Walaas, and Iversen (188) have provided biochemical evidence for GABAminergic neurons in various rat limbic areas. Anden (11) reported that the GABA transaminase inhibitor aminoxyacetic acid similarly inhibited the haloperidol-induced increase in DA turnover in the striatum and mesolimbic regions, which suggests similar endogenous GABA mechanisms in these regions.

Stevens, Wilson, and Foote (587) postulated that the ventral tegmental area (VTA) in the rat might receive GABA efferents from limbic dopaminergic tracts—that is, from nucleus accumbens septi, olfactory tubercle, and the nucleus of the stria terminalis. They injected the putative GABA-blocking agent bicuculine into the VTA or the substantia nigra of freely moving cats with stereotactically implanted cannulas. Bicuculine in the VAT rapidly produced hypervigilance, followed by staring, crouching, and the appearance of intense fear. This was followed by behavior which was cautiously and tentatively characterized as catalepsy, stereotypy, waxy flexibility, and possible hallucinations. Injection of bicuculine into the substantia nigra produced grooming, circling, and hyperesthesia. Amphetamine potentiated and haloperidol inhibited the effects of bicuculine injected into the VTA. The authors favored the conclusion that bicuculine in the VTA blocked GABA inhibition of mesolimbic dopaminergic units which mediate dopaminergic stereotyped behavior. However, they pointed out the possibility of a cholinergic influence on the VTA and of nonspecific synaptic excitant effects of bicuculine.

These GABA studies require verification and extension of the investigation of the role of GABA in mesocortical and mesolimbic dopaminergic activity.

Because GABA levels in brain increase rapidly after removal or death, direct measurement of GABA in brain is not likely to be a useful test of the GABA hypothesis of schizophrenia. However, the activity of glutamic acid decarboxylase (GAD), the enzyme which controls the synthesis of GABA, can be measured in post-mortem material. It has been repeatedly demonstrated that GABA levels and GAD activity are markedly decreased in the brains of deceased Huntington's chorea patients (359,468), a disease which sometimes presents with schizophrenic symptoms (207) and which is partially responsive to neuroleptic drugs (178,506) and GABA-minergic agents (15,374). GAD activity has not been found to be decreased in a pilot study of schizophrenic brains (361); but because of the great difficulty in interpreting results in post-mortem studies of psychiatric patients who have been treated for many years with high doses of neuroleptic drugs, who may have intercurrent illnesses at the time of death, and who may not have even been adequately diagnosed in the first place, more studies of GAD activity must be carried out. Even if no definitive decrease in total GAD activity is found in specific brain regions, this would not provide a definitive rejection of the role of GABA, because the *functional* activity of the enzyme might still have been reduced *in vivo*, or conceivably GABA inactivation might have been enhanced. Determination of GABA levels in the CSF of untreated and neuroleptic-treated schizophrenics could also be of interest. Glaeser and Hare (218) have developed a method sensitive enough to detect the low levels of GABA present in CSF. Their preliminary results indicate lower lovels in schizophrenics than in neurological control groups.*

For a more complete review of the role of GABA in schizophrenia, the recent article by Van Kammen (629) is useful.

CONCLUSIONS

The dopamine hypothesis of schizophrenia is supported by a wide variety of indirect evidence, chiefly derived from pharmacological studies. There can be little question that the ability to block DA receptors plays a major role in the antipsychotic action of neuroleptics, with the possible exception of clozapine. The hypothesis that amphetamine psychosis is dopaminergically mediated is also well supported. There is, however, scant direct evidence in support of the DA hypothesis. The recent reports from Seeman's group of increased specific DA-receptor building in the brains of deceased schizophrenics is an initial step in the provision of such evidence; but important issues of drug effects must be further investigated.

The failure of antipsychotic drugs to halt the deterioration of social functioning and to eliminate psychopathology in many chronic schizophrenics suggests the existence of important biological and social psychological factors for the phenotypic expression of schizophrenia. On the other hand, the usefulness of neuroleptics in the treatment of all the major psychoses—the acute schizophreniform psychoses, mania, depres-

---

* Glaeser, B. S., and Hare, T. A., personal communication.

sion, unspecified psychoses, and drug-induced psychoses—suggests that the fact that reduction of dopaminergic activity leads to clinical improvement cannot be used as evidence that increased dopamine activity is the cause of schizophrenia, unless one is willing to accept all these pathological states as manifestations of the same basic illness. This is unlikely from genetic data. Therefore, *it seems safest to conclude at the present time that the reduction of dopaminergic activity is a nonspecific means of alleviating psychotic symptomatology.*

Neuroendocrine Studies in Schizophrenia

Previous reviews of endocrine studies of schizophrenics in this series (78,193) have focused on possible dysfunction of the endocrine glands—such as the thyroid, adrenal, testes, or ovaries—as a possible cause or concomitant of the schizophrenic syndrome. Research along these lines has diminished greatly in the last decade, despite the vastly greater knowledge of endocrine function in man.

Nevertheless, the last five years have seen a tremendous burst of interest in the use of endocrine methods and techniques to study schizophrenia and its treatment. This new research interest is based on very strong evidence that many functions of the "master gland," the pituitary, are regulated by hypothalamic hormones whose release is dependent on neural function. Thus, hypothalamic neural activity may be monitored by studying pituitary function directly or via the function of the target organs. Because of the need to take advantage of any means available to study neural function in schizophrenia, the endocrine approach has attracted great interest.

The major foci of interest in schizophrenia research to date has been the study of prolactin and growth-hormone secretion. The secretion of both of these hormones is controlled in part by DA and 5-HT (364,369, 376,662), two neurotransmitters which figure heavily in current theories of the etiology of schizophrenia. By monitoring prolactin and growth-hormone secretion in laboratory animals, normals, and schizophrenics, both with and without drug treatment, it has been possible to increase our knowledge of dopaminergic and serotonergic neuronal activity and of the effects of drugs on these neurotransmitters. There is evidence, especially from animal studies, that other neurotransmitters—such as 5-HT and thyrotropin-releasing hormone—can affect prolactin or growth-hormone secretion. This finding means that caution must be exercised in interpreting prolactin and growth-hormone secretion only in terms of dopaminergic and serotonergic influences. However, it also offers the opportunity to utilize prolactin and growth-hormone secretion to monitor the effects of these substances or of drugs which affect these substances. It should also be noted that secretion of other pituitary hormones, such as thyroid-stimulating hormone and adrenocorticotrophic hormone, is regulated, in part, by hypothalamic neurons, so that studies similar to those to be discussed for prolactin and growth hormone can be based on monitoring the secretion of these substances.

The major determinant of prolactin secretion from the pituitary gland appears to be the tonic inhibitory influence of DA released from the tubero-infundibular DA neurons of the hypothalamus. DA may reach the pituitary via the pituitary-portal circulation and inhibits prolactin release directly. Drugs which *increase* dopaminergic activity—such as L-DOPA, apomorphine, or ergot alkaloids—all *decrease* serum prolactin levels. On the other hand, drugs which *decrease* dopaminergic activity—such as the neuroleptics—*increase* serum prolactin levels (159,352,377,597). Monoamine oxidase inhibitors, which should increase brain DA, have been reported to increase serum prolactin in man (559). This paradoxical effect will require verification and further study.

Thus, serum prolactin levels can be utilized as an indirect assay of the activity of tubero-infundibular DA neurons. This provides a powerful and noninvasive tool for studying the activity of a central DA system in man, since useful information can be obtained about brain through the study of patients' blood. Furthermore, this strategy provides a monitoring system in man and animals for assessing the effects of drugs on tubero-infundibular DA neurons. Thus, measurement of the effects of drugs on serum prolactin levels has been advocated as a method of screening drugs for possible antipsychotic activity (115). This has led to the successful testing of thiethylperazine as an antipsychotic drug (528) and to the suggestion that perlapine, a dibenzodiazepine chemically related to clozapine, may be an antipsychotic (403). However, there are at least three problems with this strategy: (1) not all drugs which increase prolactin do so by blocking DA receptors, and only those which do are likely to also be antipsychotic; (2) there is questionable need for more drugs which are antipsychotic by virtue of their ability to block DA receptors, as opposed to those which act via other mechanisms; (3) one must be cautious in extrapolating drug effects in the tubero-infundibular DA system to other DA systems, because the identity of their pharmacological responses and receptor characteristics is yet to be established, although there is suggestive evidence of their similarity (115,403,405).

Serum prolactin levels have usually been found to be normal or slightly elevated in unmedicated acute and chronic schizophrenic patients.* Only a few schizophrenics have had prolactin levels monitored during an extended period of the day (405). These patients show no excess of prolactin secretion. If there was increased DA reaching the pituitary or supersensitive DA receptors, decreased prolactin secretion would be predicted. The fact that this has not been observed does not mean that increased dopaminergic activity does not occur in other dopaminergic regions of a schizophrenic's brain. Johnstone, Crow, and Mashiter (292) found significant negative correlations between changes in serum prolactin levels in unmedicated schizophrenics and two of nine measures of psychopathology: incoherence of speech and total positive symptoms. They suggested these results are consistent with the possibility that increasing severity of schizophrenic disturbance is associated with increasing levels of DA release. The fluctuations in serum prolactin

---

* See references 292, 323, 402, 405, and 412.

levels during the brief period these were assessed were of a small magnitude. No such relationship was found by Meltzer, Sachar, and Frantz (412). However, they did find a nonsignificant negative correlation between severity of psychopathology and serum prolactin levels in twenty-two unmedicated schizophrenic patients.

It is well established that the phenothiazines raise serum prolactin levels in humans (319,402,615). This accounts for the galactorrhea (inappropriate discharge of milk from the breasts) produced by these agents in some female patients taking phenothiazines (58). Only those phenothiazines which are antipsychotic have been shown to increase serum prolactin levels in rats (115). Thioridazine, an antipsychotic phenothiazine, with relatively weak DA-receptor-blocking capacities and potent cholinolytic properties in the striatum, is able to produce large increases in serum prolactin in schizophrenics (402,413) and normals (527). Clozapine, an antipsychotic agent with properites similar to thioridazine, can elevate plasma prolactin in rats (399). Clozapine produces small increases in serum prolactin in man, far less than would be expected on the basis of its clinical potency (405). The reason for and significance of this qualitative difference between clozapine and classical neuroleptics is not known.

Serum prolactin levels in normals and schizophrenics are elevated within 30 to 60 minutes after the first oral ingestion of chlorpromazine. Serum prolactin became persistently elevated after the first oral dose of several phenothiazines in twelve of twenty schizophrenics. Possible reasons for lack of an increase in all patients include patients not taking medication, problems in absorption, rapid metabolism, or failure of the tubero-infundibular neurons to respond. After several days of phenothiazine administration, serum prolactin levels were elevated in all subjects studied by Meltzer, Sachar, and Frantz (411,412) and Meltzer and Fang (402).

Serum prolactin levels in normals and schizophrenics are elevated within 15 to 30 minutes after an intramuscular injection of 50 milligrams of chlorpromazine. There is a tendency for the increases in plasma prolactin levels to be slightly lower in the schizophrenics.* Following oral administration of doses of neuroleptics equivalent to at least 200 milligrams of chlorpromazine, twice daily, serum prolactin levels usually become persistently elevated.† The increases in males are less than those in females. As can be seen in figure 2–2 serum prolactin levels increase up to approximately 600 milligrams of chlorpromazine per day when the drug is given on a twice-a-day schedule orally, and the serum prolactin levels are measured 11 hours after the evening dose. The dose-response relationship in the linear phase reflects the strong correlation between prolactin levels and blood levels of chlorpromazine or its active metabolites (322,446). We have also demonstrated a strong correlation between serum prolactin and chlorpromazine levels in schizophrenic sera, as in figure 2–3.‡ Kolakowska et al. (323) found no correlation between plasma chlorpromazine and prolactin levels in chronic schizophrenics given 150 to 600 milligrams of chlorpromazine in divided doses. The

---

* Meltzer et al.: in preparation.
† See references 58, 59, 322, 402, and 411.
‡ Meltzer, Fang, Creese, and Snyder: unpublished data.

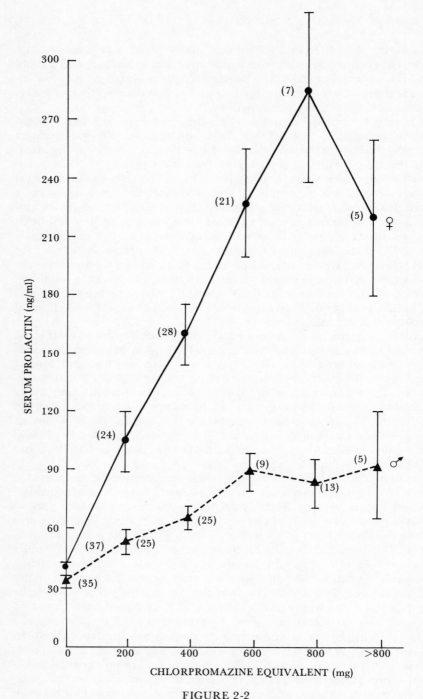

FIGURE 2-2

Effect of Neuroleptic Treatment on Serum Prolactin Levels.

Schizophrenic patients (number in parentheses) were treated with chlorpromazine, thioridazine, fluphenazine, or haloperidol on a twice-a-day schedule. Blood samples were obtained after at least one week at each dose level, 12 hours after the last dose. All dosages were converted to chlorpromazine equivalent (142). No adjustments were made for differences in subject's body weight.

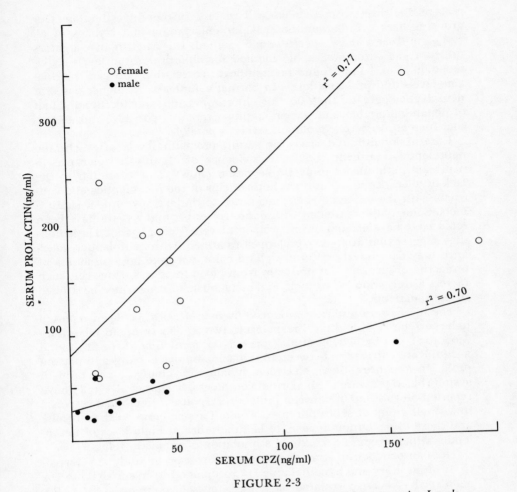

FIGURE 2-3

Correlation between Serum Prolactin and Serum Chlorpromazine Levels.

Blood samples from subjects receiving chlorpromazine (200 milligrams orally [p.o.] twice a day) were analyzed for prolactin levels by radioimmunoassay and for chlorpromazine and its active metabolites by ability to compete for dopamine-receptor binding. (I. Creese and S.H. Snyder: personal communication.)

reasons for these discrepancies will require further investigation. Our group utilizes a radioimmunoassay for chlorpromazine; Nyback et al. (447) utilizes a mass spectroscopic method; the English investigators utilize a gas chromatographic method for chlorpromazine levels. Nikitopoulou et al. (444) found no significant correlation between thioridazine levels and prolactin levels in normal volunteers. At higher doses of neuroleptics (greater than 600 mg chlorpromazine), no additional effect of dopaminergic blockade on prolactin secretion is possible, and no further increase in serum prolactin levels is possible (403).

Careful longitudinal study of serum prolactin levels after chronic neuroleptic treatment reveals no evidence of significant tolerance to neuroleptic-stimulated prolactin secretion (402). This is similar to the lack of tolerance to the antipsychotic effects of the neuroleptics and contrasts with the development of tolerance to the extrapyramidal side effects. Some patients treated with neuroleptics for many years have been reported to have normal serum prolactin levels (59,147,322). These findings suggest that after very prolonged treatment with neuroleptics, tolerance may develop, the pituitary gland cannot secrete large amounts of prolactin, or clearance of prolactin from blood increases. However, such factors as ingestion, absorption, and metabolism of drugs must be studied in these patients.

The increase in prolactin produced by neuroleptics has been reported to be correlated with clinical response in two studies from our laboratory (402,405) and by Sedvall et al. (544). Nikitopoulou et al. (444) found a significant correlation between thioridazine-induced changes in plasma prolactin and drowsiness, electroencephalogram changes, and drop in systolic blood pressure in six normal volunteers. Sachar et al. (528) have reported no correlation between prolactin response and clinical response in a small group of schizophrenics. The difference between their results and those of our group appears to be due to use of high doses of neuroleptics which produce a maximal stimulation of prolactin release.

The neuroendocrine strategy has also been used to study supersensitivity of pituitary and hypothalamic DA receptors. Supersensitivity to DA agonists has been postulated as a basis of schizophrenia (316). Behavioral, biochemical, and neurophysiological supersensitivity to DA agonists at striatal and limbic DA receptors has been frequently demonstrated in rats or mice following cessation of administration of a variety of neuroleptics or following lesions of DA neurons. (See Meltzer and Stahl [416] for additional references.) Reid has reported the same for the hypothalamus.

Studies of development of supersensitivity of DA receptors of the rat pituitary following chronic neuroleptic treatment or hypothalamic lesions have produced conflicting results (81,110,405,493). Studies of supersensitivity of pituitary hormone secretion in response to apomorphine in schizophrenics with or without tardive dyskinesia have also produced conflicting results. No difference in the increase in growth hormone or no fall in prolactin following apomorphine (0.75 mg per kg injected subcutaneously) between scrizophrenics and controls has been reported in two studies (176,405). Langer et al. (334) have found that the peak growth-hormone response to intravenous d-amphetamine was the same in eight schizophrenic patients (three chronic, five acute).

However, Rotrosen et al. (521) found relatively high growth-hormone responses to apomorphine in schizophrenics who subsequently failed to respond to neuroleptics, and relatively low growth-hormone responses to schizophrenics who did respond compared with normal controls. No such differences were seen in response to L-DOPA. These results were interpreted in terms of supersensitivity of DA receptors in the nonresponding schizophrenics. Tamminga et al. (602) found a diminished growth-hormone and prolactin response to apomorphine in chronic schizophrenics compared with normal controls. Thus, there is as yet no consensus in this important area. Standardization of test procedures, better diagnostic procedures, and assessment of clinical research are needed.

The neuroendocrine strategy in schizophrenia research will undoubtedly expand in the next decade as radioimmunoassays for the hypothalamic hormones become available, as our understanding of the biochemical mechanisms regulating hypothalamic hormone factors increases, and as new drugs to perturb these systems become available. Furthermore, the pituitary and hypothalamic hormones undoubtedly have many profound central effects, and these could be a factor in the etiology of one or more types of schizophrenia.

Dopamine-β-Hydroxylase and Schizophrenia

Stein and Wise (586) have proposed that schizophrenia may be due to endogenous production of the neurotoxin 6-hydroxydopamine (6-OHDA) within the noradrenergic neurons of the medial forebrain bundle which leads to the destruction of these neurons. On the basis of the theory that noradrenergic neurons of the medial forebrain bundle are believed to mediate rewarded or goal-directed behavior in rats (585), Stein and Wise have proposed that damage to this system in man could produce deficits in goal-directed behavior and in the capacity to experience pleasure, both of which are said to be characteristic of schizophrenia (586). However, the medial forebrain bundle is not the only brain tract which will support electrical stimulation. Breese, Cooper, and Hollister (74) have presented evidence that self-stimulation in the lateral hypothalamus of the rat can be mediated by dopamine rather than norepinephrine. Fibiger and Phillips (185) have demonstrated that both dopaminergic and noradrenergic pathways in the rat brain can support electrical self-stimulation. Both the nigro-striatal and mesolimbic dopaminergic pathways supported self-stimulation in their studies.

Numerous investigations have shown that 6-OHDA causes a selective and long-lasting depletion of NE from noradrenergic nerve terminals of the sympathetic nervous system, presumably due to a selective neurotoxic action of 6-OHDA on catecholamine-containing neurons (366, 606). However, the specificity of its neurotoxic actions for catecholamine neurons has been questioned, especially in the central nervous system (476). It appears that the effects of 6-OHDA are dose-dependent, with neurotoxic actions specific for catecholamine-containing neurons occurring at low concentration of 6-OHDA and nonspecific histopathology occurring at high concentrations of this drug. Depending on the dose of 6-OHDA or pretreatment with desimipramine, selective depletion of noradrenaline or DA can be produced (75,620).

Rats treated with 6-OHDA show a decrease in the rate of self-stimulation of the medial forebrain bundle (586). However, their methodology was strongly criticized by Antelman et al. (22), who pointed out the possibility of nonspecific drug toxicity and reversibility of the 6-OHDA effect by experimental priming of the medial forebrain bundle. Stein and Wise (586) also report that pretreatment with chlorpromazine antagonized the effect of 6-OHDA on self-stimulation, presumably because chlorpromazine might prevent the NE depletion by blocking neuronal uptake of 6-OHDA. These investigators have speculated that chlorpromazine exerts its antipsychotic effects by inhibiting the uptake of endogenously produced 6-OHDA and thereby preventing destruction of the schizophrenic's noradrenergic reward system. Such an interpretation, however, is severely limited by the lack of correlation of clinical efficacy of antipsychotic phenothiazines with their ability to inhibit amine uptake, as well as by the fact that many drugs which are potent amine-uptake blockers have no clinical effectiveness in the treatment of schizophrenia and may even exacerbate psychotic symptomatology (477).

Stein and Wise (586) proposed that 6-OHDA could be formed endogenously from dopamine in the synaptic cleft by auto-oxidation or by enzymatic reaction. They hypothesized that dopamine-β-hydroxylase (DBH) might be diminished, on a genetic basis, in schizophrenia, which might lead to release of DA rather than NE into the synaptic cleft where conversion of DA to 6-OHDA would occur. They also noted that other means of formation of 6-OHDA might be present in schizophrenia. Adams (3) proposed that 6-OHDA and other related compounds which are toxic to catecholamine neurons might be produced by DBH through the formation of dopamine-O-quinone as an intermediate. Antelman and Caggiula (21) have summarized evidence which suggests that under conditions of stress, decreased NE activity will enhance DA-dependent behaviors. Thus, decreased NE resulting from diminished DBH might synergize with increased DA in schizophrenia. Hartmann (254) has also called attention to a possible NE-DA imbalance, based on decreased DBH activity, as relevant to the pathogenesis of schizophrenia.

Wise and Stein (666) assayed post-mortem brain specimens from eighteen schizophrenic patients and twelve controls and found significant reductions in DBH activity in all regions studied, particularly the hippocampus and the diencephalon. Some studies were carried out to determine the effects of post-mortem changes, drug treatment, duration of hospitalization, cause of death, and age. These factors were felt not to be sufficient to explain the differences. Subsequently, Wise, Baden, and Stein (665) reported that the activities of lactic dehydrogenase, monoamine oxidase, and superoxide dismutase (the latter enzyme being the one which catalyzes the decay of superoxide anions, such as those produced by the auto-oxidation of 6-OHDA) were not significantly different in the brain of schizophrenics and controls. There was some evidence for decreased activity of catechol-O-methyltransferase and choline acetyltransferase (the enzyme which catalyzes the synthesis of acetyl-choline). The selective decreases in activity in three out of six enzymes was proposed as evidence that nonspecific causes of enzyme inactivation were not present.

Laduron (330) severely criticized the biochemical method used by Wise and Stein (666) for DBH assay on several grounds, including the fact that the curve presented by these authors relating DBH activity to substrate concentrations was probably invalid. Wyatt et al. (670) studied DBH activity in post-mortem brains from nine schizophrenic patients and nine controls. There was a tendency for DBH activity to be lower in schizophrenic brain, but this did not reach statistical significance and could be related to drug dosage and the elapsed time between death and freezing the brain for study. However, Laduron's criticism of the assay technique of the Wise-Stein study (666) could also be leveled against Wyatt et al. (670). More adequate biochemical studies, including one of the radioimmunoassay for DBH, in brains from young, untreated schizophrenics, will be needed to test the DBH hypothesis.

DBH is located in a variety of tissues (253). Rosenblatt, Leighton, and Chanley (514) found that two schizophrenic patients had increased DBH activity in the sympathetic neurons of the salivary glands as judged by conversion of infused tritiated DA to NE. This interesting study needs further attention to methodological issues and larger numbers of subjects.

Serum DBH activity is believed to result from the exocytosis of NE storage granules by sympathetic nerves (652). Its activity varies widely in man and is under genetic control. Serum DBH activity was studied longitudinally in schizophrenic patients and found not to vary from the acute phase to the remission phase (396). The distribution of DBH activities is not significantly different in schizophrenics and normals (165,552,655). Since serum DBH activity is under genetic control (578), if there were a genetic basis for low serum DBH activity in the brains of schizophrenics, one might expect low serum DBH as well.

The 6-hydroxydopamine theory of schizophrenia has also been reviewed by Adams (4).

Platelet Monoamine Oxidase (MAO)

As previously discussed, 5-HT, NE, and DA are neurotransmitters which have been postulated to be importantly involved in the etiology of the major psychoses or at least in the response to the currently available somatic treatments utilized in the treatment of these illnesses. Recently interest has also developed in the relationship to the major mental illnesses of other biogenic amines which occur in trace amounts and are chemically related to NE, DA, or 5-HT: for example, octopamine, tyramine, phenethylamine, and tryptamine (38,671).

NE, 5-HT, DA, and the trace amines are all substrates for one or more forms (isozymes) of MAO. Oxidative deamination by MAO is a major pathway for the catabolism of these amines, although other means of inactivation are available, including other types of enzymatic transformation or uptake by presynaptic neurons. Thus, diminished activity of MAO, either on a genetic basis or subsequent to exogenous factors, including drugs, might be expected to enhance the effects of these substrates of MAO, by increasing their availability and/or modifying the sensitivity of presynaptic and postsynaptic receptors of these bioamines. Administration of MAO inhibitors, plus 5-hydroxytryptophan (5-HTP), the precursor of the amines above, can have profound effects on animal behavior; for example, 5-HTP plus tranylcypromine can cause hyperactivity and stimulation of prolactin secretion (235,353).

Administration of MAO inhibitors to schizophrenics has been reported to have no effect on psychopathology, to bring about modest improvement in target symptoms (294,336,685), or to cause a worsening of symptomatology, especially when combined with specific amino acids such as methionine (479). These studies are of interest in understanding the role of MAO in schizophrenia, but the profound alterations in monoamine physiology to be expected by one to four weeks of treatment with drugs that produce extensive, if not complete, inhibition of MAO throughout the body are not necessarily relevant to the effect of chronic, selective, partial diminution of one or more forms of MAO in specific tissues or specific areas of the brain.

Human platelets contain a mitochondrial MAO, which is a "type B" MAO—meaning that its rate of oxidation of benzylamine and phenethylamine is significantly greater than its rate of oxidation of 5-HT or NE, which are the preferred substrates of "type A" MAO (681). DA has been thought to be a substrate *in vitro* for types A and B MAO (248,357,677). However, recent studies have suggested that *in vivo*, in the rat brain, the deamination of DA is almost entirely effected by MAO A (643). Others have proposed that there is a specific isoenzyme of MAO with a high activity toward DA in human brain (119), rat liver (681,682), and rat brain (645). Types A and B MAO differ in sensitivity to inhibitors, temperature inactivation, and a variety of other properties.* The properties of the human platelet enzyme are very similar to those of the B enzyme in other tissues.

The platelet has a mechanism for active uptake of 5-HT and storage of 5-HT in granules. The kinetic features and response to drugs of 5-HT uptake and storage by human platelets is comparable to that of rat brain synaptosomes (566). For these reasons the platelet has been utilized, perhaps too loosely by some, as a "model" for serotonergic nerve endings (580). This analogy is the basis for the as yet unconfirmed hypothesis that a genetically determined decrease in platelet MAO activity could be reflected in decreased brain MAO activity.

PREVIOUS STUDIES OF PLATELET MAO IN SCHIZOPHRENIA

In 1972, the report of Murphy and Wyatt (436) that acute and chronic schizophrenic patients had diminished platelet MAO activity sparked a tremendous interest in the role of MAO in schizophrenia and, in particular, in platelet MAO. Table 2–1 provides a comprehensive list and

---

* See references 119, 229, 291, 313, and 441.

TABLE 2-1
Platelet MAO Studies in Schizophrenia

Study	Subjects (age)	Drug Status	Assay	Results*†	Comments
Murphy and Wyatt (436)	33 chronic schizophrenics (28 ± 1.8)	medicated	^{14}C-tryptamine	2.7 ± 0.40	Significantly lower platelet MAO in chronic and acute schizophrenics. No drug effect. Sex of subjects not specified. No effect of dialysis on low platelet MAO.
	22 normals	drug-free	^{14}C-tryptamine	6.4 ± 0.86	Severity, chronicity, paranoia, catatonia, undifferentiated subgroups not significant factors.
	17 chronic schizophrenics	drug-free for 2 weeks	^{14}C-tryptamine	2.63 ± 0.61	Patients hospitalized continuously 2-15 years. Pellet protein determined.
	5 acute schizophrenics	drug-free	^{14}C-tryptamine	3.72 ± 0.86	
Wyatt et al. (672)	13 monozygotic schizophrenic twins	7 medicated 6 drug-free	^{14}C-tryptamine	3.9 ± 2.3	No significant difference between affected and nonaffected or lesser-affected twins. MAO of both schizophrenic and discordant twins significantly less than controls. Most severely ill schizophrenic twins had lowest MAO activity. No drug effect. Proposed that low platelet MAO a marker for vulnerability to schizophrenia. Pellet protein determined.
	13 co-twins of schizophrenics			4.7 ± 2.9	
	23 normals			6.4 ± 2.7	

TABLE 2-1 (Continued)

Study	Subjects (age)	Drug Status	Assay	Results*†	Comments
Nies et al. (442)	12 schizophrenics (acute–subchronic)	not stated	¹⁴C-benzylamine	schizophrenics: 19.1 ± 1.9 controls: 22.1 ± 2.8	Platelet MAO significantly lower in schizophrenics than controls only with ¹⁴C-tryptamine as substrate. Protein determined.
	12 normals		¹⁴C-tryptamine	schizophrenics: 2.6 ± 0.2 controls: 3.6 ± 0.4	
Owen, Ridges, and Cookson (460)	27 schizophrenics (probably acute) (38.5 ± 11)	not stated	¹⁴C-tryptamine	schizophrenics: 8.4 ± 5.0 controls: 20.1 ± 7.4	Patients acute to subchronic. Platelet MAO increased in one patient who improved markedly. Pellet protein determined.
	23 normals (34.8 ± 11)				
Meltzer and Stahl (415)	12 chronic (36 ± 9.4)	medicated	fluorescence assay—M-iodobenzylamine (MIB) tyramine, octopamine, tryptamine		Chronic patients significantly lower than controls with all 4 substrates. Acutes significantly lower than controls with MIB and tyramine. Results led to hypothesis that platelet MAO in schizophrenia may be different form of enzyme than controls. Pellet protein determined.
	10 acute (24 ± 9.4)				
	15 normals (29 ± 5.4)				

Study	Subjects	Drug status	Substrate	Values	Comments
Friedman et al. (196)	26 chronic schizophrenics	drug free > 7 days	^{14}C-tryptamine	1.58 ± 0.19	Schizophrenics and affectives not significantly different from controls. Pellet protein determined.
	10 affective			1.66 ± 0.33	
	23 normals			1.9 ± 0.17	
Carpenter, Murphy, and Wyatt (101)	40 acute schizophrenics	drug free > 2 weeks	^{14}C-tryptamine	5.16 ± 0.32	Acutes, chronic, and controls not significantly different. Undifferentiated and schizo-affective significantly greater than paranoid, catatonic group. Impaired reality testing, good prognosis associated with low MAO. Sex of subjects not specified. Pellet protein determined.
	4 chronic schizophrenics			4.94 ± 0.29	
	131 normals			5.24 ± 0.20	
Wyatt and Murphy (673)	68 chronic schizophrenics	receiving phenothiazines	^{14}C-tryptamine	2.86 ± 0.25	MAO in chronic patients significantly less than in controls. No male/female difference in patients or controls. No difference in platelet MAO between subtypes of schizophrenia. Platelet MAO of index patients and first-degree relatives correlated. Pellet protein determined.
	181 normals (18-40)			5.24 ± 0.20	
	first-degree relatives			Low MAO index patients: 3.22 (N=27) High MAO index patients: 5.19 (N=15)	
Zeller et al. (686)	10 schizophrenic females	not stated	metaiodobenzylamine		Schizophrenics lower than controls with all 3 substrates. MAO in normal females greater than males; no difference between schizophrenic females and males. Suggestion that form of MAO in schizophrenics is different from controls. Acute and chronic schizophrenics combined. Pellet protein determined.
	57 normal females		tyramine		
	27 schizophrenic males		p-methoxy-benzylamine		
	45 normal males				

TABLE 2-1 (Continued)

Study	Subjects (age)	Drug Status	Assay	Results*†	Comments
Shaskan and Becker (549)	24 depressed, anergic schizophrenic outpatients	drug-free	^{14}C-tryptamine		No differences between patients and normals. Activity remains stable over 5 weeks despite medication with chloropromazine and imipramine. No relationship between primary symptoms and MAO. Pellet protein determined.
	8 alcoholics				
	7 staff volunteers				
Domino and Khanna (157)	13 chronic schizophrenics	drug-free	^{14}C-tryptamine	schizophrenics: 3.4 ± 0.20	Significant difference between schizophrenics and controls. Pellet protein determined.
				normals: 7.14 ± 0.16	
Schildkraut et al. (536)	16 schizophrenics with hallucinations	not drug-free	^{14}C-tryptamine	3.5 ± 0.4	Schizophrenics with hallucinations had significantly lower platelet MAO than those without hallucinations or controls. No effect of drug dosage, previous hospitalization, or length of total illness on platelet MAO. Pellet protein determined.
	16 schizophrenics without hallucinations			6.0 ± 0.4	
	28 normals			5.7 ± 0.4	

Reference	Subjects	Drug status	Substrate	Values	Comments
Belmaker et al. (50)	18 schizophrenics, chronic; 27 manic-depressive; 19 normals	not drug-free	^{14}C-benzylamine; ^{14}C-tryptamine		No difference between schizophrenics and controls. Manics > controls. Females > males. Plasma MAO not different between groups. Platelet counts.
Wyatt and Murphy (673)	77 chronic schizophrenics; 27 acute schizophrenics; 670 normals	not all drug-free	^{14}C-benzylamine; ^{14}C-tryptamine	males: females: 7.86 7.04 / 10.68 13.85 / 11.04 13.29	Chronic schizophrenics less than acute schizophrenics who did not differ from controls. Patients were studied with platelet count method whereas controls studied with pellet protein method, and results converted (see text for discussion).
Murphy et al. (434)	22 chronic schizophrenics selected for low MAO	12 receiving drugs	^{14}C-tyramine; ^{14}C-tryptamine; ^{14}C-benzylamine		Schizophrenics lower than controls with all 3 substrates. Km of patients and controls with tryptamine not significantly different. Vmax 45% less in patients. Platelet protein determined. No evidence for difference in form of MAO in chronic schizophrenics. Activity of 3 other platelet enzymes normal in patients compared with controls.
Belmaker et al. (51)	12 chronic schizophrenics; 11 normal volunteers; 10 manic-depressives	not drug-free	electrophoresis of platelet MAO; ^{14}C-benzylamine		No difference in electrophoretic properties noted.

TABLE 2-1 (Continued)

Study	Subjects (age)	Drug Status	Assay	Results*†	Comments
White, McLeod, and Davidson (656)	12 chronic schizophrenics (37.3)	not drug-free	¹⁴C-substrate	1.8 ± 0.3	Platelet MAO of schizophrenics not significantly different. Importance of determining platelet count emphasized.
	12 normals (39.8)			2.0 ± 0.8	
Owen et al. (459)	600 chronic schizophrenics	drug-free	¹⁴C-tyramine	controls: 28.4 ± 10.0 schizophrenics: 27.5 ± 14.8	No diagnostic effect. No significant difference between patients with positive and negative symptoms. No relationship with severity of illness or other clinical features. "Considerable variation" in platelet MAO over 6 months noted. Pellet protein determined.
	700 normals		¹⁴C-tryptamine	controls: 3.6 ± 1.4 schizophrenics: 3.2 ± 1.1	
Becker and Shaskan (47)	14 acute schizophrenics (in-patient)	drug-free for 2 weeks	¹⁴C-tryptamine		No significant difference between patients and controls. Patients with low MAO (apparent point of bimodal split) had higher incidence of hallucinations than those with high MAO. 8 patients had marked decrease in platelet MAO at 4th week of hospitalization. Patients with low MAO had higher global rating of severity of illness. Glass tubes used. Pellet protein determined.
	15 chronic schizophrenics (in-patient)				
	26 schizophrenics (out-patient)				

Meltzer et al. (410)	~50 acute schizophrenics ~75 chronic schizophrenics ~50 normals	most drug-free	^{14}C-tyramine ^{14}C-tryptamine ^{14}C-benzylamine	No difference with any substrate between schizophrenics and controls except for increased platelet MAO with tyramine for acute schizophrenics. However, MAO in chronic schizophrenics with hallucinations significantly less than in those without hallucinations with benzylamine as substrate. Pellet protein with tyramine, tryptamine substrate. Platelet counts with benzylamine as substrate.
Berrettini, Vogel, and Clouse (56)	12 chronic schizophrenics 10 normal controls	not drug-free	tryptamine	Mean Km and Vmax of platelet MAO were significantly lower for chronic schizophrenics. Pellet protein determined.

*Units vary depending on assay procedure. Consult original literature.

†Raw data is omitted where complexity precludes brief summary.

selective review of the studies of platelet MAO in schizophrenia. Despite some five years of effort, the validity of Murphy and Wyatt's report is still far from certain, and its significance is still totally unestablished. The reasons for this will be discussed.

FACTORS TO BE EVALUATED IN ASSESSING PLATELET STUDIES

To be valid and useful, studies of biological "deficits" in psychiatric patients must satisfy a large number of requirements. The list, not exhaustive, includes: (1) a valid means of chemical determination which has day-to-day reproducibility; (2) satisfactory assessment of diagnosis and any other behavioral or clinical features which are to be related to the biological measure; (3) explicit determination of, and accounting for, any effects of drugs, diet, stress, biorhythms, activity, clinical state, temporal variations (432); (4) comparison with appropriate controls, both normal and disease.

By these criteria all studies of platelet MAO in schizophrenia are lacking. A probable major flaw in most studies (the ones affected are indicated in table 2–1) is the practice of measuring platelet MAO activity in relation to the amount of protein in platelet pellets (668,673), rather than determining the MAO activity of the platelet-rich plasma and counting the number of platelets. Marked variability in results occurs with platelet-pellet protein measurement because of contamination with red and white cells (656,673).*

There are other sources of error in platelet MAO studies. Most studies utilized glass tubes for blood collection. Platelets adhere to glass to a variable extent, depending on their intrinsic properties and that of the glass. Some studies utilized siliconized pasteur pipettes for removing platelet-rich plasma after initial centrifugation. Siliconizing agents can inhibit platelet MAO even with brief contact (486). Conditions of pH, substrate concentration, and extraction of metabolites were not described in detail.

Despite the methodological sources of error in these studies, all their findings or conclusions are not necessarily spurious. It is possible that in actual operation these sources of error contributed little to variance or, applied equally to all groups, permitted such factors as diagnosis, symptomatology, sex, or drugs to be assessed accurately.

SUBSTRATES OF PLATELET MAO AND OTHER
ASPECTS OF ASSAY PROCEDURE

Platelet MAO, as previously stated, is type B MAO. The optimal substrates to determine its activity are benzylamine, metaiodobenzylamine, or phenethylamine. The original study of platelet MAO in schizophrenia by Murphy and Wyatt employed tryptamine as substrate. Meltzer and Stahl (415) were the first to study multiple substrates of platelet MAO in the same patients. They found that tyramine and metaiodobenzylamine were better substrates than octopamine or tryptamine in normal controls. For schizophrenics, octopamine was the preferred substrate, and tryptamine, tyramine, and metaiodobenzylamine were less effective. Zeller et al. (686) reported that methoxybenzylamine was the best sub-

---

° G. P. Pscheidt and H. Y. Meltzer: unpublished data.

strate for platelet MAO of schizophrenics, which had relatively higher activity with this substrate compared with controls (61 percent of control activity). Iodobenzylamine was a better substrate than tyramine for controls and patients, but both substrates distinguished between patients and controls equally well.

Wyatt and Murphy (673) reported that the activity of platelet MAO with tryptamine as substrate or benzylamine as substrate were correlated 0.85 for normals (N=48) and 0.76 for schizophrenics (N=20). For the combined group, the correlation was 0.83. Belmaker et al. (49) found the correlation between MAO activities with the two substrates was 0.86. On this basis Wyatt and Murphy (673) converted all their data with tryptamine as substrate to benzylamine and incorporated this data into their subsequent reviews. The errors in this procedure are obvious. First, platelet-pellet protein was utilized in the first method and is less reliable than the platelet counts utilized in the later studies. Second, the variance (r^2) of platelet MAO for the two substrates is only 0.50, which indicates there is considerable error in converting one measure to another. Murphy et al. (434) also reported relatively low correlations between tyramine and tryptamine as substrate ($r=0.75$). In this latter study, with tryptamine, tyramine, and benzylamine as substrates, platelet MAO was significantly less in schizophrenic patients than in controls. The investigators reported that benzylamine was a better substrate than tyramine, which in turn was a better substrate than tryptamine. The approximate ratios were 12:8:1 (benzylamine:tyramine:tryptamine). These studies were carried out with platelet-protein determinations, but qualitative results are probably valid.

These studies taken together suggest that it is reasonable to employ benzylamine as the sole substrate in the study of platelet MAO in schizophrenia. Although it is not unequivocally established that the form of MAO in platelets of schizophrenics is the same as the one in normals, it is unlikely that multiple substrates are the most effective way to reveal any qualitative difference.

DIAGNOSTIC ASSESSMENT IN PLATELET MAO STUDIES

Most, but not all, studies of platelet MAO activity were done prior to the adoption of the currently accepted practice of utilizing explicitly defined criteria for the diagnosis of schizophrenia. However, a careful reading of the platelet MAO studies suggests diagnosis is not a major cause of the disagreement between studies. Those studies of chronic schizophrenics appear to have a fair uniformity of patient populations. Domino and Khanna (157) and Owen et al. (459) studied chronic schizophrenics who can be maintained drug-free more or less indefinitely without exacerbation of symptoms. They may represent unique subgroups of schizophrenics. Nevertheless, Domino and Khanna found decreased platelet MAO in their patients, whereas Owen et al. did not.

The distinction between acute and chronic schizophrenia has not been made rigorously in any study in which platelet counts were utilized except that of Meltzer et al. (410). They utilized *Research Diagnostic Criteria* (578) and found no difference in platelet MAO activities between the two subtypes of schizophrenics (although there was an association between presence of hallucinations and low MAO as will be discussed subsequently). Carpenter, Murphy, and Wyatt (101) did a study of platelet MAO in acute schizophrenia, and their attention to diagnosis and phenomenology were exemplary. Unfortunately this study utilized "platelet protein" measurement. The four chronic patients studied in that report had platelet MAO no different from controls.

HALLUCINATIONS AS A PREDICTOR OF LOW PLATELET MAO ACTIVITY

One of the most interesting findings concerning platelet MAO and schizophrenia is the evidence that schizophrenic patients who report hallucinations have lower platelet MAO activity than those without hallucinations. The hallucination factor emerged from the studies of Schildkraut et al. (536), Becker and Shaskan (46), and Meltzer et al. (410). Schildkraut et al. retrospectively divided a group of schizophrenics into those with auditory hallucinations and usually paranoid delusions and those without either. The former subgroup had significantly lower platelet MAO (per mg platelet protein) than the latter subgroup of normal controls. The problems with this study are that it was retrospective; it relied upon resident-obtained clinical data and the type of assay employed.

In the recent Becker and Shaskan (46) study the incidence of hallucinations in acute and chronic schizophrenic patients with higher MAO activity (2/15) was significantly less than that in patients with low MAO activity (24/40) (chi square = 8.345, p<.01). The presence or absence of hallucinations was determined by the research psychiatrist during an interview to complete a brief psychiatric rating scale (BPRS) (458).

Owen et al. (459) divided their population of drug-free chronic patients into those with and without positive symptoms (hallucinations, delusions, and formal thought disorder). There was no significant difference in platelet MAO between the groups. The Carpenter, Murphy, and Wyatt study previously cited also found no relationship between hallucinations and platelet MAO activity (101).

All of these studies utilized the measurement of platelet protein. This could contribute to the different results, although it is possible that errors in assessing hallucinations or genuine population differences are the entire cause of the differences.

Meltzer et al. (410) studied the relationship between hallucinations and platelet MAO activity in the following manner. Diagnostic assessment included a detailed inquiry into auditory, visual, and tactile hallucinations at admission and periodically thereafter by a research social worker and research psychologist. Information from other staff about patients' psychopathology throughout hospitalization was also utilized to classify patients as to the presence or absence of any type of hallucination during hospitalization. Utilizing these data, and assay of platelet MAO activity with ^{14}C-benzylamine as substrate and platelet counts, a strong hallucination effect was found. Further, we found significantly lower skeletal muscle MAO activity in schizophrenic patients with hallucinations than in those without.

Wyatt et al. (673) reported that in their most recent study of chronic schizophrenic patients, paranoid schizophrenics had significantly lower platelet MAO activity than acute schizophrenics. This may be comparable to the finding of Schildkraut et al. (536).

KINETICS OF PLATELET MAO OF SCHIZOPHRENICS

Murphy et al. (434) reported that the rate constant (Km) of platelet MAO of chronic schizophrenic patients and controls were not significantly different, but that Vmax, the maximum rate at which tryptamine was oxidized, was 45 percent lower in patients than controls. A recent study reported that both Km and Vmax of platelet MAO were significantly lower in schizophrenics than in normals (56). These investigators found Vmax was 41 percent less in the schizophrenics compared with the controls. They also utilized tryptamine as substrate. Because pellet protein was utilized in all these studies, it is premature to conclude there is a pathological form of platelet MAO present in schizophrenia. The decrease in Vmax and normal Km in the MAO of schizophrenics suggests that there are fewer molecules of MAO in the platelets of schizophrenics than in those of normals but that the kinetic properties of the enzyme in patients and controls are not significantly different. This is consistent with the report that the electrophoretic mobilities of solubilized platelet MAO in chronic schizophrenics and normal controls are not significantly different (48).

TEMPORAL VARIATIONS IN PLATELET MAO ACTIVITY

The studies of Meltzer et al. (410) and of Wyatt and Murphy (673) are in good agreement that platelet MAO activity is relatively constant for a given individual. Mean variations of 20 percent in platelet MAO levels in thirty individuals whose platelet MAO was studied on three or more occasions over a three-month period were found. When greater variations were found, repeated assay suggested that laboratory error accounted for the deviant values. Murphy et al. (435) studied platelet MAO with the benzylamine-PRP assay at intervals of one to two weeks and eight to ten weeks. Highly correlated results were obtained for both the one- to two-week interval (r=0.94, p<0.001, N=26) and the eight- to ten-week interval (r=0.86, p<0.001, N=42) for platelet MAO. Correlation coefficients do not provide any indication of the absolute variation over time in this sample. Stable platelet MAO activity was also reported by Owen, Ridges, and Cookson (460) in twenty-four schizophrenic patients.

On the other hand, Becker and Shaskan (47) have reported on eight schizophrenics who had platelet MAO levels greater than 2.75 millimicromoles per milligram of protein per hour (high MAO) at admission and who four weeks later had platelet MAO levels below this level (low MAO). One patient had low MAO activity initially, and it increased subsequently. In the eight patients whose platelet MAO went down, the decline was stepwise from a mean of 2.5 units to a mean of 2.0 units. The fact that the decline occurred gradually, week by week, increases the possibility that this is a real finding rather than a laboratory error. No relationship between change in clinical state and platelet MAO was noted in these eight patients, nor were they distinguishable by clinical criteria from the forty-seven other schizophrenic patients who had relatively stable platelet MAO activity. Becker and Shaskan propose that platelet MAO activity is state-dependent in relation to schizophrenia but do not expand on this hypothesis, which so far is supported mainly by their data. Owen, Ridges, and Cookson (460) reported on one acute schizophrenic whose platelet MAO activity increased markedly over a two-week period in association with clinical improvement.

LOW PLATELET, MUSCLE, AND BRAIN MAO ACTIVITIES AND CONSTITUTIONALLY "WEAK" MONOAMINERGIC SYSTEMS

Meltzer et al. (395) found low skeletal muscle MAO activity in all major subgroups of psychiatric patients we have studied: acute schizophrenics, chronic schizophrenics, bipolar and unipolar affective psychoses, and a mixed group of patients with diagnoses of borderline states, polydrug abuse, and nonpsychotic depressive illness. This non-specificity of decreased MAO at once eliminates drug effects but raises the possibility of factors such as stress, hospitalization, ward diet, etc., as possible causes. However, it also suggested the hypothesis that low MAO activity may predispose in some way to a variety of mental illnesses. Previous studies have reported platelet MAO to be decreased in chronic schizophrenics, bipolar affective disorders, and normals with a significant personal or family history of psychiatric difficulties or sociopathic deviance (84). Wiberg, Wahlstrom, and Oreland (659) have offered a similar hypothesis based on their findings of: (1) low MAO activity in the brains of alcoholic suicides (233); (2) low platelet MAO activities in alcoholics (658); (3) low concentrations of 5-HIAA in CSF of suicidal patients (27); and (4) no effect of chronic ethanol on rat brain MAO activity. Specifically, they proposed that "low platelet and brain MAO activities reflect constitutionally 'weak' monoaminergic systems which cause an increased vulnerability to, e.g., ethanol abuse or suicidal behavior" (658,659).

PLATELET MAO ACTIVITY IN NORMAL CONTROLS—HIGH-RISK STUDIES

All studies of platelet MAO activity in schizophrenia are in agreement that there is extensive overlap of platelet MAO activity in patients and normal controls, and that some normal controls have MAO activity in the lowest 5 to 10 percent of the entire sample studied. Buchsbaum, Coursey, and Murphy (84) examined this subgroup of patients for psychopathology, comparing them with normal volunteers who had relatively high platelet MAO activity. Specifically, they studied 375 college students and university employees, ages eighteen to thirty-eight. The top 10 percent and the bottom 10 percent of the sample were chosen for further study. Of these, 87 percent cooperated. Repeat determinations again demonstrated the difference between the samples. With benzylamine the low MAO males ranged from 2.4 to 8.4 units (N=19) and the high males, from 12.4 to 22.5 (N=17). The low MAO females ranged from 5.8 to 11.0 (N=18) and high MAO females from 14.9 to 28.1 (N=17). Subjects participated in a structured interview on personal and family history and were studied with perceptual and cognitive tasks, average evoked-response measures, and personality-assessment tests.

The low MAO subjects reported a twofold higher incidence of psychiatric contact: fifteen of thirty-seven low MAO subjects versus seven of thirty-four high MAO subjects (p=0.49, Fisher Exact Test, one-tailed). Three past psychiatric hospitalizations were found in the low MAO group, none in the high MAO group. Males particularly showed an association between low platelet MAO and psychosocial problems and increased incidence rate of suicide or suicide attempts in their relatives.

Murphy et al. (431) studied an additional ninety-five normal volunteers. Platelet MAO was negatively correlated with fifteen of eighteen Minnesota Multiphasic Personality Inventory (MMPI) and Zuckerman sensation-seeking scale (SSS) in males, although only three correlations were statistically significant. The MMPI and SSS correlation coefficients were positive in females. Low MAO males tended to have higher MMPI profiles than high MAO males. No association between MMPI or SSS and platelet MAO was noted with low or high MAO females. Murphy et al. (431) interpret these results to suggest a relatively greater amount of general psychopathology in low MAO males. They had T scores greater than 70 (2 standard deviation [S.D.] > normal mean) for hypomania, psychopathic deviation, and schizophrenia. This profile is found among persons with acting-out disturbances and unlawful behavior resulting from an impulse disorder. No explanation for the sex differences was offered.

These provocative studies need independent replication before their implications require incorporation into current theories of schizophrenia or other forms of mental illness. On the face of it, it seems reasonable to find this type of association if low brain MAO activity correlates with low platelet MAO in man, but there is no evidence for or against this type of association. Furthermore, low skeletal muscle MAO activity in a variety of types of psychiatric patients did not significantly correlate with platelet MAO activity even though type B is present in both platelets and muscle, and the kinetic constants are within experimental error. As we have discussed, low platelet MAO activity may be an indication of "constitutionally 'weak' monoaminergic systems," to use the phrase of Wiberg, Wahlstrom, and Oreland (659). Since platelet MAO activity is genetically determined, this may be the result of linked genes which affect other aspects of neural functioning, rather than a direct effect of low platelet MAO activity or low MAO activity of other tissues. Much additional basic research would be needed to test this hypothesis.

PLASMA AMINE OXIDASE IN SCHIZOPHRENIA AND DEPRESSION

There is a soluble form of MAO in blood which differs from platelet MAO in substrate preference, cofactor requirement, and susceptibility to inhibitors (85,358,433). Murphy and Donnelly (433) have found no significant correlation between plasma and platelet MAO activity within individuals, which suggests that the two activities may be clinically and genetically separate. Meltzer et al. (410) also found no correlation between platelet MAO and plasma MAO in schizophrenic patients.

Plasma MAO is a pyridoxal-containing protein, whereas the platelet enzyme is a flavoprotein. The plasma enzyme is inhibited by JB-516, but pargyline, phenelzine, iproniazid, and isoniazid are not effective inhibitors of plasma MAO (321,509). Kobayashi (321) reported that tranylcypromine was a potent plasma MAO inhibitor, but this was not confirmed by Robinson et al. (509). Briggs and Briggs (77) reported that oral contraceptives are potent inhibitors of plasma MAO. The biological significance of plasma MAO is not known. It may play a role in detoxifying some amines and drugs (85). It should be pointed out that histamine is a good substrate of plasma MAO (85). Thus, decreased plasma MAO levels could lead to increased blood histamine levels. As reviewed by Wyatt, Termini, and Davis (674), a number of studies have reported elevated blood histamine levels in schizophrenics.

Ehrensvard, Liljekvist, and Nilsson (170) have reported decreased plasma amine oxidase activity in chronic schizophrenics. Belmaker et al. (50) found normal levels of plasma MAO in chronic schizophrenics and manic-depressives. Plasma MAO activity just missed being significantly less in chronic schizophrenics and manics. Gershon et al. (212) found no difference in plasma MAO activities of 37 patients with primary affective illness, 105 relatives and spouses, and 37 normal controls.

Plasma MAO activity is stable over time in normals (212). Gershon et al. (212) reported that plasma MAO is heritable and does not vary as a function of sex or of age in the observed age range (eighteen to eighty-two). Similar results were reported by Belmaker et al. (50). We also found no significant sex effect.

Murphy et al. (434) reported that higher MMPI and Zuckerman sensation-seeking scale (689) scores were found in male, but not female, volunteers with lower plasma and platelet amine oxidase activities. Schooler et al. (539) found similar results and, in addition, a positive linear correlation of plasma amine oxidase activity and paranoid mood.

BRAIN AMINE OXIDASE IN SCHIZOPHRENIA, DEPRESSION, AND ALCOHOLISM

Some of the factors affecting amine oxidase activity in various regions of the brain have been studied by Robinson et al. (510). Schwartz, Arkens, and Wyatt (541), Domino, Krause, and Bowers (158), and Wise, Baden, and Stein (665) found no evidence of decreased brain MAO in schizophrenia. Gottfries et al. (233) reported decreased MAO activity in brains of alcoholic suicides, which, as discussed elsewhere, they ascribe to "constitutionally weak monoaminergic systems." There is no convincing evidence of decreased brain MAO in depressed patients (57,241,443). Animal studies reviewed by Youdim (683) indicate that there must be at least an 85 percent decrease in MAO activity before a decrease can have any physiological significance.

SKELETAL MUSCLE MAO

Previous studies have established that human skeletal muscle is mainly type B MAO and that the Km and Vmax of this enzyme are the same as that of platelet MAO (25). We have found that the mean skeletal muscle MAO activity of chronic schizophrenics, acute schizophrenics, and manic-depressives was 16 to 26 percent lower than controls (389). However, only the differences between chronic schizophrenics and controls reached statistical significance. There was no significant relationship between skeletal muscle MAO activity and the presence or the absence of hallucinations, paranoid symptoms, type or dose of medication, presence of other muscle abnormalities, or platelet MAO activity. These findings may nevertheless have some meaning for the interpretation of low platelet MAO in some schizophrenic patients as well as for the reports of low platelet MAO in some manic-depressives and normal controls. Since skeletal muscle is comparable to neural tissues in many respects, it increases the likelihood there is decreased neural MAO activity. As previously mentioned, the decrease in MAO activity would most probably have to be of the order of magnitude of at least 85 percent to have physiological significance. This is also the case for skeletal muscle, but these results could be significant as further evidence of a "constitutionally weak monoaminergic system" in the psychoses, which could predispose to psychotic decompensation or be correlated with more specific defects leading to psychiatric illness.

The Transmethylation Hypothesis

In 1952, Osmond and Smythies (456) proposed that schizophrenia might be due to an abnormality of transmethylation by which endogenous psychotogens chemically related to mescaline were formed from catecholamine precursors such as dopamine. This theory was later broadened to include methylated indoleamines which are psychotomimetics (e.g., 5-methoxy-N,N-dimethyltryptamine and N,N-dimethyltryptamine) (479, 601). Research in this area has been reviewed recently.* Here we will indicate some of the more salient recent developments.

A key issue in this area of research has been the accurate identification of these compounds in the urine, blood, or CSF of schizophrenic patients. Early studies frequently employed paper or thin-layer chromatography which frequently produced misleading results because of the inability to separate the compounds of interest. Gas chromatographic separation of chemically prepared derivatives provided some improvement, but it is only with gas chromatographic-mass spectrometric (GC-MS) methods that very highly reliable identification and quantification have been possible. N,N-dimethyltryptamine has occasionally been reported to occur in urine, whole blood, plasma, and serum of acute and chronic schizophrenics,† but the quantities are minute and the frequency of occurrence is not different from that in normal subjects, when the results of all studies are combined. However, since administered dimethyltryptamine (DMT) disappears very rapidly from blood and only traces appear in urine, this could account for the difficulty in identifying it in body fluids from schizophrenics (295).

Rodnight et al. (511) recently reported a carefully conducted study of urinary DMT in relation to psychiatric symptomatology and classification. DMT was measured by a combined thin-layer and gas chromatographic method with gas chromatography-mass spectrometric verification of selected results. Although DMT was found in a variety of

* See references 155, 194, 216, 264, 327, 515, 651, and 674.
† See references 16, 60, 100, 346, 367, 438, 439, and 672.

psychiatric patients, it was most common in schizophrenia (twenty of forty-two, 47 percent) and patients with "other nonaffective psychosis." Urinary DMT was not related to the number of symptoms present. Patients with delusions or hallucinations had DMT in urine specifically more frequently than those without such symptoms. A discriminant function analysis using Catego syndromes which distinguished best, on the basis of chi-square test, between the DMT-positive and DMT-negative patients, selected twenty-one patients from the sample of ninety-nine patients. Fifteen of the nineteen had DMT in urine. There was no specific psychiatric syndrome associated with detectable DMT excretion. Rodnight et al. (511) said that if their "results showed anything it was a general link between DMT detection and a range of psychotic 'syndromes.' "

Using a gas-liquid chromatographic method, with mass spectroscopic confirmation, Christian and colleagues have identified a subgroup of schizophrenic patients with increased levels of apparent DMT in spinal fluid (114,125). Similar findings have been made by other investigators who have also found elevated DMT levels in manic-depressive patients (327).

Friedhoff (194) has identified dimethoxyphenethylamine (DMPEA) in the urine of schizophrenics with GC-MS and carried out a clinical study with a specific isotope dilution method. He reports that 60 percent of acute drug-free schizophrenic subjects had increased concentrations of DMPEA in urine, compared with normal controls or nonschizophrenic psychiatric patients. Seventy-one percent of male and 75 percent of female paranoid-hallucinating schizophrenics were reported to have DMPEA in urine, using a thin-layer chromatographic method.

The evidence that DMT can be formed *in vitro* from enzymes present in human tissues has been reviewed elsewhere (367). However, *in vivo* synthesis of DMT in man has not been demonstrated (216). Many of the studies purportedly involving synthesis of DMT *in vitro* actually resulted in the formation of tryptolines, a class of tricyclic compounds (43,515). It is not known if these substances are formed *in vivo* or if they have any effects on behavior. They do have 5-HT-agonist and 5-HT-uptaking blocking properties (306).* Domino (156) has proposed that a useful strategy for developing new therapeutic agents for treating schizophrenics would be the identification of inhibitors of N-methyltransferase, the enzyme thought to be involved in the biosynthesis of methylated indole psychotomimetics. Several inhibitors have already been identified.

There is some evidence that neuroleptics can inhibit the synthesis or biological activity of indole hallucinogens. (See Gillin and Wyatt [217] for specific references.) A recent study found a biphasic interaction of neuroleptics and DMT. Low doses of most neuroleptics *potentiated* the inhibitory effect of DMT on electrically evoked potentials in cat visual cortex. High doses were inhibitory (428). There is other evidence that these indoles may produce at least some of their effects on animal behavior via dopaminergic neurons (187,236). Waldmeier and Maitre (646) have presented evidence that DMT is a short-acting potent MAO inhibitor and may also possess DA-releasing effects. Both these properties

---

* Fang and Meltzer: unpublished data.

could result in an indirect dopaminomimetic activity of DMT. Thus, there could be a significant relationship between the indoleamine and the DA hypotheses of schizophrenia.

Wyatt et al. (675) administered high doses of 5-hydroxytryptophan (5-HTP) and a peripheral decarboxylase inhibitor to eleven chronic schizophrenic patients for up to three months. Seven of the patients improved, two became worse, and two showed no change. On the other hand, Mendels (417) reported that methysergide, a 5-HT receptor blocker, aggravated schizophrenic symptoms in five of twelve subchronic or chronic patients. Since methysergide is an ergot alkaloid, it also has some DA agonist effects, which could account for its ability to exacerbate psychosis.

The transmethylation hypothesis in its current versions no longer occupies the preeminent position it once enjoyed among theories competing as explanations of the etiology of schizophrenia. Nevertheless, the identification of small amounts of particular methylated hallucinogens in the spinal fluid of some patients, the unexplained presence of specific methylating enzymes, the exacerbations of psychosis produced by methionine and MAO inhibitors, the emerging picture of an interrelationship between dopaminergic and indole neuronal systems all suggest further basic research is warranted in this area. Koslow (327) has pointed out that the major significance of the transmethylation hypothesis may be its focus on the one-carbon unit cycle, a defect which could lead to abnormalities in nucleic acid synthesis and hence a wide variety of processes that may lead to psychotic symptomatology.

Neuromuscular Dysfunction in Schizophrenia

Creatine kinase (creatine phosphokinase, CPK) is an enzyme whose activity is elevated in serum in a variety of diseases of skeletal muscle (175). Bengzon, Hippius, and Kanig (51) studied serum CPK levels in schizophrenic patients before and after treatment with neuroleptics to see if a drug-induced increase in serum CPK activity might signal pathological effects of these drugs on skeletal muscle. To their surprise, increased serum CPK activity was present in 50 percent of the sixty patients studied prior to any treatment. No evidence of any drug effect was noted. Enzyme levels returned to normal within several weeks' time. They postulated that the CPK might be leaking from brain, where, as in skeletal and cardiac muscle, it plays a critical role in energy metabolism. They suggested loss of CPK from brain might be significant to the etiology of schizophrenia. Somewhat early Schiavone and Kaldor (535) made a similar finding. Since then there have been numerous studies of this intriguing phenomenon.* These studies have been reviewed in detail

---

* See references 117, 135, 189, 231, 232, 247, 250, 251, 273, 281, 348, 383, 384, 385, 400, 406, 409, 461, 542, 574, 613, 614, and 650.

elsewhere (390,393,394). Here we will briefly cite some of the major aspects of this area of research.

Increased serum CPK activity is found in approximately half of all types of newly admitted *acutely* psychotic patients. It is not confined to schizophrenics; it is also found in manic-depressive and unipolar psychotic depressive patients, periodic catatonia, alcoholic psychoses, and organic psychoses (273,383,409). It is rarely ever present in newly admitted nonpsychotic psychiatric patients, nor is it present in chronic schizophrenic patients not experiencing an acute exacerbation of psychotic symptomatology. Following admission, elevated serum CPK activity almost always returns to normal within one to seven days but may remain above generally accepted upper limits of normal for a month or even throughout hospitalization (273,383). Following the return to normal, subsequent elevations may occur during an exacerbation of psychotic symptoms during hospitalization (383,390) or during outpatient treatment at expected times of recurrence of manic episodes (232). In a few cases increased serum CPK activity has preceded the onset of psychotic symptoms by a few days (231,273,383,393). Mean serum CPK activity during periods of partial remission are also elevated in psychotic patients (390). Some first-degree relatives of psychotic patients have increased serum CPK activity (406). The incidence of increased serum CPK activity (94 of 253, 37.2 percent) in first-degree relatives of patients who themselves had increased serum CPK activity was significantly greater than the incidence (7 of 61, 11.5 percent) in first-degree relatives of patients who did not have serum CPK elevations (chi square=13.699, p<.001) (393).

A number of factors which influence the probability of finding increased serum CPK activity in psychotic patients have been identified. Intramuscular injections of short-acting neuroleptics will increase serum CPK levels, but oral psychotropic drugs and subcutaneous injections of fluphenazine decanoate do not (382,408). Muscle trauma, including the effects of restraints sometimes needed for assaultive psychotic patients, may increase serum CPK activity (226). Physical activity, when severe, may increase serum CPK activity (240). Serum CPK levels in psychotic patients are not especially responsive to the effects of isometric or isotonic activity (225). Alcoholism of a very severe degree may cause muscle damage and increase serum CPK activity (448), but in the series of newly admitted alcoholic patients reported by Ikeda et al. (273), mainly those alcoholics who were psychotic had increased serum CPK activity. Starvation does not affect serum CPK activity (40). Sleep deprivation may produce small increases in serum CPK levels (329). Psychotomimetic drugs such as LSD may have some effect on serum CPK levels (251). Phencyclidine, a psychotomimetic drug, did not affect serum CPK levels in man (407), but it did potentiate the effect of stress on serum CPK levels in the rat (386). Stress is not a sufficient cause of increased serum CPK activity in man (53,500).

Increased serum CPK levels in newly admitted psychotic patients is more frequent in those in whom the onset of psychotic symptoms occurred less than one week before admission, compared with those with a longer duration of symptoms (390). There is some evidence that psychotic patients with increased serum CPK levels may have more florid psychopathology, especially greater levels of agitated motor behavior, than those with normal serum CPK levels (189,247,390).

The type of CPK in the sera of acutely psychotic patients is the skeletal muscle isoenzyme (273,383). No brain-type CPK was present. No spinal fluid (CSF) CPK activity was detected in acutely psychotic patients by several investigators (370,385), but others have reported such increases (627,642). Several reports have demonstrated brain-type CPK is unstable in sera (111,112,197). Thus, any brain-type CPK in sera, or possibly, CSF might not be detectable by routine enzymatic methods. We have recently developed radioimmunoassays for human skeletal muscle-type and brain-type CPK (179). We found increased skeletal muscle-type CPK in sera of psychotic patients with increased serum CPK activity. There was no increase in brain-type CPK activity (112).

Increased serum CPK activity has been reported in patients with hemorrhagic and thrombotic cerebrovascular disease, drug-induced coma, and encephalitis (2,163,573). Both skeletal muscle-type and brain-type CPK have been found in the sera of patients with acute brain diseases (163,573). These studies raise the possibility that, at least in some psychotic patients, increased serum CPK levels may be a reflection of acute brain disease.

The determination of the significance of elevated serum CPK activity in schizophrenia must await definitive evidence that it is not an artifact in a good proportion of cases. At present this evidence is circumstantial and will remain so until the pathophysiology is understood. Monitoring serum CPK activity at admission may have some diagnostic value providing all confounding causes previously enumerated are explored.

Finding increased skeletal muscle-type serum CPK activity in a large proportion of acutely psychotic patients led Meltzer and colleagues to study skeletal muscle fibers and subterminal motor nerves. A variety of pathological muscle fibers were observed, along with excessive branching of subterminal motor nerves; these findings are consistent with mild denervation and α-motor neuron abnormalities.* These conclusions are based on examination of large numbers of concomitantly studied normal controls as well as literature data (499). Single fiber electromyographic studies of the extensor digitorum communis muscle have revealed an increased fiber density—for example, an increase in the average number of single-muscle-fiber-action potentials belonging to the same motor unit within the uptake area of the electrode in some psychotic patients (130). These results are consistent with the findings of the skeletal-muscle-fiber and subterminal-motor-nerve studies (397,398). They suggest a long-standing abnormality of subterminal motor nerves or motor end plates. Some psychotic patients have been shown to have a decreased number of motor units and abnormalities of the recovery curve of the spinal cord electrically induced monosynaptic reflex, the so-called H-reflex (149, 226). Acute schizophrenics tended to have decreased recovery of the H-reflex, consistent with increased dopaminergic influence on the alpha-motor neuron. Chronic schizophrenics and manic-depressives had increased recovery curves, consistent with decreased dopaminergic activity. The recovery curves of the latter two groups of psychiatric patients were

---

* See references 186, 387, 389, 397, 398, and 401.

similar to those of parkinsonian patients (226). These H-reflex findings may provide a link between neuromuscular dysfunction studies and the bioamine theories of the major psychoses. The correlation between these neurophysiological abnormalities and CPK activity is limited (226). The abnormal eye tracking in schizophrenics and some manic-depressives may reflect peripheral neuromuscular dysfunction or failure of central mechanisms for integrating eye movements, or both.

Meltzer et al. (395) have found decreased skeletal muscle MAO activity in schizophrenics. As MAO inhibitors have been found to produce skeletal muscle abnormalities in rats, decreased MAO activity may prove to be a connecting link between neuromuscular dysfunction in the psychoses and the monoaminergic abnormalities which have been reported in schizophrenics. However, psychotically depressed patients treated with MAO inhibitors do not have especially abnormal skeletal muscle fibers.*

Viral Studies in Schizophrenia

The possibility that some forms of schizophrenia may be related to a slow virus has been extensively reviewed by Torrey and Peterson (607, 609). A brief overview will be provided here. In recent years unequivocal evidence has developed that some human diseases, such as Jakob-Creutzfeldt disease and kuru, are due to viruses or to viruslike agents that may be latent and asymptomatic for five to twenty years and yet subsequently lead to profound, even fatal, neurological damage. Various forms of encephalitis, particularly herpes simplex encephalitis, have been known to mimic acute or chronic schizophrenia.† There is abundant evidence that some viruses are relatively specific for the brain nuclei they attack, probably based on specific cell-surface receptors of the target cells. Examples of viral infections with specific target areas are rabies, poliomyelitis, and postencephalitic Parkinson's disease which is thought to be caused by a slow virus (68,205,290). The combination of slow onset and regional specificity of neurological involvement is clearly compatible with at least some forms of schizophrenic illness.

Torrey and Peterson proposed that the following aspects of schizophrenia are consistent with a putative viral etiology of some types: (1) the lethal catatonia syndrome (fever, vascular collapse, rigidity, and sometimes death in a catatonic schizophrenic); (2) the excessive number of stillbirths and children with congenital anomalies produced by schizophrenic women (501,572); (3) a high incidence of abnormal dermatoglyphics (finger, palm, and foot prints) (47,310); (4) abnormal capillary formations in nail beds; and (5) neurological and electroencephalograph abnormalities. The major rationale for relating these studies to the viral hypothesis of schizophrenia is that viruses have been

---

* Stanton and Meltzer: in preparation.
† See references 106, 219, 220, 259, 470, 492, 550, and 663.

known to produce similar abnormalities or these defects are likely to have developed in utero.

Variations in geographical, temporal, and seasonal incidences of schizophrenia are compatible with a viral hypothesis (609). For example, the first admission rate for schizophrenia in Ireland is over twice as high as in England (307,452,647). Studies in four Western countries have indicated an increased incidence of schizophrenia in people born in winter and spring months.*

Torrey and Peterson (609) have reviewed the evidence for protein abnormalities in CSF and serum of schizophrenics. Studies in this area have produced unusually inconsistent results, even for schizophrenia research. Some studies are consistent with a viral etiology (e.g., a large increase in one of the types of CSF immunoglobulin: IgG).†

Increased levels of antibodies to some viruses have been noted in the sera of schizophrenics by some investigators (249,365,609), but others have not found them (356,502). Rimon and Halonen (502,503,504) have demonstrated that patients with psychotic depression have unusually high antibody levels to herpes simplex virus, as do schizophrenics and patients with some other psychiatric diseases. These investigators cautiously raise the possibility of a general herpes-induced vulnerability to a wide range of psychiatric disorders. This is of interest in light of the other evidence presented in this review that there are a variety of abnormalities common to patients with the major psychoses.

The viral hypothesis of schizophrenia is most useful and generative. It is clear that a proportion of cases diagnosed as schizophrenia solely on the basis of phenomenological criteria are due to viral infections. The size of this proportion is unknown and will remain so until there are reliable methods for screening large numbers of psychiatric patients for active viral infection. The slow-virus hypothesis has a great deal of appeal because it is compatible, at least temporally, with many aspects of the schizophrenic syndrome. Were some forms of schizophrenia to be due to one or more viruses or virallike agents, the possibility of immunization against the pathogens would emerge. Although it is unlikely that the cause of most types of schizophrenia is viral, this important hypothesis deserves continuing attention.

Autoimmune Hypothesis of Schizophrenia‡

The hypothesis that schizophrenia is an autoimmune illness was proposed among others by Fessel (184) and Burch (88). In general terms the autoimmune hypothesis of schizophrenia proposes that production of autoantibodies or alterations in cellular immunity without autoantibody production may specifically alter brain function so as to lead to the

° See references 138, 252, 449, 611, and 639.
† See references 48, 537, 595, 609, and 610.
‡ This section was written by M. Strahilevitz and H. Y. Meltzer.

behavioral manifestations of schizophrenia. The alteration in brain function may be caused: (1) by primary immune-induced structural or physiological alterations in the brain—for example, by cytotoxic antibodies to neuronal cell nuclei in the septal region of the brain, as proposed by Heath et al. (255); (2) by autoimmune-induced alteration in organs or systems other than the brain which would secondarily affect brain function. An "indirect" autoimmune mechanism may, for example, be related to the etiology of pernicious anemia in some patients who are found to have antibodies against the intrinsic factor of the gastric mucosa (222).

Autoimmune mechanisms may be determined by both genetic factors and stress (184,593). Alterations in the immune system may merely be associated with another nonimmune pathogenic process and may in themselves not be of etiological significance. Thus, autoantibodies against brain antigens may not be etiological but may rather reflect alteration in antigenic structure or change in blood-brain barrier permeability induced by a nonimmune pathogenic factor, such as a virus.

The autoimmune hypothesis of schizophrenia would be supported by the following types of evidence (30,166): (1) presence of autoantibodies against central nervous system (CNS) antigens from brain areas likely to play a role in the behavioral manifestations of schizophrenia and demonstration in sera from schizophrenics of antibodies which produce behavioral or physiological (EEG) abnormalities in humans or animals that are suggestive of behavioral or physiological abnormalities observed in schizophrenics; (2) presence of autoantibodies to non-CNS organs, tissues, or body constituents; (3) abnormality in structure or functions of lymphocytes and other immune-reactive cells; (4) elevated serum immunoglobulins; (5) tissue lesions characterized by infiltration with lymphocytes, histiocytes, and plasma cells; (6) clinical and serological association with other autoimmune diseases; (7) association with enlargement of the thymus or the thymic tumor, or both; (8) ameliorating effect of corticosteroids and cytotoxic drugs; (9) production of similar diseases of an autoimmune etiology in animals. We will now briefly review evidence of these types of abnormalities in schizophrenia.

Several investigators reported presence of antibrain antibodies in schizophrenia. For example, Heath et al. (255) reported that "taraxein," a protein factor fractionated from schizophrenia serum, is an antibody against neuronal nuclei of the septal region and the caudate nucleus. However, the report of Heath et al. (255) that antibrain antibodies in the sera of schizophrenics can be demonstrated by an immunofluorescent technique could not be confirmed by Whittingham et al. (657), Logan and Deodhar (349), and Boehme et al. (69). Heath et al. (256) also reported that some schizophrenic individuals show a characteristic wave-and-spike abnormality when electrical activity is recorded from the septal region of the brain through stereotactically implanted deep electrodes.

The indirect immunofluorescent technique is technically complicated and has numerous sources of error. A new method of studying brain-binding factors was introduced by Witz et al. (667). This is an indirect radioimmunofixation method which is believed to be more quantitative and more readily controlled than the indirect immunofluorescent technique, but it has not been independently verified. Baron et al. (45) reported that with this technique, higher levels of a brain-binding factor were present in schizophrenics and their biological relatives as compared with normal controls and depressed psychiatric patients. This brain-binding factor was present in relatively high levels in approximately 2 of 117 (2 percent) of healthy controls and in 17 of 27 (63 percent) of schizophrenics and 5 of 28 (17 percent) of their relatives. It binds not only to human brains but also to human liver and to mouse brain, liver, and thymus. In view of the presence of brain-binding activity in nonclinically ill relatives of schizophrenic index cases, the authors concluded that the brain-binding factors may be a genetic marker for the vulnerability to develop schizophrenia. The etiological significance of the brain-binding factor, which is not IgG but may be another type of globulin, in schizophrenia and its relation to the immune system have yet to be determined (667).

A variety of Russian studies have reported antibrain antibodies in schizophrenics, the levels of which fluctuate with clinical state. They are also reported to occur in the first-degree relatives of schizophrenics. (See Durell and Archer [166] for references.) Vartanian (636) and Prilipko et al. (484) have reported that schizophrenic patients, as well as patients with certain neurological diseases, have a higher incidence of antibodies directed against a specific antigen isolated from brain gray matter by column chromatography. This antibody may also have contributed to the inhibition of blast transformation of lymphocytes obtained from antibody-positive schizophrenic subjects as well as to inhibition of blast transformation of lymphocytes obtained from healthy individuals following incubation with serum from schizophrenics who had significant titers of antibodies to the brain antigen. These investigators suggested that their findings indicate the possible presence of an antibody directed against shared antigenic determinants in CNS and lymphocytes. This probability is consistent with the report of Luria and Domashneva (355) that schizophrenic serum was cytotoxic to mouse thymocytes and displayed binding (as determined by indirect fluorescence) to mouse thymocytes and to mouse lymph node cells.

Autoimmune diseases are usually associated with a wide overlap of serological reactions. Mellsop, Whittingham, and Ungar (380) found no difference in the prevalence of autoantibodies to nuclear, thyroid, gastric, smooth muscle, and mitochondrial antigens in 297 female schizophrenics and a like number of age- and sex-matched controls. The schizophrenics and 100 intellectually subnormal children did have an increased prevalence of autoantibodies to nuclei of leukocytes. An increased incidence of antinuclear antibodies has been reported in schizophrenics receiving high doses of neuroleptics (487).

Alterations in immunoglobulin levels in schizophrenia have been reported by a number of researchers, but these reports have generally been inconsistent with each other. Part of this inconsistency may be related to factors such as different patient populations and drug effects (166). Recently Bock (66) reported lower serum IgM in chronic schizophrenics than in control subjects with minor psychiatric or neurologic conditions. Serum IgM levels in schizophrenics did not differ from the levels in patients with dementia of neurologic origin or endogenous depression.

Del Vecchio et al. (145) found that chronic schizophrenics with a family history of schizophrenia had a significantly higher mean serum IgA level than chronic schizophrenics without such a history.

Strahilevitz (594) suggested that this observation, in light of the findings of a familial occurrence of the Witz globulin brain-binding serum factor (45) and the previously reported increased serum IgA in schizophrenia (594), implies that the Witz brain-binding factor may be an IgA globulin.

Recently Torrey et al. (610) reported that multiple-admission schizophrenics (but not first-admission schizophrenics) had elevated CSF levels of IgA. The elevation, however, fell slightly short of statistical significance. They discussed the possibility that the abnormalities in lymphocytes, alterations in serum and CSF immunoglobulins, and the presence of autoantibodies against brain and other tissue antigens may conceivably be the result of a viral infection.

Sullivan, Stanfield, and Dackis (596) have recently called attention to a possible relationship between platelet MAO activity in schizophrenia and the autoimmune hypothesis. They cite several published studies as well as their own unpublished data indicating low activity of leukocyte oxidative enzymes, including MAO, in schizophrenic patients. They state there is evidence that these low enzyme activities could result from immunological mechanisms (221,272).

The autoimmune hypothesis of schizophrenia is thus undergoing a revival of interest based on somewhat better technical methods and possible linkage to other areas of research in schizophrenia. Nevertheless, as assessed by Durell and Archer (166), the weight of the evidence does not support the autoimmune hypothesis of schizophrenia. Strahilevitz (592) has called attention to the use of immunologic methods in psychiatric treatment.

HL-A Antigens and Schizophrenia

It has been known for many years that a graft elicits an immune response if it carries antigens which the host recognizes as foreign. Lymphocytes probably play a role in this process. Genes which play a role in graft rejection are called "histocompatibility loci," and the products determined by their alleles are "histocompatibility antigens." In man the only major histocompatibility locus, frequently referred to as the "major histocompatibility complex" (MHC), is called the "HL-A locus." These genes are located on chromosome 6. They include the serologically detectable (SD) loci A, B, and C which control cell-surface glycoproteins; the D locus which controls cell-surface antigens and is detectable in mixed lymphocyte culture (MLC); and other loci which control various components of complement and transplantation antigens (35,293). These loci are polymorphic, which implies that in some way they are of general benefit for the survival of the population, possibly as a defense against viral agents (153). As reviewed by Bach and Van Rood (35,36,37), the biological importance of the MHC may be in its participation in such processes as immune responsiveness, development, and susceptibility to disease through its determination of cell-surface structures and hence cell interactions which are significant for morphogenesis and the maintenance of individuality.

Typing of humans as to their HL-A antigens is of major importance in the study of many diseases, since it may yield pertinent clues to the genetics and the pathogenesis of the diseases in question. A number of diseases—especially multiple sclerosis, myasthenia gravis, ankylosing spondylitis, and Reiter's disease—have shown associations with specific HL-A antigens (9,35,36,37). These studies are complicated by choice of patients and controls, antisera, and statistics. Controls and patients should be matched for race and belong to the same population with the same geographical area. There are sources of error in typing. Usually the frequencies of twenty or more HL-A antigens are compared, and on an average one of these will show a significant difference at the 5 percent probability level if there is no true difference between the groups compared. This can be corrected by multiplying the p-values by the number of comparisons made. When small populations are studied, rejection of true differences is difficult to avoid. A large number of controls makes it easier to detect increased antigen frequencies in the patient group, whereas a decreased frequency can become significant only when a large number of patients are studied. These issues are discussed in detail by Svejgaard et al. (598) and Bach and Van Rood (35,36,37).

There have been several studies of the HL-A antigens in schizophrenia.[*] Smeraldi and colleagues in their first study (560) found no association between HL-A antigens and schizophrenia, except that hebephrenics had a higher incidence of HL-A than paranoid patients. However, there was no statistical correction for the number of comparisons made. A second group of patients was studied by this group (561). A reduced incidence of HL-A10 was present even after correction for number of comparisons. Eberhard et al. (168) in Sweden reported a significant, comparison-adjusted association between increased HL-A9 frequency and schizophrenia. Smeraldi et al. (561) combined their results with those of Eberhard and again found a decreased HL-A10 frequency. Ivanyi et al. (278), however, found a slightly higher incidence of HL-A10 in 148 chronic schizophrenics than in 1,200 controls in Czechoslovakia.

The inconsistency of these results is not surprising in light of the heterogeneity inherent in the schizophrenic syndrome, the difficulty in reliable diagnosis, and the problem of appropriate controls. Conceivably, the most meticulous study of the type just reviewed, involving upward of 500 patients and 2,500 controls, of the most homogeneous ethnic background, with highly reliable typing, may lead to reproducible associations between HL-A antigens and subtypes of schizophrenia. It may be much

---

[*] See references 104, 168, 278, 560, and 561.

more useful to employ a family-study method, determining if there is a linkage with schizophrenia and a particular HL-A haplotype in a family with two to three generations of affected and unaffected members, a large number of whom are informative about the linkage.

Central Nervous System Peptides

There is considerable evidence that peptides of the pituitary or the hypothalamus have behavioral effects in laboratory animals and humans which are independent of their hormonal trophic effects on target organs (347). Thus, thyrotropic hormone (TRH), adrenocorticotrophic hormone (ACTH), and smaller peptide fragments of the ACTH molecule and melanocyte stimulating hormone (MSH) have been shown to produce a variety of behavioral effects. TRH can antagonize sedatives (482), enhance locomotor activity (548), and may be antidepressant in man (483). MSH and ACTH and their analogues have a role in memory and attention (148,529). Luteinizing hormone-releasing hormone (LH-RH) can reinstate mating behavior in hypophysectomized, ovariectomized rats primed with small doses of estrogens (471). Numerous other examples could be cited. The possibility that a peptide abnormality might be a factor in the developmental, as well as the transient, functional abnormalities in schizophrenia is being explored with increasing vigor at the present time.

In recent years there has been extensive research on the endorphins which are endogenous peptides that can be identified by their opiate receptor agonist effects (224). Five endogenous peptides with morphinelike biological properties have been isolated from brain or pituitary and characterized chemically: met-enkephalin, leu-enkephalin, α, β-, and γ-endorphin. The sequence of β-endorphin and met-enkephalin can be found in β-lipotropin, a pituitary prohormone (341). The smaller penta-peptides, the enkephalins, may act as neurotransmitters or neuromodulators (191,328), while larger peptides which have a longer duration of action, particularly β-endorphins, may have a hormonal action. Studies of localization of met- and leu-enkephalin in the CNS indicate that they are present in highest concentrations in the striatum and the nucleus accumbens (171,554).

Bloom et al. (64) reported that β-endorphin produced marked, prolonged muscular rigidity in rats following intracerebroventricular injection. This effect, which they likened to catatonia, was blocked by naloxone, an opiate antagonist. They suggested that abnormalities of β-lipotropin-endorphin-regulating mechanisms might be relevant to mental illness. They further proposed that naloxone might be expected to be clinically effective in some psychiatric patients. Intraventricular injection of β-endorphin into cats produced mild excitation and "apparent fixation on phantom objects" which was likened to visual hallucination (375). Jacquet and Marks (280) also observed profound sedation and catalepsy in the rat following intracerebral injection of β-endorphin and to a lesser extent, following met- and leu-enkephalin. They proposed that these effects were analogous to those produced by neuroleptics and that a deficiency of the endorphins might be relevant to the pathophysiology of those mental illnesses where the neuroleptics are clinically effective. The report of increased levels of one endorphin fraction in the cerebrospinal fluid of four chronic schizophrenics supports the possibility of a relationship between the endorphins and schizophrenia (246). β-endorphin has been shown to inhibit striatal dopamine release *in vitro* (350).

There have since been several studies of the effects of naloxone on chronic schizophrenics. Gunne, Lundstrom, and Terenius (246) reported that 0.4 milligrams of naloxone, given intravenously, temporarily reduced or abolished auditory hallucinations in four cases of chronic schizophrenia. Similar results were reported by Barchas (42). However, two other groups found no effect at the same or higher doses in similar types of patients (141,284,285). The reasons for these discrepancies are unclear. Conceivably there are some subtypes of schizophrenia that do have functionally significant excessive endorphin levels and in whom naloxone is effective.

A recent preliminary investigation reported that intravenous administration of 1.5 to 6 milligrams of β-endorphin to three chronic schizophrenics and two depressed patients who were medicated with antipsychotics or antidepressants rapidly worsened the schizophrenics and improved the mood of the depressed patients (320). The schizophrenics showed increased cognitive and conceptual difficulties. These results could not be replicated in a second trial. However, 6 milligrams of β-endorphin did produce transient clinical improvement in one drug-free schizophrenic. Little can be concluded from this very preliminary report.

We have measured β-lipotropin levels in the sera of ten acute, ten chronic schizophrenics, and twenty normal controls using antisera provided by C.H. Li (404). No significant difference between diagnostic groups or drug effect was noted.

Conclusions

This necessarily selective and personalized review of the biochemical studies of the schizophrenic syndrome which seem to be of greatest current importance reveals that we now know a great deal more about the psychotic process, which most certainly can be ameliorated by reduction of dopaminergic activity and usually can be exacerbated by increasing dopaminergic activity. Through the neuroendocrine strategy we have a most important means of studying dopaminergic processes in patients and normal controls. *The importance of the DA hypothesis to a general understanding of schizophrenia, rather than the phase of acute psychosis which is present in some but not all forms of schizophrenia as*

well as in the affective psychoses, seems much more problematic. If
excessive DA—either through increased synthesis, decreased metabolism, supersensitive receptors, or a deficit in other neural systems which
are required to balance DA, such as acetylcholine and GABA—is not the
cause of schizophrenia but only a manifestation of a possibly stress-
induced psychotic phase, then we are left with the conclusion that we
have little certain knowledge about the causes of the schizophrenias.

In view of the myriad schizophrenics who continue to deteriorate
despite neuroleptic treatment and all efforts for social rehabilitation
through such reasonable approaches as social skills training, family and
individual therapy, it is apparent that we have not come close to identifying the cause of the disorder in these patients. For these individuals,
slow virus infections, genetically determined enzymatic deficiencies, or
loss of regulatory mechanisms may be responsible. For those patients
who have only acute schizophreniform episodes, and who are not misdiagnosed as having affective psychoses, it is not impossible that increased dopaminergic activity is the major biological factor in the pathogenesis of this disorder. If this is so, then this last decade has seen a
historic development in schizophrenia research, for it would represent
the first identification of a major subgroup of the schizophrenic syndrome
for whom pathogenesis has been partially identified. It will still be
necessary to determine how, why, and where in the brain increased
dopaminergic activity develops in these patients. This leads us back to
the critical issue of identifying the interaction between psychological
and social factors which may contribute to the pathogenesis of cerebral
dysfunction as well as be their consequence.

The major advances in schizophrenia research of the next decade will
surely rest on continued developments in the basic neural sciences on
the one hand, on precise descriptive and assessment procedures on the
other, and finally on utilization of the best available statistical methods.
It is not unreasonable to expect that within the next one or two decades,
providing research support is available at adequate rates, we will identify
the majority of the biochemical and neurophysiologic deficits which
underlie the various diseases comprising the schizophrenic syndrome.

BIBLIOGRAPHY

1. Abood, L. G. 1968. The psychotomimetic glycolate esters and related drugs. In *Psychopharmacology*, ed. D. H. Efron, Public Health Service Publication 1836 (Washington, D.C.: U.S. Government Printing Office), pp. 683–92.
2. Acheson, J.; James, D. C.; Hutchinson, E. C.; and Westhead, R. 1965. Serum-creatine-kinase
levels in cerebral vascular disease. *Lancet* 1:1306–7.
3. Adams, R. N. 1972. Stein and Wise theory of schizophrenia: A possible mechanism for 6-
hydroxydopamine formation in vivo. *Behavioral Biology* 7:861–66.
4. Adams, R. N. 1974. An overview of the 6-hydroxydopamine theory of schizophrenia. *Bulletin
of the Menninger Clinic* 38:57–69.
5. Adey, W. R., and Tokiazane, T., eds. 1967. *Structure and function of the limbic system*
(Amsterdam: Elsevier), *Progress in Brain Research*, vol. 27.

6. Aghajanian, G. K., and Bunney, B. S. 1973. Central dopaminergic neurons: Neurophysiological identification and response to drugs. In *Frontiers in Catecholamine Research*, eds. E. Usdin and S. H. Snyder (New York: Pergamon Press), pp. 643–48.

7. Agid, Y.; Javoy, F.; Glowinski, J.; Bouvet, D.; and Sotelo, C. 1973. Injection of 6-hydroxy-dopamine into the substantia nigra of the rat. II. Diffusion and specificity. *Brain Research* 58:291–301.

8. Alfredsson, G.; Wiesel, F.-A.; and Skett, P. 1977. Levels of chlorpromazine and its active metabolites in rat brain and the relationship to central monoamine metabolism and prolactin secretion. *Psychopharmacology* 58:13–18.

9. Alter, M.; Harshe, M.; Anderson, V. E.; Emme, L.; and Yunis, E. G. 1976. Genetic association of multiple sclerosis and HL-A determinants. *Neurology* 26:31–36.

10. Anden, H. 1974. Effects of oxotremorine and physostigmine on the turnover of dopamine in the corpus striatum and the limbic system. *Journal of Pharmacy and Pharmacology* 26:738–40.

11. Anden, N.-E. 1976. The interaction of neuroleptic drugs with striatal and limbic dopaminergic mechanisms. In *Antipsychotic drugs: Pharmacodynamics and pharmacokinetics*, eds. G. Sedvall, B. Uvnas, and Y. Zotterman (Oxford: Pergamon Press), pp. 217–25.

12. Anden, N.-E., and Bedard, P. 1971. Influence of cholinergic mechanisms on the function and turnover of brain dopamine. *Journal of Pharmacy and Pharmacology* 23:460–62.

13. Anden, N.-E.; Butcher, S. G.; Corrdoi, H.; Fuxe, K.; and Understedt, U. 1970. Receptor activity and turnover of dopamine and noradrenaline after neuroleptics. *European Journal of Pharmacology* 11:303–14.

14. Anden, N.-E., and Jackson, D. M. 1975. Locomotor activity stimulation in rats produced by dopamine in the nucelus accumbens: Potentiation by caffeine. *Journal of Pharmacy and Pharmacology* 27:666–70.

15. Anden, N.-E., and Stock, G. 1973. Effect of clozapine on the turnover of dopamine in the corpus striatum and in the limbic system. *Journal of Pharmacy and Pharmacology* 25:346–48.

16. Angrist, B.; Gershon, S.; Sathanathan, G.; Walker, R. W.; Lopez-Ramos, B.; Mandel, L. R.; and Van den Heuvel, W. J. A. 1976. Dimethyltryptamine levels in blood of schizophrenic patients and control subjects. *Psychopharmacology* 47:29–32.

17. Angrist, B.; Lee, H. K.; and Gershon, S. 1974. The antagonism of amphetamine-induced symptomatology by a neuroleptic. *American Journal of Psychiatry* 131:817–19.

18. Angrist, B.; Sathananthan, G.; Wilk, S.; and Gershon, S. 1974. Amphetamine psychosis: Behavioral and biochemical aspects. *Journal of Psychiatric Research* 11:13–23.

19. Angrist, B.; Sathananthan, G.; and Gershon, S. 1973. Behavioral effects of L-DOPA in schizophrenic patients. *Psychopharmacologia* 31:1–12.

20. Angrist, B.; Shopsin, B.; and Gershon, S. 1971. Comparative psychotomimetic effects of stereoisomers of amphetamine. *Nature* (London) 234:152–53.

21. Antelman, S. M., and Caggiula, A. R. 1977. Norepinephrine-dopamine interactions and behavior. *Science* 195:646–53.

22. Antelman, S. M.; Lippa, A. S.; Fisher, A. E.; Bowers, M. B.; Van Woert, M. H.; Strauss, J. S.; Carpenter, W. T.; Stein, L.; Wise, C. D. 1972. 6-hydroxydopamine, noradrenergic reward, and schizophrenia. *Science* 175:919–23.

23. Antelman, S. M., and Szechtman, H. 1975. Tail pinch induces eating in sated rats which appears to depend on nigrostriatal dopamine. *Science* 189:731–33.

24. Arbuthnott, G. W.; García-Muñoz, M.; Nicolaou, N. M.; Tulloch, I. F.; and Wright, A. K. 1976. Is the striato-nigral pathway responsible for "feed-back" control of dopamine release? *British Journal of Pharmacology* 58:272.

25. Arora, R. C. and Meltzer, H. Y. 1977. Characterization of rat skeletal muscle monoamine oxidase. *Biochemical Pharmacology* 26:45–49.

26. Asano, T.; Noma, T.; Matsuda, K.; Ikeda, H.; and Otsuki, S. 1973. Effects of L-DOPA on the hypochondriac complaints of the chronic psychotic. *Clinical Psychiatry* 15:745–51 (in Japanese).

27. Asberg, M.; Thoren, P.; Traskman, L.; Bertilsson, L.; and Ringberger, V. 1976. "Serotonin depression"—A biochemical subgroup within the effective disorders *Science* 191:478–80.

28. Asberg, M.; Traskman, L.; and Thoren, P. 1976. 5-HIAA in the cerebrospinal fluid. *Archives of General Psychiatry* 33:1193–97.

29. Ashcroft, G. W.; Dow, R. C.; and Moir, A. T. B. 1968. The active transport of 5-hydroxyindole-3-acetic acid and 3-methoxy-4-hydroxyphenyl-acetic acid from a recirculatory perfusion system of the cerebral ventricles of the unanesthetized dog. *Journal of Physiology* (London) 199:397–425.

30. Asherson, G. L. 1967. Autoimmune disease. *British Medical Journal* 3:479–82.

31. Assaf, S. Y., and Miller, J. J. 1970. Excitatory action of the mesolimbic dopamine system on septal neurones. *Brain Research* 129:353–60.

32. Axelrod, J.; Albers, W.; and Clemente, C. D. 1959. Distribution of catechol-O-methyl transferase in the nervous system and other tissues. *Journal of Neurochemistry* 5:68–72.

33. Ayd, F. G., Jr. 1967. Persistent dyskinesia: A neurologic complication of major tranquilizers. *Medical Science* 18:32–40.

34. Azima, H.; Durost, H.; and Arthurs, D. 1959. The effect of thioridazine (Mellaril) on mental symptoms: Comparison with chlorpromazine and promazine. *Canadian Medical Association Journal* 81:549.

35. Bach, F. H., and Van Rood, J. J. 1976. The major histocompatibility complex—genetics and biology. Part 1. *New England Journal of Medicine* 295:806–13.

36. Bach, F. H., and Van Rood, J. J. 1976. The major histocompatibility complex—genetics and biology. Part 2. *New England Journal of Medicine* 295:872–78.

37. Bach, F. H., and Van Rood, J. J. 1976. The major histocompatability complex—genetics and biology. Part 3. *New England Journal of Medicine* 295:927–36.

38. Baldessarini, R. J., and Fischer, J. E. 1977. Neuropsychiatric illness and the metabolism of aromatic amino acids, trace amines, and substitute neurotransmitters. In *Neuroregulators and psychiatric disorders*, eds. E. Usdin, D. A. Hamburg, and J. D. Barchas (New York: Oxford University Press), pp. 46–56.

39. Baldessarini, R. J.; Lipinski, B. F.; and Chace, K. V. 1972. Effects of amantadine HCl on catecholamine metabolism in the brain of the rat. *Biochemical Pharmacology* 21:77–87.

40. Balmer, S. E., and Rutishaure, I. H. E. 1968. Serum creatine kinase in malnutrition. *Journal of Pediatrics* 73:783–87.

41. Barbeau, A. 1969. L-DOPA therapy in Parkinson's disease: A critical review of nine years' experience. *Canadian Medical Association Journal* 101:791–800.

42. Barchas, J. D. 1977. Implications of biochemical regulatory mechanisms for behavioral states. Presented at the Society of Biological Psychiatry, Toronto, May 1977.

43. Barchas, J. D.; Elliott, G. R.; DoAmaral, J.; Erdelyi, E.; O'Connor, S.; Bowden, M.; Brodie, H. K. H.; Berger, P. A.; Renson, J.; and Wyatt, R. J. 1974. Tryptolines: Formation from tryptamines and 5-MTHF by human platelets. *Archives of General Psychiatry* 31:862–67.

44. Bargman, W., and Schade, J. P. 1963. *The rhinencephalon and related structures* (Amsterdam: Elsevier), *Progress in Brain Research*, vol. 3.

45. Baron, M.; Stern, M.; Anavi, R.; and Witz, I. P. 1977. Tissue-binding factor in schizophrenia sera: A clinical and genetic study. *Biological Psychiatry* 12:199–219.

46. Becker, R. E., and Shaskan, E. G. 1977. Platelet monoamine oxidase activity in schizophrenia patients. *American Journal of Psychiatry* 134:512–17.

47. Beckman, L., and Norring, A. 1963. Finger and palm prints in schizophrenia. *Acta Genetica* (Basel) 13:170–77.

48. Belmaker, R. H., and Ebstein, R. P. 1977. The search for genetic polymorphisms of human biogenic-amine related enzymes. In *The impact of biology on modern psychiatry*, eds. E. S. Gershon, R. H. Belmaker, S. S. Kety, and M. Rosenbaum (New York: Plenum Press), pp. 241–60.

49. Belmaker, R. H.; Ebbesen, K.; Ebstein, R.; and Rimon, R. 1976. Platelet monoamine oxidase in schizophrenia and manic-depressive illness. *British Journal of Psychiatry* 129:227–32.

50. Belmaker, R. H.; Ebstein, R.; Rimon, R.; Wyatt, R. J.; and Murphy, D. L. 1976. Electrophoresis of platelet monoamine oxidase in schizophrenia and manic-depressive illness. *Acta Psychiatrica Scandinavica* 54:67–72.

51. Bengzon, A.; Hippius, H.; and Kanig, K. 1966. Some changes in the serum during treatment with psychotropic drugs. *Journal of Nervous and Mental Disease* 143:369–76.

52. Bennert, H. W., Jr., and Betts, A. 1967. The serum CPK levels in postoperative patients over forty. *Journal of the Maine Medical Association* 58:214–18.

53. Berger, B. 1977. Histochemical identification and localization of dopaminergic axons in rat and human cerebral cortex. In *Non-striatal dopaminergic neurons*, eds. E. Costa and G. L. Gessa (New York: Raven Press), pp. 13–20.

54. Berger, P. A.; Elliot, G. R.; and Barchas, J. D. 1978. Neuroregulators and Schizophrenia. In *Psychopharmacology, A Generation of Progress*, eds. M. A. Lipton, A. A. DiMascio, and K. F. Killam (New York: Raven Press), pp. 1071–82.

55. Berger, B.; Thierry, A. M.; Tassin, J. P.; and Moyne, M. A. 1976. Dopaminergic innervation of the rat prefrontal cortex: A fluorescence histochemical study. *Brain Research* 106:133–45.

56. Berrettini, W. H.; Vogel, W. H.; and Clouse, R. 1977. Platelet monoamine oxidase in chronic schizophrenia. *American Journal of Psychiatry* 134:805–6.

57. Beskow, J.; Gottfries, C. G.; Roos, B. E.; et al. 1976. Determination of monoamine metabolites in the human brain: Post-mortem studies in a group of suicides and in a control group. *Acta Psychiatrica Scandinavica* 53:7–20.

58. Beumont, P. J. V.; Gelder, M. G.; Friesen, H. G.; Harris, G. W.; MacKinnon, P. C. B.; Mandelbrote, B. M.; and Wiles, D. H. 1974. The effects of phenothiazines on endocrine function: I. Patients with inappropriate lactation and amenorrhoea. *British Journal of Psychiatry* 124:413–19.

59. Beumont, P. J. V.; Corker, C. S.; Friesen, H. G.; Kolakowska, T.; Mandelbrote, B. M.; Marshall, J.; Murray, M. A. F.; and Wiles, D. H. 1974. The effects of phenothiazines on endocrine function: II. Effects in men and postmenopausal women. *British Journal of Psychiatry* 124:420–30.

60. Bidder, T. G.; Mandel, L. R.; Ahn, H. S.; Walker, R. W.; and Van den Heuvel, W. J. A. 1974. Blood and urinary dimethyltryptamine in acute psychotic disorders. *Lancet* 1:165.

61. Biederman, J.; Rimon, R.; Ebstein, R.; and Belmaker, R. H. 1976. Neuroleptics reduce spinal fluid cyclic AMP in schizophrenic patients. *Neuropsychobiology*, 2(5–6):324–327.

62. Blass, J. P.; Milne, J. F.; and Rodnight, R. 1977. Newer concepts of psychiatric diagnosis and biochemical research on mental illness. *Lancet* 1:738–40.

63. Bliss, E. L., and Ailon, J. 1971. Relationship of stress and activity to brain dopamine and homovanillic acid. *Life Sciences* 10:1161–69.

64. Bloom, F.; Segal, D.; Ling, N.; and Guillemin, R. 1976. Endorphins: Profound behavioral effects in rats suggest new etiological factors in mental illness. *Science* 195:630–32.

65. Blumberg, J. B.; Taylor, R. E.; and Sulser, F. 1975. Blockade by pimozide of a noradrenaline sensitive adenylate cyclase in the limbic forebrain: Possible role of limbic noradrenergic mechanisms in the niode of action of antipsychotics. *Journal of Pharmacy and Pharmacology* 27:125–28.

66. Bock, E. 1976. Biological research in schizophrenia: Protein in the blood and cerebrospinal fluid. Presented in the First International Symposium on Immunological Components in Schizophrenia, Galveston, Texas, 1976. In press.

67. Bock, E., and Rafaelsen, O. 1974. Schizophrenia: Proteins in blood and cerebrospinal fluid: A review. *Danish Medical Bulletin* 21:93–105.

68. Bodian, D. 1972. Poliomyelitis. In *Pathology of the nervous system*, ed. J. Minckler. (New York: McGraw-Hill), pp. 2323–44.

69. Boehme, D. H.; Cottrell, J. C.; Dohan, F. C.; and Hillegass, L. M. 1974. Demonstration of nuclear and cytoplasmic fluorescence in brain tissues of schizophrenic and non-schizophrenic patients. *Biological Psychiatry* 8:89–94.

70. Bowers, M. B., Jr. 1972. Acute psychosis induced by psychotomimetic drug abuse. II. Neurochemical findings. *Archives of General Psychiatry* 27:440–42.

71. Bowers, M. B., Jr. 1973. 5-hydroxyindoleacetic acid (5-HIAA) and homovanillic acid (HVA) following probenecid in acute psychotic patients treated with phenothiazines. *Psychopharmacologia* 28:309–18.

72. Bowers, M. B., Jr. 1974. Central dopamine turnover in schizophrenic syndromes. *Archives of General Psychiatry* 31:50–54.

73. Bowers, M. B., Jr., and Van Woert, M. H. 1972. 6-hydroxydopamine, noradrenergic reward and schizophrenia. *Science* 175:920–21.

74. Breese, G. R.; Cooper, B. R.; and Hollister, A. S. 1974. Relationship of biogenic amines to behavior. *Journal of Psychiatric Research* 11:125–33.

75. Breese, G. R., and Traylor, T. D. 1971. Depletion of brain noradrenaline and dopamine by 6-hydroxydopamine. *British Journal of Pharmacology* 42:88–99.

76. Brierley, J. B.; Corsellis, J. A. N.; Hierons, R.; and Nevins, S. 1960. Subacute encephalitis of later adult life mainly affecting the limbic areas. *Brain* 83:357–68.

77. Briggs, M., and Briggs, M. 1972. Relationship between monoamine oxidase activity and sex hormone concentration in human blood plasma. *Journal of Reproduction and Fertility* 29:447–50.

78. Brill, N. Q. 1969. General biological studies. In *The schizophrenic syndrome*, eds. L. Bellak and L. Loeb (New York: Grune & Stratton), pp. 114–54.

79. Brown, F., and Redfern, P. H. 1976. Studies on the mechanism of action of amantadine. *British Journal of Pharmacology* 58:561–67.

80. Brown, R. M.; Snider, S. R.; and Carlsson, A. 1974. Changes in biogenic amine synthesis and turnover induced by hypoxia and/or foot shock stress. II. The central nervous system. *Journal of Neural Transmission* 35:293–305.

81. Brown, W. A.; Drawbaugh, R.; Gianutsos, G.; Lal, H.; and Brown, G. M. 1975. Effect of apomorphine on serum prolactin level in the male rat. *Research Communications in Chemical Pathology and Pharmacology* 11:671–74.

82. Brownstein, M.; Saavedra, J. M.; and Palkovits, M. 1974. Norepinephrine and dopamine in the limbic system of the rat. *Brain Research* 79:431–36.

83. Bruno, A., and Bruno, S. 1966. Effect of L-DOPA on pharmacological parkinsonism. *Acta Psychiatrica Scandinavica* 42:264–71.

84. Buchsbaum, M. S.; Coursey, R. D.; and Murphy, D. L. 1976. The biochemical high-risk paradigm: Behavioral and familial correlates of low platelet monoamine oxidase activity. *Science* 194:339–41.

85. Buffoni, F. 1966. Histamine and related amine oxidases. *Pharmacological Reviews* 18:1163–99.

86. Bunney, B. S., and Aghajanian, G. K. 1975. Evidence for drug actions on both pre- and post-synaptic catecholamine receptors in the CNS. In *Pre- and post-synaptic receptors*, eds. E. Usdin and W. E. Bunney, Jr. (New York: Marcel Dekker).

87. Bunney, B. S.; Walters, J. R.; Kuhar, M. J.; Roth, R. H.; and Aghajanian, G. K. 1975. D & L amphetamine stereoisomers. Comparative potencies in affecting the firing of central dopaminergic and noradrenergic neurons. *Psychopharmacology Communications* 1:177–90.

88. Burch, P. R. J. 1964. Schizophrenia: Some new aetiological considerations. *British Journal of Psychiatry* 110:818–24.

89. Burt, D. R.; Enna, S. J.; Creese, I.; and Snyder, S. H. 1975. Dopamine receptor binding in the corpus striatum of mammalian brain. *Proceedings of the National Academy of Sciences of the U.S.A.* 72:4655–59.

90. Calne, D. B.; Chase, T. N.; and Barbeau, A., eds. 1975. *Advances in neurology* (New York: Raven Press), vol. 9, *Dopaminergic mechanisms*.

91. Carenzi, A.; Gillin, C.; Guidotti, A.; Schwartz, M. A.; Trabucchi, M.; and Wyatt, R. J. 1975. Dopamine-sensitive adenyl cyclase in human caudate nucleus: A study in control subjects and schizophrenic patients. *Archives of General Psychiatry* 32:1056–59.

92. Carlsson, A. 1970. Amphetamine and brain catecholamines. In *Amphetamines and related compounds*, eds. E. Costa and S. Garatini (New York: Raven Press), pp. 289–300.

93. Carlsson, A. 1971. Basic concepts underlying recent developments in the field of Parkinson's disease. In *Recent Advances in Parkinson's Disease*, eds. F. H. McDowell and C. H. Markham (Philadelphia: F. A. Davis), pp. 1–31.

94. Carlsson, A. 1975. Receptor-mediated control of dopamine metabolism. In *Pre- and post-synaptic receptors*, eds. E. Usdin and W. E. Bunney, Jr. (New York, Marcel Dekker), pp. 49–66.

95. Carlsson, A., and Lindquist, M. 1962. In vivo decarboxylation of alpha-methyl-DOPA and alpha-methyl-meta-tyrosine. *Acta Physiologica Scandinavica* 54:87–94.

96. Carlsson, A., and Lindquist, M. 1963. Effect of chlorpromazine or haloperidol on the formation of 3-methoxytyramine and normetanephrine in mouse brain. *Acta Pharmacologica et Toxicologica* 20:140–44.

97. Carlsson, A.; Persson, T.; Roos, B. E.; and Walinder, J. 1972. Potentiation of phenothiazines by α-methyltyrosine in treatment of chronic schizophrenia. *Journal of Neural Transmission* 33:83–90.

98. Carlsson, A.; Roos, B. E.; Walinder, J.; and Skott, A. 1973. Further studies on the mechanism of antipsychotic action: Potentiation of α-methyltyrosine of thioridazine effects in chronic schizophrenics. *Journal of Neural Transmission* 34:125–32.

99. Carlsson, A.; Rosengren, E.; Bertler, A.; and Nilsson, J. 1957. Effect of reserpine on the metabolism of catecholamines. In *Psychotropic drugs*, eds. S. Garattini and G. Ghetti (Amsterdam: Elsevier).

100. Carpenter, W. T.; Fink, E. B.; Narasimhachari, N.; et al. 1975. A test of the transmethylation hypothesis in acute schizophrenic patients. *American Journal of Psychiatry* 132:1067–71.

101. Carpenter, W. T.; Murphy, D. L.; and Wyatt, R. J. 1975. Platelet monoamine oxidase activity in acute schizophrenia. *American Journal of Psychiatry* 132:438–40.

102. Carpenter, W. T.; Straus, J. S.; and Bartko, J. J. 1973. Flexible system for the diagnosis of schizophrenia: Report from the WHO International Pilot Study of Schizophrenia. *Science* 182:1275–78.

103. Casey, D. E., and Denny, D. 1975. Deanol in the treatment of tardive dyskinesia. *American Journal of Psychiatry* 132:864–67.

104. Cazullo, C. L.; Smeraldi, E.; and Penati, G. 1974. The leucocyte antigenic system HL-A as a possible genetic marker of schizophrenia. *British Journal of Psychiatry* 125:25–77.

105. Cesarec, Z.; Eberhard, G.; and Nordgren, L. 1974. A controlled study of the antipsychotic and sedative effects of neuroleptic drugs and amphetamine in chronic schizophrenics. *Acta Psychiatrica Scandinavica*, supp. 249, pp. 65–77.

106. Chacon, C.; Monro, M.; and Harper, I. 1975. Viral infection and psychiatric disorder. *Acta Psychiatrica Scandinavica* 51:101–3.

107. Chalmers, J. P.; Baldessarini, R. J.; and Wurtman, R. J. 1971. Effects of L-DOPA on norepinephrine metabolism in the brain. *Proceedings of the National Academy of Sciences of the U.S.A.* 68:662–66.

108. Charalampous, K. D., and Brown, S. 1967. A clinical trial of α-methyl-paratyrosine in mentally ill patients. *Psychopharmacologia* (Berlin) 11:422–29.

109. Chase, T. N.; Schur, J. A.; and Gordon, E. K. 1970. CSF monoamine catabolites in drug-induced extrapyramidal disorders. *Neuropharmacology* 9:265–68.

110. Cheung, C. Y., and Weiner, R. L. 1976. Supersensitivity of anterior pituitary dopamine receptors involved in the inhibition of prolactin secretion following destruction of the medial basal hypothalamus. *Endocrinology* 99:914–17.

111. Cho, H. W.; Meltzer, H. Y.; Joung, J. I.; and Goode, D. 1976. Effect of incubation in human plasma on electrophoretic mobility of brain-type creatine phosphokinase. *Clinica Chimica Acta* 73:257–65.

112. Cho, H. W.; Meltzer, H. Y.; and Fang, V. S. Isozymes of CPK in sera of psychotic patients. Submitted for publication.

113. Chouinard, G.; Pinard, G.; Prenoveau, Y.; and Tetreault, L. 1973. Alpha-methyldopa-chlorpromazine interaction in schizophrenic patients. *Current Therapeutic Research* 15:60–72.

114. Christian, S. T.; Benington, F.; Morin, R. D.; and Corbett, L. 1975. Gas-liquid chromatographic separation and identification of biologically important indolealkylamines from the human cerebrospinal fluid. *Biochemical Medicine* 14:191–200.

115. Clemens, J. A.; Smalstig, E. B.; and Sawyer, B. D. 1974. Antipsychotic drugs stimulate prolactin release. *Psychopharmacologia* (Berlin) 40:123–127.

116. Clement-Cormier, Y. C.; Kebabian, J. W.; Petzold, G. L.; and Greengard, P. 1974. Dopamine-sensitive adenylate cyclase in mammalian brain: A possible site of action of antipsychotic drugs. *Proceedings of the National Academy of Sciences of the U.S.A.* 71:1113–17.

117. Coffey, J. W.; Guschwan, A.; and Heath, R. 1970. Serum creatine phosphokinase, aldolase, and copper in acute and chronic schizophrenics. *Biological Psychiatry* 2:331–40.

118. Cohen, D. J.; Shaywitz, B. A.; Johnson, W. T.; and Bowers, M. B., Jr. 1974. Biogenic amines in autistic and atypical children. *Archives of General Psychiatry* 31:845–53.

119. Collins, G. G. S.; Sandler, M.; Williams, E. D.; and Youdim, M. B. H. 1970. Multiple forms of human brain mitochondrial monoamine oxidase. *Nature* 225:817–20.

120. Connell, P. H. 1958. *Amphetamine psychosis.* Maudsley Monographs, no. 5. Institute of Psychiatry. (London: Chapman & Hall).

121. Cools, A. R.; Struyker-Boudier, H. A. J.; and Van Rossum, J. M. 1976. Dopamine receptors: Selective agonists and antagonists of functionally distinct types within the feline brain. *European Journal of Pharmacology* 37:283–93.

122. Cools, A. R., and Van Rossum, J. M. 1976. Excitation-mediating and inhibition-mediating dopamine receptors: A new concept towards a better understanding of electrophysiological, biochemical, pharmacological, functional and clinical data. *Psychopharmacologia* (Berlin) 45:243–54.

123. Cooper, J. R.; Bloom, F. E.; and Roth, R. H. 1974. *The biochemical basis of neuropharmacology,* 2nd ed. (New York: Oxford University Press).

124. Cooper, S. J. 1974. Anesthetization of prefrontal cortex and response to noxious stimulation. *Nature* (London) 254:439–40.

125. Corbett, L. 1976. Progress in schizophrenia research. *Lancet* 2:426.

126. Corrodi, H.; Fuxe, K.; Lidbrink, P.; Olson, L. 1971. Minor tranquilizers, stress and central catecholamine neurons. *Brain Research* 29:1–16.

127. Costa, E., and Gessa, G. L., eds. 1977. *Nonstriatal dopaminergic neurons* (New York: Raven Press).

128. Costall, B.; Naylor, R. J.; and Olley, J. E. 1972. On the involvement of the caudate-putamen, globus pallidus and substantia nigra with neuroleptic and cholinergic modification of locomotor activity. *Neuropharmacology* 11:317–30.

129. Crane, G. E. 1973. Persistent dyskinesia. *British Journal of Psychiatry* 122:395–405.

130. Crayton, J. W.; Stalberg, E.; and Hilton-Brown, P. 1977. The motor unit in psychotic patients: A single fibre EMG study. *Journal of Neurology, Neurosurgery and Psychiatry* 40:455–63.

131. Creese, I.; Burt, D. R.; and Snyder, S. H. 1975. Dopamine receptor binding: Differentiation of agonist and antagonist states with ³H-dopamine and ³H-haloperidol. *Life Sciences* 17:993–1002.

132. Creese, I.; Burt, D. R.; and Snyder, S. H. 1976. Dopamine receptor binding predicts clinical and pharmacological potencies of antischizophrenic drugs. *Science* 192:481–83.

133. Creese, I., and Iversen, S. D. 1975. The pharmacological and anatomical substrates of the amphetamine response in the rat. *Brain Research* 83:419–36.

134. Crow, T. J., and Gillbe, C. 1974. Brain dopamine and behavior. *Journal of Psychiatric Research* 11:163–72.

135. Cunningham, L. A.; Rich, C. L.; Woodruff, R. A., Jr.; and Olney, J. W. 1974. Creatine phosphokinase and psychiatric illness. *British Journal of Psychiatry* 124:87–91.

136. Curzon, G. 1975. CSF homovanillic acid. An index of dopaminergic hyperactivity. In *Advances in neurology*, eds. D. B. Calne, T. N. Chase, and A. Barbeau (New York: Raven Press), vol. 9, pp. 349–57.

137. Dahlstrom, A., and Fuxe, K. 1964. Evidence for the existence of monoamine-containing neurones in the central nervous system. I. Demonstration of monoamine in the cell bodies of brain stem neurons. *Acta Physiologica Scandinavica* 62, supp. 232, pp. 1–55.

138. Dalen, P. 1974. *Season of birth in schizophrenia and other mental disorders* (Göteborg: University of Göteborg).

139. Daly, J. W. 1976. The nature of receptors regulating the formation of cyclic AMP in brain tissue. *Life Sciences* 18:1349–58.

140. DaPrada, M., and Keller, H. H. 1976. Baclofen and γ-hydroxybutyrate. Similar effects on cerebral dopamine neurones. *Life Sciences* 19:1253–64.

141. Davis, G. C.; Bunney, W. E., Jr.; DeFrantis, E. G.; et al. 1977. Intravenous naloxone administration in schizophrenia and affective illness. *Science* 197:74–77.

142. Davis, J. M. 1974. Dose equivalence of the anti-psychotic drugs. *Journal of Psychiatric Research* 11:65–69.

143. Davis, J. M., and Cole, J. O. 1975. Antipsychotic drugs. In *Comprehensive textbook of psychiatry*, eds. A. M. Freedman, H. I. Kaplan, and B. J. Sadock (Baltimore: Williams & Wilkins), pp. 1921–41.

144. Davis, K. L.; Hollister, L. E.; Berger, P. A.; and Barchas, J. D. 1975. Cholinergic imbalance hypotheses of psychoses and movement disorders: Strategies for evaluation. *Psychopharmacology Communications* 1:533–43.

145. Del Vecchio, M.; Ventruto, V.; Vacca, L.; Festa, B.; Celani, T.; and Erto, P. 1975. Variazoni delle valuazioni statische. *Acta Neurological* (Naples) 30:483–96.

146. Dencker, S. J., and Malm, U. 1968. Protein pattern of cerebrospinal fluid in mental disease. *Acta Psychiatrica Scandinavica*, supp. 203, pp. 105–9.

147. De Rivera, J. L.; Lal, S.; Ettigi, P.; Hontela, S.; Muller, H. F.; and Friesen, H. G. 1976. Effect of acute and chronic neuroleptic therapy on serum prolactin levels in men and women of different age groups. *Clinica de Endocrinologia* 5:273–82.

148. De Weid, D.; Bohus, B.; Gispen, W. H.; Urban, I.; Van Wimersma Greidanus, T. B. 1976. Hormonal influences on motivational learning and memory processes. In *Hormones, behavior and psychopathology*, ed. E. J. Sachar (New York: Raven Press), pp. 1–14.

149. Diamantopoulos, S., and Zander Olsen, P. 1965. Motorneurone excitability in normal subjects and patients with abnormal muscle tone. *Proceedings of the Sixth International Congress of EMG and Clinical Neurophysiology* (New York: Elsevier), pp. 621–23.

150. Diefendorf, A. R., and Dodge, R. 1908. An experimental study of the ocular reactions of the insane from photographic records. *Brain* 31:451–89.

151. Dill, R. E., and Campbell, K. M. 1973. 3-methoxytyramine: A possible endogenous toxin of psychosis? *Research Communications in Chemical Pathology and Pharmacology* 6:975–82.

152. Divac, I.; Wikmark, R. G. E.; and Gade, A. 1975. Spontaneous alternation in rats with lesions in the frontal lobes: An extension of the frontal lobe syndrome. *Physiological Psychology* 3:39–42.

153. Doherty, P. C., and Zinkernagel, R. M. 1976. A biological role for the major histocompatibility antigens. *Lancet* 1:1406–9.

154. Dominic, J., and Moore, K. E. 1971. Depression of behavior and the brain content of alpha-methyl-norepinephrine and alpha-methyl-dopamine following the administration of alphamethyldopa. *Neuropharmacology* 10:33–44.

155. Domino, E. F. 1975. Indole alkylamines as psychotogen precursors-possible neurotransmitter balance. In *Neurotransmitter balances regulating behavior*, eds. E. F. Domino and J. M. Davis (Ann Arbor: NPP Books), pp. 185–228.

156. Domino, E. F. 1976. Search for new treatment approaches in schizophrenia: *In vitro* studies of potential n-methyltransferase inhibitors. *Archives Internationales de Pharmacodynamie et de Therapie* 221:75–86.

157. Domino, E. F., and Khanna, S. S. 1976. Decreased blood platelet MAO activity in unmedicated chronic schizophrenic patients. *American Journal of Psychiatry* 133:323–26.

158. Domino, E. F.; Krause, R. R.; and Bowers, J. 1973. Various enzymes involved with putative neurotransmitters. *Archives of General Psychiatry* 29:195–201.

159. Donoso, A. O.; Bishop, W.; Fawcett, C. P.; Krulich, L.; and McCann, S. M. 1971. Effect of drugs that modify brain monoamine concentrations on plasma gonadotropin and prolactin levels in the rat. *Endocrinology* 89:774–84.

160. Dorris, R. L., and Shore, P. A. 1971. Amine uptake and storage mechanisms in the corpus striatum of rat and rabbit. *Journal of Pharmacology and Experimental Therapeutics* 179:15–19.

161. Dorris, R. L. and Shore, P. A. 1971. Localization and persistence of metaraminol and alpha-methyl-m-tyramine in rat and rabbit brain. *Journal of Pharmacology and Experimental Therapeutics* 179:10–14.

162. Drachman, D. A., and Adams, R. D. 1962. Herpes simplex and acute inclusion-body encephalitis. *Archives of Neurology* 7:45–63.

163. Dubo, H.; Park, D. C.; Pennington, R. J. T.; Kalbog, R. M.; and Walton, J. N. 1967. Serum creatine kinase in cases of stroke, head injury and meningitis. *Lancet* 2:743–48.

164. Duby, S. E.; Cotzias, G. C.; Papavasilious, P. S.; and Lawrence, W. H. 1972. Injected apomorphine and orally administered levadopa in parkinsonism. *Archives of Neurology* 27:474–80.

165. Dunner, D. L.; Cohn, C. K.; Weinshilboum, R. M.; and Wyatt, R. J. 1973. The activity of dopamine-β-hydroxylase and metionine activating enzyme in blood of schizophrenic patients. *Biological Psychiatry* 6:215–20.

166. Durell, J., and Archer, E. G. 1976. Plasma proteins in schizophrenia: A review. *Schizophrenia Bulletin* 2:147–60.

167. Duvoisin, R. C. 1967. Cholinergic-anticholinergic antagonism in parkinsonism. *Archives of Neurology* 17:124–36.

168. Eberhard, G.; Franzen, G.; and Low, B. 1975. Schizophrenia susceptibility and HL-A antigens. *Neuropsychobiology* 1:211–17.

169. Ebstein, R. P.; Biederman, J.; Rimon, R.; Zohar, J.; and Belmaker, R. H. 1976. Cyclic GMP in the CSF of patients with schizophrenia before and after neuroleptic treatment. *Psychopharmacologia* 51:71–74.

170. Ehrensvard, G.; Liljekvist, J.; and Nilsson, H. T. 1960. Studies of human serum constituents in relation to schizophrenia. In *Molecular basis of some aspects of mental activity*, ed. O. Walaas (New York: Academic Press), vol. 1, pp. 231–40.

171. Elde, R.; Hokfelt, T.; Johansson, O.; and Terenius, L. 1976. Immunohistochemical studies using antibodies to leucine enkephaline: Initial observations in the nervous system of the rat. *Neuroscience* 1:349–51.

172. Ellinwood, E. H.; Sudilovsky, A.; and Nelson, L. M. 1973. Evolving behavior in the clinical and experimental amphetamine (model) psychosis. *American Journal of Psychiatry* 130: 1088–93.

173. El-Yousef, M. K.; Janowsky, P. S.; Davis, J. M.; and Seckerke, H. J. 1973. Reversal of antiparkinsonian drugs toxicity by physostigmine. A controlled study. *American Journal of Psychiatry* 130:141–45.

174. Enna, S. J.; Bennett, J. P.; Burt, D. R.; Creese, I.; and Snyder, S. H. 1976. Stereospecificity of interaction of neuroleptic drugs with neurotransmitters and correlation with clinical potency. *Nature* 263:338–41.

175. Eschar, J., and Zimmerman, H. J. 1967. Creatine kinase in disease. *American Journal of the Medical Sciences* 253:272–82.

176. Ettigi, P.; Nair, N. P. V.; Lal, S.; Cervantes, P.; and Guyda, H. 1976. Effect of apomorphine on growth hormone and prolactin secretion in schizophrenic patients, with or without oral dyskinesia, withdrawn from chronic neuroleptic therapy. *Journal of Neurology, Neurosurgery and Psychiatry* 39:870–76.

177. Everett, G. M., and Borscherding, J. W. 1970. L-DOPA: Effect on concentrations of dopamine, norepinephrine and serotonin in brains of mice. *Science* 168:849–50.

178. Fahn, S. 1973. Treatment of choreic movements with perphenazine. In *Huntington's chorea, 1872–1972*, eds. A. Barbeau, T. N. Chase, E. W. Paulson. (New York: Raven Press), pp. 755–64.

179. Fang, V. S.; Cho, H. W.; and Meltzer, H. Y. 1977. Radioimmunoassay for MM and BB isoenzymes of creatine kinase substantiated by clinical application. *Clinical Chemistry* 23:1898–1902.

180. Fann, W. E.; Lake, C. R.; Gerber, C. J.; and McKenzie, G. M. 1974. Cholinergic suppression of tardive dyskinesia. *Psychopharmacologia* 37:101–7.

181. Farley, I. J.; Price, K. S.; and Hornykiewicz, O. 1977. Dopamine in the limbic regions of the human brain: Normal and abnormal. In *Non-striatal dopaminergic neurons*, eds. E. Costa and G. L. Gessa (New York: Raven Press), pp. 57–64.

182. Farnebo, L.; Fuxe, K.; Goldstein, M.; Hamberger, B.; and Ungerstedt, U. 1971. Dopamine and noradrenaline releasing action of amantadine in the central and peripheral nervous system: A possible mode of action in Parkinson's disease. *European Journal of Pharmacology* 16:27–38.

183. Ferris, R. M.; Tang, F. L. M.; and Maxwell, R. A. 1972. A comparison of the capacities of isomers of amphetamine, deoxypipradrol and methylphenidate to inhibit the uptake of tritiated catecholamines into rat cerebral cortex slices, synaptosomal preparations of rat cerebral cortex, hypothalamus and striatum and into adrenergic nerves of rabbit aorta. *Journal of Pharmacology and Experimental Therapeutics* 181:407–16.

184. Fessel, W. J. 1962. Autoimmunity and mental illness. A preliminary report. *Archives of General Psychiatry* 6:320–323.

185. Fibiger, H. C., and Phillips, A. E. 1974. Role of dopamine and norepinephrine in the chemistry of reward. *Journal of Psychiatric Research* 11:135–43.

186. Fischman, D. A.; Meltzer, H. Y.; and Poppei, R. W. 1970. The disruption of myofibrils in the skeletal muscle of acutely psychotic patients. *Archives of General Psychiatry* 23:503–15.

187. Foldes, A., and Costa, E. 1975. Relationship of brain monoamine and locomotor activity in rats. *Biochemical Pharmacology* 24:1617–21.

188. Fonnum, F.; Walaas, I.; and Iversen, E. 1977. Localization of gabergic, cholinergic and aminergic structures in the mesolimbic system. *Journal of Neurochemistry* 29:221–30.

189. Foster, F. G., and Kupfer, D. J. 1973. Psychomotor activity and creatine phosphokinase activity. *Archives of General Psychiatry* 29:752–58.

190. Federiksen, P. K. 1975. Baclofen in the treatment of schizophrenia. *Lancet* 1:702–3.

191. Fredickson, R. C. A. 1977. Enkephalin pantapeptides: A review of current evidence for a physiological role in vertebrate neurotransmission. *Life Sciences* 21:23–42.

192. Freedman, D. X. 1975. *Biology of the major psychoses: A comparative analysis* (New York: Raven Press).

193. Freeman, H. 1968. Physiological studies. In *Schizophrenia: A review of the syndrome*, ed. L. Bellak (New York: Logos Press), pp. 174–215.

194. Friedhoff, A. J. 1977. Biosynthesis of endogenous hallucinogens. In *Neuroregulators and psychiatric disorders*, eds. E. Usdin, D. A. Hamburg, and J. D. Barchas (New York: Oxford University Press), pp. 557–64

195. Friedhoff, A. J., and Alpert, M. 1973. A dopaminergic-cholinergic mechanism in production of psychotic symptoms. *Biological Psychiatry* 6:165–69.

196. Friedman, E.; Shopsin, B.; Sathananthan, G.; and Gershon, S. 1974. Blood platelet monoamine oxidase activity in psychiatric patients. *American Journal of Psychiatry* 131:1392–94.

197. Frotscher, V.; Dominik, B.; Richter, R.; Zschaege, B.; Schulte-Lippern, M.; Jenelt, G.; Messerchmidt, W.; Schmidtmann, V.; and Wilbrandt, R. 1973. Die instabilitat der kreatin-phosphokinase-isoenzyme in serum. *Klinische Wochenschrift* (Berlin) 51:801–5.

198. Fuxe, K., and Hokfelt, T. 1966. Further evidence for the existence of tubero-infundibular dopamine neurons. *Acta Physiologica Scandinavica* 66:245–46.

199. Fuxe, K., and Hokfelt, T. 1969. Catecholamines in the hypothalamus and the pituitary gland. In *Frontiers in neuroendocrinology*, eds. W. Ganong and L. Martin (New York: Oxford University Press), pp. 47–96.

200. Fuxe, K.; Hokfelt, T.; Johansson, O.; Jonsson, G.; Lidbrink, P.; and Ljungdahl, A. 1974. The origin of the dopamine nerve terminals in limbic and frontal cortex: Evidence for meso-cortical dopamine neurons. *Brain Research* 82:349–55.

201. Fyro, B.; Nyback, H.; and Sedvall, G. 1972. Tyrosine hydroxylation in the rat striatum in vivo after nigral lesion and chlorpromazine treatment. *Neuropharmacology* 11:531–37.

202. Fyro, B.; Wade-Helgodt, B.; Borg, S.; and Sedvall, G. 1974. The effect of chlorpromazine on homovanillic acid levels in cerebrospinal fluid of schizophrenic patients. *Psychopharmacologia* (Berlin) 35:287–94.

203. Galey, D., and Le Moal, M. 1976. Locomotor activity after various radiofrequency lesions

of the limbic midbrain area in the rat. Evidence for a particular role of the ventral mesencephalic tegmentum. *Life Sciences* 19:677–84.

204. Galey, D.; Simon, H.; and Le Moal, M. 1977. Behavioral effects of lesions in the A10 dopaminergic area of the rat. *Brain Research* 124:83–97.

205. Gamboa, E. T., et al. 1974. Influenza virus antigen in postencephalitic parkinsonian brain: Detection by immunofluorescence. *Archives of Neurology* 31:228–32.

206. Garelis, E., and Neff, N. H. 1974. Cyclic adenosine monophosphate: Selective increase in caudate nucleus after administration of L-DOPA. *Science* 183:532–33.

207. Garron, D. C. 1973. Huntington's chorea and schizophrenia. In *Huntington's chorea, 1872–1972*, eds. A. Barbeau, T. N. Chase, and G. W. Paulson (New York: Raven Press), pp. 729–34.

208. Garver, D. L.; Schlemmer, F., Jr.; Maas, J. W.; and Davis, J. M. 1975. A schizophreniform behavioral psychosis mediated by dopamine. *American Journal of Psychiatry* 132:33–38.

209. George, W. J.; Polson, J. B.; O'Toole, A. G.; and Goldberg, N. D. 1970. Elevation of guanosine 3',5'-cyclic phosphate in rat heart after perfusion with acetylcholine. *Proceedings of the National Academy of Sciences of the U.S.A.* 66:298–403.

210. Gerlach, J., and Luhdorf, K. 1975. The effect of L-DOPA on young patients with simple schizophrenia treated with neuroleptic drugs. *Psychopharmacologia* (Berlin) 44:105–10.

211. Gerlach, J.; Reisby, N.; and Randrup, A. 1974. Dopaminergic hypersensitivity and cholinergic hypofunction in the pathophysiology of tardive dyskinesia. *Psychopharmacologia* (Berlin) 34:21–35.

212. Gershon, E. S.; Belmaker, R. H.; Ebstein, R.; and Jonas, W. Z. 1977. Plasma MAO activity unrelated to genetic vulnerability to primary affective illness. *Archives of General Psychiatry* 34:731–34.

213. Gershon, S.; Hekimian, L. J.; Floyd, A., Jr.; Hollister, L. E. 1967. α-methyl-p-tyrosine (AMPT) in schizophrenia. *Psychopharmacologia* (Berlin) 11:189–94.

214. Gianutsos, G., and Moore, K. E. 1977. Increase in mouse brain dopamine content by baclofen: Effects of apomorphine and neuroleptics. *Psychopharmacology* 52:217–21.

215. Gibbs, F. A. 1951. Ictal and nonictal psychiatric disorders in temporal lobe epilepsy. *Journal of Nervous and Mental Disease* 113:522–28.

216. Gillin, J. C.; Kaplan, J.; Stillman, R.; and Wyatt, R. J. 1976. The psychedelic model of schizophrenia: The case of N,N-Dimethyltryptamine. *American Journal of Psychiatry* 153:203–8.

217. Gillin, J. C., and Wyatt, R. J. 1977. N,N-Dimethyltryptamine and 5-methoxy-N,N-Dimethyltryptamine: Possible relationships to schizophrenia. In *Neuroregulators and psychiatric disorders*, eds. E. Usdin, D. A. Hamburg, and J. D. Barchas (New York: Oxford University Press), pp. 565–77.

218. Glaeser, B. S., and Hare, T. A. 1975. Measurement of GABA in human cerebrospinal fluid. *Biochemical Medicine* 12:274–82.

219. Glaser, G. H., and Pincus, J. H. 1969. Limbic encephalitis. *Journal of Nervous and Mental Disease* 149:59–67.

220. Glaser, G. H.; Solitare, G. B.; and Manuelidis, E. A. 1968. Acute and subacute inclusion encephalitis. *Research Publications of the Association for Research in Nervous and Mental Disease* 49:178–215.

221. Glason, K. V. 1967. Certain features of the metabolism of leucocytes in nuclear schizophrenia. In *Biological research in schizophrenia*, ed. M. Vartanian (Moscow: Ordina Lennia), pp. 210–12.

222. Goldberg, L. S.; Shuster, J.; Stuckey, M.; et al. 1968. Autoantibody activity in gastric juice. *Science* 168:1240–41.

223. Goldberg, M. E., and Salama, A. I. 1972. Tolerance to drum stress and its relationship to dopamine turnover. *European Journal of Pharmacology* 17:202–7.

224. Goldstein, A. 1976. Opioid peptides (endorphins) in pituitary and brain. *Science* 193:1081–86.

225. Goode, D. J., and Meltzer, H. Y. 1976. Effects of isometric exercise on serum creatine phosphokinase activity. *Archives of General Psychiatry* 33:1207–10.

226. Goode, D. J.; Meltzer, H. Y.; Crayton, J. W.; and Mazura, T. A. 1977. Physiologic abnormalities of the neuromuscular system in schizophrenia. *Schizophrenia Bulletin* 3:121–39.

227. Goodwin, F. K. 1972. Behavioral effects of L-DOPA in man. In *Psychiatric complications of medical drugs*, ed. R. I. Shader (New York: Raven Press), pp. 149–74.

228. Goodwin, F. K.; Murphy, D. L.; Brodie, H. K.; and Bunney, W. E. 1971. Levadopa: Alterations in behavior. *Clinical Pharmacology and Therapeutics* 12:383–96.

229. Goridis, C., and Neff, N. H. 1971. Evidence for a specific monoamine oxidase associated with sympathetic nerves. *Neuropharmacology* 10:557–64.

230. Gordon, R.; Spector, R.; Sjoerdsma, A.; and Udenfriend, S. 1966. Increased synthesis of norepinephrine and epinephrine in the intact rat during exercise and exposure to cold. *Journal of Pharmacology and Experimental Therapeutics* 153:440–47.

231. Gosling, R.; Kerry, R. J.; Orme, J. E.; and Owen, G. 1972. Creatine phosphokinase activity in newly admitted psychiatric patients. *British Journal of Psychiatry* 121:351–55.

232. Gosling, R.; Kerry, R. J.; and Owen, G. 1972. Creatine phosphokinase activity during lithium treatment. *British Medical Journal* 3:327–29.

233. Gottfries, C. G.; Oreland, L.; Wiberg, A.; and Winblad, B. 1975. Lowered monoamine oxidase activity in brains from alcoholic suicides. *Journal of Neurochemistry* 25:667–73.

234. Gozzani, J. L., and Izquerdo, I. 1976. Possible peripheral adrenergic and central dopaminergic influences in memory consolidation. *Psychopharmacology* 49:109–11.

235. Grahame-Smith, D. G. 1971. Studies *in vivo* on the relationship between brain tryptophan, brain 5-HT synthesis and hyperactivity in rats treated with a monoamine oxidase inhibitor and L-tryptophan. *Journal of Neurochemistry* 18:1053–66.

236. Grahame-Smith, D. G., and Green, A. R. 1974. The role of brain dopamine in the hyperactivity syndrome produced in rats after administration of L-tryptophan and a monoamine oxidase inhibitor. *British Journal of Pharmacology* 50:442–43.

237. Greengard, P. 1974. Biochemical characterization of the dopamine receptor in the mammalian caudate nucleus. *Journal of Psychiatric Research* 11:82–90.

238. Grelak, R. P.; Clark, R.; Stump, J. M.; and Vernier, V. G. 1970. Amantadine–dopamine interaction. Possible mode of action in parkinsonism. *Science* 169:203–4.

239. Griffiths, J. J.; Oates, J.; and Cavanaugh, J. 1968. Paranoid episodes induced by drugs. *Journal of the American Medical Association* 205:39.

240. Griffiths, P. D. 1966. Serum levels of ATP: Creatine phosphotransferase (creatine kinase), the normal range and effect of muscular activity. *Clinica Chimica Acta* 13:413–20.

241. Grote, S. S.; Moses, S. G.; Robins, E.; Hudgens, R. W.; and Croninger, A. B. 1974. A study of selected catecholamine metabolizing enzymes: A comparison of depressive suicides and alcoholic suicides with controls. *Journal of Neurochemistry* 23:791–802.

242. Guldberg, H. C.; Ashcroft, G. W.; and Crawford, T. B. B. 1966. Concentration of 5-hydroxyindole acetic acid and homovanillic acid in the cerebrospinal fluid of the dog before and during treatment with probenecid. *Life Sciences* 5:1571–75.

243. Gulmann, N. C.; Bahr, B.; Andersen, B.; and Eliassen, H. M. M. 1976. A double-blind trial of baclofen against placebo in the treatment of schizophrenia. *Acta Psychiatrica Scandinavica* 54:287–93.

244. Gumulka, S. W.; Dinnendahl, V.; Schonhoffer, P. S.; and Stock, K. 1976. Dopaminergic stimulants and cyclic nucleotides in mouse brain. *Naunyn-Schmiedeberg's Archives of Pharmacology* 295:21–26.

245. Gunne, L. M., and Anggard, E. 1973. Pharmacokinetic studies with amphetamines: Relationship to neuropsychiatric disorders. *Journal of Pharmacokinetics and Biopharmaceutics* 1:481–95.

246. Gunne, L. M.; Lundstrom, L.; and Terenius, L. 1977. Naloxone-induced reversal of schizophrenic hallucinations. *Journal of Neural Transmission* 40:13–19.

247. Guterman, A. 1973. Manifest psychopathology and serum creatine phosphokinase: A correlational study. *Diseases of the Nervous System* 33:49–53.

248. Hall, D. W. R.; Logan, B. W.; and Parsons, G. H. 1969. Further studies on the inhibition of monoamine oxidase by M + B 9302 (chorgyline). I. Substrate specificities in various mammalian species. *Biochemical Pharmacology* 18:1447–54.

249. Halonen, P. E.; Rimon, R.; Katve, A.; and Jantti, V. 1974. Antibody level to herpes simplex type I, measles and rubella viruses in psychiatric patients. *British Journal of Psychiatry* 125:461–65.

250. Harding, T. 1974. Serum creatine kinase in acute psychosis. *British Journal of Psychiatry* 125:280–85.

251. Harding, T. 1974. The effect of lysergic acid diethylamide on serum creatine kinase levels. *Psychopharmacologia* (Berlin) 40:177–84.

252. Hare, E. H.; Price, J. S.; and Slater, E. 1974. Mental disorder and season of birth. *British Journal of Psychiatry* 124:81–86.

253. Hartman, B. K. 1973. Immunofluorescence of dopamine-β-hydroxylase application of improved methodology to the localization of the peripheral and central noradrenergic nervous system. *Journal of Histochemistry and Cytochemistry* 21:312–32.

254. Hartmann, E. 1976. Schizophrenia: A theory. *Psychopharmacology* 49:1–15.

255. Heath, R. G.; Krupp, I. M.; et al. 1967. Schizophrenia as an immunologic disorder. *Archives of General Psychiatry* 16:1–33.

256. Heath, R. G., and Mickle, W. A. 1960. Evaluation of seven years' experience with depth electrode studies in human patients. In *Electrical Studies of the Unanesthetized Brain*, eds. E. R. Ramey and D. S. O'Doherty. (New York: Harper & Row), pp. 214–47.

257. Heckert, E. E., and Keup, W. 1969. Excretion patterns of tryptamine, indoleacetic acid and 5-hydroxyindole acetic acid and their correlation with mental changes in schizophrenic patients under medication with alpha-methyldopa. *Psychopharmacologia* (Berlin) 15:48–59.

258. Hess, S. M.; Connamacher, R. H.; Ozaki, M.; and Udenfriend, S. 1961. The effects of alpha-methyl-dopa and alpha-methyl-meta-tyrosine on the metabolism of norepinephrine and serotonin *in vivo*. *Journal of Pharmacology and Experimental Therapeutics* 134:129–38.

259. Himmelhoch, J.; Pincus, J.; Tucker, G.; and Detre, T. 1970. Subacute encephalitis: Behavioral and neurological aspects. *British Journal of Psychiatry* 116:531–38.

260. Hökfelt, T. 1967. The possible ultrastructural identification of tubero-infundibular dopamine-containing nerve endings in the median eminence of the rat. *Brain Research* 5:121–23.

261. Hökfelt, T., and Fuxe, K. 1972. On the morphology and the neuroendocrine role of the hypothalamic catecholamine neurons. In *Brain-Endocrine Interaction. Median Eminence: Structure and function*, eds. K. M. Knigge, D. E. Scott, and A. Weindl (Basel: S. Karger), pp. 181–223.

262. Hökfelt, T.; Fuxe, K.; Johansson, O.; Jeffcoat, S.; and White, N. 1975. Distribution of thyrotropin-releasing hormone (TRH) in the central nervous system as revealed with immuno-chemistry. *European Journal of Pharmacology* 34:389–92.

263. Hökfelt, T.; Ljungdahl, A.; Fuxe, K.; and Johansson, O. 1974. Dopamine nerve terminals in the rat limbic cortex: Aspects of the dopamine hypothesis of schizophrenia. *Science* 184:177–79.

264. Hollister, L. E. 1977. Some general thoughts about endogenous hallucinogens. In *Neuroregulators and Psychiatric Disorders*, eds. E. Usdin, D. A. Hamburg, and J. D. Barchas (New York: Oxford University Press), pp. 550–56.

265. Holzbauer, M., and Vogt, M. 1956. Depression by reserpine of the noradrenaline concentration in the hypothalamus of the cat. *Journal of Neurochemistry* 1:8–11.

266. Holzman, P. S., and Levy, D. L. 1977. Smooth pursuit eye movements and functional psychoses: A review. *Schizophrenia Bulletin* 3:15–27.

267. Holzman, P. S.; Proctor, L. R.; Levy, D. L.; Yasillo, N. J.; Meltzer, H. Y.; and Hurt, S. W. 1974. Eye-tracking dysfunctions in schizophrenic patients and their relatives. *Archives of General Psychiatry* 31:143–51.

268. Hornykiewicz, O. 1966. Dopamine (3-hydroxytyramine) and brain function. *Pharmacological Reviews* 18:925–64.

269. Hornykiewicz, O. 1972. Neurochemistry of Parkinsonism. In *Handbook of neurochemistry*, ed. A. Lajtha (New York: Plenum Press), vol. 7. pp. 465–501.

270. Hornykiewicz, O. 1973. Parkinson's disease: From brain homogenate to treatment. *Federation Proceedings* 32:183–90.

271. Horowitz, M. J., and Adamas, J. E. 1970. Hallucinations on brain stimulation: Evidence for revision of the Penfield hypothesis. In *Origins and mechanisms of hallucinations*, ed. W. Keup (New York: Plenum Press), pp. 13–22.

272. Ibrisoye, I. M. 1976. A study of the activity of the leucocyte enzymes in the blood of schizophrenic patients. *Zhurnal Nervropatologli Psikhiatrii Im. S.S. Korsakova* 76:431–36.

273. Ikeda, H.; Uefuji, K.; Noma, T.; Manabe, T.; and Nasu, M. 1977. Serum creatine phosphokinase and transaminase activities in newly admitted psychiatric patients. *Kyushu Neuropsychiatry* 22:164–68.

274. Inanaga, K.; Inoue, K.; Tachibana, H.; Oshima, M.; and Kotorii, T. 1972. Effect of L-DOPA in schizophrenia. *Folia Psychiatrica et Neurologica Japonica* 26:145–57.

275. Inanaga, K.; Nakazawa, Y.; Inoue, K.; Tachibana, H.; Oshima, M.; Kotorii, T.; Tanaka, M.; and Ogawa, N. 1975. Double-blind controlled study of L-DOPA therapy in schizophrenia. *Folia Psychiatrica et Neurologica Japonica* 29:123–43.

276. Inanaga, K.; Oshima, M.; Tachibana, H.; Nakamura, K.; and Koketsu, K. 1971. Three cases of schizophrenia treated with L-DOPA. *Kurume Medical Journal* 18:161–68.

277. Isaacson, R. L. 1974. *The Limbic System* (New York: Plenum Press).

278. Ivanyi, D.; Zemek, P.; and Ivanyi, P. 1976. HLA antigens in schizophrenia. *Tissue Antigens Newsletter*, pp. 217–20.

279. Iversen, L. 1975. Dopamine receptors in the brain. *Science* 188:1084–89.

280. Jacquet, Y. F., and Marks, N. 1976. The C-fragment of β-lipotropin: An endogenous neuroleptic or antipsychotogen? *Science* 194:632–35.

281. Janowsky, D. S., and Davis, J. M. 1974. Dopamine, psychomotor stimulants, and schizophrenia: Effects of methylphenidate and the stereoisomers of amphetamine in schizophrenia. In *Neuropsychopharmacology of monoamines and their regulatory enzymes*, ed. E. Usdin (New York: Raven Press), pp. 317–23.

282. Janowsky, D. S.; El-Yousef, M. K.; and Davis, J. M. 1973. Parasympathetic suppression of manic symptoms by physostigmine. *Archives of General Psychiatry* 28:542–47.

283. Janowsky, D. S.; El-Yousef, M. K.; Davis, J. M.; and Sekerke, H. J. 1973. Provocation of schizophrenic symptoms by intravenous administration of methylphenidate. *Archives of General Psychiatry* 28:185–91.

284. Janowsky, D. S.; Segal, D. S.; Abrams, A.; Bloom, F.; and Guillemin, R. 1977. Negative naloxone effects in schizophrenic patients. *Psychopharmacology* 53:295–97.

285. Janowsky, D. S.; Segal, D. S.; Bloom, F.; Abrams, A.; and Guillemin, R. 1977. Lack of effect of naloxone on schizophrenic symptoms. *American Journal of Psychiatry* 134:926–27.

286. Janowsky, D. S.; Segal, D. S.; and Judd, L. L. 1977. Schneiderian symptoms in amphetamine psychosis. Abstracts, Sixth World Congress of Psychiatry, Honolulu, August 1977, p. 274.

287. Jarrott, B. 1973. The cellular localization and physiological role of catechol-O-methyl transferase in the body. In *Frontiers in catecholamine research*, eds. E. Usdin and S. Snyder (New York: Pergamon Press), pp. 113–15.

288. Javoy, F.; Agid, Y.; Bouvet, D.; and Glowinski, J. 1974. Changes in neostriatal dopamine metabolism after carbachol or atropine microinjections into the substantia nigra. *Brain Research* 68: 253–60.

289. Johnson, J., and Milner, G. 1966. Psychiatric complications of amphetamine substances. *Acta Psychiatrica Scandinavica* 42:252–63.

290. Johnson, R. T. 1965. Experimental rabies: Studies of cellular vulnerability and pathogenesis using fluorescent antibody staining. *Journal of Neuropathology and Experimental Neurology* 24:662–74.

291. Johnston, J. P. 1968. Some observations upon a new inhibitor of monoamine in brain tissue. *Biochemical Pharmacology* 17:1285.

292. Johnstone, E. C.; Crow, T. J.; and Mashiter, K. 1977. Anterior pituitary hormone secretion in chronic schizophrenia—an approach to neurohumoral mechanisms. *Psychological Medicine* 7:223–28.

293. Kahan, B. D., and Reisfeld, R. A. 1972. *Transplantation antigens, markers of biological individuality* (New York: Academic Press).

294. Kamman, G. K.; Freeman, J. G.; and Lucero, R. J. 1953. The effect of 1-isonicotynl 2-isopropyl hydrazide (IIH) on the behavior of long-term mental patients. *Journal of Nervous and Mental Disease* 118:391–407.

295. Kaplan, J.; Mandel, J. R.; Stillman, R.; Walker, R. W.; Van den Heuvel, W. J. A.; Gillin, J. C.; and Wyatt, R. J. 1974. Blood and urine levels of N,N-dimethyl-tryptamine following administration of psychoactive dosages to human subjects. *Psychopharmacologia* (Berlin) 38:239–45.

296. Karobath, M., and Leitcih, H. 1974. Antipsychotic drugs and dopamine-stimulated adenylate cyclase prepared from corpus striatum of rat brain. *Proceedings of the National Academy of Sciences of the U.S.A.* 71:2915–18.

297. Karobath, M. E. 1975. Tricyclic antidepressive drugs and dopamine-sensitive adenylate cyclase from rat brain striatum. *European Journal of Pharmacology* 30:159–63.

298. Katz, R. I.; Goodwin, J. S.; and Kopin, I. J. 1969. Disposition of neurotransmitters in experimental mouse glioma. *Life Sciences* 8:561–69.

299. Kawamura, T.; Asada, N.; Kimura, N.; and Tsukue, I. 1971. Psychiatric clinical findings of L-DOPA effect, especially for psychic symptom and drug-induced parkinsonian symptom in schizophrenia. *Shinryo* 23:826–51 (in Japanese).

300. Kazamatsuri, H.; Chien, C.; and Cole, J. O. 1972. Treatment of tardive dyskinesia. I. Clinical efficacy of a dopamine-depleting agent, tetrabenazine. *Archives of General Psychiatry* 27:95–99.

301. Kazamatsuri, H.; Chien, C.; and Cole, J. O. 1972. Treatment of tardive dyskinesia. II. Short-term effiicacy of dopamine blocking agents haloperidol and thiopropazate. *Archives of General Psychiatry* 27:100–103.

302. Kazamatsuri, H.; Chien, C.; and Cole, J. O. 1973. Long-term treatment of tardive dyskinesia with haloperidol and tetrabenazine. *American Journal of Psychiatry* 130:479–83.

303. Kebabian, J. W., and Greengard, P. 1971. Dopamine-sensitive adenyl cyclase: Possible role in synaptic transmission. *Science* 174:1346–48.

304. Kebabian, J. W.; Petzold, G. L.; and Greengard, P. 1972. Dopamine-sensitive adenylate cyclase in caudate nucleus of rat brain, and its similarity to the "dopamine receptor." *Proceedings of the National Academy of Sciences of the U.S.A.* 69:2145–49.

305. Kehr, W.; Carlsson, A.; Lindquist, M.; Magnusson, T.; and Atack, C. 1972. Evidence for a receptor-mediated feedback control of striatal tyrosine hydroxylase activity. *Journal of Pharmacy and Pharmacology* 24:744–47.

306. Kellar, K. J.; Elliott, G. R.; Holman, R. B.; Vernikos-Danellis, J.; and Barchas, J. D. 1976. Tryptoline inhibition of serotonin uptake in rat forebrain homogenates. *Journal of Pharmacology and Experimental Therapeutics* 198:619–25.

307. Kelleher, M. J.; Copeland, J. R. M.; and Smith, A. J. 1974. High first admission rates for schizophrenia in the west of Ireland. *Psychological Medicine* 4:460–62.

308. Kelly, P.; Miller, R. J.; and Sahakian, B. Interaction of neuroleptic and cholinergic drugs with central dopaminergic mechanisms. *British Journal of Pharmacology* 49:430–31.

309. Kelly, P. H.; Seviour, P. W.; and Iversen, S. D. 1975. Amphetamine and apomorphine responses in the rat following 6-OHDA lesions of the nucleus accumbens septi and corpus striatum. *Brain Research* 94:507–22.

310. Kemali, D. K.; Polani, P. E.; Polani, N.; and Amati, A. 1972. Dermatoglyphics in a small sample of Italian males, mostly with paranoid schizophrenia. *Acta Neurologica* (Naples) 27:506–21.

311. Kety, S. S. 1969. Biochemical hypotheses and studies. In *The schizophrenic syndrome*, eds. L. Bellak and L. Loeb (New York: Grune & Stratton), pp. 155–71.

312. Kety, S. S., and Matthysee, S. 1972. Prospects for research on schizophrenia. *Neurosciences Research Program Bulletin* 10:370–507.

313. Kim, H. C., and D'Iorio, A. 1968. Possible isoenzymes of monoamine oxidase in rat tissues. *Canadian Journal of Biochemistry* 46:295–97.

314. Kim, J. S.; Bak, I. J.; Hasder, R.; and Okada, Y. 1971. Role of γ-aminobutyric acid (GABA) in the extrapyramidal motor system. II. Some evidence for the existence of a type of GABA-rich strio-nigral neurons. *Experimental Brain Research* 14:95–104.

315. Klawans, H. L. 1973. The pharmacology of extrapyramidal movement disorders. In *Monographs in neural sciences*, 2nd ed., ed. M. Cohen (Basel: Karger).

316. Klawans, H. L. 1973. The pharmacology of tardive dyskinesia. *American Journal of Psychiatry* 130:82–86.

317. Klawans, H. L. 1975. Amphetamine-induced dopaminergic hypersensitivity in guinea pigs. *Archives of General Psychiatry* 32:725–32.

318. Klawans, H. L.; Goetz, C.; and Westheimer, R. 1972. Pathophysiology of schizophrenia and the striatum. *Diseases of the Nervous System* 33:711–19.

319. Kleinberg, D. L.; Noel, G. L.; and Frantz, A. G. 1971. Chlorpromazine stimulation and L-DOPA suppression of plasma prolactin in man. *Journal of Clinical Endocrinology and Metabolism* 33:873–76.

320. Kline, N. S.; Li, C. H.; Lehmann, H. E.; Lajtha, A.; Laskin, E.; and Cooper, T. 1977. β-endorphin-induced changes in schizophrenic and depressed patients. *Archives of General Psychiatry* 34:1111–13.

321. Kobayashi, Y. 1966. The effect of three monoamine oxidase inhibitors on human plasma monoamine oxidase activity. *Biochemical Pharmacology* 15:1287–94.

322. Kolakowska, T.; Wiles, D. H.; McNeilly, A.S.; and Gelder, M. G. 1975. Correlation between plasma levels of prolactin and chlorpromazine in psychiatric patients. *Psychological Medicine* 5:214–16.

323. Kolakowska, T.; Wiles, D. H.; Gelder, M. G.; and McNeilly, A. S. 1976. Clinical significance of plasma chlorpromazine levels. II. Plasma levels of the drug, some of its metabolites and prolactin in patients receiving longterm phenothiazine treatment. *Psychopharmacology* 49:101–7.

324. Kolb, B.; Nonneman, A. J.; and Singh, R. K. 1974. Double dissociation of spatial impairments and persevation following selective prefrontal lesions in rats. *Journal of Comparative and Physiological Psychology* 87:772–80.

325. Kornetsky, C. 1976. Hyporesponsivity of chronic schizophrenic patients to dextroamphetamine. *Archives of General Psychiatry* 33:1425–28.

326. Korsgaard, S. 1976. Baclofen (Lioresal(R)) in the treatment of neuroleptic-induced tardive dyskinesia. *Acta Psychiatrica Scandinavica* 54:17–24.

327. Koslow, S. H. 1977. Biosignificance of N- and O-methylated indoles to psychiatric disorders. In *Neuroregulators and Psychiatric Disorders*, eds. E. Usdin, D. A. Hamburg, and J. D. Barchas (New York: Oxford University Press), pp. 210–19.

328. Kosterlitz, H. W., and Hughes, J. 1975. Some thoughts on the significance of enkephalin, the endogenous ligand. *Life Sciences* 17:91–96.

329. Kupfer, D. J.; Meltzer, H. Y.; Wyatt, R. J.; and Snyder, F. 1970. Serum enzyme changes in sleep deprivation. *Nature* 228:768–70.

330. Laduron, P. 1975. Scope and limitation in dopamine β-hydroxylase measurement. *Biochemical Pharmacology* 24:557–62.

331. Laduron, P.; De Bie, K.; and Leysen, J. 1977. Specific effect of haloperidol on dopamine turnover in the frontal cortex. *Naunyn-Schmiedeberg's Archives of Pharmacology* 296:183–85.

332. Laduron, P., and Leysen, J. 1977. Specific *in vivo* binding of neuroleptic drugs in rat brain. *Biochemical Pharmacology* 26:1003–7.

333. Langer, G.; Heinze, G.; Reim, B.; and Matussek, N. 1976. Reduced growth hormone responses to amphetamine in "endogenous" depressive patients. *Archives of General Psychiatry* 33:141–47.

334. Langer, G.; Sachar, E. J.; Green, P. H.; and Halpern, F. S. 1977. Human prolactin response to neuroleptic drugs correlate with anti-schizophrenic potency. *Nature* 266:639–40.

335. Langer, S. Z., and Trendelunburg, U. 1966. The onset of denervation supersensitivity. *Journal of Pharmacology and Experimental Therapeutics* 151:73–86.

336. Lauer, J. W. 1958. Biochemical and clinical changes resulting from administration of marsilid and tryptophan to schizophrenic patients. *Journal of Clinical and Experimental Psychopathology* supp. 1, 19:110–13.

337. Lee, T., and Seeman, P. 1977. Dopamine receptors in normal and schizophrenic brains. *Neuroscience Abstracts* 3:443.

338. Lees, A. J.; Clarke, C. R. A.; and Harrison, M. J. 1977. Hallucinations after withdrawal of baclofen. *Lancet* 1:858.

339. Lerner, P.; Nose, P.; Gordon, E. K.; and Lovenberg, W. 1977. Haloperidol: Effect of long-term treatment on rat striatal dopamine synthesis and turnover. *Science* 197:181–83.

340. Lewis, P. R., and Shute, C. C. D. 1967. The cholinergic limbic system: Projections to hippocampal formation, medial cortex, nuclei of the ascending cholinergic reticular system, and the subfornical organ and supra-optic crest. *Brain* 90:521–40.

341. Li, C. H.; Barnafi, L.; Chretien, M.; and Cheung, D. 1965. Isolation and amino-acid sequence of B-LPH from sheep pituitary glands. *Nature* 208:1093–94.

342. Lichtensteiger, W., and Keller, P. J. 1974. Tubero-infundibular dopamine neurons and the secretion of luteinizing hormone and prolactin: Extrahypothalamic influences, interaction with cholinergic systems and the effect of urethane anesthesia. *Brain Research* 74:279–303.

343. Lindvall, O., and Bjorklund, A. 1974. The organization of the ascending catecholamine neuron systems in the rat brain as revealed by the glyoxylic acid fluorescence method. *Acta Physiologica Scandinavica*, supp. 412:1–48.

344. Lindvall, O.; Bjorklund, A.; Moore, R. Y.; and Stenevi, U. 1974. Mesencephalic dopamine neurons projecting to neocortex. *Brain Research* 81:325–31.

345. Linnoila, M.; Viukari, M.; and Hietla, O. 1976. Effect of sodium valproate on tardive dyskinesia. *British Journal of Psychiatry* 129:114–19.

346. Lipinski, J. R.; Mandel, L. R.; Ahn, H. S.; Van den Heuvel, W. J. A.; and Walker, R. W. 1974. Blood and urinary dimethyltryptamine in acute psychotic disorders. Letter to Editor, *Lancet* 1:165.

347. Lipton, M. A.; Breese, G. R.; Prange, A. J., Jr.; Wilson, I. C.; and Cooper, B. R. 1976. Behavioral effects of hypothalamic polypeptide hormones in animals and man. In *Hormones, Behavior and Psychopathology*, ed. E. J. Sachar (New York: Raven Press), pp. 15–31.

348. Loebel, J. P., and Robins, A. H. 1973. Creatine phosphokinase activity in psychiatric patients. *British Journal of Psychiatry* 122:617–18.

349. Logan, D. G., and Deodhar, S. D. 1970. Schizophrenia, an immunological disorder? *Journal of the American Medical Association* 212:1703–4.

350. Loh, H. H.; Brase, D. A.; Sampath-Khanna, S.; Mar, J. B.; and Way, E. L. 1976. β-endorphin *in vitro* inhibition of striatal dopamine release. *Nature* 264:567–68.

351. Lomax, P. 1970. Drugs and body temperature. *International Review of Neurobiology* 12:1–43.

352. Lu, K. H.; Amenomori, Y.; Chen, C. L.; and Meites, J. 1970. Effects of central acting drugs on serum and pituitary prolactin levels in rats. *Endocrinology* 87:667–72.

353. Lu, K. H., and Meites, J. 1971. Inhibition by L-DOPA and monoamine oxidase inhibitors of pituitary prolactin release; stimulation by methyldopa and d-amphetamine. *Proceedings of the Society for Experimental Biology and Medicine* 137:480–83.

354. Luchins, D. 1975. The dopamine hypothesis of schizophrenia. A critical analysis. *Neuropsychobiology* 1:365–78.

355. Luria, E. A., and Domashneva, I. V. 1974. Autoantibodies to thymocytes in patients with schizophrenia. *Proceedings of the National Academy of Sciences of the U.S.A.* 71:235–36.

356. Lycke, E.; Norrby, R.; and Roos, B. E. 1974. A serological study on mentally ill patients. *British Journal of Psychiatry* 124:273–79.

357. McCauley, R., and Racker, E. 1973. Separation of two monoamine oxidases from bovine brain. *Federation Proceedings* 32:797.

358. McEwin, C. M. 1972. The soluble monoamine oxidase of human plasma and sera. *Advances in Biochemical Psychopharmacology* 5:151–65.

359. McGeer, E. G.; McGeer, P. L.; and Fibiger, H. C. 1974. The distribution in human postmortem brain tissue of enzymes concerned with neurotransmitter metabolism. *Society for Neuroscience* 4:447.

360. McGeer, P. L.; Greivaal, D. S.; and McGeer, E. G. 1974. Influence of noncholinergic drugs on rat striatal acetylcholine levels. *Brain Research* 80:211–17.

361. McGeer, P. L.; McGeer, E. G.; and Fibiger, H. C. 1973. Choline acetylase and glutamic acid decarboxylase in Huntington's chorea. *Neurology* 23:912–17.

362. McGeer, P. L.; McGeer, E. G.; Wada, J. A.; and Jung, E. 1971. Effects of globus pallidus lesions and Parkinson's disease on brain glutamic acid decarboxylase. *Brain Research* 32:425–31.

363. MacLean, P. D. 1952. Some psychiatric implications of physiological studies on the front-temporal portion of the limbic system (visceral brain). *Electroencephalography and Clinical Neurophysiology* 4:407–18.

364. MacLeod, R. M. 1975. Regulation of prolactin secretion. In *Frontiers in Neuroendocrinology*, eds. L. Martini and W. F. Ganong (New York: Raven Press), pp. 169–94.

365. Malis, G. U. 1961. *Research on the etiology of schizophrenia* (New York: Consultants Bureau; originally published in Russian in 1959).

366. Malmfors, T., and Thoenen, H., eds. 1971. *6-Hydroxydopamine and catecholamine neurons* (Amsterdam: North-Holland).

367. Mandel, L. R. 1975. Dimethyltryptamine: Its biosynthesis and possible role in mental disease. In *Neurotransmitter Balances Regulating Behavior*, eds. E. F. Domino and J. M. Davis (Ann Arbor: NPP Books), pp. 175–83.

368. Markianos, E. S.; Ruther, E.; and Gluba, H. 1976. 3,4-Dihydroxyphenylacetic acid and homovanillic acid in serum and cerebrospinal fluid of psychotic patients estimated by a gas chromatographic method. *Neuroscience Letters* 3:37–40.

369. Martin, J. B. 1975. Brain regulation of growth hormone secretion. In *Frontiers in Neuro-endocrinology*, eds. L. Martini and W. F. Ganong (New York: Raven Press), pp. 129–68.

370. Martin, W. A.; Garey, R. E.; and Heath, R. G. 1972. Cerebrospinal fluid creatine kinase in acutely psychotic patients. *Journal of Neurology, Neurosurgery and Psychiatry* 35:726–29.

371. Matthysse, S. 1973. Antipsychotic drug action: A clue to the neuropathology of schizophrenia. *Federation Proceedings* 32:200–205.

372. Matthysse, S. 1974. Dopamine and the pharmacology of schizophrenia: The state of the evidence. *Journal of Psychiatric Research* 11:107–13.

373. Matthysse, S., and Baldessarini, J. 1972. S-adenosylmethionine and catechol-O-methyltransferase in schizophrenia. *American Journal of Psychiatry* 128:130–32.

374. Mattson, B., and Boman, K. 1974. Buronil in Huntington's chorea. *Lancet* 2:1323.

375. Meglio, M.; Hosobuchi, Y.; Loh, H. H.; Adams, J. E.; and Li, C. H. 1977. β-endorphin: Behavioral and analgeric activity in cats. *Proceedings of the National Academy of Sciences of the U.S.A.* 74:774–76.

376. Meites, J., and Clemens, J. A. 1972. Hypothalamic control of prolactin secretion. *Vitamins and Hormones* 30:165–221.

377. Meites, J.; Lu, K. H.; Wuttke, W.; Webch, C. W.; Nagasawa, H.; and Quadri, S. K. 1972. Recent studies on function and control of prolactin secretion in rats. *Recent Progress in Hormone Research* 28:471–526.

378. Melamud, N. 1967. Psychiatric disorder with intracranial tumors of the limbic system. *Archives of Neurology* 17:113–24.

379. Mellsop, G. 1973. Schizophrenia or antiphrenia. *Australian & New Zealand Journal of Psychiatry* 7:6–8.

380. Mellsop, G.; Whittingham, S.; and Ungar, B. 1973. Schizophrenia and autoimmune serological reactions. *Archives of General Psychiatry* 28:194–96.

381. Meltzer, H. Y. 1968. Creatine kinase and aldolase in serum; abnormality common to acute psychoses. *Science* 159:1368–70.

382. Meltzer, H. Y. 1969. Intramuscular chlorpromazine and creatine kinase: Acute psychoses or local muscle trauma? Technical Comment. *Science* 164:727–28.

383. Meltzer, H. Y. 1969. Muscle enzyme release in the acute psychoses. *Archives of General Psychiatry* 21:102–12.

384. Meltzer, H. Y. 1970. Increased creatine phosphokinase and adolase activity in acutely psychotic patients: Case reports. *Journal of Psychiatric Research* 7:249–62.

385. Meltzer, H. Y. 1971. Factors influencing serum creatine phosphokinase levels in the general population. The role of race, activity and age. *Clinica Chimica Acta* 33:165–172.

386. Meltzer, H. Y. 1972. Muscle toxicity produced by phencyclidine and restraint stress. *Research Communications in Chemical Pathology and Pharmacology* 3:369–82.

387. Meltzer, H. Y. 1972. Central core fibers in an acutely psychotic patient: Evidence for a neurogenic basis for the muscle abnormalities in the acute psychoses. *Archives of General Psychiatry* 27:125–32.

388. Meltzer, H. Y. 1973. Creatine phosphokinase activity and clinical symptomatology: A study in acute schizophrenic patients. *Archives of General Psychiatry* 29:589–93.

389. Meltzer, H. Y. 1973. Skeletal muscle abnormalities in patients with affective disorders. *Journal of Psychiatric Research* 10:43–57.

390. Meltzer, H. Y. 1975. Neuromuscular abnormalities in the major mental illnesses. I. Serum enzyme studies. In *The biology of the major psychoses: A comparative analysis*, ed. D. X. Freedman (New York: Raven Press), pp. 165–88.

391. Meltzer, H. Y. 1976. Biological studies in schizophrenia. *Schizophrenia Bulletin* 2:11–18.

392. Meltzer, H. Y. 1976. Dopamine receptors and average clinical dose. *Science* 194:545–46.

393. Meltzer, H. Y. 1976. Neuromuscular dysfunction in schizophrenia. *Schizophrenia Bulletin* 2:106–35.

394. Meltzer, H. Y. 1976. Serum creatine phosphokinase in schizophrenia. *American Journal of Psychiatry* 133:192–97.

395. Meltzer, H. Y.; Arora, R. C.; Pscheidt, G. R.; and Goode, D. J. 1976. Decreased skeletal muscle MAO in the psychoses. *Social Biology Psychiatry Abstracts*, p. 39.

396. Meltzer, H. Y.; Cho, H. W.; Carroll, B. J.; and Russo, P. 1976. Serum dopamine-β-hydroxylase activity in the affective psychoses and schizophrenia. *Archives of General Psychiatry* 33:585–91.

397. Meltzer, H. Y. and Crayton, J. W. 1974. Subterminal motor nerve abnormalities in psychotic patients. *Nature* 249:373–75.

398. Meltzer, H. Y., and Crayton, J. W. 1975. Neuromuscular abnormalities in the major mental illnesses. II. Muscle fiber and subterminal motor nerve abnormalities. In *The biology of the major psychoses: A comparative analysis*, ed. D. X. Freedman (New York: Raven Press), pp. 189–207.

399. Meltzer, H. Y.; Daniels, S.; and Fang, V. S. 1975. Clozapine increases rat serum prolactin levels. *Life Sciences* 17:339–42.

400. Meltzer, H. Y.; Elkun, L.; and Moline, R. 1969. Serum enzyme changes in newly admitted psychiatric patients. *Archives of General Psychiatry* 21:731–38.

401. Meltzer, H. Y., and Engel, W. K. 1970. Histochemical abnormalities of skeletal muscle in patients with acute psychoses. Part II. *Archives of General Psychiatry* 23:492–502.

402. Meltzer, H. Y., and Fang, V. S. 1976. Serum prolactin levels in schizophrenia: Effect of antipsychotic drugs: A preliminary report. In *Hormones, behavior and psychopathology*, ed. E. J. Sachar (New York: Raven Press), pp. 177–92.

403. Meltzer, H. Y.; Fang, V. S.; Fessler, R.; Simonovic, D.; and Stanisic, D. Neuroleptic-stimulated prolactin secretion in the rat as an animal model for biological psychiatry. I. Comparison with anti-psychotic activity. In *Animal models of mental illness*, eds. E. Usdin and I. Hanin (New York: Academic Press), forthcoming.

404. Meltzer, H. Y.; Fang, V. S.; and Li, C. H. β-Lipotropin levels in schizophrenia. In preparation.

405. Meltzer, H. Y.; Goode, D. J.; and Fang, V. S. The effect of psychotropic drugs on endocrine function. I. Neuroleptics, precursors and agonists. In *A Review of Progress*, eds. A. DiMascio and M. Lipton (New York: Raven Press), forthcoming.

406. Meltzer, H. Y.; Grinspoon, L.; and Shader, R. 1970. Serum creatine phosphokinase and aldolase activities in acute schizophrenic patients and their relatives. *Comprehensive Psychiatry* 11: 552–58.

407. Meltzer, H. Y.; Holzman, P. S.; Hassan, S. Z.; and Guschwan, A. 1972. Effects of phencyclidine and stress on plasma creatine phosphokinase (CPK) and aldolase activities in man. *Psychopharmacologia* 26:44–53.

408. Meltzer, H. Y.; Mrozak, S.; and Boyer, M. 1970. Effect of intramuscular injections on serum creatine phosphokinase activity. *American Journal of the Medical Sciences* 259:42–48.

409. Meltzer, H. Y.; Nankin, R.; and Raftery, J. 1971. Serum creatine phosphokinase activity in newly admitted psychiatric patients. II. *Archives of General Psychiatry* 24:568–72.

410. Meltzer, H. Y.; Pscheidt, G. R.; Goode, D. J.; Piyakalmala, S.; and Dichtel, M. 1977. Platelet monoamine oxidase and plasma amine oxidase in schizophrenia. Presented at American Psychiatric Association, Toronto, May 1977.

411. Meltzer, H. Y.; Sachar, E. J.; and Frantz, A. A. 1974. Serum prolactin levels in acutely psychotic patients: An indirect measurement of central dopaminergic activity. In *Neuropsychopharmacology of monoamines and their regulatory enzymes*, ed. E. Usdin (New York: Raven Press), pp. 299–316.

412. Meltzer, H. Y.; Sachar, E. J.; and Frantz, A. A. 1974. Serum prolactin levels in unmedicated schizophrenic patients. *Archives of General Psychiatry* 31:564–69.

413. Meltzer, H. Y.; Sachar, E. J.; and Frantz, A. A. 1975. Dopamine antagonism by thioridazine in schizophrenia. *Biological Psychiatry* 10:53–57.

414. Meltzer, H. Y.; Simonovic, M.; Fessler, R.; and Fang, V. S. 1977. Effect of d- and l-amphetamine on rat serum prolactin levels. *Neuroscience Abstracts* 3:351.

415. Meltzer, H. Y., and Stahl, S. M. 1974. Platelet monoamine oxidase activity and substrate preferences in schizophrenic patients. *Research Communications in Chemical Pathology and Pharmacology* 7:419–31.

416. Meltzer, H. Y., and Stahl, S. M. 1976. The dopamine hypothesis of schizophrenia. *Schizophrenia Bulletin* 2:19–76.

417. Mendels, J. 1967. The effect of methysergide (an antiserotonin agent) on schizophrenia: A preliminary report. *American Journal of Psychiatry* 124:849–52.

418. Merrick, E. M., and Schmitt, P. P. 1973. A controlled study of the clinical effects of amantadine hydrochloride (Symmetrel). *Current Therapeutic Research* 15:552–58.

419. Miller, E., and Nieburg, H. A. 1973. Amphetamine: Valuable adjunct in treatment of parkinsonism. *New York State Journal of Medicine* 73:2657–61.

420. Miller, R. J., and Hiley, C. R. 1974. Anti-muscarinic properties of neuroleptics and drug-induced parkinsonism. *Nature* 248:596–97.

421. Miller, R. J.; Horn, A. S.; and Iversen, L. L. 1974. The action of neuroleptic drugs on dopamine-stimulated adenosine cyclic 3',5'-monophosphate production in rat neostriatum and limbic forebrain. *Molecular Pharmacology* 10:759–66.

422. Miller, R. J.; Horn, A. S.; and Iversen, L. L. 1975. Effect of butaclamol on dopamine-sensitive adenylate cyclase in rat striatum. *Journal of Pharmacy and Pharmacology* 27:212–13.

423. Mindham, R. H. S.; Lamb, P.; and Bradley, R. 1977. A comparison of piribedil, procyclidine and placebo in the control of phenothiazine-induced parkinsonism. *British Journal of Psychiatry* 130:581–85.

424. Mitsuda, H., and Fukuda, T., eds. 1974. *Biological mechanisms of schizophrenia and schizophrenia-like psychoses.* (Tokyo: Igaku Shoni), pp. 1–341.

425. Modell, W., and Hussar, A. E. 1965. Failure of dextroamphetamine sulfate to influence eating and sleeping patterns in obese schizophrenic patients. *Journal of the American Medical Association* 193:275–78.

426. Modestin, J.; Schwartz, R. B.; and Hunger, J. 1973. Zur frage der beeinflussung schizophrener symptome durch physostigmin. *Pharmakopsychiatrie* 6:300–304.

427. Moore, K. E., and Thornburg, J. E. 1975. Drug-induced dopamine supersensitivity. *Advances in Neurology* 9:93–104.

428. Moore, R. H.; Hatada, K.; and Domino, E. F. 1976. Effects of N,N-dimethyltryptamine on electrically evoked responses in the cat visual system and modification by neuroleptic agents. *Neuropharmacology* 15:535–39.

429. Mora, F.; Rolls, E. T.; Burton, M. J.; and Shaw, S. G. 1976. Effects of dopamine-receptor blockade on self-stimulation in the monkey. *Pharmacology, Biochemistry and Behavior* 4:211–16.

430. Murphy, D. L. 1973. Mental effects of L-DOPA. *Annual Review of Medicine* 24:209–16.

431. Murphy, D. L.; Belmaker, R. H.; Buchsbaum, M.; Martin, N. F.; Ciaranello, R.; and Wyatt, R. J. 1977. Biogenic amino-related enzymes and personality variations in normals. *Psychological Medicine* 7:149–57.

432. Murphy, D. L.; Belmaker, R.; Carpenter, W. T.; and Wyatt, R. J. 1977. Monoamine oxidase in chronic schizophrenia studies of hormonal and other factors affecting enzyme activity. *British Journal of Psychiatry* 130:157–58.

433. Murphy, D. L., and Donnelly, C. H. 1974. Monoamine oxidase in man: Enzyme characteristics in platelets, plasma and other tissues. In *Neuropsychopharmacology of monoamines and their regulatory enzymes*, ed. E. Usdin (New York: Raven Press), pp. 71–85.

434. Murphy, D. L.; Donnelly, C. H.; Miller, L.; and Wyatt, R. J. 1976. Platelet monoamine oxidase in chronic schizophrenia. *Archives of General Psychiatry* 33:1377–81.

435. Murphy, D. L.; Wright, C.; Buchsbaum, M.; Nichols, A.; Costa, J. L.; and Wyatt, R. J. 1976. Platelet and plasma amine oxidase activity in 680 normals: Sex and age differences and stability over time. *Biochemical Medicine* 16:254–65.

436. Murphy, D. L., and Wyatt, R. J. 1972. Reduced monoamine oxidase activity in blood platelets from schizophrenic patients. *Nature* 238:225–26.

437. Myers, R. D. 1966. Temperature regulation: Neurochemical systems in the hypothalamus. In *The hypothalamus*, eds. W. Haymaker, E. Anderson, and W. J. Nanta (Springfield, Ill.: Charles C Thomas), pp. 506–23.

438. Narasimhachari, N.; Baumann, P.; Pak, H. S.; Carpenter, W. T.; Zocchi, A. F.; Hokanson, L.; Fujimori, M.; and Himwich, H. E. 1974. Gas chromatographic-mass spectrometric identification of urinary bufotenin and dimethyltryptamine in drug free chronic schizophrenic patients. *Biological Psychiatry* 8:293–307.

439. Narasimhachari, N., and Himwich, H. E. 1973. Gas chromatographic-mass spectrometric identification of N,N-dimethyltryptamine in urine samples from drug-free chronic schizophrenic patients and its quantification by the technique of single (selective) ion monitoring. *Biochemical and Biophysical Research Communications* 55:1064–71.

440. Narotzky, R.; Griffeth, D.; Stahl, S.; Bondareff, W.; and Zeller, E. A. 1973. Effect of long-term L-DOPA administration on brain biogenic amines and behavior in the rat. *Experimental Neurology* 38:218–30.

441. Neff, N. H., and Yang, H. Y. T. 1973. Monoamine oxidase. II. Evaluation of the physiological role of type A and B enzyme of brain. *Federation Proceedings* 32:797.

442. Nies, A.; Robinson, D. S.; Harris, L. S.; and Lamborn, K. R. 1974. Comparison of monoamine oxidase substrate activities in twins, schizophrenics, depressives and controls. *Advances in Biochemical Psychopharmacology* 12:59.

443. Nies, A.; Robinson, D. S.; and Ravaris, C. L. 1971. Amines and monoamine oxidase in relation to aging and depression in man. *Psychosomatic Medicine* 33:470.

444. Nikitopoulou, G.; Thorner, M.; Crammer, J.; and Lader, M. 1977. Prolactin and psychophysiological measures after single doses of thioridazine. *Clinical Pharmacology and Therapeutics* 21:422–29.

445. Nishikawa, K.; Higasayama, I.; and Kasahara, T. 1972. L-Dopa therapy of chronic schizophrenia (with the main symptoms, lack of spontaneity and emotional blunting). *Shinryo and Shinyaku* 9:1439–50 (in Japanese).

446. Nyback, H.; Alfredsson, G.; and Sedvall, G. 1977. Plasma levels of chlorpromazine and prolactin in psychotic patients treated with chlorpromazine using different dose schedules. Abstracts, Sixth World Congress of Psychiatry, Honolulu, August 1977, p. 217.

447. Nyback, H.; Borzeck, Z.; and Sedvall, G. 1968. Accumulation and disappearance of catecholamines formed from tyrosine-^{14}C in mouse brain: Effect of some psychotropic drugs. *European Journal of Pharmacology* 4:395–403.

448. Nygren, A. 1966. Serum creatine phosphokinase activity in chronic alcoholism, in connection with acute alcohol intoxication. *Acta Medica Scandinavica* 179:623–30.

449. Odegaard, O. 1974. Season of birth in the general population and in patients with mental disorder in Norway. *British Journal of Psychiatry* 125:397–405.

450. Ohgo, S.; Kato, Y.; Chihara, K.; Imura, H.; and Maeda, K. 1976. Effect of hypothalamic surgery on prolactin release induced by 5-hydroxytryptophan (5-HTP) in rats. *Endocrinologia Japonica* 23:485–91.

451. Ogura, C.; Nakao, T.; Kishimoto, A.; Okuma, T.; Inagaki, T.; and Motoike, M. 1974. Effects of biogenic amine precursor (L-DOPA) on schizophrenia. *Japanese Journal of Clinical Psychiatry* 3:1115–24.

452. O'Hare, A., and Walsh, D. 1974. Further data on activities of Irish psychiatric hospitals and units, 1965–1969. *Journal of the Irish Medical Association* 67:57–63.

453. Olson, L. 1974. Post-mortem fluorescence histochemistry of monoamine neuron systems in the human brain: A new approach in the search for a neuropathology of schizophrenia. *Journal of Psychiatric Research* 11:199–203.

454. Olson, L.; Nystrom, B.; and Seiger, A. 1973. Monoamine fluorescence histochemistry of human post-mortem brain. *Brain Research* 63:231–47.

455. Olson, L.; Nystrom, B.; and Seiger, A. 1973. Monoamine neuron systems in the normal and schizophrenic human brain: Fluorescence histochemistry of fetal, neurosurgical and post-mortem materials. In *Frontiers in catecholamine research*, eds. E. Usdin and S. Snyder (New York: Pergamon Press), pp. 1097–1100.

456. Osmond, H., and Smythies, J. 1952. Schizophrenia: A new approach. *Journal of Mental Science* 98:309–15.

457. Otsuka, T.; Kumashiro, E.; Mizushima, S.; Maruko, K.; Koizumi, S.; and Unno, Y. 1974. The effect of L-DOPA on schizophrenia. *Japanese Journal of Clinical Psychiatry* 3:629–37 (in Japanese).

458. Overall, J. E., and Gorham, D. R. 1962. Brief Psychiatric Rating Scale (BPRS). *Psychological Reports* 10:799–812.

459. Owen, F.; Bourne, R.; Crow, T. J.; Johnstone, E. C.; Bailey, A. R.; and Hershon, H. I. 1976. Platelet monoamine oxidase in schizophrenia: An investigation in drug-free chronic hospitalized patients. *Archives of General Psychiatry* 33:1370–73.

460. Owen, F.; Ridges, A. P.; and Cookson, I. B. 1974. Monoamine oxidase activity: A genetic marker of schizophrenia? *Acta Geneticae Medicae et Gemellologiae* (Rome) 23:371–76.

461. Owen, G., and Kerry, R. J. 1974. Anesthesia during raised creatine phosphokinase activity. *British Medical Journal* 4:75–76.

462. Palmer, G. C., and Manian, A. A. 1974. Modification of the receptor component of adenylate cyclase in the rat brain by phenothiazine derivatives. *Neuropharmacology* 13:851–66.

463. Papeschi, R.; Sourkes, T. L.; Poirer, L. J.; and Boucher, R. 1971. On the intracerebral origin of homovanillic acid of the cerebrospinal fluid of experimental animals. *Brain Research* 28:527–33.

464. Paul, S. M.; Gallant, D. M.; and Mielke, D. H. 1976. 2-Dimethylaminoethanol (Deanol) in chronic schizophrenia. *Research Communications in Psychology, Psychiatry, and Behavior* 1:183–86.

465. Peaston, M. J. T.; Bianchine, J. R.; and Messiha, F. S. 1973. Effect of amantadine on L-2-^{14}C-DOPA metabolism in parkinsonism. *Life Sciences* 13:237–46.

466. Pecknold, J. C.; Ananth, J. V.; Ban, T. A.; and Lehmann, H. E. 1972. The use of

methyldopa in schizophrenia: A review and comparative study. *American Journal of Psychiatry* 128: 1207–11.

467. Perel, J. M.; Levitt, M.; and Dunner, D. L. 1974. Plasma and cerebrospinal fluid probenecid concentrations as related to accumulation of acidic biogenic amine metabolites in man. *Psychopharmacologia* 35:83–90.

468. Perry, T. L.; Hansen, S.; and Kloster, M. 1973. Huntington's chorea: Deficiency of GABA in brain. *New England Journal of Medicine* 288:337–42.

469. Persson, T., and Roos, B.-E. 1969. Acid metabolites from monoamines in cerebrospinal fluid of chronic schizophrenics. *British Journal of Psychiatry* 115:95–98.

470. Petrov, P. A. 1970. Vilyuisk encephalitis in Yakut Republic, U.S.S.R. *American Journal of Tropical Medicine and Hygiene* 19:146–49.

471. Pfaff, D. W. 1973. Luteinizing hormone-releasing factor potentiates lordosis behavior in hypohysectomized ovariectomized female rats. *Science* 182:1148–49.

472. Pfeiffer, C. C., and Jenney, E. H. 1957. The inhibition of the conditioned response and the counteraction of schizophrenia by muscarinic stimulation of the brain. *Annals of the New York Academy of Sciences of the U.S.A.* 66:753–64.

473. Pijnenburg, A. J. J., and Van Rossum, J. M. 1973. Stimulation of locomotor activity following injection of dopamine into the nucleus accumbens. *Journal of Pharmacy and Pharmacology* 25: 1003–5.

474. Pincus, J. H., and Tucker, G. J. 1974. *Behavioral neurology* (New York: Oxford University Press).

475. Pletscher, A.; Bartholini, G.; and Tissot, R. 1967. Metabolic fate of L-[^{14}C]-DOPA in cerebrospinal fluid and blood plasma in humans. *Brain Research* 4(4):106–9.

476. Poirier, L.; Langelier, P.; Roberge, A.; Boucher, R.; and Kitsikis, A. 1972. Non-specific histopothological changes induced by the intracerebral injection of 6-hydroxydopamine. *Journal of the Neurological Sciences* 16:401–16.

477. Pollack, M.; Klein, D. F.; Willner, A.; Blumberg, A.; and Fink, M. 1965. Imipramine-induced behavioral disorganization in schizophrenic patients. In *Recent advances in biological psychiatry*, ed. J. Wortis (New York: Plenum Press), vol. 3, pp. 53–61.

478. Pollin, W. 1972. The pathogenesis of schizophrenia. *Archives of General Psychiatry* 27: 29–37.

479. Pollin, W.; Cardon, P. V., Jr.; and Kety, S. S. 1961. Effects of amino acid feedings in schizophrenic patients treated with iproniazid. *Science* 133:104–5.

480. Popper, K. R. 1959. *The logic of scientific discovery* (New York: Basic Books).

481. Post, R. M.; Fink, E.; Carpenter, W. T., Jr.; and Goodwin, F. K. 1975. Cerebrospinal fluid amine metabolites in acute schizophrenia. *Archives of General Psychiatry* 32:1063–69.

482. Prange, A. J., Jr.; Breese, G. R.; Cott, J. M.; Martin, B. R.; Cooper, B. R.; Wilson, I. C.; and Plotnikoff, N. P. 1974. Thyrotropin releasing hormone: Antagonism of pentobarbital in rodents. *Life Sciences* 14:447–55.

483. Prange, A. J.; Wilson, I. C.; Lara, P. P.; Alltop, L. B.; and Breese, G. R. 1972. Effects of thyrotropin-releasing hormone in depression. *Lancet* 1:999–1002.

484. Prilipko, L. 1976. The behavior of T-lymphocytes in schizophrenia. Presented in the First International Symposium on Immunological Components in Schizophrenia, Galveston, Texas, October 28–31, 1976.

485. Prockop, L.; Fahn, S.; and Barbour, P. 1974. Homovanillic acid: Entry rate kinetics for transfer from plasma to homovanillic acid. *Brain Research* 80:435–42.

486. Pscheidt, G. R., and Meltzer, H. Y. 1976. Siliconising agent inhibits platelet MAO. *Lancet* 2:474.

487. Quasimoro, F.; Bjarnason, D. F.; Kiely, W. F.; Dubois, E. L.; and Friou, G. J. 1975. Antinuclear antibodies in chronic psychotic patients treated with chlorpromazine. *American Journal of Psychiatry* 132:1204–6.

488. Rabin, A. F., and Winder, C. L. 1969. Psychological studies. In *The schizophrenic syndrome*, eds. L. Bellak and L. Loeb (New York: Grune & Stratton), pp. 205–55.

489. Raiteri, M.; Bertollini, A.; Angelini, F.; and Levi, G. 1975. D-amphetamine as a releaser or reuptake inhibitor of biogenic amines in synaptosomes. *European Journal of Pharmacology* 34: 189–95.

490. Randrug, A., and Munkvard, I. 1968. Behavioral stereotypes induced by pharmacological agents. *Pharmakopsychiatriatrie Neuro-Psychopharmakologie* 1:1–26.

491. Randrug, A., and Munkvard, I. 1970. Biochemical, anatomical and psychological investigations of stereotyped behavior induced by amphetamines. In *Amphetamines and related compounds*, eds. E. Costa and S. Garattini (New York: Raven Press), pp. 695–713.

492. Raskin, D. E., and Frank, S. W. 1974. Herpes encephalitis with catatonic stupor. *Archives of General Psychiatry* 31:544–46.

493. Ravitz, A. J., and Moore, K. E. 1977. Effects of amphetamine, methylphenidate and cocaine on serum prolactin concentrations in the male rats. *Life Sciences* 21:267–72.

494. Ravitz, A. J., and Moore, K. E. 1977. Lack of effect of chronic haloperidol administration on the prolactin lowering actions of piribedil. *Journal of Pharmacy and Pharmacology* 29:384–85.

495. Reid, J. L. 1975. Dopamine supersensitivity in the hypothalamus? *Advances in Neurology* 9:73–80.

496. Reid, W. D.; Volicer, L.; Smookler, H.; Beaven, M. A.; and Brodie, B. B. 1968. Brain amines and temperature regulation. *Pharmacology* 1:329–44.

497. Reis, D. J. 1974. Consideration of some problems encountered in relating specific neurotransmitters to specific behaviors or disease. *Journal of Psychiatric Research* 11:145–48.

498. Reiss, D., and Wyatt, R. J. 1975. Family and biologic variables in the same etiologic studies of schizophrenia: A proposal. *Schizophrenia Bulletin* 14:64–81.

499. Reske-Nielsen, E.; Coers, C.; and Harmsen, A. 1970. Qualitative and quantitative histological study of neuromuscular biopsies from healthy young men. *Journal of the Neurological Sciences* 10:369–84.

500. Rich, C. L.; Woodrow, K. M.; and Gillin, J. C. 1977. CPK: Relation to psychological and physical stress. *Diseases of the Nervous System* 38:34–37.

501. Rieder, R. O.; Rosenthal, D.; Wender, P.; and Blumenthal, H. 1975. The offspring of schizophrenics. *Archives of General Psychiatry* 32:200–211.

502. Rimon, R., and Halonen, P. 1969. Herpes simplex virus infection and depressive illness. *Diseases of the Nervous System* 30:338–40.

503. Rimon, R., and Halonen, P. 1977. Antibody levels to viruses in psychiatric illness. In *The impact of biology on modern psychiatry*, eds. E. S. Gershon, R. H. Belmaker, S. S. Kety, and M. Rosenbaum (New York: Plenum Press).

504. Rimon, R.; Halonen, P.; Anttinen, E.; and Evola, K. 1971. Complement fixing antibody to herpes simplex virus in patients with psychotic depression. *Diseases of the Nervous System* 32:822–24.

505. Rimon, R.; Roos, B.; Rakkolainen, V.; and Alanen, Y. 1971. The content of 5-hydroxy-indoleacetic acid and homovanillic acid in the cerebrospinal fluid of patients with acute schizophrenia. *Journal of Psychosomatic Research* 15:375–78.

506. Ringel, S. P.; Guthrie, M.; and Klawans, H. C. 1973. Current treatment of Huntington's chorea. In *Huntington's chorea, 1872–1972* (New York: Raven Press), pp. 797–801.

507. Ringwall, E.; Lorinez, P.; and Wolper, M. 1977. Dopamine-receptor stimulators and neuroleptic-induced dyskinesia. Abstracts, Sixth World Congress of Psychiatry, Honolulu, August 1977, p. 876.

508. Roberts, E. 1972. An hypothesis suggesting that there is a deficit in the GABA system in schizophrenia. In *Prospects for research in schizophrenia*, eds. S. S. Kety and S. Matthysse, Neuroscience Research Program Bulletin 10:468–507.

509. Robinson, D. S.; Lovenberg, W.; Keistor, H.; and Sjoerdsma, A. 1968. Effects of drugs on human blood platelet and plasma amine oxidase activity *in vitro* and *in vivo*. *Biochemical Pharmacology* 17:109–11.

510. Robinson, D. S.; Sourkes, T. L.; Nies, A.; et al. 1977. Monoamine metabolism in human brain. *Archives of General Psychiatry* 34:89–92.

511. Rodnight, R.; Murray, R. M.; Oon, M. C. H.; Brockington, I. F.; Nicholls, P.; and Birley, J. L. T. 1976. Urinary dimethyltryptamine and psychiatric symptomatology and classification. *Psychological Medicine* 6:649–57.

512. Roffler-Tarlov, S.; Sharman, D. F.; and Tegerdine, P. 1971. 3,4-Dihydroxyphenylacetic acid and 4-hydroxy-3-methoxyphenylacetic acid in the mouse striatum: A reflection of intra- and extra-neuronal metabolism of dopamine. *British Journal of Pharmacology* 42:343–51.

513. Rolls, E. T.; Rolls, B. J.; Kelly, P. H.; Shaw, S. G.; Wood, R. J.; and Dale, R. 1974. The relative attenuation of self-stimulatory eating and drinking produced by dopamine-receptor blockade. *Psychopharmacologia* (Berlin) 38:219–30.

514. Rosenblatt, S.; Leighton, W. P.; and Chanley, J. D. 1973. Dopamine-beta-hydroxylase: Evidence for increased activity in sympathetic neurons during psychotic states. *Science* 182:923–24.

515. Rosengarten, H., and Friedhoff, A. J. 1976. A review of recent studies of the biosynthesis and excretion of hallucinogens formed by methylation of neurotransmitters or related substances. *Schizophrenia Bulletin* 2:90–105.

516. Rosengren, E. 1960. On the role of monoamine oxidase for the inactivation of dopamine in brain. *Acta Physiologica Scandinavica* 49:370–75.

517. Rosenthal, R., and Bigelow, L. B. 1973. The effects of physostigmine in phenothiazine resistant chronic schizophrenic patients: Preliminary observations. *Comprehensive Psychiatry* 14:489–94.

518. Ross, S. B.; Wetterberg, L.; and Myrhed, M. 1973. Genetic control of plasma dopamine β-hydroxylase. *Life Sciences* 12:529–32.

519. Roth, R. H.; Walters, J. R.; and Aghajanian, G. K. 1973. Effect of impulse flow on the release and synthesis of dopamine in rat striatum. In *Frontiers in catecholamine research*, eds. E. Usdin and S. H. Snyder (London: Pergamon Press), pp. 567–74.

520. Roth, R. H.; Walters, J. R.; Murrin, L. C.; and Morgenroth, V. H. III. 1975. Dopamine neurons: Role of impulse flow and presynaptic receptors in the regulation of tyrosine hydroxylase. In *Pre- and post-synaptic receptors*, eds. E. Usdin and W. E. Bunney, Jr. (New York: Marcel Dekker), pp. 5–46.

521. Rotrosen, J.; Angrist, B. M.; Gershon, S.; Sachar, E. G.; and Halpern, F. S. 1976. Dopamine receptor alteration in schizophrenia: Neuroendocrine evidence. *Psychopharmacology* 51:1–7.

522. Roufogalis, B. D.; Thornton, M.; and Wade, D. M. 1976. Specificity of the dopamine sensitive adenylate cyclase for antipsychotic antagonists. *Life Sciences* 19:927–34.

523. Routtenberg, A., and Holzman, N. 1973. Memory disruption by electrical stimulation of substantia nigra, pars compacta. *Science* 181:83–86.

524. Rutledge, C. O.; Azzaro, A. J.; and Ziance, R. J. 1973. Dissociation of amphetamine-induced release of norepinephrine from inhibition of neuronal uptake in isolated brain tissue. In *Frontiers of catecholamine research*, eds. E. Usdin and S. H. Snyder (London: Pergamon Press), pp. 973–75.

525. Rylander, G. 1969. Clinical and medico-criminological aspects of addictions to central stimulating drugs. In *Abuse of central stimulants*, eds. F. Sjoquist and M. Tottie (New York: Raven Press), pp. 251–73.

526. Sachar, E. J., ed. 1976. *Hormones, behavior and psychopathology* (New York: Raven Press), pp. 1–307.

527. Sachar, E. J.; Gruen, P. H.; Karasu, T. B.; et al. 1975. Thioridazine stimulates prolactin secretion in man. *Archives of General Psychiatry* 32:885–86.

528. Sachar, E. J., Langer, G.; and Gruen, P. H. 1977. Neuroendocrine approaches to studying neuronal receptor sensitivity in schizophrenic and normal subjects. Sixth World Congress of Psychiatry, Honolulu, August 1977.

529. Sandman, C. A.; Miller, L. H.; Kastin, A. J.; and Schally, A. V. 1972. Neuroendocrine influence on attention and memory. *Journal of Comparative and Physiological Psychology* 80:54–58.

530. Sarai, K.; Kimura, N.; Ishii, T.; Iseki, K.; Imada, H.; Kawamura, T.; Kino, M.; and Echigo, T. 1973. Possibility of amine precursor-therapy on schizophrenics by experimental study with L-Dopa. *Clinical Psychiatry* 15:189–96, (in Japanese).

531. Sathananthan, G.; Angrist, B. M.; and Gershon, S. 1973. Response threshold to L-DOPA in psychiatric patients. *Biological Psychiatry* 7:139–46.

532. Scatton, B.; Cheramy, A.; Besson, M. J.; and Glowinski, J. 1970. Increased synthesis and release of dopamine in the striatum of the rat after amantadine treatment. *European Journal of Pharmacology* 13:131–33.

533. Scatton, B.; Garret, C.; and Joulu, L. 1975. Acute and subacute effects of neuroleptics on dopamine synthesis and release in the rat striatum. *Naunyn-Schmiedeberg's Archives of Pharmacology* 289:419–34.

534. Schelkunov, E. L. 1967. Adrenergic effect of chronic administration of neuroleptics. *Nature* (London) 124:1210–12.

535. Schiavone, D. J., and Kaldor, J. 1965. Creatine phosphokinase levels and cerebral disease. *Medical Journal of Australia* 52:790–92.

536. Schildkraut, J. J.; Herzog, J. M.; Orsulak, P. J.; Edelman, S. E.; Shein, H. M.; and Frazier, S. H. 1976. Reduced platelet monoamine oxidase activity in a subgroup of schizophrenic patients. *American Journal of Psychiatry* 133:438–39.

537. Schneck, S. A., and Claman, H. N. 1969. CSF immunoglobulins in multiple sclerosis and other neurologic disease. *Archives of Neurology* 20:132–39.

538. Schneider, K. 1959. *Clinical psychopathology*, trans. M. W. Hamilton (New York: Grune & Stratton).

539. Schooler, C.; Zahn, T. P.; Murphy, D. L.; and Buchsbaum, M. S. Psychological correlates of monoamine oxidase activity in normals. Submitted for publication.

540. Schopf, J., and Hucker, H. 1977. Baclofen in the treatment of schizophrenia: A pilot study. *Pharmakopsychiatrie* 10:89–91.

541. Schwartz, M. A.; Arkens, A. M.; and Wyatt, R. J. 1974. Monoamine oxidase activity in brains from schizophrenic and mentally normal individuals. *Psychopharmacologia* 38:319–28.

542. Schweid, D. E.; Steinberg, J. S.; and Sudak, H. 1972. Creatine phosphokinase and psychosis. *Archives of General Psychiatry* 26:263–65.

543. Sedvall, G., ed. 1975. *Antipsychotic drugs: Pharmacodynamics and pharmacokinetics* (New York: Pergamon Press).

544. Sedvall, G.; Bjerkenstedt, L.; Fyro, B.; Hanryd, C.; and Wode-Helgodt, B. 1977. Biochemical effects of antipsychotic drugs in man. Abstracts, Sixth World Congress of Psychiatry, Honolulu, August 1977, p. 140.

545. Sedvall, G.; Fyro, B.; Nyback, H.; Wiesel, F.; and Wode-Helgodt, B. 1974. Mass fragmentometric determination of homovanillic acid in lumbar cerebrospinal fluid of schizophrenic patients during treatment with antipsychotic drugs. *Journal of Psychiatric Research* 11:75:80.

546. Seeman, P.; Chau-Wong, M.; Tedesco, J.; and Wong, K. 1975. Brain receptors for antipsychotic drugs and dopamine: Direct binding assays. *Proceedings of the National Academy of Sciences of the U.S.A.* 72:4376–80.

547. Seeman, P.; Lee, T.; Chau-wong, M.; and Wong, K. 1976. Antipsychotic drugs doses and neuroleptic/dopamine receptors. *Nature* 261:717–18.

548. Segal, D. S., and Mandell, A. J. 1974. Differential behavioral effects of hypothalamic polypeptides. In *The thyroid axis, drugs and behavior*, ed. A. J. Prange (New York: Raven Press), pp. 129–33.

549. Shaskan, E. G., and Becker, R. E. 1975. Platelet monoamine oxidase in schizophrenia. *Nature* 253:659–60.

550. Shearer, M. L., and Finch, S. M. 1964. Periodic organic psychosis associated with recurrent herpes simplex. *New England Journal of Medicine* 271:394–497.

551. Sheppard, H., and Burghardt, C. R. 1974. The dopamine-sensitive adenylate cyclase of rat caudate nucleus. I. Comparison with the isoproterenol-sensitive adenylate cyclase (beta receptor system) of rat erythrocytes in response to dopamine derivatives. *Molecular Pharmacology* 10:721–26.

552. Shopsin, B.; Freedman, L. S.; Goldstein, M.; and Gershon, S. 1972. Serum dopamine β-hydroxylase (DBH) activity and affective states. *Psychopharmacologia* 27:11–16.

553. Siggins, G. R.; Hoffer, B. J.; and Ungerstedt, U. 1974. Electrophysiological evidence for involvement of cyclic adenosine monophosphate in dopamine responses of caudate nerons. *Life Sciences* 15:779–84.

554. Simantov, R.; Kuhar, M. J.; Uhl, G. R.; and Snyder, S. H. 1977. Opioid peptide enkephalin: Immunohistochemical mapping in the rat central nervous system. *Proceedings of the National Academy of Sciences of the U.S.A.* 74:2167–71.

555. Singh, M. M., and Kay, S. R. 1975. A comparative study of haloperidol and chlorpromazine in terms of clinical effects and therapeutic reversal with benztropine in schizophrenia. Theoretical implications for potency differences among neuroleptics. *Psychopharmacologia* (Berlin) 43:103–13.

556. Singh, M. M., and Kay, S. R. 1975. A longitudinal therapeutic comparison between two prototypic neuroleptics (haloperidol and chlorpromazine) in matched groups of schizophrenics. Nontherapeutic interactions with trihexyphenidyl theoretical implications for potency differences. *Psychopharmacologia* (Berlin) 43:115–23.

557. Singh, M. M., and Kay, S. R. 1975. Therapeutic reversal with benztropine in schizophrenics. Practical and theoretical significance. *Journal of Nervous and Mental Disease* 169:258–66.

558. Singh, M. M., and Smith, J. M. 1973. Reversal of some therapeutic effects of an antipsychotic agent by an anti-Parkinsonian agent. *Journal of Nervous and Mental Disease* 157:50–58.

559. Slater, S. L.; Shiling, D. J.; Lippen, S.; and Murphy, D. L. 1977. Elevation of plasma prolactin by monoamine-oxidase inhibitors. *Lancet* 2:275–76.

560. Smeraldi, E.; Bellodi, L.; and Cazzulo, C. L. 1976. Further studies on the major histocompatibility complex as a genetic marker for schizophrenia. *Biological Psychiatry* 11:655–61.

561. Smeraldi, E.; Bellodi, L.; Scorza-Smeraldi, R.; Fabio, G.; and Sacchetti, E. 1976. HLA-SD antigens and schizophrenia: Statistical and genetical considerations. *Tissue Antigens* 8:191–96.

562. Smith, C. C.; Tallman, J. F.; Post, R. M.; Van Kammen, D. P.; Jimerson, D. C.; and Brown, G. L. 1976. An examination of baseline and drug-induced levels of cyclic nucleotides in the cerebrospinal fluid of control and psychiatric patients. *Life Sciences* 19:131–36.

563. Smith, R. C., and Davis, J. M. 1977. Comparative effects of d-amphetamine, l-amphetamine and methylphenidate on mood in man. *Psychopharmacology* 53:1–12.

564. Smith, R. C.; Tamminga, C.; and Davis, J. M. 1977. Effect of apomorphine on schizophrenic symptoms. *Journal of Neural Transmission* 40:171–76.

565. Smythies, J. R., and Adey, W. R. 1966. *The neurological foundations of psychiatry* (New York: Academic Press), pp. 150–57.

566. Sneddon, J. M. 1973. Blood platelets as a model for monoamine-containing neurons. *Progress in Neurobiology* 1:151–87.

567. Snyder, S. H. 1972. Catecholamines in the brain as mediators of amphetamine psychosis. *Archives of General Psychiatry* 27:169–79.

568. Snyder, S. H.; Aghajanian, G. K.; and Matthysse, S. 1972. Drug-induced psychoses. In *Prospects for research on schizophrenia*, eds. S. S. Kety and S. Matthysse, Neuroscience Research Program Bulletin 10:430–45.

569. Snyder, S. H.; Banerjee, S. P.; Yamamura, H. I.; Greenberg, D. 1974. Drugs, neurotransmitters, and schizophrenia. *Science* 184:1243–53.

570. Snyder, S. H., and Bennett, J. P., Jr. 1976. Neurotransmitter receptors in the brain: Biochemical identification. In *Biogenic Amine Receptors*, eds. L. I. Iversen, S. D. Iversen, and S. H. Snyder (New York: Plenum Press), pp. 153–75.

571. Snyder, S. H.; Greenberg, D.; and Yamamura, H. I. 1974. Antischizophrenic drugs and brain cholinergic receptors: Affinity for mescarinic sites predicts extrapyramidal effects. *Archives of General Psychiatry* 31:58–61.

572. Sobel, D. E. 1961. Infant mortality and malformations in children of schizophrenic women. *Psychiatric Quarterly* 35:60–65.

573. Somer, H.; Kasto, M.; Troupp, H.; and Konttinen, A. 1975. Brain creatine kinase in blood after acute brain injury. *Journal of Neurology, Neurosurgery and Psychiatry* 38:572–76.

574. Soni, S. D. 1976. Serum creatine phosphokinase in acute psychoses. *British Journal of Psychiatry* 128:181–183.

575. Sourkes, T. L.; Murphy, G. F.; Chavey, B.; and Zielinska, M. 1961. The action of some α-methyl and other amino acids on cerebral catecholamines. *Journal of Neurochemistry* 8:109–115.

576. Sourkes, T. L. 1973. On the origin of homovanillic acid (HVA) in the spinal fluid. *Journal of Neural Transmission* 34:153–57.

577. Spector, S.; Sjoerdsma, A.; and Udenfriend, S. 1965. Blockade of endogenous norepinephrine synthesis by α-methyl-tyrosine, an inhibitor of tyrosine hydroxylase. *Journal of Pharmacology and Experimental Therapeutics* 147:86–95.

578. Spitzer, E. L.; Endicott, J.; and Robins, E. 1975. *Research Diagnostic Criteria* (New York: New York State Department of Mental Hygiene, New York State Psychiatric Institute, Biometrics Research).

579. St. Jean, A.; Donald, M. E.; and Ban, T. A. 1963. Les effets psychophysiologiques de la methyldopa. *Union Medicale du Canada* 92:1420–22.

580. Stahl, S. M. 1977. A diagnostic and research tool for the study of biogenic amines in psychiatric and neurologic disorders. *Archives of General Psychiatry* 34:509–16.

581. Stahl, S. M.; Daniels, A. C.; Derda, D.; and Spehlamnn, R. 1975. Injection of 6-hydroxy-dopamine and hydrogen peroxide into the substantia nigra and lateral ventricle of the cat: Specific and non-specific effects on striatal biogenic amines. *Journal of Neurochemistry* 24:165–72.

582. Stahl, S. M., and Meltzer, H. Y. 1977. The human platelet as a model for the serotonergic neuron: Comparison of kinetic and pharmacologic properties of serotonin transport in platelets and neurons. *Neuroscience Abstracts* 3:416.

583. Stanton, J. R.; Meltzer, H. Y.; and Schlessinger, S. Skeletal muscle abnormalities in patients treated with anti-depressants. In preparation.

584. Stawarz, R. J.; Hill, H.; Robinson, S. E.; Settler, P.; Dingell, J. V.; and Sulser, F. 1975. On the significance of the increase in homovanillic acid (HVA) caused by antipsychotic drugs in corpus striatum and limbic forebrain. *Psychopharmacologia* (Berlin) 43:125–30.

585. Stein, L. 1971. Neurochemistry of reward and punishment: Some implications for the etiology of schizophrenia. *Journal of Psychiatric Research* 8:345–61.

586. Stein, L., and Wise, C. D. 1971. Possible etiology of schizophrenia: Progressive damage to the noradrenergic reward system by 6-hydroxydopamine. *Science* 171:1032–36.

587. Stevens, J.; Wilson, K.; and Foote, W. 1974. GABA blockade, dopamine and schizophrenia: Experimental studies in the cat. *Psychopharmacologia* (Berlin) 39:105–19.

588. Stevens, J. R. 1973. An anatomy of schizophrenia? *Archives of General Psychiatry* 29:177–89.

589. Stevens, R. W., and Lawson, D. M. 1977. The influence of estrogen on plasma prolactin levels induced by thyrotrophin releasing hormone (TRH), clonidine and serotonin in ovariectomized rats. *Life Sciences* 20:261–66.

590. Stille, G. 1971. Zur pharmakologie katatonigener stoffe. V. Die wirkun von neuroleptika. *Arzniemittel-Forschung* 21:800–808.

591. Stille, G., and Hippius, A. 1971. Kritische stellungnahme zum begriff der neuroleptika (anhand von pharmakologischen und klinischen befunden mit clozapin). *Pharmakopsychiatrie* 4: 182–91.

592. Strahilevitz, M. 1975. Immunologic methods in psychiatric treatment. *Canadian Psychiatric Association Journal* 20:513–20.

593. Strahilevitz, M. 1974. Possible interaction of environmental and biological factors in the etiology of schizophrenia. Review and integration. *Canadian Psychiatric Association Journal* 19:207–17.

594. Strahilevitz, M., and Davis, S. D. 1970. Increased IgA in schizophrenic patients. *Lancet* 2:370.

595. Strahilevitz, M.; Fleischman, J. B.; Fischer, G. W.; Harris, R.; and Narasimhachari, N. 1976. Immunoglobulin levels in psychiatric patients. *American Journal of Psychiatry* 133:772–77.

596. Sullivan, J.; Stanfield, C. N.; and Dackis, C. 1977. Platelet MAO activity in schizophrenia and other psychiatric illnesses. *American Journal of Psychiatry* 134:1098–1103.

597. Sulman, F. G. 1970. *Hypothalamic control of lactation* (New York: Springer-Verlag).

598. Svejgaard, A.; Platz, P.; Ryder, L. P.; Nielsen, L. S.; and Thomsen, M. 1975. HL-A and disease associations: A survey. *Transplantation Review* 22:3–43.

599. Svensson, T. H. 1973. Dopamine release and direct dopamine receptor activation in the central nervous system by D-145, an amantadine derivative. *European Journal of Pharmacology* 23: 232–38.

600. Symchowicz, S.; Korduba, C. A.; and Veals, J. 1973. The effect of amantadine on radiolabeled biogenic amines in the rat brain. *European Journal of Pharmacology* 21:155–60.

601. Szara, S. 1956. Dimethyltryptamine: Its metabolism in man, the relation of its psychotic effect to serotonin metabolism. *Experentia* 12:441–42.

602. Tamminga, C. A.; Smith, R. C.; Pandey, G.; Frohman, L. A.; and Davis, J. M. 1977. A neuroendocrine study of supersensitivity in tardive dyskinesia. *Archives of General Psychiatry* 36: 1199–1203.

603. Thierry, A. M.; Blanc, G.; Sobel, A.; Stinus, L.; and Glowinski, J. 1973. Dopaminergic terminals in the rat cortex. *Science* 182:499–501.

604. Thierry, A. M.; Javoy, F.; Glowinski, J.; and Kety, S. S. 1968. Effects of stress on the metabolism of norepinephrine, dopamine and serotonin in the central nervous system of the rat. I. Modifications of norepinephrine turnover. *Journal of Pharmacology and Experimental Therapeutics* 163:163–71.

605. Thierry, A. M.; Tassin, J. P.; Blanc, G.; and Glowinski, J. 1976. Selective activation of the neurocortical DA system by stress. *Nature* (London) 263:242–44.

606. Thoenen, H., and Tranzer, J. P. 1968. Chemical sympathectomy by selective destruction of adrenergic nerve endings with 6-hydroxydopamine. *Naunyn-Schmiedeberg's Archives of Pharmacology* 261:271–88.

607. Torrey, E. F., and Peterson, M. R. 1973. Slow and latent viruses in schizophrenia. *Lancet* 2:22–24.

608. Torrey, E. F., and Peterson, M. R. 1974. Schizophrenia and the limbic system. *Lancet* 2: 942–46.

609. Torrey, E. F., and Peterson, M. R. 1976. The viral hypothesis of schizophrenia. *Schizophrenia Bulletin* 2:136–46.

610. Torrey, E. F.; Peterson, M. R.; Brannon, W. L.; Carpenter, W. T.; Post, R. M.; and Van Kammen, D. P. 1977. Presented in the 1977 American Psychiatric Association Annual Meeting, Toronto, Ontario, Canada.

611. Torrey, E. F.; Torrey, B. B.; and Peterson, M. R. 1977. Seasonality of schizophrenic births in the U.S. *Archives of General Psychiatry* 34(9):1065–70.

612. Tran, N.; Laplante, M.; and Lebel, E. 1971. Decarboxylation of radioactive DOPA by erythrocytes in schizophrenia. *British Journal of Psychiatry* 118:465–66.

613. Tropeano, G.; Del Vecchio, M.; Amati, A.; Cocorullo, M.; and Kemali, D. 1972. Compartamento du liveli serici di CPK e aldolasi in pazienti psichiatrici. *Acta Neurologica* (Naples) 27: 386–94.

614. Tuason, V. B.; Oleshansky, M. A.; and Jaranson, J. M. 1974. Creatine phosphokinase in functional psychosis. *Comprehensive Psychiatry* 15:435–38.

615. Turkington, R. W. 1972. The clinical endocrinology of prolactin. *Advances in Internal Medicine* 18:363–87.

616. Ungerstedt, U. 1971. Stereotaxic mapping of the monoamine pathways in the rat brain. *Acta Physiologica Scandinavica* supp. 367:1–48.

617. Ungerstedt, U. 1971. Striatal dopamine release after amphetamine or nerve degeneration revealed by rotational behavior. *Acta Physiologica Scandinavica* supp. 267:49–67.

618. Ungerstedt, U.; Ljungberg, T.; Hoffer, B.; and Siggins, G. 1975. Dopaminergic supersensitivity in the striatum. *Advances in Neurology* 9:57–65.

619. Uretsky, N. 1974. Effect of alpha-methyldopa on the metabolism of dopamine in the striatum of the rat. *Journal of Pharmacology and Experimental Therapeutics* 189:359–69.

620. Uretsky, N. J.; Chase, G. J.; and Lorenzo, A. V. 1975. Effect of α-methyldopa on dopamine synthesis and release in rat striatum *in vitro*. *Journal of Pharmacology and Experimental Therapeutics* 193:73–87.

621. Uretsky, N. J., and Iversen, L. L. 1970. Effects of 6-hydroxydopamine on catecholamine neurones in the rat brain. *Journal of Neurochemistry* 17:268–69.

622. Usdin, E., ed. 1974. *Neuropsychopharmacology of monoamines and their regulatory enzymes* (New York: Raven Press).

623. Usdin, E., and Bunney, W. E., Jr., eds. 1975. *Pre- and post-synaptic receptors* (New York: Marcel Dekker).

624. Usdin, E.; Hamburg, D. A.; and Barchas, J. P., eds. 1977. *Neuroregulators and psychiatric disorders* (New York: Oxford University Press), pp. 1–627.

625. Usdin, E., and Snyder, S. H. 1974. *Frontiers in catecholamine research* (New York: Pergamon Press), pp. 1–1217.

626. Vaatstra, W. J., and Ergman, L. 1974. Dopamine turnover in the rat corpus striatum: *In vivo* and *in vitro* studies of the action of amantadine. *European Journal of Pharmacology* 25:185–90.

627. Vale, S.; Espejel, A.; Calcneo, F.; Ocampo, J.; and Diaz-de-Leon, J. 1974. Creatine phosphokinase: Increased activity of the spinal fluid in psychotic patients. *Archives of Neurology* 30:103–4.

628. Van Andel, H. 1959. Neuro-pharmacological studies on catatonic phenomena. In *Neuropsychopharmacology*, eds. P. B. Bradley, P. Deniker, and C. Raduoco-Thomas (Amsterdam: Elsevier), pp. 701–3.

629. Van Kammen, D. P. 1977. γ-Aminobutyric acid (GABA) and the dopamine hypothesis of schizophrenia. *American Journal of Psychiatry* 134:138–43.

630. Van Kammen, D. P. 1977. GHB and GABA. Letter to the Editor, *American Journal of Psychiatry* 134:1046.

631. Van Kammen, D. P.; Bunney, W. E., Jr.; Docherty, J.; Marder, S.; Jimerson, D.; Post, R.; Gillin, C.; and Ebert, M. 1977. Amphetamine effects in schizophrenia vs. depression. Abstracts, Sixth World Congress of Psychiatry, Honolulu, August 1977, p. 22.

632. Van Praag, H. M. 1977. The significance of dopamine for the mode of action of neuroleptics and the pathogenesis of schizophrenia. *British Journal of Psychiatry* 130:463–74.

633. Van Praag, H. M., and Korf, J. 1975. Neuroleptics, catecholamines, and psychoses: A study of their interactions. *American Journal of Psychiatry* 132:593–97.

634. Van Praag, H. M., and Korf, J. 1976. Importance of dopamine metabolism for clinical effects and side effects of neuroleptics. *American Journal of Psychiatry* 133:1171–77.

635. Van Woert, M. H.; Ambani, L.; and Bowers, M. B. 1972. Levadopa and cholinergic hypersensitivity in Parkinson's disease. *Neurology* (Minneapolis) supp. 22:86–93.

636. Vartanian, M. 1976. Humoral and cellular immune mechanisms in schizophrenia. *Presented in the First International Symposium on Immunological Components in Schizophrenia, Galveston, Texas, October 28–31, 1976.*

637. Velley, L.; Blanc, G.; Tassin, J. P.; Thierry, A. M.; and Glowinski, J. 1975. Inhibition of striatal dopamine synthesis in rats injected chronically with neuroleptics in their early life. *Naunyn-Schmiedeberg's Archives of Pharmacology* 288:97–102.

638. Versteeg, D. H. G.; Van Der Gugten, J.; DeJong, W.; and Palkovits, M. 1976. Regional concentrations of noradrenaline and dopamine in rat brain. *Brain Research* 113:563–74.

639. Videbech, T. H.; Weeke, A.; and Dupont, A. 1974. Endogenous psychoses and season of birth. *Acta Psychiatrica Scandinavica* 50:202–18.

640. Von Voigtlander, P. F.; Boukma, S. J.; and Johnson, G. A. 1973. Dopaminergic denervation supersensitivity and dopamine stimulated adenyl cyclase activity. *Neuropharmacology* 12:1081–86.

641. Von Voigtlander, P. F.; Losey, E. G.; and Triezenberg, H. J. 1975. Increased sensitivity to dopaminergic agents after chronic neuroleptic treatment. *Journal of Pharmacology and Experimental Therapeutics* 193:88–94.

642. Votolina, E. J. 1970. Spinal fluid creatine phosphokinase abnormalities following LSD usage. *Clinical Toxicology* 3:85–87.

643. Waldmeier, P. C.; Delini-Stula, A.; and Maitre, L. 1976. Preferential deamination of dopamine by an A type monoamine oxidase in rat brain. *Naunyn-Schmiedeberg's Archives of Pharmacology* 292:9–14.

644. Waldmeier, P. C., and Maitre, L. 1974. 3,4-Dihydroxyphenylacetic acid (DOPAC): A possible endogenous inhibitor of indoleamine-N-methylation in the rat brain. *Experentia* 30:456–58.

645. Waldmeier, P. C., and Maitre, L. 1976. Comparison of short and long-lasting effects of pargyline on cerebral dopamine metabolism. *Naunyn-Schmiedeberg's Archives of Pharmacology* 294:133–40.

646. Waldmeier, P. C., and Maitre, L. 1977. Neurochemical investigations of the interaction of N,N-dimethyltryptamine with the dopaminergic system in rat brain. *Psychopharmacology* 52:137–44.

647. Walsh, D., and Walsh, B. 1970. Mental illness in the Republic of Ireland—First admissions. *Journal of the Irish Medical Association* 63:365–70.

648. Walters, J. R., and Roth, R. H. 1976. Dopaminergic neurons: An *in vivo* system for measuring drug interactions with pre-synaptic receptors. *Naunyn-Schmiedeberg's Archives of Pharmacology* 296:5–14.

649. Walinder, J.; Skott, A.; Carlsson, A.; and Roos, B. E. 1976. Potentiation by metyrosine of thioridazine effects in chronic schizophrenics. *Archives of General Psychiatry* 33:501–5.

650. Warnock, D. G., and Ellman, G. L. 1969. Intramuscular chlorpromazine and creatine kinase: Acute psychoses or local muscle trauma? *Science* 164:724.

651. Weil-Malherbe, H., and Szara, S. I. 1971. *The biochemistry of functional and experimental psychoses* (Springfield, Ill.: Charles C Thomas).

652. Weinshilboum, R., and Axelrod, J. 1971. Serum dopamine-beta-hydroxylase activity. *Circulation Research* 28:307–14.

653. West, A. P. 1974. Interaction of low dose amphetamine use with schizophrenia in outpatients: Three case reports. *American Journal of Psychiatry* 131:321–22.

654. Westfall, T. C.; Besson, M.-J.; Giorguieff, M.-F.; and Glowinski, J. 1976. The role of presynaptic receptors in the release and synthesis of ^{3}H-dopamine by slices of rat striatum. *Naunyn-Schmiedeberg's Archives of Pharmacology* 292:279–87.

655. Wetterberg, L.; Aberg, H.; Ross, S. B.; and Froden, O. 1972. Plasma dopamine β-hydroxylase activity in hypertension and various neuropsychiatric disorders. *Scandinavian Journal of Clinical & Laboratory Investigation* 30:283–89.

656. White, H. L.; McLeod, M. N.; and Davidson, J. R. T. 1976. Platelet monoamine oxidase in schizophrenia. *American Journal of Psychiatry* 133:1191–93.

657. Whittingham, S.; Mackay, I. R.; Jones, I. H.; and Davies, B. 1968. Absence of brain antibodies in patients with schizophrenia. *British Medical Journal* 1:347–48.

658. Wiberg, A.; Gottfries, C. G.; and Oreland, L. 1977. Low platelet MAO activity in human alcoholics. *Medical Biology* 55(3):181–6.

659. Wiberg, A.; Wahlstrom, G.; and Oreland, L. 1977. Brain monoamine oxidase activity after chronic ethanol treatment of rats. *Psychopharmacology* 52:111–13.

660. Wiesel, F. A., and Sedvall, G. 1975. Effect of antipsychotic drugs on homovanillic acid levels in striatum and olfactory tubercle of the rat. *European Journal of Pharmacology* 30:364–67.

661. Williams, D. J.; Crossman, A. R.; and Slater, P. 1977. The efferent projections of the nucleus accumbens in the rat. *Brain Research* 130:217–27.

662. Wilson, C. A. 1974. Hypothalamic amines and the release of gonadotrophins and other anterior pituitary hormones. In *Advances in drug research*, ed. A. B. Simmonds (London: Academic Press), pp. 119–204.

663. Wilson, L. G. 1976. Viral encephalopathy mimicking functional psychoses. *American Journal of Psychiatry* 133:165–70.

664. Wilson, R. D. 1972. The neural associations of nucleus accumbens septi in the albino rat. Thesis, Massachusetts Institute of Technology.

665. Wise, C. D.; Baden, M. M.; and Stein, L. 1974. Post-mortem measurement of enzymes in human brain. Evidence of a central noradrenergic deficit in schizophrenia. *Journal of Psychiatric Research* 11:185–98.

666. Wise, C. D., and Stein, L. 1973. Dopamine-β-hydroxylase deficits in the brains of schizophrenic patients. *Science* 181:344–47.

667. Witz, I.; Anavni, R.; and Weisenbeck, H. 1977. A tissue-binding factor in the serum of schizophrenic patients. In *The impact of biology on modern psychiatry*, eds. E. S. Gershon, R. H. Belmaker, S. S. Kety, and M. Rosenbaum (New York: Plenum Press).

668. Wurtman, R. J., and Axelrod, J. 1963. A sensitive and specific assay for the estimation of monoamine oxidase. *Biochemical Pharmacology* 12:1439–40.

669. Wyatt, R. J. 1976. Biochemistry and schizophrenia. Part IV. The neuroleptics—their mechanism of action: A review of the biochemical literature. *Psychopharmaceutical Bulletin* 12:5–50.

670. Wyatt, R. J.; Erdelyi, E.; and Wise, C. D. 1975. Dopamine-β-hydroxylase activity in brains of chronic schizophrenic patients. *Science* 187:368–70.

671. Wyatt, R. J.; Gillin, W. C.; Stoff, D. M.; Majo, E. A.; and Tinklenburg, J. R. 1977. β-Phenethylamine and the neuropsychiatric disturbances. In *Neuroregulators and psychiatric disorders*, eds. E. Usdin, D. A. Hamburg, and J. D. Barchas (New York: Oxford University Press), pp. 31–45.

672. Wyatt, R. J.; Mandel, L. R.; Ahn, H. S.; Walker, H. S.; and Van den Heuvel, W. J. A. 1973. Gas chromatographic-mass spectrometric isotope delution determination of N,N-dimethyltryptamine concentrations in normal and psychiatric patients. *Psychopharmacologia* 31:265–70.

673. Wyatt, R. J., and Murphy, D. L. 1976. Low platelet monoamine oxidase activity in schizophrenia. *Schizophrenia Bulletin* 2:77–89.

674. Wyatt, R. J.; Termini, B. A.; and Davis, J. M. 1971. Biochemical and sleep studies of schizophrenia: A review of the literature—1960–1970. Part I. Biochemical studies. *Schizophrenia Bulletin* 4:10–44.

675. Wyatt, R. J.; Vaughan, T.; Galanter, M.; Kaplan, J.; and Green, R. 1972. Behavioral changes of chronic schizophrenic patients given L-5-hydroxytryptophan. *Science* 77:1124–26.

676. Yamauchi, I. 1972. The effect of L-DOPA on schizophrenia. *Clinical Psychiatry* 14:941–49, (in Japanese).

677. Yang, H. Y. T., and Neff, N. H. 1974. The monoamine oxidases of brain: Selective inhibition with drugs and the consequences for the metabolism of biogenic amines. *Journal of Pharmacology and Experimental Therapeutics* 189:733.

678. Yayura-Tobias, J. A.; Diamond, B.; and Merlis, S. 1970. The action of L-DOPA on schizophrenic patients. *Current Therapeutic Research* 12:528–33.

679. Yayura-Tobias, J. A.; Wolpert, A.; Dana, L.; and Merlis, S. 1970. Action of L-DOPA in drug-induced extrapyramidalism. *Diseases of the Nervous System* 31:60–63.

680. Yoshida, M., and Precht, O. W. 1971. Monosynaptic inhibition of neurons of the substantia nigra by caudato-nigral fibers. *Brain Research* 32:225–27.

681. Youdim, M. B. H. 1972. Multiple forms of monoamine oxidase and their properties. *Advances in Biochemical Psychopharmacology* 5:67–77.

682. Youdim, M. B. H. 1974. Physico-chemical properties, development and regulation of central and peripheral MAOs. In *Neuropsychopharmacology of monoamines and their regulatory enzymes*, ed. E. Usdin (New York; Raven Press).

683. Youdim, M. B. H. 1977. Factors influencing the deamination and functional activity of biogenic monoamines in the central nervous system. In *The impact of biology on modern psychiatry*, eds. E. S. Gershon, R. H. Belmaker, S. S. Kety, and M. Rosenbaum (New York: Plenum Press), pp. 125–36.

684. Yu, M. K.; Wright, T.; Dettbarn, W. D.; and Olson, W. H. Pargyline-induced myopathy with histochemical characteristics of Duchenne dystrophy. Abstract, *Neurology* (Minneapolis) 24:237–44.

685. Zeller, E. A.; Bernsohn, J.; Inskip, W. M.; and Lauer, J. W. 1957. On the effect of a monoamine oxidase inhibitor on the behavior and tryptophan metabolism of schizophrenic patients. *Naturwissenschaften* 44:42–44.

686. Zeller, E. A.; Boshes, B.; Davis, J. M.; and Thorner, M.: 1975. Molecular abberration in platelet monoamine oxidase in schizophrenia. *Lancet* 2:1385.

687. Zimmermann, K.; Moschke, P.; and Wieder, H.-H. 1976. Uber die ausscheidung von 3,4-dimethoxy-phenylathylamin im urin von schizophrenen. *Psychiatrie, Neurologie und Medizinische Psychologie* (Leipzig) 28:163–73.

688. Zis, A. P., and Fibiger, H. C. 1975. Neuroleptic-induced deficits in food and water regulation: Similarities to the lateral hypothalamic syndrome. *Psychopharmacologia* (Berlin) 43:63–68.

689. Zuckerman, M. The sensation-seeking motive. In *Progress in experimental personality research*, ed. B. Maher (New York: Academic Press), vol. 7, pp. 79–148.

Chapter 3

THE GENETIC STUDIES OF THE SCHIZOPHRENIC SYNDROME: A REVIEW OF THEIR CLINICAL IMPLICATIONS

Robert Cancro, M.D., Med.D.Sc.

The issue of diagnosis is directly relevant to all of the genetic studies. There can be no understanding, let alone comparison, of genetic studies without the recognition that their clinical populations have been arrived at through the process of clinical diagnosis. The method of diagnosing the population defines the group which will be studied genetically and contributes to the results obtained in that study. The scientific merit and the comparability of the genetic studies is no stronger than the rigor of the determination of the clinical groupings studied. Much of the variability in the studies to be reported later in this chapter can be attributed to differences in diagnostic criteria chosen by different investigators.

Any coherent discussion of diagnosis must start with a careful consideration of how the syndrome is conceptualized. There are many conceptions of the schizophrenic syndrome, and each has its explicit and at times even more important implicit assumptions. When applied to clinical populations, these different conceptualizations produce patient groups which are not coextensive. Furthermore, they lead to different diagnostic strategies and have very different implications for treatment. At one extreme of the spectrum of assumptions is that of schizophrenia as a brain disease. This unsupported assumption leads to a view of the schizophrenias as one or more distinct disease entities. The strategy for diagnosis becomes the search for and the identification of the pathognomonic signs of this entity. The disorder is assumed to exist in nature as a real illness, and the clinician must learn to recognize it as such. The approach taken by Kraepelin (25) is typical of the disease entity model, with its assumptions concerning specifiable etiology, natural course, and predictable outcome. Perhaps of even greater importance is that the disease entity model justifies, if not compels, the clinician to intervene therapeutically in the face of a foreign disease.

There are a variety of other conceptualizations of the schizophrenias which need not be summarized in this chapter. They include such extreme positions as that the disorder is an expansion of consciousness or a creative adaptation to an insane world, or even that it is nonexistent. The bias of this chapter is that the disorder is best thought of as a syndrome. As with all syndromes, the clinician is dealing with a collection of signs and symptoms which are present in certain cases at certain times. These symptoms are disjunctive, and the clinical picture is variable. The syndrome conceptualization recognizes that the construct of schizophrenia is a man-made imposition on the data (10). It assumes not that there is a real entity called schizophrenia but rather that the construct is an effort to organize the data of observation in a manner consistent with human thought processes. We need to organize data rationally and logically for science to proceed. Classification is an essential activity of science, but it should not be reified. The syndrome approach considers not the correctness or the truth of the conceptualization but rather its utility. This is basically the approach taken by Eugen Bleuler (1) in his classical departure from the disease entity model of Kraepelin.

The schizophrenic syndrome represents a clinical grouping. There is no independent test for this disorder. There is neither tissue nor fluid which can be sent to the laboratory. The diagnosis must be made on the basis of clinical findings. If there is no independent validation, then there is no such thing as a correct diagnosis. This point can be confusing. It can lead to the misconception that diagnosis is an unimportant process. The method for arriving at a diagnosis must be reasonable and consistent. Nevertheless, it is correct only in the sense that it consistently follows a particular clinical strategy about the utility of whose procedure there is general professional agreement. While the diagnosis can be reliable, it cannot be validated independently (9).

There are a variety of associated findings which can be thought of as contributing to validity—for example, family history of similar disorders (33). Nevertheless, these findings only demonstrate the utility of the classification; they cannot validate it in the true meaning of the term. The conclusion is inevitable. Any effort at diagnosis based exclusively on clinically defined signs must be arbitrary. The important distinction is that the criteria, while arbitrary, must not be capricious. This does not mean that any set of diagnostic criteria is as good as any other; it means rather that different nosological efforts must be compared with each other in terms of utility rather than correctness. Diagnostic criteria must be useful as well as reliable. The usefulness may, for example, be in terms of predicting outcome, or identifying appropriate treatment efforts, or increasing the homogeneity of the population in other useful ways.

The choice of diagnostic criteria utilized by different workers has been influenced not only by their conceptualization of the disorder but by their personal preferences. Some authors have preferred to derive their criteria from a theoretical position, while others have preferred a more empirical one. The work of Langfeldt (27) is illustrative of this atheoretical position. His criteria are empirically derived. They include feelings of derealization, depersonalization, and unreality as well as insidious onset, autism, emotional blunting, and clear consciousness. He diagnoses "true schizophrenia" on the basis of the presence of these symptoms. A limitation of this nosological approach is that the assessment of the Langfeldt criteria tends to be more subjective and less reliable than certain other approaches.* Furthermore, no single sign is essential, and thus any sign is as diagnostic as any other.

An equally empirical approach to diagnosis is to be seen in the work of Schneider (42). His criteria are not related to any theoretical position concerning the schizophrenic syndrome. He cites a number of symptoms which are identified as of the first rank in importance in making the diagnosis. These include:

audible thoughts, voices heard arguing, voices heard commenting on one's actions; the experience of influences playing on the body (somatic passivity experiences); thought-withdrawal and other interferences with thought; diffusion of thought; delusional perception and all feelings, impulses (drives), and volitional acts that are experienced by the patient as the work or influence of others. [pp. 133–34]

The advantage of such a position as Schneider's is that it is inherently atheoretical. The list of diagnostic criteria came from actual patients about whom there was general diagnostic agreement. These were the signs and the symptoms which were of major importance—that is, the most frequently found—in a group of patients about whom there was diagnostic consensus. The signs utilized by Schneider are easily described and reliable. *The International Pilot Study of Schizophrenia* (52), conducted by the World Health Organization, demonstrated that the Schneiderian first-rank symptoms could be agreed upon even by clinicians working in different cultural settings.

It is often forgotten that Schneider warned the practitioner that the list of first-rank symptoms was meant to serve as a guide and not as a *de fide* document. Schneider stated that there were patients who should be diagnosed as schizophrenic even though they did not show symptoms of the first rank. He argued that the practitioner should not abandon clinical judgment and rely on these symptoms exclusively. Unfortunately his warning has been ignored by many who use his first-rank symptoms mechanically without clinical acumen.

Another problem with the use of multiple diagnostic signs as the criteria for schizophrenia is that the signs tend to be weighted equally rather than differentially. Any sign is as good as any other sign for diagnostic purposes. This practice gives the signs an interchangeability which is clinically difficult to justify. Moreover, even a casual review of the preceding lists would dismay the experienced clinician. Some signs utilized by Langfeldt, such as derealization, are quite nonspecific and can be seen in a variety of disorders. There is also the likelihood that some patients with acute mania and many patients with an amphetamine psychosis would be extremely difficult to differentiate from schizophrenics if the diagnosis were made on the basis of a rigid cross-

* J. P. Leff: personal communication.

sectional application of first-rank symptoms without attention to the course of the disorder.

Eugen Bleuler developed his altered fundamental signs from a theoretical position concerning the hypothetical deficit in the schizophrenic syndrome. The altered fundamental signs have enjoyed considerable popularity since their introduction and include associational disturbance (i.e., thought disorder), affective disturbance, autism, and ambivalence. These signs are recognizable to a reliable degree, and clinicians have found Bleuler's criteria applicable for almost three-quarters of a century. Nevertheless, they do require clinical judgment and therefore do not lend themselves as readily to a checklist format. A decision has to be made as to the presence or the absence of particular signs, rather than letting the patient's response to a question become the criterion for the diagnosis. Clearly both approaches have advantages and disadvantages. Nevertheless, the present Zeitgeist has moved toward a reliance on the patient's response rather than on the clinician's inference. Although Bleuler's list is shorter than those of Langfeldt or Schneider, the criteria remain multiple. There is more than one criterion for the diagnosis even according to Bleuler. A shorter list has all of the conceptual problems of a longer list, although perhaps not to the same practical degree.

Apart from the choice of criteria utilized for making the diagnosis, the clinician must be satisfied with making one of two types of error: either overinclusion or underinclusion. Recognizing that error is inevitable, clinicians must choose the type of error they prefer. Some prefer to make the diagnosis more frequently, while others prefer to make it more cautiously. Those who make it cautiously through the use of a narrow conception will find a greater frequency of chronic and poor-prognosis patients. Those who make the diagnosis readily and use a broad conception will include more cases who show an acute and nonrecurring picture. It is impotrant that the practitioner not vacillate between different diagnostic schema which will yield different populations. It is vital that the basis for the diagnosis be communicated in any report concerning a patient, be it a case history or a scientific article.

All of the strategies cited, and most others as well, have been influenced by German psychiatry with its emphasis on symptoms. By contrast, the Moscow school of psychiatric thought, which dominates Russian psychiatry, relies almost exclusively on the direction of the clinical course over time (19). Despite Moscow's deemphasis of symptoms, its choice of course as the core criterion remains clinical in nature. The clinical picture is all that is available for the diagnostic efforts of the students of this syndrome.

The preference of this writer is not to utilize a list but rather to restrict the diagnostic scheme to a single criterion variable. The choice of a formal thought disorder as described by Eugen Bleuler has much to recommend it. The classical signs of formal thought disorder require a clinical inference, but their assessment is highly reliable (8). More important, the use of these formal signs increases the homogeneity of the sample in terms of premorbid adjustment, type of onset, presenting clinical picture, and duration of hospital stay (7). This strategy will also significantly reduce the size of the population diagnosed as schizophrenic (6).

Vulnerability

It will be helpful to discuss the concept of vulnerability prior to reviewing the genetic literature. It is well known and has been long understood that a complex disorder such as the schizophrenic syndrome cannot be transmitted directly. It has been assumed that what is transmitted is a vulnerability or weakness which allows the individual to develop the schizophrenic syndrome in the face of certain environmental stresses. The genetic vulnerability is seen as a diathesis which is necessary but not sufficient for the illness (16). It is also assumed that not everyone with the diathesis will manifest the disorder, and that only some of those who are exposed to the appropriate stresses will become ill. There is much that is attractive about this formulation; therefore it is important to reflect on its implications. The vulnerability which is transmitted is seen as a weakness. In that sense it is implicitly, if not explicitly, an abnormal trait which is transmitted. While this abnormal trait does not inevitably lead to maladaptation, it can be analogized to a time bomb. If the time bomb fails to go off, it does no harm; but under no circumstances can it be seen in a positive light or as an asset. Also implicit in the concept of vulnerability is the hope of preventing the transmission of that vulnerability through genetic counseling and/or genetic regulation.

An alternative formulation to vulnerability would see the transmitted trait as nothing more than a capacity for the form of the schizophrenic illness if the individual were to become ill (11). The transmitted trait in a potentially schizophrenic group can be seen as a normal variation of the expression of that trait in the general population. Those individuals who fall into a particular range of the distribution of the trait have the capacity for a schizophrenic illness if they become ill with a psychosis. Those who fall in a different range of the distribution do not have the capacity for a schizophrenic illness but rather will show some other form of maladaptation if they become mentally ill. An advantage of this alternative formulation is that there need not be a search for either an abnormal gene or an abnormal trait. The potential for the form of the schizophrenic illness would derive from the normal variability of the trait distribution found within the population. This formulation has a further advantage in that it would see the normal variation in the trait as multipotential in nature. Individuals who find themselves in that particular range of the trait in question need not have an abnormal outcome. Being in a statistical minority can lead to excellent as well as to poor adaptation. This interpretation merely means that individuals who have the traits which underlie the capacity for the form of the schizophrenic illness are statistically unusual both in health and in illness. These individuals are unusual in a statistical rather than in a moral sense. The preceding description refers to a single trait for purposes of clarity. The rationale holds equally well for multiple traits and for patterns of traits.

Genetic Studies

The review of the genetic literature will consist of three parts. Each part will emphasize a particular research strategy used in behavioral genetics. The strategies or research methods used in behavioral genetics are: consanguinity (or family), twin, and adoptive studies.

The consanguinity or family method is quite straightforward conceptually. The method assumes that if a genetic factor is operating, there will be a significant increase in the prevalence rate of the disorder in question in the first-degree relatives of the index cases as compared with the prevalence rate in the general population. This can be expressed in another way: the greater the degree of consanguinity vis-à-vis the index case, the higher the prevalence rate. Obviously the increase in prevalence rate must differ significantly from that found in the general population. A subsidiary expectation in consanguinity studies is that second-degree relatives of index cases will still show a higher rate of prevalence than that found in nonrelatives.

The first published study on the genetics of schizophrenia was one on consanguinity by Rüdin (41). He reported a significant increase in the prevalence rate of schizophrenia in the biological relatives of his probands or index cases. Subsequent studies done in Europe by Schultz (43) and Kallmann (21) confirmed Rüdin's report. Zerbin-Rüdin (53) summarized twelve early European studies which were quite consistent in their results. Slater (44) also reviewed some of the earlier studies and found a significantly higher prevalence rate of schizophrenia in the blood relatives of index cases than in the general population. Slater noted that this was true even in studies conducted by investigators with a markedly environmental bias. These studies also showed the expected positive relationship between degree of consanguinity and prevalence rate. The closer the relative, the more likely is there to be schizophrenia. For the parents, the siblings, and the children of schizophrenics, the prevalence rate was approximately 10 to 15 percent. This is an order of magnitude higher than the approximately 1 percent expected in the general population. These studies show that even second-degree relatives are at greater risk than the general population.

The consanguinity studies show excellent agreement that the siblings of index cases have approximately a 10 percent age-corrected risk for the disorder (29,46). Rüdin found almost equal numbers of schizophrenic and manic-depressive relatives in the families of his schizophrenic cases. The subsequent studies have not been consistent and are very much influenced by diagnostic practices. In general there was no excess of affective disorder in the siblings of schizophrenics and some evidence that the rate might actually be significantly reduced (4,24). It is safe to conclude, however, that neither schizophrenics nor affective disorders breed perfectly true to their diagnostic category—that is, to the degree that the categories can be validly identified.

There are many obvious limitations to the consanguinity studies.

While they clearly and consistently indicate that there is an increase in the prevalence rate in the families of schizophrenic index cases, they do not rule out an environmental explanation. Many things run in families which are clearly determined by social and cultural experiences. First-degree relatives share more than an increased similarity in their genetic makeup. The closer the relative, the more likely is it that environmental experiences will also be similar. In partial response to this position is a rarely cited study by Manfred Bleuler (2). He reported that relatives of schizophrenic index cases who developed schizophrenia themselves tended to have a similar type of onset, symptomatology, duration of illness, and outcome. It is difficult to explain this finding in exclusively environmental terms, because many of the relatives were geographically separated and in certain cases did not even know each other.

The second strategy in genetic research—the twin method— is more powerful. The rationale for the twin study method is also relatively simple. When genetic factors operate in the etiology of a disorder, the monozygotic-twin concordance rate is significantly higher than the dyzygotic-twin concordance rate. Concordance can mean the occurrence of either the same or a similar condition in both twins. In the case of a clinical disorder this determination must be arbitrary to some degree. If the index case, for example, has "definite schizophrenia," a decision as to concordance must be made for the co-twin who has "probable schizophrenia." Concordance rates can be calculated and are usually reported by the pairwise, casewise, or proband methods. The pairwise rate is the proportion of concordant pairs, while the casewise rate is the proportion of concordant cases. The proband rate is a casewise rate modified by defining the specific method of case ascertainment. Each of these methods will give different results on identical data. An example will clarify the differences. Given 100 monozygotic twins in which 40 pairs are concordant and 60 pairs discordant, the pairwise rate is 40 concordant pairs divided by 100 total pairs, or 40 percent. The casewise rate is 80 concordant cases (40 twin pairs) divided by 140 total cases (80 concordant plus 60 discordant), or 57 percent. The proband rate will approximate the casewise rate but will be determined by the actual method of case ascertainment. It is important, therefore, in comparing different twin studies to utilize the same method of determining concordance rates. Obviously the concordance rate is no more reliable than the diagnostic method used in making clinical judgments.

The concordance rate of schizophrenia in monozygotic twins has consistently been found to be significantly higher than the rate in dyzygotic twins. Kallmann in 1946 (22) and Slater and Shields in 1953 (45) reported large studies in which the monozygotic concordance was significantly higher than the dyzygotic rate. Unfortunately these studies had certain methodological limitations. A look at the more recent literature may help to overcome those deficiencies.

The recent studies have been extended to larger populations of dyzygotic twins, thereby including index cases who were less severely ill, and have not restricted the population to chronically hospitalized individuals. Rosenthal (39) reviewed eleven twin studies, including the more recent ones, and found that in ten the concordance rates were consistent with the predictions that would be made from genetic theory.

There are five twin studies published since 1963 which can be considered as the best available. These include three Scandinavian studies by Tienari (47, 49), Kringlen, (26), and Fischer (12), each of which was done in a different country. There are two twin studies in English-speaking countries which are included in this group. They are the studies by Gottesman and Shields (15) in England and by Pollin et al. (32) in the United States. These five studies report concordance rates in the range of 6 percent to 40 percent. Many factors operate to determine the exact concordance rate, and it is influenced significantly by the diagnostic criteria utilized. In all of these studies the concordance rate for dyzygotic twins has been no higher than that found in ordinary siblings.

Tienari in 1963 (47) reported a 0 percent concordance rate for monozygotic twins. In 1968 (48) he raised that figure to 6 percent as additional twin members became ill. Gottesman and Shields (17) reported that by the date of their article his concordance rate had risen to 16 percent. This figure would rise to 35 percent if probable schizophrenia were included and the proband method were used (17). The Kringlen study (26) showed a significant monozygotic-dyzygotic difference using a pairwise method for determining concordance. He reported a somewhat lower concordance rate than some of the earlier studies. More important, he confirmed some of Kallmann's (22) major findings. Kringlen found no significant difference between dyzygotic and regular siblings. He found neither male-female differences nor differences between same-sex and opposite-sex dyzygotes. These negative findings all support the role of a genetic factor rather than the role of gender or psychologic identification factors in the etiology of the disorder.

The study by Pollin et al. (32) was extremely useful for several reasons. First of all, it included a large number of cases; and, second, the sample was biased toward health. In order for a twin pair to enter the sample, both twins had to pass an induction physical given by the United States armed forces. This meant that early onset cases, who have the worst prognosis and probably the highest concordance rates, were excluded from the sample. Despite this bias, the results showed a significant increase in the concordance rate for monozygotic as compared with dyzygotic twins. The Tienari and Pollin studies did not include female twins. Nevertheless, the Kringlen study found no sex differences, and therefore the overall significance of the Tienari and the Pollin studies is not impaired.

The Fischer study (12) has several remarkable features. There was virtually no age correction necessary, so that the monozygotic concordance of 56 percent—arrived at through the proband method—is particularly informative. A unique feature of Fischer's work is that she studied the children born to monozygotic twins as a function of whether their parents were schizophrenic or not. The offspring of schizophrenic members of twin pairs had a 9.6 percent risk for schizophrenia, while the offspring of the discordant nonschizophrenic twins showed a 12.9 percent risk. For samples of this size—31.2 and 23.1 age-corrected offspring, respectively—this is not a significant difference. The important finding is that the offspring of discordant twins are as vulnerable to the schizophrenic illness as are the offspring of probands. Looked at from another point of view, the discordant or nonschizophrenic member of the twin pair was as likely to produce a schizophrenic child as was an individual who actually had the illness. Furthermore, Fischer studied the twins who were concordant and those who were discordant and found no significant difference in risk to their offspring.

Using the proband method, Gottesman and Shields (17) recalculated the concordance rates in these five studies. They found the monozygotic concordance rates ranged between 35 percent and 58 percent and averaged 47 percent. The dyzygotic concordance rate, using the proband method, varied between 9 percent and 26 percent and averaged 15 percent. These concordance rates are presented without age corrections.

A number of objections can be raised concerning the strength of the twin data. Jackson (20) argued the obvious psychological fact that monozygotic twins share much more than a common genome. They have a unique psychological environment in which the demarcation between one another is at best amorphous. They are often dressed alike from birth, frequently misidentified, and often seen as a unit (i.e., *the* twins) rather than as individuals. All of these factors operate to make the monozygotic-dyzygotic comparison less than an ideal experimental situation. Rosenthal, in a series of papers (34, 37), raised a number of methodological criticisms of these earlier studies. Furthermore, there are problems at the biological level. Campion and Tucker (5) reviewed some of the biological differences between monozygotic and dyzygotic twins which make the monozygotes a very special group of individuals. There is no denying that the monozygotic-dyzygotic comparison is not a perfect natural experiment. Nevertheless, monozygotic twins are not at a higher risk for schizophrenia than singletons. This finding in itself tends to be an answer to the argument that the high concordance rate in monozygotic twins is attributable to a shared psychological environment.

There are twenty-seven reported pairs of monozygotic twins separated in early life from their biological parents and reared apart from the parents and one another (17). The concordance rate for this group does not differ significantly from that which would be expected if they had been reared by their biological parents. While it is necessary to interpret twenty-seven pairs with caution, they do represent a unique population. The finding is certainly supportive of a genetic role in the transmission of the schizophrenic syndrome.

The combination of consanguinity and twin data strongly suggests the existence of a genetic role in the transmission of this disorder. Nevertheless, the data can be explained by a purely psychogenic transmission. The twenty-seven adopted identical twins who were separated from their biological families and one another early in life pose a problem to the psychogenic theory, but every theory has enough flexibility to ignore a few unpleasant facts. A major value of the adoptive studies is that they test some of the alternative environmental explanations. To the degree that they permit the refutation of environmental hypotheses, they strengthen the value of the consanguinity and twin results.

The initial strategy in the adoptive studies was to examine the offspring of schizophrenic parents reared by nonschizophrenic parents and then to study the actual versus the expected prevalence rates. Heston (18) published the first such study. He found that the prevalence rates for the disorder in the biological offspring of schizophrenic mothers was not significantly different from what would be expected if they had been reared by the biological parent. Furthermore, he found that the adopted offspring of a control group of nonschizophrenic women showed a prevalence rate which did not differ significantly from that found in the general population. Like any clinical study, this was criticized for a variety of methodological shortcomings. A deficiency which was given great weight by some observers was that the adoptive parents were informed of the mental illness of the biological mother. It was argued that this knowledge was thus a self-fulfilling prophecy.

The extensive genetic research on adoptions led by Kety, Rosenthal, and Wender have addressed most of the criticisms raised concerning Heston's earlier work (23,40). Initially this group took a large population of adopted children and separated them into those who had or had not become schizophrenic. They then ascertained the prevalence rate of the disorder in the biological relatives and compared it with the adoptive relatives of the children. They included in their first studies all children adopted in Copenhagen during a twenty-four-year period. Their results have consistently supported the existence of a genetic factor.

Since the earlier reports Kety et al. have expanded their studies in a number of elegant ways, including the use of extensive interviews with the biological and the adoptive families of both the schizophrenics and the controls (24,51). These much more refined studies have confirmed the earlier findings. There is more schizophrenia and schizophrenialike illness in the biological relatives of adoptees from schizophrenic parents than in the biological relatives of adoptees from nonschizophrenic parents. The studies are complex and have been reported upon in detail. Several conclusions appear clear. What matters for the prevalence rate of schizophrenia is who bore you and not who reared you. Many of the parents whose children subsequently became ill with schizophrenic disorders did not show their own illness until after the children were adopted. This factor certainly argues against the self-fulfilling prophecy hypothesis. Furthermore, parents who adopted a child without parental schizophrenia but who themselves developed a schizophrenic illness did not produce schizophrenic offspring. In other words, being reared by a schizophrenic parent is not in and of itself enough of a stress to produce the disorder without some other factor operating. These studies also showed that the prevalence rate was not influenced by which parent had the illness, and that the genetic factor operated as strongly when the ill parent was the father as when it was the mother. This result tends to diminish the importance of an intrauterine factor and suggests a relatively pure genetic transmission.

The behavioral sciences cannot speak of proof in a mathematical sense; they must rather use the concept of evidence. The weight of the evidence is clear. An as yet undefined genetic factor operates in the prevalence rate of this disorder. This factor is powerful enough to have its effect independently of a number of environmental conditions at least at the population, if not at the individual, level. The adoptive studies make untenable many of the environmental explanations of the consanguinity and twin studies. In that sense they powerfully strengthen the meaningfulness of the other methods while adding their own unique evidence. The total weight of the evidence, when these three lines of investigation are united, is overwhelmingly clear. Genes are involved in the transmission of the schizophrenic disorder. In retrospect, it seems strange that so much furor and so much money has been spent to arrive at such an obvious conclusion.

Modes of Genetic Action

There are many models of genetic transmission which fit reasonably well the actual data to be found in the schizophrenic syndrome. It is beyond the goals of this chapter to explore their relative merits and demerits. What is of more importance for an understanding of the clinical implications is the mode of genetic operation. Genes are nothing more than encoded potential information. They represent instructions which may or may not be activated. The forces which activate the gene and cause it to have its particular effect are nongenetic. These nongenetic or environmental factors activate genes which are both structural and regulatory, and thereby ultimately determine the effective genetic makeup of an organism. Every organism is born with many more genes than are activated during its lifetime. In this sense every individual represents multiple genetic potentialities, depending upon the accidents of environment which activate one or another set of genes. This gene-environment activity is spoken of as an "interaction" but it is best conceived of as a "biological union." It is very similar to the union of the sperm and the egg. The resulting fetus is something more than the simple sum of its so-called constituent parts. The environment is, of course, the biochemical bath in which the gene sits. This bath is influenced by a variety of social and intrapsychic events through physiological pathways. While there is no clear understanding of the pathways which translate psychic events into physiological ones, these pathways must exist. It remains the task of future research to identify the specific gene-environment interactions, the significance of the timing of those interactions, the mechanisms, and the pathways by which social events become translated into biochemical ones.

We know from our contemporary understanding of genetics that every gene is multipotential. If a particular gene is activated by a specific environment, it will produce a characteristic, or phenotype. That very same gene activated by a different environment will produce a different characteristic. This difference may be quantitative (e.g., taller or shorter) or qualitative (e.g., presence or absence of audiogenic seizure susceptibility in mice). The range of potential outcomes inherent in any given genotype is not vast but, rather, is modest. The exciting point is that the outcome has a finite range of possibilities and is not predetermined. It is an empirical question as to how much phenotypic variation can be found within any genotype as a function of environmental variation. This question can be answered by the appropriate research strategies. Looked at from this point of view, the gene or genes which contribute to the form of the schizophrenic illness in one individual can contribute to creative and highly adaptive outcomes in another individual. The gene is not necessarily inherently "bad" or immutably destined to produce a maladaptive outcome.

The other side of this equation lies in the phenotype. Any trait of interest can be arrived at from multiple genotypes. The identical trait in different individuals will be derived from different genotypes. An animal model may help to illustrate this point. There are mice which show the trait of audiogenic seizure susceptibility on the basis of disturbances in their gamma-aminobutyric acid (GABA)—glutamic acid decarboxylase (GAD) system (14). This defect is genetically transmitted but will respond to a diet rich in glutamic acid. The improvement in the GAD/GABA system results in a diminution of seizure activity. Other mice which also show seizure susceptibility, but on the basis of a different mechanism, will not respond to glutamic acid manipulation of their diet. Parenthetically, both sets of mice will respond to dilantin. It is difficult not to draw a parallel to the schizophrenic syndrome, with the neuroleptic agents performing more like dilantin and less like glutamic acid.

Different genes will combine with different environments to produce the same or different characteristics. This is the richness of biological diversity. A knowledge of the phenotype does not allow a conclusion as to the genotype any more than a knowledge of the genotype allows a prediction of the ultimate phenotype. There is plasticity in the system. This insight suggests that there is no single gene or any single environment which will inevitably produce the schizophrenic syndrome, but rather that a number of genetic patterns and evoking environmental situations can contribute to the development of this disorder.

Phenotypes can be thought of in a number of different ways. A phenotype may be conceived of as a structure—for example, a molecule whose form and/or function is controlled by gene-environment interactions. At other times a trait is better thought of quantitatively without reference to a particular structure. An example of this latter approach would be height. In behavior it is often simplest to define a trait in psychological terms, and then develop a procedure to measure that trait. The measurement then becomes used as the phenotype. An example of measurement used as the phenotype is the IQ tests used as the measure of a psychological construct called intelligence. Schizophrenia is usually treated in this latter fashion, and its diagnosis—that is, measurement— is discussed as a phenotype. It is probably less of a true phenotype than intelligence, which in itself is probably too complex and global a conceptualization to lend itself to the more discrete and atomic approach of genetics. Furthermore, as discussed earlier, it is not necessary to conceive of the phenotype, or the phenotypes, involved in the etiology of the schizophrenic syndrome as pathogenic or even abnormal. The data can be explained equally well by arguing that the so-called vulnerability merely defines the form that the illness will take if an individual has the misfortune to become ill. It may not define a group which is at increased risk for mental illness in general, but may rather define one which is at increased risk for the formal characteristics of a particular mental illness.

There is now no demonstrated true phenotype which is necessary but not sufficient for the schizophrenic syndrome. There is not even a genuine genetic marker available, although many findings in the literature are referred to as such. They would more appropriately be called biological correlates of the genetic potentiality. At this time it is best to seek a psychological phenotype which can be described and studied in afflicted individuals, normals, and their respective families. This psychological trait or characteristic should be relevant to the clinical picture of the disorder, and not arbitrary. Ideally it should be a part of the process under reasonably direct genetic control, and not a complex epiphenomenon far removed from any single gene.

Attention regulation appears to be a psychological process which may serve admirably to fulfill this role of psychological phenotype. A major function of attention regulation is to process information, differentially and efficiently, between inner and outer sources of a stimuli. This activity can be thought of as a stable cognitive control which is under genetic regulation. It is then possible to study patterns of attention-regulation distribution in health and in illness in different populations. It would be expected that this attention-regulation factor (or factors) would have a Gaussian distribution. No individual member of that distribution need be defined as abnormal; but any may be defined as statistically unusual. To use an analogy, there are short people who are not dwarfs. In fact, most short people are not dwarfs. While some cases in the extreme tails of the distribution may be on the basis of a genetic abnormality, the vast majority will be on the basis of Gaussian variation. Extreme members of any distribution are statistically unusual individuals both in health and in illness. It would not come as a surprise, therefore, that people from one part of the distribution would manifest a different form of mental illness than those from another part. Attention regulation certainly could explain the basic disturbances of cognition and object relations which characterize the group of the schizophrenias. A tendency toward preoccupation with inner percepts could easily explain the autism which has also been seen as a cardinal symptom. More important, this is a strategy which promises to carry genetic studies beyond their present level.

Conclusions

The very fact that different gene-environment combinations can produce the phenotype, or phenotypes, which are necessary but not sufficient for the schizophrenic syndrome, means that there are multiple etiologic pathways through which this syndrome can develop. This etiologic heterogeneity is biologically based and does not reflect nosological in-adequacies. The clinical syndrome is only a modestly homogeneous end state, which can be arrived at from different initial conditions through different pathways. This genetic argument is extremely important. It suggests that the search for a single etiology is unlikely to be productive, and that there is neither a single environment nor a particular genetic constellation which is schizophrenogenic.

Inasmuch as the gene-environment interactions are multiple and the mechanisms controlled by those interactions equally diverse, we would anticipate that the clinical picture of the disorder would be inherently variable. This variability would be predicted in a group of individuals labeled schizophrenic because of the different mechanisms involved. The syndrome nature of the disorder would also lead to an intraindividual variability. A particular symptom used for diagnostic purposes may be arrived at through different mechanisms, and its presence at certain times would neither prevent its absence at others nor its recurrence on a different basis. The symptoms of this disorder are disjunctive both in-traindividually and interindividually. This is another important im-plication of the genetic studies.

To the degree that the clinical course is influenced by genetic hetero-geneity, the observer would anticipate variable outcomes. This is indeed the case. The weight of the evidence, however, is that a significant por-tion of the variability in course is a function of life events and circum-stances (28). The individual with a supportive social environment will have the prognostic advantage over someone without such support.

The implications for treatment are perhaps the most important. The essential biological heterogeneity of the syndrome excludes the rational search for a preferred, let alone correct, treatment of this disorder; there can be no single treatment which is not neutral or even harmful for a number of cases. Any single treatment which is useful for certain patients will be useless for others and harmful to the remainder. This distribution of responses need not be equal, but there is no treatment that will be good for all such patients. The very heterogeneity of the syndrome precludes this possibility. We should expect a range of ef-fective treatments which reflect to some degree the range of variability among the patients. This is not to say that any treatment is appropriate for this disorder. The decision as to the efficacy of a treatment is em-pirical. If a treatment has been demonstrated to be significantly better than no treatment, it can enter the armamentarium. The genetically based conclusion concerning the need for multiple treatments holds not only for biological but for social treatment as well.

The genetic studies do not rule out social interventions. Part of the resistance to accepting the genetic studies derived from the fear that they would invalidate the utility of social interventions, including psycho-therapy. The knowledge of the value of these techniques for certain patients derives from experience and cannot be refuted by a theoretical notion. There is nothing in the genetic studies to prevent a clinician from developing an intense and honest relationship with a patient. Clinicians may choose to avoid this personal involvement, but that decision cannot be justified on the basis of the genetic studies.

BIBLIOGRAPHY

1. Bleuler, E. 1911. Dementia Praecox oder die Gruppe der Schizophrenien. In *Handbuch der Psychiatrie*, ed. G. Aschaffenburg (Leipzig: Deuticke).
2. Bleuler, M. 1941. *Krankheitsverlauf, Persönlichkeit und Verwandtschaft Schizophrener und ihre gegenseitigen Beziehungen* (Leipzig: Thieme).
3. Bleuler, M. 1972. *Die schizophrenen Geistesstörungen im Lichte langjahriger Kranken- und Familiengeschichten* (Stuttgart: Thieme).
4. Bleuler, M. 1974. The offspring of schizophrenics. *Schizophrenia Bulletin* 8:93–103 (Spring).
5. Campion, E., and Tucker, G. 1973. A note on twin studies, schizophrenia and neurological impairment. *Archives of General Psychiatry* 29:460–64.
6. Cancro, R. 1968. Thought disorder and schizophrenia. *Diseases of the Nervous System* 29: 846–49.
7. Cancro, R. 1969. Prospective prediction of hospital stay in schizophrenia. *Archives of General Psychiatry* 20:541–46.
8. Cancro, R. 1970. A classificatory principle in schizophrenia. *American Journal of Psychiatry* 126:1655–59.
9. Cancro, R. 1973. Increased diagnostic reliability in schizophrenia: Some values and limitations. *International Journal of Psychiatry* 11:53–57.
10. Cancro, R. 1975. Genetic considerations in the etiology and prevention of schizophrenia. In *Schizophrenia: Biological and psychological perspectives*, ed. G. Usdin (New York: Brunner/Mazel).
11. Cancro, R. 1976. Some diagnostic and therapeutic considerations on the schizophrenic syndrome. *Psychiatry Digest* 37:13–18.
12. Fischer, M. 1973. Genetic and environmental factors in schizophrenia. *Acta Psychiatrica Scandinavica*, supp. 238.
13. Fischer, M. 1974. Development and validity of a computerized method for diagnoses of functional psychoses (Diax). *Acta Psychiatrica Scandinavica* 50:243–88.
14. Ginsburg, B. E.; Cowen, J. S.; Maxson, S. C.; and Sze, P. Y. 1969. Neurochemical effects of gene mutations associated with audiogenic seizures. In *Progress in Neuro-Genetics*, eds. A. Barbeau and J. R. Brunette (Amsterdam: Excerpta Medica).
15. Gottesman, I. I., and Shields, J. 1966. Schizophrenia in twins: 16 years' consecutive admissions to a psychiatric clinic. *British Journal of Psychiatry* 112:809–18.
16. Gottesman, I. I., and Shields, J. 1972. *Schizophrenia and genetics: A twin study vantage point* (New York: Academic Press).
17. Gottesman, I. I., and Shields, J. 1976. A critical review of recent adoption, twin, and family studies of schizophrenia: Behavioral genetics perspectives. *Schizophrenia Bulletin* 2:360–401.
18. Heston, L. L. 1966. Psychiatric disorders in foster home reared children of schizophrenic mothers. *British Journal of Psychiatry* 112:819–25.
19. Holland, J. 1978. Schizophrenia in the Soviet Union. In *Annual review of the schizophrenic syndrome*, ed. R. Cancro (New York: Brunner/Mazel), vol. 5.
20. Jackson, D. D. 1960. A critique of the literature on the genetics of schizophrenia. In *The etiology of schizophrenia*, ed. D. D. Jackson (New York: Basic Books).
21. Kallmann, F. J. 1938. *The genetics of schizophrenia* (New York: Augustin).
22. Kallmann, F. J. 1946. The genetic theory of schizophrenia: An analysis of 691 schizophrenic twin index families. *American Journal of Psychiatry* 103:309–22.
23. Kety, S. S.; Rosenthal, D.; Wender, P. H.; and Schulsinger, F. 1968. The types and prevalence of mental illness in the biological and adoptive families of adopted schizophrenics. In *The transmission of schizophrenia*, eds. D. Rosenthal and S. S. Kety (Oxford: Pergamon Press).
24. Kety, S. S.; Rosenthal, D.; Wender, P. H.; Schulsinger, F.; and Jacobsen, B. 1975. Mental illness in the biological and adoptive families of adopted individuals who have become schizophrenic: A preliminary report based on psychiatric interviews. In *Genetic Research in Psychiatry*, eds. R. R. Fieve, D. Rosenthal, and H. Brill (Baltimore: Johns Hopkins University Press).
25. Kraepelin, E. 1899. *Psychiatrie. Ein kurzes Lehrbuch für Studierende und Ärzte*, 6th ed. (Leipzig: Barth).
26. Kringlen, E. 1967. *Heredity and environment in the functional psychoses* (London: Heinemann).
27. Langfeldt, G. 1956. The prognosis in schizophrenia. *Acta Psychiatrica Scandinavica*, supp. 110.
28. Leff, J. P. 1976. Schizophrenia and sensitivity to the family environment. *Schizophrenia Bulletin* 2:566–74.
29. Lindelius, R. 1970. A study of schizophrenia: A clinical, prognostic, and family investigation. *Acta Psychiatrica Scandinavica*, supp. 216.
30. Odegaard, O. 1972. The multifactorial theory of inheritance in pre-disposition to schizophrenia. In *Genetic factors in "schizophrenia,"* ed. A. R. Kaplan (Springfield, Ill.: Charles C Thomas).
31. Paikin, H.; Jacobsen, B.; Schulsinger, F.; Godtfredsen, K.; Rosenthal, D.; Wender, P. H.; and Kety, S. S. 1974. Characteristics of people who refuse to participate in a social and psychopathological study. In *Genetics, Environment and Psychopathology*, eds. S. A. Mednick, F. Schulsinger, J. Higgins, and D. Bell (Amsterdam: North-Holland).
32. Pollin, W.; Allen, M. G.; Hoffer, A.; Stabenau, J. R.; and Hrubec, Z. 1969. Psychopathology in 15,909 pairs of veteran twins. *American Journal of Psychiatry* 126:597–609.
33. Robins, E., and Guze, S. B. 1970. Establishment of diagnostic validity in psychiatric illness: Its application to schizophrenia. *American Journal of Psychiatry* 126:983–87.

34. Rosenthal, D. 1959. Some factors associated with concordance and discordance with respect to schizophrenia in monozygotic twins. *Journal of Nervous and Mental Disease* 129:1–10.

35. Rosenthal, D. 1960. Confusion of identity and the frequency of schizophrenia in twins. *Archives of General Psychiatry* 3:297–304.

36. Rosenthal, D. 1961. Sex distribution and the severity of illness among samples of schizophrenic twins. *Journal of Psychiatric Research* 1:26–36.

37. Rosenthal, D. 1962. Familial concordance by sex with respect to schizophrenia. *Psychological Bulletin* 59:401–21.

38. Rosenthal, D. 1962. Problems of sampling and diagnosis in the major twin studies of schizophrenia. *Journal of Psychiatric Research* 1:116–34.

39. Rosenthal, D. 1970. Genetic research in the schizophrenic syndrome. In *The schizophrenic reactions: A critique of the concept, hospital treatment, and current research*, ed. R. Cancro (New York: Brunner/Mazel).

40. Rosenthal, D.; Wender, P. H.; Kety, S. S.; Schulsinger, F.; Welner, J.; and Ostergaard, L. 1968. Schizophrenic's offspring reared in adoptive homes. In *The transmission of schizophrenia*, eds. D. Rosenthal and S. S. Kety (Oxford: Pergamon Press).

41. Rüdin, E. 1916. *Zur Vererbung und Neuentstehung der Dementia Praecox* (Berlin: Springer-Verlag).

42. Schneider, K. 1959. *Clinical psychopathology* (New York: Grune & Stratton).

43. Schultz, B. 1932. Zur Erbpathologie der Schizophrenie. *Zeitschrift für die gesamte Neurologie und Psychiatrie* 143:175–293.

44. Slater, E. 1968. A review of earlier evidence on genetic factors in schizophrenia. In *The transmission of schizophrenia*, eds. D. Rosenthal and S. S. Kety (Oxford: Pergamon Press).

45. Slater, E., and Shields, J. 1953. *Psychotic and neurotic illnesses in twins*. Medical Research Council Special Report Series no. 278 (London: Her Majesty's Stationery Office).

46. Stephens, D. A.; Atkinson, M. W.; Kay, D. W. K.; Roth, M.; and Garside, R. F. 1975. Psychiatric morbidity in parents and sibs of schizophrenics and nonschizophrenics. *British Journal of Psychiatry* 127:97–108.

47. Tienari, P. 1963. Psychiatric illnesses in identical twins. *Acta Psychiatrica Scandinavica*, supp. 171.

48. Tienari, P. 1968. Schizophrenia in monozygotic male twins. In *The transmission of schizophrenia*, eds. D. Rosenthal and S. S. Kety (Oxford: Pergamon Press).

49. Tienari, P. 1971. Schizophrenia and monozygotic twins. *Psychiatria Fennica* 2:97–104.

50. Tsuang, M. T.; Fowler, R. C.; Cadoret, R. J.; and Monnelly, E. 1974. Schizophrenia among first-degree relatives of paranoid and nonparanoid schizophrenics. *Comprehensive Psychiatry* 15:295–302.

51. Wender, P. H.; Rosenthal, D.; Kety, S. S.; Schulsinger, F.; and Welner, J. 1974. Cross-fostering: A research strategy for clarifying the role of genetic and experiential factors in the etiology of schizophrenia. *Archives of General Psychiatry* 30:121–28.

52. World Health Organization. 1975. *The international pilot study of schizophrenia* (Geneva: World Health Organization Press), vol. 1.

53. Zerbin-Rüdin, E. 1967. Endogene Psychosen. In *Humangenetik, ein kurzes Handbuch*, ed. P. E. Becker (Stuttgart: Thieme), vol. V/2.

Chapter 4

NEUROPHYSIOLOGICAL ASPECTS OF THE SCHIZOPHRENIC SYNDROME

Monte S. Buchsbaum, M.D.

Introduction

As one surveys the researches into the schizophrenic syndrome over the ten years since the last edition of this book, one sees numerous confirmations of earlier findings, using more sophisticated and rigorous approaches as well, as demonstrations of new and intriguing neurophysiological dysfunctions. Can we expect a synthesis of the cerebral blood flow, electroencephalogram (EEG), evoked potential, and neurochemical findings into a single unitary brain disease? Can this reviewer function in the manner of the famous old neurologist who astonished the medical house staff at the bedside by suggesting a single pinpoint central nervous system (CNS) lesion as uniting seemingly disparate symptoms? This hope is not only currently impossible but ultimately futile. Numerous causes of schizophrenia have already been discovered (e.g., tumors, B_{12} deficiency, etc.) and have passed out of psychiatry into other medical specialties. Davidson and Bagley (40) reviewing organic disorders associated with psychoses, concluded that "alleged distinguishing clinical features between these psychoses and 'true schizophrenia' are largely illusory."

This review begins with the premise, expressed in the last edition of this volume, that schizophrenia is not a discrete, single, unitary disease. Even if one eliminates the numerous known organic conditions (not always specifically excluded in clinical studies), there is no clear reason to consider the residual patient group homogeneous; certainly variability in drug response, clinical course, genetic transmission, and other factors suggests quite the opposite.

The schizophrenic syndrome might well be made up of a number of relatively uncommon neurophysiological and/or neurochemical disease entities, each variously exacerbated by environmental factors. Research in depression has recently indicated there may be subtypes which differ neurochemically (e.g., norepinephrine and serotonin depression) but are symptomatically indistinguishable. And in the syndrome of mental retardation more than two hundred separate genetic conditions have been described, few of which have unique behavioral symptoms. In the common research paradigm where neurophysiological measures made on small groups of patients and normals are compared by t-test statistics, we cannot expect significant results, even when as many as 30 percent to 40 percent of schizophrenics might be involved. For example, a hypothetical disorder of dreaming-sleep regulation, causing schizophrenia in 100,000 persons (of the million or more cases) in the United States, would almost certainly be missed in a ten-patient study where only one or two patients might be so affected.

Indeed, from this perspective it appears that positive studies may well be uninformative, and that negative studies may contain our best hopes. Given biological diversity, a neurophysiological finding in a large majority of patients may well reflect symptomatic response rather than causative, underlying biological factors; the finding might also be a nonspecific result related to artifacts of hospitalization, drug treatment (past or present), or chronic illness. A neurophysiological finding showing no statistically significant differences between patient and control populations but showing a few patients with extremely aberrant values may well be much more valuable in identifying causal neurophysiological deficits.

Strategies which reverse the usual dependent and independent variables may be especially useful in dealing with biological heterogeneity. Instead of beginning with hospitalized patients and normals and looking for neurophysiological deficits, a search for all individuals with the deficit, followed by behavioral and family assessment, may be a more fruitful approach. Among the pedigrees of such probands, one would expect also to find psychiatric illness assorting with the presumed deficit (179). Such an approach we have termed the "biological high-risk paradigm" (17).

Neurophysiological Research Strategy

The neurophysiological, or psychophysiological, researcher often begins with behavioral observations and psychological theories of psychopathology and attempts to study the physiology of the CNS or cardiovascular response to quantify or objectify basically psychological theories. Regrettably little research is available, however, in which the powerful neurochemical or pharmacological strategies are combined with physiological or psychophysical measures. Two areas of increased contact would seem especially promising. First, many psychopharmacological studies rely on a schizophrenic's own reports or observer ratings of his internal state to assess a neurochemical effect. But the schizophrenic's idiosyncratic or disordered verbal communications make it difficult to interpret his reports. Observable behavior, such as responding to a voice, may not occur often enough to be counted during a short-term drug trial. The psychophysiologist's approach of objectifying internal states by recording physiological variables can bypass the verbal channel. The observation can be made unobstrusively, repeated at brief intervals, and scored uniformly and automatically.

Second, physiological techniques may assist in locating neurochemical effects or deficits within the brain. If, for example, excess dopamine—in accordance with the currently leading biochemical theory of schizophrenia—occurs in only a small portion of the brain, analysis of peripheral fluids might not show higher levels of any enzyme, neurotransmitter, or metabolite. EEG, evoked potentials, or peripheral autonomic measures might be able to locate any abnormality, perhaps when used in combination with neuropharmacological manipulations. Such localized brain lesions might occur in a variety of ways, including mosaicism for neurotransmitter enzymes ("calico brain"), localized blood-brain barrier deficits following birth trauma, anomalous terminations of dopamine tracts in inappropriate areas, or developmental structural abnormalities.

This review covers human research between 1968 and 1977 and emphasizes neurophysiological measures and the effects of genetics, attention, and the dopamine system—the three greatest biological hints we have at this time about the psychobiology of the schizophrenic syndrome.

Cerebral Blood Flow

Cerebral energy metabolism and cerebral blood flow appear to be closely linked with each other and with local changes in neural activity. While it has long been attractive to postulate metabolic derangements or inactivity in specific regions of a schizophrenic's brain, technical difficulties both in the regulating of blood flow and metabolism in animals or in the measurement of regional flow in humans have previously made this hypothesis untestable. Now with the development of methods for determining local glucose consumption with C14 deoxyglucose as a tracer in animals (224), and possibly even in humans with position omission tomography*, and regional flow methods using radioactive labeled 133-xenon (171), detailed studies are possible. Early studies of psychiatric patients which used the nitrous oxide technique (118) showed no differences between schizophrenics and normals in total cerebral blood flow or oxygen consumption, although subgroup differences might exist (95). Kety et al. (118) noted, however, that local disturbances in flow might go undetected. Such localized abnormalities have been found using the 133-xenon technique. Here, the subject was injected in the

---

* Reivich, M.; Kuhl, D.; Wolf, A.; Greenberg, J.; Phelps, M.; Ido, T.; Casella, V.; Fowler, J.; Hoffman, E.; Alavi, A.; Sam, P.; Sokoloff, L. The [18 F] Flurodeoxyglucose Method for the measurement of local cerebral glucose utilization in man. *Circulation Research*, pp. 127–37 (1979).

internal carotid with labeled xenon, and thirty-two detectors were spaced over the scalp to record clearance. While normal total hemispheric blood flow was found, chronic schizophrenics tended to have low flow in frontal lobes and higher postcentral flows. Ingvar and Franzen (58, 98) speculated that these high flows in the posterior sylvian and adjacent parietal, occipital, and temporal parasensory areas might be associated with a "hypergnostic" syndrome of unusual elaboration of sensory messages and perceptual disturbance. This speculation parallels both perceptual theories of schizophrenia and possibly evoked-potential and EEG findings. While the xenon technique requires special equipment and a low but nonnegligible risk (138), the report of correlations between high local flow and increased mean scalp EEG frequency (r=0.73) (100) provides not only the opportunity to use a noninvasive measure but also a metabolic interpretation of available EEG findings.

Rheoencephalography based on noninvasive scalp recording of cerebral impedance may offer even better estimates of regional blood flow; while initially the interpretation of the recordings was controversial (129,130,167), recent high correlations with the 133-xenon clearance methods (109) and detailed clinical and physiological investigations (139) give the method greater credibility. In two studies (111,138) using frontal impedance leads, diminished cerebral blood flow was found in schizophrenics. Schizophrenics tended to decrease blood flow following electroshock therapy (EST) in contrast to depressives (140). In patients followed longitudinally, ratings of stuporousness and total disturbance were negatively correlated with cerebral blood flow (137). While these results might be partially attributable to drug effects, Jacquy et al. (110) were not able to demonstrate neuroleptic effects. Reports (27) that amphetamine increases cerebral blood flow are interesting although inconsistent with the usual and nontherapeutic action of these drugs in schizophrenia.

These studies in patients imply a consistent decrement in frontal flow. However, blood flow and mental activity are coupled and respond to tasks. In normal subjects, reading induced an increase in left hemisphere blood flow, as measured by 133-xenon flow (99) or rheoencephalographically, whereas a spatial-perception test increased flow on the right (110). Similarly, 133-xenon measures showed visual tasks giving a dominant hemisphere flow increase in visual areas, such as occipital and temperoparietal cortex, in contrast to auditory digit span backward, yielding posterior temporal, prerolandic, and frontal increases (180). Among highly psychotic schizophrenic patients, frontal blood-flow increases during visual tasks are essentially absent, although postcentral flow increased almost as much as in controls (59).

This lack of frontal-lobe activation is interpreted by Franzen and Ingvar (59) as related to a transmission failure in projection systems to the frontal granular cortex, perhaps the frontocortical medio-thalamic projection bundle. Frontal brain lesions may not only mimic some aspects of the clinical picture of schizophrenia, but they have also been created in a surgical attempt at treatment. More detailed neuropsychological investigations, perhaps using rheoencephalography and evoked potentials as well, are needed to pursue this important new direction in schizophrenia research.

Electromyographic Studies

While neurophysiological approaches to schizophrenia have generally focused on higher functions in the CNS, study of neuromuscular dysfunction appears of increasing relevance. Brain injury or disease processes, including vitamin deficiencies, hereditary metabolic disorders, and brain damage in utero, may damage upper motor-neuron input to lower motor neurons and thus bring about pathological changes in skeletal muscle fibers through tropic mechanisms (148). Evidence of muscle abnormalities in schizophrenics includes elevated skeletal-muscle-enzyme levels in serum, usually indicative of muscle fiber damage, as well as such biopsy evidence of muscle fiber abnormalities as Z-band pathology (52), scattered atrophy of individual muscle fibers, and increased terminal branching (148,149). The increased subterminal branching suggests impairment in some motor neurons, with the remaining intact neurons branching at low levels in order to reinnervate muscle fiber no longer functionally connected. Using single-fiber electromyographic (EMG) techniques, Crayton et al. (36) found increased fiber density in a group of schizophrenic patients, which they interpreted as consistent with reinnervation by collateral sprouting. Motor- and sensory-nerve induction velocities were within the normal range. This abnormal innervation could be one source of impaired motor performance in schizophrenic adults (172) and in children of schizophrenics (53,86,143), including poor reaction time (161) and even smooth-pursuit eye movements (90,212).

Alpha-motor-neuron function can also be assessed using the monosynaptic H(Hoffman)-reflex technique. This reflex can be elicited by electrically stimulating the posterior tibial nerve which innervates both the gastrocnemius and soleus muscles. Sensory fibers predominantly from muscle spindle receptors are activated, and these ascend to the cord where they synapse directly through a single synapse on the alpha motor neuron which, about 35 milliseconds after stimulation, produces a motor response that can be recorded with EMG electrodes. At higher stimulus levels a direct efferent muscle response (M-reflex) can also be recorded, appearing at about 5 milliseconds after stimulation. When two stimuli are presented in sequence, the amplitude of the second H-reflex is altered, depending on the interval between the stimuli, and a recovery curve can be constructed (similar to the technique used by Shagass [208] for evoked potentials) with the ratio of the (H_1/H_2)—first to second response—at each interstimulus interval used as a measure of alpha-motor-neuron excitability. Schizophrenic patients, especially chronics, tend to have a smaller peak of "secondary facilitation" in their H-reflex recovery curve (34,75), which tends to be reversed by phenothiazine administration (69,75). This finding, together with that of increased secondary facilitation in patients with tardive dyskinesia (35) and larger H-reflexes in patients with Parkinson's disease (163) appears to implicate the dopamine system in H-reflex regulation.

Interestingly from the viewpoint of psychological theories of schizophrenia, the H-reflex appears to be strongly modified when the subject shifts his attention. The H-reflex increases while subjects do difficult cognitive or perceptual tasks (4,11,248); it is enhanced by auditory stimuli (184); and in intraindividual analyses it fluctuates with EEG alpha parameters indicative of cortical activation (242).

Pupil Diameter

The widened pupil as a psychophysiological sign of attention was known in Renaissance times to the ladies who dilated their pupils with belladonna, and it has been studied extensively as an indicator of emotional arousal and attention (74,240). This attentional sensitivity, combined with the fact that pupillary diameter is easily measured and affected by three neurotransmitter systems, makes it an especially appropriate physiological technique in schizophrenia research. The size of the pupil is controlled by the dynamic, opposing interaction of the sympathetic adrenergic (dilatation) and parasympathetic cholinergic (constriction) portions of the autonomic nervous system. Pupillary constriction, caused by a bright light, begins with retinal stimulation; the pathway proceeds to the Edinger-Westphal nucleus in the third nerve nuclear complex. From there efferent fibers carry the constriction message to the ciliary ganglion and thence to the sphincter muscle of the iris. Pupillary dilatation pathways are less well known, probably originating in midbrain centers, parts of the cortex, and the hypothalamus and descending to the ciliospinal center in the spinal cord, to the sympathetic superior cervical ganglion, and finally to the dilator muscle of the eye. Dilatation can also occur by inhibition of the Edinger-Westphal nucleus; the pathways are poorly known but probably involve frontal areas (84). These cortical dilatory pathways are probably responsible for the opening of the pupil with arousal and attentional engagement. Sensory filtering appears coupled with dilatation; the pupil opens as information is presented during a short-term memory task, and constricts during a subject's report when sensory input would presumably need suppression (5,62,117). Thus, if schizophrenics have defective sensory filtering, we might expect the reported diminished pupillary-constriction responses to light (84,128,189,191). This characteristic may be shown even when patients are in remission (188,190), which suggests pupillary response as a genetic marker. Considering data drawn from both animal and human psychopharmacological research, Rubin and Barry (191) conclude that supranuclear inhibition of the Edinger-Westphal nucleus and defective central sympathetic outflow are important in this deficit. The importance of supranuclear inhibition would also be most consistent with attentional theories of schizophrenia; Douglas and Pribram (46), Venables (243), and Patterson (166) reviewed the links between cholinergic depletion, hippocampal and amygdaloid function, and sensory filtering deficits.

However, many psychotic patients show excessive or normal constriction, and Rubin (187) emphasized that tests of pupillary dynamics,
in revealing the adrenergic/cholinergic balance, may provide a neurochemical subtyping technique on which individualized pharmacotherapy
may be designed. Cholinergic/adrenergic imbalance as a biochemical
theory of schizophrenia was also advanced by Davis (41), who explored
behavioral effects of physostigmine in schizophrenics.

Phenothiazines also affect pupillary diameter. Both normals and
schizophrenics show smaller pupils on haloperidol (145) and chlorpromazine (192,223). Indeed, pupillometry may provide as accurate a
measure of bioavailability of chlorpromazine as direct assay of blood
levels (223). L-DOPA administered systemically and eyedrops of both
L-DOPA and dopamine cause pupillary dilatation (225,247); but as the
investigators themselves pointed out, these results do not rule out a
central effect of dopamine (see also reference 206).

These findings of attentional effects and prominent individual differences, taken together with the possible therapeutic effects of drugs
like physostigmine which are not in routine clinical use, suggest that
an important neurochemical subgroup of schizophrenics could be identified with pupilography. Combined neurochemical and psychophysiological pupil measurements are needed in therapeutic trials. Contrasts
of cholinergic and adrenergic drugs in the same patients are necessary
to demonstrate the existence of a specific physiological syndrome.

Electroencephalographic Studies

The small, constantly changing electrical potentials that can be recorded from the scalp in man with electronic amplification are termed
the electroencephalogram (EEG). These potentials, usually 1 to 100
microvolts in size and lasting 20 to 300 milliseconds, originate in the
cerebral cortex largely as slow postsynaptic potentials, but subcortical
centers are also important as pacemakers (37). The mix of EEG
frequency changes with mental state; resting subjects show a clear 10-
second sinusoidal oscillation (alpha), which may suddenly block, giving
way to higher frequencies (beta), with sensory stimulation or cognitive
tasks. Slow waves (theta) may appear with drowsiness. Such changes
may be localized. Left parietal fast beta activity is enhanced with reading (165). Nevertheless, in resting subjects, characteristic EEG frequencies emerge and are apparently under genetic control (44,244);
even monozygotic twins reared apart show marked similarities (115).
In addition to such frequency changes, abnormal electrical signs—
including focal sharp waves, high voltage spikes, dysrhythmia and B-mit-
tens—may appear. These signs are associated with specific CNS lesions—
such as tumors, epilepsy, trauma, or anoxia—and are not usually part
of the electrical repertoire of a normal subject's shifting mental tasks.

In reviewing EEG findings in schizophrenics, it may be helpful to differentiate two kinds of findings: organic pathology and functional indicators.

PATHOLOGICAL EEG SIGNS

Pathological EEG signs were early noted in higher incidence in patient populations. Despite careful diagnostic criteria, blind review of both patient and matched control sample EEG, and the use of medication-free samples, the best current studies (1,104) still show these abnormalities in as many as 6 percent to 20 percent of patients diagnosed as schizophrenic, and show high incidences of psychiatric symptoms among "medical" patients with epilepsy (222).

Efforts to relate focal signs, dysrhythmia (1), photo convulsive responses (220), or specific spike patterns to either diagnostic categories (220), schizophrenic subgroups (1), or psychological traits (152) have not been very successful, although the B-mitten pattern (231, 232) appears to differentiate process and reactive schizophrenics.

If, however, rather than beginning with a population of schizophrenics and counting EEG abnormalities, we begin with populations of individuals with EEG abnormalities and examine the appearance of psychoses, more striking findings emerge. Psychiatric patients also seem to have a higher incidence of 6-per-second spike and wave complexes (218). Comparison of fifty "spike" patients with fifty matched patients with normal EEG revealed a less chronic course with fewer suicide attempts, which suggests a spike/psychosis antagonism, which Small confirmed. Again, beginning with groups of patients with and without a specific EEG sign, Small (219) found a clear predominance of affective disorders among patients with sharp spikes. Using a related strategy, Taylor (234) examined patients with temporal lobe epilepsy (diagnoses by EEG). A high percentage showed schizophrenialike symptoms, with left hemisphere involvement carrying a particular risk, which confirmed earlier studies (54, 55). Stevens (229) has suggested that subcortical spiking may occur in some schizophrenics; he based this suggestion on recognition of a specific spectral pattern in scalp EEG seen in animal studies of cats with subcortical eliptogenic foci.

The absence of increased familial incidence of schizophrenia in relatives of temporal lobe epileptics (217) and the greater probability of a family history negative for schizophrenia among schizophrenics with abnormal EEGs (87) support the heterogeneous etiology of schizophrenia. Irritative lesions, perhaps resulting from brain trauma or viral disease, in certain brain areas may cause seizure activity and symptoms of the schizophrenic syndrome; other genetic deficits also apparently result in symptomatically indistinguishable cases. Slater (217) noted that without the EEG findings "one would have no excuse for not diagnosing the patient as schizophrenic," and that the whole range of schizophrenic subtypes was shown.

While the incidence of left temporal lobe epilepsy appears related to schizophrenia, seizure activity itself was inversely related to psychosis

(55). Small (218) also noted an apparent protective interaction with 6-per-second spike and wave phenomena. Possible neuropharmacological contrasts between anticonvulsant therapy and antipsychotic therapy have been proposed. Reynolds (176) noted the antagonistic effects of anticonvulsants on folic acid, and that vitamin B_{12} partially reverses the effects of the drugs on seizures; B_{12} metabolism defects may be related to the transmethylation hypothesis of schizophrenia.

Similarly, in the dopamine system, dopamine blockers such as phenothiazines enhance epileptic seizures in man (136,238) and animals (147), whereas dopamine agonists such as apomorphine or piribedil (147) appear to reduce seizure activity. Reviewing the evidence, Trimble (239) suggested that this reciprocal relationship may explain the apparent antagonism between seizure activity and schizophrenia.

EEG Activity

Rather than relying on visual examination, as is generally done in detecting pathological signs, one may peak resting EEG down into a series of estimates of the amount of activity at each frequency from 1 to 50 Hertz (Hz) (termed "power spectra"). New computational techniques such as the Cooley-Tukey FFT (Fast Fourier Transform) (31) and cheap minicomputers have made spectral analysis widely available, perhaps outstripping advances in understanding the neurophysiology of scalp EEG. It should be noted that such techniques can pass easily through baseline shifts, spikes, muscle activity, calibration marks, and other artifacts, so careful examination of the raw record is necessary. Further, these techniques are based on an underlying model of a number of sine-wave generators, each smoothly waxing and waning; neurophysiological theory supports no such model, and phenomena such as alpha-blocking violate important mathematical assumptions. Nevertheless, as an empirical technique for biological psychiatry, frequency analysis may be quite useful. Power-spectra profiles are stable (105,107) and highly heritable (48,141), and they have been related to specific psychotropic drug action (21,51,104). In the last ten years these sophisticated techniques have tended to confirm earlier observations of increased low-voltage, high-frequency activity in schizophrenics (termed "choppy"). Greater high-frequency activity in the beta range has been found in resting off-medication schizophrenics (104,105,133,181). More fast beta activity was also found in children of schizophrenics (102,107), which tends to rule out artifacts of illness, hospitalization, or past history of drug administration as explanations of this finding. Schizophrenics with greater-rated thought disorder also appear to have higher beta activity and less alpha (196). Slow reaction time, another psychological mark of schizophrenia, also appears in patients during epochs of low alpha, flat-spectrum EEG (229). It is interesting that Vogel (244) proposed a general model of multifactorial inheritance for diffuse beta patterns and note assortative mating—both issues raised in the discussions of the genetics of schizophrenia.

ALPHA ACTIVITY

Schizophrenia patients have generally been reported to show diminished or slower alpha activity,* although not all studies confirmed this (133,193). Alpha may decrease during schizophrenic episodes in patients followed longitudinally (205). These findings seem not to reflect effects of neuroleptics or artifacts of hospitalization, since they appear in off-medication patients (104) and in children of schizophrenic mothers (102,107). Schizophrenics also appear to show faster blocking of alpha by a stimulus (38,153), more prolonged blocking which habituates less (153), and greater effect of eye opening or closing on alpha production (160).

While the neurophysiological mechanisms of alpha generation remain in doubt, empirically enhanced alpha has been associated with relaxation, low information processing, and drug effects related to well-being and heightened mood (51).

These high-beta, low-alpha-frequency findings are consistent with the low-EEG-variability results initially reported by Goldstein et al. (70). Measuring the coefficient of variation (CV) (standard deviation as a percentage of the mean) of the integral of consecutive brief (3–20 sec) segments of EEG, several studies have confirmed low CV values in schizophrenics,† especially those high in thought disorder (196). Haloperidol appears to increase or normalize the CV (169). Intermittent bursts of slow delta activity, probably indicating drowsiness in normal resting individuals (133), or alpha bursts (155) are probably responsible for the high CV in normals. Reasonable test-retest correlations (r=.70) (73) and the finding of reduced variability in children of schizophrenics (102) suggest the measure's utility in genetic studies.

The pattern of high beta and low alpha observed in schizophrenics occurs in normal individuals when sensory stimulation is presented (64) or tasks are performed. Information-processing appears important; alpha is not blocked by light flashes presented to the bad eye of subjects with congenital defects allowing only diffuse light perception (68). Taken together, the EEG findings seem to indicate that the resting schizophrenic is in a habitual state of cortical processing, and they are consistent with the many psychological models of deficient filtering of sensory input.

PSYCHOPHARMACOLOGY AND THE EEG

It is attractive to use human psychopharmacological results and link the low alpha, high beta pattern found in schizophrenics with the dopamine theory of schizophrenia. Thus, the alpha enhancement seen with

---

* See references 65, 101, 104, 153, 181, and 205.
† See references 70, 71, 132, 133, 144, and 155.

L-DOPA administration (251) or dopamine-receptor blocking agents such as haloperidol (101), chlorpromazine (51), or fluphenazine (106) appears to support the dopamine-excess theory of schizophrenia. However, most drug studies have been carried out in patient groups—the very subjects with the postulated biochemical deficit—thus seriously affecting results. Further, as Fink points out (51), control of attention and arousal in the subjects is an essential and frequently missing ingredient in these studies. Different drug dosages may also affect EEG spectra in different ways, as noted for fluphenazine (106).

Most significant from the biological heterogeneity viewpoint of this chapter are reports (101,103) that schizophrenic patients with high-frequency beta and less alpha pretreatment showed better therapeutic response to neuroleptics than did those with rhythmical alpha activity; this suggests that EEG spectra may assist in identifying the dopamine-excess type of schizophrenic.

Evoked Potentials

Like the EEG, sensory evoked-potential (EP) components probably arise largely from postsynaptic potentials fairly close to the cortical surface. Since their size is usually from 10 percent to 50 percent of the spontaneous EEG, they can rarely be directly observed in EEG and are normally recorded with computer techniques which require the averaging of many stimulus presentations (see references 208 and 12 for details). Components coming less than 100 milliseconds after the stimulus tend to be small (2 microvolts or less), appear only over primary areas, and are usually more affected by physical characteristics of the stimulus than by psychological factors. Following these components are a sequence of positive, negative, and positive waves, which occur at 50 to 100, 110 to 140, and 160 to 200 milliseconds and are termed "P100," "N140," and "P200." These components appear in widespread cortical areas, both contralateral and ipsilateral, and are usually of very similar configuration for visual, auditory, and somatosensory stimuli. Their lack of sense-modality specificity and their widespread appearance seem to indicate that they primarily reflect activation of nonspecific cortical systems through cortico-cortico and comissural connections or nonspecific medio-thalamic connections (6). The N140 and P200 components are affected by selective attention, habituation, novelty—all psychological phenomena possibly associated with deficits in schizophrenia. At 300 milliseconds a late positive wave (termed "P300" or "P3") may appear if there is uncertainty about the nature or time of occurrence of the stimulus or even in response to the omission of a stimulus (216,233). And if the subject anticipates the arrival of a second "imperative" stimulus requiring a response (as in a constant foreperiod warned-reaction-time task) a very slow negative wave (termed "contingent negative variation" or "CNV") may follow. This CNV, which peaks at the arrival of the second stimulus, returns to baseline shortly thereafer. Early (211), middle (15), and late (185) EP components are reviewed more extensively elsewhere.

Genetic effects are prominent, with identical twins showing extremely similar EPs—both in amplitude and general waveform (18).

Functional parameters such as the amplitude/stimulus intensity slope also show significant heritability in twin and family studies (13,18,63). Fraternal twins show much lower intraclass correlations than do identical twins—approaching zero for some EP components (13), which suggests multifactorial inheritance. No EP studies in the families of schizophrenics have yet been reported, although families of patients with affective disorders (63) and learning disorders (183) have proved informative.

PHARMACOLOGICAL EFFECTS

EPs are quite sensitive to psychopharmacologic agents, and efforts have been made to relate specific patterns of component change to different drug classes (194,195,210). If specific components can be related to a neurotransmitter system, then EPs possibly could be used to identify individuals off medication with particular neurotransmitter system abnormalities and even to predict drug treatment success. The dopamine system and dopamine-receptor blockers appear especially relevant to schizophrenia. Phenothiazines tend to reduce the amplitude and increase the latency of components at 100 milliseconds and later. In chronic schizophrenics, haloperidol (201), fluphenazine (199), and thiothixene (200), all reduced somatosensory EP amplitude and increased latency, with effects on the P100–N120 component being perhaps the most consistent across studies. This pattern of changes did not appear to be unique to adult chronic schizophrenics, since it was also observed in normal volunteers given 50 milligrams of chlorpromazine (197). Corssen and Domino (33) and Sakalis et al. (192) similarly found little effect of chlorpromazine on early components but significant lengthening of the latency of components after 100 milliseconds. Nakra, Bond, and Lader (159) found prochlorperazine to lengthen N110 (N2) latency in normal volunteers, but they observed no amplitude effects.

A general sedative effect cannot clearly be invoked since minor tranquilizers (e.g., chlordiazepoxide) produced a different pattern of EP results: greater changes in early peak latency and latency decreases for the late peaks (197). CNV amplitude is also decreased by chlorpromazine (236). However, it is not clear whether these EP changes of long latency and decreased amplitude result from the dopamine-receptor-blocker properties of phenothiazines, or whether they may reflect indirect changes caused by other means. The only human study of the dopamine metabolite, homovanillic acid (HVA), in the cerebrospinal fluid (CSF) found high HVA associated with short latencies and high amplitudes (78)—the opposite direction from that expected, since phenothiazines tend to raise CSF HVA (76).

Changes in EPs with amphetamine might be in the opposite direction of phenothiazine effects due to its dopamine-releasing action. Increases in

CNV (120) and P200 of the EP in depressives (19) and hyperactive children (85) were observed, but differences between clinical responders and nonresponders (19,85) and individual differences among normals (235) are prominent. Taken together, the effect of phenothiazines on P100, CSF-HVA correlations with the 90-millisecond component (78), the phenothiazine responder/nonresponder differences for peaks at 69 milliseconds (196), and altered topography of N60 in chronic schizophrenics (214) suggest that a focus on the P100 component and its preceding negative trough might be especially useful in identifying schizophrenic patients for whom some variant of the dopamine hypothesis of schizophrenia is valid.

SENSORY STIMULATION LEVELS

Schizophrenic patients tend to produce smaller amplitude EPs than do nonschizophrenic patients or normal controls even when no active task is required, whether visual (124,173), auditory (113,196,214), or somatosensory stimuli (108,195,214) are used. High levels of sensory stimulation where stimuli are especially intense (124,173), novel (186), or uncertain (125) or are presented rapidly, as in the second number of a pair (213), are particularly effective in differentiating schizophrenics from controls. Information about stimulus arrival, which normally reduces EP amplitude, may not do so in schizophrenics (9), and EP habituation may be reduced (241).

These abnormalities are consistent with a number of theories of schizophrenia (Freud, Pavlov, Mednick, Broen and Storms, Venables) which Epstein and Coleman (50) characterize as assuming "that the basic defect in schizophrenia consists of a low threshold for disorganization under increasing stimulus input." Alternatively, the finding that EP amplitude does not increase with increasing stimulus intensity, novelty, or uncertainty could indicate the operation of compensatory neurophysiological mechanisms protecting the CNS during a period of psychotic illness—for example, stimulus-intensity control (14) or central biasing mechanism (150). The EPs might reflect the inhibitory mechanism of a back-up system, valuable in suppressing incoming sensory signals at a time when cortical cognitive systems normally operative are flooded with internally generated stimuli (154). If this were so, we might expect these protective mechanisms to operate in acute more than in chronic schizophrenics and thus to be possible indicators of prognosis. Shagass (209) found that acute schizophrenics had lower amplitudes, particularly at strong stimulus intensities, in comparison with chronics for the early components of somatosensory EPs; and Schooler, Buchsbaum, and Carpenter (203) report similar findings for P100 in the visual EP. The report that acute schizophrenics who go on to improve without pharmacological treatment are the individuals who initially have smaller amplitudes for high- rather than low-intensity stimuli (124) is also consistent with this formulation. Reduced reactivity at high intensity in comparison with low intensity is also observed in electrodermal responsiveness (42) and is consistent with interpretations of overarousal in schizophrenia (252).

ATTENTION, EXPECTANCY, AND AROUSAL

Selective attention seems to be indexed by the N120 component of the EP (204). Unfortunately no comprehensive series of experiments has yet been carried out with independent measurement of each EP component in a selective-attention paradigm. While a reduction of N100 (186) or N100–P300 (125) was observed to a greater degree under conditions of novelty or uncertainty, selective attention was not specifically manipulated in these studies. The generalized reduction in P100–N140 and P200, seen in studies where merely passive cooperation is required, also suggests that a specific N140 deficit is not present. Late positive waves at 300 milliseconds (P300) were also reduced in schizophrenics in Roth and Cannon's study (186), where rare stimuli were studied and no task was required; in Shagass's study (211), where neither task requirement nor stimulus rarity was manipulated; and in Levit's study (125), where subjects guessed equiprobable stimuli. Thus, the same kind of specific-attention deficits defined in psychophysical studies have not yet clearly been demonstrated using EPs in clinical studies of schizophrenics.

The CNV experiments more closely parallel the reaction time (RT) paradigm used so successfully in demonstrating abnormalities in schizophrenics. In a simple, warned RT task the CNV returns toward zero baseline 100 to 200 milliseconds after the stimulus, but in complex RT tasks the CNV resolution can be delayed. Several studies (142,221,237) have found smaller CNV in schizophrenics with prolonged recovery.* Prominent individual differences in CNVs, both baseline and with amphetamine (235), make it an attractive technique for isolating individuals with specific cognitive deficits. However, since current studies involve patients usually on phenothiazines, the field awaits a combined individual-difference/neuropharmacology approach.

Schizophrenics' responses to perceptual tasks do seem to vary more from trial to trial than do those of normals. High variability might account for diminished habituation seen in schizophrenics by causing continuous dishabituation. High variability might also be associated with the formation of abnormally flat stimulus-generalization gradients (146) as an adaptation to this deficit. Inability to maintain a stable response set, postulated by Shakow (215) to be a general explanation of the psychological deficit in schizophrenics, might produce inordinate variation in perceptual processing.

The EP technique appears initially as an excellent tool for studying perceptual variability. Indeed, studies have linked individual differences in EP variability to perceptual response variability (24,96), and a number of studies have reported greater EP variability in schizophrenics.†

Increased EP variability does not seem to be a product of increased electromyographic activity in schizophrenics, since analysis of the prestimulus epoch produced no variability differences (24). Nor does variability in acoustic input seem entirely crucial. Worden et al. (249) compared variability of auditory EPs in cats when stimuli were presented via overhead speaker or through fitted earphones. Variation was markedly

---

* See references 2, 29, 45, 47, and 237.
† See references 8, 30, 113, 131, 173, 196, and 198.

reduced by the excellent stimulus control achieved with earphones when EPs were obtained from the cochlear nucleus, but little if any change in variability was seen at cortical levels.

Some considerable methodological problems in the interpretation of these studies, however, make it quite unclear whether schizophrenics really have more variable EPs. The appearance of particularly high variability might arise if a subject had especially small EPs in relation to his background EEG—even though his EP was as large or larger than normal. This situation, of a low signal size in comparison with background noise, we term "low signal-to-noise ratio." Techniques for differentiating this from high variability of the individual EP trials have not been fully developed. The problem is further complicated by the possibility that background nontime-locked EEG could well change amplitude in response to a stimulus.

Coppola et al. (32) compared several techniques for estimating signal-to-noise ratio and concluded that it may be easier to measure its trial-by-trial variation than actual signal variability. Buchsbaum and Coppola (16) reported not only lower signal-to-noise ratios in schizophrenics but greater trial-by-trial variability as well. Freedman (60), noting that norepinephrine may both inhibit spontaneous (noise) response and enhance specific (signal) response and the action of fluphenazine on this system, suggested a neurophysiological mechanism linking schizophrenic perceptual disorders to catecholamine regulation through modification of CNS signal-to-noise ratios.

Another link between EP variability and catecholamine-abnormality theories of schizophrenia is the amphetamine model of psychosis. Crucial parts of the amphetamine model include stereotypy, a preoccupation with minutiae, and vigilance—all of which seem allied with decreasing perceptual variability. Whether this conflict between the observed increased EP variability in schizophrenics represents problems with the measurement of EPs or the amphetamine model will require both mathematical and psychopharmacological studies to resolve. The finding of the effect of phenothiazines on the P100 components, the decreased variability for EP components prior to 100 milliseconds (209), and a relationship of slow wave activity to N100 variability (170), all suggest that a careful estimation and characterization of variability for each component may prove valuable.

Eye Movements

Folklore has long linked eye-movement patterns (e.g., "shifty-eyed" or "couldn't look me in the eye") to internal psychological states and attentional processes. Much previous investigation has centered on "saccadic" movements—the quick jerks between steady fixation. These establish new points of regard for sharp foveal viewing, and their sequence gives hints about central processing mechanisms. The extensive dependency of such sequences on subject instruction, motivation, and details of the stimulus configuration makes this technique especially frustrating to schizophrenia researchers. Smooth pursuit movements, a type of slow tracking used in following a moving target, such as a swinging pendulum, have certain advantages which make them especially appropriate for patient studies. Since the movement cannot be generated in the absence of a physical stimulus (at least initially; see references 226 and 227), the record indicates whether the subject was actually engaged in the task. Schizophrenics show unusual deviations in eye tracking while observing a swinging pendulum.* Instead of the smooth sinusoidal pattern seen in normals, schizophrenics evidence an irregular one with many velocity arrests or places where the eye comes to a complete stop. Significantly, a high proportion of first-degree relatives of schizophrenics were also found to show this pattern (93). Within a population of twins of which at least one member was schizophrenic, higher concordances were found for eye movements than for clinical schizophrenia (89,90). While some nonschizophrenic psychiatric patients were reported to show the deficit (92,212), the specificity of the measure was improved when psychological test criteria of thought disorder, rather than clinical diagnoses, were used (93). Phenothiazines did not seem to be responsible for the effect since the medication-free relatives showed the abnormality, and secobarbital, but neither diazepam nor chlorpromazine, caused the abnormality (91). The effects of barbiturates on smooth pursuit appear to be their replacement with saccadic motion (174), rather than the kind of brief, irregular velocity arrests observed in schizophrenics. It is unclear whether this is not also what happens in fatigued normals (10), rather than a true similarity to schizophrenic movements. A specific definition of velocity arrests which separates smooth pursuit irregularities from fixations following saccades (usually thought to be necessarily over 200 msec in duration) is needed to clarify this point beyond merely arguing about tracing characteristics.

Simple fatigue or inattention appear not to be responsible for the Holzman effect, since verbally "realerting" subjects to the task does not influence velocity arrests (89). The maneuver of placing numerals on the pendulum and asking the patient to read them does seem to improve tracking (90,213), but by eliminating saccades more noticeably than the short velocity arrests. Holzman and Levy (90) postulate a disorder of "nonvoluntary attention," described as a "failure of inhibitory synchronizing or integrating systems." Eye movements require very complex integration of eye, head, and body position, with vestibular information to maintain the appearance of stability of the visual scene despite a moving retina; this stability appears better maintained during saccadic than smooth pursuit motions (226). To maintain this stability, cerebellar, brain stem and cortical centers must work together. Oscillatory movements in the velocity range of pursuit movements (termed "nystagmus") occur with lesions in these systems or with non-

* See references 10, 92, 119, 121, 202, 212, and 213.

naturalistic conditions (e.g., unilateral caloric stimulation of the laby-
rinth or observing rotating striped fields). Not only can the vestibular
system influence visual sensations, but the reverse can occur, leading to
a variety of peculiar and even bizarre sensory illusions produced by
ingenious psychophysical procedures (43). Smooth pursuit movements
are also integrated with motor control, as indicated by their generation
by subjects tracking their own hands in the dark (114); links to both
cerebellar and basal ganglia input might relate schizophrenic clumsiness
and dopaminergic excess to pursuit abnormalities.

One such integrative deficit where attentional factors could be involved is the failure to suppress the background behind the swinging
pendulum which traverses the retina in the opposite direction; this
retrograde illusory motion of the background appears with pursuit but
not saccadic movement (230). While normal individuals show little
effect of background stripes behind the swinging target, some patients
with cerebellar disease show tracking patterns not unlike those of the
schizophrenic (94), which disappear when the background is removed.
Thus, the eye-tracking deficit could be part of the larger problem of
distractibility, selective attention, and foreground/background confusion widely reported in the psychological literature.

Do some fraction of schizophrenics have a heretofore unknown and
hereditary form of cerebellar disease, while some schizophrenics show
dysrhythmic nystagmus after caloric stimulation (126)? Other distinctly
cerebellar eye signs—including lateralization of the deficit, slow drift
on lateral fixation, saccadic dysmetria, enhanced caloric response, or
deteriorated optokinetic response—have not been reported as occurring
in conjunction with the smooth pursuit abnormality. Further, the absence of correspondence between vestibular abnormalities and smooth
pursuit abnormalities, reported by Levy et al. (126), tends to rule out
posterior fossa lesions and points toward cortical integrative deficits.

Left Hemispheric Dysfunction and Schizophrenia

The possibility that left hemispheric dysfunction is related to the
schizophrenic syndrome has been suggested in recent reviews (3,56,61).
Clinical evidence includes the association of left temporal epileptic foci
(54,55,234) and left temporal brain damage (134) with schizophrenia
or psychosis. The increased incidence of left-handedness (83,135), left-
footedness (83), and poorly developed hand preference (245) in schizophrenics and psychotics is also consistent with a left hemisphere deficit, since prenatal or perinatal brain damage increases the proportion
of left-handedness (127). Crossed eye/hand dominance has been found
in some schizophrenics (162) but failed to reach statistical significance
in other studies (83,135).

Asymmetrical skin-conductance responses have been found (79,80,

81), which the authors interpreted as representing left limbic malfunction. Venables (243) reviewed these findings and central control of skin-conductance response.

Evoked-potential and EEG findings also tend to support left hemispheric dysfunction in schizophrenics or at least suggest the existence of asymmetries. Low EP waveform stability, found generally in schizophrenics, differed more between the left and the right hemispheres of schizopherics than it did in nonpsychotic patients with especially low left hemisphere stability (182). Normal right hemisphere amplitude superiority for visual EPs (177,178) was not found in schizophrenics (168). Spectral analysis of EEG showed a greater proportion of power in the fast beta (20–30 Hz) range in the left, but not in the right, temporal lobe of schizophrenics in comparison with normals (57). Changes in alpha power, normally associated with lateralized tasks, were missing (57), reduced (3), or even reversed (65), especially in temporal lobe leads. The finding of a significant increase in left temporal alpha power with L-DOPA treatment in patients with Parkinson's disease (251) may implicate the dopaminergic system in the observed alpha-regulation asymmetries. In contrast to these left-sided findings, Itil et al. (107) found a predominance of right-sided temporal EEG differences in children of schizophrenic parents when compared with matched controls.

The relationship of lateralized asymmetry to psychosis may arise from both genetic and perinatal factors. Handedness and cross-dominance appear to be under genetic control (127) and little influenced by cross-fostering (88). Lateralized effects may appear in EEGs of newborns (39). Such lateralized signs could be: (1) genetic markers linked to the "schizophrenia gene"; (2) related in some way to a cortical organization with increased psychiatric vulnerability; or (3) merely of higher incidence in a gene pool with higher frequency of schizophrenia. However, left-handedness and thus right-cortical dominance may also arise as an apparent adaptation to left hemisphere perinatal damage. Lishman and McMeekan (135) suggest that this nongenetic mechanism is the source of the excess left-handed schizophrenics in their sample, since they came primarily from exclusively right-handed families. Also suggesting a nongenetic mechanism, Hays found left-sided EEG abnormalities most prominent among schizophrenics with no family history of schizophrenia. The failure of offspring of schizophrenics to show excess left-handedness or crossed dominance when compared with their matched controls drawn from the National Institute of Neurological and Communicative Disorders and Stroke perinatal study,* despite their higher incidence of neurological soft signs, may be informative. Could the schizophrenia in left-handed schizophrenics be "localized left-hemisphere trauma schizophrenia" and could the offspring of schizophrenic mothers receive instead a genetic vulnerability to nonlocalized brain damage? The finding by Boklage (7) of greater concordance in diagnosis of schizophrenia in right-handed than in left-handed identical twin pairs studied by Gottesman and Shields (77) is also consistent with both a genetic vulnerability

---

* R. Rieder: personal communication.

mechanism (in right-handers) and a trauma or abnormal developmental mechanism (in left-handed schizophrenic twins).

Laterality effects could also arise on the basis of asymmetries in neurochemical mechanisms. Asymmetrical behavioral or psychophysiological effects of stimulants (72,156), L-DOPA (251), and chlorpromazine (72,80,207) indicate that stimulating or blocking the dopamine system can affect left-right differences. Clinically, hemispheric asymmetries in schizophrenics' auditory performance were normalized by chlorpromazine (80), and EEG voltage was observed to increase on the left side both with chlorpromazine treatment and with improvement (207). Further support for an asymmetrical effect of chlorpromazine was the correlation between dose levels (mg/kg) and differences in left-right ear auditory discrimination scores (80). The finding of a higher correlation between evoked-potential amplitude and CSF HVA for the left hemisphere EPs, whereas CSF 5-hydroxyindoleacetic acid showed higher correlations on the right (78), is an intriguing clue that peripheral biochemical indicators might index lateralized processes.

Sleep

Nowhere else in psychobiological research on schizophrenia do clinical, psychological, physiological, and neurochemical hypotheses seem to come together more than in sleep research. The analogies between schizophrenic hallucinations and dreaming sleep in normals are intuitively compelling, and the relationship between sleep stages and neuro-endocrine secretion provide neurochemical entry. Sleep studies usually require a series of all-night recordings of scalp EEG, eye movements, and electromyographic activity. Four different stages of sleep are recognized on the basis of physiological criteria; they range from light sleep (stage I) through deeper slow-wave or delta sleep (stages III and IV). Dreaming appears primarily during stage I and is characterized by loss of muscle tone and conjugate eye movements—hence the name "rapid eye movement" (REM) sleep. Cyclic changes from one sleep stage to another appear throughout the night. Because of the laborious nature of sleep research, requiring all-night monitoring and hand evaluation of sleep records, clinical studies of very small groups of schizophrenics are usually reported. And as I suggested at the beginning of this chapter, specific sleep disturbances present in only a proportion of schizophrenics cannot be detected this way. In a comprehensive review Mendelson et al. (151) concluded that investigators have "failed to establish any unique or even consistent abnormalities in the sleep of schizophrenic patients." Both Mendelson et al. and Reich et al. (175) based their negative conclusions on the contradictory nature of the series of research reports of significant increases, significant decreases, or lack of differences between controls and schizophrenics. Their evaluation is certainly reasonable, but the small sample sizes they used preclude consistent results if schizophrenics are highly heterogeneous. The variety of findings could also indicate great diversity in sleep neurophysiology of psychotic individuals, who are inconsistently diagnosed into schizophrenic or affective groups according to symptom-oriented diagnostic schemes unrelated to underlying neurophysiological deficits. Further, sampling bias due to cooperativeness, ability to remain medication-free, and local factors affecting patient assignment to sleep studies might well interact with individual differences in neurochemistry or arousal neurophysiology and confound sleep-pattern differences.

Shortened REM sleep latency may be an example of a sleep abnormality cutting across diagnostic groups. Reduced most strikingly in primary-affective-disorder patients (123), it was also reported reduced in schizophrenics in some studies (49,82,116,228). The findings that it was especially low in schizo-affectives (175), and that schizophrenic patients with low REM latency tended to require tricyclic antidepressant treatment, suggest that REM latency could index either affective symptoms or a particular biological subgroup of patients. This conclusion is directly supported by the important observation that it is the patients with high levels of homovanillic acid (HVA, dopamine's metabolic product) in their CSF who show short REM latency (122). The findings that infusion of L-DOPA delays REM onset (67), that amphetamine withdrawal increases REM latency (246), that alpha-methyl-para-tyrosine increases REM (250) and its withdrawal decreases sleep (20), all suggest the importance of catecholamines on REM sleep regulation.

If subjects are awakened systematically during REM sleep and thus prevented from having their accustomed amount of it—about 20 percent of the night—on following nights they tend to show increased REM sleep. Two studies (66,253) have found schizophrenics to lack this compensatory or "REM rebound" response. Poor REM compensation may be related to perceptual field dependence, also frequently reported in schizophrenic populations (28,66) and to other personality characteristics (158). Individual differences in amount of REM rebound are prominent (158) and appear to predict which individuals show increases and which show decreases in REM sleep when haloperidol is administered (157).

The greatly contradictory studies of REM sleep and how it is affected by phenothiazines (151) could reflect the occurrence of great heterogeneity in sleep and dopamine systems in patient populations. All these findings on REM latency, percentage, and REM rebound might well have been more impressive if the sleep measures had been used as independent variables and if neurochemical measures had been analyzed in individuals with "REM latency" disease.

The amount of delta, or stage IV, sleep may also be a significant biological indicator. Schizophrenics do tend to have increased slow-wave activity while awake, as has been discussed, but apparently they have reduced delta sleep (22,23,228). Gillin et al. (66) indicated a delta sleep increase after REM deprivation. Low-delta-sleep schizophrenics appeared also to be poor attenders on the continuous performance task (164), again illustrating important individual differences in just those measures closely tied to psychological aspects of schizophrenia.

Conclusion

A basic heterogeneity in the schizophrenic syndrome is suggested by the literature reviewed here. One group of patients appears characterized by brain damage and little family history of schizophrenia; perhaps perinatal trauma or viral etiologies are involved. Epilepsy, unilateral EEG abnormalities, poor motor control, and left-handedness are possible indicators. Another group may be those patients with a stronger genetic pattern and characteristic psychological deficits without the previous neurological features; perhaps an assortment of neurochemical abnormalities are responsible. Yet another group may have uncommon developmental or anatomical deficits associated with psychosis, like Kleinfelter's chromosomal abnormalities or partial agenesis of the corpus callosum. Distinctive clinical symptoms are largely lacking to differentiate these major divisions, and patients are rarely screened by karyotyping, pneumoencephalography, or other expensive, low-yield clinical tests.

At present it may be that EEG features and abnormal lateralization will prove useful for separating out patients with brain trauma etiology and permitting psychopharmacological experiments to be done on the residual. Sleep, pupilometry, and evoked-potential techniques may be most valuable for identifying the dopamine or other neurotransmitter types of schizophrenia and for separating possible mesolimbic, mesocortical, and other dopamine system deficits (148). Especially fruitful if individual etiologies are being explored may be the reversal of the usual independent (clinical) and dependent (biological) variables: "short REM latency psychosis" may be a syndrome more tractable to the biological approach than "withdrawn — bizarre — hallucinating psychosis."

The biological heterogeneity observed is not a cause for despair that biological factors in the schizophrenic syndrome can never be isolated. Instead, it relieves the researcher of the burden of trying to integrate all the conflicting data into a single unitary etiology. So freed, the researcher must apply new strategies to understand each individual's neurobiological and psychosocial problem.

BIBLIOGRAPHY

1. Abenson, M. H. 1970. EEGs in chronic schizophrenia. *British Journal of Psychiatry* 116: 421–25.
2. Abraham, P.; McCallum, W. C.; and Gourlay, J. 1976. The CNV and its relation to specific psychiatric syndromes. In *The responsive brain*, eds. W. C. McCallum and J. R. Knott (Bristol: John Wright), pp. 144–49.
3. Alpert, M., and Martz, M. J., Jr. 1977. Cognitive views of schizophrenia in light of recent

studies of brain asymmetry. In *Psychopathology and brain dysfunction*, eds. C. Shagass, S. Gershon, and A. J. Friedhoff (New York: Raven Press), pp. 1–13.

4. Bathien, N. 1971. Reflexes spinaux chez l'homme et niveaux d'attention. *Electroencephalography and Clinical Neurophysiology* 30:32–37.

5. Beatty, J., and Kahneman, D. 1966. Pupillary changes in two memory tasks. *Psychonomic Science* 5:371–72.

6. Beck, E. C. 1975. Electrophysiology and behavior. *Annual Review of Psychology* 26:233–62.

7. Boklage, C. E. 1977. Schizophrenia, brain asymmetry development, and twinning: Cellular relationship with etiological and possibly prognostic implications. *Biological Psychiatry* 12:19–35.

8. Borge, G. F. 1973. Perceptual modulation and variability in psychiatric patients. *Archives of General Psychiatry* 29:760–63.

9. Braff, D. L.; Callaway, E.; and Naylor, H. 1977. Very short-term memory dysfunction in schizophrenia. *Archives of General Psychiatry* 34:25–30.

10. Brezinova, V., and Kendell, R. E. 1977. Smooth pursuit eye movements of schizophrenics and normal people under stress. *British Journal of Psychiatry* 130:59–63.

11. Brunia, C. H. M. 1971. The influence of a task on the Achilles tendon and Hoffmann reflex. *Physiology and Behavior* 6:367–73.

12. Buchsbaum, M. S. 1970. Average evoked response: Technique and applications. *Schizophrenia Bulletin* 1(3):10–18.

13. Buchsbaum, M. S. 1974. Average evoked response and stimulus intensity in identical and fraternal twins. *Physiological Psychology* 2:365–70.

14. Buchsbaum, M. S. 1976. Self-regulation of stimulus intensity: Augmenting/reducing and the average evoked response. In *Consciousness and self-regulation*, eds. G. E. Schwartz, and D. Shapiro (New York: Plenum Press), pp. 101–35.

15. Buchsbaum, M. S. 1977. The middle evoked response components and schizophrenia. *Schizophrenia Bulletin* 3:93–104.

16. Buchsbaum, M. S., and Coppola, R. Signal-to-noise ratio and response variability in affective disorders and schizophrenia. In *Evoked brain potentials and behavior*, ed. H. Begleiter (New York: Plenum Press), forthcoming.

17. Buchsbaum, M. S.; Coursey, R. D.; and Murphy, D. L. 1976. The biochemical high risk paradigm: Behavioral and familial correlates of low platelet monoamine oxidase activity. *Science* 194:339–41.

18. Buchsbaum, M. S., and Gershon, E. S. Genetic factors in EEG, sleep and evoked potentials. In *Human consciousness and its transformations*, eds. J. Davidson, R. J. Davidson, and G. E. Schwartz (New York: Plenum Press), forthcoming.

19. Buchsbaum, M. S.; Van Kammen, D. P.; and Murphy, D. L. 1977. Individual differences in AER to d- and l-amphetamine with and without lithium carbonate in depressed patients. *Psychopharmacology* 51:129–35.

20. Bunney, W. E., Jr.; Kopanda, R. T.; and Murphy, D. L. 1977. Sleep and behavioral changes possibly reflecting central receptor hypersensitivity following catecholamine synthesis inhibition in man. *Acta Psychiatrica Scandinavica* 56:189–203.

21. Caille, E. J. 1974. Psychotropic drug-induced EEG changes based on power spectrum analysis. In *Psychotropic drugs and the human EEG*, ed. T. M. Itil (Basel: Karger), pp. 99–116.

22. Caldwell, D. F. 1969. Differential levels of stage IV sleep in a group of clinically similar chronic schizophrenic patients. *Biological Psychiatry* 1:131–41.

23. Caldwell, D. F., and Domino, E. F. 1967. Electroencephalographic and eye movement patterns during sleep in chronic schizophrenic patients. *Electroencephalography and Clinical Neurophysiology* 22:414–20.

24. Callaway, E. 1975. *Brain electrical potentials and individual psychological differences* (New York: Grune & Stratton).

25. Callaway, E., and Halliday, R. A. 1973. Evoked potential variability: Effects of age, amplitude and methods of measurement. *Electroencephalography and Clinical Neurophysiology* 34:125–33.

26. Callaway, E.; Jones, R. T.; and Donchin, E. 1970. Auditory evoked potential variability in schizophrenia. *Electroencephalography and Clinical Neurophysiology* 29:121–428.

27. Carlsson, C.; Hagerdal, M.; and Siesjo, B. K. 1975 Influence of amphetamine sulphate on cerebral blood flow and metabolism. *Acta Physiologica Scandinavica* 94:128–29.

28. Cartwright, R. D.; Monroe, L. J.; and Palmer, C. 1967. Individual differences in response to REM deprivation. *Archives of General Psychiatry* 16:297–303.

29. Chouinard, G.; Annable, L.; and Dongier, M. 1977. Differences in psychopathology in schizophrenic patients with normal and abnormal postimperative negative variation (PINV). *Comprehensive Psychiatry* 18:83–87.

30. Cohen, R. 1973. The influence of task-relevant stimulus variations on the reliability of auditory evoked responses in schizophrenia. In *Average evoked responses and their conditioning in normal subjects and psychiatric patients*, eds. A. Fessard and G. LeLord (Paris: Inserm), pp. 373–88.

31. Cooley, J. W., and Tukey, J. W. 1965. An algorithm for the machine calculation of complex fourier series. *Mathematics of Computation* 19:297–301.

32. Coppola, R.; Tabor, R.; and Buchsbaum, M. S. 1978. Signal-to-noise ratio and response variability measurements in single-trial evoked potentials. *Electroencephalography and Clinical Neurophysiology*, 44(2):214–22.

33. Corssen, G., and Domino, E. F. 1964. Visually evoked responses in man: A method for measuring cerebral effects of preanesthetic medication. *Anesthesiology* 25:330–41.

34. Crayton, J. W.; Meltzer, H. Y.; and Goode, D. J. 1977. Motorneuron excitability in psychiatric patients. *Biological Psychiatry* 12:545–61.

35. Crayton, J. W.; Smith, R. C.; Klass, D.; Chang, S.; and Ericksen, S. E. 1977. Electrophysiological (H-reflex) studies of patients with tardive dyskinesia. *American Journal of Psychiatry* 134:775–81.

36. Crayton, J. W.; Stalberg, E.; and Hilton-Brown, P. 1977. The motor unit in psychotic patients: A single fibre EMG study. *Journal of Neurology, Neurosurgery and Psychiatry* 40:455–63.

37. Creutzfeldt, O., ed. 1974. The neuronal generation of the EEG. In *Handbook of EEG and clinical neurophysiology*, ed., A. Redmond, vol. 2, part C (Amsterdam: Elsevier), pp. 5–55.

38. Cromwell, R. L., and Held, J. M. 1969. Alpha blocking, latency and reaction time in schizophrenics and normals. *Perceptual and Motor Skills* 29:195–201.

39. Crowell, D. H.; Jones, R. H.; Kapuniai, L. E.; and Nakagawa, J. K. 1973. Unilateral cortical activity in newborn humans: An early index of cerebral dominance? *Science* 180:205–8.

40. Davidson, K., and Bagley, C. R. 1969. Schizophrenia-like psychoses associated with organic disorders of the central nervous system: A review of the literature. In *Current problems in Neuropsychiatry*, ed. R. N. Herrington (Ashford, Kent: Headley Bros.).

41. Davis, J. M. 1975. Critique of single amine theories: Evidence of a cholinergic influence in the major mental illnesses. In *Biology of the major psychoses: A comparative analysis*, ed. D. X. Freedman (New York: Raven Press), pp. 333–46.

42. Depue, R. A., and Fowles, D. C. 1976. Electrodermal activity and schizophrenia: The problem of stimulus intensity modulation. *Psychological Bulletin* 83:192–93.

43. Dichgans, J., and Brandt, T. 1972. Visual-vestibular interaction and motion perception. *Biblioteca Ophthalmologica* 82:327–38.

44. Dieker, H. 1967. Untersuchungen zur genetik besonders regelmabiger hoher alpha-wellen im EEG des menschen. *Humangenetik* 4:189–216.

45. Dongier, M.; Dubrovsky, B.; and Garcia-Rill, E. 1974. Les potentiels cérébraux lents en psychiatrie. *Canadian Psychiatric Association Journal* 19:177–83.

46. Douglas, R. J., and Pribram, K. H. 1966. Learning and limbic lesions. *Neuropsychologia* 4:197–220.

47. Dubrovsky, B., and Dongier, M. 1976. Evaluation of event-related slow potentials in selected groups of psychiatric patients. In *The responsive brain*, eds. W. C. McCallum and J. R. Knott (Bristol: John Wright), pp. 150–53.

48. Dumermuth, G. 1968. Variance spectra of electroencephalograms in twins. In *Clinical electroencephalography of children*, eds. P. Kellaway and I. Petersen (New York: Grune & Stratton), pp. 119–54.

49. Durrigl, V.; Buranji, I.; and Stojanovic, V. 1973. Characteristics of paradoxical sleep in schizophrenic patients. In *Sleep: Physiology, biochemistry, psychology, pharmacology, clinical implications*, First European Congress of Sleep Research, eds. W. P. Koella et al. (Basel: Karger), pp. 587–91.

50. Epstein, S., and Coleman, M. 1970. Drive theories of schizophrenia. *Psychosomatic Medicine* 32:113–40.

51. Fink, M. 1974. EEG profiles and bioavailability measures of psychoactive drugs. In *Psychotropic drugs and the human EEG*, ed. T. M. Itil (Basel: Karger).

52. Fischman, D. A.; Meltzer, H. Y.; and Poppei, R. W. 1970. Disruption of myofibrils in the skeletal muscle of psychotic patients. *Archives of General Psychiatry* 23:503–15.

53. Fish, B., and Hagin, R. 1973. Visual motor disorders in infants at risk for schizophrenia. *Archives of General Psychiatry* 28:900–904.

54. Flor-Henry, P. 1969. Psychosis and temporal lobe epilepsy. A controlled investigation. *Epilepsia* 10:363–95.

55. Flor-Henry, P. 1969. Schizophrenic-like reactions and affective psychoses associated with temporal lobe epilepsy: Etiological factors. *American Journal of Psychiatry* 126:399–505.

56. Flor-Henry, P. 1974. Psychosis, neurosis, and epilepsy. *British Journal of Psychiatry* 124:144–50.

57. Flor-Henry, P.; Koles, Z. J.; Bo-Lassen, P.; and Yeudall, L. T. 1975. Studies of the functional psychoses: Power spectral EEG analysis. *IRCS Medical Science; Biomedical Technology; Neurology and Neurosurgery; Psychiatry and Clinical Psychology* 3:87.

58. Franzen, G.; and Ingvar, D. H. 1975. Abnormal distribution of cerebral activity in chronic schizophrenia. *Journal of Psychiatric Research* 12:199–214.

59. Franzen, G., and Ingvar, D. H. 1975. Absence of activation in frontal structures during psychological testing of chronic schizophrenics. *Journal of Neurology, Neurosurgery and Psychiatry* 38:1027–32.

60. Freedman, R. 1977. Interactions of antipsychotic drugs with norepinephrine and cerebellar neuronal circuitry: Implications for the psychobiology of psychosis. *Biological Psychiatry* 12:181–97.

61. Galin, D. 1974. Implications for psychiatry of left and right cerebral specialization. A neurophysiological context for unconscious processes. *Archives of General Psychiatry* 31:572–83.

62. Gardner, R. M.; Beltramo, J. S.; and Krinsky, R. 1975. Pupillary changes during encoding, storage, and retrieval of information. *Perceptual and Motor Skills* 41:951–55.

63. Gershon, E. S., and Buchsbaum, M. S. 1977. A genetic study of average evoked response augmenting/reducing in affective disorders. In *Psychopathology and brain dysfunction*, eds. C. Shagass, S. Gershon, and A. J. Friedhoff (New York: Raven Press), pp. 279–90.

64. Giannitrapani, D. 1971. Scanning mechanisms and the EEG. *Electroencephalography and Clinical Neurophysiology* 30:139–46.

65. Giannitrapani, D., and Kayton, L. 1974. Schizophrenia and EEG spectral analysis. *Electroencephalography and Clinical Neurophysiology* 36:377–86.

66. Gillin, J. C.; Buchsbaum, M. S.; Jacobs, L. S.; Fram, D. H.; Williams, R. B., Jr.; Vaughan, T. B., Jr.; Mellon, E.; Snyder, F.; and Wyatt, R. J. 1974. Partial REM sleep deprivation, schizophrenia and field articulation. *Archives of General Psychiatry* 30:643–62.

67. Gillin, J. C.; Post, R. M.; Wyatt, R. J.; Goodwin, F. K.; Snyder, F.; and Bunney, W. E., Jr. 1973. REM inhibitory effect of L-dopa infusion during human sleep. *Electroencephalography and Clinical Neurophysiology* 35:181–86.

68. Glass, J. D. 1977. Alpha blocking: Absence in visubehavioral deprivation. *Science* 298:59–60.

69. Glotzner, F. L., and Mattke, D. J. 1972. The action of neuroleptic drugs on the motor system in man. *Pharmakopsychiatry* 5:82–93.

70. Goldstein, L.; Murphree, H. B.; Sugerman, A. A.; Pfeiffer, C. C.; and Jenney, E. H. 1963. Quantitative electroencephalographic analysis of naturally occurring (schizophrenic) and drug-induced psychotic states in human males. *Clinical Pharmacology and Therapeutics* 4:10–21.

71. Goldstein, L., and Pfeiffer, C. C. 1969. Quantitative electroencephalographic correlates of the psychological status in schizophrenics. In *Schizophrenia: Current concepts and research*, ed. D. V. Siva Sankar (New York: PJD Publications), pp. 236–55.

72. Goldstein, L., and Stoltzfus, N. W. 1973. Psychoactive drug-induced changes of inter-hemispheric EEG amplitude relationships. *Agents and Actions* 3:124–32.

73. Goldstein, L.; Sugerman, A. A.; Stolberg, H.; Murphree, H. B.; and Pfeiffer, C. C. 1965. Electro-cerebral activity in schizophrenics and non-psychotic subjects: Quantitative EEG amplitude analysis. *Electroencephalography and Clinical Neurophysiology* 19:350–61.

74. Goldwater, B. C. 1972. Psychological significance of pupillary movements. *Psychological Bulletin* 77:340–55.

75. Goode, D. J.; Meltzer, H. Y.; Crayton, J. W.; and Mazura, T. A. 1977. Physiologic abnormalities of the neuromuscular system in schizophrenia. *Schizophrenia Bulletin* 3:121–38.

76. Goodwin, F. K., and Post, R. M. 1975. Studies of amine metabolites in affective illness and in schizophrenia: A comparative analysis. In *The biology of the major psychoses: A comparative analysis*, ed. D. X. Freedman (New York: Raven Press), pp. 299–332.

77. Gottesman, I. I., and Shields, J. 1972. *Schizophrenia and genetics—A twin study vantage point* (New York: Academic Press).

78. Gottfries, C. G.; Perris, C.; and Roos, B. E. 1974. Visual average evoked responses (AER) and monoamine metabolites in cerebrospinal fluid (CSF). *Acta Psychiatrica Scandanavica* 255:135–41.

79. Gruzelier, J. 1973. Bilateral asymmetry of skin conductance orienting activity and levels in schizophrenics. *Biological Psychology* 1:21–41.

80. Gruzelier, J., and Hammond, N. 1976. Schizophrenia: A dominant hemisphere temporal-limbic disorder? *Research Communications in Psychology, Psychiatry and Behavior* 1:33–72.

81. Gruzelier, J., and Venables, P. 1974. Bimodality and lateral asymmetry of skin conductance orienting activity in schizophrenics: Replication and evidence of lateral asymmetry in patients with depression and disorders of personality. *Biological Psychiatry* 8:55–73.

82. Gulevich, G.; Dement, W.; and Zarcone, V. 1967. All-night sleep recordings of chronic schizophrenics in remission. *Comprehensive Psychiatry* 8:141–49.

83. Gur, R. E. 1977. Motoric laterality imbalance in schizophrenia. *Archives of General Psychiatry* 34:33–37.

84. Hakerem, G., and Lidsky, A. 1975. Characteristics of pupillary reactivity in psychiatric patients and normal controls. In *Experimental approaches to psychopathology*, eds. M. L. Kietzman, S. Sutton, and J. Zubin (New York: Academic Press), pp. 61–72.

85. Halliday, R.; Rosenthal, J. H.; Naylor, H.; and Callaway, E. 1976. Averaged evoked potential predictors of clinical improvement in hyperactive children treated with methylphenidate: An initial study and replication. *Psychophysiology* 13:429–40.

86. Hanson, D. R.; Gottesman, I. I.; and Heston, L. L. 1976. Some possible childhood indicators of adult schizophrenia inferred from children of schizophrenics. *British Journal of Psychiatry* 129:142–54.

87. Hays, P. 1977. Electroencephalographic variants and genetic predisposition to schizophrenia. *Journal of Neurology, Neurosurgery and Psychiatry* 40:753–55.

88. Hicks, R. E., and Kinsbourne, M. 1976. Human handedness: A partial cross-fostering study. *Science* 192:908–10.

89. Holzman, P. S.; Kringlen, E.; Levy, D. L.; Proctor, L. R.; Haberman, S. J.; and Yasillo, N. J. 1977. Abnormal-pursuit eye movements in schizophrenia. *Archives of General Psychiatry* 34:802–5.

90. Holzman, P. S., and Levy, D. L. 1977. Smooth pursuit eye movements and functional psychoses: A review. *Schizophrenia Bulletin* 3:15–27.

91. Holzman, P. S.; Levy, D. L.; Uhlenhuth, E. H.; Proctor, L. R.; and Freedman, D. X. 1975. Smooth-pursuit eye movements, and diazepam, CPZ, and secobarbital. *Psychopharmacologia* (Berlin) 44:111–15.

92. Holzman, P. S.; Proctor, L. R.; and Hughes, D. W. 1973. Eye-tracking patterns in schizophrenia. *Science* 181:179–81.

93. Holzman, P. S.; Proctor, L. R.; Levy, D. L.; Yasillo, N. J.; Meltzer, H. Y.; and Hurt, S. W. 1974. Eye-tracking dysfunctions in schizophrenic patients and their relatives. *Archives of General Psychiatry* 31:143–51.

94. Hood, J. D. 1975. Observations upon the role of the peripheral retina in the execution of eye movements. *Journal for Oto-Rhino-Laryngology and its Borderlands* 37:65–73.

95. Hoyer, S., and Oesterreich, K. 1975. Blood flow and oxidative metabolism of the brain in patients with schizophrenia. *Psychiatria Clinica* 8:304–13.

96. Inderbitzen, L. B.; Buchsbaum, M. S.; and Silverman, J. 1970. EEG-averaged evoked response and perceptual variability in schizophrenics. *Archives of General Psychiatry* 23:438–44.

97. Ingvar, D. H. 1974. Distribution of cerebral activity in chronic schizophrenia. *Lancet* 2:1484–86.

98. Ingvar, D. H., and Franzen, G. 1974. Abnormalities of cerebral blood flow distribution in patients with chronic schizophrenia. *Acta Psychiatrica Scandanavica* 50:425–62.

99. Ingvar, D. H., and Schwartz, M. S. 1974. Blood flow patterns induced in the dominant hemisphere by speech and reading. *Brain Research* 97:273–88.

100. Ingvar, D. H.; Sjolund, B.; and Ardo, A. 1976. Correlation between dominant EEG frequency, cerebral oxygen uptake and blood flow. *Electroencephalography and Clinical Neurophysiology* 41:268–76.

101. Itil, T. M. 1974. Computerized EEG findings in schizophrenia and effects of neuroleptic drugs. In *Biological mechanisms of schizophrenia and schizophrenia-like psychoses*, eds. H. Mitsuda and T. Fukuda (Tokyo: Igakushoin).

102. Itil, T. M. 1977. Qualitative and quantitative EEG findings in schizophrenia. *Schizophrenia Bulletin* 3:61–79.

103. Itil, T. M.; Marasa, J.; Saletu, B.; Davis, S.; and Mucciardi, A. N. 1975. Computerized EEG: Predictor of outcome in schizophrenia. *Journal of Nervous and Mental Disease* 160:188–203.

104. Itil, T. M.; Saletu, B.; and Davis, S. 1972. EEG findings in chronic schizophrenics based on digital computer period analysis and analog power spectra. *Biological Psychiatry* 5:1–13.

105. Itil, T. M.; Saletu, B.; Davis, S.; and Allen, M. 1974. Stability studies in schizophrenics and normals using computer-analyzed EEG. *Biological Psychiatry* 8:321–35.

106. Itil, T. M.; Saletu, B.; Hsu, W.; Kiremitci, N.; and Keskiner, A. 1971. Clinical and quantitative EEG changes at different dosage levels of fluphenazine treatment. *Acta Psychiatrica Scandinavica* 47:440–51.

107. Itil, T. M.; Saletu, B.; Hsu, W.; and Mednick, S. 1974. Computer EEG and auditory evoked potential investigations in children at high risk for schizophrenia. *American Journal of Psychiatry* 131:892–900.

108. Ivanitsky, A. M., and Strelets, V. B. 1973. Comparative study of somatosensory evoked potentials in patients with reactive psychosis and schizophrenia. *Zhurnal Nevropathologii Psikhiatrii* 73:79–82.

109. Jacquy, J.; Dekoninck, W. J.; Piraux, A.; Calay, R.; Bacq, J.; Levy, D.; and Noel, G. 1974. Cerebral blood flow and quantitative rheoencephalography. *Electroencephalography and Clinical Neurophysiology* 37:507–11.

110. Jacquy, J.; Piraux, A.; Jocquet, P.; Lhoas, J. P.; and Noel, G. 1977. Cerebral blood flow in the adult blind: A rheoencephalographic study of cerebral blood flow changes during braille reading. *Electroencephalography and Clinical Neurophysiology* 43:325–29.

111. Jacquy, J.; Wilmotte, J.; Piraux, A.; and Noel, G. 1976. Cerebral blood flow patterns studied by rheoencephalography in schizophrenia. *Neuropsychobiology* 2:94–103.

112. Jones, R. T.; Blacker, K. H.; Callaway, E.; and Layne, R. S. 1965. The auditory evoked response as a diagnostic and prognostic measure in schizophrenia. *American Journal of Psychiatry* 122:33–41.

113. Jones, R. T., and Callaway, E. 1970. Auditory evoked responses in schizophrenia—a reassessment. *Biological Psychiatry* 2:291–98.

114. Jordan, S. 1970. Ocular pursuit movement as a function of visual and proprioceptive stimulation. *Vision Research* 10:775–80.

115. Juel-Nielsen, N., and Harvald, B. 1958. The electroencephalogram in uniovular twins brought up apart. *Acta Genetica et Statistica Medica* 8:57–64.

116. Jus, K.; Bouchard, M.; Jus, A. K.; Villeneuve, A.; and Lachance, R. 1973. Sleep EEG studies in untreated, long-term schizophrenic patients. *Archives of General Psychiatry* 29:386–90.

117. Kahneman, D., and Beatty, J. 1966. Pupil diameter and load on memory. *Science* 154: 1583–85.

118. Kety, S. S.; Woodford, R. B.; Harmel, M. H.; Freyhan, F. A.; Appel, K. E.; and Schmidt, C. F. 1948. Cerebral blood flow and metabolism in schizophrenia. *American Journal of Psychiatry* 104:765–70.

119. Klein, R. H.; Salzman, L. F.; Jones, F.; and Ritzler, B. 1976. Eye tracking in psychiatric patients and their offspring. *Psychophysiology* 13:186.

120. Kopell, B. S.; Wittner, W. K.; Lunde, D. T.; Wolcott, L. J.; and Tinklenberg, J. R. 1974. The effects of amphetamine and secobarbital on the contingent negative variation amplitude. *Psychopharmacologia* 34:55–62.

121. Kuechenmeister, C. A.; Linton, P. H.; Mueller, T. V.; and White, H. B. 1977. Eye tracking in relation to age, sex, and illness. *Archives of General Psychiatry* 34:578–79.

122. Kupfer, D. J., and Bowers, M. B., Jr. 1972. REM sleep and central monoamine oxidase inhibition. *Psychopharmacologia* (Berlin) 27:183–90.

123. Kupfer, D. F., and Foster, F. G. 1975. The sleep of psychotic patients: Does it all look alike? In *Biology of the major psychoses: A comparative analysis*, ed. D. X. Freedman (New York: Raven Press), pp. 143–64.

124. Landau, S. G.; Buchsbaum, M. S.; Carpenter, W.; Strauss, J.; and Sacks, M. 1975. Schizophrenia and stimulus intensity control. *Archives of General Psychiatry* 32:1239–45.

125. Levit, R. A.; Sutton, S.; and Zubin, J. 1973. Evoked potential correlates of information processing in psychiatric patients. *Psychological Medicine* 3:487–94.

126. Levy, D. L.; Holzman, P. S.; and Proctor, L. R. 1978. Vestibular responses in schizophrenia. *Archives of General Psychiatry* 35(8):972–81.

127. Levy, J. 1975. A review of evidence for a genetic component in the determination of handedness. *Behavior Genetics* 6:429–53.

128. Lidsky, A.; Hakerem, G.; and Sutton, S. 1971. Pupillary reactions to single light pulses in psychiatric patients and normals. *Journal of Nervous and Mental Disease* 153:286–91.

129. Lifshitz, K. 1963. Rheoencephalography: I. Review of the technique. *Journal of Nervous and Mental Disease* 136:388–98.

130. Lifshitz, K. 1963. Rheoencephalography: II. Survey of clinical applications. *Journal of Nervous and Mental Disease* 137:285–96.

131. Lifshitz, K. 1969. Intra- and inter-individual variability and the averaged evoked potential in normal and chronic schizophrenic subjects. *Electroencephalography and Clinical Neurophysiology* 27:688–89.

132. Lifshitz, K., and Gradijan, J. 1972. Relationships between measures of the coefficient of variation of the mean absolute EEG voltage and spectral intensities in schizophrenic and control subjects. *Biological Psychiatry* 5:149–63.

133. Lifshitz, K., and Gradijan, J. 1974. Spectral evaluation of the electroencephalogram: Power and variability in chronic schizophrenics and control subjects. *Psychophysiology* 11:479–90.

134. Lishman, W. A. 1966. Psychiatric disability after head injury: The significance of brain damage. *Proceedings of the Royal Society of Medicine* 59:261–66.

135. Lishman, W. A., and McMeekan, R. L. 1976. Hand preference patterns in psychiatric patients. *British Journal of Psychiatry* 129:158–66.

136. Logothetis, J. 1967. Spontaneous epileptic seizures and electroencephalographic changes in the course of phenothiazine therapy. *Neurology* 17:869–77.

137. Lovett-Doust, J. W. 1976. Cerebral circulation and EEG frequency in relation to daily fluctuations in psychotic behavior. *Journal of Nervous and Mental Disease* 162:158–68.

138. Lovett-Doust, J. W.; Kolesar, G. S.; and Dixon, L. M. 1976. Carotid-vertebral artery blood transit time: Results in healthy subjects and patients with schizophrenia and brain disease. *Biological Psychiatry* 11:697–707.

139. Lovett-Doust, J. W., and Lovett-Doust, J. N. 1975. Aspects of the cerebral circulation during non-REM sleep in healthy controls and psychiatric patients, as shown by rheoencephalography. *Psychophysiology* 12:493–98.

140. Lovett-Doust, J. W., and Raschka, L. B. 1975. Enduring effects of modified ECT on the cerebral circulation in man. *Psychiatria Clinica* 8:293–303.

141. Lykken, D. T.; Tellegen, A.; and Thorkelson, K. 1974. Genetic determination of EEG frequency spectra. *Biological Psychology* 1:245–59.

142. McCallum, W. C., and Abraham, P. 1973. The contingent negative variation in psychosis. In *Event-related slow potentials of the brain: Their relations to behavior*, eds. W. C. McCallum and J. R. Knott (New York: Elsevier).

143. Marcus, J. 1974. Cerebral functioning in offspring of schizophrenics. *International Journal of Mental Health* 3:57–73.

144. Marjerrison, G.; Krause, A. E.; and Keogh, R. P. 1968. Variability of the EEG in schizophrenia: Quantitative analysis with a modulus voltage integrator. *Electroencephalography and Clinical Neurophysiology* 24:35–41.

145. Mattke, Von D. J., and Wisuschil, W. 1976. Eine Methode zur Untersuchung der Pupillomotorik unter dem Einfluß Neuroleptischer Medikation [A method of examining pupillomotorics under the influence of neuroleptic medication]. *Arzneien-Forsch* [Drug Research] 26:946–50.

146. Mednick, S. A. 1955. Distortions in the gradient of stimulus generalization related to cortical brain damage and schizophrenia. *Journal of Abnormal Psychology* 51:536–42.

147. Meldrum, B.; Anlezark, G.; and Trimble, M. 1975. Drugs modifying dopaminergic activity and behavior, the EEG and epilepsy in Papio Papio. *European Journal of Pharmacology* 32:203–13.

148. Meltzer, H. Y. 1976. Neuromuscular dysfunction in schizophrenia. *Schizophrenia Bulletin* 2:106–35.

149. Meltzer, H. Y., and Crayton, J. W. 1974. Muscle abnormalities in psychotic patients. II. Serum CPK activity, fibre abnormalities and branching and sprouting of sub-terminal nerves. *Biological Psychiatry* 8:191–208.

150. Melzack, R. 1973. The puzzle of pain (New York: Basic Books).

151. Mendelson, W. B.; Gillin, J. C.; and Wyatt, R. J. 1977. *Human sleep and its disorders* (New York: Plenum Press).

152. Milstein, V., and Small, J. G. 1971. Psychological correlates of 14 and 6 positive spikes, 6/second spike-wave, and small sharp spike transients. *Clinical Electroencephalography* 2(4):206–12.

153. Milstein, V.; Stevens, J.; and Sachdev, K. 1969. Habituation of the alpha attenuation response in children and adults with psychiatric disorders. *Electroencephalography and Clinical Neurophysiology* 26:12–18.

154. Mirsky, A. F. 1969. Neurophysiological bases of schizophrenia. *Annual Review of Psychology* 20:321–48.

155. Murphree, H. B., and Schultz, R. E. 1969. Computer time-series frequency analysis of the electroencephalograms of male nonpsychotic and chronic schizophrenic subjects. In *Schizophrenia: Current concepts and research*, ed. D. V. S. Sankar (Hicksville, N.Y.: PJD Publications).

156. Murphy, E. H., and Venables, P. H. 1971. The effects of caffeine citrate and white noise on ear asymmetry in the detection of two clicks. *Neuropsychologia* 9:27–32.

157. Nakazawa, Y.; Kotorii, M.; Kotorii, T.; Ohshima, M.; and Hasuzawa, H. 1977. Individual variations in response of human REM sleep to amitryptyline and haloperidol. *Electroencephalography and Clinical Neurophysiology* 42:769–75.

158. Nakazawa, Y.; Kotorii, M.; Kotorii, T.; Tachibana, H.; and Nakano, R. 1975. Individual differences in compensatory rebound of REM sleep, with particular reference to their relationship to personality and behavioral characteristics. *Journal of Nervous and Mental Disease* 161:18–25.

159. Nakra, B. R. S.; Bond, A. J.; and Lader, M. H. 1975. Comparative psychotropic effects of metoclopramide and prochlorperazine in normal subjects. *Journal of Clinical Pharmacology* 17:449–54.

160. Nideffer, R. M.; Deckner, W.; Cromwell, R. L.; and Cash, T. F. 1971. The relationship of alpha activity to attentional sets in schizophrenia. *Journal of Nervous and Mental Disease* 152:346–52.

161. Nuechterlein, K. H. 1977. Reaction time and attention in schizophrenia: A clinical evaluation of the data and theories. *Schizophrenia Bulletin* 3:373–428.

162. Oddy, H. C., and Lobstein, T. J. 1972. Hand and eye dominance in schizophrenia. *British Journal of Psychiatry* 120:331–32.

163. Olsen, P. Z., and Diamantopoulos, E. 1967. Excitability of spinal motor neurones in normal subjects and patients with spasticity, Parkinsonian rigidity, and cerebellar hypotonia. *Journal of Neurological and Neurosurgical Psychiatry* 30:325–31.

164. Orzack, M. H.; Hartmann, E. L.; and Kornetsky, C. 1977. The relationship between attention and slow-wave sleep in chronic schizophrenia. *Psychopharmacology* 13:59–60.

165. Osborne, K., and Gale, A. 1976. Bilateral EEG differentiation of stimuli. *Biological Psychology* 4:185–96.

166. Patterson, T. 1976. Skin conductance recovery and pupillometrics in chronic schizophrenia. *Psychophysiology* 13:189–95.

167. Perez-Borja, C., and Meyer, J. S. 1964. A critical evaluation of rheoencephalography in control subjects in proven cases of cerebrovascular disease. *Journal of Neurology and Neuro-Psychiatry* 27:66–72.

168. Perris, C. 1974. Averaged evoked responses (AER) in patients with affective disorders. *Acta Psychiatrica Scandinavica*, supp., 255:89–98.

169. Pfeiffer, C. C.; Goldstein, L.; and Sugerman, A. A. 1968. Effects of parenteral administration of haloperidol in man. II. Male chronic schizophrenics: Quantitative EEG findings. *Journal of Clinical Pharmacology* 8:89–94.

170. Pfurtscheller, G. 1976. Variability of cortical evoked responses in man related to slow wave activity. *European Journal of Physiology* 362:193–99.

171. Posner, J. B. 1972. Newer techniques of cerebral blood flow measurement. *Stroke* 3:227–37.

172. Quitkin, F.; Rifkin, A.; and Klein, D. F. 1976. Neurologic soft signs in schizophrenia and character disorders. *Archives of General Psychiatry* 33:845–53.

173. Rappaport, M.; Hopkins, H. K.; Hall, K.; Belleza, T.; and Hall, R. A. 1975. Schizophrenia and evoked potentials: Maximum amplitude, frequency of peaks, variability and phenothiazine effects. *Psychophysiology* 12:196–207.

174. Rashbass, C. 1961. The relationship between saccadic and smooth tracking eye movements. *Journal of Physiology* 159:326–38.

175. Reich, L.; Weiss, B. L.; Coble, P.; McPartland, R.; and Kupfer, D. J. 1975. Sleep disturbance in schizophrenia. *Archives of General Psychiatry* 32:51–55.

176. Reynolds, E. H. 1968. Epilepsy and schizophrenia: Relationship and biochemistry. *Lancet* 1(7539):398–401.

177. Rhodes, L. E.; Dustman, R. E.; and Beck, E. C. 1969. The visual evoked response: A comparison of bright and dull children. *Electroencephalography and Clinical Neurophysiology* 27: 364–72.

178. Rhodes, L. E.; Obitz, F. W.; and Creel, D. 1975. Effect of alcohol and task on hemispheric asymmetry of visually evoked potentials in man. *Electroencephalography and Clinical Neurophysiology* 38:561–68.

179. Rieder, R. O., and Gershon, E. S. 1978. Genetic strategies in biological psychiatry. *Archives of General Psychiatry* 35(7):866–73.

180. Risberg, J., and Ingvar, D. H. 1973. Patterns of activation in the grey matter of the dominant hemisphere during memorizing and reasoning. *Brain* 96:737–56.

181. Rodin, E.; Grisell, J.; and Gottlieb, J. 1968. Some electrographic differences between chronic schizophrenic patients and normal subjects. In *Recent advances in biological psychiatry*, ed. J. Wortis (New York: Plenum Press), vol. 10.

182. Roemer, R. A.; Shagass, C.; Straumanis, J. J.; and Amadeo, M. 1977. Pattern evoked potential measurements suggesting lateralized hemispheric dysfunction in chronic schizophrenics. *Biological Psychiatry* 12:221–35.

183. Ross, J. J.; Childers, D. G.; and Perry, N. W. 1973. The natural history and electrophysiological characteristics of familial language dysfunction. In *The disabled learner*, eds. P. Satz and J. J. Ross (Rotterdam: Rotterdam University Press).

184. Rossignol, S., and Jones, G. M. 1976. Audio-spinal influence in man studied by the H-reflex and its possible role on rhythmic movements synchronized to sound. *Electroencephalography and Clinical Neurophysiology* 41:83–92.

185. Roth, W. T. 1977. Late event-related potentials and psychiatry. *Schizophrenia Bulletin* 3: 105–20.

186. Roth, W. T., and Cannon, E. H. 1972. Some features of the auditory evoked response in schizophrenics. *Archives of General Psychiatry* 27:466–71.

187. Rubin, L. S. 1976. Sympathetive-parasympathetic imbalance as a diagnostic concomitant of schizophrenia: Implications for pharmacotherapy. *Research Communications in Psychology, Psychiatry and Behavior* 1:73–89.

188. Rubin, L. S., and Barry, T. J. 1970. Dysautonomia in schizophrenic remission. *Psychosomatics* 11:506–12.

189. Rubin, L. S., and Barry, T. J. 1972. The effects of conjunctival instillation of erserine and homatropine on pupillary reactivity in schizophrenics. *Biological Psychiatry* 5:257–69.

190. Rubin, L. S., and Barry, T. J. 1972. The reactivity of the iris muscle as an index of autonomic dysfunction in schizophrenic remission. *Journal of Nervous and Mental Disease* 155: 265–76.

191. Rubin, L. S., and Barry, T. J. 1976. Amplitude of pupillary contraction as a function of intensity of illumination in schizophrenia. *Biological Psychiatry* 11:267–82.

192. Sakalis, G.; Curry, S. H.; Mould, G. P.; and Lader, M. H. 1972. Physiological and clinical effects of chlorpromazine and their relationship to plasma level. *Clinical Pharmacology and Therapeutics* 13:931–46.

193. Salamon, I., and Post, J. 1965. Alpha blocking and schizophrenia. *Archives of General Psychiatry* 13:367–74.

194. Saletu, B. 1974. Classification of psychotropic drugs based on human evoked potentials. In *Psychotropic drugs and the human EEG*, ed. T. M. Itil (Basel: Karger).

195. Saletu, B. 1977. The evoked potential in pharmacopsychiatry. *Neuropsychobiology* 3:75–104.

196. Saletu, B.; Saletu, M.; and Itil, T. M. 1971. Auditory evoked response, EEG, and thought process in schizophrenics. *American Journal of Psychiatry* 128:336–44.

197. Saletu, B.; Saletu, M.; and Itil, T. M. 1972. Effect of minor and major tranquilizers on somatosensory evoked potentials. *Psychopharmacologia* (Berlin) 24:347–58.

198. Saletu, B.; Saletu, M.; and Itil, T. M. 1973. The relationships between psychopathology and evoked responses before, during, and after psychotropic drug treatment. *Biological Psychiatry* 6:46–74.

199. Saletu, B.; Saletu, M.; Itil, T. M.; and Hsu, W. 1971. Changes in somatosensory evoked potentials during fluphenazine treatment. *Pharmakopsychiatrie Neuro-Psychopharmakologie* 4(3): 158–68.

200. Saletu, B.; Saletu, M.; Itil, T. M.; and Jones, J. 1971. Somatosensory-evoked potential changes during thiothixene treatment in schizophrenic patients. *Psychopharmacologia* (Berlin) 20: 242–52.

201. Saletu, B.; Saletu, M.; Itil, T. M.; and Marasa, J. 1971. Somatosensory-evoked potential changes during haloperidol treatment of chronic schizophrenics. *Biological Psychiatry* 3(4):229–307.

202. Salzman, L. F.; Klein, R. H.; and Strauss, J. S. Pendulum eye-tracking in remitted psychiatric patients. *Journal of Psychiatric Research*, in press.

203. Schooler, C.; Buchsbaum, M. S.; and Carpenter, W. T. 1976. Evoked response and

kinesthetic measures of augmenting/reducing in schizophrenics: Replications and extensions. *Journal of Nervous and Mental Disease* 163:221–32.

204. Schwent, V. L.; Snyder, E.; and Hillyard, S. A. 1976. Auditory evoked potentials during multichannel selective listening: Role of pitch and localization cues. *Journal of Experimental Psychology* 2:313–25.

205. Scott, D. F., and Schwartz, M. S. 1975. EEG features of depressive and schizophrenic states. *British Journal of Psychiatry* 126:408–13.

206. Sears, M. L. 1975. Catecholamines in relation to the eye. In *Handbook of physiology. Endocrinology,* eds. R. O. Greep and E. B. Astwood (Washington, D.C.: American Physiological Society).

207. Serafetinides, E. A. 1972. Laterality and voltage in the EEG of psychiatric patients. *Diseases of the Nervous System* 33:622–23.

208. Shagass, C. 1972. *Evoked brain potentials in psychiatry* (New York: Plenum Press).

209. Shagass, C. 1973. Evoked response studies of central excitability in psychiatric disorders. In *AER and their conditioning in normal subjects and psychiatric patients,* eds. A. Fessard and G. LeLord (Paris: Inserm).

210. Shagass, C. 1974. Effects of psychotropic drugs on human evoked potentials. In *Psychotropic drugs and the human EEG,* ed. T. M. Itil (Basel: Karger).

211. Shagass, C. 1977. Early evoked potentials. *Schizophrenia Bulletin* 3:80–92.

212. Shagass, C.; Amadeo, M.; and Overton, D. A. 1974. Eye-tracking performance in psychiatric patients. *Biological Psychiatry* 9:245–60.

213. Shagass, C.; Roemer, R. A.; and Amadeo, M. 1976. Eye-tracking performance and engagement of attention. *Archives of General Psychiatry* 33:121–25.

214. Shagass, C.; Straumanis, J. J.; Roemer, R. A.; and Amadeo, M. 1977. Evoked potentials of schizophrenics in several sensory modalities. *Biological Psychiatry* 12:221–35.

215. Shakow, D. 1977. Segmental set—The adaptive process in schizophrenia. *American Psychologist* 32:129–39.

216. Simson, R.; Vaughan, H. G.; and Ritter, W. 1976. The scalp topography of potentials associated with missing visual or auditory stimuli. *Electroencephalography and Clinical Neurophysiology* 40:33–42.

217. Slater, E. 1969. The schizophrenia-like illness of epilepsy. In *Current problems in neuropsychiatry schizophrenia, epilepsy, the temporal lobe,* ed. R. N. Herrington (Ashford, Kent: Headley Bros.).

218. Small, J. G. 1968. The six per second spike and wave: A psychiatric population study. *Electroencephalography and Clinical Neurophysiology* 24:561–68.

219. Small, J. G. 1970. Small sharp spikes in a psychiatric population. *Archives of General Psychiatry* 22:277–84.

220. Small, J. G. 1971. Photoconvulsive and phytomyoclonic responses in psychiatric patients. *Clinical Electroencephalography* 2:78–88.

221. Small, J. G., and Small, I. F. 1971. Contingent negative variation (CNV) correlations with psychiatric diagnosis. *Archives of General Psychiatry* 25:550–54.

222. Small, J. G.; Small, I. F.; and Hayden, M. P. 1966. Further psychiatric investigations of patients with temporal and nontemporal lobe epilepsy. *American Journal of Psychiatry* 123:303–10.

223. Smolen, V. F.; Murdock, H. R., Jr.; and Williams, E. J. 1975. Bioavailability analysis of chlorpromazine in humans from pupilometric data. *Journal of Pharmacology and Experimenttal Therapeutics* 195:404–15.

224. Sokoloff, L.; Reivich, M.; Potlock, C. S.; Pettigrew, K. D.; DesRosiers, M.; and Kennedy, C. 1974. The 14C-deoxyglucose method for quantitative determination of local cerebral glucose consumption. *Transactions of American Society of Neurochemistry* 5:85.

225. Spiers, A. S. D.; Calne, D. B.; Vakil, S. D.; and French, T. M. 1971. Action of thymoxamine on mydriasis induced by levodopa and dopamine. *British Medical Journal* 2:438–39.

226. Steinbach, M. J. 1976. Pursuing the perceptual rather than the retinal stimulus. *Vision Research* 16:1371–76.

227. Steinman, R. M., and Skavenski, A. A. 1969. Voluntary control of smooth pursuit velocity. *Vision Research* 9:1167–71.

228. Stern, M.; Fram, D. H.; Wyatt, R.; Grinspoon, L.; and Tursky, B. 1969. All-night sleep studies of acute schizophrenics. *Archives of General Psychiatry* 20:470–77.

229. Stevens, J. R. 1976. Computer analysis of the telemetered EEG in the study of epilepsy and schizophrenia. *Acta Neurochirurgica,* supp. 23:71–84.

230. Stoper, A. E. 1973. Apparent motion of stimuli presented stroboscopically during pursuit movement of the eye. *Perception and Psychophysics* 13:201–11.

231. Struve, F. A., and Becka, D. R. 1968. The relative incidence of the b-mitten EEG pattern in process and reactive schizophrenia. *Electroencephalography and Clinical Neurophysiology* 24:80–82.

232. Struve, F. A.; Becka, D. R.; and Klein, D. F. 1972. B-mitten EEG pattern and process and reactive schizophrenia. *Archives of General Psychiatry* 26:189–92.

233. Sutton, S. 1967. Information delivery and the sensory evoked potential. *Science* 155:1436–38.

234. Taylor, D. C. 1975. Factors influencing the occurrence of schizophrenia-like psychosis in patients with temporal lobe epilepsy. *Psychological Medicine* 5:249–54.

235. Tecce, J. J., and Cole, J. O. 1974. Amphetamine effects in man: Paradoxical drowsiness and lowered brain activity (CNV). *Science* 185:451–53.

236. Tecce, J. J.; Cole, J. O.; and Savignano-Bowman, J. 1975. Chlorpromazine effects on brain activity (contingent negative variation) and reaction time in normal women. *Psychopharmacologia* (Berlin) 43:293–95.

237. Timsit-Berthier, M.; Delaunoy, J.; Koninckx, N.; and Rousseau, J. C. 1973. Slow potential changes in psychiatry. I. Contingent negative variation. *Electroencephalography and Clinical Neurophysiology* 35:355–61.

238. Toone, B. K., and Fenton, G. W. 1977. Epileptic seizures induced by psychotropic drugs. *Psychological Medicine* 7:265–70.

239. Trimble, M. 1977. The relationship between epilepsy and schizophrenia: A biochemical hypothesis. *Biological Psychiatry* 12:299–304.

240. Tryon, W. W. 1975. Pupilometry: A survey of sources of variation. *Psychophysiology* 12: 90–93.

241. Tueting, P., and Levit, R. A. 1977. Long-term changes in evoked potentials of normals, psychotic depressives and schizophrenics. In *Progress in clinical neurophysiology*, ed. J. Desmedt (Basel: Karger).

242. Van Boxtel, A. 1976. The relation between monosynaptic spinal reflex amplitudes and some EEG alpha activity parameters. *Electroencephalography and Clinical Neurophysiology* 40:297–305.

243. Venables, P. H. 1977. The electrodermal psychophysiology of schizophrenics and children at risk for schizophrenia: Controversies and developments. *Schizophrenia Bulletin* 3:28–48.

244. Vogel, F. 1970. The genetic basis of the normal human electroencephalogram (EEG). *Humangenetik* 10:91–114.

245. Walker, H. A., and Birch, H. G. 1970. Lateral preference and right-left awareness in schizophrenic children. *Journal of Nervous and Mental Disease* 151:341–51.

246. Watson, R.; Hartmann, E.; and Schildkraut, J. J. 1972. Amphetamine withdrawal: Affective state, sleep patterns, and MHPG excretion. *American Journal of Psychiatry* 129:39–45.

247. Weintraub, M. I.; Gaasterland, D.; and Van Woert, M. H. 1970. Pupillary effects of levodopa therapy. *New England Journal of Medicine* 283:120–23.

248. Willer, J. C.; Bathien, N.; Singer, B.; and Lavallard, M. C. 1975. A propos d'un cas d'épilepsie électivement déclenchée par la lecture: Effets de tests d'attention et d'épreuves de lecture sur l'EEG et sur le réflexe "H." *Electroencephalography and Clinical Neurophysiology* 39: 421–24.

249. Worden, F. G.; Marsh, J. T.; Abraham, F. D.; and Whittleley, J. R. B. 1964. Variability of evoked auditory potentials and acoustic input control. *Electroencephalography and Clinical Neurophysiology* 17:524–30.

250. Wyatt, R. J.; Chase, T. N.; Kupfer, D. J.; Scott, J.; Snyder, F.; Sjoerdsma, A.; and Engel, K. 1971. Brain catecholamines and human sleep. *Nature* 233:63.

251. Yaar, I. 1977. EEG power spectral changes secondary to L-dopa treatment in Parkinsonian patients: A pilot study. *Electroencephalography and Clinical Neurophysiology* 43:111–18.

252. Zahn, T. P. 1977. Autonomic nervous system characteristics possibly related to a genetic predisposition to schizophrenia. *Schizophrenia Bulletin* 3:49–60.

253. Zarcone, V.; Azumi, K.; Dement, W.; Gulevich, G.; Kraemer, H.; and Pivik, T. 1975. REM phase deprivation and schizophrenia. *Archives of General Psychiatry* 32:1431–36.

Chapter 5

STUDIES OF PSYCHOLOGICAL
FUNCTIONS IN SCHIZOPHRENIA

A. I. Rabin, Ph.D., Stuart L. Doneson, M.A., and
Ricky L. Jentons, M.A.

Studies of schizophrenia in general, and psychological studies in particular, show the tendency toward "sprawl" which was observed in our previous review (349). Although, as will be seen subsequently, some areas are currently stressed to a lesser extent while others show a proliferation of studies, the general outline of the present report will not differ markedly from that of the previous one. Excluded from this chapter are "family studies," which receive detailed attention in chapter 7 in this volume.

In his epilogue to the last volume on the schizophrenic syndrome, Bellak (25) felt "fairly certain that purely psychogenic factors will be demonstrated to play the primary role in the etiology and pathogenesis in about 50 percent of all schizophrenic pathology." One might have hoped that many psychologists would rise to this challenge and direct their efforts to understanding the "failure of psychogenic ego development" and to the investigation of "poor superego structure." However, these tasks were undertaken by an extremely limited number of investigators whose theoretical perspective is consonant with the variables just mentioned (23,24,25).

Experimental psychologists involved in schizophrenia research have for the most part shown that schizophrenics, as compared with normals, have a greater tendency toward stimulus avoidance, an inability to maintain set or attention, a deficit in generalizing and categorizing ability, and poor involvement in experimental tasks (especially those involving social stimuli) and, are socially withdrawn and subject to disturbed autonomic nervous system functioning. This summary reported in a recent National Institute of Mental Health monograph (302) is appropriately capped by the statement that "major questions remain about variability, reliability and etiological significance of the findings." Essentially much of this research extends and deepens, and also objectifies, the description of the syndrome but does not clearly point to causality. The studies are for the most part cross-sectional rather than longitudinal (or even retrospective). The latter direction is a trend we proposed and wished to encourage in our previous review of the schizophrenic syndrome (349).

Indirectly many of the experimental studies are concerned with "failure of psychogenic ego development," but they hardly fit into any kind of unitary conceptual framework—a desideratum stressed also in Bannister's (14) theoretical article on schizophrenia.

Intellectual Functioning

There has been a considerable decline in the number of reports that deal with intellectual functioning based on standard intelligence tests. A trend to the study of cognitive functioning by means of special methods has to a great extent replaced the more conventional approaches, as we shall see in the subsequent sections of this review.

Developmental trends of IQs in schizophrenics have interested several investigators. Upon a reassessment of earlier findings, Lane and Albee (239) found a decline in the intellectual function from early to later childhood in persons who later became schizophrenic. Studies by Offord and coworkers (320,321) indicate that schizophrenics with low IQs in childhood tend to have an earlier onset, perform more poorly in school, and are institutionalized for longer periods than schizophrenics of average intelligence. There are also marked sex differences in IQ and early school performance, favoring the females. Finally, it was interesting to note that the IQs of children of schizophrenics are significantly higher than those of their parents (240).

As might be expected, and consonant with earlier reports, reactive schizophrenics score higher on intelligence tests than process schizophrenics (373,376). This sort of result is not surprising in view of some of the data reported in the previous paragraph.

Comparisons of intellectual functioning of schizophrenics with organics, using tests from the Halstead battery, indicated that the brain-damaged are significantly inferior to the schizophrenics and medical patients, while no significant differences were noted between the latter two groupings. On the other hand, variability in performance in several Wechsler Intelligence Scale for Adults (WAIS) subtests did not discriminate between schizophrenics and organics (469).

A recent review (167) of studies of WAIS patterns and comparative intellectual functioning in subgroups of schizophrenic and other disorders does not conclude with an optimistic note. The authors feel that

it is doubtful that anything will be accomplished by comparing groups composed of wide ranges of whatever gross characteristic is being explored (e.g., schizophrenia, organicity, personality disorder, etc.) which are also accompanied by wide ranges of demographic variables. Not only are these characteristics not diagnostic specific, but they are not present to the same degree in patients who carry the same diagnosis. [p. 324]

It appears that the road to understanding the schizophrenic syndrome as well as to its better definition is less via the ready-made tests and more in the direction of the investigation of more specialized processes described in subsequent sections of this review. This is not to deny the usefulness of patterns, scatter, and microanalysis of responses in the individual case study.

Cognitive Processes

Of all the subareas of psychological research into schizophrenia, none has received more lavish attention than that of language and cognitive processes. In spite of a proliferation of variables, methods, and designs that render careful comparisons of findings embarrassingly difficult, there is solid evidence that some investigators have grown increasingly sophisticated in their appreciation of the logical and methodological requirements of such research (14,75). In addition, there is a pervasive trend away from the more global study of "thought disorder" and "schizophrenic language" toward the molecular analysis of stable behavior deficits as the royal road to identifying the specific mechanisms involved in schizophrenic cognitive and linguistic performance. Operating on the assumption that science proceeds not by mere accumulation of data, but by the assimilation and integration of programatic research into increasingly differentiated theories, atheoretical pieces and "one shot" opportunistic raids on the domain will be largely disregarded in this review. But regardless of whether data are selected at the so-called molar or molecular levels, this discussion will highlight the theoretical frameworks and guiding hypotheses which undergird specific studies.

DEVELOPMENTAL THEORIES OF COGNITION

While clinical work is often conceptualized in terms of developmental regressions of various kinds (145), these concepts have proved refractory to empirical testing. Mindful of the slipperiness and ambiguity of the wholesale use of regression theories, several current lines of research have attempted to arrive at more adequate theoretical restatements of the regression hypothesis and to develop more subtle and sophisticated ways of putting them to experimental test.

PSYCHOANALYTICALLY ORIENTED STUDIES

Operating within a theoretical framework that draws heavily on psychoanalytic ego psychology and object relations theorizing, as well as on academic psychologies of cognitive development, Blatt and his associates* have called attention to the vicissitude of object constancy and

---

° See references 40, 41, 42, 43, 50, 51, 347, and 348.

boundary disturbance as an important key to schizophrenic thought and language disorder. In a series of studies they have focused on the schizophrenic's inability to differentiate, articulate, and represent boundaries. They theorize that the incapacity to maintain separation between independent objects and the representations of these objects, between internal experience and external objects and events, results in various degrees of fusion, merging, and contamination in the structural aspects of thought and perception. By ordering these varying degrees of boundary disturbance on a developmental continuum, it has been possible to discriminate three levels of boundary confusion on the Rorschach, corresponding to three types of formal primary-process thinking within the psychotic range. In order of increasing severity these are "fabulized combinations," "confabulations," and "contaminations." Patients with greater disturbance in representing boundaries on the Rorschach (i.e., with higher proportion of contaminations) showed significantly less cognitive and affective control, greater use of overinclusive and underinclusive thinking, less interpersonal involvement and disruptive behavior, and more disruptions of representations of human figures. In a related study (51) the manifest dream content of schizophrenic subjects was reported to exhibit a greater degree of boundary disruption (specifically contaminations and also confabulations, and fabulized combinations) than did the manifest dreams of nonschizophrenic patients.

In another study (40) Werner's (470) developmental principles of "differentiation," "articulation," and "integration" were used to analyze the formal properties of object representation in normal and schizophrenic patients. When analyzed in these terms, the human-figure references on the Rorschach exhibited consistent positive change with development as well as differential impairment related to the severity of psychopathology. Patients' representations of human figures were significantly more distorted, partial, and inaccurately perceived. In addition, they were seen as inert or involved in unmotivated, nonspecific, and malevolent activity. Malevolent content was related to realistic perceptions; more benevolent content was associated with unrealistic perceptions.

These studies constitute an ongoing program of research that combines a lively interest in clinical phenomena with an appreciation of the interplay of empirical research and theory building. If anything, some of these studies suffer from characteristic design failures that beset so much research in this area. For one thing, there is little indication of whether nonmedicated subjects were used. For another, in some instances schizophrenic patients are compared to normals without always controlling for effects of hospitalization or presence of disturbance in other pathological groups.

PIAGETIAN STUDIES

Since a recurring complaint about research on schizophrenic thought concerns the continuous proliferation of "data" without commensurate theoretical integration, it is not surprising that some investigators have chosen Piaget's theory of cognitive development as a framework broad enough to encompass schizophrenic functioning as well as normal cognitive development. If anything, it is surprising that in the past more attention has not been given to this potentially fruitful approach.

In an attempt to provide a theoretical explanation for the reported cognitive differences between process and reactive schizophrenics, it was hypothesized that the former would use less complex and advanced cognitive structures than the latter (217). Using the Lunger Analogies Test—a Piagetian instrument designed to measure the formal operations of normal adult thought—it was found that normals scored significantly higher than reactive subjects, who in turn did significantly better than process subjects. These differences held up even when WAIS vocabulary scores were statistically controlled.

Another Piagetian study (424) focused on the relationship between concrete operational thinking and the pattern of schizophrenic psychopathology. On several tests of conservation and on geometric drawings, acute subjects outperformed chronic nonparanoid subjects. However, differences between chronic paranoids and nonparanoids were not significant. Both of these studies suffer from failure to provide information about current medication. In addition, the latter study is weakened by an unsystematic method of assigning subjects to schizophrenic subtypes. In spite of these limitations it would appear that Piagetian concepts and methods hold the promise of playing a larger integrating role in future research in schizophrenic cognitive development.

OTHER STUDIES OF THE DEVELOPMENTAL AND REGRESSION HYPOTHESIS

Even in the absence of specific allegiances to an overarching theoretical framework, research continues to be generated on the assumption that process and reactive schizophrenics are at different levels of maturation in some or all modes of functioning (343). DeWolfe (110) presented a careful review of eleven well-controlled studies of schizophrenic cognitive functions bearing on the regression hypothesis. He proposed that while process schizophrenics are idiosyncratic and underdeveloped in their thinking, the cognitive deficit of reactive schizophrenics is due to the fragmentation of relatively normal thinking under stress conditions—resulting in cognitive performance regressing to the level of process schizophrenics or below. While the studies DeWolfe reviewed provided tentative support for his hypothesis, he acknowledged the necessity for further research on the differential effects of stress as well as for "greater conceptual differentiation" of dimensions of cognitive performance.

In another study Dewolfe (110) showed that paranoid schizophrenics gave significantly fewer responses typical of children in the Gottesman Forced Choice Word Association technique than did nonparanoid schizophrenics. This finding was taken to support the hypothesis that paranoid schizophrenics are less regressed than nonparanoid schizophrenics. It is of interest that these results did not hold up for the process-reactive subgroupings, which suggests the importance of the paranoid-nonparanoid dimensions. In this connection Witkin's report (477) that paranoid schizophrenics are more field independent than nonparanoids, as well as the theorizing of Freeman et al. (144), Zucker (488), and Blatt and Wilds (42) theorizing about the rigidity of ego boundaries in paranoid pathology, provide additional conceptual differentiation of DeWolfe's finding. However, with the exceptions of field articulation, an extensive study of cognitive controls and psychopathology (326) failed to find distinctively different organizations of cognitive controls between schizophrenics and other psychiatric patients, regardless of whether schizophrenics were grouped according to paranoid-nonparanoid, process-reactive, or acute-chronic dimensions. Rather, the authors attributed differences in subclasses of schizophrenics to each person's enduring response characteristics that antedate the manifestation of pathology. In this sense, cognitive style variables represent underlying traits reflecting individual consistencies, rather than the specific effects of schizophrenic disorganization. The relationship between the degree of regression and the state of schizophrenic disorganization within specific cognitive styles has yet to be experimentally clarified. In spite of its longevity, the regression hypothesis, or one of its variants, provides a conceptual toehold on the theoretical issues raised by Holzman's thoughtful and clarifying analysis (188).

LOSS OF ABSTRACT THINKING

Since the seminal studies in the loss of abstract thinking by Vygotsky and Goldstein the investigation of concept-formation deficits has promised to provide the key to understanding schizophrenic cognition. Although numerous criticisms have been leveled at imprecision in both the methods and the interpretation of such studies (275), research continues to appear using the abstract-concrete dimension as a critical variable. Several studies report that the capacity to respond abstractly is related to intelligence and not diagnosis (136,172). More interesting have been the alternative hypotheses advanced to reinterpret the rich clinical data reported by Goldstein and others. Thus, one line of research[*] has provided evidence that the deficiencies of schizophrenics on proverbs tests can be better accounted for by autistic, bizarre, and idiosyncratic interpretations than by concrete literalness. Some data suggest that while process schizophrenics are more concrete than reactives (172,463), reactives are more autistic than process schizophrenics. However, measures of conceptual plasticity (metalog test) did not correlate with the process-reactive dimension (66).

THE OVERINCLUSION HYPOTHESIS

There seems to be no abatement in the flow of studies dealing with the "overinclusion hypothesis"—that is, the tendency to respond to a larger number of objects than properly belong to a given set (originally described by Cameron and Payne). Consistent with other research de-

[*] See references 172, 357, 405, 408, 463, 465, and 466.

velopments in the area of schizophrenia cognition, the most conspicuous trends in the past decade were the attempts to criticize and refine the concept of overinclusion; to compare and contrast the effects of alternative methodologies; and to examine the differential use of overinclusive thinking by various subtypes of schizophrenics.

Thus, Lloyd (254) criticized Payne's use of proverb word count as an adequate indication of so complex a phenomenon as overinclusion. Similarly, the concept of overinclusion has been taken to task as too broad and heterogeneous, as giving inadequate attention to the performance requirements embedded in the experimental tasks (202,343, 355). Other researchers (174) have distinguished three types of overinclusion based on the different phenomena studied by different experimental tasks—namely, "behavioral overinclusion," "conceptual overinclusion," and "stimulus overinclusion." More recent investigations suggest that this latter is principally a deficit in attention rather than in concept formation (172,173). Behavioral overinclusion—based on the quantitative aspects of the subject's overt behavior (e.g., the number of objects sorted in an object-sorting test)—was correlated at both the acute phase and the posthospital phase of treatment for schizophrenic as well as nonschizophrenic patients. Schizophrenics did not differ from nonschizophrenics at either point (59). Moreover, differences have been found in the discriminating power of behavioral versus conceptual overinclusion; that is, in addition to the number of objects sorted, the concepts used by the subject also involve overinclusive thinking (174), with conceptual overinclusion significantly more frequent in acute schizophrenics than in nonschizophrenic patients, and behavioral overinclusion more frequent in schizophrenics but also found in many acute nonschizophrenic patients. These findings also suggest some slippage between the experimental operation and the underlying thought process it purports to measure, and thereby raises questions about the use of behavioral overinclusion as an important index of schizophrenic thought disorder. High energy, drive, and attendant overactivity (174), as well as overresponsiveness, have been proposed as alternative hypotheses for behavioral overinclusion (176) (compare references 75, 86, and 87).

Other studies have concentrated upon the relationships between overinclusive thinking as it relates to the different subtypes of schizophrenia. Thus, "classical" schizophrenic patients showed more overinclusive thinking at the time of hospital admission than did latent and nonschizophrenic patients. However, another study (403) found that schizophrenic patients did not experience significantly more stimulus overinclusion than did other patients. Similarly, manic patients were found to exhibit significantly more overinclusive thinking than schizophrenic patients on two of the three tests of Payne's battery (6). Although schizophrenics were more overinclusive than normal controls, overinclusiveness per se does not appear to be specific to schizophrenia (2).

The evidence for the relationship between paranoid delusions and overinclusive thinking remains inconclusive (178). In two studies Foulds and his coworkers (137,138) found that paranoid schizophrenics performed more abnormally than nonparanoid schizophrenics on the Payne

Object Classification task, thus supporting Payne's original hypothesis that overinclusion is the basis for delusional thinking. Unfortunately other research has not fully borne this out (254).

It appears that an adequate assessment of the relations between subtypes of schizophrenics and the forms of overinclusion still remain a task for future research.

THE "LOOSE CONSTRUING" HYPOTHESIS

Among investigators, Bannister (13,14) has long argued for the scientific importance of using well-articulated theoretical frameworks to guide research and to meaningfully organize data, instead of relying on ad hoc notions and minitheorems. Taking his own advice, Bannister and his associates have used George Kelly's (215) personal construct theory as a means of coordinating the common clinical features of schizophrenic thought disorder. Specifically Bannister has proposed that thought-disordered schizophrenics lack the stable constructs necessary to predict regularities in events. Failure to show consistencies in using constructs—what Bannister called "loose construing"—has distinguished thought-disordered schizophrenics from nonthought-disordered schizophrenics as well as from other pathological groups and from normals (13,14,15,16). As in so many other areas of research in schizophrenia, more recent studies of loose construing have attempted further to differentiate, refine, and criticize the dimensions of the concepts and methods involved (145,198,269,471). The upshot has been heated controversy regarding the alleged interrelationships among intensity, consistency, social deviation, element consistency, and element allocation on the Bannister-Fransell Grid Test. That this ongoing debate—especially in British journals—might rest on differential performances of different subgroups of schizophrenics remains an intriguing possibility.

Another major focus of Bannister's work has been to demonstrate that thought-disordered schizophrenics differ from normals in the consistency of their construal of people but show no differences in construing inanimate objects (180,268,270,271). This finding is consonant with Bannister's "serial invalidation" hypothesis concerning the nature of schizophrenic thought disorder—namely, that the schizophrenic has had a history of repeated invalidations in predicting from his construal systems, in spite of attempts to alter them, so that his constructs become "loose" and idiosyncratic, especially when construing other (important) people (13,272). In this regard Bannister's findings dovetail with the body of research reporting that schizophrenics demonstrate greater thought disorder with affective and interpersonal stimuli than with neutral and solitary ones (5,74,345) (but compare reference 168). Although there is considerable evidence to support this claim, the overall picture is muddied by failures to match the complexity and difficulty of affective and neutral stimuli. Nevertheless, the possibility that all or some subgroups of schizophrenics respond differentially to affective stimuli is too important a finding to let slip away due to faulty methodology.

PSYCHOLINGUISTIC THEORIES

Inevitably studies of schizophrenic cognition must rely on the language and/or behavior of schizophrenics as the source of data. Psycholinguistic approaches may be characterized by their special concern with the grammar of schizophrenic language, with specific interest in its semantic and syntactic dimensions. Of such studies the research program of Freedman and his associates has been the most ambitious, the most productive, and the most interesting.*

LANGUAGE CONSTRUCTION STUDIES

In a series of studies based on assumptions derived from Piaget's and Chomsky's discussions of language, Steingart and Freedman have described a method for analyzing the formal aspects of language behavior as it develops toward syntactic maturity (431). To put it simply, they code language into four subcategories based on a hypothesized developmental sequence moving from a "fragmented language code," a "narrative language," a "complex portrayal language," to a "complex conditional language." These subcategories are viewed as progressing in complexity from simple descriptions of essentially unintegrated events to complex patterned relationships established by a conditional contingency framework. By analyzing the language behavior of different clinical subgroups according to their formal coding system, these authors have been able to demonstrate important differences in the way subgroups of schizophrenic individuals linguistically structure their experience.

In one study (157) chronic schizophrenic patients were divided into two groups on the basis of their relative solitariness or isolation and their relative assertiveness or belligerence in interpersonal behavior. This division was thought to reflect relatively stable forms of social adaptation as well as differing levels of ego regression in the face of aggressive wishes. On various tests of relative capacities to represent objects linguistically (i.e., transform experience into verbal form), isolated patients performed significantly more poorly than belligerent subjects: they did less well on a linguistic encoding task; they utilized simpler forms of language construction (simple narrative sentences vs. complex conditional sentences); and they employed more gestures unrelated to speech which appear to be associated with encoding difficulties. These findings are taken as evidence of the difficulties isolated patients have in using verbally encoded thought to represent their experience, with the attendant problems in integrating thought and action. The authors drew on recent psychoanalytic theorizing to interpret these findings as defensive reactions to the threats which the subject's aggression poses to important objects: the isolated patient loses the ability to represent objects, and the belligerent patient is able to maintain some contact, albeit hostile, with objects.

* See references 143, 156, 157, 158, 435, 436, and 437.

Another study (436) compared the organization of body-focused kinesic behavior and language construction in schizophrenic and depressed states. Although the two groups did not differ in overall incidence of body stimulation or verbal productivity, they did manifest different forms of body stimulation and language construction. Depressed patients employed more articulated body touching along with articulated narrative language. Schizophrenic patients used less articulated forms of self-stimulation (finger and hand motions), together with fragmented language syntax. These findings were interpreted as reflecting the differential intactness of the "formal representational substrate" of communicative behaviors which can be assessed independently of the content of representations. Moreover, the identification of units of self-stimulation as they relate to linguistic productions provides a method of describing the organizational status of self-representations and levels of narcissism in different psychopathological conditions. Thus, schizophrenics reveal a level of communicative dedifferentiation involving a noncohesive and nonstable narcissistic organization in their linguistic and kinesic pattern; while depressed patients show a more stable articulated form of narcissism, reflected in the increased complexity of narrative language and cohesive representational structures of self and object.

Regrettably, this study remains more provocative than conclusive. The small number of subjects used (four in each group), as well as the failure initially to distinguish paranoid from nonparanoid chronic schizophrenics, appears to have reduced the significance of the comparison of language-construction variables (although not of kinesic variables) between the schizophrenic and depressed patients to strong trends (p < .10) in the predicted directions.

In another study by the same authors (158), syntactically less-differentiated chronic schizophrenic patients did more poorly on a verbal-encoding task (the Stroop Color-Word Interference Test) than did more-differentiated chronic schizophrenic patients. These results, which are consistent with previous findings, are discussed in terms of the hypothesized role of language construction in attention regulation, with greater evidence of complex conditional language in broadened attention dispersal and vice versa.

Making use of the same coding systems (425), another study by these authors (437) demonstrated how differences in the linguistic and the kinesic organization of communication are reflected in the representation of anxiety in chronic schizophrenia. Thus, the forms of anxiety expression, evinced by high organization of communication in chronic schizophrenics, are more developmentally advanced than that of low organization of communication subjects. Where the former express more guilt anxiety, the latter express more diffuse, undifferentiated forms of anxiety.

Taken together, these studies constitute an impressive demonstration that certain aspects of language construction and kinesics represent stable and important indices of the cognitive organization of communication—indices capable of shedding light on the similarities and differences in the syntactic behavior subtypes of schizophrenics, as well as of differentiating schizophrenics from other pathological and normal groups of subjects.

LANGUAGE-RECEPTION STUDIES

This work of Freedman and his associates takes on added significance when viewed against the background of the long and spirited debate over the question whether schizophrenics are sensitive to syntactic structure. Early evidence suggested that schizophrenics' speech reception exhibited difficulties in using the grammatical structure of language to understand language (76,265,386). In particular they showed less improvement than controls in recall of word lists as grammatical structure of test passages was increased. While some of these findings were not restricted to schizophrenics (251), the thrust of this line of research remained unchallenged until Gerver (151) changed the experimental procedure to one of presenting syntactically acceptable but semantically anomalous sentences. He found that the presence of syntactic rules aided correct perception, retention, and recall of speech in chronic schizophrenics at least as well as in normals.

Using an embedded click technique to study sentence recall, other investigators (366,367) also concluded that schizophrenics use syntax as a basis of information processing and sentence decoding. Indeed, some evidence (161) suggests that, due to greater susceptibility to interference, schizophrenics exhibit a stronger dependence on sentence structure than do normals.

As is so often the case in the research literature on schizophrenia, different investigators using different experimental paradigms arrive at diametrically opposing conclusions. Just as in the present case, these contradictions often prove more apparent than real, as they rest on the ambiguities entailed in using the same terms to designate different phenomena or aspects of phenomena. Thus, there is the suggestion that the early findings based on Miller and Selfridge's (291) passages were confounded by the uncontrolled influence of semantic considerations. Similarly, the seeming disjunction between the language-construction studies that suggest syntactic regressions in schizophrenia and the embedded click paradigm studies that suggest syntactic equality is based on two crucial ambiguities. On the one hand, the former line of research focuses on the structure of speech production, while the latter concentrates on speech reception. And while it will require further empirical study to determine whether schizophrenics exhibit deficits specific to speech production and not to speech reception, it is equally necessary not to overlook that the sharp distinctions of four syntactic levels made in the language-construction studies is not matched by a similarly painstaking set of distinctions in the click paradigm research. In any event, at present this entire body of research appears to be complementary, not contradictory. It is likely to profit from further conceptual refinements which will facilitate more sensitive experimental studies with potentially greater theoretical yield.

This debate is far from over. Indeed, the explanatory potential of developments in psycholinguistics to illuminate schizophrenic cognitive functioning promises to make this area a battleground for some time to come. Thus, in a well-known article Roger Brown (60) denied the existence of a distinctive schizophrenic speech deficit while acknowledging the presence of *thought* disorder. Rising to the bait, a linguist took issue with Brown's conclusion and proposed that schizophrenic speech exhibited six definable features (73). In another article Fromkin (147) attempted to refute the proposal of definable features of schizophrenic speech by pointing to evidence suggesting that nonlinguistic aberrations (i.e., thought) are reflected in disconnections of discourse. Regrettably, this particular controversy is more impressive for its vitality than for its incisiveness. All three reports rely on relatively casual, uncontrolled observations from very small samples of subjects. Moreover, little effort is made systematically to define terms, to control for kinds of subjects, to select levels of analysis, etc. In short, these reports suffer more than most from the well-known sins besetting research in this area. It is to be hoped that future linguistic approaches will follow on the heels of these one-man—or one-woman—raids and remain long enough to seriously join the battle.

Associative Processes

STRONG MEANING AND CONTEXTUAL CONSTRAINT AS EXCESSIVE YIELDING TO NORMAL BIAS

Since Bleuler anomalies in the associative processes of schizophrenics have been regarded as a "primary symptom" of thought disorder. Chapman and his coworkers have attempted to explain this "cognitive symptom" by proposing that "schizophrenics respond excessively to those stimuli that normal subjects are biased to choose" (75). Strictly speaking, this principle of "excessive yielding to normal biases" is less an explanation than a description which attempts to link a variety of seemingly diverse phenomena. In any case, based on this perspective, Miller and Chapman (75) found that schizophrenics make more "halo errors"—that is, they show a greater predisposition than normal subjects to emphasize the correlation between two not necessarily related evaluative dimensions. By extension it was reasoned that on word-interpretation tasks schizophrenics would produce the more common, or "strong" meaning of words even in contexts requiring the correct but less common, nonpreferred, or "weaker" meaning. In addition to the original support for this position (76), other studies (28,300) provided further evidence that schizophrenics are somewhat more inclined to prefer "strong meaning" responses than are control subjects—especially for ambiguous words.

Subsequent experimentation, while failing unequivocally to endorse Chapman's principle, has helped clarify the scope and limits of its applicability. Thus, one study (39) found support for Chapman's hypothesis only for disorganized schizophrenics, and only when the ambiguous element was syntactic rather than semantic. This finding was supported in a study comparing chronic and acute schizophrenics with normal persons. Only the chronic schizophrenic patients showed exaggerated "strong meaning" response bias (443).

The specificity of these data is useful to bear in mind when assessing the reports of negative results. Several studies failed to replicate the findings that schizophrenics neglect the context in responding to the strong meaning of words (309,310,350). A more serious challenge to the contextual constraint hypothesis came from Chapman's laboratory. In a carefully controlled study it was found that schizophrenic subjects actually scored lower than normal subjects in regard to contextual constraint. This result is diametrically opposed to the direction of differences found in previous studies. It is noteworthy that the authors drew the conclusion that the original support for their position was probably artifactual, and that schizophrenics' deficit in recall is actually decreased by increasing contextual constraint. This is the exact opposite of the original principle!

There is ample documentation that the associative processes of (chronic) schizophrenics are susceptible to greater distractions, disruptions, and intrusions than other patients and normals; the greater the distraction, the greater the number of associative errors.* Similarly, schizophrenic subjects exhibit "looser" and more idiosyncratic associations than other patients (46,134,328). Some investigators have attempted to relate these findings to differences in schizophrenic subtype (103), to sex differences (112), and to length of hospitalization (319). These studies are limited in the experimental measures employed as well as by conceptual ambiguities surrounding the term "looseness"; with the exception of the effects of hospitalization, they failed to find differences between the experimental groups.

An important caveat concerning many of the findings regarding the associative processes of schizophrenics—at least those measured by word-association tests—was raised by a study showing that schizophrenics displayed significantly more auditory misperceptions of stimulus words than did normal controls (297). Since these subjects showed normal auditory acuity when given standard hearing tests, the authors attributed their mishearing to a failure to attend selectively to stimulus words. As a result schizophrenic associative deviancy may reflect mishearing as much as it does disordered thinking.

Several studies focused on schizophrenics' problems with, or associative intrusion into, goal-directed thought processes (441). Contrary to predictions, chronic schizophrenic subjects did not utilize primitive precausal thought processes in explaining nonaffective events (35). And while they exhibited more faulty deductive reasoning with emotional material, they were similar to normals when reasoning with symbolic material (187). Ho (187) concludes that schizophrenic thought pathology results from functional disturbances rather than from concreteness or faulty deductive processes. This confirms a similar finding

---

* See references 279, 353, 357, 365, and 448.

in two studies of means-end thinking (200,201) which found that the
logical competence of schizophrenics is only slightly inferior to that of
normals on special problem-solving tasks.

To test the hypothesis, based on response-interference theory, that
personal, idiosyncratic, preexisting associative habits intrude on the
performance of schizophrenics, Storms and Broen (441) employed an
association task and a concept-identification task. On both measures
schizophrenics produced or responded to significantly more idiosyncratic associations than did nonschizophrenic patients. However, these
findings provides only questionable support for the authors' response-
interference theory. On the one hand, schizophrenics did show the predicted errors attributable to the intrusion of pre-existing associates to
the stimulus situation. On the other hand, the high reliability of associative errors to the same word on different testings does not support the
predictions of instability based on a theory of collapsed-response
hierarchies.

In another attempt to test Storms and Broen's proposition that a response that is nondominant for normal subjects can never become
dominant for schizophrenics, Boland and Chapman (44) found that the
latter chose more close associates than correct responses. This result
was consistent with Chapman's response-bias principle, but not with
Broen and Storms' Hullian-derived learning theory (58).

THE IMMEDIACY HYPOTHESIS

Operant learning theory provides the theoretical background for
Salzinger's "immediacy hypothesis" of schizophrenic language behavior
(385,387). In simplest terms the hypothesis states that schizophrenic
behavior is largely controlled by the stimuli which are "immediate" (i.e.,
most recently occurring) in the environment (386). Thus, Salzinger
and his colleagues attempted to show that to a greater extent than for
normals, schizophrenics' verbal behavior is controlled by those words
occurring more immediately or recently in their speech and less so by
more distant words. They found that with increasing context, judges
could more easily predict an omitted word from the language of a
normal speaker than of a schizophrenic speaker. However, with very
brief contexts, judges could do no better in estimating an omitted word
from schizophrenic utterances than they could from normal utterances.
It is not clear to what extent this finding supports the immediacy hypothesis. If anything, the latter finding confutes the notion that schizophrenic language is more easily predicted from more recently occurring
words than is normal language (276).

In a very interesting study Blaney (39) attempted to amplify both the
immediacy hypothesis as well as the contextual constraint hypothesis
(that schizophrenics don't respond to the context of meaning) by considering syntactic sources of ambiguity in addition to the traditional
semantic (lexical) aspects of ambiguity. No differences were found for
the total sample of schizophrenic patients versus normal subjects or
nonschizophrenic patient control group. However, when schizophrenics
were compared along the dimensions of long- and short-term hospitaliza-

tion, or degree of florid psychotic disorganization, then differences appeared. As a result, florid psychotic schizophrenics showed a stronger meaning bias on the lexical ambiguity task, while the more compensated schizophrenics showed a stronger meaning bias on the syntactical ambiguity task. Similarly, the long-term hospitalized group had less of a strong meaning bias on the lexical ambiguity task, while the short-term hospitalized group had a stronger meaning bias on the syntactic ambiguity task. Blaney construed these results as providing qualified support for the contextual-constraint hypothesis for the subgroup of disorganized schizophrenics when the ambiguous element is semantic. When the effect was limited to the semantic task, the finding that schizophrenics are disproportionately constrained by proximal semantic elements was compatible with the immediacy hypothesis.

THE SELF-EDITING HYPOTHESIS

Broadly speaking, the studies of the anomalies of the associative processes of schizophrenics considered thus far have attempted to delineate this phenomenon by adducing some property—or some deficiency—intrinsic to the associative process itself—whether this be described in terms of excessive yielding to normal bias or to control by the most immediate stimuli in the environment, etc. By contrast, Cohen and his colleagues (81) proposed a two-stage model of a speaker's referential processes. The first, or sampling, stage entails generating associations. The second, or self-editing, stage involves comparing associations and editing out nondiscriminating or irrelevant elements. From this vantage point they argue that schizophrenics are deficient not in their repertoire of associations but rather in their self-editing capacity.

Contending that performance on recall tasks requires both sampling and comparing, while recognitions require only comparing, Nachmani and Cohen (301) found that schizophrenics were less accurate than normal subjects on a recall, but not on a recognition, task. This finding was in line with the experimental hypothesis and was taken as is in support for the two-stage model (compare references also, 20 and 421). In a more direct test of the hypothesis that schizophrenics sample from an adequate underlying repertoire of nondeviant associations, but that their self-editing deficiencies result in the production of deviant responses, Lisman and Cohen (252) asked schizophrenic and normal subjects to provide "free" and "idiosyncratic" associations to stimulus words. Consistent with their hypothesis, schizophrenics produced more common associations than normals under "idiosyncratic" instructions. These findings appear to contradict the one-stage model of word-associative performances which would predict more rather than less schizophrenic idiosyncratic associations to the "idiosyncratic" instructions. In another study, early, acute nonparanoid schizophrenics performed normally in a color-discrimination task when the hues were highly dissimilar and postulated self-editing tasks were minimal. When the hues increased in similarity, the accuracy of the schizophrenics dropped below, while their utterance length and reaction times rose above, normal subjects (82). The authors attributed these results to the collapse of the comparative, self-editing phase when the common associative response was not adequate to the task. At that point the schizophrenic speaker evinces the perseverative and chaining tendencies as predicted by the disattention (47) and immediacy hypotheses. When these findings were later replicated for chronic schizophrenic subjects (208), the authors concluded that deficits in communicative accuracy of schizophrenics, regardless of subtype, result from failures in the self-editing stage of the communicative process. In a similar fashion Davis and Blaney (99) showed that while overinclusion appears to be associated with a high degree of schizophrenic disorder, self-editing deficit—or as these authors interpreted it, role-taking deficit—appeared to correlate with all levels of schizophrenic pathology.

Although the self-editing hypothesis has been productive of a stimulating line of research, it is still necessary to ask how much is really explained by attributing schizophrenic communicative deficit to a negative symptom—namely, the failure of hypothesized self-editing function (75). It is something akin to accounting for disordered behavior by lacunae in the superego. Rather than invoking a generalized breakdown in higher-level mechanisms, one wishes better to understand the specific vulnerabilities and modes of adaptation positively operating in different schizophrenic subtypes. Thanks to the work of Cohen and his coworkers, perhaps we have a clearer picture of what still needs to be explained.

Attention and Perception

It has become an increasingly popular gambit for experimental psychopathologists to turn to models of attention in order to account for the frequent observation that (under certain conditions) schizophrenics do not process information with the same facility as do normal subjects or even other pyschiatric patients. Indeed, the terms "attention" and "perception" confer a misleading distinctiveness and clarity upon processes which are anything but clear, distinct, and impermeable (264). Mindful of the hazards of illusory precision inherent in undefined terms, Venables (455) has suggested replacing "disorders of attention and perception" with the ungainly but more accurate phrase "input dysfunction." Such considerations place in sharp relief some of the conceptual dilemmas inherent in artificially segmenting the terminology of different cognitive processes. Moreover, it is arguable that such conceptual "woolliness" is at least partly responsible for the fragmentation that characterizes much of the empirical yield of the research in this area.

These caveats notwithstanding, many researchers have hoped to locate the explanation of the cognitive, linguistic, and perceptual deviances manifested by schizophrenics in the underlying disorders of selective attention (330). To accomplish this task, two leading approaches to attention have been pressed into service: one derives from the work of Gardner et al. (150) on cognitive controls; the other stems from Broadbent's analysis of the role of the "filter" in the human organism conceived as an information-processing system (52).

SIZE-ESTIMATION STUDIES

The construct of "cognitive controls" refers to the stable patterns of regulating cognitive structures that are hypothesized to intervene between perceptual tests (stimuli) and cognitive-perceptual behaviors (responses). In a seminal analysis Silverman (411,412) proposed that the differences found in the visual size-estimation performance of good versus poor premorbid schizophrenics could be attributed to the attention styles of extensive versus minimal scanning, respectively. (Extensive scanners are those who repeatedly look about the visual field and consequently have more frequent eye movements; minimal scanners have fewer eye movements.)

Subsequent studies of eye movement and scanning styles using size-estimation paradigms have produced mixed results. By considering premorbid adjustment as well as the presence of paranoid symptomatology, Davis, Cromwell, and Held (98) found that good premorbid paranoid patients were the only ones to underestimate size differences, while nonparanoid patients with poor premorbid status overestimated size—with increasing degrees of overestimation for poor paranoids, good nonparanoids, and poor paranoids (305).

In an attempt to clarify the effect of eye movements on size estimation, Neale and Cromwell (305) found that, contrary to Silverman's predictions, mean size estimation under a 10-second exposure was higher than under a 100-millisecond exposure for all groups—normal, good premorbid paranoids, and poor premorbid nonparanoids. But if eye movements were the crucial factor, then greater size-estimation deviations would be expected with the 10-second presentation. However, good premorbid paranoids manifested their greatest errors in the 100-millisecond condition, in which the possibility for repeated visual fixations was eliminated. Consequently the eye-movement explanation of size-estimation deviances appears to have suffered an important setback.

Additional studies of the relation between eye movement, scanning styles, and size estimation has resulted in a much more complex pattern of relationships than the one originally proposed by Silverman (411). One study (413) found that for normal subjects, eye movements were inversely related to level of size estimation. The reverse relationship was found for schizophrenics, where eye movement was positively related to size estimation. To further complicate the picture, Silverman and King (414) found that correlations between size estimation and extensiveness of scanning occurred in opposite directions for male and female subjects in both normal and schizophrenic groups. Similarly, MacKinnon and Singer (267), employing the same methods as Silverman, found that nonmedicated, nonparanoid schizophrenics showed greater size underestimation than did nonmedicated paranoids. The reverse was found to be the case for the medicated subjects. Although medicated patients showed lower eye-movement and eye-fixation rates than nonmedicated patients and controls, there were no significant differences attributable to schizophrenia.

Analysis of the psychological requirements in performing size-estimation tasks has resulted in an expanded list of variables which have not been routinely controlled in the research on size estimation and attention. Contrary to previous findings, when such factors as pupil size, affective content, and visual acuity were considered along with the standard controls for subtype and premorbid history, no significant differences were found in regard to level of size estimation between normals, acute good premorbid paranoids, acute poor premorbid paranoids, chronic good premorbid paranoids, and chronic poor premorbid paranoids (306). By contrast, thematic content proved to be a significant determinant of size-estimation performance for all subjects. Tree, bush, and dominance scenes were overestimated, while square, acceptance, overprotection, and rejection scenes showed increasing degrees of underestimation.

In a like manner, another study found a "schizophrenic subject × thematic content × trials effect" (442). These results may be compared with studies that have attempted to relate differences in size estimation to drive arousal as measured by skin resistance. In such studies, acute poor schizophrenics exhibited the highest basal level of skin resistance, while chronic good premorbids exhibited the lowest, with paranoids in both groups exhibiting a higher basal level than nonparanoids. By interpreting skin-resistance levels as a measure of drive, it was found that for acute poor and chronic good subgroups of schizophrenics, size estimation was negatively related to drive for nonparanoids and positively related for paranoids. In the chronic poor subgroup, paranoids were found to exhibit a negative size-estimation-drive relationship. Magaro (273) interpreted these results by viewing size estimation as a function of increased drive level in the acute poor and chronic good paranoid subgroups, with the reverse relationships exhibited in the nonparanoid groups.

Part of the difficulty in comparing these studies stems from the asymmetry between the concepts and the methods employed in each, which makes any conclusion tentative at best (231). Thus, the striking conflict between Neale's results and Silverman's may be attributable to the former's employment of an artificial pupil for his subjects, as well as the greater distance between subject and stimuli than had been the case in earlier studies. Further, the finding of Neale et al. that thematic content was a significant performance variable for schizophrenics as well as for normals casts doubt on an affective-arousal interpretation of schizophrenia. But as long as the hypothesized relationships between skin resistance, drive, affective arousal, and scanning style remain unclarified, all of these variables upon size estimation still remain as no more than very promising leads to future research.

ATTENTION

The model of a defective filtering mechanism (52, 53, 54) has been invoked by a variety of studies that have attempted to gain purchase on the attentional deficit in schizophrenia.* Studies bearing on the delineation of specific deficits in the filtering phase of information processing include evidence that chronic nonparanoid schizophrenics show a more restricted range of sensitivity to peripheral sensory channels than acute paranoid schizophrenics (57); that schizophrenics perform more poorly than controls on span-of-apprehension tests with irrelevant noise present, but show no difference from normals when there are no irrelevancies;† and that schizophrenics perform more poorly on tasks involving switching attention between stimulus modalities as well as discrimination shifts.‡ However, a multivariate analysis of five leading tasks employed in studying attentional dysfunction—reaction time, size estimation, vigilance, object sorting, and proverbs—found that these tests did not intercorrelate highly, sharing little common variance (231). That these different tasks are not measuring the same process is the obvious implication. Moreover, there is evidence to suggest that the selective attention of various subgroups of schizophrenics is adversely affected by content, interactive, social, and motivational variables; for example, process types screen threats from awareness while reactives seem overattuned to threats (388) (compare references 257, 273, 275, and 439).

Such perplexing findings call attention to chronic failures in making the conceptual discriminations necessary for the precise measurement operations and perceptual task analyses which would effectively rule out competing interpretations of reported deficits. Among the sobering conclusions of their review of research on attention and schizophrenia, Neale and Cromwell (305) underlined the "definitional looseness" of the attention construct itself. Mindful that in research, as on the wards, overinclusive thinking breeds confusion and disarray, Zubin (487) attempted to organize the experimental data on attention in schizophrenia by articulating a more differentiated model of attention consisting of three dimensions: (1) *selection* for focusing, (2) *maintenance* of focus, and (3) *shift* of focus. Evidence was presented which suggested that schizophrenics deviate primarily in the area of shifting attention, and that other reports of deviance are attributable to motivational and social variables. Similarly, a review of the research based on Broadbent's model of attention and information processing concluded that a failure to differentiate consistently between the "filtering" and the "pigeonholing" subphases of attention has produced an indeterminate experimental yield (182). One inescapable conclusion is that rigorous theoretical analyses of the operative variables and psychological processes underlying the experimental measures is a prerequisite for meaningful progress in this field (274,487).

Numerous studies reported that schizophrenics exhibited simple and complex perceptual deficits over a wide range of dimensions and measures. Subgroups of schizophrenics were found to differ in their reactions to sensory deprivation and sensory overload (258); in response to some perceptual illusions (247); in their general nonverbal performances (75); in the speed of their perceptual functioning (233,481); in pro-

---

* See references 176, 182, 183, 264, 332, 333, 398, and 400.
† See references 4, 71, 97, 211, 304, 307, 324, and 383.
‡ See references 235, 312, 313, 314, 315, 460, and 476.

ducing visual afterimages (216,422,423); for perceptual memory for numerousness (225); and in auditory threshold and sensitivity (122, 206,300).

Fairly consistent errors in time estimation have been reported for schizophrenic subjects, with respect to the accuracy, overestimation, and variability of their predictions.* However, studies of the effects of crowding (336) and anxiety (378) on increasing errors in time judgments of different nosological groups—not to mention the effect of different drug regimens—suggests that reported differences on temporal estimation cannot be attributed to nosological differences alone.

Laboratory measures of reaction times continue to exert special appeal to researchers concerned with the assessment of the subtle deficits of schizophrenics occurring at the "molecular level" of behavior.† Rodnick and Shakow (368) had reported that regularity and length of the preparatory interval, or PI (the time between the warning and the presentation of the stimulus), had an important effect on the performance of schizophrenics: when predictable preparatory intervals were increased to over 4 seconds, the reaction time went down for schizophrenics and went up for normals. This is the so-called crossover effect. More recently the crossover effect has been shown to be restricted to process schizophrenics (26, 456). Further clarification of the crossover effect was found by studying the influence of the preparatory interval or the PPI (i.e., the preparatory interval on the immediately previous trial). It was found that when the PPI was greater than the PI, the reaction times of schizophrenics were slower, and vice versa (483). Additional studies suggested that the durability of the crossover effect on regular trials could not be accounted for by contextual factors (26,27,431,432). Because process schizophrenics do worse with regular trials than with irregular ones, these authors argued that their results were more compatible with an explanation in terms of inhibitory deficit due to information redundancy than with one of such a deficit due to an inability to maintain a set (399). An intriguing implication of this line of research is that contrary to general expectations, a deficit in the capacity to anticipate, rather than slowed reaction times per se, emerges as the most sensitive and important indicator of schizophrenic pathology (311).

Psychomotor Functions

The comment made ten years ago in *The Schizophrenic Syndrome* that "schizophrenics have been studied primarily in terms of fine psychomotor performance with very little research on gross abilities" holds true for the period covered in the present report as well. There is still a trend to differentiate schizophrenics from others on reaction time under a variety of conditions.

° See references 69, 115, 153, 154, 255, 317, 325, 374, and 375.
† See references 68, 92, 209, 282, 283, 284, and 373.

Some aspects of the proprioceptive hypothesis concerned with the deficit in the reception of stimuli which affects motor behavior have been tested in a series of studies by Ritzler and associates (362,363,364). They confirmed previous results that schizophrenics show "significantly elevated thresholds at the light weight intensity" in a weight-judgment task, that normals received larger kinesthetic figural aftereffects than acute and chronic schizophrenics, and that in a variation of the weight-discrimination task the schizophrenic deficit was also demonstrated. Along with the proprioceptive deficit explanation, a signal-detection interpretation, due to the nature of the task, was given. The authors suggested that cognitive dysfunction and body image disturbances might be influenced by the proprioceptive deficit.

Interest has also been generating around the effect of external factors, such as noise, room light, or other experimental conditions, on the reaction time of schizophrenics. Raskin (352) compared anxious, hallucinating, and severely ill schizophrenics on a reaction-time task with background conversation, during darkness, or a normal presentation of the stimulus. Schizophrenics with recent auditory hallucinations had a slower reaction time when there was background conversation; anxious subjects gave elevated reaction times when the room lights were extinguished; while severely ill patients did equally poorly under the three conditions. Storms and Acosta (440) replicated a study which found that dynamometer tension led to performance deficits at the training stimulus for patients with high MMPI (Minnesota Multiphasic Personality Inventory) schizophrenic scores. Their results confirmed the earlier findings of a tension-produced decrement only on the training stimulus (440).

Individual studies assessing previously reported findings and examining different aspects of psychomotor functioning have begun to appear in the literature. One example is the study conducted by Borinsky et al. (45) which investigated Venables's (455) arousal theory. They used both the two-flash threshold technique and a yes-no signal-detection theory to evaluate arousal in schizophrenics and normals. Contrary to Venables's results, Borinsky et al. found the yes-no procedure effective in showing that schizophrenics performed similarly to, and at a lower sensitivity level than, normals. Hustmyer (196) looked at the relationship of eye movement to the process-reactive dimension in schizophrenia. The study was marred by the uncontrolled effects of drugs on the patients. A negative correlation between drug treatments and eye movements was reported, though. Douglas and Sara (119) made clinical observations of the handwriting of schizophrenic and organic patients. Decorating the paper, writing nonsense, adding or deleting words from phrases, and drawing lines or figures were examples of writing styles. No specific characteristic was unique to either group, as both schizophrenic and organics varied considerably from individual to individual. It was suggested that a constellation attitude be employed when rating handwriting styles. Begelman and Hersen (21) analyzed the discrepancy between verbal responses and motor behavior in schizophrenics and normals, using a self-report and approach task toward a feared object (snake). The normal subjects were consistent in their motor measures and verbal responses. Schizophrenics who rated themselves as definitely afraid of snakes approached the snake more readily than was expected. A second presentation of the verbal measure revealed that the discrepancy was reduced. A couple of explanations were considered: one was that schizophrenics are unable to make accurate predictions; the other was that behavior is a more appropriate measure for assessing certain human reactions. Earlier work on establishing cognitive sets led McCormack, Phelan, and Tang (260) to reconsider that topic. In tasks involving arithmetic, digit symbols, anagrams, and cancellations of letters, both normals and schizophrenics established and used cognitive sets more frequently than chance. Normals established sets more readily and intelligently than the schizophrenics, however.

Some of the more recent studies have attempted to move away from the traditional reaction-time designs, as evidenced by the preceding research endeavors. The reaction-time studies have shed considerable light on psychomotor function, but the variety of explanations given to describe the consistent results leaves one a bit skeptical. Ventures to standardize research designs and procedures, to increase the accuracy of measurement techniques, and to examine a broader range of psychomotor functioning need to be considered.

Learning

The number of learning studies has been on the increase in recent years. This increase stems in part from the more systematic and operational techniques available for examining specific behavioral responses (i.e., ward behavior). Also there is strong desire among psychologists to increase and improve treatment modalities. An approach involving learning procedures appears to meet some of their needs. In this section the major forms of learning and/or conditioning will be discussed in relation to their effectiveness with the schizophrenic population.

Operant conditioning is the process of giving some kind of reward or reinforcement to increase the likelihood of obtaining a certain behavioral response from an organism. In tasks ranging from word association to the reinstatement of speech in mute psychotics, schizophrenic subjects have been seen to produce more appropriate responses or behavior with positive reinforcements as a contingency.* The reinforcements have varied from verbal praise to tangible rewards such as candy, or tokens, which could be traded in. Meiselman (289) reported that nonparanoid schizophrenics could improve on tasks involving more than one sensory modality when contingent reinforcement and feedback were utilized in the design. A few studies have found that when the reinforcement is withdrawn, as in the case of an ABA (nonreinforcement-reinforcement-nonreinforcement) design, the designated behavior will be seen to return to a level similar to its baseline performance (296,473).

---

* See references 29, 80, 219, 315, 473, and 474.

Following Premack's principle that a freely occurring high-frequency response can act as a reinforcer, Mitchell and Stoffelmayr (295) used "sitting" as a reward for doing more chores in the hospital when schizophrenic patients wouldn't accept and respond to other tangible rewards. Ciottone and McCarthy (78) looked at the sequential effects of praise and censure on learning in a response-contingent paradigm. Contrary to predictions, the sequence of praise-to-censure led to the most efficient performance relative to the baseline measure, for schizophrenics.

Streiner (444) found that schizophrenics performed faster on tasks involving verbal evaluation and varying degrees of complexity when they were censured rather than praised. Another study reported that receiving punishment instead of decreasing the positive reward resulted in faster learning for schizophrenics (318). Defining regressive behavior as temporal, nonspecific withdrawal, Schenck and Surber (392) reported an increase in withdrawal behavior under conditions of verbal censure of their schizophrenic subjects. Other work conducted by Panek (327) showed that both praise with tokens, and removal of tokens and no praise, were equally as effective in learning a word-association task. Mitchell, Mowart, and Stoffelmayr (294) looked at the social contact sought for by chronic, male schizophrenics. After the subjects had been socially deprived (isolation for 45 minutes), they sought social contact more than avoided it. However, after some schizophrenics had a 10-minute undemanding conversation with the experimenter, they avoided any further social contact. Still other researchers reported that specific behavior changes could not be observed under a variety of contingencies (312,391,461). Questions can be raised as to the types of tasks asked to be performed, a patient's mental and physical state, what constitutes reinforcement, etc., in an attempt to understand the different findings. The study by Miller and Heckel (292), in which schizophrenics and normals did not perform differently on intentional-learning tasks, raises another issue. They posited that if the schizophrenic's response set is congruent with the specific demands of the task, learning will occur faster and at a higher performance level.

A good deal of time and energy has been spent on word-association tasks which incorporate an affective component, meaningfulness, social stimulus value, and other relevant factors in an effort to see if any particular response patterns are evident in schizophrenic populations. Some workers (111,204) found that their reactive schizophrenic subjects exhibited quicker and more accurate learning to positive words than did the process patients they were compared with. In another study involving word-reversal shifts as a measure of discrimination learning, again reactive patients learned faster and made more reversal shifts than did process schizophrenics when tested (323). From the data reported it appears that a reactive-process distinction is relevant in learning tasks.

However, in studies not controlling for the reactive-process distinction, other results have been presented. For instance, Wischner and Glade (475) reported that schizophrenics learned to form associations with aversive words more easily than with neutral words. Rychlak et al. (382) found that schizophrenics tended to learn word associations to triagrams with negative reinforcement value quicker than those with a positive reinforcement value. The opposite trend was seen in the normal control group. Another approach was to examine the social stimulus value of words. Sutker, Sutker, and Gil (447) observed that schizophrenics learned low-stimulus-value words faster than high-stimulus-value ones. Their normal subjects learned faster overall, and without reference to the stimulus value. A study comparing paranoid and nonparanoid schizophrenics, and nonpsychiatric patients, revealed that the verbal recall of neutral material was better for paranoids, no matter what level of contextual constraint was employed. A paired-associate learning task with concrete and abstract variations showed that schizophrenics performed more poorly than nonpsychotic patients on mixed (AC and CA) pairings, and also performed worse on mixed lists than on concrete-concrete pairings (408). A comparison between normal subjects and chronic schizophrenics on the learning of evaluative (ugly, altruistic), potent (cowardly, feminine), and active (careless, erratic) words showed that normals learned faster and recalled more evaluative words. Schizophrenics recalled a significantly greater number of potency words as compared with active and evaluative words (390). Increasing the "meaningfulness" of word lists from low to high was shown to relate to a faster paired-associate learning in schizophrenics (446). Two studies by Mourer (299,300) provided evidence that on tests of generalization schizophrenics made significantly more errors to words that shared strong meanings than did normal controls.

In general, the research literature on learning in schizophrenics tends to support the view that schizophrenics learn slower and perform at a lower level of efficiency than the normal or nonschizophrenic populations they are compared with.* Other studies assessing the learning differences among the subtypes of schizophrenia add more information to the field (62,328). However, some psychologists have focused their interest on the possible processes that underlie these differences. One hypothesis that has attracted the attention of researchers is that of interference and distraction. The reasoning behind this hypothesis is that a schizophrenic individual is unable, or is limited in his ability, to concentrate on the immediate stimuli presented. Other stimuli in the setting, along with previous memories or associations, interfere with the ability to focus on the task at hand; the result is a poorer performance due to the diffuse stimulation (19,287,430). Another hypothesis is that of a response hierarchy disorganization, in which a partial collapse of the response hierarchy in schizophrenics occurs due to increased interference from competing responses (34,58). The memory process, especially short-term, has been considered a factor in the learning of schizophrenics. It is felt that schizophrenics have loose mnemonic organization, which impedes them from structuring ideas and thoughts clearly. In turn, they have difficulty performing well on tasks that involve organizational properties.†

Research in learning with schizophrenics has also gone one step further. Experimenters and researchers have attempted to teach learning techniques to schizophrenics, so that the subjects themselves can

---

* See references 152, 220, 221, 338, 375, and 433.
† See references 20, 222, 223, 224, 226, 377, 420, and 468.

assist in their learning process (288,342,458). In the self-instruction technique employed by Meichenbaum and Cameron (288) an instructor gave a problem or question to the subject and then explained the steps taken (cognitive guidance) to solve such a problem accurately. Emphasis was placed on having the subject rehearse the pattern in his head. Meichenbaum and Cameron found that schizophrenic subjects using this technique performed better on digit symbol substitution, digit recall, and proverb interpretation than control subjects not utilizing the method. The strategy used in solving problems can be a factor, as was discussed earlier and in a few other studies (49,277). Brengelmann and Goldsmith (49) found that practice improved the scores of normal and brain-damaged subjects on a serial learning task but did not affect schizophrenic performance. Maier and Ray (277) observed that schizophrenics used a "successive scanning" strategy, while normal subjects employed a more systematic approach in an attempt to discover four letters over fifty trials. Utilizing the appropriate strategy instead of a random approach can facilitate the performance in the task.

As can readily be seen, various aspects of the learning process in schizophrenics have been examined. The incoming data has shed some light upon possible treatment modalities, such as token economies, behavioral contracts, and operant conditioning of functional behavior. However there are areas which deserve further attention. These include the subject's definition of what constitutes reinforcement, generalization from one setting to another, the demands of the task, the subjective experience to the stimulus, or stimuli, presented, sequential effects of reinforcement, and the motivation of the individual. Additional information in these areas might help explain the variety of results presented in the literature.

Psychophysiological Aspects

Some studies concerned with physiological aspects and their psychological concomittants merit inclusion. Most of the following are concerned with "arousal" as the central variable.

Hustmyer (195) found that reactive schizophrenics displayed more horizontal eye movement than process patients to tasks involving the observation of dots and pictures. The generally smooth eye-tracking patterns of normals was not observed in schizophrenics (189). It was suggested that oculomotor involvement may relate to perceptual difficulties in schizophrenia. A schizo-affective group was significantly differentiated from acute and latent schizophrenics using REM intensity and latency measures during sleep (356). A reduction in the amplitude of the delta wave component, as measured by electroencephalogram (EEG), was observed in chronic schizophrenics but not in normal controls. Also 40 percent of the schizophrenic subjects failed to manifest any stage IV sleep (high voltage and slow activity) (63).

Measures, such as the galvanic skin response (GSR), heart rate, skin conductance, and EEG have been used as indications of arousal states. Bernstein (30,31) found that after both normals and schizophrenics had habituated to a given stimulus intensity, rearousal of the GSR resulted when the stimulus change involved an increase in intensity. Chronic schizophrenics had to receive a substantial increase in stimulation (presentation of different tones) to raise their GSR levels after the initial habituation (31). Directions of both stimulus change and degree of change appear to be important factors in triggering the GSR orienting response. In a study looking at comparisons between chronic paranoid, acute paranoid, undifferentiated, and chronic undifferentiated schizophrenics, and normal controls, chronic paranoid patients tended to have higher GSR than normals to critical (high-stimulating) and to control (low-stimulating) words (207). Stephen (438) found that there was less of an orienting response to neutral sounds and light stimuli in process schizophrenics than in nonprocess patients. A classical conditioning paradigm was used in another study to examine the different GSRs in normals and schizophrenics. It was reported that the normals showed GSR conditioning to a specific tone, while schizophrenics exhibited no conditional GSR differentiation (11). A drop in performance and increase in GSR resulted for schizophrenics when the sorting task took on an affective component (55). Depue and Fowles (105) reviewed the research on electrodermal activity and observed two trends consistently: habituation of responses at levels during periods of minimal stimulation, and frequency of spontaneous electrodermal responses regardless of stimulus conditions for schizophrenics. Further support for the spontaneous fluctuations was reported by Gruzelier and Venables (163).

A study by Krooth (236), using EEG as a measure of arousal, revealed that schizophrenics were more consistently aroused and showed less variation than normals to twelve high-commonality stimulus words. Many researchers, however, have begun to use multiple measures to assist in determining the level of arousal. Under conditions of auditory and visual stress both chronic and reactive schizophrenics had a higher heart rate, faster respiration, more muscle activity as measured by electromyogram (EMG), and more nonspecific GSR and basal skin conductance than normals (131). During hallucinations a schizophrenic's telemetered skin potential increased significantly, while there was no change in heart rate. When angry, though, the heart rate decelerated, then increased, while skin potential remained the same (248). Ax (10) observed impaired orienting responses (GSR), higher palmar skin conductance, and no change in skin potential for schizophrenics during a classical conditioning experiment, in which a variety of tones and corresponding shock intensities were used. Using different methods of stress and multiple measures of arousal, Van Zood and McNulty (454) reported that generally normals and reactive schizophrenics showed greater increments of arousal to the stressful conditions except for their heart rates and skin resistance. Process patients displayed less reactivity. Other studies have also employed multiple measures of arousal, as evidence of the physiological changes during different conditions of stress, and were relatively successful (13,104,114,159).

A miscellany of reports using those measures discussed previously and additional ones—such as gustatory acuity, cutaneous sensitivity, two-flash threshold, and lateral asymmetry—has supplemented the information currently found in the literature.* However, more work needs to be conducted in these latter areas in order to confirm the initial physiological findings. One question that comes up is whether the response detected is due to the present state of the individual or is evidence of his general response pattern. The varying reports on arousal level raise some issues concerning the sensitivity of the measures and/or the attentional component of the subject (164). Another concern that follows from the attentional factor is how much control the subject has of his physiological reactions (401). These and other issues must be considered in the attempt to link psychological behavior with physiological responsivity.

Personality Processes

In recent years a number of studies have been conducted in an attempt to link body concept disturbances with schizophrenia. Some of the variables employed to define body concept are contamination, penetration, fabulized combinations, and barrier scores. One study, using low barrier and high penetration scores as indicative of vague boundary definition, reported that barrier scores increased significantly after somatic exercises (96). Questions concerning the length of the effect and the relation of body ego to other areas of behavior were raised. Mazekari and Kreiger (286) did not find an alteration in body boundary definiteness of chronic schizophrenics as a result of inducing internal and external somatic awareness.

Shukla (409) found that schizophrenics received relatively higher scores on penetration than normals or psychoneurotics. The results were interpreted as indicating more disturbance and a perception of body image boundary as diffuse and fragile. Another study also reported a large number of penetration responses to the presentation of subliminal aggressive stimuli (416).

Other researchers have found contaminations and fabulized combinations to be more frequent among schizophrenics. Quinlan and Harrow (347) reported that Rorschach responses for schizophrenics and latent schizophrenics possessed more of the factors mentioned above than did depressives. In this study, barrier and penetration responses were not strongly related to schizophrenia or to features associated with disturbed thinking as in schizophrenia. It was suggested that these responses (barrier and penetration) assess emphasis on types of content that may be related more to underlying personality differences than to current level of psychopathology.

Another approach to body image disturbances has been to administer the Draw-A-Person test to different nosological groups. It has been shown that hospitalized schizophrenics demonstrate more omissions of arms/

* See references 56, 133, 162, 165, 166, and 184.

hands and legs/feet than normals (227). Cancro (67) developed a
Sophistication of Body Concept (SOBC) technique and tried to use it for
discriminating process from reactive schizophrenics. The linear correlation between premorbid adjustment and SOBC was near zero. Questions
were raised concerning the appropriateness of using the SOBC with
schizophrenics, since it was originally developed for a normal population.
Also a reactive-process classification may not be related to differentiation
of the body concept.

Dimond (116), in a study using the Secord Homonym test, reported
that paraplegics expressed more body involvement than schizophrenics.
This finding cast doubt on the assumed isomorphism between ego and
body boundary, and on the assumption of disturbed imagery in schizophrenia. Quinlan and Harrow (347) noted the difficulty in evaluating
the boundary hypothesis. The many ways of defining boundary disturbances and examining the hypothesis (Rorschach, Object Sorting
Test, Draw-A-Person, etc.) have led to a looseness in its application.
However, schizophrenic pathology has continuously shown more signs
of low barrier scores and high penetration ratings and a markedly higher
incidence of contaminations than other diagnostic groups.

The lack of affect, or flat affect, has been used to aid in detecting
schizophrenic behavior. McPherson (272) found a lack of affect in
paranoid and nonparanoid schizophrenics. Flattening of affect, as rated
by two psychiatrists experienced in assessing schizophrenics, was significantly associated with a relative failure to use constructs descriptive
of personality and emotional states. No mention was made of a paranoid-
nonparanoid distinction. In a study examining premorbid adjustment
and affective expression, significant differences were found between
reactive and process schizophrenics on profiles developed from MMPI
clinical scales. The results showed that process schizophrenics were
generally more clinically disturbed, affectively flattened, and less responsive to a variety of affectively laden stimuli (101).

Rosenman and Drennan (371) were unable to find a difference between schizophrenics, neurotics, and normals on the Literature Empathy
Test. However, schizophrenics were reported to respond in a more idio-
graphic manner than the two other groups. In a study comparing normals
and schizophrenics on the recall of pleasant and unpleasant, affect-laden
words, schizophrenics had a lower recall of pleasant words than normals
(212). They had the same recall on unpleasant words.

Farina and Holzberg (129) reported that the anxiety level of their
good, premorbid schizophrenics increased when moving from an individual to a group situation as compared with poor, premorbid schizophrenics and controls, whose anxiety decreased. Dominance of and
conflict with the parents was not shown to increase the anxiety level of
the subjects (129). In relation to the findings the authors raised questions concerning the appropriateness of the measures, the experimental
situation, and severity of the subjects' condition. Anxiety has also been
looked at as a factor affecting the process of therapy with schizophrenia
(8). Anxiety over one's self-image can lead to a destruction of the inner
self. It has been suggested that the patient may be willing to reaccept an
unbearable self-image and its accompanying anxiety if he feels the
therapist is sharing that anxiety.

Different results have been found in the literature concerning sex role identification, gender, and consistency and conformity of behavior. Marsella and Murray (281) found less consistency in conforming behaviors for paranoid schizophrenics when compared with manic-depressives and normals on a perceptual judgment and attitude-change conformity task. Ecker (121) found no differences between schizophrenics and normals on the Role Preference and Body Parts tests. Evidence of disturbed sexual identification in schizophrenics was displayed on the Humor Test: schizophrenics were less adequate than normals in comprehending cartoons involving abnormal or ambiguous sex roles.

Kokonis (227), using the Machover Draw-A-Person and other measures of sex-role identification, found no significant relationships between gender of the first drawing and sex-role identification for schizophrenics or normals. In another study (229) he found that schizophrenics with both parents expressing dominant styles, scored lower than normal counterparts on a sex-role-identification measure. The results were in accordance with the schizophrenic hypothesis derived from the psychoanalytic theory. McClelland and Watt (259) reported another variation in sex-role identification: in their study schizophrenics showed sex-role alienation with a repressed self-image.

Hurvich and Bellak (197), in an attempt to define and differentiate ego boundaries from body boundaries in schizophrenia, developed ten factors which they put under the heading "ego functioning." They included reality testing; sense of reality; regulation and control of drives, affects, and impulses; object relations; thought processes; adaptive regression in service of the ego; defensive functions; autonomous functioning; stimulus barrier; and synthetic-integrative functioning. The list was used during interviews, on standardized tests, and in laboratory experiments. A small pilot study produced results reflecting the differences between schizophrenics and other groups (197). This line of investigation was expanded in a later publication (23).

A later study by Bellak and Hurvich (22) showed statistically significant differences in adequacy of ego functioning. An additional two factors of judgment and mastery-competence were included in the list (24). Since that time profiles of behavior have been developed. Patterns of behavior and individual differences can be examined. Quantitative and qualitative differences have been noted, which have implications for therapeutic intervention (23,24).

Using ego functioning to address etiological components of schizophrenia, King (218) proposed the blurring of ego focus and the double-bind phenomena as leading to schizophrenia. Many other authors, researchers, and therapists have supported that hypothesis or some form of it. King emphasized the mother-child relationship and the development of the ego through object relations. Landis (237) in a similar manner found the collapse of ego boundaries to be evident in schizophrenia.

In a Japanese study using semantic structure as an indication of ego functioning, schizophrenics were differentiated from undergraduates on seven concepts. Scale-checking styles were related to personality variables (322).

A coping-with-dissonance technique was employed with schizophrenics and control subjects (232). Results indicated that diagnostic category, level of dissonance, situational content, and order of presentation were all important variables in determining one's strategy. Richtberg (360) found a reduced cognitive rigidity in schizophrenics as compared with normals using the Luchins tests. However, schizophrenics tend toward rigidity in social relationships. The findings were discussed in terms of the overinclusion concept of ego defense.

Locus of control studies have attracted attention as a means of assessing ego functioning and reality testing. Cash and Stack (72) used Rotter's Internal-External Control Scale and the Sc, Pa, and K scales of the MMPI with schizophrenic and other hospitalized psychiatric patients. They found a positive relationship between external control and degree of psychological disturbance (Sc and Pa scales). Paranoid subjects accounted for most of the externality in the schizophrenic sample. Acute schizophrenics were found to be significantly more external than chronics (72). In another study using Rotter's Internal-External Control Scale, process schizophrenics scored significantly more external than did reactive schizophrenics (256). An attempt was made to predict posthospital adjustment in the community for schizophrenic patients from the Rotter Scale. A significant negative correlation between externality scores and independence scores was seen for subjects living in apartments (434). Schlosberg (393) used the construct "time perspective" in looking at schizophrenics. He defined time perspective as concern with the whole personality, memories of past events, hopes, ambitions, and expectations of future events. In comparing schizophrenics and tuberculous patients, he found total and future time perspectives to be shorter for the schizophrenics.

The ethical self-presentation of schizophrenics, prisoners, and normals was looked at by Watson (461). Using a multiple-choice ethics inventory, he found that process schizophrenics presented themselves as less antisocial than normals. The ethical standards of schizophrenics as a group were reported to be more inconsistent than normals. And the standards of process schizophrenics showed more instability than those of reactives.

Altered states of consciousness and the fantasies of schizophrenics have also been examined by researchers. One technique was to look at the death concerns of schizophrenic patients compared with normals. Female schizophrenics did not produce fantasies similar to those of dying females (246). There was no reported difference between schizophrenics and nonschizophrenics in death concerns. Hypnosis was also used in an attempt to examine altered states of consciousness. Psychotic subjects were found to achieve a level of hypnosis comparable with normals (160). In another study chronic schizophrenics were significantly more suggestible than nonpsychotics on a standard hypnotic scale (155). Lavoie (242) found that schizophrenics had a lower frequency of high Stanford Hypnosis Susceptibility Scale scores but were higher in posthypnotic amnesia.

The dreams of schizophrenics were employed in considering fantasies. In a laboratory experiment depressed patients were able to recall 51 percent of their dreams, while schizophrenics had 71 percent recall. The emotional lives and continuity of mental life differed for the two groups (234). Children with symptoms of borderline and psychotic character revealed deficits in dream conception, particularly in areas dependent upon internal-external boundary formations (127). This is a similar finding to the boundary disturbances found in schizophrenics who took the Rorschach, mentioned earlier in this section. Brenneis (51) did not find a higher incidence of distortions in the representation of body boundaries for schizophrenics. He felt that too much emphasis was placed on loss of body integrity versus evidence of a thought disorder. Contaminations, confabulations, and fabulized combinations do appear more frequently and consistently in the dreams of schizophrenics. The waking and dream thought processes are believed to be continuous in schizophrenia (50). It is easier to agree upon the role of ego deficits in the thought processes than to agree upon or assess what data actually give evidence of an ego deficit.

Phenomenology

The phenomenological experience of schizophrenics has proved to be an interesting and challenging task for many experimenters. It is difficult to perform worthwhile and respectable research in this area. Such research is particularly susceptible to validity and reliability problems simply because the basic data are by definition subjective (251). This is not to say that work in this area should be terminated, but a more systematic approach must be developed in order to enhance the study of phenomenology. The following studies made an attempt to use standardized procedures but still ran into problems.

Hallucinatory experiences is one topic which has received considerable attention. Mintz and Alpert (293) found that schizophrenics with auditory hullucinations tended to have higher vividness of auditory imagery than nonpsychotic controls and schizophrenics without auditory hallucinations. This finding was assessed by having each subject imagine that a record was playing for 30 seconds and then having each one rate his experience. Hallucinating subjects also displayed the greatest inability to assess auditory perception. Lowe (257) looked at the number and the type of hallucinations and Rorschach responses of manic-depressives, organic patients, and paranoid schizophrenics in his study. His work showed that schizophrenics gave a larger number of Rorschach responses and reported more than three hallucinations, on all modalities, including the most rare—hallucination of the self. The hallucinations were reported to originate within the body, to show considerable inconstancy, and to have clearly specified causes. These findings, along with those of Mintz and Alpert (293), provide additional data concerning hallucinatory experiences. Cartwright (70) examined the fantasy content of actively hallucinating patients (during the day) during REM and non-REM sleep, and reported no differences in content between sleep periods. Even with the results of the preceding studies, there are still questions concerning the self-report measures employed to observe and detect hallucinations. There are no definitive tests available for distinguishing reported imaginings and hallucinations from actual phenomenal experiences or perceptions (257,389).

Is a schizophrenic aware of his immediate environment, and to what degree has the awareness been used in trying to understand the phenomenological experience? Zlotowski and Cohen (486) reported that a change in the hospital environment had an effect on both poorly and well-adjusted schizophrenics: poorly adjusted patients showed a significant decrease in behavior pathology, while better-adjusted subjects showed an increase in behavior pathology under conditions of moderate and maximum environmental change. The results suggest that the patient's perception of the treatment environment is an important factor and will have an effect on how he responds to a change in that situation (396,486). Another study, based on the results of the Family Relations Test, indicated that schizophrenics had a more accurate perception of their illness and patient role than their parents did (293). Using a stressful situation to assess physiological and psychological responsiveness, it was found that paranoid schizophrenics evidenced greater heart-rate response to the stressful stimuli than did nonparanoids (402). However on the verbal ratings, paranoid subjects underrated their autonomic response while nonparanoids overrated it (402). Reilly, Harrow, and Tucker (357) reported a variation in the free verbalizations of schizophrenics depending upon whether or not they were in an acute phase. The acute phase was marked with a vivid, overwhelming flood of details, while at a later time the patients were not overinvolved, shifted toward future concerns, and became more coherent with the passage of time (357). The results of these studies support the view that schizophrenics are in touch with their surroundings, but that awareness fluctuates depending upon the situation, the individual's state, and other intervening factors.

Some researchers have investigated the relationship between how a schizophrenic feels about his experience and what impact this might have on future growth and adjustment. Much of this work has been classified under the heading "integration." An integrative individual is one who places a high value on insight into solving ongoing problems, who tends to put blame on oneself, who regards psychotic symptoms as a part of life, and who displays a flexible attitude toward illness; a disintegrative person manifests the opposite characteristics (266,426). Researchers have found that schizophrenic patients with a positive integrative attitude had a better posthospital adjustment (426). Those schizophrenics with a disintegrative attitude tended not to strive toward understanding, maintained a negative view of their illness, and did not place experiences into a life perspective (266,341).

From the preceding studies, it is evident that thoughtful attempts are being made to examine the phenomenological experiences of schizophrenics. However, investigators will need to expand their modes of examination in order to explore the numerous personal experiences of the schizophrenic population. These modes can include self-reports, clinical and/or therapeutic data, statements from guardians or parents, physiological and neurological testing, etc. And these modes should not be employed in isolation or opposition to each other. Rather there should be a concerted effort to combine and utilize various approaches. Employing different techniques to tap the phenomenological experiences can aid in determining the validity and the reliability of the reported data. They can also help in defining what modalities of experience the subject is and is not in touch with (402).

Creativity Studies

In spite of popular opinion—aided and abetted by the work of R. D. Laing—which links creativity and madness, there is a surprising paucity of research in this area. Moreover, of the published research, the majority are case studies or phenomenological descriptions rather than quantitative or experimental. (That the former are likely to be done in non-English-speaking European countries, while the latter stem chiefly from the United States, is an interesting footnote on the geography and sociology of knowledge.)

The descriptive studies tend to feature either the content or the form of schizophrenic art work. The former include studies of patients' drawings of hallucinations (280) and fantasy (339) as representing symbolic content (123,124,125,126). The latter include attempts to trace the schizophrenic disintegration and reintegration of boundaries of self, time, space, motion, and perspective, as reflected in art.*

Quantitative research on schizophrenia and creativity has approached the issues of differentiating schizophrenic from nonschizophrenic art works as well as comparing the creativity of schizophrenics, artists, and normals. In one study, college graduates were no more accurate than psychologists in detecting schizophrenic drawings from those of college graduates. Another study showed that judges were able to rate whether paintings were done by schizophrenic or nonschizophrenic painters (244). Comparisons of the creative aptitudes of schizophrenics and normals found schizophrenics scoring lower on tests of divergent thinking (427). Moreover, creative normals showed greater tolerance than chronic schizophrenics for incongruity in information input (94). Similarly, when fifteen creative writers were compared with fifteen manic and fifteen schizophrenic patients, the writers and the manic patients showed more behavioral and conceptual overinclusion, while schizophrenics tended to be underinclusive and to show less bizarreness and conceptual richness than writers or manics (7). Finally, a study comparing the color choices in the painting of ten schizophrenic patients and nine normal subjects showed the schizophrenics used much more white, yellow, and violet than red, black, gray, and brown. At the same time their contrast values and levels of brightness were higher than that of normals.

* See references 36, 37, 48, 179, and 359.

At best, these studies point to an intrinsically interesting and potentially fruitful topic of study, one that has received insufficient attention from serious researchers. More often, however, they lack most what they purport to be most interested in—namely, creativity.

Interpersonal Relationships

This section has points which overlap with personality process and family attitudes and relationships. An attempt will be made to focus primarily on social aspects which are not specifically based on the familial environment.

The literature on schizophrenia is filled with studies and theories concerning the withdrawn behavior exhibited by psychotic patients. In a study looking at the high school behavior of individuals before they became schizophrenic, it was found that these subjects were less involved with student council, with language, academic, or special interest clubs, and with student publications (17,394). There was some concern expressed based on the comparison between the controls and schizophrenic individuals. Social class was not held constant. Also, some questions were raised as to whether social activities are independent of intelligence and academic achievement. Recent studies, using spatial distance and/or behavior as a technique to examine isolated and withdrawn behavior, have reported results conflicting with the preceding ones. Tolor (449), using a modification of Kuethe's social schemata technique, found no differences between schizophrenics and normals for placing neutral or social stimuli. Normals actually placed neutral stimuli farther apart. It was suggested that process schizophrenics do not indicate alienation or a wish for withdrawal from human contacts. Aronow et al. (9) reported evidence that supported Tolor's results. They found no indication that process schizophrenics were more interpersonally distant than reactive patients or normal controls. Howowitz (192) found that schizophrenic patients preserve unusually great space between self and others, especially during the acute phase of their illness. An environmental orientation study revealed that reactive schizophrenics were "approach-oriented," while process patients were "avoidance-oriented" (186)—in contrast to the reports of Tolor and Aronow. Duke and Mullens (120) looked at the relationship between interpersonal distance and locus-of-control orientation. They reported that schizophrenics were more externally oriented than nonschizophrenic patients and normals.

Different forms of communication—such as verbal communication, visual interaction, body orientation—have been employed to examine interpersonal relationships. Clark and Cullen (79) used two self-report scales to assess the type of communication people receive and what support systems are available. Their results support the hypothesis that there is an association between conflicting communications and schizophrenia. Visual-interaction studies have been rather consistent in their findings. Most report that schizophrenics look at the interviewer less than do other groups with which they are compared (244,379,380). Male process patients were found to look less at female interviewers (244). Shimkunas (406) reported that schizophrenics were markedly delusional and autistic in response to a demand that they reveal their feelings about several emotion-laden topics. Using a proverb test as a measure of interpersonal communication, Watson (465) observed that autism, or the loss of ability to abstract, in adult schizophrenics does not increase with the amount of interpersonal interaction in the task.

There has been much discussion about whether schizophrenics have control over how they present themselves in different situations. Recent work in impression management has resulted in some interesting findings. Kelley, Farina, and Mosher (214) gave their schizophrenic subjects the Phillips Scale for good-poor premorbid adjustment and then asked them to create favorable or unfavorable impressions. The schizophrenic women were capable of performing the task without receiving instructions on what constitutes good or bad behavior. Good premorbid schizophrenics showed a tendency to act in either fashion more easily than poor premorbid subjects. In cases where hospitalization, discharge, or the presence of a prominent figure was at stake, behaviors were seen to vary. Schizophrenic patients presented more organized, healthy appearances or more aloof, bizarre, and unstable conditions, depending upon how they viewed the situation. Tumer (452) conducted a study in which both chronic "good" and acute "poor" premorbid schizophrenics performed poorly to guarantee their stay in the hospital. However, chronic poors acted in a healthier fashion to enhance their chances for discharge. Braginsky and Braginsky (47) also reported that schizophrenics can appear healthy or sick depending on the type of interview being conducted. Watson (464), using a videotape of a waiting room, observed more abnormal behavior in schizophrenic patients when the staff psychologist was absent than when he was present. In a later study Watson (467) found that other diagnostic groups, neurotics and those with alcoholic character disorder, were also capable of impression management. These results argue against the hypothesis that schizophrenics are peculiarly capable of impression management.

There is some question about what kind of verbal and behavioral stimuli schizophrenics are responsive to, and to what degree. Watson (465), looking at interpersonal contact and verbal content of interacting with schizophrenics and normals, found that the abstract-thinking deficits in schizophrenics were more prominent with tasks including verbal stimuli.

The original hypothesis—that the loss of ability to think abstractly in adult schizophrenics would increase as the amount of interpersonal interaction increased—was not supported. A study (199) that used tape recordings of different patterns of parental dominance and had subjects respond with a task which was based on the pattern heard had provocative findings. Poor premorbid schizophrenics tended to support a maternal figure regardless of whether she was dominant, while good premorbid subjects tended to support the dominant figure, and the controls supported the parental figure who was not dominating the interaction. Pishkin and Bourne (340) reported that newly admitted schizophrenics were deficient in using social information and were more likely to be influenced by normal stooges' cues on a concept-identification task than other schizophrenics giving out information. Tasks employing censure techniques have also been employed in this area. Allen (3) found that normals and reactive schizophrenics improved their cognitive performance after interpersonal censure. Process schizophrenics got worse, on the other hand. Another study using a censure task and including the examiner's sex as a factor revealed that reactive males were more sensitive to the sex of the examiner than were process subjects (245). Schizophrenics and normals were asked to rate the "average American man," an unfavorably described individual, and a favorably described individual on fifteen trait-pair scales, both hypothetically and realistically (370). All subjects were fairly certain of their ratings for the favorably described individual; however, schizophrenics gave lower ratings than normals for the apparent personality of the "average American man" and the real personality of the unfavorably described individual.

Schizophrenics have been observed under competitive situations, hostile-friendly environments, hard-easy tasks, etc., to see how these conditions affect their performance. In two competitive situation studies the schizophrenics performed better after the incentive was added (87, 89). In one study specifically, schizophrenics exhibited less bizarre behavior after competition (89). It was felt that with results such as these promising behavior-modification programs might be forthcoming in the future. Fontana and Klein (135) found evidence to support the findings of Craig (87). They found that schizophrenics who were in a group that was evaluated by the researchers increased their performance on a reaction-time task, while schizophrenics in the nonevaluative group remained constant or decreased in performance. In a study looking at performances in accepting, hostile, or neutral settings, schizophrenics did worst in the hostile condition, and process subjects performed worse than reactives (55). The best results were found under the neutral setting.

Experimental work has been conducted to test the practicality of some of the findings concerning interpersonal contact and schizophrenic behavior. Spugel et al. (428), found no evidence of patient improvement as a result of student visitation of regressed schizophrenics. In a classical conditioning study using a tone-shock procedure, with and without the presence of a social agent, schizophrenics were found to increase their heart rate during tone-shock administration and a social interaction. Normals reduced their heart rate under the same conditions (149). Videotaping was used to measure the stability of interpersonal reactions of schizophrenics and chronic brain patients. Both groups showed stability in their interpersonal reactions over the two taping sessions (117). However, no comparison was made between the groups. It was suggested that the small sample sizes and individual differences may have minimized the nosological differences. Ravensborg (354) used money, praise, money and praise together, and a no-reward situation to increase the name recall and picture identification in schizophrenics. The group receiving money and praise together as a reinforcement showed the greatest change in mean score.

Finally, Frattner and Howard (140) examined the behavior of therapists toward schizophrenic patients, based on the work of Betz (32,33) and Rosenthal (372). They found that type A therapists did better with process patients, while type B therapists did better with neurotic outpatients. Type A therapists were reported to be biased toward patients of low social competence—a bias that was reflected in variations in a therapist's voice (140). Obviously a therapist's attitude can affect the treatment process and/or outcome. Findings such as these should be used as steppingstones for further research in exploring the behavior and biases of therapists as well as those of their patients.

Epilogue

After wending one's way through the mass of reported data concerning psychological studies of schizophrenia, it would be folly to attempt any sort of summary or conclusion. To some extent these were made in the beginning of this chapter. It is difficult to discern, in the cacophony of numerous voices, a particular tone, pattern, melody, or guiding principle. There is a welter of sundry bits of information, but little crystallization of knowledge.

Some of the shortcomings that have plagued schizophrenia research have not disappeared; they still persist. First is the matter of controls in investigation. Many studies do not report whether the patients were medicated; and there is not much systematic psychopharmacological information regarding the effects of the different drugs employed, and the effects of their different dosages. Furthermore, adequate controls for sex, age, socioeconomic status, and length of hospitalization are often lacking or are not reported.

The second shortcoming is the large number of "single shot" studies which are casual forays into the field and are not integrated with an available body of information or a clearly enunciated theoretical stance. The few outstanding exceptions to this trend made a contribution in their programatic pursuit of integrated sets of variables.

Third is the problem with the control groups employed in studying the alleged characteristics of schizophrenics; in a way this is an extension of the control issue. If "normals" only are used as controls, or normals and organics, still lacking are comparisons with groups where the problem of differential diagnosis is most salient.

Fourth, the typology within schizophrenia, although useful, leaves much to be desired. Methods by means of which classifiers arrive at "process-reactive," "good" or "poor premorbid," "paranoid" versus "nonparanoid" are far from uniform and remain a significant source of error.

Fifth, much psychological research deals not with direct observation or phenomenological reporting but with inferences from limited empirical samples of response which depend on interpretive hypotheses that are themselves in need of further confirmation. This is a "bootstrap" operation. Perhaps more systematic, prolonged, and longitudinal observations in naturalistic settings should be encouraged.

Finally, ideally we could avoid this "sprawl" of publication, which is not cumulative, if we had a stable theory of the *normal* personality and its developmental antecedents. Such a theory could then point to the relevant aspects to be studied in the several patterns of deviation—including the schizophrenic syndrome.

BIBLIOGRAPHY

1. Adler, D., and Harrow, M. 1974. Idiosyncratic thinking and personally overinvolved thinking in schizophrenic patients during partial recovery. *Comprehensive Psychiatry* 15(1):57–67.

2. Al-Issa, I. 1972. Stimulus generalization and overinclusion in normal and schizophrenic subjects. *Journal of Consulting and Clinical Psychology* 39(2):182–86.

3. Allen, P. G. 1974. The effect of interpersonal censure on the cognitive performance of acute process and reactive schizophrenic patients. *Journal of Psychology* 87(1):103–6.

4. Alumbaugh, R. V., and Stoney, A. B. 1973. Application of any information model to schizophrenia: Relationship to relevancy and irrelevancy. *Psychological Reports* 32(2):519–29.

5. Andorfer, J. C.; Shimkunas, A. M.; and Sciauni, J. W. 1975. Neutralization of affective concepts on schizophrenia. *Journal of Abnormal Psychology* 84(6):722–25.

6. Andreasen, N. J., and Powers, P. S. 1974. Overinclusive thinking in mania and schizophrenia. *British Journal of Psychiatry* 125:452–56.

7. Andreasen, N. J., and Powers, P. S. 1975. Creativity and psychosis: An examination of conceptual style. *Archives of General Psychiatry* 32(1):70–73.

8. Arieti, S. 1973. Anxiety and beyond in schizophrenia and psychotic depression. *American Journal of Psychotherapy* 27(3):338–45.

9. Aronow, E.; Reznikoff, M.; and Tryon, W. W. 1975. The interpersonal distance of process and reactive schizophrenics. *Journal of Consulting and Clinical Psychology* 43(1):94.

10. Ax, A. F., et al. 1970. Autonomic condition in chronic schizophrenia. *Journal of Abnormal Psychology* 76(1):140–54.

11. Baer, P. E., and Fuhrer, M. J. 1968. Cognitive factors in differential conditioning of the GSR: Use of a reaction time task as the UCS c/normals and schizophrenics. *Psychophysiology* 4(4):501.

12. Bannister, D. 1960. Conceptual structure of thought-disordered schizophrenics. *Journal of Mental Science* 106:1230–49.

13. Bannister, D. 1962. The nature and measurement of schizophrenic thought disorder. *Journal of Mental Science* 108:825–42.

14. Bannister, D. 1977. The logical requirements of research into schizophrenia. *Schizophrenia Bulletin* 4:72–77.

15. Bannister, D., and Fransella, F. 1966. A grid test of schizophrenic thought disorder. *British Journal of Social and Clinical Psychology* 5:95–102.

16. Bannister, D.; Frith, C. D.; and Lillie, F. J. 1972. Critiques of the concept of "loose construing": A reply. *British Journal of Social and Clinical Psychology* 11(4):412–14.

17. Barthell, C. N., and Holmes, D. S. 1968. High school yearbooks: A nonreactive measure of social isolation in graduates who later became schizophrenic. *Journal of Abnormal Psychology* 73:313–16.

18. Bassos, C. A. 1973. Affective content and contextual constraint in recall by paranoid, nonparanoid, and nonpsychiatric patients. *Journal of Consulting and Clinical Psychology* 40(1):126–32.

19. Bauman, E., and Kolisnyk, E. 1973. Input and output interference in schizophrenic short-term memory. *Proceedings of the 81st Annual Convention of the American Psychological Association* (Montreal, Canada), 8:467–68.

20. Bauman, E., and Murray, D. J. 1968. Recognition versus recall in schizophrenia. *Canadian Journal of Psychology* 22(1):18–25.

21. Begelman, D. A., and Hersen, M. 1973. An experimental analysis of the verbal-motor discrepancy in schizophrenia. *Journal of Clinical Psychology* 29(2):175–79.

22. Bellak, L., and Hurvich, M. 1969. A systematic study of ego functions. *Journal of Nervous and Mental Disease* 148(6):569–85.

23. Bellak, L.; Hurvich, M.; and Gediman, H. 1973. *Ego functions in schizophrenics, neurotics and normals* (New York: John Wiley).

24. Bellak, L.; Hurvich, M.; Gediman, H.; and Crawford, P. J. 1970. Study of ego functions in the schizophrenic syndrome. *Archives of General Psychiatry* 23(4):326–36.

25. Bellak, L., and Loeb, L., 1969. *The schizophrenic syndrome* (New York: Grune & Stratton).

26. Bellissimo, A., and Steffy, R. A. 1972. Redundancy—associated deficit in schizophrenic reaction time performance. *Journal of Abnormal Psychology* 80(3):299–307.

27. Bellissimo, A., and Steffy, R. A. 1975. Contextual influences on crossover in the reaction time performance of schizophrenics. *Journal of Abnormal Psychology* 84(3):210–20.

28. Benjamin, T. B., and Watt, N. F. 1969. Psychopathology and semantic interpretation of ambiguous words. *Journal of Abnormal Psychology* 74:706–14.

29. Bergman, R. L., and Ranz, J. 1975. Model-facilitated cooperative behavior in regressed schizophrenics. *Perceptual and Motor Skills* 40(3):894.

30. Bernstein, A. S. 1968. The orienting response and direction of stimulus change. *Psychonomic Science* 12(4):127–28.

31. Bernstein, A. S. 1970. Phase electrodermal orienting responses in chronic schizophrenia: II. Response to auditory signals of varying intensity. *Journal of Abnormal Psychology* 75(2):146–56.

32. Betz, B. J. 1963. Differential success rates of psychotherapists with process and nonprocess schizophrenic patients. *American Journal of Psychiatry* 119:1090–91.

33. Betz, B. J. 1967. Studies of the therapist's role in the treatment of the schizophrenic patient. *American Journal of Psychiatry* 123:963–71.

34. Bible, G. H., and Magaro, P. 1971. Response hierarchy disorganization for chronic and acute schizophrenia. *Journal of Genetic Psychology* 119(1):119–26.

35. Biles, P. E., and Heckel, R. V. 1968. "Awareness" in chronic schizophrenia: II. Awareness of causal factors in recent events. *Psychological Reports* 22(1):255–58.

36. Billig, O. 1969. Structures of schizophrenic expressive forms. *Confinia Psychiatrica* 12(1): 1–22.

37. Billig, O. 1971. Is schizophrenic expression art? A comparative study of creativeness and schizophrenic thinking. *Journal of Nervous and Mental Disease* 153(3):145–64.

38. Billig, O. 1973. The schizophrenic "artists" expression of movement. *Confinia Psychiatrica* 16(1):1–27.

39. Blaney, P. H. 1974. Two studies on the language behavior of schizophrenia. *Journal of Abnormal Psychology* 83(1):23–31.

40. Blatt, S. J.; Brenneis, C. B.; Schimek, J. G.; and Glick, M. 1976. Normal development and psychopathological impairment of the concept of the object on the Rorschach. *Journal of Abnormal Psychology* 81(4):364–73.

41. Blatt, S. J., and Ritzler, B. A. 1974. Thought disorder and boundary disturbances in psychosis. *Journal of Consulting and Clinical Psychology* 421:370–81.

42. Blatt, S. J., and Wild, C. M. 1976. *Schizophrenia: A developmental analysis* (New York: Academic Press).

43. Blatt, S. J.; Wild, C. M.; and Ritzler, B. A. 1975. Disturbances of object representations in schizophrenia. In *Psychoanalysis and Contemporary science*, ed. D. Spence (New York: International Universities Press), vol. 4, pp. 235:90.

44. Boland, T. B., and Chapman, L. 1971. Conflicting predictions from Broen's and Chapman's theories of schizophrenic thought disorder. *Journal of Abnormal Psychology* 78(1):52–58.

45. Borinsky, M.; Neale, J. M.; Fox, R.; and Cromwell, R. L. 1973. Two flash thresholds in normal and subclassified schizophrenic groups. *Perceptual and Motor Skills* 36(3):911–15.

46. Braatz, G. A. 1970. Preference intrasensitivity as an indicator of cognitive slippage in schizophrenia. *Journal of Abnormal Psychology* 75(1):1–6.

47. Braginsky, B. M., and Braginsky, D. D. 1967. Schizophrenic patients in the psychiatric interview: An experimental study of their effectiveness of manifestation. *Journal of Consulting Psychology* 31(6):143–47.

48. Breakey, W. R., and Goodell, H. 1972. Thought disorder in mania and schizophrenia evaluated by Bannister's Grid Test for schizophrenic thought disorder. *British Journal of Psychiatry* 120(557):391–95.

49. Brengelmann, J. C., and Goldsmith, R. W. 1971. Effects of practice, exposure time and difficulty on the learning of abnormals. *Archiv für Psychologie* 123(2):120–28.

50. Brenneis, C. B. 1971. Factors affecting diagnostic judgements of manifest dream content in schizophrenia. *Psychological Reports* 29(3):311–18.

51. Brenneis, C. B. 1971. Features of the manifest dream in schizophrenia. *Journal of Nervous and Mental Disease* 153(2):81–91.

52. Broadbent, D. E. 1958. *Perception and communication* (New York: Macmillan).

53. Broadbent, D. E. 1971. *Decision and stress* (London: Academic Press).

54. Broadbent, D. E. 1977. Hidden preattentive processes. *American Psychologist* 32(2):109–18.

55. Brodsky, M. J. 1968. Sorting behavior and arousal level. *Proceedings of the 76th Annual Convention of the American Psychological Association*, 3:537–38.

56. Broekma, V., and Rosenbaum, G. 1975. Cutaneous sensitivity in schizophrenics and normals under two levels of proprioceptive arousal. *Journal of Abnormal Psychology* 84(1):30–35.

57. Broen, W. E., and Nakamura, C. Y. 1972. Reduced range of sensory sensitivity in chronic nonparanoid schizophrenics. *Journal of Abnormal Psychology* 79(1):106–11.

58. Broen, W. E., and Storms, L. H. 1966. Lawful disorganization: The process underlying a schizophrenic syndrome. *Psychological Review* 73:265–79.

59. Bromel, E., and Harrow, M. 1973. Behavioral overinclusion as a prognostic index in schizophrenic disorder. *Journal of Abnormal Psychology* 82(2):345–49.

60. Brown, R. 1973. Schizophrenia, language and reality. *American Psychologist* 28(5):395–403.

61. Bullock, G. M., and Johnson, B. S. 1970. A study of differences in causal thinking between schizophrenic and nonschizophrenic patients. *Nursing Research* 19(2):129–34.

62. Bustinova, L. 1972. Verbal conditioning in simple and paranoid forms of schizophrenia. *Studia Psychologica* 14(2)183–85.

63. Caldwell, D. F., and Dommo, E. F. 1967. Electroencephalographic and eye movement pat-

terns during sleep on chronic schizophrenic patients. *Electroencephalography and Clinical Neurophysiology* 22(5):414–20.

64. Calhoun, J. F. 1970. Changing schizophrenic conceptualization by enrichment. *British Journal of Social and Clinical Psychology* 9(2):185–86.

65. Calhoun, J. F. 1971. Comment on differentiating paranoid from nonparanoid schizophrenics. *Journal of Consulting and Clinical Psychology* 36(1):104–5.

66. Cancro, R. 1969. Conceptual plasticity and prognosis in acute schizophrenia. *Proceedings of the 77th Annual Convention of the American Psychological Association* 4(part 2):571–72.

67. Cancro, R. 1971. Sophistication of body concept in process-reactive schizophrenia. *Perceptual and Motor Skills* 32(2):567–70.

68. Cancro, R.; Sutloy, S.; Keir, J.; and Sugerman, A. A. 1971. Reaction time and prognosis in acute schizophrenia. *Journal of Nervous and Mental Disease* 153(5):351–59.

69. Carlson, V., and Feinberg, I. 1968. Individual variation in time judgment and the concept of an internal clock. *Journal of Experimental Psychology* 77:631–40.

70. Cartwright, R. D. 1972. Sleep fantasy in normal and schizophrenic persons. *Journal of Abnormal Psychology* 80(3):275–79.

71. Cash, T. F.; Neale, J. M.; and Cromwell, R. L. 1972. Span of apprehension in acute schizophrenics: Full-report technique. *Journal of Abnormal Psychology* 79(3):322–26.

72. Cash, T. F., and Stack, J. J. 1973. Locus of control among schizophrenics and other hospitalized psychiatric patients. *Genetic Psychology Monographs* 87(1):105–22.

73. Chaika, E. 1974. A linguist looks at "schizophrenic" language. *Brain and Language* 1:257–76.

74. Chapman, L. J. 1961. Emotional factors in schizophrenic deficit. *Psychological Reports* 9:564.

75. Chapman, L. J., and Chapman, J. P. 1973. *Disordered thought in schizophrenia* (New York: Appleton-Century-Crofts).

76. Chapman, L. J.; Chapman, J. P.; and Miller, G. A. 1964. A theory of verbal behavior in schizophrenia. In *Progress in experimental personality research*, ed. B. A. Maher (New York: Academic Press), vol. 1.

77. Cicchetti, D. V. 1969. Cortical review of the research relating mother dominance to schizophrenia. *Proceedings of the 77th Annual Convention of the American Psychological Association* 4(2):557–58.

78. Ciottone, R. A., and McCarthy, J. F. 1969. Sequential effects of praise and censure upon learning in schizophrenics. *Proceedings of the 77th Annual Convention of the American Psychological Association* 4(2):495–96.

79. Clark, A. W., and Cullen, W. E. 1974–75. Social support: A counter to pathogenic communication. *Interpersonal Development* 5(11):50–59.

80. Cliffs, M. J. 1974. Reinstatement of speech in mute schizophrenics by operant conditioning. *Acta Psychiatrica Scandinavica* 50(6):577–85.

81. Cohen, B. P., and Camhi, J. 1967. Schizophrenic performance in a word communication task. *Journal of Abnormal Psychology* 72:240–46.

82. Cohen, B. P.; Nachmani, G.; and Rosenberg, F. 1974. Referent communication disturbance in acute schizophrenia. *Journal of Abnormal Psychology* 83(1):1–13.

83. Comalli, P. E. 1973. Perceptual regression in schizophrenics. *Journal of Clinical Psychology* 29(4):433–37.

84. Court, J. H., and Garwoli, E. 1968. Schizophrenic performance on a reaction-time task with increasing levels of complexity. *British Journal of Social and Clinical Psychology* 7(3):216–23.

85. Craig, R. J. 1970. Relationship between severity of illness and overinclusive thinking in schizophrenia. *Psychological Reports* 26(1):251–54.

86. Craig, R. G. 1970. Significant intercorrelations among measures of overinclusive thinking. *Psychological Reports* 26(3):571–74.

87. Craig, R. J. 1971. Absolute and relative performance of schizophrenics under competition. *Journal of Consulting and Clinical Psychology* 37(1):75–79.

88. Craig, R. J. 1971. Overinclusive thinking and schizophrenia. *Journal of Personality Assessment* 35(3):208–23.

89. Craig, R. J. 1973. Interpersonal competition, overinclusive thinking, and schizophrenia. *Journal of Consulting and Clinical Psychology* 40(1):9–14.

90. Cressen, R. 1975. Artistic quality of drawings and judges' evaluations of the DAP. *Journal of Personality Assessment* 39(2):132–37.

91. Cromwell, R. L. 1968. Stimulus redundancy and schizophrenia. *Journal of Nervous and Mental Disease* 146(5):360–75.

92. Cromwell, R. L. 1975. Assessment of schizophrenia. *Annual Review of Psychology* 26:593–620.

93. Cromwell, R. L., and Dohecki, P. R. 1968. Schizophrenic language: A disattention interpretation. In *Developments in applied psycholinguistic research*, eds. S. Rosenberg and J. H. Koplin (New York: Macmillan).

94. Cropley, A. J., and Sikand, J. S. 1973. Creativity and schizophrenia. *Journal of Consulting and Clinical Psychology* 40(3):462–68.

95. Dant, R. L., and Chapman, L. J. 1974. Object sorting and the heterogeneity of schizophrenia. *Journal of Abnormal Psychology* 83(5):581–84.

96. Darby, J. A. 1970. Alterations of some body image indices in schizophrenics. *Journal of Consulting and Clinical Psychology* 35(1):16–121.

97. Davidson, G. S., and Neale, J. M. 1974. The effects of signal-noise similarity on visual information processing of schizophrenics. *Journal of Abnormal Psychology* 83(6):683–86.

98. Davis, D.; Cromwell, R. L.; and Held, J. M. 1967. Size estimation in emotionally disturbed children and schizophrenic adults. *Journal of Abnormal Psychology* 72:395–401.

99. Davis, K. M., and Blaney, P. H. 1976. Overinclusion and self-editing in schizophrenia. *Journal of Abnormal Psychology* 85(1):51–60.

100. Davis, W. E.; Beck, S. J.; and Ryan, T. 1973. Race-related and educationally-related

MMPI profile differences among hospitalized schizophrenics. *Journal of Clinical Psychology* 29(4): 478–79.

101. Davis, W. E., and DeWolfe, A. S. 1971. Premorbid adjustment and affectual expression in schizophrenia. *Journal of Abnormal Psychology* 78(2);198–201.

102. Davis, W. E.; Dizzonne, M. F.; and DeWolfe, A. S. 1971. Relationships among WAIS subtest scores, patient's premorbid history, and institutionalization. *Journal of Consulting and Clinical Psychology* 36(3):400–403.

103. Deckner, C. W., and Cromwell, R. L. 1970. Commonality of word association responses in schizophrenia as a function of premorbid adjustment, chronicity, and paranoid status. *Psychological Reports* 26:503–9.

104. Depue, R. A. 1974. The specificity of response interference to schizophrenia. *Journal of Abnormal Psychology* 83(5):529–32.

105. Depue, R. A., and Fowles, D. C. 1973. Electrodermal activity as an index of arousal in schizophrenics. *Psychological Bulletin* 99(4):233–38.

106. Depue, R. A., and Fowles, D. C. 1974. Conceptual ability, response interference, and arousal in withdrawn and active schizophrenics. *Journal of Consulting and Clinical Psychology* 42: 509–18.

107. DeWolfe, A. S. 1968. Self-reports and case histories of schizophrenic patients: Reliability and validity of Phillips scale ratings. *Journal of Clinical Psychology* 24(4):415–18.

108. DeWolfe, A. S. 1971. Cognitive structure and pathology in associations of process and reactive schizophrenics. *Journal of Abnormal Psychology* 78:148–53.

109. DeWolfe, A. S. 1973. Premorbid adjustment and the sex of the patient: Implications of Phillips scale ratings for male and female schizophrenics. *Journal of Community Psychology* 1(1): 63–67.

110. DeWolfe, A. S. 1974. Are there two kinds of thinking process and reactive schizophrenics? *Journal of Abnormal Psychology* 83(3):285–90.

111. DeWolfe, A. S., and Konieczny, J. A. 1973. Premorbid adjustment and short-term recall in schizophrenia. *Journal of Clinical Psychology* 29(1):14–16.

112. DeWolfe, A. S., and McDonald, R. K. 1972. Sex differences and institutionalization in the word associations of schizophrenics. *Journal of Consulting and Clinical Psychology* 39:215–21.

113. DeWolfe, A. S., and Youkilis, H. D. 1974. Stress and word associations of process-reactive schizophrenics. *Journal of Clinical Psychology* 30:151–53.

114. DeWolfe, A. S.; Youkilis, H. D.; and Konieczny, J. A. 1975. Psychophysiological correlates of responsiveness in schizophrenia. *Journal of Consulting and Clinical Psychology* 43(2):192–97.

115. Dilling, C., and Rabin, A. I. 1967. Temporal experience in depressive states and schizophrenia. *Journal of Consulting Psychology* 31:604–8.

116. Dimond, R., and Hirt, M. 1973. Body involvement among schizophrenics, normals and paraplegics. *Social Behavior and Personality* 1(1):33–34.

117. Dinoff, M.; Taylor, G. E.; Lyman, R.; and Reynolds, R. 1971. Stability of interpersonal reaction via videotape: Comparisons of organics and schizophrenia. *Psychological Reports* 9(3): 1313–14.

118. Dokecki, P. R.; Cromwell, R. L.; and Polidoro, L. G. 1968. The premorbid adjustment and chronicity dimensions as they relate to commonality and stability of word associations in schizophrenia. *Journal of Nervous and Mental Disease* 146(4):310–11.

119. Douglas, D. G., and Sara, D. 1975. Handwriting in schizophrenia: Some clinical observations. *Diseases of the Nervous System* 36(10):561–67.

120. Duke, M. P., and Mullens, C. 1973. Preferred interpersonal distance as a function of locus of control orientation in chronic schizophrenics, nonschizophrenic patients, and normals. *Journal of Consulting and Clinical Psychology* 41(2):230–34.

121. Ecker, J.; Levine, J.; and Zigler, E. 1973. Impaired sex-role identification in schizophrenia expressed in the comprehension of humor stimuli. *Journal of Psychology* 83(1):67–77.

122. Emmerich, D. S., and Levine, F. M. 1970. Differences in auditory sensitivity of chronic schizophrenic patients and normal controls determined by use of a forced choice procedure. *Diseases of the Nervous System* 31(8):552–57.

123. Enachescu, C. 1967. Psychological contributions concerning models and sculptures of schizophrenic patients. *Annales Medico-Psychologiques* 2(4):541–60.

124. Enachescu, C. 1968. The psychopathological analysis of plastic expressions in familial schizophrenia. *Neuropsychiatria* 24(2):392–419.

125. Enachescu, C. 1971. Contribution to the study of drawing disturbances in schizophrenia of the adolescent. *Neurologia, Pschiatria, Neurochirurgia* 16(5):431–44.

126. Enachescu, C. 1972. The dynamics of art expressed by schizophrenics. *Neurologia, Pschiatria, Neurochirurgia* 17(3):259–74.

127. Evans, R. C. 1973. Dream conception and reality testing in children. *Journal of the American Academy of Child Psychiatry* 12(1):73–92.

128. Farina, A., and Holzberg, J. 1967. Attitude and behaviors of fathers and mothers of male schizophrenics. *Journal of Abnormal Psychology* 72(5):381–87.

129. Farina, A., and Holzberg, J. 1970. Anxiety level of schizophrenic and control patients and their parents. *Journal of Abnormal Psychology* 75(2):157–63.

130. Feinsilver, D. 1970. Communication in families of schizophrenic patients: Describing common objects as a test of communication between family members. *Archives of General Psychiatry* 22(2):143–48.

131. Fenz, W. D., and Velner, J. 1970. Physiological concomitants of behavioral indices in schizophrenia. *Journal of Abnormal Psychology* 76(1):27–35.

132. Ferry, W. P., and Velner, J. 1970. Physiological concomitants of behavioral indices in schizophrenia. *Journal of Abnormal Psychology* 76(1):27–35.

133. Fischer, R.; Ristine, L. P.; and Wisecup, P. 1969. Increase in gustatory acuity and hyperarousal in schizophrenia. *Biological Psychiatry* 1(3):209–18.

134. Flekkoy, K. 1975. Changes of associative performance in hospitalized schizophrenics: A 16-year follow-up. *Acta Psychiatrica Scandinavica* 52:330–35.

135. Fontana, A. F., and Klein, E. B. 1968. Self-presentation and the schizophrenic "deficit." *Journal of Consulting and Clinical Psychology* 32(3):250–56.

136. Forrest, A. D.; Hay, A. J.; and Kushner, A. W. 1969. Studies in speech disorder in schizophrenia. *British Journal of Psychiatry* 115(24):833–41.

137. Foulds, G. A.; Hope, K.; McPherson, F. M.; and Mayo, R. R. 1967. Cognitive disorder among the schizophrenics: II. Differences between the subcategories. *British Journal of Psychiatry* 113(505):1369–74.

138. Foulds, G. A.; Hope, K.; McPherson, F. M.; and Mayo, R. R. 1968. Paranoid delusions, retardation and overinclusive thinking. *Journal of Clinical Psychology* 24(2):177–78.

139. Fowles, D. C.; Watt, N. F.; Maher, B. A.; and Grimspoon, L. 1970. Autonomic arousal in good and poor premorbid schizophrenics. *British Journal of Social and Clinical Psychology* 9(2):135–47.

140. Frattner, J. H., and Howard, K. I. 1970. A preliminary investigation of covert communication of expectancies to schizophrenics. *Journal of Abnormal Psychology* 75(3):245–47.

141. Freedman, B. 1974. The subjective experience of perceptual and cognitive disturbances in schizophrenia: A review of autobiographical accounts. *Archives of General Psychiatry* 30(3):333–40.

142. Freedman, B., and Chapman, L. J. 1973. Early subjective experience in schizophrenic episode. *Journal of Abnormal Psychology* 82(1):46–54.

143. Freedman, N., and Steingart, I. 1975. Kinesic internalization and language construction. In *Psychoanalysis and contemporary science*, ed. D. Spence (New York: International Universities Press), vol. 4, pp. 355–403.

144. Freeman, T.; Cameron, J. L.; and McGhie, A. 1966. *Studies on psychosis* (New York: International Universities Press).

145. Freud, S. 1915. Instincts and their vicissitudes. In *Standard edition of the complete psychological works of Sigmund Freud*, ed. J. Strachey (London: Hogarth Press, 1947), vol. 14, pp. 117–40.

146. Frith, C. D., and Lillie, F. J. 1972. Why does the repertory grid test indicate thought disorder? *British Journal of Social and Clinical Psychology* 11:73–78.

147. Fromkin, V. A. 1975. A linguist looks at "A linguist looks at schizophrenic language." *Brain and Language* 2(4):498–503.

148. Furth, H. G., and Youniss, J. 1968. Schizophrenic thinking on nonverbal conceptual discovery, and transfer tasks. *Journal of Nervous and Mental Disease* 146(5):376–83.

149. Galtozzi, R. E. 1971. The effect of person on a conditional emotional response of schizophrenic and normal subjects. *Conditional Reflex* 6(4):181–90.

150. Gardner, R. W.; Holzman, P. S.; Klein, G. S.; Linton, H. B.; and Spence, D. P. 1959. Cognitive control: A study of individual consistencies in cognitive behavior. *Psychological Issues* 1:4.

151. Gerver, D. 1967. Linguistic rules and the perception and recall of speech by schizophrenic patients. *British Journal of Social and Clinical Psychology* 6(3):204–11.

152. Glades, M. 1967. Retention of verbal paired associates by schizophrenic subjects. *Psychological Reports* 21(1):241–6.

153. Goldstone, S., and Goldfarb, J. L. 1962. Time estimation and psychopathology. *Perceptual and Motor Skills* 15:28.

154. Goldstone, S. 1975. The variability of temporal judgement in psychopathology. In *Experimental approaches to psychopathology*, eds. M. L. Kietzman, S. Sutton, and J. Zubin (New York: Academic Press).

155. Gordon, M. C. 1973. Suggestibility of chronic schizophrenics and normal males matched for age. *International Journal of Clinical and Experimental Hypnosis* 21(4):284–88.

156. Grand, S.; Freedman, N.; and Steingart, I. 1973. A study of the representation of objects in schizophrenia. *Journal of the American Psychoanalytic Association* 21:399–434.

157. Grand, S.; Freedman, N.; Steingart, I.; and Buchwald, C. 1975. Communicative behavior in schizophrenia: The relation of adaptive styles to kinetic and linguistic aspects of interview behavior. *Journal of Nervous and Mental Disease* 161(5):293–306.

158. Grand, S.; Steingart, I.; Freedman, N.; Buchwald, C. 1975. Organization of language behavior and cognitive performance in chronic schizophrenia. *Journal of Abnormal Psychology* 84(6):621–28.

159. Gray, A. L. 1975. Autonomic correlates of chronic schizophrenia: A reaction time paradigm. *Journal of Abnormal Psychology* 84(3):189–96.

160. Greene, J. T. 1969. Hypnotizability of hospitalized psychotics. *International Journal of Clinical and Experimental Hypnosis* 17(2):103–8.

161. Grimes, C., and McGhie, A. 1973. Stimulus overload in schizophrenia. *Canadian Journal of Behavioral Science* 5:101–9.

162. Gruzelier, J. H. 1973. Bilateral asymmetry of skin conductance orienting activity and levels in schizophrenics. *Biological Psychology* 1(1):21–41.

163. Gruzelier, J. H., and Venables, P. H. 1972. Skin conductance orienting activity in a heterogeneous sample of schizophrenics. *Journal of Nervous and Mental Disease* 155(4):277–87.

164. Gruzelier, J. H., and Venables, P. H. 1973. Skin conductance responses to tones with and without attentional significance and nonschizophrenic psychiatric patients. *Neuropsychologia* 11(2):221–30.

165. Gruzelier, J. H., and Venables, P. H. 1974. Bimodality and lateral asymmetry of skin conductance orienting activity in schizophrenics: Replication and evidence of lateral asymmetry in patients with depression and disorders of personality. *Biological Psychiatry* 8(1):55–73.

166. Gruzelier, J. H., and Venables, P. H. 1974. Two-flash threshold, sensitivity, and B in normal subjects and schizophrenics. *Quarterly Journal of Experimental Psychology* 26(4):594–604.

167. Guertin, W. H.; Ladd, C. E.; Frank, G. H.; Rabin, A. I.; and Hiester, D. S. 1971. Research with the Wechsler Intelligence Scales for Adults: 1965–1970. *The Psychological Record* 21:239–89.

168. Hamlin, R. M., and Lorr, M. 1971. Differentiation of normals, neurotics, paranoids, and nonparanoids. *Journal of Abnormal Psychology* 77:90–96.

169. Harmatz, M. G.; Mendelsohn, R.; and Glassman, M. L. 1975. Gathering naturalistic objec-

tive data on the behavior of schizophrenic patients. *Hospital and Community Psychiatry* 26(2):83–86.

170. Harris, J. G. 1975. An abbreviated form of the Phillips Rating Scale of Premorbid Adjustment in Schizophrenia. *Journal of Abnormal Psychology* 84(2):129–37.

171. Harrison, A. W.; Spellman, M. S.; and Mellsop, G. W. 1972. The proverbs test for disorder of thinking in schizophrenia and mania. *Australian and New Zealand Journal of Psychiatry* 6(1):52–56.

172. Harrow, M.; Adler, D.; and Hanf, E. 1974. Abstract and concrete thinking in schizophrenia during the prechronic phase. *Archives of General Psychiatry* 31(1):27–33.

173. Harrow, M.; Bromet, E., and Quinlan, D. 1974. Predictors of posthospital adjustment in schizophrenia: Thought disorders and schizophrenic diagnosis. *Journal of Neurosis and Mental Diseases* 158(1):25–36.

174. Harrow, M.; Tucker, G.; Hummelhoch, J.; and Putman, N. 1972. Schizophrenic "thought disorders" after the acute phase. *American Journal of Psychiatry* 128(7):824–29.

175. Hartwich, P. 1971. Study of colors used in the paintings of schizophrenics. *Zeitschrift für Psychotherapie and Medizinische Psychologie* 21(2):64–73.

176. Hawks, D. V., and Marshall, W. L. 1971. A parsimonious theory of overinclusive thinking and retardation in schizophrenia. *British Journal of Medical Psychology* 44(1):75–83.

177. Hawks, D. V., and Payne, R. W. 1972. Overinclusive thinking and concept identification in psychiatric patients and normals. *British Journal of Medical Psychology* 45(1):57–69.

178. Haynes, E. T., and Phillips, J. P. 1973. Inconsistency, loose constructs and schizophrenic thought disorder. *British Journal of Psychiatry* 123:209–17.

179. Hearturch, W., and Know, W. 1969. Experiences with groups who faint during psychiatry. *Psychiatrie, Neurologie und Medizinische Psychologie* 21(11):421–27.

180. Heather, N. 1976. The specificity of schizophrenic thought disorder: A replication and extension of previous findings. *British Journal of Social and Clinical Psychology* 15:131–37.

181. Heilbrun, A. B. 1973. *Aversive maternal control* (New York: John Wiley).

182. Helmsley, D. E. 1975. A two-state model of attention in schizophrenic research. *British Journal of Social and Clinical Psychology* 14(1):81–89.

183. Helmsley, D. E. 1976. Attention and information processing on schizophrenics. *British Journal of Social and Clinical Psychology* 15:199–211.

184. Hieatt, D. J., and Tong, J. E. 1969. Differences between normals and schizophrenics on activation-induced change in two-flash fusion threshold. *British Journal of Psychiatry* 115(521):477–78.

185. Higgins, J. 1968. Commonality of word association responses in schizophrenia as a function of chronicity and adjustment: A response to Dokecki, Cromwell and Polidero. *Journal of Nervous and Mental Disease* 146(4):312–13.

186. Higgins, J. 1968. Process-reactive schizophrenia and environmental orientation. *Journal of Schizophrenia* 2(2):72–80.

187. Ho, D. Y. 1974. Modern logic and schizophrenic thinking. *Genetic Psychology Monographs* 89(1):145–65.

188. Holzman, P. S. 1970. Perceptual dysfunction in the schizophrenic syndrome. In *The schizophrenic reaction*, ed. R. Lanero (New York: Brunner/Mazel), pp. 216–32.

189. Holzman, P. S.; Proctor, L. R.; and Hughes, D. W. 1973. Eye teaching patterns in schizophrenia. *Science* 181(4095):179–81.

190. Honers, T., and Nichols, K. A. 1975. Types of overinclusion and emotional arousal. *Perceptual and Motor Skills* 38(3):933–34.

191. Hope, K.; McPherson, F. M.; and Mayo, R. R. 1967. Cognitive disorder among the schizophrenics: II. The validity of some tests of thought-process disorder. *British Journal of Psychiatry* 113(505):1361–68.

192. Horowitz, M. J. 1968. Spatial behavior and psychopathology. *Journal of Nervous and Mental Disease* 146(1):24–35.

193. Houpt, J. L.; Tucker, G. J.; and Harrow, M. 1972. Disordered cognition and stimulus processing. *American Journal of Psychiatry* 128(12):1505–10.

194. Huber, R. J., and Stiggins, R. J. 1970. Double-aspect perception and social interest. *Perceptual and Motor Skills* 30(2):387–92.

195. Hustmyer, F. E. 1969. Eye movement consistency and relationship to the process-reactive dimension in schizophrenia. *Perceptual and Motor Skills* 29(2):448–50.

196. Hustmyer, F. E. 1970. Eye movements, intelligence and field dependency in schizophrenics. *Perceptual and Motor Skills* 30(3):703–6.

197. Hurvich, M., and Bellak, L. 1968. Ego function patterns in schizophrenics. *Psychological Reports* 22(1):299–308.

198. Ivison, D. J. 1972. Overinclusion and short-term memory. *British Journal of Social and Clinical Psychology* 11(3):298–99.

199. Jackson, N. L. 1970. Sex and dominance cues in good-poor premorbid schizophrenia. *Journal of Abnormal Psychology* 75(1):78–82.

200. Jerome, E. A., and Young, M. L. 1971. Means-end thinking of schizophrenics. *Psychological Reports* 29(3):855–62.

201. Jerome, E. A.; Young, M. L.; and Bostwick, S. B. 1969. Reality testing by schizophrenics. *Journal of Abnormal Psychology* 74:148–56.

202. Johnson, J. E., and Breliauskas, L. A. 1971. Two measures of overinclusive thinking in schizophrenia: A comparative analysis. *Journal of Abnormal Psychology* 77(2):149–54.

203. Johnson, J. E., and Petzel, T. P. 1971. Temporal orientation and time estimation in chronic schizophrenics. *Journal of Clinical Psychology* 27(2):194–96.

204. Johnson, J. E.; Petzel, T. P.; and Figueroa, P. 1973. The effects of positive versus negative social stimuli on the learning of process and reactive schizophrenics. *Journal of Social Psychology* 89(2):251–56.

205. Jones, G. 1973. Prediction of locus of control from performance on a perceptual recognition task. *Perceptual and Motor Skills* 36(1):99–102.

206. Jonson, C. O., and Sjostedt, A. 1973. Auditory perception in schizophrenia: A second study of the intonation test. *Acta Psychiatrica Scandinavica* 49(5):560–88.

207. Kantor, W.; Langdon, B.; Watts, W.; and Maltzman, I. 1968. Semantic conditioning and generalization of the orienting reflex in schizophrenics. *Proceedings of the 76th Annual Convention of the American Psychological Association* 3:505–6.

208. Kantorowitz, D., and Cohen, B. D. 1977. Referent communication in chronic schizophrenia. *Journal of Abnormal Psychology* 86(1):1–9.

209. Karras; A. 1973. Effects of competing and complex responses on the reaction time of acute psychiatric groups. *Journal of Abnormal Psychology* 82(1):134–38.

210. Karris, E., and Muzekari, L. H. 1973. Concept identifications in chronic schizophrenics. *Journal of Clinical Psychology* 29(4):439–40.

211. Kay, S. R., and Singh, M. M. 1974. A temporal measure of attention in schizophrenia and its clinical significance. *British Journal of Psychiatry* 125:146–51.

212. Kayton, L., and Koh, S. D. 1975. Hypohedonia in schizophrenia. *Journal of Nervous and Mental Disease* 161(6):412–20.

213. Kelley, F. D. 1973. Paralinguistic indicator of patient's affect: Attitudinal significance of length of communication. *Psychological Reports* 32(3):1223–26.

214. Kelley, F. S.; Farina, A.; and Mosher, D. L. 1971. Ability of schizophrenic women to create a favorable or unfavorable impression on an interviewer. *Journal of Consulting and Clinical Psychology* 36(3):404–9.

215. Kelly, G. A. 1955. *The psychology of personal constructs* (New York: W. W. Norton).

216. Kelm, H. 1968. Visual figural aftereffect in schizophrenic and nonschizophrenic patients. *Journal of Abnormal Psychology* 73(3):273–75.

217. Kilburg, R. R., and Siegel, A. W. 1973. Formal operations in reactive and process schizophrenics. *Journal of Consulting and Clinical Psychology* 40(3):371–76.

218. King, P. D. 1970–71. Ego development and the hypnosis theory of schizophrenia. *Psychoanalytic Review* 57(4):647–56.

219. Klein, B. 1971. Reinforcement and learning in schizophrenics. *Psychological Reports* 29(3): 785–86.

220. Klibanoff, L. S.; Phelan, J. G.; and Kiker, V. L. 1973. Performance of male schizophrenics on an anagram solution task: An application of an S-R medication model. *Perceptual and Motor Skills* 36(2):535–40.

221. Klingman, A.; Ban, T. A.; and Lehmann, H. E. 1972. Transference, discrimination and reversal: A comparison between normals and pathological groups. *Conditional Reflex* 7(4):216–25.

222. Koh, S. D., and Kayton, L. 1971. Free recall learning by nonpsychotic schizophrenics. *Proceedings of the Annual Convention of the American Psychological Association* 6:11–12.

223. Koh, S. D., and Kayton, L. 1974. Memorization of "unrelated" word strings by young nonpsychotic schizophrenics. *Journal of Abnormal Psychology* 83(1):14–22.

224. Koh, S. D.; Kayton, L.; and Berry, R. 1973. Mnemonic organization in young nonpsychotic schizophrenics. *Journal of Abnormal Psychology* 81(3):299–310.

225. Koh, S. D., and Peterson, R. A. 1974. Perceptual memory for numerousness in "nonpsychotic schizophrenics." *Journal of Abnormal Psychology* 83(3):215–26.

226. Koh, S. D.; Kayton, L.; and Schwarz, C. 1974. The structure of word storage in the permanent memory of nonpsychotic schizophrenics. *Journal of Consulting and Clinical Psychology* 42(6):879–87.

227. Kokonis, N. D. 1972. Body image disturbance in schizophrenia: A study of arms and feet. *Journal of Personality Assessment* 36(6):573–75.

228. Kokonis, N. D. 1972. Choice of gender on the DAP and measures of sex-role identification. *Perceptual and Motor Skills* 35(3):727–30.

229. Kokonis, N. D. 1973. Parental dominance and sex-role identification in schizophrenia. *Journal of Psychology* 84(2):211–18.

230. Kopfstein, J. H., and Neale, J. M. 1971. Size estimation in schizophrenic and nonschizophrenic subjects. *Journal of Consulting and Clinical Psychology* 36(3):430–35.

231. Kopfstein, J. H., and Neale, J. M. 1973. Performance profile of hospitalized psychiatric patients. *Perceptual and Motor Skills* 36(3):739–44.

232. Kops, V., and Anker, J. M. 1973. Normal and schizophrenic performance in coping with dissonance. *Proceedings of the 81st Annual Convention of the American Psychological Association* (Montreal, Canada), 8:465–66.

233. Korboot, P., and Yates, A. J. 1973. Speed of perceptual functioning in chronic nonparanoid schizophrenics: Partial replication and extension. *Journal of Abnormal Psychology* 81(3):296–98.

234. Kramer, M., and Roth, T. 1973. A comparison of dream content in laboratory dream reports of schizophrenic and depressive patient groups. *Comprehensive Psychiatry* 14(4):325–29.

235. Kristofferson, M. W. 1967. Shifting attention between modalities: A comparison of schizophrenics and normals. *Journal of Abnormal Psychology* 72:388–91.

236. Krooth, D. M. 1971. Cortical arousal in paranoid schizophrenics as a function of a word association task. *Journal of Nervous and Mental Disease* 153(5):366–76.

237. Landis, B. 1970. Ego boundaries. *Psychological Issues* 6:1–172.

238. Lane, E. A. 1968. The influence of sex and race on process-reactive ratings of schizophrenia. *Journal of Psychology* 68(1):15–20.

239. Lane, E. A., and Albee, G. W. 1968. On childhood intellectual decline of adult schizophrenics: A reassessment of an earlier study. *Journal of Abnormal Psychology* 73(2):174–77.

240. Lane, E. A.; Albee, G. W.; and Doll, L. S. 1970. The intelligence of children of schizophrenics. *Developmental Psychology* 2(3):315–17.

241. Langevin, R., and Hutchins, L. M. 1973. An experimental investigation of judges' ratings of schizophrenics and nonschizophrenics painting. *Journal of Personality Assessment* 37(6):537–43.

242. Lavoie, G.; Sabourin, M.; and Langlois, J. 1973. Hypnotic susceptibility, amnesia, and IQ in chronic schizophrenia. *International Journal of Clinical and Experimental Hypnosis* 21(3):157–68.

243. Lawson, J. S.; McGhie, A.; and Chapman, J. 1964. Perception of speech in schizophrenia. *British Journal of Psychiatry* 110:375–80.

244. Lefcourt, H.; Rotenberg, F.; Buckspan, S.; and Steffy, R. 1967. Visual interaction and performance of process and reactive schizophrenics as a function of examiner's sex. *Journal of Personality* 35(4):535-46.

245. Lefcourt, H.; Steffy, R. A.; Buckspan, S.; and Rotenberg, F. 1968. Avoidance censure by process and reactive schizophrenics as a function of examiner's sex and type of task. *Journal of General Psychology* 79(1):87-96.

246. Lester, D., and Schumacher, J. 1969. Schizophrenia and death concern. *Journal of Projective Techniques and Personality Assessment* 33(5):403-5.

247. Letourneau, J. E. 1974. The Oppel-Kundt and the Muller-Lyer illusions among schizophrenics. *Perceptual and Motor Skills* 39(2):775-78.

248. Levine, F. M., and Grinspoon, L. 1971. Telemetered heart rate and skin potential of a chronic schizophrenic patient especially during periods of hallucination and periods of talking. *Journal of Consulting and Clinical Psychology* 37(3):345-50.

249. Levine, F. M., and Whitney, N. 1970. Absolute auditory threshold and threshold of unpleasantness of chronic schizophrenic patients and normal controls. *Journal of Abnormal Psychology* 75(1):74-77.

250. Levine, J., and Feinstein, A. 1972. Differences in test performance between brain-damaged, schizophrenic, and medical patients. *Journal of Consulting and Clinical Psychology* 39(3):508-11.

251. Levy, R., and Maxwell, A. E. 1968. The effects of verbal context on the recall of schizophrenics and other psychiatric patients. *British Journal of Psychiatry* 114:311-16.

252. Lisman, S. A., and Cohen, B. P. 1972. Self-editing deficits in schizophrenia: A word association analogue. *Journal of Abnormal Psychology* 79:181-188.

253. Livingston, P. B., and Blum, R. A. 1968. Attention and speech in acute schizophrenia: An experimental study. *Archives of General Psychiatry* 18(3):373-81.

254. Lloyd, D. M. 1967. Overinclusive thinking and delusion in schizophrenic patients: A critique. *Journal of Abnormal Psychiatry* 72(5):451-53.

255. Locke, S. A. 1974. Temporal discrimination of brief auditory stimuli by schizophrenics, neurologically impaired, and normals. *Perceptual and Motor Skills* 39(3):1111-20.

256. Lottman, T. J., and DeWolfe, A. J. 1972. Internal versus external control in reactive and process schizophrenics. *Journal of Consulting and Clinical Psychology* 39(2):344.

257. Lowe, G. R. 1973. The phenomenology of hallucination as an aid to differential diagnosis. *British Journal of Psychiatry* 123 (577):621-33.

258. Ludwig, A. M., and Stark, L. H. 1973. Schizophrenia, sensory deprivation and sensory overload. *Journal of Nervous and Mental Disease* 157(3):210-16.

259. McClelland, D. C., and Watt, N. F. 1968. Sex-role alienation in schizophrenia. *Journal of Abnormal Psychology* 73(3):226-39.

260. McCormack, J. H.; Phelan, J.; and Tang, T. 1967. Experimental studies of cognitive and motor sets: An aspect of psychological deficit in schizophrenia. *Journal of Clinical Psychology* 23(4):443-46.

261. McCreary, C. P. 1974. Comparison of measures of social competencies in schizophrenics and the relation of social competence to socioeconomic factors. *Journal of Abnormal Psychology* 3(2):124-29.

262. McDowell, D.; Reynolds, B.; and Magaro, P. 1975. The integration deficit in paranoid and nonparanoid schizophrenics. *Journal of Abnormal Psychology* 84(6):629-36.

263. McFadyen, M., and Foulds, G. A. 1972. Comparison of provided and elicited grid content in the Grid Test of Schizophrenic Thought Disorder. *British Journal of Psychiatry* 121(560):53-57.

264. McGhie, A. 1970. Attention and perception in schizophrenia. In *Progress in experimental personality research*, ed. B. A. Maher (New York: Academic Press).

265. McGhie, A., and Chapman, J. 1961. Disorders of attention and perception in early schizophrenia. *British Journal of Medical Psychology* 34:103-16.

266. McGlashan, T. H.; Levy, S. T.; and Carpenter, W. T. 1975. Integration and sealing over. *Archives of General Psychiatry* 32(10):1269-72.

267. MacKinnon, T., and Singer, G. 1969. Schizophrenia and the scanning cognitive control: A re-evaluation. *Journal of Abnormal Psychology* 74:242-49.

268. McPherson, F. M.; Armstrong, J.; and Heather, B. B. 1975. Psychological construing, "difficulty," and thought-process disorder. *British Journal of Medical Psychology* 48:303-15.

269. McPherson, F. M.; Blackbuss, I. M.; Draffan, I. W.; and McFadyen, M. 1973. A further study of the brief test of thought disorder. *British Journal of Social and Clinical Psychology* 12(4):420-27.

270. McPherson, F. M., and Buckley, F. 1970. Thought process disorder and personal construct subsystems. *British Journal of Social and Clinical Psychology* 9(4):380-81.

271. McPherson, F. M.; Buckley, F.; and Draffan, J. 1971. "Psychological" constructs and delusions of persecution and "nonintegration" in schizophrenia. *British Journal of Medical Psychology* 44(3):277-80.

272. McPherson, F. M., et al. 1970. Flattening of affect and personal constructs. *British Journal of Psychiatry* 116(537):39-43.

273. Magaro, P. A. 1967. Perceptual discrimination performance of schizophrenics as a function of censure, social class and premorbid adjustment. *Journal of Abnormal Psychology* 72(5):415-28.

274. Magaro, P. A. 1974. Theories of the schizophrenics performance deficit: An integration theory synthesis. In *Progress in experimental personality research*, ed. B. Maher (New York: Academic Press).

275. Maher, B. A. 1966. *Principles of psychopathology* (New York: McGraw-Hill).

276. Maher, B. A. 1972. The language of schizophrenia: A review and integration. *British Journal of Psychiatry* 120:3-17.

277. Maier, S., and Ray, E. R. 1974. An experimental study of strategy learning in schizophrenic patients. *Psychologische Forschung* 36(4):359-74.

278. Maller, O. 1974. A motivation evaluation rating scale for chronic impaired schizophrenics (MERS). *Psychiatria Clinica* 7(6):347-57.

279. Marchbanks, G., and Williams, M. 1971. The effect of speed on comprehension in schizophrenia. *British Journal of Social and Clinical Psychology* 10(1):55–60.

280. Marinow, A. 1971. Case study: A schizophrenic patient draws his hallucinations. *American Journal of Art Therapy* 11(1–2):45–47.

281. Marsella, A. J., and Murray, M. D. 1974. Diagnostic type, gender and consistency vs. specificity behavior. *Journal of Clinical Psychology* 30(4):484–88.

282. Marshall, W. L. 1973. Cognitive functioning in schizophrenia: I. Stimulus analysis and response selection processes. *British Journal of Psychiatry* 123(575):413–23.

283. Marshall, W. L. 1973. Cognitive functioning in schizophrenia: II. Conceptual performance under unpaced, speeded and slowed conditions. *British Journal of Psychiatry* 123(575):423–28.

284. Marshall, W. L. 1973. Cognitive functioning in schizophrenics: III. The relationship between conceptual performance and information processing capacities. *British Journal of Psychiatry* 123(575):428–33.

285. Mattsoon, N. B., and Gerard, R. W. 1968. Typology of schizophrenia based on multidisciplinary observational vectors. Public Health Service Publication no. 1584, pp. 507–34.

286. Mazekari, L. H., and Kreiger, P. 1975. Effects of inducing body awareness in chronic schizophrenics: Body boundary changes. *Journal of Consulting and Clinical Psychology* 43(3):435–36.

287. Mefferd, R. B., et al. 1969. Influence of distraction on the reproduction of spoken words by schizophrenics. *Journal of Nervous and Mental Disease* 149(6):504–9.

288. Meichenbaum, D., and Cameron, R. 1973. Training schizophrenics to talk to themselves: A means of developing attentional controls. *Behavior Therapy* 4(4):515–34.

289. Meiselman, K. C. 1973. Broadening dual modality via utilization in chronic nonparanoid schizophrenia. *Journal of Consulting and Clinical Psychology* 41(3):447–53.

290. Miller, B. 1974. Semantic misinterpretations of ambiguous communications in schizophrenia. *Archives of General Psychiatry* 30(4):435–40.

291. Miller, G. A., and Selfridge, J. A. 1950. Verbal context and the recall of meaningful material. *American Journal of Psychology* 63:176–85.

292. Miller, P. M., and Heckel, R. V. 1969. "Awareness" in chronic schizophrenics: III. Incidental versus directed learning. *Psychological Reports* 24(3):783–86.

293. Mintz, S., and Alpert, M. 1972. Imagery vividness, reality testing and schizophrenic hallucinations. *Journal of Abnormal Psychology* 79(3):310–16.

294. Mitchell, W. S.; Mowat, E. M.; and Stoffelmayr, B. E. 1975. Effects of social deprivation and satiation on the reinforcing properties of social stimulation in chronic male hospitalized schizophrenics. *Journal of Abnormal Psychology* 84(5):494–97.

295. Mitchell, W. S., and Stoffelmayr, B. E. 1973. Application of the Premack Principle to the behavioral control of extremely inactive schizophrenics. *Journal of Applied Behavior Analysis* 6(3):419–23.

296. Mitchell, W. S., and Stoffelmayr, B. E. 1974. The effects of contingent social stimulation on severely withdrawn chronic schizophrenic patients. *Psychological Record* 24(4):515–21.

297. Moon, A. F.; Mefferd, R. B.; Wieland, B. A.; Pokorny, A. D.; and Falconer, G. A. 1968. Perceptual dysfunction as a determinant of schizophrenic word associations. *Journal of Nervous and Mental Disease* 146(1):80–84.

298. Morikawa, S. 1967. A study of concept formation in schizophrenics. *Journal of Clinical Psychology* 6(1):21–29.

299. Mourer, S. 1971. Some issues regarding semantic generalization in schizophrenics. *Proceedings of the Annual Convention of the American Psychological Association* 6:449–50.

300. Mourer, S. 1973. A prediction of patterns of schizophrenic error resulting from semantic generalization. *Journal of Abnormal Psychology* 81(3):250–54.

301. Nachmani, G., and Cohen, B. P. 1969. Recall and recognition—free learning in schizophrenics. *Journal of Abnormal Psychology* 74:511–16.

302. National Institute of Mental Health. 1975. *Research in the service of mental health.* Report of the Research Task Force of the NIMH (Rockville, Md.), DHEW Publication no. (ADM) 75–237.

303. Neale, J. M. 1968. Size estimation in schizophrenics as a function of stimulus presentation time. *Journal of Abnormal Psychology* 73(1):44–48.

304. Neale, J. M. 1971. Perceptual span in schizophrenia. *Journal of Abnormal Psychology* 77(2):196–204.

305. Neale, J. M., and Cromwell, R. L. 1970. Attention and schizophrenia. In *Progress in experimental personality research*, ed. B. Maher (New York: Academic Press).

306. Neale, J. M.; Davis, D.; and Cromwell, R. L. 1971. Size estimation in schizophrenia: Some additional controls. *Perceptual and Motor Skills* 32(2):363–67.

307. Neale, J. M.; McIntyre, C. W.; Fox, R.; and Cromwell, R. L. 1969. Span of apprehension in acute schizophrenics. *Journal of Abnormal Psychology* 74(5):593–96.

308. Neufeld, R. W. 1975. A multidimensional scaling analysis of schizophrenics' and normals' perceptions of verbal similarity. *Journal of Abnormal Psychology* 84(5):498–507.

309. Neuringer, C.; Fiske, J. P.; and Goldstein, G. 1969. Schizophrenic adherence to strong meaning associations. *Perceptual and Motor Skills* 29(2):394.

310. Neuringer, C.; Fiske, J. P.; Schmidt, M. W.; and Goldstein, G. 1972. Adherence to strong verbal meaning definitions in schizophrenics. *Journal of Genetic Psychology* 121(2):315–23.

311. Nideffer, R. M.; Neale, J. M.; Kopfstein, J. H.; and Cromwell, R. L. 1971. The effect of previous preparatory intervals upon anticipatory responses in the reaction time of schizophrenic and nonschizophrenic patients. *Journal of Nervous and Mental Disease* 153(5):360–65.

312. Nolan, J. D. 1960. Reversal and extradimensional shifts in abstract and concrete schizophrenics. *Journal of Abnormal Psychology* 73:330–35.

313. Nolan, J. D. 1970. Effects of overtraining on reversal and extradimensional shifts in schizophrenics. *Journal of Abnormal Psychology* 75:323–28.

314. Nolan, J. D. 1974. A within subject analysis of discrimination shift behavior in schizophrenics. *Journal of Abnormal Psychology* 83(5):497–511.

315. Nolan, J. D., and Anderson, D. 1973. Effect of excessive overtraining and aversive feed-

back on reversal and extradimensional shifts in schizophrenics. *Journal of Abnormal Psychology* 81(1):27–35.

316. Nori, G. 1967. Painting and drawing in the rehabilitation of chronic schizophrenics. *Psychotherapy and Psychosomatics* 15(1):48.

317. Normington, C. 1967. Time estimation in process-reactive schizophrenia. *Journal of Consulting Psychology* 31:222.

318. O'Brien, B. A., and McCarthy, R. 1967. Schizophrenia performance under reward and punishment on tasks yielding varying degrees of information. *Journal of Experimental Research in Personality* 2(3):220–25.

319. O'Connell, M. J. 1969. Institutionalization and cognitive functioning of schizophrenics. *Psychological Reports* 25(2):621–22.

320. Offord, D. R. 1974. School performance of adult schizophrenics, their siblings and age mates. *British Journal of Psychiatry* 125:12–19.

321. Offord, D. R., and Cross, L. A. 1971. Adult schizophrenia with scholastic failure or low IQ in childhood: A preliminary report. *Archives of General Psychiatry* 24(5):431–36.

322. Oishi, K. 1974. A comparison of semantic structure among college students, junior high school boys, and schizophrenic patients. *Japanese Journal of Psychology* 45(1):21–32.

323. O'Keefe, G. S., and DeWolfe, A. S. 1973. Reversal shift preferences in process and reactive schizophrenic, brain damaged, and control group patients. *Journal of Abnormal Psychology* 82(3):390–98.

324. Oltmanns, T. F., and Neale, J. M. 1975. Schizophrenic performance when distractors are present: Attentional deficit or differential task difficulty? *Journal of Abnormal Psychology* 84(3):205–9.

325. Orme, J. 1966. Time estimation and the nosology of schizophrenia. *British Journal of Psychiatry* 112:37–39.

326. Otteson, J. P., and Holzman, P. S. 1976. Cognitive controls and psychopathology. *Journal of Abnormal Psychology* 85(2):125–39.

327. Panek, D. M. 1970. Word association learning by chronic schizophrenics on a token economy word under conditions of reward and punishment. *Journal of Clinical Psychology* 26(2):163–67.

328. Pavy, D. 1968. Verbal behavior in schizophrenia: A review of recent studies. *Psychological Bulletin* 70(3):164–78.

329. Pavy, D.; Grinspoon, L.; and Shades, R. I. 1969. Word frequency measures of verbal disorders in schizophrenia. *Diseases of the Nervous System* 30(3):553–56.

330. Payne, R. W. 1966. The measurement and significance of overinclusive thinking and retardation in schizophrenic patients. In *Psychopathology of schizophrenia*, eds. P. Hoch and J. Zubin (New York: Grune & Stratton).

331. Payne, R. W. 1971. Cognitive defects in schizophrenia: Overinclusive thinking. In *Cognitive studies: II. Defects in cognition*, ed. J. Hellmuth (New York: Brunner/Mazel).

332. Payne, R. W., and Caird, W. K. 1967. Reaction time, distractability and overinclusive thinking in psychotics. *Journal of Abnormal Psychology* 72:112.

333. Payne, R. W.; Hochberg, A. C.; and Hawks, D. V. 1970. Dichotic stimulation as a method of assessing disorder of attention in overinclusive schizophrenic patients. *Journal of Abnormal Psychology* 76(2):185–93.

334. Payne, R. W., and Van Alen, R. K. 1969. The relationship between overinclusive thinking, perceptual rigidity and the discrimination learning of new concepts. *Canadian Journal of Behavioral Science* 1(3):193–203.

335. Peters, U. M. 1975. Word-field disturbance and sentence-field disturbance: Interpretation of a schizophrenic language phenomenon by structuralistic means. *Archiv für Psychiatrie and Nervenkrankheiten* 217(1):1–10.

336. Petzel, T. P., and Johnson, J. E. 1972. Time estimation of process and reactive schizophrenics under crowded and uncrowded conditions. *Journal of Clinical Psychology* 28(3):345–47.

337. Petzel, T. P., and Johnson, J. E. 1973. Formation of concepts of varying degrees of dominance by process and reactive schizophrenics. *Journal of Consulting and Clinical Psychology* 41(2):235–41.

338. Phelan, J. G.; Levy, H. C.; and Thorpe, J. W. 1967. Concept learning in schizophrenics and normals: Selection and addition of cues; effect of amount and style of memory information. *Journal of Psychology* 67(2):503–11.

339. Pickford, R. W. 1968. Disguise in the expression of fantasy: The "art work" in painting. *Bulletin of Art Therapy* 7(4):167–84.

340. Pishkin, V., and Bourne, L. E. 1968. Relevant and irrelevant social dimensions in concept identification of schizophrenics and normals. *Proceedings of the 76th Annual Convention of the American Psychological Association* 3:509–10.

341. Pishkin, V., and Thome, F. C. 1973. A factorial study of existential state reactions. *Journal of Clinical Psychology* 29(4):392–402.

342. Platt, J. J., and Spivack, G. 1973. Studies in problem-solving thinking of psychiatric patients: I. Patient-control differences: II. Factorial structure of problem-solving thinking. *Proceedings of the 81st Annual Convention of the American Psychological Association* (Montreal, Canada) 8:463–64.

343. Price, R. H. 1970. Task requirements in tests of schizophrenic overinclusion. *British Journal of Clinical and Social Psychology* 9(1):60–67.

344. Prior, M. R. 1973. Overinclusion in chronic schizophrenia. *Psychological Reports* 32(2):426.

345. Putterman, A. H. 1975. Referential speaker processes in male and female process-reactive schizophrenics. *Journal of Nervous and Mental Disease* 160(5):354–58.

346. Putterman, A. H., and Pollack, H. B. 1976. The developmental approach and process-reactive schizophrenia: A review. *Schizophrenia Bulletin* 2(2):198–208.

347. Quinlan, D. M., and Harrow, M. 1974. Boundary disturbances in schizophrenia. *Journal of Abnormal Psychology* 83(5):533–41.

348. Quinlan, D. M.; Harrow, M.; Tucker, G.; and Carlson, K. 1972. Varieties of "disordered" thinking on the Rorschach: Findings in schizophrenic and nonschizophrenic patients. *Journal of Abnormal Psychology* 79(1):47–53.

349. Rabin, A. I., and Winder, C. L. 1969. Psychological studies. In *The schizophrenic syndrome*, eds. L. Bellak and L. Loeb (New York: Grune & Stratton).

350. Raeburn, J. M., and Zong, J. E. 1968. Experiments on contextual constraints in schizophrenics. *British Journal of Psychiatry* 114(506):43–52.

351. Rappaport, M. 1968. Attention to competing voice measages by nonacute schizophrenic patients: Effects of message load, drugs, dosage levels and patient background. *Journal of Nervous and Mental Disease* 146(5):404–11.

352. Raskin, A. 1967. Effect of background conversation and darkness on reaction time in anxious, hallucinating, and severely ill schizophrenics. *Perceptual and Motor Skills* 25(2):353–58.

353. Rattan, R., and Chapman, L. J. 1973. Associative intrusions in schizophrenic verbal behavior. *Journal of Abnormal Psychology* 82(1):169–73.

354. Ravensborg, M. R. 1972. An operant conditioning approach to increasing interpersonal awareness among chronic schizophrenics. *Journal of Clinical Psychology* 28(3):411–13.

355. Rawling, P. J. 1975. Overinclusion as a nominalist definition of the schizophrenic thought disorder. *Australian Psychologist* 10(1):64–74.

356. Reich, L., et al. 1975. Sleep disturbance in schizophrenia: A revisit. *Archives of General Psychiatry* 32(1):51–55.

357. Reilly, F. E.; Harrow, M.; and Tucker, G. J. 1973. Language and thought content in acute psychosis. *American Journal of Psychiatry* 130(4):411–17.

358. Reiss, D. 1967. Individual thinking and family interaction: II. A study of pattern recognition and hypothesis testing families of normals, character disorders and schizophrenics. *Journal of Psychiatric Research* 5(3):193–211.

359. Rennert, H. 1969. The vertical displacement of the visual angle in drawings by schizophrenics. *Psychiatrie, Neurologie und Medizinische Psychologie* 21(9):325–29.

360. Richtberg, W. 1973. Schizophrenia and rigidity: Results of an experimental-psychological investigation. *Psychiatria Clinica* 6(3):150–70.

361. Rice, J. K. 1970. Disordered language as related to autonomic responsivity and the process-reactive distinction. *Journal of Abnormal Psychology* 76(1):50–54.

362. Ritzler, B., and Ebner, E. 1973. Contrast and stimulus intensity in kinesthetic figural aftereffects with normal and schizophrenic subjects. *Perceptual and Motor Skills* 37(3):927–35.

363. Ritzler, B., and Rosenbaum, G. 1974. Bilateral transfer of inhibition in the motor learning of schizophrenics and normals. *Journal of Motor Behavior* 6(3):205–15.

364. Ritzler, B., and Rosenbaum, G. 1974. Proprioception in schizophrenics and normals: Effects of stimulus intensity and interstimulus interval. *Journal of Abnormal Psychology* 83(2):106–111.

365. Roberts, M. A., and Schuham, A. I. 1974. Word associations of schizophrenics and alcoholics as a function of strength of associative distracter. *Journal of Abnormal Psychology* 83(4):426–31.

366. Rochester, S. R. 1973. The role of information processing in the sentence decoding of schizophrenic listeners. *Journal of Nervous and Mental Disease* 157(3):217–23.

367. Rochester, S. R.; Harris, J.; and Seeman, M. 1973. Sentence processing in schizophrenic listeners. *Journal of Abnormal Psychology* 82(2):350–56.

368. Rodnick, E. H., and Shakow, D. 1940. Set in the schizophrenic as measured by a composite reaction time index. *American Journal of Psychiatry* 97:214–25.

369. Rosenberg, S., and Cohen, B. D. 1966. Referential processes of speakers and listeners. *Psychological Review* 73:208–31.

370. Rosenman, M. F. 1970. Impression formation in schizophrenics and normals. *Perceptual and Motor Skills* 31(3):867–77.

371. Rosenman, M. F., and Drennan, W. T. 1967. Empathy in schizophrenics, neurotics, and normals. *Psychological Reports* 21(3):863–64.

372. Rosenthal, R. 1966. *Experimenter effects in behavioral research* (New York: Appleton-Century-Crofts).

373. Royer, F. L. 1973. Reaction time of process and reactive schizophrenics to multi-dimensional visual stimuli. *Newsletter for Research in Mental Health and Behavioral Sciences* 15(3):27–29.

374. Royer, F. L., and Friedman, S. 1973. Scanning time of schizophrenics and normals for visual design. *Journal of Abnormal Psychology* 82(2):212–19.

375. Royer, F. L., and Friedman, S. 1973. Scanning time of schizophrenics and normals for visual design. *Newsletter for Research in Mental Health and Behavioral Sciences* 15(2):33–36.

376. Royer, F. L., and Jonowich, L. 1973. Performance of process and reactive schizophrenics in a Symbol Digit Substitution test. *Newsletter for Research in Mental Health and Behavioral Sciences* 15(2):31–33.

377. Russell, P. N.; Bannatyne, P. A.; and Smith, J. F. 1975. Associative strength as a mode of organization in recall and recognition: A comparison of schizophrenics and normals. *Journal of Abnormal Psychology* 84(2):122–28.

378. Rutschmann, J. 1973. Time judgments of magnitude estimation and magnitude production and anxiety: A problem of comparison between normal and certain schizophrenic patients. *Journal of Psychology* 85(2):187–223.

379. Rutter, D. R. 1973. Visual interaction in psychiatric patients. *British Journal of Psychiatry* 123(57):193–202.

380. Rutter, D. R., and Stephenson, G. M. 1972. Visual interaction in a group of schizophrenic and depressive patients. *British Journal of Social and Clinical Psychology* 11(1):57–65.

381. Rutter, D. R.; Wishner, J.; and Callaghan, B. A. 1975. The prediction and predictability of speech in schizophrenic patients. *British Journal of Psychiatry* 126:571–76.

382. Rychlak, J. F.; McKee, D. B.; Schneider, W. E.; and Abramson, Y. 1971. Affective evaluation in the verbal learning styles of normals and abnormals. *Journal of Abnormal Psychology* 77(3):247–57.

383. Sacuzzo, D. P.; Hirt, M.; and Spencer, T. J. 1974. Backward masking as a measure of attention in schizophrenia. *Journal of Abnormal Psychology* 83(5):512–22.

384. Sakamoto, Y. 1969. A study of the attitude of Japanese families of schizophrenics toward their ill members. *Psychotherapy and Psychosomatics* 17(5–6):365–74.

385. Salzinger, K. 1971. An hypothesis about schizophrenic behavior. *American Journal of Psychotherapy* 25:601–14.

386. Salzinger, K.; Portnoy, S.; Pisoni, D. B.; and Feldman, R. S. 1970. The immediacy hypothesis and response-produced stimuli in schizophrenic speech. *Journal of Abnormal Psychology* 76: 258–64.

387. Salzinger, K., and Salzinger, S. 1973. Behavior theory for the study of psychopathology. In *Psychopathology: Contributions from the social, behavioral, and biological sciences*, eds. M. Hammer, K. Salzman, and S. Sutton (New York: John Wiley), pp. 111–26.

388. Sappington, J. 1973. Perception of threatening stimuli in process and reactive schizophrenics. *Journal of Consulting and Clinical Psychology* 41(1):48–50.

389. Sarbin, T. R. 1967. The concept of hallucination. *Journal of Personality* 35(3):359–80.

390. Sattler, J. M., and Nordmark, T. 1971. Verbal learning in schizophrenics and normals. *Psychological Record* 21(2):241–48.

391. Schalock, R. L., and Walker, K. A. 1967. An attempt to promote behavioral change in paired schizophrenics by reinforcing associative behavior. *Psychological Reports* 21(3):904.

392. Schenck, H. U., and Surber, C. 1974. Regression in schizophrenics as a function of censure, reinforcement cues, and response habit hierarchies. *Journal of Genetic Psychology* 124(1):69–77.

393. Schlosberg, A. 1969. Time perspective in schizophrenics. *Psychiatric Quarterly* 43(1):22–34.

394. Schwarz, J. C. 1970. Comment on "high school yearbook: A nonreactive measure of social isolation in graduates who later become schizophrenic." *Journal of Abnormal Psychology* 75(3): 317–18.

395. Schwarz, J. C. 1971. High school yearbook: Further explanation and reply to Meehl. *Journal of Abnormal Psychology* 78(2):145–47.

396. Scott, R. D. 1973. The treatment barrier: II. The patient as unrecognized agent. *British Journal of Medical Psychology* 46(1):57–67.

397. Serban, G., and Gidynaki, C. B. 1975. Differentiating criteria for acute-chronic distinction in schizophrenia. *Archives of General Psychiatry* 32(6):705–12.

398. Shakow, D. 1962. Segmental set. *Archives of General Psychiatry* 6:1–17.

399. Shakow, D. 1963. Psychological deficit in schizophrenia. *Behavioral Science* 8:275–305.

400. Shakow, D. 1977. Segmental set. *American Psychologist* 32:129–39.

401. Shean, G., and Faia, C. 1975. Autonomic control, selective attention, and schizophrenic subtype. *Journal of Nervous and Mental Disease* 160(3):176–81.

402. Shean, G.; Faia, C.; and Schmaltz, E. 1974. Cognitive appraisal of stress and schizophrenic subtype. *Journal of Abnormal Psychology* 83(5):523–28.

403. Shield, P. H.; Harrow, M.; and Tucker, G. 1974. Investigation of factors related to stimulus overinclusion. *Psychiatric Quarterly* 48(1):109–16.

404. Shimkunas, A. M. 1970. Reciprocal shifts in schizophrenic thought processes. *Journal of Abnormal Psychology* 76(3):423–26.

405. Shimkunas, A. M. 1972. Conceptual deficit in schizophrenia: A reappraisal. *British Journal of Medical Psychology* 45(2):149–57.

406. Shimkunas, A. M. 1972. Demand for intimate self-disclosure and pathological verbalization in schizophrenia. *Journal of Abnormal Psychology* 80(2):197–205.

407. Shimkunas, A. M., and Murray, D. R. 1974. Assessment of change in conventional vs. unconventional thought processes of schizophrenia. *Journal of Personality Assessment* 38(1):32–40.

408. Shimkunas, A. M., and Young, J. M. 1973. Abstract-concrete concept shifts and learning deficit in schizophrenia. *Proceedings of the 81st Annual Convention of the American Psychological Association* (Montreal, Canada) 8:469–70.

409. Shukla, T. R. 1972. Perception of penetration of body-image-boundary in schizophrenia. *Psychologia: An International Journal of Psychology in the Orient* 15(4):240–42.

410. Silverman, G. 1972. Psycholinguistics of schizophrenic language. *Psychological Medicine* 2(3):254–59.

411. Silverman, J. 1964. Scanning control and cognitive filtering. *Journal of Consulting Psychology* 71:385.

412. Silverman, J. 1964. The problem of attention in the research and theory of schizophrenia. *Psychological Review* 71:352.

413. Silverman, J., and Gaarder, K. 1967. Rates of saccadic eye movement and size judgments of normals and schizophrenics. *Perceptual and Motor Skills* 25:661–67.

414. Silverman, J., and King, C. 1970. Pseudoperceptual differentiation. *Journal of Consulting and Clinical Psychology* 34(1):119–23.

415. Silverman, L. H. 1971. An experimental technique for the study of unconscious conflict. *Journal of Medical Psychology* 44(1):17–25.

416. Silverman, L. H., and Candell, P. 1970. On the relationship between aggressive activation, symbiotic merging, intactness of body boundaries, and manifest pathology in schizophrenics. *Journal of Nervous and Mental Disease* 150(5):387–99.

417. Silverman, L. H.; Candell, P.; Pettit, T. F.; and Blum, E. A. 1971. Further data on effects of aggressive activation and symbiotic merging on ego functioning of schizophrenics. *Perceptual and Motor Skills* 32(1):92–94.

418. Silverman, L. H.; Pettit, T. F.; and Dunne, E. J. 1971. On the relationship between self-object differentiation, symbiotic experiences and pathology reduction in schizophrenia. *Journal of Nervous and Mental Disease* 152(2):118–28.

419. Silverman, L. H., and Spero, R. H. 1968. The effects of subliminal, supraliminal and vocalized aggression on the ego functioning of schizophrenics. *Journal of Nervous and Mental Disease* 146(1):50–61.

420. Smith, E. E. 1969. Short-term memory impairment in chronic schizophrenics. *Canadian Journal of Psychology* 23(2):114–26.

421. Smith, E. E. 1970. Associative and editing processes in schizophrenic communication. *Journal of Abnormal Psychology* 75:182–86.

422. Smith, G. J., and Ruuth, E. 1973. Effects of extraneous stimulation on visual afterimage serials produced by young schizophrenics. *Scandinavian Journal of Psychology* 14(1):34–38.

423. Smith, G. J.; Sjoholm, L.; and Wielzen, S. 1974. Sensitive reaction and afterimage varigation. *Journal of Personality Assessment* 38(1):41–47.

424. Solod, R., and Lapidus, L. B. 1977. Concrete operational thinking, diagnosis and psychopathology in hospitalized schizophrenics. *Journal of Abnormal Psychology* 86(2):199–202.

425. Sonnenber, S. M.; Stern, M. J.; and Lieberman, R. P. 1972. A profile for rating depressive and schizophrenic behavior. *Comprehensive Psychiatry* 13(1):25–31.

426. Soskis, D., and Bowers, M. B. 1969. The schizophrenic experience: A follow-up study of attitude and posthospital adjustment. *Journal of Nervous and Mental Disease* 149(6):443–49.

427. Soueif, M. I., and Farag, S. E. 1971. Creative thinking aptitudes in schizophrenics: A factorial study. *Sources de l'Ael* 8(1):51–60.

428. Spugel, D.; Keith-Speigel, P.; Zugules, J.; and Wine, D. B. 1971. Effects of student visits on social behavior of regressed schizophrenic patients. *Journal of Clinical Psychology* 27(3):396–400.

429. Starr, B. J.; Leibowitz, H. W.; and Lundy, R. M. 1968. Size constancy in catatonia. *Perceptual and Motor Skills* 26(3):747–52.

430. Stedman, J. M. 1967. Mediation on the A-B, A-B¹ transfer paradigm for schizophrenic and control subjects. *Journal of Experimental Research in Personality* 2(3):212–19.

431. Steffy, R. A., and Galbraith, K. A. 1974. A comparison of segmental set and inhibitory deficit explanations of the crossover pattern in process schizophrenic reaction time. *Journal of Abnormal Psychology* 83(3):227–33.

432. Steffy, R. A., and Galbraith, K. 1975. Time-limited impairment in schizophrenic reaction time performance. *Journal of Abnormal Psychology* 84(4):307–14.

433. Steinberg, H. R. 1969. Hyperamnesia and schizophrenia. *Psychological Reports* 25(1):195–98.

434. Steinberg, T.; Yu, J.; Brenner, H.; and Krieger, P. 1974. Locus of control and community adjustment among schizophrenic patients. *Journal of Clinical Psychology* 30(1):101.

435. Steingart, I., and Freedman, N. 1972. A language construction approach for the examination of self/object representation in varying clinical states. In *Psychoanalysis and contemporary science: An annual of integrative and interdisciplinary studies*, eds. R. R. Holt and E. Peterfreund (New York: Macmillan), vol. 1.

436. Steingart, I., and Freedman, N. 1975. The organization of body-focused kinesic behavior and language construction in schizophrenic and depressed states. In *Psychoanalysis and contemporary science*, ed. D. Spence (New York: International Universities Press), vol. 4, pp. 423–52.

437. Steingart, I.; Grand, S.; Margolis, R.; Freedman, N.; and Buchwald, C. 1976. A study of representation of anxiety in chronic schizophrenia. *Journal of Abnormal Psychology* 85(6):535–42.

438. Stephen, J. H.; Brown, C.; Forster, J. W.; and Klein, H. G. 1967. Orienting responses in "process" and "nonprocess" schizophrenics. *Conditional Reflex* 2(2):166.

439. Stilson, D. W.; Walsmith, C. R.; and Penon, N. E. 1971. Effects of content on schizophrenics' ability to process information. *Psychological Reports* 28(2):571–74.

440. Storms, L. H., and Acosta, F. X. 1974. Effects of dynamometer tension on stimulus generalization of schizophrenic and nonschizophrenic patients. *Journal of Abnormal Psychology* 83(2):204–7.

441. Storms, L. H., and Broen, W. E. 1972. Intrusion of schizophrenics' idiosyncratic associations into their conceptual performance. *Journal of Abnormal Psychology* 79(3):280–84.

442. Strauss, M. E. 1970. Thematic content and trials effects in the size estimation of meaningful stimuli. *Journal of Abnormal Psychology* 76(2):276–78.

443. Strauss, M. E. 1975. Strong meaning-response bias in schizophrenia. *Journal of Abnormal Psychology* 84(3):295–98.

444. Streiner, D. L. 1969. Effects of task complexity and verbal evaluation on the learning of normals and schizophrenics. *Journal of Abnormal Psychology* 74(5):606–11.

445. Suchotliff, L. C. 1970. Relation of formal thought disorder to the communication deficit in schizophrenics. *Journal of Abnormal Psychology* 76(2):250–57.

446. Sutker, P. B., and Cauthen, N. R. 1970. Paired-associate CVC learning with varied meaningfulness in schizophrenic males. *Perceptual and Motor Skills* 30(2):579–81.

447. Sutker, P. B.; Sutker, L. W.; and Gil, S. H. 1971. Serial learning of CVC combination with high and low social content ratings by schizophrenics and normals. *Perceptual and Motor Skills* 33(3):1035–39.

448. Taylor, J. F., and Hirt, M. 1975. Irrelevance of retention interval length and distractor-task similarity to schizophrenic cognitive interference. *Journal of Consulting and Clinical Psychology* 43(3):281–85.

449. Tolor, A. 1970. Fallacy of schizophrenic deficit in the interpersonal sphere. *Journal of Consulting and Clinical Psychology* 35(2):278–82.

450. Trunnell, T. L., and Pasnau, R. O. 1968. Thought disturbance, psychopathology and behavior in schizophrenia. *Journal of Nervous and Mental Disease* 145(4):326–35.

451. Truscott, I. P. 1973. Contextual constraint and the language function of schizophrenic outpatients. *Journal of Consulting and Clinical Psychology* 41(3):468.

452. Tumer, T. 1973. Effects of chronicity and premorbid adjustment on impression management. *Proceedings of the 81st Annual Convention of the American Psychological Association* (Montreal, Canada), 8:475–76.

453. Turner, R. J., and Zabo, L. J. 1968. Social competence and schizophrenic outcome: An investigation and critique. *Journal of Health and Social Behavior* 9(1):41–51.

454. Van Zood, B. L., and McNulty, J. A. 1971. Autonomic functioning in process and reactive schizophrenia. *Canadian Journal of Behavioral Sciences* 3(4):307–23.

455. Venables, P. H. 1964. Input dysfunction in schizophrenia. In *Progress in experimental personality research*, ed. B. A. Maher (New York: Academic Press).

456. Vermaak, V. J. 1969. Presentation of self in mental illness. *Journal of Behavioral Science* 1(1):33–36.

457. Wagener, J. M., and Hartsough, D. M. 1974. Social competence as a process-reactive dimension with schizophrenics, alcoholics, and normals. *Journal of Abnormal Psychology* 83(2): 112–16.

458. Wagner, B. W. 1968. The training of attending and abstracting responses in chronic schizophrenics. *Journal of Experimental Research in Personality* 3(1):77–88.

459. Wahl, O., and Wishner, J. 1972. Schizophrenic thinking as measured by developmental tests. *Journal of Nervous and Mental Disease* 155(4):232–44.

460. Waldbaum, J. K.; Sutton, S.; and Kerr, J. 1975. Shift of sensory modality and reaction time in schizophrenia. In *Experimental approaches to psychopathology*, eds. M. L. Kietzman, S. Sutton, and J. Zubin (New York: Academic Press).

461. Watson, C. G. 1972. A comparison of the ethical self-presentations of schizophrenics, prisoners and normals. *Journal of Clinical Psychology* 28(4):479–83.

462. Watson, C. G. 1972. Relationships of anhedonia to learning under various contingencies. *Journal of Abnormal Psychology* 80(1):43–48.

463. Watson, C. G. 1973. Abstract thinking deficit and autism in process and reactive schizophrenics. *Journal of Abnormal Psychology* 82(3):399–403.

464. Watson, C. G. 1973. Conspicuous psychotic behavior as a manipulative tool. *Journal of Clinical Psychology* 29(1):3–7.

465. Watson, C. G. 1973. Roles of interpersonal contact and verbal contact in abstract thinking deficits in schizophrenics. *Psychological Reports* 32(3):1023–32.

466. Watson, C. G. 1974. Effects of content verbalness and intangibility on schizophrenics' deficits in abstract thinking. *Psychological Reports* 34(3):1115–18.

467. Watson, C. G. 1975. Impression management abilities in psychiatric hospital samples and normals. *Journal of Consulting and Clinical Psychology* 43(4):540–45.

468. Weinberger, E., and Cermak, L. S. 1973. Short-term retention in acute and chronic paranoid schizophrenics. *Journal of Abnormal Psychology* 82(2):220–25.

469. Wentworth-Rohr, I., and Macintosh, R. 1972. Psychodiagnosis with WAIS intrasubtest scatter of scores. *Journal of Clinical Psychology* 28(1):68.

470. Werner, H. 1948. *Comparative psychology of mental development* (New York: International Universities Press).

471. Williams, E. 1971. The effect of varying the elements in the Bannister-Fransella Grid Test of Thought Disorder. *British Journal of Psychiatry* 119:207–12.

472. Williams, E., and Quirke, C. 1972. Psychological construing in schizophrenics. *British Journal of Medical Psychology* 45(1):79–84.

473. Wincze, J. P.; Leitenberg, H.; and Agros, W. S. 1970. A sequential analysis of the effects of instructions and token reinforcement in the modification of delusional verbal behavior in chronic psychotics. *Proceedings of the Annual Convention of the American Psychological Association* 5: 737–38.

474. Wincze, J. P.; Leitenberg, H.; and Agros, W. S. 1972. The effects of token reinforcement and feedback on the delusional verbal behavior of chronic paranoid schizophrenics. *Journal of Applied Behavior Analysis* 5(3):247–62.

475. Wischner, G. J., and Glades, M. 1969. Rate of formation of associations by schizophrenic and normal subjects as a function of stimulus or response placements of aversive components. *Psychological Reports* 25(2):599–605.

476. Wishner, J., and Wahl, O. 1974. Dichotic listening in schizophrenia. *Journal of Consulting and Clinical Psychology* 42(4):538–46.

477. Witkin, H. A. 1965. Psychological differentiation and the forms of pathology. *Journal of Abnormal Psychology* 70:317–36.

478. Wolfgang, A.; Pishkin, V.; and Rosenbush, E. S. 1968. Concept identification of schizophrenics as a function of social interaction, sex and task complexity. *Journal of Abnormal Psychology* 73(4):336–42.

479. Wright, D. M. 1973. Impairment in abstract conceptualization and Bannister and Fransella's grid test of schizophrenic thought disorder. *Journal of Consulting and Clinical Psychology* 41(3):474.

480. Wright, D. M. 1974. Payne's object classification nonabstract scores and Lovibond's measure of schizophrenic thought disorder. *Psychological Reports* 35(3):1284.

481. Yates, A. J., and Korboot, P. 1970. Speed of perceptual functioning in chronic nonparanoid schizophrenics. *Journal of Abnormal Psychology* 76(3):453–61.

482. Youkilis, H. D., and DeWolfe, A. S. 1975. The regression hypothesis and subclassifications of schizophrenia. *Journal of Abnormal Psychology* 84(1):36–40.

483. Zahn, T. P.; Rosenthal, D.; and Shakow, D. 1963. Effects of irregular preparatory intervals in reaction time in schizophrenia. *Journal of Abnormal and Social Psychology* 67:44–52.

484. Zigler, E., and Levine, J. 1973. Premorbid adjustment and paranoid-nonparanoid status in schizophrenia: A further investigation. *Proceedings of the 81st Annual Convention of the American Psychological Association* (Montreal, Canada), 8:477–78.

485. Zigler, E., and Phillips, L. 1962. Social competence and the process-reactive distinction in psychopathology. *Journal of Abnormal Psychology* 65:215–22.

486. Zlotowski, M., and Cohen, D. 1968. Effects of environmental change upon behavior of hospitalized schizophrenic patients. *Journal of Clinical Psychology* 24(4):470–75.

487. Zubin, J. 1975. Problem of attention in schizophrenia. In *Experimental approaches to psychopathology*, eds. M. L. Kietzman, S. Sutton, and J. Zubin (New York: Academic Press).

488. Zucker, L. 1958. *Ego structure in paranoid schizophrenia: A new method of evaluating projective material* (Springfield, Ill.: Charles C Thomas).

Chapter 6

CHILDREN AT RISK

Ronald O. Rieder, M.D.

Studies of children at risk for schizophrenia may be defined as prospective studies of children selected on the basis of a characteristic indicating an increased probability of schizophrenia in later life. The characteristic which has been most widely used for this selection is schizophrenic psychopathology in the parent. There are other ways of defining and selecting children at risk, but consideration of these other types of "risk studies" will be postponed here until the studies of the offspring of schizophrenic parents have been reviewed.

Studies of children at risk, as defined above, were begun with the observation of infants of schizophrenic parents by Fish (10,12,17) and by Sobel (85). Such studies later shifted to older children entering the age of risk for schizophrenia and proliferated under the term "high-risk studies" put forth by Mednick and McNeil (52). There are numerous current projects in this field; Garmezy (23,24) catalogued twenty in his recent comprehensive review, which included many preliminary reports on the collected data. This chapter will not attempt to duplicate Garmezy's excellent effort; rather it will focus on some selected issues in this area and on the few research projects which have reported their follow-ups and their analyses of the factors which preceded the development of schizophrenia.

How Much Risk and Risk for What?

The term "high risk," when applied to children having *one* schizophrenic parent, might be considered a misnomer in that calculations from previous family studies indicate that the risk for schizophrenia in this group is only 11 to 12 percent (range 6.8–19.4 percent) (8). However, when Mednick and McNeil chose this term, they hypothesized that 50 percent would become "seriously deviant," some with schizophrenia and others with various psychiatric disorders. They based this 1968 calculation on previous studies by Heston (35), Kallman (40), and Reisby (64). In Heston's follow-up of foster-home-reared children of chronic schizophrenic mothers, he found that 55 percent had a significant psychiatric disability. Besides the 10.6 percent with schizophrenia (age-corrected = 16.6 percent), he found some other illnesses among these offspring, most notably sociopathic personalities (27 percent of the males) and neurotic personalities (28 percent of the total group). He also found that 8.5 percent of these offspring had a mental deficiency (IQ < 70; see table 6–1).

TABLE 6-1

Differences in Adulthood Between Foster-Home-Reared Children
of Schizophrenic and Nonschizophrenic Mothers

Diagnosis	Foster-home-reared Children of Schizophrenic Mothers	Foster-home-reared Children of Nonschizophrenic Mothers	Fisher Exact Probability
Number	47	50	
Schizophrenia	5	0	0.024
Sociopathic personality	9	2	0.017
Neurotic personality disorder	13	7	0.052
Mental deficiency (IQ < 70)	4*	0	0.052

Source: Adapted from L. L. Heston, "Psychiatric Disorders in Foster Home Reared Children of Schizophrenic Mothers," *British Journal of Psychiatry* (1966) 112:174.
*One mental defective was sociopathic; another was schizophrenic.

Heston noted the similarity of his findings to those of Kallman (40), who had used the term "schizoid psychopath" in describing one of the various types of "schizoidia" that he found among the offspring of schizophrenics. Kallman diagnosed 32.6 percent of these offspring as having schizoidia of some type, in addition to the 16.4 percent morbidity risk for schizophrenia—rates which he combined to produce a 43.7 percent figure for his "schizophrenic disease complex."

Reisby (64) studied a large Danish sample of children of schizophrenic mothers (N = 349) but did not have personal interview information or a control group for comparison. As in the other two studies, he found a wide range of psychopathology among his subjects, including twice as many cases of schizophreniform psychosis than cases of "clearly established schizophrenia." His age-corrected risk for both these schizophrenic types was 10.4 percent. Without personal interviews it was not possible to calculate from his data accurate risk figures for other types of illness.

Studies over the past decade have supported the hypothesis of an increased risk for other disorders besides schizophrenia among these high-risk offspring, but the results have not been consistent about the types of illness to be found, or about the overall degree of risk.

Manfred Bleuler (2) stated that his sample of schizophrenics' children contained "many more normal children and far fewer eccentrics, psychopaths, and schizoid psychopaths" than previous investigations (37,40,62). He found a 9.4 percent risk for schizophrenia, similar to the figures above, but he classified only 18 percent of the sample as "unfavorable personality developments and eccentrics." This 18 percent was, however, significantly greater (p < .005) than his control rate of 5 percent.

Rosenthal, Kety, and Wender (42,76,90) used the term "schizophrenia spectrum" in their 1968 publications—a term which has come to include chronic schizophrenia, probable schizophrenia, borderline schizophrenia, and personality disorders with schizophrenialike features (schizoid, paranoid, inadequate), but *not* antisocial personality and not recovered (acute) schizophrenia. The latest report from Rosenthal's study of the adopted-away children of schizophrenics (table 6–2) diagnosed 4.7 percent as schizophrenic, 15.6 percent as borderline schizophrenic, and 12.5 percent as schizophrenic personalities, which would combine to 32.8 percent (not age-corrected) with "schizophrenia spectrum disorders" (32).

TABLE 6-2

Consensus Diagnoses of Adopted-away Offspring of
Schizophrenic Parents and Control Adoptees

Diagnosis	Adopted-away Offspring of Schizophrenic Parents	Adopted-away Controls
Number*	64	64
Chronic schizophrenia	3	0
Borderline schizophrenia	10	7
Schizoid, paranoid inadequate personality	8	9
Other personality disorders	11	15
Affective disorders	6	4
No diagnosis	22	27

Source: Adapted from R. Haier, D. Rosenthal, and P. H. Wender, "MMPI Assessment of Psychopathology in the Adopted-away Offspring of Schizophrenics," *Archives of General Psychiatry* (1978) 35:174. Copyright 1978, American Medical Association.

*These columns do not total 64 because a few cases with diagnoses other than those listed are not included in the table.

In considering the sizable rates of these spectrum disorders in Rosenthal's study, it should be noted that the control group contained approximately equal percentages for spectrum categories other than schizophrenia. This analysis thus produced results somewhat different from previous analyses (76,77) in which the total of all spectrum disorders was greater for index cases than for controls. In considering these comparisons, one must recognize that the control parents, especially in adoption studies, do not represent a random sample from the population. High rates of psychiatric illness among the control offspring may relate to (undiagnosed) illness among the control parents. Thus, using these "ill controls" may lead to underestimating the degree of increased risk among the offspring of schizophrenics (just as nonrandom mating, discussed below, may lead to overestimating the risk).

H. Schulsinger (83) has recently performed a thorough clinical evaluation of 173 offspring of schizophrenics, most raised by their own parents, as part of a high-risk study by Mednick and F. Schulsinger. Data from this evaluation will later be considered in more detail, but we are concerned here with the types of diagnosis made in this sample compared with controls. There were many more "borderline states" among the high-risk offspring, regardless of whether the interviewer's clinical diagnosis or computerized systems (CAPPS/DIAGNO and PSE/CATEGO) were used. The consensus diagnoses, derived by agreement between two of the three diagnostic methods, found 31.8 percent borderline states in the high-risk group versus 4.4 percent for controls (see table 6–3). The

TABLE 6-3

Consensus Diagnoses of High-risk and Low-risk
Subjects at Ten-Year Follow-up

Diagnosis*	High-risk Subjects		Low-risk Subjects		x^2 p-value
Number	173		91		
	N	%	N	%	
Schizophrenia	15	8.7	1	1.1	$< .02$
Borderline states (including schizoid and paranoid personality disorders)	55	31.8	4	4.4	$< .001$
Psychopathy	5	2.9	4	4.4	NS
Other personality disorders	22	12.7	9	9.9	NS
Neuroses	30	17.3	33	36.3	$< .001$
Nonspecific conditions	13	7.5	11	12.0	NS
No mental disorder	25	14.5	27	29.7	$< .005$
Other conditions (including affective and paranoid psychoses)	1	0.6	0	0	NS
Disagreement among the three diagnoses	7	4.1	2	2.2	NS

Source: Adapted from H. Schulsinger, "A Ten-Year Follow-up of Children of Schizophrenic Mothers: Clinical Assessment," *Acta Psychiatrica Scandanavica* (1976) 53:371-386.

*Consensus diagnoses represent agreement of two of the three diagnostic measures (Interviewer, CAPPS, PSE).

borderline state category is not well defined and differed somewhat across diagnostic systems. However, it included schizoid and paranoid personality disorders plus some borderline schizophrenic conditions, the same entities that are in Rosenthal, Kety, and Wender's schizophrenia spectrum.

Neurotic and sociopathic personality disorders, which had been found by Heston to be elevated among the high-risk offspring, were not found in increased numbers by Schulsinger, though there had been evidence of an increase in number of crimes in this sample (44). Rosenthal (78), too, did not find any increase in sociopathy.

It is obvious that "how much risk?" is inseparably connected with the question of "risk for what?" When reliable standardized diagnoses of the schizophrenialike conditions are established, which is now occurring (87), and large-scale family studies are performed, it will be possible to determine which diagnoses are more prevalent in these families, and to what degree. Meanwhile we only know that there is an increased risk for schizophrenia, probably for "borderline states" and possibly for "some other things," in the offspring of a schizophrenic.

Along with the risk for schizophrenia and other forms of psychopathology as adults, there appears to be an increased risk for childhood disability among these "children at risk." This topic was reviewed by this author previously (66), and only recent reports will be noted here. Perinatal mortality (69), delayed motor development,* inconsistency in test performance (33), soft neurological signs (48), attentional dysfunction (6,9,30,79) reading disability with perceptual dysfunction (18), and psychiatric disorders (14), including hyperactivity (68), have been described. Again the degree of risk is determined by the outcome measure which has been chosen, but the rate of these disorders appears considerable. Previously this author estimated that in 20 percent of the cases where a child has one schizophrenic parent there will be significant social and psychological maladjustment (66).

Determinants of the Risk

The selection of the offspring of schizophrenics for high-risk studies may appear to involve the assumption of the genetic transmission of schizophrenia, but environmental factors could also be responsible for this increased risk, in whole or in part; and in fact Mednick hypothesized just such environmental influences in the early stages of his risk-research planning (49). Unequivocal evidence of the role of genetic factors awaited the adoption studies of Heston (35), Kety (43), Rosenthal (77), and Wender (91).

Heston (30) noted that his age-corrected rate for schizophrenia of 16.6 percent was a finding "consistent with Kallmann's 16.4 percent." In other words, the risk for the adopted-away high-risk offspring was equal to that for offspring reared with the schizophrenic parent— implying that genetic factors account for *all* of the risk. In the Rosenthal study, three of sixty-four index cases were diagnosed as schizophrenic (4.7 percent), and this would translate into 9.6 percent for age-corrected morbidity risk.† This figure, though lower than Heston's, is still close to the mean for studies of children of schizophrenics reared in their natural

---

* See references 6, 14, 33, 53, and 54.
† For comparison purposes the borderline schizophrenic parents should be excluded, making the rate of definitely schizophrenic offspring three of forty-four (6.8 percent), before age correction. The calculation of an age-corrected figure is somewhat problematic for this data in that such corrections have been derived on hospitalized cases, and two of the three schizophrenic cases in Rosenthal's sample were diagnosed by the interviewer, without having been hospitalized.

homes and is practically the same as Reisby's finding (10.4 percent), which was determined for the same period in the same country. Wender found a low incidence of schizophrenia spectrum disorders among the children of normal parents who had been adopted-away and reared in a family with a schizophrenic parent (91). Taken together, these studies are strong evidence against a hypothesis that the transmission of schizophrenia comes through contact with the ill parent.

What role then does the rearing relationship play in the adoption studies? Rosenthal et al. have considered this, calculating an overall correlation of the parent-child relationship with psychopathology of about 0.30 for all offspring in the study (78). However, this correlation was higher for the subjects who were not born of schizophrenic parents (0.37) than for the offspring of schizophrenics (0.23). They concluded, "These findings suggest that rearing patterns have only a modest effect on individuals who harbor a genetic background for schizophrenia, but an appreciable effect on persons without such a background."

The role of family relations could be discussed in more detail if space permitted, for this factor cannot be evaluated entirely on the basis of adoption studies. There is evidence that parental criticism, hostility, and overprotectiveness can cause exacerbation of a psychosis if not the schizophrenic condition itself (3,88). The influence of parental communication patterns is discussed below in the review of Goldstein et al.'s study, and is discussed in this volume and elsewhere by Wynne (92). The influence of this factor in children having a schizophrenic parent, however, has not been adequately demonstrated.

PERINATAL COMPLICATIONS

The importance of environmental factors in the etiology of schizophrenia is evidenced by the twin studies, which show that the concordance rate for monozygotic twins is only about 50 percent (29). However, "environment" is a broad category, and factors other than family relations need to be considered, including nongenetic biological variables such as dietary, infectious, toxic, and traumatic influences. There has not been much study of these possibilities except in one area—the exposure to adverse perinatal events. McNeil and Kaij (47) stated that their extensive review of this literature "suggest[s] that obstetric complications are a risk-increasing factor to be taken seriously in the etiology of schizophrenia." Nevertheless, there is evidence against concluding that the transmission of schizophrenia from parent to child is through an adverse perinatal influence. As McNeil and Kaij noted, the majority of studies show (1) no differences in birth weights for offspring of schizophrenics versus controls, and (2) no differences in the rates of various types of perinatal complications (pregnancy, birth, neonatal, combined) in reproductions by schizophrenics compared with controls. Moreover, the Danish adoption studies found a high rate of schizophrenia in the paternal half siblings of the adopted-away schizophrenic, and the relationship between the proband and these ill relations was only genetic. They had different mothers and thus different intrauterine and postnatal environments.

What possible role for perinatal factors is left then in the transmission of illness to the children of schizophrenics? The remaining possibility is of some type of genetic-environmental interaction in which perinatal events, though not more frequent in the pregnancies of schizophrenic women, have a greater influence when they occur, due to a genetic susceptibility on the part of the child. Three separate studies, by Mednick (54,55), Rieder (67), and Schachter (82), have suggested such an interaction, but each has focused on different perinatal variables and different outcome measures. The difficulty of demonstrating this type of role for perinatal variables can be seen by the arguments of Heston (36) and Fish (13) in their discussions of Mednick's study, in which they both concluded that his data were more supportive of a purely genetic than an interactive influence. They argued that low birth weight and early developmental deviations are more likely to reflect the influence of the schizophrenic genotype than a traumatic influence of pregnancy complications.

There are some other studies which relate perinatal variables and schizophrenia. McNeil and Kaij (47) noted that "Four studies show some apparent increase in fetal and neonatal deaths and malformations in reproductions by schizophrenic parents (especially mothers), but this may not be characteristic only of schizophrenics." The four studies referred to are those by Sobel (86), Paffenbarger (63), Rieder (69), and Hanson (33). An increase in perinatal deaths suggests, but of course does not prove, that perinatal factors increase the risk for the surviving children and, as Sameroff and Zax have found, the offspring of chronically ill depressed women may be as much at risk as the offspring of schizophrenics (80,93).

The high-risk studies by Mednick and by Fish have both analyzed perinatal influences, and their data will be discussed below along with their other findings.

ILLNESS IN THE CO-PARENT

Just as perinatal variables may have a complex interactive effect on the risk for the children of schizophrenics, rather than a simple causative or addictive effect, so the genetic determinants of the risk may be complex in their nature. Data have been recently collected on the issue of nonrandom mating by schizophrenics, and how this might influence the psychiatric status of the offspring.

Fowler and Tsuang (21) evaluated the spouses of male and female schizophrenics and controls; blind as to each index case's diagnosis. They found an "excess of illness," especially an excess of personality disorder, at least when compared with the spouses of affective-disordered subjects. These personality disorders were not described in detail but were labeled "unspecified," and it was stated that "schizoid-like qualities were not noted." Besides personality disorders, alcoholism was found more frequently in the spouses of schizophrenics than in the spouses of manics. One reason for the importance of studying the spouses of schizophrenics is to evaluate the possibility that some of the disorders among the children relate more to the co-parent's illness than to the index parent's schizophrenia. Fowler and Tsuang believed that the personality disorders seen in the children of schizophrenics, especially the sociopathic personalities found by Heston, may relate to the personality disorders and alcoholism they found in their co-parent study.

Kirkegaard-Sorensen and Mednick (44) examined Mednick and Schulsinger's high-risk sample for criminality (conviction with a sentence greater than a fine). They found more criminality in the male co-parents of the female schizophrenics than would be expected on the basis of rates from the Danish population. They also found more registered crimes among the male children in the high-risk group than among the controls or in the population at large. In an analysis of the parent and child data together, they concluded, "If the father is not criminal, the schizophrenia in the mother does not heighten the level of criminality in the children."

TABLE 6-4

Offspring Diagnosis According to the Diagnosis of the Co-parent
When All Index Parents are Chronic Schizophrenics

Co-parent Diagnosis	Diagnosis of Offspring	
	Schizophrenic Spectrum	Not Spectrum
Schizophrenic spectrum	5	3
Not spectrum	1	10

Source: Adapted from D. Rosenthal, 1975. Discussion: Subschizophrenic disorders. In *Genetic research in psychiatry*, eds. R. R. Fieve, D. Rosenthal and A. Brill (Baltimore: John Hopkins University Press) p. 207.

p = 0.024 (Fisher Exact Probability).

Recalling that Rosenthal did not find many sociopathic personalities in his adoption studies, but that he did find a high rate of schizophrenia spectrum disorders, it is perhaps not surprising that in his own co-parent study he found more schizophrenic spectrum disorders than sociopathy (75). He found that when the schizophrenic parent was female, 28 percent of the co-parents were given a spectrum diagnosis, and 28 percent, a diagnosis of sociopathic disorder. When the schizophrenic parent was male, 45 percent of the female co-parents were given a spectrum diagnosis. Thus, approximately half of the co-parents were diagnosed, and most were spectrum cases. The influence this may have is demonstrated in table 6-4, which shows that there were many more spectrum cases from the chronic schizophrenia x spectrum matings. This is again evidence that the co-parent diagnosis has a significant influence on the type and degree of risk of the high-risk children.

The one study which more than any others has recognized the importance of psychopathology in the co-parent is the high-risk study begun by Erlenmeyer-Kimling, which includes a study of children of two schizophrenic parents.* Using data from older studies, she has estimated the

° See references 5, 6, 7, 8, 9, and 79.

risk for schizophrenia to be about 39 percent for the offspring of two schizophrenics, so this will indeed be a study of children at high risk for schizophrenia itself.

Models for Risk and Genetic Counseling

Though genetic factors have been shown to be operating in the transmission of schizophrenia, the mode of this genetic transmission is unknown. Polygenetic models, monogenic models with limited penetrance, and heterogeneity models each have their adherents. Understanding the risk for schizophrenia in a specific individual awaits the unraveling of this genetic influence, but even our limited data gives us some basis for estimating relative risk and for using this knowledge in genetic counseling. The following conclusions have been drawn by Kety, Matthysse, and Kidd (41) and by Erlenmeyer-Kimling (7), who are currently working on methods of counseling schizophrenic patients and their families:

1. Risk figures have been developed almost entirely from studies in which there was a chronic schizophrenic illness in the parent; such figures are probably lower for other types of schizophrenia (borderline, schizoaffective) that are often diagnosed as schizophrenia in the United States.
2. The risk of illness applies most appropriately to a child not yet born; the empirical risk will be affected by the age and the psychological status of the offspring. At age forty-five the remaining risk is small.
3. The risk increases both with the number of relatives having definite schizophrenia and with the closeness of their genetic relationship.
4. Some risk estimates—such as the risk of having another affected child, given affected children in the family—are strongly influenced by the model chosen (polygenic vs. monogenic), while other risk estimates are relatively independent of the model.
5. There has been an increase in the reproduction rates for schizophrenic women and men since the 1930s.
6. Most parents who will have a schizophrenic child cannot be recognized beforehand (i.e., only 20 percent of schizophrenics have a schizophrenic parent or sibling).
7. Currently there are no concrete measures of known benefit that could be taken by a prospective parent to minimize the risk, other than refraining from having children.

(Nearly) Completed Studies of High-Risk Children

Of the many studies of children of schizophrenic parents, there are two which are complete to the point where measures collected at an earlier stage of life have been related to the later development of schizophrenia.

These two studies—the first by Fish and her colleagues, the second by Mednick and co-workers—will be summarized and examined here in some detail, so that the nature, promise, and problems of this type of research can be illustrated.

FISH: "NEUROINTEGRATIVE DEFECT"

Fish's study has received less recognition than it warrants, perhaps because it began with infants in 1952 and has followed them prospectively into childhood and adolescence, but has not yet had "adult schizophrenia" as its outcome measure. Fish and her collaborators have published descriptions of the project at its inception (10,11,12,17), after the ten-year follow-up (15,18,19,20), and recently after the addition of some new data collected at age eighteen (14,16).

TABLE 6-5
Diagnoses at Age Ten of High-risk
Offspring and Controls

Children's Diagnoses	Offspring of Schizophrenic Mothers	Controls
Number	12	12
Childhood schizophrenia	2	0
Personality disorder		
Severe	3	1
Moderate	5	2
Mild or no symptoms	2	9

Source: Adapted from B. Fish, "Biologic Antecedents of Psychosis in Children," in *The Biology of the Major Psychoses: A Comparative Analysis*, ed. D. X. Freedman, (New York: Raven Press), p. 49-80.

The ten-year and eighteen-year follow-up evaluations were composed of a blind psychiatric diagnostic interview and a psychological battery, including intelligence, projective, and perceptual-motor testing. The psychiatric diagnoses for the index cases and controls at age ten are listed in table 6–5. Of the twelve index cases, there are ten children regarded as psychiatrically ill, and two as having childhood schizophrenia (see table 6–5). This is a strikingly high rate of childhood psychopathology, and especially of childhood schizophrenia in this small sample. Fish has indicated that her later follow-up confirmed the diagnoses of the two schizophrenics, though one is now in a partial remission or residual state. She has published case history information for the two children that supports her diagnoses and allows for independent judgments.*

Fish analyzed her sample for early developmental patterns of the

* See references 10, 14, 15, 16, 17, 18, 19, and 20.

type she had postulated should discriminate preschizophrenic infants. She concluded (16):

> Analysis of the developmental curves points to an early biologic disorder in the two childhood schizophrenics. Both infants had a major disorganization of neurologic maturation that involved postural-motor, visual-motor, and physical development as early as the first month of life. There was no fixed neurologic deficit, but rather a disorder of the timing and integration of neurologic maturation. [p. 1303]

This project has focused upon measures of irregularities of development. At each of the repeated examinations of the infant, his growth and abilities were compared to norms for different areas of development (physical, postural-motor, visual-motor) and a "development quotient" (DQ) was calculated for each of these areas. If there were deceleration and recovery of the DQs on successive exams, or if there were a wide range of developmental quotients on any one exam with a profile of passes and failures different from that found in organic brain disorder ("scatter"), neurological development was considered uneven. In an earlier article Fish (18) focused upon scatter in postural-motor and visual-motor development as a predictor of later psychopathology. She also found one visual-motor task—"failure of hand-to-hand integration" between four and nine months—to be highly correlated with subsequent emotional impairment. However, in her latest analysis she turned her attention back to the delays in physical growth and motor performance which she had observed and reported upon when these subjects were infants (10,11). She has coined the term "pandevelopmental retardation," meaning intermittent retardation of physical development as well as postural-motor and/or visual-motor development, and stated (16):

> This "pandevelopmental retardation" was related to psychiatric morbidity at 10 years of age. It was most severe in the two preschizophrenic infants. . . . Children in whom pandevelopmental retardation was milder and shorter were ranked just below the schizophrenic children in the severity of their psychiatric disturbance at 10 years. Children who had no retardation of physical growth had still milder psychiatric disorders at ten years. . . . [p. 1304] [See table 6–6]

Though Fish found a high rate of psychological disturbance, perceptual dysfunctions (18), and pandevelopmental retardation in her high-risk sample, she found a low rate of complications of pregnancy and birth, and no association could be established between perinatal complications and later psychopathology. Fish (16) stated that the type of developmental abnormalities found in this high-risk sample "were distinctly different from the patterns seen following pregnancy and birth complications." She also admitted, however, that for several mothers adequate records of the first trimester of pregnancy were not available.

One other factor besides pandevelopmental retardation which appeared to differentiate the schizophrenic children in this study is early environmental conditions. The two schizophrenics were raised in what Fish called "the most impoverished environments"—one for four years in a foundling institution, the other by a "disorganized maternal grandmother."

Fish's study is the oldest ongoing prospective study of children of schizophrenic parents. Like most beginning efforts, it has aspects of its design that are not ideal: (1) The sample was collected by combining

TABLE 6-6

"Pandevelopmental Retardation" and Psychiatric Outcome
at Ten Years within the High-risk Sample

Number*	Type of Developmental Disorder	Lowest Motor DQ, Birth to 2 Years	Diagnoses at 10 Years
2	Pandevelopmental retardation (growth and motor lags)	<79	2 with schizophrenia
5	Pandevelopmental retardation (growth and motor lags)	80-89	2 with severe personality disorder 3 with moderate personality disorder
3	Motor lag only	80-89	2 with moderate personality disorder 1 with mild symptoms
1	No motor lag	>90	1 with mild symptoms

Source: Adapted from B. Fish, "Neurobiologic Antecedents of Schizophrenia in Children: Evidence for an Inherited, Congenital Neurointegrative Defect," *Archives of General Psychiatry* (1977) 34:1305; plus personal communication.

*One child excluded because of lack of developmental data.

a sample from the Bellevue Hospital well-baby clinic with a later-born sample of children of hospitalized mothers. Most (all but two) of the high-risk children came from the latter group, while the controls came from the former. (2) Though some data have been collected carefully and prospectively, such as the developmental quotients, other important data, such as pregnancy complications, were obtained from prenatal and obstetrical records. (3) The ratings of development were not made by someone blind to the parent's illness, and the reliability of these ratings has not been established. (4) The sample is in fact only at the beginning of the age of risk for schizophrenia, and who in the sample will be schizophrenic as an adult remains in question. (5) The sample is too small to determine the harmful or beneficial effect of certain variables, such as the impact of early environmental conditions. (6) The sample is atypical in that such a high percentage of children are diagnosed as having a personality disorder or childhood schizophrenia.

Regardless of these weaknesses, Fish's study in its major outlines has prospectively related early developmental observations to later psychopathology. It has supported the hypothesis that the genes which transmit schizophrenia have an observable effect in infancy, a "neurointegrative defect" manifested by pandevelopmental retardation.

MEDNICK AND SCHULSINGER

Mednick and Schulsinger, working in Denmark, selected 207 children with a chronic schizophrenic mother and 104 controls, aged nine to twenty, for their study in 1962. At that time, the subjects were examined with a battery of psychological and psychophysiological tests; they and their parents or guardians were interviewed; the midwife's report on a subject's gestation and delivery was sought; and a report was collected from the teachers concerning school behavior. Information on each mother's illness was obtained through hospital and other agency records.

By 1967, Mednick and Schulsinger were able to identify 20 individuals from the high-risk group whom they believed had had a psychiatric or a social breakdown. They called this group of 20 the "Sick Group" in their reports (50,55) and found that certain variables could distinguish this group from the other high-risk subjects. These variables were: (1) hospitalization of the mother relatively early in life, (2) reports by the teacher of disturbing, aggressive behavior in school, (3) a rapid rate of recovery of the GSR (galvanic skin response) following the peak response, (4) pregnancy and/or birth complications, and (5) associative drift on a word-association test.

The members of the 1967 Sick Group, however, were not all sick with schizophrenia. In 1972 there began a comprehensive reassessment of the sample, when the average age was 25.1 years (range 18 to 30). This 1972–74 reassessment, which forms the basis for the new analyses of the Mednick-Schulsinger study, focused on schizophrenia (83) and was referred to earlier in discussing the types of illness in the high-risk offspring (table 6–3).

The diagnostic evaluation was centered around a lengthy interview, lasting about three hours, by a research psychologist. A structured interview format, using both the Present State Exam (PSE) of Wing and the Current and Past Psychopathology Scale (CAPPS) of Spitzer and Endicott, was used during part of the interview, and during this part the interviewer was blind as to the subjects' status. Hospital records were also obtained, and a Minnesota Multiphasic Personality Inventory (MMPI), which has not yet been reported upon, was administered.

The return rate was 86 percent of the subjects living at the time of the assessment. Of the original 207, 34 were lost to the study including 8 who had died, compared to none in the control group. Of these deaths 4 or perhaps 5 were suicides, and 2 of these individuals were considered schizophrenic on the basis of previous information and hospital records. H. Schulsinger (83) reported in detail the level of agreement of the various diagnostic instruments and stated that

when the three sets of diagnoses (PSE, CAPPS, Interviewer's diagnoses) were summarized into "consensus" diagnoses based on agreement between two of the three, there were 15 schizophrenics in the high-risk group . . . [and] . . . to this could be added two of the deceased subjects. . . . [p. 382]

Mednick et al. have now begun to determine which variables discriminate these schizophrenics from the other high-risk subjects. This group is quite different from the Sick Group of the previous reports. Only six of the twenty in the Sick Group were diagnosed schizophrenic in 1972, and three of these committed suicide. The first report on this new "schizophrenic group" used the fourteen *interviewer-diagnosed* schizophrenics and compared them to all other high-risk subjects (57):

The 14 high-risk subjects who were diagnosed schizophrenic (schizophrenic group) had mothers whose illness began while the mother was relatively young. She was also younger at the time of her first hospitalization. This suggests that the mothers of the schizophrenic group had a more chronic and serious illness.

The birth of the schizophrenic group was relatively difficult. The period of labor was longer and was characterized by more complications. It should also be mentioned that the mothers of the schizophrenics were more frequently unmarried. . . .

No significant differences were observed on individual items relating to early infant behavior or parental attitudes or behavior. It was noticed that the schizophrenic group did evidence marginally greater deviance on a number of items reflecting infant behavior. However, not one of these differences was statistically significant. . . . It should be pointed out that of the 14 schizophrenics only 2 had been raised in an intact family.

Except for the perinatal data (based on midwife reports), all of the results above are based on retrospective reports. . . . The school teacher who rated the behavior of the subjects, however, bases his or her report on the current behavior of the subject . . . or on the basis of relatively short-term retrospection.

On the whole the schizophrenic group separated itself sharply from the other groups in the teacher's judgements. They were reported as being very easily angered and upset and very slow in calming down from such upsets. The schizophrenic group disturbed the class with inappropriate behavior, was characterized as being violent and aggressive and a disciplinary problem for the teacher. . . . [pp. 244–45]

This portion of Mednick et al.'s report is quoted at length for two reasons. First, it is a summary of important findings, and each statement has implications for our understanding of the etiology or the natural history of schizophrenia. Second, however, the relevant analyses of the data are referred to but not presented by Mednick, and thus we have only his interpretations to consider. The statistical significance of these effects, their independence or interrelatedness, and the extent to which they differentiate the schizophrenic group were not presented and cannot be reviewed here.

There are some recent reports from this project which are more detailed, but they, too, leave questions unanswered. Mednick (51) reported on the psychophysiological functioning of thirty-four high-risk subjects who had been diagnosed as chronic, acute, or borderline schizophrenics. (These thirty-four were chosen from the previously mentioned fifteen schizophrenics and fifty-five with borderline states on the basis of their having had psychiatric evaluation or treatment.) He reported that the electrodermal recovery rates of these thirty-four subjects, measured in 1962, were more rapid than the rest of the high-risk sample, but that there was considerable variability within the group on this measure.

The latest analysis (58) focused upon sex differences in the factors which discriminate the schizophrenics. It used a form of path analysis, LISREL, which involves the establishment of "constructs" from the variables which have been collected. The constructs which this analysis employed were: (1) mother's age of onset of illness, (2) parental separation in the first five years of life, (3) pregnancy and birth complications, (4) autonomic nervous system recovery rate and responsiveness, (5) socioeconomic status, and (6) schizophrenia in the high-risk child. Each construct had two or more items which entered into it. For example, parental separation was defined by (1) amount of separation from father, (2) amount of separation from mother, and (3) amount of time in children's homes. These constructs, which were regarded as more reliable than any individual item defining them, were then used as the elements in the path analysis.

The results of the analyses are reproduced in figures 6–1 and 6–2. Mednick et al.'s summary of the findings is as follows:

> Figure [6–1] presents the path diagram for men. Significant path coefficients (and their probability levels) are indicated. Insignificant path coefficients were estimated but omitted from Figures 1 and 2 for purposes of clarity. Note that pregnancy and birth complications have no direct effect on schizophrenia; their effect is mediated by the ANS construct. Childhood separation and the ANS construct are directly related to later schizophrenia in high-risk men, as hypothesized. Also as hypothesized, the ANS factors are rather well predicted by pregnancy and birth complications. Childhood separation is predicted by an early age of onset of the mother's schizophrenia which does not evidence a direct relation to schizophrenia. [p. 185]

and:

> Figure [6–2] presents the path diagram for the women. In this path diagram the only construct which is significantly directly related to the development of schizophrenia is the age of onset of the mother's schizophrenia. The pattern for the women is quite different from that seen in Figure [6–1] for men. The ANS construct (a reliable predictor for men) is not significantly related to schizophrenia in women, nor is childhood separation. Comparison of the path diagrams strongly suggests that some aspects of the etiology of schizophrenia are quite different in high-risk men and women. [pp. 185–6]

The appropriate interpretation of these findings is not obvious. LISREL is an adaptation of path analysis which allows one to develop causal multivariate models (39). However, it remains basically a correlational technique; causal statements can be suggested but not proved by it. The statistically significant relationships in figures 6–1 and 6–2 do not prove the importance of any of the predispositional variables, because other variables, which are not in the analysis, may be causative, and the identified variables may in reality be mediators or secondary effects of the causative factors. Also, variables not in the analysis may be more important mediators than the mediators analyzed. In other words, we do not know that the age of onset of a schizophrenic mother's illness is directly causative of schizophrenia in her daughter, because both of these variables may be the result of another variable which was not specified, such as the degree of genetic predisposition to schizophrenia. Similarly, we cannot conclude that the age of onset of the mother's illness is related to illness in her son only through parental separation, when we have not evaluated other factors that might provide a link to schizophrenia in the child—for example, early developmental deviations or misbehavior in school.

The construct which was most conspicuously absent in this analysis was a measure of genetic factors. Of course, it was not possible to identify with certainty those parents or children who have a greater genetic loading, but a reasonable construct for such loading could be made which would include family history of schizophrenia, the severity of illness in the mother, and schizophrenic traits in the father. Among the available constructs the closest thing to a measure of genetic factors was age of onset of illness in the mother, which in fact had a relationship to schizophrenia in both sexes.

These criticisms are not meant to imply that the LISREL analysis is

FIGURE 6-1
Path Diagram for Men

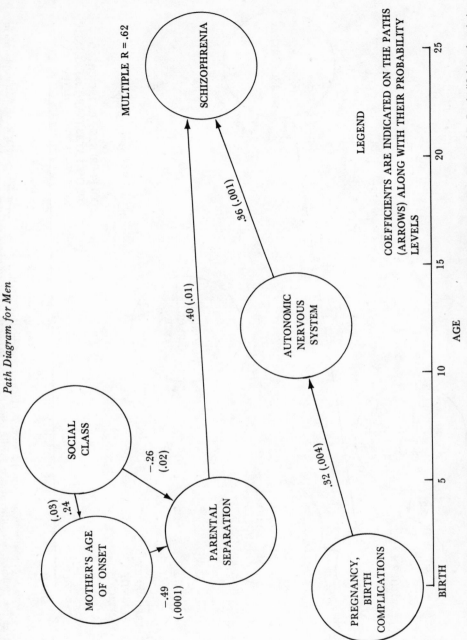

MULTIPLE R = .62

LEGEND

COEFFICIENTS ARE INDICATED ON THE PATHS
(ARROWS) ALONG WITH THEIR PROBABILITY
LEVELS

Source: Reprinted with permission from S. A. Mednick, F. Schulsinger, T. W. Teasdale, P. Venables, and R. Rock, "Schizophrenia in High-risk Children: Sex Differences in Predisposing Factors," in *Cognitive Defects in the Development of Mental Illness*, ed. G. Serban (New York: Brunner/Mazel, 1978), p. 187.

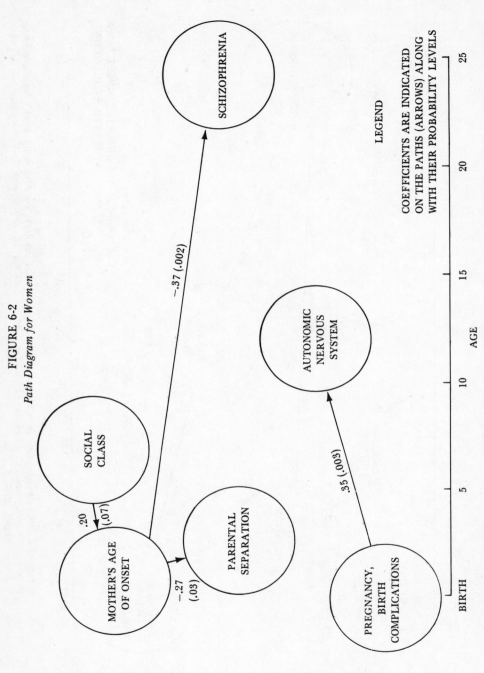

FIGURE 6-2

Path Diagram for Women

LEGEND

COEFFICIENTS ARE INDICATED
ON THE PATHS (ARROWS) ALONG
WITH THEIR PROBABILITY LEVELS

Source: Reprinted with permission from S. A. Mednick, F. Schulsinger, T. W. Teasdale, P. Venables, and D. Rock, "Schizophrenia in High-risk Children: Sex Differences in Predisposing Factors," in *Cognitive Defects in the Development of Mental Illness*, ed. G. Serban (New York: Brunner/Mazel, 1978), p. 187.

not appropriate for the analysis of these data and data from other high-risk studies. However, the results of this very useful analytic procedure are influenced and limited by the constructs entered into it. The fact that this is a first attempt at defining the antecedents of schizophrenia by this method, and that it is limited to these data and to these constructs, is well recognized by Mednick and his co-workers. The criticisms above are directed to readers of their work and to other investigators, who will need to become more aware of both the power and the limits of this method as it is used in future studies.

In the context of these caveats, there are some findings in this study which are important and interesting. There were two groupings of constructs which link to schizophrenia among the males and one among the females. In the males the first grouping linked parental separation quite strongly to schizophrenia (0.40), and this was explained in part, but not all, by early onset of the mother's illness. Since separation from father entered into "parental separation," it is possible that this variable reflected the importance of the father's psychopathology, more among the males than among the female offspring. It is of interest also to see how social class, which has often been linked to schizophrenia (45), is correlated with these other variables and may be linked to schizophrenia through them.

The ANS construct of Mednick was a product of GSR recovery rate and "responsiveness," the percentage of measurable responses during the whole exam. This construct showed a moderately high relationship with schizophrenia among the males, but in both sexes it is independent of the previous grouping. If, as discussed earlier, the previous grouping reflects genetic factors, and the ANS construct does not, then this analysis has begun to specify and measure nongenetic influences, at least in males. This interpretation is supported by finding the perinatal complication-ANS path. Before accepting a causative role for perinatal complications, however, it would be important to know what specific perinatal complications discriminated the schizophrenics from controls, because earlier versions of the complications scale (60) included low birth weight, which cannot be regarded as a traumatic perinatal event, independent of the genotype of the child. Finding perinatal complications linked to schizophrenia in males only is not entirely unexpected, given that males show a greater susceptibility to perinatal injury in general. The ANS construct is Mednick's counterpart to Fish's pandevelopmental retardation, in that (in males) it appears to be an indicator of the predisposition to schizophrenia. However, this may be a congenital, nongenetic defect rather than a genetic one.

Other Risk Studies

As mentioned in the first paragraph of this chapter, other characteristics than schizophrenia in a parent could be used to select children at high risk for schizophrenia. One group of investigators, at UCLA, led by Goldstein and Rodnick (27), have chosen to follow up adolescents seen at the UCLA Psychology Clinic. They hypothesized that certain types of adolescent psychopathology and that parental communication disturbance represent risk factors for schizophrenia. Their typology of adolescent psychopathology included four groups: (1) aggressive, antisocial, delinquent; (2) actively hostile to parents and internally distressed, but not delinquent; (3) passively negative and hostile to parents; and (4) withdrawn, socially isolated. Note that these were nonpsychotic adolescents. On the basis of previous studies of adolescent disturbances preceding schizophrenia, they predicted that types 2 and 4 would be at higher risk than the other two types. Measures of family communication deviance based on TAT (Thematic Apperception Test) responses have followed the work of Wynne and Singer (92). Even before the follow-up began, analysis of the data revealed that the types of communication and thought disturbances characterizing the parents of schizophrenics were found more often among the parents of group 2 and group 4 adolescents than among the parents of the other groups (38).

In 1976 Goldstein et al. (28) presented their first five-year follow-up report. It was on only twenty-three cases, but, according to personal communication with Goldstein, the addition of more cases recently has only strengthened these earlier findings. The assessment at the five-year follow-up was thorough, with efforts made to ensure blind ratings. Diagnoses were made using the Research Diagnostic Criteria (RDC), plus the Diagnostic Interview for Borderlines developed by Gunderson (31). Many of Goldstein et al.'s results were reported in terms of "schizophrenia spectrum cases," using Gunderson's interview schedule to diagnose the "probable" and "definite borderlines" in the spectrum. It is questionable and, according to recent evidence (87), probably unlikely that borderlines diagnosed in this way are the same as the "borderline schizophrenics" of Wender et al. (90), though they were equated by Goldstein. However, two out of the twenty-three cases had a schizophrenic or schizo-affective psychosis, and there presumably would be less diagnostic dispute about these, since the RDC were used.

The conclusions from this study, based as mentioned on "schizophrenia spectrum diagnoses" (SSD), were that: (1) severity of adolescent psychopathology predicts later SSD; (2) parental communication deviance, measured when the child was an adolescent, relates to SSD as a young adult; and (3) the absence of parental communication deviance is associated with improvement in the child's clinical status over time. The discriminating features of the two schizophrenic cases were: (1) they both came from the seven adolescents judged as type 2 above; and (2) they both were among the twelve with high levels of parental communication deviance.

It is evident that this type of high-risk study is much more oriented toward determining the predictive utility of adolescent psychopathology than toward determining an underlying manifestation of the genetic predisposition to schizophrenia. In this way Goldstein's study is similar to the follow-up studies by Robins (70) and others, which might also be considered high-risk studies. It relates also to the follow-back studies of Ricks (65), Watt (89), and others, which began with schizophrenics and reviewed childhood records, asking questions about the natural history and predictive behavioral discriminators of schizophrenia. This line of research has reported with remarkable consistency that many male schizophrenics have had adolescent behavior disorders that are similar to Goldstein's type 2. Watt concluded (89):

> With age, the preschizophrenic boys became quite unpleasant, aggressive, self-centered, and defiant of authority. In short, they became adolescent "behavior problems" rather than "wall flowers," a finding consistent with that of Ricks and Berry and Robins. [p. 164]

These other types of high-risk studies have been considered in more detail previously (23,24). To complete this limited review of this area, Garmezy's table outlining the characteristics of the many on-going projects is reproduced here (table 6–7).

Promises, Problems

The exciting promise of the high-risk studies is to be able to sit with data collected years previously and evaluate prior hypotheses on what leads to a schizophrenic breakdown. This has seemed to many to be a way to unlock the areas of etiology, prediction, and prevention of schizophrenia. As these studies have progressed, however, there has been some dampening of the initial enthusiasm. Reports questioning the theoretical basis, the feasibility, and the generalizability of these studies have recently appeared (26,34,74,84); they have raised the following arguments against the basic assumption of these studies that measurements previously made on those individuals who later break down will lead to understanding the causes of schizophrenia:

1. There may be so much heterogeneity of the transmitted predisposing genotypes that there will be no common manifestation of the predisposition to schizophrenia.
2. Many individuals who do not break down, even after long follow-up, may yet have the genetic predisposition to schizophrenia, so comparisons of the breakdown cases with the others are confounded and may not reveal early manifestations of the genotype.
3. Causative environmental factors and manifestations of the predisposing genotype will obviously not be discovered unless they are included as variables, but most of the high-risk studies have not focused on deviant family interaction or on biochemical abnormalities, both of which hold leading places in environmental and genetic theories of the etiology of schizophrenia.
4. Physiological and neuropsychological measures which predict illness cannot be assumed to be "precursors" of illness if in fact behavioral abnormalities are already present in the children or adolescents examined. These measures may reflect the *effects* of illness, much as such measures are influenced by manifest schizophrenia.

The feasibility of drawing firm conclusions from the high-risk studies has also been questioned:

1. Different studies are employing different measures, sometimes slightly different and sometimes completely different. The reliability of these

TABLE 6-7
Current Programs of Prospective Research on Children
at Risk for Schizophrenia and Related Disorders

Investigator(s)	Locale	Age Range of Children	Criteria for Risk Group Selection
Anthony, E. J.	St. Louis, Mo.	Preschool School age Adolescence Early adulthood	Schizophrenic mother or father
Erlenmeyer-Kimling, L., and Rainer, J.	New York, N.Y.	School age	Schizophrenic mother or father Two schizophrenic parents
Erlenmeyer-Kimling, L., and Rainer, J.	New York, N.Y.	Adolescence Early adulthood	Two schizophrenic parents
Fish, B.	New York, N.Y., and Los Angeles, Calif.	Infancy	Schizophrenic mother
Garmezy, N., and Devine, V.	Minneapolis, Minn.	School age	Schizophrenic mother
Grunebaum, H. V.	Boston, Mass.	Infancy Preschool School age	Psychotic mother

Criteria for Control Group Selection	Central Variables	Effort at Intervention	Central Reference*
Parent with physical disorder Parents free of mental or physical disorder	Clinical assessment Home visits Information processing Neurological assessment Piagetian tasks (egocentrism) Play behavior Psychophysiology	Yes	Anthony (1)
One or two parents non-schizophrenic with psychiatric disorder Normal control parents	Attentional tasks Home visits Neurological assessment Physical development Psychiatric assessment Psychological assessment Psychophysiology School evaluations Social behavior	No	Erlenmeyer-Kimling (6)
Schizophrenic mother; nonschizophrenic psychiatric dis-ordered mother	Attentional measures Birth data Developmental data Electrophysiology Neurological assessment Personality assessment Psychiatric records Psychophysiology School records Visual motor tasks	No	Erlenmeyer-Kimling (9)

	Developmental tasks:
	   arousal
	     autonomic functioning
	     vestibular functioning
	Neurological assessment
	Visual-motor tasks
	Psychological assessment
		Yes	Fish and Hagin (18)
			Fish et al. (20)

Depressive mother Acting-out child Withdrawn child Matched and random normal controls hyperactive child	Attentional and vigilance tasks Competence measures Information processing School records Sociometric measures Teacher ratings	No	Garmezy (22)
Nonpsychotic mother	Attentional and vigilance tasks Cognitive styles Competence measures Mother-child interaction Psychological assessment	Yes	Grunebaum et al. (30)

TABLE 6-7 (Continued)

Investigator(s)	Locale	Age Range of Children	Criteria for Risk Group Selection
McNeil, T. F., and Kaji, L.	Malmo, Sweden	Prenatal and infancy	Schizophrenic mother
Marcus, J., and colleagues	Israel	Infancy	Schizophrenic mother or father
Mednick, S. A., and Schulsinger, F.	Copenhagen, Denmark	Adolescence Early adulthood	Schizophrenic mother
Mednick, S. A., and Schulsinger, F.	Copenhagen, Denmark	Infancy School age	Schizophrenic mother or father
Mednick, S. A., Schulsinger, F., and Venables, P.	Mauritius, Indian Ocean	Preschool	Specific psychophysiological patterns of the child
Miller, D.	San Francisco, Calif.	School age	Psychiatric disorder in parents

Criteria for Control Group Selection	Central Variables	Effort at Intervention	Central Reference*
Matched nonpsychiatric mother Manic-depressive mother Atypical endogenous psychosis—mother	Birth and obstetrical data Infant temperament Maternal attitudes toward pregnancy Mother-infant interaction Neurological assessment Psychophysiology	No	McNeil and Kaji (46)
Other psychiatric disorders in mother or father Normal control parents	Attentional (visual) tasks Biochemical measures catecholamine metabolism Infant temperament Mother-infant interaction Neurological-behavioral assessment Sleep studies	Yes (projected)	Marcus (48)

Matched control nonpsychiatric mother	Birth and obstetrical records
	Clinical assessments:
	  Personality
	  Significant life events
	  Positive aspects of personality functioning
	Psychophysiology
	School records
	Word-association tasks
		No	Mednick and Schulsinger (55)

Character disordered mother and father Normal control mother and father	Assessment and vigilance tasks Birth and obstetrical data Home ratings Neurological assessment Pediatric assessment Psychological assessment Psychophysiology School ratings Social competence measures	No	Mednick et al. (53)
"Normal" psychophysiological pattenrs	Operant conditioning Peer relationships Play behavior Psychophysiology Social competence Socialization pattenrs	Yes	Mednick and Schulsinger (56)
Felons (parents) Welfare recipients (parents) Normal controls (parents)	Clinical assessment Court records School functioning Social agency records Social competence	Yes	Miller (59)

TABLE 6-7 (Continued)

Investigator(s)	Locale	Age Range of Children	Criteria for Risk Group Selection
Rodnick, E. H., and Goldstein, M. J.	Los Angeles, Calif.	Adolescence Early childhood	Differential symptom patterns in disturbed adolescents: (a) aggressive, antisocial (b) active family conflict (c) passive-negative (d) withdrawn, socially isolated
Rolf, J. E., and colleagues	Burlington, Vt.	Preschool	Schizophrenic parent
Rosenthal, D., Nagler, S., Marcus, J., and colleagues	Israel	School age Adolescence	Schizophrenic mother or father (rearing in kibbutz or nuclear family)
Sameroff, A. J., Zax, M., and Babiqian, H.	Rochester, N.Y.	Infancy Preschool	Schizophrenic mother
Schachter, J.	Pittsburgh, Pa.	Infancy	Schizophrenic mother

Criteria for Control Group Selection	Central Variables	Effort at Intervention	Central Reference*
Acutely ill schizophrenic patients for contrast purposes	Clinical assessment Coping behavior Family process variables Psychophysiology Social communication patterns Therapeutic change measures	Yes	Goldstein et al. (27)
Economically deprived parents Unsocialized aggressive children	Epidemiological survey of early behavior disorders Intellectual competence Peer interaction Play behavior Psychological assessment Social competence	Yes	Rolf and Harig (71)
Nonschizophrenic mother or father (rearing in kibbutz or nuclear family)	Neurological assessment Psychological assessment Psychophysiology Sensory-integration tasks Social competence Word-association tests	No	Rosenthal (73)
Depressive mother Personality disordered mother Normal control mother	Attachment behavior Birth and obstetrical records Conditioning studies Developmental schedules Home observations Infant temperament Maternal attitudes Maternal anxiety Mother-child relationships Object conservation Psychophysiology Social development Stranger anxiety	No	Sameroff and Zax (80)
Other maternal psychiatric disorders Normal control mother	Bayley developmental tests Developmental data Physical growth studies Electrophysiology Home environment studies Maternal care Psychophysiology	No	Schachter (81)

TABLE 6-7 (Continued)

Investigator(s)	Locale	Age Range of Children	Criteria for Risk Group Selection
Weintraub, S., and Neale, J. M.	Stony Brook, N.Y.	School age	Schizophrenic mother or father
Wynne, L. C., Cromwell, R. L., and colleagues	Rochester, N.Y.	Preschool School age	Schizophrenic mother

Source: Reprinted with permission from N. Garmezy, "The Experimental Study of Children Vulnerable to Psychopathology," in *Child Personality and Psychopathology—Current Topics*, ed. A. Davids (New York: John Wiley, 1975), vol. 2, pp. 186-91.

Criteria for Control Group Selection	Central Variables	Effort at Intervention	Central Reference*
Depressive mother or father Normal control parents	Attentional tasks Information processing Psychiatric assessment (parents) Psychological assessment (parent and child) Referential communication School assessments Social competence Social interaction tasks	No	Neale and Weintraub (61)
Other functional psychiatric disorders in mother	Assessments: diagnostic and personality (parent and child) Conditioning and habituation Electrophysiology Family process interaction Genetic linkage studies Information processing Mother (father) child play interaction Piagetian tasks (role-taking; egocentrism) Potential genetic markers Biochemical Eye tracking Psychophysiology Referential communication (mother and child) School adaptation School competence Sensory-integration tasks	No	Cromwell and Wynne (4)

*A more complete set of references can be found in Garmezy and Streitman (23) and Garmezy (24). The single reference cited in this table typically provides an overview of the project.

measures has often not been established. Thus the replication of findings across samples is inhibited.

2. Follow-up through the age of risk is essential, but few investigators have such persevering spirits and stable funding to be able to do this. If long-term follow-up is not done, the schizophrenics in the sample will be biased toward early onset cases, while others with a schizophrenic future may be counted as controls.

3. In many studies there are small samples, which adversely affect or prevent statistical analysis of multiple variables.

With regard to the generalizability of the studies, arguments are set forth that:

1. Most schizophrenics do not have a schizophrenic parent, and precursors or predictors of schizophrenia found among the offspring of schizophrenics cannot be assumed to be applicable to schizophrenia at large.

2. The type and the severity of parental schizophrenia, as well as the presence of illness in the spouse and biological relatives, indicate differential risks for schizophrenia in the offspring. Thus, variance in the parental samples may limit the generalizability of findings even to the offspring of certain types of schizophrenics.

From the vantage point of the material covered in this review, some other evaluative comments can be made:

1. It is clear that the schizophrenic breakdowns will occur in many different forms, allowing for many different types of correlations and analyses. Hypotheses that fit with schizophrenia spectrum cases may not fit with schizophrenia, and among the schizophrenics the early onset cases may be quite different from those occurring later. While consensus schizophrenia may seem the best outcome measure, because it is diagnosed most reliably and is the illness that prompted this research, there will be many other subjects who are ill and must be taken into account.

2. If the high-risk studies are to identify environmental factors which contribute to schizophrenia, then genetic-biologic factors need to be controlled or systematically varied. In studies of monozygotic twins it can be assumed that differences are the result of environmental variation. However, not all high-risk children have inherited the predisposing genotype from their ill parent, and highly significant environmental differences between ill and well children may be etiologically meaningless or the result of genetic-environmental covariation. This problem is recognized by the high-risk investigators and may be overcome. One way which offers possibilities is the type of analysis used by Mednick et al. (39,58), which can simultaneously estimate the importance of many factors ("constructs") and the interaction between them. As mentioned above, even with this improved type of analysis, it is still difficult to incorporate a construct of the genetic predisposition when there is no known measurement of it. Therefore, the promise of high-risk studies may have to await the determination of some measurable genetic risk factors, so that the interaction of environment and other genetic influences with the specified genetic factor can be studied. To say that risk factors have to be identified *before* high-risk studies may seem to be "passing the buck," but in fact it is not unreasonable to assume that studies of patients, of specific pedigrees, and of populations selected for biochemical abnormalities will identify genetic variables which appear to increase the risk for schizophrenia. Using the high-risk method on schizophrenics and their offspring who have these abnormalities may avoid some of the problems listed above.

This area is one of innovation and development. Many other studies, each with its own modification of the method, could have been reviewed. What the next version of this chapter ten years from now will contain is certainly an open question and an exciting one.

BIBLIOGRAPHY

1. Anthony, E. J. 1972. A clinical and experimental study of high-risk children and their schizophrenic parents. In *Genetic factors in schizophrenia*, ed. A. R. Kaplan (Springfield, Ill.: Charles C Thomas), pp. 380–406.

2. Bleuler, M. 1974. The offspring of schizophrenics. *Schizophrenia Bulletin* 8:93–107.

3. Brown, G. W.; Birley, J. L. T.; and Wing, J. K. 1972. The influence of family life on the course of schizophrenic disorders: A replication. *British Journal of Psychiatry* 121:241–58.

4. Cromwell, R. L., and Wynne, L. C. 1974. The University of Rochester child and family study: Development of competence and vulnerability in families at high-risk for schizophrenia. Rochester, N.Y. Mimeographed.

5. Erlenmeyer-Kimling, L. 1968. Studies on the offspring of two schizophrenic parents. In *The transmission of schizophrenia*, eds. D. Rosenthal and S. S. Kety (New York: Pergamon Press), pp. 65–83.

6. Erlenmeyer-Kimling, L. 1975. A prospective study of children at risk for schizophrenia: Methodological considerations and some preliminary findings. In *Life history research in psychopathology*, eds. R. D. Wirt, G. Winokur, and M. Roff (Minneapolis: University of Minnesota Press), vol. 4.

7. Erlenmeyer-Kimling, L. 1976. Schizophrenia: A bag of dilemmas. *Social Biology* 23:123–34.

8. Erlenmeyer-Kimling, L. 1977. Issues pertaining to prevention and intervention of genetic disorders affecting human behavior. In *Primary prevention of psychopathology*, vol. I: *The issues*, eds. G. W. Albee and J. M. Joffee (Hanover, N.H.: University Press of New England).

9. Erlenmeyer-Kimling, L., and Cornblatt, B. 1978. Attentional measures in a study of children at high-risk for schizophrenia. *Journal of Psychiatric Research*, in press.

10. Fish, B. 1957. The detection of schizophrenia in infancy: A preliminary report. *Journal of Nervous and Mental Disease* 125:1–24.

11. Fish, B. 1959. Longitudinal observations of biological deviations in a schizophrenic infant. *American Journal of Psychiatry* 116:25–31.

12. Fish, B. 1963. The maturation of arousal and attention in the first months of life: A study of variation in ego development. *Journal of the American Academy of Child Psychiatry* 2:253–70.

13. Fish, B. 1971. Discussion: Genetic or traumatic developmental deviation? *Social Biology* 18: S117–S119.

14. Fish, B. 1975. Biologic antecedents of psychosis in children. In *The biology of the major psychoses: A comparative analysis*, ed. D. X. Freedman, Association for Research in Nervous and Mental Disease, publication no. 54 (New York: Raven Press), pp. 49–80.

15. Fish, B. 1976. An approach to prevention in infants at risk for schizophrenia: Developmental deviations from birth to 10 years. *Journal of the American Academy of Child Psychiatry* 15: 62–82.

16. Fish, B. 1977. Neurobiological antecedents of schizophrenia in children: Evidence for an inherited, congenital neurointegrative defect. *Archives of General Psychiatry* 34:1297–313.

17. Fish, B., and Alpert, M. 1962. Abnormal states of consciousness and muscle tone in infants born to schizophrenic mothers. *American Journal of Psychiatry* 119:439–45.

18. Fish, B., and Hagin, R. 1973. Visual-motor disorders in infants at risk for schizophrenia. *Archives of General Psychiatry* 28:900–4.

19. Fish, B.; Shapiro, T.; Halpern, F.; and Wile, R. 1965. The prediction of schizophrenia in infancy. III. A ten-year follow-up report of neurological and psychological development. *American Journal of Psychiatry* 121:768–75.

20. Fish, B.; Wile, R.; Shapiro, T.; and Halpern, F. 1966. The prediction of schizophrenia in infancy: II. A ten-year follow-up report of predictions made at one month of age. In *Psychopathology of schizophrenia*, eds. P. H. Hoch and J. Zubin (New York: Grune & Stratton), pp. 335–53.

21. Fowler, R. C., and Tsuang, M. T. 1975. Spouses of schizophrenics: A blind comparative study. *Comprehensive Psychiatry* 16:339–42.

22. Garmezy, N. 1973. Competence and adaptation in adult schizophrenic patients and children at risk. In *Schizophrenia: The first ten dean award lectures*, ed. S. R. Dean (New York: MSS Information Corporation), pp. 168–204.

23. Garmezy, N., and Streitmen, S. 1974. Children at risk: The search for the antecedents of schizophrenia. Part I. Conceptual models and research methods. *Schizophrenia Bulletin* 8:14–90.

24. Garmezy, N. 1974. Children at risk: The search for the antecedents of schizophrenia. Part 2: Ongoing research programs, issues, and intervention. *Schizophrenia Bulletin* 9:55–125.

25. Garmezy, N. 1975. The experimental study of children vulnerable to psychopathology. In *Child personality and psychopathology—Current topics*, ed. A. Davids (New York: John Wiley), vol. 2, pp. 171–216.

26. Garmezy, N. 1977. On some risks in risk research. *Psychological Medicine* 7:1–6.

27. Goldstein, M. J.; Judd, L. L.; Rodnick, E. H.; Alkire, A. A.; and Gould, E. 1968. A method for studying social influence and coping patterns within families of disturbed adolescents. *Journal of Nervous and Mental Disease* 147:233–51.

28. Goldstein, M. J.; Rodnick, E. H.; Jones, J. E.; McPherson, S. R.; and West, K. C. 1976. Familial Precursors of Schizophrenia Spectrum Disorders. Presented at the Second Rochester (N.Y.) International Conference on Schizophrenia, 1976.

29. Gottesman, I. I., and Shields, J. 1972. *Schizophrenia and genetics: A twin study vantage point* (New York: Academic Press).

30. Grunebaum, H.; Weiss, J. L.; Gallant, D.; and Cohler, B. J. 1974. Attention in young children of psychotic mothers. *American Journal of Psychiatry* 131:887–91.

31. Gunderson, J. G., and Kolb, J. 1978. Discriminating features of borderline patients. *American Journal of Psychiatry* 135(7):792–96.

32. Haier, R.; Rosenthal, D.; and Wender, P. H. 1978. MMPI assessment of psychopathology in the adopted-away offspring of schizophrenics. *Archives of General Psychiatry* 35:171–75.

33. Hanson, D. R.; Gottesman, I. I.; and Heston, L. C. 1976. Some possible childhood indicators of adult schizophrenia inferred from children of schizophrenics. *British Journal of Psychiatry* 129:142–54.

34. Hanson, D. R.; Gottesman, I. I.; and Meehl, P. E. 1977. Genetic theories and the validation of psychiatric diagnoses: Implications for the study of children of schizophrenics. *Journal of Abnormal Psychology* 86:575–88.

35. Heston, L. L. 1966. Psychiatric disorders in foster home reared children of schizophrenic mothers. *British Journal of Psychiatry* 112:819–25.

36. Heston, L. L. 1971. Discussion: Schizophrenia in infancy? *Social Biology* 18:S114–S116.

37. Hoffmann, H. 1921. Die Nachkommenschaft bei Endogenen Psychosen. *Monograph aus Gesamtgebiete der Neurologie und Psychiatrie* (Berlin: Julius Springer), vol. 26.

38. Jones, J. E.; Rodnick, E. H.; Goldstein, M. J.; McPherson, S. R.; and West, K. L. 1977. Parental transactional style deviance as a possible indicator of risk for schizophrenia. *Archives of General Psychiatry* 34:71–74.

39. Jöreskog, K. G., and Van Thello, M. 1972. LISREL—A general computer program for estimating a linear standard equation system involving multiple indicators of unmeasured variables. Princeton, N.J.: Educational Testing Service. *Research Bulletin* 72–56.

40. Kallmann, F. J. 1938. *The genetics of schizophrenia* (New York: J. J. Augustin).

41. Kety, S. S.; Matthysse, S.; and Kidd, K. K. 1978. Genetic counseling for schizophrenic patients and their families. In *Controversy in psychiatry*, ed. H. K. H. Brodie (New York: W. B. Saunders).

42. Kety, S. S.; Rosenthal, D.; Wender, P. H.; and Schulsinger, F. 1968. The types and prevalence of mental illness in the biological and adoptive families of adopted schizophrenics. In *The transmission of schizophrenia*, eds. D. Rosenthal and S. S. Kety (Oxford: Pergamon Press), pp. 345–62.

43. Kety, S. S.; Rosenthal, D.; Wender, P. H.; Schulsinger, F.; and Jacobsen, B. 1975. Mental illness in the biological and adoptive families of adopted individuals who have become schizophrenic: A preliminary report based upon psychiatric interviews. In *Genetic research in psychiatry*, eds. R. Fieve, D. Rosenthal, and H. Brill (Baltimore: Johns Hopkins University Press), pp. 147–65.

44. Kirkegaard-Sorensen, L., and Mednick, S. A. 1975. Registered criminality in families with children at high-risk for schizophrenia. *Journal of Abnormal Psychology* 84:197–204.

45. Kohn, M. L. 1973. Social class and schizophrenia: A critical review and a reformulation. *Schizophrenia Bulletin* 7:60–79.

46. McNeil, T. F., and Kaij, L. 1973. Obstetric complications and physical size of offspring of schizophrenic, schizophrenic-like, and control mothers. *British Journal of Psychiatry* 123:341–48.

47. McNeil, T. F., and Kaij, L. 1976. Obstetric factors in the development of schizophrenia. Presented at the Second Rochester (N.Y.) International Conference on Schizophrenia, 1976.

48. Marcus, J. 1974. Cerebral functioning in offspring of schizophrenics: A possible genetic factor. *International Journal of Mental Health* 3:57–73.

49. Mednick, S. A. 1958. A learning theory approach to research in schizophrenia. *Psychological Bulletin* 55:315–27.

50. Mednick, S. A. 1970. Breakdown in individuals at high risk for schizophrenia: Possible predispositional perinatal factors. *Mental Hygiene* 54:50–63.

51. Mednick, S. A. 1976. Berkson's fallacy and high-risk research. Presented at the Second Rochester (N.Y.) International Conference on Schizophrenia, 1976.

52. Mednick, S. A., and McNeil, T. F. 1968. Current methodology in research on the etiology of schizophrenia: Serious difficulties which suggest the use of the high-risk-group method. *Psychological Bulletin* 70:681–93.

53. Mednick, S. A.; Mura, M.; Schulsinger, F.; and Mednick, B. 1971. Perinatal conditions and infant development in children with schizophrenic parents. *Social Biology* 18:S103–S113.

54. Mednick, S. A.; Mura, E.; Schulsinger, F.; and Mednick, B. 1973. Erratum and further analysis: Perinatal conditions and infant development in children with schizophrenic parents. *Social Biology* 20:111–12.

55. Mednick, S. A., and Schulsinger, F. 1968. Some premorbid characteristics related to breakdown in children with schizophrenic mothers. In *The transmission of schizophrenia*, eds. D. Rosenthal, and S. S. Kety (Oxford: Pergamon Press), pp. 267–91.

56. Mednick, S. A., and Schulsinger, F. 1973. Studies of children at high risk for schizophrenia. In *Schizophrenia: The first ten dean award lectures*, ed. S. R. Dean (New York: MSS Information Corporation), pp. 247–93.

57. Mednick, S. A.; Schulsinger, H.; and Schulsinger, F. 1975. Schizophrenia in children of schizophrenic mothers. In *Child personality and psychopathology—current topics*, ed. A. Davids (New York: John Wiley), vol. 2, pp. 217–53.

58. Mednick, S. A.; Schulsinger, F.; Teasdale, T. W.; Schulsinger, H.; Venables, P.; and Rock, D. 1978. Schizophrenia in high-risk children: Sex differences in predisposing factors. In *Cognitive defects in the development of mental illness*, ed. G. Serban (New York: Brunner/Mazel).

59. Miller, D. 1966. Alternatives to mental patient rehospitalization. *Community Mental Health Journal* 2:124–28.

60. Mizrahi-Mirdal, G. K.; Mednick, S. A.; Schulsinger, F.; and Fuchs, F. 1974. Perinatal complications in children of schizophrenic mothers. *Acta Psychiatrica Scandanavica* 50:553–68.

61. Neale, J. M., and Weintraub, S. 1972. Selecting variables for high-risk research. Position paper. Conference on Risk Research, Dorado Beach, Puerto Rico, October 1972.

62. Oppler, W. 1932. Zum Problem der Erbprognosebestimmung über die Erkrankungsaussichten der direkten nachkommen von Schizophrenen in Schlesien. *Zeitschrift für die gesamte Neurologie und Psychiatrie* 141:549–616.

63. Paffenbarger, R. S.; Steinmetz, C. H.; Pooler, B. G.; et al. 1961. The picture puzzle of the postpartum psychoses. *Journal of Chronic Disease* 13:161–69.

64. Reisby, N. 1967. Psychoses in children of schizophrenic mothers. *Acta Psychiatrica Scandinavica* 43:8–20.

65. Ricks, D. F., and Berry, J. C. 1970. Family and symptom patterns that precede schizophrenia. In *Life history in psychopathology*, eds. M. Roff, and D. F. Ricks (Minneapolis: University of Minnesota Press), pp. 31–50.

66. Rieder, R. O. 1973. The offspring of schizophrenic parents: A review. *Journal of Nervous and Mental Disease* 157:179–90.

67. Rieder, R. O.; Broman, S. H.; and Rosenthal, D. 1977. The offspring of schizophrenics. II: Perinatal factors and IQ. *Archives of General Psychiatry* 34:789–99.

68. Rieder, R. O., and Nichols, P. Offspring of schizophrenics. III: Behavioral disorders and neurological soft signs. *Archives of General Psychiatry*. In press.

69. Rieder, R. O.; Rosenthal, D.; Wender, P.; and Blumenthal, H. 1975. The offspring of schizophrenics: Fetal and neonatal deaths. *Archives of General Psychiatry* 32:200–211.

70. Robins, L. N. 1966. *Deviant children grown up* (Baltimore: Williams & Wilkins).

71. Rolf, J. E., and Harig, P. T. 1974. Etiological research in schizophrenia and the rationale for primary prevention. *American Journal of Ortho-psychiatry* 44:538–54.

72. Rosenthal, D. 1970. *Genetic theory and abnormal behavior* (New York: McGraw-Hill).

73. Rosenthal, D. 1971. A program of research on heredity in schizophrenia. *Behavioral Science* 16:191–201.

74. Rosenthal, D. 1974. Issues in high risk studies of schizophrenia. In *Life history research in psychopathology*, eds. D. F. Ricks, A. Thomas, and M. Roff (Minneapolis: University of Minnesota Press), vol. 3, pp. 25–41.

75. Rosenthal, D. 1975. Discussion: Subschizophrenic disorders. In *Genetic research in psychiatry*, eds. R. R. Fieve, D. Rosenthal, and A. Brill (Baltimore: Johns Hopkins University Press), pp. 199–208.

76. Rosenthal, D.; Wender, P. H.; Kety, S. S.; Schulsinger, F.; Welner, J.; and Ostergaard, L. 1968. Schizophrenics' offspring reared in adoptive homes. In *The transmission of schizophrenia*, eds. D. Rosenthal and S. S. Kety (Oxford: Pergamon Press), pp. 377–91.

77. Rosenthal, D.; Wender, P. H.; Kety, S. S.; Welner, J.; and Schulsinger, F. 1971. The adopted away offspring of schizophrenics. *American Journal of Psychiatry* 128:307–11.

78. Rosenthal, D.; Wender, P. H.; Kety, S. S.; Schulsinger, F.; Welner, J.; and Rieder, R. O. 1975. Parent-child relationships and psychopathological disorder in the child. *Archives of General Psychiatry* 32:466–76.

79. Rutschmann, J.; Cornblatt, B.; and Erlenmeyer-Kimling, L. 1977. Sustained attention in children at risk for schizophrenia. *Archives of General Psychiatry* 34:571–75.

80. Sameroff, A. J., and Zax, M. 1973. Perinatal characteristics of the offspring of schizophrenic women. *Journal of Nervous and Mental Disease* 157:191–99.

81. Schachter, J. 1974. The vulnerable child in infancy. Paper presented at the meetings of the International Association for Child Psychiatry and Allied Professions, Philadelphia, July 1974.

82. Schachter, J.; Kerr, J.; Lachin, J. M.; and Faer, M. 1975. Newborn offspring of a schizophrenic parent: Cardiac reactivity to auditory stimuli. *Psychophysiology* 12:483–92.

83. Schulsinger, H. 1976. A ten-year follow-up of children of schizophrenic mothers: Clinical assessment. *Acta Psychiatrica Scandanavica* 53:371–86.

84. Shields, J. 1977. High risk for schizophrenia: Genetic considerations. *Psychological Medicine* 7:7–10.

85. Sobel, D. E. 1961. Children of schizophrenic patients: Preliminary observations on early development. *American Journal of Psychiatry* 118:512–17.

86. Sobel, D. E. 1961. Infant mortality and malformations in children of schizophrenic women. *Psychiatric Quarterly* 35:60–65.

87. Spitzer, R. L.; Endicott, J.; and Gibbon, M. Crossing the border into borderline personality and borderline schizophrenia: The development of criteria. *Archives of General Psychiatry*, in press.

88. Vaughn, C. E., and Leff, J. P. 1976. The influence of family and social factors on the course of psychiatric illness: A comparison of schizophrenic and depressed neurotic patients. *British Journal of Psychiatry* 129:125–37.

89. Watt, N. F. 1978. Patterns of childhood social development in adult schizophrenics. *Archives of General Psychiatry* 35:160–70.

90. Wender, P. H.; Rosenthal, D.; and Kety, S. S. 1968. A psychiatric assessment of the adoptive parents of schizophrenics. In *The transmission of schizophrenia*, eds. D. Rosenthal and S. S. Kety (Oxford: Pergamon Press), pp. 235–50.

91. Wender, P. H.; Rosenthal, D.; Kety, S. S.; Schulsinger, F.; and Welner, J. 1974. Crossfostering: A research strategy for clarifying the role of genetic and experiential factors in the etiology of schizophrenia. *Archives of General Psychiatry* 30:121–28.

92. Wynne, L. C.; Singer, M. J.; and Bartko, J. J. 1975. Schizophrenics and their families: Recent research on parental communication. In *Psychiatric research: The widening perspective*, ed. J. M. Tanner (New York: International Universities Press).

93. Zax, M.; Sameroff, A. J.; and Babigian, H. M. 1977. Birth outcomes of mentally disordered women. *American Journal of Orthopsychiatry* 47:218–30.

Chapter 7

FAMILY STUDIES

Lyman C. Wynne, M.D., Ph.D., Margaret L. Toohey, M.A.,
and Jeri Doane, Ph.D.

The year 1968 is the starting point for this critique of studies of families with a schizophrenic member. From the perspective of a decade later, that year appears to have been a turning point, a time of assessment and recognition of the accomplishments and the limitations of earlier approaches and of moving on to new orientations, strategies, and methods. In this chapter we shall first comment on several influential reviews of family studies and then identify trends of the past decade, possible reasons for their emergence, and their current status.

The term "family studies" will be restricted to clinical and experimental research on family relationships when a family member is, has been, or is at risk for becoming schizophrenic in adolescence or young adulthood. The families of childhood psychotics will not be discussed, because they would involve consideration of different kinds of diagnostic, conceptual, and methodological issues. Clearly the family is highly relevant to many aspects of the schizophrenic disorders that are discussed in this volume under other headings, notably genetics, epidemiological and sociocultural factors, psychodynamic studies, psychosocial treatment, and prevention; those approaches to understanding the families of schizophrenics are explicitly outside the scope of this chapter. Furthermore, we shall refer the reader elsewhere for studies of families in which schizophrenia is not a major issue; thus, we shall not emphasize research on "disturbed" and psychiatrically "abnormal" families when schizophrenia in a family member has not been explicitly diagnosed.

A Review of Reviews

MISHLER AND WAXLER (50)

During the mid-1950s clinical and conceptual studies of schizo-phrenics began to emphasize the whole family as a unit. Gradually more systematic research was undertaken on family patterns of inter-action and communication concurrent with active illness in a family member. A significant retrospective review of this work was published in 1968 by Mishler and Waxler. Their book, *Family Processes and Schizophrenia*, reprinted a 1965 review of the early clinically based theories. Three groups of theories were given special attention in this critique: namely, those of the "Bateson group" in Palo Alto, a group often identified with the double-bind concept; the "Lidz group" at New Haven, which was viewed as extending and applying psychoanalytic concepts to the family triad; and the "Wynne group" at the National Institute of Mental Health, which was viewed as drawing upon social-psychological and developmental concepts and linking schizophrenic thought disorder and family interaction patterns. The book reprinted commentaries by Bateson, Lidz, Wynne, and Spiegel, as well as illustra-tive studies that used experimental methods of dyadic interaction of the parents of schizophrenics, triads of parents with a schizophrenic off-spring, and tetrads of parents with a schizophrenic offspring and a "well" offspring.

The Mishler-Waxler critique wrapped up a phase of preliminary broad theory building and pointed toward a need for more specific and sys-tematic hypothesis testing, but it did not yet chart what the new directions might be.

RISKIN AND FAUNCE (71)

The major issues, methods, and dimensions of quantifiable family interaction research were definitively reviewed by Riskin and Faunce. Their evaluation of 286 studies dissected the complex issues and pitfalls in designing and carrying out family interaction studies. They pointed out that sensible interpretations of the findings from such studies are possible only after painstaking scrutiny of the methods and measures used and of the samples selected. All too often investigators have used terms such as "dominance," "conflict," "acknowledgment," and "inter-ruptions" with vague, inconsistent, or unspecified meaning in relation to their actual methods and to hypotheses and theory. Unwary readers (including investigators and reviewers of the literature) frequently have taken the original author's terminology at face value. As a result they often have concluded erroneously that various studies have confirmed or disconfirmed one another, when in fact they usually have been simply irrelevant both to one another and to any current viable theory. It has been fashionable for reviewers to deplore a lack of methodological rigor in family studies, but by failing to examine the underlying logic and meaning of the data from different studies, they often have misjudged both the strengths and the weaknesses of this field.

The Riskin-Faunce critique has provided the most noteworthy corrective to these difficulties in assessing family-interaction research. At the same time that they set forth sobering guidelines for careful, pragmatic research design and conceptualization, they also underlined the point that schizophrenic researchers by and large have failed to utilize and apply the interdisciplinary methodological knowledge that has been gained in interaction studies with families in which schizophrenia is *not* the focal concern. Although some of the early methods in the family-interaction field were devised in order to study the families of schizophrenics, by 1972 this field had moved far beyond schizophrenia. Riskin and Faunce appended a useful glossary of terms as used by different investigators; much misleading debate could have been—and still could be—avoided by reference to their definitions.

HIRSCH AND LEFF (29)

In a 109-page review of the literature on the "role of parents in the aetiology of schizophrenia," Hirsch and Leff included many aspects of parental "abnormalities" that are not relevant to the issues considered in this chapter on family relationships, communication, and interaction. They classified studies into five groups:

1. *Clinical studies relying on case study review.* After briefly surveying the early retrospective clinical family studies that had been assessed by Mishler and Waxler (50), Hirsch and Leff included in this group a conceptually heterogeneous set of nonretrospective clinical reports using follow-back, follow-up, twin and adoption methods in which family relationships and the family as a social unit were not studied.
2. *Questionnaire family studies.* These attitudinal and child-rearing reports, nearly all published before 1968, have contributed little to understanding the families of schizophrenics. As Hirsch and Leff pointed out, they were fragmentary and "heterogeneous," and were not followed by efforts to replicate or to "reach agreement on the definition of the concepts being studied."
3. *"Small group interaction studies."* Readers interested in these methods for studying families will find that the Riskin-Faunce review of 1972 (71) is more up-to-date, comprehensive, and systematic, partly because Riskin and Faunce extensively and personally interviewed the researchers in order to clarify the concepts and methods used.
4. *"Psychological tests of abnormal thought processes."* Here Hirsch and Leff dealt not with family relationships as such, but with presumed genetic similarities in "allusive thinking," chiefly measured, rather unsatisfactorily, with the Object Sorting Test.
5. *"Abnormalities of communication and language."* This section was a review of a mid-sixties segment of the work on communication deviance by Wynne and Singer and a portion of the empirical work on double-bind theory; Hirsch and Leff's review essentially ends with reports of 1969. More recently, as we shall discuss later, the communication deviance research has been greatly extended by Goldstein, Rodnick, J. Jones, Hassan, Wild, Singer, and Wynne. Conceptually Hirsch and Leff were concerned with linear causes and effects that hypothetically stem from "abnormalities" of individual parents; they did not review the literature from the orientation of family systems theory or developmental psycho-

pathology in which concepts of circular or, more accurately, spiral causality are used to examine reciprocal relationships and transactional processes within families.

JACOB (31)

Jacob surveyed direct observation studies (through 1973) and compared family interaction in families of schizophrenics, psychiatrically disturbed nonschizophrenics, and nonpatients ("normals"). Thirty of these studies involved families of schizophrenics (ten reported in 1968 or later). Jacob usefully tabulated the methodological characteristics of the studies. He went on to subsume the studies under the "domains" of "dominance, conflict, affect, and communication clarity." He concluded that "one must notice the considerable variability and inconsistency among the results reflected by different investigators," particularly in the domains of conflict, dominance, and affect. His view of "communication clarity and accuracy" was more positive. He noted that the available data "suggest that schizophrenic families communicate with less clarity and accuracy than do normal families."

In our view Jacob stepped into some of the conceptual traps that had been identified by Riskin and Faunce, especially by accepting at face value the definitions of constructs by different investigators and lumping them together in his four domains. For example, when one author had defined high "conflict" by frequency of interruptions and simultaneous speeches, a "process" measure in which content is disregarded, and another author had defined "conflict" by rate of disagreements judged by content, Jacob failed to re-examine whether these two measures should have been regarded as equivalent. Actually interruptions and simultaneous speech have been found to characterize lively "normal communication" (47); surely such measures of family "process" should not be regarded as an unambiguous index of "conflict," though classified as such by Jacob in his review. Our assessment is that *both* negative and positive conclusions in this literature need more detailed scrutiny, with reformulation of the constructs reported in the original studies; each measure needs to be carefully examined to see whether it is a reasonable indicator of a given construct.

DOANE (9)

Doane recently attempted such a critique of the family-interaction research literature, including most of the studies covered by Jacob. From a systems-oriented perspective she reformulated dimensions along which psychiatrically disturbed and nondisturbed ("normal") families differ. When the empirical methods of measurement were re-examined in relation to underlying constructs (often disregarding the labels used by various authors), then several areas of consistency in the literature were found that led to conclusions differing from those of Jacob. These included: family coalition patterns, patterns of conflict, flexibility versus rigidity, problem-solving effectiveness and efficiency, and deviant styles of communication.

Although measures of several such constructs, especially communication deviance, reliably discriminate "normal" families from families with a psychiatrically disturbed member, how much the findings are specific for schizophrenia is blurred by the pervasive unclarity of diagnostic criteria. As noted elsewhere in this volume, only in recent years has the diagnostic issue begun to be examined systematically. To be sure, this problem of inconsistent and unsystematic diagnoses of research subjects, which complicates the interpretation of the relevance of family studies to schizophrenia, is not very different from that found, for example, in biochemical studies.

In addition, Doane noted that a variety of other variables limit the comparability and generalizability of family studies (e.g., age, sex, and premorbid functioning of the identified patient, developmental stage of the family, and socioeconomic status). The problems of interpreting the family-interaction literature have been discussed in a response to Doane's review by Jacob and Grounds (31) and in a reply by Doane (10).

GOLDSTEIN AND RODNICK (23)

As of 1978 the most up-to-date review that has focused explicitly on assessing "the family's contribution to the etiology of schizophrenia" was by Goldstein and Rodnick. With the aid of access to doctoral dissertations, especially from their own program, they assessed the status of studies of family communication concurrent with, and prior to, the onset of schizophrenic illness diagnosed in an offspring. They concluded that the evidence, on balance, shows "robust trends" supporting the first of three assumptions: that "families of schizophrenics are discriminably different from those containing other offspring with other types of disturbances." They emphasized the evidence that "strongly supported" this assumption from the series of studies carried out by Wynne and Singer on attentional-communicational deviance in families of schizophrenics and in comparison groups.

Goldstein and Rodnick went on to describe the preliminary evidence for a second assumption: that "these differences occur early enough in the life experience of the potential schizophrenic to have a significant impact on his development." Despite earlier speculations on this issue, only now is evidence emerging through predictive, prospective research using the "high-risk" model (see chapter 6). Such research has included three classes of risk variables: (1) child or adolescent attributes identified before the onset of schizophrenic symptoms; (2) parental schizophrenia, placing the offspring at presumed genetic risk; and (3) family attributes, such as communicational styles and interaction patterns, risk variables that can be identified in the absence of parental schizophrenia and prior to the onset of psychosis in an offspring. Goldstein and Rodnick reported that a sample of psychiatrically troubled but nonschizophrenic adolescents with parents showing high communication deviance, used as a family risk variable, had been followed up for five years; schizophrenia and schizophrenia-spectrum disorders were beginning to emerge in this sample despite the lack of evidence of genetic risk in these families.

A third assumption would constitute an etiological statement: that "disordered family relationships are a necessary but not sufficient condition for the development of schizophrenia." As noted by Goldstein and Rodnick, writers of the 1970s seem in agreement that longer-term follow-up in the high-risk programs will be required in order to assess this third hypothesis.

LEFF (36)

Julian Leff has provided an overview of a series of English studies of family influences on the course of schizophrenic illness. Turning away from the possible precursor contributions of the family in schizophrenic disorders, Brown and his colleagues (6,7) and more recently Vaughn and Leff (100,101) have studied the influence of family members on the course of schizophrenia, specifically the relapse rate nine months after a key admission. In summary, these studies indicate that ratings made from interviews with parents or spouse of a schizophrenic show a high number of critical comments (rated on content and tone of voice), hostile rejection of the patient as a person, and emotional over-involvement or "unusually marked concern about the patient." These three measures have been called "expressed emotion" (EE). Low family EE was followed by a low relapse rate whether or not the patient was on drugs. If EE was high in a relative with whom the patient returned to live, then a few hours of face-to-face contact reduced the relapse rate. When face-to-face contact was over thirty-five hours per week with a high EE relative, the relapse rate was highest and major tranquilizers seemed to be necessary to reduce the relapse rate.

Trends of 1968–78

The diversity of the preceding literature reviews should convey that family studies related to schizophrenia have not been neatly packaged. Several developments during the past decade have made this field full of rich promise for the future but have produced a shift in the kind of research that has been reported.

EMERGENCE OF FAMILY THERAPY

During the past decade, family therapy, as an orientation to the family unit and as a set of techniques in which family members meet conjointly, has emerged as a treatment approach of importance in its own right. Earlier, conjoint therapy with families of schizophrenics had been a prime source of research data and hypotheses. However, such therapy 'has been increasingly fused with other psychosocial therapies and with pharmacotherapy (see chapter 12). Also, family therapy generally, including therapy with families of schizophrenics, has become much more problem-oriented and crisis-oriented, often with an emphasis on education of families and building of social skills of ambulatory (aftercare) patients in the family setting. This action-oriented ambience has been beneficial for therapeutic appropriateness and effectiveness but has gradually turned family therapy into a less rich source for research hypotheses and concepts about interaction in the families of schizophrenics.

An effort to bring together the divergent viewpoints of family researchers and family therapists was made in a 1967 conference, with the published report appearing in 1972 (16). The proceedings revealed marked differences between the experiential orientation of the therapists and the measurement interests of the systematic researchers. Subsequently there have been few serious efforts to bring these two approaches together. Part of the difficulty lies in expectable differences in the personalities of the leading figures in the therapy and research fields, with only a few people attempting work in both spheres. A second source of difficulty has been the lack of interest, or disdain, on the part of family therapists in individually based diagnostic issues, so that topics such as schizophrenia have been less studied by family therapists who are more concerned with disturbances of relationships within the family system. Third, family-interaction researchers have reorganized and reformulated their work during the past decade, so that they are less dependent upon therapeutic assessments. Longitudinal, multivariate studies are now integrating family-interaction variables into a broader framework that includes measures of individual symptoms and competence, as well as attentional, cognitive, psychophysiological, and genetic variables (123). Most such research uses the "high-risk" research strategy in longitudinal studies (see chapter 6) (18,19,20).

Early intervention and prevention with families was discussed in a World Health Organization conference (1975) and has been introduced as a component of several of the longitudinal research programs (4,25,34,48). Because ethical and "informed consent" issues require consideration of when and how early treatment should be offered to subjects at high risk, and because a therapeutic relationship provides opportunities for intensive study of family relationships, future longitudinal family studies no doubt will combine preventive efforts and prospective research. The complications of this combination for the design of research on outcome will require constant attention but do not appear insurmountable.

Although clinical studies of families have not been a prolific source of ideas during the past decade, compared with the previous one, a number of generative contributions continued to appear. Building upon many years of earlier clinical research, Lidz (37,38,39,40) has synthesized his formulations into a theory "that the serious disturbances of family settings derived from the profound egocentricity of one or both parents; that the disturbances of language and thought that form the critical attribute of schizophrenic disorders are largely types of egocentric cognitive regressions to developmental stages described by Piaget and Vygotsky; and that the parents' disturbed styles of communication, which are manifestations of their egocentricities, are essential precursors of the patient's cognitive regression that occurs when he cannot surmount the essential developmental tasks of adolescence" (38,39).

As part of a series of formulations, Stierlin* has described schizophrenia as a "derailed delegating process" in which "a vulnerable individual, as a delegate of his parents or forebears, may become overburdened, possibly to the breaking point and, therefore, fail in age-appropriate individuation-separation and, eventually, in his socialization."

Wynne (118,119,120,122) has emphasized from several conceptual standpoints that the predisposition or vulnerability to schizophrenic psychopathology also carries with it the potentiality for alternative, nonsymptomatic, sometimes positive, developmental outcomes. This point of view provides a basis for conceptual integration of findings from both genetics and family dynamics. (Also see references 88 and 124.)

Scott and Ashworth (81) have described families in which there is a history of mental illness in a close relative that can be interpreted alternatively from the standpoint of genetics and/or family-communication processes. Scott presents clinical evidence from twenty-three families suggesting that those particular family members who become ill bear a "shadow of an ancestor": a parent has perceived the patient, but not other offspring, "in terms of his experience with the mad relative." The parent sometimes "literally saw the patient as the 'same as' the relative and destined for the same fate. The evidence was against the image of the ill relative being merely an activation product of the patient's illness." This image, or expectation, appeared to have influenced the parent's attitude toward the potential patient in the pre-illness period, though it was often concealed as a secret fear and was not reported in standard psychiatric histories.

In the decade after 1956 much attention was given to the double-bind hypothesis in relation to schizophrenia. More recently, Sluzki and Ransom (90) have assembled a thoughtful collection of papers reassessing this notion. Difficulties in research testing of the double-bind hypothesis were discussed, as well as the evidence that the concept is relevant in families other than those with a schizophrenic member. Current emphasis is upon a broader communicational theory in which the double-bind hypothesis is embedded. The concept of paradox rather than the double bind is more central in recent theories of this tradition.

The preceding references illustrate some of the trends in the clinical literature on family relationships during the past decade. Other examples include papers by Ackerman (1), Alanen (2), Conran (8), Fleck (15), Laing (35), Meissner (49), Mosher (56), Mueller and Orfanidis (58), Parker (60), Rubinstein (74), Sander (76), Schatzman (77,78), and Slipp (89).

---

* See references 93, 94, 95, 96, 97, and 98.

DEVELOPMENTS IN RESEARCH METHODS FOR SAMPLING FAMILY PATTERNS

The reviews that were outlined earlier describe much of the new methodology in systematic family research during the past decade. As we have indicated, both problems of research design and of linking measures to constructs continue to plague this work. Additionally, research methods for studying family interaction are no longer focused on the families of schizophrenics as a primary special problem group. In addition to the literature cited in the reviews, a number of more recent methodological studies are noteworthy. Illustrative is the work on sampling issues by Wild, Shapiro, and Abelin (109); they specifically show how family-oriented selection criteria attenuate research samples to a dismaying degree.

Usually starting with the concept of the family as a social unit or small social system, two main alternative strategies for sampling data about family relationships at a given time have been used during the past decade. First, some studies have called for the examination of communicational patterns of key relatives (parents or spouse) of schizophrenics. This strategy is based on the hypothesis that enduring patterns of communication and relationships sampled in tests or interviews with key relatives can be *inferred* or will be significant indicators of the relatives' behavior when they are with the identified patient or the subject at risk. This work has emphasized two constructs: "communication deviance," thus far studied as a possible parental precursor of schizophrenia in an offspring; and "expressed emotion," studied as a parent or spouse predictor of later relapse of schizophrenia.

Second, members of the entire family, or at least the triad of the parents and the identified patient offspring, have been studied in *direct* interaction and communication with one another (see references 115, 116, and 124 for a more extended discussion of this distinction). This approach overlaps conceptually with the studies of individual communication deviance but samples a broader range of communication patterns—including repeated sequences, coalitions, efficiency in reaching closure, positive and negative expressions of affect, etc.,—in which the impact of family members on one another is not inferred but is observed directly.

STUDIES OF COMMUNICATION PATTERNS OF KEY RELATIVES OF SCHIZOPHRENICS

Communication Deviance Studies Wynne, Singer, Bartko, and Toohey (124) recently confirmed earlier work on individual "communication deviance" (CD). (A synonym for "communication deviance" is the term "transactional style deviance" [33].) The concepts underlying this work (85,88,116) particularly made use of the formulation that how persons learn to share foci of attention and derive meaning from external stimuli is related to basic, repeated components of parent-child exchanges during the formative years. As growth and development proceed, this learning experience could, it was hypothesized, contribute to disturbed thinking and communication of children who were trying to relate to parents with highly deviant styles or patterns of communication. Singer, Wynne, and Toohey (88) found that thirty-two categories of these communication deviances, identified as especially frequent in individual Rorschach records of the parents of schizophrenics, significantly differentiated them from the parents of neurotic patients and normal subjects. However, an important point is that the parents of "borderline" subjects overlap with both the more disturbed and the less disturbed groups. Thus, this measure is not *specific* for the parents of typical schizophrenics; that is, it is not exclusively limited to these parents.

Although the communication of members of these families was sampled individually in their Rorschach protocols, the data were analyzed and compared from a family-wide standpoint: not only the individual parents but also the parental pairs, the index offspring, and their siblings were compared across groups (identified by diagnosis of the index offspring). These comparisons revealed a continuum in CD frequencies for persons in all family roles, whether or not they were symptomatically schizophrenic.

Interestingly, the CD scores of the index offspring (who were frankly psychotic) were *lower* than for their nonschizophrenic parents. If one hypothesizes that communication deviances in one family member may engender similar deviances in other family members, this finding suggests that the primary direction of effects would be from the parents to the offspring, not the reverse. This finding is in contrast to the common assumption that disturbed communication of schizophrenics may induce deviance in parental communication. At any rate, the findings do underline an important point, that the communication-deviance measure is not the same as measures of clinical psychopathology. This finding was confirmed in a multivariate analysis of communication deviance carried out by Wynne et al. (124), who showed that ratings of parental psychopathology can be statistically distinguished from the frequency of parental CD; parental psychopathology and parental CD *both* "predict" severity of offspring psychopathology, when *either* of these parental variables is held constant.

Hirsch and Leff (28,29) carried out a study which attempted to replicate the Wynne et al. study, but the former differed in important respects. First, while the Wynne et al. study involved 114 families and offspring in five diagnostic groups, ranging from normal to neurotic, to borderline, to remitting schizophrenics, and to nonremitting schizophrenics, the Hirsch-Leff study involved only two groups of 20 families in which the offspring was neurotic and 20 families in which the offspring was an acute schizophrenic. The Wynne et al. data were reported after five or more years of clinical follow-up in order to confirm the diagnosis, whereas the Hirsch-Leff sample of schizophrenics were assessed diagnostically only at the time of first admission and without follow-up. These patients clearly were less chronically and severely disturbed than the hebephrenic and paranoid "process," nonremitting varieties of schizophrenics included in the Wynne et al. sample. Also, the Hirsch-Leff sample of neurotics consisted mostly of depressives who, as Holzman (30) suggested, probably would have been diagnosed as "borderline" in the United States—given their degree of disturbance with depressive symptoms leading to hospitalization in early adulthood.

These diagnostic issues were discussed by Rutter (75) and Wynne (121).

Despite the ambiguity about sample comparability, the results of the Hirsch-Leff study showed significant differences at the p < .05 level for the Initial Viewing portion of the parental Rorschachs. However, there was some overlap in the communication-deviance scores of the two groups of parents, reminiscent of the overlap found in the borderline group in the Wynne et al. series. For the Inquiry portion of the Rorschach, the methods of test administration by Hirsch and Leff were markedly different and produced drastically different CD scores from the first half compared with the second half of their sample (29). Both halves differed from the procedure used by Wynne et al., so that the Inquiry portion of the data cannot be compared in the two studies (121). Problems in the method of statistical analysis used by Hirsch and Leff have been raised by Woodward and Goldstein (113).

In an initial interpretation of their data Hirsch and Leff (28) speculated that sheer word count of the parents of schizophrenics may account for differences in frequency of communication deviances. However, as they acknowledged later (29), word count could not account for the findings in the Wynne et al. data. With word count statistically controlled, the frequency of CD in the parents of the schizophrenics continued to differentiate very strongly such parents from the other groups of parents (124). These findings on the nonsignificance of word count also have been supported by findings from another sample of parents in fifty-nine families scored by Singer but independently tested in Houston.

For some years Wynne and Singer had conceptualized CD as a broad group of patterns which should in principle be discernible in diverse kinds of communication samples. Their original manual for use with individual Rorschach and TAT (Thematic Apperception Test) protocols (1966) was further developed by J. E. Jones (33) (1977) for use with TATs. Parent TAT protocols from the same sample of parents studied by Wynne and Singer with Rorschachs were scored by Jones, in addition to a sample of forty-four families at UCLA in which the index offspring was a nonschizophrenic adolescent who had presented for behavioral problems at a university clinic. A factor analysis of the TAT scores by Jones showed that *total* CD scores from the TATs discriminated the parents of schizophrenics from those of nonschizophrenics less well than had been true with Rorschach CD scores. However, two of the factors in the TAT scores were significant discriminators of the parents of schizophrenics, and the best discrimination occurred when the scores of fathers and mothers were taken together as pairs.

The use of the TAT measure of CD was followed up five years later in the UCLA risk research program. The results indicate that parental communication deviance predicts later development of schizophrenia and schizophrenia-spectrum disorders in the adolescent offspring who were nonschizophrenic when the parents originally were tested (21,24, 34). The authors of these studies also presented evidence that the CD variable interacts with other variables, such as the severity of the adolescent behavior and the type of family relationships as assessed clinically. Apparently a composite of individual and family-communication variables is likely to provide the best indicator of risk for later schizophrenia in families in which there is no known genetic risk factor.

Expressed Emotion Studies A different approach to the study of family relationship was introduced by George Brown and his colleagues in 1962 (7), with replications in the current decade in 1972 (6) and 1976 (100,101). This work, described earlier in connection with Leff's review (36), began with the study of families during acute hospitalized illness and was concerned with the familial influences on subsequent course rather than with the precursor factors in the family. As with individual parental Rorschach or TATs used to study CD, the English researchers who have studied expressed emotion (EE) hypothesized that patterns that are sampled in interaction with a key relative also occur in that relative's relationships directly with the patient. In studying EE, the investigators examined tape recordings of lengthy, semi-structured interviews in which the relative was asked to discuss the patient. The raters then made global ratings of hostility, warmth, and emotional overinvolvement of the relative with the patient, plus a count of the frequency of critical comments by the relative about the patient, with criticalness defined in terms of both content and tone of voice. Whereas the families in the CD studies have involved index patients who were offspring in the family, in the EE studies the index patient has been *either* an offspring or a spouse of the key relative. Vaughn and Leff (100,101) reported that the relative's critical comments about the patient referred not mainly to symptoms that had developed during the acute psychosis but instead to long-standing patient attributes. Thus, it may be that the EE in the relative has been part of a long-standing pattern and may be a precursor of the illness. However, this possibility has not been studied explicitly thus far. Rather, the later course of the illness has been examined. The findings, as described in Leff's review (36) show that patients whose relatives have high EE tend to relapse more frequently than those whose relatives have low EE. When the relative is either a spouse or a parent, critical comments and hostility global ratings are good predictors of relapse over the nine-month period after key admission. Emotional overinvolvement is a strong predictor with the parents of schizophrenics but not with spouses.

The need for cross-cultural study of family emotional interaction is suggested by a report from Finland by Niskanen (59). In an interview study (method not clearly specified) with key relatives of ninty-eight schizophrenics, his findings did not "support the hypothesis that the unfavourable attitudes of family members lead to the patient's admission to hospital more readily or to his becoming institutionalized in the long run."

An important problem that has not yet been empirically studied is the relationship between the concepts of communication deviance and expressed emotion. Among the CD categories, both in the Rorschach and the TAT manuals, categories and factors have been identified which include derogatory and critical remarks that are very similar qualitatively to the dimensions studied in the EE procedure. However, until the same families are studied with both methods, it is not possible to say whether there actually is an overlap between these two broad constructs.

Family Relationship Test Another research approach to familial factors in the course of schizophrenic illness has been carried out in a series of studies by R. D. Scott and colleagues (80,82,83). This work draws upon psychodynamic concepts and in these aspects is closely related to the clinical studies of such workers as Lidz. However, Scott's goal was essentially the same as that in the EE research: to study course and outcome rather than pathogenesis and etiology. He made a distinction between "tenable" home settings leading to "home-based" or "community-based" course, and "untenable" home settings leading to a "hospital-based" course with more than 70 percent of the first two years of illness spent in the hospital.

Scott and his colleagues employed a Family Relationship Test in which attributions in interpersonal perceptions among family members were scored, using an adjective checklist. The relationships within the family were scored in dyadic, reciprocal patterns, as if the family members were in interaction, without analyzing interaction *directly* within the family. Scott and his colleagues found that the patients who were hospital-based saw their parents as "ill," whereas the patients who were home- or community-based saw their parents very much as the parents expected to be seen—namely, with the identity of "well parents." Tenability in the parent-patient relationship was found to depend upon whether or not the patient confirmed this parental identity. Especially if a parent has had experience with mental illness in a close relative, the parent is likely to fear that lack of confirmation of the role of being a "well parent" threatens his or her loss of identity or even madness. In conclusion, Scott et al. found:

> if patients do not accept their role in the family as 'patients,' but either, (a) insist on seeing themselves as 'well' in similar terms to how they see their parents, or, (b) insist upon seeing their parents as 'patients' similarly to how they, the patients, see themselves; these patients have violated the family role structure and are likely to be Hospital-centred in their lives. [p. 59]

Correct predictions were made for thirty out of thirty-three patients on the basis of the Family Relationship Test results obtained within three months of admission for all first admissions from parental families, with these predictions made as to whether the patient would be community-(home-) or hospital-centered two years after the first admission (82).

Scott (80) has gone on to emphasize the abruptness of the change in family relationships that takes place at the time when the patient has been officially identified as a patient. This "closure" about the patient's identity as a patient appears to be associated with the development of "untenability" in the home setting. Twelve out of thirteen patients in untenable home settings, typically associated with closure about the patient's identity as a patient at the time of admission, were found to have a poor outcome in terms of social and work ratings two years later. In the patients with a tenable home setting, fifteen out of twenty-seven had good or intermediate outcomes; most of those twelve with poor outcomes in the tenable group were "deeply embedded in their families, having only tenuous, or no connections, with the outside world." These findings thus appear to be very similar to the conclusions about emotional overinvolvement and negative views of the patient by the parents, as found in the expressed emotion studies and as reported for many years by family therapists. What Scott's important, but unfortunately overlooked, work shows is that the *reciprocal* perceptions within the family, including the patient's perception of the parents, is significant in affecting family relationships and outcome. The expressed emotion technique studies the key relative's view of the patient, whereas Scott's and other family system approaches emphasize as well the patient's contribution to the difficulties within the family.

STUDIES OF DIRECT COMMUNICATION BETWEEN FAMILY MEMBERS

A major trend in family research in relation to schizophrenia can be found in a diverse group of studies in which family members are observed while in direct communication with one another, rather than during interviews or tests with a researcher. Going beyond data that can be obtained from individual family members, these conjoint family-interaction procedures tap patterns of intrusion and disruptiveness, of coalitions and leadership, of corrections or aggravations made by one family member following deviant communication by another. On the other hand, a methodological difficulty with conjoint methods is to provide the family with a task in which they may feel free and comfortable enough to communicate in a "natural" manner likely to be representative of enduring family patterns. Most of the investigators have found that procedures in which family members meet together without an interviewer present are superior to those with an interviewer in the room, especially if the task presented to the family can be absorbing and interesting enough to involve them in lively interaction.

The methods that have been used with the families of schizophrenics during the past decade in which conjoint family interaction is directly sampled can be loosely classified into three groups:

1. *Revealed differences methods.* Adapting a technique devised by Strodtbeck (99), researchers first discover differences in viewpoints of family members through individual answers to a questionnaire; then they reveal these differences to the family and ask them to discuss and reconcile the differences. Multiple codes for rating the Revealed Differences interaction have been devised, most notably by Mishler and Waxler (52). Results of studies using this approach have been reported by Mishler and Waxler (53,54), by Waxler and Mishler (104,105), and by Farina and Holzberg (11,12). A similar method called "confrontation interaction" has been used by the family-research group at UCLA.*

2. *Consensus Rorschach and related procedures.* Another group of procedures involves a task in which the family members are asked to discuss their viewpoints about a task in which prior differences are not revealed to them, but discussion is needed to discover their viewpoints and then see if they can reach a consensus—for example, in their percepts of a Rorschach inkblot. This technique, as applied to the families of schizophrenics, was described by Loveland, Wynne, and Singer (45), with further details supplied by Loveland (44), Singer (85), and Wynne (115). Reports using this approach have been made by Behrens, Rosenthal, and Chodoff (5), Rosenthal, Behrens, and Chodoff (73), Wynne (118), Mosher et al. (57), Shapiro and Wild (84), Herman and Jones (27), Wild, Shapiro, and Abelin (110), and Singer, Wynne, and Toohey (88). A report on the use of Consensus Proverb interpretation with families of schizophrenics was made by Sojit (91). Friedman and

---

° See references 22, 24, 46, 47, and 72.

Friedman (17) used a TAT picture of an adult family scene to stimulate joint family storytelling. The family members were asked to agree on a single story, similar to the instructions for the Consensus Rorschach. Ferreira and Winter (14) asked families to discuss and jointly agree on answers to a questionnaire.

Watzlawick (102) described a structured family interview that included instructions to focus discussion on particular topics, not necessarily requiring a consensus. One of Watzlawick's questions to marital couples is "How, out of all the millions of people in the world, did the two of you get together?" Research analyzing responses to this question have been reported by Hassan (26). Lieber (41) has examined data from videotaped feedback in which family members were instructed to talk about their own behavior seen on a videotape.

3. *Structured problem-solving tasks.* Reiss has devised a series of methods for asking family members to cooperate with each other in solving various problems of pattern recognition and information exchange. By limiting the channels of communication for the family, Reiss was able to use an online computer for recording the data in the communication, and thus obtained detailed and complete information about the steps and processes by which the family members went about the problem-solving task.* A Map Task with a problem-solving approach to eliciting family interaction has been reported by Sølvberg and Blakar (92). Feinsilver (13) devised an object-identification task for conjoint family interaction. This method also was adapted for use by Liem (42,43). Still another technique of studying family problem-solving makes use of the Twenty Questions Task as developed for family research by Mosher and Hornsby (55). Studies using this method with the families of schizophrenics have been reported by Waxler (103), Wild, Shapiro, and Goldenberg (111), Wild and Shapiro (108), and Wild, Shapiro, and Abelin (110).

Obviously detailed reports on these many methods for studying interaction in the families of schizophrenics are beyond the scope of this chapter. For discussion of methodological issues, the reader is referred to the reviews by Riskin and Faunce (71), Jacob (31), and Doane (10). It should be noted that most of the studies thus far have been on small samples of families so that present results must be regarded as preliminary. The methods are complicated to carry out if good interrater reliability is sought; also, they are time-consuming and often expensive. Nevertheless they seem conceptually sound, and the early findings suggest that further work along these lines is highly warranted, both on methodological and substantive levels.

A few illustrative examples of the kinds of findings that have emerged will suffice here to indicate their nature and direction. Wild, Shapiro, and Goldenberg (111) used the family interaction taking place around the problem solving of the Twenty Questions Task to compare families of schizophrenics, psychiatrically hospitalized nonschizophrenic controls, and normal controls. The patient or index family member was a son aged fifteen to thirty-six. The authors scored tape recordings using constructs that had been developed with quite different methods of sampling communication, such as the individual Rorschach. The authors established that the families of the schizophrenics could best be differentiated from other families by looking at parental behavior in terms of complementary roles: the mothers of the schizophrenics showed an amorphous vagueness in focusing attention on the task. Complementary

---

° See references 61, 62, 63, 64, 65, 66, 67, and 69.

to the mothers, the fathers took over in an arbitrary, often irrational, controlling fashion in which they went ahead and reached conclusions without discussion with the rest of the family, contrary to task instructions. The theoretical importance of this study particularly lies in its support for a view of family systems made up of differentiated roles, not the same from one family member to the other, but fitting together in complementary relationships. This conceptual framework means that ordinarily one should not expect similarities between family members, except in very gross terms. Such data are also difficult to explain by nonsystems theory—for example, by neither a simple psychological theory of transmission by identification nor genetic transmission of individual characteristics.

Thus far the literature has few studies in which alternative methods of studying family communication have been examined with the same families. Such work with multiple procedures is essential in the validation of underlying constructs. One such study is reported by Herman and Jones (27); in it they examined the construct of "lack of acknowledgment." Communication deviance in the parents was assessed in accord with the scoring system developed by Singer and Wynne (87), here applied to the TAT and to Zulliger inkblots. The Consensus Family Rorschach was used with triads of the family members—parents and an offspring—and scored with a code measuring "lack of acknowledgment," earlier used by Mishler and Waxler with the Revealed Differences procedure (52). From the results with these and other scoring codes, the authors concluded that communication deviance, assessed in individual parents as an index of risk for schizophrenia in an offspring, taps the same domain of behavior as "lack of acknowledgment" in conjoint interaction of the same families. Conceptually communication deviance is a broad group of variables, while lack of acknowledgment is a narrower construct.

Another study comparing differing family-communication variables with the same families was reported by Lieber (41). She explored the view that communication deviance (or transactional style deviance) can be tapped in such diverse procedures as individual parental TAT protocols and in videotape playback of families discussing their reactions to viewing themselves interacting on a videotape. *Positive* patterns of establishing and maintaining a focus of attention helped to identify those families which were at *low* risk, as judged by the individual TAT measure. Further work on the overlap and differences between such constructs is needed, but the methodology now seems available for these more detailed studies.

Behrens, Rosenthal, and Chodoff (5) used the Consensus Family Rorschach in the home setting with families, all of lower socioeconomic status, divided into three groups, those with a black schizophrenic offspring, a white schizophrenic offspring, and a black control. The authors found that several methods of scoring the Family Rorschachs blindly from tape recordings enabled them to differentiate with high statistical significance between the schizophrenic lower-class families, both black and white, and the black control lower-class families. These findings are contrary to a frequently expressed speculation that disturbed patterns of communication may be an undifferentiated aspect of disad-

vantaged socioeconomic status. Also in the same study, 46 percent of
the families were not intact and had no biological father present, but a
variety of other adult males in the home. Factors such as broken homes
and differences in educational achievement and in social mobility failed
to show significant differences in the scores of family attentional and
communication disorder; for example, these factors were not related
to the family's ability or inability to maintain and share a focus of
attention on the designated task.

FAMILY PATTERNS AND THE PROBLEM OF CAUSALITY

Most family researchers have agreed during the past decade that the
study of differences between families of schizophrenic patients and other
families provides an important starting point for identifying family
variables but cannot answer questions about the place of the family
variables in causal sequences. Indeed, the major trend during the past
decade to incorporate family studies within a risk research paradigm
stems primarily from recognition of this point (20).

Earlier, before the risk research studies were begun, the question of
direction of effects was discussed by Mishler and Waxler (51). They
distinguished an "etiologic" interpretation in which the family patterns
existed prior to the development of schizophrenia, a "responsive" interpretation in which the family behaviors followed and appeared to be
adaptive to the illness, and a "situational" interpretation dependent upon
differential orientations of families to the hospital, the investigator, or
the research setting. Mishler and Waxler's concept of "etiology" was not
spelled out and appeared to include both precipitating and predisposing
"causes"; most current theoreticians, we believe, would not regard
precipitating factors as etiological. The three interpretations outlined
by Mishler and Waxler all involve a linear concept of causality and need
to be differentiated from a transactional or field theory, in which causality is understood in terms of reciprocal determinants and feedback
models viewed within an unfolding developmental context. Mishler and
Waxler argued that the limitations of simpler, unidirectional causal
models should be studied empirically before turning to a transactional
point of view and to longitudinal studies, and that efforts to learn as
much as possible from families seen at one point in time should continue, mainly because of the time, expense, and difficulty of carrying
out prospective longitudinal studies.

One cross-sectional approach tried out by Waxler and Mishler (105)
used their Revealed Differences data to compare parental patterns with
patient offspring and with nonpatient offspring. They formulated an
"etiologic" hypothesis that family-interaction patterns involving a patient offspring, if contributory to the illness, should differ when the
patient versus the sibling is present, should have preceded the illness,
and should still be evident after the illness has been diagnosed. Using
two rather limited sets of measures in the domains of interpersonal
power and affective expressiveness, they found that the patient sessions
did differ significantly between the schizophrenic and the control groups.
However, sessions of the parents with the well sibling produced more

inconsistency. The variance in the sibling sessions was so great that, within each subtype of families, differences between patient and the well-sibling sessions were not significant. They concluded that the findings could not clarify the question of an etiological versus a responsive interpretation of communication by the parents of schizophrenics.

Still, dealing with families after the illness already had developed in an offspring, Waxler (103) constructed "artificial families" in order to study short-term direction of effects. The Twenty Questions Task was given to these artificial families, each consisting of a parents-offspring triad. The parents were unacquainted with the adolescent or young adult offspring, some of whom were schizophrenic and some normal. The key finding was that the "normal" parents facilitated improved cognitive performance of the schizophrenic offspring. This report underlined the importance of studying corrective aspects of family interaction and fits with much clinical and experimental data that suggest that schizophrenic performance can be "normalized" under appropriate conditions. All hypotheses about the possible effects of parents on an offspring, or the impact of schizophrenic offspring upon the parents, have specified that the effects should be expected only within the context of long-term, repetitious relationships; it would be far-fetched to hypothesize that schizophrenia or schizophrenialike functioning could be engendered in one-hour experimental sessions such as were used in the study of "artificial families."

In another artificial family study using tape-recorded exchanges of communication rather than the actual family interaction of Waxler's study, Liem (42, 43) "discovered" that schizophrenic sons, compared with normal sons, were harder for all parents to understand. Although she interpreted this finding as supporting a "responsive" versus an "etiologic" hypothesis about family variables, it is not reasonable to regard this experiment as relevant to the long-term developmental issue of etiology. She did find that parents of schizophrenics communicate with their own sons more adequately than they do with stranger sons. This finding supports the view that transactional or reciprocal learning may have occurred within the family, but it can throw no light on the precursors of the schizophrenic disorder.

Another approach to the etiological versus responsive question using cross-sectional family data was carried out by Wild and Shapiro (108). These authors used a conceptual task, the Twenty Questions, first individually with each family member and then with the family as a unit. Performance of each individual and family unit was compared for problem-solving efficiency and conceptual level. In contrast with the control sons, far more of the schizophrenic sons performed better individually than they did subsequently with their families. When such deterioration took place, it also was found that the parents had difficulty attending to and making use of "competent" information from the schizophrenic son, even though this information would have improved the effectiveness of the family performance. Also, the fathers of the schizophrenics typically dominated the family task and closed off discussion without appearing to grasp corrective or alternative strategies of problem solving offered by other family members. Wild and Shapiro acknowledged that their study could not answer the question whether this current behavior of families was etiological or responsive, but the evidence did suggest that the current impact of the family context was to impair competencies of the offspring that were apparent outside the family. The implications for future course and for treatment are more evident from all cross-sectional family studies than for issues of etiology and precursors.

Mishler and Waxler also had raised a question whether situational factors in the research situation itself might account for family-communication problems, quite apart from longer-standing etiological or responsive factors. A study of this issue by Schopler and Liftin (79) was carried out with the families of child psychotic patients (in that respect this study is not within the scope of this review, because it is questionable whether families of psychotic children can be grouped with families of early adolescent and young adult schizophrenics). One group of parents of psychotic children were first interviewed about their success in rearing a normal sibling of the psychotic child and then were given the Object Sorting Test (OST). A second group of parents of psychotic children were tested in connection with anxiety-provoking interviews relevant to psychotherapy for their psychotic child. Whereas the normal control group showed 12 percent with high conceptual impairment scores, using Lovibond's scoring method, 30 percent of the parents in the "non-anxious" psychotic group and 40 percent in the "anxious" psychotic group showed such impairment. The difference between the parents in the two psychotic groups was not statistically significant; thus it is not clear evidence of the effects of test anxiety (though this paper has been erroneously cited to that effect elsewhere in the literature). In any event, the OST appears to be a rather unsatisfactory method for sampling family communication because, unlike the Rorschach, it is sensitive to educational differences and does not supply meaningful results for subjects who have less than a high school education (112).

Probably more relevant to the question of situational anxiety is evidence from studies of Wynne et al., (124) in which a normal control group was compared with a group of parents who had very seriously ill but nonschizophrenic hospitalized offspring, many of them believed by the parents to be schizophrenic but not so regarded by research diagnosticians. The parents of this hospitalized neurotic group had every reason to be situationally anxious as the parents of the borderline and schizophrenic patients who were in a similar symptomatic situation at the time of testing, but the parents of hospitalized neurotics had markedly lower CD scores than the parents of schizophrenics but essentially no difference from the scores of parents of the normal controls.

Still another approach to untangling "causality" with cross-sectional data lies in the adoption methodologies. Unfortunately no adoption study has included family-conjoint-interaction techniques of the kinds discussed here. However, individual parental Rorschachs were obtained in a Maryland adoption study (not to be confused with the Danish adoption studies) reported by Wender, Rosenthal, and Kety (106). This method involved a comparison of three groups of parents, those who had adopted and reared a child who later became schizophrenic (AS), biological parents who had reared a schizophrenic (BS), and an adoptive normal control group (AN). Wynne, Singer, and Toohey (125) reported on the blind assessment of the individual parental Rorschach protocols provided to them by Wender, Rosenthal, and VanDyke. They found that the biological and adoptive parents of the schizophrenics were indistinguishable on the Rorschach communication-deviance measure and that sixteen parental pairs with a schizophrenic offspring (regardless of whether they were BS or AS) were perfectly separable from the nine parental pairs in the adoptive normal control offspring group. Wender et al., (106) previously had found in these three groups that the BS parents showed the most severe clinical psychopathology, the AS parents less, and the AN parents the least. Comparing their findings with those by Wynne, Singer, and Toohey on the same families, one can conclude that the measure of communication deviance and the clinical ratings of psychopathology tap different aspects of parental functioning, a finding in accord with other work reported by Wynne, Singer, Bartko, and Toohey (124). The results are consistent with a gene-environment interaction viewpoint whereby both experiential and genetic factors may provide the developmental preconditions for schizophrenia.

Wender et al., (107) attempted a replication of this adoption study on a sample of parents in New York. Unfortunately they used a "scale of psychopathology" in assessing parental Rorschachs, not the CD procedure developed by Singer and Wynne (87) for use with such protocols. This way of assessing Rorschachs failed to reveal significant differences between the three groups of parents. Because of the major methodological differences and also because of apparent differences in sampling of the families, it is not possible to conclude whether their results are a disconfirmation of the report by Wynne, Singer, and Toohey (125). In any event, the study of adoptive families in which an offspring has already become schizophrenic cannot provide a definitive answer to the question of etiological versus responsive determinants. The nature of the reciprocal impact between a schizophrenic and an adoptive parent over the years prior to onset of the disorder must remain speculative without prospective longitudinal study.

Thus, during the last decade there have been various efforts to use cross-sectional data to make inferences about etiological, responsive, or situational aspects of family-interaction patterns, but family researchers have by and large increasingly abandoned such efforts. Instead, they are turning to the high-risk research paradigm and to prospective studies that may illuminate the possible role of family relationships in later schizophrenia. Anthony's high-risk research has especially emphasized extensive home visits in studying family relationships prospectively (3,4). The current status of efforts with other methods has been reviewed by Garmezy (19,20) and in part by Rieder (see chapter 6). As described earlier, the first prospective longitudinal study in which standardized family-communication measures were used predictively at initial evaluation is the UCLA risk research program that began with fifteen-year-old adolescents seen in a university outpatient clinic. Similar and additional family measures have been used in a study of families at Rochester, New York. In these families a parent has been hospitalized for schizophrenic or depressive illness; both genetic and family-communication risk variables are examined in relation to intermediate outcomes for index four-, seven-, and ten-year-old sons in these families.

Longitudinal studies that incorporate family communication variables should contribute to our understanding of both developmental psychopathology (compare reference 17) and the pathogenesis of schizophrenic disorders. However, such studies should not be inappropriately expected to answer directly questions about specific (necessary) etiological factors. Wynne (116,117) and Wynne et al., (124) have conceptualized family-relationship variables as "intermediate" in developmental sequences between genetic endowment and symptomatic breakdown. Reiss and Wyatt (70) and Reiss (68) have also hypothesized possible links between family and biological variables. Family relationships may contribute to an acquired component of vulnerability or predisposition (122). If so, the place of these or similar experiential factors could be highly significant for the emergence of fully symptomatic schizophrenia, though probably in complex interaction with biological variables.

BIBLIOGRAPHY

1. Ackerman, N. W. 1969. The affective climate in families with psychosis. In *Problems of psychosis*, eds. P. Doucet and C. Laurin (Amsterdam: Excerpta Medica Foundation), pp. 129–39.

2. Alanen, Y. 1968. From the mothers of schizophrenic patients to interactional family dynamics. *Journal of Psychiatric Research* 6(supp. 1):201–12.

3. Anthony, E. J. 1968. The developmental precursors of adult schizophrenia. *Journal of Psychiatric Research* 6(supp. 1):293–316.

4. Anthony, E. J. 1974. A risk-vulnerability intervention model for children of psychotic parents. In *The child in his family: Children at psychiatric risk*, eds. E. J. Anthony and C. Koupernik (New York: John Wiley), vol. 3, pp. 99–122.

5. Behrens, M. I.; Rosenthal, A. J.; and Chodoff, P. 1968. Communication in lower-class families of schizophrenics: II. Observations and findings. *Archives of General Psychiatry* 18:689–96.

6. Brown, G. W.; Birley, J. L. T.; and Wing, J. K. 1972. Influence of family life on the course of schizophrenic disorders: A replication. *British Journal of Psychiatry* 121:241–58.

7. Brown, G. W.; Monck, E. M.; Carstairs, G. M.; and Wing, J. K. 1962. Influence of family life on the course of schizophrenic illness. *British Journal of Preventative and Social Medicine* 16:55–68.

8. Conran, M. B. 1976. Schizophrenia as incestuous failure. Theoretical implications, derived from transference observations of the young male schizophrenic and his mother, concerning the mother-infant relationship. In *Schizophrenia 75: Psychotherapy, family studies, research*, eds. J. Jørstad and E. Ugelstad (Oslo, Norway: Universitetsforlaget), pp. 203–10.

9. Doane, J. A. 1978. Family interaction and communication deviance in disturbed and normal families: A review of research. *Family Process* 17:357–376.

10. Doane, J. A. 1978. Questions of strategy: Rejoinder to Jacob and Grounds. *Family Process* 17:389–394.

11. Farina, A., and Holzberg, J. D. 1968. Interaction patterns of parents and hospitalized sons diagnosed as schizophrenic or nonschizophrenic. *Journal of Abnormal Psychology* 73:114–118.

12. Farina, A., and Holzberg, J. D. 1970. Anxiety level of schizophrenic and control patients and their parents. *Journal of Abnormal Psychology* 75:157–163.

13. Feinsilver, D. 1970. Communication in families of schizophrenic patients. Describing common objects as a test of communication between family members. *Archives of General Psychiatry* 22:143–148.

14. Ferreira, A. J. and Winter, W. D. 1968. Information exchange and silence in normal and abnormal families. *Family Process* 7:251–76.

15. Fleck, S. A. 1976. A general systems view of families of schizophrenics. In *Schizophrenia 75: Psychotherapy, family studies, research*, eds. J. Jørstad and E. Ugelstad (Oslo, Norway: Universitetsforlaget), pp. 211–28.

16. Framo, J. L., ed. 1972. *Family interaction: A dialogue between family researchers and family therapists* (New York: Springer Publishing).

17. Friedman, C. J., and Friedman, A. S. 1970. Characteristics of schizophrenic families during a joint story-telling task. *Family Process* 9:333–53.

18. Garmezy, N., and Streitman, S. 1974. Children at risk: The search for the antecedents of schizophrenia. I: Conceptual models and research methods. *Schizophrenia Bulletin* 8:14–90.

19. Garmezy, N. 1974. Children at risk: The search for the antecedents of schizophrenia. II: Ongoing research programs, issues, and intervention. *Schizophrenia Bulletin* 9:55–125.

20. Garmezy, N. 1978. Current status of a sample of other high-risk research programs. In *The nature of schizophrenia*, eds. L. C. Wynne, R. Cromwell, and S. Matthysse (New York: John Wiley) pp. 473–483.

21. Goldstein, M. J., and Jones, J. E. 1977. Adolescent and familial precursors of borderline and schizophrenic conditions. In *Borderline personality disorders: The concept, the syndrome, the patient*, ed. P. Hartocollis (New York: International Universities Press), pp. 213–29.

22. Goldstein, M. J.; Judd, L. L.; Rodnick, E. H.; Alkire, A.; and Gould, E. 1968. A method for studying social influence and coping patterns within families of disturbed adolescents. *Journal of Nervous and Mental Disease* 147:233–56.

23. Goldstein, M. J., and Rodnick, E. H. 1975. The family's contribution to the etiology of schizophrenia: Current status. *Schizophrenia Bulletin* 14:48–63.

24. Goldstein, M. J.; Rodnick, E. H.; Jones, J. E.; McPherson, S. R.; and West, K. L. 1978. Familial precursors of schizophrenia spectrum disorders. In *The nature of schizophrenia*, eds. L. C. Wynne, R. Cromwell, and S. Matthysse (New York: John Wiley), pp. 487–98.

25. Grunebaum, H.; Weiss, J. L.; Cohler, B. J.; Hartman, C. R.; and Gallant, D. H. 1975. *Mentally ill mothers and their children* (Chicago: University of Chicago Press).

26. Hassan, S. A. 1974. Transactional and contextual invalidation between the parents of disturbed families: A comparative study. *Family Process* 13:53–76.

27. Herman, B. F., and Jones, J. E. 1976. Lack of acknowledgment in the family Rorschachs of families with a child at risk for schizophrenia. *Family Process* 15:289–302.

28. Hirsch, S. R., and Leff, J. P. 1971. Parental abnormalities of verbal communication in the transmission of schizophrenia. *Psychological Medicine* 1:118–27.

29. Hirsch, S. R., and Leff, J. P. 1975. *Abnormalities in parents of schizophrenics* (London: Oxford University Press).

30. Holzman, P. 1976. Schizophrenia: The family medium may not transmit the message. *Contemporary Psychology* 21:416–17.

31. Jacob, T. 1975. Family interaction in disturbed and normal families: A methodological and substantive review. *Psychological Bulletin* 2:33–65.

32. Jacob, T., and Grounds, L. 1978. Confusions and conclusions: A response to Doane. *Family Process* 17:377–387.

33. Jones, J. E. 1977. Patterns of transactional style deviance in the TAT's of parents of schizophrenics. *Family Process* 16:327–37.

34. Jones, J. E.; Rodnick, E. H.; Goldstein, M. J.; McPherson, S. R.; and West, K. L. 1977. Parental transactional style deviance as a possible indicator of risk for schizophrenia. *Archives of General Psychiatry* 34:71–74.

35. Laing, R. D. 1969. *The politics of the family*. Massey Lectures (Toronto: Canadian Broadcasting Corporation Publications).

36. Leff, J. P. 1976. Schizophrenia and sensitivity to the family environment. *Schizophrenia Bulletin* 2:566–74.

37. Lidz, T. 1972. Schizophrenic disorders: The influence of conceptualizations on therapy. In *Psychotherapy of schizophrenia*, eds. D. Rubinstein and Y. O. Alanen (Amsterdam: Excerpta Medica Foundation), pp. 9–24.

38. Lidz, T. 1973. Egocentric cognitive regression and a theory of schizophrenia. In *Psychiatry: Proceedings of Vth world congress of psychiatry*, eds. R. de la Fuente and M. Weisman (Amsterdam: Excerpta Medica Foundation), pp. 1146–52.

39. Lidz, T. 1973. *The origin and treatment of schizophrenic disorders* (New York: Basic Books).

40. Lidz, T. 1978. Egocentric cognitive regression and the family setting of schizophrenic disorders. In *The nature of schizophrenia*, eds. L. C. Wynne, R. Cromwell, and S. Matthysse (New York: John Wiley), pp. 526–33.

41. Lieber, D. J. 1977. Parental focus of attention in a videotape feedback task as a function of hypothesized risk for offspring schizophrenia. *Family Process* 16:467–75.

42. Liem, J. H. 1974. Effects of verbal communications of parents and children: A comparison of normal and schizophrenic families. *Journal of Consulting and Clinical Psychology* 42:438–50.

43. Liem, J. H. 1976. Intrafamily communication and schizophrenic thought disorder: An etiological or responsive relationship? *Clinical Psychologist* 29:28–30.

44. Loveland, N. T. 1967. The relation Rorschach: A technique for studying interaction. *Journal of Nervous and Mental Disease* 145:93–105.

45. Loveland, N. T.; Wynne, L. C.; and Singer, M. T. 1963. The family Rorschach: A method for studying family interaction. *Family Process* 2:187–215.

46. McPherson, S. R. 1970. Communication of intents among parents and their disturbed adolescent child. *Journal of Abnormal Psychology* 76:98–105.

47. McPherson, S. R.; Goldstein, M. J. and Rodnick, E. H. 1973. Who listens? Who communicates? How? *Archives of General Psychiatry* 28:393–99.

48. Mednick, S. A.; Mura, E.; and Schulsinger, F. et al. 1973. Erratum and further analysis: perinatal conditions and infant development in children with schizophrenic parents. *Social Biology* 20:111–112.

49. Meissner, W. W. 1970. Sibling relations in the schizophrenic family. *Family Process* 9:1–25.

50. Mishler, E. G., and Waxler, N. E. 1968. *Family processes and schizophrenia: Theory and selected experimental studies* (New York: Science House).

51. Mishler, E. G., and Waxler, N. E. 1968. Family interaction and schizophrenia: Alternative frameworks of interpretation. *Journal of Psychiatric Research* 6(supp. 1):213–22.

52. Mishler, E. G., and Waxler, N. E. 1968. *Interaction in families: An experimental study of family processes and schizophrenia* (New York: John Wiley).

53. Mishler, E. G., and Waxler, N. E. 1970. Functions of hesitations in the speech of normal families and families of schizophrenic patients. *Language and Speech* 13(part 2):102:17.

54. Mishler, E. G., and Waxler, N. E. 1975. The sequential patterning of interaction in normal and schizophrenic families. *Family Process* 14:17–50.

55. Mosher, F. A., and Hornsby, J. R. 1966. On asking questions. In *Studies in cognitive growth*, eds. J. Bruner, R. Olwer, and P. Greenfield (New York: John Wiley).

56. Mosher, L. R. 1969. Schizophrenogenic communication and family therapy. *Family Process* 8: 43–63.

57. Mosher, L. R.; Wild, C.; Valcov, A.; and Feinstein, A. E. 1972. Cognitive style, schizophrenia, and the family: Methodological implications of contextual effects. *Family Process* 11:125–46.

58. Mueller, P. S., and Orfanidis, M. M. 1976. A method of co-therapy for schizophrenic families. *Family Process* 15:179–91.

59. Niskanen, P. 1972. A survey of family attitudes of schizophrenic inpatients and outpatients. *Psychiatria Fennica* 3:193–97.

60. Parker, B. 1972. *A mingled yarn: Chronicle of a troubled family* (New Haven: Yale University Press).

61. Reiss, D. 1967. Individual thinking and family interaction. I. Introduction to an experimental study of problem solving in families of normals, character disorders, and schizophrenics. *Archives of General Psychiatry* 16:80–93.

62. Reiss, D. 1967. Individual thinking and family interaction. II. A study of pattern recognition and hypothesis testing in families of normals, character disorders, and schizophrenics. *Journal of Psychiatric Research* 5:193–211.

63. Reiss, D. 1968. Individual thinking and family interaction. III. An experimental study of categorization performance in families of normals, those with character disorders and schizophrenics. *Journal of Nervous and Mental Disease* 146:384–403.

64. Reiss, D. 1968. Family problem solving: Two experiments on the relationship between family interaction and individual thinking in families of schizophrenics, normals, and character disorders. *Journal of Psychiatric Research* 6(supp. 1):223–34.

65. Reiss, D. 1969. Individual thinking and family interaction. IV. A study of information exchange in families of normals, those with character disorders, and schizophrenics. *Journal of Nervous and Mental Disease* 149:473–90.

66. Reiss, D. 1970. Individual thinking and family interaction. V. Proposals for the contrasting character of experiential sensitivity and expressive form in families. *Journal of Nervous and Mental Disease* 151:187–202.

67. Reiss, D. 1971. Varieties of consensual experience. III. Contrasts between families of normals, delinquents, and schizophrenics. *Journal of Nervous and Mental Disease* 152:73–95.

68. Reiss, D. 1976. The family and schizophrenia. *American Journal of Psychiatry* 133:181–185.

69. Reiss, D., and Sheriff, W. H. 1970. A computer-automated procedure for assessing some experiences of family membership. *Behavioral Science* 15:431–43.

70. Reiss, D., and Wyatt, R. J. 1975. Family and biologic variables in the same etiologic studies of schizophrenia: A proposal. *Schizophrenia Bulletin* 14:64–81.

71. Riskin, J., and Faunce, E. E. 1972. An evaluative review of family interaction research. *Family Process* 11:365–455.

72. Rodnick, E. H., and Goldstein, M. J. 1974. A research strategy for studying risk for schizophrenia during adolescence and early adulthood. In *The child in his family—Children at psychiatric risk*, eds. E. J. Anthony and C. Koupernik (New York: John Wiley), vol. 3, pp. 507–26.

73. Rosenthal, A. J.; Behrens; M. I.; and Chodoff, P. 1968. Communication in lower class families of schizophrenics. I. Methodological problems. *Archives of General Psychiatry* 18:464–70.

74. Rubinstein, D. 1972. Clinical issues in family therapy of schizophrenia. In *Psychotherapy of schizophrenia*, eds. D. Rubinstein and Y. O. Alanen (Amsterdam: Excerpta Medica Foundation), pp. 159–68.

75. Rutter, M. 1978. Communication deviance and diagnostic differences. In *The nature of schizophrenia*, eds. L. C. Wynne, R. Cromwell, and S. Matthysse (New York: John Wiley), pp. 512–16.

76. Sander, F. M. 1971. T. S. Eliot's *The family reunion*—"Schizophrenia" reconsidered. *Family Process* 10:213–28.

77. Schatzman, M. 1971. Paranoia or persecution: The case of Schreber. *Family Process* 10: 177–212.

78. Schatzman, M. 1973. *Soul murder: Persecution in the family* (New York: Random House).

79. Schopler, E., and Loftin, J. 1969. Thought disorders in parents of psychotic children: A function of test anxiety. *Archives of General Psychiatry* 20:174–81.

80. Scott, R. D. 1976. "Closure" in family relationships and the first official diagnosis. In *Schizophrenia 75: Psychotherapy, family studies, research*, eds. J. Jørstad and E. Ugelstad (Oslo, Norway: Universtitetsforlaget), pp. 265–81.

81. Scott, R. D., and Ashworth, P. L. 1969. The shadow of the ancestor: A historical factor in the transmission of schizophrenia. *British Journal of Medical Psychology* 42:13–32.

82. Scott, R. D.; Ashworth, P. L.; and Casson, P. D. 1970. Violation of parental role structure and outcome in schizophrenia. A scored analysis of features in the parent-patient relationship. *Social Science Medicine* 4:41–64.

83. Scott, R. D., and Montanez, A. 1972. The nature of tenable and untenable patient-parent relationships and their connection with hospital outcome. In *Psychotherapy of schizophrenia*, eds. D. Rubinstein and Y. O. Alanen (Amsterdam: Excerpta Medica Foundation), pp. 226–42.

84. Shapiro, L. M., and Wild, C. M. 1976. The product of the consensus Rorschach in families of male schizophrenics. *Family Process* 15:211–24.

85. Singer, M. T. 1968. The Consensus Rorschach and family transaction. *Journal of Projective Techniques and Personality Assessment* 32:348–51.

86. Singer, M. T. 1977. The Rorschach as a transaction. In *Rorschach psychology*, ed. M. A. Rickers-Ovsiankina (Huntington, N.Y.: Robert E. Krieger Publishing), pp. 455–58.

87. Singer, M. T., and Wynne, L. C. 1966. Principles for scoring communication defects and deviances in parents of schizophrenics: Rorschach and TAT scoring manuals. *Psychiatry* 29:260–88.

88. Singer, M. T.; Wynne, L. C.; and Toohey, M. L. 1978. Communication disorders and the families of schizophrenics. *The nature of schizophrenia,* eds. L. C. Wynne, R. Cromwell, and S. Matthysse (New York: John Wiley), pp. 499–511.

89. Slipp, S. 1973. The symbiotic survival pattern: A relational theory of schizophrenia. *Family Process* 12:377–98.

90. Sluzki, C. E., and Ransom, D. C., eds. 1976. *Double bind: The foundation of the communicational approach to the family* (New York: Grune & Stratton).

91. Sojit, C. M. 1971. The double bind hypothesis and the parents of schizophrenics. *Family Process* 10:53:74.

92. Sølvberg, H. A., and Blakar, R. M. 1975. Communication efficiency in couples with and without a schizophrenic offspring. *Family Process* 14:515–34.

93. Stierlin, H. 1969. *Conflict and reconciliation: A study in human relations and schizophrenia* (Garden City, N.Y.: Anchor Books).

94. Stierlin, H. 1972. Family dynamics and separation patterns of potential schizophrenics. In *Psychotherapy of schizophrenia,* eds. D. Rubinstein and Y. O. Alanen (Amsterdam: Excerpta Medica Foundation), pp. 169–79.

95. Stierlin, H. 1972. The impact of relational vicissitudes on the life course of one schizophrenic quadruplet. In *Genetic factors in "schizophrenia,"* ed. A. R. Kaplan (Springfield, Ill.: Charles C Thomas), pp. 451–63.

96. Stierlin, H. 1974. Psychoanalytic approaches to schizophrenia in the light of a family model. *International Review of Psychoanalysis* 1:169–79.

97. Stierlin, H. 1974. *Separating parents and adolescents* (New York: Quadrangle).

98. Stierlin, H. 1978. The transmission of irrationality reconsidered. In *The nature of schizophrenia,* eds. L. C. Wynne, R. Cromwell, and S. Matthysse (New York: John Wiley), pp. 517–25.

99. Strodbeck, F. 1951. Husband-wife interaction over revealed differences. *American Sociological Review* 16:468–73.

100. Vaughn, C. E., and Leff, J. P. 1976. The influence of family and social factors on the course of psychiatric illness: A comparison of schizophrenic and depressed neurotic patients. *British Journal of Psychiatry* 129:125–37.

101. Vaughn, C. E., and Leff, J. P. 1976. The measurement of expressed emotion in the families of psychiatric patients. *British Journal of Social and Clinical Psychology* 15(part 2):157–65.

102. Watzlawick, P. 1966. A structural family interview. *Family Process* 5:256–71.

103. Waxler, N. E. 1974. Parent and child effects on cognitive performance: An experimental approach to the etiological and responsive theories of schizophrenia. *Family Process* 13:1–22.

104. Waxler, N. E., and Mishler, E. G. 1970. Sequential patterning in family interaction. A methodological note. *Family Process* 9:211–20.

105. Waxler, N. E., and Mishler, E. G. 1971. Parental interaction with schizophrenic children and well siblings. *Archives of General Psychiatry* 25:223–31.

106. Wender, P. H.; Rosenthal, D.; Kety, S. S. 1968. A psychiatric assessment of the adoptive parents of schizophrenics. *Journal of Psychiatric Research* 6(supp. 1):235–50.

107. Wender, P. H.; Rosenthal, D.; Rainer, J. D.; Greenhill, L.; and Sarlin, M. B. 1977. Schizophrenics' adopting parents. Psychiatric status. *Archives of General Psychiatry* 34:777–84.

108. Wild, C. M., and Shapiro, L. 1977. Mechanisms of change from individual to family performance in male schizophrenics and their parents. *Journal of Nervous and Mental Disease* 165:41–56.

109. Wild, C. M.; Shapiro, L. N.; and Abelin, T. 1974. Sampling issues in family studies of schizophrenia. *Archives of General Psychiatry* 30:211–15.

110. Wild, C. M.; Shapiro, L. N.; and Abelin, T. 1977. Communication patterns and role structure in families of male schizophrenics: A study using automated techniques. *Archives of General Psychiatry* 34:58–70.

111. Wild, C. M.; Shapiro, L. N.; and Goldenberg, L. 1975. Transactional communication disturbances in families of male schizophrenics. *Family Process* 14:131–60.

112. Wild, C. M.; Singer, M. T.; Rosman, B.; Ricci, J.; and Lidz, T. 1965. Measuring disordered styles of thinking. *Archives of General Psychiatry* 13:471–76.

113. Woodward, J. A., and Goldstein, M. 1977. Communication deviance in the families of schizophrenics: A comment on the misuse of analysis of covariance. *Science* 197:1096–97.

114. World Health Organization. 1975. *Primary prevention of schizophrenia in high-risk groups* (Copenhagen: World Health Organization).

115. Wynne, L. C. 1968. Consensus Rorschachs and related procedures for studying interpersonal patterns. *Journal of Projective Techniques and Personality Assessment* 32:352–56.

116. Wynne, L. C. 1968. Methodological and conceptual issues in the study of schizophrenics and their families. *Journal of Psychiatric Research* 6(supp. 1):185–99.

117. Wynne, L. C. 1969. Family research in the pathogenesis of schizophrenia. Intermediate variables in the study of families at high risk. In *Problems of psychosis,* eds. P. Doucet and C. Laurin (Amsterdam: Excerpta Medica Foundation), pp. 401–23.

118. Wynne, L. C. 1970. Communication disorders and the quest for relatedness in the families of schizophrenics. *American Journal of Psychoanalysis* 30:100–114.

119. Wynne, L. C. 1972. The injection and concealment of meaning in the family relationships and psychotherapy of schizophrenics. In *Psychotherapy of schizophrenia,* eds. D. Rubinstein and Y. O. Alanen (Amsterdam: Excerpta Medica Foundation), pp. 180–93.

120. Wynne, L. C. 1976. On the anguish and creative passions of not escaping double binds: A reformulation. In *Double bind: The foundation of the communicational approach to the family,* eds. C. Sluzki and D. C. Ransom (New York: Grune & Stratton), pp. 243–50.

121. Wynne, L. C. 1978. Concluding comments: Section on family relationships and communication. In *The nature of schizophrenia,* eds. L. C. Wynne, R. Cromwell, and S. Matthysse (New York: John Wiley), pp. 534–42.

122. Wynne, L. C. 1978. From symptoms to vulnerability and beyond: An overview. In *The*

nature of schizophrenia, eds. L. C. Wynne, R. Cromwell, and S. Matthysse (New York: John Wiley), pp. 698–714.

123. Wynne, L. C.; Cromwell, R.; and Matthysse, S. eds. 1978. *The nature of schizophrenia* (New York: John Wiley).

124. Wynne, L. C.; Singer, M. T.; Bartko, J. J.; and Toohey, M. L. 1977. Schizophrenics and their families: Recent research on parental communication. In *Developments in psychiatric research,* ed. J. M. Tanner (London: Hodden & Stoughton), pp. 254–86.

125. Wynne, L. C.; Singer, M. T.; and Toohey, M. L. 1976. Communication of the adoptive parents of schizophrenics. In *Schizophrenia 75: Psychotherapy, family studies, research,* eds. J. Jørstad and E. Ugelstad (Oslo, Norway: Universitetsforlaget), pp. 413–52.

PART II

Clinical Aspects

Chapter 8

DIAGNOSTIC ISSUES IN SCHIZOPHRENIA

William T. Carpenter, Jr., M.D. and John S. Strauss, M.D.

Introduction

The nosology of schizophrenia was firmly established around the turn of the century when Kraepelin combined three syndromes (catatonia, hebephrenia, and paranoia) into a single disease concept termed "dementia praecox" (32). In his 1911 monograph (7) Bleuler recognized that this illness was not a dementia. In most of his writings (but not in all; see reference 59), Bleuler—like most workers before and since—assumed a somatic etiology but defined a basic psychological defect (weakening of associative thinking) and attempted to understand the manifest psychopathology of schizophrenia by integrating clinical observations into a coherent theoretical framework. Bleuler described a fourth syndrome (simple schizophrenia) and referred to the disease, or diseases, as the "group of schizophrenias." The label "schizophrenia" emphasized the fundamental psychological defect—the splitting of associative processes.

Since 1911 the nosological picture has undergone relatively little change. There has been the addition of an important, but confusing, subtype—"schizo-affective" schizophrenia. Equally confusing, but less important, is the presumptive subtype—"latent" schizophrenia. There no doubt is such a clinical phenomenon as "prepsychotic" schizophrenia, but it seems far wiser to reserve the term "schizophrenia" for patients who manifest highly distinguishing symptoms of the illness, symptoms which are psychotic in nature. "Residual" schizophrenia simply describes a phase following a psychotic episode and has little descriptive and no important conceptual value as a subtype. Other modifications and additions have ranged from the overinclusive (e.g., "pseudoneurotic" schizophrenia) to the atomistic subtyping of Fish, Kleist, and Leonhard (22,31,33).

With relative nosological stability over the years, the major developments related to classification have been primarily concerned with determining optimal diagnostic criteria. Major disagreement exists between those diagnostic schools that rely on highly discriminating psychotic symptoms (e.g., special forms of hallucinations and delusions) and those more concerned with disordered thinking and the interpersonal consequences of the illness. Each approach has left an important, unresolved problem in its wake. The former can provide relatively clear and reliable criteria for diagnosis but fails to classify many patients whose presenting psychopathology does not lend itself to crisp classification. There is a current tendency to assume that these patients suspected of having schizophrenia (but failing to meet stringent criteria) are atypical affective disorder patients. However, if equally stringent criteria for major affective disorders are applied, it becomes obvious that a large number of psychotic patients do not fit neatly into any nosological niche.

On the other hand, diagnostic approaches which pay less attention to highly discriminating delusions and hallucinations and emphasize disordered thinking and disturbed interpersonal relating, have a different problem. A broader range of patients can be diagnosed as schizophrenic, but this results in greater within-class heterogeneity, less reliability, and more difficulty in description. While there is little doubt that the first approach has the greater reliability, it is yet to be determined which is more valid. It is, in fact, the dissonance between these two approaches to classification that has spawned the developments of recent years. This chapter provides an opportunity to review the progress of this decade critically, and to address the complex issue of how to identify most effectively and productively patients with an illness, or illnesses, which we call schizophrenia.

It is no longer essential to deal with the preliminary question as to whether schizophrenia exists, since there is little scientific merit or clinical sense to the argument that this syndrome is a myth. On the contrary, recent investigations have provided increasing data in support of conceptualizing schizophrenia within the general framework of a biopsychosocial model of medical illness. The term schizophrenia is not sacrosanct, and there is little reason to think that schizophrenia, as presently defined, is a single illness. Regardless of the inexact nature of present classification, the concept of the "group of schizophrenias" has considerable communicative value and validity. Patients so diagnosed have remarkable similarity across cultures (70); there is a within-patient consistency of psychopathological manifestations across distinct psychotic episodes (72); a genetic contribution has been established in at least some subgroups of schizophrenia;* differential psychopharmacology has made the diagnosis a useful, but not absolute, guide to drug selection in pharmacotherapy (10,19,30,51); and some subgroups of schizophrenia show a certain degree of uniformity in course and outcome (e.g., chronic or process schizophrenia), which suggests similar pathogenic processes (1,4,57,58).

For the reader who is unfamiliar with recent psychiatric history, it may be worth pointing out that twenty-five years ago the diagnosis of schizophrenia was of little help in making treatment choices, it was not established that such illness occurred in all cultures, genetic contribu-

---

* See references 9, 28, 34, 46, and 47.

tions were not firmly established, and it was unclear to what extent patients diagnosed schizophrenic in different centers would actually manifest similar symptomatology. Despite the considerable progress that has been made, the etiology, the pathogenesis, and the treatment of schizophrenic patients remains enigmatic. It is from this perspective that this chapter is written. We will focus on recent trends and progress relevant to the classification of schizophrenic patients, with minimal reliance on theory and primary emphasis on scientifically sound clinical investigations. However, before describing recent developments in nosology, it is necessary to adumbrate the earlier conceptual frameworks which have shaped current interests and investigative styles.

Conceptual Models of Schizophrenia

In the latter part of the nineteenth century, Kraepelin (32) pulled together the seemingly disparate syndromes of hebephrenia, paranoia, and catatonia. He noted common features, such as the deteriorating course of the illness, the manifestation of bizarre thought disturbances, the frequent presence of paranoid and grandiose delusions, the occurrence of auditory and other hallucinatory experiences, and a pervasive reduction in cognitive and affective capacities. Kraepelin's description of the psychopathology associated with dementia praecox has undergone relatively little important modification over the years, although most students of schizophrenia would now regard Kraepelin's descriptions as defining process, or poor-prognosis, schizophrenia and as having less complete relevance to the acute and remitting forms of schizophrenia.

In 1911, Bleuler's monograph, entitled *Dementia Praecox, or the Group of Schizophrenias*, was published (7). This remarkable work extended Kraepelin's clinical observations into the realm of psychology in an attempt to understand the meaning and the mechanisms of psychosis. Bleuler corrected the major conceptual defect inherent in the term "dementia praecox." He observed schizophrenia to be a chronic and usually deteriorating condition; but he noted that it was not a dementia, and that onset was not invariably early in life. The critical role of a clear sensorium in distinguishing organic and toxic psychoses from the functional psychoses was established.

Bleuler postulated dissociative thinking as primary in schizophrenia, in that this symptom alone could not be explained by other observable schizophrenic phenomena. Hence, he took dissociative thinking as the basic defect in schizophrenia, and attempted to account for much of the remaining psychopathology as a consequence of this process. Bleuler assumed that a somatic etiology gave rise to the dissociative thinking, a proposition for which there is considerable rationale, but which is still not scientifically established.

Bleuler used concepts from the new field of psychoanalysis to ascribe meaning and to develop understanding of symptomatology in schizophrenic patients. This use of psychoanalytic concepts, plus the complexity of many of Bleuler's own concepts, has created ambiguity regarding the phenomenology of schizophrenia. Until recently Bleuler's teachings have been more influential than Kraepelin's in the United States, in large measure because of the influence of psychoanalysis in this country, and partially because of the contributions of Adolf Meyer and Harry Stack Sullivan. During this period (the middle third of the twentieth century) many centers of European psychiatry emphasized careful description of clinical phenomena, thus providing fertile soil for the German phenomenologists.

Jaspers (29), a key figure among the phenomenologists, believed that a principle defect in the makeup of the schizophrenic was the inability to establish empathetic bonds. This is a complex concept, but the essence of its application in schizophrenia led to the belief that experiences of schizophrenic patients were "un-understandable" since the listener could not comprehend through empathy the experiences being reported.* Perhaps one contribution to this theory was the belief that the observing clinician could not share a sense of how the schizophrenic patient came to have his experience, and that, therefore, the bizarre manifestations of schizophrenia did not make sense to any observer. Thus the "un-understandability" of schizophrenic phenomena placed the emphasis on description rather than on meaning. This is contrary to psychoanalytic theory which stresses meaning rather than overt content and has led, in the United States particularly, to attempts to find meaning and psychodynamic significance in schizophrenic phenomena (with a reduced interest in careful description of the manifest psychopathology).

Kurt Schneider (49) emerged as the most influential representative of the German phenomenological school. His approach to a clinical definition of schizophrenia was pragmatic. He sought diagnostic criteria based on psychopathological manifestations that occurred frequently in schizophrenia and could be reliably evaluated by clinicians. Most important, the association of these manifestations with the illness in question must be as particular as possible. Schneider gave diagnostic primacy to a few symptoms which he believed met these criteria. These first rank symptoms were regarded as pathognomonic of schizophrenia in the absence of an organic psychosyndrome. Schneider assumed a somatic etiology in schizophrenia but was otherwise atheoretical regarding the function and meaning of these symptoms. These were symptoms of first rank because they were specific indicators of the presence of schizophrenia, not because they could be used to explain secondary phenomena or because a theoretical construct suggested their primacy. The presence of these first rank symptoms simply meant schizophrenia, except for their occasional occurrence in organic psychosyndromes. According to Schneider, there are many other manifestations of schizophrenic psychopathology important as experiences to the patient and relevant to the diagnosis of the illness. However, these second rank symptoms and

---

* The clinician could, of course, empathize in the usual sense of the word. Jaspers's emphasis was on two modes of informative communication: the language-oriented cognitive communication and the relationship-oriented empathetic communication. It is this latter form which he felt was unavailable to the schizophrenic. The interested reader should study Jaspers's concept to avoid misunderstanding on this point.

psychic experiences do not have the unique relationship to schizophrenia as do symptoms of the first rank.

First rank symptoms, as defined by Schneider (49) and summarized by others (16,38), include three *special forms of auditory hallucintion*: (1) the patient hears voices speaking his thoughts aloud; (2) the patient is the subject about whom hallucinatory voices are arguing or discussing; (3) the patient hallucinates voices describing his activity. A fourth symptom, *delusional percept*, is a two-stage phenomenon consisting of a normal perception followed by a delusional interpretation of special and highly personalized significance. This phenomenon occurs infrequently and should be distinguished from delusional misinterpretations which so often comprise part of the psychotic state. Delusional percepts are apophanous phenomena with a sudden and unexpected delusional explanation of ordinary occurrences.

Other symptoms of first rank can be conceptualized as defects in the barrier separating self from environment. In *somatic passivity* the patient is a passive and reluctant recipient of externally imposed bodily sensation. In *thought insertion* the patient experiences thoughts as though they were put in his mind by an outside force. In *thought withdrawal* the patient believes that his thoughts are being removed from his mind by an outside agent. *Thought broadcast* is the passive experience of one's thoughts being magically transmitted to others. The remaining first-rank symptoms consist of *affect, impulses, or motor activity experienced as imposed and controlled from outside one's body*. These symptoms are to be distinguished from somatic passivity, which is a hallucinated somesthetic experience, attributed to outside sources.*

If the German phenomenologists (Mayer-Gross, Kleist, Leonhard, Schneider, and others† represent an extension, and to some extent a narrowing, of Kraepelin's descriptive work, then Adolf Meyer, Harry Stack Sullivan, and psychoanalytic clinicians‡ can be said to have extended, and to some extent broadened, the work of Bleuler. Thus, ten years ago there were four relatively distinct conceptual approaches to the diagnosis of schizophrenia based on the contributions of Kraepelin and Bleuler, with phenomenological, psychodynamic, and interpersonal revisions. Kraepelin had emphasized the early onset and deterioration; Bleuler, the underlying dissociations; Schneider, the pragmatic, symptom-oriented diagnosis; and psychoanalytic workers emphasized interpersonal and intrapsychic psychopathology. In contrast to the other three, the psychoanalytic approach emphasized psychopathological manifestations within the spheres of interpersonal relatedness and intrapsychic con-

---

* It is an asset that Schneider's approach lends itself to systematic evaluation. However, Schneider's major proposals were extant for almost fifty years before clinical investigations were designed to test his findings. Mellor (38) first reported that first rank symptoms occurred in schizophrenic patients with sufficient frequency to have utility in the diagnostic process; his findings supported the clinical experience of others. Using patients from the Washington Center of the International Pilot Study of Schizophrenia and from the National Institute of Mental Health Clinical Center, we reported that first rank symptoms could be reliably observed, occurred frequently, and were highly discriminating diagnostically. However, these symptoms also were found in depressed and manic patients (16). If taken as absolute indicators of schizophrenia, first rank symptoms could be seriously misleading. Similar findings have since been reported from several sources (5,13,35,43, 52,68,70), although there remains disagreement as to interpretation. Taylor (64) stands alone in confirming Schneider's pathognomonic claim, but his work was based on nonsystematic clinical assessments in the old records of a Veterans Administration hospital.

† See references 22, 31, 33, 36, and 49.

‡ See references 2, 8, 17, 24, 39, 50, and 63.

flict. Attention to process was natural in this approach. Psychodynamic understanding was emphasized, and it was assumed that accurate diagnosis was neither difficult nor of primary importance.

Similarity between diagnoses guided by the Bleulerian and the Schneiderian models is only superficial. Dissociative thinking could be considered the first rank symptom of schizophrenia in the senses that it was considered specific or unique to schizophrenia, and that it was assumed to be omnipresent and reliably observed in schizophrenic patients. In point of fact, however, dissociative thinking is not easily operationalized as a clinical criterion, and little attention was paid to adequately defining the concept to permit reasonable reliability among clinicians. Also, patients manifesting other psychotic phenomena generally associated with schizophrenia are often simply assumed to have dissociative thinking—an assumption not established with clinical observation. To some extent, emphasis on loosening of the associative processes has pervaded all psychodiagnostic schools and may have had greater pedagogical than clinical significance. Virtually everyone was prepared to teach that dissociative thinking is critical to the psychopathology of schizophrenia, but few were prepared to restrict the use of the term "schizophrenia" to patients in whom dissociative thinking could be reliably judged to be present.

An important result of these conceptual trends is the uncertainty in communication between centers. Your cohort of fifty schizophrenic patients might or might not resemble my schizophrenic cohort. Since study reports rarely included adequate descriptions of psychopathology, a reader could not make his own judgment regarding another's cohort. This situation has been a particular problem in the United States, where Bleuler's concepts and psychodynamic formulation were emphasized; and it was clarified emphatically by the United States-United Kingdom study examining diagnostic approaches of New York and London psychiatrists (18,44). Using research diagnoses as a standard (specified symptom criteria more representative of British and European concepts), New York patients were "overdiagnosed" as schizophrenic. This conclusion received support from the fact that many New York "schizophrenics" were actually being treated with drugs appropriate for major affective disorders. Sandifer (8) doubts that this New York sample adequately represents the United States, but it was certainly established that important clinical differences are achieved with different conceptual approaches.

Recent Developments

During the 1950s and 1960s psychiatry was increasingly challenged to establish itself firmly on scientific principles. The field was the butt of comparisons with other areas of medicine where etiology, pathogenesis, and specific treatments were rapidly being discovered, aided by the advances in scientific technology related to biology and chemistry. By comparison, psychiatry seemed circular rather than cumulative in its pursuit of knowledge. Although psychiatric nosology was stable, the diagnostic process had serious problems in both reliability and validity. The field of therapeutics faced a profound disappointment when the exaggerated hopes engendered by the explanatory theories of psychodynamic psychiatry were not fulfilled. On the other hand, the development of other treatment techniques was painfully slow, and psychiatrists often felt trapped with a sense of embarrassment in their somatic therapies. We still do not understand the principles governing the therapeutic efficacy of convulsive therapies. The widespread application of psychosurgery to schizophrenic patients was ill conceived and tragic. And it was only in the second half of the twentieth century that effective and differential pharmacotherapy began its ascent to the forefront of psychiatric therapeutics. Even now these treatments are empirically derived rather than etiologically and pathogenetically based.*

This atmosphere of frustration and disappointment in our therapeutic capacities and scientific advances fostered a search for sophistication in clinical methodology that could provide the foundation for multiple scientific disciplines to explore the puzzles of schizophrenia. The development of statistical and mathematical concepts, the availability of computer technology, and a new interest in systematic and methodologically sound clinical investigations promised to provide progress in diagnostic research. Studies of diagnosis revealed that psychiatrists all too frequently failed to reach the same conclusion from the same set of clinical data. It became apparent that diagnostic reliability was inadequate, and that the reliable observation of commonplace psychopathological manifestations had to be established rather than assumed. Concepts such as autism and pathological ambivalence, although theoretically important and clinically meaningful, were found to mean different things to different clinicians. On the other hand, it was shown that certain important symptoms could be reliably assessed. Clinicians tended to agree when a patient experienced his movements as being controlled by an outside force. Large-scale studies were able to demonstrate that the diagnosis of schizophrenia was often made in the absence of an observed thinking disorder, and that patients could manifest certain psychopathology believed to be highly discriminating of schizophrenia, without simultaneously manifesting dissociative thinking. These and related findings that important phenomenological changes have occurred over time in several psychiatric syndromes (27) suggest that a new descriptive look at the psychoses is warranted.

The development and the application of structured interview techniques, such as the Present State Examination (67) and the Current and Past Psychopathology Scale (20), were clearly suited to advance

---

* It should be noted that even the impressive pharmacological advances are now being viewed with some disappointment in relation to their value for treating schizophrenia. Dopamine-blocking antipsychotic drugs have a therapeutic effect in nonschizophrenic conditions and hence are not specifically antischizophrenic. They have an incomplete therapeutic effect in schizophrenia, being most efficacious in reduction of certain symptoms and preventing psychotic relapse. Their merit in altering the social psychopathology and the deterioration of intrapsychic functioning is not established, and many patients remain in a deteriorated state regardless of treatment. The high incidence of tardive dyskinesia associated with the long-term use of these drugs has become a major factor in the risk-benefit ratio.

diagnostic work within a pragmatic framework. Development of clinical research instruments relevant to intrapsychic and interpersonal aspects of schizophrenia has been less impressive, and complex diagnostic concepts based on interpersonal and intrapsychic theory are consequently receiving less attention.

The various scientific and medical sociopolitical forces in the evolution of diagnostic practice can only be partially understood, but the result is the rapid acceleration of sound clinical investigations relevant to nosology, investigations clearly biased toward a pragmatic model of schizophrenia. The advances are noteworthy for their substantive and methodological contributions; but in reviewing this work, we will also note that certain shortcomings have been accentuated in the process.

Results of Recent Progress—The Schizophrenic Patient Viewed Through Currently Attractive Diagnostic Systems

The result of the preceding developments has been the proliferation of a number of diagnostic systems in which the criteria are specified and, in some instances, operationalized. In many parts of Europe there has been a trend (e.g., the adoption in the *British Glossary of Mental Disorders* [26] of a Schneiderian approach) toward using a limited number of highly discriminating symptoms of schizophrenia as criteria for its diagnosis. The development of a computerized diagnostic system (44,55,67,70) provided an opportunity for patients to be diagnosed by precise rules, with 100 percent reliability; that is, one can know precisely how judgments are to be made, and if identical data are passed through the system multiple times, the same classification will always be designated. In the United States a group of workers at the Washington University in St. Louis undertook a series of diagnostic studies. The results of many years of work were summarized in a report and have become widely known as the "Feighner criteria" (21). The criteria relevant to schizophrenia are shown in table 8–1. The emphasis is on a few discriminating symptoms, but a duration of symptomatology criteria is provided to preclude acute psychotic conditions from being diagnosed as schizophrenia.

The work of the Washington University group led to the Research Diagnostic Criteria developed by Spitzer et al. (56, pp. 1–34). These criteria are specified in table 8–2 and provide a means of enhancing reliability and definition of schizophrenia. They have become popular with research investigators and provide some comparability of method for defining study populations. These criteria have been more widely used than the theoretically derived and somewhat more cumbersome approach of the New Haven Schizophrenia Index (3). This latter scale is based on concepts of schizophrenia that emphasize the primacy of the thinking disorder (table 8–3); as such, it appears to define schizophrenia as

TABLE 8-1

Diagnostic Criteria for Schizophrenia According to Feighner et al.

For a diagnosis of schizophrenia, A through C are required.

A. Both of the following are necessary: (1) A chronic illness with at least six months of symptoms prior to the index evaluation without return to the premorbid level of psychosocial adjustment. (2) Absence of a period of depressive or manic symptoms sufficient to qualify for affective disorder or probable affective disorder.

B. The patient must have at least one of the following: (1) Delusions or hallucinations without significant perplexity or disorientation associated with them. (2) Verbal production that makes communication difficult because of a lack of logical or understandable organization. (In the presence of muteness the diagnostic decision must be deferred.)

C. At least three of the following manifestations must be present for a diagnosis of "definite" schizophrenia, and two for a diagnosis of "probable" schizophrenia: (1) Single. (2) Poor pre-morbid social adjustment or work history. (3) Family history of schizophrenia. (4) Absence of alcoholism or drug abuse within one year of onset of psychosis. (5) Onset of illness prior to age forty.

Source: From J. Feighner et al., "Diagnostic Criteria for Use in Psychiatric Research," *Archives of General Psychiatry* (1972) 26: 57-63; Copyright 1972, American Medical Association.

understood by many American psychiatrists, but provides a broader definition of the syndrome than do the Research Diagnostic Criteria.

By far the most ambitious project undertaken relevant to nosology in psychiatry is the International Pilot Study of Schizophrenia (IPSS) (70,71). This study, sponsored by the World Health Organization, the National Institute of Mental Health, and participating centers, involved investigators from Geneva and the nine nations collaborating in it. The very questions this study addressed reflected the methodological developments of the 1960s. The first of these questions was whether it was possible to undertake similar clinical assessment of psychotic patients with different clinicians in diverse cultures. Second, if patients were identified as schizophrenic in all these cultures, could one describe important similarities and differences? Third, could data so collected cast light on diagnostic and prognostic issues relevant to schizophrenia?

This nine-nation investigation was able to demonstrate that a sound clinical instrument (the Present State Examination) could be applied by many clinicians of varying backgrounds to the systematic assessment of psychiatric patients. In the application of this evaluation technique, encouraging reliability was obtained in assessing a large number of symptoms and signs of psychopathology. The reliability within each center was, of course, greater than the reliability between centers. Also, reliability in evaluating elicited symptomatology was generally more adequate than the reliability in evaluating observed behavior or signs of psychopathology. In a separate study we were able to show that cross-sectional symptom data elicited in a research interview compared favorably with that obtained in a lengthy clinical diagnostic evaluation including multiple informants. However, the research interview was too brief

TABLE 8-2
Research Diagnostic Criteria for Schizophrenia

There are many different approaches to the diagnosis of schizophrenia. The approach taken here avoids limiting the diagnosis to cases with a chronic or deteriorating course. It includes subjects who would not be considered schizophrenic by many, particularly those subtyped as "acute." However, the criteria are designed to screen out subjects frequently given clinical diagnoses such as: borderline schizophrenia, brief hysterical or situational psychoses, and paranoid states. Subjects with a full depressive or manic syndrome which overlaps active psychotic symptoms are excluded and are diagnosed as either schizo-affective disorder, major depressive disorder, or manic disorder. If the symptoms in A occur only during periods of alcohol or drug use or of withdrawal from them, the diagnosis should be unspecified functional psychosis.

A through C are required for the period of illness being considered.

A. During an active phase of the illness (may or may not now be present) at least two of the following are required for definite and one for probable:

1. Thought broadcasting, insertion, or withdrawal.
2. Delusions of being controlled (or influenced), other bizarre delusions, or multiple delusions.
3. Somatic, grandiose, religious, nihilistic, or other delusions without persecutory or jealous content lasting at least one week.
4. Delusions of any type if accompanied by hallucinations of any type for at least one week.
5. Auditory hallucinations in which either a voice keeps up a running commentary on the subject's behaviors or thoughts as they occur, or two or more voices converse with each other.
6. Nonaffective verbal hallucinations spoken to the subject.
7. Hallucinations of any type throughout the day for several days or intermittently for at least one month.
8. Definite instances of marked formal thought disorder accompanied by either blunted or inappropriate affect, delusions or hallucinations of any type, or grossly disorganized behavior.

B. Signs of the illness have lasted at least two weeks from the onset of a noticeable change in the subject's usual condition (current signs of the illness may not now meet criterion A and may be residual symptoms only, such as extreme social withdrawal, blunted or inappropriate affect, mild formal thought disorder, or unusual thoughts or perceptual experiences).

C. At no time during the *active* period (delusions, hallucinations, marked formal thought disorder, bizarre behavior, etc.) of illness being considered did the subject meet the full criteria for either probable or definite manic or depressive syndrome to such a degree that it was a *prominent* part of the illness.

Source: From R. L. Spitzer, J. Endicott, and E. Robins, *Research Diagnostic Criteria*, Biometric Research Unit, New York State Department of Mental Hygiene, New York State Psychiatric Institute (1975).

TABLE 8-3
Criteria for Schizophrenia According to the
New Haven Schizophrenia Index

Checklist of Symptoms

A. *Symptoms*

1. (a) Delusions (not specified or other than depressive)
   (b) Hallucinations (auditory)
   (c) Hallucinations (visual)
   (d) Hallucinations (other)

2. Crazy thinking and/or thought disorder
   Any of the following:
   (a) Bizarre thinking
   (b) Autism or grossly unrealistic private thoughts
   (c) Looseness of association, illogical thinking, overinclusion
   (d) Blocking
   (e) Concreteness
   (f) Derealization
   (g) Depersonalization

3. Inappropriate affect

4. Confusion

5. Paranoid ideation (self-referential thinking, suspiciousness)

6. Catatonic behavior
   (a) Excitement
   (b) Stupor
   (c) Waxy flexibility
   (d) Negativism
   (e) Mutism
   (f) Echolalia
   (g) Stereotyped motor activity

Scoring System

To be considered part of the schizophrenic group, the patient *must* score on either Item 1 or Items 2a, 2b, 2c and must attain a total score of at least 4 points.

He can achieve a maximum of 4 points on Item 1: 2 for the presence of delusions, 2 for hallucinations.

On Item 2—he can score 2 points for *any* symptoms *a* through *c*, 1 point for either or both symptoms *d* through *e*, and 1 point each for *f* and *g*. He can thus score a maximum of 5 points on Item 2.

Items 3, 4, 5 and 6 each receive 1 point.

Note: Where the 4th point necessary for inclusion in the sample is provided by 2d or 2e, these symptoms are not scored.

Note: Reprinted with permission of the publisher from B. Astrachan et al., "A Checklist for the Diagnosis of Schizophrenia," *British Journal of Psychiatry* (1972) 121: 530.

an observation period to be adequately informative as to observed signs of psychopathology (12).

Concerning the second question, schizophrenic subjects were identified in all nine nations, and there was a very considerable degree of similarity in patients so identified across cultures. There was also important similarity in the symptomatology most helpful in differentiating schizophrenic from nonschizophrenic patients across all nine centers.

Concerning the third question, many diagnostic issues can be addressed by the International Pilot Study of Schizophrenia. The interested reader is again referred to the main reports, since only selected studies will be described in this chapter (70,71,72). A large-scale multicenter study like the IPSS has several critical methodological advantages for such investigations. In the first place, it is possible to generate large patient cohorts, thus providing a numerical advantage over smaller studies. In the second place, when patients and clinicians from diverse backgrounds participate, the chance is minimized of local patient artifact or clinician bias appearing as an important clinical variable. For example, if a study is conducted in a center subscribing to the belief that a diagnosis of schizophrenia must be based upon the presence of a manifest thought disorder, then it will not be surprising to find that the thinking disturbance is a hallmark of schizophrenia if only patients diagnosed in that center are studied. However, should other participating centers not accept the criterion of the necessary presence of a thought disorder, then that criterion will appear less critical in the multicenter study. Hence, diagnostic studies emanating from one center have a greater likelihood of representing the particular diagnostic biases held therein or of reflecting other local artifacts that may affect the patient's clinical presentation but not be central to pathogenesis.

In work carried out in the Washington Field Research Center, we evaluated the implications for several diagnostic systems, using the data from the nine nations of the IPSS. We accepted the principle that findings shared across cultures be given more weight than findings specific to one or two centers. Likewise, reliable observations were preferred to less reliable data. Selecting statistical approaches suitable to these principles, we analyzed clinical data from the nine nations of the IPSS to determine which signs and symptoms best discriminated between schizophrenic and nonschizophrenic patients.* There were a large number of signs and symptoms which were differentially associated with the diagnosis of schizophrenia. Table 8–4 lists many of the variables that have a statistically significant association with a diagnosis of schizophrenia in contrast to a nonschizophrenic diagnosis (15).

The aim of this inquiry was not simply to determine what aspects of the manifest psychopathology were valuable in differential diagnosis, but also to apply an adaptation of Schneider's conceptual model to a nosological investigation. We adopted Kurt Schneider's diagnostic model

---

* Details of the IPSS methods are provided in the references cited. Briefly stated, some 1,202 patients were studied in nine centers. Patients were evaluated with the Present State Examination and other instruments shortly after admission to a facility. Patients were included if they showed suggestive signs of psychosis (excluding suspected organic psychosyndromes), were ages fifteen to forty-four, and were still considered in acute, subacute, and subchronic phases of illness (i.e., long-established chronicity was an exclusion criteria). In this patient cohort, 811 received a clinical diagnosis of schizophrenia.

TABLE 8-4

Signs and Symptoms Significantly Associated with the
Schizophrenic Diagnosis in Contrast to a Nonschizophrenic Diagnosis

Preoccupied, inattentive	Preoccupied with delusions	Poor rapport
Irrelevance	Lack of affective reaction to disordered thoughts	Denies delusions though present
Perseveration	Audible thoughts	Made feelings and/or made impulses
Vagueness	Thought alienation	Made volition
Blocking	Thought broadcast	Widespread delusions
Incomprehensibility	Thought withdrawal	Bizarre delusions
Unreliable information	Thought insertion	Nihilistic delusions
Idiosyncratic speech	Apophany	Nonverbal auditory hallucinations
Incoherent speech	Remoteness from reality	Voices speak to patient
Neologisms	Stereotypic	Hallucinated voices speak sentences
Abnormal explanations	Apathy	Hallucinated voices sound human
Persecutory ideas	Restricted affect	Voices argue or discuss patient
Suspiciousness	Poor insight	Voices comment on patient's activity

Source: From W. T. Carpenter, Jr., J. S. Strauss, and J. J. Bartko, "Use of Signs and Symptoms for the Identification of Schizophrenic Patients: A Report of the International Pilot Study of Schizophrenia," *Schizophrenia Bulletin* (1974) 11: 37-49.

in the sense of trying to determine empirically which variables, taken together in a diagnostic system, could most effectively discriminate schizophrenic from nonschizophrenic patients. Like Schneider, our emphasis was on reliable, frequently occurring signs and symptoms that would have the simple pragmatic advantage of being highly discriminating of schizophrenia. The result was a reduction of data initially arrayed as 443 overlapping variables into twelve readily understandable and reliably applied signs and symptoms of particular relevance to discriminating schizophrenia patients from psychiatric patients with other diagnoses often confused with schizophrenia (14).

Table 8–5 lists these twelve symptoms, the seventeen Present State Examination inquiries on which judgments are based, and the interrater reliability coefficients.

Table 8–6 shows the results of using these twelve discriminating signs and symptoms to make diagnostic assessments. The nine signs and symptoms most prevalent in schizophrenia are scored one point each when present, and the three symptoms (waking early, depressed facies, and elation) more prevalent in the nonschizophrenic group are scored one point each when absent. Thus, the most stringent criteria for a diagnosis of schizophrenia would be a total score of twelve based on the presence of nine symptoms and the absence of the other three. A meaningful split between schizophrenic and nonschizophrenic diagnosis results when one determines that five to seven points are present. At

TABLE 8-5

Twelve Signs and Symptoms Found Most Effective in Differentiating Schizophrenia from Other Psychoses.

Items from the Present State Examination (PSE) corresponding to the twelve signs or symptoms are listed together with their intraclass correlation coefficient reflecting interrater reliability.

Sign or Symptom	PSE Observations or Question	r*
Restricted affect	Blank, expressionless face.	.62
	Very little or no emotion shown when delusion or normal material is discussed which would usually bring out emotion.	.63
Poor insight	Overall rating of insight.	.85
Thoughts aloud	Do you feel your thoughts are being broadcast, transmitted, so that everyone knows what you are thinking?	.95
	Do you ever seem to hear your thoughts spoken aloud? (Almost as if someone standing nearby could hear them?)	.74
Waking early (−)	Have you been waking earlier in the morning and remaining awake? (Rate positive if 1 to 3 hours earlier than usual.)	.83
Poor rapport	Did the interviewer find it possible to establish good rapport with patient during interview?	.86
	Other difficulties in rapport.	.75
Depressed facies (−)	Facial expression sad, depressed.	.73
Elation (−)	Elated, joyous mood.	.67
Widespread delusions	How widespread are patient's delusions? How many areas in patient's life are interpreted delusionally?	.74
Incoherent speech	Free and spontaneous flow of incoherent speech.	.74
Unreliable information	Was the information obtained in this interview credible or not?	.73
Bizarre delusions	Are the delusions comprehensible?	.69
Nihilistic delusions	Do you feel that your body is decaying, rotting?	None†
	Do you feel that some part of your body is missing, for example, head, brain, or arms?	.70
	Do you ever have the feeling that you do not exist at all, that you are dead, dissolved?	.71

NOTE: Reprinted with permission of the publisher from W. T. Carpenter, Jr., J. S. Strauss, and J. J. Bartko, "A Flexible System for the Identification of Schizophrenia: A Report from the W. H. O. International Pilot Study of Schizophrenia," *Science* (1973) 182: 1276.

*Interrelater reliability coefficient.

†Insufficient variability to determine intraclass r.

TABLE 8-6

Results of Applying Twelve-Symptom Differential Diagnostic System to Cohort A Patients and Results of Replication Attempt with a Different Patient Group (Cohort B)

Values are percentages of patients diagnosed schizophrenic or nonschizophrenic who are included when a particular number of points are required. The number of patients in each category in cohort A and cohort B is given in parentheses. A χ^2 comparison of the results with the initial study group (cohort A) and the replication group (cohort B) revealed no significant differences.

	Number of Points		
Percentage of Patients	**5 or More**	**6 or More**	**7 or More**
Cohort A			
Schizophrenic			
patients (N = 407)	80	66	44
Nonschizophrenic			
patients (N = 152)	13	4	1
Cohort B			
Schizophrenic			
patients (N = 404)	81	63	39
Nonschizophrenic			
patients (N = 156)	22	6	1

Source: Adopted from Carpenter, Strauss, and Bartko, "A Flexible System for the Identification of Schizophrenia," *Science* (1973) 182:1275-78, and Carpenter, Strauss, and Bartko, "Use of Signs and Symptoms for the Identification of Schizophrenic Patients," *Schizophrenia Bulletin* (1974) 11:37-49.

these levels of stringency, a substantial number of diagnosed schizophrenic patients would be judged schizophrenic, as well as a small portion of the nonschizophrenic population. For example, if a patient with six or more points is automatically assigned to a schizophrenic category, one might expect that two-thirds of the patients receiving an ordinary clinical diagnosis of schizophrenia would fit into the schizophrenia group. On the other hand, only about 5 percent of presumed nonschizophrenic psychotic patients would be assigned to the schizophrenic group. The latter point is important in that it provides a rough estimate of the "false-positive" schizophrenic diagnoses. This serves to guide the clinician in using the system and also reminds us that no conclusions regarding the diagnosis of schizophrenia are above question and the possibility of error.

There are several advantages in using a flexible system such as the one described. In the first place, the signs and symptoms are operationalized, and reliable judgments regarding their presence or their absence can be made. Second, the system is simple enough to encourage widespread use among clinicians and researchers alike. Third, since one can choose the stringency level to meet specific needs, the system can be applied in a busy emergency room as effectively as by a research team attempting to select a small number of patients for a special project. In any case the system *must be used* as only one diagnostic tool within the overall context of a clinical psychiatric evaluation. In this way silly errors can be avoided, and the overall diagnostic impression can be based on the maximum amount of information supplemented by a special diagnostic procedure. For example, in such a clinical context a patient with an manic-depressive history would not be judged schizo-phrenic simply by scoring six points in this system. This approach should be used rather to ascertain degree of confidence in diagnosis and to provide a description of criteria, not to replace a comprehensive clinical diagnostic method.

A replication study has supported the usefulness of this system, and a variety of manipulations provide reason to think that these particular twelve signs and symptoms are more advantageous in the diagnostic process than are other similar groupings of symptoms. Weighting these variables does not appreciably enhance their value. Decreasing the number below twelve seriously hinders the effectiveness of the system, while the addition of other highly discriminating variables adds little to its diagnostic discriminating power (15).

Subtypes of Schizophrenia

We have already mentioned that most workers assume that schizophre-nia refers to several illnesses. While these cannot yet be definitively specified, the acute versus chronic and the process versus reactive dichotomies seem promising. However, a backward glance suggests an-other possibility. Was Kraepelin misled by the similarities between three distinct illnesses when he proposed one nosological class for hebephrenia, paranoia, and catatonia? Do the traditional subtypes in fact represent separate diagnostic entities?

This question appears to be answered in the negative. In the first place, many attempts to validate these subtypes as psychobiologically distinct have had minimal success. Clinical observations are even more to the point. We often observe psychopathological manifestations of several subtypes simultaneously in a patient. Also, many patients mani-fest psychopathology suggestive of one subtype in one episode and of another subtype in a subsequent episode. These simple observations make it unlikely that any of the traditional subtypes of schizophrenia represent specific illnesses readily distinguishable from one another, and that the search for etiologically relevant subgroups of schizophrenics should be guided by these subtypes.

These conclusions are reinforced by findings in the IPSS (70). In a substudy of the IPSS, we constructed descriptive profiles of patients who had received one of six subtypes—simple, hebephrenic, catatonic, paranoid, acute, and schizo-affective (11). The profiles were based on twenty-seven psychopathological dimensions (see table 8–7). The di-

TABLE 8-7
Twenty-seven Psychopathological
Dimensions Used for Profile Comparison

The number of Present State Examination items
included in each dimension and the reliability
of each dimension is listed.

Dimension	Intraclass Reliability	Number of PSE* Items
1. Depression	.92	24
2. Anxiety	.84	4
3. Restlessness	.74	6
4. Psychomotor retardation	.89	9
5. Hypomania/mania	.92	15
6. Somatic concerns	.78	1
7. Belligerence	.86	4
8. Obsessions	.78	3
9. Unkempt appearance	.59	1
10. Disorientation	.33	1
11. Lack of insight	.79	1
12. Depersonalization-derealization	.86	10
13. Paranoid delusions	.93	17
14. Grandiose delusions	.93	5
15. Delusions of passivity	.92	7
16. Depressive and nihilistic delusions	.85	7
17. Other delusions	.84	3
18. Visual hallucinations	.82	1
19. Auditory hallucinations	.92	3
20. Other hallucinations	.92	5
21. Bizarre behavior	.81	16
22. Withdrawal	.82	6
23. Incomprehensibility	.83	16
24. Nonsocial speech	.76	4
25. Restricted affect	.65	3
26. Labile affect	.59	1
27. Incongruous affect	.66	1

Note: Reprinted with permission of the publisher from W. T. Carpenter, Jr., et al., "Another View of Schizophrenia Subtypes: A Report from the International Pilot Study of Schizophrenia," *Archives of General Psychiatry* (1976) 33:511; Copyright 1976, American Medical Association.

*Present State Examination.

mensions were scored according to symptomatology elicited with the Present State Examination. The results (based on visual comparison and profile analysis of variance) were surprising. A broad range of presenting symptomatology failed to differentiate four of the subtypes from each other. Only the simple and catatonic subtyped were distinguished in the expected manner (see figures 8–1 and 8–2). Flagrant psychotic manifestations were minimal in the simple subtype, while several behavioral dimensions showed greater disturbance in the catatonic subtype.

In another study of schizophrenia subtypes Tsuang and Winokur (66,69) examined a chronic-patient population and found evidence for a clinical differential between hebephrenic and paranoid schizophrenia. The latter were characterized symptomatically by a preoccupation with well-organized delusions or hallucinations. The hebephrenic patients had disorganized thought, affect changes, and behavior symptoms (i.e., hebephrenic or catatonic movements or bizarre behavior).

Inconsistent findings among these studies may be accounted for by chronicity. In the early phases of psychosis there is little evidence for distinct traditional clinical subtypes. In more chronic populations relatively distinct symptom patterns may emerge. The acute paranoid patient usually has multiple psychotic symptoms, but the chronic paranoid may be preoccupied with his delusional system to the exclusion of other symptom manifestations. Traditional subtypes may not be the best key to etiologically distinct subgroups of schizophrenia, but there may be descriptive validity for some subtypes in the chronic stages of the illness. There will always be disagreement between "lumpers" and "splitters," but these observations lend some support to those (e.g., Schneider) who speak of schizophrenia as a whole without much interest in traditional subtypes.

A more recently defined subtype, schizo-affective schizophrenia, is being intensively scrutinized with respect to nosology. Evidence has been brought forward suggesting that this subtype is an atypical affective disorder, or that it stands as a syndrome distinct from both schizophrenia and affective disorders (25,26). From this latter point of view, one considers schizo-affective illness in relationship to the reactive psychoses and the episodic-behavior dyscontrol syndromes.*

Using the same descriptive profile approach, we were able to ask the subtype question anew—this time based on the principles of cluster analysis (6,23,53,61). Using a mathematical approach to search for naturally occurring subgroups free of a priori assumptions, we were able to define four new subgroups of schizophrenia (11). The largest cluster is similar in profile to the hebephrenic, acute, schizo-affective, and paranoid subtypes shown in figures 8–1 and 8–2. However, three smaller subgroups are remarkably different in terms of descriptive profiles. While similar to the "typical" subgroup in certain features distinguishing of schizophrenia (e.g., characteristic hallucinations), they are distinctive in other features. Figures 8–3, 8–4, 8–5, and 8–6 show the profiles and list the discriminating features. These subgroups may be useful subdivisions of schizophrenia (e.g., relevant to etiology, treat-

---

* See references 37, 40, 41, 42, and 45.

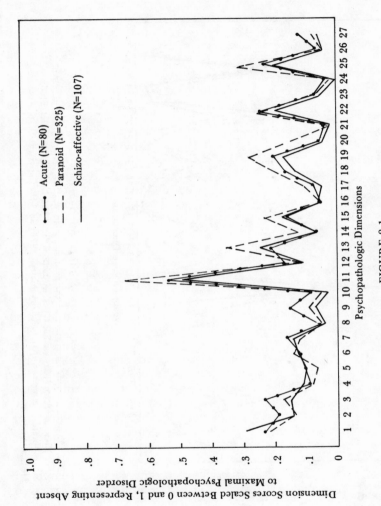

FIGURE 8-1

Profiles of Three Schizophrenic Subtypes

NOTE: Reprinted with permission of the publisher from W.T. Carpenter, Jr., et al., "Another View of Schizophrenic Subtypes: A Report from the International Pilot Study of Schizophrenia," *Archives of General Psychiatry* (1976) 33:512; Copyright 1976, American Medical Association.

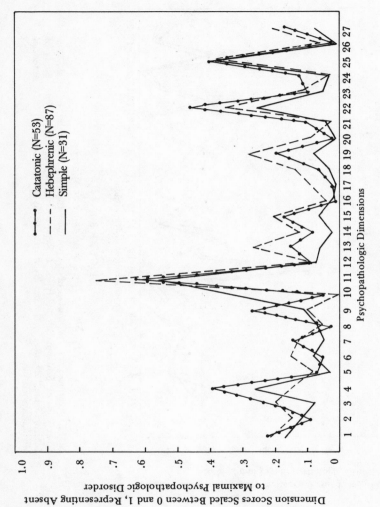

FIGURE 8-2

Profiles of Three Schizophrenic Subtypes

NOTE: Reprinted with permission of the publisher from W.T. Carpenter, Jr., et al., "Another View of Schizophrenia Subtypes: A Report from the International Pilot Study of Schizophrenia," *Archives of General Psychiatry* (1976) 33:510; Copyright 1976, American Medical Association.

ment, or course), but replication and validation studies have yet to be carried out.

Critique of Recent Developments

There has been considerable progress in our clinical science during this past decade, some of which is illustrated in the preceding review. In the first place, the scientific methodology currently being applied in descriptive psychiatry is far superior to that extant ten years ago. In the second place, we have learned a great deal during the past ten years about the manifest psychopathology of schizophrenia, the extent to which it is diagnostically discriminating, and the feasibility of using certain criteria for identifying patients as schizophrenic.

There are significant shortcomings in the present emphasis on practical models of diagnosis. In the first place, we have not achieved a satisfactory degree of homogeneity among patients diagnosed as schizophrenic. Regardless of the emphasis on stringent diagnostic criteria, we continue to identify a wide range of psychopathologies and, presumably, multiple illness syndromes under the rubric "schizophrenia." When the homogeneity is increased by using criteria other than cross-sectional psychopathology (e.g., chronicity requirements), diagnosed patients naturally become more similar, at least on that dimension.

A second problem arising from emphasis on practical diagnostic systems is that only modest understanding of the patients or their therapeutic requirements is provided by the diagnosis. Such diagnosis may be particularly well suited for guiding choice of a somatic treatment, but it gives precious little information about other requirements and therapeutics. This is especially noteworthy in schizophrenia where the intrapsychic and interpersonal manifestations of the disorders are most critical to the long-term course.

Finally, many pragmatic approaches to diagnosis raise a problem by excluding many patients from a diagnosis of schizophrenia. This is a mirror image of the earlier problem of overinclusion. Some of the diagnostic systems described earlier fail to identify as schizophrenic many patients who receive that clinical diagnosis. To the extent that such exclusion eliminates "erroneous" diagnoses, its advantage is clear. On the other hand, the narrow diagnosis of schizophrenia has been associated with a tendency to use nonstringent, ill-defined criteria for affective disorders (including heavy reliance on weak discriminating psychopathological manifestations, such as depression and psychomotor agitation or retardation). It would appear that we are in the process of creating a problem within the affective disorders similar to that previously created in schizophrenia, with broad definition and ill-defined criteria for inclusion. This has no scientific advantage, although it may be less harmful to patients, since the social stigma and the therapeutic risks involved are not so severe in the affective disorders as in the schizophrenias.

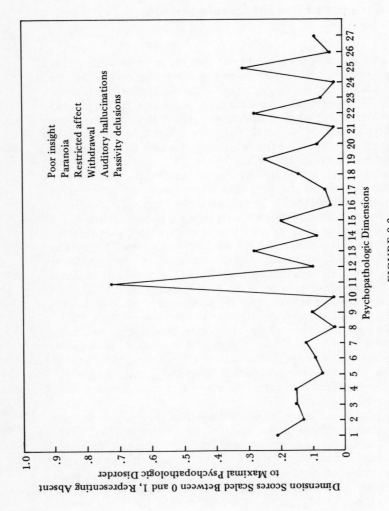

FIGURE 8-3

Profile of Cluster 1 (N = 439, Typical Schizophrenia, with Characteristic Symptoms Listed

NOTE: Reprinted with permission of the publisher from W.T. Carpenter, Jr., et al., "Another View of Schizophrenia Subtypes: A Report from the International Pilot Study of Schizophrenia," *Archives of General Psychiatry* (1976) 33:512; Copyright 1976, American Medical Association.

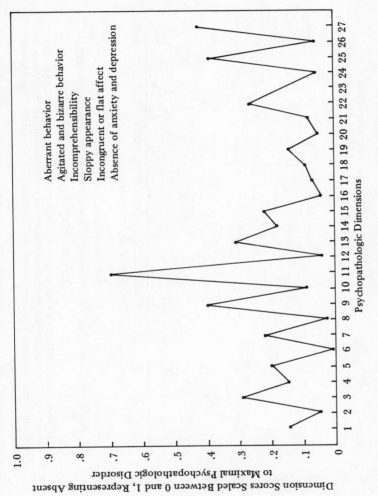

FIGURE 8-4

Profile of Cluster 2 (n = 25), Flagrant Schizophrenia, with Distinguishing Symptoms Listed.

NOTE: Reprinted with permission of the publisher from W.T. Carpenter, Jr., et al., "Another View of Schizophrenia: A Report from the International Pilot Study of Schizophrenia," *Archives of General Psychiatry* (1976) 33:513; Copyright 1976, American Medical Association.

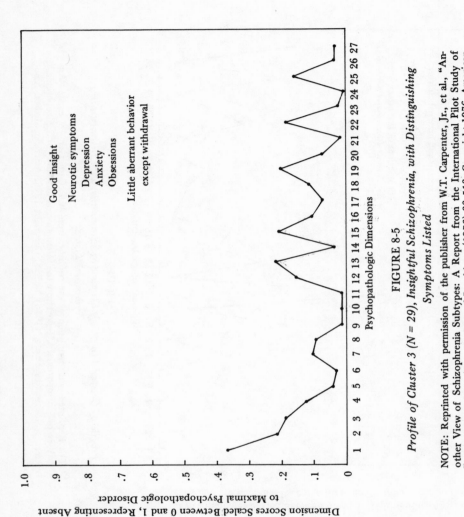

Good insight

Neurotic symptoms
  Depression
  Anxiety
  Obsessions

Little aberrant behavior
  except withdrawal

FIGURE 8-5

*Profile of Cluster 3 (N = 29), Insightful Schizophrenia, with Distinguishing
Symptoms Listed*

NOTE: Reprinted with permission of the publisher from W.T. Carpenter, Jr., et al., "Another View of Schizophrenia Subtypes: A Report from the International Pilot Study of Schizophrenia," *Archives of General Psychiatry* (1976) 33:513; Copyright 1976, American Medical Association.

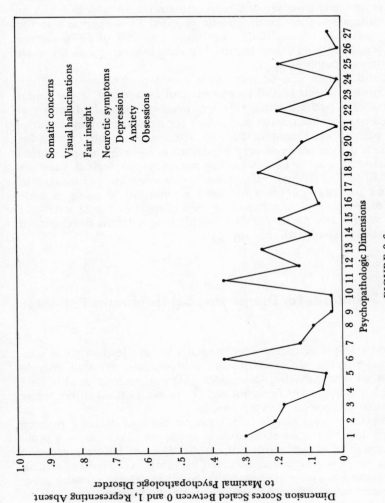

Somatic concerns
Visual hallucinations
Fair insight
Neurotic symptoms
Depression
Anxiety
Obsessions

Psychopathologic Dimensions

Dimension Scores Scaled Between 0 and 1, Representing Absent to Maximal Psychopathologic Disorder

FIGURE 8-6

Profile of Cluster 4 (N = 80), Hypochondriacal Schizophrenia, with Distinguishing Symptoms Listed.

NOTE: Reprinted with permission of the publisher from W.T. Carpenter, Jr., et al., "Another View of Schizophrenia Subtypes: A Report from the International Pilot Study of Schizophrenia," *Archives of General Psychiatry* (1976) 33:514; Copyright 1976, American Medical Association.

One method of coping with the inadequacies of current diagnostic procedures in describing individual patients receiving increasing attention is the multiaxial diagnostic approach (60,62). This approach can be conceptualized in one of two ways. Once may view diagnosis as being based on the simultaneous evaluation of a number of axes. For example, symptomatology, social competence, intellectual achievement, and family history of psychiatric disorder can represent four axes which would be applied simultaneously in the diagnostic process. This approach to the multiaxial system is conceptually appealing, but difficult. We cannot presently escape the need to use identifying symptomatology as the basis for diagnosing schizophrenia.

A multiaxial system can be used as a two-step phenomenon. First, highly discriminating signs and symptoms can be applied to the initial classification of a patient. Once this has been accomplished, one can specify other axes which require evaluation for a more complete description of the patient. For example, if a patient meets symptom criteria for schizophrenia, it then becomes very important to describe his premorbid social adjustment, course of illness, the role of psychological stressors in onset of illness, etc. Such an approach can combine advantages of practical and process systems. One has the potential of using reliable criteria for diagnosis and simultaneously describing functional attributes of patients within any particular diagnostic class. Current development of DSM-III is consistent with this approach.

Current Standards for Diagnosing Schizophrenic Patients

A review and critique of recent developments should lead to some conclusions regarding the process of classifying patients. We will provide this, but not without advising the reader that conclusions in this field are not simple extensions of facts but rather are synthesized through any author's particular biases and experiences.

The diagnostic process should be the pivotal point of decision making in psychiatry. It is no longer acceptable to approach diagnosis as a process to go through in order to rule out certain diseases before beginning one's favorite therapy—or, as has occurred too often in the case of schizophrenia, to assume a stance of therapeutic nihilism. The diagnostic process should result in an intimate familiarity with the patient's experiences and functioning, including those areas not directly reflecting psychopathology. While a cross-sectional approach to symptomatology is productive regarding positive (or expressive) symptoms, it is inadequate as a base for behavioral observation (12,67) and is not suitable for evaluating data relevant to the more subtle personality disturbances so critical to the schizophrenic process. We wish this did not require comment, but all too often diagnosis and major treatment are determined before any real attempt is made: (1) to establish rapport (and through that process assess a patient's interpersonal functioning); (2) to engage the patient in an attempt to understand the immediate setting and social consequences of his decompensation (and by this means assess capacity for insight and treatment collaboration); (3) to permit patient and family to observe the clinician's interest in and benign attitude toward psychopathology (and thus encourage a more complete disclosure of the psychotic experience).

Other illustrations could be given, but the point is simple. The current proclivity to rapid diagnosis based on a few conspicuous psychopathological manifestations, followed (or often preceded) by narrowly and automatically derived treatment decisions, is a reprehensible model for the psychiatric clinician and serves the needs of none but the third-party payer. A symptom orientation has pragmatic advantages in classification, but it is sorely abused when our clinical concepts and maneuvers become preoccupied only with flagrant psychotic symptoms. We have reached the low point where virtually every patient receiving a diagnosis of schizophrenia is urged to accept long-term drug therapy as the only rational basis for treatment (since antipsychotic drugs modify symptom status) while ignoring the intrapsychic and interpersonal consequences of the illness so familiar to Kraepelin and Bleuler (7,32).

The diagnostic process, then, should involve the clinician in a longitudinal, interpersonal process with the patient and serve as a basis for a wide range of relevant clinical judgments. It is critical that the clinician assess symptomatic status and past history, which provide the basis for conceptualizing the illness within the framework of nosology relying in important degree on highly discriminating symptom features. The same diagnostic approach can yield the critical information on which prognosis and treatment should be based. The clinical relationship established in the process may be therapeutic in itself, and it certainly is the *optimal* base from which to engage the patient in the myriad considerations essential to a comprehensive therapeutic approach.

The desired data for diagnosis include a wealth of clinical data such as patterns of illness in biologic relatives, symptomatic expression in present and past illness episodes, subtle attributes of relating during and between episodes, premorbid physical and psychosocial development, psychosocial and organic precipitating factors, patterns of pharmacological responsivity, and many others. The clinician will weigh various features differently case by case, but within a nosological structure which can guide diagnostic decisions sufficiently to permit reliability and descriptive validity to the diagnosis of schizophrenia, on the one hand, and full clinical richness to the diagnostic process, on the other.

BIBLIOGRAPHY

1. Achte, K. A. 1967. *On Prognosis and Rehabilitation in Schizophrenia and Paranoid Psychoses* (Copenhagen: Munksgaard).

2. Arieti, S. 1974. An overview of schizophrenia from a predominantly psychological approach. *American Journal of Psychiatry* 131(3):241–49.

3. Astrachan, B. M.; Harrow, M.; Adler, D.; Brauer, B.; Schwartz, A.; Schwartz, C.; and Tucker, G. 1972. A checklist for the diagnosis of schizophrenia. *British Journal of Psychiatry* 121:529–39.

4. Astrup, C., and Noreik, K. 1966. *Functional psychoses. Diagnostic and prognostic models* (Springfield, Ill.: Charles C Thomas).

5. Baron, J. 1977. Linkage between an X-chromosome marker (Deutan color blindness) and bipolar affective illness. *Archives of General Psychiatry* 34:721–25.

6. Bartko, J. J.; Strauss, J. S.; and Carpenter, W. T. 1971. An evaluation of taxometric techniques for psychiatric data. *Bulletin of the Classification Society* 2:2–28.

7. Bleuler, E. 1950. *Dementia praecox, or the group of schizophrenias*, trans. J. Zinkin (New York: International Universities Press).

8. Burnham, D. L.; Gladstone, A. I.; and Gibson, R. W. 1969. *Schizophrenia and the need-fear dilemma* (New York: International Universities Press).

9. Cancro, R. 1975. Genetic considerations in the etiology and prevention of schizophrenia. In *Schizophrenia: Biological and psychological perspectives*, ed. G. Usdin (New York: Brunner/Mazel).

10. Carlsson, A. 1975. Pharmacological approach to schizophrenia. In *Schizophrenia: Biological and psychological perspectives*, ed. G. Usdin (New York: Brunner/Mazel).

11. Carpenter, W. T., Jr.; Bartko, J. J.; Langsner, C. A.; and Strauss, J. S. 1976. Another view of schizophrenia subtypes: A report from the international pilot study of schizophrenia. *Archives of General Psychiatry* 33:508–16.

12. Carpenter, W. T., Jr.; Sacks, M. H.; Strauss, J. S.; Bartko, J. J.; and Rayner, J. N. 1976. Evaluating signs and symptoms: Comparison of structured interview and clinical approaches. *British Journal of Psychiatry* 128:397–403.

13. Carpenter, W. T., Jr.; and Strauss, J. S. 1974. Cross-cultural evaluation of Schneider's first rank symptoms of schizophrenia: A report from the international pilot study of schizophrenia. *American Journal of Psychiatry* 131:682–87.

14. Carpenter, W. T., Jr.; Strauss, J. S.; and Bartko, J. J. 1973. A flexible system for the identification of schizophrenia: A report from the international pilot study of schizophrenia. *Science* 182:1275–78.

15. Carpenter, W. T., Jr.; Strauss, J. S.; and Bartko, J. J. 1974. Use of signs and symptoms for the identification of schizophrenic patients: A report of the international pilot study of schizophrenia. *Schizophrenia Bulletin* 11:37–49.

16. Carpenter, W. T., Jr.; Strauss, J. S.; and Muleh, S. 1973. Are there pathognomonic symptoms in schizophrenia? An empiric investigation of Kurt Schneider's first rank symptoms. *Archives of General Psychiatry* 28:847–52.

17. Chodoff, P., and Carpenter, W. T. 1975. Psychogenic theories of schizophrenia. In *Schizophrenia: Biological and psychological perspectives*, ed. G. Usdin (New York: Brunner/Mazel).

18. Cooper, J. E.; Kendell, R. E.; Gurland, B. J.; Sharpe, L.; Copeland, J. R. M.; and Simon, R. J. 1972. *Psychiatric diagnosis in New York and London: A comparative study of mental hospital admissions*. Maudsley Monograph 20 (London: Oxford University Press).

19. Davis, J. M. 1975. Overview maintenance therapy in psychiatry: I. Schizophrenia. *American Journal of Psychiatry* 132:1237–45.

20. Endicott, J., and Spitzer, R. L. 1972. Current and past psychopathology scale (CAPPS): A rationale, reliability and validity. *Archives of General Psychiatry* 27:678–82.

21. Feighner, J.; Robins, E.; Guze, S.; Woodruff, R., Jr.; Winokur, G.; and Munoz, R. 1972. Diagnostic criteria for use in psychiatric research. *Archives of General Psychiatry* 26:57–63.

22. Fish, F. J. 1962. *Schizophrenia* (Bristol: John Wright).

23. Fleiss, J. E., and Zubin, J. 1969. On the methods and theory of clustering. *Multivariate Behavior Research* 4:235–50.

24. Fromm-Reichman, F. 1950. *Principles of Intensive Psychotherapy* (Chicago: University of Chicago Press).

25. Garver, D. L.; Ericksen, S.; Casper, R.; Pandey, G. N.; and Davis, J. M. 1977. Schizophrenia of good prognosis: A distinct syndrome? *Proceedings of the American Psychiatric Association* 130: 22–23.

26. Great Britain General Registrar's Office Sub-Committee on Classification of Mental Diseases. 1968. *A glossary of mental disorders based on the international statistical classification of diseases: Injuries and causes of death*, 8th ed. (London: Her Majesty's Stationery Office).

27. Grinker, R. 1973. Changing styles in psychotic and borderline states. *American Journal of Psychiatry* 130:151:52.

28. Heston, L. L. 1973. Genes and schizophrenia. In *Biological psychiatry*, ed. J. Mendels (New York: John Wiley).

29. Jaspers, K. 1963. *General psychopathology*, trans. J. Hoenig and M. W. Hamilton (Chicago: University of Chicago Press).

30. Klein, D. F., and Davis, J. M. 1969. *Diagnosis and drug treatment of psychiatric disorders* (Baltimore: Williams & Wilkins).

31. Kleist, K. 1960. Schizophrenic symptoms and cerebral pathology. *Journal of Mental Science* 106:246–55.

32. Kraepelin, E. 1919. *Dementia praecox*, trans. R. M. Barclay (Edinburgh: E. S. Livingston).

33. Leonhard, K. 1959. *Aufteilung der Endogen Psychosen* [Classification of the endogenous psychoses], 2nd ed. (Berlin: Akademie Verlag).

34. McCabe, M. S.; Fowler, R. C.; Cadoret, R. J.; and Winokur, G. 1971. Familial differences in schizophrenics with good and poor prognosis. *Psychological Medicine* 1:326–32.

35. McCabe, M. S., and Strömgren, E. 1975. Reactive psychoses: A family study. *Archives of General Psychiatry* 32:447–54.

36. Mayer-Gross, W.; Slater, E.; and Roth, M. 1969. *Clinical psychiatry* (Baltimore: Williams & Wilkins).

37. Meduna, L. J. 1950. *Oneirophrenia, "The confused state"* (Urbana: University of Illinois Press).

38. Mellor, C. S. 1970. First rank symptoms of schizophrenia: I. The frequency in schizophrenics on admission to hospital; II. Differences between individual first rank symptoms. *British Journal of Psychiatry* 117:15–23.

39. Meyer, A. 1951. Collected Papers of Adolf Meyer, ed. E. E. Winters. (Baltimore: Johns Hopkins University Press), vols. 1–3.

40. Mitsuda, H., ed. 1967. *Clinical genetics in psychiatry: Problems in nosological classification* (Tokyo: Igaku Shoin).

41. Monroe, R. R. 1970. *Episodic behavioral disorders: A psychodynamic and neurophysiologic analysis* (Cambridge: Harvard University Press).

42. Monroe, R. R. 1974. Episodic behavioral disorders: An unclassified syndrome. In *American Handbook of Psychiatry*, vol. III, eds. S. Arieti and E. B. Brody (New York: Basic Books), pp. 237–254.

43. Newmark, C. S.; Falk, R.; Johns, N.; Boren, R.; and Forehand, R. 1976. Comparing traditional clinical procedures with four systems to diagnose schizophrenia. *Journal of Abnormal Psychology* 85:66–72.

44. Professional Staff of the United States-United Kingdom Cross-National Project. 1974. The diagnosis and psychopathology of schizophrenia in New York and London. *Schizophrenia Bulletin* 11:80–102.

45. Rodin, E. A., et al. 1957. Relationship between certain forms of psychomotor epilepsy and schizophrenia. *Archives of Neurology and Psychiatry* 77:449.

46. Rosenthal, D. 1971. Two adoption studies of heredity in the schizophrenic disorders. In *The origin of schizophrenia*, eds. M. Bleuler and A. J. Bern (Switzerland: Hans Huber), pp. 23–34.

47. Rosenthal, D., and Kety, S. S., 1968. *The transmission of schizophrenia* (Oxford: Pergamon Press).

48. Sandifer, M. G., Jr. 1972. Psychiatric diagnosis: Cross-national research findings. *Proceedings of the Royal Society of Medicine* 65:497–500.

49. Schneider, K. 1959. *Clinical psychopathology*, trans. Hamilton, M. (New York: Grune & Stratton).

50. Searles, H. F. 1965. *Collected Papers on Schizophrenia and Related Subjects* (New York: International Universities Press).

51. Shader, R. I., 1975. *Manual of psychiatric therapeutics* (Waltham, Mass.: Little, Brown).

52. Silverstein, M. L., and Harrow, M. 1977. First rank symptoms in the post-acute schizophrenic: A follow-up study. Presented at the 130th Annual Meeting of the American Psychiatric Association, Toronto, Canada, May 2–6, 1977.

53. Sokal, R. R., and Sneath, P. H. A. 1973. *Numerical taxonomy* (San Francisco: W. H. Freeman).

54. Spitzer, R. L., and Endicott, J. 1968. Diagno: A computer program for psychiatric diagnosis utilizing the differential diagnostic procedure. *Archives of General Psychiatry* 18:746–56.

55. Spitzer, R. L., and Endicott, J. 1969. Diagno II: Further developments in a computer program for psychiatric diagnosis. *American Journal of Psychiatry* 125:12–21.

56. Spitzer, R. L.; Endicott, J.; and Robins, E. 1975. *Research Diagnostic Criteria*. Biometric Research Unit, New York State Department of Mental Hygiene, New York State Psychiatric Institute.

57. Stephens, J. H. 1978. Long-term prognosis and follow-up in schizophrenia. *Schizophrenia Bulletin*, in press.

58. Stephens, J. H., and Astrup, C. 1963. Prognosis in "process" and "non-process" schizophrenia. *American Journal of Psychiatry* 119:945–53.

59. Stierlin, H. 1967. Bleuler's concept of schizophrenia: A confusing heritage. *American Journal of Psychiatry* 123:996–1001.

60. Strauss, J. 1974. *Towards a Multiaxial System for the Diagnosis of Adult Psychopathology*. Presented at the 127th Annual Meeting of the American Psychiatric Association, Detroit, Michigan.

61. Strauss, J. S.; Bartko, J. J.; and Carpenter, W. T. 1973. The use of clustering techniques for the classification of psychiatric patients. *British Journal of Psychiatry* 122:531–40.

62. Strauss, J. S., and Carpenter, W. T., Jr. 1975. The key clinical dimensions of the functional psychoses. In *Biology of the major psychoses: A comparative analysis*, ed. D. X. Freedman (New York: Raven Press), pp. 9–18.

63. Sullivan, H. S. 1953. *The interpersonal theory of psychiatry* (New York: W. W. Norton).

64. Taylor, M. 1972. Schneiderian first-rank symptoms and clinical prognostic features in schizophrenia. *Archives of General Psychiatry* 26:64–67.

65. Tsuang, M. T. 1975. Schizophrenia and affective disorders: One illness or many? In *Biology of the major psychoses: A comparative analysis*, ed. D. X. Freedman (New York: Raven Press), pp. 27–39.

66. Tsuang, M. T., and Winokur, G. 1974. Criteria for subtyping schizophrenia: Clinical differentiation of hebephrenic and paranoid schizophrenia. *Archives of General Psychiatry* 31:43–47.

67. Wing, J. K.; Cooper, J. E.; and Sartorius, N. 1974. *The measurement and classification of psychiatric symptoms* (London: Cambridge University Press).

68. Wing, J. K., and Nixon, J. 1975. Discriminating symptoms in schizophrenia: A report from the International Pilot Study of Schizophrenia. *Archives of General Psychiatry* 30:853–59.

69. Winokur, G. 1975. Paranoid vs. hebephrenic schizophrenia: Clinical and familial (genetic) heterogeneity. *Psychopharmacological Communications* 1(6):567–77.

70. World Health Organization. 1973. *International Pilot Study of Schizophrenia*, vol. 1 (Geneva: World Health Organization Press).

71. World Health Organization. 1975. *Schizophrenia: A multi-nation study* (Geneva: World Health Organization Press).

72. World Health Organization. *International Pilot Study of Schizophrenia*, vol. 2 (Geneva: World Health Organization Press), forthcoming.

Chapter 9

PHARMACOLOGICAL TREATMENT
OF SCHIZOPHRENIA

Morris A. Lipton, Ph.D., M.D. and Gordon B. Burnett, M.D.

Introduction

Acceptable forms of treatment for the psychoses have always reflected the conflict between different concepts about the nature and the cause of mental illness. Even in ancient times the question of whether madness was a disease of the brain or a disease of the soul was reflected in different cultures by the choice of trephination or the administration of folk potions versus the use of exorcism and prayer. As religious influence waned and medicine became "scientific," the nature of infectious and deficiency diseases was discovered, and treatments successful for these types of illness were quickly applied to the treatment of insanity. Although most psychotic patients failed to respond to such treatments, the early demonstration that even the psychological symptoms of general paresis responded to fever or malaria therapy led to the hope that other types of mental illness might also respond to other types of anti-infectious treatment. A residue of this thinking exists in the recent suggestion that schizophrenia might be caused by a slow virus (101), or that it might be associated with human leucocyte antigenic types (HL-A) (64). When the mental as well as the physical symptoms of pellagra were found to respond to treatment with niacin, there were attempts to treat other forms of mental illness nutritionally. A residue of this concept remains with those psychiatrists who treat schizophrenia with megavitamins (54,56). It is also reflected in the recent suggestion that schizophrenia might be associated with prostaglandin deficiency which might be treatable with arachadonic acid, an essential fatty acid required for prostaglandin synthesis (62). In the early thirties, when schizophrenia and epilepsy were thought to be incompatible, convulsive therapy with electric shock or with metrazol was extensively used. When schizophrenia was considered to be a product of central nervous system hyperactivity, insulin coma was introduced (95). When a toxin adrenal steroid was postulated, some adrenalectomies were done (7). When defective neural circuitry was suspected, lobotomies were extensively performed (85). As experience was gained with these treatments, it became clear that results were erratic and frequently useless and had seriously damaging side effects. Concurrent laboratory investigations failed to demonstrate anatomical or chemical lesions in schizophrenia.

The failure to find demonstrable biological pathology and the many manifest failures with somatic treatments led to a resurgence of the idea of psychogenesis, a concept which implies that schizophrenia is a disease of the mind, not of the brain. The "moral treatment" of Pinel early in the nineteenth century implied a mental condition which was curable in an appropriate psychological and social environment. To this was added the insights of psycholanalysis in the twentieth century. Pinel's strong recommendation for case studies and the scientific assessment of treatments of large numbers of patients was ignored (77). In this country, under the influence of Sullivan, Fromm-Reichman, Rosen, Searles, Will, Arieti, and others, intensive psychotherapy based upon psychoanalytic principles became the most highly valued form of treatment. It was considered to be aimed at the etiological psychogenic causes and hence as capable of producing a true cure by correction of these factors. Somatic treatments were downgraded to be merely symptomatic and were employed along with sedatives for the large number of institutionalized patients who had few resources and who were considered incurable. There is little doubt that up until a quarter of a century ago psychogenesis as a cause and psychotherapy as a treatment dominated psychiatric thinking in this country. Even though Kallmann, Slater, and others were accumulating evidence that there was a genetic component to schizophrenia and that this implied some sort of biological diathesis, their work was largely ignored by practitioners, perhaps because they felt it not clinically relevant, since they considered the action of genes unalterable and the best possible treatment one that enhanced the adaptive function of the individual through insight psychotherapy.

The picture changed rather dramatically around 1950. As a result of some curiously convoluted thinking, lithium salts were tested and reported to be effective in the treatment of psychotic excitement by Cade in 1949 (21). Cade reasoned that manic-depressive illness was analogous to thyrotoxicosis-myxedema, and that mania was a "state of intoxication [caused] by a normal product of the body circulating in excess." This product he believed could be found in urine, and after tests on animals he concluded that it might be urea. Although he could demonstrate no differences in urea or uric acid in the urine of manics versus controls, he administered uric acid salts which he believed would "protect" against urea effects. He found that lithium urates reduced the startle reaction of guinea pigs. Wisely he used lithium carbonate also and found that it produced similar effects. After trying it on his own person and demonstrating no serious toxic effects, he conducted a limited trial of lithium carbonate on manic patients, with impressive therapeutic results (22). At least a decade passed before the value of this treatment was generally accepted for mania. Rauwolfia serpentina (snakeroot), used for centuries in India for the treatment of madness and many other ills, became the subject of pharmaceutical investigation in 1931, but it was not until 1954 that its active principle, reserpine, was chemically isolated and identified. A year later Kline and Stanley reported that it was useful in the treatment of psychotic states (71).

Phenothiazines had been synthesized for the dye industry in the late nineteenth century. Many derivatives of the phenothiazine nucleus were made, and some were found to be antihistaminic or antiparasitic. Amine derivatives of the phenothiazines were found to have strong effects on the central nervous system (CNS). These were investigated initially for the treatment of surgical shock and later as potentiators of anesthetics. In 1950 chlorpromazine was synthesized and found to be devoid of anti-histaminic effects, while possessing powerful CNS effects manifested as diminished fear without major changes in consciousness. It was first used in surgery, but very quickly thereafter it was subjected to clinical trial on psychiatric patients. Delay, Daniker, and Harl in 1952 in France (38) and Lehman and Hanrahan in 1954 in Canada (76) reported its effectiveness in psychomotor excitement and manic states. Chlorproma-zine was then widely introduced into clinical psychiatry as an aid to management of seriously disturbed and disruptive inpatients. Over a period of years it was found to be effective not only in the management of excited psychotic states but also in the reduction of aggressiveness, delusions, hallucinations, and, indeed, of all of the primary and sec-ondary symptoms of schizophrenia. These conclusions about the broad-ranging therapeutic effects of the phenothiazines were reached only after multihospital trials with large numbers of patients and with objec-tive measures of behavioral changes (26,86).

It is noteworthy that the major antipsychotic drugs were discovered accidentally or at best serendipitously. They were not found as a result of a search for a treatment based upon the correction of a hypothesized etiological defect; but rather they were the product of a search for sub-stances that would diminish psychotic symptoms. They were derived pragmatically, and their results were demonstrated empirically. Rather than being derived from theory, they have altered theory. Their intro-duction and broad use has resulted in what has been called a "psychiatric revolution" (43).

To some extent this term is appropriate because their discovery acti-vated the long-standing conflict between those who saw schizophrenia as a manifestation of mental phenomena generated by early psychological trauma or deprivation which required psychological correction, and those who believed that there was clearly a defect in the functioning of the brain which could be corrected by drugs. At one extreme, drugs were seen as stupefying chemical straitjackets to be avoided because they interfered with the necessary work of psychotherapy. At the other ex-treme, correction of the brain defect by available drugs (or better ones still to come) was seen as sufficient. The absurdity of both extremities can perhaps best be illustrated by an analogy. Suppose, for example, that there were some children with learning difficulties from some un-diagnosed cause. Conscientious teachers would make special efforts and would develop innovative curricula with special instruments to correct these difficulties. Suppose, now, that an ophthalmologist appeared and discovered that the children had correctible visual defects. One would hardly expect the teachers to oppose the children's use of eyeglasses because the glasses interfered with the arduously developed special teaching devices. Nor would one expect the ophthalmologist to claim that the students no longer needed to go to school. Yet something like this happened for more than a decade in the treatment of schizophrenia between those who opposed drugs as interfering with psychotherapy and those who felt drugs to be sufficient, making psychological treatment unnecessary.

Two other major consequences followed the introduction of psychotropic drugs on a large scale. The first was the deinstitutionalization of patients, which led to a dramatic decrease in the population of state hospital patients from a maximum of more than 500,000 in 1950 to less than 200,000 today (15). Simultaneously the length of hospitalization for a psychotic episode dropped by about two-thirds. The establishment of community mental health centers was, as Leighton points out (77), a resurgence of Pinel's principles of moral treatment, modernized by the addition of drugs and psychodynamic insights. These centers have not been generally successful for the psychotic. Rates of readmission of discharged hospitalized patients have more than doubled in state hospitals, and many discharged patients live in nursing homes or primitive boarding houses (15). It is a point of debate whether the fault is with the limited power of the drugs or the failure to recognize the degree to which schizophrenics need social support systems. Probably both are true. Whatever the reasons, the fact remains that when measured by standards of employment, family life, education, or integration into the community, the plight of the chronic schizophrenic is far from happy. Lehmann (74) points out that the number of fully and permanently recovered patients has not increased significantly since the introduction of psychotropic drugs. On the other hand, about 60 percent of the patients hospitalized for an acute episode of schizophrenia will be socially recovered five years later; 30 percent will show some psychopathology but will live in the community; only 10 percent will be rehospitalized.

The other consequence of the revolution was that a generation of clinician scientists was born. Basic scientific investigations of the mode of action of the neuroleptic drugs have led to great advances in our knowledge of brain structure and function. Clinicians working with methods developed by basic scientists have obtained new insights into the pathobiology of schizophrenia and the other major mental illnesses. Measurement of baseline pathological behavior and of change associated with the introduction of drugs on other-dependent variables has become feasible, and much which was long considered unmeasurable is now measured routinely. Diagnosis has become more precise, and its utility in the interest of selectively effective treatment is very clear.

Studies of the mode of antipsychotic drug action have involved many investigators in this country and abroad and have resulted in a voluminous literature which is reviewed elsewhere in this volume. Carlsson (23) has put it very succinctly: "These various drugs have only one basic pharmacological property in common, namely an inhibitory action on dopaminergic neurotransmission. In fact not only do all antipsychotic agents appear to possess antidopaminergic activity but it also appears that all antidopaminergic agents possess antipsychotic activity." From

FIGURE 9-1
Structural Relationships of Some Phenothiazines

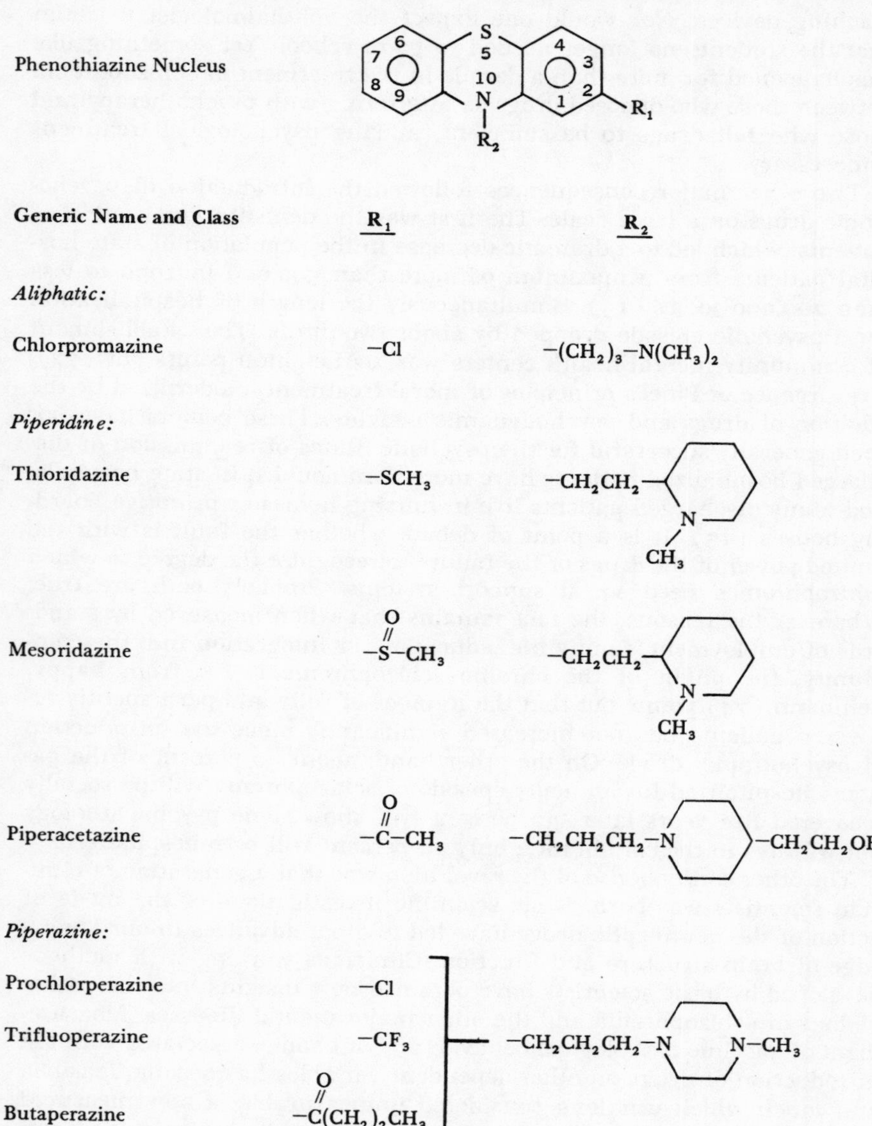

Phenothiazine Nucleus

Generic Name and Class	R_1	R_2
Aliphatic:		
Chlorpromazine	$-Cl$	$-(CH_2)_3-N(CH_3)_2$
Piperidine:		
Thioridazine	$-SCH_3$	
Mesoridazine	$-\overset{\overset{\textstyle O}{\|\|}}{S}-CH_3$	
Piperacetazine	$-\overset{\overset{\textstyle O}{\|\|}}{C}-CH_3$	$-CH_2CH_2CH_2-N$ $-CH_2CH_2OH$
Piperazine:		
Prochlorperazine	$-Cl$	
Trifluoperazine	$-CF_3$	$-CH_2CH_2CH_2-N$ $N-CH_3$
Butaperazine	$-\overset{\overset{\textstyle O}{\|\|}}{C}(CH_2)_2CH_3$	
Perphenazine	$-CL$	
Fluphenazine	$-CF_3$	$-CH_2CH_2CH_2-N$ $N-CH_2CH_2OH$

this conclusion there has been derived the dopamine hypothesis of schizophrenia, which rests almost entirely on the studies of the mode of action of antipsychotic drugs on the brains and behavior of animals.

Current Drugs

For many years only the phenothiazines were used in the United States. Now butyrophenones, thioxanthenes, dihydroindoles, dibenzoxazepines, dibenzodiazepines, diphenylbutylpiperidines, and others are available in most countries.

The structural relationships of the phenothiazines in most common use are summarized in figure 9–1. These drugs are all variants of the phenothiazine structure and are divided into aliphatic, piperidine, and piperazine families.

The aliphatic and piperidine drugs are usually regarded as low-potency phenothiazines. The piperazines are usually high-potency drugs. Piperacetazine shares the same structure with the piperazines but is classed technically within the piperidines.

FIGURE 9-2

Structural Relationships of the Thioxanthenes

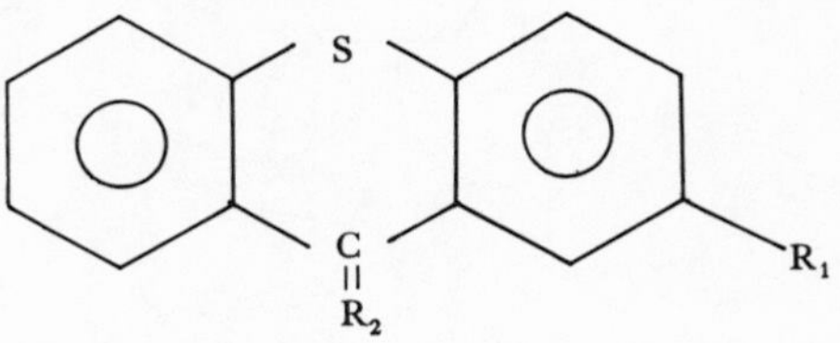

	R_1	R_2
Chloroprothixene	Cl	$CHCH_2CH_2-N(CH_3)_2$
Thiothixene	$-SO_2 \cdot N(CH_3)_2$	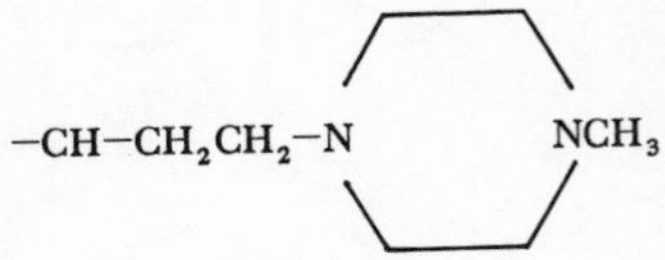 $-CH-CH_2CH_2-N \qquad NCH_3$

The thioxanthenes are structurally related to the phenothiazines and differ only in having a carbon atom at the C_{10} position instead of a nitrogen atom (see figure 9–2). Substitutions at the R_1 and R_2 positions are made to give roughly analogous compounds to the substituted phenothiazine families.

Chlorprothixine is a structural homologue of chlorpromazine with some loss in potency. Thiothixene, which is also less potent than its phenothiazine homologue thioproperazine, is still more potent than the aliphatic and piperidine phenothiazines. Only its cis-isomer has pronounced therapeutic efficacy.

The butyrophenones, represented usually by haloperidol, are variations of the phenylpiperidinol configuration and resemble the diphenylbutyl piperidines, of which pimozide and penfluridol are family members (see figure 9–3). In fact, the butyrophenones and diphenylbutylpiperidines share the piperidine ring with the nitrogen atom always in the same position regardless of other substitutions.

FIGURE 9-3

Structural Relationships of the Butyrophenones and Diphenylbutylpiperidines

Butyrophenone

Haloperidol

Diphenylbutylpiperidine

Pimozide

Penfluridol

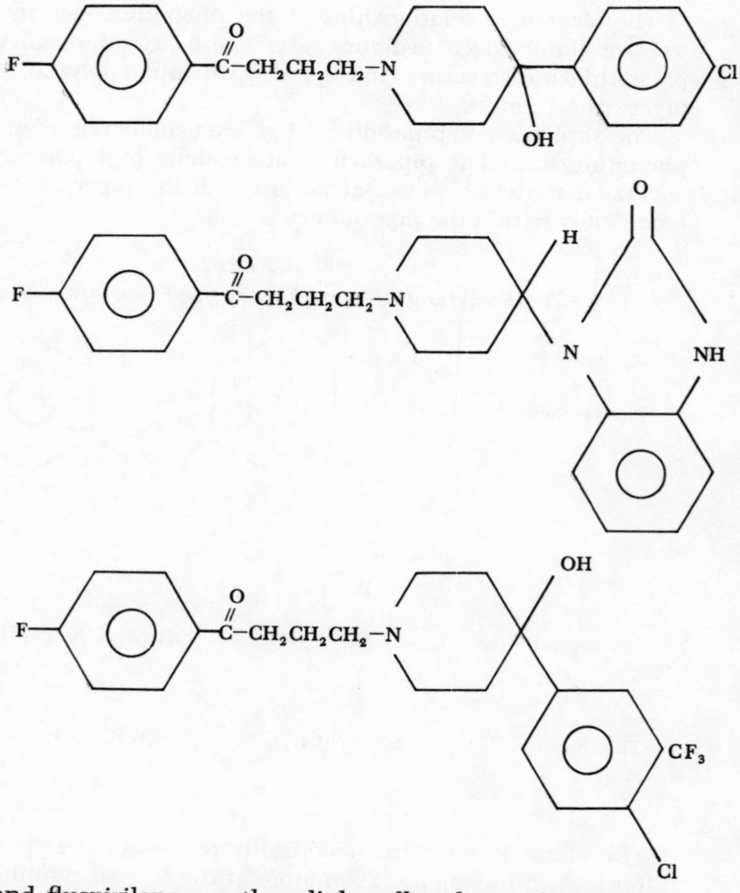

Penfluridol and fluspirilene, another diphenylbutylpiperidine, are remarkably similar to pimozide in structure and are slowly metabolized, by virtue possibly of their fluoride moieties. They are as a result possessed of long activity following oral dosages and would complement the range of potent parenteral, long-acting drugs such as fluphenazine and its thioxanthene analogue, flupenthixol.

Clozapine, a drug which has been widely studied in Europe, has, it is claimed, moderate potency and possesses few extrapyramidal side effects (EPS). Its introduction into the United States has been delayed because of reports of agranulocytosis, and it may yet be withdrawn worldwide (51).

FIGURE 9-4

*Representative Structures of a Dihydroindole
and a Dibenzoxazepine*

Dihydroindole

Molindone

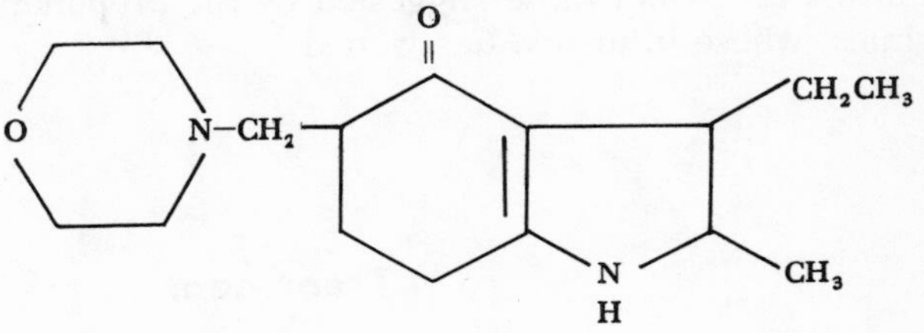

Dibenzoxazepine

Loxapine

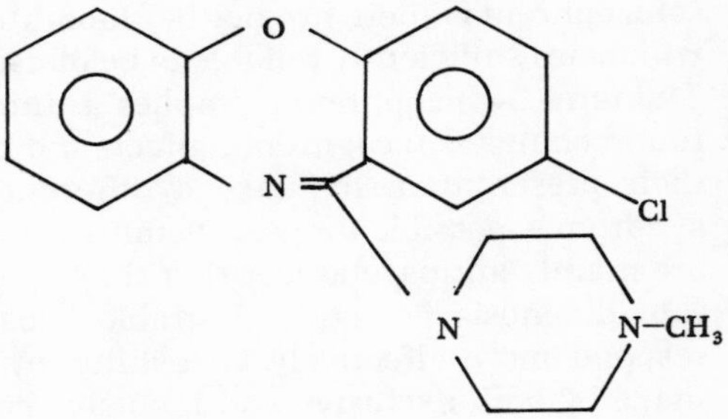

The most recent introductions to the United States, molindone and loxapine, a tricyclic compound (see figure 9–4), may not represent any clear advance over other neuroleptics (35), although it remains to be seen whether newer members of their drug classes will offer advantages in pharmacotherapy. Molindone has the reputation of being the only neuroleptic which does not induce obesity in clinical practice, and it does not block the antihypertensive effect of guanethidine (35).

Although particular target symptoms are claimed by drug manufacturers to be uniquely responsive to their particular brand of antischizophrenic medication, it does not seem likely at this time that important therapeutic differences exist among neuroleptics (28,35,61). Therefore, the choice of neuroleptic tends in the minds of most clinicians to be arbitrary and comes down usually to a choice between sedative antipsychotic drugs, such as chlorpromazine, or the piperidines, thioridazine and mesoridazine, for excited hyperactive patients. Frequently employed for

[handwritten annotations in top margin: stelazine, haldol, prolixin, trilafon]

the early treatment of the retarded apathetic patient are the piperazines, such as trifluoperazine, fluphenazine, and perphenazine, or the newer drugs, such as butyrophenones, dibenzoxazepines, or indolic agents. The European literature suggests that pimozide may be very useful in treating this second group. When in doubt as to choice of a specific drug, a good rule to follow is to use that drug with which one is familiar and which has been shown to be effective in the past. In the early stages of treatment it is better to exceed the minimum required dose than to remain below it. Table 9–1 shows the relative doses and the relative potencies of neuroleptics in common use today. Most of these dosages are higher than one would have used in the past, but they are much more conservative than those suggested by the proponents of megadosage regimes, whose influence has waned.

Treatment

THE NEED FOR DIAGNOSIS

Proper treatment depends upon accurate diagnosis. In the case of the schizophrenias there are neither laboratory tests nor biological indicators which are sufficiently reliable to be of assistance in making the diagnosis. The term "schizophrenia" implies a uniquely human condition with profound changes in cognition, affect, and behavior sufficiently consistent in their presentation to make a differentiation from other psychological syndromes possible in most instances. Even though the neuroleptic drugs are mainly antipsychotic rather than specifically antischizophrenic, accurate diagnosis is highly desirable because other psychotic states may respond more effectively to a different treatment. Diagnosis should be made by both exclusive and inclusive criteria. Organicity, metabolic disorders, criteria for probable or definite manic or depressive syndromes, and drug-induced psychotic states should be ruled out by history and examination. Inclusive criteria should include:

1. At least two of the following: Disorders of the form of thought which makes communication difficult because of a lack of logical or understandable connection; delusions of control; other bizarre delusions or multiple delusions; thought broadcasting, insertion, or withdrawal (alienation of thought); delusions other than persecutory, or jealousy lasting at least one week; delusions of any type or accompanied by hallucinations of any type for at least one week; auditory hallucinations forming a running commentary on the subject's behavior or thoughts as they occur, or two or more voices conversing with each other (dichotomous thinking); nonaffective verbal hallucinations spoken to the subject; hallucinations throughout the day for several days or intermittently for at least one month; obvious catatonic motor behavior;
2. A period of illness of at least two weeks (44,97).
   Diagnosis should never be made retrospectively solely on the basis of a patient's satisfactory response to previous neuroleptic and possible nonspecific treatment (63).

TABLE 9-1
Generic Names, U.S. Trade Names, and
Conversion Factors for Doses of Neuroleptic
Drugs in Relation to Chlorpromazine

Generic Name	U.S. Trade Name	Conversion Factor*
Phenothiazines		
Aliphatic		
Chlorpromazine	Thorazine	1:1
Promazine	Sparine	1:1
Triflupromazine	Vesprin	1:4
Piperazine		
Acetophenazine	Tindal	1:5
Butaperazine	Repoise	1:10
Carphenazine	Proketazine	1:4
Fluphenazine	Permitil	1:50
	Prolixin	
Perphenazine	Trilafon	1:10
Prochlorperazine	Compazine	1:6
Thiopropazine	Dartal	1:10
Trifluoperazine	Stelazine	1:20
Piperidine		
Mesoridazine	Serentil	1:2
Piperacetazine	Quide	1:10
Thioridazine	Mellaril	1:1
Butyrophenones		
Haloperidol	Haldol	1:50
Thioxanthenes		
Chlorprothixene	Taractan	1:1
Thiothixene	Navane	1:25
Dihydroindolone		
Molindone	Moban	1:5

*Estimated dosage ration in relation to chlorpromazine. For example: a dose of 10 mg of perphenazine (Trilafon) is equivalent to 100 mg of chlorpromazine (Thorazine), since it is 10 times as potent.

Note: Reprinted with permission of author and publisher from H. E. Lehmann, "Psychopharmacological Treatment of Schizophrenia," *Schizophrenia Bulletin* (1975) 13:30.

There is a tendency in the United States to diagnose schizophrenia more often than in Europe. This is because Americans tend to be over-inclusive in diagnosis; those who are not diagnosed as schizophrenic in Europe are diagnosed as having affective disorders (53). It should be borne in mind that severe anxiety reactions with dissociative features may resemble some aspects of schizophrenia and will usually respond rapidly to the benzodiazepines or other anxiolytic agents. The severe depressions, including those with psychotic features, will often respond better to antidepressant medication than to neuroleptics. Psychotic manic states respond to phenothiazines but are generally better main-tained on lithium. In any case where a diagnosis of schizo-affective schizophrenia, excited type, is suspected, a trial of lithium carbonate should be attempted, because some patients may be responsive, and long-term neuroleptic regimes with their attendant risk of tardive dyskinesia can be avoided (61).

Lehman (75) has noted that there are four principal indications for the use of neuroleptic drugs. These are: (1) symptomatic tranquilization of any pathological excitement, (2) treatment of acute psychotic dis-order, (3) treatment of chronic schizophrenic conditions, and (4) main-tenance treatment of schizophrenic patients in remission. The first condition is essentially that of emergency care.

TREATMENT OF PATHOLOGICAL EXCITEMENT

Although recent work has indicated that some psychotic patients, per-haps as many as 30 percent, will spontaneously remit within a few days in an appropriate milieu (25), the fact remains that severely excited patients are difficult to manage and are at risk to themselves and to others. The goal of treatment for such patients is the very limited one of excitement reduction. Thus, treatment with neuroleptics may be very brief, and hence side effects and complications from long, continued use are minor considerations. When a neuroleptic is administered appropri-ately in proper dosage, its calming effects will usually be noted within an hour or two. The usual doses are approximately 100 milligrams, in-tramuscularly, of chlorpromazine or an equivalent dose of another neu-roleptic. If it is given by mouth, about twice that amount is needed to achieve behavioral changes, which usually precede toxic symptoms. If this dosage is not adequate, the drug should be given again at about half the level of the initial dose, this dosage should be repeated thereafter until there is an adequate behavioral response. Treatment must be con-sidered as a medical emergency, and the physician or his team should be in continuous physical and also verbal contact until the emergency is over. Treatment should be continued until there is appropriate reduction of the pathological excitement; one should bear in mind that oral and intramuscular routes of drug administration are slower than intravenous ones, which cannot be used with neuroleptics. Thus, parenteral drugs can reasonably be expected to take effect within about twenty to thirty minutes. The oral drugs are remarkably safe, and the only serious ad-verse reaction is orthostatic hypotension, which is more pronounced with the drugs of lower relative potency. This autonomic response can be readily handled by having the patient lie down. Other acute side effects of neuroleptics include tachycardia, laryngospasm, and EPS reactions. It should always be borne in mind that neuroleptics potentiate CNS depressants, including narcotics and alcohol, and also act additively if they possess an anticholinergic profile with other anticholinergic agents. Large intramuscular doses of haloperidol (5 to 20 mg in a single dose and up to 100 mg orally per day) have been specifically recommended for excited assaultive patients. (103).

TREATMENT OF ACUTE SCHIZOPHRENIC DISORDERS

Treatment of symptomatic presentations other than in the emergency situation routinely consists of the prescription of 300 to 1,000 milligrams per day in divided doses of chlorpromazine or its equivalent. A dose of less than 300 to 400 milligrams per day is seldom used these days in the United States, and also it is probable that reliable therapeutic blood levels are not obtainable unless one is in a daily dose range of greater than 400 milligrams (36).

Routinely dosage tends to be equated with clinical improvement which may be delayed for two to three weeks with respect to arousal symptoms (e.g., psychomotor excitement, restlessness, irritability, and insomnia). Affective symptoms (anxiety, depression, and apathetic behaviors) tend to take longer and remit usually after two to five weeks of treatment. Symptoms related to perceptual and cognitive aspects of cerebration—such as delusional percepts, hallucinations, and formal thought disorders—usually take longer and may persist for six to eight weeks of treatment (75).

Most acute treatment failures appear to be due to the use of insufficient medication doses and to too rapid changes in medication (75). It is better, therefore, to exceed the minimal required dose than to remain below it. Also there are a few patients who appear to respond better to one drug than to another. As larger populations are studied, it may be possible in the future to identify more clearly such specific drug-patient responders.

So far as we know, there is no a priori way of determining who these patients are or to what degree they will respond. Therefore, at this time the rule of thumb seems to be that six to eight weeks of gradually increasing dosages of medication should be tried on the assumption that the patient takes the medicine and the absorption of medication occurs. Should the patient show continued behavioral impairment after such a time, and if compliance is not a problem, conversion to another neuroleptic should be considered. However, it is important to bear in mind that different patients respond to different doses, owing undoubtedly to wide variations in absorption, rates of metabolism, and excretion of neuroleptic drugs. In many studies a one-hundredfold variation of blood levels of chlorpromazine and a greater than thirtyfold variation for another phenothiazine, butaperazine, have been reported between different patients on the same dosages (36). Some people metabolize the drug so rapidly that they achieve very low blood levels unless they are given ultrahigh doses. Some slow metabolizers may achieve toxic brain levels on what would customarily be regarded as low-dosage regimens. Three groups of workers have reported good results in patients much of whose drug, it is suspected, is metabolized in the gut wall, and in whom parenteral administration has bypassed this source of clinical error (33,63,79). Therefore, it is important that at some point drug nonresponders be given parenteral medications before the doctor concludes that they have derived little benefit from their particular medication.

The use of estimations of blood levels of neuroleptics has not yet found its way into clinical practice, as most neuroleptics, with the exception of haloperidol, produce many active metabolites; although some may also be therapeutically inactive—for example, inactive (ring) sulfoxides. With those neuroleptics that have been analyzed by electron capture and other gas chromatographic techniques, no strict correlation between neuroleptic blood levels and therapeutic efficacy has been adduced, although correlations between side effects and blood levels have been partly achieved (36,65).

An indirect measure of neuroleptic blood levels—namely, the haloperidol-equivalent technique—has been devised by Creese, Snyder, and Burt. In this technique tritiated butyrophenones (H^3-spiroperidol, for example) are used to determine dopamine-receptor-blocking activity in a sample of a patient's blood (30,31). This method has been studied in schizophrenics, but the exact relationship to neuroleptic dosage has not been fully established, although the correlation is positive (20). The next step would require standardized dose-response studies with various commonly used antipsychotic drugs to ascertain the clinical relevance of this promising, but as yet experimental, research technique.

It is also possible that antiparkinsonian anticholinergic drugs adversely affect blood levels—at least for chronic paranoid schizophrenics (CPS) (3,94)—perhaps by reducing gastrointestinal motility and hence absorption of drugs. This possibility would, therefore, support the conclusion of Hollister (61) and others that to give anticholinergics routinely in early treatment, as a prophylactic measure to those on neuroleptics known to cause EPS symptoms, limits the clinician's opportunity to test the drug at therapeutic blood levels and to know that he has at least achieved blood levels capable of affecting the EPS. Much of the earlier empirical clinical studies with respect to dose and clinical response will require to be reworked as and when reliable blood-level techniques have been established and shown to possess clinical utility.

In order to obtain adequate blood levels in terms of our current available knowledge, divided doses tend to be given in the first few days of treatment. As symptoms remit, it is probably equally effective to give single dosages, and most physicians now prescribe these at night. Even in multiple-dosage regimens most of the medication is commonly given at night, which ensures an improvement in nighttime sedation and reduces EPS side effects, such as dystonias and pseudoparkinsonian rigidity which are typically ameliorated by sleep, by mechanisms that are as yet obscure. Occasionally with those drugs which possess more potent extrapyramidal side effects, an antiparkinsonian drug may be required to be given. Benztropine mesylate (cogentin), 2 to 4 milligrams orally in individual doses per day, may then be given for the first few days; but such prescriptions of an anticholinergic drug should be as few as possible because of a possible reduction of neuroleptic blood levels and dangerous augmentation of anticholinergic side effects if a sedative anticholinergic neuroleptic is being given. A better technique is to use once-only treatment to attempt amelioration in EPS symptoms. Diphenhydrate maleate (50 milligrams intramuscularly) intravenous caffeine sodium benzoate (500 mg) or an antiparkinsonian anticholinergic (given intramuscularly) may be employed (61). By this means, there will be minimal variations in blood level; and if the dose of medication is further increased, as should occur in normal practice, a breakthrough to a new plateau of absence of EPS is often achieved (5).

In contrast to the preceding guidelines, at least two groups of workers advocate rapid escalation of dosage, usually beginning with 10 to 20 milligrams of fluphenazine or haloperidol—equivalent to 500 to 1,000 milligrams of chlorpromazine (34)—and increasing daily by 10 to 20 milligrams until adequate symptom control is reached. This technique has been described as analogous to "digitalization" (40). Final doses of 50 to 100 milligrams of fluphenazine are usually achieved, which is high indeed and corresponds to 2,500 to 5,000 milligrams of chlorpromazine. When a patient no longer has sleep disturbances, begins to show signs of sedation, or demonstrates a significant clinical response, he is considered to have achieved a therapeutic drug level. An antiparkinsonian agent, 2 to 4 milligrams of benztropine daily in divided dosage, is routinely given as a prophylactic against extrapyramidal side effects. Further EPS are treated as necessary with additional antiparkinsonian or antihistaminic anticholinergic drugs.

Most clinicians would question the use of high-dosage regimes as not producing an initial tissue-saturation effect in any case and as giving a graded response (61). They would also question the advisability of subjecting large numbers of people to high-dosage medication for the possible goal of shortened hospital stay for the few who might otherwise be treatment-resistant. In any case high-dosage schedules have not been conclusively shown to be more advantageous (35). Most authors would, however, agree with the view that for some treatment-resistant patients, higher doses than the recommended range of total daily dose should be tried as a final resort. The only exception to this would seem to be thioridazine, which should not exceed 800 milligrams daily because of dosage-related retinal pigmentation and subsequent partial or total blindness.

MAINTENANCE TREATMENT

Once symptomatic remission becomes evident, most clinicians maintain their patients on a once-daily nighttime dosage to achieve improved compliance, better absorption, and few, if any, EPS. This route of administration is also cheaper, as many drugs are now marketable in single-dose forms. Once this state is achieved, maintenance therapy should continue for at least six to eight weeks for an adequate trial of the medication. After this time, if remission continues and the patient is able to return to the community, an attempt should be made to maintain the patient on as low a dosage as is possible without relapse. This method is preferable to an arbitrary reduction in medication and should reduce the possibility of postpsychotic apathy which may be contributed to by too-high drug levels. Over the longer haul of weeks or months the patient should be seen in an outpatient situation or day-hospital clinic and followed up regularly and attentively by his primary physician and not "passed along" to an anonymous group of outpatient personnel. If other physicians are to provide follow-up, the patient should have previous exposure to them in order to achieve some therapeutic expectation and/ or rapport. At some point after three or four months, at which time most patients will relapse if they have not complied with their medication schedule, they can be allowed greater control of their medication requirements and may have occasional drug holidays if they are compliant and responsible. The choice of which patient will benefit from a drug holiday is unclear, but with good social support and a positive social-emotional climate his or her chances of avoiding relapse can be improved. Should the patient be returned to a negative social climate, the chances of relapse are increased (19). Many patients will excuse themselves from 100 percent drug compliance and will limit their drug dosage to certain days of the week. Other patients, as yet an undefined group, will maintain themselves on low-dosage neuroleptic medications—for example, taking 2 milligrams of trifluoperazine per day for years. Whether this is necessary is not known, but the practice is common and is consistent with the notion that the process schizophrenic patient, and frequently the patient with late onset reactive illness, is chronically handicapped. Experience with currently available drugs has shown that the majority of patients will form a residual schizophrenic cohort, requiring maintenance levels of medications, and efforts at rehabilitation should, therefore, be conceptualized in terms of a chronic disease paradigm. This situation is analogous to treating hypertension in various forms or chronic anemias or arthritis in medical outpatient or aftercare clinics (69).

LONG-ACTING PHENOTHIAZINES

In the past decade long-acting depot phenothiazines have become available for routine outpatient use (9,67). The residual schizophrenic is clearly less socially adaptable following repeated readmissions, which are believed to result in a downhill clinical progression (75). Therefore, in most centers vigorous efforts are made to reduce the possibility of drug failures through poor patient compliance, which in many schizophrenic and, indeed, other patient populations is about 25 percent to 50 percent (61). Parenteral depot preparations, such as fluphenazine enanthate and decanoate, require less frequent administration than oral drugs and usually are given by intramuscular injection once every two to four weeks. Treatment is usually begun with ½ to 1 cubic centimeter (12.5–25 mg) fluphenazine decanoate, intramuscularly; this dose is repeated every one to two weeks in most centers. In very disturbed patients higher doses are frequently given. For most patients, however, ½ cubic centimeter every two weeks is probably sufficient after hospital treatment is completed and change to depot preparations has been made. With some inpatients for whom this drug regimen has been chosen, it can be combined with oral neuroleptic dosages (29). This method of management in the acute state of illness may have a place for those who obtain poor symptomatic relief with oral medications alone.

Although earlier studies indicated that these regimens showed promise in preventing relapse (9), more recent work suggests that a significant number of patients either do not respond with continued clinical improvement or are daunted by reason of severe and often later development of EPS (75). In one study the therapeutic differences between oral and parenteral routes of administration of fluphenazine were ambiguous, and with respect to the parenteral preparation more akinetic presentations were found (92). In a recent review of the whole issue of maintenance intramuscular schedules, akinesia may appear late in treatment after several weeks or months and be more pervasive than was formerly thought (9,92). Such presentations of postpsychotic apathy and akinesia will respond to a low-dose parenteral anticholinergic, antiparkinsonian drug, such as benztropine (2 mg), often dramatically enough to suggest its use as a diagnostic test for akinesia (92). A further disadvantage with respect to the wholesale use of depot preparations in those who comply with their administration is the development of serious and sometimes suicidal mood changes. This side effect has been well documented since the first report by Benassi and co-workers in 1966 (17).

The thioxanthene analogue of fluphenazine, flupenthixol, which has —it was claimed in one uncontrolled trial—an antidepressant profile, may offer some advantage over fluphenazine in the future (102). Recently penfluridol, an oral long-acting neuroleptic, was introduced in Europe; it is a dephenylbutylpiperidine whose action lasts approximately one week after one dose of 40 to 160 milligrams (45).

ADRENERGIC BETA-BLOCKING AGENTS AND SCHIZOPHRENIA

Propranolol is currently the only adrenegic beta blocker available for clinical use in the United States. Since the initial reports of early improvement in psychotics treated with this drug (7,98), other workers have suggested, usually in uncontrolled studies, that this agent may have a therapeutic effect in certain patients (8,96,109). This could be an important discovery or simply another treatment to add to a huge list of unverified but tantalizing leads in therapeutics. One recent controlled trial suggests that in conjunction with neuroleptics, patients might respond better to a combination of high-dose propranolol (4 g per day in some cases) and phenothiazines than to phenothiazines alone (108). This study requires replication, for even in inpatient settings the use of propranolol is not without serious drawbacks. Propranolol can precipitate heart failure and is potentially dangerous to asthmatics. Also, its use may predispose to hypoglycemia, hypotension, occasionally hypertension, and, in large doses, to ataxia and visual hallucinations.

ALCOHOL AND ALCOHOL-RELATED SCHIZOPHRENIA

It is a common clinical impression, and one that we share, that patients frequently discontinue their medication some weeks or months after hospital discharge, while they increase their consumption of alcohol, often to the point of abuse. The impression that alcohol aggravates a schizophrenic relapse is widespread (14).

In view of the many heavy drinkers (12 percent) and alcoholics in the United States (estimated to be between 5 million and 9 million persons) (105) and of a prevalence of schizophrenia of 0.3 to 1.0 percent in the population, it is not surprising that many schizophrenics abuse alcohol or are dependent on it. Recent human and animal studies suggesting that low doses of alcohol induce motor restlessness and euphoria which in turn are related to increased catecholamine synthesis are consonant with the catecholamine hypothesis of alcoholism (1,24). This hypothesis would support a theory of alcohol-induced aggravation and relapse of schizophrenia. Since the problems of treating the chronic alcoholic are as formidable as those of treating the chronic schizophrenic, the combination of the two illnesses represents a major public health problem.

It has been suggested that alcohol-induced euphoria can be prevented by concomitant-use of 2,000 to 4,000 milligrams of alpha-methyl-para-tyrosine (AMT), a compound which inhibits tyrosine hydroxylase, the rate-limiting enzyme of catecholamine synthesis (1). It has also been suggested that nicotinamide may prevent alcohol-induced exacerbations in schizophrenics (14). Like AMT, nicotinamide has been tried in the treatment of schizophrenia with little or no success. However, it is yet possible that these compounds may have clinical utility when added to neuroleptics in the treatment of alcohol-aggravated schizophrenia, although so far no clinical data support this possibility.

ACUTE TOXICITY AND SIDE EFFECTS

It seems likely that all neuroleptics share to a greater or a lesser extent unwanted effects, commonly called side effects, which represent an extension or an exaggeration of their pharmacological actions as well as hypersensitivity and idiopathic reactions (61,75). The toxicity of neuroleptic drugs is remarkably low within a wide therapeutic margin. The nature and frequency of adverse reactions are summarized in table 9–2. Overdose with sedation is most frequently seen with aliphatic and piperidine phenothiazines; hence they are often referred to as the "sedative neuroleptics." This is so particularly in children—where are seen most fatalities with these drugs in overdose.

The more potent neuroleptics—namely, the piperazines, the butyrophenones, and some of the newer drug families—produce less sedation than the former more anticholinergic neuroleptic groups. They are, however, more likely to produce extrapyramidal effects and variants of the parkinsonian syndrome, such as acute dystonias and dyskinesias and akathisia. Akathisia is a syndrome of uncomfortable and uncontrolled muscular restlessness, manifested by constant, seemingly random hand and limb fidgeting and by constant random pacing, and it is often mistaken for agitation. Severe dystonic reactions may present as wry neck, or torticollis, as truncal distortions, and as oculogyric eye movements. Excessive salivation, or sialorrhea, may be particularly distressing for some patients. Most of these symptoms will respond to anticholinergic medication, with the exception of akathisia, which may last for weeks while neuroleptics are given. Extrapyramidal symptoms occur usually in approximately 30 percent of patients on sedative phenothiazines or

TABLE 9-2

Nature and Frequency of Adverse Reactions to Various Types of Neuroleptic Drugs*

Adverse Reactions	Phenothiazines			Thixoanthenes	Butyrophenones
	Aliphatic Derivatives	Piperazine Derivatives	Piperidine Derivatives		
Behavioral					
Oversedation	+++*	-	+++	+++	-
Extrapyramidal					
Parkinson's syndrome	++	+++	+	++	+++
Akathisia	++	+++	++	++	+++
Dystonic reaction	+	++	+	+	++
Autonomic					
Postural hypotension	+++	+	+++	++	++
Anticholinergic effects	+++	++	+++	++	+
Genitourinary					
Inhibition of ejaculation	++	++	+++	-	-
Cardiovascular					
EKG abnormalities	+	+	++	-	-
Hepatic					
Cholestatic jaundice	++	+	+	+	+
Hematological					
Blood dyscrasias	++	+	+	+	++
Ophthalmological					
Lenticular pigmentation	++	+	-	-	-
Pigmentary retinopathy	-	-	++	-	-
Dermatological					
Allergic skin reaction	++	+	+	+	+
Photosensitivity reaction	++	+	++	+	+
Skin pigmentation	++	-	-	-	-

*Modified and expanded from *Medical Letter* (1970).
+++ = common; ++ = uncommon; + = rare.

Note: Reprinted with permission of the author and publisher from H. E. Lehman, "Psychopharmacological Treatment of Schizophrenia," *Schizophrenia Bulletin* (1975) 13:40.

thioxanthenes and in greater than 50 percent of those on other neuroleptics (75). In a survey of 3,775 patients treated with various neuroleptics, extrapyramidal reactions occurred in 38.9 percent, and parkinsonism was found in 15.4 percent; akathisia, in 21.2 percent; and dystonic
reactions, in 2.3 percent. Although to some extent dose-dependent, the
occurrence of such symptoms was largely idiosyncratic, as more than
60 percent of the patients did not develop any neurological symptoms.

Concomitant use of other medications, such as tricyclics and anticholinergics, will infrequently lead to a central anticholinergic syndrome,
particularly when they are used with the sedative neuroleptics, which
have an anticholinergic profile. The following couplet describes the symptoms of the central anticholinergic syndrome: "Mad as a hatter, dry as
a bone, red as a beet, and blind as a stone" (100). Another striking feature of this syndrome is profound memory loss (48). Patients also develop hyperpyrexia, severe delirium, and often acutely agitated behavior.
The central anticholingeric syndrome is temporarily arrested by an anticholinergic drug which crosses the blood brain barrier—namely, phy-
sostygmine, in a dosage of 1 to 3 milligrams, which is infused slowly
intravenously while the patient is on a cardiac monitor (55). The treatment regimen must be carried out cautiously to avoid a cholinergic crisis.
Not every patient requires physostigmine, and its use may also be contraindicated for those with heart disease, asthma, hyperthyroidism, pep-
tic ulcer, pregnancy, and a history of previous allergy to physostigmine,
to name a few exceptions. Cautious supportive nonpharmacological
treatment may be all that is necessary for life support or all that may
be given in the event of contraindications to drug use.

Other presentations of neuroleptic overdosage include hypotension,
induced seizures, hypothermia, and cardiac arrhythmias.

Hypotension can be particularly unnerving for the patient, particularly for the elderly on the more sedative neuroleptics, unless its likely
occurrence is explained beforehand. Alterations in posture to a supine
position, elastic stockings, lower-limb isometric exercises, and reassurance will help relieve lightheadedness. On rare occasions an acute hypo-
tensive crisis will require immediate supportive treatment with bed rest,
elevation of the foot of the bed, occasionally the use of a plasma ex-
pander, and, if these are insufficient, a norepinephrine infusion. Since
the hypotension results from alpha-adrenergic blockage, epinephrine
should not be used as it has a beta-adrenergic stimulant effect which can
further lower blood pressure.

The peripheral anticholinergic effects seen commonly with the more
sedative phenothiazines present as an atropinic syndrome of dry mouth,
blurred vision, tachycardia, constipation, urinary hesitation; and rarely
these drugs may precipitate closed angle glaucoma, bladder retention,
and, more seriously, paralytic ileus. For these reasons, and perhaps because of the frequent unanticipated production of these symptoms, many
clinicians today will tend to select phenothiazines with minimal peripheral or central anticholinergic profiles in early management.

Thioridazine has been particularly implicated in the production of
reversible, prolonged ventricular depolarization with prolonged "Q-T"
intervals and prominent "U" waves in the electrocardiogram. This effect
is exaggerated especially in patients who show evidence of low serum

potassium or in whom cellular potassium shifts may be undetected before serum changes appear (2).

Sudden death has rarely been reported with phenothiazines, and the pathogenesis is not known at present (61,75). All phenothiazines have a slight bone-marrow depressant effect which may progress, but rarely does, to agranulocytosis (61). Although an initial leucocyte count may be useful for the identification of patients at high risk, sudden leucocytopenia may occur. Careful clinical observation of symptoms, such as afebrile sore throat or intercurrent infections, rather than repeated blood studies, must serve at this time as warning of developed leucopenias. Pigmentary retinopathies produced by thioridazine appear to be dose-related, particularly in patients exposed to doses in excess of 800 milligrams per day for variable lengths of time (61). Chlorpromazine has also been implicated in the production of skin pigmentary deposits, corneal or lens opacities, and photosensitivity. It is possible that toxicity reports with the newer neuroleptics may increase as they become more widely used. There appear to be fewer reports than there were several years ago of cholestatic hypersensitivity jaundice. This condition, which is accompanied by fever, eosinophilia, and rashes, was mostly prevalent with the earlier use of chlorpromazine. A much-ignored side effect, possibly because patients may be inhibited about discussing it, is ejaculatory disturbance in sexually active men, a condition which causes considerable apprehension. It is frequently associated with thioridazine use. Reduction of dosage or change to another medication is often sufficient for complete reversal of this symptom. All neuroleptics may produce seizures in some patients, especially those with a history of epilepsy (61).

TARDIVE DYSKINESIA

Tardive, or late-onset, dyskinesias (TDs) have, since the publication of a position statement by the American College of Neuropsychopharmacology in 1973 (3), received widespread publicity as a late consequence of neuroleptic therapy. Presently available evidence suggests that up to 1972 at least, among 28,000 long-stay psychiatric patients, there was a mean prevalence of 15 percent (42). It is highly possible, therefore, that prolonged neuroleptic medication over many years is a cause of tardive dyskinesia, as TD is probably three to twenty times more prevalent among those on drugs than among those not on drugs, and most prevalent among geriatric patients. (11).

The fact that not all long-term patients on neuroleptic medications develop TD suggests to us that there is possibly a predisposed subgroup of patients who are at risk. What this predisposition may be is not clear at this time. Duration of therapy as well as the age of the patient may possibly also be correlated with the severity of TD (88). It has been suggested that TD may be associated with preexisting organic brain disease, as many treated and untreated schizophrenic patients have overt or hidden neuropathological changes (32). However, dyskinesias are also reported in neurologically intact and nonpsychotic patients receiving neuroleptics on a chronic basis (72,80). It has also been suggested that the drugs most likely to be implicated are chlorpromazine and thioridazine (46), but in most studies patients have been on so many mixtures of neuroleptics and other medications that it is impossible to ascribe TD to any particular drug. Newer antischizophrenic drugs, including halo-peridol and thiothixene, have also been associated with dyskinesias (87). It is not known for certain whether changes in medication from one neuroleptic to another are therapeutic or otherwise, for by changing to another drug it is possible to mask the appearance of TD. Recent work by our group indicates also that concurrent use of anticholinergic, anti-parkinsonian medication increases the likelihood of TD, presumably by striatal dopaminergic potentiation (20). This work confirms several other reports to this effect (18,47,66,68).

The available evidence thus suggests a strong association between drug use and TD. Whether or not predisposing organicity relates to the development of TD is of little relevance to the patient and his clinician who are faced with disfiguring and health-impairing oro-facial dyskinesia (11). Rehabilitation of such patients is frequently most difficult, and treatment often is unavailing. The development of involuntary bucco-linguo-facial tics, tongue "fly-catching" movements, grunting and other peculiar sounds, smacking and sucking lip movements, chewing and jaw deviations, furrowing of the forehead, rapid perseverative eye blink-ing, and choreoatheototic movements of the trunk and extremities should be anticipated in all patients on long-term neuroleptic regimes (73)— especially in those who are to be maintained on neuroleptics for longer than three months (10). Probably for all such patients informed con-sent, and/or relatives' consent for those who are refractory to treatment of their psychosis, should be obtained if neuroleptic treatment is to be continued for more than three months (10). Reasonable standards of prevention would appear to include the reduction of drug dosages, drug holidays, and periodic reevaluation of the necessity for continued drug prescriptions.

The whole question of irreversibility of TD is at present under inves-tigation. The most parsimonious interpretation of currently available evidence seems to be that for most patients if TD is diagnosed early enough, it is clinically reversible provided neuroleptic medication is dis-continued. However, there is at least one report (27) of brain histopatho-logical changes in a patient who had received neuroleptic drugs and who showed signs of TD; such changes were of gliosis in the midbrain and cell degeneration in the substantia nigra. Although at least one animal study suggests this association, to our knowledge the human post-mortem study has not been replicated.

With respect to definitive treatment of established TD, currently under study are agents which reverse the underlying neurotransmitter imbal-ance in the striato-nigral system; that is, agents which reverse the rela-tively high dopamine and low acetylcholine (possibly also low serotonin) levels might be beneficial. Substances which show early promise are lithium, which may lower dopamine levels postsynaptically (90,91), and procholinergic agents such as choline chloride (up to 5 g per day) (37, 99) and lecithin (106,107). The TD situation would appear to be the reverse of that of Parkinson's disease, where irreversible anatomic dam-age exists, yet chemotherapy with L-DOPA effectively treats the symp-toms in a majority of patients. The recent reports of some benefit in the use of cholinergic agents for the treatment of established TD are therefore most timely.

RECENT TREATMENTS OF UNCERTAIN VALUE

MEGAVITAMIN THERAPY

Theories of the pathogenesis of schizophrenia and treatments based on these theories continue to abound. Most of these theories run counter to the mainstream of existing concepts of the nature of the disorder. Perhaps the most popular deals with orthomolecular psychiatry. The hypothesis for this theory, stated by Linus Pauling, is that a disordered or less than optimum molecular environment for the brain will lead to a variety of types of behavioral pathology, particularly schizophrenia. This hypothesis does not define an optimum molecular environment. More important, it claims that this disordered molecular environment can be corrected nutritionally by the intake of "mega" quantities of nutrients, particularly water-soluble vitamins and trace element minerals. The claims of the megavitamin proponents are based upon an attractive hypothesis and upon numerous case reports and testimonials from patients and their relatives. Hoffer and his co-workers have emphasized the need for vitamins in huge doses (56). Niacin, for example, is recommended at doses ten to two hundred times the average daily estimated requirement. Pfeiffer (89) has recommended large oral doses of zinc, because he finds evidence of a copper and/or zinc imbalance in schizophrenia.

The claims of the orthomolecular psychiatrists have been carefully examined by many psychiatrists and have been found seriously lacking. An American Psychiatric Association task force was seriously critical (4). The Canadian Mental Health Association (12) and a multidisciplinary task force established by the Minister of Social Services and Community Health of the Province of Alberta, Canada (84), were equally so. There are several reasons for these criticisms:

1. The theoretical basis for the use of megavitamins and minerals is internally not consistent.
2. No laboratory evidence of vitamin deficiency has ever been demonstrated in schizophrenic patients maintained on average diets.
3. Controlled clinical trials with niacin and vitamin B_6 therapy have failed to find any therapeutic advantage to their use in megadoses (13), and some patients became worse.

The fact is that in actual usage "megavitamin therapy" is somewhat of a misnomer. Although proponents claim that there are genetic vitamin deficiencies which are corrected by administration of the vitamins in megadoses with resultant cure, in actual fact such practitioners—who initially decried the use of neuroleptic drugs—now use those drugs and even electroconvulsive therapy extensively and claim that the addition of megavitamins enhances the drug and shock treatment. Furthermore, these practitioners now use many more vitamins, plus hormones and minerals and electroconvulsive shock, in a fashion that they say is individualized for every patient. This individualized treatment is claimed to be based on laboratory evidence of deficiency, but we are not told how such deficiencies are documented. A consequence of such varied practices is that it is extraordinarily difficult for other investigators to duplicate the work, and most of the attempts at replication do not exactly follow the individualized treatments of the megavitamin practitioners. One may therefore conclude that the burden of proof is on the orthomolecular psychiatrists who must perform controlled studies with rigorous designs that will generate convincing data. Since their position is that they have an effective treatment and that withholding the megavitamins in blind trials would be withholding treatment and hence be unethical, it is not likely that they will perform such studies. Thus, it seems proper at this time to judge that the treatment is of no general value in schizophrenia. The possibility that there is a subgroup of schizophrenics who require megavitamin therapy must not be ignored. But if there is such a group, it must be quite small because among the many patients who have been studied by critical investigations in replicative studies, none has been found to respond as dramatically as would be expected if a vitamin deficiency truly existed. The subject of megavitamin therapy was thoroughly reviewed in 1973 (4) and more recently by Ban (13).

OTHER SOMATIC TREATMENTS OF UNCERTAIN VALUE

In the last few years claims for the sucess of several innovative treatments have been made. For each of these there is a plausible rationale and some empirical clinical evidence. For example, there have been claims that wheat gluten ingestion exacerbates schizophrenia and that its elimination abates it (39). And recently it has been asserted that wheat gluten might contain in its large protein molecule a morphinelike fragment. It has been suggested that pepsin in the stomach may cleave or release endorphin from gluten, and that this derived opioid then binds to receptors in brain.*

Some orthomolecular psychiatrists have joined with some allergists who claim that cerebral allergy to certain ingested foods or minerals exacerbates schizophrenia, and that removal of these allergens from the diet is therapeutic (78). Wheat products and some meats have been implicated as allergens.

A recent report states that hemodialysis is effective in the treatment of fifteen out of sixteen chronic schizophrenics (104), which implies that schizophrenics have manufactured an endogenous psychotogen which can be dialyzed out by an artificial kidney but is apparently not cleared by the normal kidney. A very recent report by the same investigators† suggests that this compound may be a leucine endorphin which, they say, has been partially identified in the dialysate from schizophrenics' blood. Such an endorphin might be a mutant, because naturally occurring endorphin contains methionine in the position where leucine has been claimed to be found in schizophrenic dialysates. A separate and independent study of the dialysates, however, failed to show any endorphin activity by radioimmunoassays or rat behavioral tests.‡ This report is nevertheless intriguing because another group has reported that

---

* Reported in *Medical World News* (January 9, 1978), pp. 86 ff.
† R. Palmour, F. Ervin, and H. Wagemaker: unpublished results.
‡ Reported in *Medical World News* (January 9, 1978), pp. 86 ff.

the intravenous administration of naturally occurring beta-endorphin dramatically and rapidly improved several schizophrenics (70). This finding is of special interest because beta-endorphin is an endogenous peptide which binds to the opiate receptor. Conceivably there is deficiency in endorphin production in schizophrenia, with perhaps an abnormal endorphin being produced instead.

None of these treatments has been tested with the tight experimental design and rigorous control demanded by modern clinical research. Therefore, despite their plausibility the effectiveness of such treatments is unproven and will remain so until adequate clinical trials are conducted.

Major problems in the ethics of science and medicine are posed by the publication and the popularization of therapeutic claims based on inadequate evidence. On the one hand, rapid publication of hopeful treatments for major illnesses is called for by the social need for more effective treatment and by the highly competitive nature of modern research and its funding. Furthermore, there is intrinsic merit in rapid dissemination of promising results, for if a treatment turns out to be actually valuable, the public benefits from its early introduction.

On the other hand, popularization leads to demands for implementation among some sections of the public, and apparently physicians can always be found to supply the treatment. Most radically innovative treatments turn out to be worthless or to have very limited value. Fortunately those which are clearly beneficial can have their effectiveness shown ultimately in rigorous clinical trials. Unfortunately it is much more difficult to prove that a treatment has value than to claim its efficacy. Typically, those who propose a new treatment are the least likely to test their claims rigorously, and it becomes the task of other clinical researchers to make such tests. This is both time-consuming and expensive for the consumer, who initially pays for the treatment and ultimately for the research costs. Many examples may be given, The cost of coronary by-pass surgery to the consumer is in the billions of dollars, and its value is currently under question. The cost of laetrile for cancer or of vitamin C for the common cold is very high, and the cost of clinical research to accurately assess their value is also very high. Food additives, particularly dyes and the antioxidant food preservatives, have been claimed to be implicated in hyperkinesis and learning disability.* Millions of dollars and thousands of research hours will undoubtedly be spent to investigate the truth of this claim.

The practitioner, the patient, his family, and society are faced with a real dilemma when they fail to obtain adequate therapeutic results with existing methods that are generally effective. Sometimes beneficial results, probably in the nature of a placebo response, are obtained when novel treatments are employed. In psychiatric conditions particularly, identification with and acceptance of a charismatic figure and his group may be helpful, but more often short-term benefits are followed by long-term disappointments. In the end, therapeutics must be scientifically based, with carefully controlled clinical trials, if they are to have general

---

° B. Feingold: personal communication.

applicability and long-term value. Until the innovative treatments are subject to such trials, they remain exciting curiosities.

DRUGS AND PSYCHOSOCIAL TREATMENTS COMBINED

Not only do most medical illnesses which have unknown etiology require medical or pharmacological treatment, but patients with such illnesses must also receive support and assistance in a variety of psychosocial dimensions (41). For example, not only does the hypertensive require antihypertensive drugs, but he must also be assisted in losing weight, controlling his salt intake, diminishing his smoking, increasing his exercise, and altering his work patterns and his interpersonal relationships. If these changes are not made, the efficacy of the antihypertensive drugs is limited, and the patient's prognosis for health and longevity is seriously compromised. Similar consideration should be given to the treatment of schizophrenia with drugs. It is naïve to think that drugs alone can effectively treat this illness. Even if the chemical pathology that apparently exists in the brain of a schizophrenic were totally remedied by drugs, it is highly likely that his coping skills would be compromised because of past life experiences. It is also likely that the pathological defenses that were employed prior to the onset of illness and subsequent to it would require corrective reeducation. The genetic diathesis rendering a schizophrenic susceptible to further episodes will remain forever. It is a part of the patient's heritage. Its expression as psychotic behavior can, however, be minimized by maintenance medication and with the acquisition of new, learned styles of coping behavior.

The dramatic and relatively rapid benefits of the neuroleptic drugs when compared with psychological treatments generated the opinion, which prevailed by the end of the 1960s, that treatment of schizophrenia without pharmacotherapy was unjustifiable. In large measure this opinion followed a comprehensive study by May (81) which compared drugs alone, psychotherapy alone, milieu therapy alone, drugs plus psychotherapy and electroshock therapy (EST). From data like length of hospital stay and rates of relapse following discharge from the hospital, it was clear that drugs were the most powerful in determining outcome. Some disagreement with this point of view was quickly generated by those that argued that the experience of the psychotherapist, and hence the quality of the psychotherapy, was inadequate in May's experiment. Although this point may be debated, it should be emphasized that May offered both the quantity and the quality of psychotherapy that was practical and feasible in a state hospital. Furthermore, Grinspoon et al. (49) conducted a similar experiment at the Massachusetts Mental Health Center and used highly trained psychotherapists, with similar results. Reviewing the literature in 1975, May concluded that the bulk of available evidence suggested that drug treatment during a patient's initial hospital stay and its contiuued use following discharge resulted in more satisfactory recovery and follow-up (82,83).

Hogarty and co-workers (60) also demonstrated significantly improved recovery rates among those who had received early drug treatments. This finding was in agreement with two earlier studies which had shown that the earlier the treatment was begun with drugs, the less likely were major symptoms and delusions to develop. However, these same studies carried out in multicenter trials by Hogarty revealed that when major role therapy (MRT), which consists of psychosocial and vocational rehabilitation programs, was added onto continuing neuroleptic treatment, it contributed to the well-being and improved the social and interpersonal adjustments of the patients. The results were particularly striking after an elapsed time of eighteen months from discharge. These studies strongly suggested that a clinic in which MRT is not offered as part of the overall treatment program does not provide optimal therapy. However, even with optimal therapy, there was a relapse rate of about 30 percent over an extended time. Recent work by Hogarty showed that this relapse rate was not due to discontinuation of drugs, since it apparently occurred with patients on long-acting phenothiazines (58).

Some very recent work suggests that not all acute schizophrenics require neuroleptic drug treatment. In a study from the National Institute of Mental Health well-diagnosed young schizophrenic patients were admitted to a research ward with an excellent milieu and were not given drugs for at least a month (in order to obtain drug-free biological baseline data). About 30 percent of the patients remitted. These patients apparently had good premorbid personalities and few paranoid characteristics. However, the characteristics of these patients are not so well delineated that it is yet possible to predict which of them could safely be treated without drugs (52). This finding has once again raised the issue of pharmacotherapy versus psychosocial therapy. If indeed a significant number of schizophrenic patients do not require drugs and respond well to concurrent group and individual psychosocial therapies in a supportive milieu, then it is clearly imperative to develop methods for detecting these patients. This emphasizes the need for further research on prediction of outcome. Furthermore, if drugs are not to be employed, there is an increasing need to investigate therapist-patient interactions, and there is now evidence that therapists can be objectively evaluated in terms of their positive or negative characteristic styles of responding to patients (52). It is likely that the most significant positive variable in this regard may boil down to enthusiastic and highly motivated treatment personnel. Indeed, Bellak has suggested anecdotally that enthusiastic nonprofessional or lay persons can become powerful therapists for schizophrenic patients, and that their active participation should be encouraged in therapeutic settings (16). This observation seems borne out by the reported results from Soteria House in which schizophrenic patients without drugs and with highly motivated nonprofessional "buddies" seem to do as well as similar patients who enter a comprehensive community mental health center, where they are given neuroleptics while hospitalized, and are then maintained on drugs and conventional psychotherapy in a mental health clinic.

The findings, which must be considered preliminary, nonetheless raise the question of the degree to which psychosocial interventions can be therapeutically substituted for pharmacotherapy. It is debatable whether they should be substituted or used as coequal partners in the treatment and rehabilitation of the schizophrenic, but certainly the evidence is very strong that drugs alone are insufficient for the optimal management of the schizophrenic patient. This situation may point to significant deficiencies in the types of drugs we now employ. Such deficiency unquestionably exists and may be a consequence of the fact that all available drugs are developed in tests on animals for substances to blockade dopamine. It is possible that rational drug combinations affecting more than one neurotransmitter system may be useful in the future. It is also possible that new biological treatments based on rationales other than dopamine-receptor blockade will be forthcoming. Some of these have been briefly described in the section on innovative treatments, but it is not yet possible to predict what they will be or the rate of their development. At the present time the most conservative treatment remains the use of neuroleptic drugs in the context of an adequate psychosocial support system. We have attempted to offer guidelines for the proper use of drugs in this condition.

Conclusion

AN ASSESSMENT OF THE VALUE OF DRUGS IN SCHIZOPHRENIA

It is often said that the neuroleptic drugs do not cure schizophrenia. While this is true, one should consider the meaning of the term "cure" and what the neuroleptic drugs actually do. It has been noted elsewhere that the term "cure" is used in medicine in a somewhat casual fashion (50). In its strictest sense, "cure" means elimination of the etiological agent and the return to total health. The highest levels of cure in medicine are achieved with the infectious diseases like diphtheria, poliomyelitis, or smallpox, where exposure to an attenuated virus or bacterium in small doses causes a brief infection followed by permanent immunity. Another level of "cure" is achieved with antibiotics, where the etiological agent is eliminated, but immunization is not obtained, and the illness can recur. The term "cure" is even employed when the initial infection is eliminated but residual damage remains, as, for example, when cardiac or renal lesions remain after a streptococcal infection.

Most often in modern therapeutics cures are not achieved, but instead symptoms are eliminated or markedly attenuated, and the progression of the illness is stopped or retarded. In illnesses like hypertension, diabetes, or rheumatoid arthritis, where the etiology is not known and may indeed be multivalent, drug treatments which control symptoms are accepted and are commonly employed, while research goes on seeking better understanding, better treatment, and, perhaps ultimately, cure.

In the management of schizophrenia drugs certainly do not cure in the sense that the patient who has remitted completely can be considered immunized against any further attacks. On the other hand, drugs are an effective treatment, since in most cases all of the primary and the secondary symptoms are attenuated, and in some cases they disappear entirely when treatment is adequately prolonged. Unfortunately many patients are not entirely well when on drugs; and when drug treatment is stopped, it becomes clear that some asymptomatic patients have not been cured because frequently the illness may recur. For example, several researchers have shown that up to 70 percent of the patients who have had at least one schizophrenic episode will relapse within a year if they are not on medication, whereas only 32 percent relapse who are continuing to receive chlorpromazine (57). This is strong evidence that drugs are better than placebo for acute treatment and maintenance, but the same data also show that about 30 percent of patients relapse within a year while on maintenance neuroleptics. Prediction of relapse is difficult. One study shows that many patients did well for up to a period of ten months and then relapsed rapidly and without warning (59). Furthermore, although the data are not adequate for absolute certainty, there is reason to supect that even among those patients who do not relapse and require rehospitalization, there is less than an optimum social adjustment. Lehmann (74), for example, states that "about 60 percent of patients hospitalized for an attack of acute schizophrenia will be socially recovered five years later and will have been employed for more than half of that time." This statement can be interpreted also to signify that there is approximately 50 percent unemployment for what he calls the group of "socially recovered" schizophrenics. If this is indeed the case, it is not possible to pinpoint its cause. Perhaps it reflects the continued social stigma attached to schizophrenia. More likely it implies that some residual symptoms remain, insufficient to warrant rehospitalization but sufficient to render the schizophrenic unemployable. Probably many of these patients do not have optimum drug management. But some would likely continue to have residual symptoms even with better drug management; and for these, better drugs or drug combinations or new forms of treatment must be sought. For still other patients, there is ample reason to suspect that many psychosocial support systems fail to retrain and rehabilitate them adequately.

It is also worth noting that in those experiments which showed a 70 percent relapse rate in a year among schizophrenics who received placebo as outpatients, 30 percent did not relapse—which implies that they did not require maintenance medication (57). Since it is not yet possible to predict with accuracy which patients will require maintenance medication and which can do without, the clinician still faces a difficult decision. On the one hand, he may elect a course of indefinite medication, perhaps for many years, and will risk iatrogenic neurological disease as well as the cost of continued medical treatment. On the other hand, the social and economical risks of a second or third breakdown are so great—with attendant stigmatization, loss of job, dismissal from school, or alienation from family—that a conservative approach of continued medication is often warranted. The decision about length of treatment must include factors like the premorbid history, the degree to which the patient is socially successful while on the drugs, and the nature of the social support systems that are available to him. If all of these factors are favorable—as they frequently are for first-admission, middle-class, and well-educated patients, who can afford careful and continued scrutiny by a psychiatrist or another professional mental worker—then the risk may well be worth it. At the very least a drug holiday is warranted. However, if the patient's premorbid history is poor, if he is socially disadvantaged, has limited education, and lives with poor social support systems or in a highly destructive family milieu, then maintenance medication is indicated. Lehmann notes that in his experience the first schizophrenic attack should be treated with maintenance medication for at least two or three years, the second for five years, and if the patient has three or more relapses, he should be treated indefinitely, perhaps even for a lifetime.

The prospect that patients with diagnosed schizophrenia may require neuroleptics for prolonged periods is sobering, especially in view of the increasing recognition of adverse neurological effects, some of which may be irreversible. The problem must be viewed in cost-benefit terms, with constant attempts to reduce the costs and increase the benefits. There is by now adequate recognition that the milieu in which the schizophrenic lives and the social supports offered will significantly affect outcome. But the precise nature of this milieu for individual patients has not been determined. Moreover, the generation of such support systems will not be simple, given our social structure and the nature of our health-care delivery systems. Furthermore, the evidence is persuasive that medication is required as a prelude for most patients so that they may benefit from psychosocial support. The pharmacological problem then is to improve the medical treatment of these patients.

Prospects for such improvement are good, but additional research is essential. Although the general rule that most neuroleptics have the same clinical efficacy seems valid, the fact remains that individual patients frequently do badly on one drug and well on another. The reason for this is not known; but in view of the great variance already noted among patients and the complex metabolism of these drugs, it seems likely that blood-level measurements will provide some clue. Such levels will also assist in assuring compliance and in selecting doses which will maximize therapeutic effects while minimizing the adverse ones. Although previous attempts to select drugs on the basis of patient symptoms have not been encouraging, newer drugs are appearing that suggest that greater specificity may yet be achieved. A major problem exists with the chronic patient with residual symptoms for whom oral, long-acting drugs may be the treatment of choice. Such drugs are not yet available in the United States, though they are used in Europe.

Finally, it should be emphasized that all available neuroleptics have the common property of blocking dopamine neurotransmitter systems. The blunderbuss action of these drugs follows from the fact that they inhibit dopamine systems not only in the mesolimbic system, where such blockade is desirable, but also in the dopaminergic striatal and tubero-infundibular systems. These latter inhibitions lead to undesirable extrapyramidal and neuroendocrine side effects. Fewer adverse reactions may be obtained by developing agents which specifically alter the mesolimbic system or which can protect the dopaminergic systems involved in movement and neuroendocrine function. Alternatively it should be recalled that the dopamine hypothesis of schizophrenia is inferred almost entirely from the beneficial effects of drugs which block this system. Such an inference may be incorrect. The primary pathogenetic lesion may be elsewhere, with hyperdopaminergic activity as a result. Should this prove to be the case, entirely new treatments may yet become available.

BIBLIOGRAPHY

1. Ahlenius, S.; Carlsson, A.; Engel J.; et al. 1973. Antagonism by alpha-methyl tyrosine of the ethanol-induced stimulation and euphoria in man. *Clinical Pharmacological Therapeutics* 14:586–92.
2. Alvares-Mena, S. C., and Frank M. J. 1973. Phenothiazine-induced T-wave abnormalities. *Journal of the American Medical Association* 222:1730–33.
3. American College of Neuropsychopharmacology. 1973. Neurological syndromes associated with antipsychotic drug use. *Archives of General Psychiatry* 28:463–66.
4. American Psychiatric Association. 1973. Megavitamin and orthomolecular therapy in psychiatry. Task Force Report no. 7, Washington, D.C.
5. Anden, N-E. 1976. The interaction of neuroleptic drugs with striatal and limbic dopaminergic mechanisms. In *Antipsychotic drugs: Pharmacodynamics and pharmacokinetics*, eds. G. Sedvall, B. Uvnas, and Y. Zotterman (Oxford: Pergamon Press), pp. 217–25.
6. Apter, N. S. 1958. Bilateral adrenalectomy in chronic schizophrenia patients: Six years after. *American Journal of Psychiatry* 115:55–59.
7. Atsmon, A., and Blum, I. 1970. Treatment of acute porphyria variegata with propranolol. *Lancet* 1:196.
8. Atsmon, A.; Blum, I.; Wijsenbeck, H.; et al. 1971. The short-term effects of adrenergic-blocking agents in a small group of psychotic patients. *Psychiatria Neurologica, Neurochirurgia* 74:251–54.
9. Ayd, F. J., Jr. 1975. The depot fluphenazines: A reappraisal after 10 years' clinical experience. *American Journal of Psychiatry* 132:491–500.
10. Ayd, F. J., Jr. 1977. Ethical and legal dilemmas posed by tardive dyskinesia. *International Drug Therapy Newsletter* 12:29–36.
11. Baldessarini, R. J. 1974. Tardive dyskinesia: An evaluation of the etiologic association with neuroleptic therapy. *Canadian Psychiatric Association Journal* 19:551–54.
12. Ban, T. A. 1971. Nicotinic acid in the treatment of schizophrenia. Canadian Mental Health Association, Toronto, Canada.
13. Ban, T. A. 1978. Current status of orthomolecular therapy in schizophrenia. *Weekly Psychiatry Update Series* 2:5.
14. Ban, T. A., and Lehmann, H. E. 1977. Myths, theories and treatment of schizophrenia. *Diseases of the Nervous System* 38:665–71.
15. Bassuk, E. L., and Gerson, S. Deinstitutionalization and mental health services. *Scientific American* 238(2):46–53.
16. Bellak, L. A. 1977. A drug-free week after admission. *Schizophrenia Bulletin* 3:342–43.
17. Benassi, P.; Bertolotti, P.; and Pecorari, T. 1966. Clinical experience with a phenothiazine derivative with prolonged action. *Rivista Sperimentale di Freniatria e Medicina Legale delle Alienazioni Mentale* 90:51–75.
18. Birket-Smith, E. 1974. Abnormal involuntary movements induced by anticholinergic therapy. *Acta Neurologica Scandinavica* 50:801–11.
19. Brown, G. W.; Birley, J. L. T.; and Wing, J. K. 1972. Influence of family life on the course of schizophrenic disorders: A replication. *British Journal of Psychiatry* 121:241–58.
20. Burnett, G. B.; Prange, A. J., Jr.; Wilson, I. C.; et al. Paper presented at the Sixth World Congress of Psychiatry (1977), in press.
21. Cade, J. F. J. 1949. Lithium salts in the treatment of psychotic excitement. *Medical Journal of Australia* 36:349–52.
22. Cade, J. F. J. 1970. The story of lithium. In *Discoveries in Biological Psychiatry*, ed. F. J. Ayd, Jr., and B. Blackwell (Philadelphia: J. B. Lippincott), pp. 218–29.
23. Carlsson, A. 1978. Antipsychotic drugs, neurotransmitters and schizophrenia. *American Journal of Psychiatry* 135:164–73.
24. Carlsson, A., and Lindquist, M. 1973. Effect of ethanol on the hydroxylation of tyrosine and tryptophan in rat brain in vivo. *Journal of Pharmacy and Pharmacology* 25:437–39.
25. Carpenter, W. T.; McGlashan, T. H.; and Strauss, J. S. 1977. The treatment of acute schizophrenia without drugs: An investigation of some current assumptions. *American Journal of Psychiatry* 134:14–20.
26. Casey, J. F.; Bennett, I. F.; Lindley, C. J.; et al. 1960. Drug therapy in schizophrenia. *Archives of General Psychiatry* 2:210–20.
27. Christensen, E.; Moller, J. E.; and Faurbye, A. 1970. Neuropathological investigation of 28 brains from patients with dyskinesia. *Acta Psychiatrica Scandinavica* 46:14–23.

28. Cole, J. O. 1977. Pharmacotherapy of psychosis. In *Psychopharmacology in the practice of medicine*, ed. M. E. Jarvik (New York: Appleton-Century-Crofts), p. 207.

29. Cole, J. O.; Chien, C-P.; and Goldberg, H. 1973. Fluphenazine enanthate in community mental health in the United States. In *The future of pharmacotherapy: New drug delivery systems*, ed. F. J. Ayd, Jr. (Baltimore: International Drug Therapy Newsletter), pp. 33–35.

30. Creese, I.; Burt, D. R.; and Snyder, S. H. 1976. Dopamine receptor binding predicts clinical and pharmacological potencies of antischizophrenic drugs. *Science* 192:481–83.

31. Creese, I., and Snyder, S. H. 1977. A simple and sensitive radioreceptor assay for antischizophrenic drugs in blood. *Nature* 270:180–82.

32. Curren, T. P. 1973. Tardive dyskinesia, side effect or not? *American Journal of Psychiatry* 130:406–10.

33. Curry, S. H., and Adamson, D. 1972. Double-blind trial of fluphenazine decanoate. *Lancet* 2:543–44.

34. Davis, J. M. 1976. Comparative doses and costs of antipsychotic medication. *Archives of General Psychiatry* 33:858–61.

35. Davis, J. M. 1976. Recent developments in the drug treatment of schizophrenia. *American Journal of Psychiatry* 133:208–14.

36. Davis, J. N.; Erickson, S.; and Dekirmenjian, H. 1978. Plasma levels of antipsychotic drugs. In *Psychopharmacology: A generation of progress*, eds. M. A. Lipton, A. DiMascio, and K. F. Killiam (New York: Raven Press), pp. 905–15.

37. Davis, K. L.; Berger, P. A.; and Hollister, L. E. 1975. Choline for tardive dyskinesia. *New England Journal of Medicine* 293:152.

38. Delay, J.; Deniker, P.; and Harl, J. M. 1952. Utilization en thérapeutique psychiatrique d'une phenothiazine d'action centrale élective. *Annals of Medical Psychology* 110–12.

39. Dohan, F. C.; Grasberger, J. C.; Lowell, F. M.; et al. 1969. Relapsed schizophrenics: More rapid improvement on a milk- and cereal-free diet. *British Journal of Psychiatry* 115:595–96.

40. Donlon, P. T., and Tupin, J. P. 1974. Rapid "digitalization" of decompensated schizophrenics with antipsychotic agents. *American Journal of Psychiatry* 131:310–12.

41. Engel, G. L. 1977. The need for a new medical model: A challenge for biomedicine. *Science* 196:129–36.

42. Fann, W. E.; Davis, J. M.; and Janowsky, D. S. 1972. The prevalence of tardive dyskinesias in mental hospital patients. *Diseases of the Nervous System* 33:182–86.

43. Fieve, R. R. 1977. The revolution defined: It is pharmacologic. *Psychiatric Annals* 7(10): 10–18.

44. Fish, F. 1962. *Schizophrenia* (Baltimore: Williams & Wilkins), pp. 18–57.

45. Gallant, D. M.; Mielke, D. H.; Spirtes, M. A.; et al. 1974. Penfluridol: An efficacious long-acting oral antipsychotic compound. *American Journal of Psychiatry* 131:699–702.

46. Gardos, G., and Cole, J. O. 1977. Paper presented at Sixth World Congress of Psychiatry.

47. Gerlach, J.; Reisby, N.; and Randrup, A. 1974. Dopaminergic hypersensitivity and cholinergic hypofunction in the pathophysiology of tardive dyskinesia. *Psychopharmacologia* (Berlin) 34:21–35.

48. Granacher, R. P., and Baldessarini, R. J. 1975. Physostigmine: Its use in acute anticholinergic syndrome with antidepressant and antiparkinson drugs. *Archives of General Psychiatry* 32:375–80.

49. Grinspoon, L.; Ewalt, J.; and Shader, R. I., eds. 1972. *Schizophrenia: Pharmacotherapy and psychotherapy* (Baltimore: Williams & Wilkins).

50. Group for the Advancement of Psychiatry. *Pharmacotherapy and psychotherapy: Paradoxes, problems, and progress*. GAP Publication no. 93, vol. 9 (March 1975), pp. 279–81.

51. Guirguis, E.; Voineskos, G.; Gray, J.; and Schlieman, E. 1977. Clozapine (lepones) vs. chlorpromazine (largactil) in acute schizophrenia: A double blind study. *Current Therapeutic Research* 21:708.

52. Gunderson, J. G. 1977. Drugs and psychosocial treatment of schizophrenia revisited. *Journal of Continuing Education in Psychiatry* (December 1977), pp. 25–40.

53. Gurland, B. J.; Sharpe, L.; Simon, R. J.; et al. 1972. On the use of psychiatric diagnosis for comparing psychiatric populations. *Psychiatric Quarterly* 46:461–73.

54. Hawkins, D., and Pauling, L. 1973. *Orthomolecular psychiatry: Treatment of schizophrenia* (San Francisco: W. H. Freeman).

55. Heiser, J. R., and Gellin, J. C. 1971. The reversal of anticholinergic drug-induced delirium and coma with physostigmine. *American Journal of Psychiatry* 127:1050–52.

56. Hoffer, A. 1962. *Niacin therapy in psychiatry* (Springfield, Ill.: Charles C Thomas).

57. Hogarty, G. E. 1977. Treatment and the course of schizophrenia. *Schizophrenia Bulletin* 3: 587–99.

58. Hogarty, G. E. 1978. Trial of maintenance antipsychotic therapy: Psychopharmacological roulette. *American Journal of Psychiatry*, in press.

59. Hogarty, G. E., and Goldberg, S. C. 1973. Drugs and social therapy in aftercare of schizophrenic patients. *Archives of General Psychiatry* 28:54–64.

60. Hogarty, G. E.; Goldberg, S. C.; Schooler, N. R.; and Ulrich, R. F. 1974. Drug and sociotherapy in the aftercare of schizophrenic patients. II: Two-year relapse rates. *Archives of General Psychiatry* 31:603–608.

61. Hollister, L. E. 1977. Antipsychotic medications and the treatment of schizophrenia. In *Psychopharmacology, from theory to practice*, eds. J. F. Barchas, P. A. Berger, R. D. Ciaranello, and G. R. Elliott (New York: Oxford University Press), pp. 121–50.

62. Horrobin, D. F. 1977. Schizophrenia as a prostaglandin deficiency disease. *Lancet* 1:936–37.

63. Itil, T. M.; Keskiner, A.; and Fink, M. 1966. Therapeutic studies in therapy-resistant schizophrenic patients. *Comprehensive Psychiatry* 7:488–93.

64. Jersild, C. 1976. The HL-A system and CNS disease with special reference to multiple sclerosis. Presented at the First International Symposium on Immunological Components in Schizophrenia, Galveston, Texas, 1976.

65. Kane, J.; Rifkin, A.; Quitkin, F.; and Klein, D. 1975. Antipsychotic drug blood levels and clinical outcome. In *Progress in psychiatric drug treatment*, eds. D. F. Klein and R. Gittelman-Klein (New York: Brunner/Mazel), vol. 2, pp. 399–408.

66. Kiloh, L. G.; Smith, J. S.; and Williams, S. E. 1973. Antiparkinson drugs as causal agents in tardive dyskinesia. *Medical Journal of Australia* 2:591–93.

67. Kinross-Wright, J.; Vogt, A. H.; and Charalampous, K. D. 1963. A new method of drug therapy. *American Journal of Psychiatry* 119:779–80.

68. Klawans, H. L., and Rubovits, R. 1974. Effect of cholinergic and anticholinergic agents on tardive dyskinesia. *Journal of Neurology, Neurosurgery and Psychiatry* 37:941–47.

69. Klerman, G. L. 1974. Pharmacotherapy of schizophrenia. *Annual Review of Medicine* 25:199–217.

70. Kline, N. S.; Li, C. H.; Lehmann, H. E.; et al. 1977. β-endorphin induced changes in schizophrenic and depressed patients. *Archives of General Psychiatry* 34:1111–13.

71. Kline, N. S., and Stanley, A. M. 1955. Use of reserpine in a neuropsychiatric hospital. *Annals of the New York Academy of Science* 61:85–91.

72. Kobayashi, R. M. 1976. Orofacial dyskinesia: Clinical features, mechanisms, and drug therapy. *Western Journal of Medicine* 125:277–88.

73. Kobayashi, R. M. 1977. Drug therapy of tardive dyskinesia. *New England Journal of Medicine* 296:257–60.

74. Lehmann, H. E. 1975. In *Comprehensive textbook of psychiatry*, eds. A. M. Freedman, H. I. Kaplan, and B. J. Sadock (Baltimore: Williams & Wilkins), pp. 890–923.

75. Lehmann, H. E. 1975. Psychopharmacological treatment of schizophrenia. *Schizophrenia Bulletin* 13:27–45.

76. Lehmann, H. E., and Hanrahan, G. E. 1954. Chlorpromazine, a new inhibiting agent for psychomotor excitement and manic states. *AMA Archives of Neurology and Psychiatry* 71:227–37.

77. Leighton, A. H. 1978. The compass and the troubled sea. *Psychiatric Annual* 8(2):43–54.

78. Lesser, M. 1977. Statement on orthomolecular medicine and orthomolecular psychiatry. Presented to the Hearing on Nutrition, Mental Health and Mental Development, United States Senate Select Committee on Nutrition and Human Needs, June 22, 1977.

79. Lewis, D. M.; Curry, S. H.; and Samuel, G. 1971. Long-acting phenothiazines in schizophrenia. *British Medical Journal* 1:671–72.

80. Marsden, C. D.; Tarsy, D.; and Baldessarini, R. J. 1975. Spontaneous and drug-induced movement disorders in psychotic patients. In *Psychiatric aspects of neurological disease*, eds. D. F. Benson and D. Blumer (New York: Grune & Stratton), pp. 219–66.

81. May, P. R. A. 1968. *Treatment of schizophrenia: A comparative study of five treatment methods* (New York: Science House).

82. May, P. R. A. 1974. Treatment of schizophrenia: I. A critique of reviews of the literature. *Comparative Psychiatry* 15:179–85.

83. May, P. R. A. 1975. Schizophrenia: Overview of treatment methods. In *Comprehensive textbook of psychiatry*, eds. A. M. Freedman, H. I. Kaplan, and B. J. Sadok (Baltimore: Williams & Wilkins), pp. 923–38.

84. *Megavitamin therapy.* Final report of the Joint University Megavitamin Therapy Review Committee to the Minister of Social Services and Community Health, Alberta, Canada, December 1976.

85. Moniz, E. 1936. *Tentatives opératoires dans le traitement de certaines psychoses* (Paris: Masson et Cie).

86. National Institute of Mental Health Psychopharmacology Service Center Collaborative Study Group. 1964. Phenothiazine treatment in acute schizophrenia. *Archives of General Psychiatry* 10:246–61.

87. Parkes, J. D. 1976. Clinical aspects of tardive dyskinesia. In *Biochemistry and neurology*, eds. H. F. Bradford and C. D. Marsden (London: Academic Press), pp. 47–55.

88. Paulson, G. W. 1975. Tardive dyskinesia. *Annual Review of Medicine* 26:75–81.

89. Pfeiffer, C. C.; Iliev, V.; and Goldstein, L. 1973. Blood histamine basophil counts and trace elements in the schizophrenias. In *Orthomolecular psychiatry: Treatment of schizophrenia*, eds. D. Hawkins and L. Pauling (San Francisco: W. H. Freeman).

90. Prange, A. J., Jr.; Wilson, I. C.; Morris, C. E.; et al. 1973. Preliminary experience with tryptophan and lithium in the treatment of tardive dyskinesia. *Psychopharmacological Bulletin* 9:36–37.

91. Reda, F. A.; Scanlaw, J.; Kemp, K.; et al. 1974. Treatment of tardive dyskinesia with lithium carbonate. *New England Journal of Medicine* 291:850.

92. Rifkin, A.; Quitkin, F.; and Klein, D. F. 1975. Akinesia—A poorly recognized drug-induced extrapyramidal behavioral disorder. *Archives of General Psychiatry* 32:672–74.

93. Rivera-Calimlim, L.; Castañeda L.; and Lasagna, L. 1973. Effects of mode of management on plasma chlorpromazine in psychiatric patients. *Clinical Pharmacological Therapy* 14:978–86.

94. Rivera-Calimlim, L.; Nastrallah, H.; Strauss, J.; et al. 1976. Clinical response and plasma levels: Effects of dose, dosage schedules and drug interactions on plasma chlorpromazine levels. *American Journal of Psychiatry* 133:646–52.

95. Sakel, M. 1938. *The pharmacological shock treatment of schizophrenia* (New York: Nervous and Mental Diseases Publishing Co.).

96. Shopsin, B.; Hirsch, J.; and Gershon, S. 1975. Visual hallucinations and propranolol. *Biological Psychiatry* 10:105–107.

97. Spitzer, R. L.; Endicott, J.; Robins, E.; et al. 1975. Preliminary report of the reliability of research diagnostic criteria applied to psychiatric case records. In *Predictability in psychopharmacology*, eds. A. Sudilovsky, S. Gershon, and B. Beer (New York: Raven Press), pp. 1–47.

98. Steiner, M.; Blum, J.; Wijsenbeck, H.; and Atsmon, A. 1972. Results of the treatment of psychoses with propranolol. *Kupat Holim Yearbook* 2:201.

99. Tamminga, C. A.; Smith, R. C.; Ericksen, S. E.; et al. 1977. Cholinergic influence in tardive dyskinesia. *American Journal of Psychiatry* 134:769–74.

100. Tinklenberg, J. R., and Berger, P. A. 1977. Treatment of abusers of nonaddictive drugs. In *Psychopharmacology, from theory to practice*, eds. J. D. Barchas, et al. (New York: Oxford University Press), p. 398.

101. Torrey, E. F., and Peterson, M. R. 1976. The viral hypothesis of schizophrenia. *Schizophrenia Bulletin* 2:136–46.

102. Trueman, H. R., and Valentine, M. G. 1974. Flupenthixol decanoate in schizophrenia. *British Journal of Psychiatry* 124:58–59.

103. Tupin, J. P. 1975. Management of violent patients. In *Manual of psychiatric therapeutics*, ed. R. I. Shader (Boston: Little, Brown), p. 134.

104. Wagemaker, H., and Cade, R. 1977. The use of hemodialysis in chronic schizophrenia. *American Journal of Psychiatry* 134:684–85.

105. Woodruff, R. A., Jr.; Goodwin, D. W.; and Guze, S. B. 1974. *Psychiatric diagnosis.* (London: Oxford University Press).

106. Wurtman, R. J., and Fernstrom, J. D. 1978. Dietary influences on brain neurotransmitter synthesis. Presented at the Kellogg Nutrition Symposium, Toronto, Canada, March 20–21, 1978.

107. Wurtman, R. J.; Hirsch, M., and Growdon, J. H. 1977. Lecithin consumption raises serum-free choline levels. *Lancet* 2:68–75.

108. Yorkston, N. J.; Gruzelier, J. H.; Zaki, S. A.; et al. 1977. Propranolol as an adjunct to the treatment of schizophrenia. *Lancet* 2:575–78.

109. Yorkston, N. J.; Zaki, S. A.; Malik, M. K. U.; et al. 1974. Propranolol in the control of schizophrenic symptoms. *British Medical Journal* 4:633–35.

Chapter 10

EST AND OTHER SOMATIC THERAPIES OF SCHIZOPHRENIA

Max Fink, M.D.

Schizophrenia is a complex group of disorders undergoing continual redefinition. From generation to generation the criteria for diagnosis change with the attitudes of the cataloguers and the successes of new therapies. As fever therapy was replaced by penicillin therapy for dementia paralytica, whole populations of "schizophrenics" disappeared. As lithium therapy relieved the symptoms of manic patients, another segment of "schizophrenics" were lost by redefinition. The problem of diagnosis in an amorphous disorder allows observers to see or not to see "schizophrenics" almost at will. The complex symptoms may be as vague as a Rorschach image, allowing each observer as much play in interpretation as allowed by a Rorschach card. From these shifting foundations, is it any wonder that the therapies of "schizophrenia" are so poorly defined? Is it any surprise that every presumed treatment of the mentally ill has been applied to "schizophrenics," and that since the population is so poorly defined, some patients improved, some remained the same, and some got worse? Thus, almost all recently introduced somatic therapies had their early trials on "schizophrenic patients"— fever therapy, insulin coma, Metrazol (pentylenetetrazol) and electroshock, psychosurgery, vitamin therapy, and the whole range of psychoactive drugs from sedatives and stimulants to hallucinogens, deliriants, and opiates.

The past decade is a reflection of the many that went before it. The insulin coma and psychosurgery therapies that were so prominent in the 1940–50 era were quickly replaced by drug therapies when these were found to be more effective, safer, easier to use, and more economical. For example, the discontinuation of insulin coma therapy was assured by the results of two carefully done, random assignment studies of insulin coma and chlorpromazine (8,24) and barbiturates (2), which confirmed clinicians' beliefs that pharmacotherapy was safer, easier to administer, and less costly than insulin coma.

Interest in electroshock (EST), insulin coma, and psychosurgery in schizophrenia has waned, reflecting the apparent success of the anti-psychotic drugs. The increasing acceptance of genetic theories for the origin of schizophrenia has diverted more attention to the identification of patients at risk and to the principles of prophylaxis. But a genetic view of schizophrenia also leads to therapeutic pessimism: a common view is that no therapy can be successful in a genetic disorder other than palliative rehabilitation or psychotherapy. The lack of interest in biological therapies is reflected in the 1976 review of progress in schizophrenia research issued by the Center for Studies of Schizophrenia of the National Institute of Mental Health (40). In an extensive fifty-six-page report, only one paragraph of fewer than three hundred words is dedicated to "Treatment."

Awareness that patients receiving antipsychotic drugs may yet pay an unanticipated price in extensive motor dyskinesia is leading to a reassessment of pharmacotherapy. In the beginning, only hypotension and parkinsonism were considered risks of the drug therapies; later un-usual eye findings and retinopathy became matters of concern; and lately tardive dyskinesia has occupied the attention of researchers. The increased frequency, the earlier age of onset, and shorter exposures to antipsychotic drug treatment impress readers that irremediable tardive dyskinesia is a significant risk of antipsychotic drug therapy. In this period of anxiety perhaps there is some justification for reviewing the role of convulsive therapy in schizophrenia—a treatment which has been poorly tested but seems to be effective.

Electroshock (EST), or convulsive therapy (ECT), was introduced as a treatment for schizophrenia in the mistaken belief that the concentra-tion of cerebral glial cells was less in schizophrenic patients than in nor-mal subjects and other mentally ill. In 1939, Meduna (50) noted that patients with epilepsy had increased cerebral gliosis, and it occurred to him that repeated seizures may increase cerebral gliosis and thereby relieve the symptoms of schizophrenia. He first used camphor injections, and then introduced Metrazol (pentylenetetrazol). Cerletti and Bini (12) showed an electrical induction to be feasible. Soon seizures were found to be therapeutic not only for "schizophrenic" patients, but for those with depressive psychoses as well. In the following decades, EST was shown to be effective in depressive psychoses, its variations were de-fined, and its place in the therapy of the mentally ill was established (22). Despite much study, the role of EST in schizophrenia remains a matter of debate (23).

A reviewer of the therapy of schizophrenia is faced with a difficult task of interpretation. The diagnosis of schizophrenia is subjective and depends on the education of the physician who identifies the case, selects the treatment, and assesses the outcome. The schizophrenias may be divided into a number of classes which have heuristic value: "acute" and "chronic" reflect the duration and the severity (intensity) of the dis-turbances in motility and thought processes. Chronic schizophrenia is often described by such terms as "hebephrenic," "paranoid," "catatonic," and "simple," but these have less utility in these assessments.

An important variable in assessing the efficacy of EST is the number, frequency, and type of seizures induced. For example, a dictum in

Redlich and Freedman (58) may preclude adequate therapy in some schizophrenic patients:

Electric convulsive therapy is still employed in the treatment of schizophrenia. It has not been very effective. Even critical proponents of the method do not recommend it in general, but specifically for the treatment of stuporous and hyperactive catatonic patients. Remissions in pure catatonics may occur after a few shocks, but experienced therapists generally suggest a full course of treatment, consisting of twelve to twenty shocks. Very massive treatment with one or more shocks daily in our opinion, is not justified. It regresses the patient, makes him apathetic, and produces temporary deficit states. [pp. 512–513]

This opinion contrasts with the report by Kalinowsky (36), who summarized an experience with 1,500 patients treated with EST and stated:

Stress is placed on the efficacy of electric convulsive therapy in cases of acute schizophrenia where a sufficient number of convulsions is administered; discontinuation of treatment after the usual early improvement leads almost invariably to relapse and is the most important reason for failure of this method in treatment of schizophrenia. [p. 660]

In defining the efficacy of EST in schizophrenia, we must consider the problems of diagnosis (and heterogenicity of samples), type of outcome evaluation, and dosage (number and frequency of seizures). This review of EST includes reports of the repeated induction of cerebral seizures by electrical or chemical (flurothyl, pentylenetetrazol) means and excludes the subconvulsive therapies and insulin coma.

Efficacy of EST in Schizophrenia

Few clinical studies of EST meet our present standards for an evaluation of therapeutic efficacy. Most reports are case studies, with little description of the previous or concurrent therapy and without adequate follow-up. The studies frequently lack contemporaneous controls or comparison groups (59).

EST is recommended for the treatment of acute and chronic schizophrenia (18,37,56,62). Its efficacy is proportional to the patient's length of illness (17,38,70) and to the number and the frequency of seizures (3,36). EST is effective in acute schizophrenia (illnesses of less than two years' duration and acute onset), but the results are inversely proportional to the length and the severity of the illness, particularly in disorders of long duration with slow, insidious onset.* The results are better with more intensive treatment.†

---

* See references 10, 36, 51, 53, and 60.
† See references 3, 20, 27, 35, 41, and 52.

ACUTE SCHIZOPHRENIA

In the open clinical studies done before the advent of psychotropic drugs, 75 percent of cases treated exhibited a reduction in symptoms and shorter hospitalization.* Zeifert (70) found improvement rates of 84 percent with Metrazol and 80 percent with EST. EST-treated samples showed better discharge rates, improved symptom evaluations, and fewer relapses than patients treated by psychotherapy, milieu therapy, or sedatives (28,46,55,69). In studies using a historical control, EST exhibited an improvement rate of 50 percent to 70 percent, contrasted with a rate of 10 percent to 30 percent for the earlier period.† In a follow-up of hospitalized patients treated by psychotherapy, EST, or insulin coma therapy, Rachlin et al. (57) found shorter hospitalization periods and better discharge rates for EST.

With the advent of psychotropic drugs, the interest in assessments were mainly in camparisons of EST with drug therapy, either alone‡ or combined (15,42,65).

Comparisons between EST and phenothiazines in first-admission or acute schizophrenic patients found the treatments to be equivalent in short-term results.§ Patients receiving from twelve to twenty electroshocks or from 300 to 1,200 milligrams a day of chlorpromazine exhibited equivalent reductions in symptom ratings by "blind" raters, on nurses' ward observations, and improved discharge evaluations (44,48).

No difference was found between EST alone and EST combined with chlorpromazine in symptom ratings; but EST either with or without chlorpromazine showed more improvement than either fluphenazine (20 mg per day) or chlorpromazine (1 g per day) alone (15). Smith et al. (65) found greater short-term (one to three weeks) improvement scores for patients treated by EST plus chlorpromazine (400 mg per day) than by EST alone; in later assessments (six weeks, six months, one year) the therapies were equivalent.

CHRONIC SCHIZOPHRENIA

In many open clinical studies EST was effective in discharging 10 percent to 20 percent of the long-term mentally ill (11,36,64). Symptom reduction, particularly decreases in excitement and the need for restraints, was often described. In open comparisons of EST with milieu, drug, and insulin coma therapies, little difference among the treatments was reported.¶ There was no difference in short-term evaluations of improvement between EST, insulin coma, and psychotherapy (30), while a follow-up study found better clinical results for EST than for insulin coma or psychotherapy alone (57).

Controlled clinical trials found little difference among various treat-

---

* See references 4, 17, 29, 31, 43, and 70.
† See references 9, 16, 19, 30, and 32.
‡ See references 4, 15, 44, 47, 48, and 49.
§ See references 4, 15, 42, 44, and 47.
¶ See references 13, 14, 25, 30, 61, and 67.

ments of chronic schizophrenia (34,59). Miller et al. (51) compared the effects of EST, anesthesia alone, EST and anesthesia, and subconvulsive currents in the chronic mentally ill and found each equally ineffective. Brill et al. (10) studied EST alone, EST and succinylcholine, EST and thiopental, thiopental alone, and nitrous oxide in chronic, hospitalized psychotic veterans and found no differences among the treatments. They concluded that EST was ineffective in chronic schizophrenia. May (47), May and Tuma (48), May et al. (49) assigned "middle prognosis" schizophrenic patients (many of whom were readmissions) to EST, milieu therapy, psychotherapy, psychotropic drugs, or psychotherapy combined with psychotropic drugs. The short-term results for the drug therapies were superior to EST and to other therapies; but in the long term (more than three years) they found that patients treated with EST joined those treated by drug therapies in the better results: they had shorter stays in the hospital before discharge and shorter rehospitalizations after their initial release.

The efficacy of EST in chronic scizophrenia is clearly dependent on the duration of illness as well as on the number and rate of treatments. The longer the duration of illness, the poorer the therapeutic results and the greater the number of treatments needed for symptom relief. Relief is estimated as 50 percent to 70 percent in patients who have been ill for less than one year, but it is reduced to less than 20 percent in patients who have been ill more than three years.* Courses of treatments with fewer than twenty seizures are less effective than longer courses.† Baker et al. (3) compared the efficacy of twelve seizures with twenty seizures and found greater benefits with the latter.

Some physicians increased the frequency of seizures to daily treatments or to a few treatments a day, which led to "regressive therapy" (27,35,41). In uncontrolled studies, the efficacy rates were greater for schizophrenic patients treated with multiple treatments than for those treated three times a week (17,27). But the severity and persistence of the organic mental syndrome and the availability of antipsychotic drugs led to this treatment's disuse. Recently Murillo and Exner (20,52) reexamined the efficacy of intensive EST and found a superiority of this treatment in such long-term indices as work record, number and duration of rehospitalizations, and need for further treatment when compared with drug therapy or standard courses of EST.

MAINTENANCE TREATMENT

Another application of EST in schizophrenia is in sustaining clinical improvement or preventing relapse with treatments given monthly, biweekly, or even weekly for extended periods. The assessments of such treatments are few, and the results inconclusive. Geoghegan and Stevenson (26) administered monthly treatments to thirteen psychotic patients for five years after a course of EST. In three years there were

---

* See references 10, 17, 36, 38, 51, 53, and 60.
† See references 3, 20, 27, 35, 41, and 52.

no rehospitalizations in this group, compared with eleven readmissions among eleven patients who did not agree to receive prophylactic treatments. In the next two years two of the thirteen were readmitted despite continued treatment (66). Karliner and Wehrheim (39) offered maintenance treatment to 210 patients. Fifty-seven accepted, receiving an average of one treatment a month, and 12 percent relapsed; while of 153 patients who received no maintenance treatments, 79 percent relapsed within a six-year observation period. Barton, Mehta, and Snaith (5) compared the effects of two extra treatments for those who ended a course of EST as soon as improvement was established. They found no additional benefit for two extra treatment at two-, six-, and twelve-week evaluations.

Safety of EST in Schizophrenia

Death, brain damage, memory impairment, and spontaneous seizure are the principal complications of EST; they are derived from the direct effects of the seizure and the convulsive, the anesthesia, and the anxiety and fear of "shock therapy." Memory impairment and other aspects of an organic mental syndrome are of special concern when schizophrenic patients are given an intensive treatment schedule or an extended number of treatments. In addition, fracture (particularly of the spine), fear, panic, and headache were reported with sufficient frequency to be considered risks of the treatment.

Any survey of EST since its inception in the late 1930s must consider the significant technical advances which mark the treatment (22,23). In the first few years neither anesthesia nor muscle relaxants were routine; and anoxia was not only accepted but encouraged. "Missed seizures" (incomplete inductions) were common and contributed both to the anxiety and the fear of the treatment and to its mortality and morbidity. Spontaneous seizures were frequently reported, and "brain damage" was a complication which was often cited. Treatment modifications introduced since 1953 have reduced the complication rate significantly. Anesthesia and muscle paralysis (using succinylcholine) are now routinely used. Anoxia is no longer acceptable, as hyperoxygenation and supported ventilation are commonly prescribed. Attention to electrode placement and to current characteristics, in addition to oxygenation, anesthesia, and muscle relaxation, have reduced to negligible dimensions the complications of fracture, brain damage, death, spontaneous seizure, panic, and fear. Brain pathology after EST has not been examined since 1956, since these changes were introduced, and we lack any evidence that these treatments induce persistent brain damage. This optimistic summary is particularly true for the use of EST in the depressive psychoses, where the treatment response is notoriously rapid and few (4 to 8) seizures often suffice (22).

Whether such a sanguine therapeutic outlook is justified in schizophrenia is unclear. The clinical response is often laggard, so that many treatments are prescribed. Some therapists find intensive (daily) treatments effective, often eliciting an organic mental syndrome. It is difficult at this juncture to evade the conclusion that the EST process in schizophrenia differs from that in depressive psychoses, insofar as the number and frequency of seizures are important variables and a more intensive course, stimulating in most cases of an organic mental syndrome, is required for efficacy. If this be true, then the question, how safe is EST in schizophrenia? may best be rephrased, "What is the safety of extensive EST in schizophrenia?" To answer this question, one would have to reassess the long-term consequences of regressive EST. In the early published studies, the extensive mental syndromes resolved; but pathologic studies are lacking (another evidence of relative safety of regressive EST?). Exner and Murillo (20,52) have failed to find evidence of a persistent mental syndrome in their cases treated with intensive EST.

Multiple monitored electroconvulsive treatment (MMECT) is another intensive EST treatment (7). Blachly and Gowing (7) proposed that four to six seizures be given in one session; and they suggested that clinical efficacy is high, and that mental changes did not occur. But Abrams and Fink (1) and Strain and Bidder (68) found that some depressive subjects sustained transient severe mental syndromes with MMECT.

Other modifications of the EST process have been developed during the past decade, including unilateral electrode placement and selection of minimal currents to elicit a seizure. The reviews of the comparative efficacy of unilateral electrode placement compared with bilateral electrode placement emphasize the equivalence of the two applications for efficacy in depressive psychoses (with differences in the incidence of memory defects); but no data are available on the efficacy of unilateral EST in schizophrenia. Similarly, the principal emphasis in the use of minimal currents is to reduce the incidence of an organic mental syndrome and memory deficits; and no evidence in schizophrenia is available.

The assessment of the hazards of EST must also consider the hazards of the drug therapies where tardive dyskinesia, lenticular opacities, organic psychosis, hepatic dysfunction, and cardiac toxicity are major consequences which have only recently been well documented (33).

Discussion

Both acute and chronic schizophrenia patients receive some benefit from EST. For the acutely ill the benefits are at least equal to pharmacotherapy, and even for the chronically ill EST elicits some benefits for some patients, provided the treatment is given intensively. The modern induction of seizures is safe, and the intensive treatment, while not fully evaluated, may yet prove to be safe with minimal hazards. This is particularly important since the alternate therapies for schizophrenia, other than pharmacotherapy, are largely ineffective; and pharmacotherapy is a treatment whose risks have yet to be defined. A review of the assessments of EST in schizophrenia is plagued not only by the problems of diagnosis and classification defined earlier, but by the general reluctance of practitioners to accept multiple treatments as particularly useful in schizophrenia. The expectation—encouraged by experiences with patients with endogenous phychoses—that patients will respond to four to eight seizures remains unfulfilled in the treatment of many schizophrenic patients. More treatments, more intensively given, are often necessary in schizophrenia—an indication that the underlying pathology is indeed different from the endogenous depressions.

When insulin coma and psychosurgery were recommended for patients with schizophrenia, better results after insulin coma were obtained in patients who had sustained a prolonged coma—an organic mental syndrome which occasionally supervened during a normal treatment. Recovery from the mental syndrome was often accompanied by improvement in the underlying psychosis. Similar results were reported in patients treated with psychosurgery, where retreatment with a greater degree of brain damage was considered useful in ameliorating symptoms in some patients. It is probable that the degree of brain dysfunction is an important factor in the improvement in symptoms after the use of any of these "organic" treatments in schizophrenia.

There is much to be learned regarding the role of EST in the treatment of schizophrenia (23). What is the role of the organic mental syndrome in the therapeutic process? Can the therapeutic benefits be sustained by maintenance EST or equally well by maintenance pharmacotherapy? EST is a way to stimulate hypothalamic function in depressive psychoses (22). What is the role of hypothalamic stimulation in the schizophrenic process? What behavioral predictors are useful in prognosticating the efficacy of EST in schizophrenic patients? What is the relative efficacy of MMECT and regressive EST, and how do comparisons of these two modes of EST help us understand the EST process and the psychopathology of schizophrenia? These are a few questions posed by the EST data. It is necessary to reassess the exclusion of interest in the biological therapies reflected in the 1976 review by the National Institute of Mental Health committee responsible for stimulating research into the causes and cure of schizophrenia. It is time to reassess the usefulness of EST in schizophrenia.

A special note about the role of other biological treatments of schizophrenia: neither insulin coma nor psychosurgery are now used systematically in treating the mentally ill. The recent review by the National Commission for the Protection of Human Subjects of Biomedical and Behavioral Research (54) of the role of psychosurgery in treating the mentally ill failed to find evidence for the efficacy of psychosurgical procedures in patients with symptoms of schizophrenia. Neither did Bernstein, et al. (6), nor did Shobe and Gildea (63) in their reviews. Nevertheless, the commission encouraged further study, and it is in the public interest to consider carefully monitored and well-controlled studies of psychosurgery in patients with symptoms of schizophrenia.

Summary

A review of the literature on the efficacy and the safety of biological treatments in schizophrenia finds EST to be as effective as pharmacotherapy in acute schizophrenia. In chronic schizophrenia the efficacy is limited, but inadequate dosage may contribute to the poor findings. Except for intensive EST, where an organic mental syndrome may be a significant consequence, the risks of EST, using modern methods of medication, compare favorably with pharmacotherapy in the reviewer's opinion.

Despite the limited nature of the comparative assessments, EST may be considered as an alternate therapy in schizophrenia. A major need is for comparative assessments of EST and other therapies using modern, controlled methods of evaluation, with special emphasis on the role of intensive therapy on outcome.

Insulin coma, psychosurgery, electronarcosis, and sleep therapy are no longer viable therapies of schizophrenia.

[handwritten note: nothing and ne at compliance, or rela of combined thy; ie c psychmed rx; yet absolutely no evidence that ECT "cure" rely by itself]

BIBLIOGRAPHY

1. Abrams, R., and M. Fink. 1972. Clinical experiences with multiple electroconvulsive treatments. *Comprehensive Psychiatry* 13:115–21.

2. Ackner, B.; Harris, A.; and Oldham, A. J. 1957. Insulin treatment of schizophrenia: Controlled study. *Lancet* 2:607–11.

3. Baker, A. A.; Bird, G.; Lavin, N. I.; and Thorpe, J. G. 1960. E.C.T. in schizophrenia. *Journal of Mental Science* 106:1506–11.

4. Baker, A. A.; Game, J. A.; and Thorpe, J. G. 1960. Some research into the treatment of schizophrenia in the mental hospital. *Journal of Mental Science* 106:203–13.

5. Barton, J. L.; Mehta, S.; and Snaith, R. P. 1973. The prophylactic value of extra ECT in depressive illness. *Acta Psychiatrica Scandinavica* 49:386–92.

6. Bernstein, I. C.; Callahan, W. A.; and Jaronson, J. M. 1975. Lobotomy in private practice. *Archives of General Psychiatry* 32:1041–47.

7. Blachly, P. H., and Gowing, D. 1966. Multiple monitored electroconvulsive treatment. *Comprehensive Psychiatry* 7:100–109.

8. Boardman, R. H.; Lomas, J.; and Markowe, M. 1956. Insulin and chlorpromazine in schizophrenia: Comparative study in previously untreated cases. *Lancet* 2:487–94.

9. Bond, E. D. 1954. Results of psychiatric treatments with control series. *American Journal of Psychiatry* 110:561–66.

10. Brill, N. O.; Crumpton, E.; Eiduson, S.; Grayson, H. M.; Hellman, L. I.; and Richards, R. A. 1959. Relative effectiveness of various components of electroconvulsive therapy. *Archives of Neurology and Psychiatry* 81:627–35.

11. Brussel, J. A., and Schneider, J. 1951. The E.S.T. in the treatment and control of chronically disturbed mental patients. *Psychiatric Quarterly* 25:55–64.

12. Cerletti, U., and Bini, L. 1938. Un nuevo metodo di shockterapie "L'elettroshock." *Bollettino della Accademia Medica di Roma* 64:136–38.

13. Chafetz, M. E. 1943. An active treatment for chronically ill patients. *Journal of Nervous and Mental Disease* 98:464–73.

14. Cheney, C. O., and Drewry, P. H. 1938. Results of non-specific treatment in dementia praecox. *American Journal of Psychiatry* 95:203–17.

15. Childers, R. T. 1964. Comparison of four regimens in newly admitted female schizophrenics. *American Journal of Psychiatry* 120:1010–11.

16. Currier, G. E.; Cullinan, C.; and Rothchild, D. 1952. Results of treatment of schizophrenia in a state hospital. *Archives of Neurology and Psychiatry* 67:80–88.

17. Danziger, L., and Kendwall, J. A. 1946. Prediction of the immediate outcome of shock therapy in dementia praecox. *Diseases of the Nervous System* 7:229–303.

18. Detre, T. P., and Jarecki, H. G. 1971. *Modern psychiatric treatment* (Philadelphia: J. B. Lippincott).

19. Ellison, E. A., and Hamilton, D. M. 1949. The hospital treatment of dementia praecox. *American Journal of Psychiatry* 106:454–61.

20. Exner, J. E., and Murillo, L. G. 1977. A long term follow-up of schizophrenics treated with regressive ECT. *Diseases of the Nervous System* 38:162–68.

21. Fink, M. 1977. CNS sequellae of EST: Risks of therapy and their prophylaxis. In *Psychopathology and brain dysfunction*, eds. A. Friedhoff, S. Gershon, and C. Shagass (New York: Raven Press), pp. 223–39.

22. Fink, M. 1978. Efficacy and safety of induced seizures (EST) in man. *Comprehensive Psychiatry* 19(1):1–18.

23. Fink, M. Is EST a useful therapy in schizophrenia? In *Controversy in psychiatry*, eds. J. P. Brady and H. K. H. Brodie (Philadelphia: W. B. Saunders), forthcoming.

24. Fink, M.; Shaw, R.; Gross, G. E.; and Coleman, F. C. 1958. Comparative study of chlorpromazine and insulin coma in therapy of psychosis. *Journal of the American Medical Association* 166:1846–50.

25. Funk, J. C.; Shatin, L.; Freed, E.; and Rockmore, L. 1955. Somatopsychotherapeutic approach to long-term schizophrenic patients. *Diseases of the Nervous System* 12:423–37.

26. Geoghegan, J. J., and Stevenson, G. H. 1949. Prophylactic electroshock. *American Journal of Psychiatry* 105:494–96.

27. Glueck, B. C.; Reiss, H.; and Bernard, L. E. 1957. Regressive electric shock therapy. *Psychiatric Quarterly* 31:117–35.

28. Goldfarb, W., and Kiene, H. 1945. The treatment of psychotic-like regressions of combat soldiers. *Psychiatric Quarterly* 19:555–65.

29. Goller, E. S. 1960. A controlled trial of reserpine in chronic schizophrenia. *Journal of Mental Science* 106:1408–12.

30. Gottlieb, J. S., and Huston, P. E. 1951. Treatment of schizophrenia. A comparison of three methods: Brief psychotherapy, insulin coma, and electric shock. *Journal of Nervous and Mental Disease* 113:237–46.

31. Guttman, E.; Mayer-Gross, W.; and Slater, E. T. O. 1939. Short distance prognosis of schizophrenia. *Journal of Neurology, Neurosurgery and Psychiatry* 2:25–34.

32. Hamilton, D. M., and Wall, J. H. 1948. The hospital treatment of dementia praecox. *American Journal of Psychiatry* 105:346–52.

33. Hartshorn, E. A. 1974. Interactions of CNS drugs—Antidepressants. *Drug intelligence and Clinical Pharmacy* 8:591–606.

34. Heath, E. S.; Adams, A.; and Wakeling, P. L. G. 1964. Short courses of ECT and simulated ECT in chronic schizophrenia. *British Journal of Psychiatry* 110:800–807.

35. Jacoby, M. G., and Van Houten, Z. 1960. Regressive shock therapy. *Diseases of the Nervous System* 21:582–83.

36. Kalinowsky, L. B. 1943. Electric convulsive therapy, with emphasis on importance of adequate treatment. *Archives of Neurology and Psychiatry* 50:652–60.

37. Kalinowsky, L. B., and Hippius, H. 1972. *Pharmacological, convulsive and other treatments in psychiatry* (New York: Grune & Stratton).

38. Kalinowsky, L. B., and Worthing, H. J. 1943. Results with electroconvulsive therapy in 200 cases of schizophrenia. *Psychiatric Quarterly* 17:144–53.

39. Karliner, W., and Wehrheim, H. K. 1965. Maintenance convulsive treatments. *American Journal of Psychiatry* 212:1113–15.

40. Keith, S. J.; Gunderson, G. G.; Reifman, A.; Buchsbaum, S.; and Mosher, L. R. 1976. Special report: Schizophrenia, 1976. *Schizophrenia Bulletin* 2:509–65.

41. Kennedy, C. J. C., and Anchel, D. 1948. Regressive electric-shock in schizophrenia refractory to other shock therapies. *Psychiatric Quarterly* 22:317–20.

42. King, P. 1960. Chlorpromazine and electroconvulsive therapy in the treatment of newly hospitalized schizophrenics. *Journal of Clinical and Experimental Psychopathology* 21:101–5.

43. Kino, F. F., and Thorpe, F. T. 1946. Electrical convulsion therapy in 500 selected psychotics. *Journal of Mental Science* 92:138–45.

44. Langsley, D. G.; Enterline, J. D.; and Hickerson, G. X. 1959. A comparison of chlorpromazine and ECT in treatment of acute schizophrenic and manic reactions. *Archives of Neurology and Psychiatry* 81:384–91.

45. Laurell, B. 1970. Flurothyl convulsive therapy. *Acta Psychiatrica Scandinavica*, supp. 213: 5–79.

46. McKinnon, A. L. 1948. Electric shock therapy in a private psychiatric hospital. *Canadian Medical Association Journal* 58:478–83.

47. May, P. R. 1968. *Treatment of schizophrenia* (New York: Science House).

48. May, P. R., and Tuma, A. H. 1976. Follow-up study of the results of treatment of schizophrenia. In *Evaluation of psychological therapies*, eds. R. Spitzer and D. F. Klein (Baltimore: Johns Hopkins University Press), pp. 256–84.

49. May, P. R.; Tuma, A. H.; Yale, C.; Potepan, P.; and Dixon, W. J. 1976. Schizophrenia—A follow-up study of results of treatment. *Archives of General Psychiatry* 33:481–86.

50. Meduna, L. 1939. Die Konvulsionstherapie der Schizophrenia. Rückblick und Ausblick [The convulsive therapy of schizophrenics: Retrospect and Prospect]. *Psychiatrisch-neurologische Wochenschrift* 41:165–69.

51. Miller, D. H.; Clancy, J.; and Cummings, F. 1953. A comparison between undirectional current non-convulsive electrical stimulation, alternating current electroshock and pentothal in chronic schizophrenia. *American Journal of Psychiatry* 109:617–20.

52. Murillo, L. G., and Exner, J. E., Jr. 1973. The effects of regressive ECT with process schizophrenics. *American Journal of Psychiatry* 130:269–73.

53. Naidoo, D. 1956. The effects of reserpine (Serpasil) on the chronic disturbed schizophrenic:

A comparative study of rauwolfia alkaloids and electroconvulsive therapy. *Journal of Nervous and Mental Disease* 123:1–13.

54. National Commission for the Protection of Human Subjects of Biomedical and Behavioral Research. 1977. *Psychosurgery—Report and recommendations.* DHEW Publications OS 77-0001 (Washington, D. C.: U.S. Government Printing Office).

55. Palmer, D. M.; Sprang, H. E.; and Hans, C. L. 1951. Electroshock therapy in schizophrenia: A statistical survey of 455 cases. *Journal of Nervous and Mental Disease* 114:162–71.

56. Paterson, A. S. 1963. *Electrical and drug treatments in psychiatry* (Amsterdam: Elsevier).

57. Rachlin, H. L.; Goldman, G. S.; Gurvitz, M.; Lurie, A.; and Rachlin, L. 1956. Follow-up study of 317 patients discharged from Hillside Hospital in 1950. *Journal of Hillside Hospital* 5:17–40.

58. Redlich, F., and Freedman, D. X. 1966. *The theory and practice of psychiatry* (New York: Basic Books).

59. Riddell, S. A. 1963. The therapeutic efficacy of ECT. *Archives of General Psychiatry* 8:546–56.

60. Ross, J. R., and Malzberg, B. 1939. A review of the results of the pharmacological shock therapy and the Metrazol convulsive therapy in New York State. *American Journal of Psychiatry* 96:297–316.

61. Rouleau, Y.; Nadeau, G.; Delage, J.; Coulombe, H.; and Bonchard, M. 1955. An appraisal of histamine therapy in schizophrenia. *Journal of Clinical and Experimental Psychopathology* 16:1–9.

62. Sargant, W., and Slater, E. 1964. *An introduction to physical methods of treatment in psychiatry* (Baltimore: Williams & Wilkins).

63. Shobe, F. O., and Gildea, M. 1968. Long-term follow-up of selected lobotomized private patients. *Journal of the American Medical Association* 206:327–32.

64. Shoor, M., and Adams, I. H. 1950. The intensive electroshock therapy of chronic disturbed psychotic patients. *American Journal of Psychiatry* 107:279–82.

65. Smith, K.; Surphilis, W. R. P.; Gynther, M. D.; and Shimkunas, A. 1967. ECT-chlorpromazine and chlorpromazine compared in the treatment of schizophrenia. *Journal of Nervous and Mental Disease* 144:284–90.

66. Stevenson, G. H., and Geoghegan, J. J. 1951. Prophylactic electroshock. *American Journal of Psychiatry* 107:743–48.

67. Stinson, B.; Kempff, N.; Lilly, V.; and G. Schmidt. 1972. Prediction of response to electroshock therapy in chronic mental patients. *Diseases of the Nervous System* 33:123–25.

68. Strain, J. J., and Bidder, T. G. 1971. Transient cerebral complication associated with multiple monitored electroconvulsive therapy. *Diseases of the Nervous System* 32:95–100.

69. Wolff, G. E. 1955. Electric shock treatment. *American Journal of Psychiatry* 111:748–50.

70. Zeifert, M. 1941. Results obtained from the administration of 12,000 doses of Metrazol to mental patients. *Psychiatric Quarterly* 15:772–78.

Chapter 11

INDIVIDUAL PSYCHOTHERAPY

John G. Gunderson, M.D.

Historical Development

As a young psychiatrist who in 1903 strongly embraced the psychoanalytic approach to understanding mental illness being described by Freud, Carl Jung made the first recorded effort to apply this method to a schizophrenic patient (49). The patient himself was a young psychiatrist who had been hospitalized at the Burghölzli Sanitarium in Switzerland. After nine months of intensive therapy with Jung, the patient escaped from the hospital and was subsequently reported to have died by suicide three years later. Through this and other efforts Jung and his associates, under the guidance of Bleuler, developed and tested experimentally the idea that the symbolic communications of schizophrenic patients could be understood (11).

Freud himself had limited access to hospitalized schizophrenic patients, and thus his contributions are extrapolated from his theoretical formulations in working with paranoid, but not clearly schizophrenic, patients and from his efforts to understand the autobiographical accounts of Schreber (25). Freud's contributions include the concepts of primary narcissism, his view of delusions and hallucinations as restitutive phenomena, and his outline of the dynamics of projection. Although in his early writings Freud viewed schizophrenia as on a continuum with nonpsychotic mental disorders, he later concluded that some aspects of schizophrenia were beyond a purely psychological understanding. This rather pessimistic conclusion, based on rather sparse observations, nevertheless influenced psychoanalysis away from psychotherapeutic work with schizophrenics. With a few notable exceptions, such as the Burghölzli Sanitarium, schizophrenia has remained a psychiatric disease entity which to most Europeans is inaccessible to psychotherapeutic interventions. Among these exceptions are Paul Federn, who contributed the concepts of ego boundaries, and more recently the theoretical constructs by Melanie Klein and the clinical implications noted by her followers.

In America, however, Adolph Meyer provided a much different climate in which to approach schizophrenia, by virtue of his emphasis upon understanding psychiatric disorders as logical but maladaptive reactions to common life events. In this climate flowered Sullivan's inspirational efforts to view schizophrenia as a human process and to develop a scholarly approach to understanding schizophrenic communications and interactional styles. Sullivan openly inspired the hope that schizophrenic persons could be successfully treated with individual psychotherapy.

Many of Sullivan's students working out of Chestnut Lodge subsequently expanded and popularized psychotherapeutic approaches to schizophrenia. Prominent among these was Frieda Fromm-Reichmann who emphasized the importance of addressing and using the patient's ego in a firm task-oriented approach to individual psychotherapy. This approach was set in stark contrast to that of John Rosen's dramatic "direct analytic technique" which purported to address the id. His work suggested the possibility that an intensive and active short-term approach could bring about far-reaching changes in this most serious of psychiatric disorders. Although subsequent research failed to demonstrate any lasting results from Rosen's approach (9,47), the conflicting but optimistic reports of that period generated a great deal of excitement and interest. As a result many departments of psychiatry began to make the teaching of individual psychotherapy for schizophrenics part of their training for residents.

Emerging from this period was a third generation of prolific and articulate psychotherapists, which included representatives from the mainstream of psychoanalysis, such as Arlow, Brenner, Jacobson, Wexler, and Boyer, and from the mainstream of academic psychiatry, such as Pious, Semrad, Lidz, and Arieti. Among the contributions of these therapists has been the effort to adapt a psychoanalytic approach suitable for office practice and the greater recognition of the role social context has in creating or reducing schizophrenic psychopathology. No one, however, attracted a wider interest and following than Harold Searles, who detailed the countertransference problems encountered during his growth as a psychotherapist with these patients and contributed the concept of the therapeutic symbiosis to the understanding of their psychotherapy. At the same time Otto Will eloquently articulated the problems in attachment commonly encountered in intensive work with schizophrenic patients, and helped to recognize the therapeutic potentials available within regressed states. Both Searles and Will have helped to encourage the application of intensive individual psychotherapy to include those persons more chronically afflicted and seriously disabled.

Outcome Studies

CONTROLLED RESEARCH

The current pessimism about the efficacy of individual psychotherapy for schizophrenics can be traced to the results of controlled-outcome studies done in the 1960s. During the 1960s there were four efforts to compare schizophrenic patients treated with psychotherapy with those treated by other methods (19). The turnabout in attitude which occurred during the period of these studies is illustrated by the fact that at the initiation of one of these studies it was considered unethical to have a control group which did not receive individual psychotherapy, while at the conclusion of another study it was considered unethical to have a control group which received only psychotherapy. The two studies which have received the most attention were both largely negative in their results, whereas two other studies which had less rigorous designs had more positive results.

In the study done at the Massachusetts Mental Health Center, chronic schizophrenic patients had been transferred from a state hospital into an intensive milieu (36). For ethical reasons all of the patients in the intensive milieu received intensive psychotherapy, and half of them also received drugs. The psychotherapists were all experienced, analytically oriented therapists who saw patients at least twice a week for a two-year period. This design isolated the effects of drugs—not of the psychotherapy—yet the general failure of patients in both conditions to show much improvement has been interpreted as demonstrating the limitations of psychotherapy. Among the problems with this interpretation is the fact that this was a highly treatment-resistant group of patients for whom two years might not reasonably be expected to show dramatic turnabouts. Moreover, the milieu in which the treatment of both groups took place did not, as Greenblatt has pointed out, incorporate progressive expectations which would encourage manifest behavioral changes. Since a similar group of patients had previously been transferred from the same state hospital to an intensive milieu at the Massachusetts Mental Health Center with resulting improvement (31), the failure of the patients in this study to improve suggests that countertherapeutic forces were operating within the milieu.

A second and even more influential study concerned middle-prognosis schizophrenics treated with individual psychotherapy in a California state hospital (67). Here the therapists were inexperienced, and each saw the patient for about two hours a week over a six-month period of hospitalization. The psychotherapy was provided both in the presence and in the absence of drug therapy, and there were also comparison groups of patients who received neither psychotherapy nor drugs. While some slight advantages were noted for those receiving psychotherapy plus drugs over those who received drugs alone, the differences were not significant. Psychotherapy without drugs was significantly less effective than either of the drug conditions. This study has frequently been quoted as demonstrating the failure of individual psychotherapy to have a meaningful impact during the inpatient phase of hospitalization with good- to medium-prognosis schizophrenic patients. The major problem with this study and therefore with this conclusion is the quality of the psychotherapy. The therapy was nonintensive; it was provided by inexperienced therapists who had inexperienced supervisors (102) and no expectation that it would be an enduring relationship which would exceed the boundaries of the hospitalization. It is doubtful that such a constricted psychotherapeutic approach could support an open-ended type of exploration. Moreover, only an extremely sensitive measure of ego functions could detect personality changes which could be expected after six months of such treatment. Nevertheless, it was at the conclusion of the inpatient phase of this study that it was argued that it would be unethical to conduct a study on psychotherapy of schizophrenia in which drugs were withheld.

Two other concurrent studies tested the efficacy of psychotherapy with schizophrenics and had more positive results, although they received less attention. One of these, at Michigan State, found dramatically positive results on a small number of apparently poor-prognosis patients who were randomly assigned to therapists with varying amounts of experience (50,51). The psychotherapy was initially provided three to five times a week and was followed by once-a-week treatment for up to a year. The results suggested that experienced therapists did better overall then inexperienced therapists, and that specific and significant improvement occurred in the extent of the thought disorder for those treated with psychotherapy. Because of a number of uncontrolled variables—such as different settings in which patients were seen, the uncertain drug treatment status, and the differing types of therapy and experience of the therapists—the interpretation and the credibility of these results have been subject to debate (68).

Another study, at the University of Wisconsin, employed therapists who were inexperienced in the treatment of schizophrenia to work with a group of chronic patients over a two-and-a-half-year period at two hours a week (80). Despite the fact that about half the patients were believed by the therapists themselves never to have gotten into a therapeutic relationship, some favorable results emerged after a year and a half for those who received the psychotherapy. The changes noted were that those who received psychotherapy demonstrated a decreased need to deny their own experience and a greater appropriateness in emotional expression. They also spent more of their time out of the hospital.

Taken together, these controlled-outcome studies neither prove psychotherapy ineffective nor provide strong evidence for its helpfulness. Although these and many other studies have demonstrated the usefulness of drugs in treating schizophrenia in the short term, no comparable statement can be made about the role of psychotherapy. As a result these studies have seemed to limit interest and enthusiasm for individual psychotherapy. Yet they have spoken far more convincingly to those who are unaccustomed to spending long hours with individual patients than to those who are already involved in this treatment.

CASE REPORTS

The controlled-outcome studies can neither account for nor substantially discount those case reports—which have appeared sporadically over the last thirty years—in which an individual psychotherapeutic intervention, largely in the absence of other forms of treatment, has brought about a dramatic resolution of severe schizophrenic psychopathology. Clinicians who are involved in sitting with schizophrenic persons find in the case reports of therapists such as Sullivan, Will, Sechehaye, French and Kasanin, Fromm-Reichmann, Arieti, Searles, Schwing, Wexler, Schulz, Foster, Ekstein, and even Laing, familiar and comprehensible examples of the interactions they experience with their own patients.

To those who are looking for objective and replicable data about efficacy, these case reports seem idiosyncratic, exceptional, and perhaps dispensable as sources of evidence. Thus, it is of interest that two more recent reports have also suggested that the efficacy of individual psychotherapy might not be limited to only a few rare cases treated by particularly gifted therapists. Rubenstein's (82) follow-up on patients five years after discharge from Yale Psychiatric Institute showed them to have a generally excellent level of social functioning, despite the fact that they retained largely negative memories of their therapeutic experience. Kayton (52) had a similar experience with a series of selected patients who were given long-term individual psychotherapy and long-term hospitalizations at Michael Reese in Chicago and had surprising recoveries despite markedly poor prognoses prior to treatment. Although the authors of these reports believed that individual psychotherapy was the essential ingredient in bringing about these favorable outcomes, it is not possible to isolate the therapy from the many other inputs during the hospitalizations.

At the present time a reasonable conclusion to draw from the available evidence is that individual psychotherapy is not dramatically successful over a short period of time for most schizophrenic patients, but that it occasionally and perhaps not infrequently may lead to major differences in some schizophrenic patients who are as yet not easily recognizable in advance.

OUTCOME MEASURES

A major ongoing problem for those who would evaluate the effectiveness of individual psychotherapy is to develop outcome measures which are specific to this form of treatment. Both drugs and group therapies are known to affect symptom level and social functioning, which in turn are the major determinants of hospitalizations and recidivisms. Thus, for the patient who receives these treatments in conjunction with individual psychotherapy, which is almost always the case, measures of symptom level and social functioning and hospitalization cannot be expected to reflect the impact of individual psychotherapy alone. Bellak (8) and Semrad et al. (93) have attempted to develop such measures by looking at ego functions. Schulz (84) has approached this by trying to measure levels of self-object differentiation. None of these efforts has yet been tested adequately to demonstrate that patients receiving individual psychotherapy will compare preferentially.

Systematic follow-up interviews with a series of nonchronic schizophrenic patients, some of whom have been treated with intensive psychotherapy, have suggested some outcome variables which may be more specific to this form of treatment (42). Among these are the following: (1) the patient recognizes that his past, including his psychosis, is part of a coherent evolution into the present; (2) the patient can have constant impressions of, and be able to acknowledge appreciation for, specific others; (3) the patient recognizes a need for people and feels drawn toward letting them do things for him; (4) the patient recognizes but does not act upon his tendency to see internal conflicts externally; (5) the patient frequently observes himself even as he is engaged in talking or acting; (6) the patient shows a capacity for uncertainty, not knowing, and helplessness; (7) the patient experiences a widened range of affects on a regular basis; (8) the patient recognizes his limitations as having deprived him of satisfaction in the past and as likely to influence his future. Many of these variables were reiterated on the basis of extensive clinical experience in a review of this issue by Schulz (85). To delineate the contributions of individual psychotherapy to the overall treatment of schizophrenia, future outcome studies will need to determine whether these or other outcome measures can discriminate between those patients who received successful intensive individual psychotherapy and those who did not.

Conditions of Psychotherapy

SETTING

One of the important determinants of the possibility and the nature of individual psychotherapy with a schizophrenic person is whether the patient is seen in a hospital and, if so, whether it is for a short or a long term; or whether the patient is seen in an outpatient clinic or an office. Therapists who initiate individual psychotherapy within a short-term hospital setting will need to initiate contact early and to see the patient frequently to establish an alliance sufficient to sustain the relationship when the patient leaves the hospital. In outpatient settings the therapist must be actively involved in the patient's drug management, and he must secure the support and trust of the family with whom he must have a long-term alliance. Within a long-term hospitalization a more flexible schedule of involvement and the use of other personnel to work with the patient's family and administrate other aspects of the patient's treatment program will help the therapeutic relationship become established. Because the family situation is often an unreliable source of environmental support for the schizophrenic person, both halfway houses and partial hospital programs greatly enhance the possibilities of establishing a meaningful therapeutic relationship. The failure to provide adequate environmental supports for the schizophrenic patient will result in a precocious rigidity in both thinking and relating which frequently precludes the possibilities of individual psychotherapy.

SELECTION OF PATIENTS

The following description summarizes the impression of some twenty-five experienced psychotherapists about the selection of schizophrenic patients for individual psychotherapy:

Schizophrenic patients who tend to profit the most from individual psychotherapy are young and intelligent, reactive, and present during their first break in an acute manner. They have a past history of achievement at work and in other creative activities as well as some success in interpersonal relationships. They tend to experience "pain," or the sense of a "struggle" and definitely see themselves in need of help. They often appear to be striving actively for higher levels of functioning and exhibit some degree of the following capacities: self-observation, problem solving, integrating experience, self-control, and delay. [38, p. xxi]

For the most part neither the past history of hospitalization nor the symptomatic presentation at time of admission was considered significant. In a further approach to this problem the following five factors persisted in importance: (1) sudden onset, (2) known precipitant, (3) the psychosis is ego-dystonic, (4) patient displays pain or depression, and (5) employment or academic success outside of the nuclear home (44). Although these five factors may be useful, they do not add much to widely recognized good prognostic signs for treatment of all types. Among the patients who seem most difficult to engage in psychotherapy are the severe chronic paranoid patients or those with severe concurrent antisocial problems. This does not mean that on behavioral measures such patients may not look good; it means that their engagement in, and chances of gain from, a meaningful psychotherapy is extremely unlikely. In contrast, withdrawn, isolated, hallucinating patients with limited object ties often utilize individual psychotherapy very well indeed. Here it is most frequently the psychotherapist who forms an unwarranted, initial pessimistic conclusion about psychotherapeutic prospects. These patients may use psychotherapy differently, however, from the acute reaction schizophrenic. Initial statements by a patient or impressions of an evaluator about a schizophrenic insight into his illness or motivation for therapy are highly misleading indicators for the selection of a patient. More important is the degree to which a patient tends to internalize rather than to externalize in explaining events. This capacity includes issues of curiosity and psychology-mindedness. Thus, if a patient who is asked why he was hospitalized relates his hospitalization to past life events and especially to relationships, however inaccurate or farfetched, he is more likely to engage in psychotherapy than is the patient who relates his hospitalization to impersonal factors such as tiredness or to a nonspecifically malevolent environment.

MATCHING WITH A THERAPIST

The best-known effort to distinguish the characteristics of those therapists who work well with schizophrenics from those who do not is found
in the work of Whitehorn and Betz (105). In retrospective studies on
schizophrenic persons treated by residents on whom follow-up data were
available, they found that those therapists who scored highly on the
Strong Vocational Interest Inventory as having an aptitude for law or
accounting were particularly effective in working with schizophrenics.
In contrast, those therapists who scored high in their aptitude as printers
or as mathematics and physical science teachers were particularly ineffective. The effective therapists were designated "Type A," and the
ineffective ones "Type B." Despite the limitations of this original study,
a great deal of subsequent research attention has been given to this
intriguing typology. At the conclusion of these further studies the
validity of the typology remains controversial, and its clinical meaningfulness remains obscure (79).

Subsequently a group of distinguished therapists articulated the qualities in therapists they felt augered well for such patients (26). Among
these qualities is a deep personal need or enthusiasm for intensive work
with sick patients. Although suggesting omnipotence and rescue fantasies, such a quality should be well integrated into the personality of
the therapist so as to be reasonable and manageable. Friedman et al.
also emphasized a need for such therapists to have suffered painful life
experiences that tended to render them honest or real persons who have
themselves experienced a struggle to attain a strong sense of their own
identity. Among the outstanding qualities of therapists who work poorly
with schizophrenics are being guilt-ridden, tending to feel sorry for
people, or being overly perfectionistic and rigid.

It is generally believed that the personality dimensions of the therapist are increasingly important as the ego strength of the patient decreases. This was confirmed in the Menninger psychotherapy study (53)
and also more specifically in the work with schizophrenics by Rogers et al.
(80). Personality dimensions are also particularly important during the
early phase of treatment. A research study has attempted to evaluate
whether clinically derived hypotheses about what kind of therapist personality will match particularly well or poorly with a specific patient
personality can have predictive strength (41, 43). The following are
those personality-matching characteristics which were found to be particularly good indications of both whether a therapeutic relationship
will form and even of whether there will subsequently be overall clinical
improvement found in the patient:

1. An anxious schizophrenic patient is likely to work particularly well with
   a composed, contained, and stable therapist and particularly poorly with
   a therapist who is himself frenetic or disorganized.
2. A hostile, belligerent, and assaultive schizophrenic patient is particularly likely to work well with a therapist who is himself comfortable
   with aggression, either in the style of an unthreatening Grandma Moses
   or as a domineering, autocratic Napoleon.
3. The seductive schizophrenic patient (that is, one involved with sexual,
   id, or bodily matters) does particularly well with a "grandfatherly"

psychotherapist who can accept id material without excitement or judgment, and will do particularly poorly with a therapist who is himself either puritanical or seductive.

4. The schizophrenic patient who is particularly depressed will do well with a therapist who is comfortable with depression—that is, one who has himself experienced and understands depression.

5. The burned-out or poor-prognosis schizophrenic will do particularly poorly with a therapist who is optimistic or grandiose or even charismatic; such patients will do better with a more pessimistic therapist.

The overall conclusion of this study is that the therapist's capacity to be involved with and accepting of the dominant affective characteristics (sexual, depressive, angry, or anxious) of a schizophrenic patient may be the central ingredient to patient-therapist matching. This capacity may in fact represent the "A" typology (29). Although this work suggests that the matching variable can be quite important in determining the value of psychotherapy for schizophrenia, further prospective work is required to determine whether these or other clinical guides can be developed.

A related question about matching concerns evaluation of whether a therapeutic relationship develops. A working therapeutic relationship with a schizophrenic patient should include talks about meaningful aspects of the patient's past and references to the immediate interaction with the therapist. If these aspects of a therapeutic relationship are not present at six months with most schizophrenic patients or within a year for a severely disturbed schizophrenic patient who has had a past history of psychotherapeutic failures, it is frequently time for a new psychotherapist to be assigned to the case. This, it should be understood, is a guideline to be applied under circumstances where the motivation and the interest of the therapist are not in question. A review of the psychotherapy experience at McLean Hospital in Framingham, Massachusetts, during the 1960s suggested that such changes of therapist are too often resisted or delayed (13). There is a general error in the direction of working fruitlessly for too long a time with a patient and of simply ascribing the failure to the schizophrenic patient's recalcitrance.

A second guideline which may help evaluate the match between patient and therapist concerns the similarities and the differences between the personalities of the therapist, the patient, and the patient's parents. A recently hospitalized schizophrenic patient frequently chooses to attach him to someone similar to the person whose loss precipitated the psychosis, whether that person was a parent or, as is frequently the case, someone of the opposite sex. Insofar as the therapist resembles in his personality or gender aspects of the lost person, the psychotic patient will experience him as familiar and more readily substitute him for the absent internal object representation. However, as the psychosis recedes, the qualities in the therapist's personality which are similar to the patient's are more likely to sustain the relationship. At this stage when the therapist's self-knowledge is sufficient, these similarities may allow for greater empathy. (In this context further differentiation can be the result for the patient.) However, if the therapist is intolerant and/or ignorant of those aspects of himself which are similar to the patient's, then a change of therapist may be required.

INTERACTION WITH DRUGS

Many individual psychotherapists were originally suspicious about the possibility that drugs might interfere with the development and the understanding of a therapeutic relationship. These suspicions have diminished with a growing awareness of the helpful role drugs can play in reducing disorganizing anxiety. This awareness has developed especially with the expansion of individual psychotherapy into outpatient settings where drugs have helped ameliorate regressive responses to external stresses. Bellak (6) has suggested that drugs allow many patients to engage in the symbolic verbal operations required for psychotherapy.

During inpatient treatment of chronic schizophrenics Grinspoon et al. (36) found that the discontinuation of drugs led to a rapid reversion to previous levels of psychopathology despite the continuation of individual psychotherapy. As with the May study (67) there was little evidence to suggest that any specific benefits of psychotherapy were enhanced by drugs. The interaction of drugs and a supportive therapy provided twice monthly by social workers during the outpatient phase of treatment has also been studied. Hogarty et al. (45) found that drug treatment appeared to make patients more accessible to psychotherapeutic intervention. By itself the social work counseling could have toxic effects, which they attributed to its being overstimulating—that is, it demanded too much responsibility for symptomatic patients (30). This study points to the complicated nature of the drug and psychotherapy interaction. At the same time it suggests that psychotherapeutic intervention can be helpful to nonsymptomatic patients on or off drugs, but that it appears to be harmful to the symptomatic patient. Under these latter circumstances drugs appear necessary to prevent an individual therapeutic interaction from being harmful.

There remains, however, a body of evidence to suggest that the major tranquilizers can interfere with learning (76) and with some of the cognitive functions* of schizophrenic persons. Moreover, some recent research has suggested that drugs may be detrimental to the effectiveness of psychosocial interventions (40). On balance there may be some benefits to attempting psychotherapy in the absence of drugs for hospitalized patients. In prolonged periods of serious disturbance, or when brief hospitalization is required, drugs should be tried. When a therapeutic relationship has been established or the period of acute disturbance is over, a trial off drugs can and perhaps should be attempted.

CONTRACTS AND GOALS

Another condition which should be established early in an individual psychotherapy has to do with common goals to which the patient will agree. This contract can range from agreement to help a patient feel better or leave the hospital to a more far-reaching goal of helping the patient understand himself. One essential ingredient is that the patient

---

* H. Spohn: cited in "Special Report: Schizophrenia, 1976," *Schizophrenia Bulletin* (1976), vol. 2, no. 4, p. 553.

be engaged at whatever level in a joint task. The less circumscribed these goals are, the greater the therapist's commitment must be in terms of availability. It makes no sense to undertake an open-ended exploration in a time-limited therapy. Regular hours should be established as early as possible. The patient should be encouraged to think about the content of the hours between meetings. Of particular use with some schizophrenic patients is to enlist their help in establishing a chronology to their lives which will be written down and discussed. It should also be clear that confidentiality is a matter of the therapist's discretion, and that under no circumstances should it be assured. In the course of a treatment with schizophrenic persons most therapists will be called upon to take responsibility for making communications on behalf of the patient, either with other treatment personnel or with the family.

Processes of Psychotherapy

This section will provide an overview of the major issues within psychotherapy with schizophrenics and the varying opinions therapists have taken about the proper approach to these issues. These opinions draw heavily from discussions with the participants in a program sponsored by the National Institute of Mental Health (26). The most significant controversies are found in the following areas: (1) content (What? What is the area of principal investigation and discussion in the interviews?); (2) technique (How? What methods does one employ to pursue the psychotherapeutic goals?). The debates are often clearer in the abstraction of discussions than in actual practice, where the questions become more matters of emphasis, priorities, or sequence.

CONTENT

The controversies about focus largely concern the initial stage of psychotherapy. Differences can be seen in terms of particular periods in the patients' lives and in terms of differing ego structures being addressed.

PAST VERSUS PRESENT VERSUS FUTURE

Some therapists focus on a patient's past, others focus on the immediate present, and others orient their approach toward the future.

Those who focus on the past would ask the patient, "What happened?" This approach emphasizes the importance of integrating the precipitating circumstances. The therapist sees the patient's distortions and projections as avoidance techniques and asks the patient to remember his painful but real life crisis. In this more limited sense of recent history this approach was first advocated by Whitehorn (104) and employed by Semrad (92). The experience of other therapists leads them to question whether many schizophrenic patients are either unaware of their precipitating crisis or unwilling to deal with it early in treatment.

Using an attitude-toward-illness questionnaire, Soskis and Bowers (96) differentiated two recovery styles from psychosis. In one, the schizophrenic patients seemed to have integrated their illness with the rest of their lives and to have recognized the importance of factors within themselves and their social environment which were related to it. In the other recovery style, patients isolated their psychosis and viewed it more negatively. Patients who followed the first pattern were significantly better in their social functioning and symptom remissions. More recently McGlashan et al. (64) have labeled the second recovery style "sealing over" and described the unfolding of these two distinct patterns. They also suggested that patients who integrate their psychosis benefit from this process. In addition to patient factors, they feel a psychotherapist's readiness to attend to this integration process will determine whether it occurs.

In a broader sense the approach to the past seeks to explore all past developmental history relevant to the patient's presenting problem (85). It is necessary for a patient to recognize himself in terms of his entire past and to see his present as a continuation of that experience. In this instance the precipitating crisis must be reexperienced and worked through in the relationship to the therapist. Other therapists feel that too much emphasis on the past involves the danger that the therapist may impose too much of his own theory and expectations on the patient, and not follow the patient closely enough.

The second approach, focus on the present, would address a different question in the initial phase: "What are you experiencing?" This draws the patient's attention to his immediate reality and emphasizes the importance of the interaction with the therapist in ultimately coming to understand himself. Advocates see this process as critical in helping the patient define his psychological (60) and his biological (66) selves. This approach would directly take up the patient's feelings and their connection with the therapist. There would be an effort to understand the function served by the patient's operating defenses. This process might be likened to that used in ego or character analysis. Opponents of this approach say it addresses the patient's presenting psychopathology not as a reaction but as a part of his usual personality. Because it may overlook a loss precipitant, this approach may encourage the therapist to function as a substitute for a lost object, and thus postpones grief work—which might bring about earlier recompensation—until terminal phases of treatment.

The third orientation would focus on the patient's future. The question is: "What do you want for yourself?" This question appeals to the patient's need to make decisions, to plan, and to organize. This would draw the patient's attention to the aimless course of his life and to the maladaptive aspects of being psychotic. It avoids the psychotic productions and sets aside past experiences, at least for the time being, while openly supporting the patient's developing autonomy by pursuing what he wants independently of family expectations. Hence the phrase "for yourself" is a way of saying that the patient is master of his own destiny and needs to define himself in terms of his wants. Proponents of this approach (70,86) point to its antiregressive function and emphasize the importance of providing support for the patient's development of competence and sense of efficacy through the use of his problem-solving capacities (103). This approach seems vulnerable, however, to the criticism that internal satisfaction depends on more than leaving home, being competent, and pursuing what one wants; such satisfaction requires interpersonal-relatedness. In fact, the achievement of competence and efficiency may be of use only insofar as it is rewarded by feeling loved; it may also cause a patient to feel that his passive and dependent wishes are unacceptable to the therapist.

It may be that each approach is most appropriate for different schizophrenic patients. For example, the approach that stresses integration of the precipitant may be useful only for patients with histories of a clear precipitant (acute-reactive patients), while the ego-organizing adaptational approach of the last type (future-oriented) may be best for those whose schizophrenic condition might be considered chronic. It may also be that for a given patient these different approaches will be most appropriate at different phases of recovery.

REALITY VERSUS FANTASY

Another issue of focus is how much attention should be paid to dreams and fantasies and how much to realities. The real life approach views the schizophrenic's dreams and fantasies as avoidance techniques by someone who is already too likely to avoid and distort what is real. The schizophrenic, in this view, is aided by more structure, by being reminded of the discrepancy between reality and his fantasies and dreams, and by the therapist's role as a reality anchor (53,59). This view contrasts with the Jungian (77) and with Schulz's recommendation (85) that interpretations of dreams is a central aspect of psychotherapy with schizophrenics whose disrupting effects have been exaggerated. The concern with fantasies follows from where the patient is "at," and movement toward reality must stem from the patient's initiative. This emphasis on fantasy is criticized for involving the danger of providing intellectual depth without practical, reality-based connectedness to improve social adaptation.

AFFECTS

Many therapists feel that the schizophrenic disorganization is frequently a regressive response from intolerable affects (87,92). Often these intolerable affects occur in response to the loss of some important relationship. A follow-up study supports the view that the capacity to sustain and deal with loss differentiates schizophrenic patients who do well from those who do not (70). Opinions vary, however, as to exactly what affects the schizophrenic encounters in the process of loss which he primarily needs help in learning to deal with. Some clinicians see the patient's primary difficulty as recognizing and managing his aggression and its affective derivative, anger (35,97). By encouraging the patient to express anger directly, they hope to avert the need for projection and eventually to modify basic concerns about his omnipotent destructiveness which are accentuated when loss is encountered. Some research evidence supports this idea: that therapists who focus on a patient's aggression tend to have better results (94).

Other therapists focus on the patient's need to remember the pain involved in the loss itself. This requires the patient to recognize what was positive or "loved" in the relationship which is now no longer available and is being missed. The primary affect called upon in this process is sadness, and this process is not dissimilar to mourning. Here the patient's aggressive presentation and concerns about destructiveness are seen as defenses to avoid the real pain of dealing with what was once valued but is gone. Searles (88) has concluded along this line that the hateful expressions he chronicled in his early writing are basically "subsidiary to love," and "that such an ugly emotion as vindictiveness is basically a reaction against such positively oriented emotions as separation, anxiety, and grief." Similarly, Wynne et al. (110) has singled out a group of families he calls "pseudohostile," in which constant bickering is used to avoid the threatening affectionate interactions.

Regardless of the nature of a specific affect, it is generally valued as an indicator of where to focus. In itself any affect allows a therapist to help a schizophrenic patient label his feelings and connect them to his life experience, regardless of whether the feelings are past, present, or anticipated (106).

PSYCHOTIC CONTENT

The older debate about emphasis on psychotic productions seems all but settled. Few clinicians feel that active exploration of and interest in the content of a patient's hallucinations and delusions is of much therapeutic worth. While no one says they are of *no* worth or interest, they are seen as a low-yield and low-priority area of focus. In this respect Fromm-Reichmann's mandates seem to have survived better than those of Rosen. Both Arieti (2) and Schulz (85) have felt that hallucinations are primarily useful as signals of some immediate stress—that is, as defenses against the expected distress, which should be attended to. Consistent with this development, there seems to be little interest in the early suggestion that therapists enter into and go along temporarily with the patient's hallucinatory or delusional world. Almost all of the approaches seem to have in common, as an initial goal, helping the patient define himself, whether this is in terms of past experiences, psychobiological boundaries, feelings, wishes, or goals.

TECHNIQUES

Whereas the problem of focus concerns mainly the content of the therapeutic interaction, the issues involved in technique concern how a therapist interacts with schizophrenic patients.

EXPLORATION VERSUS RELATIONSHIP

The process of exploration can be described as a mutual patient-therapist effort to investigate and understand the causes for the patient's dilemma; and it is closely related to insight. To acquire insight, Stanton

(98) has suggested that special emphasis must be given to expanding the schizophrenic patient's use of his often-neglected power of self-observation. The goal of this process might be defined simply as understanding oneself; and, in general, it is felt that this understanding will allow change, growth, and improvement. The therapist's ability to maintain objectivity in his observations of the patient is considered important for this process. While a relationship inevitably develops between patient and therapist, this is viewed as necessary for the investigative task but not as primarily therapeutic in itself.

There are therapists, however, who feel that this process is less valuable with schizophrenic patients than with other patients. They feel that the emphasis on investigation implies that the schizophrenic's problems are predominantly intrapsychic, and does not give due weight to their interpersonal or contextual origins. They emphasize that what is most helpful to schizophrenic patients is the development of a real relationship (34). In this view the therapist's value is less as objective inquirer and more as subjective participant. The therapist's consistency and concern facilitate his internalization (101). It is the experience of trusting and being cared about that diminishes the patient's previous distrust and improves his low self-esteem. The growing closeness of this relationship then provides a vehicle by which the patient's expectations of being hurt or rejected are modified—that is, an ego-corrective experience. Although such changes may, in turn, ultimately permit the exploration of past life and defense operations in a way similar to that with neurotics, this remains a secondary phase of secondary importance. Such observations led Rosen and Fromm-Reichmann to debate in the 1950s whether a schizophrenic patient actually needed two therapists: one for beginning therapy and one for analysis.

Some of those who consider exploration to be the primary vehicle of change feel that a real trusting relationship is developed only after the patient is able to see what interferes with his getting close to someone else. Such a relationship is fostered by the therapist's active interest in having the patient share with the therapist what the patient has avoided by himself, or by the analysis of his defenses against such closeness. In any event, the importance of the relationship is predominantly (or only) its usefulness in either allowing investigation or being the subject of investigation.

A third position, perhaps somewhere in between these two, would emphasize the importance of the investigation of the ongoing relationship (106). The therapist's objective use of his subjective responses to the patient are important tools to aid both the patient's understanding and the developing relationship (88).

INTERPRETATION VERSUS SUPPORT

Closely related to a debate about exploration and relating is the relative importance given to interpretative and supportive techniques. Interpretations have traditionally been considered a therapist's tool for allowing the patient's experience to be enlightened with a new perspective, such as facilitating the movement of avoided material into awareness. By this model the interpretation is followed by insight and a learning experience. However, this "interpretation" of what results from interpretation with schizophrenic patients has been questioned. Less interpretative psychotherapists see the danger that interpretation may bring premature closure or cause undue regression (53). Even if we allow that an interpretation may be beneficial, a new explanation of why it is is needed for psychotics, since there is alleged to be no unconscious in psychosis and frequently no alliance with a reasonable self-observing ego (33,111). Therefore, the benefit may arise either out of nonverbal accompaniments to the interpretation (e.g., sincerity, empathy, affection) or from the relief in discovering that the uncovered material can be understood and accepted. Paul Federn was perhaps the strongest critic of being overly interpretative with schizophrenics (17). He pointed out that these patients require greater repression, not less, and that interpretation could prevent the maintenance of a positive transference. He recognized the essential role of a supportive environmetal context for psychotherapy, and he utilized a nurse co-therapist, M. Schwing, to help provide this.

Support is delivered in a ingenious variety of ways and in greatly varying amounts to schizophrenic patients. Behavioral methods include the actual provision of token supports such as candy, cigarettes, and even lodging. These nonverbal responses are thought to be responsive to preverbal needs. Common forms of verbal support include support of executive ego functions such as advice, problem solving, and reality testing, and support of self-esteem by reassurance and encouragement. A third type of support (neither verbal nor behavioral) arises from the therapist's consistency, dependability, interest, and enthusiasm.

Even if conflicts could be fully verbalized, many therapists believe that supportive techniques help establish contact and build a positive relationship necessary for later interpretive work. Less-supportive therapists feel that such supports may sometimes be harmful "acting out," and that supports too often underestimate the patient's strengths (especially his capacity to form an alliance and to verbalize conflict), unnecessarily infantalize the patient, and unfairly limit the potential for growth or, at best, greatly prolong treatment. Searles (89) suggests that such activities stem from a therapist's unconscious need to curtail the schizophrenic's aggression. As with other variables, the two sides to the interpretation support dichotomy are not incompatible, and invariably the advocates for either extreme do more of the other's technique than they may at first acknowledge.

ACTIVITY VERSUS PASSIVITY

"Activity" here refers to the therapist's role in initiating anxiety, defining himself, confronting defenses, pursuing hypotheses, giving support, getting a history, or otherwise selecting the focus. Activity imposes the therapist's preconceptions on the content. Thus, too much activity may keep the content too confined to the present and not permit free expression of other, possibly deeper areas of conflict. This risk is weighed against the belief that such activity may greatly abbreviate unnecessary and prolonged symptomatic distress for the patient. Active therapists may feel that past experience allows them rather quickly to formulate the origins of the patient's problems and thus justify their role in selecting content.

"Passivity," of course, refers to the therapist's nonimposition on the patient's associations. The belief here is that by following the patient's own associations, a therapist has a greater chance of finding out what is most important as the patient experienced it and, in any event, of avoiding the danger that activity may prematurely lead to such experiences before the patient is ready or able to deal with them. This belief also implies less verbal activity and more opacity for the patient. Such passivity is criticized for encouraging projection, increasing separation, and not providing enough ego support.

Sometimes an active therapist may be replicating a pathogenic family relationship which a patient experiences as instrusive. Schulz (85) advocates directing the activity at how the patient evokes this parental response. It is also true that passivity may mimic the parental posture experienced as neglect by a patient.

A phase of recovery with specific technical controversies concerning activity is the postpsychotic depression or neurasthenic phase (63). Psychotherapists generally recognize the temptation to discontinue psychotherapy during this period but seem to agree that this is a critical phase to stay with a patient however recalcitrant and negativistic he appears. There is debate about whether the proper technique involves persistent and active efforts to get the patient to pay attention, plan his future, and relinquish old ways. The danger is that the patient will further withdraw and feel suicidal. The alternative view involves maintaining an accepting presence which may need to survive long periods of silence and passivity. Other therapists have found that confrontation, limits, and exhortation are needed to terminate this phase (18,20). Kayton (52) has pointed out that the issue may be one of timing—that is, that the pressure to change can be successful only after there has been evidence of activation in the patient's concentration and interests.

REGRESSION

Perhaps more than any other topic in the area of psychotherapy of schizophrenia, "regression" has come to be charged with affect and disagreement. Signals of the extent of these feelings can be seen in the rhetoric used by opposing camps to describe the other's treatment. Treatment that takes active measures to oppose regression is described as "manipulative" and "inhuman." Therapists who attempt to prevent regression are called "impatient," "intrusive," "doers" who are "intolerant of psychoses and affects" and who have been "poorly analyzed." Treatment that is permissive of regression is described by its enemies as "infantalizing" and "outdated." The therapist who accepts regression is caricatured as an "indecisive," "inassertive" sitter who is "only interested in the patient's pathology" and/or attaining "infantile gratifications" of his own unresolved dependency and power needs.

In a more positive sense, each point of view can present a consistent approach with a persuasive rationale. Those who are permissive and accepting of the patient's psychotic regression see the patient as re-creating the unresolved infantile disorder that must be "lived through" and grown out of in order to attain a stable, higher level of ego integration. The unfolding of a primitive transference to the therapist and the formation of a symbiotic relationship require the therapist's permissive acceptance.

The resolution of this symbiosis is a process of self-object differentiation by which the patient leaves the previous level of object relations and develops true autonomy. There is disagreement as to whether this re-emergence ("rebirth," as Jungians term it; "inner voyage" for the existentialists) is a healing process that follows naturally, given an accepting atmosphere, or whether it occurs as the result of a conscious process of learning and conflict resolution, as others suggest (101). The first approach emphasizes that the therapist's attitudes—for example, accepting, hopeful—are more important than the particular type of verbal engagement. Psychosis naturally "lived through" is believed by some to offer an opportunity not just for return to premorbid function, but for growth (73,96). The latter approach stresses the importance of the therapist's verbalizations and has seen the application of traditional psychoanalytic techniques to psychotic patients, including the use of the couch.

Therapists who favor active intervention against regression—which might include structured milieu, maintaining contact with family, lending support to defenses, and sometimes ataraxic drugs—stress the importance of the patient's using his ego strengths in the service of integration. The therapist would not do anything for the patient that the latter could do for himself. The therapist has expectations of maximal performance from the patient and attentively addresses the patient's higher ego functions with the aim of getting the patient to observe himself. Too much disorganization and primary-process thinking makes working with the patient impossible.

Therapists who oppose long regressions view the existence of a psychotic transference by schizophrenic patients as unnecessary, often unanalyzable, and potentially leading to either the transfer of patients to another therapist or chronicity. The psychotic transference referred to is that where the therapist comes to be seen delusionally—not, for example, as being *like* mother but rather as actually *being* mother. The process of such a delusional attachment is fostered by the therapist's passivity, by his reluctance actively to confront the patient's projections and distortions, and by his reluctance to be real. According to this view, the therapist must make it clear that he is not a mother, and that he will not take care of the patient in any real sense. The logical extension of this view is that a therapist should not in any way take any physical care of a patient, even if he is willing, since this is not possible over the long run and sets up unrealistic life expectations. Jacobson (48), for example, has criticized Searles' use of symbiotic relatedness as involving the danger of the therapist's regression and of a nontherapeutic impasse.

Therapists who are permissive about regression often say that the power to prevent regression is an exaggerated claim, and that a psychotic transference is, if not desirable, at least inevitable. The activity, the structuring, and the participant functions required by a therapist to prevent regression make proper analysis of the infantile vicissitudes of the maternal transference impossible to investigate and grow out of. In response, those who use such active measures to control regression acknowledge that their goal is not the prevention of all regression, but rather modulation of regression within limits that allow the patient to integrate the regressive content, that do not unduly separate the patients

from the important people and the business of his life, and that dis-
courage unnecessary periods of psychotic distress. Within this context,
they feel there is still room for regression that is in the service of ego
growth. The difference is in the emphasis on keeping this regression
within proscribed limits—that is, what is reversible within the context
of the psychotherapy.

THERAPEUTIC PROCESSES

One of the implications of the recent outcome research is that a great
deal more needs to be known about what are the critical variables within
a psychotherapeutic interaction which determine whether it has therapeutic effects. No means of identifying and quantifying such variables
have yet been developed. The variables described in this section all reflect clinical impressions.

INSIGHT

Stanton (98) has suggested that some of the target areas for the development of insight in the psychotherapy of schizophrenic patients are
different from those for other patients usually treated by psychoanalysis.
After citing the initial need to strengthen the patient's capacity for self-
observation, he notes the following areas where insight should be attained with schizophrenics: (1) enlarging the patient's grasp of context
and the recognition of its relevance, (2) discovery of undesirable patterns of interpersonal behavior and how they come about, and (3) the
nature of patient's difficulties in accepting new information about himself. Other areas related to the use of insight in the therapy of schizophrenic patients include the integration of the psychotic experience,
which has been described, and the integration of dissociative aspects of
the self. Many seriously disturbed patients actively keep out of their
awareness whole bodies of memories and feelings associated with prior
experiences. Meaningful recovery and integration of these memories and
feelings can come about only in the context of an ongoing intensive
relationship which has no predetermined time limitations. Insightful
experience of all kinds requires verbalization of issues, but with a schizophrenic patient this may specifically require the verbalization of issues
which he had not previously been able to articulate.

IDENTIFICATION

"Identification" is used here in a general sense to refer to the way a
schizophrenic person internalizes or introjects aspects of the therapist
into the growing sense of self during psychotherapy. Here the therapist's
choice of treatment technique probably influences the nature of the
identification a patient makes. A therapist with more active interpretative methods encourages aggressive identification, whereas a therapist who is supportive may foster ego-ideal identification. In both
instances a patient adopts the therapist's strengths and may utilize them,
in the first instance, for understanding internal conflict and, in the latter
instance, for managing external situations. In contrast, a therapist who
is quite passive may be confronted with a more projective identification.

In this case the identification process must be treated as a transference phenomenon to be analyzed.

AUTONOMY

Autonomy is recognizable in successful psychotherapy as the growing recognition by a patient that the past has been at least partly determined by himself, and that accepting this fact implies that the future is also his responsibility. Within psychotherapy autonomy comes about by virtue of the therapist's respect for the patient's secrets, the therapist's nonintrusiveness, his recognition of his as well as the patient's own needs for distance, and the therapist's willingness to allow failures. This frequently is tested in the context of psychotherapy by regressions which a therapist experiences as unnecessary as the patient flagrantly denies what he has previously appeared to learn. If the therapist joins with the patient in the latter's devaluation of the previous work, the patient may abandon treatment; whereas the therapist's recognition of the patient's wish and right to assert his independence in even this perverse way will act further to support his autonomy.

INTIMACY

Intimacy grows gradually out of the common task and shared experience of psychotherapy. It correlates directly with the degree of self-revelation which occurs in therapy independent of the insight which accompanies or facilitates this process of revelation. It includes but is not limited to a mutual dependability and predictability which evolves over time. It begins with the undesirable recognition of the therapist's importance and progressively includes recognition of the therapist's unique qualities. It is a unique aspect of intensive psychotherapy and can coexist with serious regressions in the patient. It may even be that only during an apparent regression will a schizophrenic patient allow himself the first acknowledgment of his positive attachment to the therapist without an accompanying experience of shame.

The four process variables cited in this section are only a partial list of those ingredients of psychotherapy which clinicians might point to as being critical in determining therapeutic effectiveness. It is clear, however, that any such list includes variables which relate to the patient's heightening awareness of self and concurrently to his having ego-corrective or original experiences with the therapist which modify past patterns and expectations.

COMMENT

There has been some narrowing of the practice of individual psychotherapy for schizophrenia. Nevertheless, there are major differences among therapists about where it is most useful to focus in content, when to permit or prevent regression, and how to conceptualize the factors producing change. Therapists often have a unique and sometimes surprising admixture of the techniques of therapy described here. It would seem probable, for instance, that therapists stressing exploration would also emphasize the importance of interpretation and tend to be more

active—and vice versa. Yet this is frequently not the case. A more pervasive trend is that most therapists find "relationship therapy," "support," and "activity" more useful early in treatment, and that they move
in their own distinctive styles toward less activity, more interpretations,
and more exploration with time. The conclusion seems inescapable that
the varying forms of psychotherapeutic practice are not simply logical
derivatives of clinical observations, but to some degree each is an extension of the personality of the therapist. This is consistent with the importance of the therapist's personality and of his being real, and making
contact with and relating to people diagnosed as schizophrenic.

Theoretical Derivatives

FREUD'S LEGACY

Disputes about the metapsychology of schizophrenia have traditionally
focused on the question whether schizophrenia is best understood as a
disorder of deficit or as a disorder of defense (i.e., conflict). A derivative
argument has concerned the schizophrenic as qualitatively different
from other people or, as in the conflict model, the schizophrenic as being on a continuum with other people. Both the conflict and the deficit
theoretical models can trace their beginnings to Freud. Those who adhere to a conflict view are in sympathy with Freud's early formulations
on schizophrenia (23,24), those who further the deficit view cite
Freud's later formulations, beginning with his analysis of the Schreber
bibliography (25).

In the earlier formulations Freud described the decathexis of the object
world and subsequent investment of object libido in the ego—a state
called "primary narcissism." This process and the concurrent emergence
of primary-process thinking were believed to be defensive processes. In
this context both the projection characterisic of paranoia and the hallucinations characteristic of schizophrenia proper are efforts toward recovery by regaining contact with the object world. Pao (74) has pointed out
that this theory neither really explains symptoms themselves nor allows
for the ongoing conflict regarding the maintenance of those symptoms.

In later formulations Freud emphasized the ego's conflict with reality
resulting in the use of denial ("disavowal") of reality as a central characteristic of schizophrenia. He attributed this denial to an abnormal or,
by inference, a defective ego. This theory emphasized a defective ego
which Freud felt could not be explained by psychological means. Several
authors (10,74) have noted that Freud's efforts to complete a structural
theory for schizophrenia remained incomplete. Federn subsequently
expanded the concept of the ego and revised Freud's theory by postulating that the defect was due not to the ego's denial of reality but to its
permeable and flexible boundaries which allowed the creation of a false

reality (75). Federn's view has itself been developed further in the work of Freeman, Cameron, and McGhie (22).

The subsequent development of these two disparate theoretical views have come to incorporate more modern psychoanalytic thinking. Changes in the theoretical concepts of schizophrenia since Freud largely parallel the growth of psychoanalytic theory in general. Thus, while Freud's early formulations stress the topographic model (i.e., conscious-unconscious systems) and the vicissitudes of intrapsychic energies (i.e., cathexis-decathexis), later theorists have emphasized structural components of intrapsychic life and, more recently, the dependence of intrapsychic structure on object relations. These theoretical developments have been subjected to a number of reviews.* This review will summarize this traditional theoretical debate and attempt to describe some new developments which may hint at future theoretical positions.

DEFICIT THEORIES

Prominent among the efforts to take up the deficit banner where Freud left off are the contributions by Wexler (101). His hypotheses about the vulnerability of those who become schizophrenic to the loss of their internal object representations is founded in the conceptual framework prepared by Freud in the Schreber case and in "Mourning and Melancholia." It remains a broadly accepted and widely cited psychoanalytic formulation of schizophrenia. In brief, this theory states that the preschizophrenic child, because of a deficient perceptual apparatus, central organization, or learning capacity, does not normally internalize from his early parental experiences a stable sense of self. Thus, in times of later stress these brittle internalizations evaporate, leaving the schizophrenic "selfless." This overwhelming experience leads the schizophrenic to attempt object restitution (and thus self-restitution) in ways that constitute the familiar clinical symptoms of schizophrenia—hallucinations, delusions, and so on. The emphasis here is upon the defect in central organization which is believed to be organic in nature.

Among the reasons that this theoretical position is generally accepted is that it allows for but does not require an organic or a genetic base to schizophrenia. Moreover, it focuses attention on an internal developmental deficit that recurs catastrophically in the adult schizophrenic and thus is consistent with or explains much of the dramatic clinical phenomenology of schizophrenia. Finally, it uses familiar language and is closely wedded to early psychoanalytic traditions. Yet, despite these strengths, this formulation is also vulnerable to the following criticisms:

1. It does not specify the nature of the deficit or why the schizophrenic has his particular deficit of memory traces, learning, or internalization. In other words, it describes the what, but not the how and why of a deficit, and not whether it is specific to schizophrenia (vs. other disorders).
2. It fails adequately to consider the role of nonmaternal family members or the nonfamily environment.

* See references 7, 21, 37, 39, 61, 62, 75, and 83.

3. The concept of internal object representation is not well defined—that is, some feel that what is really unstable are those object representations that have become self-representations; it is not well understood developmentally and is not a readily recognized inference from clinical observations—that is, like all metapsychology, it is at least a second-order inference).

4. This theory does not adequately explain the social inadequacy or gradual onset found in many severe schizophrenics.

Multiple variations of deficit theories have been advocated. Arieti (1) earlier used a conflict model to explain schizophrenia, but more recently he has preferred to talk of "deficient internalization," which may involve nonpsychological factors (3). Federn (17) felt the problem was a weak cathexis of the ego which was irreversible. Rado (78) provided a theoretical view of schizophrenia specifically based on the presence of a genetically determined "schizotype" personality. Kessler (56) postulated that the genetically determined deficit is an exaggerated "inhibitory defense"—that is, a neurologically determined inability to repress selectively. Aronson (5) has attempted to modify Wexler's deficit view by introducing the controlled observations from animal experiments done by Harlow and Lorenz. The principal impact of these studies on Aronson's revision of the deficit theory is the increased emphasis given to the strength and adaptive quality of the vulnerable infant's learned responses to his early frustration experiences. These response patterns become maladaptive when confronted with other demands in life. This modification would help explain the deeply ingrained characterologic pathology of the adult schizophrenic, in addition to the more acute fulminating symptomatology explained by Wexler. Searles (89) has presented further critical comments of the deficit view. He believes the readiness to see deficits in schizophrenic persons is accountable by the therapist's unresolved countertransference which has led him to write off the possibility of dealing with his own bad mothering experiences.

DEFENSE THEORIES

For the purposes of simplicity, the devolpment in the conflict theories of schizophrenia can be divided into three models: object relations, ego defect, and affect intolerance. All these models incorporate a much more central place for aggressive drives in the pathogenesis of schizophrenia than did Freud's defensive theory, which stressed only libidinal drive alterations.

The first of these, and the one most frequently and vociferously argued about by those who do not accept deficit models, is derived from the observations of children by Melanie Klein (58) and has subsequently been elaborated on from psychotherapeutic work with schizophrenic patients by her followers Segal (90) and Rosenfeld (81). This theoretical position stresses the importance of internal-external, good-bad, part-object splitting during early infancy. Like the deficit theory, it posits a defective process of early internalization (called "introjection" by Kleinians) but does so without hypothesizing that this is due to a constitutional deficit. Rather, the core conflict in internal object images occurs when the three- to six-month-old infant experiences predominantly destructive impulses toward the mother. This provides a prototypical confusion between good and bad or love and hate. This phase was termed "schizoid position" by Klein (57) and renamed "paranoid position" later by Fairbairn (16). It is considered a normal phase of development. The infant who is unable to surmount (i.e., bear) the fear of being hurt which results from his destructive impulses is vulnerable to later development of schizophrenia. The paranoid-schizoid position is reactivated in adult life when there is a danger of internalizing whole objects. This occurs when the vulnerable person loses an object who has been the target of his split-off (projected) badness, or when he becomes attached to an object on whom he cannot project his badness (i.e., some form of intimacy is called for). The flight from internalizing his own badness (from becoming a whole object) and the ensuing loss of internal object representation is thus an active rather than passive defensive process by the ego. This formulation pinpoints the particular intrapsychic conflict that explains why a person becomes psychotic at a particular time in his life. It is less useful for the more insidious onset forms of schizophrenia. It also helps to explain how and why a paranoid person clings to, and depends upon having, persecutors in his environment, as he is commonly observed to do.

This viewpoint has been criticized both for the inferences Klein drew from childhood observation and for the predominant role given very early experience while comparatively neglecting the impact of later environmental conditions. The concepts and the language defy ready correlation with clinical observations and lead even sophisticated metapsychologists to admit they are not sure they understand a particular position. Freeman (21) complained that this theory failed to account for similar psychopathological content appearing in organic and toxic psychoses. Furer (27) felt that this theory underestimated the contribution of the seriously impaired early mothering required to create a paranoid-schizoid fixation. Moreover, for better or worse, the Kleinian metapsychology can be adapted to include possible genetic predispositional factors. Greenson (32) criticized the technical implications derived from Kleinian theory.

The second development in the conflict theory of schizophrenia is attributable largely to the work of Arlow and Brenner (4), who renounced the topographic model as used by Freud and placed the responsibility for schizophrenia squarely on the shoulders of a defective ego. This defective ego, however, is not to be confused in their formulation with the presence of some deficiency which would be inexplicable by environmental determinants. In their view the psychosis is a defensive effort involving regression and serving to avoid the emergence of anxiety from inner conflicts which usually are about aggressive impulses. These defenses differ only in the degree of disruption of reality contact they cause, not in any qualitative difference.

Semrad (92) extended this ego psychology view of schizophrenia. He saw the schizophrenic psychosis as a defensive operation designed to avoid intolerable affects including, but not limited to, anxiety. The defenses (denial, projection, distortion, and identification with the aggressor) become habitual means of warding off the pain that had accompanied depriving or overindulgent early childhood relationships. By not attending to unpleasant percepts, the child prevents internal turmoil from occurring. This produces severe handicaps in later life when internal affect is handled as if it were an external danger. (This closely parallels the Kleinian formulation, which also notes how all experiences of unpleasure are consistently attributed to persecutory objects (91). Therefore, in children who rely on these defenses, the capacities to delay responses, to bear painful experiences, and to dissipate tension within the body are developed only to a limited extent. The preschizophrenic thus avoids relationships as a means of controlling the danger of developing intense affects. Ego decompensation, regression, and clinical psychosis occur in later periods of intensification of affect. At such times the impossible pain of the early relationship to a parent is evoked. Like Arlow and Brenner's, this theory emphasizes the defective ego structure and quantitative—not qualitative—differences in the defenses used by the schizophrenic. But it also goes farther by stressing the central role of affects in the pathological childhood development which predispose to later schizophrenic psychoses.

The theory of affect intolerance can be commended for its coherence and its close affiliation with clinical observation. Many others have noted the importance of affect intolerance in schizophrenia. Most commonly the affect which is implicated has been anger (35,97). In some respects the role of anger resembles the central role given flight from destructive impulses in the formulations about schizophrenia by Searles (88), by Arlow and Brenner (4), and by Kleinian theory. Yet this theory, like most others, can be viewed as descriptive rather than etiological. Thus, it fails to explain either why one child and not another develops pathological defenses against affects, or why one affect may be particularly unbearable as opposed to another for a given schizophrenic patient. Like the Kleinian theory, this theory also requires a grossly disturbed early parent-child relationship as the explanatory basis for the disturbed relationship that the adult schizophrenic shows toward a therapist. But retrospective reconstructions of early mother-child relationships remain unconfirmed hypotheses, awaiting prospective evaluations. This theory lacks specificity: that is, it uses an inability to integrate aggression and express it effectively to explain, for example, borderline psychopathology and obsessive compulsive disorders as well as schizophrenia.

It may be readily appreciated that all of these theories, both deficit and conflict, have in common a reliance upon the metapsychological language of psychoanalysis that has been derived from observations in the analytic situation. None of the traditional theories of schizophrenia has taken into consideration, for example, the newer observations about schizophrenia which have arisen out of the community movement and the widespread employment of antipsychotic drugs. London (61) and Holzman (46) were critical of the limitations of data derived solely from the analytic situation, and they questioned the applicability and appropriateness of psychoanalytic metapsychology to schizophrenia. Holzman argued that the language of psychoanalysis is based on conflict and can be useful only when applied to the clinical phenomena of schizophrenia which reflect restitutive efforts; it is ill suited for the phenomena of etiology. Other, newer theories about schizophrenia employ new data bases, and all try to avoid the traditional controversy of deficit versus conflict viewpoints.

RECONCILIATORY THEORIES

One means by which recent theorists have sought to overcome the old split between conflict and deficiency is to delineate central or organizing issues which may be viewed with equal comfort either as a cause of defective structure or as being superimposed on and perhaps caused by weak structure. In this respect, Burnham et al. (12) emphasized the need-fear dilemma and linked it to specific aspects of weak internal structure—namely, the systems for self-control and self-regulation which are either too tenuous or too rigid, and which the person has difficulty maintaining autonomously.

Similarly, and more broadly, Mahler (65) stressed the central role of separation-individuation in normal and pathological development. Like Klein, her theoretical constructs derive primarily out of childhood observations. Stierlin (99), Schulz (84), Searles (88), Jacobson (48), and Freeman (21) employ Mahler's developmental axis as a central organizing theoretical construct to explain adult schizophrenia. In brief, this theoretical position states that there are normally occurring autistic and symbiotic phases in the relationship of the infant to its mother. During these phases the infant has a poor sense of itself as independent from the mother, and it is only through a gradual process of separation that individuation occurs, with its accompanying formation of a stable and assured sense of self. This process is seen as largely dependent upon the libidinal availability of the mother. Failure to emerge successfully from these developmental phases predisposes such children to later development of schizophrenia.

Even with the widespread use of Mahler's theory, it has been criticized. Stierlin (100) was dissatisfied with the prominent role this theory gives the dyadic symbiotic experience. Likewise, Searles (89) criticized Mahler's formulation as underestimating the degree of interpersonal, intrafamilial trauma that schizophrenic patients suffer despite a relatively normal genetic endowment. The result of this, according to Searles, is an underestimation of the role of aggression in a schizophrenic. From a different vantage point, the self-object differentiation formulation can be criticized as not being specific to schizophrenia and as being descriptive rather than an explanatory theory. From the point of view of Kleinian theory, Mahler's proposal rests too heavily on the disturbed reality of the infant and does not attend sufficiently to the infant's active ego capacity to distort reality through fantasy.

TRANSACTIONAL THEORY

A second major trend in new theories of schizophrenia has stemmed from the recognition that the schizophrenic develops his pathological vulnerability over an extended period of time and in circumstances that are extended beyond the early infantile parent-child relationship. This recognition has meant that theoretical formulations must allow for, if not actively include, the impact of the interpersonal network and social climate in which the individual has developed far beyond the first year or two of life. This line of theory can be traced to Sullivan and is pursued by existential theory and the social perspective of Laing. For example, several studies have demonstrated that the father's psychopathology may be just as influential on development of schizophrenia as the mother's (14). Growing out of the active and relatively new research and therapeutic interest in the families of schizophrenics has come the first, albeit preliminary, theoretical formulations of milieu transaction. One of the difficulties required in moving out of the dyadic relationship—as postulated as occurring in early development and as recapitulated in the analytic situation—has been the need to develop a new language along with new metapsychological concepts.

Wynne (108) has formulated schizophrenia as a disorder of psychological and emotional transaction between people, not as a process located exclusively within a person. The infant learns to interact in his family and particularly with the mother. If this primordial experience is disrupted, either because of the mother's distractions (a failure to teach) or because the child, for organic and probably genetic reasons, is unresponsive (or responds idiosyncratically), a failure to learn to use language meaningfully takes place. Thus, response dispositions interact with interpersonal (particularly intrafamilial) transactional processes to create the schizophrenia-vulnerable person. Wynne has speculated that the nature of the disturbed response disposition may be a genetically determined difficulty in relating to the object world. The nature of the defect impaired by disturbed interpersonal processes, he feels, may be an inability to focus attention. Such families tend to interact in rigid, oversimplified, and distant ways in which any readjustment to accommodate growth or change is not tolerated. Thus, schizophrenic symptomatology is reflective of a crisis in development which requires change or intimacy.

In extending this interactional conception of schizophrenia, Stierlin (99) has focused on the centripetal and centrifugal forces within normal family constellations and has applied concepts derived from his observation of them to the schizophrenic family. In this context he borrowed the concepts of self-object differentiation and formulated the development of schizophrenia in terms of degree, amount, and type of distance of differentiation the index child is permitted from his parents. Although this concept owes something to the concept of self-object differentiation, the language is transformed into the language of transactional systems.

SYSTEMS THEORY

In a more ambitious effort to expand theoretical formulations of schizophrenia beyond the infantile experience, Grinker (35) has employed "systems" theory. This systems theory, like Hughling Jackson's theory of neurological development, views the organism as the product of an unfolding logical progression whose course is influenced in succession by constitutional, nurturing, familial, economic, social, and interpersonal factors. According to Grinker, we know that all of these factors are involved in the ontogeny of schizophrenic disturbance as well as in so-called healthy development. The schizophrenic state can then be viewed as a system composed of difficulties in heredity, in early family systems of communication, in early peer experiences, with trauma, etc. This view means that we are not able to focus on any one factor in our concern for the various etiologies of schizophrenia, but we must note that all factors are necessary in varying combinations. There is no such thing as spontaneous change; we are just not now able to pinpoint the factors in the schizophrenic's system which can explain his changes. Holzman (46) pointed out that this view of development, and more specifically of schizophrenia, takes into account the considerable contributions of nonpsychological factors (e.g., genetic, biochemical, and neurological) which he views as necessary in light of current scientific understanding of schizophrenia; yet as comprehensive as the systems theory appears to be, it provides little specificity for the problem of schizophrenia. Despite its ability to account for the unique concatenation of factors which can lead to schizophrenia, it does not readily account for schizophrenia's more universal characteristics. Thus, it fails to provide testable hypotheses, guides to clinical practice, and predictions for course and behavior. Holzman employs systems theory mainly as a prescription and rationale for further systematic observations before expanding psychological theory. In this sense it is closer to describing the criteria for a theory of schizophrenia than to actually providing such a theory.

FUTURE CHALLENGES

The more recent developments in the clinical theories about schizophrenia have in common the impulse to encompass observations from sources other than the analytic situation. In the effort to do this, no theory has emerged which is both sufficiently specific to schizophrenia to provide predictions readily and thus testable hypotheses, or general enough to encompass known information about schizophrenia. It is certain that among the criteria for a modern theory of schizophrenia are the following:

1. It must encompass what is known from the clinical phenomena in the schizophrenic as a patient (i.e., the patient's style of relating or transference.)
2. It must draw viable implications from such phenomena to conform with what is known about the schizophrenic's early childhood development.
3. It must incorporate nontransference phenomena, including information about the schizophrenic's response to drugs, community, and family.
4. It must allow for and hopefully embody a role for constitutional or biological factors in at least some members of the schizophrenic group.
5. It must encompass factors derived from nondyadic interactions, including social circumstances, drug precipitants, and spontaneous remissions.

It is noteworthy that the two most widely used concepts since Freud's formulations are those introduced by Klein and Mahler, both of which were derived from systematic observation of normal and disturbed child development. This circumstance may reflect the limitations of theory building based on reconstructions inferred from adult patients. Fortunately, there is currently under way a group of studies of children at risk for subsequent development of schizophrenia. These studies are looking at and systematically assessing early development, including areas such as interpersonal relatedness, mother-child interaction, use of language, and ability to express affects. Since a fraction of these children (about 10 to 15 percent) will later develop schizophrenia, there will be a chance to test the validity of some of these theoretical models and to delineate a better-informed concept. Risk children have now been differentiated from others by prolonged separation of mother and child, the difficulty of dealing with positive affect in three-year-olds, the compliance of female versus hostility of male preschizophrenics in school, etc. (28,72).

But it is noteworthy that clinical theorists have thus far shown little interest in this highly relevant literature. An exception here is Kernberg (54), who has made at least a preliminary effort to relate the observations from the psychoanalytic stiuation to studies of infancy and perceptual deficit. Hence he has stated:

> Schizophrenic patients may present lowered thresholds to perceptual input leading to information input overload and excessive arousal, and/or lowering of anxiety thresholds or excessive arousal leading to diffuse, massive affective reactions, and secondary cognitive disorganization. A biological disequilibrium in autonomic reactivity may underlie both types of lowered thresholds (perceptual and affective); lowered thresholds, in turn, may determine excessive reactivity, protective withdrawal, and disorganization under the impact of affect-laden interactions. All these defects may *interfere* with the building up of the "all good" interpersonal experiences and their corresponding intrapsychic "all good self-object image" and bring about a pathological predominance of aggressively determined "all bad self-object images." [pp. 237–38]

This formulation allows for and even suggests some specific psychobiological vulnerability in the infant, while it attempts to explain how that vulnerability might interact with the interapsychic phenomena observed in adult patients. Although not very developed, such a formulation is refreshingly original.

Even more difficult is the task of connecting metapsychological concepts of schizophrenia with the burgeoning literature on the nature of a constitutional deficit in schizophrenia. This difficulty is largely due to the current absence of a unified, generally accepted biochemical, neurological, or genetic theory of schizophrenia. Yet biochemical theorists like Kety are taking some steps toward distinguishing symptoms that might be attributable to one biochemical hypothesis from clinical phenomena that cannot be explained in that way. Likewise, an essentially neurological hypothesis like Shakow's (95), that schizophrenia is due to an inability to sort out relevant stimuli, lends itself to metapsychological extrapolation. Indeed, Wynne (110) and Will (106) have tried to employ this model. Even conflict theorists need to attend to the interface between biology and psychology. Here, for example, Mednick (69) has suggested and provided some empirical substantiation for the ideas that the autonomic nervous system is unstable in those children who later develop schizophrenia, and that this instability is the product of environmental events like separations from mother.

Unfortunately the findings from both the high-risk studies and the searches for organic substrates are still sufficiently weak that specific etiological factors can not yet be incorporated into a theory. Despite the speculative nature of metapsychological correlations with such results, bridging this gap between biological and psychological is the most important step lacking in most current metapsychological theories. This step must be taken to make any theory comprehensive and usefully predictive and to change descriptive metapsychological theories into true etiological theories.

Current Status

Currently the psychotherapy of schizophrenia is largely at an impasse. There are no widely debated controversies about methods, there is no bevy of new and charismatic spokesmen, and there is little evidence of new theories developed out of the experience of psychotherapists. Nor has acceptance of psychotherapy as a useful modality with schizophrenic persons—which grew modestly but consistently from 1930 to 1960— continued to expand. Though there are reasons outside of the mental health field—such as the limitations on reimbursement for psychotherapy—the current impasse is most attributable to developments within the field itself. Amongst these reasons are: (1) decline in the importance of psychoanalytic preceptors in training programs, (2) the prevailing trend toward short-term hospitalization, which places a necessary emphasis on closure of conflicts, (3) the prevailing pessimism about the efficacy of this form of treatment. This impasse provides a good opportunity to assess the past progress of psychotherapy and to specify some directions that are likely in the future.

It would be difficult to do justice to the problems of doing a definitive study about the efficacy of this, or perhaps any, form of psychosocial intervention. The problem of finding an appropriate measure for outcome was reviewed earlier. Yet even if such an instrument is reliably developed to measure those results which can be attributed to an individual psychotherapy, there will still be the problem of interpreting why one patient has a favorable outcome and another has not. The task of outcome research would be assisted if there was some known means of identifying the patients and/or the therapists who are most suited to undertake this work. Unfortunately this problem is unlikely to yield to any simple formula. Curiously, I believe the importance of and the nature of appropriate therapists has been attended to even better than have issues concerning selection of patients. This trend was seen in the Whitehorn-Betz work (105); it was further noted by Shader et al. (94); it has been especially emphasized by Dyrud and Holzman (15); and it has been given further substantiation by recent research (41).

Even more complicated than the selection of appropriate therapists and appropriate patients is defining the nature of the psychotherapy itself. Psychotherapy consists of many elements which themselves are independent variables worthy of investigation. Each in turn is in need of isolation and quantification in order to locate those elements which are particularly critical in determining outcome. This would include, but is not limited to, processes such as identification, unique experiences of sharing, insight, and conflict resolution. There are no current means to identify or to quantify these variables.

There has been some narrowing of the practice of individual psychotherapy for schizophrenia. There is less polarization of opinion about the necessity and the value of regression and prolonged hospitalization, with some recognition of the shortcomings to any generalization. There is also some narrowing of the therapist's technique in the direction away from direct id interpretation and away from behavioral provision of nurturance for patients. In keeping with this development, there seems to be a trend toward acknowledging that real relationships are needed, but that they are insufficient by themselves, without analysis of the transference aspects. The therapists of schizophrenics generally appear sober and businesslike in their approach to psychotherapy and do not tend to romanticize their chosen work, as is evident in their taking less interest in pathology and symptomatology and more interest in practical issues regarding adaptation. They put less emphasis on the schizophrenic as victim of deprivation and more on his role as perpetuator of his difficulties.

There is also evidence of some narrowing in the conceptualization about schizophrenia derived from intensive work with adult schizophrenics. The following definition of schizophrenia was, for example, suggested by and agreeable to a group of therapists who had otherwise diverse theoretical positions:

> Schizophrenia is a disorder of ego functioning caused by developmental, parent-child experiences (which may include biological-constitutional elements) which results in an inability to separate out and maintain accurate internal mental representations of the outside real world. This inability, in turn, causes the production of restitutional symptoms (delusions, hallucinations) which are most prominent when the individual is confronted with the stresses of developing independent, mature, trusting adult relationships. [26, p. 675]

As has been noted, there have been many recent reviews about development of the psychoanalytic theories of schizophrenia. These reviews reflect efforts to resolve old and no longer productive debates, such as the deficit/defense division, and they presage new developments in the metapsychology of schizophrenia. Some of these developments already under way utilize observations drawn from animal experiments, longitudinal studies of children who develop schizophrenia subsequent to evaluation at birth, and studies of the cognitive and family functioning of already diagnosed schizophrenics. The persisting diversity of theory reflects a recognition that our understanding of schizophrenia is incomplete, and that the enormous research efforts from other perspectives about the nature and etiology of schizophrenia have still failed to be very useful in explaining the clinical phenomena observed in intensive psychotherapy.

The intense emphasis given to diverse theoretical positions by experienced psychotherapists is not mirrored by any predictable use of techniques in clinical practice. This raises the question whether the theoretical construct is most important insofar as it allows a therapist to organize and systematize his observations and not particularly by virtue of its accuracy or inaccuracy.

It would be incomplete to close a review on individual psychotherapy for schizophrenic patients without noting or commenting on the symbolic significance attached to the controversies about its efficacy. Those who advocate or practice this form of treatment place themselves at one extreme in the humanist tradition in psychiatry. By their efforts they suggest that even the most extreme forms of human psychopathology are accessible to the healing efforts of well-conceived interaction with fellow human beings, and that, whatever the impact of constitutional genetic factors, schizophrenia is in some measure an understandable mode of adaptation to a disturbing human environment. Will (107) has stated this position succinctly: "We might through our science and improved methods of control do away with schizophrenia—and be left with the problem of schizophrenia; that is, the willful nature of man himself." Viewed in this light, the individual therapist is a researcher who may illuminate less about those factors specific to schizophrenia than about those perverse elements of humanity common to us all. The interest throughout the mental health field in the psychotherapy of schizophrenics has always far exceeded the small number of people who actually seriously engage in this work. This discrepancy, I believe, is explained by the universally hopeful message contained in this undertaking: that those socially maladaptive or personally shameful or inflexibly limited aspects of ourselves could, if the conditions were right, be exposed, understood, and maybe even modified. It is unlikely that the mental health field will ever wish to foreclose this possibility even if it is scientifically established as a rarity.

BIBLIOGRAPHY

1. Arieti, S. 1955. *Interpretation of schizophrenia* (New York: Robert Brunner).
2. Arieti, S. 1962. Hallucinations, delusions, and ideas of reference treated with psychotherapy. *American Journal of Psychotherapy* 16:1,52–60.
3. Arieti, S. 1971. Schizophrenia. *American Journal of Psychiatry* 128:3.
4. Arlow, J., and Brenner, C. 1964. *Psychoanalytic concepts and the structural theory* (New York: International Universities Press).
5. Aronson, G. 1972. Defense and deficit models of schizophrenia. Presented at the fall meeting of the American Psychoanalytic Association, December 1, 1972.
6. Bellak, L. 1963. Methodology and research in the psychotherapy of psychoses. *Psychiatric Research Reports of the American Psychiatric Association* 17:162–75.
7. Bellak, L., and Loeb, L. 1969. *The schizophrenic syndrome* (New York: Grune & Stratton).
8. Bellak, L.; Hurvich, M.; and Gediman, H. 1973. *Ego functions in schizophrenia, neurotics and normals* (New York: John Wiley).
9. Bookhammer, R. S.; Meyers, R. W.; Schober, C. C.; and Piotrowski, A. Z. 1966. A five year followup study of schizophrenics treated by Rosen's "direct analysis": Compared with controls. *American Journal of Psychiatry* 123:602–4.
10. Boyer, B., and Giovacchini, P. L. 1967. *Psychoanalytic treatment of characterological and schizophrenic disorders* (New York: Science House).
11. Brill, A. A. 1938. *The basic writings of Sigmund Freud* (New York: Random House), pp. 3–34.
12. Burnham, D.; Gladstone, A.; and Gibson, R. 1969. *Schizophrenia and the need-fear dilemma* (New York: International Universities Press).

13. Cain, A. 1971. Psychotherapy at McLean: The case for modesty. Paper presented at the McLean Hospital Academic Conference, Framingham, Massachusetts, May 14, 1971.

14. Cheek, F. E. 1965. The father of the schizophrenic. *Archives of General Psychiatry* 13:336-45.

15. Dyrud, J. E., and Holzman, P. S. 1975. Evaluation of psychotherapy. In *Psychotherapy of schizophrenia*, eds. J. G. Gunderson and L. R. Mosher (New York: Jason Aronson), pp. 269-80.

16. Fairbairn, W. D. 1952. *Psychoanalytic studies of the personality* (London: Tavistock). Also published as *An object relations of personality* (New York: Basic Books, 1954).

17. Federn, P. 1952. *Ego psychology and the psychoses* (New York: Basic Books).

18. Feinsilver, D. B. 1977. The symbiotic block. *International Journal of Psychoanalytic Psychotherapy* 6:131-144.

19. Feinsilver, D. B., and Gunderson, J. G. 1972. Psychotherapy of schizophrenia: Is it indicated? A review of the relevant literature. *Schizophrenia Bulletin* 6:11-23.

20. Foster, B. 1975. The recapitulation of development during regression: A case report. In *Psychotherapy of schizophrenia*, eds. J. G. Gunderson and L. R. Mosher (New York: Jason Aronson), pp. 67-111.

21. Freeman T. 1969. *Psychopathology of the psychoses* (New York: International Universities Press).

22. Freeman, T.; Cameron, J.; and McGhie, A. 1964. *Chronic schizophrenia* (New York: International Universities Press).

23. Freud, S. 1894. Neuro-psychoses of defense. In *The Standard Edition of the Complete Psychological Works of Sigmund Freud* (hereafter: *Standard Edition*), ed. J. Strachey (London: Hogarth Press, 1953), vol. 3, pp. 41-68.

24. Freud, S. 1896. Further remarks on the neuropsychoses of defense. *Standard Edition* (London; Hogarth Press, 1953), vol. 3, pp. 157-185.

25. Freud, S. 1911. Psychoanalytic notes on an autobiographical account of a case of paranoia. *Standard Edition* (London: Hogarth Press, 1958), vol. 12, pp. 3-82.

26. Friedman, R. J.; Gunderson, J. G.; and Feinsilver, D. B. 1973. The psychotherapy of schizophrenia: An NIMH program. *American Journal of Psychiatry* 130:674-77.

27. Furer, M. 1977. Psychoanalytic dialogue: Kleinian theory today. *Journal of the American Psychoanalytic Association* 25:371-86.

28. Garmezy, N., and Streitman, S. 1974. Children at risk: The search for antecedents of schizophrenia. *Schizophrenia Bulletin* 8:14-90.

29. Geller, J. D., and Berzins, J. I. 1976. A-B distinction in a sample of prominent psychotherapists. *Journal of Consulting and Clinical Psychology* 44(1):77-82.

30. Goldberg, S.; Schooler, N.; Hogarty, G.; et al. 1977. Prediction of relapse in schizophrenic outpatients treated by drug and sociotherapy. *Archives of General Psychiatry*, 34:171-84.

31. Greenblatt, M.; Soloman, M.; Evans, A.; et al. 1965. *Drug and social therapy in chronic schizophrenia* (Springfield, Ill.: Charles C Thomas), vol. 3.

32. Greenson, R. R. 1975. The limits of an interpretive approach. In *Psychotherapy of schizophrenia*, eds. J. G. Gunderson and L. R. Mosher (New York: Jason Aronson), pp. 205-7.

33. Greenson, R. R. 1965. The working alliance and the transference neurosis. *Psychoanalytic Quarterly* 34:155-81.

34. Greenson, R. R., and Wexler, M. 1969. The non-transference relationships in the psychoanalytic situation. *International Journal of Psychiatry* 50:27-39.

35. Grinker, R. 1973. Changing styles in psychoses and borderline states. *American Journal of Psychiatry* 130:151-52.

36. Grinspoon, L.; Ewalt, J.; and Shader, R. 1972. *Schizophrenia: Pharmacotherapy and psychotherapy* (Baltimore: Williams & Wilkins).

37. Grotstein, J. S. 1975. A theoretical rationale for psychoanalytic treatment of schizophrenia. In *Psychotherapy of schizophrenia*, eds. J. G. Gunderson and L. R. Mosher (New York: Jason Aronson), pp. 175-204.

38. Gunderson, J. G. 1975. Introduction. In *Psychotherapy of schizophrenia*, eds. J. G. Gunderson and L. R. Mosher (New York: Jason Aronson), pp. xiii-xlii.

39. Gunderson, J. G. 1975. The current metapsychology of schizophrenia. In *Psychotherapy of schizophrenia*, eds. J. G. Gunderson and L. R. Mosher (New York: Jason Aronson), pp. 145-60.

40. Gunderson, J. G. 1976. Recent research on psychosocial treatments of schizophrenia. In *Schizophrenia '75: Psychotherapy, family studies, research*, eds. J. Jørstad and E. Ugelstad (Oslo, Norway: Universitetsforlaget), pp. 307-26.

41. Gunderson, J. G. 1978. Patient-therapist matching: A research evaluation. *American Journal of Psychiatry* 135[10]1193-1197, 1788.

42. Gunderson, J. G. 1978. Psychotherapy of schizophrenia: The nature of outcome. In preparation.

43. Gunderson, J. G.; Feinsilver, D.; and Schulz, C. 1975. Matching therapists with schizophrenic patients. In *Psychotherapy of schizophrenia*, eds. J. G. Gunderson and L. R. Mosher (New York: Jason Aronson), pp. 343-59.

44. Gunderson, J. G., and Hirschfeld, R. 1975. Factors influencing the selection of patients for individual psychotherapy. In *Psychotherapy of schizophrenia*, eds. J. G. Gunderson and L. R. Mosher (New York: Jason Aronson), pp. 293-303.

45. Hogarty, G. E.; Goldberg, S. C.; Schooler, N. R.; and Ulrich, R. F. 1974. The collaborative study group: Drug and sociotherapy in the aftercare of schizophrenic patients II. Two Year Relapse Rates. *Archives of General Psychiatry* 31:603-8.

46. Holzman, P. S. 1975. Problems of psychoanalytic theories. In *Psychotherapy of schizophrenia*, eds. J. G. Gunderson and L. R. Mosher (New York: Jason Aronson), pp. 209-22.

47. Horwitz, W.; Polatin, P.; Kolb, L.; and Hoch, P. 1958. A study of cases of schizophrenia treated by direct analysis. *American Journal of Psychiatry* 114:780-83.

48. Jacobson, E. 1967. *Psychotic conflict and reality* (New York: International Universities Press).

49. Jones, E. 1963. *The Life and Work of Sigmund Freud* (New York: Doubleday-Anchor).

50. Karon, B. P., and O'Grady, P. 1969. Intellectual test changes in schizophrenic patients in the first six months of treatment. *Psychotherapy: Theory, Research and Practice* 6:88–96.

51. Karon, B. P., and VandenBos, G. R. 1970. Experience, medication and the effectiveness of psychotherapy with schizophrenics: A note on Drs. May and Tuma's conclusions. *British Journal of Psychiatry*, 116(533):427–28.

52. Kayton, L. 1975. Clinical features of improved schizophrenics. In *Psychotherapy of schizophrenia*, eds. J. G. Gunderson and L. R. Mosher (New York: Jason Aronson), pp. 361–95.

53. Kernberg, O. F. 1972. Clinical observations regarding the diagnosis, prognosis, and intensive treatment of chronic schizophrenic patients. Paper presented at the Follow-up Conference on Schizophrenia: The Implications of Research Findings for Treatment and Teaching, Los Angeles, California, March 26–27, 1972.

54. Kernberg, O. F. 1972. Early ego integration and object relations. *Annals of the New York Academy of Sciences*, 193:233–47.

55. Kernberg, O. F.; Burstein, E.; Coyne, L.; Applebaum, A.; Horwitz, L.; and Voth, H. 1972. Psychotherapy and psychoanalysis: Final report of the Menninger Foundation Psychotherapy Research Project. *Bulletin of the Menninger Clinic* 36(1,2):87–275.

56. Kessler, M. 1969. Use of familiar dynamic considerations to explain the schizophrenic process. *Dynamische Psychiatrie* 2:40–49.

57. Klein, M. 1946. Notes on some schizoid mechanisms. *International Journal of Psycho-Analysis*, 27(3,4):99–110.

58. Klein, M. 1948. *Contributions to psychoanalysis* (London: Hogarth Press).

59. Kolb, L. C. 1968. *Modern clinical psychiatry*, 7th ed. (Philadelphia: W. B. Saunders).

60. Laing, R. D. 1960. *The divided self* (London: Tavistock).

61. London, N. J. 1973. An essay on psychoanalytic theory: Two theories of schizophrenia. I. Review and critical assessment of the development of the two theories. *International Journal of Psycho-Analysis* 54:169–78.

62. London, N. J. 1973. An essay on psychoanalytic theory: Two theories of schizophrenia. II. Discussion and restatement of the specific theory of schizophrenia. *International Journal of Psycho-Analysis* 54:179–93.

63. McGlashan, T. H., and Carpenter, W. T. 1976. An investigation of the postpsychotic depressive syndrome. *American Journal of Psychiatry* 133(1):14–19.

64. McGlashan, T. T.; Levy, S. T.; and Carpenter, W. T. 1975. Integration and sealing over. *Archives of General Psychiatry* 32:1269–72.

65. Mahler, M. S. 1968. On human symbiosis and the vicissitudes of individuation. In *Infantile Psychosis* vol. 1 (New York: International Universities Press).

66. Mann, J., and Semrad, E. V. 1959. Conversion as process and conversion as symptoms in psychosis. In *On the mysterious leap from the mind to the body*, ed. F. Deutsch (New York: International Universities Press), pp. 131–54.

67. May, P. R. A. 1968. *Treatment of schizophrenia: A comparative study of five treatment methods* (New York: Science House).

68. May, P. R. A., and Tuma, A. H. 1970. Methodological problems in psychotherapy research: Observations on the Karon-VandenBos study of psychotherapy and drugs in schizophrenia. *British Journal of Psychiatry* 117(540):569–70.

69. Mednick, S. A., and Schlusinger, F. 1968. Some premorbid characteristics related to breakdown in children with schizophrenic mothers. In *The Transmission of Schizophrenia*, eds. D. Rosenthal and S. Kety (London: Pergamon Press Ltd.), pp. 213–22.

70. Merrifield, J.; Carmichael, W. G.; and Semrad, E. V. 1971. Recovery patterns 15 years after acute psychosis. Paper presented at the 124th Annual Meeting of the American Psychiatric Association, Washington, D.C., May 1–5, 1971.

71. Mosher, L. R. 1972. Implications of family studies for the treatment of schizophrenia. Read at the Symposium on the Treatment of Schizophrenia, University of California at Los Angeles, March 18, 1972.

72. Mosher, L., and Gunderson, J. 1973. Special Report on Schizophrenia, 1972. *Schizophrenia Bulletin* 7:10–52.

73. Mosher, L. R.; Menn, A. Z.; and Matthews, S. M. 1975. Soteria: Evaluation of a home-based treatment for schizophrenia. *American Journal of Orthopsychiatry* 45(3):455–67.

74. Pao, P. 1972. Notes on Freud's theory of schizophrenia. Presented at the fall meeting of the American Psychoanalytic Association, December 1, 1972.

75. Pao, P. 1975. The place of Federn's "Ego Psychology" in a contemporary theory of schizophrenia. *International Review of Psycho-Analysis* 2(4):467–80.

76. Paul, G. L.; Tobias, L. L.; and Holly, B. L. 1972. Maintenance psychotropic drugs in the presence of active treatment programs. *Archives of General Psychiatry* 27:106–15.

77. Perry, J. W. 1962. Reconstitutive process in the psychopathology of the self. *Annals of the New York Academy of Sciences* 96:853–76.

78. Rado, S. 1962. Theory and therapy: The theory of Schizotypal organization and its application to the treatment of decompensated schizotypal behavior. In *Psychoanalysis of Behavior*, vol. 2, ed. S. Rado (New York: Grune & Stratton, Inc.), pp. 127–40.

79. Razin, A. M. 1971. The "A-B" variable in psychotherapy: A critical review. *Psychological Bulletin* 75(1):1–21.

80. Rogers, C. R.; Gendlin, E. G.; Kiesler, D. J.; and Truax, C. B. 1967. *The therapeutic relationship and its impact: A study of psychotherapy with schizophrenics* (Madison: University of Wisconsin Press).

81. Rosenfeld, H. 1966. *Psychotic states: A psychoanalytic approach* (New York: International Universities Press).

82. Rubenstein, R. 1972. Mechanisms for survival after psychosis and hospitalization. Paper presented at the Annual Meeting of the American Psychoanalytic Association (Dallas, Texas), April 27–30, 1972. Available through author, Mt. Zion Hospital, San Francisco, California 94115.

83. Rubins, J. G. 1972. Schizophrenia as conflict and defense: Implications for therapy and research. In *Research and relevance*, vol. 21 of *Science and psychoanalysis*, ed. J. Masserman (New York: Grune & Stratton).

84. Schulz, C. G. 1975. Self and object differentiation as a measure of change in psychotherapy. In *Psychotherapy of schizophrenia*, eds. J. G. Gunderson and L. R. Mosher (New York: Jason Aronson), pp. 305–16.

85. Schulz, C. G. 1975. An individual psychotherapeutic approach with the schizophrenic patient. *Schizophrenia Bulletin* 13:46–69.

86. Schulz, C. G., and Kilgalen, R. K. 1969. *Case studies in schizophrenia* (New York: Basic Books).

87. Schwartz, D. P. 1959. The integrative effect of participation. *Psychiatry* 22:81–86.

88. Searles, H. F. 1965. *Collected papers on schizophrenia and related subjects* (New York: International Universities Press).

89. Searles, H. F. 1975. Countertransference and theoretical model. In *Psychotherapy of schizophrenia*, eds. J. G. Gunderson and L. R. Mosher (New York: Jason Aronson), pp. 223–28.

90. Segal, H. 1951. Some aspects of the analysis of a schizophrenic. *International Journal of Psycho-Analysis* 31:285.

91. Segal, H. 1977. Psychoanalytic dialogue: Kleinian theory today. *Journal of the American Psychoanalytic Association* 25:363–70.

92. Semrad, E. V. 1969. A clinical formulation of the psychoses. In *Teaching psychotherapy of psychotic patients*, ed. D. Van Buskirk (New York: Grune & Stratton), pp. 5–17.

93. Semrad, E. V.; Grinspoon, L.; and Feinberg, S. E. 1973. Towards the development of the ego profile scale. *Archives of General Psychiatry* 28:70–77.

94. Shader, R. I.; Grinspoon, L.; Harmatz, J. S.; et al. 1971. The therapist variable. *American Journal of Psychiatry* 127:1009–12.

95. Shakow, D. 1963. Psychological deficit in schizophrenia. *Behavioral Science* 8:275–305.

96. Soskis, D. S., and Bowers, M. B. 1969. The schizophrenic experience. A follow-up study of attitude and posthospital adjustment. *Journal of Nervous and Mental Disease* 149:443–49.

97. Spotnitz, H. 1969. *Modern psychoanalysis of the schizophrenic patient* (New York: Grune & Stratton).

98. Stanton, A. H. 1978. The significance of ego interpretive states in insight-directed psychotherapy (Harry Stack Sullivan Colloquium). *Psychiatry* 41, no. 2:129–40.

99. Stierlin, H. 1975. Schizophrenic core disturbances. In *Psychotherapy of schizophrenia*, eds. J. G. Gunderson and L. R. Mosher (New York: Jason Aronson), pp. 317–22.

100. Stierlin, H. 1975. Some therapeutic implications of a transactional theory of schizophrenia. In *Psychotherapy of schizophrenia*, eds. J. G. Gunderson and L. R. Mosher (New York: Jason Aronson), pp. 317–22.

101. Wexler, M. 1971. Schizophrenia: Conflict and deficiency. *Psychoanalytic Quarterly* 40:82–99.

102. Wexler, M. 1975. Comment on the five treatment comparative study. In *Psychotherapy of schizophrenia*, eds. J. G. Gunderson and L. R. Mosher (New York: Jason Aronson), pp. 431–33.

103. White, R. W. 1965. The experience of efficacy in schizophrenia. *Psychiatry* 28:199–211.

104. Whitehorn, J. C. 1944. Guide to interviewing and clinical personality study. *Archives of Neurology and Psychiatry* 52:197–216.

105. Whitehorn, J. C., and Betz, B. J. 1954. A study of psychotherapeutic relationships between physicians and schizophrenic patients. *American Journal of Psychiatry* 111:321–31.

106. Will, O. A. 1967. Psychological treatment of schizophrenia. In *Comprehensive textbook of psychiatry*, eds. A. M. Freedman and H. I. Kaplan (Baltimore: Williams & Wilkins), pp. 649–61.

107. Will, O. A. 1975. The conditions of being therapeutic. In *Psychotherapy of schizophrenia*, eds. J. G. Gunderson and L. R. Mosher (New York: Jason Aronson), pp. 53–66.

108. Wynne, L. C. 1970. Communication disorders and the quest for relatedness in families of schizophrenics. *American Journal of Psychoanalysis* 30:100–114.

109. Wynne, L. C. 1976. Schizophrenics and their families: Research on parental communication. In *Developments in psychiatric research*, ed. J. M. Tanner (Sevenoaks, Kent: Hodder & Stoughton).

110. Wynne, L. C.; Ryckoff, I.; Kay, J.; et al. 1958. Pseudomutuality in the family relations of schizophrenics. *Psychiatry* 21:205–20.

111. Zetzel, E. R. 1970. *The capacity for emotional growth* (London: Hogarth Press).

Chapter 12

GROUP, FAMILY, MILIEU, AND COMMUNITY SUPPORT SYSTEMS TREATMENT FOR SCHIZOPHRENIA*

Loren R. Mosher, M.D. and John G. Gunderson, M.D.

Introduction

A brief note is in order to orient readers to the authors' philosophical position. For us, the tendency of mental health workers, family, and society to withdraw from personal involvement with mad persons is understandable and often reinforced by mad persons themselves and the current social context. Nonetheless, we find it regrettable. Whatever one chooses to use as the defining characteristics of schizophrenia, there is little doubt that most persons receiving this label have extraordinary difficulty establishing and maintaining human relationships. Given this fact, it seems self-evident that it is important for others *not* to mirror their tendency to withdraw from, or drive away, other human beings. It is to this aspect of schizophrenia that psychosocial treatments can address themselves. Even the seemingly mechanistic approach of behavior modification requires the presence of at least two persons—the client and his treater. Despite the relative lack of research evidence to document the efficacy of specific psychosocial treatments, we will not rationalize a position of "why bother, if it can't be shown to do any good?" While perhaps supportable as an academic research view, we feel it has no place in the day-to-day contact with severely disturbed persons. It can too easily be used as justification for our withdrawal. It is clear the withdrawal of interest on the part of "helping" persons will be responded to by withdrawal on the part of these patients. When the

* The opinions expressed in this chapter are those of the authors and do not necessarily represent any official position of the National Institute of Mental Health.

The authors would like to acknowledge the assistance of Ms. Kathy Beck, Ms. Sherry Buchsbaum, Ms. Constance Durrett, Ms. Susan Matthews, and Ms. Lynne Montcrieff for their invaluable assistance in the preparation of this manuscript.

mutual withdrawal is sufficiently great and fixed in character, we are apt to label the patient a "chronic, unremitting, backward schizophrenic." Continued human involvement is the only known treatment that can prevent this from occurring.

The psychosocial treatment of schizophrenia is a book-length topic by itself. Therefore, several caveats are in order with regard to this chapter so that unrealistic reader expectations are not engendered or reinforced. Space limitations will not allow us to address the following important considerations in detail:

1. *Heterogeneity of individuals labeled "schizophrenic."* For example, we recognize that a person receiving this diagnosis at age seventeen after spending four years as a recluse at home is very different from one so labeled at age thirty-five who has been working productively and raising a family for a number of years. Although it is our *belief*, based on clinical experience, that the goals, types, and responsiveness to psychosocial treatments are likely to be quite different for these two individuals, there is no space to describe a series of prototypical patients and prototypical appropriate psychosocial treatments. In addition, the research evidence on which to base these differential treatment assignments is meager—*at best*. For the most part our discussion will assume that the patients are not very long-term, chronically hospitalized, or backward. Where feasible, we will discuss this type of patient separately.

2. *Heterogeneity of psychosocial treatments.* This chapter will not be an encyclopedic discussion of all types of psychosocial treatments given schizophrenic patients. We will discuss only four broad categories: group and family psychotherapy, milieu treatment, and community support systems. The first two can be viewed as specific types of psychosocial treatment. Within each category there are numerous major variations in theory and practice. Our attempt will be to take a "middle of the road" position: that is, for example, we will discuss what we consider a "modal" type of group therapy offered schizophrenic patients. Again, as is the case with patient heterogeneity, there is very little other than personal bias on which to base a preference for one theory or practice of group therapy over another.

We subscribe to Frank's view (40) that all psychosocial treatments—whether or not clearly defined as entities like individual psychotherapy—share common nonspecific elements: an emotionally charged relationship with a helping person; a plausible explanation of the causes of distress; provision of some experiences of success; and use of the therapist's personal qualities to strengthen the client's expectation of help.

The last two types of psychosocial intervention (milieu and community support systems) are generally seen as nonspecific treatments. They tend to be viewed by many as background conditions onto which the "real" treatments (e.g., neuroleptics, individual therapy) are overlaid. We believe this view is incorrect, and there are some data to support our position (34,173); that is, it seems to be becoming clearer and clearer that despite their relative nonspecificity, these two social contextual "treatments" can have powerful positive or negative effects on individuals. Inclusion of these less specific approaches in a chapter on psychosocial treatment is a departure from previous editions of this book and most other similar chapters (e.g., reference 103). However, by including them, we are consonant with the current emphasis on community-based treatment. In addition, by highlighting them, we hope to direct more attention to these undervalued aspects of psychosocial treatment.

3. *The facilitative, neutral, or interfering interactions of neuroleptic drugs with psychoscial treatments.* At this time, whether we like it or not, neuroleptics are a fact of life for almost everyone labeled schizophrenic. Some patients will have them only briefly, while others will have been maintained on them for years—but schizophrenics who have never received these drugs are very scarce in the current mental health treatment system. When, where, how, with whom, and with which psychosocial treatment or treatments neuroleptics may add, detract, or exert no effect, remains unknown (51). For purposes of this chapter we will assume that most participants in the various psychosocial treatments have had or are currently receiving neuroleptics. We will also assume that they are being or have been prescribed in a thoughtful, responsive, nonobtunding manner. In our experience this assumption is often not "reality"; however for psychosocial treatments to have any prospect of helpfulness, a patient must not be made into a zombie by his medication. We will assume neuroleptics are a relatively neutral background variable unless there is evidence to the contrary.

4. *Belief systems, social contexts, and the quality of psychosocial treatment.* Clinicians will generally agree that there are competent and incompetent individual, group, and other kinds of therapists. The defining qualities of the two types are much less agreed upon. Although there is considerable literature on therapist characteristics (70,139,143,144) —especially for individual psychotherapy—space does not allow us to discuss them in detail. We will assume that therapists giving the treatments described in this chapter are at least of average competence— not especially gifted, charismatic persons and not inexperienced, untrained, uninterested ones.

Because the potential for effectiveness of psychosocial treatments relies heavily on mutual commitment of patient and therapist, it is important that the therapist believe in what he is doing. Belief does not mean overwhelming, uncritical zealotry, rather, it means sufficient interest, investment, and involvement to stay with what may often be a draining, unrewarding endeavor. Such belief is difficult to maintain over long periods without some type of reinforcement. To prevent therapists from becoming excessively dependent on their patients for this reinforcement, the social context within which therapists work must share and support this belief. For the purposes of this discussion we will assume this to be the case. For example, we will presume that therapists involved in group therapy are not doing so in a treatment setting that sees such therapy as a waste of time and medication as the only treatment of value for schizophrenics.

The number of caveats and assumptions we have made in order to simplify our task may seem excessive or unimportant to some readers. In each instance we have done so only out of our conviction of their importance to, and relevance for, the extraordinary complexities of psychosocial treatments. Although we could often not address them definitively, even with unlimited space, they do let the reader know what factors should be considered when psychosocial treatments are discussed and studied.

Each section that follows will have a common format: historical background, definition of the treatment, current status of research, new developments, and practical clinical guidelines.

In reviewing the last decade of research, we have been selective. In general, we have included research that makes some attempt to address most of six widely accepted design characteristics (39,114).

1. *Theory and technique.* The nature of the treatment to be delivered must be adequately defined. Moreover, definition should coincide with reality; that is, the treatment should relate in a coherent and meaningful way to the theory underlying it. As is well known, what we say (and believe) we are doing may be very different from what we really *are* doing.

2. *Patient characteristics.* The patient group should be adequately defined. Since diagnostic difficulties with schizophrenia are notorious (and it is clearly a "wastebasket" term), each researcher's criteria must be made explicit (i.e., based on behavioral items that can be rated reliably) to permit replication and comparison across studies.

3. *Therapist characteristics.* In studies of psychological intervention the therapist, as well as his patients, must be the object of study. At a minimum he should be categorized according to level of experience, theoretical orientation, enthusiasm, and type of patient-therapist relationship that evolves. In studies of group or milieu therapy his role as a leader should obviously be part of any research evaluation.

4. *The process.* Research addressing primarily the *result* of interpersonal interactions cannot ignore these processes themselves. Unfortunately our tools for evaluating a transacting dyad are inadequate. While the individual roles of both patient and therapist have been studied extensively (e.g., reference 143), the transactional flow *between* them has received little attention. This area is vitally in need of new methods.

5. *The context.* Psychological interventions are very sensitive to the context within which they are delivered. It is therefore crucial to understand the attitudes, the belief systems, and the demand characteristics of the settings in which treatment is carried out.

6. *Outcome.* Criteria measuring outcome should be carefully defined and do justice to the treatment being tested. In assessing individual psychotherapy, for example, measures of personality change and insight are clearly more relevant than mere symptom reduction. These criteria should also allow for a long-range view. Interactional techniques are generally slower than somatic treatments, but their effects may be relatively enduring and may intensify over time.

Although we evaluated each study in terms of these criteria, we did not apply these criteria too strictly. We frequently compromised these "ideal" research design qualities in accepting studies for inclusion. However, totally inadequate studies have not been included.

Group Psychotherapy

HISTORY

As far as its history is determinable, group psychotherapy appears to have grown out of the observation that patients with similar medical or psychological problems could receive benefit from each other as well as from the doctor. A recent review by Gomes (46) has described the origins of group therapy for hospitalized patients. Originally it consisted of lectures for mental reeducation (82,100). Since then group treatment of schizophrenia has diversified into many forms—supportive therapy, psychodynamic therapy, activity groups. Neither the early didactic techniques, designed to instill understanding of the psychological mechanisms underlying behavior through classroom presentations and lectures (4,13,72), nor the strictly psychoanalytic approaches introduced during the same period (1,153,176) remain in wide use with schizophrenic patients today.

The use of group treatment flowered particularly after World War II in Veterans Administration hospitals, where it was often the only expedient means of dealing with the large numbers of returning veterans with psychological problems. In fact, the Veterans Administration sponsored one of the earliest studies of its efficacy with schizophrenics, and this resulted in the widely influential book by Powdermaker and Frank (135).

While the primary aim in most traditional group therapies is facilitation of insight into personal and interpersonal problems, much group work with schizophrenics is oriented toward providing support, an environment in which patients can develop social skills, or a format that allows friendships to begin and be sustained. Therapy is not always limited to verbal interaction. Hypnosis (60), play therapy (41), and Gestalt games (17) have been attempted. Occasionally treatments conducted in a group context involved individual body awareness (144) or play with symbol-laden infantile objects (88) rather than interaction among group members.

Early enthusiasts saw group therapy as more economical, more widely applicable, simpler, and perhaps more effective than individual treatment. Group therapy was promoted as an alternative to individual therapy. But this overly optimistic view has had to be considerably modified in the light of clinical and research experience. Group psychotherapy has definite contraindications and limitations and can be just as expensive and may be as difficult and demanding as any other psychotherapy technique. A more realistic assessment views it not as a replacement for individual psychotherapy, but rather as offering different techniques for the more effective treatment of some patients and particular problems.

DEFINITION

Group therapy has been defined as anything ranging from a casual kaffee klatsch to psychoanalysis-in-groups. Part of the confusion stems from the failure to distinguish between groups that are therapeutic (including self-help groups—e.g., Alcoholics Anonymous, Synanon, Recovery, Inc.; activity groups—e.g., Great Books, Parent-Teacher Associations, Boy Scouts; and training groups—e.g., T-Group, group institutes) and psychotherapy groups. There are basic dynamic differences between these two types of group, both of which may be therapeutic, yet achieve similar goals through quite dissimilar means. Powles* suggests three useful criteria for defining group psychotherapy: (1) that there be a group of troubled people gathered for some therapeutic goal; (2) that there be present a professional or an expert leader to assist the group; and (3) that the relationships and interactions among group members be exploited as tools for clarification, motivation, or behavior change. Clearly, self-help, social, and training groups may be therapeutic although not purposefully psychotherapy. Other group activities such as social group work, occupational-recreational therapy groups, and diagnostic intake groups may have both educational and therapeutic elements which merge into group therapy. Thus, the distinctions between types of group activities may sometimes be arbitrary. The nature of the group may change during the course of group experience, or various aspects may be present simultaneously in the same group. Finally, there are a wide range of explicit psychotherapy groups varying from ward milieu group therapy to psychoanalysis-in-groups. The difference in techniques is so great that group psychotherapy per se is not one technique but many. However, almost all group therapy attempts to enhance social interaction.

A convenient method for categorizing the type of therapy group is derived from Levine's (85) four categories of therapeutic interaction: suppressive, supportive, relationship, and expressive insight. Each type of interaction may occur within the same group over time, but one type of interaction will probably be typical of a given group.

RESEARCH

In addition to the chapter in the previous edition of this book, there are a multiplicity of reviews of the group therapy outcome literature up to 1968 (10,105,128,164). It is fair to say that, based on the data available to them, these reviewers generally concluded that most controlled evaluations of group therapy showed meager, if any, therapeutic benefit for schizophrenics (especially long-term inpatients) from groups. There were individual instances of special benefits from group treatment, but design problems—such as lack of follow-up, inappropriate control groups, and insufficient duration of treatment—made firm conclusions, either pro or con, difficult to draw. Our focus will be the 1966–76 decade of research. This review is adapted, with modifications, from Parloff and Dies (125).

In addition to the criteria listed in the introduction, we asked that the research design permit the inference that the changes observed in patients were due primarily to the effects of group psychotherapy. How-

---

° Powles, W. E. Varieties and uses of group psychotherapy. *Canadian Psychiatric Association Journal* 9:196–201, 1964.

ever, this and our other criteria were compromised to permit the inclusion of those studies that: (1) systematically controlled for the effects of time, suggestion, and expectation and/or compared the effects of alternate treatment forms, and (2) included reasonable diagnostic and other criteria as well as before- and after-treatment measures. The studies have been classified according to the treatment setting: hospital or posthospital.

STUDIES WITH HOSPITALIZED PATIENTS

GROUP PSYCHOTHERAPY COMPARED WITH THE USUAL HOSPITAL TREATMENT PROGRAM

Hospital settings almost always provide a wide range of treatment modalities:—for example, recreational and occupational therapy, music therapy, and medication. Therefore, group psychotherapy offered in inpatient settings is an "add-on" rather than an exclusive treatment form. In each of the six studies of "group therapy versus no-group therapy" patients selected for their predicted suitability for group therapy were randomly assigned to either group therapy or a no-group therapy hospital treatment control group. Unfortunately, as is so often the case, diverse measures of outcome were used with little overlap between studies, so that direct comparison was difficult.

Boe et al. (12) and Pattison et al. (129) compared patients receiving the usual hospital services with patients who also received two to three months of group psychotherapy. The dropout rate was high in both studies—32 percent and 40 percent, respectively—but was similar for both experimental and control conditions. Both studies failed to show any consistent improvements attributable to the effects of group therapy on either a wide range of self-report measures or on observer ratings of patient change. Boe et al. reported that control patients described themselves as gaining in social dominance, whereas group-treated patients tended to see themselves as increasingly unassertive and more indulgent of others. These changes in self-perception are difficult to evaluate, because it is not possible to tell whether they were realistic self-appraisals, that is, whether they involved changed levels of social interaction. In addition, it is difficult to decide whether the control or experimental group changes were more positive—that is, a goal of the therapy. Pattison et al.'s study (129) examined the effectiveness of ten to twelve weeks of *analytically oriented* group therapy. Of the twelve patients who remained in group therapy, three concurrently received individual therapy, while of the twelve in the no-group condition, six received individual therapy. Patients in group therapy tended to show less improvement than did the hospital control group on a wide range of measures, including self-acceptance, personality change, symptoms, and hospital adjustment.

An analysis of the trends revealed by the subsamples, who had been exposed to various combinations of group and individual therapy, led the authors to conclude that patients in individual therapy tended to demonstrate greater improvement than did patients in group therapy alone. Pattison and his associates concluded that it is probably unwise to use psychoanalytically oriented group treatment for relatively short-term hospital inpatients for whom the goal is immediate reconstitution and return to the community. Before this conclusion is accepted, however, it should be noted that only one therapist conducted the analytic group psychotherapy. Ergo, it is not in fact possible to determine whether the effects observed are attributable to group therapy or to the therapist.

Lipton et al. (91) compared the effectiveness of twice-a-week group therapy focused on increasing "general insight and socialization" with two once-a-week ward "gripe session" meeting control groups. Discussion of personal problems on the two "gripe session" control wards was discouraged and referred to private discussion with the physician during the nine-month treatment period. Although the 180 male Veterans Administration hospital subjects were demographically similar, one control ward contained more patients judged to be sicker by the psychiatrist. These investigators failed to show any advantage for group psychotherapy on measures of admission to closed wards or discharge rates. Because insight and socialization were not assessed directly, however, it is not possible to know whether outcome for the group-treated patients was better than that for controls on these dimensions.

Haven and Wood (57) compared recidivism among patients treated in twice-a-week group therapy with that found among patients afforded only the usual hospital treatment program. The group therapy was described as eclectic but directive and reality-oriented, and duration of treatment was determined by the "patient's readiness for release." The median number of sessions for the thirty-four patients assigned to groups was sixteen, and there were from eight to twenty-two sessions. At the end of a twelve-month follow-up period the study failed to show any difference between group and not-group-treated schizophrenic patients on measures of rates of hospital discharge, readmissions, non-readmissions, and non-hospital release.

Vitalo (174) compared the relative impact of three treatments: group psychotherapy, type unspecified; hospital milieu control; and a special training program emphasizing Rogerian dimensions of interpersonal relationships, empathy, positive regard, and genuineness. Twenty-nine patients were randomly assigned to one of the three treatment forms. Following treatment, patients in group therapy showed less clinical pathology than did patients in either the training group or the ward control group. As predicted, the group that received special training in recognizing and expressing empathy, positive regard, and genuineness scored higher on instruments presumed to measure these skills. However, such training effects did not appear to be translated into personality changes. The nature and degree of socialization were similar for patients in the group therapy and the special training condition and superior to the ward milieu control group.

Olson and Greenberg (123) compared three groups of patients who received: (1) "incentive group therapy" (2 hours per week) which was focused on rewarding patients for developing mutual responsibility for doing specific tasks; (2) an interaction control group (2 extra hours of problem-focused group therapy); and (3) a "usual" hospital control group. "Usual," in this setting, included weekly nurse-led group therapy. The incentive group subjects were not allowed to see the professional staff (e.g., psychiatrists, psychologists, or social workers) individually. Seventy-four male Veterans Administration hospital patients (80 percent schizophrenic) were divided into three matched groups that received the incentive, interaction, or usual treatments over a four-month period. Inhospital adjustment, activity levels, and extrahospital adjustment were measured before, during, and for four months after termination of the treatment program. No differences were found between treatment groups in terms of patient interaction levels or a patient activity checklist. On the dimension of patients' hospital social adjustment, however, the nurses described patients in both the "usual" and the "interaction" groups as showing better adjustment than patients treated with incentive therapy, who, in fact, were rated by nurses as having "gotten worse." Yet patients receiving incentive therapy attended more scheduled activities, spent more time away from the hospital, and obtained more town passes during the four-month follow-up period than did the other comparison groups. These latter two studies suggest that focused interventions aimed at producing specific effects (e.g., Rogerian interpersonal and incentive therapy) can achieve their very clearly defined outcomes.

In summary, of the six comparisons of group therapy of schizophrenics against a no-group therapy hospital condition, four failed to reveal any unique or impressive contribution assignable to "group psychotherapy." It should be noted, however, that the studies with positive results (123,197) were better designed in terms of length of treatment and outcome measures that addressed the investigators' hypotheses directly.

GROUP PSYCHOTHERAPY COMBINED WITH OTHER PSYCHOSOCIAL INTERVENTIONS, COMPARED WITH UNAUGMENTED THERAPY

Corder et al. (27) compared the effects of group therapy alone and group therapy in combination with a dyadic social interaction. The experimental condition required that each patient spend a minimum of thirty minutes daily with an assigned patient-partner in a discussion of personal problems. The tapes of the experimental dyadic sessions were compared with the tapes of group therapy sessions conducted by the same experimenter with a matched control group. Results showed that group therapy patients who also met with their assigned partners manifested more reality contact, greater intimacy, a deeper level of emotional material, and more verbal interaction with fellow patients than did patients in group therapy alone.

Coons and Peacock (26) also addressed the question whether prescribed social interaction among patients usefully augments group psychotherapy. Predominantly schizophrenic patients were assigned at random to one of four treatment conditions, each of which lasted six weeks: group psychotherapy plus random ward interaction; group therapy plus organized ward interaction; random ward interaction alone; and organized ward interaction alone.

Group psychotherapy was aimed at fostering intragroup transactions in a warm, accepting, and permissive atmosphere. The organized ward interaction group involved assigning patients to groups of seven members each that maintained its identity throughout most of the daily

hospital activities. In addition, the hospital staff was involved in planning, conducting, and supervising the organized ward interactions but
not the random ward activities.

It was found that increments in tested intelligence were associated
with participation in group therapy independent of the form of ward
activity. However, patients in group psychotherapy plus organized ward
interaction were described by the ward staff as showing significantly
better hospital adjustment than patients in group therapy combined with
random ward condition. Positive change on the Rorschach test was
associated with the combination of group therapy plus random ward
interaction. The data suggested that on all three criterion measures, the
combination of group psychotherapy plus either formal or informal ward
interactions produced significantly greater positive change than did
either ward condition alone.

Coons and Peacock speculate that the findings regarding hospital
adjustment, which were based on ratings by the ward staff, may reflect
a bias in favor of those programs in which the ward staff was actively
involved. Thus, organized ward activities directed by the staff were
judged by them to be more useful than unorganized ward activities in
which they were not involved. Patient change on independent measures
of intelligence and personality did not appear consistent with staff
ratings of institutional adjustment. Whether this discrepancy is indeed
an artifact of rater bias, as suggested by the investigators, cannot be
assessed on the basis of this research design. Taken in conjunction
with apparently similar rater-based discrepancies found by Olson and
Greenberg (123) these findings point out an important methodological
question—that is, that therapy outcome may indeed be contingent upon
who evaluates improvement.

Roback (141) compared a form of group therapy aimed at encouraging patient-to-patient interactions with a more insight-oriented group
therapy and with a control group. In addition, a treatment group which
combined both interaction and insight approaches was studied. No
statistical differences on a wide range of behavioral and psychometric
measures were found between either the insight or the interaction
forms of therapy offered separately. However, the combined treatment
form was consistently superior to either treatment alone, or to the
control group, on measures of personal functioning within the institution. No differences in terms of days spent out of the hospital were
found among any of the treatments tested.

The effects of group psychotherapy alone versus group therapy plus
alternate sessions (authorized meetings of the group held in the absence
of a therapist) were investigated by Truax et al. (169). They found that
patients who participated in the alternate sessions had developed significantly *less* adequate self and ideal-self descriptions, and these patients tended to describe themselves as deflecting more from experts'
depictions of positive mental health after treatment than they had before
group therapy began. This shift was not found in patients treated in the
"group therapy only" condition. Changes on the Minnesota Multiphasic
Personality Inventory (MMPI) were compatible with these findings in
that patients having alternate sessions showed less improvement on the
paranoia and schizophrenia scales than patients taking part only in the

regular group sessions. It was concluded that alternate sessions may have a disruptive rather than a facilitative effect on chronic schizophrenic patients.

During the past decade the use of pharmacological agents has become a standard part of most hospital regimes for the treatment of schizophrenics and the severely mentally disturbed. One study appropriate for inclusion in this section of the review involved the combination of drug and group therapy. Borowski and Tolwinski (14) compared the effects of chlorpromazine alone and in combination with twice-weekly group psychotherapy for two groups of forty paranoid-schizophrenic patients over a period of two months. Treatment included reassurance, persuasion, discussion, clarification, and in some cases manipulation of family situations.

The patients treated by a combination of chlorpromazine and group therapy showed greater symptomatic improvement than did patients treated by the drug alone. Equally important was the finding that patients in the combined treatment condition showed more rapid reduction of clinical pathology than did patients in drug treatment alone. Delusional thinking, for example, lessened in 61 percent of the patients in combined treatment groups by the third or fourth week, while in the same period only 14 percent of the patients in the drug-treatment-alone condition were free of delusional thinking.

Robinson (142) attempted to determine whether group psychotherapy combined with videotape feedback was more useful to seriously disordered inpatients than group therapy alone. Forty patients—selected by hospital staff members as meeting the criteria of being in good contact with reality, having adequate verbal facility, and not having been hospitalized for longer than eighteen months before the study—were divided into six groups. All patients received group psychotherapy, which was videotaped during the experimental period. Three therapy groups were offered one hour of videotape feedback immediately following each session. The remaining three therapy groups were offered one hour of postgroup discussion, but the videotape was not shown. The entire experimental period was limited to six hours over two weeks.

Two criteria of change were employed: judges' ratings of the frequency of adaptive and maladaptive behaviors manifested in the first and the fifth videotaped therapy sessions, and patients' own ratings of their adaptive behavior. The judges reported that the patients in the focused feedback condition showed significantly greater increase in behaviors that had been sanctioned by the therapist than did patients in the control group. There was, however, no significant difference between treatment forms in effecting a decrease of behaviors that were cited by the therapists as "maladaptive." Patients' self-reports failed to reveal any differences attributable to either treatment approach.

In brief, five of the six studies which tested group therapy in combination with another treatment approach reported that the combination —be it drug, videotape feedback, ward activity, or dyadic social interaction—was superior to the treatment forms offered singly.

Integrating the results of these two types of inhospital studies is difficult for a number of reasons; the patient groups are often noncomparable, the outcome measures varied widely and frequently did not address the specific effects sought by the treatment, and many of the studies involved short treatment periods. This problem is especially relevant when the subjects were long-term patients. Yet positive results were found in those studies that carefully defined the behaviors or attitudes they wished to change, and used outcome measures that taped them. In addition, it appears that the more structured the activity (i.e., Osmond and Greenberg's "incentive therapy," Corder et al.'s required dyadic interaction, and Robinson's videotape feedback), the more likely there is to be a positive result.

Although this interpretation is admittedly speculative, it is consistent with the types of milieu therapy found to be most useful for chronic patients.

AFTERCARE TREATMENT STUDIES

The treatment of schizophrenics has been revolutionized during the past fifteen years. Extended hospitalization has given way to early release. Treatment is increasingly provided in general hospitals and outpatient settings rather than in large mental hospitals. Patients are discharged into the community, to their families, to halfway houses, or to foster homes with increasing frequency. As this community treatment emphasis has grown, it has become increasingly apparent that psychosocial interventions are required to aid the patient in maintaining community adjustment; drugs do not teach individual social and interpersonal skills. Group psychotherapy has been used as a treatment modality aimed at maintaining the posthospital discharge patient in the community by enhancing social and interpersonal skills.

During the past decade six major studies have appeared which attempted to test the relative efficacy of some form of group therapy contrasted with an alternative treatment form or a no-therapy control group in the treatment of posthospitalization patients. Four of these studies tested the relative value of group therapy and individual therapy with reference to rehospitalization.

Levene et al. (84), O'Brien et al. (122), and Herz et al. (59) reported no differences in terms of recidivism in the effects of individual and group psychotherapy programs which ranged from one to two years. Purvis and Miskimins (137), in contrast, found that group and individual therapy patients, who had attended at least five therapy sessions, differed significantly in rehospitalization rates, with group therapy patients showing the advantage (19 percent versus 50 percent for individual therapy). In addition, 34 percent of the patients in their no-treatment control group returned to the hospital, a rate that is reliably greater than that for the group-therapy-treated sample.

Shattan et al. (156) reported mixed results. Group-treated patients showed fewer readmissions and a greater number of absolute discharges after one year of conditional discharge, but did not differ from the no-group-therapy control group in number of months out of the hospital during the trial discharge period or in employment after the twelve-month probationary period. The no-group patients received only approximately half as many clinic contacts following their hospital release. The findings on vocational adjustment were corroborated by Purvis and Miskimins, however. In their study, too, group-treated patients did not show any better work adjustment. This is of particular interest since the study by Purvis and Miskimins was specifically directed at enhancing vocational adjustment.

Only two of the studies contained in this review of discharged patients incorporated measures of social effectiveness. O'Brien et al. reported that group-treated patients were rated as more socially adept than their individually treated cohorts. In contrast, Levene et al. observed that the relatives' ratings of patient behavior showed significantly more improvement for patients treated individually than for those treated in group therapy. Four other measures of social adjustment in the Levene et al. study failed to discriminate between the patients treated individually and those treated in groups; neither treatment form gave impressive results.

In terms of reduced psychopathology, Herz et al. found no differences in the relative effectiveness of group and individual therapy as judged either by mental health experts or by the patients themselves.

Claghorn et al. (23) tested the effects of thiothixene and chlorpromazine alone or in combination with six months of weekly, structured, practical problem-oriented group psychotherapy. Both medications effected positive symptom change to an approximately equal degree, but group therapy did not appear to contribute significantly to the effects of either drug in reducing patient symptomatology. There was evidence, however, that the group-therapy-treated patients achieved a greater appreciation of their own disability, in that they perceived *others* as "healthier" in terms of their being more dominant and affiliative. Group-treated patients also reported their own basic intentionality—as measured by the MMPI, Psychopathic deviate (Pd) and Masculinity/femininity (Mf) scales—as having shifted to a much more dominant position, although their affiliation scores on this measure did not change significantly over the treatment period.

In summary, recent studies of group psychotherapy, as an undefined treatment given heterogenous groups of posthospital schizophrenics, have not yielded strong or consistent evidence that this form of treatment reduces rates of rehospitalization, improves vocational adjustment, diminishes psychopathology, or enhances social effectiveness. However, in each instance, the evidence was contradictory, so that it is not possible to conclude that outpatient group therapy is not useful for schizophrenics. In fact, a treatment whose principal aim is to promote socialization and enhance interpersonal skills should probably not be expected to have a striking effect on rehospitalization or vocational adjustment. Two of the three studies that addressed the most relevant outcome variable (O'Brien et al. and Claghorn et al.) showed a positive effect from group treatment. The negative findings of Levene et al. were based on relatives' ratings, whereas the positive findings of the other two came from research raters and the patients themselves. Thus, the same methodological issue addressed in attempting to interpret the inpatient group therapy studies—that is, the influence of who does the ratings on the assessment of outcome—is raised by these outpatient studies. It should also be noted that both O'Brien et al. and Herz et al. reported that both group patients and therapists retrospectively reported more favorable feelings about the treatment experience than did the individually treated patients and their therapists. These morale-enhancing, affiliative effects are likely to be very important and certainly need further research, because they are particularly difficult issues with long-term, community-based patients.

RECENT INNOVATIONS

Because groups have had a long history of innovations in their use, we could not identify any really "new" approaches. However, certain trends, while not new, are beginning to receive increasing emphasis. Two are worth mentioning. First, legitimate group leadership has been spread more widely than ever before: nurses, social workers, para-professionals, etc., now lead groups on a regular basis. This is consistent with the current trend toward proletarianization of the therapist role. Second, groups in short-term residential settings (where most inpatient treatment of schizophrenia now takes place) are more often *task-* rather than therapy-focused; that is, ward groups to deal with passes and privileges, discharge, etc., are now commonplace. They generally amalgamate group therapy and therapeutic community principles and may fit the definition of groups that "may be therapeutic" better than group therapy. In any case, they are consonant with the current short-hospitalization emphasis in being specifically task-focused and devoting relatively little attention to developing, discussing, and using group process—something that requires stable, longer-term groups.

CLINICAL GUIDELINES

The present authors' clinical experience agrees with O'Brien's (121) conclusions about the practical utility of group therapy. Hence, much of what follows is adapted from his article. Like O'Brien, we believe inpatient groups are not feasible in today's short-term hospitals. He reasons that there is insufficient time for the development of group process—a point with which we agree. Taking it a step further, we believe that groups of all types (i.e., task-focused, community meetings, etc.) should not be used with *newly* admitted *acutely disorganized* schizophrenics. Our reasoning is that persons undergoing the fragmentation, disintegration, and loss of sense of self characteristic of acute psychosis will be overwhelmed by the complexities of groups with ten to twelve persons they know only minimally. The result can be yet another blow to their already impaired self-esteem. We recommend that these patients not be required to attend ward groups until such time as the attentional disorder, confusion, and acute disorganization have subsided sufficiently to allow their real participation in groups. Instead of inclusion in groups or other formal therapeutic endeavors, we recommend that they receive close one-to-one contact with staff or other patients to provide support, certainty, and protection. As the psychosis abates, patients can then be assigned to group therapy. Ideally the same groups would be continued after discharge.

Although not conclusive, research evidence is accumulating to support the use of groups as an important postdischarge therapeutic experience for many schizophrenic patients. Whether seen as providing a structured, regular opportunity for socializing or as a way of enhancing medication compliance (122), of improving social functioning (31,101), or of building staff morale (59,101,122), there does seem to be a valuable role for group therapy with outpatient schizophrenics.

PATIENT SELECTION AND RECRUITMENT

Almost all patients require a thorough explanation of outpatient groups. This explanation may entail several visits and should be presented by a therapist who is committed to a group approach. Too often, in a busy clinic with a low staff-to-patient ratio, the patient and his family gain the impression that group therapy is stressed because there are not enough therapists to go around. The fact that group treatment is a unique experience—one that seems to provide some things that individual therapy does not—is the aspect that should be stressed. In addition, there is no reason to believe group treatment interferes with other types of concurrent treatment.

GROUP COMPOSITION

We believe it is wise to have groups balanced on a number of relevant patient characteristics. There should be a mix of ages, with adolescents being considered a separate category. There should be about equal numbers of men and women. There should not be so many verbal, assertive members as to dominate the interaction and prevent less verbal or more withdrawn patients from participating. And there should be some range of overt disturbance; that is, a group composed exclusively of very disturbed individuals will make it more difficult for any one of them to learn from another member how to cope more effectively. We would recommend that sociopaths be excluded from groups of current or ex-psychotics to avoid the risk of their being exploited by the character-disordered patient. We also prefer that groups be relatively homogeneous in terms of cultural background and values, as it makes the selection of therapist or therapists easier.

THERAPISTS

The co-therapy team approach has several advantages. The therapists may interact with one another and thus provide a model of interpersonal relations for the patients. They provide useful support for one another during discouraging phases of the group's development; this is especially true when groups are just getting started. The team approach also provides a valuable opportunity for an inexperienced therapist to work with a more experienced one. But the therapists may, of course, be equals in experience. The roles and the statuses of both therapists should be clearly defined to avoid unnecessary confusion for the patients.

A male-female team has the unique advantage of re-creating aspects of the parental roles in the group. Patients may exhibit patterns of relating to each therapist which can be interpreted or used as information during therapy.

It is always important that supervision or consultation be available for treatment teams. Subtle aspects of group dynamics may not become apparent until the sessions are discussed with a supervisor or a consultant. The supervisor should be an experienced group therapist from any of several disciplines. If a majority of the patients are on medication, it is convenient (but not necessary) to have a psychiatrist as one co-therapist.

There are no published studies comparing the effectiveness of a single group therapist versus that of co-therapy teams, but good results can certainly be obtained by either approach. We generally recommend teams if staffing permits, however, because of the advantages already cited.

The best training for group therapy with schizophrenics is supervised experience with individual schizophrenic patients and a period of apprenticeship as a co-therapist. Of course, the therapist or the apprentice should be a mature, stable individual who can tolerate the stress of having to deal with chaotic thinking from all directions. We have found that even relatively inexperienced therapists can get good results with schizophrenic patients in group therapy. What they lack in experience they may make up in enthusiasm and optimism. The period of apprenticeship with an experienced group therapist and the availability of regular supervisory sessions are important, however.

Although there is no research evidence to support it, our contention is that groups are easier to get started and become more rapidly self-sufficient (i.e., the therapists no longer have to make the major effort to stimulate and sustain interaction) when the therapists share the cultural background and values of the patients in the groups. Use of co-therapists allows for somewhat greater group heterogeneity of cultural background, if each can be chosen to match a segment of the group members' backgrounds. We believe the shared therapist-patient cultural experience is important, because it gives them a common idiomatic language and noncontrived subjects of mutual relevance and importance, it facilitates the development of interaction between patients and therapists as equals, and it mitigates against the normal hesitancy and mistrust of a "powerful" stranger.

There is now considerable literature describing psychological characteristics thought to be important for therapists, although the relationship of these characteristics to outcome is less well documented. Nevertheless, the consistency of the descriptions in the literature leads us to conclude that they deserve consideration in selection of therapists for groups. The characteristics most often cited as important for "good" therapists address three related aspects of personality: ego or sense of self, affect, and cognitive-attitudinal dimensions. Although the terms vary considerably, most writers describe good therapists as strong, having good self-esteem, and persevering. Affectively they are described as warm, empathic, and sensitive. Cognitively they are tolerant, flexible, open-minded, and nonjudgmental.

FREQUENCY, LENGTH OF SESSIONS, GROUP SIZE, AND OPEN AND CLOSED MEMBERSHIPS

These will probably be determined initially by local custom. However, it is difficult to believe that groups that are larger than ten or twelve, or that meet less than once a week for an hour, can be expected to have much therapeutic benefit.

Whatever local custom dictates should be seen only as a starting point. Thereafter there should be considerable flexibility on the part of the therapist with regard to both length and frequency of meetings. By being flexible and responsive to the group's wishes, the therapist may be able to transmit these useful qualities to excessively rigid or self-centered clients. As soon as the group begins to have even minimal cohesiveness, the therapist should begin to seek individual's views on issues of duration and frequency. For example, if one group member is having a particularly rough time, others in the group may decide they would like to try and be of more support to him by meeting more frequently or longer. The therapist should try to accommodate their wishes, and if it is impossible for him to meet with them, he should be sure that their regular meeting place is available, and he should raise the issue of whether they want to elect one of their members to lead the extra sessions, or be leaderless. After its formation the group should also be able to decide whether they want to add to its membership, and if so, whom. The general principle being described here is fairly simple: decision-making power to the members, as soon as and as much as possible. This process can, in and of itself, be very therapeutic in terms of the promotion of autonomy and independence, enhancement of self-esteem, and provision of opportunity for successful experiences.

PROMOTING INTERACTION

In general, the job of the therapist is to promote interaction among patients, who look to him for wisdom, guidance, support, and approval. The communication diagram for a new schizophrenic group is shown in figure 12–1. One of the objectives of the therapist is to transform the situation to something similar to that shown in figure 12–2, where the patients are less oriented toward the therapist; they freely interact with one another and do not wait for permission from the therapist to speak.

Nonverbal Interaction. Although various techniques may be used to encourage interaction, sensitivity techniques featuring touching and confrontation should be introduced with care, as they may be too frightening for some of the members, especially early in the group's life.

Bowers et al. (17), however, have described the use of some nonverbal exercises that are not excessively provocative when used in a group whose members have begun to develop some trust in the therapist and in each other. Exercises that are focused on a here-and-now situation are selected. They are frequently designed to help a group member who is having difficulty in becoming aware of his feelings even though they seem apparent to other members and therapists.

An example of nonverbal techniques for promoting interaction would be the rearrangement of chairs so that the members do not sit in the

FIGURE 12-1

Communication Diagram for a New Schizophrenic Group

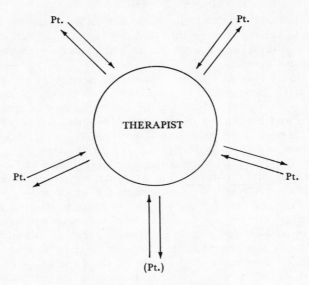

FOCUS ON THERAPIST

[1]Patient (Pt.)

Source: From C. P. O'Brien, "Group Therapy for Schizophrenia: A Practical Approach," *Schizophrenia Bulletin* (1975) 1(13): 119-130.

FIGURE 12-2

Communication Diagram for an Intermediate Schizophrenic Group*

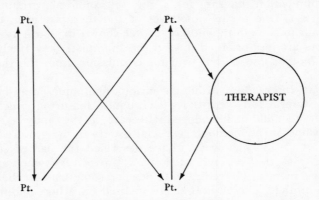

FOCUS ON INTERPATIENT INTERACTION

[1]Patient (Pt.)

Source: From C. P. O'Brien, "Group Therapy for Schizophrenia: A Practical Approach," *Schizophrenia Bulletin* (1975) 1(13): 119-30.

same pattern each week; a break in the pattern often causes a shift in communication and helps to get the group out of a rut. When two members are angry with one another but are not expressing their hostility, the following exercise may be employed (17): the two members are instructed to face each other and clasp both hands palm to palm; at a signal from the therapist, both begin pushing. This exercise often facilitates the verbal expression of anger in individuals who have had great trouble in even becoming aware of emotion.

Food is often an excellent means of stimulating interaction among withdrawn patients. Masnik et al. (101) have described a technique called "Coffee and . . ." which uses coffee and cookies to promote conversation. The clinic may supply the coffee, but the patients should be encouraged to bring in their own cakes and cookies. Something very similar was independently described by Parras (126). The "Coffee and . . ." technique can be enlarged upon to provide an experience of sharing and pride. One can speculate theoretically about the need to gratify exaggerated oral-dependent strivings in regressed schizophrenics. But from a practical point of view, our concern is with a healthy social experience. When people interact in a group, whether verbally or through the sharing of food, they find the process easier the next time. One social interaction leads to another in a progressive fashion.

Medication can be another important focus for withdrawn patients. If one of the therapists is a physician, prescription writing may be an important part of a withdrawn group session (133). The medication ritual, including the discussion of side effects, may actually facilitate group interaction. Medication is something the patients have in common. It is a concrete, here-and-now subject.

It should be emphasized that groups are not designed simply as a convenient mechanism to keep patients medicated. Actually group therapy may permit a lower dose of medication and perhaps a shorter period of treatment.

Verbal Interaction. The importance of patient-toward-patient interaction cannot be overemphasized; it is the immediate objective of group treatment. While nonverbal techniques, as previously described, have their place, most of the therapist's efforts center upon verbal methods.

The "go around" is a simple but time-tested method to get people to talk. The therapist asks each member to give his opinion on a particular subject. The subject may be something that has just occurred in the session, or it may relate to something in a member's personal life. Often the "go around" stimulates interaction among group members, who comment on each other's comments. Withdrawn patients, however, may refuse to respond at all or may simply say, "I don't know." Pressuring a withdrawn patient to commit himself usually fails. The therapist should move on to the next member without calling undue attention to the fact that the previous patient failed to contribute anything.

Not all therapists would approach withdrawn patients as actively as we are suggesting here. Ward (175), for example, tells of letting a group sit in total silence for fifty minutes in order for the members to feel responsibility to be active on their own. Although this was described as a successful technique, most therapists would probably consider it extreme. On the other hand, when the therapist is too active, the responsibility to interact may be taken away from the group members. All this touches on one of the differences of opinion alluded to previously. Actual outcome studies comparing very active therapists with very passive ones are not available. Presumably extremes in either direction are counter-productive.

Another technique for stimulating expression in schizophrenic groups is to organize a simplified form of psychodrama, a *structured dialogue*. The patients are first given a story in the form of a dialogue, which they act out under the direction of the co-therapists. Later they are given themes and asked to make up their own dialogue. The structured dialogue takes up only the first fifteen minutes or so of the session. The group can then discuss the dialogue and the feelings expressed by the "actors." Once warmed up, the group finds it easier to start discussing problems.

Role playing is another technique that can be borrowed from psychodrama. A patient may be asked to rehearse a difficult task such as a job interview during a group session. Another member will play the role of interviewer. The interview may be repeated with a third member playing the role of applicant, so the first patient can see how someone else might handle the situation. Similarly other members can be asked to play the role of parents, siblings, spouse, or landlord—to name a few —and to aid in working out other problems. *Role reversal*, in which group members play one another, is usually difficult in predominantly withdrawn groups. It may be possible, however, if the therapist is sufficiently enthusiastic. This technique may help greatly in working out angry conflicts within the group by enabling patients to see things from each other's point of view. It is also useful for teaching appropriate assertiveness.

These techniques require no special equipment or meeting room. Rearranging chairs may be helpful, not only during role playing but at any time the group seems to be stuck in a set pattern. If special equipment such as a tape recorder or a videotape system is available, it can be quite useful in loosening up withdrawn members in a gentle way. Playing back segments of a meeting is a great stimulus for expression.

GROUP ACTIVITIES

Opinion varies about the possible value and problems associated with social contacts outside of the group. We believe such contacts should be encouraged but *not legislated* by the therapist. It should be made explicit that phone calls, ride sharing, and dating between group members is approved of by the therapist, but that members should not feel *obligated* to socialize. We also believe that the therapist should be allowed to participate in and generate outside-the-group activities, although he should be under no obligation to do so. Basically the greater consonance there is between rules governing therapist and patient, the easier it will be for either to initiate and maintain interaction.

In capsule form, we believe that therapy with groups of patients composed predominantly of schizophrenics should operate on the two middle positions of our therapeutic continuum—that is, as supportive and relationship groups. The focus for both therapist and patients will be on day-to-day problems of real life, on the sharing of relevant experiences, on offering new perspectives on a situation, on learning to listen and be sensitive to the feelings of others, on asking exploratory questions, on encouraging the expression of contrary opinions without fear of reprisal, and on keeping the topic in focus until some sort of closure is reached —to name but a few key therapeutic processes. At the most general level the therapist should do whatever is necessary to promote group cohesion. Initially the therapist may find himself being very active in order to exemplify these processes for the group. With the passage of time he will become a more nearly equal participant, as members gradually learn or rediscover these interpersonal skills. The therapist's role is similar to that of a teacher, but only until the "students" begin to learn the material sufficiently well to teach other, less adept members of the group. The therapist will evolve from leader to fellow "student" at differing rates with different individuals, and he might remain a teacher in some respects to some "students" for prolonged periods.

Family Therapy

HISTORICAL BACKGROUND

The family did not come under the scrutiny of psychiatrists until the late 1940s and early 1950s—some forty years after social workers and child guidance clinics had begun to deal with it as an important aspect of the treatment of individual patients. Frieda Fromm-Reichmann's 1948 paper (42) on the schizophrenogenic mother—a conceptual parent to the later hypothesized schizophrenogenic family—was the first in this vein to receive widespread attention in the psychiatric literature. Since that time, research work on and with families has been carried out at a number of American centers, principally Palo Alto, Bethesda, Philadelphia, New York, New Haven, Boston, Denver, and Galveston; important contributions have also been made by a London-based group. This body of family research is discussed elsewhere in this book (see chapter 7).

The major influence of the study of the family on contemporary psychiatry has been to broaden conceptual "sights." Once focused almost exclusively on the intrapsychic pathology of the individual patient, psychiatrists are increasingly coming to view the *family context* as relevant to the problems of afflicted individuals. The contention that the patient can be treated in isolation from major parts of his social environment— especially the family—grows daily less tenable. Indeed, some theorists no longer conceptualize the problem of "schizophrenia" as residing in the designated patient but as being inexorably intertwined with his family and the wider social context. As an outgrowth of this position, the important unit in therapy is not the single patient, or the transacting psychotherapeutic dyad, but the patient's family and perhaps also the relevant social network. In "network" therapy (161), for example, thirty or more persons, including some without biological relationships, may be seen simultaneously. Thus, the family has, to greater and lesser extents, penetrated the psychiatric consciousness of practitioners, who variously hold that the family cannot be *disregarded* in treatment or that it should be the principal *object* of treatment. But whether seen as a contributing or a preeminent factor, the family has undeniably emerged as an element to be contended with in the treatment of schizophrenic patients.

There is one baffling aspect of the new focus of attention on the family in psychiatric research and practice—namely, the remarkable gap between research on families, on the one hand, and the translation of these research findings into treatment principles. It would not seem unreasonable to expect in two decades' research on families having a schizophrenic member might have identified a number of principles important in the day-to-day practice of treating schizophrenic patients. Yet the findings of this research have not, in fact, been systematically translated into the treatment of schizophrenia—even when carried out by *family therapists!* Intrigued by this most interesting and surprising state of affairs, Mosher (113) hypothesized that this lack of communication between the—one would have thought—closely related fields of family therapy and family research exists because the former grew out of the individual and group therapy tradition, while the latter has its roots in sociology and experimental psychology.

DEFINITION

"Family therapy" is defined in myriad ways; in practice, it ranges from individual psychoanalysis focused on the family relations of individual patients to group meetings involving large social networks of thirty to forty persons. Although we will describe several innovations that extend our own definition, for the purpose of this discussison "family therapy" refers to a meeting between a therapist or therapists and two or more family members with an explicit focus on *family* problems. Meetings with various family members that *may* have incidental therapeutic value (e.g., social work intake interviews) are excluded.

RESEARCH

Family therapy is now two decades old. Does it work? If so, with what types of patients (or families) and in conjunction with which other treatment modalities? These questions are easy to pose but notoriously difficult to answer. Indeed, questions about efficacy may be premature; that is, until "family therapy" is itself better defined, we cannot hope to know whether "it" works. Applying the individual patient diagnostic system will not allow us to say whether "it" works, until we have defined what we mean by "schizophrenia." Unfortunately even if this term were defined in a generally acceptable way, it might not be applicable to families. The family literature is in dire need of a family typology, for, with a few exceptions (e.g., reference 140), terminology derived from studies of individuals has been applied willy-nilly to family research/treatment. If the position taken by many (ourselves included) is accurate that a family is more than the sum of its parts, a typology of individuals will inevitably do the family an injustice.

Only three controlled studies of the outcome of family therapy include substantial numbers of schizophrenics. Wynne (180) has pessimistically suggested that such research may not be possible because of the tremendous variety of influences, in addition to family therapy, to which the hospitalized patient is subjected. This criticism is, of course, applicable to all treatment studies. Evaluations of the outcome of family therapy with schizophrenic patients have been generally limited to anecdotal accounts of a therapist's experiences with a single case or to global comparisons of the progress made by various families treated with the same techniques. We will review uncontrolled studies that include more than a few cases. Single case reports are excluded.

UNCONTROLLED STUDIES

Using therapy techniques aimed at undoing schizophrenic patterns of family communication, Esterson et al. (36) treated twenty male and twenty-five female hospitalized schizophrenics between the ages of fifteen and thirty-five. All of the patients spent less than one year in the hospital, and only 17 percent were readmitted in the subsequent year. Among a large sample of patients in the same age range who had less than one year of psychiatric hospitalization, readmissions averaged 52 percent in the year following discharge. Since the patients treated with family therapy could have differed from the control population in countless dimensions, these discharge statistics are at best suggestive of the potential utility of the Esterson et al. treatment program, as opposed to undefined "average" hospital procedures.

Jackson and Weakland (61) attempted to disrupt the homeostatic systems of family interaction in eighteen families with schizophrenic members. Although their patients were in approximately the same age range as those of Esterson et al., they had spent longer periods in psychiatric hospitals (up to 6 years) and included only four patients experiencing their first acute break. After periods of family treatment ranging from three to forty-one months, six of the seven patients who had been hospitalized at the onset had returned to the community. Among the nine adolescent patients who had previously been restricted to the home or had functioned very inadequately outside the home, seven improved sufficiently to begin working, to achieve some success in school, or at least to go out unaccompanied. The remaining two patients, who had also been restricted to the home, were able to move about the community unaccompanied after therapy. The authors felt that half of the parents and siblings had made some improvement. Of great theoretical interest for family systems theorists was their report that two mothers and one sibling seemed to be worse after treatment. This aspect of the study supports the widespread impression that if a patient-designate gets "well," another family member may experience "breakdown."

Bowen (15,16) integrated the entire family of the schizophrenic into the treatment process by insisting that family members live on the hospital ward and assume primary responsibility for the patient's care. In addition to three mother-patient dyads and seven entire families treated as inpatients for up to thirty-five months, Bowen saw eight families of schizophrenics in outpatient therapy for up to thirty months. Six of the eighteen families terminated therapy without change or in greater disharmony. Among the remaining families, improvement was largely limited to symptom reduction, rather than involving reorganization of the underlying pathological relationships. Indeed, Bowen (16) eventually decided that schizophrenic patients probably lack any capacity to differentiate themselves from a family system in which individuality cannot be tolerated. However, as Lidz (89) has suggested, Bowen's practice of hospitalizing the entire family along with the schizophrenic member may actually have impeded the patient's efforts to separate himself from the family system.

Rather than hospitalize either the schizophrenic or other family members, MacGregor et al. (98) chose to treat the schizophrenic family with an intensive two- to three-day outpatient evaluation, designed to point out the problems in family interactions and to attempt rapid restructuring of family relationships. This "multiple impact" method included a series of interviews with individuals and varying subgroups of family members. After the initial evaluation, continued progress in altering family interactions was monitored through follow-up appointments in the home and in the therapists' offices. Among the six families of schizophrenics treated with this technique, five of the adolescent patients were able to resume school work at a level appropriate for their ages. Although all of the mothers seemed to have redirected their activities sufficiently to prevent resumption of an exploitative relationship with the patient, only one father showed constructive personality changes. Furthermore, the investigators expressed some doubts about the durability of the changes.

UNCONTROLLED STUDIES OF MULTIPLE FAMILY THERAPY

Some family therapists have chosen to meet with groups of families rather than with a single family with a schizophrenic member. The historical background, development, techniques, goals, comparison with conjoint family therapy, and evaluation of results have been recently reviewed by Strelnick (165). As there are no controlled evaluations of this variant of family therapy, only representative examples of results reported will be detailed here.

Laqueur et al. (80) treated 100 families of hospitalized patients ("mostly" schizophrenics) in groups of 4 to 6 families. According to self-evaluations completed by 80 families, 67 percent felt that they had definitely made improvements in communication and mutual understanding. Therapists observed that 46 percent of the 80 families showed marked improvement, and 32 percent, some improvement. However, the contribution of family therapy in effecting these changes was unclear, since half of the patients also received drugs, insulin, or electroshock, and all were involved in a "therapeutic community."

Lassner and Brassea (81) supplemented group therapy for seven hospitalized chronic schizophrenics with weekly group sessions attended by patients and family members. After one year of active-directive therapy the investigators observed improvements in patients' physical appearances, increased conversation among patients, and decreased need for ataractic drugs. Five years after treatment six of the seven patients were living in the community. The institution of day care programs and halfway houses after the completion of the study was also felt to have helped to increase the frequency of reintegration into the community.

The conflict between the patients' drives for independence and the parents' reluctance to relinquish control was explored in multiple family therapy for recently discharged, young adult (eighteen to twenty-five years old) schizophrenics (97). After one year of weekly sessions, including groups of five to six families, none of the seventeen patients who had been specially selected for family treatment was rehospitalized.

CONTROLLED RESEARCH

The first controlled investigation of outpatient family therapy with patients who otherwise would have been hospitalized was conducted by Langsley and his collaborators (75,76,77,78). In this study the relative merits of outpatient family intervention were compared with those of hospitalization for the member experiencing an acute psychiatric crisis. From a group of 300 families requesting emergency treatment for a family member in acute distress, half of the disturbed family members were randomly assigned to inpatient hospital care including individual group therapy, milieu treatment, and ataractic drugs, and half to family therapy aimed at quickly reducing the level of tension, so that family resources could be garnered to cope more effectively with the crisis situation. Crisis intervention included approximately five office visits, one home visit, and several telephone conversations over two and one-half to three weeks. If long-term therapy seemed necessary after the immediate crisis had been resolved, referrals to other facilities were made.

Follow-up family interviews by an independent psychiatric social worker six, twelve, and eighteen months after treatment revealed that patients who received family crisis therapy were less likely to be hospitalized later and spent fewer days in the hospital than did control patients. Although these differences between therapy and control patients were smaller at each successive evaluation, it appeared that outpatient family therapy prevented rather than postponed hospitalization. Although patients who received family therapy showed greater capacity to manage a crisis than control patients (particularly at the six-month evaluation), the two groups of patients showed comparable levels of improvement in both social adjustment and personal functioning (adequacy of role performance, general health, and absence of psychiatric symptoms). A subanalysis (79) contrasting the crisis management skills of fifty schizophrenic and fifty nonschizophrenic patients revealed that only the *nonschizophrenics* who had received family therapy improved in their ability to deal with stressful events. The results of this study show that schizophrenics can be handled successfully on an outpatient basis, but reveal no advantage over hospitalization per se for schizophrenics.

In the one other controlled comparative study in print at this writing (August 1977), Ro-Trock et al. (146) compared family with individual therapy in two small groups, fourteen in each, of randomly assigned hospitalized adolescents. Sixteen of the twenty-eight adolescents (mean age about 17) were diagnosed as schizophrenic; ten were in the family therapy condition, and six in individual therapy. Two experienced co-therapist teams each treated seven families; two experienced individual therapists treated seven adolescents each. Both groups received ten therapy sessions. The family therapy was intended to promote clear communication and to shift the balance of maladaptive relationships within the family, so that new, more adaptive forms of relating would be possible. The individual therapy was focused on helping the patient develop solutions and problem-solving skills in dealing with life conflicts. Outcome measures included family problem solving (Strodtbeck's Revealed Differences), self-report, community adjustment, and rehospitalization.

There were a number of complex pre-post treatment changes on variables derived from the family interaction measure, but few on the self-reports. Although this would indicate that both treatments (and different therapists) exerted influence, the patterns were difficult to interpret. On follow-up three months after discharge, no family-therapy-treated subjects had been rehospitalized, whereas six of fourteen individually treated subjects had been ($p < .025$). In addition, family therapy subjects required significantly fewer days to return to functioning in the community. The study is noteworthy for its attention to methodological details (such as including the therapists as an independent variable in the design) and its sophisticated data analytic techniques. As the authors themselves noted, the lack of *strong, consistent* effects on their interaction and self-report measures might have been due to their being repeated only at the end of treatment rather than at the three-month follow-up period when the most impressive outcome differences were found. Other problems with the study are the small number of subjects in the samples, the limited number of sessions (10), and the lack of information on psychotropic drug use in the two groups. Finally, it would have been desirable to have had the data from the two groups of schizophrenics analyzed separately from the data for the nonschizophrenic adolescents.

The most recent comparative outcome study of family therapy, whose final results are as yet unpublished, was conducted by Goldstein* et al. (45). In this study, 104 consecutive first-admission schizophrenic patients discharged from brief inpatient stays (mean = twelve days) were randomly assigned to one of four treatment settings: (1) Low-dose (0.25 cc. every other week) injectable neuroleptic plus family therapy; (2) low-dose injectable neuroleptic without family therapy; (3) moderate-dose (1.5 cc. every other week) injectable neuroleptic plus family therapy; and (4) moderate-dose injectable neuroleptic without family therapy. The family therapy consisted of six two-hour sessions given weekly, beginning in the first postdischarge week. The therapy is described as "crisis-oriented" with four major goals: (1) accepting the occurrence of the psychosis; (2) identifying precipitating stresses; (3) looking at possible future similar stressful events; (4) developing strat-

* M. Goldstein 1977: personal communication.

egies for avoiding, minimizing, and coping with these stresses. Pre-post treatment and six-month follow-up data on symptomatology and community adjustment were collected. Significant family therapy effects were identified at six weeks (end of family treatment). By six months, however, the positive family therapy effects on community adjustment and relapse rates had endured only in the portion of the sample characterized as having "good premorbid" adjustment—an effect that was seemingly independent of drug dose level. Poor premorbid patients, on the other hand, showed a significant drug effect at six months in that relapse rates in the high-dose group were significantly lower—independently of the presence or the absence of family therapy. More definite and complete interpretation of this study must await publication, but its findings indicate that brief (six-session) posthospital family therapy is helpful for at least some schizophrenics.

SUMMARY

Although some evidence for the efficacy of family therapy with schizophrenics is beginning to emerge, it can hardly be called an impressive body of literature—especially when looked at in terms of the treatment of schizophrenia per se. One would hope the sophisticated approach to neuroleptic drugs and subgroup analysis of Goldstein et al. could be combined with the family interaction methodology and inclusion of therapists as variables, as was the case in the Ro-Trock et al. study, in a design that includes direct assessment of community psychosocial functioning in a substantial sample of schizophrenic patients and their families treated for six to twelve months and followed for one to two-years after treatment. The current group of comparative outcome studies focused on brief family therapy do not adequately test the ability of family therapy to alter the basic intrafamilial psychopathology found to be associated with the occurrence of schizophrenia in an offspring (see chapter 7).

INNOVATIONS

A recent innovation that bears noting is Speck's use of network therapy (161). His first report, in 1967, was of the treatment of a mother-son pair who had been symbiotically and pathologically united since the death of the child's father. When the mother and son, who had successfully resisted every previous attempt at treatment, first came to Speck, he asked them to bring in a set of "parents" to be involved in the treatment. At his encouragement the therapy group was continually expanded with friends and relatives until it totaled about forty persons. The son eventually moved away from his mother and found relationships with peers, while the mother's gratifications began to accrue from the reestablishment of her relationships with her own family. This approach, which reconstructs the extended kinship networks (although it is not confined to kin), seems especially appropriate to a society which has, for the most part, devalued them. Unfortunately as the extended kinship family has been replaced by the present-day nuclear configuration, very few grassroots institutions have grown up to serve the functions of the extended kinship network of yesteryear. In addition to Speck's network therapy, there are other examples of surrogate family (or pseudo-family) treatment. One form of such surrogate family therapy sprang up spontaneously in communes, and there have also been other group-living treatment settings (e.g., Soteria House, Kingsley Hall), which are designed to incorporate some elements of the family —a homelike setting, sharing of household tasks, parent figures, peer relationships, etc. Such treatment approaches seem to be responses to an urgent need. Where can one get human support, involvement, and caring in times of crisis? Clearly the social welfare and medical systems (which seem to be our attempts at replacing social networks) have not, probably cannot, and in all likelihood will not provide this involvement. It is interesting to speculate whether government-sponsored programs like Welfare and Medicaid have failed to replace these functions because they are externally introduced systems which may not fit grassroots needs. Clearly locally developed, responsive community support systems are needed—hence the concluding section of this chapter.

CLINICAL GUIDELINES

Family therapy for schizophrenics has undergone extensive rethinking and reevaluation in recent years. Likewise, family research is undergoing major changes, and this development merits a brief note. The original family studies were usually conceived of as addressing etiology. Recently, however, with the development of increasing methodological sophistication, the difficulties inherent in attributing causal significance to findings in families with an already manifest schizophrenic have become more widely known. The inability of traditional family studies to distinguish families' responses to disorder in one of their members from the basic causes of the disorder has led many investigators to turn to the prospective study of individuals at high risk for development of schizophrenia.

Traditional family research may never identify familial etiological factors; it can, however, contribute to our knowledge and to our treatment armamentarium by elucidating family interactional patterns which maintain illness in the patient-designate. For example, by planning our treatment to take into account the deficiencies in communication and the negatively charged overinvolvement found in these families, we may maximize the possibility of the designated patient's being able to change and grow and evolve from his position of the "crazy one" in the family. If we do not, the family will be unable to do other than maintain (for complex unconscious reasons) its most affected member as a "career" patient. Or it will permit him or her to become a "chronic" inmate in a mental hospital—an institution which often uses mechanisms similar to those seen in the family to maintain illness in the patient-designate.

The initial wave of enthusiasm which led to overly optimistic claims for the effectiveness of family therapy in treating schizophrenia has now been tempered by experience and time. This more sober view seems to be reflected in a recent book reviewing developments in family therapy in which only four of fifty-two papers are devoted specifically to schizo-phrenia and the family (148).

Although there was a time when strong advocates of family therapy believed that their approach was the treatment of choice for schizo-phrenia, some family therapists (ourselves included) have come to believe that family therapy that includes the patient-designate is ordi-narily contraindicated during acute psychosis (i.e., disorder requiring residential care) (54). The data of Gould and Glick (47) tentatively supports such a position, as do the clinical observations summarized as follows.

1. Severe disruption of ordinary cognitive and attentional processes is almost always seen in acute psychosis. Thus, the psychotic individual will have difficulty dealing effectively with even the simplest, *least* affectively charged situation. Because the conjoint family group is neither simple nor affectively neutral, participation by the labeled patient is likely to result in his feeling overwhelmed, incompetent, and a failure. This type of experience can only intensify already present feelings of inadequacy and confusion—to his detriment.

2. Family members are frequently frightened and made defensive by material brought up by the patient-designate. This material might be primary process in nature—for example, the patient's telling his father that he would like to kill him; or it might be very insightful data on the nature of his family's interactions—for example, "Dad, you always do what Mom says and never stick up for your point of view." In either case it will almost inevitably make other family members defensive and likely to withdraw from the patient. Although the therapist can attempt to lessen the impact of such exchanges by reinterpreting in a more acceptable vein, etc., it may make him appear to be siding with the patient against the family members and, by implication, to be blaming them. Unless the therapist can circumvent this very tricky situation, he will be likely to lose the family from treatment. The easiest way to avoid such an eventuality is to exclude the patient until he is able to participate as an equal.

3. At the point of hospitalization both patient and family have usually exhausted their tolerance for one another. What seems to make most sense clinically is a short time-out for both parties. Therefore, bringing a hostile patient into forced contact with his already guilty, subtly furious family seems to be an unnecessary exercise in futility—probably destined to drive patient, therapist, and family farther apart and, in turn, to make an eventual reconciliation more difficult.

Along with the position of no conjoint therapy during the acute psy-chosis, there has also developed the belief that family therapy is crucial to the reintegration of the patient with his family and the community. For married schizophrenics, conjoint therapy with the spouse should be considered as soon as the acute psychosis abates. It should probably be preceded by an assessment of the spouse's role in the precipitation of the episode as well as of the kinds of difficulties presented by the labeled patient to his or her spouse; the early resumption of the patient's role in the family is ordinarily the primary consideration.

One way of encouraging the maintenance of the patient-spouse's role function is through the use of "couples" therapy groups. This approach is now fairly common throughout the country and seems very effective in helping maintain function during hospitalization (after the most severe symptoms have subsided); in providing the nonpatient spouses a supportive atmosphere within which they can voice their concerns; in helping resolve some of the issues between the couples (which often precipitated the psychotic episode); and in providing a smoother transition back to the family. Although this approach could be called "group," rather than "family," therapy, the group's homogeneity (i.e., all couples) and its strong focus on family problems are obviously closely allied with family therapy.

In this same vein, Laqueur et al. (80) and others have begun to pay special attention to parents of patients. Many inpatient settings now have group therapy sessions for parents only, excluding the psychotic offspring. This approach is quite congruent with the position stated in the preceding paragraphs, in that it seems to provide a supportive atmosphere in which groups of parents can share concerns about their children; have an opportunity to express their feelings of anger, guilt, and responsibility (and hear similar feelings from the others); and, finally, develop sources of much-needed social gratification. Again these groups call to mind Speck's network approach. It would seem that parents' groups are best suited to the inpatient and immediate post-hospital phases of treatment, whereas the network approach is most useful with families containing a child who has returned home—for whatever reason—after his hospital discharge.

Unmarried schizophrenics who have not achieved independence of their families of origin present a special problem. To begin with, these unmarried patients (especially those with early onset) account for most of the schizophrenics who go on to chronic hospitalization (73). As an extremely high-risk group they deserve special attention. Rapid return to their families is usually unwise, partly because of the level of mutual disenchantment which almost always precedes hospitalization, but basically because it may be inadvisable for such a patient to return home to live at all. There is evidence (19, 67) that unmarried schizophrenics who return home do worse than those who go to some alternative-care facility or are able to live with peers or alone (67). Thus, work with these families might best be focused on helping parents separate from their offspring, rather than on discussing their particular problems or attempting to change their behavior with the patient offspring. Unfortunately, however, few supportive living arrangements are available to discharged schizophrenics, so clinicians often have little choice but to work with the family conjointly, striving to aid the process of reintegration and prevent exacerbations by changing family interactional patterns. But if alternative living arrangements can be secured, many therapists feel the family should be worked with without the patient offspring. In this situation the family therapist's goal should be to help parents deal with the realignments that will likely occur in their marital relationship and with the "loss" of their offspring and help them find alternative sources of gratification. For example, modification of Speck's network approach could be useful in facilitating the reestablishment of social bonds with significant others (e.g., friends, neighbors, relatives).

The question of whether, and at what ages, sibs should be included in family therapy sessions remains open to a variety of positions. We believe that sibs over age twelve, living at home, should be seen, at a minimum, for family-assessment purposes. They often provide the "sanest" point of view available as to what transpired just before the onset of psychosis. If the patient-designate is to return home (and therefore to be included in sessions), then it is crucial that available sibs be involved. They provide a more dispassionate view of the family situation, are frequently supportive of patient sib (in part because they are of the same generation), and can learn about how separation difficulties operate in their family in a way which may prevent their undergoing serious psychological difficulties when they are ready to leave home. We routinely exclude children under twelve from sessions, because they are not able to operate on the same cognitive levels as most adolescent sibs and the parents. When we have attempted to include them, our experience has been that they feel inadequate to deal with the situation and tend to be too frightened to participate actively. Of course, an immature sixteen-year-old might also need to be excluded. In practice we never apply our twelve-year-old "rule" in the ten-to-fourteen age group without carefully assessing an individual child's abilities.

If conjoint family therapy is undertaken in the posthospital phase of treatment, it is probably best conducted with a principal focus on communication; that is, according to current evidence (see chapter 7), the family's contribution to the occurrence and the maintenance of schizophrenia revolves around unusual patterns of cognition, attention, and communication which have been described as a "transactional thought disorder" (158,181). Although aspects of these problems have been described in a variety of ways, the simplest view is that families of schizophrenics do not communicate clearly—especially with each other—but also with outsiders. This approach to family therapy and its rationale has been described in greater detail elsewhere (113,115). Its essence will be detailed here.

Before the actual family therapy is begun, it is useful to seek answers to three questions during initial sessions:

1. *The specificity question.* Does the family evidence the types of peculiar communication that have been reported in families with an already manifest schizophrenic member? This question is crucial to the whole issue of family diagnosis, as it addresses itself to the ways in which families with a schizophrenic child are different from those with neurotic or character-disordered offspring.
    a. If present, how does communication deviance work in this family, and how does the patient-designate respond?
    b. What are the lines of communication (who in the family spoke to whom)?
    One might expect the patient to be the partner in most of the communicatively peculiar transactions and to respond to them in a way which could be viewed as a "symptom" of schizophrenia.
2. *The selection question.* What are the splits and alignments in the family that might account for one member being seen as "sick" and the others "well"? How and why was a particular member "selected" (this does not imply conscious selection) to be the patient? That is, what is the major motivation for the patient's being "special" in this family? Further, which of the parents was most involved in this process of singling him out?
3. *The maintenance question.* How was the patient maintained in his unique position in the family? This question involves consideration of

biological and psychological dependency, in addition to consideration of the characteristics of the particular family as a social subsystem.

Careful consideration of the answers to these three questions will allow the therapist to modify his technique to suit the particular needs of the family in question. Note particularly that the answers to questions 2 and 3 may be similar for several types of family, whereas the answers to question 1 shoud vary depending on the diagnostic category.

Essentially we advocate a type of conjoint family therapy focused on the formal structural aspects of communication, which strives *actively* to enhance communicational clarity by:

1. Seeking more information about issues that are confusing to *any* of the participants (including the therapist).
2. Continuing to focus attention on a particular topic until its meaning is shared by all.
3. Encouraging and asking questions that provide a clearer contextual framework ("metacommunication") for the subject under discussion.
4. Correcting distortions, misrepresentations, projections, and denial manifest among members.
5. Attempting to define and validate a consensual family "reality."
6. Attending to contradictory expectations held until they become congruent with the family and individual "realities."

This approach usually requires a great deal of activity on the part of the therapist or therapists, especially early in the course of treatment.

Although the *principal* focus of this approach is communicational, it does not mean that affective-motivational psychodynamic factors are excluded; it means merely that they receive less emphasis. We base our views in this regard on the research evidence that indicates that affective-motivational factors vary greatly in schizogenic families and have considerable overlap (i.e., are nonspecific) with those found in other types of families with psychiatric patient members. In contrast, the communicational difficulties found in schizogenic families appear to be reasonably specific to that diagnostic group (62).

In addition, it is these communicational difficulties that make it so difficult for persons labeled schizophrenic to cope with the demands of a complex technological society. They therefore warrant special attention.

Our position with regard to the numbers, training, and background of therapists for family therapy is essentially the same as for other types of group therapy (see p. 402). The clinical approach described is our own and is not necessarily the most widely accepted in the field.

Beels (11) has described a comprehensive family-oriented approach to more chronic patients that embodies, but expands, much of what is described here. It is highly recommended.

As illustrated by the preceding discussion, a far more refined assessment of indications for conjoint family therapy is being made by family therapists than was formerly the case. This reevaluative process has naturally involved a certain amount of disillusion among family therapy's strongest advocates, who once believed their approach a veritable panacea. For some, though, it reflects an increasing level of clinical sophistication and realism about the use, and the potential abuse, of this relatively young technique.

Milieu Therapy

HISTORICAL BACKGROUND

"Milieu therapy" refers to the specifically designed environment intended to be therapeutic for the psychiatric patient. The belief that a patient's environment can greatly affect the course of his illness is traceable to such pioneers in psychiatric reform as Vincenzo Chiarugi in Italy, William Tuke in England, and Philippe Pinel in France, who in the late eighteenth century introduced the concepts of moral treatment. Their common belief that severely disturbed patients could profit from being treated with support and respect within the confines of a structured living situation (112) was put into practice in a group of private mental hospitals established in the United States in the early nineteenth century. The prevailing optimism about moral treatment of the insane provided a fertile background for Dorothea Dix's devoted efforts to persuade state governments to construct mental hospitals for the care of the mentally ill. The original state institutions were small, and patients remained in them for a limited time; if they did not improve, they were returned to their homes or to almshouses. Dix's perseverance eventually led to the establishment of at least thirty state mental hospitals (124). Yet even before the conclusion of the nineteenth century these small asylums had grown into large custodial institutions to house the chronically ill with a minimum of therapeutic intent. Ozarin (124) traces this transformation to the decline both of publicly financed support for the increasingly heavy burden of patients, and of the cult of curability which had characterized the initial development of psychiatric facilities. The decline of this positive view was probably also related to the first waves of non-Anglo-Saxon immigration to the United States, to rapid industrialization, and to the advent of social Darwinism as an influential philosophy of man (30). The original mandate to provide safety and support, and thereby allow natural healing processes to occur, had become a mandate simply to provide safety. In the process the mentally ill were apparently isolated from those relationships which may have been therapeutic, for by 1925 over 50 percent of patients admitted to state psychiatric facilities were never discharged.

In this bleak period were initiated more systematic approaches to the study of the design and the effects of milieu upon patient outcome. Sullivan (166) began such experiments with a unit for the treatment of acute young schizophrenic males, and his efforts inspired a more hopeful approach to the treatment of schizophrenia within specially designed milieus. Introducing the notion of carefully individualized programing, Menninger (106) developed explicit recipes for prescribed environments which were contingent upon the patient's diagnosis.

Another important contribution was made by Rowland (147), who initiated the first careful description of the subcultures within state hospital organizations. Then in 1952, by being a concealed participant-observer, Caudill (22) illustrated how differing expectations and belief systems of patients and staff lead to therapeutic impasses. A more microscopic view of the therapeutic or antitherapeutic implications of milieu was taken by Stanton and Schwartz (162) at Chestnut Lodge. They described how problems in communication and social organization can enhance or interfere with but, in any case, directly influence the behavior and course of treatment for schizophrenic and other patients.

Although Stanton and Schwartz, Caudill, Rowland, and later Edelson (32) carefully analyzed the characteristics of milieus, their contributions were largely descriptive. These efforts did not in themselves elevate the milieu to a therapeutic modality in its own right nor did they develop the idea that the optimal milieu can provide therapeutic functions for patients which go beyond those inherent in moral treatment—namely, support and protection.

Arising in the late 1940s out of experience in shorter-term units with less ill patients was the idea of the *therapeutic community*. First introduced by Main (99) based on his experience with neurotic patients at the Cassel Hospital in England, it was subsequently popularized by his English contemporary, Maxwell Jones (63,64,65), who employed its principles with sociopathic inpatients. The therapeutic community embodied the notion that a milieu could in itself provide a highly active and specific type of treatment which was not merely supplementary to other treatments but actively engaged the patients' assets in a communal effort toward rehabilitation. Unlike its predecessors, this milieu approach is not prescriptive but required active collaboration by patients. The critical elements of the therapeutic community include: (1) a flattening of the hierarchical distribution of authority, (2) blurring of role definitions, and (3) open communication minimizing differences between social life within the hospital and outside society (28,145). Aspects of this form of milieu treatment have subsequently been used with schizophrenic patients in a large number of community mental health centers, teaching hospitals, and short-term general hospital units.

During the last fifteen years another major development in milieu therapy has been the implementation of token economies using the principles of behavior modification. Such units have drawn attention to the refined and creative ways in which rewards can be manipulated to alter social behavior. Their effectiveness was first described and provided with a conceptual basis by Ayllon and Azrin (6,7). Originally used almost exclusively with the chronic populations found in large state hospitals, token economy units have recently been gaining popularity in Veterans Administration psychiatric wards. These units have heightened awareness that operant conditioning is a central ingredient, often employed unknowingly and sometimes harmfully, in all psychiatric milieus (2).

As the principles of therapeutic communities and token economies have become more widely recognized, so has the viewpoint that the milieu can exert direct and specifically therapeutic effects which surpass the mandates of moral treatment. Cumming and Cumming (29) expanded this awareness by articulating the ways in which a therapeutic milieu can bring about alterations in patients' ego functioning.

CURRENT STATUS OF RESEARCH

In a recent review of research on milieu therapy of schizophrenic patients, Van Putten and May (172) stated, "Milieu therapy has increasingly become an ideology rather than a defined method of treatment sustained to a large extent not by scientific evaluation but by a steady flow of rhetoric and by humanitarian and emotional justifications." They further stated that "the evidence from controlled studies suggests that milieu therapy does not add much to the treatment of schizophrenia once adequate chemotherapy is used and gross neglect corrected." The research evidence to which they refer was largely obtained in custodial or intensive milieus where chronic schizophrenics were treated with or without drugs. More recent findings based on work with both acute and chronic schizophrenics suggest that this pessimistic conclusion may require re-evaluation.

In reviewing this research area, we will use some simplified terms to describe differing milieu approaches. The first is "custodial," which refers to a passive interpersonal treatment approach directed at providing safe, clean room and board. This custodial approach is generally found in large units with a small staff, where neuroleptic drugs are usually the only form of active treatment. The second type of milieu, called "intensive," involves active and intrusive interpersonal efforts to mobilize patients and to prepare them for discharge. Such milieus generally have more staff per patient and smaller wards and, to varying degrees, involve group meetings and graded privileges. "Therapeutic communities" and "token economies" are two specific subvarieties of intensive milieu approaches that will be cited when they are the focus of particular studies. Since most milieu outcome research has separated chronic and nonchronic schizophrenic patients, we will review studies on these two groups separately.

MILIEU RESEARCH ON THE CHRONIC PATIENT

Three major controlled outcome studies have been concerned with the use of milieu treatment for the chronically hospitalized schizophrenic patient: those of Greenblatt et al. (49), Grinspoon et al. (50), and Paul and Lentz (130). In the original study by Greenblatt et al. (49), a group of chronic schizophrenic patients were transferred from a custodial milieu in the Boston State Hospital to a very intensive milieu at the Massachusetts Mental Health Center. Comparable groups of medicated and unmedicated patients were then compared over a six-month period of treatment. Patients receiving drugs in either of the milieus showed the greatest improvement. When the patients who did not receive drugs in the intensive milieu were compared with their unmedicated counterparts in the custodial milieu, no significant differences emerged. When the patients receiving drugs in the intensive milieu were compared with those receiving drugs in the custodial milieu, however, there were some advantages for those in the intensive milieu in terms of their earlier discharge and clinical status at a twelve- to eighteen-month follow-up evaluation. Greenblatt et al. therefore concluded that the effects of intensive milieu therapy were additive to the effects of chemotherapy, and that the advantages of the milieu approach emerged over the long run.

Grinspoon et al. (50) subsequently repeated this study and used a smaller number of patients who were also transferred from the Boston State Hospital custodial unit to an intensive treatment unit at Massachusetts Mental Health Center. They found that patients in the intensive milieu showed no demonstrable advantages after a two-year period of treatment over those in the custodial unit. A follow-up on these patients at three and five years also revealed no differences in their social adjustment and mental status (107). There was, however, a nonsignificant trend suggesting that the patients who had been treated in the intensive milieu for the initial two years had consistently lower psychotic symptomatology, and more of them (65 percent) lived outside of the hospital than did those who had been treated in the custodial institution (37 percent). The disparity of this result from that previously reported by Greenblatt et al. is not readily explainable. Van Putten and May (172) have attributed the advantages of the intensive milieu, shown in the study of Greenblatt et al., not to the milieu itself but to the useful role served by active social workers assisting community placements. On the other hand, Greenblatt (48) has noted that the intensive milieu to which patients were transferred in the study of Grinspoon et al. may have contained less-effective rehabilitation programs than those available in the custodial milieu, and that the intensive milieu itself may have contained too much stimulation and too few expectations of the patients.

Paul et al. (131) and Paul and Lentz (130) have transferred two groups of chronically hospitalized schizophrenic patients, of twenty-eight each, from a custodial milieu to two differing intensive milieus: one a therapeutic community, and the other a social learning milieu based on behavior-modification principles. They found that patients who were transferred to intensive milieus were significantly better after four months of treatment than those who stayed in custodial units. Moreover, patients in the intensive milieus who had been randomly and blindly withdrawn from drugs improved more than those maintained on neuroleptics. After this original four-month period, 85 percent of the patients in the intensive milieus were withdrawn from all medications, whereas all the patients in the custodial milieu remained on drugs, mostly in high dosages. In a three-year follow-up it was found that being on drugs was a significant negative predictor of improvement and of release. Patients treated in active milieu programs, whether they were on or off drugs, showed significantly more discharges, less recidivism, and better symptom remission than the group given continued maintenance drug treatment in a custodial setting (see table 12–1).

In comparing the two types of milieu treatment, Paul and Lentz found a consistent advantage for the social learning program in terms of release to the community, learning of greater numbers of socially adaptive behaviors, and suppression of bizarre and symptomatic behaviors. Of great practical significance was the social learning program's effectiveness in dealing with dangerous and aggressive acts, whereas the therapeutic community milieu had no effect whatsoever on these very problematic behaviors.

The study is remarkable for several reasons: it is the first to compare

TABLE 12-1
Milieu Type

	Social Learning	Therapeutic Community	Custodial
Release to community	97.5%	71%	44.8%
Release to independent functioning	10.7%	7.1%	0%
Rehospitalization (2 years)	3%	3%	0%

Source: From G. L. Paul and R. J. Lentz, *Psychosocial Treatment of Chronic Mental Patients: Milieu vs. Social-Learning Programs* (Cambridge: Harvard University Press, in press).

two varieties of intensive milieus; it took great pains to equate enthusiasm in the two programs; the milieus were carefully defined and monitored; and patients continued treatment in the community for six months after discharge. Because they have also developed training manuals and an implementation strategy, the Paul and Lentz study is likely to have a substantial impact on the treatment of chronic patients over the next decade or more.

However, before this treatment approach is hailed as a "cure" for chronic schizophrenia, it would be wise to heed Paul and Lentz's data on independent functioning (see table 12–1) in these patients. They have clearly shown that patients can be gotten out of hospitals and can *remain* in the community but are still functioning only marginally. Based on these data, our expectations can certainly be positive but they should not be exaggerated.

This study by Paul and Lentz confirms the observations of Greenblatt et al. about the advantage of an intensive milieu for chronic patients over custodial treatment. It also tends to support Greenblatt's contention that the intensive milieu employed in the Grinspoon study contained countertherapeutic elements. Why drug treatment seemed to interfere with the effects of the intensive milieu for chronic patients is not obvious, but such a conclusion is somewhat supported by an earlier study conducted by Hamilton et al. (56). Hamilton found that unmedicated chronic patients treated in an intensive milieu emphasizing group processes did as well as comparable drug-treated patients in a custodial milieu. When the drugs and the intensive milieu were used together, however, there were no further advantages. The Paul and Lentz findings are also consistent with the animal literature where neuroleptics have been shown to interfere with learning.

On balance, these studies (49,56,130) suggest that intensive milieu treatment can offer substantial advantages for chronic schizophrenic patients when it is carefully tailored to their needs.

Token economies have been used increasingly since their introduction in 1963 by Ayllon and Azrin. Several comprehensive reviews of the use of behavior-modification principles in the treatment of chronic schizophrenia are available (55,86,87). This review will focus only on the application or behavior-modification techniques to entire wards, not on their use with individual cases. In token economy milieus the patient earns coinlike objects which can be exchanged for a variety of privileges and "desirable" items (e.g., cigarettes). Earning these rewards is contingent upon adopting socially appropriate behaviors, since the token economy approach is particularly effective in reversing "the social breakdown syndrome" (52) that develops in custodial settings. The use of such economies in a variety of hospital settings has been shown to be dramatically helpful in improving the level of performance, diminishing symptom levels, and increasing discharge rates among chronic patients.* Unfortunately until the Paul and Lentz study, none of the studies addressed the problem of their generalizability and maintenance of gains achieved in posthospital community environments where reinforcements are less immediate and less apparent to the partially rehabilitated chronic patient.

MILIEU RESEARCH ON THE NONCHRONIC PATIENT

Three recent studies have examined the treatment of nonchronic schizophrenic patients in intensive milieus with and without drugs. In the first of these, Carpenter et al. (21) studied the effectiveness of an intensive milieu at the National Institute of Mental Health, which made extensive use of a medical model, professional staff, and the adjuncts of formal individual and group therapy. In this NIMH milieu, patients given drugs were found to be similar to unmedicated patients on measures of mental status and prognosis. At the conclusion of the patients' four-month residential stay, no difference was found in the outcome of those treated with and those treated without drugs. This finding suggests that drugs may be unnecessary within this type of intensive milieu treatment. When all the patients treated in the intensive NIMH milieu were compared with medicated patients treated at local hospitals with short-term stays and good neuroleptic drug treatment, the NIMH patients were significantly better in both mental status and social functioning. This study supports a conclusion that a relatively long stay in an intensive, structured, well-organized, hierachical psychosocial milieu exerted favorable effects, both with and without neuroleptic drugs, which exceeded those found in patients treated briefly in less well-defined programs in community hospital wards.

Mosher and co-workers (116, 119, 120) have focused a research study on a type of milieu (called Soteria House) located in a house in the community. The program's ingredients that distinguish it from the comparison facility and most other settings treating acute schizophrenics are: reliance on specially trained nonprofessional staff as the primary therapists; no neuroleptic drug treatment for at least six weeks; small size (six patients at a time); prolonged stays (median stay of four and one-half months); a psychoeducational philosophy that focuses on learning, growth, and natural healing processes rather than on symptoms and dysfunction; and normalization of the experience and the treatment of

---

* See references 5, 25, 33, 92, and 152.

schizophrenia to reduce their potentially disruptive and stigmatizing effects.

Newly diagnosed, young (sixteen to thirty), unmarried schizophrenic patients deemed in need of hospitalization were compared with similar patients assigned to a well-staffed, medically oriented community mental health center with a rapid turnover and strong reliance upon pharmacotherapy. Their two-year, postadmission follow-up report revealed that Soteria-treated patients had fewer readmissions (52 vs. 68 percent) despite the fact only 10 percent as compared with 60 percent of control patients were maintained on neuroleptics continuously. The data also indicated that patients treated in Soteria House are more likely than controls to be living away from their nuclear families, to have more positive views of their treatment experience, to be working at higher levels of occupation, and to have more friends and social memberships.*

The nonsignificant difference in readmission rates seems at first to mitigate the stronger data on psychosocial adjustment that support the usefulness of the Soteria program. However, since it is well known that readmission is markedly reduced by maintenance neuroleptic drug treatment, the fact that a readmission rate opposite to what would have been predicted from other data (i.e., the non-drug-maintained Soteria subjects should have had a *higher* readmission rate) makes even this aspect of the results stronger. These results, like the Carpenter et al. study (21), above indicate that nonchronic schizophrenics can be treated without drugs in the presence of an intensive psychosocial milieu.

Rappaport et al. (138) studied a hospital milieu which in some ways was similar to Soteria House. Within this experimental setting, acute schizophrenic male patients were randomly assigned to receive drugs or placebo. The milieu was staffed by specially trained and experienced nonprofessionals who believed strongly in the value of interpersonal contacts and had developed special skills for working with unmedicated psychotic patients. In a three-year follow-up, patients given placebo were found to have lower rates of recidivism and higher levels of social functioning than drug-treated patients; they were also somewhat, though not significantly, better in ratings of severity of illness. Patients who were originally assigned to drugs but stopped them after discharge also did worse than those who received no drugs at all. Although this study does not isolate the effect of the milieu treatment per se, it does indicate that in a well-staffed intensive milieu, drug treatment may not only be unnecessary for acute schizophrenics but may actually diminish their receptivity or ability to learn from the milieu treatment experience.

All three of these studies demonstrate that in the presence of an intensive milieu drugs are unnecessary for nonchronic schizophrenics, and suggest that there may be some advantages to not using them. A curious source of support for this conclusion comes from the NIMH collaborative study of 299 acute schizophrenics treated in a variety of hospital settings (155). This study found that those patients who were treated with placebo were less likely to be rehospitalized than patients in any of the three drug conditions in a one-year follow-up. The authors speculated that these placebo patients may have received a more inten-

---

* L. R. Mosher 1977: personal communication (June 28).

sive milieu experience to compensate for their greater distress, and that this experience might have had lasting advantages for them.

How can the effectiveness of the milieu programs in the absence of drugs, demonstrated by Rappaport et al., Carpenter et al., and Mosher and Menn, be reconciled with the results from earlier studies which showed milieu to be relatively ineffective for nonchronic schizophrenics in the absence of drugs? The most influential of these studies was that done by May (102) in which 228 first-admission, nonchronic schizophrenics were divided into groups exposed to five different treatment conditions. Those patients who received milieu treatment were found to be less improved both at the end of the six-month treatment period and at three-year follow-up (104) than those who received similar milieu treatment plus drugs. The discrepancy of this result with those of Rappaport et al., Carpenter et al., and Mosher and Menn may be explainable by the possibility that the type of milieu provided by the state hospital in which May's study was carried out lacked the necessary characteristics to make it therapeutic. Although milieu therapy in this study had a high staff-to-patient ratio, May's study gave no details concerning patient participation, use of groups, or the attitudes and expectations of staff. Greenblatt (48) noted that May conceived of the milieu as a limited resource without using "active promulgation of progressive expectations or goals for improvement."

If it is reasonable to explain the relative ineffectiveness of milieu treatment in May's work on the basis of the quality of that milieu, it is more difficult to explain why the milieu treatment used in the recent studies of Rappaport et al., Carpenter et al., and Mosher and Menn was so effective with acute patients, when its success is contrasted with the impotence of a more comparable intensive milieu employed by Spadoni and Smith (160). Spadoni and Smith also had a small, well-staffed, highly enthusiastic unit which believed in the value of employing psychosocial efforts without drugs. However, they found that only twenty-one of the forty-three patients were able to be discharged after six months, and that ten of these relapsed within six months. The fact that only seven of the seventeen patients who were transferred to a state hospital and received drug treatment were discharged after an additional six months in that setting suggests that the original patient sample was a worse prognosis group than intended, and that the poor results are not easily attributable to the specific milieu approach. Moreover, the use of a relatively small, poorly described sample in the absence of a control group makes the results difficult to interpret. Almond (3) has suggested that Spadoni and Smith's unit failed to supplement its therapeutic community approach with sufficient use of control and structure to be effective for schizophrenics. Their results do, however, suggest caution about too readily embracing the practices used so promisingly by Rappaport et al., Carpenter et al., and Mosher and Menn.

The recent studies reviewed here which indicate that milieu treatment can be efficacious have all used intensive milieu approaches with nonchronic patients. That negative results are possible in milieu therapy of nonchronic patients has also been demonstrated by May and by Spadoni and Smith. As with the controlled studies on chronic patients, these studies taken together draw our attention to the facts that not all intensive milieu treatments are effective, and that there must be critical ingredients which distinguish between those which are and those which are not therapeutic for nonchronic schizophrenic patients.

Although the three milieus that produced positive results were different in many respects, they do seem to share a number of characteristics: relatively small units, high staff-to-patient ratios, primarily research settings, average stays of three to five months, positive expectations on the part of staff, real staff and patient involvement in decision making, and belief that interpersonal processes can be as effective as—or even more than—neuroleptic drugs in producing recovery from psychosis. Although selection of these characteristics is somewhat speculative, they are consistent with those found in research on the following milieu processes.

RESEARCH ON MILIEU PROCESSES

In addition to the preceding outcome studies there have been three major investigative efforts to define the active therapeutic ingredients of treatment milieus. The conclusions reached are based on correlational studies between outcome variables and the characteristics of a wide variety of milieus that were evaluated. Although these studies do not control for any particular patient population, they do include systematic, quantitative, and replicable assessments of ingredients within the milieus studied.

A recent review by Ellsworth (34) has focused attention on two ingredients of successful milieus. The first of these is that *high interaction between patients and staff* correlates with improved psychosocial adjustment in those who are discharged, when compared with milieu treatments with low staff-to-patient interaction. This conclusion affirms the earlier report by Kellam et al. (69) which initially drew attention to the importance of the amount of this interaction. Linn (90) has also found that high staff-to-patient interaction within the milieu correlates with higher release rates. The second major ingredient highlighted by Ellsworth, *the degree to which patients and staff are involved in decisions and share responsibilities*, correlates with lower readmissions and increased psychosocial adjustment among discharged patients, compared with those who come from milieus in which there is low involvement by patients and staff in decision making and unequal sharing of responsibility.

Moos (109), like Ellsworth, has quantified basic characteristics of treatment environments and has begun to examine which of these can be used to predict various indices of treatment outcome. With Shelton and Petty, Moos (111) found that treatment environments which produce particularly good community tenure tend to be high on the following five characteristics: *autonomy, practical orientation, order and organization, focus on personal problems,* and *open expression of angry feelings.* These characteristics emphasize aspects of the treatment programing in a milieu as opposed to either development of relationships or administrative structure of the milieus. Interestingly, Moos has also found that staff control relates positively to community tenure on large wards but negatively to community tenure on small wards.

Smith and King (159) have conducted a large-scale analysis of eighteen hospitals in the United States and correlated organizational variables of the milieus with outcome measures. Allocation of staff and resources was found to be the most important factor in promoting community adjustment. Pointing to the benefits of decentralized decision making, Smith and King concluded that administrative support of middle-level staff in a relatively democratic but structured decision-making process was important in promoting milieu effectiveness. Also, positive staff expectations were more predictive of community adjustment than was diagnosis.

Ellsworth and Moos both found that the factors which correlated with length of stay in the community after discharge were somewhat different from those which are correlated with rapid release. For Ellsworth et al. (35) faster discharge rates were associated with a patient's perception of staff's inaccessibility and with the nursing staff's feeling unappreciated by the professionals. Moos (109) found such units low on support and high in practical orientation. That these variables differ from those associated with community tenure strongly indicates that the criterion of length of stay is a poor one around which to design a milieu if one is interested in more long-term indices of patient welfare.

Fairweather et al. (38) randomly assigned ninety-six patients to four different treatment programs ranging from custodial care to an intensive group-living situation. Although chronic schizophrenic patients did worse in the more intensive therapy programs, the more acute schizophrenics did better in this environment. Patients in the most intensive therapy program also showed the greatest variance in ward behavior and outcome, which indicates that such programs may have the potential of making some patients better and some worse. These results are consistent with those reported previously in indicating that intensive milieu therapy can have favorable effects with nonchronic schizophrenics. They also help explain why Van Putten and May reached such pessimistic conclusions about the role of milieu therapy, since the studies they reviewed were almost exclusively done on chronic patients or with nonintensive forms of milieu.

Ellsworth (34) cited a number of studies indicating that high interaction with other patients and with staff is a particularly critical process variable in the treatment of chronic schizophrenic patients and patients who have withdrawal as part of their symptomatology. Even more specifically, it is suggested that such patients do better when interaction is based on a social learning model that emphasizes planned modification of specific behaviors, rather than on a socialization model (130,149). Along this same line Ludwig and Marx (95) have introduced in a controlled way the elements of "attention" and "structure" into a custodial care situation and found that most chronic patients over a six-week period of study were improved by exposure to these elements. Attention consisted of unfocused small group meetings and fifteen-minute individual talks with staff. Structure consisted of clearly defined staff expectations with a hierarchical privilege system. In other experiments Ludwig and co-workers showed that the introduction of a more active group program into a ward or the introduction of a "buddy" system generally improved the behavior and symptom level of chronic patients (94,96). Like Fairweather et al., they also found that for some of the sickest chronic patients the introduction of more intensive milieu techniques had a worsening effect.

NEW DEVELOPMENTS

One feature of many newer milieu approaches to schizophrenia is their reliance on specially selected and trained nonprofessionals for working with schizophrenic inpatients. This trend can be seen in the development of "technician" skills on behavior-modification units and of "being with" skills on the special units for treating unmedicated acute schizophrenics. The effectiveness of such experimental approaches is extremely significant both for cost-effective deployment of mental health resources and for the potential of these special personnel for helping patients develop psychosocial skills that will allow them to function more effectively in posthospital community environments. Another new development in the milieu treatment of schizophrenia emerged from the three recent studies using intensive milieus for nonchronic schizophrenia. An important principle that all three shared was that the psychotic experience should be accepted and understood. This approach, although recently popularized by Laing (74), has a long history in this country— dating back to Meyer (108) and Sullivan (168) and their followers, especially among psychoanalysts. Bullard (20), for example, urged "an environment in which the patient may be sick and unpunished for it." The affirmation of this principle in the milieus employed by Mosher and Menn and by Rappaport et al. stands in contrast to the control-conscious, drug-oriented approaches to schizophrenia which dominate short-term psychiatric milieus at the current time.

Within the recent studies of milieu therapy where drugs were not used, an interesting and confusing phenomenon has been repeatedly demonstrated. These studies indicate that drugs can be either unnecessary or actually harmful to schizophrenic patients who are receiving intensive milieu therapy. Hamilton et al. (56) had previously shown with chronic patients that an intensive milieu seemed to be as effective as drugs, but that the two treatments were not additive when given in combination. Under what conditions a therapeutic milieu and drugs— which are generally found to be therapeutic—interact beneficially, not at all, or harmfully and with what types of patients is a major and still-unanswered question. On the surface it is difficult to understand the two approaches not being additive. Perhaps drug treatment has a dulling effect which precludes the intense commitment to interpersonal healing that is required for schizophrenic patients to become involved with those who are treating them; perhaps the drugs exert physiological handicaps toward interpersonal learning; perhaps the absence of drugs leads staff to behave in therapeutic ways which would not seem necessary if they were relying on drugs as the major form of therapy; and, finally, perhaps attempting an iconoclastic treatment gives a missionary zeal to staff or provides an imaginary enemy against which staff and patients can collaborate more effectively. These possibilities and others require careful examination.

Another recent development derives from the accumulating experience in treating schizophrenics in therapeutic communities or in expressive, noncoercive milieu environments. This involves a growing recognition of the limitations and risks inherent in this approach. Studies have shown these "opening-up" methods can be misapplied to both acute schizophrenics (160) and chronic schizophrenics (83,93). Several observers (3,53,157) have also suggested that it is too simple to recommend a noncoercive, accepting, and expressive environment and expect that this will sufficiently embody the necessary therapeutic qualities for treatment of most schizophrenic inpatients. Such a recommendation underestimates the containment and the structure which are usually needed during periods of inpatient treatment. Not only can there be "revolving door" phenomena associated with underestimation of pathology, but there may be increased risks of suicide or accidental death.

The major recent development in the treatment of the chronic patient has been the application of the principles of behavior modification to his rehabilitation. The study by Paul and Lentz (130) can be expected to encourage greater use of social learning programs based on operant-conditioning principles. The experience that patients discharged from token economies frequently relapse, however, also requires more attention. Thus, one frontier area for the application of operant conditioning to chronic patients remains in helping the socially adjusted inpatient maintain his gains while making the transition into the community. Behavior-modification principles have, for example, been applied to day hospitals (87), to a halfway house (58), and to community lodges (37). Another major frontier involves the application of operant-conditioning techniques to milieus treating nonchronic forms of schizophrenia. There have been suggestions that token economies are not useful for acute patients (46). The less sick or recovering schizophrenic patient can be given too much control and structure, and thus negative therapeutic reactions can result which could lead to a new variation of the social breakdown syndrome characterized by alienated nonautonomous compliance with environmental dictates. Here again it seems that excessive dependence upon, and disregard for, containment and structure may both be critical process variables in the milieu treatment of schizophrenia.

The issue of fit between therapeutic milieu design and the nature of the schizophrenic patient's psychopathology can be illuminated by further comparative outcome research. Paul and Lentz have eloquently demonstrated how different types of active milieu approaches can be compared when applied to similar patient populations. Another design would involve carefully selected but different patient samples treated in the same milieu as was done by Fairweather et al. (38). Other studies employing these designs can help answer the many remaining questions about the nature of the optimal milieu treatment for both chronic and nonchronic schizophrenic patients. The Ward Atmosphere Scale (WAS) by Moos and the Perceptions of Ward (POW) scale by Ellsworth have provided relatively simple means of objectively evaluating different milieus. These instruments allow a milieu to be compared with other milieus whose efficacy with schizophrenic patients is known, and can point to specific alterations which are suitable for the patient population being treated.

One issue of obvious relevance to the issue of "fit" would be when and how milieus can be too stimulating or too demanding for schizophrenic patients. This issue of too much intensity in a milieu has been repeatedly cited by Van Putten as being harmful to schizophrenics (171,172). Yet those milieus which have seemed particularly useful for treatment of both chronic or nonchronic patients have all shared a therapeutic enthusiasm and high level of staff-patient *or* patient-patient interaction. "A traditional hospital environment with emphasis on rest, medication, and simple communication" (172) seems dangerously close to the custodial approach, whose disadvantages have been convincingly and repeatedly illustrated (9,52). This approach is probably only optimal for acutely agitated patients. The issue of intensity must certainly involve the more subtle question of: At what point in the patient's treatment can what forms of stimulus demand be helpful? It seems, for example, that highly demanding stimulations from graded-reward systems or intensive staff talks are useful for many chronic schizophrenics. It also seems that demanding stimulations, such as self-government participation and group attendance, are useful for the schizophrenic patient who has recovered from an active psychotic phase. Examples of harmful stimulation might include mandatory groups or discussions of privileges for the acute psychotic, or low or inconsistent expectations for the chronic patient.

This issue of stimulus intensity is only one example of the necessity of conceptualizing the underlying principles which determine whether or not a milieu characteristic is useful. The need for deeper analytic understanding of the therapeutic ingredients common to all wards was cited twenty-five years ago by Stanton and Schwartz (162) and has been pointed up since then by the work of Cumming and Cumming (29) and Edelson (32). Almond (3) recently attempted to describe the interaction between the forms of power employed on milieus and the forms of involvement employed by patients. For example, a patient whose involvement is based on obedience will only be served by a staff whose power is based on coercions. Likewise, the only patients responsive to symbolic (nonmaterial) power will be those whose involvement is based on moral beliefs. Between these extremes is the use of remunerative power for patients whose involvement is calculative.

Gunderson (53) recently has defined five therapeutic functions which social organizations can utilize: containment, support, structure, involvement, and validation. Each function has different purposes or goals, and they are hierarchical in order of complexity and in increasing demands for patient participation. The functions are to varying degrees offered by milieus and are differentially needed and utilized by patients. For example, chronic schizophrenic patients require long-term approaches in which milieus provide structure; the more acute patient requires both containment and, eventually, involvement; and the paranoid patient will particularly require validation. There remains a continuing need to define therapeutic processes or activities that exist within milieus and to specify which of these are particularly needed by what schizophrenic patients.

CLINICAL GUIDELINES

Emerging from the extensive clinical experience in milieu treatment of schizophrenic patients and from the burgeoning research data are some practical clinical guidelines which provide a framework for designing an optimal milieu for treating schizophrenic patients.

The first principle that a milieu, which intends to treat most of the broad range of schizophrenic patients, should incorporate is clarity. This principle would encompass the need for order and organization noted by Moos (109) and the need for clear communications noted by Stanton and Schwartz (162). The need for clarity is especially important with schizophrenic patients because of their idiosyncratic interpretations and periods of confusion. Stanton and Schwartz illustrated the perverse effects on schizophrenic inpatients when there is poor communication among staff members or to patients. This principle of clarity also would extend to reasonably clear role definitions, explicitly presented treatment programs and plans, and the importance of a consistent and common approach to an individual patient by various members of the staff.

A second critically important ingredient in milieus which treat schizophrenic patients is hope (Moos's and Ellsworth's "involvement," Smith and King's "positive expectations"). To a large extent the attitudes within a milieu can be affected by the leadership on the ward. Within the context of an overall hopeful attitude, three ingredients can be separated out: a positive but realistic long-term perspective, respect, and enthusiasm. It is essential that the staff comprehend the seriousness and long-term nature of the schizophrenic patient's difficulties, and that they understand that their efforts are part of what is a slow and generally partial rehabilitation compared with what they may have in mind as ideal. It is distinctly harmful for a staff to convey to the schizophrenic patient that there is any simple, easy, or complete solution to his life difficulties. On the other hand, to overfocus on his disabilities and dysfunction may be just as harmful. Even within shorter-term-treatment situations, a longer-term realistic perspective accompanied by sufficient attention to a patient's areas of accomplishment and normality will lead to more careful transition and disposition planning. It cannot be emphasized too strongly that, like other persons, given a proper context, schizophrenic patients are able to interact, utilize, and expand previous areas of competence. The major contribution of the community mental health and therapeutic community movements within milieu treatment has been to stress the role of a firm expectation that no matter how disturbed patients feel, they can and eventually will behave as socially appropriate and functional human beings. A final ingredient of the overall hopeful attitude is that of enthusiasm. "Enthusiasm" refers here to the eagerness and pleasure which are attained from working with and getting to know schizophrenic persons and which are *not* contingent upon therapeutic impact.

A third important element of milieu treatment for schizophrenia is an emphasis upon relationship building. The importance of this is alluded to in studies such as that by Kellam et al (69), which show the importance of high staff-to-patient interaction and the importance of smallness (159). This element addresses the central issue of the schizophrenic person's impoverished relatedness and attempts, through the development of friendships or other enduring relationships built on consistency and continuity, to provide ego-corrective experiences. Such milieus would rate high on Moos's (109) dimensions of involvement, support, and spontaneity. The milieus in which relatedness is developed over negotiations about privileges and reward also provide a type of relationship building for schizophrenic individuals. Relationship building takes time, tolerance, and genuine acceptance of the patient. It also usually requires initiative on the part of staff. These qualities depend, in turn, upon having an adequate staff-to-patient ratio. Relationship building can be facilitated for schizophrenic patients if the unit is relatively small, if it contains some patients with greater interactive skills, and if it facilitates involvement through common day rooms and groups.

The fourth ingredient of a milieu which intends to be successful with schizophrenic patients is *flexibility* of roles, relationships, and responses. The concept of flexibility involves an ongoing capacity for, and readiness to, change both among staff members and patients and within milieu structures themselves. It does not, of course, refer to being ambiguous or unstructured. If one conceptualizes the schizophrenic's difficulties in terms of an inability to manage change, it makes sense to place him within a system which expects change but provides some continuity of support and a practical, down-to-earth problem-solving approach. It seems patently antitherapeutic to place the schizophrenic patient in a rigid system where his passive tendencies to conform or to negate would unwittingly be encouraged. Flexibility is also a necessary quality for the individualization of programs and is required by the diversity of problems presented by schizophrenic patients. The implementation of these rather obvious guidelines is a matter of serious difficulty and great complexity. Unfortunately the extent to which these qualities can be provided for schizophrenic patients is determined by institutional and community needs, resources, and attitudes and only to a limited degree by what is best for patient care.

SUMMARY

The past decade has seen considerable progress in the definition of, clarification of, and research on what constitutes a "therapeutic" milieu (177). Specific milieu typologies have been developed from new instruments that allow systematic assessment (110). Clinically the differing characteristics of milieus for acute as compared with chronic patients have been described. Acute patients are felt to require an accepting, supportive, stimulus-decreasing environment (at least early in treatment), and chronic patients, a structured, organized, high-expectation, specific behavior, change-oriented one. Recently four milieu characteristics associated with increased community tenure have been identified by several different investigators. They are: small size, positive expectations on the part of staff, active involvement and investment of line staff in the treatment process and decision making (resulting in high morale), and a practical, down-to-earth problem-solving orientation (34,68,136,159).

It is notable that these important milieu characteristics have only recently become apparent after more than a decade of research that could find no, or little, relationship between inhospital milieu characteristics and posthospital adjustment.

The research findings are notable for their consistency, replicability, and obvious clinical relevance—and they can be implemented, with appropriate modification, in settings dealing with either acute or chronic patients or a mixture thereof.

Community Support Systems

In the past decade there has been a gradual emergence of interest in a variety of community-based resources that, taken together, provide important support to patients designated schizophrenic. At least nine different potential elements of community support programs have been identified (170). Some of these resources include cooperative apartments, halfway houses, and psychosocial rehabilitation centers such as Fountain House and Thresholds (43). These community support systems are in part a response to the progressive nuclearization of the family and are intended to fill the support functions lost by the dissolution of extended kinship networks.

Unfortunately these community resources are still relatively rare; they can accommodate only a small portion of potential clients; and they remain largely isolated and little known, as most are the result of efforts of one or two concerned enthusiastic persons in the particular locale. Generally they are a private sector response to failures of the medical and social welfare systems to provide adequately for the needs of patients.

Their efficacy, beyond their a priori humanitarian importance, remains largely untested. Although the efficacy of particular community supports (e.g., psychosocial rehabilitation centers) is not well established, several studies lead one to expect community support systems will receive even greater emphasis in the next decade. Results from data from the five-year follow-up of schizophrenic patients in the International Pilot Study of Schizophrenia (151) are quite relevant to the issue of community support. This careful longitudinal research studied more than one thousand patients in eight countries on admission and two and five years later. It found, to everyone's surprise, that the outcomes of patients in "developing" countries (Nigeria, India, Colombia) were significantly better than those of patients from "developed" countries (United States, USSR, United Kingdom, Denmark, Czechoslovakia). Although this finding is open to a variety of interpretations, one having to do with the presence of extended kinship networks to provide support is consistent with the family organizations in developing countries. A related explanation of these results also fits the community support model; that is, these less complex societies are less stressful on individuals. It has been shown for medical illness (24,66) that social support is protective against the development of illness and aids recovery from it when it is related to life stress. Thus, one parsimonious explanation is that in developing countries, for whatever stress there is, greater protection is available to individuals from their natural social support systems. This case is even more persuasive when taken in conjunction with the data of Brown and Birley (18), which indicate that schizophrenics do experience greater life stress than others in the three-week period prior to onset of overt symptomatology.

Although they have not generally been conceptualized as "community support systems," the various alternatives to hospitalization that have been studied can be thought of as providing support systems for individuals undergoing the severe personal distress and crisis that comes to be labeled "schizophrenia." Thus, Stein and Test's "Training in Community Living" (163), Langsley et al.'s "Family Crisis Intervention" (75, 79), Pasamanick et al.'s visiting nurse program (127), Sanders et al.'s Enablers Program (150), Polak's Family Foster Care (134), Fairweather et al.'s Lodges (37), and the Soteria program (117) can be viewed as examples of the intentional provision of a support program in lieu of the support inherent in hospital care. The results of these divergent programs, utilized with various patient types, have been uniformly similar. Each found that severely disturbed persons who would otherwise have been hospitalized, can be maintained in nonhospital settings if sufficient support and protection is made available to the patients and their caretakers. However, with the exception of Stein and Test (163), the simultaneous and subsequent use of other available relationships and services by individuals in these programs have not been subject to systematic scrutiny.

Taken as a whole, this body of research appears to substantiate the usefulness of community-based support systems for ameliorating and treating schizophrenia. What remains to be learned has to do with the necessity of various specific and nonspecific ingredients in facilitating positive outcome. This new focus in psychiatry is somewhat belated in receiving greater emphasis; that is, community support networks should have received greater attention as soon as the shift from institutional to community-based care got under way more than fifteen years ago. However belated, this new focus is highly laudable.

BIBLIOGRAPHY

1. Abrahams, J. 1948. Preliminary report of an experience in the group psychotherapy of schizophrenics. *American Journal of Psychiatry* 104:613–17.
2. Almond, R. 1974. *The healing community* (New York: Jason Aronson).
3. Almond, R. Overview: Concepts and new developments in milieu treatment. In *Principles and Practices of Milieu Therapy*, eds. O. Will, J. G. Gunderson, and L. Mosher (New York: Jason Aronson, Inc.). In press.
4. Altshuler, J. M. 1940. One year's experience with group psychotherapy. *Mental Hygiene* 24:190–96.
5. Atthowe, J. M., and Krasner, L. 1968. Preliminary report on the application of contingent reinforcement procedures (token economy) on a "chronic" psychiatric ward. *Journal of Abnormal Psychology* 73:37–43.
6. Ayllon, T., and Azrin, N. H. 1965. The measurement and reinforcement of behavior of psychotics. *Journal of the Experimental Analysis of Behavior* 8:357–83.
7. Ayllon, T., and Azrin, N. H. 1968. *The token economy* (New York: Appleton-Century-Crofts).

8. Azima, H.; Wittkower, E. D.; and LaTendresse, J. 1958. Object relations therapy in schizophrenic states. *American Journal of Psychiatry* 115:60–62.

9. Barton, R. 1959. *Institutional neurosis* (Bristol: John Wright).

10. Bednar, R. L., and Lawlis, G. F. 1971. Empirical research in group psychotherapy. In *Handbook of psychotherapy and behavior change: An empirical analysis*, eds. A. Bergin and S. Garfield (New York: John Wiley).

11. Beels, C. 1975. Family and social management of schizophrenia. *Schizophrenia Bulletin* 1(13):97–118.

12. Boe, E. E.; Gocka, E. F.; and Kogan, W. S. 1966. The effect of group psychotherapy on interpersonal perceptions of psychiatric patients. *Multivariate Behavioral Research* 1:177–87.

13. Boisen, A. T. 1954. Group therapy: The Elgin plan. *Pastoral Psychology* 5:33–38.

14. Borowski, T., and Tolwinski, T. 1969. Treatment of paranoid schizophrenics with chlorpromazine and group therapy. *Diseases of the Nervous System* 30:201–2.

15. Bowen, M. 1961. Family psychotherapy. *American Journal of Orthopsychiatry* 31:40–60.

16. Bowen, M. 1965. Family psychotherapy with schizophrenia in the hospital and in private practice. In *Intensive family therapy*, eds. I. Boszormenyi-Nagy and J. Framo (New York: Harper & Row).

17. Bowers, P. F.; Banquer, M.; and Bloomfield, H. H. 1974. Utilization of nonverbal exercises in the group therapy of outpatient chronic schizophrenics. *International Journal of Group Psychotherapy* 24:13–24.

18. Brown, G. W., and Birley, J. L. T. 1968. Crises and life changes and the onset of schizophrenia. *Journal of Health and Social Behavior* 9:203–14.

19. Brown, G. W.; Bome, M.; Dalison, B.; and Wing, J. K. 1966. *Schizophrenia and social care.* Maudsley Monograph no. 17 (London: Oxford University Press).

20. Bullard, D. M. 1940. The organization of psychoanalytic procedure in the hospital. *Journal of Nervous and Mental Disease* 91:697–703.

21. Carpenter, W. T.; McGlashan, T. H.; and Strauss, J. S. 1977. The treatment of acute schizophrenia without drugs: An investigation of some current assumptions. *American Journal of Psychiatry* 134(1):14–20.

22. Caudill, W. 1958. *The psychiatric hospital as a small society.* (Cambridge: Harvard University Press).

23. Claghorn, J. L.; Johnstone, E. E.; Cook, T. H.; and Itschner, L. 1974. Group therapy and maintenance treatment of schizophrenics. *Archives of General Psychiatry* 31:361–65.

24. Cobb, S. 1976. Social support as a moderator of life stress. *Psychosomatic Medicine* 38:300–314.

25. Cochran, B. 1969. Conference report: Behavior Modification Institute, May 12–14, 1969, Tascaloosa, Alabama. *Hospital and Community Psychiatry* 20:16–18.

26. Coons, W. H., and Peacock, E. P. 1970. Interpersonal interaction and personality change in group psychotherapy. *Canadian Psychiatric Association Journal* 15:347–55.

27. Corder, B. F.; Corder, R. F.; and Hendricks, A. 1971. An experimental study of the effect of paired-patient meetings in the group therapy process. *International Journal of Group Psychotherapy* 21:310–18.

28. Crocket, R. W. 1973. Doctors, administrators, and therapeutic communities. In *The therapeutic community*, eds. J. J. Rossi and W. J. Filstead (New York; Behavioral Publications), pp. 153–68 (reprinted from *Lancet*).

29. Cumming, J., and Cumming, E. 1962. *Ego and milieu* (New York: Atherton Press).

30. Dain, N. 1964. *Concepts of insanity in the United States 1789–1865* (New Brunswick, N. J.: Rutgers University Press).

31. Donlon, P. T.; Rada, R. T.; and Knight, S. W. 1973. A therapeutic aftercare setting for refractory chronic schizophrenic patients. *American Journal of Psychiatry* 130:682–84.

32. Edelson, M. 1964. *Ego psychology, group dynamics, and the therapeutic community* (New York: Grune & Stratton).

33. Ellsworth, R. B. 1969. Reinforcement therapy with chronic patients. *Hospital and Community Psychiatry* 20:238–40.

34. Ellsworth, R. B. Characteristics of effective treatment settings. In *Psychiatric milieu and the therapeutic process*, eds. O. A. Will, J. G. Gunderson, and L. R. Mosher, forthcoming.

35. Ellsworth, R. B.; Maroney, R.; Klett, W.; Gordon, H.; and Gunn, R. 1971. Milieu characteristics of successful psychiatric treatment programs. *American Journal of Orthopsychiatry* 41:427–41.

36. Esterson, A.; Cooper, D.; and Laing, R. 1962. Results of family-oriented therapy with hospitalized schizophrenics. *British Medical Journal* 2:1462–65.

37. Fairweather, G.; Sanders, D.; Cressler, D.; and Maynard, H. 1969. *Community life for the mentally ill: An alternative to institutional care* (Chicago: Adline Publishing).

38. Fairweather, G.; Simon, R.; Gebhard, M.; Weingarten, E.; Holland, J. L.; Sanders, R.; Stone, G. B.; and Reahl, G. E. 1960. Relative effectiveness of psychotherapeutic programs. *Psychological Monographs* 74(1–492).

39. Fiske, D. W.; Luborsky, L.; Parloff, M. B.; Hunt, H. F.; Orne, M. T.; Reiser, M. F.; and Tuma, A. H. 1970. Planning of research on effectiveness of psychotherapy. *American Psychologist* 25:727–37.

40. Frank, J. D. 1961. *Persuasion and healing: A comparative study of psychotherapy* (Baltimore: Johns Hopkins University Press).

41. Freedman, N.; Warshaw, L.; Engelhardt, D. M.; Blumenthal, I. J.; and Hankoff, L. D. 1959. The effect of various therapies upon fecal incontinence in chronic schizophrenic patients. *Journal of Nervous and Mental Disease* 128:562:65.

42. Fromm-Reichmann, F. 1948. Notes on the development of treatment of schizophrenia by psychoanalytic psychotherapy. *Psychiatry* 11:263–73.

43. Glasscote, R. M. 1971. *Rehabilitating the mentally ill in the community: A study of psychosocial rehabilitation centers.* Joint Information Service of the American Psychiatric Association and the National Association for Mental Health, Washington, D.C.

44. Goertzel, W.; May, P. R.; Salkin, J.; and Schoop, T. 1965. Bodyego technique: An Approach to the schizophrenic patient. *Journal of Nervous and Mental Disease* 141:53–60.

45. Goldstein, M. J.; Rodnick, E. H.; Evans, J. R.; and May, P. R. A. 1975. Long-acting phenothiazine and social therapy in the community treatment of acute schizophrenia. In *Drugs in combination with other therapies*, ed. M. Greenblatt (New York: Grune & Stratton).

46. Gomes, B. 1975. Psychotherapy outcome with schizophrenics: A review of the literature. Paper presented at the Sixth Annual Meeting of the Society for Psychotherapy Research, Boston, Massachusetts, 1975.

47. Gould, E., and Glick, I. D. 1977. The effects of family presence and family therapy on outcome of hospitalized schizophrenic patients. *Family Process* 16(4):503–10.

48. Greenblatt, M. 1972. Foreword in *Schizophrenia: Pharmacotherapy and psychotherapy*, eds. L. Grinspoon, J. R. Ewalt, and R. I. Shader (Baltimore: Williams & Wilkins).

49. Greenblatt, M.; Solomon, M.; Evans, A. S.; and Brooks, G. W. 1965. *Drug and social therapy in chronic schizophrenia* (Springfield, Ill.: Charles C Thomas).

50. Grinspoon, L.; Ewalt, J. R.; and Shader, R. I. 1972. *Schizophrenia: Pharmacotherapy and psychotherapy* (Baltimore: Williams & Wilkins).

51. Group for the Advancement of Psychiatry. 1976. *Pharmacotherapy and Psychotherapy: Paradoxes, Problems, and Progress* (New York: Brunner/Mazel).

52. Gruenberg, E. M., and Bennett, C. L. 1969. Preventing the social breakdown syndrome. *Social Psychiatry* 67:179–95.

53. Gunderson, J. G. 1978. Defining the therapeutic process in psychiatric milieus, *Psychiatry* 41: 327–35.

54. Guttman, H. 1973. A contradiction for family therapy. *Archives of General Psychiatry* 29: 352–55.

55. Hagen, R. L. 1975. Behavioral therapies and the treatment of schizophrenics. *Schizophrenia Bulletin* 1(13):70–96.

56. Hamilton, M.; Hordern, A.; Waldrop, F. N.; and Lofft, J. 1963. A controlled trial on the value of prochlorperazine, trifluoperazine and intensive group treatment. *British Journal of Psychiatry* 109:510–22.

57. Haven, G. A., and Wood, B. S. 1970. The effectiveness of eclectic group psychotherapy in reducing recidivism in hospitalized patients. *Psychotherapy: Theory, Research, Practice* 7:153–54.

58. Henderson, J., and Scoles, P. E. 1970. A community-based behavioral operant environment for psychotic men. *Behavior Therapy* 1:245–51.

59. Herz, M. I.; Spitzer, R. L.; Gibbon, M.; Greenspan, K.; and Reibel, S. 1974. Individual versus group aftercare treatment. *American Journal of Psychiatry* 131:808–12.

60. Illovsky, J. 1962. Experiences with group hypnosis on schizophrenics. *Journal of Mental Science* 108:685–93.

61. Jackson, D. D., and Weakland, J. H. 1961. Conjoint family therapy: Some considerations on theory, technique and results. *Psychiatry* 24:30–45.

62. Jacob, T. 1975. Family interaction in disturbed and normal families: A methodological and substantive review. *Psychological Bulletin* 82:33–65.

63. Jones, M. 1953. *The therapeutic community* (New York: Basic Books).

64. Jones, M. 1968. *Beyond the therapeutic community: Social learning and social psychiatry* (New Haven: Yale University Press).

65. Jones, M. 1976. *Maturation of the therapeutic community* (New York: Behavioral Publications).

66. Kaplan, B.; Cassel, J.; and Gore, S. 1977. Social support and health. *Medical Care* 15:47–58.

67. Kayton, L. 1975. Toward an integrated treatment of schizophrenia. *Schizophrenia Bulletin* 1(12):60–70.

68. Kellam, S. G. Ward atmosphere, continuity of therapy and the mental health system. In *Psychiatric milieu and the therapeutic process*, eds. O. A. Will, J. G. Gunderson, and L. R. Mosher, forthcoming.

69. Kellam, S. G.; Goldberg, S. C.; Schooler, N.; Berman, A.; and Schmelzer, J. L. 1967. Ward atmosphere and outcome of treatment of acute schizophrenia. *Journal of Psychiatric Research* 5: 145–63.

70. Kiesler, D. J. 1973. *The process of psychotherapy: Empirical foundations and systems of analysis* (Chicago: Aldine Publishing).

71. Kirby, K., and Priessman, S. 1957. Values of a daughter and mother therapy group. *International Journal of Group Psychotherapy* 7:281–88.

72. Klapman, J. 1946. *Group psychotherapy: Theory and practice* (New York: Grune & Stratton).

73. Klorman, R.; Strauss, J.; and Kokes, R. 1977. The relationship of demographic and diagnostic factors to measures of premorbid adjustment in schizophrenia. Part III. *Schizophrenia Bulletin* 3(2):214–25.

74. Laing, R. D. 1967. *The politics of experience* (New York: Ballantine Books).

75. Langsley, D. G.; Flomenhaft, K.; and Machotka, D. 1969. Follow-up evaluation of family crisis therapy. *American Journal of Orthopsychiatry* 39:753–59.

76. Langsley, D. G.; Kaplan, D. M.; Pittman, P. S.; Machotka, P.; Flomenhaft, K.; and DeYoung, C. D. 1968. *The treatment of families in crisis* (New York: Grune & Stratton).

77. Langsley, D. G.; Machotka, P.; and Flomenhaft, K. 1968. Family crisis therapy—results and implications. *Family Process* 7:145–58.

78. Langsley, D.; Machotka, P.; and Flomenhaft, K. 1971. Avoiding mental hospital admission: A follow-up study. *American Journal of Psychiatry* 127:1391–94.

79. Langsley, D. G.; Pittman, F.; and Swank, G. 1969. Family crisis in schizophrenics and other mental patients. *Journal of Nervous and Mental Disease* 149(3):270–76.

80. Laqueur, H. P.; Laburt, H. A.; and Morong, E. 1964. Multiple family therapy: Further developments. *International Journal of Social Psychiatry*, Congress Issue:70–80.

81. Lassner, R., and Brassea, M. 1968. Family centered group therapy with chronic schizophrenic patients: A five year follow-up study. *Group Psychotherapy* 21:247–58.

82. Lazell, E. W. 1921. The group treatment of dementia praecox. *Psychoanalytic Review* 8: 168–79.

83. Letemendia, F. J., and Harris, A. D. 1967. Chlorpromazine and the untreated chronic schizophrenic: A long-term study. *British Journal of Psychiatry* 113:959–71.

84. Levene, H. I.; Patterson, V.; Murphey, B. G.; Overbeck, A. L.; and Veach, T. L. 1970. The aftercare of schizophrenics: An evaluation of group and individual approaches. *Psychiatric Quarterly* 44:296–304.

85. Levine, M. 1961. Principles of psychiatric treatment. In *The impact of freudian psychiatry*, eds. F. Alexander and H. Ross (Chicago: University Chicago Press).

86. Liberman, R. P. 1972. Behavioral modification of schizophrenia: A review. *Schizophrenia Bulletin* 1(6):37–48.

87. Liberman, R. P. 1976. Behavior therapy for schizophrenia. In *Treatment of schizophrenia, progress and prospects*, eds. L. J. West and D. E. Flinn (New York: Grune & Stratton).

88. Liberman, R. P.; King, L. W.; and DeRisi, W. 1976. Behavior analysis and modification in community mental health. In *Handbook of behavior modification and Behavior Therapy*, ed. H. Leitenberg (New York: Appleton-Century-Crofts).

89. Lidz, T. 1973. *The origin and treatment of schizophrenic disorders* (New York; Basic Books).

90. Linn, L. 1970. State hospital environment and rates of patient discharge. *Archives of General Psychiatry* 23:346–51.

91. Lipton, S. M.; Fields, R. J.; and Scott, R. A. 1968. Effects of group psychotherapy upon types of patient movement. *Diseases of the Nervous System* 29:603–5.

92. Lloyd, K. E., and Abel, L. 1970. Performance on a token economy psychiatric ward: A two year summary. *Behavior Research and Therapy* 8:1–10.

93. Ludwig, A. M., and Farrelly, F. 1966. The code of chronicity. *Archives of General Psychiatry* 15:562–68.

94. Ludwig, A. M., and Marx, A. J. 1969. The buddy treatment model for chronic schizophrenics. *Journal of Nervous and Mental Disease* 148:528–41.

95. Ludwig, A. M., and Marx, A. J. 1971. The effects of attention and structure in the treatment of chronic schizophrenics. *British Journal of Psychiatry* 118:447–50.

96. Ludwig, A. M.; Marx, A. J.; Hill, P. A. et al. 1967. Forced small group responsibility in the treatment of chronic schizophrenics. *Psychiatry Quarterly Supplement* 41:262–80.

97. Lurie, A., and Ron, H. 1971. Multiple family group counseling of discharged schizophrenic young adults and their parents. *Social Psychiatry* 6:88–92.

98. MacGregor, R.; Ritchie, A.; Serrano, A.; Shuster, F.; McDonald, E.; and Goolashian H. 1964. *Multiple impact therapy with family* (New York: McGraw-Hill).

99. Main, T. F. 1946. The hospital as a therapeutic institution. *Bulletin of the Menninger Clinic* 19:66–70.

100. Marsh, L. C. 1933. Experiments in group treatment of patients at Worcester State Hospital. *Mental Hygiene* 17:396–416.

101. Masnik, R.; Bucci, L.; Isenberg, D.; and Normand, W. 1971. "Coffee and . . .": A way to treat the untreatable. *American Journal of Psychiatry* 128:164–67.

102. May, P. R. A. 1968. *Treatment of schizophrenia* (New York: Science House).

103. May, P. R. A. 1975. Schizophrenia: Overview of treatment methods. In *Comprehensive textbook of psychiatry*, eds. A. Freedman, H. Kaplan, and B. Sadock (Baltimore: Williams & Wilkins).

104. May, P. R. A., and Tuma, A. H. 1976. A follow-up study of the results of treatment. *Archives of General Psychiatry* 33:474–78, 481–86.

105. Meltzoff, J., and Konieich, M. 1970. *Research in psychotherapy* (New York: Atherton Press).

106. Menninger, W. 1939. Psychoanalytic principles in psychiatric hospital therapy. *Southern Medical Journal* 32:348–54.

107. Messier, M.; Finnerty, R.; Botvin, C.; and Grinspoon, L. 1969. A follow-up study of intensively treated chronic schizophrenic patients. *American Journal of Psychiatry* 125:1123–27.

108. Meyer, A. 1948–52. *Collected papers of Adolf Meyer*, 4 vols. (Baltimore: Johns Hopkins University Press).

109. Moos, R. H. 1974. *Evaluating treatment environments: A social ecological approach* (New York: John Wiley).

110. Moos, R. H. 1975. *Evaluating correctional and community settings* (New York: John Wiley).

111. Moos, R. H.; Shelton, R.; and Petty, C. 1973. Perceived ward climate and treatment outcome. *Journal of Abnormal Psychology* 82:291–98.

112. Mora, G. 1975. Historical and theoretical trends in psychiatry. In *Comprehensive textbook of psychiatry*, eds. A. Freedman, H. Kaplan, and B. Sadock (Baltimore: Williams & Wilkins), vol. 1, pp. 1–76.

113. Mosher, L. R. 1969. Schizophrenogenic communication and family therapy. *Family Process* 8:43–63.

114. Mosher, L. R. 1972. Research design to evaluate psychosocial treatments of schizophrenia. In *Psychotherapy of schizophrenia*, eds. D. Rubinstein and Y. Alanen (Amsterdam; Excerpta Medica Foundation).

115. Mosher, L. R. 1976. Implications of family studies for the treatment of schizophrenics. *Irish Medical Journal* 69:456–63.

116. Mosher, L. R., and Menn, A. Z. 1976. Dinosaur or astronaut? One year follow-up data from Soteria Project. *American Journal of Psychiatry* 133:919–20.

117. Mosher, L. R., and Menn, A. Z. Community residential treatment for schizophrenia: Two year follow-up data. *American Journal of Psychiatry*, in press.

118. Mosher, L. R., and Menn, A. Z. 1978. The surrogate "Family", an alternative to hospitalization. In *Schizophrenia: Science and Practice*, ed. S. C. Shershow (Cambridge: Harvard University Press), pp. 223–39.

119. Mosher, L. R.; Menn, A. Z.; and Matthews, S. M. 1975. Soteria: Evaluation of a home-based treatment for schizophrenia. *American Journal of Orthopsychiatry* 45(3):455–67.

120. Mosher, L. R.; Reifman, A.; and Menn, A. Z. 1973. Characteristics of non-professionals serving as primary therapists for acute schizophrenics. *Hospital and Community Psychiatry* 24:391–96.

121. O'Brien, C. P. 1975. Group therapy for schizophrenia: A practical approach. *Schizophrenia Bulletin* 1(13):119–30.

122. O'Brien, C. P.; Hamm, K. B.; Ray, B. A.; Pierce, J. F.; Luborsky, L.; and Mintz, J. 1972. Group vs. individual psychotherapy with schizophrenics: A controlled outcome study. *Archives of General Psychiatry* 27:474–78.

123. Olson, R. P., and Greenberg, D. J. 1972. Effects of contingency-contracting and decision-making groups with chronic mental patients. *Journal of Consulting and Clinical Psychology* 38:376–83.

124. Ozarin, L. D. 1973. Moral treatment and the mental hospital. In *The therapeutic community*, eds. J. J. Rossi and W. J. Filstead (New York: Behavioral Publications).

125. Parloff, M. B., and Dies, R. R. 1977. Group psychotherapy outcome research 1966–1975. *International Journal of Group Psychotherapy* 27:281–319.

126. Parras, A. 1974. The lounge: Treatment for chronic schizophrenics. *Schizophrenia Bulletin* 1(10):93–96.

127. Pasamanick, B.; Scarpitti, F. D.; and Dinitz, S. 1967. *Schizophrenics in the community* (New York: Appleton-Century-Crofts).

128. Pattison, E. M. 1965. Evaluating studies of group psychotherapy. *International Journal of Group Psychotherapy* 15:382–97.

129. Pattison, E. M.; Brissenden, A.; and Wohl, T. 1967. Assessing specific effects of inpatient group psychotherapy. *International Journal of Group Psychotherapy* 17:283–97.

130. Paul, G. L., and Lentz, R. J. 1977. *Psychosocial treatment of chronic mental patients: Milieu vs. social-learning programs* (Cambridge: Harvard University Press).

131. Paul, G. L.; Tobias, L. L.; and Holly, B. L. 1972. Maintenance psychotropic drugs in the presence of active treatment programs. A "triple-blind" withdrawal study with long-term mental patients. *Archives of General Psychiatry* 27:106–15.

132. Payn, S. B. 1965. Group methods in the pharmacotherapy of chronic psychotic patients. *Psychiatric Quarterly* 39:258–63.

133. Payn, S. B. 1974. Reaching chronic schizophrenic patients. *International Journal of Group Psychotherapy* 24:25–31.

134. Polak, P. R., and Kirby, M. W. 1976. A model to replace psychiatric hospitals. *Journal of Nervous and Mental Disease* 162:13–22.

135. Powdermaker, F., and Frank, J. 1953. *Group psychotherapy* (Cambridge: Harvard University Press).

136. Price, R. H. Knowledge into practice: Assessment and change in treatment environments. In *Psychiatric milieu and the therapeutic process*, eds. O. A. Will, J. G. Gunderson, and L. R. Mosher, forthcoming.

137. Purvis, S. A., and Miskimins, R. W. 1970. Effects of community follow-up on post-hospital adjustments of psychiatric patients. *Community Mental Health Journal* 6:374–82.

138. Rappaport, M.; Hopkins, H. K.; Hall, K.; et al. Schizophrenics for whom phenothiazines may be contraindicated or unnecessary. In *Controversy and psychiatry*, eds. H. K. H. Brody, and P. Brady (Philadelphia: W. B. Saunders), forthcoming.

139. Razin, A. M. 1971. A-B variable in psychotherapy: A critical review. *Psychological Bulletin* 75:1–21.

140. Reiss, D. 1971. Varieties of consensual experience: III. Contrasts between families of normals, delinquents and schizophrenics. *Journal of Nervous and Mental Disease* 152:73–95.

141. Roback, H. B. 1972. Experimental comparison of outcomes in insight and non-insight-oriented therapy groups. *Journal of Consulting and Clinical Psychology* 38:411–17.

142. Robinson, M. B. 1970. A study of the effects of focused video-tape feedback in group counseling. *Comparative Group Studies* 1:47–75.

143. Rogers, C. R.; Gendlin, E. G.; Kiesler, D. J.; and Truax, C. B. 1967. *The therapeutic relationship and its impact* (Madison: University of Wisconsin Press).

144. Rosen, J. N. 1969. Psychotherapy and schizophrenia. *International Journal of Psychiatry* 8:748–52.

145. Rossi, J. J., and Filstead, W. J. 1973. Therapeutic milieu, therapeutic community, and milieu therapy: Some conceptual and definitional distinctions. In *The therapeutic community*, eds. J. J. Rossi, and W. J. Filstead (New York: Behavioral Publications).

146. Ro-Trock, G. K.; Wellisch, D. K.; and Schoolar, J. C. 1977. A family therapy outcome study in an inpatient setting. *American Journal of Orthopsychiatry* 47:514–22.

147. Rowland, H. 1938. Interaction processes in the state mental hospital. *Psychiatry* 1:323–37.

148. Sager, C. J., and Kaplan, H. S. 1972. *Progress in group and family therapy* (New York: Brunner/Mazel).

149. Sanders, R.; Smith, R. S.; and Weinman, B. S. 1967. *Chronic psychosis and recovery* (San Francisco: Jossey Bass).

150. Sanders, S. H.; Williamson, D.; Akey, R.; and Hollis, P. 1976. Advancement to independent living: A model behavioral program for the intermediate care of adults with behavioral and emotional problems. *Journal of Community Psychology* 4:275–82.

151. Sartorius, N.; Jablensky, A.; and Shapiro, R. 1978. Crosscultural differences in the short-term prognosis of schizophrenic psychoses. *Schizophrenia Bulletin* 4(1):102–13.

152. Schaefer, H. H., and Martin, P. L. 1966. Behavior therapy for "apathy" of hospitalized schizophrenics. *Psychological Reports* 19:1147–58.

153. Schilder, P. 1936. The analysis of ideologics as a psychotherapeutic method, especially in group treatment. *American Journal of Psychiatry* 93:601–17.

154. Schniewind, H. E.; Day, M.; and Semrad, E. V. 1969. Group psychotherapy of schizophrenics. In *Schizophrenic Syndrome*, eds. L. Bellak, and L. Loeb (New York: Grune & Stratton).

155. Schooler, N.; Goldberg, S.; Boothe, H.; and Cole, J. 1967. One year after discharge: Community adjustment of schizophrenic patients. *American Journal of Psychiatry* 123:986–99.

156. Shattan, S. P.; Dcamp, L.; Fujii, E.; Fross, G. G.; and Wolff, R. J. 1966. Group treatments of conditionally discharged patients in a mental health clinic. *American Journal of Psychiatry* 122: 798–805.

157. Shershow, J. C. 1976. Disestablishing a therapeutic community. Presented at the 129th Annual Meeting of the American Psychiatric Association, Miami, Florida, May 1976.

158. Singer, M. T., and Wynne, L. C. 1965. Thought disorder and family relations of schizophrenics: III. Methodology using projective techniques. IV. Results and implication. *Archives of General Psychiatry* 12:187–212.

159. Smith, C. G., and King, J. A. 1975. *Mental hospitals: A study in organizational effectiveness* (Lexington, Mass.: Lexington Press).

160. Spadoni, A. J., and Smith, J. A. 1969. Milieu therapy in schizophrenia. *Archives of General Psychiatry* 20:547–51.

161. Speck, R. V., and Attneave, C. L. 1973. *Family network* (New York: Pantheon Books).

162. Stanton, A. H., and Schwartz, M. S. 1954. *The mental hospital* (New York: Basic Books).

163. Stein, L. I., and Test, M. A. 1976. Training in community living: One year evaluation. *American Journal of Psychiatry* 133:917–18.

164. Stotsky, B. A., and Zolik, E. S. 1965. Group psychotherapy with psychotics: 1921–1963—A review. *International Journal of Group Psychotherapy* 15:321–44.

165. Strelnick, A. H. 1977. Multiple family group therapy: A review of the literature. *Family Process* 16:307–25.

166. Sullivan, H. S. 1931. Socio-psychiatric research: Its implication for the schizophrenia problem and for mental hygiene. *American Journal of Psychiatry* 10:977–91.

167. Sullivan, H. S. 1931. The modified psychoanalytic treatment of schizophrenia. *American Journal of Psychiatry* 11:519–40.

168. Sullivan, H. S. 1962. *Schizophrenia as a human process* (New York: W. W. Norton).

169. Truax, S. B.; Wargo, D. G.; Carkhuff, R. R.; Kodman, F.; and Moles, E. A. 1966. Changes in self-concepts during group psychotherapy as a function of alternate sessions and vicarious therapy pretraining in institutionalized mental patients and juvenile delinquents. *Journal of Consulting Psychology* 30:309–14.

170. Turner, J. C. 1977. Comprehensive community support systems for severely mentally disabled adults: Definitions, components and guiding principles. Unpublished manuscript.

171. Van Putten, T. 1973. Milieu therapy: Contraindications. *Archives of General Psychiatry* 29: 640–43.

172. Van Putten, T., and May, P. R. A. 1976. Milieu therapy of the schizophrenias. In *Treatment of schizophrenia, progress and prospects*, eds. L. J. West and D. E. Flinn (New York: Grune & Stratton).

173. Vaughn, C. E., and Leff, J. P. 1976. The influence of family and social factors in the course of psychiatric illness: A comparison of schizophrenic and depressed neurotic patients. *British Journal of Psychiatry* 129:125–37.

174. Vitalo, R. L. 1971. Teaching improved interpersonal functioning as a preferred mode of treatment. *Journal of Clinical Psychology* 27:166–71.

175. Ward, J. T. 1974. The sounds of silence: Group psychotherapy with non-verbal patients. *Perspectives in Psychiatric Care* 12:13–19.

176. Wender, L. 1936. Dynamics of group therapy and its application. *Journal of Nervous and Mental Disease* 84:54–60.

177. Will, O. A.; Gunderson, J. G.; and Mosher, L. R., eds. *Principles and Practices of Milieu Therapy* (New York: Jason Aronson, Inc.), in press.

178. Wincze, J. P.; Leitenberg, H.; and Agras, W. S. 1972. The effects of token reinforcement and feedback on the delusional verbal behavior of chronic paranoid schizophrenics. *Journal of Applied Behavior Analysis* 5:247–62.

179. Wing, J. K., and Brown, G. W. 1970. *Institutionalism and schizophrenia* (New York: Cambridge University Press).

180. Wynne, L. 1974. Family and group treatment of schizophrenia: An interim view. In *Strategic intervention in schizophrenia*, eds. R. Cancro, N. Fox, and L. Shapiro (New York: Behavioral Publications).

181. Wynne, L. C., and Singer, M. T. 1963. Thought disorder and family relations of schizophrenics: I. A research strategy. II. A classification of forms of thinking. *Archives of General Psychiatry* 9:191–206.

Chapter 13

COMMUNITY PSYCHIATRIC TREATMENT

Israel Zwerling, M.D., Ph.D.

Introduction

The community mental health movement has clearly been a dominant trend in American psychiatry over the last two decades, and one consequence has been the shift in the "career" of schizophrenic patients from long-term institutional residence with occasional brief stays in the community, to long-term community residence with occasional brief stays in mental hospitals. Chapters by Musto, Ewalt, Langsley, and Yolles in Barton and Sanborn's recent volume (6) are among a number of excellent reviews of the history of this development, and still another summary seems unnecessary. For the present purpose, the bottom line is the fact that the resident population of mental hospitals in the United States has fallen from a high of 558,922 in 1955 to under 200,000 in 1976 (6); and since there is no evidence whatsoever that either the incidence or the prevalence of schizophrenia has decreased in this period, the hundreds of thousands of persons diagnosed as schizophrenic who are not in mental hospitals are patently enough somewhere in the "community." Precisely where they are, why they are where they are, what they are doing, and what difference the change in locus makes or can make, are the questions to which this chapter is addressed. It is perhaps best to indicate at the outset that the answers which can at present be provided are tentative and uncertain. At the same time there are few questions which arouse as much partisan heat and passion as do alternative views on these issues.

Part of the tentativeness and uncertainty derives from the many unresolved questions regarding the term "schizophrenia." It is quite evident, for one thing, that the issues one would pursue in organizing a community treatment program for schizophrenic patients would be rather different if one felt oneself to be dealing with an essentially organic disorder of the central nervous system, instead of with a dysfunctional state which is perceived primarily as a developmental disturbance at the psychodynamic or sociocultural level of integration. Thus, Wender et al. (53) concluded from their research that their "study again confirms the role of genetic factors and fails to show an environmental component in the etiology of schizophrenia." In a similar vein Davis et al. (15) observed that their "data clearly pointed to schizophrenic recurrence and episodes as occurring without notable external precipitants," and that "endogenous problems proved to be the most important single item differentiating failure from success. . . . Surprisingly, interpersonal problems were comparatively more prevalent among successes and were not closely related to rehospitalization." In the opposite vein, Beels (8) notes as a characteristic of the illness that "schizophrenia gets worse as a result of stress . . . we need to go beyond our present individual diagnostic approach to the classification of patients, and to classify instead the *lives* of patients in family, economic, and treatment contexts."

A question separate and independent from that of organic versus psychosocial factors in the etiology of schizophrenia is the uncertainty about whether schizophrenia is a single entity or a heterogeneous group of entities. A growing consensus appears to be emerging in favor of at least two distinct subgroups, with different premorbid histories, different responses to hospital treatment, and different prognoses in the community. Leff (37) stated:

> It was possible to identify the patients with a good prognosis by a number of distinguishing characteristics. They were patients with a good premorbid personality experiencing a first attack of schizophrenia with an acute onset, the illness being characterized by marked depressive symptoms in addition to typical schizophrenic symptoms. [p. 464]

Wing (55) questioned whether chronic schizophrenia always begins as acute schizophrenia. It appears that the traditional view—that chronicity in schizophrenia is entirely an iatrogenic product of the custodial warehousing and desocialization of patients—must be modified, at least in part, to accommodate the predictably different courses of illness traversed by a cohort of patients. Hargreaves et al. (25), in a study contrasting the outcome of short versus long hospitalization, concluded: "This study should dispel the notion that hospitalization for as long as four months in an active ward milieu leads to 'institutionalization.' Our data rather clearly show that the long-term subjects do not function worse in the community than do the short-term subjects." Shader (50) noted that 20 percent to 30 percent of patients with an initial episode of schizophrenia "restitute promptly, and have no further episodes," whereas a similar number prove to be refractory to treatment and become "chronic." Leff (37) noted the latter group as constituting 7 percent; and Beckett (7), the same group as 10 percent to 20 percent. Setting aside for a moment the numbers, virtually all cohort studies reported a fraction of patients as unresponsive, and another fraction as highly responsive, to whatever treatment is provided.

If, indeed, there are two or more distinct illnesses, some with a good and others with a poor prognosis, then outcome studies of hospital or community treatment programs which do not indicate how many patients of which category were studied are rather meaningless. Although, as has been indicated, the data appear to support the existence of at least the two broad categories of schizophrenic patients, there is by no means universal agreement concerning the identity of the "good prognosis group" with the "good premorbid adjustment group." Evans et al. (19) reported that "the good-premorbid schizophrenic not only showed signs of more rapid recovery from psychopathological symptoms while an inpatient but also a continuous process of social recovery over the course of the one-year follow-up period." Spohn et al. (51), on the contrary, reported that "premorbid social-sexual adjustment was not found to be related to behavioral, psychophysiological, and therapeutic response variance."

We are then in the position, in assessing reports concerning the treatment of schizophrenic patients in the community, of not being certain about whether we are dealing with one or several illness states; whether, if there are two or more "schizophrenias," they can be differentiated with regard to prognosis at the time treatment plans must be made; whether the disability associated with the one or two or several schizophrenias is fundamentally "endogenous" or maintained by exposure to definable stresses; and whether or not there is any relationship between the kind and duration of hospital treatment and the subsequent course in the community. It may be that it is precisely because these uncertainties are so formidable that proponents for one or another treatment modality present their arguments with so much passion and zeal.

Community Treatment Programs

The literature abounds in reports of follow-up studies of schizophrenic patients discharged from mental hospitals or from alternative crisis intervention programs; a recent review (5), designed to develop the issues with regard to deinstitutionalization, contains citations to 326 references, and the author cautioned, in her preface, that "the bibliography is extensive, but it is not 'complete' . . . I have selected for inclusion those writings—both professional and lay—which support or illustrate points I wish to make in the analytical review." The same writer, in another publication (4), pointed out that follow-up studies tend to be limited in terms of numbers and types of subjects, to be brief and variable in the duration of the follow-up period, to be undifferentiated with regard to patients discharged with careful follow-up programs versus those who sign out without any posthospital plan, and to be limited to recidivism and employment status as the only criteria for success or failure. Rehospitalization rates are of questionable reliability because of the many factors other than severity of illness which have been demonstrated to play determining roles in decisions to hospitalize: these include, in part, number of previous admissions, relative availability of beds, social class, and capacity of family and community to tolerate deviant behavior. Employment status is equally unreliable, because it is difficult to define, it cannot reasonably be applied as a criterion of recovery to patients not in the labor market, and it varies with general economic conditions. Data with reference to the outcome of community treatment programs are therefore to be read with considerable caution.

GENERAL STUDIES

Anthony et al. (1) have provided a most valuable summary of results reported in studies of community treatment programs. Table 13–1 from their report offers an overall compilation of "base-rate" studies—that is, of those programs using only patients who received "the traditional hospital regimen of drug treatment and perhaps some form of individual or group psychotherapy," to serve as a comparison base for programs offering special rehabilitative procedures. The data are subject to all the flaws noted earlier—for example, the outcome criteria for judging success or failure are recidivism and employment—but they are the best data available and merit replication. The authors noted that the type of treatment offered during hospitalization does not seem to matter:

TABLE 13-1
Suggested Base-rate Data for Recidivism and Employment

Time since Discharge	Recidivism (%)	Full-time Employment (%)
6 months	30-40	30-50
12 months	40-50	20-30
3-5 years	65-75	25

Source: From W. A. Anthony, G. J. Buell, S. Sharratt, and M. E. Althoff, "Efficacy of Psychiatric Rehabilitation," *Psychological Bulletin* (1972) 78:449.

eclectically oriented group therapy; psychoanalytically oriented individual or group therapy; individual or group therapy; or drugs, shock, individual or group therapy. Regardless of the type of traditional therapy patients receive, their recidivism and employment rates are not differentially affected. [p. 449]

With regard to special hospital treatment programs, including Total Push Therapy, they noted, "While all these approaches have been able to demonstrate positive effects on within-hospital behavior, they have as yet not demonstrated their effects on measures of community adjustment, such as rehospitalization rates."

One potential difficulty in comparing future outcome studies of community treatment programs with past or current studies is that the composition of a future cohort of discharged patients will necessarily be different. Weinstein and Patton (52) have pointed out that in New York State the proportion of "chronic" patients (i.e., those with two years or longer of continuous hospitalization) only declined from 78 percent to 76 percent over the fourteen years from 1955 to 1969—a period during which the percentage of patients admitted to the mental hospitals who became chronic (i.e., who stayed for two or more continuous years) fell from 28 percent to 9 percent. However, over the past eight years pressure has mounted on the states to empty their mental hospitals—a movement sparked chiefly by the fact that federal support for the maintenance of discharged patients is more liberal than for hospitalized patients. As a result the principal criterion for discharge is no longer that the patient has received optimal benefit from hospitalization, but only that symptoms have sufficiently subsided so that the patient *can* be treated in the community. At the same time the residual "chronic" population of the hospitals has been reduced to a hard core of patients most difficult to discharge. As a result an ever greater percentage of those discharged from hospitals consists of schizophrenic patients who have previously had one or more brief hospital admissions, and an ever lower percentage of patients who have had two years or more of continuous hospitalization.

THE ROLE OF PSYCHOPHARMACOLOGICAL AGENTS

Issues regarding the pharmacological treatment of schizophrenia have been reviewed in detail in chapter 9 of this volume. My present purpose is to summarize those studies which have been devoted particularly to the application of pharmacotherapy to community treatment programs. Crane (14) has traced the fascinating way in which "psychopharmacology and community psychiatry, which began as two separate developments, have become dependent on one another." Bennett (9) pointed out that in both England and Norway the process of discharging large numbers of schizophrenic patients from mental hospitals had already begun prior to the introduction of the phenothiazines, as a consequence of the change in the social organization of hospitals and in the management of patients. However, this is in no way to deny the powerful impact of the neuroleptic drugs upon community treatment programs; Wing (55) stated flatly, "No discussion of recent advances in our knowledge of the social causes of schizophrenia, or of the social aspects of treatment, is complete unless it gives due acknowledgment to the fact that the course and outcome are markedly altered by drug treatment." While this statement is generally accepted, there is limited agreement about *how* outcome is altered, and for how many patients, and at what cost.

A number of studies have demonstrated the statistical reliability of the advantage with regard to recidivism to schizophrenic patients in community programs treated with drugs versus placebos. Hogarty (26) and Hogarty et al.* have published a number of reports of a carefully executed long-term follow-up study of 374 schizophrenic patients randomly assigned to chlorpromazine or placebo therapy after an initial two-month period in which all patients were "stabilized" on a chlorpromazine regimen. Their data are compelling: "cumulative relapse rates at one year were 67 percent for placebo and 31 percent for drug" (30). Further (28):

The average time that chlorpromazine-treated patients survive in the community during the two years of study is 17.4 months, but only 10.3 months for placebo-treated patients. In that all patients were taking active medication for

* See references 27, 28, 29, 30, and 31.

the first two months following discharge, the mean survival time while receiving placebo is closer to eight months. By 24 months, 80% of placebo-
treated patients have relapsed, but only 48% of drug-treated patients. [p. 605]

In their most recent report (30) these writers offered a more refined
statistical device—a monthly risk of relapse—and noted that even after
three years the risk of relapse on placebo is three times that for drugs
(9.6 percent as against 2.9 percent); and they concluded that "the best
global estimate of the superiority of maintenance chemotherapy in forestalling relapse over a three year period is 2½ to 3 times that of placebo."
"Relapse" was defined by these writers as "unequivocal clinical deterioration of such magnitude that rehospitalization was imminent" (30).

An equally careful study—the more impressive with reference to the
issue of the effectiveness of psychoactive drugs because this was a peripheral issue in their study—was reported by Pasamanick et al. (43).
A total of 148 schizophrenic patients judged in need of hospital treatment at the Louisville General Hospital in Kentucky were divided randomly into a home care drug group, a home care placebo group, and a
hospitalized control group. The primary object of the study was to test
the feasibility of home care for schizophrenic subjects, and the drug
versus placebo issue was of secondary interest. Their finding was that
"over 77 percent of the drug home care patients but only 34 percent of
the placebo cases remained in the community throughout their participation in the project."

It must be noted, however, that Hogarty et al. (27) could find no advantage for their drug over their placebo treatment group with regard to
their measures of the extent of the improved *adjustment* of patients,
as reported by the patients themselves and their relatives and as reflected
in employment. They concluded that "the 'medication' clinic that simply
offers 'pills' will do little to improve the adjustment of patients beyond
forestalling relapse." Crane (14) made the same point in noting that
"major drug studies have shown that at most 50 percent of schizophrenics derive some benefit from neuroleptics. Those who improve do not
show anything approaching a recovery from the disease." Leff (37)
pointed out that one-third of patients relapse within a year despite active
drug treatment, which is consistent with the Hogarty et al. report cited
earlier (30) of a relapse rate of 31 percent in the first year for patients
on drug therapy. In the same direction, Bockoven and Solomon (10)
reported a comparative five-year follow-up study of 100 patients discharged from the Boston Psychopathic Hospital in 1947 and a similar
group discharged from the Solomon Center in 1967. They noted that:

> The most unexpected finding of this study is that the outcome of schizo-
> phrenic patients at Solomon Center today is not very different from that
> reported 20 years ago for schizophrenic patients at Boston Psychopathic
> Hospital. . . . The finding of no substantial change in the outcome of schizo-
> phrenic patients was not expected in view of the absence of psychotropic drugs
> during the entire 5 years of the Boston Psychopathic Hospital follow-up period,
> compared with the extensive use of psychotropic drugs at Solomon Center for
> both initial treatment on admission and the entire period of aftercare. This
> finding suggests that the attitudes of personnel toward patients, the socio-
> environmental setting, and community helpfulness guided by citizen organiza-
> tions may be more important in tipping the balance in favor of social recovery
> than are psychotropic drugs. The distinctive value of the drugs may well be

limited in most instances to their capacity to alleviate the distress of acute emotional decompensation. [p. 799]

A further series of contributions tending to promote caution in the use of the psychoactive drugs concern their undesired side effects, particularly those associated with their long-term administration. Crane's review (14) is particularly troubling. He stated that

> manifestations of tardive dyskinesia can be observed in 30 to 50% of patients who have been treated with drugs for several years. . . . A number of homeostatic mechanisms of the central and autonomic nervous system are also impaired by the continued exposure to neuroleptics. . . . Next to the nervous system, the cardiovascular organs are the most vulnerable to neuroleptics . . . electrocardiographic changes due to electrolyte imbalance often persist for as long as the patient is on medication. Epidemiological studies comparing the incidence of cardiovascular disorders in treated and untreated populations have not been carried out; hence little is known about the seriousness of these complications. [p. 646]

Unsupported statements affirming the safety of long-term administration of the neuroleptic drugs continue to appear; for example, Claghorn and Kinross-Wright (12) wrote that "many studies have supported the prolonged use of maintenance doses of psychotropic drugs, dispelling old fears of addiction and side effects and pointing out that patients can be safely kept on maintenance therapy, with minimal danger of complications"; unfortunately they cited no references to any of the "many studies."

A final set of cautions regarding the use of psychotropic drugs in the community treatment of schizophrenic patients derives from reports of apparently paradoxical results in interactive studies of drug-plus-psychotherapy programs. Cottman and Mezey (13) campared high and low users of outpatient services, and one finding was that "of the patients receiving phenothiazines, 50 percent had residual or psychotic symptoms at follow-up compared with 27 percent of the remaining 15 not receiving phenothiazines." One of the observations of Hogarty et al. (27) was that "among patients treated in the community, those treated with combined drug and sociotherapy adjust better than those taking the drug alone; to a greater extent, those receiving placebo alone adjust better than those receiving placebo and sociotherapy." Goldstein et al. (23) reported that "the highest rate of treatment failure was in the low-dose, no family therapy group, and the least in the low-dose, family therapy group. Both high-dose groups show a moderate rate of treatment failure which fell between the rates of the other two." In each instance, variables concerning the selection of subjects, the kind of psychosocial therapy, the ability of the therapists, etc., make any conclusions about these findings speculative; for example, it is not unlikely that more severely ill patients will be given higher drug dosages, and the association between high dosage and residual symptoms may be explained by the severity of the illness. However, the possibility must also be entertained that prolonged administration of psychotropic drugs, in some schizophrenic patients, *impairs* adjustment in the community.

A summary of conclusions which may be drawn at this juncture regarding the use of psychotropic drugs in community treatment of schizophrenic patients would then include:

1. A comparison of a random population of patients treated with drugs, with patients given no drugs, may reliably be expected to demonstrate a highly significant advantage in favor of the drugs with regard to rehospitalization rates.
2. There will be no significant differences between the two groups with regard to the quality of adjustment in the community.
3. Even with careful monitoring of drug use, 25 percent to 35 percent or more of patients in the drug group will be rehospitalized within a year following discharge.
4. A significant number of patients on maintenance drug therapy for any extended period of time will have undesired side effects—for example, from 10 percent up to 30 percent may have the symptoms of tardive dyskinesia; and some patients may adjust less well than they might without drugs.

THE ROLE OF FAMILY THERAPY

Studies of the role of the family in the etiology and the pathogenesis of schizophrenia, and of the role of family therapy in treatment programs, have been summarized in chapter 7 of this volume. Few studies, however, have been devoted specifically to the issue of the role of the family in community treatment programs, and these merit separate review.

Langsley et al. have reported a study conducted between 1964 and 1969 at the Colorado Psychiatric Hospital in a monograph (34) and in a series of publications including an eighteen-month follow-up (35). Their object was to test the feasibility of family-crisis therapy as a substitute for inpatient treatment in the case of patients judged to be in need of immediate hospitalization. At the six-month follow-up twice as many control patients, who had been hospitalized at the time of their entry into the project, had been rehospitalized (39 of the 1,950) as had patients initially receiving family-crisis therapy who were hospitalized for the first time during the same period (19 of the 1,950); further, the average length of stay among all those who had been hospitalized during the six months was twice as long for the control group. At eighteen months, however, the two populations were almost equal with regard to rehospitalization. The authors put it that the advantage noted during the first six months was "somewhat reduced," but the advantage remaining to the family-crisis group (17 of 126 patients, as against 15 of 99 patients initially hospitalized) was not statistically significant. The study was carefully planned and executed, and the data provide an impressive demonstration of the effectiveness of direct supportive intervention in the families of schizophrenic patients in maintaining the patients in the community even at the time of an acute psychotic episode. Although the two studies were somewhat different in design, the Langsley data are very comparable with the results reported by Pasamanick et al. (43) cited earlier. In both unfortunately follow-up data indicated that the group initially treated by family intervention in the community became indistinguishable from the group initially hospitalized, and in both instances the follow-up data were well within the base-rates reported by Anthony et al. (1) for patients who received traditional treatment. In an ironic way, the loss of the advantage when family intervention in the community is discontinued provides its own evidence of the superiority of this approach over traditional hospital and outpatient treatment, in terms of maintaining schizophrenic patients in the community.

Brown et al. (11) have offered an index of a family's interaction with a schizophrenic patient—"expressed emotion" (EE)—which they have reported to be highly predictive of the rate of relapse of patients in the community. The higher the EE index, the more the emotional overinvolvement of the family with the patient, the more overt the hostility, and the more frequent the critical comments about the patient. A follow-up study nine months after discharge revealed that 58 percent of the patients whose families had been rated high on the EE index at the time of admission to the hospital had relapsed, but only 16 percent of the patients from low EE families had relapsed. Of special interest in relation to the studies of the effectiveness of pharmacotherapy in maintaining schizophrenic patients in the community is Brown et al.'s finding that drug therapy had no effect upon relapse rates in patients from low EE families (14 percent for patients taking drugs and 15 percent for those not taking drugs) but made a significant difference in patients from high EE families (46 percent relapsed of those on drugs, and 66 percent of those not on drugs). Again the data are impressive, indicating that about four times as many schizophrenic patients in the community from high EE families as from low EE families may be expected to relapse in nine months following hospitalization. Leff (37) cited studies which have demonstrated that a majority of the critical comments about patients by members of high EE families refer not to their symptomatic behavior but to long-standing personality traits; he concluded that

it is reasonable to suppose that poor relationships of long standing are more difficult to alter than adverse reactions to acute symptoms of illness. For this reason the focus of a programme of management for schizophrenics living with relatives should be on increasing the social distance between patient and relative rather than attempting to change the relative's attitude. [p. 467]

He further suggested, "In some cases it might be feasible to remove the patients from their home altogether, by finding them an alternative accommodation such as a hostel."

Beels (8) has described a program of family treatment for schizophrenic patients based in a state mental hospital. Although the locus of treatment was on the wards assigned to his unit, staff teams retained responsibility for a patient and family after the patient's discharge. Attention is called to this contribution for the following reasons: its synthesis of theoretical approaches to the role of the family in schizophrenia; its success in establishing a family and social model for treating schizophrenia in the very citadel of the medical model—a hospital; its focus on complete continuity of care between inpatient and outpatient phases of treatment (including the formation of treatment groups composed of both hospitalized and discharged patients); and its detailed illustrative case histories which involve the use of virtually every type of community resource in the efforts of the therapists to stabilize their patients. Beels's contribution is one of the finest illustrations which has been published of the use of a state mental hospital as a base for a community psychiatric program.

COMMUNITY SUPPORT PROGRAMS

Few mental health professionals today can remain unaware of the enormous gap between the promise of deinstitutionalization and the actuality of community life for the largest numbers of schizophrenic patients. Mosher and Feinsilver (40) pointed out "the fact that only 15 to 40 percent of schizophrenics living in the community achieve what might be termed an average level of adjustment (that is, being self-supporting or successfully functioning as a housewife)"; other researchers (32) place this proportion at between 5 percent and 10 percent. Reich and Siegel (45) reported that no fewer than 25,000 ex-patients were living in single-room-occupancy welfare hotels in New York City, and that most of them by far lacked even anyone to see that they left their rooms for meals. In many areas zoning laws have jealously guarded resident populations from an influx of patients in boarding or foster homes or halfway houses or psychiatric day care centers in their communities. Beneath the surface unanimity of concern for the care of our mentally ill brothers and sisters, a battle rages between the elected representatives of society who devise strategies for making the mentally ill invisible and for keeping the cost of this process at a minimum and a rather small band of mental health workers who keep busy devising counterstrategies for making possible a reasonable quality of life in the community for mental patients. If one conceives of the gap between normal family life and hospital life as a continuum in space and time, the central counterstrategy for the care and treatment of schizophrenic patients in the community has been the creation of intermediate facilities for residence, recreation and socialization, employment, and treatment. Some facilities—for example, Horizon House in Philadelphia (47)—aim to serve concurrently in all four areas; most are more limited in their goals. It is not possible in a brief review to do full justice to the wide range of innovative programs that have been reported, virtually all of which have demonstrated some success in improving the adjustment of schizophrenic patients and/or in decreasing rehospitalization. Rather than attempt a complete review, the present effort will be to select some representative programs in each of the areas noted, so that the salient issues can be elucidated. The artificiality of identifying these programs as illustrative of only one of these rehabilitative areas must be acknowledged at the outset; in each instance more than one purpose was sought in the programs reviewed below.

RESIDENTIAL PROGRAMS

Many schizophrenic patients ready to be discharged from mental hospitals have no families, and the longer the period of hospitalization, the more likely is this circumstance. Other patients have been firmly extruded from their families; relatives can be located but refuse to accept the patients upon discharge. Still others return to families and promptly establish a tense and hostile interaction with their relatives which forebodes an early return to the hospital. Provision must then be made for the residential requirements for an uncertain, but clearly large, fraction of schizophrenic patients discharged from hospitals; estimates by Leaf (36) and by Cole (32) in the United States, and by Brown et al. (11) in England, indicate that this fraction is well over 25 percent. As one consequence of the slogans of the deinstitutionalization movement—and undoubtedly even more pointedly because recent changes in social security legislation made possible a transfer of fiscal responsibility for discharged patients from local (county and state) to federal sources—the strategy devised by most states to deal with this has been simply to dump patients into "the community," with subsistence provided by the welfare system, and into whatever residential resources could be contrived. Reference was made earlier to the report of Reich and Siegel (45) that some 25,000 ex-patients were holed up in single-room-occupancy hotels in New York City; Segal (48) reported a parallel finding of 11,000 ex-patients living in boarding homes under similar circumstances in Los Angeles; and probably no major urban center in the United States has failed to adopt some variant of this "solution," including machinery for facilitating the "revolving door" transfer of patients between the mental hospitals and their totally unsupervised and almost universally substandard housing.

The most troubling aspect of the situation is that there is no lack of information about preferable alternatives. A recent volume by Lamb et al. (33) provides summaries of the techniques available to make a wide range of alternatives to isolated individual residential placements supportive for schizophrenic patients, including boarding homes, foster homes, halfway houses, and cooperative patient group homes. The latter perhaps represent a less familiar technique and may merit a brief discussion.

Dewhurst et al. (16) have described the Oxford group-home program in some detail; Cole (32) and Zwerling (57) have described similar efforts in Boston and in the Bronx. Essentially small groups of from three to six patients are selected for their expectable compatibility, based upon observations of their interactions while in the hospital. They are then moved as a unit into an apartment which is leased by an agency allied with the hospital (the League of Friends in Oxford; the Pibly Fund in the Bronx); tenants—that is, the patients—pay rent to the agency, which is essentially self-supporting. The purpose of this arrangement is to protect both landlords and tenants from the possibility that a recurrence of illness requiring rehospitalization would leave the rent partly unpaid. Cole (32) described an active role for the landlords; they were initially screened by the staff and took some responsibility for teaching the patients how to keep house. All three reports are extremely positive with regard to the effectiveness of the technique; Dewhurst et al. (16) believed that the greater reduction in inpatient population in Oxford over the national average (45 percent between 1954 and 1969, as against 31 percent for the entire country) was in part due to the group-home program.

SOCIAL AND RECREATIONAL PROGRAMS

Schizophrenic patients are generally extremely deficient in social skills, and a variety of community programs for the treatment of schizophrenic patients direct some effort toward the goal of enhancing social and recreational capabilities and practices. There is a level at which this issue is seen by some researchers as at the heart of the problem of "treatment." Dr. Mosher, in chapter 12, has reviewed those approaches which view schizophrenia as a human experience organized as a withdrawal response to a grossly disordered social context, and which therefore approach treatment as a rehumanizing (or resocializing) process. The present purpose is to highlight some of the techniques devised by more traditional therapists, with the more limited goal of breaking down the isolation of patients in the community and improving the quality of their lives through an enriched social and recreational milieu.

A short report by Parras (42) touched upon the crucial issues in this area. The Lounge began as a medication clinic, where patients could gather weekly and, while waiting for their prescription renewals, could play pool or cards, or participate in an arts and crafts program, or listen to music, or just hang around. It was gradually taken over by the patients as a social center—unstructured (as against the traditional milieu therapy programs), unpressured (as against the many programs which find it useful to prescribe activities for patients), unscheduled (patients could come and go as they pleased, as against the many programs which find it necessary to control who may do what, and when, in order not to overwhelm limited resources), and open to inpatients, outpatients, and any guests the patients chose to bring. The success of the Lounge program is attested to by the fact that after a year a Lounge room was established which was open every day, all year, and operated without staff supervision. The model created by Parras at the Maimonides Community Mental Health Center has been replicated by the Metropolitan Hospital and by the Metropolitan Unit of the Manhattan State Hospital in New York City.

The more familiar socialization programs are those conducted by the large rehabilitation agencies: Fountain House in New York City, Horizon House in Philadelphia, Thresholds in Chicago, Hill House in Cleveland, and Council House in Pittsburgh are perhaps the best known. Dincin (17), director of the Thresholds, has provided a brief but comprehensive summary of the operation of these agencies. It is instructive to note that the major impetus for their development came initially from a group of ex-patients, supported almost immediately by two nonprofessional, nongovernmental groups—the National Council of Jewish Women and the regional mental health associations. Fountain House, the pioneer among these centers, originally functioned entirely as a social club, but it has— as have the others in this group—added vocational and treatment programs to its socialization program. Although, as Dincin pointed out, these agencies attempt to retain an atmosphere of informality, their very size and the complexity of their many programs inevitably necessitates a degree of structure which is quite unlike the informality of the Lounge: schedules, step systems for tracking the progress of patients, charts and attendance records are essential; though it is recognized that they may generate the pressure of high expectations upon a population which is highly sensitive to pressure. This matter is of central importance and is further discussed in the concluding section.

VOCATIONAL REHABILITATION

Many patients experience their first pyschotic episode before they obtain their first job; many find work a source of stress and are unable to stay on a job; others cannot find work because of the lack of marketable skills; still others are denied employment because of the bias on the part of many employers against ex-mental patients. In a period where unemployment is in general high, these factors patently become the more severe. The most implacable index of the failure of schizophrenic patients to adapt successfully in the community, consequently, has been the low rate of employment; recall that the base-rate reported by Anthony et al. (1) three years after discharge is 25 percent. A major thrust in both hospital and community treatment of schizophrenia has been the development of vocational habilitation and rehabilitation programs. The range of intermediate facilities devised for these programs extends from prevocational training, industrial therapy, work-for-pay programs, and sheltered workshops for inpatients to similar extramural facilities and to programs designed to protect patients who are working against the usual reasons for their losing their jobs.

Dincin (17) has summarized the vocational rehabilitation program of the Thresholds in Chicago, and Rutman (47) the parallel program of Horizon House in Philadelphia. The latter is particularly extensive and includes industrial, building-maintenance, food-service, and clerical workshops, as well as "work adjustment training" which is concerned with general preparation of patients for work situations. Both programs include placement as well as job-retention services, to help find appropriate jobs for patients and to help them through the period of initial adjustment to their jobs. Most crucially, in the view of this writer, vocational-rehabilitation programs vary in being time-limited or not and in tending toward a high or a low expectation of productivity from their subjects.

Fairweather et al. (20) have described a particularly innovative approach to the problem of job retention. To begin with, their seventy-five subjects were housed in a variant of the cooperative patient residence, the Lodge, which was completely operated by the patients and which thus could provide sheltered employment for some of their number. If a resident with outside employment was, for a brief period, incapable of working, he could be given a temporary assignment in the Lodge, and replaced by a more "together" resident until he could resume outside employment; in this way the job could be retained for the Lodge and thus for that resident. The Fairweather group is particularly insistent upon separating away psychotic symptoms from the issue of work. Mosher (39) repeated their anecdote about a resident who constantly hallucinated and responded vocally to the voices he heard while in the Lodge; on the job his supervisor announced each day, "We don't allow any talking here," and this resident's hallucinations, as well as his responses, would stop until he got into the truck to return to the Lodge.

TREATMENT PROGRAMS

The issues that emerge from a review of the range of intermediate facilities between home and hospital which have been devised for the treatment of schizophrenic patients in the community are the most familiar to mental health professionals. The intensity of the treatment effort, the modalities of treatment available, the accessibility of the facility, and the relevance of the program to the needs of the patients are the most crucial considerations.

Treatment intensity varies from the once-a-month "medication clinic," which is an almost omnipresent feature of community mental health centers, to day centers and day or partial hospitals. The latter attempt to provide in full all the treatment resources of a hospital during weekday, day-shift hours; at night and on weekends, when active treatment efforts in most hospitals are in any event at a low ebb, patients are at home. Zwerling and Wilder (58) have described the use of a day hospital in place of traditional twenty-four-hour hospitalization; two-thirds of patients judged in need of psychiatric hospitalization can be successfully treated in a day hospital. A psychiatric day center program more closely resembles a socialization center than a hospital but includes treatment programs. Gootnick (24) has described such a center with a range of group-treatment and group-recreation approaches and emphasizes the value to patients of discovering that others share their problems, of establishing friendships, and of learning to use the center's supportive legal, financial, and educational resources.

A host of practical issues about the organization of outpatient services are of direct import to their effectiveness—their location and accessibility; the availability of therapists who speak the language of the patient; the ease of entry permitted by the intake process; the range of therapists and therapies available. Some problems bedevil community treatment programs for schizophrenic patients which are rare or even unheard of in other programs. For example, schizophrenic patients tend to be difficult to locate in their communities: they move a great deal; they have great difficulty in using public transportation; and they prefer to be invisible. As a consequence, as Fisch (21) pointed out, it is necessary to obtain the addresses of three or more collateral relatives or friends at the time of first contact or referral, as well as to have an aggressive policy of tracking down patients who fail to keep appointments. May—who is generally regarded as the spokesman for pharmacotherapy in the hospital treatment of schizophrenia, and who grudgingly accepts that "in certain rare situations where cost and length of stay are of no consequence, the addition of psychotherapy may be justifiable, despite the slight chance of additional benefit"—nevertheless has this to say about the referral process (38):

> If I had to select the phase of treatment most in need of improvement, it would be the release phase, the transition of the patient from hospital to community. Weeks or months of hard work can be quickly undone by failure in such simple matters as providing drugs and instructions about how they should be taken, eliciting family cooperation, and arranging for the patient to return for follow-up interviews . . . aftercare should start by establishing a follow-up relationship when the patient is first admitted. . . . Every possible administrative device is needed to strengthen continuity of care and to support the patient and his family during the discharge period.

Only passing reference can be made here to the role of the para-professional therapist in the community treatment of schizophrenia, an issue which would require a volume of its own for its full elucidation. Data with regard to this question are scarce; anecdotal reports and opinions are plentiful and range from horror stories of great harm done by intrusive and untrained meddlers to near magical cures effected by gifted and talented indigenous mental health workers. It is my impression that, in the community treatment programs I have visited, para-professionals are more underused than overused. Mosher and Menn's (41) argument for staffing Soteria with nonprofessionals is one I would endorse in establishing a balanced personnel complement for a community program:

We believe that relatively untrained, psychologically unsophisticated persons can assume a phenomenological stance vis-à-vis psychosis more easily than highly trained persons (e.g., M.D.'s or Ph.D.'s) because they have learned no theory of schizophrenia, whether psychodynamic, organic, or a combination of both. This allows them freedom to be themselves, to follow their visceral responses, and to be a "person" with the psychotic individual.

Some Conclusions

A review of so broad an area as the community psychiatric treatment of schizophrenia almost necessarily leaves one with an awareness of the diffusion of the efforts and interests which have marked the research programs of the last decade. Two conclusions and one caveat seem to this writer to be of sufficiently compelling importance to merit special attention.

First, it is incontrovertibly the case that the technology now exists for completely reversing the current gloomy enterprise of community treatment and making successful integration of schizophrenic patients into the community the rule and not the exception. In 1971, Hogarty (26) noted that "the chasm between the treatment services possible and the actual treatment experiences of schizophrenics in many programs continues to expand, apparently for want of adequate funding to provide appropriate services." Davis et al. (15), in the sober light of their finding that five years of traditional practice had wiped out the initial advantage of their experimental public health nursing-family treatment program, poignantly conclude that there is:

a need for the structuring of community mental health services on an intensive, aggressive basis, if we are to do anything more than transfer custodial care to the community. . . . It is not an unreasonable possible assumption to make, that if ITC care had been continued, no deterioration in behavior of functioning would have occurred. It is even possible that if more intensive care—including day hospitals, sheltered workshops, hostels, and vocational, marital and personal guidance—were available, with respected and well-paid jobs as part of the program of community mental health care, as well as the other components described, total functioning might very well have improved instead of deteriorating or remaining constant.

The point is, of course, not that we know all we wish to know either about schizophrenia or about community treatment; the point is rather that we already know all we need to know to make effective community treatment a reality for the greatest number of schizophrenic patients. The political decision to condemn schizophrenic patients to SRO hotel rooms, to a rehospitalization rate of 70 percent over a three-year period, and to an unemployment rate of 75 percent (not 7.5 but 75 percent) is no less a decision by virtue of its emerging as a consequence of the low priorities and the gross underfinancing of community treatment programs than if it were a consequence of setting these statistics as a deliberate national goal. An instructive and humbling exercise is to read, one after the other, the brief articles by Aviram and Segal (3) on the strategies used by communities, and by Wilder (54) on the strategies used by mental health professionals, to exclude the chronic schizophrenic patient. There can be no more abhorrent self-fulfilling prophecy than that of a legislature which, having ensured the failure of its community mental health programs by an initial and gross underfinancing, then points to this failure as a reason for further cutting the community mental health budget.

A second compelling conclusion concerning the community psychiatric treatment of schizophrenic patients is that a good deal of the problem is a direct and immediate consequence of the irrational ambition of mental health professionals. John Wing (55) has, in his characteristic way, made the point most simply: "The most important and most difficult requirement . . . is to be realistic." We discover that low-expectation messages (e.g., "You're not ready yet") are heard by some patients as "You are sick," and that high-expectation messages (e.g., "I expect you to complete this program") stimulate some patients to greater efforts toward recovery; we then institutionalize these discoveries into a system of time-limited "steps" or "phases," into which patients must fit or else be extruded from our programs. I have on another occasion, in this regard, commented (57):

> It is important to emphasize that any point along the continuum of autonomy and independence may come to represent a resting place for a chronic psychotic patient; to insist on an all-or-none division into hospital vs. fully independent community life is simply unrealistic. This may appear to be a pessimistic note, implying a recognition that the chronic psychotic patient will never be totally "cured" and rendered capable of living like the rest of us. . . . I rather see this as *our* problem—the problem of the observers—rather than that of the chronic psychotic patients we are observing. It has been demonstrated that the presentation of a wooden facsimile of a monkey will terrify a colony of monkeys. In a related experiment, a fish trapped in a plastic bubble and released back into his school to swim his wobbly course will scatter the other fish in apparent terror. I am suggesting that much of our behavior is like that of the monkeys and the fish: we cannot abide the more wobbly swimmers and more wooden ones among us, and our panic becomes translated into an urgent need to make them just like ourselves. I have the feeling that if we make provision in the community for a range of wobbliness and woodenness, we will in the end, paradoxically, move further toward our present goal of "cure" than insistence upon polarizing humanity into the "sick" and the "well" will permit.

Finally, attention must be called to a caveat concerning some of the uncertain and presently unpredictable bio-psycho-social consequences of the community treatment of schizophrenia which will increasingly confront us as these programs increase in number and effectiveness. The greater the number of schizophrenic patients in the community, the larger the gene pool for susceptibility to schizophrenia among reproducing adults; the greater the expectable frequency with which families—including infants and young children—will be exposed to the crises of an acute schizophrenic episode; and the more likely it is that pressure from deviant behaviors will be added to the pressures of modernization and social change that alter the fabric of community life. In this arena there are as yet few data, but extrapolation from these few are already extant. Thus, Arnhoff (2) has recently noted that:

> As the traffic between home and hospital multiplies, a point must be reached when the mental health needs of the community as a whole conflict with the mental health needs of individual patients. . . . Supposed benefits for the patient alone can no longer suffice as determinants of policy when the data so strongly indicate potential iatrogenic effects on others.

One can readily enough dismiss this particular argument: in the face of the overwhelming data from clinical studies of community programs, he characterized the benefits to patients as "supposed"; on the contrary, in the face of the very limited data from the few relevant studies of family and of the social costs of community treatment, these data can "so strongly indicate" only the bias of Dr. Arnhoff. However, the problem does not thereby go away. Rieder et al. (46) for example, recently reported that the seven-year old children of schizophrenic parents "were found to have a slightly lower IQ than their matched controls." The difference was found only among male children, and a statistical review of the data from other studies indicated a negative correlation between the IQ of the children and "certain perinatal events" in chronic schizophrenic patients. However, more studies, and more and better data, can be expected in pursuit of the hypotheses that there are indeed bio-psycho-social costs associated with maintaining schizophrenic patients in the community:—for example, the effects on children, on illness rates in family members, and on family finances. In many instances we can expect that these costs will appear prohibitive.

Ultimately this is a political issue, and the hope is that political decisions will be based upon the most careful assessment of the most reliable information about how to achieve the greatest good for the largest number of the polity. In the face of the evidence at hand at the moment, the full support and the recognition of the highest priority for community psychiatric treatment for schizophrenic patients is urgently indicated. Mental health professionals may well ask, with Rabbi Hillel, "If not now, then when?"

BIBLIOGRAPHY

1. Anthony, W. A.; Buell, G. J.; Sharratt, S.; and Althoff, M. E. 1976. Efficacy of psychiatric rehabilitation. *Psychological Bulletin* 78:447–56.

2. Arnhoff, F. N. 1975. Social consequences of policy toward mental illness. *Science* 188:1277–81.

3. Aviram, U., and Segal, S. 1973. Exclusion of the mentally ill. *Archives of General Psychiatry* 29:126–31.

4. Bachrach, L. L. 1976. A note on some recent studies of released mental hospital patients in the community. *American Journal of Psychiatry* 133:73–75.

5. Bachrach, L. L. 1976. *Deinstitutionalization: An analytical review and sociological perspective.* DHEW Publication no. (ADM) 76-315 (Washington, D.C.: U.S. Government Printing Office).

6. Barton, W. F., and Sanborn, C. J. 1977. *An assessment of the community mental health movement* (Lexington, Mass.: Lexington Books, D. C. Heath).

7. Beckett, G. S. 1970. Home or hospital for chronic schizophrenia? *Journal of the Irish Medical Association* 63:149–52.

8. Beels, C. C. 1975. Family and social management of schizophrenia. *Schizophrenia Bulletin* 13:97–118.

9. Bennet, D. H. 1975. The management of schizophrenia. *British Journal of Psychiatry* Special no. 9:48–54.

10. Bockoven, J. S., and Solomon, H. C. 1975. Comparison of two five-year follow-up studies: 1947–1952 and 1967–1972. *American Journal of Psychiatry* 132:796–801.

11. Brown, G.; Marck, E.; Carstairo, G. M.; and Wing, J. 1962. The influence of family life on the course of schizophrenic illness. *British Journal of Preventive Social Medicine* 16:55–68.

12. Claghorn, J. L., and Kinross-Wright, J. 1971. Reduction in hospitalization of schizophrenics. *American Journal of Psychiatry* 128:344–47.

13. Cottman, S. B., and Mezey, A. G. 1976. Community care and the prognosis of schizophrenia. *Acta Psychiatrica Scandinavica* 53:95–104.

14. Crane, G. E. 1974. Two decades of psychopharmacology and community mental health: Old and new problems of the schizophrenic patient. *Transactions of the New York Academy of Sciences* 36:644–62.

15. Davis, A. E.; Dinitz, S.; and Pasamanick, B. 1972. The prevention of hospitalization in schizophrenia: Five years after an experimental program. *American Journal of Orthopsychiatry* 42:375–88.

16. Dewhurst, K.; McKnight, A. L.; and Leopoldt, H. 1974. The Oxford group-home scheme for psychiatric patients. *Practitioner* 213:195–204.

17. Dincin, J. 1975. Psychiatric rehabilitation. *Schizophrenia Bulletin* 13:131–47.

18. Dunham, H. W. 1977. Schizophrenia: The impact of sociocultural factors. *Hospital Practice* 12:61–68.

19. Evans, J. R.; Goldstein, M. J.; and Rodnick, E. H. 1973. Premorbid adjustment, paranoid diagnosis and remission. *Archives of General Psychiatry* 28:666–72.

20. Fairweather, G. W.; Sanders, D. H.; and Maynard, H. 1969. *Community life for the mentally ill* (Chicago: Aldine).

21. Fisch, M. 1967. Post-hospital contacts with schizophrenics. *Current Psychiatric Therapies* 7:221–24.

22. Freeman, H. L. 1968. Management of schizophrenia in the community. *British Medical Journal* 4:371–73.

23. Goldstein, M. J.; Rodnick, E. H.; Evans, J. R.; and May, P. R. A. 1975. Long-acting phenothiazine and social therapy in the community treatment of acute schizophrenics. *Psychopharmacology Bulletin* 11:37–38.

24. Gootnick, I. 1971. The psychiatric day center in the treatment of the chronic schizophrenic. *American Journal of Psychiatry* 128:485–88.

25. Hargreaves, W. A.; Glick, I. D.; Drues, J.; Showstack, J. A.; and Feigenbaum, E. 1977. Short vs. long hospitalization: A prospective controlled study. *Archives of General Psychiatry* 34:305–11.

26. Hogarty, G. E. 1971. The plight of schizophrenics in modern treatment programs. *Hospital and Community Psychiatry* 22:21–27.

27. Hogarty, G. E.; Goldberg, S. C.; and Schooler, N. R. 1974. Drug and sociotherapy in the aftercare of schizophrenic patients. *Archives of General Psychiatry* 31:609–18.

28. Hogarty, G. E.; Goldberg, S. C.; Schooler, N. R.; and Ulrich, R. F. 1974. Drug and sociotherapy in the aftercare of schizophrenic patients. II. Two-year relapse rates. *Archives of General Psychiatry* 31:603–8.

29. Hogarty, G. E.; Guy, W.; Gross, M.; and Gross, G. 1969. An evaluation of community-based mental health programs: Long-range effects. *Medical Care* 7:271–2801.

30. Hogarty, G. E., and Ulrich, R. F. 1977. Temporal effects of drug and placebo in delaying relapse in schizophrenic outpatients. *Archives of General Psychiatry* 34:297–301.

31. Hogarty, G. E.; Ulrich, R.; Goldberg, S.; and Schooler, N. 1976. Sociotherapy and the prevention of relapse among schizophrenic patients: An artifact of drug? In *Evaluation of psychological therapies*, eds. R. L. Spitzer and D. F. Klein (Baltimore: Johns Hopkins University Press).

32. Cited in Huey, K. ed. Special Report. Alternatives to Mental Hospital Treatment. Highlights from a Conference in Madison, Wisconsin. *Hospital and Community Psychiatry* 27:186–92, March 1976.

33. Lamb, H. R., et al. 1976. *Community survival for long-term patients* (San Francisco: Jossey-Bass).

34. Langsley, D. G.; Kaplan, D. M.; Pittman, F. S.; et al. 1968. The treatment of families in crisis (New York: Grune & Stratton).

35. Langsley, D. G.; Machotka, P.; and Flomenhaft, K. 1971. Avoiding mental hospital admission: A follow-up study. *American Journal of Psychiatry* 127:1391–94.

36. Leaf, P. 1977. Patients released after Wyatt: Where did they go? *Hospital and Community Psychiatry* 28:366–69.

37. Leff, J. P. 1976. The maintenance and management of schizophrenia. *Journal of the Irish Medical Association* 69:464–68.

38. May, P. R. A. 1969. Modifying health-care services for schizophrenic patients. *Hospital and Community Psychiatry* 20:363–68.

39. Mosher, L. R. 1972. Recent trends in psychosocial treatment of schizophrenia. *American Journal of Psychoanalysis* 32:9–15.

40. Mosher, L. R., and Feinsilver, D. 1973. Current studies on schizophrenia. *International Journal of Psychiatry* 11:7–52.

41. Mosher, L. R., and Menn, A. 1975. Soteria: An alternative to hospitalization for schizophrenia. *Current Psychiatric Therapies* 15:287–96.

42. Parras, A. 1974. The lounge: Treatment for chronic schizophrenics. *Schizophrenia Bulletin* 10:93–97.

43. Pasamanick, B.; Scarpitti, F. R.; and Dinitz, S. 1967. *Schizophrenics in the community* (New York: Appleton-Century-Crofts).

44. Ramon, S. 1975. Culture change and schizophrenia: Exploring the case of three Israeli subcultures. University of Bradford.

45. Reich, R., and Siegel, L. 1975. Psychiatry under siege: The chronically mentally ill shuffle to oblivion. *Psychiatric Annals* 3:35–55.

46. Rieder, R. O.; Broman, S. H.; and Rosenthal, D. 1977. The offspring of schizophrenics. *Archives of General Psychiatry* 34:789–99.

47. Rutman, I. D. 1976. Position paper: Adequate residential and community-based programs for the mentally disabled. Horizon House Institute for Research and Development, Philadelphia, Pennsylvania.

48. Segal, S. P. 1974. Life in board and care. In *Where is my home?* ed. Stanford Research Institute (Proceedings of a conference at the closing of State Mental Hospitals), pp. 141–50.

49. Serban, G.; Gidynski, C. B.; and Zimmerman, A. 1975. The role of informants in community oriented mental health programs for schizophrenics. *Diseases of the Nervous System* 36:215–19.

50. Shader, R. I. 1976. Discussion: Sources of variance in studies of drugs and other therapies. In *Evaluation of psychological therapies*, ed. K. Spitzer (Baltimore: Johns Hopkins University Press).

51. Spohn, H. E.; Lacoursiere, R. B.; Thompson, K.; and Coyne, L. 1977. Phenothiazine effects on psychological dysfunction in chronic schizophrenics. *Archives of General Psychiatry* 34:633–44.

52. Weinstein, A. S., and Patton, R. E. 1970. Trends in "chronicity" in the New York State mental hospitals. *American Journal of Public Health* 60:1071–80.

53. Wender, P. H.; Rosenthal, D.; Rainer, J. D.; Greenhill, L.; and Sarlin, M. B. 1977. Schizophrenics' adopting parents. *Archives of General Psychiatry* 34:777–84.

54. Wilder, J. F. 1972. The "dumping" syndrome; Causes and treatment. *American Journal of Psychiatry* 128:1445–49.

55. Wing, J. K. 1977. The social context of schizophrenia. Institute of Psychiatry, London. Presented to American Psychiatric Association, May 1977.

56. World Health Organization. 1975. *Schizophrenia. A Multinational Study* (Geneva: World Health Organization Press).

57. Zwerling, I. 1977. Community-based treatment of chronic psychotic patients. In *Long-term treatments of psychotic states*, C. Chiland and P. Bequart (New York: Human Sciences Press).

58. Zwerling, I., and Wilder, J. F. 1964. An evaluation of the applicability of the day hospital in treatment of acutely disturbed patients. *Israel Annals of Psychiatry and Related Disciplines* 2:162–85.

Chapter 14

THE PROGNOSIS OF SCHIZOPHRENIA

John S. Strauss, M.D. and William T. Carpenter, Jr., M.D.

Introduction

Determining prognosis has always been considered an important aspect of understanding any disorder. Prognosis is significant not only for such practical purposes as informing the patient and his relatives about the likelihood of recovery or of prolonged disorder, but also for providing a baseline expectation against which treatment effectiveness can be gauged. For many, such as Robins and Guze (77), who believe that diagnosis should indicate the natural history associated with a disorder, prognosis is also a key aspect of diagnostic concepts.

But it has been difficult to achieve a clear picture of the prognosis of schizophrenia. The introduction to the corresponding chapter of this volume ten years ago noted that very little had been learned over the previous decade about prognosis and outcome (47). In another publication appearing about the same time, Stromgren (103) reached a similar conclusion. Now, ten years later, it is still not possible to predict definitively the outcome of a person with schizophrenia; nevertheless, over this period much has been learned about the prognosis of this disorder. This knowledge has been of two kinds: a growing and sometimes discouraging appreciation of the complexity of prognostic processes, and a beginning understanding of the patterns that might characterize these processes. In this review we shall describe these advances.

Recent Methodological Progress

Most of the advances of the last decade in understanding prognosis are the result of improved research methods. Past reviews have decried methodological faults of the earlier outcome studies, including inadequate diagnostic procedures, failure to define outcome criteria, and incomplete description of demographic characteristics. Because of these shortcomings it had been difficult to compare results across studies or to evaluate conflicting findings.

These problems also had many ramifications outside of the study of prognosis itself. Investigations of treatment effectiveness were often marred by failure to evaluate and control key prognostic characteristics of the patients involved. It was not possible to determine accurately whether a treatment was particularly effective if the prognosis of the patient groups without the treatment had not been established. For example, one statement frequently seen in the treatment literature was that patients who received treatment early in their disorder had a better response. Such a statement indicated a failure to recognize the fact that a major predictor of outcome in schizophrenia is prior duration of illness. Patients with a shorter previous duration of disorder have better prognosis, generally speaking, no matter what treatment is given, or even if no treatment is given.

Another criticism of prognostic studies in the past has been that most were carried out retrospectively rather than prospectively. Retrospective studies provide clues to prognostic patterns, but they involve numerous problems of bias, such as retrospective falsification. They are also marred by the unavailability of important data from the early stages of illness. In the past ten years a number of prospective studies have been carried out.*

Given both the importance of prognosis and the limits of earlier outcome research, methodological improvements developed in the past several years are especially significant. Instruments such as structured interviews and rating scales for data collection have been devised to provide increased reliability in assessing prognostic, diagnostic, and outcome variables.† Although not appearing dramatic, the development of such basic psychiatric yardsticks for assessing clinically relevant characteristics has had the profound effect of allowing comparisons of findings and clarification of discrepancies across studies. Through use of such methods, for example, it has been possible to evaluate different aspects of outcome function (85,94) to compare outcomes of patients designated as schizophrenic by various diagnostic criteria (39,88,95) to show that different informants provide different kinds of information about patient function (46,98), and to detect certain types of bias, as in the study by Harty and Horwitz (38) which suggested that therapists overestimate patients' improvement.

Besides the increasing availability of various reliable data-collection techniques, another important methodological advance has been the development of statistical approaches to deal with special technical problems and to determine the relationships among the variables assessed in prognostic studies. For example, prospective study designs face the probable loss of subjects from the initial sample over time. While not completely satisfactory, techniques such as life table analysis (110) and reverse cohort analysis (62) are promising approaches to solving such problems.

---

* See references 1, 4, 17, 39, 41, 85, 87, 97, 102, and 114.
† See references 25, 50, 98, 109, and 114.

Several statistical approaches now exist that have assisted in understanding relationships among the many variables involved in prognostic studies. These methods include multiple regression (17,96), path analysis that permits analysis of the contribution made by variables occurring sequentially over time (11), and stratification analysis (26). This last technique recognizes that many characteristics may have different predictive values at different levels. For example, it has been shown that in medical illness, blood pressure within a rather wide range has minimal utility for predicting later coronary heart disease. However, above a certain level the prognostic importance of this variable increases considerably. Recognizing these different "strata" permits more accurate understanding of the relationships between predictors and outcome variables.

Recent Progress in Understanding Prognosis

It has been said that for every problem there is an answer that is clear, concise, simple—and wrong. It is no longer possible to claim that there is a concise, simple way to describe the prognosis of schizophrenia. In fact, increasingly, schizophrenia is seen not as a single pathological entity with a uniform outcome, but as a syndrome probably with multiple determinants, a wide range of possible outcomes, and many characteristics of prognostic importance.

Recognizing this complexity is already an important advance, in spite of the fact that it renders confusing a topic sometimes considered simple in the past. But there are also more positive advances that have been made in the study of prognosis. These are best described under six headings: (1) the probabilistic nature of prognostic statements about schizophrenia; (2) the several aspects of outcome in schizophrenia; (3) the wide range and variation of outcome; (4) stages in the longitudinal pattern or "course" of disorder; (5) overlap of outcome in schizophrenia with outcome in other disorders; and (6) the several characteristics useful as predictors of outcome.

THE PROBABILISTIC NATURE OF PROGNOSTIC STATEMENTS

For many clinicians and investigators who do not specialize in this area, prognosis sometimes appears to be absolute and fatalistic. However, with schizophrenia, as in any type of disorder, a definitive statement about outcome in the individual case is impossible. Some patients recover from illnesses that are supposedly fatal. Other patients with supposedly benign conditions may develop complications and die. In schizophrenia, too, prognosis is often problematic. Ever since Kraepelin described the poor prognosis of dementia praecox and then noted that some patients recovered, theories about prognosis in schizophrenia have had to reconcile apparently contradictory findings.

The recognition of the probabilistic nature of predicting outcome in schizophrenia deals with these conflicting findings by emphasizing how misleading is the question, What is the prognosis of schizophrenia? The more accurate questions are, What is the range of possible outcomes in schizophrenia, and what factors are important in determining where in this range a particular individual is likely to be? This restatement of the prognosis question provides a more realistic basis than the absolute view for understanding the processes involved.

This view also suggests that deteriorating course should not be considered an essential feature of schizophrenia. Previously some students of this disorder postulated that recovery meant schizophrenia was incorrectly diagnosed (48,54). While this view reinforced Langfeldt's important concept of a variable outcome disorder, schizophreniform psychosis, in contrast to a poor outcome disorder, true schizophrenia (52), recent evidence suggests that no highly specific relationships between symptom type and outcome have been found to support such a dichotomy.*

CHARACTERISTICS OF OUTCOME IN SCHIZOPHRENIA

One of the major advances in knowledge about the prognosis of schizophrenia has been an improved understanding of the characteristics of outcome. Although Kraepelin had defined various "end states" from the time schizophrenia (dementia praecox) was first described, many subsequent studies have classified outcome only in global quantitative terms, such as the four levels: deterioration, moderate impairment, improvement, and recovery. Such global estimates of outcome have the advantage of using the clinician's capacity to integrate all available data regarding the patient. However, these terms are rarely defined adequately and almost never subjected to reliability assessment.

In the past ten years several studies have showed that no single outcome measure is as informative as the consideration of several aspects of outcome in schizophrenia (46,85,94). The basis for this conclusion is the repeated finding that there is only a moderate level of correlation among various aspects of outcome functioning. Readmission rates or duration of hospital stay have often been used as the only measure of outcome in comparative treatment studies earlier in this past decade. This information is easily obtained, reliably judged, and readily validated. However, even this measure, because of its limited correlation with other outcome characteristics, is inadequate for the task of accurately reflecting the outcome of schizophrenia.

For understanding the entire outcome state, four relatively independent characteristics appear to be particularly important. These are: duration of hospitalization, severity of symptomatology, level of social relations function, and level of work function. Failure to consider each of

* See references 14, 39, 87, 95, and 115.

these characteristics can readily lead to misperception of outcome functioning. Since the correlation among these variables is limited, outcome measurement of readmission, for example, tells about readmission, but not necessarily about levels of social relationships or work function.

There are other aspects of outcome also of considerable practical as well as theoretical importance. For example, Rodnick et al. (78) have studied recovery of mothering function in women who have experienced schizophrenic episodes. Death as an outcome also must not be ignored. Babigian and Odoroff (9) noted, for example, that early death from all causes is more common in schizophrenia than in a comparison group of individuals. Some, but apparently not all, of this increased death rate is a result of increased incidence of suicide among schizophrenics (56, 105).

RANGE OF OUTCOME

The range of outcomes in schizophrenia is wide, depending to some extent at least on the diagnostic criteria used. Elsewhere in this volume (chapter 8) the considerable differences in the current diagnostic approaches to schizophrenia are described. Obviously diagnostic systems, in which the diagnosis of schizophrenia is changed if the patient recovers, automatically restrict the range of outcomes possible for the disorder as conceptualized by those approaches.

But other diagnostic criteria also influence the range of outcomes likely in the patients they include as schizophrenic. To the extent that prognostic variables based on previous history of functioning, such as established duration of illness, are included as diagnostic criteria, the range of outcomes likely in a given diagnostic system is diminished. It is, in fact, the inclusion of such prognostic variables as diagnostic criteria that influences the range of outcomes likely in patients designated as schizophrenic.

Attempts have been made to use certain symptoms as diagnostic criteria to identify so-called nuclear schizophrenia with poor prognosis. A common error in the past has been the assumption that nuclear schizophrenia (as defined by highly discriminating symptom criteria) is synonymous with process schizophrenia (defined by premorbid adjustment and/or chronic course of illness). Methodological advances have permitted symptom and premorbid functioning criteria to be carefully separated, and recent studies have demonstrated that stringent symptom criteria are useful for reliable diagnosis but not for establishing prognosis. Patients designated as schizophrenic by narrow symptom criteria, such as those of Schneider and Langfeldt, have about the same outcome as patients designated schizophrenic by broader symptom criteria, such as those of the Diagnostic and Statistical Manual of Psychiatric Disorders II (DSM-II) (39,63).

Given the various approaches to diagnosing schizophrenia and measuring outcome, it is not surprising that considerable disagreement remains regarding the distribution pattern of outcome in schizophrenia. Many studies using first-admission patients have suggested that about one-third of the patients recover, one-third remain at some level of disability, and about one-third have a grave prognosis (15,43,95). Other studies, such as those by Silverstein and Harrow (87), Astrachan et al. (5), and Soskis et al. (90), have suggested that schizophrenic patients often remain severely symptomatic over an extended follow-up period. Since all these studies have used structured evaluation techniques and carefully defined diagnostic and outcome criteria, they reflect important methodological progress. However, to resolve the contradictions generated by these studies, it will be necessary for several research groups to evaluate routinely nondiagnostic prognostic variables and to use a common set of outcome and diagnostic criteria.

COURSE OF DISORDER

In contrast to outcome, which generally refers to a particular moment in some period following an episode of illness, "course of disorder" implies the pattern by which the disorder unfolds or resolves over time. Measuring "outcome" is particularly useful when studying large numbers of patients, and when detailed assessment of course is impractical. In such outcome studies it is assumed that idiosyncratic time-related findings from individual patients will be canceled out by data from a large number of subjects. However, for many purposes, and especially when few patients are involved, only course assessment can fairly reflect the progress of disorder. To understand the course of individual patients requires continuous monitoring over time.

There has been an increasing trend over the past twenty years to focus on patterns of hospitalization as a criterion for evaluating course in schizophrenia. Such a criterion provides readily available data in many centers and therefore is particularly appealing. However, it excludes social functioning and intrapsychic variables. For that reason studies using this criterion must be interpreted with care, especially since current treatment practices are oriented to prevent or shorten hospital stay, sometimes with limited assessment of the impact of such decisions on the quality of life or the capacity for functioning of nonhospitalized schizophrenic patients.

But some studies have evaluated several measures of function to investigate the course of schizophrenia. One group of these has attempted to plot course of disorder by carrying out occasional serial evaluations over an extended period of time to answer the question, Is the evolution of schizophrenic disorder, when followed over a short period, valuable for predicting long-term outcome? It has been suggested, for example, that schizophrenia evolves in such a way that following patients for one or two years may give a very poor estimate of eventual outcome. There is now evidence suggesting that one-year and two-year levels of function are actually very good indicators of longer-term (five to fifteen years) outcome (3,97). Although the consistency of outcome over extended periods of time appears to be true in group statistics, for individual cases such continuity is not always found. Manfred Bleuler (12) has followed 208 patients over four decades. He noted that the course of disorder generally is defined by five years with little unexpected change thereafter. However, he has also shown that patients who have been severely disordered for many years may recover, at least partially, later in life. These observations have been both questioned (28) and supported (6). In any case, they serve as ample reminder that we have little reason to be fatalistic regarding the final outcome in individual patients, even when there is reason to consider the prognosis to be guarded.

Current investigative trends are moving away from long-term evaluation of course in schizophrenia. This trend may be explained by greater impatience among today's clinical scientists, but it is probably more a result of improved methods for intensive longitudinal research on short-term changes, increasingly interesting findings about short-term course, and the increasing demand that follow-up studies be prospective, together with the logistical problems associated with the fact that neither patients nor research clinicians tend to stay within the same institutional framework for the ten to thirty years necessary for long-term longitudinal study.

The reawakening of interest in short-term study of course has focused especially on the processes of decompensation and recovery. For example, Wittenbotn (112) has shown differential patterns of symptom change. Huber et al. (43) have shown a dissociation between "characteristic symptoms" of schizophrenia (reversible) and defect symptoms, such as withdrawal and flatness of affect, which tend to persist. In still more detailed studies, Kayton (45) and Sacks et al. (82) have described phases of recovery from schizophrenia. It appears from these and related investigations that patients recovering from schizophrenic episodes may follow several qualitatively different patterns of recovery in which thought disorder diminishes and perceptual and cognitive connections with consensually defined reality are reestablished. The patterns described include those patients who experienced a stage of depression following a psychotic episode, those who contrast in terms of the dimension integration/sealing over, and those who pass through a series of regular steps in recovery from psychosis.

A postpsychotic depressive state may be one crucial stage marking the short-term course of many patients. This state complicates adjustment after hospital discharge and causes significant treatment problems. The characteristics of this syndrome have been reviewed (59) and include apathy, lack of motivation, depression, and a sense of emptiness and hopelessness following remission of psychotic symptoms. The relationship between the affective component (depression) and the cognitive (delusional) and perceptual (hallucinations) manifestations that might be revealed by more intensive study of these processes suggests that this syndrome is a particularly important focus for further investigation. Roth (81) and others (58) have already carried out preliminary work in this area.

Another important aspect of the course of disorder that can be readily studied over a short time is the differentiation of styles of recovery. This area can be readily pursued with laboratory-based procedures, such as average evoked-response patterns to flashing lights (51), or with the study of descriptive attributes, such as integration and sealing over. In the integrative style, the psychotic episode is given perspective within the individual's life; in sealing over, denial is prominent, and psychotic experiences are "forgotten." Studies of these two styles of recovery are only beginning to be carried out in a systematic fashion, but they may have important therapeutic and prognostic implications (55,60,65).

Finally, Docherty et al. (23) have investigated sequential stages through which patients pass during periods of decompensation and recovery. He found that six such stages could be described: integration, overextension, restricted consciousness, disinhibition (prepsychosis), psychotic disorganization, and psychotic organization.

It seems likely that further clarification of the types of microprocess in the evolution of schizophrenia, as in the studies described in this section, will provide a major increment to the understanding of prognosis in this disorder.

COMPARISON OF OUTCOME IN SCHIZOPHRENIA WITH OTHER PSYCHIATRIC DISORDERS

Outcome differences between schizophrenia and other disorders are important for two major reasons. First, the more that diagnostic groups differ in their outcomes, the more validity there is in viewing them as distinctive disorders. Second, the more similarity of outcome there is across diagnostic groups, the more likely it is that variables other than diagnostic characteristics represent the key prognostic factors.

Surprisingly, very few careful investigations directly comparing the outcome of different diagnostic groups have been carried out. Perhaps diagnostic categories have seemed so separate that such comparisons appeared irrelevant. Recently, as part of the International Pilot Study of Schizophrenia (IPSS), such comparisons have been made (115). Findings from the IPSS suggested that outcome in schizophrenia is in fact somewhat worse than outcome in other types of disorder, but that there is significant overlap of outcome across various diagnostic categories. As part of the IPSS, we assessed the outcome of various domestic groups in the Washington center, using an outcome scale of demonstrated reliability (95). The findings were essentially the same as those for the entire IPSS sample, schizophrenics having somewhat worse outcome than the other diagnostic groups, but with considerable overlap between groups. Sampling methods in these studies were such that these findings must be considered tentative. If replicated, however, a primary implication of these results is that even major diagnostic classes have some, but limited, prognostic validity.

To resolve this issue more definitively, more representative patient samples will be required. Sampling is critical, because course and outcome vary greatly as a function of many nondiagnostic characteristics of patients. For example, if the patient group is mixed in terms of previous duration of symptoms, the outcome in schizophrenia will be worse than outcome in affective disorders. On the other hand, if first-episode schizophrenic patients are selected, then outcome is more heterogeneous and not as readily distinguishable from other major psychiatric disorders.

Besides the more general considerations, the prognosis of specific diagnostic subtypes has also been evaluated. Literature in the past has often suggested that of the traditional subtypes, catatonics have better outcome than other schizophrenic patients. Abrams and Taylor (2) and Morrison (64) have produced further evidence to support this claim. However, previous history characteristics of the catatonic patients may have been the major factor determining their results. A study by Guggenheim and Babigian (35) suggested that catatonics do not have a superior prognosis. However, these investigators utilized diagnoses from a psychiatric case register in which operational criteria had not been used.

An alternative to the traditional subtype categories has been offered by Leonhard, who described in detail a large number of subtypes of (presumed) chronic schizophrenia (54). In utilizing this system, Astrup (7) has suggested that the criteria defined by Leonhard do in fact define subtypes of schizophrenia, each of which has a relatively distinctive and homogeneous outcome. However, methodological difficulties involved in studies using Leonhard's criteria, such as failure in some instances to establish their reliability or failure in others to use a prospective research design, prevent these findings from being definitive. Furthermore, the complexity of using so many descriptive subgroups restricts their clinical applicability.

At the moment one major diagnostic subdivision seems compelling prognostically: the outcome of acute, good premorbid schizophrenia is remarkably better than the outcome of chronic, poor premorbid schizophrenia. But this prognostic difference is at least partly a function of using diagnostic characteristics other than symptoms. The prognostic role of these nonsymptom characteristics will be described next.

PREDICTORS OF OUTCOME

Many characteristics have been considered to be important prognostically in schizophrenia. Some of those most commonly found to be of predictive value have been described in reviews by Vaillant (107) and Stephens (91). These reviewers noted that premorbid and illness onset variables were of more prognostic significance than symptom variables. For example, characteristics such as poor social adjustment prior to the occurrence of psychosis and insidious onset of illness without precipitating stresses identified poor-prognosis schizophrenia.

In more recent studies the prognostic importance of such characteristics has been confirmed. Prior length of disorder, especially if associated with lengthy hospitalization, may be one of the most powerful predictors of outcome (73,96). The most consistent variable of prognostic importance is premorbid social relations functioning. Data on this fact from studies such as those carried out by Gittelman-Klein and Klein (29), Longabaugh and Eldred (57), and Strauss and Carpenter (97) have been reviewed elsewhere (101).

One particular set of predictive measures—one that is weighted heavily on the variable of premorbid social relations function previously described—is the process-reactive dichotomy, "process" patients having poorer premorbid adjustment than "reactive" patients. Higgins (40) has reviewed the vast body of process-reactive literature, which reflects one of the most widely substantiated sets of prognostic findings in psychiatry. More recently an issue of *Schizophrenia Bulletin* (84) has been devoted to a thorough review of methods, concepts, and findings on the premorbid-adjustment component of this topic. Although many of the areas discussed in that issue are summarized in this chapter, a detailed review of various prognostic scales described in that series (50) is not feasible in this context. It is important to note here, however, the trend toward developing increasingly differentiated scales of premorbid adjustment. The scales constructed recently are derived from the earlier work of Phillips (72) and Wittman (113), but assess more specifically the levels of premorbid adjustment at various life stages. This addition may increase the predictive validity of these measures as well as clarify some of the major issues in understanding stages of change in function as precursors to the development of psychopathology and chronicity.

As noted earlier, prior duration of illness and social relations competence are crucial to prognosis, but other predictive characteristics have also been suggested. These include premorbid work function (15,96), acuteness of onset, presence of confusion, family history of affective illness, depression, precipitating factors, concern with death (107), marital status, IQ, and absence of emotional blunting (91). Although each of these variables has been prognostically valuable, they do not show the consistent potency demonstrated for the variables, previous duration of illness and premorbid social adjustment.

Several studies have shown that symptoms viewed cross-sectionally have limited prognostic value (8,61,66,86). Symptoms considered characteristic of schizophrenia signify that a patient group is likely to have somewhat greater impairment in outcome functioning than a group of affectively ill patients, but there is considerable variation in the outcome of patients in either case (19). The prognostic value of groups of symptoms as diagnostic criteria does not appear to improve considerably if different sets of schizophrenic symptoms are considered (39). Even time-honored prognostically valuable symptoms such as anxiety and depression bode well for the schizophrenic only when contrasted with a case of established chronicity and restricted affective expression: they do not help define prognosis among early cases (19).

About other prognostic characteristics, the data are more conflicting. While Cancro (17) has suggested that thinking disorder is indicative of poor prognosis, the work of Reed (75) and Harrow et al. (37) suggests that this is not the case. Low IQ, especially low-performance IQ, may be indicative of poor prognosis (31), but the data on this variable are incomplete.

There are conflicting findings regarding the prognostic relevance of demographic characteristics. Although some studies suggest that low social class is associated with poor outcome (70,106), others suggest this is not the case (68). Although at least one study suggests that males have worse outcome than females, this finding may be an artifact, as suggested by the work of Brodsky (13), which shows the difficulties of assessing impairment of outcome functioning of housewives. The problem of assessment of functioning may cause housewives to be judged as functioning more adequately than they would be if engaged in a paid occupation. Although marital status has been suggested as another demographic characteristic with prognostic value, this finding may be a result primarily of correlation between marital status and premorbid social function (30,49).

Recently a number of investigations have attempted to discover biological and psychophysiological predictors of outcome in schizophrenia. Some positive results have been obtained, but in most instances too recenty to be replicated. Cancro et al. (18) have evaluated reaction time and found some correlation between prolonged reaction time and prognosis. Unfortunately this study involves a relatively small sample (N = 30), so that the findings are somewhat tentative. Autonomic arousal and abnormal electroencephalogram patterns have been tentatively related to prognosis (44,104).

An attempt to define genetic markers associated with outcome of illness has only recently begun (77). Other biological characteristics have been investigated as possible prognostic indicators, including eye tracking (42) and platelet monoamine oxidase (21). Interpretation of findings from these studies must await further development and replication.

The Patient's Environment Following Onset of Illness

The preceding characteristics of prognostic value are features of the individual either before the onset of his disorder or as part of the disorder itself. However, environmental factors (including treatment) also influence prognosis. In fact, Gurel and Lorei (36) have pointed out that any prognostic model for schizophrenia that does not consider the patient's environment following the onset of disorder is incomplete. For example, the patient's living situation following onset has considerable impact on outcome. The extreme example of this impact is demonstrated by the literature on institutionalism (10,22,32,111), which indicates the degree to which a prolonged stay at institutions serving primarily as psychiatric warehouses promotes deterioration in the form of withdrawal and loss of skills and initiative.

Diagnostic labeling is another factor with prognostic implications that is an aspect of the patient's environment after the onset of disorder. Scheff (83) and others have suggested that the process of labeling the patient as schizophrenic in itself sets up a chain of expectations that influences the way the patient is treated not only by medical personnel, but by families, employers, and others. It is believed that these expectations and behaviors in the case of schizophrenia contribute to chronicity and deterioration. There is much controversy about this view (34), and final evidence is not conclusive on either side. Perhaps one of the major problems with labeling theory, and many of its refutations, is the tendency to overstate the arguments by suggesting that labeling primarily accounts for psychiatric disorder, on the one hand, or that it has no impact, on the other. It seems likely that both arguments are inaccurate. The question may be not whether labeling causes schizophrenia but whether having a psychotic experience classified as schizophrenia alters the responses of a patient's environment in a deleterious manner. There are many reasons to conclude that it does. Recent work by Rosenhan (80) suggests that the harmful responses of the patient's social network are often subtle and unwitting. A poignant statement recently published in the *Schizophrenia Bulletin* (71) by a medical student diagnosed as schizophrenic provides further valuable description of how the diagnosis of schizophrenia might have repercussions on one so labeled. From these reports it appears likely that the labeling process may be one among many environmental factors promoting chronicity and interfering with recovery.

The family environment is another factor that partially determines course of illness. Fascinating research in this area has been carried out during this decade. Freeman and Simmons's early work (27) indicated that patients' bizarre behavior—not inadequate instrumental performance or family rejection, as originally hypothesized—was an important immediate precipitant of rehospitalization. In more recent and more detailed studies of the impact of the family environment on course of disorder, Brown et al. (16) and Vaughn and Leff (108) conducted a particularly well-controlled series of investigations to evaluate the effect that personal relationships within the family have on the exacerbation of schizophrenia. After first noting that patients living alone were less likely to relapse, they found that "emotional expressiveness" in family members was a key factor associated with recurrence of schizophrenic symptoms. With further methodological refinement, these workers have shown that only certain kinds of emotional expression are associated with increased likelihood of exacerbation. Critical attitudes, hostility, and overprotectiveness by family (parents or spouse) are related to high relapse rates. Intrafamilial warmth, if not overintrusive, appears to decrease relapse vulnerability. The intrafamilial interaction variables were more important to relapse than whether or not antipsychotic medication was being used. These results are similar to less controlled findings reported earlier in Taiwan by Rin (76), who noted that in families with a better attitude, patients had a better outcome.

The improved accuracy in specifying what type of family communication is related to higher relapse rates is important because of a common belief that schizophrenics do poorly in any but a bland context. The work of Brown et al. (16) at first suggested that in families emotional expressiveness of any kind was deleterious to the course of a schizophrenic's disorder. From the later studies, however, it is now clear that only certain kinds of noxious expressiveness appear to have unfortunate prognostic implications. The findings of the institutional and family investigations have been interpreted as suggesting that following a schizophrenic episode the individual is in a state in which too little stimulation will cause "defect" symptoms, such as withdrawal and apathy, and too much, especially noxious, stimulation will contribute to a recurrence of the psychotic process.

Treatment

A comprehensive review of studies investigating the treatment of schizophrenia cannot be included in this chapter on prognosis. Nevertheless, custom to the contrary, prognosis cannot be discussed without considering the role of treatment in determining outcome. Because of the close relationship between understanding prognosis and treatment effects, however, a major problem is immediately encountered: how can the effects of treatment be teased apart from the effects of multiple prognostic and environmental factors?

One approach to this problem is to evaluate evidence of how the level of outcome in schizophrenia is changed by modern treatment. This apparently simple issue, surprisingly enough, has rarely been addressed. Treatment studies have tended to focus more on showing a statistically significant frequency of treatment impact rather than on evaluating the amount of effect. The overlap of various treatments given to all patients and the need to consider several types of outcome function make the question particularly difficult to answer.

These problems are augmented by the facts that customarily studies of prognosis do not evaluate comparative treatment, and treatment studies deal with nontreatment predictors either by failing to evaluate them carefully or by holding them constant. The problem of comparing the impact of prognostic and treatment variables is complicated still further by the fact that these variables often interact.

The work of Goldstein et al. (33) and a National Institute of Mental Health group (67) demonstrate that treatment effectiveness may actually depend on patients' subtype in terms of their premorbid status, and in this sense treatment effectiveness and premorbid status are inseparable. Leff and Wing (53) have noted that antipsychotic medications may be most helpful for schizophrenic patients who are in the mid-range prognostically. Clearly more studies dealing with prognostic and treatment variables are required—a series of investigations perhaps that would utilize certain basic measures of level of disorder and change, so that results from different premorbid function and treatment groups could be systematically compared.

Interaction of Characteristics Determining Prognosis

Having noted that several types of variables are partial predictors of outcome in schizophrenia, the next and obvious issue is, How do these variables combine to determine prognosis? Is the net effect of all the prognostic characteristics on an individual just the sum of the individual effects? Or, as with treatment and prognostic characteristics, does a more complex interaction determine key prognostic processes? For example, do some prognostic variables counteract others or have specific potentiating effects? Given the large number of variables identified as having prognostic significance, the number of possible interactions is practically infinite. Before treatment effects or other specific aspects of outcome prediction can be understood, it is clearly essential that a more focused attempt be made to deal with the obvious multivariate nature of the prognosis of schizophrenia.

The studies of Brown et al. (16), Leff and Wing (53), and Goldstein et al. (33), which evaluated interactions between environmental stimulation and outcome and between prognostic status, treatment, and outcome, can be viewed as important beginnings to investigating the interaction of three different outcome determinants; premorbid levels of adjustment, antipsychotic medication, and level of environmental stress following the schizophrenic episode. Another approach to understanding complex prognostic processes has been taken by Strauss and Carpenter (96), who have analyzed prognostic data to determine whether the various aspects of outcome have specific antecedents. Results of several analyses from follow-up studies (96,97,100) suggested the existence of several predictor-outcome processes. Previous level of social relations functioning was the best predictor of social relations functioning at follow-up. Previous level of occupational functioning was the best predictor of occupational functioning at follow-up. And prior duration of hospitalization was the best predictor of hospitalization at follow-up. Together, these findings, supported by other literature (e.g., reference 85) were interpreted as suggesting that basic prognostic processes consisted of several open-linked systems. Each of the separate processes was individually identifiable and yet related to the others. These findings provided support for the construction of a multiaxial diagnostic system in which these prognostic systems were component axes (93).

Other relationships among various prognostic variables have also been studied, although the findings have not been replicated and are therefore more open to question. Nuttall and Solomon (69), for example, have suggested that there is an interaction of various predictors with social class. The role of other demographic characteristics, such as age and sex, occasionally suggested as having prognostic importance, may someday also be established, perhaps in combinations—still to be discovered—with other prognostic variables. It may be just such undiscovered combinations that account for the erratic results obtained so far in studies of these variables.

Obviously the task of defining prognostic processes is just beginning. It is to be hoped that the next edition of this volume will be able to describe prognostic patterns more completely, including interactions not only between premorbid function variables and between these variables and treatment, but considering interactions with biological characteristics as well.

The Universality of Prognostic Processes: Cultural Factors

One issue that has been of paramount interest since dementia praecox was first defined by Kraepelin is the relationship of culture to manifest illness. Some aspects of this issue are discussed elsewhere in this volume, but its counterpart for prognosis also exists: namely, are prognostic processes culture-specific, or can they be shown to occur in diverse cultural settings? The methodological problems involved in answering this question are even greater than those involved in studying prognosis within a given culture. Nevertheless, several studies suggest that the most powerful prognostic factors do in fact transcend specific cultural environments.

Raman and Murphy (74) found that, although some culturally specific prognostic indicators seem to exist, one variable, work functioning, had significant predictive power for all groups evaluated from the multi-cultural population of Mauritius. The prognostic importance of this variable has also been demonstrated in European and American cultures. In studies of Norwegian and American patients, comparable prognostic factors have been identified by Stephens et al. (92). In the World Health Organization's International Pilot Study of Schizophrenia, it has been shown that several similar prognostic variables, including social isolation, are important in patients from the nine participating centers, which represent developed and developing countries in Europe, North and South America, Asia, and Africa (114). In a study comparing predictors of outcome in patients from Taiwan and the United States and using prognostic and outcome instruments of demonstrated reliability, it was found that major prognostic factors in a sample of American patients, social relations function, and occupational function were also found to operate in Taiwan (99). These data supported earlier findings by Rin (76). A study in Nigeria (25) showed that premorbid social functioning was an important prognostic characteristic, as it has proved to be in so many parts of the world.

Universality of Prognostic Processes across Diagnostic Groups

Are the same characteristics of prognostic value for many types of psychiatric disorder? Several studies evaluating predictors of outcome have been carried out to see whether these transcend specific diagnostic categories. Investigations by Bromet et al. (14) and Rosen et al. (79) suggested that predictors of outcome in schizophrenia, such as poor social functioning prior to onset of disorder, did not predict outcome in other types of psychopathology. The work of Strauss et al. (100), studying a heterogeneous group of first admissions, however, suggests that this is not the case. Other investigations have also indicated that prognostically significant variables in schizophrenia are important for various other diagnostic groups, including neuroses (89) and borderline patients (20).

Although comparability of prognostic variables across diagnostic groups is suggested by these studies, conflicting results exist, and the question whether prognostic factors transcend psychiatric disorders remains to be solved. This question is important because it suggests that certain prognostic processes may transcend diagnostic categories and require evaluation and perhaps treatment in many types of psychopathology. On the other hand, the demonstration of marked differences between predictors of outcome in schizophrenia and other types of psychiatric disorder would suggest the differences of prognostic and pathological processes involved in the various disorders.

Conclusions

During the past ten years understanding of prognosis in schizophrenia has moved away from predicting outcome in general terms and has begun to explore more systematically the specifics and the complexities involved. Increasing concern with methodological issues and a new generation of clinical research techniques have provided the basis for new information.

Although discoveries of the complexities involved have discouraged hope of finding simple answers, the work of many investigators has begun to define prognostic patterns and establish a broader conceptual basis for understanding. Perhaps the findings are best summarized as follows:

1. Schizophrenia is best viewed as having not just a "bad" or "good" prognosis, but a wide range of potential outcomes.
2. The outcome to be predicted is not a global state but is comprised of several somewhat independent areas of function. These include symptom severity, level of social relations function, level of work functioning, and need for hospitalization.
3. The range of outcomes in schizophrenia is considerable. Although the prognosis is often guarded, the range of possible outcomes extends apparently from complete recovery to severe deterioration and perhaps even contributing to early death. This wide range arises partly from the likelihood that schizophrenia is a syndrome comprised of a heterogeneous group of disorders and also from the number of predictors, not usually included as part of the diagnostic entity, that contribute to outcome.
4. The longitudinal pattern, or course, of schizophrenia is only beginning to be studied systematically with reliable techniques. It is too early to anticipate results, but further explorations of postpsychotic depression, integration and/or sealing over, and stages of recovery and remission seem likely to provide much valuable information about the nature and determinants of outcome.

5. Although there is a wide range of outcome in schizophrenia, statistically its prognosis compares unfavorably with that of many other psychiatric diagnoses. Prognosis in schizophrenia, however, is not established effectively by a diagnosis based on symptom criteria alone, regardless of their stringency. For the diagnosis of schizophrenia to have optimal predictive power, diagnostic criteria that may predict poor outcome for most disorders (e.g., duration of illness exceeding one year) must be included.

There are several nondiagnostic variables of prognostic importance. Most of these are related to functioning in the period prior to the psychiatric evaluation. They include previous duration of symptoms, previous level of social relationships, and previous level of work function. Environmental and treatment conditions occurring after the onset of diagnosable illness are also of prognostic importance.

It is beginning to appear that combinations of these variables may define consistent prognostic patterns. Combinations of characteristics that relate to withdrawal and understimulation, on the one hand, or to excessive stimulation, on the other, are suggested as having maximum prognostic impact. There also appear to be specific longitudinal prognostic processes—social relations function, work function, and symptom duration or length of institutionalization. Each of these processes, while related to the others, may have many specific determinants and require specific treatment.

Finally, to speculate on the prognosis of prognosis: over the next several years, with the growing sophistication in patient evaluation, sampling, and data analysis, there should be a considerable increase in the ability to predict outcome in the various types of disorder encompassed in the schizophrenic syndrome. Most probably this knowledge will be obtained through multidisciplinary investigations of prognostic processes, marked by collaboration among psychiatrists, developmental psychologists, neurobiologists, and sociologists.

BIBLIOGRAPHY

1. Abrams, R., and Taylor, M. A. 1973. First-rank symptoms, severity of illness, and treatment response in schizophrenia. *Comprehensive Psychiatry* 14:353–55.

2. Abrams, R., and Taylor, M. A. 1976. Catatonia: A prospective clinical study. *Archives of General Psychiatry* 33:579–81.

3. Achte, K. A., and Apo, M. 1967. Schizophrenic patients in 1950–1952 and 1957–1959: A comparative study. *Psychiatric Quarterly* 41:422–41.

4. Affleck, J. W.; Burns, J.; and Forrest, A. D. 1976. Long-term follow-up of schizophrenic patients in Edinburgh. *Acta Psychiatrica Scandinavica* 53:227–37.

5. Astrachan, B., et al. 1974. Symptomatic outcome in schizophrenia. *Archives of General Psychiatry* 31:155–60.

6. Astrup, C. 1974. Long-term prognosis of the functional psychoses. In *Biological mechanisms of schizophrenia and schizophrenia-like psychoses*, eds. H. Mitsuda and T. Fukuda (Tokyo: Igaku Shoin).

7. Astrup, C. 1975. Predicted and observed outcome in followed-up functional psychoses. *Biological Psychiatry* 10(3):323–28.

8. Astrup, C.; Dalgard, O. S.; and Holmboe, R. 1967. A prolonged follow-up of acute schizophrenic and schizophreniform psychoses. *Acta Psychiatrica Scandinavica* 43:432–43.

9. Babigian, H. M., and Odoroff, C. L. 1969. The mortality experience of a population with psychiatric illness. *American Journal of Psychiatry* 126(4):52–62.

10. Barton, R. 1959. *Institutional neurosis* (Bristol, Eng.: Wright).

11. Blalock, H. M. 1961. *Causal inferences in nonexperimental research* (Chapel Hill: University of North Carolina Press).

12. Bleuler, M. 1974. The long-term course of the schizophrenic psychoses. *Psychological Medicine* 4:244–54.

13. Brodsky, C. 1968. The social recovery of mentally ill housewives. *Family Process* 7(2):170–83.

14. Bromet, E.; Harrow, M.; and Kasl, S. 1974. Premorbid functioning and outcome in schizophrenics and nonschizophrenics. *Archives of General Psychiatry* 30:203–7.

15. Brown, G. W. 1966. Schizophrenia and social care. In *Institute of Psychiatry*, Maudsley Monograph no. 17, eds. G. W. Brown, M. Bone, B. Dalison, and J. K. Wing (London: Oxford University Press).

16. Brown, G. W.; Birley, J. L. T.; and Wing, J. K. 1972. The influence of family life on the course of schizophrenic disorders: A replication. *British Journal of Psychiatry* 121(562):241–58.

17. Cancro, R. 1969. Prospective prediction of hospital stay in schizophrenia. *Archives of General Psychiatry* 20:541–46.

18. Cancro, R.; Sutton, S.; Kerr, J.; et al. 1971. Reaction time and prognosis in acute schizophrenia. *Journal of Nervous and Mental Disease* 153:351–59.

19. Carpenter, W. T., Jr.; Bartko, J. J.; Strauss, J. S.; et al. 1976. Do symptoms really predict outcome? Presented at the Annual Meeting of the American Psychiatric Association, Miami, Florida, May 1976.

20. Carpenter, W. T., Jr.; Gunderson, J. G.; and Strauss, J. S. 1977. Considerations of the borderline syndrome: A longitudinal comparative study of borderline and schizophrenic patients. In *Borderline personality disorders, the concept, the syndrome, the patient*, ed. P. Hartocollis (New York: International Universities Press).

21. Carpenter, W. T., Jr.; Murphy, D. L.; and Wyatt, R. J. 1975. Platelet monoamine oxidase activity in acute schizophrenia. *American Journal of Psychiatry* 132:438–41.

22. Caudill, W. 1958. *The psychiatric hospital as a small society* (Cambridge: Harvard University Press).

23. Docherty, J. P.; Siris, S. G.; Marder, S. R.; et al. Stages of onset of schizophrenic psychosis. Presented at the 129th Annual Meeting of the American Psychiatric Association.

24. Endicott, J., and Spitzer, R. L. 1977. A diagnostic interview: The schedule for affective disorders and schizophrenia. Presented at the Annual Meeting of the American Psychiatric Association, Toronto, Ontario, 1977.

25. Erinosho, O. A. 1975. Sociopsychiatric attributes and therapeutic structures as predictors of posthospital performance—A study of two psychiatric centres in Nigeria. Unpublished thesis abstract, July 1975.

26. Feinstein, A. R. 1972. Clinical biostatistics. XV. The process of prognostic stratification. *Clinical Pharmacology and Therapeutics* 13(3):442–57.

27. Freeman, H. E., and Simmons, O. G. 1963. *The mental patient comes home* (New York: John Wiley).

28. Gabriel, E. 1974. Der langfristige Verlauf schizophrener Späterkrankungen im Vergleich mit Schizophrenien aller Lebensalter. [The long-term course of late-life schizophrenia compared to those of all ages.] *Psychiatrica Clinica* 7:172–80.

29. Gittelman-Klein, R., and Klein, D. 1969. Premorbid asocial adjustment and prognosis in schizophrenia. *Journal of Psychiatric Research* 7:35–53.

30. Gittelman-Klein, R., et al. 1968. Marital status as a prognostic indicator in schizophrenia. *Journal of Nervous and Mental Disease* 147(3):289–96.

31. Glick, I. D., and Sternberg, D. 1969. Performance IQ as predictor of hospital treatment outcome. *Comprehensive Psychiatry* 10(5):365–68.

32. Goffman, E. 1961. *Asylums*, (Garden City, N.Y.: Doubleday, Anchor).

33. Goldstein, M. J.; Judd, L. L.; and Rodnick, E. H. 1969. Psychophysiological and behavioral effects of phenothiazine administration in acute schizophrenics as a function of premorbid status. *Journal of Psychiatric Research* 6:271–87.

34. Gove, W. R. 1972. Labelling and mental illness: A critique. In *The labelling of deviance: Evaluating a perspective*, ed. W. R. Gove (New York: Halsted Press).

35. Guggenheim, F. G., and Babigian, H. M. 1974. Catatonic schizophrenia: Epidemiology and clinical course. *Journal of Nervous and Mental Disease* 158(4):291–305.

36. Gurel, L., and Lorei, T. W. 1972. Hospital and community ratings of psychopathology as predictors of employment and readmission. *Journal of Consulting and Clinical Psychology* 39(2):286–91.

37. Harrow, M.; Bromet, E.; and Quinlan, D. 1974. Predictors of posthospital adjustment in schizophrenia: Thought disorders and schizophrenic diagnosis. *Journal of Nervous and Mental Disease* 158(1):25–36.

38. Harty, M., and Horwitz, L. 1976. Therapeutic outcome as rated by patients, therapists, and judges. *Archives of General Psychiatry* 33:957–61.

39. Hawk, A. B.; Carpenter, W. T., Jr.; and Strauss, J. S. 1975. Diagnostic criteria and 5-year outcome in schizophrenia: A report from the international pilot study of schizophrenia. *Archives of General Psychiatry* 32:343–47.

40. Higgins, J. 1969. Process-reactive schizophrenia: Recent developments. *Journal of Nervous and Mental Disease* 149:450–72.

41. Hogarty, G.; Goldberg, S. C.; and Schooler, N. R. 1974. Drug and sociotherapy in the aftercare of schizophrenic patients. III. Adjustment of nonrelapsed patients. *Archives of General Psychiatry* 31:609–18.

42. Holzman, P. S.; Levy, D. L.; and Proctor, L. R. 1976. Smooth pursuit eye movements, attention, and schizophrenia. *Archives of General Psychiatry* 33:1415–20.

43. Huber, G.; Gross, G.; and Schuttler, R. 1975. A long-term follow-up study of schizophrenia: Psychiatric course of illness and prognosis. *Acta Psychiatrica Scandinavica* 52:49–57.

44. Itil, T. M.; Marasa, J.; Saletu, B.; et al. 1975. Computerized EEG: Predictor of outcome in schizophrenia. *Journal of Nervous and Mental Disease* 160(2):188–203.

45. Kayton, L. 1973. Good outcome in young adult schizophrenia. *Archives of General Psychiatry* 29:103–10.

46. Kenniston, K.; Boltax, S.; and Almond, R. 1971. Multiple criteria of treatment outcome. *Journal of Psychiatric Research* 8:107–18.

47. Kind, H. 1969. Prognosis. In *The schizophrenic syndrome*, eds. L. Bellak and L. Loeb (New York: Grune & Stratton).

48. Kleist, K. 1960. Schizophrenic symptoms and cerebral pathology. *Journal of Mental Science* 106:246–53.

49. Klorman, R.; Strauss, J. S.; and Kokes, R. F. 1977. The relationship of demographic and diagnostic factors to premorbid adjustment. *Schizophrenia Bulletin* 3(2):214–25.

50. Kokes, R. F.; Strauss, J. S.; and Klorman, R. 1977. Measuring premorbid adjustment: The instruments and their development. *Schizophrenia Bulletin* 3(2):186–213.

51. Landau, S. G.; Buchsbaum, M. S.; Carpenter, W. T., Jr.; et al. 1975. Schizophrenia and stimulus intensity control. *Archives of General Psychiatry* 32:1239–45.

52. Langfeldt, G. 1969. Schizophrenia: Diagnosis and prognosis. *Behavioral Science* 14(3):173–182.

53. Leff, J. P., and Wing, J. K. 1971. Trial of maintenance therapy in schizophrenia. *British Medical Journal* 3:599–604.

54. Leonhard, K. 1966. The question of prognosis in schizophrenia. *International Journal of Psychiatry* 2:633–35.

55. Levy, S. T.; McGlashan, T. H.; and Carpenter, W. T., Jr. Integration and sealing over as recovery styles from acute psychosis. *Journal of Nervous and Mental Disease* 161(5):307–12.

56. Lindelius, R., ed. 1970. A study of schizophrenia. *Acta Psychiatrica Scandinavica* supp. 216.

57. Longabaugh, R., and Eldred, S. H. 1973. Premorbid adjustments, schizoid personality, and onset of illness as predictors of post-hospitalization functioning. *Journal of Psychiatric Research* 10:19–29.

58. McGlashan, T. H., and Carpenter, W. T., Jr. 1976. An investigation of the post-psychotic depressive syndrome. *American Journal of Psychiatry* 133:14–19.

59. McGlashan, T. H., and Carpenter, W. T., Jr. 1976. Post-psychotic depression in schizophrenia. *Archives of General Psychiatry* 33:231–39.

60. McGlashan, T. H., and Levy, S. T. 1977. Sealing-over in a therapeutic community. *Psychiatry* 40:55–65.

61. Mandelbrote, B. M., and Trick, K. L. K. 1970. Social and clinical factors in the outcome of schizophrenia. *Acta Psychiatrica Scandinavica* 46:24–34.

62. May, P, R. A.; Tuma, A. H.; and Dixon, W. J. 1976. Schizophrenia—A follow-up study of results of treatment. I. Design and other problems. *Archives of General Psychiatry* 33:474–78.

63. Mellor, C. S. 1970. First-rank symptoms of schizophrenia. *British Journal of Psychiatry* 17:15–23.

64. Morrison, J. R. 1974. Catatonia: Prediction of outcome. *Comprehensive Psychiatry* 15(4):317–24.

65. Mosher, L. R.; Menn, A.; and Matthews, S. 1975. Soteria: Evaluation of a home-based treatment for schizophrenia. *American Journal of Orthopsychiatry* 45:455–67.

66. Muller, C., and Ciompi, L. 1976. The relationship between anamnestic factors and the course of schizophrenia. *Comprehensive Psychiatry* 17(3):387–93.

67. National Institute of Mental Health Psychopharmacology Research Branch Collaborative Study Group. 1968. Short-term improvement in schizophrenia: The contribution of background factors. *American Journal of Psychiatry* 124:60–69.

68. Niskanen, P., and Achte, K. A. 1973. Outcome similar in schizophrenia in upper and lower classes. *Psychiatria Fennica* 30–31.

69. Nuttall, R. L., and Solomon, L. F. 1965. Factorial structure and prognostic significance of premorbid adjustment in schizophrenia. *Journal of Consulting Psychology* 29(4):362–72.

70. Nuttall, R. L., and Solomon, L. F. 1970. Prognosis in schizophrenia: The role of premorbid social class and demographic factors. *Behavioral Science* 15:255–64.

71. On being diagnosed schizophrenic. 1977. *Schizophrenia Bulletin* 3.4.

72. Phillips, L. 1953. Case history data and prognosis in schizophrenia. *Journal of Nervous and Mental Disease* 117:515–25.

73. Pokorny, A. D.; Thornby, J.; and Kaplan, H. B. 1976. Prediction of chronicity in psychiatric patients. *Archives of General Psychiatry* 33:932–37.

74. Raman, A. C., and Murphy, H. B. M. 1972. Failure of traditional prognostic indicators in Afro-Asian psychotics: Results of a long-term follow-up survey. *Journal of Nervous and Mental Disease* 154(4):238–47.

75. Reed, J. L. 1971. The relationship between results on some psychological tests and outcome in schizophrenia. *Acta Psychiatrica Scandinavica* 47:223:29.

76. Rin, H. 1967. A family study of Chinese schizophrenic patients: Loss of parents, sibling rank, parental attitude, and short-term prognosis. *Journal of the Formosan Medical Association* 66(9):461–69.

77. Robins, E., and Guze, S. 1970. Establishment of diagnostic validity in psychiatric illness. *American Journal of Psychiatry* 126:107–11.

78. Rodnick, E. H., and Goldstein, M. J. 1974. Premorbid adjustment and the recovery of mothering function in acute schizophrenic women. *Journal of Abnormal Psychology* 83(6):623–28.

79. Rosen, B.; Klein, D. F.; Levenstein, S.; et al. 1969. Social competence and post-hospital outcome among schizophrenic and nonschizophrenic psychiatric patients. *Journal of Abnormal Psychology* 74(3):401–4.

80. Rosenhan, D. L. 1973. On being sane in insane places. *Science* 179:250–57.

81. Roth, S. 1970. The seemingly ubiquitous depression following acute schizophrenic episodes, a neglected area of clinical discussion. *American Journal of Psychiatry* 127:51–58.

82. Sacks, M.; Carpenter, W. T., Jr.; and Strauss, J. S. 1974. Recovery from delusions: Three phases documented by patients' interpretation of research procedures. *Archives of General Psychiatry* 30(1):117–20.

83. Scheff, T. J. 1974. The labelling theory of mental illness. *American Sociological Review* 39: 444–52.

84. *Schizophrenia Bulletin* 3(2). 1977.

85. Schwartz, C. C.; Myers, J. K.; and Astrachan, B. M. 1976. Concordance of multiple assessments of outcome of schizophrenia. *Archives of General Psychiatry* 32:1221–27.

86. Serban, G. 1975. Mental status a poor predictor of readmission. *British Journal of Social and Clinical Psychology* 14:291–301.

87. Silverstein, M., and Harrow, M. 1976. Psychosis in the recovered schizophrenic. Presented at the Annual Meeting of the American Psychiatric Association, Miami, Florida, May 1976.

88. Silverstein, M., and Harrow, M. First-rank symptoms in the post-acute schizophrenic: A follow-up study. Unpublished manuscript.

89. Sims, A. 1975. Factors predictive of outcome in neurosis. *British Journal of Psychiatry* 127: 54–62.

90. Soskis, D. A.; Harrow, M.; and Detre, T. P. 1969. Long-term follow-up of schizophrenics admitted to a general hospital psychiatric ward. *Psychiatric Quarterly* 43(3):525–34.

91. Stephens, J. H. 1970. Long-term course and prognosis in schizophrenia. *Seminars in Psychiatry* 2(4):464–85.

92. Stephens, J. H.; Astrup, C.; and Mangrum, J. C. 1967. Prognosis in schizophrenia: Prognostic scales cross-validated in American and Norwegian patients. *Archives of General Psychiatry* 16: 693–98.

93. Strauss, J. S. 1975. A comprehensive approach to psychiatric diagnosis. *American Journal of Psychiatry* 132(11):1193–97.

94. Strauss, J. S., and Carpenter, W. T., Jr. 1972. Prediction of outcome in schizophrenia. I. Characteristics of outcome. *Archives of General Psychiatry* 27:739–46.

95. Strauss, J. S., and Carpenter, W. T., Jr. 1974. Characteristic symptoms and outcome in schizophrenia. *Archives of General Psychiatry* 30:429–34.

96. Strauss, J. S., and Carpenter, W. T., Jr. 1974. Prediction of outcome in schizophrenia. II. Relationships between predictor and outcome variables. *Archives of General Psychiatry* 31:37–42.

97. Strauss, J. S., and Carpenter, W. T., Jr. 1977. Prediction of outcome in schizophrenia. III. Five-year outcome and its predictors. A report from the International Pilot Study of Schizophrenia. *Archives of General Psychiatry* 34:159–63.

98. Strauss, J. S.; Carpenter, W. T., Jr.; and Nasrallah, A. 1978. How reliable is the psychiatric history? *Comprehensive Psychiatry* 19(3):213–19.

99. Strauss, J. S., and Chen, C. C. 1977. Cross-cultural predictors of outcome in schizophrenia. Presented at the annual meeting of the World Congress of Psychiatry, Honolulu, September 1977.

100. Strauss, J. S.; Kokes, R. F.; Carpenter, W. T., Jr.; et al. The course of schizophrenia as a developmental process. In *Nature of schizophrenia: New findings and future strategies*, eds. L. C. Wynne, R. L. Cromwell, and S. Matthysse (New York: John Wiley), forthcoming.

101. Strauss, J. S.; Kokes, R. F.; Klorman, R.; et al. 1977. The concept of premorbid adjustment. *Schizophrenia Bulletin* 3(2):182–85.

102. Strauss, J. S.; Kokes, R. F.; and Ritzler, B. A. 1976. Patterns of disorder in first admission psychiatric patients. Presented at the Annual Meeting of the American Psychiatric Association in Miami, Florida, May 1976.

103. Stromgren, E. 1961. Recent studies of prognosis and outcome in the mental disorders. In *Comparative epidemiology of the mental disorders*, eds. P. Hoch and J. Zubin (New York: Grune & Stratton).

104. Struve, F. A.; Becka, D. R.; and Klein, D. F. 1972. B-mitten EEG pattern and process and reactive schizophrenia. *Archives of General Psychiatry* 26:189–92.

105. Tsuang, M. T., and Winokur, G. 1977. A combined thirty-five year follow-up and family study of schizophrenia and primary affective disorders: Sample selection, methodology of field follow-up, and preliminary mortality rates. In *The origins and course of psychopathology*, eds. J. S. Strauss, H. M. Babigian, and M. Roff (New York: Plenum Press).

106. Turner, R. J. 1968. Class and mobility in schizophrenic outcome. *Psychiatric Quarterly* 42: 712–25.

107. Vaillant, G. E. 1962. The prediction of recovery in schizophrenia. *Journal of Nervous and Mental Disease* 135:534–43.

108. Vaughn, C. E., and Leff, J. P. 1976. The influence of family and social factors on the course of psychiatric illness: A comparison of schizophrenic and depressed neurotic patients. *British Journal of Psychiatry* 129:125–37.

109. Weissman, M. 1975. The assessment of social adjustment: A review of techniques. *Archives of General Psychiatry* 32:357–65.

110. Weissman, M. M. 1977. Controlled vs. naturalistic experiments: Application of the life table method. In *The origins and course of psychopathology*, eds. J. S. Strauss, H. M. Babigian, and M. Roff (New York: Plenum Press), pp. 7–22.

111. Wing, J. K., and Brown, G. W. 1970. *Institutionalism and schizophrenia* (Cambridge, Eng.: Cambridge University Press).

112. Wittenborn, J. R. 1977. Stability of symptom ratings for schizophrenic men. *Archives of General Psychiatry* 34:437–40.

113. Wittman, P. 1941. Scale for measuring prognosis in schizophrenic patients. *Elgin State Hospital Papers* 4:20–33.

114. World Health Organization. 1973. *The International Pilot Study of Schizophrenia* (Geneva: World Health Organization Press), vol. 1.

115. World Health Organization. *The International Pilot Study of Schizophrenia* (New York: John Wiley, forthcoming), vol. 2.

Chapter 15

PREVENTION IN SCHIZOPHRENIA

E. James Anthony, M.D.

Bower (12) has likened the content and substance of prevention to the amorphous pudding that Winston Churchill refused to eat "because it had no theme." Had Churchill been asked to define schizophrenia, he might very appropriately have used his description of the Russian mind as "a riddle wrapped in a mystery inside an enigma." To have to discuss prevention in schizophrenia is like being put in the double Churchillian quandary of being served with a gelatinous dish containing unknown and to a great extent unknowable ingredients. It is not in the nature of mental health workers to throw anything away, in the nature of either theory or practice; and so the challenge is to structure the concept of prevention and, to some extent at least, to demystify the phenomenon of schizophrenia. By the end of this chapter it will be apparent how difficult this combined task is going to be.

The Theme of Prevention

The first attempt to structure the content of prevention was to segment it along a spectrum ranging from a primary form (before the disorder makes itself manifest), a secondary form (when the disorder is still in a very early stage of development), and a tertiary form (when the disorder has reached a moderate or advanced state, hardly susceptible to being reversed). It is highly questionable whether tertiary prevention has any right to be included in the prevention spectrum; and until recently primary prevention was thought to be only a heuristic conception rather than a proved entity. Today, especially with regard to the primary prevention of serious mental disorders like schizophrenia, there are partisans for both points of view: some regard it as a useful fiction, and others as an operational fact. According to Goldston (19) "primary prevention is the misunderstood, undersupported, and neglected aspect of mental health work." Nonetheless, its allure, excitement, and promise tend to reinforce the graphic analogy in which primary prevention is compared to the Okefenokee Swamp: "If one explores and survives, the area becomes compelling, even addictive" (23). Those who favor its recognition as a specific set of actions directed toward specific populations tend (like the goddess Hygeia) to subdivide primary prevention into two parts: (1) specific prophylactic measures directed toward the target disorder; (2) general health promotion aimed at improving the quality of life and the general level of health.

Goldston (19) has attempted to bring these two together in an operational definition of primary prevention that runs as follows:

Primary prevention encompasses activities directed toward specifically identified vulnerable high-risk groups within the community who have not been labeled psychiatrically ill and for whom measures can be undertaken to avoid the onset of emotional disturbances and/or to enhance their level of positive mental health. Programs for the promotion of mental health are primarily educational rather than clinical in conception and operation, their ultimate goal being to increase people's capacities for dealing with crises and for taking steps to improve their own lives. [p. 20]

The spectrum of prevention has been extended to include the activities in figure 15–1.

FIGURE 15-1
Spectrum of Prevention

1	2	3	4	5
Health promotion	Specific protection	Screening Early diagnosis Prompt treatment	Disability limitations	Rehabilitation

Note: Reprinted with permission of the publisher from E. Bower, "Mythologies, Realities, Possibilities," in *Primary Prevention of Psychopathology*, eds. G. W. Alkee and J. M. Joffe (Hanover, N. H.: University Press of New England, 1977).

When one comes later to consider the spectrum of schizophrenia, it may be possible to interlink preventive measure and morbidity or premorbidity.

Other workers have expressed doubt and even skepticism with respect to the present feasibility of primary prevention, and dismiss it as illusional, woolly, magical, nebulous, and chancy. The general feeling of such polemicists tends to be that the complexity of the human condition, coupled with the complexity of the individual psyche, constitutes an endless source of unknown variables which make preventive work a fishing expedition that nets only a miniscule number of the myriad fish involved. The general conclusion is that we lack the knowledge to prevent even more than we lack the knowledge to treat. A sample of quotations will bear out this attitude.

What, then, shall we say about primary prevention when the major variables of family and social structure produce such highly diverse outcomes? It would seem more appropriate if we did not presume to use the word "prevention," for it holds greater promise than our mental health disciplines can fulfill. It also suggests a historical basis for our assumption that we know the variables that produce disorder and can stay their action. What is the source of this complacent belief that the factors for programming primary prevention efforts are known to us? [18, pp. 104–5]

Fish (17) had this to say: "We will need far more knowledge than we have at present before we can design a rational program for prevention of schizophrenia." When one thinks of primary prevention in a more limited and specific sense of preventing some particular disorder, like schizophrenia, Garmezy and Fish's statements clearly make sense, even though the heart may not allow the mind to wait on knowledge. As Bower (12) put it, prevention, in its restricted sense, may be difficult if not impossible to carry out, but in a more general connotation of promotion, it does seem possible. In the course of attempting to prevent schizophrenia, we may prevent a great deal of human suffering related or unrelated to it. This point of view, with which the author of this chapter agrees, has been cogently formulated by Bower (12).

Prevention and promotion in mental health have in the past been so tightly tied to mental illnesses that any foolhardy or misguided adventurer who stumbled into this arena was continually plagued by the question—does what you do prevent mental illness? Unfortunately, mental illnesses are only one of the many end points in human failure . . . the modes and roads to human failure are many and varied. Preventive and promotion programs need to be tied into the human condition in all its manifestations. [p. 556]

The general or nonspecific aspect of primary prevention should not only provide a basis for specific preventive programs but work together with them in the double harness of a total program.

If we go the preventive route, what we need to seek are not ways of defending life but of activating it, of enhancing or extending the mediational or ego processes of people. We want to develop in people the kind of fierce awareness that makes living an adventure in helping oneself and others to explore their own possibilities. Thus our preventive goal is not the avoidance of disabilities but the creation of positive strengths. [12, p. 556]

It may be true that the "effectiveness of techniques for preventing new cases is largely unproven" (30), but can we do better than to concentrate all that we know, both nonspecifically and specifically, in this most promising of areas? "The whole idea of curing the human mind after it has fallen ill corresponds to that stage of agriculture in which worms are removed from individual apple cores instead of spraying the trees" (5). It is up to us at this present stage to construct and keep constructing preventive models in different settings. What the field needs are even small indications of success to stimulate others to go and do likewise and not hold back in the expectation of some momentous breakthrough. For the present we should be satisfied with good enough, ad hoc explanations and procedures which meet at least minimal scientific criteria and are capable of evaluation, confirmation, or disconfirmation (4,5,6,8).

The Theme of Schizophrenia

It should be conceded that we are still some scientific distance away from arriving at an acceptable definition of schizophrenia that would satisfy both American and European clinicians. Judging from the criteria in use in both continents, it would seem that different disorders are being discussed, and that different conclusions around life history and prognosis are being reached. It remains not only mystifying and enigmatic but as much of an amorphous pudding as prevention—a psychiatric ragbag comprising a miscellaneous assortment of "reactions" which increase each decade in spite of the curbing efforts of a succession of editions of the *Diagnostic and Statistical Manual of Mental Disorders*. With characteristic restraint, Manfred Bleuler (11) has remarked that "the concept of schizophrenia is nowadays much misused"—the single most succinct understatement in the literature on psychosis. When he goes on to say that he adheres to the view of his father (and the majority of contemporary psychiatrists) that schizophrenia is a "true mental disease," many influential workers in different parts of the world would beg respectfully to differ. Alanen et al. (1), for example, consider that the common characteristic of the schizophrenias is the presence of comparatively grave disturbances in the functions of the ego, and they suggest that the concept of schizophrenia as a specific disease entity, separate from other mental disorders, should be abandoned in favor of a concept that regards it as the most serious manifestation of a general tendency toward the development of mental disorders in certain types of families. Like other family-oriented investigators, such as Lidz and his collaborators (26), Alanen et al. put stress not on the facultative changes in cognition, memory, feeling, and judgment but on the familial atmosphere pervaded by paralogic modes of thought and behavior that impede the process of separation-individuation.

In considering schizophrenia in the context of prevention, etiological and outcome opinions appear to determine positive or negative attitudes toward preventive interventions, but the discrepancy is not as marked as it was a few years ago. At that time those with a genetic-organic outlook were generally gloomy, while environmentalists (especially of the familial variety) were relatively optimistic. Earlier on, prognosis was related to the view of schizophrenia as a single nosological entity as opposed to a heterogeneous group of conditions with possibly a *Grundstörung*; to the European (process) as opposed to an American (reactive) standpoint; to a genetic-organic as opposed to a psychosocial set of causes; and to the study of schizophrenia in mental institutions as opposed to its treatment in outpatient and office settings. As long as one is seeing and treating many cases of schizo-affective, pseudo-neurotic, borderline, and "acute" forms of schizophrenia, the possibilities of recovery, of remission, and of prevention can be entertained with more conviction.

Life history studies have helped to soften prognostic beliefs and consequently to encourage some mode of prevention. According to Manfred Bleuler (11), for example, about half of the chronic schizophrenics in his sample showed some variability over the course of time, with stable states alternating with acute psychotic episodes. A third of the cases had one or more acute episodes that cleared up completely between attacks, and in another third the intervening periods were characterized by much milder disturbances. A mildly chronic course occurred in about 20 percent, and a severely chronic course in less than 10 percent of the patients. The illness tended to improve spontaneously in most cases after five or ten years from its onset, even in cases with severe chronic disablement.

Genetic studies have also added some element of hopefulness to the prognostic-preventive picture. In the light of our present knowledge it would appear that the very high earlier concordance rates of schizophrenia in identical as opposed to fraternal twins was an overestimate. With hardly more than a 50 percent expectancy in identical twins and less than 19 percent for fraternal twins, it is a moot point whether the differences report a genetic or an environmental hypothesis. In his retrospective intergenerational genetic studies, Karlsson (21) alluded to individuals who, he felt, were "genetic carriers with thought disorders," and who seemed "not infrequently to be persons of unusual ability, such as leaders in society or creative persons with performance records suggestive of a superior capacity for associative thinking"; and he raised the question whether some highly creative individuals were nonpenetrant schizophrenics upon whom society was dependent for social and scientific progress. This suggestion was compatible with the observation that on certain psychological tests the same type of response was given by both creative persons and schizophrenic patients. The difference often appeared to be (as indicated by the Minnesota Multiphasic Personality Inventory) the strength or the weakness of the ego. Heston and Denny (20) found that a certain number of the infants born to schizophrenic mothers (and placed away from them shortly after birth) not only exhibited no significant psychosocial impairment but were also extremely successful adults in comparison with a control group, in that they were leading more colorful lives, doing more creative jobs, interviewing more spontaneously, and occupying themselves altogether more imaginatively. McNeil (27) has offered some preliminary supportive evidence indicating that in their adoptee group creative ability was found to be related to mental illness rates among the adoptees and their biological relatives but not to the rates of the adopting relatives. Anthony (2) in his studies found that from 8 percent to 11 percent of children at high genetic risk for schizophrenia showed unusual degrees of creativity, originality, and divergent thinking; and he referred to these children as "superphrenics." In summing up the evidence, Garmezy (18) made the point that even in the presence of a markedly deleterious family environment, the outcomes for children were not by any means invariant—a common finding that led several workers to postulate the existence of "invulnerability" and to suggest that subjects manifesting such immunity must possess or must have developed techniques for surviving the onslaught of serious mental disorder. Was it possible, they questioned, that strategies of primary prevention could be learned from a study of such individuals?

Many other factors influence the "natural history" of schizophrenic illness: it is clearly highly susceptible to the world in which it manifests itself. It is never exactly the same in any period of history or in any culture or society. For instance, there seem to be no more cases with an acute onset evolving into a chronic phase without remission, and chronic schizophrenic states have become altogether much less severe. On the other hand, acute cases running a fluctuating course appear to be relatively more common today. Other factors have been found to militate against a favorable outcome: an abnormal premorbid state; "broken" homes in which human relations are grossly disturbed or disrupted (about 50 percent of all schizophrenic families according to Bleuler [11]); unfavorable relations with the mother, particularly in women who later become schizophrenic; domineering, rigid, cold, and controlling fathers; and typical transactional patterns and transactional modes in which the child is bound to his parents affectively in an infantile way, cognitively and interpersonally. In such families the child, as Stierlin (32) put it, acts as a delegate in "missions" intended to gratify his parents. All these distorting parental maneuvers are unconscious and based on the projective needs and investments of parents and children, with each influencing the other. Since premorbid schizoid features and these grossly disturbed family relations and functions often coexist, it must be assumed that both interpenetrate and evolve together. As Meehl (28) postulated years ago, what is inherited is not schizophrenia itself but "a subtle neurointegrative defect" which he termed "schizotaxia"; and subjects with this genetic endowment may remain well-compensated "schizotypes" without any signs of mental disorder except for minimal evidence of "cognitive slippage" and soft neurological signs on very careful examination.

All these considerations led to a spectrum concept of schizophrenia that can now be considered in its various forms. Meehl's schizotaxic disposition or the schizophrenic diathesis postulated by Kety and Rosenthal (31) anticipates a spectrum of psychiatric disturbances, both in probands and in first-degree relatives as in figure 15–2.

FIGURE 15-2
Schizophrenic Spectrum of Disorders

1	2	3	4	5
Apparently normal adjustment with tests disclosing thought disorder	Inadequate somewhat schizoid personalities but not markedly abnormal	Borderline state Pseudo-neurotic schizophrenia Ambulatory schizophrenia Severe schizoid personality	Acute undifferentiated schizophrenia Schizo-affective psychosis Acute paranoid reaction Homosexual panic	Chronic undifferentiated schizophrenia Process schizophrenia

Source: From *The Transmission of Schizophrenia*, eds. D. Rosenthal and S. S. Kety (New York: Pergamon Press), p. 356.

The spouse of the proband can be classified under the same headings, so that in any given family the amount of genetic transmission and the amount of environmental contagion or transaction of a schizophrenic kind can be roughly gauged. The interplay of genetic and experiential factors that give individuals good feeling, good thinking, and good reality testing on one side of the spectrum and poor or inadequate feeling, inadequate thinking, and limited reality testing on the other side probably follow multidimensional pathways.

Several different studies have looked retrospectively at the childhood of patients who became schizophrenic in adult life, and have come up with roughly the same kind of spectrum, as in figure 15–3.*

FIGURE 15-3
Spectrum of Childhood Disorders in Adult Schizophrenics

1	2	3	4	5
Outstanding "Superphrenic"	Average adjustment Docile Model behavior Normal rapport Friendly and pleasant	Maladjusted Excitable Nervous Immature Timid	Shut-in "Schizoid" Inactive Apathetic	Peculiar Odd Eccentric Bizarre

One might assume that the more preventable types would lie to the left side of the spectrum.

The Theme of the High-Risk Subject

In the early days of high-risk research, the spectrum of reactions was not unlike an amorphous pudding in being somewhat athematic, but with the acceleration of risk research in the past decade, the "theme" has become much more evident and susceptible to the spectrum approach. In discussing any high-risk population of children, a number of pertinent questions at once suggest themselves:

1. At high risk for what? In the present context, it would be schizophrenia.
2. Placed at high risk by what? In this instance, the intergenerational incidence of schizophrenia may be in part accounted for genetically through some inherited neurochemical or other imbalance and in part by the evidence that schizophrenia creates familial conditions that vary in severity and persistence.
3. Not all children with a schizophrenic diathesis or reared in a schizophrenic environment develop schizophrenia. To what extent can environment mitigate a genetic tendency, and to what extent can genetics mitigate an environmental influence? Is it possible to screen for sus-

* See references 5, 14, 22, 25, and 33.

ceptibility and resilience, as one is able to screen for early manifestations of disorder?

4. To what degree can poor or deviant parenting be held responsible for subsequent specific and nonspecific disorder?

5. Is it possible that schizophrenia is not the only possible adult deviant outcome that may develop among the children of schizophrenics?

6. Is it not possible that a variety of disturbances may characterize the childhood of high-risk subjects as much as they characterize the childhood of adult schizophrenics, and that these antecedent disturbances may or may not be related to a specifically schizophrenic diathesis or environment?

7. Is it possible that within the same family the interplay of genetic and environmental factors may lead one child to become a schizophrenic; another to become a criminal; another, an alcoholic; while a fourth may escape all these consequences?

8. Is it possible that nonspecific disturbances resulting from a schizophrenic environment, and specific antecedent disturbances stemming from early manifestations of the schizophrenic diathesis may both be preventable at the stage of childhood and so prevent the subsequent onset of adult mental disorders?

9. Is it possible that the only kinds of schizophrenia that are preventable are those developing in the high-risk children of schizophrenics, when the risks and vulnerabilities are detected in childhood and preventive measures instituted at this stage?

It has been suggested, within the epigenetic framework, that the pathways to the schizophrenic spectrum of disorders may be traced through the case study method. Although this method lacks rigor, relies excessively upon the subjective, is unable to furnish a basis for generalizing to larger populations, and has problems in regard to repeatability and validity, it can generate many testable hypotheses and reveal common patterns of behavior, central themes that are replicated in different cases, and the phenomenon as understood within a network of relationships and as a developmental process. From all this, it would seem that in order to understand the mechanisms activated in prevention, a follow-through of cases respectively is highly desirable. The prospective study of prevention may provide information on the stages of prevention, the stages at which prevention is effective, the stages at which vulnerabilities are acute, and some understanding of right and wrong turns along the pathway to madness (figure 15–4).

FIGURE 15-4

The Spectrum of Disorders in Subjects at High Risk for Schizophrenia

1	2	3	4	5
Outstanding Creative Imaginative "Superphrenics"	Reactive maladjustments with externalizing or internalizing symptom clusters	Contact disorders and "contagions" Folie à deux	Persistent schizoid-paranoid traits with micro-psychotic episodes	Severe undifferentiating primitivizations

Once again the left-hand side of the spectrum is more preventable from the point of view of childhood disorders, adolescent turbulences and "breakdowns," and eventual adult schizophrenic spectrum disorders.

The Preventive Functioning of the Ego

Children under stress and children otherwise at high risk appear to develop certain ego capacities that can be subsumed under the general rubric of "preventive." The ego appears to become hardened through repeated exposures to taxing experiences, and it can learn to withstand traumata to which the untried ego may succumb. The development of resilience over time can be observed and is derived in part from acquired defensive mechanisms, coping skills, problem-solving techniques, self-recuperative capacities, good reality testing, precociousness, and a variety of competencies, including organizational abilities, interpersonal skills, and a particular form of representational competence that allows the individual to categorize his experiences and predicaments and create a comprehensive frame of reference by which to understand and predict.

The preventive ego becomes more knowledgeable, more realistic, more self-confident, more competent, and therefore less vulnerable. The analysis of the preventive ego might help us to comprehend vulnerability and invulnerability and to devise better preventive programs. Those who work with disturbed children are usually aware that time is on their side, and that development itself may take care of certain disorders and disturbances: thus, development has a preventive aspect to it.

Models of Prevention in Schizophrenia

As reasoned earlier, a comprehensive model of prevention in schizophrenia should contain both health-promotional and specific preventive components operating in a variety of significant life settings, such as the home, the school, the community, or mental health centers in the community. According to Caplan and Grunebaum (16) the aims are to modify the environment and to strengthen individual capacities to cope with situations in order, they say, to reduce the incidence of new cases of mental disorder and disability in a population. Today this latter objective would be regarded as limited and, in fact, unlikely to succeed unless the promotion of good mental and physical health were included in the program. The curious fact is that some approaches restrict themselves to the general aspect of the program, some to one setting and not to others, and some concentrate their efforts at supporting and strengthening the vulnerable ego at stake.

Apart from general health-promotion endeavors, a comprehensive model of prevention in schizophrenia should be constructed on reasonably sound and up-to-date knowledge of the genetic and psychic transmission of schizophrenia and of its relation to the exigencies of family life and to detrimental environmental conditions, to the detection of vulnerable cases at high risk but not showing any psychopathology, to the screening of the earliest manifestations of disorder, and to the rate of remissions and recoveries in acute and chronic illness. The model should also incorporate the wide range of support systems that exist in some communities but, sad to say, are absent in others. It is important to warn the would-be preventionist that the elegance of the model is no guarantee of its effectiveness, and that all models, constructed for human use, are more likely to work if infused with energy, enthusiasm, dedication, persistence, and endurance—virtues that make for success in all branches of human endeavor. Furthermore, like any program designed to improve the human lot, preventive programs work best when they are centered on the family rather than on the individual, when they are continued over time, and when they make use of "primary agents of socialization," such as parents, siblings, peers, and teachers (15). Above all, like any program constructed by humans for humans, there is a need to work through humanizing rather than bureaucratic processes.

THE BOWER MODEL (12,13)

Based on what he calls an "ecological epigenetic concept of human institutions," Bower has elaborated a complex preventive strategy which he refers to somewhat whimsically as "KISS," an acronym derived from the phrase "key integrative social systems," and which is focused on the four areas of health services (especially to prospective mothers and young children): families, formal and informal peer play arrangements, and schools. Since even under the conditions of an optimal KISS, the developing child may show minor and transient crises of maladjustment, this health system is linked to an early and periodic screening, diagnosis, and treatment program similar to the one mandated under the Medicaid program but referred to by Bower by a second acronym "AID" (ailing-in-difficulty). Finally, if this is not enough to handle the situation, the child is passed on to "ICE" (illness-correctional environments) which, as Bower points out, "can do little but serve as depositories for reinforcing human failure" (13). This is not truly a spectrum of preventive interventions because it includes at one extreme such anti-preventive institutions as prisons, training schools, and mental hospitals, and it does not address itself specifically to the problem of schizophrenia. Bower adds some important components to the operation of his model. In a well-running preventive system like KISS, the child is provided with a good chance of experiencing a mediating adult who is "able to lure and connect affective bridges with children over which all kinds of important cognitive-affective traffic can pass . . . and provides the conceptual glue by which the child joins these sensory data to affective-cognitive concepts" (12, p. 559). In the time between being passed from one mediating person to another, a child needs to play within a peer system, and the experience of play will help him to develop a capacity for fantasy. Play is an important preventive measure for the child. Bower is skeptical, and even cynical, about the way in which mental health screening is being used at the present time. He does not see the purpose of screening out the "case" and adding to the abundance of "cases" about which nothing is being done for the most part. He would use screening within the context of the KISS model and locate it at points of transition between one institution and the next—in the neonatal, the nursery, or the kindergarten situation. His aim is again to achieve optimal health: the screening is used not for mental health problems, etc., but to find "positive linkages in child and parent on which to build school success." At the heart of KISS, it has a Growth Center in which a group of health professionals, parents, and parent surrogates could be identified and used by children as mediators. The Growth Center would also provide play space and life space through which a child could move as aggressively and as regressively as he chose, guided by the plan for helping him to integrate and mature his personality.

THE RISK-VULNERABILITY MODEL (6,8)

This model is concerned more specifically with the prevention of disorders that stem from a schizophrenic diathesis and environment. The model is constructed so as to be testable, which means that assessments of change are built into it. Six areas have been delineated: an area of risk is defined as something affecting the psychological organization from the outside. It is never a single factor, but always a combination of factors and ratings are made on genetic, reproductive, constitutional, developmental, physical, environmental, and traumatic loadings. A "total risk score" is derived from these ratings, and changes in it occur because of unusual circumstances, such as death, illness, residential changes, or traumatic experiences. The risks are sequential and do not occur simultaneously, but clearly their impact may be cumulative. They represent a mixture of psychological and biological factors, ratings of which still require to be investigated. There is a spectrum of risk, but subjects are allocated at an arbitrarily derived point to high or low categories. Vulnerability, on the other hand, is defined as a combination of factors which affect the psychological organization and focus on what pertains specifically to a psychotic disposition or experience. It represents a dynamic state of unsteady equilibrium which in turn generates a state of mind registered as a sense of vulnerability. It is probably closely associated with the postulated ego function conducing to feelings of safety and security or the reverse. The subject is evaluated in clinical and nonclinical spheres in terms of weaknesses and strengths and rated psychiatrically on a vulnerability rating scale (of suggestibility, submissiveness, and involvement and identification with the sick parent) and psychologically on ratings derived from a battery of tests that furnish a sum of clinical disturbance ratings. It has been found that high scores on the vulnerability rating scale are correlated with higher ratings of disturbance across fourteen of the psychological ratings and with more serious prognostic scores made independently.

The third area has to do with competence and with the capacity to master difficulties, to solve problems, and to overcome obstacles in an effective way. It is scored on performance at school, on special tests, on the rating of interpersonal skills, and on the individual's capacity "to construct a working model of the problem and understand its dimensions within this frame of reference." A total competence rating can then be made.

The fourth area deals with the level of adjustment at which the individual starts, so that we have a baseline from which to measure change. This is assessed on a seven-point rating scale ranging from "superior" to "adjustment difficulties requiring hospitalization."

The fifth area has to do with prediction, again rated on a seven-point scale, with regard to outcome during childhood, during adolescence, and during adult life. This prediction is derived from scores on risk, vulnerability, competence, and adjustment. Extreme ratings on the prediction scale occur with high risk, high vulnerability, low competence, and high maladjustment.

The last area has to do with outcome, which is defined in two ways: changes in test scores and changes in clinical status following intervention. The intervention program has both a health-promotional and a specific intervention section. In the promotional part various nonspecific procedures are aimed at building up the preventive ego—strengthening self-confidence, bringing the child into contact with benevolent figures and agencies, and offering helpful experiences, such as tutoring, camping, "Big Brother" contacts, recreational and creative opportunities, with special emphasis on play. Classical interventions are so called because they use psychotherapy as a preventive and not as a therapeutic device. In practice this turned out to be the most effective of all the interventions put into operation. Cathartic interventions were also used to abreact some of the intense feelings generated by the environment of schizophrenia and by interchanges with the psychotic parent. In this intervention it seemed that the family group provided a more supportive atmosphere for catharsis than did the individual situation. The procedure appeared to work only during the acute phase of the parent's illness when the defenses were still fluid. A set of corrective interventions represented an attempt to deal specifically with areas that would be regarded as vulnerable to the psychotic process. Here again the basic intention was to strengthen the capacity of the preventive ego, by helping with the process of self-differentiation, with object differentiation, with "demystification" of some of the incongruities presented by psychotic phenomena, and with the organization of experience in which the child was invited to order and classify his material, schedule his work efforts, bring together parts to construct a whole, carry out problems of reversibility, and restore lawful tidiness in a messy, chaotic field situation. These so-called ego exercises did seem to raise the competence of the child, but their more enduring effect was to increase his self-confidence in his competence.

AN IMMUNIZATION MODEL

This model is derived from public health and preventive medicine, although over the years it has been included within the general hygiene program from which the community as a whole benefits. In some instances screening devices are available for the detection of susceptibles, whose vulnerabilities are then diminished through the process of active or passive immunization. The mental health field has its susceptibles, but there are also "carriers" who may, as Bellak (10) has suggested, catalyze an emotional epidemic. These catalysts or contaminants may not display manifest disturbances that are clinically obvious, but they may still be "schizophrenogenic." The schizophrenic parent may also be a powerful source of contagion, generating *folie à deux* responses in vulnerable children in his or her proximity (3). The interesting fact is that not all those in contact with the contaminant develop contact disturbances. In parents who have repeated psychotic breaks, a certain number of the children appear to become "immunized" to the disturbing influence. To what extent might it be possible to expose likely susceptibles to graduated experiences of psychosis in order to create immunities? This would raise all kinds of ethical and legal problems which at present seem insurmountable. In the "living-in experiences" with schizophrenic families described by Anthony (7), the resident observers would frequently develop a wide variety of symptoms in relation to critical developments within the family, but a number of the members themselves remained apparently unaffected.

MODELS BASED ON THE USE OF CHANGE AGENTS

In a good "preventive community" there are many antipsychotic factors which can be used in the service of prevention. The exposure to rational and reasonable human behavior, to good reality testing, to nondeviant communications, and to positive interactions by, for example, the "adoption" of a psychotic family by a normal family, may bring about a correction of distorted hostile beliefs and offer nonthreatening models for benign relationships. One of the most powerful change experiences for the younger child is in peer play, where the differentiation between fantasy and reality can be repeatedly demonstrated, so that the child is able to learn by observation and participation the judicious management of internal and external worlds.

THE PREVENTION-BY-PREVENTION MODEL

We do not yet know enough about human genetics, especially in the area of psychosis, to utilize genetic counseling and the prohibition of procreation. Genetic expectancies tend to vary widely from investigator to investigator, and each case appears to run its own epigenetic course. Likewise, we do not know whether separation from a schizophrenic parent and surrogation, fostering, or adoption will prevent the development of schizophrenia in adult life; but in many cases it appears obvious to the experienced clinician that living in a schizophrenic environment can be extremely noxious for certain children. Anthony (7) has produced some evidence that what he terms "involving" psychoses (reactive, schizo-affective, chaotic, acutely paranoid types) do generate a large number of internalizing and externalizing symptoms in children, and that these, together with *folie à deux*, tend to subside and even to disappear when the child is removed from the environment. The use of this model has certain drawbacks: it may create as many separation disturbances as it solves in the way of contact disturbances; furthermore, some schizophrenic parents, in between attacks, are not only quite nice people but good enough parents. The removal of the children during attack periods constitutes a reasonable procedure for this group.

ESOTERIC HELP MODELS

In our search for good community experiences we have frequently been struck by the fact that in the more dilapidated, "drifting" schizophrenic families, the children often respond positively to esoteric religious experiences, such as Jehovah's Witnesses, Scientology, fundamentalist groups, and certain charismatic groups where they not only find community feeling but also a high degree of tolerance for eccentric attitudes and behavior: they can speak with voices and hear voices and have ideas of special references that are not considered alienating. (In one striking instance, in one of our schizophrenic families, two of the children remained well and flourishing, subscribing to Jehovah's Witnesses and Scientology respectively, while two had early decompensations, having rejected the fundamentalist religion of their parents and not finding anything to take its place.) Various studies have shown that psychotic and borderline individuals are drawn to esoteric religious groups, but no study has yet been made on the extent to which families and children have remained free from disturbances and disorders.

One should add that although no definite operational models have yet emerged, systematic intervention in the schizophrenic mother-child relationship has been attempted, using videotape of interactions as a basis for counseling sessions with the mother. The idea is to help the mother focus on mothering concerns and skills, while keeping her psychotic preoccupations out of the dyad. This is not an easy task for the intervener and depends largely on the establishment of a trusting, nonthreatening, noncritical relationship with the mother and on empathizing with, strengthening, and supporting whatever maternal feelings she has. Anthony and McGinnis (9) have tried to carry out preventive work with schizophrenic parents. At best the counselors can provide a buffer between the parental psychosis and the child. This means that continuous contact must be maintained with the family, so that confidence in the intervener can grow.

It is important to know what influence the prevailing disturbance in the parent has on the different children—to what extent they feel uncertain and insecure, confused and mystified, guilty and ashamed, angry and resentful, or tearful and apprehensive. He must also know to what extent the well parent helps or harms the situation for the children. In seriously disturbed families, the parents are in perpetual conflict with each other; the children may be used as spies for rival camps. Older children may have special problems: they may be used as surrogate parents or as surrogate spouse in an incestuous or near-incestuous way, or they may lead family movements to exclude the sick parent. One has also to bear in mind the children's age and sex since each developmental phase has its own vulnerabilities, with differences for boys and girls, depending on the sex of the sick parent. [9, pp. 335–336]

This quotation exemplifies some of the numerous problems involved in preventive intervention—whether primary, secondary, or tertiary— with schizophrenic parents, especially, one must add, when they are deeply and systematically paranoid.

Conclusions

It has almost become a truism that it takes three generations to make a schizophrenic. This may give us time to intervene, but it requires knowledge of the transmission processes, both genetic and environmental, before the destructive cycle of psychosis can be ended. The most hopeful approach to primary prevention of schizophrenia seems to be through a high-risk channel, but this group is a relatively small one within the total population of schizophrenia, the genetic expectancy ranging between 8 percent and 15 percent. Kringlen (24) has reported that 21.8 percent of the offspring of schizophrenic mothers became schizophrenic, while only 9.1 percent of children of schizophrenic fathers turned out to be schizophrenic. This contradicts a great deal of evidence that attributes a statistically higher rate of psychopathology to fathers with schizophrenia. A great deal depends on whether the diagnoses of offspring are made without being blind to the diagnoses of the parents. There is no doubt, however, that intrafamilial variables enhance the severity of any schizophrenic illness that develops, and that nongenetic factors are critical. This means that family therapy, instituted early, could have a preventive role and at least mitigate any illnesses that ensued. In work with the families there are certain qualities that need to be brought out and developed in the schizophrenic parent or, failing that, in the well spouse (bearing in mind that the "well" spouse is frequently "unwell," alcoholic, criminal, paranoid, borderline, or psychopathic in some form: homogamous mating is frequent). These qualities are present in normal families and include the role of the parent in mediating good experiences for the children, in differentiating the children clearly to themselves so that they feel differentiated, in reconciling small conflicts, confusions, and incompatibilities that go on in family life, in modeling some degree of equanimity of response to critical events, and, when adolescence approaches, in relinquishing the children without trying to entrap them within the psychotic enclave. Letting go is usually not easy for the schizophrenic mother: she either refuses to let go of the children or gives them up with a catastrophic show of rejection.

What one hopes most for the children of schizophrenic parents is that they become, to quote Murphy and Moriarty (29), "good copers," able to deal with new situations, unusual demands, peculiar stresses, and bizarre incongruities and to reorganize a situation or put an end to what they do not like. The vulnerable children, described in this section, have to learn both types of coping described by Murphy and Moriarty: coping I, having to do with the environment, and coping II, having to do with internal integration. Coping I allows children to cope with the many frustrations and threats that the schizophrenic environment presents, and coping II allows them to manage their internal thoughts and feelings in an integrated way. Both capacities could be subsumed under our concept of a preventive ego function. What we found was what Murphy and Moriarty found: that the best copers among boys and girls were those with the widest range of coping resources and those who had both "masculine" and "feminine" skills or resources. The coping devices included the capacity to delay, tolerance of frustration, "ascending power," and "healthy narcissism—devices which often tend to get exaggerated on the pathological side in high-risk children. The susceptibility to deterioration of the power to function under stress, by exposure to psychosis or to normal developmental and environmental stresses, must be recognized as early as possible, so that children can be monitored and helped whenever necessary. The basic aim of all the preventive programs is to develop the preventive ego or the "good coper":

> Some children develop self-protective preventive devices or compensatory measures to manage such problems: timing rest; ability to limit or fend off excessive stimulation; ability to control the impact of the environment through strategic withdrawal, delay and caution; and the ability to select or to restructure the environment. Involved here as prerequisites were realistic appraisal of the environment, acceptance of people, clear differentiation of fantasy from reality, and many cognitive coping capacities. . . . Some aspects of the child's self-feeling and relation to his home helped the child to cope with vulnerability. These included the adequacy of the child's self-image, security and positive orientation to life along with related items; the mother's enjoyment of the child, encouragement or support of the child and active help to the child in coping were also significantly related to coping capacity.

It is these "self-protective preventive devices or compensatory measures" that occur in our "invulnerable" or immune group that we must study in their formation and then help inculcate in the vulnerable group. The secret of a good preventive program is to learn as much as possible from the "invulnerables."

The proof of the pudding is in the eating: in eating one begins to discover the themes.

BIBLIOGRAPHY

1. Alanen, Y. O.; Rekola, J.; Stewen, A.; Takela, K.; and Tuovinen, M. 1966. The family in the pathogenesis of schizophrenia and neurotic disorders. *Acta Psychiatrica Scandinavica* 42 (supp. 189).

2. Anthony, E. J. 1968. The developmental precursors of adult schizophrenia. *Journal of Psychiatric Research* 6(supp. 1):293–361.

3. Anthony, E. J. 1970. The influence of maternal psychosis on children—Folie à deux. In *Parenthood*, eds. E. J. Anthony and T. Benedek (Boston: Little, Brown), pp. 571–93.

4. Anthony, E. J. 1972. The contagious subculture of psychosis. In *Progress in group and family therapy*, eds. C. Sager and H. Kaplan (New York: Brunner/Mazel).

5. Anthony, E. J. 1972. Primary prevention with school children. In *Progress in community mental health*, eds. H. Barten and L. Bellak (New York: Grune & Stratton), vol. 2.

6. Anthony, E. J. 1974. A risk-vulnerability intervention model for children of psychotic parents. In *The child in his family: Children at psychiatric risk*, eds. E. J. Anthony and C. Koupernik (New York: John Wiley), vol. 3, pp. 99–121.

7. Anthony, E. J. 1975. Primary prevention with school children. In *Emergencies in child psychiatry*, ed. G. Morrison (Springfield, Ill.: Charles C Thomas), pp. 43–78.

8. Anthony, E. J. 1977. Preventive measures for children and adolescents at high risk for psychosis. In *Primary prevention of psychopathology*, eds. G. W. Albee and J. M. Joffe (Hanover, N.H.: University Press of New England).

9. Anthony, E. J., and McGinnis, M. 1978. Counseling very disturbed parents. In *Helping parents help their children*, ed. L. E. Arnold (New York: Brunner/Mazel).

10. Bellak, L. 1969. Community mental health as a branch of public health. In *Progress in community mental health*, eds. H. Barten and L. Bellak (New York: Grune & Stratton), vol. 1.

11. Bleuler, M. 1977. Schizophrenia: Course and outcome. In *Encyclopedic handbook of medical psychology*, ed. S. Krauss (London: Butterworths).

12. Bower, E. M. 1972. K.I.S.S. and kids: A mandate for prevention. *American Journal of Orthopsychiatry* 42:566–65.

13. Bower, E. 1977. Mythologies, realities, possibilities. In *Primary prevention of psychopathology*, eds. G. W. Albee and J. M. Joffe (Hanover, N.H.: University Press of New England).

14. Bower, E.; Shellhamer, T.; and Daily, J. 1960. School characteristics of male adolescents who later became schizophrenic. *American Journal of Orthopsychiatry* 30:712–29.

15. Bronfenbrenner, U. 1974. Is early intervention effective? *Day Care and Early Education* (November):15–19.

16. Caplan, G., and Grunebaum, H. 1967. Perspectives on primary prevention. *Archives of General Psychiatry* 17:331–46.

17. Fish, B. 1976. An approach to prevention in infants at risk for schizophrenia. *Journal of Child Psychiatry* 15(1):62–82.

18. Garmezy, N. 1971. Vulnerability research and the issue of primary prevention. *American Journal of Orthopsychiatry* 41:11.

19. Goldston, S. 1977. Defining primary prevention. In *Primary prevention of psychopathology*, eds. G. W. Albee and J. M. Joffe (Hanover, N.H.: University Press of New England).

20. Heston, L., and Denny, D. 1969. Interactions between early life experiences and biological features in schizophrenia. In *Transmissions of schizophrenia*, eds. D. Rosenthal and S. S. Kety (Oxford: Pergamon Press).

21. Karlsson, J. 1966. *The biologic basis for schizophrenia* (Springfield, Ill: Charles C Thomas).

22. Kasanin, J., and Veo, L. 1932. A study of the school adjustments of children who later in life became psychotic. *American Journal of Orthopsychiatry* 2:212.

23. Kessler, M., and Albee, G. 1975. Primary prevention. *Annual Review of Psychology* 26:557–91.

24. Kringlen, E. 1977. Comments. In *Proceedings of Rochester International Conference on Schizophrenia*, ed. L. Wynne (New York: John Wiley).

25. Kunkel, C. 1920. Die Kindheitsentwicklung der Schizophrenen [The Childhood Development of Schizophrenia]. *Monatsshrift fuer Psychiatrie and Neurologie* 48:256.

26. Lidz, T.; Fleck, S.; and Cornelison, A. 1966. *Schizophrenia and the family*. (New York: International Universities Press).

27. McNeil, T. 1969. The relationship between creative ability and recorded mental illness. Paper presented at Southeastern Psychological Society.

28. Meehl, P. 1962. Schizotaxia, schizotypy, schizophrenia. *American Psychologist* 17:827–38.

29. Murphy, L., and Moriarty, A. 1976. *Vulnerability, coping and growth* (New Haven: Yale University Press).

30. Roberts, C. 1968. *Primary prevention of psychiatric disorders*, eds. F. C. Chalke and J. J. Day (Toronto: University of Toronto Press).

31. Rosenthal, D., and Kety, S. 1969. *The transmissions of schizophrenia* (Oxford: Pergamon Press).

32. Stierlin, H. 1973. The adolescent as delegate of his parents. *Australian and New Zealand Journal of Psychiatry* 7:249–56.

33. Wittman, M., and Steinberg, D. L. 1944. A study of prodromal factors in mental illness with special reference to schizophrenia. *American Journal of Psychiatry* 100:811–16.

Chapter 16

CHILDHOOD SCHIZOPHRENIA
AND AUTISM:
A SELECTIVE REVIEW

Paulina F. Kernberg, M.D.

In the last decade efforts toward further delineation and precision in the description of the various diagnostic syndromes subsumed under childhood schizophrenia have proceeded at a fast pace. The main contributing factor to these advances has been the multidisciplinary approach to research, diagnosis, and treatment. Of particular import has been the establishment of diagnostic criteria for the syndrome of autism, with criteria stemming from genetic and biochemical research.

In 1971 the *Journal of Autism and Childhood Schizophrenia* began to publish regularly the rapidly accumulating research in the field. Genetic, biochemical, and congenital factors are now considered to be more crucial determinants of childhood schizophrenia and autism than social-psychological factors. In assessing the relative contributions of environment and heredity, for example, Rosenthal et al. (146) reported that although the quality of the relationship between the child and his adoptive parents does affect the development of psychopathology, hereditary factors affect the production and the outcome of psychopathology to a significantly greater extent.

The controversy over the continuity between autism and childhood schizophrenia goes on. The current trend, however, is to consider childhood schizophrenia as having continuity with adult schizophrenia, and autism as possibly being a distinct syndrome. Other early and late onset psychoses are postulated in addition to autism and childhood schizophrenia. Although prognosis is still guarded, there has been substantial progress in primary prevention, psychoanalytic psychotherapy, educational approaches, and residential treatment.

In light of the current progress in autism, this chapter will focus on autism, its diagnosis, etiology, and treatment and offer some points of comparison with childhood schizophrenia. The research of Caparulo and

Cohen (32), DeMyer (50), Ritvo et al. (144), and Rutter et al. (153) will be cited on the biological-socioepidemiological side. The writings of Mahler (117) and Tustin (175) on the psychoanalytical ego and object relations side will in turn be used for describing the subjective nature of these childhood psychoses. Both points of view seem essential for an understanding of childhood psychosis, the umbrella term covering childhood schizophrenia, autism, and other psychoses of childhood. The current revision of the *Diagnostic and Statistical Manual* refers to yet another umbrella term—"pervasive developmental disorders."

A Brief Historical Note

Leo Kanner, in his recent historical overview of childhood psychosis (97), outlined the early beginnings of research with Maudsley, who in 1867 included a chapter on "Insanity in Early Life" in his book *Physiology and Pathology of Mind.* Although Maudsley was severely criticized for daring to talk about insanity in childhood, he retained the chapter in the edition of his book from the 1880s and in fact stressed how "these anomalies may set the inquirer on new and fruitful paths of research." Kanner then cited DeSautis, who in 1906 was the first to study the relation between mental retardation and dementia praecox, and who identified a syndrome called "dementia praecoxissima." Almost sixty years later the same subject was systematically studied and the relation between autism and mental retardation was established (52,54,149,154).

Through the years various attempts have been made at further delineation of childhood psychoses (54,97). Kanner (98) described the syndrome of early infantile autism in 1943, and in 1952 Mahler (116) introduced the concept of autistic and symbiotic psychosis. In the early 1950s Rank (135) coined the term "atypical child" for those children presenting ego fragmentation attributed to maternal psychopathology—a term which tended to blur the distinctions between the various childhood psychoses and borderline conditions. The relation between these various terms will be further discussed in our consideration of autism.

Childhood Schizophrenia

GENERAL INCIDENCE

Schizophrenia in children is included in the category of childhood psychosis, which appears to be a relatively uncommon disorder. Epidemiological data represent approximate values, as these are influenced by unclear diagnostic categories and policies of the reporting institution. According to Clarizio (39), the incidence is 4 to 4.5 per 10,000 children in the general population. In outpatient clinics the incidence is 8 to 9 per 100,000 boys and 3 per 100,000 for girls in the age range five to fourteen. Of hospitalized patients, data based on first admissions reveal that less than 0.5 percent of all patients in state and county hospitals are childhood psychotics under fifteen years of age. Reported psychotic conditions in youth are most common in the fifteen- to seventeen-year-old range (23.6 per 100,000 males and 17.6 per 100,000 females) and least common in the category under five years of age (1.6 per 100,000 males and 0.7 per 100,000 females). Whereas the rates of psychotic youth indicate a sex ratio of three boys to one girl, the rates in adulthood become equalized.

CLINICAL INDICATIONS

Ekstein (62) described childhood schizophrenia as characterized by such conditions as a break with reality, severely impaired reality testing, thought disorders of a primary nature (auditory and visual hallucinations, delusions, language systems in which there is often no clear separation between thought, act, and impulse), constant returns to fusion states, and temporary, complete autistic withdrawals. The symptoms are similar to adult schizophrenic conditions except that in most cases the states of mental disorganization fluctuate and are thus often mistaken for borderline conditions.

From a very early age the schizophrenic child suffers from extreme sensitivity and quickly regresses under stress. He is extremely vulnerable to separation, mild forms of rejection, and parental malfunctioning. Vulnerability depends more on the child than on the intensity or timing of the trauma, thus indicating the link with physiological and biological givens.

Ragins et al. (134) reported that in the first year and one-half of life the offspring of schizophrenic women suffered from more developmental problems and more severe ones than infants of normal mothers. These problems occurred in the area of sleep, eating, elimination, responsivity, grasping skill, sense of well-being, physical growth (as reflected in fluctuating weight), accidental injuries, recurrent infectious and allergic illnesses not requiring hospitalization, delayed reflex maturation, and erratic patterns of relatedness to mother, other persons, or toys. Unpredictable, hostile aggressive behavior was observed, as well as less spontaneous, imitative vocal and verbal activity.

In another study of infants born of schizophrenic mothers, Fish (71) found significant deviations in the development of preschizophrenic infants who show

a fluctuating dysregulation of maturation or 'pandevelopmental retardation' involving physical growth, gross motor, visual motor and cognitive development; proprioceptive and vestibular responses to caloric stimulation, muscle tone and possibly arousal. [p. 1297]

Fish (69) has also found a high correlation between uneven neurological development characterized by unusual combinations of retardation and precocity during the first year of life and schizophrenic illness in middle childhood and adolescence.

Kolvin et al. (109) outlined the similarity with adult schizophrenia. He stated that the onset of childhood schizophrenia may be as early as seven years or even earlier. (Such an early designation of pathology is probably related to the diagnostic abilities of the clinician and the perceptiveness of the parents.)

Kolvin found a disorder of thought associations in three-fifths of children with a psychosis beginning in later childhood, thought blocking in the same proportion, and most often paranoid delusions. Eighty percent had auditory hallucinations, almost 50 percent had bodily or visual hallucinations, but no child had the latter without the former. Disturbances of mood were usual, and initial perplexity was highly characteristic. Blunting of affect was present in two-thirds of the cases. Mannerisms, grimacing, and ambitendency occurred in three-fifths of the children.

Bakwin and Bakwin (4) pointed out that during childhood an abrupt beginning is rare except in prepuberty. Typically the presenting symptoms are extreme anxiety and withdrawal of interest from everyday living (parents, friends, school). Dressing and grooming habits are sometimes neglected, and persons are often treated as though they were inanimate objects. Special interests are present, and philosophical abstractions may be obsessively pursued. These children live in a world of their own.

Hypoactivity alternates with hyperactivity; endless repetitive drawing or sitting may alternate with rocking, swinging from a bar, or bizarre hand movements. The overactivity is purposeless, repetitive, and rhythmic.

Speech is not primarily used for communication purposes; the voice is often flat, reflecting the flatness of affect; the meaning of words may be strangely distorted. Patients report "introjected bodies": devils or other beings inside their stomach, lungs, or head, who guide their thoughts and are responsible for their misbehavior. This symptom shows a mix of coenesthesic and auditory pseudo-hallucinations. True hallucinations, both visual and auditory, may follow, as well as coenesthesic hallucinations, such as changes in body image. Delusions of influence may be present.

There is extreme clinging to the parent and resistance to entering new situations and relations with people. In other instances schizophrenic children may be extremely submissive. Severe temper tantrums are common, as is repressive behavior, including self-destructive behavior. Compulsive and phobic reactions are frequent, intense, and often of a bizarre nature. Excessive sexual preoccupation with compulsive masturbation is often present. Sexual confusion and preoccupation with suicide and death may also appear (8).

In summary, preschizophrenic manifestations described by various authors (34,134) confirm Garmezy's (77) report of studies indicating that the one who may become schizophrenic is psychologically and physically more vulnerable to common traumatic experiences (e.g., moving, death of a relative), more sensitive, less happy, less social, and less independent than his healthy siblings. He is more susceptible to infectious disease, is more likely to have physical handicaps (especially hearing defects), and often shows soft neurological signs. Antisocial behavior, more prevalent in boys, may also be a precursor of schizophrenia.

PSYCHOLOGICAL TEST RESULTS

As summarized by Bakwin and Bakwin (4), the Goodenough-Draw-A-Man tests show disturbed spatial relations of the body image (e.g., elongations, protrusions, omissions), in particular overemphasis on the extremities, which are drawn with bizarre detail while the remainder of the figure is neglected. Transparency effects appear, showing the incorporation into the body of objects from the outside world.

On the Wechsler Intelligence Scale for Children (WISC) the mean IQ is 86. There is subtest scatter, relatively slow comprehension on arithmetic and picture-completion tests, and a low similarity score with a higher vocabulary score. Verbal scores tend to be higher than performance scores, and block design scores higher than average performance scores. Schizophrenic children may fail easy tasks while succeeding in relatively difficult ones on the same subtest. They often bring irrelevant materials or add some bizarre qualifications and inappropriate affect to their answers to test items. Bland, thoughtless answers on the information and vocabulary tests may occur.

On the Children's Apperception Test (CAT), stories do not have any apparent relevance to the picture presented. Frequently themes concerning the origins of life, death, God, or the devil are described. The child tends to interpret the pictures as referring to himself.

THEORIES OF ETIOLOGY

Theories of etiology will be considered jointly with autism, as most researchers have heterogeneous groups in their samples. None of the biological parameters studied to date (biogenic amines, pink spot or mauve factor in the urine, bufotenine, histamine, serum factors, chromosomal abnormalities, endocrinological changes, or other metabolic factors) have been proven to be causally related to the etiology of childhood psychosis (85).

Childhood Autism

A DEFINITION

Ornitz and Ritvo (128) have comprehensively outlined the "syndrome of autism." They included Kanner's (97,98) "autistic disturbances of affective contacts" under the rubric "early infantile autism," a term indicating that symptoms begin in early infancy. Synonyms are "childhood autism," "primary autism," "infantile autism," and "symbiotic psychosis."

Ornitz (127) stated that the terms "infantile autism" and "symbiotic psychosis" refer to children who are similar in many ways, especially in their emotional unresponsiveness. In children with symbiotic psychosis, behavior may alternate between isolation and withdrawal and clinging tenaciously to their parents. These two states do not necessarily constitute a different disorder, but rather they may be two facets of progression and regression in the same child. The more general terms, such as "infantile psychosis," "childhood psychosis," and "early onset psychosis," emphasize psychological damage to the developing personality of the child and may or may not overlap with autism. What is clinically important is the variability of symptoms in each child as compared with others in the same diagnostic category; moreover, the same symptoms vary in the same child over time.

GENERAL INCIDENCE

Autism is not as rare a condition as was once thought. Ritvo et al. (144) reported that already in 1966 Lotter found 4.5 autistic children per 10,000 among eight- to ten-year-olds in Middlesex County, England, and that Treffert in 1970 found 0.7 autistic children per 10,000 children between three and eleven years of age in Wisconsin. These are considered low estimates, as the condition is frequently misdiagnosed. The proportion of boys to girls is 3.5 to 4.1 to 1. On Rimland's (140) checklist true cases of early infantile autism constitute 118 out of the sample of 2,218 psychotic children.

CLASSIFICATION

Eisenberg (60) and Rutter (149) believe the attempts to delineate some of the subgroups within childhood psychosis are of crucial importance for research and treatment purposes.

Classification efforts, as described by Miller (124), cover a wide range. From a psychoanalytic ego-psychological approach, Wenar and Ruttenberg (179) proposed a behavior-rating instrument. They established scales in five core areas: nature and degree of relationship to an adult as a person, communication, drive for mastery, vocalization and expressive speech, and psychosexual development. Others, such as Creak et al. (47), have established symptom checklists. Although the symptom checklist and ego-psychological behavioral approaches seem to differ, descriptively they coincide.

Creak's criteria continue to be used and have been further refined. Metcalf (123) added to the symptom checklist the importance of age of onset and severity of initial symptoms. Rimland (140) has developed the E2 score, a questionnaire instrument for research purposes. The need for such an instrument is clearly stated by Rimland: "a child called autistic or said to have autism by a first diagnostician has less than a chance in four of being so diagnosed by a second diagnostician." Rimland's E-2 questionnaire correlates with Kanner's (97,98) diagnosed cases and also seems to correlate with laboratory markers—namely, increased 5-hydroxyhyptamine efflux from blood platelets (20).

A specific classification of autism, differentiating it from mental subnormality in particular, is offered by DeMyer et al. (54). It is as follows:

SUBNORMAL, NONPSYCHOTIC, GENERAL, OR SPECIFIC LEARNING DISORDER

The child's relations with adults are overly dependent or negative but not consistently withdrawn. Behavior is like that of a younger child. Speech may be absent; if present, it is used for communication. If the child cannot speak, he can pantomime consistently with his mental age. Use of toys and body is commensurate with mental age; repetitive use of toys is minimal. Intelligence test performance is variable.

HIGH AUTISM

Symptoms appear before age three. The child shows withdrawn islets of response to affectionate gestures and can give affection at times. There is some communicative speech, but also echolalia and disordered rhythm, emphasis, and tone. One sees pronominal reversal in the child's repeating the question to ask a question. Only simple signaling is used for nonverbal communication. The child uses his body in a repetitive, ritualistic manner. There is a nonfunctional use of toys and pretend play is minimal. Intelligence tests show various peaks and valleys on performance and verbal curves. Generally the child does best with fitting and assembly tasks; he may have a splinter skill such as reading, but his abstraction is low.

MIDDLE AUTISM

Symptoms appear before age three. The child is withdrawn most of the time. He may cling physically to mother or laugh when chased. He shows little response to affection and does not initiate affectionate gestures. No speech is used for communication beyond an occasional word; he may have immediate or delayed echolalia; and there is only simple nonverbal signaling. As in high autism, pretend play is absent. Intelligence test performance is as in high autism, except that the performance mental age is higher than the low verbal mental age. The child has at least one splinter skill.

LOW AUTISM

Symptoms appear before age three. Relations with adults, speech and nonverbal communication, and use of toys and body are as in middle autism. Verbal and performance scores are low, with no splinter skills. Gross motor behavior often is the only peak of the performance curve. The parents generally seek medical attention when the child is two to three years of age (the range is from two months to six to seven years), depending on their capacity to observe and their need to deny the problem. As indicated earlier, the illness is generally detectable before the third year of life (150). The most frequent initial complaint is that of a delay in speech (144,154).

CLINICAL INDICATIONS

In the first year of life the mother may sense a certain difference in her infant: there is an absence of babble, lack of modulation of voice, lack of social smile, and gaze aversion. The infant may show little visual pursuit of objects and people, and little reaching when left alone (120). He does not use a pointing gesture. Disruption in eye contact with mother can be seen in microfilm analysis; the baby squints at light, people, objects. The infant does not show stranger or separation anxiety. He does not raise his arms in anticipation of being picked up, nor does he try to mold into mother's arms.

In addition, the baby changes abruptly from intense irritability with overreactivity to quiet periods when he is self-absorbed and requires no companionship or stimulation. Abrupt changes may also occur in the motor area, as seen in fluctuations between rigidness and limpness when the infant is held. Stereotypic hand motions may be observed.

The rhythmic responsiveness observed in infants as young as one week of age to the language patterns of adults seems to be lacking in autistic children. The autistic infant shows no pleasure at mealtime ministrations. The only recognizable pleasure is in locomotion.

From the preceding description we have gained a general picture of the early indications of autism. At this point, then, it seems important to examine certain signs and symptoms in greater detail.

DISTURBANCES IN DEVELOPMENTAL RATE

The sequence of normal development is disrupted in the motor and language areas and in social-interaction milestones. Precociousness, delays, and deviations are characteristic; special abilities in an otherwise retarded, autistic child illustrates this point (127).

DISTURBANCES IN PERCEPTION

The lack of modulation of sensory input makes the autistic child appear hyperresponsive or hyporesponsive. He may behave as if he were deaf, or he may startle easily at loud and sudden noises. Similarly, the patient may show no visual reaction to new persons or objects and thus may walk into objects as if he did not see them. On the other hand, he may be so sensitive to visual stimuli presented sequentially that he seeks to avoid or erase them by twirling. (For this reason these children frequently cannot watch television.) Alternations also occur in response to painful tactile stimuli. In contrast to the normal toddler who is generally insensitive to pain when he gets bruised or receives an injection, the autistic child may react with inappropriate intensity. His pain threshold fluctuates from high to low, and acute distress may suddenly appear to stimuli which earlier had made no impression (81,175).

The autistic child seems actively to seek auditory, visual, vestibular, and proprioceptive stimulation as he whirls, rolls his head, rocks, rubs and flicks his ears, and bangs himself. However, the child's intolerance for abrupt sensory stimulation is evidenced by his distress, for example, upon hearing loud noises, such as sirens, or on being exposed to sudden illumination; the child then cups his ears or eyes to protect himself. A similar intolerance for rough-textured foods causes a marked delay in the acceptance of solid foods. Vestibular stimulation when not initiated by the child causes profound aversion; roughhousing and riding in a car or an elevator are therefore avoided.

According to Schopler (157), the autistic child characteristically prefers proximal (touch, smell, and taste) to distant receptors (hearing and seeing). The registration of perception tends to depend on feedback from the child's own motor responses (130). In addition, the tolerance for perceptual stimulation is greater if the child spontaneously initiates the receptivity.

DISTURBANCES OF MOTILITY

Peculiar mannerisms and patterns of motility give autistic children their strange and bizarre appearance. The most prominent motility disturbance involves the hands and arms. The hands are usually moved within the visual field; hand flapping and oscillating occur at the same frequency over time, and different groups of patients flap at the same rate. Toe walking may be intermittent or continuous. In the trunk and body, motility disturbances include lunging and darting movements, body rocking and swaying, head rolling or head banging. Interspersed there are periods of immobility and posturing. A child of three years or younger may show opistotonus—that is, he arches his back and extends his neck for several minutes at a time. In the examination of the child the sight of a spinning top will frequently elicit motility disturbances, such as hand flapping, posturing, and twirling. For an autistic child playing ball is awkward or impossible. Autistic children also cannot imitate body movements or facial expressions—signs which are helpful in diagnostic assessments. Campbell (25) reported a high incidence of ambidexterity: 59 percent in her sample in contrast to 20 percent for the non-autistic siblings.

DISTURBANCES IN RELATING

In terms of relations to people, there is poor or deviant eye contact, delayed or absent social smile, and delayed or absent anticipatory response to being picked up. The child shows apparent aversion to physical contact, and the relationship to whole persons is lacking. People are treated as if they were partial objects—a hand, a lap, someone who offers food. The child also shows a delayed or absent reaction to strangers or overactive anxiety with strangers (117).

With inanimate objects, the autistic child tends to flick, twirl, and spin toys rather than use them for their functional or symbolic meanings. In terms of the child's contact with the environment as a whole, the symptom of preservation of sameness serves multiple functions. One function is to protect the child from different perceptual sets which upset or confuse him by giving him a sense of discontinuity between external and internal reality; the child does not perceive a boundary between the two (175). Later this rigidity and inflexibility will influence negatively the use of play material, social interaction with peers, and responsiveness to parents.

DISTURBANCES OF SPEECH AND LANGUAGE

There is a total absence of speech and language development in 58 percent of the cases. The rest have partial disturbances. If functional speech exists, it is atonal and arrhythmic, lacking inflection and failing to communicate subtle emotions. These nonverbal components of speech persist into adulthood even if communicative language develops.

Because of the problems in language communication and in the use of symbols, it is important for the understanding of the deficits of autistic children to keep in mind the normal paradigms of language and speech development (138). In their paper Ricks and Wing (138) refer to the following definitions: "Language" means the symbolization of concepts for self-communication regarding past, present, and future events and for interpersonal communication, the latter involving both reception and expression. In order to be called "language," the symbols used must have a systematic relationship to each other, allowing for the *creation* of an infinite number of messages which are understandable to all those with an adequate command of that language. The system of symbols making up a language can be received or expressed in various nonvocal forms as well as in sounds. Inner language is a speech for one's self which helps one to orient, to understand, and to overcome difficulties.

"Speech" is "the use of systematized vocalizations to express verbal symbols or words." Speech may also refer to the processes of articulation, so it is necessary to make this distinction clear when discussing a speech disorder. In addition, when working with autistic children, it is appropriate to distinguish between "spontaneous speech," which will be used here to denote the vocalization of concepts generated by the speaker, and "echolalic speech," which is the production of words that are an exact or partial copy of those originally spoken by another person. This echoing may be immediate or delayed.

"Communication" is a more general term than language or speech and refers to the transmission of information by any means, not only through a system of symbols. An aspect of communication, which is very important in working with autistic children, is that its activity is intentionally directed toward another for the purpose of evaluating the response of the target and modifying one's behavior accordingly. Communication includes both language and signals which are not sufficiently systematized to be classified as language. These signals are often referred to as "nonverbal communication." Elements or nonverbal communication include bodily contact, proximity, orientation, the angle at which people sit or stand in relation to each other, and appearance—clothing, posture, head nods, facial expression, gestures, looking (eye contact). Nonverbal aspects of speech may also be produced by variations in pitch, stress, timing, and volume.

Nonverbal communication has three different functions: (1) to communicate attitudes and emotions and to manage the immediate social situation; (2) to support and complement verbal communication with, for example, head nods, emphatic gestures, or appropriate pauses while speaking; and (3) to replace language, for example, with meaningful looks or gestures of greeting and good will made from a distance. Nonverbal communication can be symbolic or concrete: an example of the former would be pointing to an object from a distance to indicate interest in it or a desire to hold it; an example of the latter would be pushing away or striking another person.

Development of Nonverbal Communication. By six months the normal infant can be seen to respond appropriately to the mother's tone of voice through utterances conveying affection, irritation, or an invitation to play. By about nine months, and during the first year, a normal baby is able to attract attention, express emotion, and engage in social exchanges with familiar adults. Thus, the baby during his first year of life is able to smile, point, wave, lift his arms before being picked up, make excited noises, and look around to attract the attention of mother. The vocalizations used by infants, aged eight months to one year, to indicate request, frustration, greeting, and pleasant surprise seem to be universal and inbuilt; they are not learned, as they do not vary among babies with different native languages.

Now the contrast with autistic children. During the first year of life, according to Ricks and Wing (138), ten out of twenty-seven autistic children in a retrospective study did not lift their arms to ask to be picked up. Autistic children show little response to the sound of mother's voice and do not point out things for their parents to look at. Although autistic children are able to express frustration, greeting, surprise, and demand, they do so in an idiosyncratic way. They do not use the expressive noises common to normal babies. In terms of facial expression, autistic children are usually able to smile, laugh, weep, and show fear and anger, but they tend to show only extremes of emotion. Shadings of feelings, such as doubt, slight embarrassment, or mild annoyance, are rarely seen.

About half of the autistic children in Ricks and Wing's sample were mute. Unlike children who are deaf or who have developed mental-receptive speech disorders, however, *autistic children do not use gestures as a substitute for speech*. Nodding and shaking of the head to mean yes and no are rarely seen either as substitutes for or as accompaniments of speech. The use of gesture changes very little with increasing age, although comprehension of gesture tends to improve. The inability of these children to mimic gestural behaviors contributes to their apparent poverty of social response.

In terms of the nonverbal aspects of speech itself, in autistic children vocal delivery tends to be jerky, with poor control of pitch and volume and odd intonation. In contrast to normal children, autistic children do not use facial expression, hand movements, and bodily posture to accompany speech—a feature which lends a wooden quality to their social interaction.

Comprehension of nonverbal communication is also disturbed. Sometimes an autistic child will hold an adult's face with his hands while gazing intently, as if seeking a meaning which eludes him. Social graces are an almost impossible task for the autistic child, as he lacks the ability to read reactions in others, such as boredom or annoyance, and thus cannot respond accordingly. Exaggerated expressive movements are required for understanding other people. In order to teach motor skills to a young autistic child, for instance, it is necessary literally to move his limbs through speech or gesture.

Development of Speech. Normal babies begin to understand the meaning of words relating to familiar objects and events by the end of the first year. They also develop the capacity to obey very simple instructions when accompanied by gestures. In addition to the noises expressing emotion, babble—the use of vowel and consonant combinations of increasing complexity—develops through the first year. Following babble, special consonant and vowel combinations are used by the baby to indicate specific objects, although they are not conventionally accepted words. These are described as "sound labels." In this manner the baby generalizes certain sounds in an attempt to form his own concept. The first sound labels are used by the child with enthusiasm and zeal. When the baby hears his own sound labels used by his parents, his alertness is markedly increased.

Again the contrast with autistic children: The parents of autistic children in Ricks and Wing's study (138) reported that their children had not developed normal conversational babble in their first year. If there is babble in autistic children, it tends to be monotonous—like that of a normal baby falling asleep. In addition, autistic children do not consistently use sound labels or words. They do not show the exuberant joy in producing sound labels which Ricks and Wing described in normal children. Lack of generalization was also evident.

Echolalia. Echoing is found normally in young children, but this is a temporary phase, not lasting beyond two and one-half years. Normally the young child translates a sentence to fit the particular set of grammatical rules with which he is operating at the time, or skips the part he is as yet unable to handle. In marked contrast, when autistic children first begin to speak, they echo in a patternlike, meaningless way, with no show of interest in what they are saying. Words are often spoken with the inflection of the original speaker, exactly imitating any original or foreign accent.

Echoing may be immediate or delayed. Usually words which have been spoken loudly and with emphasis are likely to be repeated, such as scoldings and expletives—these may cause considerable social embarrassment when repeated in public. Pronoun reversal is a consequence of echolalia.

Development of Grammar and Abnormalities in Spontaneous Speech. By the age of five most normal children are able to use the basic grammatical structures. The rules of grammar are demonstrably not learned by a process of conditioning, which suggests that the human brain is organized to extract certain types of rules which may be fundamental to the capacity for any human language.

In spontaneous speech autistic children show peculiar uses of grammar, such as adding verb endings to a noun. Prepositions, conjunctions, and pronouns are dropped. Letter ordering or word order in sentences may be confused. There is a tendency to contract phrases and even words to the barest possible minimum; for instance, "home after bread" may mean "Can we go home after we have bought some bread?" Even those few autistic children who acquire the rules of grammar are still peculiarly restricted in the range of their conversation, showing how much they rely on stereotyped phrases and repetition when they talk. Ricks and Wing pointed out that conversing with these children is rather like holding a discussion with a well-programed computer. Understanding of speech is extremely low. The most that is understood is for simple, practical purposes. Idiomatic expressions confuse these patients, and humor is out of their grasp.

Development of Inner Language. The beginnings of inner language can be seen in the normal child around twelve months of age, when he is starting to understand a few words in context. At this stage he shows that he understands the use of everyday objects, for example, by brushing his own hair with a brush. By eighteen months he uses objects appropriately in relation to other people or pets, and by age two he is able to use correctly miniature objects, such as a doll's tea set. Further development of inner language can be seen as play becomes more and more complex.

In contrast, the lack of inner language is an important characteristic of autistic children. Most autistic children handle toys and other objects as if they are seeking sensory stimuli. They do not use them for their proper purpose or for imaginary play. They may be able to do a jigsaw puzzle and assemble construction toys, so long as these require only visual, spatial, or mechanical skills and not imaginative understanding. Brighter autistic adolescents do not show any appropriate planning for future or any interest in the realities of adult life. This kind of foresight depends upon the existence of inner language, which can be used for thinking and planning.

INTELLIGENCE TEST RESULTS

The IQs of autistic children can be measured and are predictive of the child's future functioning (50,144). DeMyer (50) found that autistic children tend to have abnormal intelligence (IQ less than 68) and more signs of neurological dysfunction than subnormal controls. In this study test data were reviewed to see which subtests differentiated a group of sixty-six autistic children from a group of twenty-nine children with subnormal intelligence. High-functioning autistic children were as a group similar to subnormal children on verbal subtests. However, subnormal children were superior to autistic children in some performing areas—for example, ball play.

PHYSICAL EXAMINATION

NEUROLOGICAL EXAMINATION

Most neurological examinations of autistic children are unremarkable. However, "soft neurological signs" are reported in 40 percent to 75 percent of patients according to Ornitz and Ritvo (128). Other findings in this area will be discussed later under "Theories of Etiology."

ELECTROENCEPHALOGRAM

Various studies indicate that autistic infants show immature electroencephalographic tracings, similar to those of premature infants. Also the REM activity of REM sleep is reduced in autistic children similar to that found in normal infants, Suggesting a maturational defect (127). Some researchers indicated 50 percent to 80 percent abnormalities in the electroencephalogram, which is characterized by focal and diffuse spikes, slow-wave or paroxysmal spike-and-wave patterns. Other authors have reported lower incidences. The use of computerized electroencephalography points to differences between autistic and normal children. Tanguay (172) studied auditory evoked responses recorded over the right and the left sides of the scalp in ten two- to five-year-old autistic children and in ten four-month to five-year-old normal children. All ten normal children showed larger evoked responses over right hemisphere during REM sleep, similar to the adult pattern; whereas no consistent hemispheric differences were found in autistic children.

COURSE AND PROGNOSIS

Approximately 75 percent of all autistic children are classified as mentally retarded throughout life. Specific organic brain dysfunction, cognitive deficits, low IQ, seizures, and failure to develop communicative language by age five correlate highly with poor prognosis, as does failure to develop the capacity to use toys. The minority of autistic children who show relatively normal cognitive and motor development and have developed communicative language before age five, have a somewhat different prognosis.

Most patients are later classified as schizoid personalities. At best, autistic adults who are able to live alone and obtain employment have a significant residual personality and cognitive impairment (aloofness, literal ways of interpreting language, and gestures which show lack of social judgment and empathy). This relatively more benign prognosis, however, corresponds to no more than 2 percent to 5 percent of autistic children.

Differential Diagnosis of Autism

RELATION TO CHILDHOOD SCHIZOPHRENIA

As mentioned in the beginning of this chapter, the controversy over the continuity between autism and childhood schizophrenia continues. Bender (8), Fish (69), and Goldfarb (78), for instance, have implied that there is a continuum of schizophrenic illness. Bender proposed that a maturational lag causes autism if the illness begins prior to three years of age; it causes childhood schizophrenia if it begins between three years and adolescence; and it causes adult schizophrenia if the onset of illness is in adolescence or later. Longitudinal and retrospective studies, such as those by Goldfarb (80) and Fish (71), support this thesis.

In contrast, Rutter (150) and Kolvin (105) believed that childhood autism is a separate disease entity which manifests itself during the first three years of life. They saw the early age of onset and the symptoms, natural history, and cause of the disease as differentiating it from childhood schizophrenia. In particular, the fact that the age of onset of psychosis in childhood shows two peaks, one at three years and one at eleven years, suggests a discontinuity between infantile autism and schizophrenia. Psychoses with onset between three and six years of age are rare, according to Rutter (150). The distinction is crucial for treatment planning. Autistic children suffer from severe language disturbances and thus respond best to behavior therapy and education. The thought and affective disorders typical of childhood schizophrenia, on the other hand, respond best to a combination of psychotropic medication, psychotherapy, and milieu therapy (79).

The course of the two conditions can in fact be seen to differ in several respects:

1. Remissions and relapses occur in schizophrenia but not in autism.
2. Autistic children do not have delusions or hallucinations, even as adults. In contrast, psychoses with onset after the age of five to seven closely resemble schizophrenia as seen in adults. Loose associations and blocking are observed in 60 percent of children, hallucinations in 80 percent, and delusions in 40 percent; blunting of affect, disturbance of mood, and ambivalence are common (105).
3. Perinatal complications and epilepsy are common in autism. When schizophrenics are epileptic, they usually have temporal lobe epilepsy, which is not the case in autism.
4. Schizophrenia is rare in parents and siblings of children with early-onset psychosis, but occurs in about 10 percent of parents of schizophrenic children with onset after five to seven years.
5. A high proportion of the parents of autistic children are of above average intelligence and of superior socioeconomic status; whereas the parents of schizophrenics with onset after five to seven years have the same background as that of the general population (153).
6. Mental retardation occurs commonly in early onset psychosis (65 percent) but is much less frequently associated with schizophrenia.
7. Sex distribution is different: autism shows a four to one preponderance of boys over girls, whereas in schizophrenia the incidence is the same for both sexes.

The differentiation of autism as a distinct entity began with Kanner (97,98), who described autism as beginning before age two and as characterized by extreme isolation, lack of communicative language, need to maintain sameness, and fascination with objects which are handled with skill. DeMyer (55,56) listed the following criteria for infantile autism: (1) emotional withdrawal from people before age three, (2) lack of speech for communication, (3) nonfunctional, repetitive use of objects, and (4) failure to engage in role play alone or with other children. The child has to fulfill all four criteria to be described as autistic. If perceptual motor performances or other aspects of his performance are approximate to chronological age, the classification will be secondary or higher-functioning autism. If perceptual motor performance is flat or below age level, the label will be primary or lower functioning autism. In addition to being called primary autism, all features delineated by Kanner have to be present.

DeMyer (55,56) has also described the criteria for diagnosing early childhood schizophrenia. There are islands of normal relatedness or emotional dependency in a background of emotional withdrawal and flat affect. Some communicative speech exists with speech abnormalities such as echolalia, stereotypy, bizarre fantasies, and failure to answer questions. However, although this clinical picture may evolve from a background of more normal behavior, it may also evolve from a typical infantile autism symptom pattern, and regression may occur to an autistic pattern.

It seems important to note here that the various scales for autism and childhood schizophrenia overlap in 35 percent of the cases. In fact, the British Working Party's term "schizophrenia" correlates to a great extent with the term "autism" as used by other authors. Recent research, however, points to the possibility of biological markers. Rimland (142), for instance, has found a correlation between serotonin efflux from platelets and autism. Cohen and Young (44) suggest that in certain autistic children monoamine oxidase and hematocrit correlate negatively—a relationship not found in control groups. These and other neurophysiological findings are discussed in greater detail under "Theories of Etiology."

The preceding presentation characterizes infantile autism as a distinct entity. This conclusion, however, *does not exclude the presence of other psychoses of early infancy.* Rutter and Hersov (153), for example, have described a group of conditions under the term "disintegrative psychosis" or "regressive psychosis." The early onset is by the age of three or four, at which time there is a profound regression and behavioral disintegration, after an apparent normal development. Rutter and Hersov (153) saw the clinical picture in terms of irritability, restiveness, and anxiety with initial impoverishment and then loss of speech and language. Although language comprehension deteriorates and intelligence may decline, an intelligent facial expression is usually retained. Stereotypies and mannerisms develop as social skills and interest in surroundings and interpersonal relationships are lost. The cause often reveals some kind of organic cortical degeneration (measles, encephalitis, lipoidosis, leucodystrophies). Prognosis is very poor, with some children ending in death after a progressive deterioration. Otherwise the children remain without speech and severely mentally handicapped.

In summary, the following categories of early onset psychosis (before three years) would be interchangeable: Kanner's primary autism (97, 98), Mahler and Furer's infantile autism (119), Tustin's abnormal primary autism (175), DeMyer et al.'s autism (55), and Kanner's secondary autism (97,98), would correspond to Mahler's symbiotic psychosis (117), Tustin's encapsulated secondary autism (175), and DeMyer and Churchill's early childhood schizophrenia (55). These latter categories correspond to early onset psychoses differing from early infantile autism by the presence of islands of normal relatedness or emotional dependence in a background of emotional withdrawal, with some speech for communication in the midst of other speech abnormalities.

RELATION TO MAJOR SENSORY DEFICITS

Otological and audiological defects of blindness may cause symptomatic or secondary autism. The psychotic syndrome produced by sensory deficits has been referred to variously under the concepts of disintegrative psychosis (153), early onset psychosis (105), and childhood schizophrenia (80).

"Blindisms," however, do not have the repetitive stereotypy characteristic of the hand flapping of classical autism, and they occur in response to environmental stimuli. Blind children, in fact, become interested in the environment and may develop quite normally with adequate education. Although the blind child may seek photic stimulation by pressing his eyeballs or vestibular stimulation by head shaking or lying with his head down, these mannerisms do not necessarily indicate a preference for nonhuman over human relatedness. Given a choice, the nonautistic blind child prefers people to things (33).

In her study of children who had had congenital rubella and also had one or more sensory deficits, Chess (33) found that the nonautistic children used alternate modes of perceiving with appropriate responses in the intact modes of reception. Deaf children, for example, exhibited visual alertness; visually impaired children compensated with auditory or tactile responsiveness. These children sought affectionate bodily contact, whereas autistic children failed to explore alternative modalities and did not manifest appropriate responsiveness. In addition, Chess found that nonautistic children, after getting used to auditory support devices, used them adaptively. In contrast, it was difficult to test the degree of hearing impairment with autistic children, as their use of devices was unpredictable, and they showed no clear improvement.

In view of these findings, one could assume that since retrolental fibroplasia is associated with generalized brain damage, autism in these cases may result from the central nervous system impairment and not from the visual damage per se (33,127). Congenital rubella is not only a cause of sensory deficits, but it is also an important etiological factor in autism. Eight to 10 percent of children with congenital rubella had the complete autistic syndrome—that is, 400 times the incidence present in the general population. In studying rubella children, Chess found that in the children with sensory defects, neither visual defects nor hearing defects nor retardation *alone* presented a complete syndrome of autism. The hearing defect seems to be an important contributor to the development of autistic syndrome in rubella children in combination with either visual defects or mental retardation.

RELATION TO DEVELOPMENTAL APHASIA*

Abnormal response to sound, delay in acquisition of language, difficulties with articulation, and difficulties with relating are present in both developmental aphasia and autism. The capacity to relate nonverbally is present in developmental aphasia but *absent* in autism. Perceptual

---

* Based on Ornitz (127) and DeMyer (50).

disturbances occur in autism but not in developmental aphasia. Hyper-activity or hypoactivity appears in both developmental aphasia and autism. The child with developmental aphasia can point toward desired objects and learns to communicate intent and emotion when speech is acquired; these abilities are not present in autism. When speech is acquired, delayed echolalia is present in autism and absent in developmental aphasia. As seen in this parallel outline, the problems are more severe and more deviant in autism than in aphasic children.

RELATION TO MENTAL RETARDATION

Sixty-six to 75 percent of the cases overlap, according to DeMyer and colleagues (52,54). Mentally retarded children do show stereotypic and perseverative behavior, although this in itself is not an exclusive sign of autism. The existence of "special abilities" in a background of general retardation may, however, differentiate autistic children.

It is of interest that in autopsies conducted on thirty-three patients diagnosed as having had an autistic syndrome, Darby (48) found three cases of Schilders disease, one of Heller's syndrome, one of cerebral lipidoses, and one of phenylketonuria. Although the course of these various encephalopathies is different, in general they show normal development at first, with subsequent rapid and progressive deterioration. Heller's syndrome, for instance, is described as beginning in the third and fourth year of life after normal development. It is characterized by increasing malaise and rapid diminution of interests, with loss of speech and sphincter control. This stage is followed by complete "idiotic regression," although the patient retains an intelligent physiognomy and adequate motoric functioning. Heller's syndrome may be differentiated by the age of onset (three to five years) from early-onset psychosis (before three years) and late-onset psychosis (five years or older). Although etiology is likely to be organic (105) social and psychological factors may also contribute. (This description overlaps with Rutter and Hersov's [153] concept of disintegrative psychosis.)

Phenylketonuria (PKU) may also be mistaken for an autistic syndrome. It differs from autism in that microcephaly is present in 50 percent of PKU patients; one-third of untreated individuals have eczema; and patients tend to have lighter complexion and hair than other members of their families. Metabolic tests show plasma phenylalanine above 20 milligrams (normal 2.4 mgs.), with normal levels of tirosinemia. In the urine phenylalanine acid is increased and is responsible for the positive ferric chloride tests. Parents of phenylketonuric children have a diminished tolerance blood curve for phenylalanine, which is inherited through autosomal recessive mechanisms.

RELATION TO SEIZURE DISORDERS

Autism and seizure disorders frequently coexist (128). Ornitz and Ritvo (128) stated that two sleep tracings are required to evaluate this possibility. In one study 25 percent of the autistic children developed seizures between eleven and nineteen years of age (grand mal and psychomotor seizures); most of them had previously shown normal results on neurological examinations and electroencephalograms.

RELATION TO MATERNAL DEPRIVATION

Deficient human stimulation—for example, maternal or environmental deprivation—may produce serious developmental disturbances, but it does not produce the syndrome of autism. Deprived children show a uniform delay in acquisition of motor skills, speech, and adaptive use of toys. In contrast, in autistic children motor and speech development is uneven, with spurts and lags.

Deprived children show athetoidlike movements of the hands, in contrast to the repetitive hand flapping of autistic children. The latter show whirling, toe walking, lunging movements—none of which are present in deprived children. Both deprived and autistic children show body rocking and hand posturing. In deprived children, however, these movements can be interrupted, whereas in autistic children these movements are much more intractable. In their use of toys, deprived children flick at toys, drop them, or fail to develop an interest in them; in contrast, autistic children frequently use toys in peculiar ways—spinning, feeling, or sighting them.

Deprived children show intense visual contact with adults, while autistic children show gaze aversion. There is a delayed but present interest in playing, which is rarely seen in autistic children. In deprived children speech is delayed, but recovery is possible with normal tone rhythm and expression and no echolalia or pronoun reversal. Even if autistic children acquire speech, their speech lacks the normal tone rhythm and expression, and echolalia and pronoun reversal are present.

RELATION TO ANACLITIC DEPRESSION

After six months an interruption of an adequate mother-child relationship produces the following constellation of symptoms. Within a few weeks the child shows psychomotor retardation, delay in development of language, weight loss, and persistent crying. After two or three months these signs are replaced by quiet whimpering, facial rigidity, lethargy, and apathy. These children do not, however, show the perceptual disturbances, language disturbances, or motility disturbances present in autistic children. There is no developmental spurt or lag. Their mood is of sadness or loneliness, in contrast to the aloofness or aloneness of the autistic child as perceived by an observer.

RELATION TO ATYPICAL DEVELOPMENT

Atypical children suffer from perceptual dysfunction, lack of modulation of anxiety, disturbed social relations, problems with attention and regulation of state. The differences from autistic children are that motor skills are slower to develop, social relations may be characterized by immaturity rather than aloofness, and verbal and nonverbal communication skills are present albeit idiosyncratic. According to Cohen (41),

atypical children may be conceptualized as the 'milder' region of the autistic spectrum, from another, as forming the more extremely deviant of the 'minimal cerebral dysfunction' phenotype in which children have difficulties in attention, cognitive phrases, motor organization and personality development.

Theories of Etiology

Some authors talk about childhood autism exclusively; others include autism as part of the spectrum of schizophrenia when they present theories on etiology. The range of theories is quite broad. For example, from Kanner's citation of the lack of affective contact, various authors have developed unitary theories to explain the autistic syndrome, such as chronic overarousal (94), chronic underarousal (139), or failure of adequate vestibular modulation of perception and motility (126). Bettelheim (13) has designated the parents as etiological agents, while Hermelin and O'Connor (88) postulate a general problem of manipulating symbols. Other theorists like Bender (8) and Cohen (41) emphasize neurophysiological and biochemical causes. The current trend, however, is to see autistic children as suffering from multiple impairments, in their affection, comprehension and use of gesture, auditory and visual perception, control of skilled movements, autonomic functioning, and certain aspects of social development which depend on subtle nonverbal cues.

THE PARENT-CHILD RELATIONSHIP

THE PSYCHOANALYTIC VIEW

The most widely accepted theory is Mahler and Furer's (119) postulation that the crucial disturbance is the infant's lack or loss of the ability to utilize the mother during early life as a complement to and as an organizer of maturation. The result is the absence of "a human beacon of orientation" both in the world of reality and in the infant's own inner world; hence the gross impairment of the ego in its integrating, synthesizing, and organizing functions. Mahler and Furer stated that most frequently constitutional limitations determine the child's inability to use the mothering function. Maternal depression, although prevalent, remains to be proved a sufficient or necessary etiological factor.

THE EFFECT OF PARENTAL PSYCHOPATHOLOGY

In cases of psychiatrically ill parents with disturbed children, according to Rutter and Koupernick (154), the psychiatrically ill parent is most often the mother. She shows high anxiety, somatic symptoms, and personality disturbance symptoms directly involving the child, such as overt hostility to the child. In 36 percent of the cases, she had a sick spouse and a long-lasting illness. In contrast, in a survey of psychiatrically ill parents with well children, the psychiatric patient was most often the father. His anxiety was not as high, he had no somatic symptoms, he did not have diagnosis of personality disturbance, his symptoms did not involve the child, and there was no overt hostility toward the child. He did not have a sick spouse, and his illness was not long-lasting.

Anthony (3) has commented on parapsychosis, an environmentally determined syndrome in high-risk children. The conditions favoring this syndrome include a symbiotic relationship between mother and child, a lower-than-average intelligence in the child, a close identification with the sick parent, a high degree of suggestibility, especially in relation to bodily feelings, objectlike passivity and submissiveness, and a marked involvement in the psychotic manifestations of the parents. Unlike pre-psychotic reactions, reactions tend to disappear altogether when the child is permanently separated from the parents. The impact of a delusional system on a family of children can be roughly predicted from measures of identification and involvement, such as stability and submissiveness. Conviction regarding the delusion may vary from child to child and in any particular child, depending on the presence or the absence of other reality-oriented figures, such as the father.

From studies of institutionalized youngsters, Yarrow as summarized by Garmezy (77) suggested that a critical period of high vulnerability occurs between three and twelve months of age. The type and duration of the mother-child separation necessitated by the mother's admission to a mental hospital appears most likely to have serious developmental implications in the period between the child's earliest differentiation of the mother as a specific object (three to four months) and in the time when he can use locomotion and language to effect some control over his environment (fifteen to eighteen months). Significantly, joint hospitalizations of mothers and their infants have been found to be most useful precisely during that critical period when a prolonged separation of mother and child would be most harmful.

Mednick and Schulsinger (121) have indicated that the mothers who were lost to their children at an earlier age were also more severely schizophrenic when ill. Furthermore, children separated earlier were more likely to have subsequent hospitalizations.

THE RELATIVE IMPORT OF FAMILY INTERACTION

Most of the research on the import of family interaction has been concerned with schizophrenia in general. In their adoption studies, Rosenthal and his collaborators (146) found that environmental factors accounted for only 9 percent of the variance in terms of incidence of schizophrenia. They concluded that although the degree of illness correlated with the quality of relationship between the child and his adoptive parents, the amount of variance explained by rearing tended to be low. They suggested that rearing patterns have only a modest effect on individuals with a genetic background for schizophrenia. In the case of individuals with more normal genetic background—namely, without familial schizophrenia—rearing patterns play a greater role in producing normal or psychopathological behavioral characteristics, presumably because there is no specific genetic interference with the shaping of behavior by different rearing patterns.

It is of note that an appreciable number of investigators nevertheless have taken the position that familial or parent-child relationships are major determinants of schizophrenia (13,83,110,120). Rosenthal et al. pointed to the child's inability to develop the kinds of skills or strengths necessary to maintain his psychological integrity: (1) failure at socialization, (2) failure at cognitive integration, and (3) failure to contain anxiety. Authors, such as Lidz (110) and Bettelheim (13), saw these deficits as stemming from the parent-child relationship.

The UCLA project (77) showed that predisposition to schizophrenia may arise from a general pattern of family disorganization, even though explicit identifying signs of schizophrenia in a parent may be absent. Parental-communication deviance appears to be a far more consistent indicator of schizophrenic symptomatology in an offspring than does actual parental symptomatology. These parental deviances predate the offspring's symptomatology and should constitute a good device for identifying schizophrenic families. The simpler notions of parental dominance and parent-child conflicts are thus being replaced by more subtle aspects of communication networks (120).

FAMILY BACKGROUND AND AUTISM

Although most of the preceding studies deal with schizophrenia, a few studies pertaining more directly to autism are of interest and will be briefly mentioned.

A comparative study of infantile autism and specific developmental receptive language disorder by Cox et al. (46) does not support the notion that parents of autistic children are uninterested in people, emotionally cold or refrigerated, perplexed, or lacking in communicative clarity.

Currently the effects on the parents of having an autistic child are being studied. Schopler and Reichler (158) have found that a child's perceptual difficulties induce maternal confusion and in turn increase the disturbance in the child. This maternal confusion may be compounded by the fact that there is a significantly higher proportion of firstborn among autistic children (25), thus adding the factor of maternal inexperience to the faulty interaction between mother and child.

SOCIAL CLASS AND AUTISM

Ornitz (127) has found that autism is not correlated with parental social class. However, Allen et al. (1) and Campbell (25) have confirmed that there is some relation with social class, and that these parents have a significantly higher intelligence and degree of education than those of children who are born mentally retarded or belong to the general population.

GENETIC THEORIES

In relation to autism most studies have failed to show an increased incidence of schizophrenia or a history of autism among nontwin siblings of autistic children. However, twin studies suggest that monozygotic pairs are likely to be concordant for and dizygotic pairs discordant for autism (166).

CONGENITAL FACTORS

There is increasing evidence of congenital factors in the development of autism. Autistic children show an increased incidence of soft or hard neurological signs (50,152) as well as the presence of abnormal electroencephalographic findings (54). Many have average IQs. Perceptual and motor disorders are similar to those found in patients with clear evidence of central nervous system impairment, thus relating infantile autism to various diseases such as rubella (33,48), toxoplasmosis, syphilis, and retrolental fibroplasia (48), celiac disease (127), and hypsarrhythmia (171).

The relation between rubella and autism in particular has been detailed in an excellent study by Chess (33). The 1964 epidemics of rubella in the United States left 20,000 to 30,000 children with congenital defects (cataracts, heart defects, deafness). Fetal infection often continuing in infancy may also leave diverse neurological abnormalities. Eighty-one percent of the infants had neurological abnormalities up to one year of age. In the 243 children studied by Chess 10 children were found to have autism, and 8 more, a partial syndrome of autism. Compared with the normal prevalence of autism of 0.7 per 10,000 or 2.1 per 10,000 for the entire childhood population, the rubella group had a prevalence of 412 per 10,000 for the core syndrome, of 329 for the partial syndrome of autism, giving a combined autism rate of 741 per 10,000 for the complete and partial syndrome. The particular deficits were distributed as follows: 3 percent of these children showed no defect; visual defects were present in 32.9 percent; hearing defects in 72 percent; neurological hard signs were present in 44 percent, and 24 percent presented neurological soft signs.

Further indirect support for a viral etiology comes from recent research by Stubbs (168), who has made a preliminary study indicating that autistic children do not show a titer rise increase of antibodies upon the administration of the rubella vaccination or booster injects. Also Stubbs and Crawford (169) showed that autistic children have a depressed lymphocyte-transformation response to phytohemagglutinin stimulation of lymphocyte cultures, as compared with control subjects ($p < 0.01$), which indicated an altered immune response to the viral antigen.

PREGNANCY AND BIRTH COMPLICATIONS

Here we will first consider the influence of these factors on schizophrenia. In 1970 in Garmezy (76), Mednick reported on pregnancy and birth complications in high-risk subjects who were beginning to show signs of breakdown. He indicated that while no single complication significantly differentiated his groups, 70 percent of the sick group had suffered one or more serious pregnancy or birth complications. This contrasted with the 15 percent of the well group and 33 percent of the control group with perinatal complications. The perinatal complications included anoxia, prematurity, prolonged labor, placenta difficulties, umbilical cord complications, mother's illness during pregnancy, multiple births, and breech presentations. Careful perusal of these data brought out an additional striking relationship within the sick group and the entire high-risk group. There was a marked correspondence between perinatal complications and anomalous electrodermal behavior. All the perinatal complications seemed to damage the modulatory control of the baby's stress-response mechanisms which may be genetically determined. Perinatal complications were also associated with rapid response onset, poor habituation of response —that is, cardiac rate—and poor extinction of the conditioned electrodermal response. This lack of modulation may be viewed as an important etiological factor in the development of mental illness, especially schizophrenia.

Mednick and Schulsinger (121) have also conducted longitudinal studies of children born of schizophrenic parents for whom excellent perinatal data were available. The children were examined at five days and at one year of age. The indexed children tended to have lower birth weights, a finding that obtained in cases where either mother or father was the patient. Difficulties in the pregnancy were suggested by the greater number of X-rays ordered by the obstetrician during the last month of pregnancy in the case of the schizophrenic mothers. In the five-day neonatal examination, children of the schizophrenic group continued to show more abnormalities, whereas even those children born to normal or character disorder parents who had shown abnormalities at birth no longer exhibited signs of disturbance. At one year of age, despite a marked loss of data (presumably due to the failure of schizophrenic mothers and character disorder fathers to return with the infant for later examination), the most outstanding feature was the retarded motor development of the children born of schizophrenic parentage and the superior rate of development evidenced by the children of character disorder fathers.

Perinatal factors have also been found in cases of monozygotic twins who are discordant for schizophrenia. In studies by Polin and Mosher in Garmezy (77), the schizophrenic twin was lighter in weight at birth, and 73 percent showed central nervous system abnormalities as compared with only 9 percent of the nonschizophrenic twins.

We shall now turn to autism. There is a consensus that premature birth is not significantly associated with autism. In fact, Mednick and Schulsinger (121) in a prospective study indicated that the one factor significantly associated with autism is hermorrhage in the second trimester of pregnancy.

NEUROPHYSIOLOGICAL AND BIOLOGICAL THEORIES

In the following sections emphasis will be on etiological theories of autism, as theories of schizophrenia are the subjects of other chapters in this book.

Ornitz (126) emphasized the abnormal perceptual experience in autism, which he took as the point of departure for explaining the development of the syndrome. He assumed that the disturbance in perception is based on a common underlying neuropathological physiological process common to all autistic patients. The consequences are (1) failure of adequate modulation of external sensory input (8,126); (2) a distortion of the normal receptor preferences—close receptors are preferred to distant receptors; and (3) impaired ability to use internal sensory input to make discriminations in the absence of feedback from motor responses. Ornitz postulated an imbalance between excitatory and inhibitory influences in the central nervous system as underlying the disturbances in stable images, in the capacity to imitate, and in the capacity to distinguish self from nonself—an imbalance which leads to language and relating disturbances. Experiments conducted by Hermelin and O'Connor (89) also strongly suggested that the disturbed relations with people may stem from the disturbances in perception. Ritvo et al. (144) further believed that the disturbances in motility can be best understood as an expression of a central nervous system dysfunction, as they occur with the same frequency over time and at the same rate in different patients and are unaffected by the presence of persons or toys.

In his book on autism, Ornitz (127) offered the model in figure 16–1 for the etiology of autism. This is a valuable schema for conceptualizing how idiopathic or known organic disturbances associated with autism may produce a central nervous system dysfunction which ends in autism. The known organic disturbances associated with autism—like phenylketonuria, congenital rubella, and seizure disorders—may also produce other central nervous system dysfunctions causing intellectual deficiency and motor retardation. Nonorganic factors—whether idiopathic or known (maternal deprivation, anaclitic depression, hospitalization, or psychotic parent)—lead to fixed, regressed, or deviant ego development and end in a nonorganic psychosis which is secondarily complicated by intellectual, perceptual, and motor retardation, but which is not coincidental with autism.

BRAIN-STEM DISTURBANCES

Advances have been made in attempting to specify further the nature of the central nervous system dysfunction postulated by Ornitz in the preceding schema. DeMyer (50), for instance, referred to the many theories of childhood autism which have focused on possible malfunction of subcortical structures and abnormal processing of sensory inputs.

DeMyer indicated that asphyxia, the most ubiquitous accident during the birth process, may bring about brain-stem sensory nuclei focal lesions, for example, in the auditory system (inferior colliculi), which is most likely to be affected because of its peculiarly high oxygen requirements. Since its myelinization is completed at birth, the damage caused by asphyxia is *irreversible*. The tectum, or inferior colliculus is a major center for selective attention and orientation to sounds and visual stimuli; ablation of the tectorium and its connections with higher centers (the medial geniculates and temporal lobes) suggests that this is one area of the auditory system that could be involved in environmental awareness and social behavior. Of the thirty-three cases of child psy-

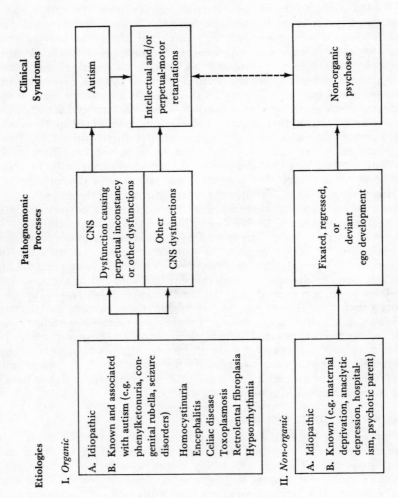

FIGURE 16-1
Etiology of Autism

Etiologies

I. *Organic*

A. Idiopathic

B. Known and associated with autism (e.g. phenylketonuria, congenital rubella, seizure disorders)

Homocystinuria
Encephalitis
Celiac disease
Toxoplasmosis
Retrolental fibroplasia
Hypsorrhythmia

II. *Non-organic*

A. Idiopathic

B. Known (e.g. maternal deprivation, anaclytic depression, hospitalism, psychotic parent)

Pathognomonic Processes

CNS Dysfunction causing perpetual inconstancy or other dysfunctions

Other CNS dysfunctions

Fixated, regressed, or deviant ego development

Clinical Syndromes

Autism

Intellectual and/or perpetual-motor retardations

Non-organic psychoses

Source: Adapted from E. R. Ritvo and B. J. Freeman, eds., *Autism—Diagnosis, Current Research and Management* (New York: Spectrum Publications, 1976).

chosis with anatomicopathological studies (48), none have specifically referred to the study of these centers.

DeMyer (50), quoted Brown, who found that if large lesions to the colliculi were made in monkeys, the animals looked mute with totally expressionless faces. All the mime responses characteristic of monkeys were absent. The eyes did not fix and looked, only approximately, in the direction of the object. The monkeys appeared totally unaware of events in the environment. No motor defects were seen, except for motor fixation. The main defect was in the reactivity of the organism, which was reduced in all aspects of externally directed behavior. Other experimenters, such as Jane and Windle, quoted by DeMyer (50), have noted similar findings in cats and monkeys submitted to asphyxia. DeMyer further observed that the lesions in the inferior colliculi and other brainstem nuclei can be reproduced in a predictable order by inducing a brief episode of asphyxia at birth in monkeys, and that the resultant behavioral symptoms parallel those observed in Kanner's syndrome. In addition, the inferior colliculi may be vulnerable not only to hypoxia but also to exposure to any other abnormal metabolites (phenylketonuria, uricaciduria, drug addiction).

Further evidence has been found to implicate a brain-stem disturbance involving the central connections of the vestibular system. Autistic children demonstrate a consistent suppression of vestibular nystagmus due to an anomalous interaction between the visual and the vestibular systems. Vestibular stimulation during REM sleep does not influence the rapid eye movement in autism as it does in normals.

DISORDERS IN CENTRAL NERVOUS SYSTEM
MATURATION AND FUNCTION

Rapid-eye movement (REM) in autistic children two to five years old during dreaming sleep is similar to that found in infants six to twelve months old, which suggests a maturational defect (127). The normal tendency of REM to cluster into bursts is also reduced. Other deficits in other reflexes have been found; an inadequate galvanic response to auditory and visual stimuli has been demonstrated in autistic children, compatible with the clinical observation of these children's lack of startle response. Furthermore, a defect in cross-modal associations is found between visual and auditory systems, vestibular and motor systems, visual and tactile systems. DeMyer (50) confirmed Birch and Hertzig's (15) findings of a defect in processing intermodal perceptual information, which varies from child to child. All autistic and schizophrenic children, however, show a specific deficiency in transferring visual information to their motor systems. These children imitate an action much more frequently when the action is in relation to an object and thus leaves traces in the visual field serving as a concrete reference point (i.e., covering a doll with a blanket), than when the action is without object (i.e., clapping hands). Imitation of pure motor function without an object requires a transfer of visual memory to the motor system; in order to achieve this, the child must have adequate visual memory and a clear body image. Because of this deficit, these children cannot make sense of the cues from the motions of their parents and cannot use movement for communicative purposes. Compounding these problems, the autistic child has a language impairment.

Another neurological factor was pointed out by Hutt and Hutt (94), who suggested that hyperactivity of the reticular activating system leads to a reactive effort to reduce sensory input by social withdrawal, stereotyping, and gaze avoidance.

Another theory of etiology of early infantile autism was based on the autistic child's inability to comprehend or to use communicative speech. Rutter and Bartak (151) postulated that autistic children suffer from a central cognitive defect which presumably prevents them from using language. There is little doubt that autistic children may have considerable difficulty in encoding or decoding information in the auditory, and to a lesser extent, in the visual mode. Frith (74) has shown that when autistic children who can speak are presented with short sentences made up solely of random words, their recall may be as good as that of normal children matched for mental age. However, when presented with sentences in which the same words have been rearranged into a meaningful message, the recall rate of autistic children does not increase, while that of normal children does markedly. Similarly, investigations by Shapiro et al. (160,161) have suggested that when autistic children do learn speech, their morphological competence is often in advance of their communicative competence. Autistic adolescents preserved their childhood style of deviance, with constraint in length of utterance, echoing, syntactic disturbance, semantic concreteness, context, inappropriateness, and disorders of prosody. Two published studies further suggest that autistic children may have special difficulty in processing material when the information is encoded in a sequential or linear pattern: Hermelin and O'Conner (89) showed autistic children to be quite insensitive to temporally patterned visual material; while DeMyer et al. (54) showed that autistic children are unable to reproduce a sequence of bodily movements.

In relation to these findings, it is well to bear in mind that some autistic children may retain certain "islands of function" amid their handicaps. Autistic children may score comparatively well on certain subtests of the Wechsler Intelligence Scale for Children: namely, digit span, block design, and object assembly (110). They may also show a remarkable ability to perceive, store, and reproduce "meaningless" phrases or "useless" information, seemingly by rote. Hermelin and Frith (88) demonstrated that autistic children may do relatively well in organizing material within a spatial frame of reference. To some, these observations suggest that autistic children are better able to process information in a holistic fashion without regard to any sequential code of information which may be present in the material.

Moving into the subject of hemispheric specialization, Tanguay (172) pointed out that

these observations may appear especially interesting. Specifically, the handicaps of the autistic child (i.e., his language deficits and his inability to process information in a linear fashion) involve functions whose gradient is predominantly in the left hemisphere. In contrast, the abilities of the autistic child involve functions whose gradients are predominantly in the right hemisphere. This does not imply that autistic children have lesions which affect

the left hemisphere. We know, however, that differentiation of function between the two hemispheres develops within the first few years of life, and
that, at first, both hemispheres may function in a more-or-less similar manner.
It appears possible that this early functioning involves a holistic rather than
a linear mode of processing information. Thus, it may be suggested that
autistic children fail to develop hemispheric specialization in the normal
manner; they are left with two sides of the brain which remain relatively
immature and plastic, able at best to process information in a relatively
holistic and spatially oriented manner. [pp. 79–80]

Recent electrophysiological studies carried out in Tanguay's (172)
laboratory are of interest in regard to this hypothesis.

BIOGENIC AMINE METABOLISM

Although research on the roles of serotonergic and dopaminergic
systems does not speak directly to etiology, the findings may indicate
biological correlates of the syndrome and thus open the way for more
precise diagnosis subgroups and for monitoring effects of medication
and other treatments.

Boullin et al. (20) for instance, found that the efflux of 5-HIAA
(serotonin) from platelets was increased in autism. They postulated
that a serotonin platelet-binding defect might parallel a serotonin
neuron-binding defect. Indeed, the efflux of ^{14}C-5 hydroxytryptamine
from blood platelets taken from a mixed diagnostic group of children
was used as the basis for prediction of the existence of primary autism.
The prediction correlated with Rimland's E-2 score criteria for a positive
or negative diagnosis of primary infantile autism (20).

According to Cohen et al. (41), the most direct available method for
studying biogenic amine metabolism in the human brain involves
sampling of cerebrospinal fluid (CSF) for catecholamines (such as
dopamine) and indoleamines (such as serotonin), which are found in
low concentration, or for their major metabolites (homovanillic acid
[HVA] and 5-hydroxyindoleacetic acid [5-HIAA], respectively). HVA
and 5-HIAA are actively excreted into the CSF. When membrane transport is inhibited by administration of probenecid, the egress of these
acid metabolites from the CSF is inhibited, and their concentrations increasingly reflect amine turnover in the brain during a specified period
of time (e.g., ten to eighteen hours).

Most studies of adult schizophrenic and depressed patients using the
probenecid method have reported a ratio of 5-HIAA/HVA between 0.5
and 0.7. For autistic children, the ratio is at the lower end of this range,
reflecting in part the finding of relatively higher HVA levels in child
patients and a weak, but statistically significant, negative relation between CSF HVA/log probenecid and age in years (between three and
twenty-one years).

One intriguing finding across diagnostic groups is a difference between children with childhood autism and children (matched for age)
with nonautistic, early onset psychosis (severe atypical development or
childhood schizophrenialike youngsters). The autistic children had lower
levels of CSF 5-HIAA (41). More noteworthy, however, was the finding
of a subgroup within the autistic population with especially elevated
levels of HVA, both absolutely and in comparison with 5-HIAA (as
reflected in 5-HIAA/HVA ratios). This subgroup was behaviorally dis-

tinguished by the greatest degree of stereotypic, repetitive behavior (flapping, twirling, finger flicking, and the like) and was overall the most severely afflicted group.

A special opportunity for investigating these relations was offered by a set of monozygotic twins concordant for primary childhood autism. In this twinship, one twin was consistently more hyperactive and stereotypic. Both with and without the use of the probenecid method, the more active, repetitive child had higher CSF HVA levels than his twin. Both were therapeutically treated with haloperidol, a potent inhibitor of dopaminergic activity. The more stereotypic, active child, with the higher concentrations of CSF HVA, tolerated a larger dose of haloperidol before displaying toxicity, which was manifested by walking in circles and heightened irritability, reflecting interference with dopaminergic systems.

The most convincing evidence to date on CNS catecholamine functions in psychotic and attentionally disturbed children is seen in the effects of pharmacological intervention. The therapeutic response of autistic and similar children to psychoactive medication is similar in type, although unfortunately different in degree, to the response of adults with schizophrenia. Medications which inhibit dopaminergic functioning (phenothiazines and butyrophenones) reduce the severity of the autistic syndrome in certain children—evidenced by decreased self-destructive repetitive actions (such as hand biting), decreased stereotypic behavior, reduced bizarre behavior, and reduced overall anxiety. With treatment, social relatedness and availability to behavior modification and special education may improve.

On the basis of the preceding CSF studies, Cohen et al. (41,42) have postulated that certain manifestations of the autistic syndrome (such as stereotypic behavior) are positively related with dopaminergic over-activity, and that there is a reciprocal relation between dopaminergic and serotonergic functioning. In this reciprocal relation serotonin, which generally plays an inhibitory role in CNS metabolism, appears to modulate catecholamine activity—a relationship which has been observed in various experimental paradigms involving both specific surgical lesions and neurochemical interventions. Serotonin appears to be responsive to environmental input, with increased sensory intake leading to increased serotonin turnover, and may be associated with a child's greater responsivity to the environment or decreased tuning out of external sensory bombardment (43).

In summary, the roles of dopaminergic and serotonergic systems in childhood psychosis are suggested by a confluence of basic and neuropsychopharmacological observations, as well as by theoretical considerations. A relatively lower CSF 5-HIAA has been found in autistic, as compared with less-impaired, nonautistic (e.g., early onset psychotic) children. Relatively higher HVA concentrations (in relation to 5-HIAA) appear in autistic children with greater stereotype and activity. A negative relation has been found between CSF HVA and 5-HIAA in children studied without probenecid loading. Finally, there is evidence of improvement in certain children treated with dopamine-inhibiting medication and of dramatic exacerbation of symptomatology in other children following treatment with medications which increased dopaminergic functioning.

Primary Prevention

With the increasing knowledge of early development it may be possible to work with young infants at risk for schizophrenia and autism.

Fish (70) cited the regular retardation of motor development and disturbances of body image in preschizophrenic children. She reported on a child who, because of poor motor control, was still anxious, with an unsteady equilibrium, even when supported erect at eleven months of age; at nineteen months he was still unable to imitate circular and vertical pencil strokes. However, he did respond at his age level after his hand was guided in one movement. She stated that it appeared that he had insufficient awareness of his own body image to translate the visual picture of another person's performance into similar actions by himself, although he was capable of repeating the movement. This case illustrates DeMyer's hypothesis of problems in cross-modal transfer.

Other characteristics of infants at risk are poor posture and poor motoric control, causing a secondary sensory deprivation which may interfere with the infant's capacity to explore the environment and develop a sense of his body, thus delaying eye-hand integration and contributing to disordered perceptions and a disturbed body image. Infantile apathy and anhedonia, oversensitivity, and symbiosis are additional characteristics. Transient pandevelopmental retardation, with lag and disorganization in posture and visual-motor development, accompanied by retardation in physical growth, identifies the infants with the most severe psychiatric disorders. Targets for primary intervention are the disturbed acquisition of motor skills, inadequate body image, poor integration of perception, lack of patterning, abnormal states of arousal (underresponsiveness or overresponsiveness), and the disturbance in affective and social development. When primary intervention is properly introduced, parents are on the whole very accepting of it.

In relation to autism, primary prevention and early diagnosis are aimed at establishing a parental-child bond and counteracting the autistic behavior. Howlin et al. (93), for example, have begun a project of a home-base approach to the treatment of autistic children, which emphasizes the need for early treatment and treatment approaches that include the mother-child pair.

Treatment

PSYCHOTROPIC DRUGS

As has been mentioned, certain psychotropic drugs have proven effective in the treatment of childhood schizophrenia and autism. Ornitz (127) recommends drug therapy for target symptoms such as aggressiveness, sleep disorders, or hyperactivity. However, the various psychopharmacological agents used in the treatment of childhood autism and childhood schizophrenia have the disadvantage of inducing excessive sedation at therapeutic levels (25,26,27,128). Here it is important to note the physiological differences between children and adults in the metabolism of psychotropic drugs (129):

1. The serum-albumin binding capacity is different from adults, so that children may have more unbound active drug available in their blood.
2. The rate at which the liver metabolizes drugs may be twice as fast as in adults and thus the half-life of a drug may be reduced in children.
3. The drug absorption rates from the gastrointestinal tract or intramuscular injection may be the same in children; for example, diazepam, given orally or intramuscularly, is absorbed into the blood stream at about the same rate.
4. The fat compartment in children is 70 percent less than that in adults. The fat compartment serves as a buffer or temporary storage area for drugs. Since children have less of this fat as buffer, an overdosage of medication is more dangerous for them than it is for an adult, as most of the overdosage will stay active in the blood stream.

It is therefore generally recommended that medication be given to children in divided dosages. If undivided dosages are given, there is the risk of increased side effects because of the initial high peak or inefficient low blood levels at a later time in the day, depending on the half-life of the drug. The long-term effects of medication in children are still unknown. One should thus begin at the lowest dosage possible, increase the medication gradually, and evaluate on an ongoing basis the minimum drug amount necessary.

The following drug profiles stem from White's review (182):

Chlorpromazine is the prototype of phenothiazine. It is the most widely used compound in child psychiatric patients. There is considerable degree of sedation produced when the medication is first started. While the sedative effect is almost immediate, the antipsychotic effect of the drug may take several weeks to develop fully. All of the major neuroleptic drugs inhibit the reuptake of norepinephrine, hydroxytriptamine, and serotonin. As a consequence of the administration of these drugs, there is a slowing of the electroencephalogram pattern, an increased quantity of beta waves, and occasionally a few bursts of spiking. The seizure threshold is also lowered. Phenothiazines, therefore, must be used with caution in patients with epileptic disorders.

Chlorpromazine, like all the phenothiazine derivatives, is indicated primarily in the treatment of psychotic symptomatology. Target symptoms such as motor agitation, as well as severe anxiety, usually respond favorably and as a result render the patient more responsive to psychotherapy and other therapeutic measures.

The side effects described for adults may also occur in children. For instance, there may be orthostatic hypertension with a feeling of dizziness, faintness, drowsiness, nasal stuffiness, constipation, or blurred vision. Other side effects include marked weight gain and menstrual irregularities. Three to 4 percent of child patients may develop jaundice with elevated alkaline phosphate and high plasma bilirubin concentrations. Leukopenia and urticaria occur in approximately 5 percent of patients and are reversible on discontinuation of the drug. Photosensitivity may result in severe sunburn with minimal exposure. Long-term use of phenothiazines in higher doses may produce an abnormal pigmentation in the skin, manifested by gray-blue coloration in regions exposed to the sun.

The most severe side effect of the prolonged administration of phenothiazine is tardive dyskinesia, which tends to occur more commonly with the piperazine derivative of phenothiazine. However, it can also occur with chlorpromazine. In contrast to the so-called buccolingual-facial dyskinesia produced in adults, in children the picture is more one of involuntary movement with ataxia and choreiform movements of the upper extremities. The movement disorder usually does not appear until withdrawal of the drug. The syndrome disappears when the drug is reinstituted. Tardive dyskinesia does not respond to antiparkinsonian medication, unlike acute dystonic reactions which may be rapidly relieved by such drugs. Tardive dyskinesia is probably related to a hypersensitivity of dopamine receptors which occurs because of the prolonged blockade. When the medication is reduced or discontinued, then very small amounts of dopamine produce exaggerated movements which are again blocked by increases in the amount of phenothiazine medication.

Polizoes et al. (131) found that fourteen out of thirty-four outpatient childhood schizophrenics showed similar involuntary movements, primarily in the extremities, trunk, and head, associated with ataxia after withdrawal of neuroleptics such as haloperidol and thiothixene. Both abrupt total withdrawal and gradual withdrawal with weekly reductions of dosage in about 25 percent of cases gave the same results. The relationships of this syndrome to persistent tardive dyskinesia in adults has not yet been determined.

The usual dosage of chlorpromazine for children ages five to twelve, according to White is between 75 and 300 milligrams; for children over twelve it is between 75 and 1,000 milligrams. The recommended approach to administration for a child under twelve years of age, with mild anxiety and/or agitation, is 10 milligrams, three to four times a day, with increases of 10 milligrams in each dosage until the symptom is controlled. A larger dose may be given at bedtime to produce a more sedating effect; this is usually twice the afternoon dosage. For a child under twelve years of age, with moderate to severe anxiety and agitation, the starting dosage is 25 milligrams, two to four times daily, with an increase in the total daily dosage by 50 milligrams every two to three days until the symptoms are controlled. Again a larger dosage, usually twice the magnitude of the afternoon dose, may be given at bedtime for the sedating effect. For the child over twelve years of age, for mild symptoms, the starting dosage is 5 milligrams three to four times daily, with gradual increases until the symptoms are controlled.

In severely agitated children who need prompt control, chlorpromazine has the advantage that it can be administered intramuscularly. An initial intramuscular dose in a child under twelve years of age should not be more than 10 milligrams. If this is inadequate, then the child may be given 25 milligrams. The intramuscular dosage for a child over twelve years of age is 25 milligrams; if this dosage is inadequate, it may be increased to 50 milligrams. Intramuscular medication may be used every four to six hours until the patient's symptoms are controlled. The change to oral medication, however, should be made as soon as possible to avoid the tissue irritation of the intramuscular injection.

For childhood psychosis it produces a lower incidence of adverse reactions than do the other drugs, and it has been shown to lessen aggressive behavior, outbursts of rage, and anxiety as well as to improve attention span. Thioridazine less frequently causes movement disorders compared with the other phenothiazine derivatives. A frequent symptom is, however, nasal stuffiness. One side effect, which is possibly dose-related, seems to be peculiar to thioridazine—namely, inhibition of ejaculation in male patients who have reached pubescence. This side effect should be explained to the adolescent, who may be unwilling to reveal to the physician the fact that he has failed to ejaculate during masturbation.

Thiothixene is another derivative of phenothiazine which has essentially similar effects to chlorpromazine with some quantitative differences. The only indication for thiothixene in children and adolescents is in the treatment of childhood or adolescent schizophrenia. It has been found useful on both an inpatient and an outpatient basis, producing significant improvement in sleeping, concentration, eating, communication, and control of motor activity and stereotyped behavior. While it produces less sedation and fewer hypertensive effects, it causes extrapyramidal symptoms more frequently than does thioridazine.

The dosage range for children under twelve and over six years of age is 10 to 24 milligrams per day in divided doses. Adolescents require more or less adult dosages, in the range of 6 to 60 milligrams a day.

Trifluoperazine is presented here as an example of a piperazine derivative. Its pharmacological actions are similar to chlorpromazine, but trifluoperazine is far less sedating than chlorpromazine and several times more potent in the same dosage. The main indication is psychotic disorders of childhood, especially in mentally retarded children. There is an improvement of the psychosis as well as of social and intellectual functioning. Trifluoperazine, however, is not approved for use in children under six years of age. The side effects are similar to those for chlorpromazine. Although trifluoperazine has a lesser tendency to produce oversedation, the incidence of extrapyramidal signs is higher.

Total dosage for children between the ages of six and twelve generally ranges from 1 to 20 milligrams daily and for children over twelve, from 4 to 14 milligrams daily. The dosage must be titrated, starting with a small amount and gradually increasing it. Children should be allowed drug-free periods at regular intervals, for example, during weekends. It is also advisable to discontinue the medication for intervals of six months to a year and observe the child's responses.

Thioridazine (Mellaril) is a primary drug in the category of piperidine derivatives of phenothiazine. Its pharmacological properties are essentially similar to those of chlorpromazine, thioridazine appears to be only a weak antagonist of dopamine in certain regions of the brain.

Of the butyrophenone drugs only two are in common usage: (1) *droperidol,* used in anesthesia for its sedating effect, and (2) *haloperidol,* used primarily in the treatment of psychosis. Haloperidol is considered an effective alternative to phenothiazines in the treatment of psychosis. Butyrophenones share many of the properties of phenothiazines, even though they are structurally different. They block dopamine and its effects. Haloperidol has potent antipsychotic properties and can be used to treat schizophrenia as well as the manic phase of manic-depressive illness. While haloperidol calms excited and agitated patients, it induces far less sedation than does chlorpromazine. In particular, haloperidol has been proven valuable in the control of violent and aggressive behavior in children, especially in the severely self-destructive child. As regards severely disturbed and psychotic children, haloperidol may be a reasonable alternative for those patients who have experienced allergic or other serious adverse reactions to phenothiazines (D. C. Renchaw, as quoted by White [182]). In general, haloperidol should be reserved for severe manifestations of childhood or adolescence psychosis and Gilles de la Tourette syndrome (182).

Extrapyramidal side effects occur up to 80 percent more frequently with haloperidol than with phenothiazine drugs. Sedation, however, is seldom a problem; nor is ocular damage, liver dysfunction, severe orthostatic hypotension, or phototoxicity. There is an increase in theta waves in the electroencephalogram, and the seizure threshold may be lowered (this side effect, however, may be counteracted by adjusting the anticonvulsant medication).

Tardive dyskinesia may also be a significant side effect when the drug is used for extended periods of time. For this reason, frequent drug holidays should be observed, and the dosage should be kept at an absolute minimum.

Antiparkinsonian drugs are not recommended in children when side effects occur during treatment with phenothiazines, as the former decrease blood levels of thorazine. It is better to decrease the thorazine levels—a measure which may in itself reduce the side effects (27). The most frequently used drug is diphenhydramine (Benadryl, Parke Davis), 25 to 50 milligrams intramuscularly, especially for acute dystonic reactions. For more prolonged conditions the two most frequently used are trihexybenadryl hydrochloride (Artane, Lederle) and benztropine-mesylate (Congentin, Merck Sharpe & Dohme).

At this point certain remarks concerning the *comparative effectiveness of specific medication for autism* are in order. Antidepressant drugs such as imipramine are, on the whole, not beneficial for autistic children. Although there are some isolated cases of improvement, over three-fourths of the children on imipramine become worse with the treatment. Nor are mild sedative drugs effective in autistic children. However, diphenhydramine (Benadryl), which is an antihistamine, is effective as a mild sedative. Although Thorazine (chlorpromazine) is the major drug for older schizophrenic children who have more advanced speech and development, this drug is not as effective for young, autistic children. Trifluoperazine (Stelazine), which has less prominent sedative effects than Thorazine, is more effective for severely retarded, autistic children with verbal IQs below 70. Of the butyrophenones, Haldol is the most frequently used in autism.

Fish (as quoted by Campbell [26]) reported that many autistic children react differently to drugs as they grow older. Some who need stimulating drugs when young may react poorly to the same drugs when older. By eight or nine they may need a drug like chlorpromazine which had not helped when they were younger.

Lithium has not proven to be very effective. It has fewer antipsychotic properties than chlorpromazine and is more difficult to regulate. There are indications that the more evidence there is of mental retardation, the more sensitive the children are to very low dosages of lithium. Megavitamins have also not proven effective.

In a study of the effects of tri-iodothyronine (T_3) in twenty autistic children, all but three of the twenty improved in a trial of three months (28). T_3 seems to be as effective as the best major neuroleptics. The children were not clinically hyperthyroid before treatment, and the mechanism of T_3's therapeutic action needs to be further clarified. The problem with T_3 is its potential effect on retardation of growth.

No available drug or any other treatment will result in dramatic improvement in a severely impaired, young autistic child or in a school-age child or adolescent who has continuously shown severely deviant development and behavior since earliest life (154). In Campbell's experience, patients seem to respond more to drug therapy in the early stages of illness (26).

In summary, pharmacotherapy for autistic and schizophrenic children should be one aspect of the overall treatment plan, which must be individualized. Pharmacological treatment offers improvement for certain target symptoms of the psychosis and thus renders the child more amenable to environmental education and psychotherapeutic approach. Pervasive anxiety, evidenced in panic attacks, and temper outbursts are the most easily managed target symptoms, and their control makes the patient more effectively responsive and better able to benefit from training in communication skills. If hallucinatory behavior is present, according to White (182), it may also be diminished by psychotropic agents. It seems important that, according to Campbell (26), it has been shown clinically that drug-induced positive behaviors and developmental gains can be retained even after drug withdrawal.

RESIDENTIAL TREATMENT

Goldfarb (80) provided a model for residential treatment in his follow-up studies of schizophrenic children admitted to the Ittleson Center. In this particular therapeutic environment, whose approach has been termed "corrective socialization," the children undergo treatment aimed at correcting adaptive deficits by a responsive human environment which is specifically and uniquely suited to meeting the ego needs of each child. Precise efforts, for example, are made to improve such characteristics as attachment behavior, ego control, attention, persistence, accessibility to auditory and visual stimuli, and more specific functional capacities, such as perceptual ability, orientation, educational achievement, speech, and communication. To achieve these goals, Goldfarb reported the use of an extensive range of therapeutic instruments, including individual psychotherapy, milieu therapy, group therapy, family therapy, and education, including specialized remedial work and more recently a program to improve the children's capacity to communicate.

Forty characteristics were selected by Goldfarb for his longitudinal assay. The characteristics were subgrouped into two categories: (1) areas where improvement might be expected on the basis of maturation and (2) areas where changes reflected with strong certainty the primary influences of the social and educational experience. The first group of characteristics included perception, conceptualization, psychomotor performance, integration of multiple sensory stimuli, balance, and postural adjustment. In the second group improvement in the essentials of reading, writing, arithmetic, and social competence was considered to be a product of environmental input.

The children studied showed significant improvement in most functions which normally mature in childhood. They grew in level of perceptual response, conceptual behavior, orientation, ability to communicate, psychomotor ability, motor strength, and a variety of neurological functions embodying locomotor balance, inhibition of motor overflow, integration of multiple stimuli, and motor coordination. They also improved in educational achievement and social competence. Change and improvement, rather than fixity and arrest, in these functional capacities were thus typical of schizophrenic children. However, in most instances, while the schizophrenic children improved in functions which develop in normal childhood as well as in all those functions reflecting educational and social influence, they tended to remain below normal levels in group averages in these functions at each of the ages studied between admission (age seven average) and final observation (three years later).

Globally speaking, untestable children (15 percent of the sample) tended to be individually unchanging in absolute level of adaptive capacity. They had stopped growing significantly at extremely early levels of ego organization. In contrast, the testable children (85 percent) continued to manifest growth and responsiveness to educational and socializing influences throughout the period of observation.

Although as a group the children improved significantly in most of the characteristics (thirty-five out of forty evaluated over a three-year period of observation), they did not improve in the following five variables: (1) muscle tone, (2) activity level, (3) auditory startle, (4) delayed auditory feedback, (5) double simultaneous stimulation (homologous stimuli given with eyes open). Most impressive was the continuing deviation in receptor input behavior. The finding of persistent deficiency in auditory self-monitoring of speech by the schizophrenic children is of considerable interest, since it coincides with clinical and therapeutic observations. The schizophrenic child's restrictions on auditory information limit his potentiality for attaining normal levels and patterns of communication and verbal-symbolic response. He lacks the essential instrument for fitting his cognitive and communicative behavior to standard expectations. Indirectly, Goldfarb proposed that this deficiency in self-monitoring is the primary factor in contributing to the child's failures in perceiving and thus constructing reality and in attaining a well-articulated self-awareness.

EDUCATIONAL APPROACHES

For children who have severe disturbances in cognitive functions, educational approaches require a high ratio of one to one or one to two. Educational approaches follow a developmental perspective: namely, children are encouraged to go through the various stages of the developmental ladder in a particular line of development through behavior-modification techniques, appropriate to the particular child. For example, food rewards might be used to condition the youngster to eye contact. After that level of attention was achieved, the next step would be social imitation, with the child imitating gestures and hand movements. The next step would be the use of expressive language and, finally, the transfer of these expressive skills to other social situations. The same procedure would apply to verbal communication.

Gallagher and Wiegerink (75) have summarized certain basic educational strategies. The *reduction of extraneous stimuli* seems to be a general principle of education. A bare room with few extraneous elements seems to be required in the initial stages of training, so that only the stimulus presented is responded to. If two stimuli are to be linked, they must be *presented at the same time*. This strategy is to counteract a defect of short memory, which is frequent in autistic children. Thus, parental affection must be given simultaneously with the application of food, not sometime before or sometime after. In addition, the auditory stimulus should be provided at the same time as the visual stimulus. The autistic child appears generally to avoid auditory and kinesthesic sequential stimulus. The dimension of visual stimuli seems to have the least impairment from a receptive standpoint, and presentation of learning materials via visual materials may be preferentially used.

Activities aimed at improving the difficulty in attention deployment on the part of the child can be implemented in an educational approach calling for interruptions, and in reciprocity in a particular sequence of behaviors. In particular cases sign language may be a more accessible mode of communication than verbal communication.

BEHAVIOR MODIFICATION

For autism in particular, whether on an outpatient or an inpatient basis, behavior-modification techniques growing out of operant conditioning principles have proven useful. Training is also provided to parents and siblings, so that treatment can extend beyond the hours of actual instruction.

Helm (87), in a review and comparison of psychodynamic and behavior-modification approaches to the treatment of infantile autism, pointed out that in the practical handling of the therapeutic hour it is crucial for the therapist to resort to both behavior-modification and psychodynamic approaches. However, a major contribution of the behavior-modification approach is its elucidation of effective techniques in helping the child develop mastery of skills and appropriate behavior.

The behavior-modification approach has also made an important contribution in its description of behavioral goals in terms of substages toward which parents can work. This delineation of attainable goals permits the parents to maintain a sense of hope and direction, which in itself is a positive affective state, beneficially influencing the mother-child relationship.

Freeman and Ritvo (72) described the expanding role of parents as paraprofessionals. Training parents of autistic children to administer behavior therapy at home has recently emerged as a major approach to management. Parents can also help in the treatment of autistic children by participation in social advocacy. For instance, in a presentation by the National Association of Autistic Children on Advocacy for the Autistic Child, an informed parent of an autistic child recommended that professional interventions with the child be at the child's level, that behaviors be well understood before intervention, that encouragement be given to parents to take risks with the child, and that not every behavior be interpreted in the light of autism.

PSYCHOTHERAPEUTIC APPROACHES

This section will include special tasks in casework with parents, as well as the integration of the parents in the psychoanalytic psychotherapy of the child—what Mahler and Furer (119) have called the "tripartite approach." Lastly, I will discuss the individual psychoanalytic psychotherapy of autistic and schizophrenic patients, with their particular conflicts and primitive defenses.

CASEWORK WITH PARENTS

Schopler (157) has classified the major problem of casework with parents into three categories: (1) parental confusion, (2) erroneous expectations, and (3) conflicting social roles of parent and professional.

Parental Confusion. When a parent learns that his child shows the peculiar characteristics of the autistic syndrome, he is automatically subjected to the theoretical approaches that are in vogue or at least are accepted by the diagnostician. None of the hypothetical psychogenic etiological factors have proved to be more than partial contributing factors. Thus, theories underlining the role of parental personality and psychopathology, faulty communication, or unfavorable emotional climate do not account for the syndrome. Professionals have compounded the problem by withholding from the parents the precise profile of the child's strengths and liabilities, including his level of intellectual functioning. Parental confusion can be reduced by discussing in an appropriate yet direct and frank manner the results of the evaluation. The parental shock at unpleasant information has never been as great as parental confusion resulting from professional attempts to gloss over findings.

Erroneous Expectations. In his clinical and research evaluations

Schopler was able to confirm that parents can assess their child's level in the areas of sociability, cognition, language, self-help sufficiency, motor coordination, and overall development in a way that correlates highly and significantly with test results. However, the import of these results in terms of their present as well as their long-term future implications was difficult for the parents to assess. The lack of appropriate services and resources in what will necessarily mean a lifelong support system for the child makes the situation more complicated. Irrational expectations can be cleared out by sharing with the parents the results of their child's intelligence testing (especially in clarifying areas of scatter and the coexistence of islands of high abilities and marked deficits). Currently the consensus is that there are no untestable children; it is a matter of finding the appropriate test for each child. Autistic children in an IQ range under 50 tend to remain stable over time, while children with IQs upward of 50 tend to be more variable, depending on their education and experience.

Schopler and Reichler (158) have developed a psychoeducational profile which sorts out the tasks that the child is doing correctly, the ones that he refuses to do or does incorrectly, and the ones that are in a partial or peculiar fashion present, demonstrating some sense of emerging skills.

Conflicting Social Roles of Parent and Professional. The autistic syndrome is a particular treatment situation in which the parent and the specialist have to intermingle in their roles of responsibility and authority. Both of them have to work in a closely connected fashion to share responsibility in developing special service programs, schooling, sheltered workshops, and other environmental supports. The parent should be helped to acquire the same skills that the therapist or the educator uses during the sessions and to extend them into the daily activities of the home. In addition, help should be available to the parents in presenting their child to the teachers and other persons responsible for the child. For instance, the autistic parent tends to dread regression inflicted by adults who may be unresponsive or relatively insensitive to the needs of their child. The parent thus generally reacts with a sense of accusation to the teacher, which tends to decrease the likelihood of an empathic reaction on the part of the teacher toward the child.

Another problem is that the parent tends to infantilize the child and to be an accomplice in the child's tendency to preserve sameness. This may be a mutual reinforcement due to the facts that, on one hand, the child communicates distress and panic which need to be forestalled at any cost, and that, on the other hand, the preservation of sameness permits a relative yet a stagnant respite.

PSYCHOANALYTIC PSYCHOTHERAPY

As space does not permit description of the process in particular cases (10,61,147,175), I will instead abstract some of the general principles of the tripartite approach as well as discuss the general principles underlying individual psychoanalytically oriented psychotherapy of autistic patients.

In *tripartite therapy* the target of the treatment is the relationship between mother and child. An attempt is made to resolve pathological forms of symbiosis and problems in separation-individuation through the empathic presence of the therapist, who acts as an auxiliary, observing ego to the pair. The therapist provides support to the mother in working with her child and facilitates the appropriate, empathic maternal reactions by clarifying the child's cues to the mother, by modeling to the mother, and by supporting the mother in a noncritical manner. The therapist has to be tuned to the mother's needs, which sometimes are as strong and regressed as those of the child.

In terms of specific techniques, baby games and role playing of symbiotic and early stages of separation-individuation are amply used. A mirror may serve as an important source of confirmation of the child's identity and self-concept constancy. Symbiotic experience may be corrected by the judicious use of touching and physical containment in the arms of the therapist or mother. Lap sitting may also be used to provide body stimulation and the enveloping feeling of containment. In all play interactions, verbal communication is an important aspect of work, combining an educational approach with psychological interpretation.

In terms of *individual psychotherapy* several issues deserve special attention. The intense turmoil of a child suffering from autism or schizophrenic illness necessitates that he receive appropriate psychological understanding and deep empathy for his predicament, so that he can emerge as far as possible from his psychotic state. Psychopharmacological and behavior-modification techniques may aid this process. Certain limitations, however, affect all these approaches. Medications may help correct target symptoms, such as rage outbursts, hallucinations, or withdrawal; but this is only the beginning of the work with the distorted, bizarre representational world of the child (156). Behavior therapy allows the child to learn appropriate behaviors. However, if the child does not have the age-appropriate capacity to assimilate his experiences of the external and the internal worlds, or the capacity to accommodate realistically to external and internal environments, behavior modification is likely to have transitory effects. In a similar fashion, because psychotherapeutic approaches ultimately rely on the cognitive capacity to interact, to express, and to verbalize, psychotherapy is indicated only for those children with an IQ above 50.

SPECIFIC ANXIETIES

Tustin (175) has enumerated typical anxieties that need to be resolved in work with these patients:

The *sense of separateness* is experienced by the psychotic child as a break in body continuity, a disconnectedness and fragmentation which is reacted to by body stiffness. In this respect, it is of interest that Tustin portrayed the autistic barrier in its subjective aspect as a pathological overdevelopment of the natural tendency to use one part of the body to protect another, such as hands over ears or eyelids over eyes. The child grows without the ordinary nurturing experiences obtained from a mother it recognizes as separate and alive. Daily routines are experienced as protective wrappings which ensure bodily survival, protecting from the sense of not-me, the unknown, and strangeness.

The *fear of falling* infinitely is a primitive anxiety described by Winnicott (184). In fact the fear of falling seems to be an inborn behavior mechanism already apparent in the prelocomotor infant. In the experiments of the "visual cliff" (177), for example, an infant was placed on a flat checkered surface, where there was an optical illusion that the checkerboard went down on another level. The infant would stop short right at the edge of the visual cliff. Fears of emptiness, darkness, solitude, and silence are associated with fear of falling.

That the autistic child with his unpredictable motor controls, hypotonia, or hypertonia is constitutionally vulnerable to the fear of falling is not surprising. The holding function of the mother's arms as well as the supportive holding function of her primary maternal preoccupation with the infant are important factors in allaying this anxiety. The persistent presence of this anxiety therefore indicates environmental deficiencies in the nurturing figures or impediments in the child which do not allow him to use the maternal care to fulfill his needs of support. Most frequently there is an interweaving of these factors.

Fear of loss of body boundaries and of the sense of separateness is expressed concretely in the fear that the body self and the psychological self will be dispersed and fragmented in the environment. The experience is that of a break in bodily continuity, as if the child had a hole in his body. Panic and rage accompany this particular anxiety; affect is experienced as a bodily explosion. Another variation of this fear is a fantasy that the body self and the fragmented self images are made of fluid: for example, the fear of loss of one's boundaries by emptying oneself through a body orifice or a scratch in the skin. In contrast to the neurotic castration anxiety, this anxiety is related to explosive body disintegration or multiple mutilation.

The loss of continuity with the mother through the nipple is felt as a black hole in the mouth. Some behavior, such as mutism, may be understood as an effort to have a closed mouth, to avoid the black hole; or the child may put all his fingers into his mouth to bridge the gap. Displacement of this black hole into other parts of the body, such as the anus or the vagina, may occur. There may also be a dread of looking at the black holes of other people's eyes. Saliva, urine, or feces may be smeared in an effort to fill up the hole. The sense of hole is a disaster that separates the child from the mother and affects both simultaneously because of the characteristic state of undifferentiation between self and object.

One autistic child insisted on being kissed if he sustained the most minute injury to his skin. He also expected his mother to snap his pants and refused to touch them himself. After laborious work, his anxieties about being emptied through whatever minute hole existed were relieved, as was his fear that by snapping his pants he would also snap his skin (he had not differentiated his clothing from his skin). Both activities had actually been preserved by the mother, who could not understand the anxieties underlying this behavior. As the child had a normal IQ, it was possible to explain these fantasies to him, to his great relief.

Anxieties about the integrity of the self require the development of a second "skin." This can be expressed by muscular rigidity and stereotypic behavior or by making clothing part of the outer limit of the self. Mahler (117) has described how once the "autistic armour" has been pierced, the child becomes particularly vulnerable to emotional frustration, helplessness, and despair.

The incapacity to develop a body image brings secondary complications, as the awareness of separateness is inseparable from awareness of space and of outside and inside. Without a body image the autistic child cannot develop a full inner life, which accounts for the impression the autistic child gives of emptiness and vacancy. According to Tustin, the child's autistic self is a primitively omnipotent one, in which he has the illusion of permeating the environment with his fluid body stuff and in that way controlling the mother in fantasy or involving the mother underneath the layer of the autistic barrier.

Further anxiety ensues if *the not-me experience is abrupt and traumatic*. In order to deal with this abrupt traumatic separateness, the child produces the autistic object. The normal transitional object is recognized by the child as being separate from his body and as partly representing the mother; the autistic object is not so recognized. The function of the autistic object is to obviate completely any awareness of the not-me because it is felt to be unbearably threatening. The autistic object is felt to fill the gap in mothering in a specific bizarre way, to fill up a vacuum or a discontinuity experienced as a hole in the body self. Animate and inanimate objects may become condensed and indistinguishable from each other. Animate objects may be deanimated; and, vice versa, inanimate objects may contain part object representations and part self-representations.

OEDIPAL CONFIGURATIONS

In spite of the severe psychopathology, autistic children may present oedipal struggles, albeit distorted ones. Tustin (175) described a case of a recovering autistic child who had reached the stage of being able to dream. The child described seeing a bowl of creamy milk in which there suddenly appeared a tuft of male pubic hair, at the sight of which he felt sick and terrified. This vignette illustrates primitive and bizarre oedipal constellations in the world of rudimentary object relations of these children.

HALLUCINATIONS

According to Tustin (175) the appearance of hallucinations indicates an antecedent stage to remembering; in turn, negative hallucinations may be precursors of ignoring and forgetting. Thus, if hallucinations or negative hallucinations appear during treatment, they may indicate that the child is in the process of transition to words and will eventually replace these hallucinations with more advanced forms of ego functioning, such as imaging, remembering, and thinking.

DEFENSE MECHANISMS

Specific defenses are used which do not form part of the general spectrum of defenses at a higher level of pathology. First, there is the defense of deanimation, described by Mahler (117). Here the world of persons is experienced as inanimate as a protection from dangerous projections. Tustin mentioned that animism and autism seem to be opposite modes of operation of the primitive mind. The child may smash objects or his clothes to destroy the painful, anxiety-producing, fragmented parts of himself. His falling and biting himself may be similarly interpreted. Spinning may be a defense blotting out bad objects and at the same time enhancing the sense of the body by the regular kinesthetic stimulation. Attempts at preservation of sameness give security and help to stabilize the explosiveness of the child's representational world. The child may also use his body as an autistic object, sucking in his cheeks or listening to the beating of his own heart to reassure himself of his integrity. Or the child may move his hands in a stereotypic fashion through space, as if the separateness of the fingers was a way of dealing with the dread of separateness.

THE PSYCHOTHERAPEUTIC TECHNIQUE

The question of intervention in psychotherapy of psychotic children is crucial, for one of its goals is to dissolve the autistic barrier—even though the breakage of this barrier induces panic in the child and an intense countertransference guilt in the therapist or the parents. What is crucial is that the intervention be well modulated and yet relentless. The therapist must share his reactions to the child with the mother, so that mother and therapist can learn jointly from and support each other against the child's inducements to allay his own distress at any cost.

Several specific aspects of technique should be noted at this point. With the autistic child, the setting of the psychotherapy, more than for any other kind of child, should be constant. Therapy should be on a regular schedule, at a minimum of two and preferably four times a week. The child should be provided with a place or a box where his belongings can be put and protected. The child needs to be held by the therapist's constant attention. The therapist should not leave the room or answer the telephone or move suddenly. He must be perfectly predictable and consistent. His interpretations should be short, brief, and promptly made.

The therapist, through his interpretations, should provide a link between behavior and verbal contact. Sometimes verbal contact is completely experienced by the child as an invasion of his boundaries, as if the words were solid objects. This experience in itself needs to be clarified to the child. The therapist also must have a capacity for imaginative reconstruction of primitive experiences, if he is to understand some of these fantasies.

Any withdrawal from contact should be transformed into a reciprocal relationship by the therapist—including solitary play and stereotypic behaviors. Tustin mentioned that the child may deal with the therapist as if the latter were a dead thing, which in turn causes further frustration for both. A brief vignette illustrates one way of handling such a situation.

An autistic child had been playing on his own, lying on the floor with his head at the same level as some rubber monsters that he pretended were fighting each other, biting and swallowing each other. This play became interactional after a few sessions. The patient dared to pretend to bite and eat parts of the therapist's body indirectly through the rubber monsters. In the process of "eating the therapist up" and enjoying it, the "dead therapist, nonexistent therapist" became a good, alive thing, worth eating up and becoming now a part of himself, who was equally more alive.

Another function of the therapist, which overlaps with that of the educator, is to use games to foster cognitive development. This aim is systematically built into as many interventions as possible. Attention deployment, mutual gazing, interplay between distancing and closeness in the spatial distribution and sitting arrangements of the hour can then be exercised innumerable times. Thus, the resolution of primitive fantasies, primitive defenses, and primitive impulses, in conjunction with the strengthening and developing ego, apparently follows the same principles of interpretation and goals as psychoanalytic psychotherapy of borderline conditions and neurotic cases.

Conclusion

This chapter has selectively reviewed literature focused on the advances in the understanding of childhood schizophrenia, especially in the syndrome of autism, of the last decade, when most of the advances have been made. The details of an autistic child's life provide opportunities for understanding the relations between social and cognitive domains, as they appear during the first years of life and as they are increasingly structured by maturation and education throughout the life cycle (41).

Recent developments in psychopharmacological, educational, and psychotherapeutic approaches offer promise for treating these children.

Undoubtedly the next decade will further clarify subgroups within childhood schizophrenia and autism and will bring a re-evaluation of programs for early intervention as well as further explication of a multidisciplinary treatment approach to this disease entity.

BIBLIOGRAPHY

1. Allen, J.; DeMyer, M. K.; Norton, J. A.; et al. 1971. Intellectuality in parents of psychotic, subnormal and normal children. *Journal of Autism and Childhood Schizophrenia* 1(3):311–26.
2. American Psychiatric Association. 1977. *Diagnostic and statistical manual of mental disorders*, 3rd ed.
3. Anthony, E. J. 1974. A risk: vulnerability intervention model for children of psychotic parents. In *Children at psychiatric risk*, eds. E. J. Anthony and C. Koupernik (New York: John Wiley), pp. 91–121.
4. Bakwin, H., and Bakwin, R. 1972. Schizophrenia. In *Behavior disorders in children* (Philadelphia: W. B. Saunders), pp. 633–49.
5. Bartak, L., and Rutter, M. 1976. Differences between mentally retarded and normally intelligent autistic children. *Journal of Autism and Childhood Schizophrenia* 6(2):109–120.

6. Bartak, L.; Rutter, M.; and Cox, A. 1975. A comparative study of infantile autism and specific developmental receptive language disorder. I. The children. *British Journal of Psychiatry*, 126:127–145.

7. Bartolucci, G., and Albers, R. 1974. Deictic categories in the language of autistic children. *Journal of Autism and Childhood Schizophrenia* 4(2):131–142.

8. Bender, L. 1969. The nature of childhood psychosis. In *Modern perspectives in international child psychiatry*, ed. J. G. Howells (Edinburgh: Oliver and Boyd), pp. 649–84.

9. Bender, L. 1974. The family patterns of 100 schizophrenic children observed at Bellevue 1935–1952. *Journal of Autism and Childhood Schizophrenia* 4(4):279–92.

10. Bergmann, A. 1971. "I and you." The separation-individuation process in the treatment of a symbiotic child. In *Separation-individuation. Essays in honor of Margaret S. Mahler*, eds. J. B. McDevitt and C. F. Settlage (New York: International Universities Press), pp. 325–355.

11. Berlin, I. N. 1973. A clinical note on the reversibility of autistic behavior in a twenty-month-old child. In *Clinical studies in childhood psychosis*, eds. S. A. Szurek and I. N. Berlin (New York: Brunner/Mazel), pp. 529–539.

12. Berlin, I. N. 1973. Lessons from failure in ten years of psychotherapeutic work with a schizophrenic boy and his parents. In *Clinical studies in childhood psychosis*, eds. S. A. Szurek and I. N. Berlin (New York: Brunner/Mazel), pp. 697–768.

13. Bettelheim, B. 1967. *The empty fortress* (New York: Free Press).

14. Bick, E. 1968. The experience of the skin in early object relations. *International Journal of Psychoanalysis* 49:484–86.

15. Birch, H., and Hertzig, M. 1967. Etiology of schizophrenia: an overview. In *Proceedings of the First Rochester International Conference.* Exerpta Medica International Congress Series No. 151, pp. 92–110.

16. Blatt, S. J., and Wild, C. M. 1976. *Schizophrenia, a developmental analysis* (New York: Academic Press).

17. Bleuler, M. 1974. The offspring of schizophrenics. *Schizophrenia Bulletin* 8:93–107.

18. Block, M.; Freeman, B. J.; and Montgomery, J. 1975. Systematic observation of play behavior in autistic children. *Journal of Autism and Childhood Schizophrenia* 5(4):363–73.

19. Bosch, G. 1970. *Infantile autism* (New York: Springer Verlag).

20. Boullin, D. J.; Coleman, M.; O'Brien, R. A.; and Rimland, B. 1971. Laboratory predictions of infantile autism based on 5 hydroxytryptamine efflux from blood platelets and their correlation with the Rimland E-2 score. *Journal of autism and Childhood Schizophrenia* 1(1):63–71.

21. Bower, T. G. R. 1965. Stimulus variables determining space perception in infants. *Science* 149:88–89.

22. Brazelton, B. T.; Young, G. C.; and Bullowa, M. 1971. Inception and resolution of early developmental pathology. In *Infant psychiatry. A new synthesis*, eds. E. Rexford, L. Sandler, and T. Shapiro (New Haven: Yale University Press), pp. 301–334.

23. Brierley, M. 1944. Notes on metapsychology as process theory. *Journal of the International Psychoanalytic Association* 25:103–4.

24. Call, J. 1963. Prevention of autism in a young infant in a well-child conference. *Journal of American Academy of Child Psychiatry* 2:451.

25. Campbell, M. 1977. The siblings of autistic children. Presentation Annual Meeting American Academy of Child Psychiatry, Dallas, Texas.

26. Campbell, M. 1977. Personal communication, Annual Meeting American Academy of Child Psychiatry, Dallas, Texas.

27. Campbell, M. 1977. Treatment of childhood and adolescent schizophrenia. In *Psychopharmacology in childhood and adolescence*, ed. J. Weiner (New York: Basic Books), pp. 101–18.

28. Campbell, M.; Fish, B.; David, R.; et al. 1972. Response to triiodothyronine and dextroamphetamine: A study of preschool schizophrenic children. *Journal of Autism and Childhood Schizophrenia* 2(4):343–58.

29. Campbell, M.; Fish, B.; Korein, J.; et al. 1972. Lithium and chlorpromazine: A controlled crossover study of hyperactive severely disturbed young children. *Journal of Autism and Childhood Schizophrenia* 2(3):234–63.

30. Campbell, M.; Fish, B.; Shapiro, T.; and Floyd, A. 1971. Imipramine in preschool autistic and schizophrenic children. *Journal of Autism and Childhood Schizophrenia* 1(3):267–82.

31. Campos, J. J.; Langer, A.; and Krowitz, A. 1970. Cardiac responses on the visual cliff in prelocomotor human infants. *Science* 170:196–97.

32. Caparulo, B. K., and Cohen, D. S. 1977. Cognitive structure, language, and emerging social competence in autistic aphasic children. *Journal of the American Academy of Child Psychiatry* (4): 620–45.

33. Chess, S. 1971. Autism in children with congenital rubella. *Journal of Autism and Childhood Schizophrenia* 1(1):33–47.

34. Chess, S. 1977. Follow-up report on autism in congenital rubella. *Journal of Autism and Childhood Schizophrenia* 7(1):81.

35. Chess, S., and Rosenberg, M. 1974. Clinical differentiation among children with initial language complaints. *Journal of Autism and Childhood Schizophrenia* 4(2):99–110.

36. Chmiel, A. J., and Mattsson, A. 1975. Heller's syndrome: A form of childhood psychosis of multicausal origin: Case report and review of literature. *Journal of American Academy of Child Psychiatry* 14:337–47.

37. Churchill, D. W. 1972. The relation of infantile autism and early childhood schizophrenia to developmental language disorders of childhood. *Journal of Autism and Childhood Schizophrenia* 2(2):182–97.

38. Clancy, H., and McBride, G. 1969. The autistic process and its treatment. *Journal of Child Psychology and Psychiatry* 10:233–44.

39. Clarizio, H., and McCoy, F. G. 1976. Childhood psychosis. In *Behavior disorders in children*, eds. H. Bakwin and R. Bakwin (New York: Thomas Y. Crowell), pp. 333–82.

40. Clark, P., and Rutter, M. 1977. Compliance and resistance in autistic children. *Journal of Autism and Childhood Schizophrenia* 7(1):33–48.

41. Cohen, D. J.; Caparulo, B. K.; and Shaywitz, B. A. 1977. *Neurochemical developmental models of childhood autism.* The Kittay Scientific Foundation. (New York: International Universities Press).

42. Cohen, D. J.; Caparulo, B. K.; Shaywitz, B. A.; and Bowers, M. B. 1977. Dopamine and serotonin metabolism in neuropsychiatrically disturbed children. *Archives of General Psychiatry* 34: 545–50.

43. Cohen, D. J., and Johnson, W. T. 1977. Cardiovascular correlates of attention in normal and psychiatrically disturbed children. *Archives of General Psychiatry* 34:561–67.

44. Cohen, D. J., and Young, J. G. 1977. Neurochemistry and child psychiatry. *Journal of the American Academy of Child Psychiatry* 16(3):331–411.

45. Colby, K., and Parkison, C. 1977. Handedness in autistic children. *Journal of Autism and Childhood Schizophrenia* 7(1):3–9.

46. Cox, A.; Rutter, M.; Newman, S.; and Bartak, L. 1975. A Comparative Study of Infantile Autism and Specific Developmental Receptive Language Disorder: II. Parental Characteristics. *British Journal of Psychiatry* 126:146–59.

47. Creak, M., et al. 1961. Schizophrenic syndrome in child progress report of a working party. *British Medical Journal* 2:889.

48. Darby, J. K. 1976. Neuropathologie aspects in psychosis in children. *Journal of Autism and Childhood Schizophrenia* 6(4):339–52.

49. Davids, A. 1975. Childhood psychosis: The problem of differential diagnosis. *Journal of Autism and Childhood Schizophrenia* 5(2):129–38.

50. DeMyer, M. K. 1975. The nature of neuropsychological disability in autistic children. *Journal of Autism and Childhood Schizophrenia* 5(2):109–28.

51. DeMyer, M. K. 1976. Research in infantile autism: A strategy and its results. In *The annual progress in child psychiatry and child development,* eds. S. Chess and A. Thomas (New York: Brunner/Mazel), vol. 9, pp. 392–415.

52. DeMyer, M. K.; Alpern, G. D.; Barton, S.; et al. 1972. Limitation in autistic, early schizophrenic and non-psychotic subnormal children. *Journal of Autism and Childhood Schizophrenia* 2(3):264–87.

53. DeMyer, M. K.; Barton, S.; DeMyer, W. E.; et al. 1973. Prognosis in autism: A follow-up study. *Journal of Autism and Childhood Schizophrenia* 3(3):199–246.

54. DeMyer, M. K.; Barton, S.; and Norton, J. A. 1972. A comparison of adaptive, verbal and motor profiles of psychotic and non-psychotic subnormal children. *Journal of Autism and Childhood Schizophrenia* 2(4):359–77.

55. DeMyer, M. K.; Churchill, D. W.; Pontius, W.; and Gilkey, K. M. 1971. A comparison of five diagnostic systems for childhood schizophrenia and infantile autism. *Journal of Autism and Childhood Schizophrenia* 1(2):175–89.

56. DeMyer, M. K.; Norton, J. A.; and Barton, S. 1971. Social and adaptive behavior of autistic children as measured in a structured psychiatric interview. In *Infantile autism: Proceedings of the Indiana University Colloquium,* eds. D. W. Churchill, G. D. Alpern and M. K. DeMyer (Springfield, Ill.: Charles C Thomas), pp. 29–70.

57. DeMyer, M. K.; Pontius, W.; et al. 1972. Parental practices and innate activity in normal, autistic and brain-damaged infants. *Journal of Autism and Childhood Schizophrenia* 2(1):49–66.

58. Despert, J. L. 1968. *Schizophrenia in children* (New York: R. Brunner).

59. Diatkine, R.; Lang, J. L.; et al. 1977. Therapeutic experience with psychotic children. In *Long term treatments of psychotic states,* eds. C. Colette, and P. Bequart (New York: Human Sciences), pp. 250:64.

60. Eisenberg, L. 1972. The classification of childhood psychosis reconsidered. *Journal of Autism and Childhood Schizophrenia* 2:388–442.

61. Ekstein, R. 1971. *The challenge: Despair and hope in the conquest of inner space* (New York: Brunner/Mazel).

62. Ekstein, R. 1975. Functional psychosis in children. In *Comprehensive textbook of psychiatry,* eds. A. M. Freedman, H. Kaplan, and B. Sadock (Baltimore: Williams & Wilkins), vol. 2, p. 2191.

63. Ekstein, R.; Bryant, K.; and Friedman, W. S. 1958. Childhood schizophrenia and allied conditions. In *Schizophrenia: A review of the syndrome,* ed. B. K. Leopold (New York: Grune & Stratton).

64. Engelhardt, D. M.; Polizoes, P.; et al. 1973. A double blind comparison of fluphenazine and haloperidol in outpatient schizophrenic children. *Journal of Autism and Chidhood Schizophrenia* 3(2):128–37.

65. Erikson, E. H. 1959. *Identity and the life cycle. Psychological issues* (New York: International Universities Press), pp. 1–71.

66. Escalona, S. K., and Corman, H. H. 1974. Early life experience and the development of competence. *International Review of Psychoanalysis* 1:151.

67. Feinsilver, D. B., and Gunderson, J. 1972. Psychotherapy for schizophrenia. Is it indicated? A review of the relevant literature. National Institute of Mental Health. *Schizophrenia Bulletin* 6: 11–23.

68. Fischer, M. 1971. Psychosis in the offspring of schizophrenic monozygotic twins and their normal co-twins. *British Journal of Psychiatry* 118:43–52.

69. Fish, B. 1971. Contributions of developmental research to a theory of schizophrenia. In *Exceptional infant: Studies in abnormalities,* ed. J. Hellmuth (New York: Brunner/Mazel), vol. 2, pp. 473–82.

70. Fish, B. 1976. Approach to prevention in infants at risk for schizophrenia: Developmental deviation from birth to 10 years. *Journal of American Academy of Child Psychiatry* 15(1):62–82.

71. Fish, B. 1977. Neurobiologic antecedents of schizophrenia in children. *Archives of General Psychiatry* 34:1297–313.

72. Freeman, B. J., and Ritvo, R. E. 1976. Parents as paraprofessionals. In *Autism,* ed. E. Ritvo (New York: Spectrum Publications), pp. 227–85.

73. Freeman, T. 1976. *Childhood psychopathology and adult psychosis* (New York: International Universities Press), pp. 1–34. 236–78.

74. Frith, V. 1970. Studies in pattern detection in normal and autistic children. I. Immediate recall of auditory sequence. *Journal of Abnormal Psychology,* 76:413–20.

75. Gallagher, J. J., and Wiegerink, R. 1976. Educational strategies for the autistic child. *Journal of Autism and Childhood Schizophrenia* 6(1):15–26.

76. Garmezy, N. 1973. Children at risk: The search for the antecedents of schizophrenia. Part I: Conceptual models and research methods. National Institute of Mental Health. *Schizophrenia Bulletin* 8:14–90.

77. Garmezy, N. 1974. Children at risk: The search for the antecedents of schizophrenia. Part II: Ongoing research programs, issues and intervention. National Institute of Mental Health. *Schizophrenia Bulletin* 9:55–125.

78. Goldfarb, W. 1961. *Childhood Schizophrenia.* (Cambridge, Massachusetts: Harvard University Press).

79. Goldfarb, W. 1971. Therapeutic management of schizophrenic children. In *Modern perspectives in international child psychiatry,* ed. J. G. Howells (New York: Brunner/Mazel), pp. 685–703.

80. Goldfarb, W. 1974. *Growth and change of schizophrenic children: A longitudinal study* (Washington, D. C.: V. H. Winston).

81. Goldfarb, W.; Goldfarb, N.; et al. 1972. Speech and language faults of schizophrenic children. *Journal of Autism and Childhood Schizophrenia* 2(3):219–33.

82. Goldfarb, W.; Mintz, I.; Stroock, K.; et al. 1969. *A time to heal; Corrective socialization: A treatment approach to childhood schizophrenia* (New York: International Universities Press).

83. Goldfarb, W.; Spitzer, R. L.; and Endicott, J. 1976. A study of psychopathology of parents of psychotic children by structured interview. *Journal of Autism and Childhood Schizophrenia* 6(4): 327–38.

84. Goldfarb, W.; Yudkovitz, E.; and Goldfarb, N. 1973. Verbal symptoms to designate objects. An experimental study of communication in mothers of schizophrenic children. *Journal of Autism and Childhood Schizophrenia* 3(4):281–98.

85. Guthrie, R. D., and Wyatt, R. D. 1975. Biochemistry and schizophrenia. A review of childhood psychosis. *Schizophrenia Bulletin* 12:19–29.

86. Hauson, D. R., and Gottesman, T. T. 1976. The genetics, if any, of infantile autism and childhood schizophrenia. *Journal of Autism and Childhood Schizophrenia* 6(3):209–34.

87. Helm, D. 1976. Psychodynamic behavior modification approaches to the treatment of infantile autism: Empirical similarities. *Journal of Autism and Childhood Schizophrenia* 6(1):27–42.

88. Hermelin, B., and Frith, V. 1971. Psychological studies of childhood autism. Can autistic children make sense of what they see and hear? *Journal of Special Education* 5:107–17.

89. Hermelin, B., and O'Connor, N. 1970. *Psychological experiments with autistic children* (Oxford: Pergamon Press).

90. Hertzig, M. E., and Walker, H. A. 1975. Symptom formation as an expression of disordered information processing in schizophrenic children. *Journal of Autism and Childhood Schizophrenia* 5(1):13–24.

91. Holmes, L.; Moser, H.; et al. 1972. *Mental retardation. An Atlas of diseases with associated physical abnormalities* (New York: Macmillan).

92. Holter, F. R., and Ruttenberg, B. A. 1971. Initial interventions in psychotherapeutic treatment of autistic children. *Journal of Autism and Childhood Schizophrenia* (2):206–14.

93. Howlin, P.; Marchant, R.; et al. 1973. A home-based approach to the treatment of autistic children. *Journal of Autism and Childhood Schizophrenia* 3(4):308–36.

94. Hutt, S., and Hutt, C. 1970. *Behaviour studies in psychiatry* (Oxford: Pergamon Press).

95. Isaacs, S. 1940. The nature and function of fantasy. *International Journal of Psychoanalysis* 29(2):73–97.

96. Jones, F. H.; Simmons, J. Q.; and Frankel, F. 1974. An extinction procedure for eliminating self-destructive behavior in a nine-year-old autistic girl. *Journal of Autism and Childhood Schizophrenia* 4(3):241–50.

97. Kanner, L. 1971. Childhood psychosis: A historical overview. *Journal of Autism and Childhood Schizophrenia* 1(1):14–19.

98. Kanner, L. 1971. Follow-up study of eleven autistic children originally reported in 1943. *Journal of Autism and Childhood Schizophrenia* 1(2):119–45.

99. Kanner, L. 1973. *Childhood psychosis: Initial studies and new insights* (New York: Halsted Press).

100. Kanner, L.; Rodriquez, A.; and Ashenden, B. 1972. How far can autistic children go in matters of social adaptation? *Journal of Autism and Childhood Schizophrenia* 2(1):9–33.

101. Kernberg, O. 1976. *Object relations theory and clinical psychoanalysis* (New York: Jason Aronson).

102. Kety, S. S.; Rosenthal, D.; Wender, P. H.; and Schulsinger, F. 1968. Types and prevalence of mental illness in the biological and adoptive families of adopted schizophrenics. In *The transmission of schizophrenia,* eds. D. Rosenthal and S. S. Kety (Oxford: Pergamon Press), pp. 345–62.

103. King, D. P. 1975. Early infantile autism: Relation to schizophrenia. *Journal of the American Academy of Child Psychiatry* 14(4):666–82.

104. Koegel, R., and Schreibman, L. 1976. Identification of consistent responding to auditory stimuli by a functionally "deaf" autistic child. *Journal of Autism and Childhood Schizophrenia* 6(2): 147–56.

105. Kolvin, J.; Ounsted, C.; Humphrey, M.; et al. 1971. Studies in the childhood psychoses. II. The phenomenology of childhood psychosis. *British Journal of Psychiatry* 118:385–95.

106. Kupferman, K. 1971. The development and treatment of a psychotic child. In *Separation-individuation. Essays in honor of Margaret S. Mahler,* eds. J. B. McDevitt and C. F. Settlage (New York: International Universities Press).

107. Laufer, M. W., and Gair, D. S. 1969. Childhood schizophrenia. In *The schizophrenic syndrome,* eds. L. Bellak and L. Loeb (New York: Grune & Stratton), pp. 378–461.

108. LaVigna, G. W. 1977. Communication training in mute autistic adolescents using the written word. *Journal of Autism and Childhood Schizophrenia* 7(2):135–49.

109. Lichstein, K. L., and Schreibman, L. 1976. Employing electric shock with autistic children: A review of side effects. *Journal of Autism and Childhood Schizophrenia* 6(2):163–74.

110. Lidz, T. 1973. *Origin and treatment of schizophrenic disorders* (New York: Basic Books).

111. Lifton, M. A., and Smolen, E. M. 1966. Group psychotherapy with schizophrenic children. *International Journal of Group Psychotherapy* 16.23–41.

112. Lockyer, L., and Rutter, M. 1970. A five to fifteen year follow-up study of infantile psychosis. IV. Patterns of cognitive ability. *British Journal Society of Clinical Psychology* 91:152–63.

113. Lotter, V. 1974. Social adjustment and placement of autistic children in Middlesex: A follow-up study. *Journal of Autism and Childhood Schizophrenia* 4(1):11–32.

114. Lotter, V. 1974. Factors related to outcome in autistic children. *Journal of Autism and Childhood Schizophrenia* 4(3):263–77.

115. McAndrew, J. B.; Quentin, C.; et al. 1972. Effects of prolonged phenothiazine intake on psychotic and other hospitalized children. *Journal of Autism and Childhood Schizophrenia* 2(1):75–91.

116. Mahler, M. S. 1952. On child psychosis and schizophrenia: Autistic and symbiotic infantile psychosis. In *The psychoanalytic study of the child,* eds. R. S. Eissler, et al. (New York: International Universities Press), vol. 7, pp. 286–94.

117. Mahler, M. S. 1968. *On human symbiosis and the vicissitudes of individuation* (New York: International Universities Press).

118. Mahler, M. S. 1976. Longitudinal study of the treatment of a psychotic child with the "tripartite design." *Journal of the Philadelphia Association for Psychoanalysis* 3(3):21–42.

119. Mahler, M. S., and Furer, M. 1972. Child psychosis. A theoretical statement and its implications. *Journal of Autism and Childhood Schizophrenia* 2(3):213.

120. Massie, H. N. 1975. The early natural history of childhood psychosis. *Journal of the American Academy of Child Psychiatry* 14:683–707.

121. Mednick, S., and Schulsinger, F. 1974. Studies of children at high risk for schizophrenia. In *Genetics, environment and psychopathology,* eds. S. A. Mednick, F. Schulsinger, et al. (New York: American Elsevier).

122. Meltzer, D.; Bremmer, J.; et al. 1975. *Explorations in autism.* The Roland Harris Educational Trust. (Scotland: Clunie Press).

123. Metcalf, A. 1973. An experience with the Rimland check-list for autism. In *Clinical studies of childhood psychosis,* eds. S. A. Szurek and I. N. Berlin (New York: Brunner/Mazel). pp. 464–477.

124. Miller, T. R. 1975. Childhood schizophrenia: A review of selected literature. In *Annual progress in child psychiatry and child development,* eds. S. Chess and A. Thomas (New York: Brunner/Mazel), pp. 357–401.

125. O'Gorman, G. 1970. *The nature of childhood autism* (New York: Appleton-Century-Crofts).

126. Ornitz, E. M. 1971. Disorders of perception common to early infantile autism and schizophrenia. In *The schizophrenic syndrome annual review,* ed. R. Cantro (New York: Brunner/Mazel), pp. 652–71.

127. Ornitz, E. M. 1976. *Medical assessment in autism–Diagnosis, current research and management* (New York: Spectrum Publications).

128. Ornitz, E. M., and Ritvo, E. R. 1976. The syndrome of autism: A critical review. *American Journal of Psychiatry* 133:609–26.

129. Perel, C. 1975. Lecture at Albert Einstein College of Medicine, Department of Child and Adolescent Psychiatry, unpublished.

130. Piaget, J. 1954. *The construction of reality in the child* (New York: Basic Books).

131. Polizoes, P.; Engelhardt, D. M.; Hoffman, S. P.; and Waizer, J. 1973. Neurological consequences of psychotropic drug withdrawal in schizophrenic children. *Journal of Autism and Childhood Schizophrenia* 3(3):247.

132. Prior, M., and McMillian, B. M. 1973. Maintenance of sameness in children with Kanner's syndrome. *Journal of Autism and Childhood Schizophrenia* 3(2):154–67.

133. Prior, M.; Perry, D.; and Gajzago, C. 1975. Kanner's syndrome or early onset psychosis: A taxonomic analysis of 142 cases. *Journal of Autism and Childhood Schizophrenia* 5(1):71–80.

134. Ragins, N.; Schacter, J.; et al. 1975. Infants and children at risk for schizophrenia: Environmental and developmental observations. *Journal of the American Academy of Child Psychiatry* 14(1):15–177.

135. Rank, D., and MacNaughton, D. 1950. A clinical contribution to early ego development. In *The psychoanalytic study of the child,* eds. R. S. Eissler, et al. (New York: International Universities Press), vol. 5, pp. 53–57.

136. Rees, S. C., and Taylor, A. 1975. Prognostic antecedents and outcome in a follow-up study of children with a diagnosis of childhood psychosis. *Journal of Autism and Childhood Schizophrenia* 5(4):309–22.

137. Reichler, R., and Schoplar, E. 1971. Observations on the nature of human relatedness. *Journal of Autism and Childhood Schizophrenia* 1(3):283–96.

138. Ricks, D. M., and Wing, L. 1975. Language, communication, and the use of symbols in normal and autistic children. *Journal of Autism and Childhood Schizophrenia* 5(3):191–222.

139. Rimland, B. 1964. *Infantile autism* (New York: Appleton-Century-Crofts).

140. Rimland, B. 1971. The differentiation of childhood psychosis: An analysis of checklists for 2,218 psychotic children. *Journal of Autism and Childhood Schizophrenia* 1(2):161–74.

141. Rimland, B. 1973. Review of L. Kanner's *Childhood psychosis: Initial studies and new insights. Journal of Autism and Childhood Schizophrenia* 3(1):88–92.

142. Rimland, B. 1976. Platelet uptake and efflux of serotonin in subtypes of psychotic children. *Journal of Autism and Childhood Schizophrenia* 6(4):379–82.

143. Ritvo, E. R.; Cantwell, D.; Johnson, F.; et al. 1971. Social class factors in autism. *Journal of Autism and Childhood Schizophrenia* 1(3):297–310.

144. Ritvo, E. R.; Freeman, B. J.; et al., eds. 1976. *Autism–Diagnosis, current research and management* (New York: Spectrum Publications).

145. Ritvo, E. R.; Yuwiler, A.; Geller, E.; et al. 1971. Effects of L-Dopa in autism. *Journal of Autism and Childhood Schizophrenia* 1(2):190–205.

146. Rosenthal, D.; Wender, P. H.; Kety, S. S.; et al. 1975. Parent-child relationships and psychopathological disorder in the child. *Archives of General Psychiatry* 32:466–88.

147. Ruttenberg, B. A. 1976. A psychoanalytic understanding of infantile autism and its treatment. In *Infantile autism: Proceedings of the Indiana University Colloquium*, eds. D. Churchill, D. Alpern, and M. K. DeMyer (Springfield, Ill.: Charles C Thomas), pp. 145–184.

148. Ruttenberg, B. A.; Dratman, M.; et al. 1966. An instrument for evaluating autistic children. *Journal of American Academy of Child Psychiatry* 5:453–78.

149. Rutter, M. 1972. Childhood schizophrenia reconsidered. *Journal of Autism and Childhood Schizophrenia* 2(4):315–37.

150. Rutter, M. 1975. The development of infantile autism. In *Annual progress in child psychiatry and child development*, eds. S. Chess and A. Thomas (New York: Brunner/Mazel), pp. 327–56.

151. Rutter, M., and Bartak, L. 1971. Causes of infantile autism: Some considerations from recent research. *Journal of Autism and Childhood Schizophrenia* 1(1):20–32.

152. Rutter, M.; Bartak, L.; and Newman, S. 1971. Autism. A central disorder of cognition and language? In *Infantile autism: Concepts, characteristics and treatment*, ed. M. Rutter (Edinburgh: Churchill and Livingstone).

153. Rutter, M., and Hersov, A., eds. 1977. *Psychiatry: modern approaches* (Philadelphia: J. B. Lippincott).

154. Rutter, M., and Koupernick, C., eds. 1970. A pathogenic approach to infantile autism. In *Infantile autism: Concepts, characteristics and treatment*, ed. M. Rutter (Edinburgh: Churchill and Livingstone).

155. Sandler, J., and Nagera, H. 1963. Aspects of the metapsychology of fantasy. *The psychoanalytic study of the child*, eds. R. S. Eissler, et al. (New York: International Universities Press), vol. 18, pp. 159–94.

156. Sandler, J., and Rosenblatt, B. 1962. The concept of the representational world. *The psychoanalytic study of the child*, eds. R. S. Eissler, et al. (New York: International Universities Press), vol. 17. 128–45.

157. Schopler, E. 1976. Toward reducing behavior problems in autistic children. *Journal of Autism and Childhood Schizophrenia* 6(1):1–14.

158. Schopler, E., and Reichler, R. J. 1971. Parents and co-therapists in the treatment of psychotic children. *Journal of Autism and Childhood Schizophrenia* 1(1):87–102.

159. Schopler, E., and Reichler, R. J. 1972. How well do parents understand their own psychotic child? *Journal of Autism and Childhood Schizophrenia* 2(4):387–400.

160. Shapiro, T., and Huebner, H. F. 1976. Speech patterns of five psychotic children now in adolescence. *Journal of American Academy of Child Psychiatry* 15(2):278–93.

161. Shapiro, T.; Huebner, H. F.; and Campbell, M. 1974. Language behavior and hierarchic integration in a psychotic child. *Journal of Autism and Childhood Schizophrenia* 4(1):71–90.

162. Simeon, J., and Itil, T. M. 1975. Computerized electroencephalogram. *Journal of Autism and Childhood Schizophrenia* 5(3):247–65.

163. Simon, N. 1976. Echolalic speech in childhood autism. Consideration of possible underlying loci of brain damage. In *Annual progress in child psychiatry and child development* (New York: Brunner/Mazel), pp. 471–90.

164. Simons, J. M. 1974. Observations on compulsive behavior in autism. *Journal of Autism and Childhood Schizophrenia* 4(1):1–10.

165. Small, J. G. 1975. E.E.G. and neurophysiological studies of early infantile autism. *Biological Psychiatry* 10(4):385–97.

166. Spence, A. M. 1976. Genetic studies. In *Autism*, ed. E. Ritvo (New York: Spectrum Publications), pp. 109–74.

167. Steg, J. P., and Rapoport, J. L. 1975. Minor physical abnormalities in normal, neurotic, learning disabled, and severely disturbed children. *Journal of Autism and Childhood Schizophrenia* 5(4):299–308.

168. Stubbs, E. G. 1976. Autistic children exhibit undetectable hemagglutination-inhibition antibody titers despite previous rubella vaccination. *Journal of Autism and Childhood Schizophrenia* 6(3):269–74.

169. Stubbs, E., and Crawford, M. L. 1977. Depressed lymphocyte responsiveness in autistic children. *Journal of Autism and Childhood Schizophrenia* 7(1):49–55.

170. Szurek, S. A., and Berlin, I. N., eds. 1973. *Clinical studies in childhood psychosis* (New York: Brunner/Mazel).

171. Taft, L., and Cohen, H. 1971. Hysarrhythmia and infantile autism. A clinical report. *Journal of Autism and Childhood Schizophrenia* 1(3):327–36.

172. Tanguay, P. E. 1976. Clinical and electrophysiological research. In *Autism—Diagnosis, current research and management*, eds. E. R. Ritvo and B. J. Freeman (New York: Spectrum Publications), p. 80.

173. Tanguay, P. E.; Ornitz, E. M.; et al. 1976. Rapid eye movement (R.E.M.) activity in normal and autistic children during R.E.M. sleep. *Journal of Autism and Childhood Schizophrenia* 6(3):275–88.

174. Torrey, E. F.; Hersh, P. S.; et al. 1975. Early childhood psychosis and bleeding during pregnancy. *Journal of Autism and Childhood Schizophrenia* 5(4):287–97.

175. Tustin, F. 1972. *Autism and childhood psychosis* (New York: Science House).

176. Waizer, J.; Polizoes, P.; et al. 1972. A single blind evaluation of thiothixene with outpatient schizophrenic children. *Journal of Autism and Childhood Schizophrenia* 2(4):378–86.

177. Walk, R. D., and Gibson, E. J. 1961. A comparative and analytical study of visual depth perception. *Psychological Monographs* 75, no. 15.

178. Walker, H. A., and Birch, H. G. 1974. Intellectual patterning in schizophrenic children. *Journal of Autism and Childhood Schizophrenia* 4(2):143–61.

179. Wenar, C., and Ruttenberg, B. A. 1976. The use of BRIAC for evaluating therapeutic effectiveness. *Journal of Autism and Childhood Schizophrenia* 6(2):175–92.

180. Wenar, C.; Ruttenberg, B. A.; Dratman, M.; and Wolf, E. G. 1967. Changing autistic behavior. *Archives of General Psychiatry* 17:26.

181. Werner, E.; Bierman, J. M.; et al. 1968. Reproductive and environmental casualties: A report on the 10-year follow-up of the children of the Kauai pregnancy study. *Pediatrics* 42:112–27.

182. White, J. H. 1977. *Pediatric psychopharmacology* (Baltimore: Williams & Wilkins), pp. 27–47, 134–70.

183. Wing, L., and Wing, J. K. 1971. Multiple impairments in early childhood autism. *Journal of Autism and Childhood Schizophrenia* 1(3):256–66.

184. Winnicott, D. W. 1958. Metapsychological and clinical aspects of regression within the psycho-analytical set up. In *Collected Papers* (New York: Basic Books), pp. 278–94.

185. Wynne, L. C., and Singer, M. T. 1974. Principles for scoring communication defects and deviances of parents of schizophrenics in psychological testing. In *Annual Report; Mental Health Intramural Research Programs, Division of Clinical and Biochemical Research* (Bethesda, Maryland: N.I.M.H.), vol. 2, pp. 11–13.

186. Yuwiler, A.; Ritvo, E.; et al. 1975. Uptake and efflux of serotonin from platelets of autistic and non-autistic children. *Journal of Autism and Childhood Schizophrenia* 5(2):83–98.

Chapter 17

LEGAL AND ETHICAL DEVELOPMENTS

Alan A. Stone, M.D.

Introduction

The past decade has witnessed massive and unparalleled legislative reform and constitutional litigation intended to place new constraints on the confinement of the mentally ill (25). The thrust of legal change has been both to make it more difficult to initiate involuntary confinement and to limit its duration. The impact of this legal reform has been augmented by administrative and psychiatric policy that now opts for community treatment and short-term hospitalization whenever possible. Custodial care in a hospital setting has been repudiated both by recent legal decisions (51) and, to a large extent, by prevailing administrative mental health policy. Since patients with schizophrenia represented a large portion of those involuntarily confined and a large portion of those traditionally provided custodial care, the changes of the past decade have had a particularly profound impact on them (48).

Legal reform is, of course, not directed at patients with a particular diagnosis or syndrome. Furthermore, the extensive literature that now records these reforms is largely composed of judicial opinions and law review articles. That literature is couched in the arcane jargon of law and must be translated for the prospective readers of this volume.

Given these limitations, I have chosen to focus on the major themes that are readily comprehensible rather than on the abstruse minutiae of law. Thus, the reader will find that the organization of this chapter derives not from the bibliographer's interest in assessing additions to the literature, but rather from the author's judgment of what constitutes the crucial themes and conflict that determine the relationship between legal intervention and the patients whose diagnosis places them within the schizophrenic syndrome.

The traditional subject matter of forensic psychiatry deals with the insanity defense, competency to stand trial, testamentary and contractual capacity, and other related issues in which the psychiatrist is asked to resolve certain kinds of questions posed by a court (52). The central theme of those questions is: Should the court treat this person like everyone else, or are there compelling reasons to make some exception? The implicit assumption of the law was that these exceptions somehow benefited the person for whom they were made. The typical assumption of the forensic psychiatrist who attempted to answer these questions was that a diagnosis of schizophrenia was enough to justify a confident assertion that the person was entitled to any such legal exception.

During the past decade serious challenges have arisen both to the legal assumption that being an exception benefits someone (19,34,75), and also to the psychiatric assumption that a diagnosis of schizophrenia is enough to decide any of these legal questions.* But even more important than these challenges to the traditional field of forensic psychiatry has been the intrusion of law into the daily decision-making processes of all mental health facilities. Civil libertarians have begun to challenge every aspect of the legal status of the mentally ill, and the interface between law and psychiatry has taken on an entirely new political and constitutional dimension (70). It is this new dimension, affecting the provision of mental health care not only for schizophrenics, but for all mentally disabled persons, which will be discussed in this chapter. The recent considerable developments in traditional forensic psychiatry cannot adequately be addressed here.† Though important in their own right, they are less relevant to the everyday treatment, management, and clinical situation of patients who manifest the symptoms of schizophrenia. The now-famous case of Kenneth Donaldson (23) illustrates many of the new issues that have become central legal and ethical considerations in psychiatry.

Mr. Donaldson was involuntarily confined in the Chatahoochee State Hospital in Florida for fourteen years with a diagnosis of paranoid schizophrenia. Although the available evidence suggested delusional ideation, there was no indication of major ego disintegration or massive disability. There was also no evidence to suggest that Mr. Donaldson would at any time cause physical injury to himself or others.‡

Chatahoochee, like many large state hospitals in the decades of the fifties and sixties, was grossly overcrowded and understaffed. During Mr. Donaldson's stay the ratio of patients per staff psychiatrist ranged from 560 to 1 up to 1,000 to 1 (2). Hospitals like Chatahoochee were often staffed by physicians who were recent émigrés from foreign countries. It is impossible to assess the training or competence of this diverse group. Many, of course, were excellent clinicians; but clearly a significant percentage had difficulty with the English language, and that, along with their different social and cultural perspective, created problems of communication with patients. Furthermore, since many could obtain licensure only in state hospitals, necessity rather than personal motivation may have determined their choice of professional speciality. But even with the participation of these foreign medical graduates, many of whom gave excellent service, staffing was grossly inadequate at most institutions (47).

---

* See references 59, 60, 63, 74, and 86.
† For such recent development, se Slovenko (65), particularly chaps, 1, 2, 3, 5, and 6.
‡ See the opinion of Justice Stewart in *O'Connor* v. *Donaldson* (51).

There seems in retrospect no way to justify the appalling living conditions or the impossibility of obtaining treatment in such "hospitals." Competent psychiatrists and other competent professionals who chose to work in that context faced an ethical dilemma: should they stay on and try to improve conditions, or should they leave rather than be part of such degrading institutions. Many, of course, failed even to recognize the dilemma either because they assumed custodial care was all that could be provided patients with chronic schizophrenia and other chronic conditions, or because they had become inured to these conditions, or perhaps because they believed society would never do more and they at least were doing something.

Donaldson v. O'Connor

Mr. Donaldson repeatedly petitioned various courts to release him from Chatahoochee State Hospital during his fourteen-year confinement (3). All of the state and federal judges ignored or rejected his plea. He made a number of attempts to find alternatives to the state hospital, but the staff and particularly Dr. O'Connor, the superintendent, rejected these alternatives. Their rejection was apparently based on their conviction that Mr. Donaldson was a chronic paranoid and the kind of troublemaker who needed custodial care. Under the existing conditions at the hospital the only treatment that might have been available was psychotropic medication, but Mr. Donaldson allegedly rejected that, at least from time to time, claiming to be a Christian Scientist.

This standoff came to an end when a new hospital superintendent, apparently more aware of contemporary psychiatric management of chronic schizophrenic patients, discharged Mr. Donaldson in 1971. But by then, with the assistance of the American Civil Liberties Union, the Mental Health Law Project, and Dr. Morton Birnbaum, a legally trained physician and a pioneer in right-to-treatment litigation, Mr. Donaldson had initiated a lawsuit against his former physicians in the Federal District Court. He claimed that his physicians, acting under color of law, had deprived him of his constitutional rights, specifically of his right to treatment. The applicable law is §1 of the Civil Rights Act of 1871, passed in the years immediately following the Civil War. It is now known as 4 USC §1983. A §1983 action has teeth as far as psychiatric liability for monetary damages is concerned. Mr. Donaldson asked for both compensatory and punitive damages: that is, that the jury order his doctors to pay him money as compensation for any damages that had resulted from his confinement without treatment, and an additional sum beyond that amount to punish the doctors for their actions.

Before discussing the results of that particular trial and the subsequent legal developments that led up to the Supreme Court and back down again, it might be useful to look at the more general legal and ethical implications of Mr. Donaldson's situation, many aspects of which were never dealt with by the various courts that concerned themselves with certain narrow questions.

I shall assume that the diagnosis of Mr. Donaldson as a chronic paranoid schizophrenic was correct, since credible evidence was never introduced to indicate that it was not; and further, if he was not mentally ill, there can be no reason to raise any legal or ethical questions, since the answers would all be obvious.

Legal Criteria for Civil Commitment

The first question is: Should a diagnosis of chronic paranoid schizophrenia be enough to justify involuntary confinement? At this time the answer is obviously no. Even the older civil commitment statutes required that, in addition, the patient must be in need of treatment: that is, the patient must be mentally ill, plus something else (8). The something else is usually one of four criteria: (1) dangerous to self, (2) dangerous to others, (3) gravely disabled, (4) in need of treatment. This last criterion is the pure "medical model"; mental illness plus need for treatment. Given the facts we know about Mr. Donaldson, this was the only basis under which he could have been confined. However, as this basis for civil commitment has been applied in Donaldson's case and in hundreds of thousands of other instances, neither courts nor psychiatrists asked whether treatment was in fact available, or whether the mental illness was treatable(58).

Thus, physicians, with judicial approval, committed patients to hospitals like Chatahoochee where little or no treatment was available. Given the way civil commitment operated in the real world, in many instances the diagnosis was in fact all that mattered. Rarely, if ever, did the courts specify which one of the four criteria in addition to mental illness applied. Psychiatrists often stretched the concept of dangerousness to include "troublemakers" like Donaldson, and thus the specific criteria, when used at all, were applied in ambiguous fashion. Based on what we now know about the social breakdown syndrome and the other dehumanizing effects of total institutions, there can be no medical justification for such commitments. What we have witnessed is better described as the "convenience model" (see reference 71, chap. 4), and not the medical model. Chronic schizophrenics, along with other mentally disabled persons, have been confined in substandard institutions with grossly inadequate medical care for the convenience of their families and for the convenience of a society that neither tolerated the presence of the mentally ill nor allocated adequate resources to care for them in decent, humane surroundings.

Most of the legal reform (28) directed at correcting these abuses of the confinement process has attacked the medical model and the unreliability of diagnostic "labeling." But the legal reform meant to replace the medical model is ill conceived and fails to address the real problems, or even to meet its own objections to diagnostic labels. All of the legal reforms retain the basic medical criterion: the alleged patient must still be mentally ill. Second, the courts and the legislatures, seeking to clarify ambiguity, have emphasized that the alleged patient must be dangerous (compare reference 38) and they have been increasingly stringent about proof of dangerousness (70). A great deal of empirical evidence has been accumulated to suggest that neither psychiatrists nor any other behavioral scientist can predict dangerousness.* Thus, courts, if they wish to commit, must either wait until some harmful act has occurred or rely on predictions that have no scientific validity. But the most important shortcoming of such legal requirements is that they still fail to consider whether the patient is treatable and will get treatment. Confining dangerous persons who are not treatable in a hospital is surely a bankrupt exercise of legal authority. It amounts to little more than preventive detention, a practice that is anathema to civil libertarians (18,20). Furthermore, the presence of a critical mass of such dangerous and uncooperative persons transforms the best of hospitals into a prison. Thus, to the extent that state hospitals might be or have been improved through allocation of resources, this new patient population destroys the possibility of a therapeutic milieu.

Perhaps even more troubling to the mental health professions is the fact that the treatment of these patients forces the caretakers into the roles of warden and prison guard. And as I shall more fully discuss, these patients typically require that we force treatment on them against their will.

Reform-oriented lawyers look at civil commitment as a procedure that should rarely be invoked, and when it is, only to protect society from a dangerous madman (24). Their model is one of social control compatible with the police power of the state. The role allotted to the psychiatrist in that model makes him the agent of the state responsible for social control of the patient, and in my view it is incompatible with medical ethics and competence. A good psychiatrist ought to look at civil commitment as a procedure rarely to be invoked, and only when a seriously mentally ill patient is suffering as a result of his illness, and because of delusions, disorientation, or dementia is unwilling or unable to accept available treatment. That is the constellation of factors that would justify the designation "medical model." (See references 71, chap. 4, and 53.) Its implementation would signify a rejection by psychiatry of its role conflicts; the psychiatrist would be repudiating the role of policeman, warden, or social control agent in favor of the role of therapist. Legally the former role is justifiable under the doctrine of *parens patriae* (66), a doctrine that is being attacked on all sides by legal reformers. Unfortunately the view of the legal reformers prevails in most jurisdictions, and there is already evidence to suggest that as the criteria for civil commitment have been "reformed," hospitals have been forced to absorb a critical mass of untreatable and dangerous patients.

Few schizophrenic patients are dangerous; those who do enter state

---

* See references 4, 40, 54, 67, 68, and 69.

hospitals are apt to be the helpless victims of this new legally created dangerous and oppressive milieu.

I shall not specifically discuss the criteria of "dangerous to self" or "gravely disabled." The most radical new statutes require suicidal patients to be released from involuntary confinement in a month (California) (11) or less (Washington) (78,79). "Gravely disabled" has been narrowly construed to mean unable to feed and clothe oneself (see reference 71, chap. 4). The criterion of "mentally ill and in need of treatment" is rapidly becoming archaic (28). The developments I have described have not occurred in every state, nor have they been given the imprimatur of the Supreme Court as a result of constitutional litigation. They do reflect a definitive trend in legal reform: erecting legal barriers to involuntary hospitalization.

Whether one applied the legal model of social control now being introduced, or the criteria of the medical model outlined by me, there is in hindsight no justification for the fourteen years involuntary confinement of Kenneth Donaldson and hundreds of thousands like him. They all were victims of the convenience model of civil commitment, the perverted tradition of custodial care, and the failure of society to provide adequate resources.

The Right to Refuse Treatment: Legal and Ethical Aspects

A second important legal and ethical issue raised by the Donaldson case is the right of a chronic paranoid schizophrenic patient to refuse treatment. Donaldson had been hospitalized prior to his Chatahoochee confinement. On that previous occasion he had been given electroshock treatment, which he apparently disliked. He certainly was wary of somatic treatment, and one of his alleged delusions involved being poisoned. Let us assume that he was a sincere Christian Scientist, and he offered that as the basis of his refusal to accept somatic treatment. What is the legal and ethical responsibility of the psychiatrist in such a case? The federal courts in New York dealt with just such a case (80) and concluded that to impose somatic treatment over the religious objections of a patient is a violation of the patient's constitutional rights. The trial court did not award monetary damages to the patient, who had in fact been treated with medication over her religious objections; but there is now law on the subject, and psychiatrists should exercise proper caution in this regard.

However, the religious issue is rarely the question; it simply allows us to begin to reflect on the considerations that judges have in mind when they examine the right of a psychotic patient to refuse treatment.

The civil libertarian argument goes much farther than the clash between religious tenets and good medical practice. Civil libertarians

would raise the principle of individual autonomy to the same constitutional status as that guaranteed religious belief by the First Amendment. Since the mind is the source of mentation, and since freedom of
speech originates in mentation, to influence anyone's mind against his
or her will is a violation of that person's First Amendment rights: so
goes the most radical legal argument (64). Nor do these legal critics
of psychiatry accept the view of many clinicians that the schizophrenic
lacks the personal autonomy they seek to protect. They would assert
that every person is presumptively competent to exercise individual
autonomy, and that the burden should be on the physician or the state
to overcome that presumption (38).

There is little doubt that the writings of Szasz (74,75,76) and, to a
lesser extent, of Laing (35,36), have had an influence on those proposing these legal arguments asserting a constitutional right to refuse
psychiatric treatment. Szasz is the apostle of autonomy and has inspired
much of the legal writing. Laing's epistemological relativism implies
that each of us is free to construct our own reality (36). The necessary
corollary of that relativism is a constraint on interference based on
some sounder or more reasonable judgment about reality. Becker (5)
has expressed Laing's relativism as it applies to deviance:

> Deviance is not a quality of the act a person commits, but rather a conse-
> quence of the application by others of rules and sanctions to an offender; the
> deviant is one to whom that label has been successfully applied; deviance is
> behavior that people so label.*

In Szasz's world everyone has autonomy; in Laing's world there is no
distinction between rational and irrational; and in Becker's world good
and evil, sick and well are entirely categories of social convention. When
this ideology is joined to the prevalent and widespread distrust of
authority, it becomes difficult indeed to demonstrate that the presumptively competent person is incompetent to refuse treatment.

Individual autonomy is an important value in a democratic society,
and it is important to consider what values are served by allowing
autonomy to be overridden. The most obvious value is the relief of
needless suffering. There are patients, particularly schizophrenics, whose
suffering can be relieved, but whose mentation is so disturbed that they
cannot choose to accept the treatment that will help them.

Second, although it is usually ignored in the libertarian calculus, the
suffering and the behavioral manifestations of the mentally ill do have
a deleterious effect on those around them, even when there is no physical
injury. The courts have long been willing to acknowledge the reality of
psychic trauma, and that construct should not be excluded here.
Mentally ill persons do cause psychic trauma to family and friends. A
psychotic parent may cause as much damage to children as does a
child batterer.

The third consideration is related to the second. When a mentally ill
patient is admitted to a hospital, his or her presence has an impact on
the other patients and their treatment. Allowing a patient to disturb
other patients needlessly as a result of a refusal to accept treatment
may make it impossible to treat others.

° Cited in Stone (71), p. 6, note 8.

There are other explicitly utilitarian rationales for imposing treatment—for example, refusal of treatment results in greater economic dependency and unnecessary waste of limited resources.

However, I would concede that none of the values I have brought forward either singly or conjointly are sufficient to overcome the value of autonomy. Certainly we would not require a person who was not mentally ill to have surgery for cancer, even if his refusal meant needless suffering for him and for his family and friends and a greater expenditure of limited resources. The only convincing argument for me is that the patient we would treat against his autonomous choice has no capacity to exercise that choice; that is to say, the values of freedom of mentation, freedom of choice, and all that autonomy implies, are not sacrificed when we impose reasonable treatment on a person who is unable to exercise his or her autonomy. Even John Stuart Mill, in his famous essay on liberty, recognized the existence of these exceptions (43).

There is another libertarian argument that acknowledges the possibility of these exceptions but asserts that if law once recognizes such exceptions, the way is open to abuse such that government will use involuntary psychiatric treatment to suppress dissidents or for other political purposes.* There seems to be no totally convincing answer to that charge. But there are considerations that mitigate its import.

First, despite the ideological rhetoric, there is little historical evidence that involuntary psychiatric treatment has been used to political ends in the United States. The abuses of psychiatry have been inflicted on no one political group, religion, or sect. Certainly there has been racism and discrimination within the mental health system, but those factors have operated so as to withhold treatment rather than to impose it.

Second, legal procedures are not an absolute protection against abuse of political power by government officials, and involuntary psychiatric treatment is not the only available alternative for that abuse. The American criminal justice system is built on procedural safeguards, but because of the discretionary powers of government officials, it is still possible to have political abuses.

Lastly, a system of law, that is too far tilted toward protecting citizens from those who might govern badly, will inevitably interfere with those who would govern well.

Taking all of these problems into consideration, the task that confronts the mental health professions is to articulate criteria that define those who lack autonomy, while being cognizant of the potential for abuse. Below I shall suggest such criteria.

RECENT LEGAL DEVELOPMENTS IN THE RIGHT TO REFUSE TREATMENT

Unfortunately the only widely reported judicial decision that touched on these difficult issues concerned experimental psychosurgery (31). The situation involved a man indefinitely committed as a sexual psycho-

---

* A. Dershowitz: personal communication.

path who consented to an amygdallotomy meant to reduce his violent proclivities. The court was asked to consider whether this man could consent to such a treatment. In their convoluted decision they emphasized three aspects: (1) that consent must be *knowing;* (2) that it must be *voluntary,* not coerced in any way; and (3) that the person must have the mental *capacity* to consent.

As to the first criterion, the court seemed to suggest that, given the experimental nature of this procedure, where risks and benefits could not be clearly defined, it was unlikely that consent could ever be knowing. As to the second, they concluded that within the coercive environment of indefinite confinement it was unlikely that the man had voluntarily consented. They made no clear ruling on whether he had the capacity. They did discuss with seeming approval the radical theory that connects mentation and First Amendment constitutional rights. Although this decision (*Kaimowitz* v. *Michigan Department of Mental Health*) has no great constitutional significance as precedent, it is frequently cited by legal commentators (7) who favor a constitutional right to refuse all psychiatric treatment.

Questions of consent, though not of constitutional dimensions, frequently arise in the medical malpractice area, and there is therefore a substantial body of tort law on this subject (77). Currently there are two separate standards defining what the courts will consider "knowing" consent. A majority of jurisdictions essentially require the physician to tell the patient what other doctors tell their patients in similar situations (10). A majority of jurisdictions require the physician to tell the patient all risks, benefits, and alternatives to a proposed treatment that a reasonable patient in that situation would want to know. This is the so-called Canterbury standard (12,26). There is typically in both types of jurisdiction an exception that allows the physician to withhold information whose revelation would cause harm to the patient (17). A physician who does not obtain the patient's informed consent as specified will be liable for damages for risks not revealed that in fact materialize (12). The doctor may thus be negligent, even if the treatment was appropriate in every other respect. Thus, the law of malpractice has historically acknowledged the right of patients to refuse treatment (except in emergencies) (17). Where patients are incompetent to consent, and there is no emergency, the next of kin's consent should be obtained.

Another source of law on the subject of consent is the result of a beginning trend of state legislatures to enact statutes controlling psychiatric treatment. Much of the lobbying for such statutes comes from the Church of Scientology and others who have particular reasons to object to somatic treatment. Typical of these statutes and the lobbying process is the California statute AB 4481, the so-called Vasconcellos Bill, which regulated electroshock therapy and psychosurgery (22). At one time in its legislative history the bill included neuroleptics as well. Although the Vasconcellos Bill focuses on informed consent as though its concern was for the autonomy of the decision maker, there is every reason to believe that its purpose is to make it more difficult to give those somatic treatments that the sponsors of the bill disfavor. Similar informed consent statutes regulating abortion were erected in some states, not because the legislature was concerned about autonomy or a woman's freedom to choose, but rather because they were concerned about the morality of abortion (73). Whether psychiatric patients need such statutory protection from those who treat them with somatic methods is debatable, but such statutes are problematic for other reasons. Once voted on, they become law, and rarely can such laws anticipate all of the complex issues of enforcement and application. Even if some obvious change is required, a vote of the legislature may be necessary and may be stalled for reasons that have nothing to do with its merits.

A more flexible alternative being implemented in many states is regulation of psychiatric treatment by the Department of Mental Health, which at least allows the rapid substitution of more workable methods. Federal regulatory agencies (the Department of Health, Education, and Welfare and the Food and Drug Administration) and the Joint Commission on Accreditation of Hospitals have also begun to concern themselves with consent procedures and protection of patients' rights (33,73).

PRACTICAL IMPLICATIONS OF THE RIGHT TO REFUSE TREATMENT

Despite, or perhaps because of, all this law and legal regulation there are no clear and simple answers about a patient's right to refuse treatment. He may not as yet have a constitutional right to refuse a treatment, but he may have a right to sue his physician for damages if something goes wrong and if neither patient nor next of kin has consented to the treatment. But the preeminent problem in psychiatry is deciding whether the patient is competent to consent to begin with. What the psychiatrist confronts every day can be conceptualized as a four-cell diagram (figure 17–1).

Cell B, the incompetent consent, is the situation that seems most to concern legal reformers who press for more explicit and detailed informed consent procedures. Cell D, the incompetent refusal, is the chief concern of practicing psychiatrists who are in the bind of being the responsible physician for a patient who refuses needed treatment.

Unfortunately treating such patients in a hospital setting further complicates this analysis, as in figure 17–2.

This complexity arises because legally a patient's confinement status

FIGURE 17-1

	Competent	Incompetent
Consent	A Competent consent	B Incompetent consent
Refusal	C Competent refusal	D Incompetent refusal

FIGURE 17-2

	Competent	Incompetent
Consent	A Competent consent—voluntary	B Incompetent consent—voluntary
	C Competent consent—involuntary	D Incompetent consent—involuntary
Refusal	E Competent refusal—voluntary	F Incompetent refusal—voluntary
	G Competent refusal—involuntary	H Incompetent refusal—involuntary

does not necessarily determine his competency status (62). Had Mr. Donaldson been legally confined involuntarily, it would not necessarily follow legally that he was incompetent to make choices about treatment. These disjunctures between legal confinement status and competency become more tangible problems as we move toward a system of civil commitment emphasizing dangerousness. Although some psychiatrists might disagree, it seems to me that most of the dangerous sociopaths may be fully capable of weighing the risks and the benefits of a proposed treatment. Such a patient would fall into cell G of the diagram. These are the dangerous persons law reformers have focused on as appropriate for civil confinement, but the most radical of these law reformers would not allow such patients to be treated against their will—that is, their competent refusal of treatment (42). Mr. Donaldson might also be in that category, since at least some chronic paranoid schizophrenics would be able to meet the legal test of competency.

Cell B presents a malpractice risk for the psychiatrist if it can be demonstrated at trial that the patient was incapable of informed consent under the stricter *Canterbury* (12) standard.

Cell D is the kind of situation that psychiatrists have traditionally considered to present no legal or ethical problems. They have failed to recognize the developing disjuncture between involuntary status and incompetency. Thus, unless they obtain consent of the next of kin, they may be treating without adequate legal authority.

Cells E and F are medically the most troublesome. The patients have voluntarily entered the treatment facility but refuse the treatment. How can one force treatment on a voluntary patient? However one resolves that question, there seems to be no rational medical reason to confine a patient in a hospital who refuses treatment. Recently a federal judge in Massachusetts issued a temporary restraining order allowing patients at a state hospital to refuse treatment. The chaos that resulted is summarized in a brief prepared by the Massachusetts Psychiatric Society:

"Tension seems to fill the air at the Austin Unit twenty-four hours a day." One wing has been destroyed by fire, set by a patient. One female patient attempted to burn a staff member, to choke a patient, and to strangle herself with a ripped dress. She smashed a window, threatened to kill several staff members, attacked, kicked, and spat at them. At another time she was "screaming, threatening, deluded, beat staff, grabs them, incited another disturbed patient to violence by inviting him to her bed and defying staff to deal with him. This other patient becomes so threatening that the night staff sent Dr. G. a letter signed by all informing him that they could not and would not work under these conditions."

Another female Austin Unit patient punched a social worker and several patients, cut herself with fliptops, and "gouged her face with her fingernails until she bled; this continued almost daily throughout the month of June." A schizophrenic male patient who has refused medication since the grant of the temporary restraining order has had sexual intercourse with at least three different patients who are either retarded or are severely and chronically regressed. He has also broken a window, kicked a patient, and grabbed and threatened two female staff members. The incidence of assaultive behavior by Austin patients has also increased as the administration of medication has declined in deference to their wishes.

Patients in the May Unit have experienced similar problems. One woman, while refusing medication, became psychotic and left the hospital in anger, lived on a doorstep without changing her clothes for two weeks, was twice returned to the hospital by police, and twice set herself on fire in her room. In the May, as in Austin Unit, "since the issuance of the temporary restraining order, tensions, threats, agitation and acts of violence have increased." [6, pp. 22–23; Statements in quotation marks are taken from hospital records.]

To avoid this disastrous scenario it is imperative that the decision to confine and the decision to treat be made in conjunction. The current structure of the law does not readily allow for this, since it is predicated on the establishment of separate legal criteria for confinement and for incompetence. Elsewhere (reference 71, chap. 4) I have developed the so-called *thank you theory* of involuntary confinement and treatment which is meant to meet both legal demands and medical rationality.

The Thank You Theory: A Five-step Procedure for Involuntary Confinement and Treatment

Reliable diagnosis of severe mental illness. Reliability, of course, means no more than that several diagnosticians would agree on a label. It does not mean that such a label is a valid indicator. But if diagnostic categories like schizophrenia and its subtypes have any validity in clinical psychiatry, it is because they indicate something about prognosis and treatability. The legal system should be particularly interested in prognosis and treatability as relevant to the imposition of involuntary treatment in the first instance. Involuntary treatment should be limited to severe pathology where good reliability can be demonstrated.

The short-term prognosis absent treatment must include profound anxiety, depression or other painful affects, deterioration of the personality, or the proliferation or intensification of symptoms. Where mental illness is the result of toxic conditions such as delirium tremens, prognosis must include evidence that failure to treat may result in brain damage or death.

The next step is to ask the hospital and the responsible physician if treatment is available, and, if so, what kind and how effective. I have emphasized that mental health practitioners cannot predict dangerousness, but they can keep records of previous treatment for patients in similar diagnostic categories—its duration and effectiveness. (Indeed, the Professional Standards Review Organization—see 42 USC §401 et seg.—requires a similar establishment of records and procedures.)

What the psychiatrist would do in this system then is first make his diagnosis. If it cannot readily be demonstrated that this is a reliable diagnosis of a severe condition, the process would go no further. Reliability and severity could be challenged and/or demonstrated by independent psychiatric examination.

Diagnosis is the product of a present evaluation and not a future prediction. It does not ask the psychiatrist to do something he is unable to accomplish. Treatability of any psychiatric patient, of course, is, like dangerousness, a predictive judgment. But at least the actuarial tables already exist, or the data to make such tables exist. And although it is a prediction, it is a different kind of prediction. The prediction is: if the psychiatrist is allowed to treat this patient in a hospital where he, the psychiatrist, can control the social context, what will happen to the patient's mental state based on his own considerable experience in similar cases?

Severe illness reliably diagnosed and a prognosis of suffering and treatability are, however, not enough to justify involuntary treatment. It must also be shown that the alleged patient's decision to refuse treatment is an incompetent refusal.

I suggest the following tests of incompetent refusal:

1. There should be a burden on the reliably diagnosed severely ill person to articulate a reason for refusing treatment.
2. That patient who is unwilling or unable to consent or object, the so-called nonprotesting patient, should be considered as having made an incompetent refusal.
3. If the alleged patient is able or willing to state a reason for objecting to treatment, the psychiatrist should be asked to demonstrate that the refusal is irrational and is based on or related to the diagnosed illness; for example, "the voices tell me the doctors are going to transplant my brain"; "the doctors are really F.B.I. men who are part of the conspiracy against me"; "I am radioactive and no one should come near me"; "I have to kill myself because everyone thinks I am a homosexual"; "I don't deserve to be treated, I am worthless."
4. If the patient has a reason that is not a product of his illness—for example, "I have been a Christian Scientist all my life. I do not believe in medicine or doctors"—even though a doctor might consider this irrational, such a refusal is not based on the patient's current misperception of reality, and it should therefore be considered a competent refusal.

Obviously under these procedures only seriously psychotic—irrational—patients would be involuntarily treated. No patient with a personality disorder, neurosis, or behavior problem would be incompetent to refuse. The same would be true of alcoholics and addicts, in the absence of toxic syndromes.

The questions a court would be asked to consider are as follows:

1. Do the psychiatrists make a convincing diagnosis of serious illness?
2. Is the patient suffering?
3. Is treatment available and how long will it take?
4. Does the patient's objection to treatment seem irrational and based on his illness?

If these four questions are answered in the affirmative, the court would turn to the last step.

Would a reasonable man accept the treatment being offered in that hospital? Might a reasonable man object to a proposed treatment method, even though the alternative is more costly to the state and/or less likely to be successful?

The balancing test I propose then is: Would a reasonable person who could exercise autonomy be willing, given the patient's illness and suffering, to accept a treatment that in similar cases produces a specific range of results? Such a test should take into account the quality of life and the treatment provided in the given treatment facility, and it *means* that a person diagnosed as schizophrenic might be involuntarily treated in one institution and not in another. It *means* that perhaps no one could be involuntarily treated in some state and county hospitals, given the conditions and treatment that are now available.

It is my contention that the criteria of serious, reliably diagnosed mental illness, incompetent refusal, reasonable expectation of treatment in a decent institution are the essential ingredients that give moral content and legal justification to involuntary confinement and treatment of the mentally ill.

It is also my contention that those criteria, if followed, would moot the many metaphysical arguments about the ambiguous line between schizophrenia and eccentricity, political and ideological dissent, religious conversion, etc. It would moot those arguments at the empirical level, because in cases where those metaphysical arguments can be raised convincingly, the criteria of suffering and severity cannot be met.

This is the *thank you theory:* It asks the psychiatrist to focus his inquiry on illness and treatment, and it asks the law to guarantee that treatment before it intervenes in the name of *parens patriae.* It is radical in the sense that it insists that society fulfill its promise of benefit when it trenches on human freedom. It is also radical in that it divests civil commitment of a police function; the control of dangerous behavior should be returned to the province of criminal law. Only someone who is irrational, treatable, and incidentally dangerous would be confined in the mental health system. Mr. Donaldson would not have been involuntarily confined and treated at Chatahoochee under the thank you theory.

The thank you theory applies to newly admitted patients; it asks the court to give its imprimatur not only to the deprivation of liberty, but also to the course of treatment and length of stay. It avoids a number of unfortunate results of past and present practices, as exemplified by Mr. Donaldson's case. It prevents the unnecessary involuntary confinement of untreatable patients. It deals with the right to treatment and the right to refuse treatment before rather than after the courts deprive persons of their freedom. Its strict application would require courts to confront the crucial distinction between preventive confinement, meant to protect society, and civil commitment, meant to benefit the person being confined. Such strict application would also force psychiatrists to confront the distinction between productive hospitalization and confinement for the convenience of society, a distinction too frequently blurred.

The Right to Treatment

The thank you theory attempts to confront questions of treatment at the time of initial confinement. Unfortunately the current historical context presents a residue of institutions like Chatahoochee where the misuse of civil commitment has left a legacy of chronic schizophrenic patients whose mental illness is complicated by institutional neglect. Legal efforts aimed at improving conditions in these hospitals were initiated during the past decade. Indeed, Kenneth Donaldson began his lawsuit as a class action right to treatment and only subsequently amended it as an individual suit for damages.

The first significant legal decision dealing with the right to treatment was *Rouse* v. *Cameron* (61), which is often cited as the first holding by a court that the right to treatment has the force of a constitutional right. The case involved a man who claimed he was receiving no treatment after being confined subsequent to a finding of not guilty by reason of insanity. The legal analysis of the ruling is complicated. Judge Bazelon found the right to treatment in the statute but indicated there might be a constitutional right as well; he alluded to questions of due process, cruel and unusual punishment, and equal protection. Judge Fahy, in his concurring opinion, went farther and relied on the constitutional arguments. The *Rouse* decision, in addition to suggesting these constitutional implications, extended the importance of the right to treatment by stating that continued failure to provide treatment cannot be justified by an insufficiency of resources. The court, however, did not articulate general judicial criteria for acceptable treatment. It did not demand cure, or even improvement, or that the treatment used was the best possible. It asked only for a bona fide effort to provide an individualized treatment program with periodic evaluation.

The next important legal case came in the category of confinement due to incompetency to stand trial. In *Nason* v. *Superintendent of Bridgewater State Hospital* (46), the court clearly saw a constitutional right to treatment on grounds of due process and equal protection, and threatened to free the patient-defendant, absent treatment.

These were the ground-breaking cases in the history of the legal right to treatment. They had little impact at first, although they articulate the right to treatment and provide a legal and constitutional rationale for it. (32). No one was discharged because of lack of treatment, and the courts gave little specific guidance to the psychiatrists or to the legislatures as to the general standard of treatment required. At best, Judge Bazelon in *Rouse* had demanded a bona-fide effort and hinted at a possible case-by-case review, an ambiguous standard reiterated in *Nason*. The American Psychiatric Association produced a strong position paper in response to the *Rouse* decision (1). Organized psychiatry at that time apparently viewed such judicial intervention as trenching on the domain of the clinician. Whatever the reasoning may have been, the psychiatric establishment recoiled rather than commit itself to working through the courts to accomplish improvements in the situation of patients.

The case of *Wyatt* v. *Stickney* (83) pushed the right to treatment farther in every respect and at last directed attention to the plight of the large group of mentally ill patients, most with the diagnosis of schizophrenia, who were involuntarily confined in less than adequate state hospitals.

Wyatt v. *Stickney* was a class action suit brought by guardians of patients involuntarily confined at Bryce Hospital, a state facility in Alabama. Civil commitment in that state took place in the context of minimal procedural safeguards, and the promise of treatment was properly considered a paramount consideration. A constitutional principle of due process was clearly stated by Judge Johnson: "To deprive any citizen of his or her liberty upon the altruistic theory that the confinement is for humane and therapeutic reasons and then fail to provide adequate treatment violates the very fundamentals of due process." (See reference 83, at 785.)

Since *Wyatt* was a class action, Judge Johnson went much farther than his predecessors and attempted to spell out standards of adequate treatment for all patients in the facility; he indicated a willingness, at least in his court, to attempt to identify and supervise the vagaries and complexities of institutional psychiatric care and treatment. That complexity is superimposed upon a critical legal entanglement—namely, the separation of powers. How far can the judiciary go in setting standards of institutional practice that will require the legislature and the executive branch to raise new tax revenues or reorder the fiscal priorities of social needs as they have been established through executive and legislative decision making (27)?

If one focuses on the constitutional aspect of the various cases that have now spawned similar litigation all over the country,* one can decipher a series of cutting points for legally enforced change.

The first is cruel and unusual punishment: that is, does confinement without treatment constitute unconstitutional punishment without even a criminal charge being filed? Here we rely on the Eighth Amendment.

This rationale is perhaps the simplest to demonstrate. Courts have held that even the most humane incarceration may constitute punish-

---

* See references 16, 45, 49, 50, and 56.

ment (15). And confinement without treatment may be regarded as punishment for a mere status—mental illness—over which the patient has virtually no control, a punishment of the type declared unconstitutional by the Supreme Court in *Robinson* v. *California* (57). Or nontherapeutic confinement of the nondangerous mentally ill may be regarded as cruel and unusual under the standards of "pointless and needless," "degrading to the dignity of human beings," or "unrelated to any valid legislative purpose" set forth recently by the Justices of the Supreme Court in capital punishment. Finally, and most simply, state mental institutions cannot be allowed to perpetuate conditions like those that have already been declared unconstitutionally cruel in *prisons*.

It is my view that if the simplest standard of cruel and unusual punishment were applied in existing total institutions, some would still be found to fall well below it. Even if the right to treatment were only constitutionally justified when the conditions of confinement were cruel and unusual on a scale developed for prisons, considerable reform could be accomplished. The Supreme Court has recently cast some doubt on the applicability of the Eighth Amendment to this situation. The court dealing with corporal punishment in schools held that the Eighth Amendment was not applicable, since it was intended to control the conditions of criminal confinement (29). Whether they would follow a similar logic as to civil commitment is unknown.

Judge Johnson recognized that Eighth Amendment argument but sought a higher standard based in due process and equal protection. That standard would seek to do more than prevent destructive conditions; it would ensure adequate treatment. This is the second cutting edge.

Thus, the *Wyatt* order detailed minimum "medical and constitutional" requirements to be met with dispatch. The decree set forth standards guaranteeing basic patient rights to privacy, presumption of competency, communication with outsiders, and so forth. Requirements were established governing staff-to-patient ratios, floor space, education, sanitation, and nutrition. The court also ordered that individual treatment plans be developed, that written medication and restraint orders be filed, and that these be periodically reviewed. Outside citizens' committees were appointed to monitor enforcement of patients' rights under the order (84).

The *Wyatt* decree was far from a generalized array of commands arbitrarily arrived at. It was formulated from study of the testimony of institutional personnel, outside experts, and representatives of national mental health organizations appearing as *amici*. Most of the specifics of the order were taken from a memorandum of agreement signed by the parties. The most critical specifics—the model staffing ratios—approximate those last recommended by the American Psychiatric Association. However, the case proceeded without the participation of organized psychiatry, but with the participation of other mental health professional groups. Not surprisingly, the court's decree did include language allowing qualified nurses, psychologists, and social workers the authority to take clinical responsibilities that had traditionally been limited to physicians. (See reference 84, at 383, standard 24.) This dethronement of the psychiatrist as the head of the mental health team has been emulated in subsequent litigation and legislation (16).

The third compelling legal question is whether one can go farther than Judge Johnson and demand *effective* therapeutic conditions as a third level of the right to treatment.

In at least twenty-four states the statutes altruistically promise to provide treatment to those who are in need of it. (See reference 8, tables 3–1–3–20.) Therefore, it might be argued that due process demands that such a promise be honored. In addition, where only the need for treatment is invoked to justify commitment, due process is compromised when the state fails to require weighing of relevant factors, such as the amenability of the patient to treatment, the capacity of the existing institutions to deal with his infirmity, and the term of confinement that for his specific malady may arguably be effectively therapeutic (30).

Beyond destructive conditions, adequate treatment, and effective treatment within a total institution, there is a fourth-level argument: namely, that confinement should not be continued if alternative treatment outside the institution would be preferable (13,82). This is the thrust of a lawsuit successfully brought against St. Elizabeths Hospital in the District of Columbia (9,21).

The right-to-treatment cases all deal with the problems of those already confined. Often the court is trying to remedy conditions in institutions where years of neglect and resulting patient deterioration are involved. The briefs in *Wyatt* read like a description of the Augean stables. As tragic as the fate of the chronic mentally ill may be, it should not deflect our attention from considering the right to treatment of those who might become the next chronic generation.

In this regard, the case of *Legion* v. *Weinberger* (37), though unsuccessful, is particularly interesting. *Legion,* as its pseudonymous title suggests, was a class action, brought by medically indigent patients who had been involuntarily committed to state mental institutions. The plaintiffs charged that Medicaid violated their equal protection rights in that ample benefits were conferred on the already more fortunate voluntary patients in the psychiatric wards of general hospitals, while it provided no benefits for the involuntary patients of state and county mental hospitals, where the poor and minority groups are overrepresented. The Supreme Court summarily affirmed the lower court's dismissal of the suit. Had the suit succeeded, the federal government would have been obliged to share with the states the cost of treating the indigent schizophrenics and other psychotics, just as they now do for all other kinds of illness.

The Impact of Donaldson

More will be offered on the impact of right-to-treatment suits, but here it is appropriate to return to Kenneth Donaldson whose lawsuit was contemporaneous with *Wyatt* v. *Stickney.* Donaldson's lawyer had argued that his physicians, and particularly Dr. O'Connor, had engaged in bad faith mistreatment, in fact depriving Donaldson of his constitutional right to treatment. His lawyers were particularly outraged by Dr. O'Connor's unwillingness to permit Donaldson to be discharged to the care of a friend or to a halfway house, and by his refusal to grant ground privileges and other opportunities for socialization. They suggested that Dr. O'Connor had some particular animosity toward Mr. Donaldson. Only that animosity could explain the treatment decisions, they argued. Dr. O'Connor, having suffered a heart attack and coronary disease to which he later succumbed, did not appear in court. His legal defense was provided by the State of Florida, and in my opinion it was inadequate.

Donaldson's lawyers called as expert witnesses psychiatrists who essentially advocated the community mental health "revolving door" policy. They testified, in line with that policy, that Donaldson should have been given ground privileges, should have generally been treated differently than custodial care would imply. Based on that testimony and on a great deal of other evidence that attested to the horrid conditions that Mr. Donaldson and other patients endured at Chatahoochee, the jury found Dr. O'Connor and another physician liable and awarded Mr. Donaldson some $38,500 in compensatory and punitive damages (3).

This decision was immediately appealed to the Fifth Circuit Court of Appeals, the same federal court that had for more than a year been deliberating the *Wyatt* decree that had been appealed by the State of Alabama.

Florida had terrible state hospitals; so did Alabama. In Florida the lawsuit awarded damages to the patient, holding that the psychiatrist had been personally responsible for the lack of treatment. The Alabama suit placed that responsibility on the state, thus pitting the power of the federal court against Governor Wallace, his administration, and other elected officials. The Florida case presented no such sensitive political questions. The Court of Appeals, not surprisingly, seized on the Florida case, holding that there was a constitutional right to treatment (23). Then immediately using that precedent, they resolved *Wyatt* (85), the Alabama case that had been in abeyance for over a year. Thus, the Fifth Circuit was firmly on the record in support of the right to treatment. Because of the constitutional right to treatment, a state might be forced to devote more money and resources, and a psychiatrist could be liable for damages for withholding treatment.

The State of Florida appealed the Donaldson case to the Supreme Court, with the American Psychiatric Association for the first time appearing on the scene to offer an *amicus* brief. The APA. position was that there should be a constitutional right to treatment, but that psychiatrists who work in understaffed, underfunded hospitals such as Chatahoochee should not be liable when that treatment is not available. The APA brief (3) pointed out the historical disjuncture between custodial care and the community mental health approach. They emphasized the impossible staff-patient ratios, and that psychiatrists should not be liable under such conditions for depriving patients of rights that courts have not yet declared to exist. "A constitutional right to treatment was little more than a gleam in the eye of its most ardent proponent during Mr. Donaldson's confinement" (3).

These arguments were meant to attack the theory that Dr. O'Connor had acted in bad faith. How could he maliciously deprive a patient of a right that he did not know existed? How could a psychiatrist know that what he was doing was wrong when so many courts, including the Fifth Circuit and the Supreme Court, had denied relief to Donaldson in his many previous legal appeals? Unfortunately the APA. was forced to make the kind of arguments in its brief that the State of Florida should have made in the original trial. The appellate courts, including the Supreme Court, are in theory limited to considering essentially those factual arguments presented to the trial court.

O'Connor v. *Donaldson* (*Donaldson* v. *O'Connor* became *O'Connor* v. *Donaldson* on appeal) came to the Supreme Court with great fanfare. It was the first time that the United States Supreme Court has dealt with the constitutional rights of the hundreds of thousands of American citizens who are civilly committed each year. Advocates of the right to treatment hoped that the Supreme Court would give its imprimatur to the right to treatment, making it necessary for all the states to improve treatment facilities. Civil libertarians described it as the case that would empty the mental hospitals. Psychiatrists worried that a major precedent would establish the liability of all psychiatrists working in the public sector. If Kenneth Donaldson had been deprived of his right to treatment by his psychiatrist, then surely there were thousands of other patients who would be entitled to make similar claims.

The Supreme Court has in the eyes of many close observers become a more conservative tribunal during the years Chief Justice Burger has presided with other Nixon appointees. Therefore, some reformers worried that the Court might strike down the right to treatment, thus overturning the decisions of many lower courts.

None of these hopes or fears came to pass; instead, the Court found a way to avoid every single important issue. Justice Stewart, writing for the unanimous Court, declared that the case raised only one narrow issue: could a state continue to confine a person like Kenneth Donaldson who, though diagnosed schizophrenic, was not dangerous to himself or others, could survive outside the hospital, and was not receiving treatment? The answer to that very narrow, almost trivial question was a unanimous no. Unfortunately the Court did not define "treatment," "survive," or "dangerous." But it is safe to infer that custodial care, even if euphemistically described as milieu treatment, will probably not be considered treatment.

Perhaps historians will describe this case as marking the end of legal acquiescence to involuntary custodial care. Since custodial care was the fate of many chronic schizophrenics, it also is a benchmark in the history of their treatment.

As to the liability of Dr. O'Connor, the Supreme Court remanded that question to the Fifth Circuit Court of Appeals to reconsider in light of an intervening case, *Wood* v. *Strickland* (81). That case had held that there should be certain limitations on retroactive liability—that is, on making an official liable for a right that had not yet been clearly established as a constitutional right. The Fifth Circuit, with little ceremony, passed that buck down to the Federal District Court in Florida. After some preliminaries the estate of Dr. O'Connor agreed to pay Mr. Donaldson $10,000 as a settlement of his claim without any admission of wrongdoing. The claim against another physician was similarly settled. Thus, the great legal struggle of Mr. Kenneth Donaldson ended not with a bang but a whimper. No meaningful precedent was established as to the liability of psychiatrists. No new law was made on the right to treatment, although the Supreme Court in an unusual move declared that *Donaldson,* as decided by the Fifth Circuit, was not precedent for the right to treatment. This means that other courts cannot rely on it as the good precedent basis of their future decisions. Justice Burger, in a separate concurring opinion to the unanimous decision, let the judges in the lower courts know that he for one would view with skepticism the kind of theorizing used to justify the right to treatment by the Fifth Circuit.

When the Supreme Court vacated the precedential significance of *Donaldson* on the right to treatment, they left the *Wyatt* case in a kind of legal limbo. *Wyatt* had already been upheld by the Fifth Circuit on the basis of a precedent that the Supreme Court had overturned. Nonetheless, it is a decided case and remains in effect, since it was never appealed to the Supreme Court.

Effects of Right-to-Treatment Litigation

Despite the Supreme Court's caution, the lower federal courts have continued to support litigation on the right to treatment. The present trend is for the federal district courts to avoid formulating a solution themselves and instead to force the state in question to negotiate with attorneys for the patient (57). The resulting so-called consent decrees then established the pattern of future mental health policy for the institution or institutions involved (71,72). These consent decrees have become increasingly complex and sophisticated, establishing conditions for deinstitutionalization as well as setting standards within the facility (41).

Despite these developments, it has become increasingly apparent that court-ordered improvements are difficult to implement, even when the responsible psychiatrists make every reasonable effort to do so. Tragically the difficulties of implementation occur even when state officials and the mental health department consent to the judicial decree and help to formulate it. Apparently neither the courts nor the litigants have yet faced up to the magnitude of costs and resources required actually to implement the right to treatment for chronic schizophrenics and other chronic mentally disabled persons. Nor have the parties to the consent decrees anticipated the involvement of other elements of the state bureaucracy, which for their own reasons resist change and throw up roadblocks in the form of endless delay and red tape.

In at least two states lengthy and detailed court decrees on the right to treatment have not produced the specified changes, despite long delays. Therefore, the plantiffs have requested the court to hold physician-defendants and state officials in contempt. This has occurred in *Davis* v. *Watkins* (16) and *New York Association for Retarded Children* v. *Rockefeller* (50). Does anyone believe that this most recent development will make it easier to recruit professional staff, as the court orders require? Will placing the entire hospital system in receivership improve the quality of care?

These problems are not unique to psychiatry; they occur in every case in which federal courts try to force progress on recalcitrant local governments. Thus, the federal district courts, in taking on the right to treatment, have taken on a burden comparable to, but in the details of its implementation even greater than, the burden they bear in the school-desegregation situation. Whether courts can effectively shoulder such burdens and force the states to do what is constitutionally required, to expend vast sums in an era of fiscal crisis, only time will tell.

The Least Restrictive Alternative

St. Elizabeths Hospital, the major psychiatric facility of the District of Columbia, had a large group of patients, many of them chronic schizophrenics, who were involuntarily confined solely because there was no alternative, less restrictive facility available for them. Although community mental health had been the brainchild of the National Institute of Mental Health, the District of Columbia has never been provided with adequate community facilities. The same can be said of most cities around the country.

The suit (21) attempted, by means of the legal theory of least restrictive alternative, to force the District to provide those community facilities (e.g., nursing homes, day care centers, foster care) that are an integral part of the community mental health concept. Presumably if such facilities were available, patients who needed limited services would have access to them, rather than be forced to enter or remain in a total institution. Furthermore, these are the kinds of services needed by the growing number of patients who have already been deinstitutionalized.

The courts found for the plaintiffs; but despite the passage of time, little has been accomplished. Alternative facilities in sufficient numbers simply cannot be developed overnight, if at all. Many of the nursing homes to which chronic schizophrenic patients might be transferred are having their own legal problems. Deinstitutionalization, even with the blessings and authority of the courts, is not easily achieved (14,41,55).

Conclusion

The legal developments of the past decade have had a profound impact on schizophrenic patients. These patients are less likely to be confined involuntarily, their hospital stay is likely to be brief, and their right to refuse treatment, particularly somatic treatment, is becoming a significant legal question. These developments, together with the right-to-treatment litigation, have hastened the demise of the old state hospital system. Changing legal standards for admission have made the atmosphere of many of the remaining state mental hospitals more dangerous and oppressive for those schizophrenics who are treated in such settings, be it voluntarily or involuntarily.

Families who now seek to use legal intervention to control schizophrenic relatives will get little assistance. Certainly the convenience model of civil commitment has come to an end. That there are costs in all these reforms is attested by the growing number of schizophrenic patients who now wander the city streets or live in welfare hotels which are the new back wards of this decade of legal progress.

BIBLIOGRAPHY

1. *American Journal of Psychiatry.* (1967) 123:1458. Position Statement on the Question of Adequacy of Treatment.
2. American Psychiatric Association. 1973. Brief amicus curiae, Supreme Court of the United States, October Term, 1973, nos. 74–8.
3. American Psychiatric Association. 1974. Brief amicus curiae, October Term, 1974.
4. American Psychiatric Association. 1974. *Task force report: Clinical aspects of the violent individual* (Washington, D.C.: American Psychiatric Association).
5. Becker, H. 1969. Deviance and the response of others. In *Delinquency, crime, and social process*, eds. D. R. Cressey and D. A. Ward (New York: Harper & Row), pp. 585–89.
6. Beyer, H., and Guttmacher, J. 1976. Preliminary draft of amicus curiae brief of the Massachusetts Psychiatric Society in *Rogers* v. *Macht*, Boston, January 1976.
7. *Boston University Law Review* (1973) 54:301. *Kaimowitz* v. *Michigan Department of Mental Health*: A right to be free from experimental psychosurgery.
8. Brakel, S., and Rock, R., eds. 1971. *The mentally disabled and the law* (Chicago: University of Chicago Press).
9. *Brewster* v. *Dukakis*, C.A. no. 76-4423F (D. Mass.).
10. *California Law Review* (1967) 55:1396. Comment: Informed consent in medical malpractice.
11. California Welfare and Institutions Code, §§5000 et seq.
12. *Canterbury* v. *Spence*, 464 F.2d 772 (D.C. Cir., 1972).
13. Chambers, D. 1972. Alternatives to civil commitment of the mentally ill: Practical guides and constitutional implications. *Michigan Law Review* 70:1107.
14. Council for Community Action Planning, Inc., California. 1971. To the lowest bidder. Mimeographed.
15. *Cross* v. *Harris*, 418 F.2d 1095 (D.C. Cir. 1969).
16. *Davis* v. *Watkins*, 384 F. Supp. 1196 (N.D. Ohio 1974).
17. Dawidoff, D. 1973. *The malpractice of psychiatrists* (Springfield, Ill.: Charles C Thomas).
18. Dershowitz, A. 1969. On preventive detention. *New York Review of Books*, March 13, 1969, p. 22.
19. Dershowitz, A. 1969. The psychiatrist's power in civil commitment: A knife that cuts both ways. *Psychology Today* (February 1969), p. 43.

20. Dershowitz, A. 1973. Preventive confinement: A suggested framework for constitutional analysis. *Texas Law Review* 51:1306.

21. *Dixon* v. *Weinberger*, 405 F. Supp. 974, 1975.

22. *Doe* v. *Younger*, Civ. No. 14407 (Calif., 4th App. Dist., Apr. 23, 1976).

23. *Donaldson* v. *O'Connor*, 493 F.2d 507 (5th Cir. 1974).

24. Ennis, B. 1972. *Prisoners of psychiatry* (New York: Harcourt Brace Jovanovich).

25. Ennis, B., and Friedman, P., eds. 1973. *Legal rights of the mentally handicapped* (New York: Practicing Law Institute), vols. 1–3.

26. Glass, E. 1970. Restructuring informed consent: Legal therapy for the doctor-patient relationship. *Yale Law Journal* 79:1533.

27. *Harvard Law Review* (1973) 86:1282. *Wyatt* v. *Stickney* and the right of civilly committed mental patients to adequate treatment.

28. *Harvard Law Review* (1976) 87:1190. Developments in the law—Civil commitment of the mentally ill.

29. *Ingraham* v. *Wright*, 97 S.C. 1401, 1977.

30. *Jackson* v. *Indiana* 406 U.S. 715, 732–733, 1972.

31. *Kaimowitz* v. *Michigan Department of Mental Health*, Civ. no. 73-19434-AW, Cir. Ct. Wayne County, Michigan, July 10, 1973.

32. Katz, J. 1969. The right to treatment: An enchanting legal fiction. *University of Chicago Law Review* 36:755.

33. Katz, J. 1972. *Experimentation with human beings* (New York: Russell Sage Foundation).

34. Kittrie, N. 1971. *The right to be different* (Baltimore: Johns Hopkins University Press).

35. Laing, R. 1960. *The divided self* (London: Tavistock Publications).

36. Laing, R. 1967. *The politics of experience* (New York: Ballantine Books).

37. *Legion* v. *Weinberger*, U.S. Supreme Court, No. 73-5467 (1973), *Legion* v. *Richardson*, 354 F. Supp. 456 (S.D.N.Y. 1972), summarily aff. 94 S. Ct. 564 (1973).

38. *Lessard* v. *Schmidt*, 349 F. Supp. 1078 (E.D. Wisc. 1972); vacated and remanded 94, S. Ct. 713 (1974).

39. Levick, M., and Werner, A. 1974–75. Advances in mental health: A case for the right to refuse treatment. *Temple Law Quarterly* 48:354–83.

40. Livermore, J.; Malmquist, C.; and Meehl, P. 1968. On the justification for civil commitment. *University of Pennsylvania Law Review* 117:75.

41. Lottman, M. 1976. Enforcement of judicial decrees: Now comes the hard part. *Mental Disability Law Reporter* 1(1):69–76.

42. *Loyola University of Chicago Law Journal* (1974) 5:578. Note, The involuntarily confined mental patient and informed consent to psychiatric treatment.

43. Mill, J. S. 1961. On liberty. In *The philosophy of John Stuart Mill*, ed. M. Cohen (New York: Random House, Modern Library), p. 296.

44. Moore, M. 1975. Some myths about "mental illness." *Archives of General Psychiatry* 32: 1483–97.

45. *Morales* v. *Turman*, 364 F. Supp. 166 (E.D. Texas 1973).

46. *Nason* v. *Superintendant of Bridgewater State Hospital*, 233 NE 2d 908 (Mass. 1968).

47. National Institute of Mental Health. 1973. Staffing of state and county mental hospitals, United States 1973. Statistical Note no. 109, Division of Biometry, National Institute of Mental Health, Rockville, Maryland. August 1974.

48. National Institute of Mental Health. 1975. Changes in the age, sex, and diagnostic composition of the resident population of state and county hospitals, United States, 1964–1973. Statistical Note no. 112, Division of Biometry, National Institute of Mental Health, Rockville, Maryland, March 1975.

49. *Nelson* v. *Heyne*, 491 F.2d 352 (7th Cir. 1974).

50. *New York State Association for Retarded Children* v. *Rockefeller*, 357 F. Supp. 752 (E.D.N.Y. 1973).

51. *O'Connor* v. *Donaldson*, 95 S.C. 2486 (1975).

52. Overholser, W. 1953. *The psychiatrist and the law* (New York: Harcourt Brace).

53. Peszke, M. 1975. Is dangerousness an issue for physicians in emergency commitment? *American Journal of Psychiatry* 132:823–28.

54. Rappeport, J., ed. 1967. *The clinical evaluation of the dangerousness of the mentally ill* (Springfield, Ill.: Charles C Thomas).

55. Reich, R., and Siegel, L. 1973. The chronically mentally ill: shuffle to oblivion. *Psychiatric Annals* 3:35.

56. *Ricci* v. *Greenblatt*, Civ. Action 72-469 (D. Mass. 1973) (consent judgment).

57. *Robinson* v. *California*, 370 U.S. 660, 1962.

58. Rock, R., et al. 1968. *Hospitalization and discharge of the mentally ill* (Chicago: University of Chicago Press).

59. Rosenhan, D. 1973. On being sane in insane places. *Science* 179:250–58.

60. Roth, R.; Dayley, M.; and Lerner, J. 1973. Into the abyss: Psychiatric reliability and emergency commitment statutes. *Santa Clara Lawyer* 13:400–446.

61. *Rouse* v. *Cameron*, 373 F.2d 451 (D.C. Cir. 1966).

62. *St. Louis University Law Review* (1975) 20:100. Note, Forced drug medication of involuntarily committed mental patients.

63. Shah, S. 1967. Crime and mental illness: Some problems in defining and labeling deviant behavior. *Mental Hygiene* 53:21.

64. Shapiro, M. 1974. Legislating the control of behavior control: Autonomy and the coercive use of organic therapies. *Southern California Law Review* 47:237.

65. Slovenko, R. 1973. *Psychiatry and law* (Boston: Little, Brown).

66. *State ex rel Hawks* v. *Lazaro*, 202 SE 2d 109 (1974).

67. Steadman, H. 1973. Some evidence on the inadequacy of the concept and determination of dangerousness in law and psychiatry. *Journal of Psychiatry and Law* 1:409.

68. Steadman, H., and Keveles, G. 1972. Community adjustment and criminal activity of the Baxstrom patients: 1966–1970. *American Journal of Psychiatry* 129:304.

69. Stone, A. 1973. Comment on "Is Dangerousness an Issue for Physicians in Emergency Commitment?" by M. Peszke. *American Journal of Psychiatry* 132:829–31.

70. Stone, A. 1975. *Mental health and law: A system in transition* (Washington, D.C.: Government Printing Office).

71. Stone, A. 1975. Overview: The right to treatment—Comments on the law and its impact. *American Journal of Psychiatry* 132:1125–34.

72. Stone, A. 1977. Recent mental health litigation: A critical perspective. *American Journal of Psychiatry* 134:273–79.

73. Stone, A. The history and future of litigation in psychopharmacologic research and treatment. In *Psychopharmacology: A review of progress, 1967–1977*, ed. D. Gallant, forthcoming.

74. Szasz, T. 1961. *The myth of mental illness* (New York: Delta Books).

75. Szasz, T. 1963. *Law, liberty and psychiatry* (New York: Macmillan).

76. Szasz, T. 1970. *The manufacture of madness* (New York: Harper & Row).

77. Waltz, J., and Scheuneman, T. 1970. Informed consent to therapy. *Northwestern University Law Review* 64:628.

78. *Washington Law Review* (1974) 49:617. Note, Progress in involuntary commitment.

79. Washington Revised Code §71.05.200(1)71.05230 (1973).

80. *Winters v. Miller* 446 F.2d 65 (2nd Cir. 1971).

81. *Wood v. Strickland* 94 S.C. 1932.

82. Wormuth, F., and Mirkin, H. 1964. *The doctrine of the reasonable alternative. Utah Law Review* 9:254–307.

83. *Wyatt v. Stickney*, 325 F. Supp. 781 (M.D. Ala. 1971).

84. *Wyatt v. Stickney*, 344 F. Supp. 373, 379–385 (M.D. Ala. 1972).

85. *Wyatt v. Stickney*, sub nom. Wyatt v. Aderholt, 503 F. 2d 1305, (5th Cir. 1974).

86. *Yale Law Journal* (1974) 83:1237–70. Mental illness: A suspect classification?

THE SCHIZOPHRENIC SYNDROME:
WHAT THE CLINICIAN CAN DO UNTIL
THE SCIENTIST COMES

Leopold Bellak, M.D.

Every week outstanding authorities present Grand Rounds lectures, and not infrequently the topic is schizophrenia. These lectures range from biochemical studies to psychodynamic considerations, and the wide ground between. As I listen to more of these lectures, I often identify with the first-year psychiatric residents who are concerned with the care of their patients on the ward, and I ask myself what they can possibly take back with them to the wards, what they can translate into the understanding and care of individual schizophrenic patients. The answer is, I am afraid, very little or nothing.

Until we have hard scientific data about various aspects and probably about various subgroups of the schizophrenic syndrome, the clinician must pay attention to whatever seems specifically contributory to an individual patient's personality and problems. If some reasonable support can be found for a specific etiological or pathogenic process, it may be helpful for both treatment and prognosis. A careful history is still the key to success, especially if listened to with some heuristic hypotheses in mind. These hypotheses must be held with a grain of salt, however, and should be changed or discarded if they are not subsequently supported.

The main emphasis has to be on understanding one's patient as an individual, as a human being who is not only the sum, but the configuration, the Gestalt of many interacting factors. To reach this understanding, one should take an extensive personal and family history, in a careful and open-minded manner. In taking such a history, one must pay particular attention to the developmental factors. One must attempt to be aware of all the input that made the patient the person that he or she is, as he or she sits opposite one. That means an understanding of the geographic, cultural, ethnic, and economic dimensions of the patient and his family in their social setting, as well as of the biological and psychodynamic factors we are more used to thinking about.

A systematic approach should not lead one to ignore the patient's highly individualistic aspects. For example, how old were his siblings while he was growing up? What roles did they play in each other's lives? What was the state of the parents' minds, individually and collectively, when this child was born and what was going on in their lives then? Don't be afraid of being concrete in trying to understand such matters. Try to imagine how your patient looked, acted, and felt in his specific environment, when he was four or twelve or at other ages.

Personality is that comprehensive configuration which derives from the impact of all of the experiential factors on the biological matrix or Anlage. It is, therefore, not enough to have an intimate, but solely abstract knowledge of the patient's significant experiential input. It is important to know that this particular person was rather small or large for his age, awkward or pretty, robust or sickly. *For history is destiny.*

Hoping that this brief reminder of the importance of fully understanding the experiences of a person will suffice, it is time to turn to the importance of learning as much as possible about the individual's Anlage. Long ago, and rather futilely, I was interested in the anthropometric aspects of schizophrenia (5). Though our experimental findings then were negative, my interest remains. Spitz's work (13) suggested that the physical constitution can be dramatically influenced by an infant's early experience. Fries and Woolf (10) suggested that congenital activity types may determine the choice of defenses—that is, whether they will be mainly alloplastic or autoplastic ones. If correct, this may have a definite bearing on the clinical picture of schizophrenia, as those with a childhood history of an active activity type might be expected to choose alloplastic defenses (such as delusions and hallucinations), while schizophrenics who were more passive children may become withdrawn and display flatness of affect. There is some suggestive evidence that the former group has a better prognosis, and the latter group a worse one. This hunch, though not yet well supported, also ties in with my belief that a highly rated evaluation of "mastery competence" cuts clear across all other psychopathology as an excellent prognosticator of outcome and responsiveness to treatment. It also coincides with Ciompi and Müller's finding (9) that a certain "personality type" (both as reported as premorbid and as seen during morbidity) is critical in determining the outcome of the schizophrenic syndrome—judging from their extremely large longitudinal study. It is Ciompi's belief* that this personality style is closely related to mastery and competence.

Of course, we want to know a great deal about the patient's family history. Even if it were solely a matter of "educational" transmission, we would want to know how the parents and siblings were faring. The evidence is mounting, however, that genetic factors play at least *some* role in *some* subgroups of the schizophrenic syndrome.

There is no solid evidence that schizophrenics with a positive family history for schizophrenia present a more chronic picture or suffer a

---

* L. Ciompi: personal communication.

worse prognosis. Ciompi and Müller belong to those who, in fact, found negative evidence for this hypothesis (9). However, with respect to individuals who present withdrawal, flat affect, a poor premorbid personality, with perhaps some hebephrenic features, and with more than a customary number of schizophrenics in their immediate family, I personally would tentatively keep in mind a genetic Anlage and a relatively unfavorable prognosis. If I were employing my "sifting" research technique, which I mentioned in my introduction, I would investigate such individuals especially for biochemical and neurophysiological abnormalities. As a clinician, I would not tend to think of them as good candidates for psychotherapy, and I would tend to think of pharmacotherapy, halfway houses, community support systems, and even the possibility of custodial care in the very long run. All this, though, is only as a heuristic hypothesis, not a foreclosed issue.

Long ago, when I still saw quite a few children and adolescents, I thought that I saw a good many with histories, including incidents of high febrile episodes (1), which were suggestive of encephalitides. In these children and adults, problems of impulse control seemed to play a particular role in their psychopathology. Clinically, such a history suggests that one should pay special attention to impulses; from a research standpoint, it suggests that one should study neurological factors.

It is true that some schizophrenic patients have heartbreaking personal histories. It may well be that there are also people with similar histories who are not schizophrenic: we will hardly ever know with certainty, though, because life histories and their individual significance will not readily lend themselves to meaningful quantification. The fact remains, however, that in such schizophrenics the blighted personal history seems sufficient to explain the presence of the entire disturbance—though it may be that some x of a biological Anlage is required to produce the phenotype. In such patients psychotherapy should play an outstanding role. These patients seem usually to be psychologically sensitive—for example, to their own psychiatric status—and to have many painful symptoms. They also seem to be especially sensitive to the side effects of phenothiazines. Goldstein's work (11) suggests that patients with some awareness ("insight" seems too optimistic a term) of their illness often do not fare well on phenothiazines. In my own experience also, such patients seem frequently to suffer from feelings of depersonalization and derealization when on phenothiazines.

In my introduction I singled out another subgroup—one with the coexistence of the schizophrenic syndrome and the syndrome of minimal brain dysfunction (MBD). I have described elsewhere (2,3) the details of psychopathology and treatment of such individuals. In short, they often suffer from disturbances of the self image, lack of impulse control, and a low stimulus barrier and probably respond better to imipramine, amytrypilin, methylphenidate, or diazepam than to phenothiazines, which often make them clinically worse.

The moral of this long story is that a clinical anamnesis is important in trying to understand what might play a primary role in the problems of the patient, even before we have solid scientific facts, and in indicating how one might best help. For all patients, however, a good human milieu is extremely important, as Ciompi and Müller also suggested.

I do believe that a diagnosis is useful and important (6), provided it is stated as a heuristic hypothesis. In that case, the limitations of the diagnostic hypothesis must be clear, and the attitude toward the use of the diagnostic concept must be flexible: that is, the diagnosis should not represent an item of dogma, but it must be judged by its usefulness. In that same spirit, Carpenter et al. (8) and Strauss and Gift (14) suggested a flexible use of variables for making diagnoses for different purposes (see chapter 8). I have based my use of the nomothetic label "schizophrenic syndrome" on the fact that, however diverse individuals may appear, they share enough intragroup similarities and intergroup differences to make that label useful. I agree that, regrettably, labeling tends to lead to stereotypes, to self-fulfilling prophecies, and to social abuse, and I am in favor of doing everything possible to minimize these effects of diagnostic labeling.

I believe that both patients and psychiatric science may best be served by utilizing several diagnoses for each patient on four levels, in hierarchical order.

1. For a *nomothetic* label I am quite willing to use "schizophrenic syndrome."

2. For strictly *descriptive* purposes, the characterizations planned for the third edition of the *Diagnostic and Statistical Manual of Mental Disorders* (which were originally meant to be operational but turned into merely descriptive labels) may yet have some limited usefulness. Perhaps it is helpful to describe somebody as suffering from an "acute episode" or a "residual syndrome," though there is no research evidence that such a descriptive label is of any therapeutic or prognostic value. It may possess some real communicative value and facilitate communication from one clinician to another. If so, I am in favor of a good descriptive term, as well defined as possible, following the initial label "schizophrenic syndrome."

3. After, first, the nomothetic syndrome and, second, the descriptive label, I would like to record the *diagnostic etiological hunches* mentioned earlier, and others as they emerge—for example, neurophysiological factors such as MBD or conditions possibly related to encephalitides. Notations could be used, such as "familial characteristics—possible genetic factors" or "primarily psychogenic, experiential factors." Many other such diagnostic hunches might be recorded and would be useful as long as they are treated heuristically and taken into consideration for treatment.

4. I have suggested for some time now that another level of strictly individual assessment may be a useful tool: that is, *ego function assessment* (EFA) (3,6,7).

My suggestions for the clinician are then to understand each patient in terms of his individual history and makeup; to subsume the patient, if appropriate, under the label "schizophrenic syndrome"; and then to add hierarchical diagnostic hunches and ego function assessment as guidelines for treatment and prognosis.

For the clinician to do this successfully, I would also emphasize the importance of not immediately medicating a patient when he comes to the emergency room, is admitted to the ward, or comes to the office (4). I have compared this practice of immediate medication with giving everybody who has any kind of severe abdominal pain a shot of morphine. I suggest at least one week of observation without drugs, so that their effects do not complicate the picture.

Careful diagnosis and prognostication should decrease the "revolving door" phenomenon. It is neither humane nor good socioeconomic sense to send patients who need custodial care into the community, while we recognize, of course, that patients who can do better outside the regressive setting of a hospital should certainly be sent to an appropriate community setting.

The relevance of psychotherapy should not be forgotten. Many of us have treated patients with "chronic brain syndromes" who may show signs of neurological impairment, and have then found that forgetfulness, confusion, and even hallucinations and delusions can disappear if one uncovers and treats a coexistent depression. I, therefore, do not care at all whether some schizophrenic patient may have genetic, biochemical, neurophysiological, constitutional, or other biological problems. The cognitive apparatus is still responsive to input. Psychotherapy is a skilled form of input which attempts to restructure certain maladaptive processes. The schizophrenic syndrome is a maladaptive process in response to biological, psychological, and other environmental factors, including socioeconomic, cultural, and perhaps even meteorological ones (see chapter 1) in various interactions.

As skilled psychoanalytically oriented psychotherapy is often not readily available and is costly in time and effort, it generally does not represent a realistic treatment option. This fact should not stand in the way of at least utilizing dynamic insights and employing intensive therapy when it is available.

Meanwhile, pharmacotherapy, other somatic therapies, group therapy, and other forms of nonsomatic therapy and support systems have to be employed, with indications as precise as possible. Patients with body image disturbances should have exercises to help them restore self-boundaries (12). Those with loss of affect might profit from music and dance therapies. Those with problems in object relations may profit from group therapy and milieu therapy. But milieu therapy will not help people with self-image disturbances, and patients with a severe thought disorder and little synthetic-integrative functioning will not profit from psychoanalytic therapy.

The clinician has to postulate as good a hypothesis about what ails a particular patient as he can on the basis of a careful study of the patient. He must then prescribe a therapeutic program—possibly *in stages*—which makes sense in terms of the diagnosis. The diagnostic hunches must serve as prognostic indicators in the sense of allowing for some kind of differentiation of planning and disposition and, when necessary, of triage.

That is as much as we can do at present. We should do no less, however. When the researchers come with more specific hypotheses about etiologies, pathogeneses, and therapeutic rationales, we can do more. I hope I will be able to report such progress in the next volume ten years from now.

BIBLIOGRAPHY

1. Bellak, L. 1949. A multiple-factor psychosomatic theory of schizophrenia. *Psychiatric Quarterly* 23:738–55.

2. Bellak, L. 1976. A possible subgroup of the schizophrenic syndrome and implications for treatment. *American Journal of Psychotherapy* 30:194–205.

3. Bellak, L. 1977. Psychiatric states in adults with minimal brain dysfunction. *Psychiatric Annals* 7:575–89.

4. Bellak, L. 1977. At issue: A drug-free week after admission. *Schizophrenia Bulletin* 3:342–44.

5. Bellak, L., and Holt, R. R. 1948. Somatotypes in relation to dementia praecox. *American Journal of Psychiatry* 104:713–24.

6. Bellak, L.; Hurvich, M.; and Gediman, H. 1973. *Ego functions in schizophrenics, neurotics, and normals* (New York: John Wiley).

7. Bellak, L., and Sheehy, M. 1976. The broad role of ego function assessment. *American Journal of Psychiatry* 133:1259–64.

8. Carpenter, W. T.; Strauss, J. S.; and Bartko, J. J. 1973. A flexible system for the diagnosis of schizophrenia: Report from the WHO International Pilot Study of Schizophrenia. *Science* 182:1275–78.

9. Ciompi, L., and Müller, C. 1976. *Lebensweg und Alter der Schizophrenen. Eine katamnestische Langzeitstudie bis ins Senium* [Course of life and Senescense of schizophrenics: A catamnestic long-term study into old age]. (Heidelberg: Springer).

10. Fries, M., and Woolf, P. 1953. Some hypotheses on the role of the congenital activity type in personality development. In *The psychoanalytic study of the child*, eds. R. Eissler et al. (New York: International Universities Press), vol. 8, pp. 48–62.

11. Goldstein, M. J. 1970. Premorbid adjustment, paranoid status, and patterns of response to phenothiazine in acute schizophrenia. *Schizophrenia Bulletin* 3:24–37.

12. May, P.; Wexler, M.; Salkan, J.; and Schoop, T. 1963. Non-verbal techniques in the reestablishment of body image and self identity—A preliminary report. *Psychiatric Research Report* 16:68–82.

13. Spitz, R. 1945. Hospitalism. In *The psychoanalytic study of the child*, eds. R. S. Eissler et al. (New York: International Universities Press), vol. 1, pp. 53–74.

14. Strauss, J. S., and Gift, T. E. 1977. Choosing an approach for diagnosing schizophrenia. *Archives of Psychiatry* 34:1248–53.

APPENDIX

EDITOR'S NOTE: In order to decrease the usual publication lag—between the writing of a manuscript and its appearance in print—we invited all contributors to send us material which they had overlooked or which had appeared since they wrote their chapters. The material below is published in response to this request. No effort is being made here for uniformity.

Appendix to Chapter 1 by E. Fuller Torrey

Book's 1949 study of schizophrenia in Northern Sweden, in which he found a schizophrenia prevalence rate three times that of the rest of Sweden, was confirmed in a re-study of the same area in 1975 (Book, J. A., et al., Schizophrenia in a north Swedish population, 1900–1975, *Clinical Genetics* 13:110, 1978).

Many new developments have taken place on the seasonality of schizophrenic births. Editorials in *Lancet* (Seasonality of birth in schizophrenia) and the *British Medical Journal* (Birth season and schizophrenia), both appearing on March 4, 1978, proclaimed the new-found respectability of this line of inquiry. Seasonality of schizophrenic births was reported in a tenth country, the Phillipines (Parker, G., and Balza, B., Season of birth and schizophrenia—An equatorial study, *Acta Psychiatrica Scandinavica* 56:143–146, 1977). The importance of the study was the magnitude of the excess schizophrenic births during the coolest months (15 percent) and the fact that, compared to Scandinavia or the northern United States, there are comparatively few seasonal temperature variations in the Phillipines.

The 91 percent excess of June schizophrenic births reported in this volume for South Carolina was found to be an artifact. Admitting officers in the state hospital apparently developed a custom of putting June as the birth month on admission sheets when the month was not known.

The fact that there have been shifts in schizophrenic birth seasonality was confirmed by Hare for England and Wales (Variations in the seasonal distribution of births of psychotic patients in England and Wales,

British Journal of Psychiatry 132:155–158, 1978), and also by E. F. Torrey, et al., for Missouri (A shifting seasonality of schizophrenic births, for publication). In the latter the peak for the 1920s was February, for the 1930s March and April, and for the 1940s April and May.

Additional theories to explain the seasonality of schizophrenic births were put forth, although no firm evidence has been forthcoming to support any given theory. Summer patterns of conception (and therefore winter and spring births) were proposed, with one observer suggesting that "in the summer people wear fewer clothes in bed and that a schizoid spouse is more likely then to notice his (or her) co-spouse there and accordingly to initiate sexual behavior" (James, W. H., Letter, *Lancet*, March 25, 1978). Another suggested that patients in mental hospitals, who are likely to give birth to more schizophrenic offsprings, have more opportunity for cohabitation in the summer months (Dawson, D. F., Personal communication). Additional biological theories were also proposed, including a "greater perinatal risk of Vitamin D deficiency and hypocalcemia in winter months [which] could be responsible for the increased risk of schizophrenia" (Moskovitz, R. A., Letter, *Lancet*, March 25, 1978).

Appendix to Chapter 10 by Max Fink

Since this chapter was first written, no new data regarding the efficacy or application of ECT in schizophrenia has emerged. But the controversy as to the role of ECT was joined in a number of publications and conferences. Erwin and Thompson (1978) focus on the problem of the proper diagnosis of schizophrenia and suggest that any favorable results in patients with ECT may be the result of diagnostic imprecision, resulting in the improper inclusion of catatonic and depressed patients among the schizophrenic patients treated with ECT. Brodie (1978), in commenting on this report and on that which I wrote in the same volume (Fink, 1978), noted that "Probably both contributors . . . would agree that ECT is appropriate therapy for the acute schizophrenic with an affective disturbance who has had an adverse reaction to neuroleptics."

At a conference reviewing the efficacy of ECT sponsored by NIMH, Salzman (in press) concluded that the literature reporting therapeutic efficacy for ECT in schizophrenia was unacceptable; that ECT has been completely replaced by pharmacotherapy, although ECT reduces acute schizophrenic symptoms and is an excellent treatment for catatonic withdrawal or excitement; that ECT offers little hope for lasting improvement in chronic schizophrenic patients; and that considering the quality of life of the schizophrenic patient, there is little evidence that ECT helps the patient live a more gratifying, less lonely and frightened life even if discharged from a hospital.

The report of the Task Force on Convulsive Therapy of the American Psychiatric Association went to press as Report No. 14 and in its recommendations ECT is not cited directly in cases of schizophrenia. The Task Force recommends that it finds ECT to be effective in cases of severe depression, severe psychoses characterized by behavior which is a threat to the safety and well-being of the patient or others, severe catatonia, and severe mania.

In the past year, I have continued my review of the indications and mode of action of ECT and have concluded anew that the evidence for efficacy of ECT in schizophrenia is poor, but no less well documented than the efficacy of antipsychotic drugs (Fink, in press). In view of the long term toxicity of antipsychotic drugs, particularly as these drugs affect tardive dyskinesia, cardiovascular, and ocular symptoms, it seems that the balance may well be shifting to a better therapeutic index for ECT than for drugs in cases of acute schizophrenia. I have also reviewed the theories of the mode of action of ECT and concluded that the mechanisms which seem to operate in the depressive psychoses and catatonia are insufficient explanations for the efficacy in schizophrenia. This theoretic discussion is particularly useful in suggesting that catatonia is best viewed as an independent syndrome not directly tied to the syndrome of schizophrenia.

In the discussions cited, including Erwin and Thompson (1978), Brodie (1978), Salzman (in press), and Fink (in press), there is a demand for further research and study of the role of ECT in schizophrenia.

BIBLIOGRAPHY

Brodie, H. K. H. 1978. Comment on electroconvulsive therapy in the management of schizophrenia. In *Controversy in psychiatry*, eds. J. P. Brady and H. K. H. Brodie (Philadelphia: W. B. Saunders), pp. 194–196.
Erwin, C. W., and Thompson, E. M. 1978. ECT in schizophrenia: A study in nosologic imprecision. *Ibid.* 165–182.
Fink, M. 1978. Is ECT a useful therapy in schizophrenia? *Ibid.* 183–193.
Fink, M. 1979. *Convulsive therapy: Theory and practice* (New York: Raven Press, 1979).
Salzman, C. 1978. ECT treatment in schizophrenia. Paper presented at the NIMH Conference "*ECT: Efficacy and Impact*", New Orleans, February, 1978.

Appendix to Chapter 11 by John G. Gunderson

A recent outcome study by Rubins at the Karen Horney Clinic in New York has been reported (1976).* In this study young nonchronic schizophrenic patients were transferred to a day care program after

* Rubins, J. L. Five-year results of psychoanalytic therapy and day care for acute schizophrenic patients. *American Journal of Psychoanalysis* 36:3–26, 1976.

hospitalizations. In addition to the intensive day care milieu program, ancillary uncontrolled use of psychotropic medications were employed. All patients received 2 to 3 hours of psychoanalytic psychotherapy per week. Of the sixty-three patients who began the program, forty-two stayed for more than six months. Most of these patients showed major improvements in psychotic symptoms, attitudes toward themselves and others, and in autonomy and competence. These changes occurred slowly and were most impressive in the third year of treatment. Although this study's design precludes making strong statements about the value of individual psychotherapy per se, it does indicate that important and enduring psychological changes may be possible for a considerable number of schizophrenic patients but that such changes occur slowly.

Appendix to Chapter 13 by Israel Zwerling

The principal conclusions regarding the assessment of community treatment of schizophrenic patients as well as the recommendations offered in the present chapter are in very substantial accord with the findings and recommendations of the Committee on the Chronic Mental Patient of the American Psychiatric Association, reported by Dr. John Talbott to the annual convention of the APA in May, 1978. The report cites the systematic underfunding of community programs, the absence of a continuum of community services and facilities for social support (housing, employment, recreation) as well as for treatment, and the low level of interest in the care of the chronic patient on the part of psychiatrists as prime reasons for the overall failure of community treatment programs. The central appeal in the report, "that there must be a stated public policy of responsibility and accountability on the part of the government for chronic mental patients," is again entirely in accord with the thrust of the present chapter.

No reports of new approaches to the treatment of schizophrenia in the community have come to my attention during the past year, nor have there been reports which substantially alter the data reported in the chapter concerning such treatment. It is becoming clear that a major impediment to the study of schizophrenia in the United States has been the tendency to overdiagnose this illness. A number of studies* have indicated that many chronic patients diagnosed as schizophrenic, upon careful study are rediagnosed as having bipolar affective psychoses or chronic organic psychoses. It remains true, in any event, that we as a nation continue to not fund programs for the treatment of schizophrenia in the community despite compelling demonstration of the potential effectiveness of such programs.

---

* Taylor, M. A., and Abrams, R. 1978. The prevalence of schizophrenia: A reassessment using modern diagnostic criteria. *American Journal of Psychiatry* 135:945.

The Contributors

The Editor

LEOPOLD BELLAK, M.D., is currently Clinical Professor of Psychiatry, Albert Einstein College of Medicine, and Clinical Professor of Psychology, post-doctoral program in psychotherapy, New York University. He trained in both medicine and psychoanalysis in Vienna and New York, studied psychology at Harvard Graduate School, and served his residency at St. Elizabeth's Hospital in Washington, D.C. He graduated from the New York Psychoanalytic Institute.

Among other things, Dr. Bellak studied somatotypes among schizophrenics during his residency and wrote his first comprehensive review of schizophrenia in 1946. This volume is consistent with his announced plan at that time to review the field every decade. Aside from studies of schizophrenia, he has played an active role in community psychiatry. As Director of Elmhurst General Hospital, he started the first twenty-four-hour walk-in clinic, The Trouble Shooting Clinic, in 1958 as part of a community mental health center in a general hospital. Another major interest has been in projective techniques, especially the T.A.T. and he originated the C.A.T. and the S.A.T. He has attempted to study psychoanalytic concepts and processes through experiments. His 27 books and 150 papers reflect these different interests.

He has been President of the Westchester Psychoanalytic Society and the Society for Projective Techniques and the Rorschach Institute. In 1964 he received the Annual Merit Award of the New York Society of Clinical Psychologists, and in 1976 he received an award for his contribution to the theory and practice of community psychiatry from the Psychiatric Outpatient Centers of America. Elected to the American College of Psychoanalysts, Dr. Bellak is also a Fellow of the American Psychiatric Association, the American Psychological Association, and the American Psychoanalytic Association, as well as of numerous other societies. In addition, he holds a variety of appointments as consultant.

Other Contributors

E. JAMES ANTHONY, M.D., came to the United States in 1958 to occupy the Blanche F. Ittelson Chair in Child Psychiatry at the Washington University School of Medicine in St. Louis, Missouri, where he is also the Director of the Edison Child Development Research Center.

He received his training in psychiatry, child psychiatry, and psychoanalysis (adult and child) in Britain, where he was for eight years Senior Lecturer at the Institute of Psychiatry in London and Consultant to the Maudsley and Bethlehem Royal hospitals. He received training in child development in Geneva under Jean Piaget. He is now a training and supervising analyst at the St. Louis Psychoanalytic Institute.

In 1970–71, Dr. Anthony was at the Center for Advanced Study in the Behavioral Sciences in Palo Alto and from 1970 to 1974 he was President of the International Association for Child Psychiatry and Allied Professions. From 1974 on he has been Chairman of an International Study Group exploring psychiatric risk and vulnerability in children around the world. He has written or edited eight books, and he has written over 200 scientific papers.

MONTE S. BUCHSBAUM, M.D., is Chief of the Unit on Perceptual Cognitive Studies of the Biological Psychiatry Branch, Intramural Research Program, National Institute of Mental Health. He received his undergraduate training at the University of Pittsburgh and his M.D. from the University of California in San Francisco.

Beginning his research interests in behavioral sciences during a summer fellowship at the Jackson Laboratory in Bar Harbor while an undergraduate, he did research on evoked potentials (EP) during medical school. After an internship at Moffit Hospital in San Francisco, he came to the Laboratory of Psychology at the National Institute of Mental Health to start a program on psychological correlates of evoked potentials in psychiatric patients. His interests in individual differences in neurophysiology led to studies first of EP correlates of perceptual style and recently to differences in psychopharmacological response and neurotransmitter enzyme levels.

Dr. Buchsbaum is an editor of *Physiological Psychology* and of the *Schizophrenia Bulletin* and a member of the Society for Psychiatric Research, the Society for Psychophysiological Research, the American Psychosomatic Society. He has written nearly one hundred publications on individual differences.

GORDON B. BURNETT, M.D., received his medical training in Aberdeen, Scotland, where he graduated M.B., Ch.D., in 1964. After an internship in medicine and surgery he trained in psychiatry at the Royal Edinburgh Hospital and obtained his D.P.M. from the University of Edinburgh in 1968. After two years as a Research Fellow in the Department of Psychiatry, University of Edinburgh, he proceeded to the Medical Reserve Corps in Psychiatry at the Royal College of Psychiatrists in 1972 and in that same year he came to the United States. In 1976 he obtained his M.D. degree for Clinical research. He is Associate Professor of Psychiatry at the University of North Carolina at Chapel Hill and Director of the Psychopharmacology Clinic, North Carolina Memorial Hospital, Chapel Hill. He teaches and conducts research in psychopharmacology and neuroendocrinology at the University of North Carolina and at the university's Biological Sciences Research Center of the Child Development Institute.

ROBERT CANCRO, M.D., MED.D.SC., is Professor and Chairman of the Department of Psychiatry at New York University Medical College. He received his education in New York City and earned his M.D. and Med.D.Sc. from the State University of New York, Downstate Medical Center. After spending several years at the Menninger Foundation, as Director of Research Training Program, Dr. Cancro became Professor of Psychiatry and Director of Residency Training at the University of Connecticut Health Center, Department of Psychiatry (1970–76).

He has long had an interest in the role of attentional mechanisms and other cognitive factors in the group of the schizophrenias and has recently been involved in the study of the genetic transmission of these cognitive traits and their implications for the development of this disorder. He has written extensively on the schizophrenic syndrome.

Dr. Cancro is a member of a number of national organizations and serves as a consultant to the National Institute of Mental Health. He is editor of the *Journal of Psychiatric Education* and is on the editorial board of a number of other professional journals.

WILLIAM T. CARPENTER, JR., M.D., is Professor of Psychiatry and Director of Research in the Department of Psychiatry at the University of Maryland School of Medicine, and Director of the Maryland Psychiatric Research Center.

He received his M.D. from Bowman-Gray School of Medicine in 1962 and pursued psychiatric training at the University of Rochester Medical Center, Rochester, New York. In 1966 he joined the Adult Psychiatry Branch of the National Institute of Mental Health's Intramural Research Program and remained there as Research Psychiatrist until 1975. During this period he received psychoanalytic training at the Washington Psychoanalytic Institute. His investigative interests include biological, phenomenological, and psychological investigations of schizophrenia and affective disorders. During this same period Dr. Carpenter utilized neuroendocrine techniques to investigate major affective disorders. He then worked as a collaborating investigator and, later, as co-chief collaborating investigator in the Washington Field Research Center of the International Pilot Study of Schizophrenia. From 1971 to 1974 he was responsible for a clinical research unit devoted to psychobiologic and diagnostic investigations of acute schizophrenia patients. From 1975 to 1976 he held the position of Professor of Psychiatry and Director of Schizophrenia Research, Department of Psychiatry at Albert Einstein College of Medicine.

In his present position Dr. Carpenter directs multidisciplinary work investigating the major psychoses, with particular emphasis in the identification of treatment-relevant and potentially etiologically-relevant subgroups of psychotic patients.

JERI DOANE, PH.D., received her Ph.D. from the University of Rochester and is Postdoctoral Fellow in the Department of Psychology at the University of California in Los Angeles.

STUART L. DONESON, M.A., received his M.A. from the University of Chicago. He is a Ph.D. candidate in clinical psychology at Michigan State University and an intern at McLean Hospital, Belmont, Massachusetts.

MAX FINK, M.D., has been since 1972 Professor of Psychiatry at the Health Sciences Center, State University of New York at Stony Brook. Concurrently he is Consultant to the Veterans Administration at Northport, New York, and Director, Division of Clinical Science, of the Long Island Research Institute.

He received his M.D. from New York University and studied psychiatry at Montefiore Hospital, Bellevue Psychiatric Hospital, and Hillside Hospital and graduated from the William Alanson White Institute of Psychiatry and psychoanalysis.

Dr. Fink began his research career as a Fellow of the National Foundation for Infantile Paralysis. In 1954 he became the first Director of the Department of Experimental Psychiatry at Hillside Hospital and in 1962 he became the first Director of the Missouri Institute of Psychiatry in St. Louis. In 1966 he returned to New York as Professor of Psychiatry at the New York Medical College. Between 1966 and 1972 he established studies of opiate dependence, heroin, narcotic antagonists, and cannabis.

Dr. Fink has published extensively in experimental psychiatry and has edited volumes on the psychobiology of convulsive therapy, the effects of anticholinergic drugs on behavior, and so forth.

A former President of the Nassau Neuropsychiatric Society and the American Psychopathological Association, Dr. Fink has been a member of numerous advisory boards. He has received the A. E. Bennett Award of the Society of Biological Psychiatry, the research award of the Electroshock Research Association, and the Hamilton Award of the American Psychopathological Association.

JOHN G. GUNDERSON, M.D., received his M.D. from Harvard Medical School in 1967. After completing residency training at Massachusetts Mental Health Center, he served as Assistant Chief to the Center for Studies of Schizophrenia in the Clinical Research Branch at the National Institute of Mental Health from 1971 to 1973. In this capacity he coordinated a national program that reviewed the current status of the psychotherapy of schizophrenia field. He continues as a consultant to the Clinical Research Branch.

Most of Dr. Gunderson's publications have concerned the understanding and treatment of borderline and schizophrenic patients. He has co-edited books on psychotherapy and milieu therapy. In addition, he is an active member of the editorial boards of *Psychiatry*, *The Schizophrenia Bulletin*, and *The McLean Journal*.

Currently Dr. Gunderson is an Assistant Professor of Psychiatry at Harvard Medical School. His research activities are complemented by clinical functions as director of an inpatient unit and director of the psychotherapy program at McLean Hospital. He is a fellow of the American Psychiatric Association, a member of the Group for the Advancement of Psychiatry, and an advanced analytic candidate at the Boston Psychoanalytic Institute.

RICKY L. JENTONS, M.A., received his M.A. from Boston University and is a candidate for a Ph.D. in clinical psychology at Michigan State University.

PAULINA F. KERNBERG, M.D., is Director, Child and Adolescent Psychiatry, New York Hospital-Cornell Medical Center, Westchester Division, in White Plains. From 1973–79 she was Associate Professor of Psychiatry, Albert Einstein College of Medicine of Yeshiva University and Director of Child and Adolescent Psychiatry, Bronx Municipal Hospital Center, Albert Einstein College of Medicine, where she was in charge of their therapeutic nursery, a program geared to early childhood psychosis. In addition, she is a lecturer in psychiatry at Columbia University and a training and supervising analyst.

A native of Santiago, Chile, Dr. Kernberg received her M.D. from the University of Chile, Santiago. She was a resident and post-residency Fellow in Adult Psychiatry at the C. F. Menninger Memorial Hospital, where her interest in the intensive treatment of psychotic patients began. From 1971 to 1973 she was Director of Therapy, Children's Division, the Menninger Foundation.

She is certified in general and child psychiatry by the American Board of Psychiatry and Neurology. She graduated from the Topeka Institute for Psychoanalysis in both child and adult analysis. Dr. Kernberg has written on "The Problem of Organicity," "Referral of Hospitalized Patients for Psychotherapy," "Object Relations in Borderline and Psychotic Children," "Childhood Psychosis; a Psychoanalytic Perspective," and "Borderline Conditions: Child and Adolescent Aspects."

MORRIS A. LIPTON, PH.D., M.D., is Sarah Graham Kenan Distinguished Professor of Psychiatry at the University of North Carolina, Chapel Hill. He is also Director, Biological Sciences Research Center, University of North Carolina, Child Development Research Institute, and Professor, Department of Biochemistry, University of North Carolina.

He received his Ph.D. in biochemistry from the University of Wisconsin and was awarded an M.D. by the University of Chicago. From 1963 to 1970 he was Professor of Psychiatry and Director of Research Development at the University of North Carolina, and in 1965–66 he was Visiting Scientist at the National Heart Institute's Laboratory of Clinical Biochemistry, Bethesda, Maryland. Dr. Lipton was Chairman of the Department of Psychiatry at the University of North Carolina from 1970 to 1973.

He is certified by both the American Board of Psychiatry and Neurology and the American Board of Internal Medicine. Among his many honors and awards he was Visiting Scientist at the Laboratory of Clinical Science, National Institute of Mental Health, and President of the American College of Neuropsychopharmacology (1977). Dr. Lipton served as Chairman of the Psychopharmacology Study Section, National Institute of Mental Health (1964–67); Consulting Editor, *Neuropharmacology and Psychopharmacology* (1969–70); Chairman, Neuropharmacology Advisory Committee, Federal Drug Administration (1970–73); Consultant, Federal Drug Administration, Bureau of Drugs (1973–   ); Chairman, National Advisory Committee on Hyperkinesis and Food Additives (1975–   ). In addition to his many activities, Dr. Lipton has published 161 papers.

HERBERT Y. MELTZER, M.D., is currently Professor in the Department of Psychiatry, University of Chicago Pritzker School of Medicine. He received his M.D. from Yale University in 1963. He trained at Massachusetts Mental Health Center and from 1966 to 1968 was Clinical Associate, Laboratory of Clinical Science, National Institute of Mental Health, Bethesda, Maryland. Since 1975 Dr. Meltzer has been Director of Adult Services and the Laboratory of Biological Psychiatry, Illinois State Psychiatric Institute, Chicago, Illinois.

Among the many honors and awards Dr. Meltzer has received are the Arnold Adlard Levenberg Prize in Chemistry (Cornell), the General Electric Fellowship in Chemistry (Harvard), and the Dean's Scholarship, Yale University School of Medicine. He is a member of numerous professional organizations and has published over 120 papers, primarily in the area of biochemical investigations relevant to psychiatry.

LOREN R. MOSHER, M.D., has been since 1968 Chief of the Center for Studies of Schizophrenia in the Clinical Research Branch of the National Institute of Mental Health's Extramural Research Division.

Dr. Mosher was born in California, obtained his undergraduate education at Stanford University, received his M.D. from Harvard, and took his residency training at the Massachusetts Mental Health Center. He then spent two years as a Clinical Associate in the section on Twin and Sibling Studies in the Adult Psychiatry Branch of the National Institute of Mental Health's Intramural Research Program.

Dr. Mosher started the *Schizophrenia Bulletin* and is its Editor-in-Chief. His personal research interests are focused on treatment evaluation, especially the use of residential alternatives to psychiatric hospitalization for schizophrenia.

ALBERT I. RABIN, PH.D., is Professor of Psychology at Michigan State University, Consultant to the Veterans Administration and Department of Corrections of the State of Michigan.

He was educated at Harvard and Boston universities and subsequently served as Chief Psychologist at the New Hampshire State Hospital and Mental

Hygiene clinics, as research psychologist at Michael Reese Hospital in Chicago, and for thirteen years (1948–61) as Director of the Psychological Clinic at Michigan State University. Dr. Rabin also served as guest professor at the Hebrew University, Jerusalem, and at Bar-Ilan University, Israel (1962). He was visiting professor at the City University of New York (1964–65) and at the University of Aarbus in Denmark (1970).

Dr. Rabin's early work was concerned with perserveration and patterns of intellectual functioning in schizophrenia and manic depressive psychoses, and he contributed the same chapter for the previous volumes, *Schizophrenia* and *The Schizophrenic Syndrome*. He has also supervised numerous M.A. theses and Ph.D. dissertation research on schizophrenia and related topics. His later work deals with temporal experience and personality as well as with the effects of early childhood experience upon personality and development. He is co-editor of *Projective Techniques With Children* (Grune & Stratton, 1960), author of *Growing Up in the Kibbutz* (Springer, 1965), and editor of *Projective Techniques in Personality Assessment* (Springer, 1968). In addition to several other books, he has also written over one hundred articles, chapters in books, and book reviews.

RONALD O. RIEDER, M.D., is Research Psychiatrist at the Laboratory of Psychology and Psychopathology, National Institute of Mental Health. He was born in Trenton, Michigan, and attended Harvard College and Harvard Medical School, where he received his M.D. degree (cum laude) in 1968. He was then an intern in pediatrics at Johns Hopkins Hospital and a resident in psychiatry at Albert Einstein College of Medicine, Bronx, New York. In 1971 he joined the National Institute of Mental Health as a Research Associate and in 1973 became Research Psychiatrist.

He is a member of the Behavior Genetics Association, the American Psychopathologic Association, and the American Psychiatric Association. His primary research interests have been in the genetics of schizophrenia, and he has been engaged since 1971 in a study of the offspring of schizophrenics.

ALAN A. STONE, M.D., is Professor of Law and Psychiatry in the Faculty of Law and the Faculty of Medicine, Harvard University, and President-Elect of the American Psychiatric Association. He received his M.D. degree at Yale Medical School and served as resident in adult psychiatry at McLean Hospital and resident in child psychiatry at the James Jackson Putnam Children's Center. Dr. Stone is a graduate of the Boston Psychoanalytic Institute and has been an instructor there. He was Director of Resident Education at McLean Hospital.

Dr. Stone was awarded the American Psychiatric Association's Manfred Guttmacher Prize for his outstanding contribution to psychiatry and law. He currently serves as Vice President of the American Psychiatric Association. His publications include *Mental Health and Law: A System in Transition*, two other books, and numerous articles.

JOHN S. STRAUSS, M.D., is Professor of Psychiatry at Yale Medical School and Director of the Yale Psychiatric Institute. A graduate of Swarthmore College and Yale Medical School, Dr. Strauss also spent a year of special studies with Professor Jean Piaget's group at the University of Geneva. Following his psychiatric residency at McLean and Beth Israel hospitals in Boston, Dr. Strauss served as a Clinical Associate in the Adult Psychiatry Branch of the National Institute of Mental Health and then as Chief of the Psychiatric Assessment Section. He was Professor of Psychiatry at the University of Rochester Medical School before assuming his current position, and he has also served as a Chief of the United States Center in the International Pilot

Study of Schizophrenia, as Consultant to the American Psychiatric Association's Task Force on Nomenclature and Statistics, and as member of a task force for the President's Commission on Mental Health.

In addition to many other articles, he is author of "A Comprehensive Approach to Psychiatric Diagnosis" (*American Journal of Psychiatry*) and senior author of a series of papers on the prediction of outcome in schizophrenia (*Archives of General Psychiatry*).

Dr. Strauss is a Fellow of the American Psychiatric Association and a member of the American Psychopathological Association and the Psychiatric Research Society. He is a former Chairman of the Society for Life History Research in Psychopathology.

MARGARET L. TOOHEY, M.A., is a co-author with Lyman C. Wynne of several recent papers and is a candidate for a Ph.D. at the University of Rochester. She is Research Coordinator, Division of Family Programs, in the Department of Psychiatry, University of Rochester.

E. FULLER TORREY, M.D., is a psychiatrist and general practitioner on the staff of St. Elizabeth's Hospital, Washington, D.C. Educated at Princeton, McGill, and Stanford universities, he received graduate training in medicine, psychiatry, and anthropology. He has practiced medicine in Ethiopia, the South Bronx, and among the Aleuts in Alaska, and received the United States Public Health Service Commendation Medal for the last. For five years he was at the National Institute of Mental Health where he carried out research on both epidemiological and immunological aspects of schizophrenia, work that is still in progress. He is the author of over seventy professional publications, including *The Mind Game*, *The Death of Psychiatry*, *Why Did You Do That?*, and the forthcoming *Schizophrenia and Civilization*.

LYMAN C. WYNNE, M.D., PH.D., is currently Chairman and Professor, Department of Psychiatry, University of Rochester School of Medicine and Dentistry; Psychiatrist-in-Chief, Strong Memorial Hospital, Rochester, New York (part-time 1971–72; full-time 1972–77); Director, Division of Family Programs, Department of Psychiatry, 1973– . Dr. Wynne received his M.D. and a Ph.D. in social psychology from Harvard University, where he graduated Alpha Omega Alpha and was a Rantoul Fellow in Psychology.

From 1957 to 1967 he was Chief of the Section on Family Studies, Adult Psychiatry Branch, National Institute of Mental Health. Since 1965 he has been Special Consultant to the Director-General of the World Health Organization, Geneva, Switzerland; Chief Collaborative Investigator for U.S. Field Center, WHO International Pilot Study of Schizophrenia (1966–67); and Collaborating Investigator (1968–).

Dr. Wynne has received the Commendation Medal (1965) and the Meritorious Service Medal (1966), United States Public Health Service; the Frieda Fromm-Reichmann Award for Schizophrenia Research, American Academy of Psychoanalysis (1966); the Hofheimer Prize for Research, American Psychiatric Association (1966); and the Fourteenth Annual Stanley R. Dean Research Award, American College of Psychiatrists and Fund for the Behavioral Sciences (1976). His most recent award was the McAlpin Award, Research Achievement Award, Mental Health Association (1977). He is a member of the editorial advisory board of many publications and a member of numerous professional organizations.

ISRAEL ZWERLING, M.D., PH.D., is currently Professor and Chairman of the Department of Mental Health Sciences, Hahnemann Medical College and

Hospital, Philadelphia, Pennsylvania, and Visiting Professor of Psychiatry at the Albert Einstein College of Medicine, Bronx, New York.

He received his Ph.D. in psychology at Columbia University and earned his M.D. from the State University of New York, Downstate Medical Center. From 1958 to 1966, Dr. Zwerling was Director of the Division of Social and Community Psychiatry, Department of Psychiatry, Albert Einstein College of Medicine. From 1964 to 1973 he was Professor of Psychiatry at Albert Einstein College of Medicine and, concurrently, Director of the Bronx State Hospital. From 1970 to 1972 he was Executive Chairman of the Department of Psychiatry at Albert Einstein.

Dr. Zwerling is a member of numerous professional organizations, and his many honors and awards include Sigma χ, Alpha Omega Alpha, and membership in the World Health Organization's Expert Advisory Panel on Mental Health (1974–79). He has published over fifty papers, primarily in the area of community psychiatry.

Name Index

Subject Index